Exam Ref AZ-104 Microsoft Azure Administrator Certification and Beyond

Master Azure administration and pass the AZ-104 exam with confidence

Donovan Kelly

<packt>

Exam Ref AZ-104 Microsoft Azure Administrator Certification and Beyond

Third Edition

Copyright © 2024 Packt Publishing

All rights reserved. No part of this book may be reproduced, stored in a retrieval system, or transmitted in any form or by any means, without the prior written permission of the publisher, except in the case of brief quotations embedded in critical articles or reviews.

Every effort has been made in the preparation of this book to ensure the accuracy of the information presented. However, the information contained in this book is sold without warranty, either express or implied. Neither the authors, nor Packt Publishing or its dealers and distributors, will be held liable for any damages caused or alleged to have been caused directly or indirectly by this book.

Packt Publishing has endeavored to provide trademark information about all of the companies and products mentioned in this book by the appropriate use of capitals. However, Packt Publishing cannot guarantee the accuracy of this information.

Author: Donovan Kelly

Reviewers: Ricardo Cabral and Mesut Aladağ

Publishing Product Manager: Sneha Shinde

Senior Development Editor: Ketan Giri

Development Editor: Akanksha Gupta

Digital Editor: M Keerthi Nair

Presentation Designer: Salma Patel

Editorial Board: Vijin Boricha, Megan Carlisle, Simon Cox, Ketan Giri, Saurabh Kadave, Alex Mazonowicz, Gandhali Raut, and Ankita Thakur

First Published: May 2019

Second Edition: July 2022

Third Edition: September 2024

Production Reference: 1300924

Published by Packt Publishing Ltd.
Grosvenor House
11 St Paul's Square
Birmingham
B3 1RB

ISBN: 978-1-80512-285-2

www.packtpub.com

Contributors

About the Author

Donovan Kelly is a principal architect and team leader with extensive experience in engineering, sales, and architecting in Azure. He has over 11 years of experience in the public cloud space and has worked in and with international organizations, specializing in both solution and technical architecture.

Donovan has many Microsoft Azure certifications, including AZ-900, AZ-103, AZ-104, AZ-303, AZ-304, and AZ-500, as well as the **Microsoft Certified Trainer** (**MCT**) certification. His passion for training and sharing knowledge with others culminated in his work on this book, which he hopes will inspire those who read it to find value in its pages and learn from the invaluable experiences of others who work in this field.

Donovan is an innovative thinker and embraces new challenges head-on. One of his favorite quotes is from Robert Frost: *"Two roads diverged in a wood; I took the one less traveled by, and that has made all the difference."*

With deep gratitude to God, who has blessed me with the inspiration and strength to complete this work. All glory to Jesus Christ, my Savior, who guides my every step.

My heartfelt thanks to my beloved wife for her endless patience, love, and sacrifices – this book wouldn't exist without you. To Tyler and Bella, my precious children - your laughter, enthusiasm, and unconditional love are my greatest treasures. Thank you to my parents for instilling in me the values of gratitude and love.

I am also grateful to those who have believed in me and pushed me to grow. And special thanks to Riaan, whose belief in me ignited this writing journey.

About the Reviewers

Based in Portugal, **Ricardo Cabral** is a licensed Computer Engineering professional and Microsoft Certified Trainer (MCT) with 20+ years of experience in IT management, development, and projects working in both administration and development roles. Through this work, he has developed proficiency in Microsoft 365, Microsoft Azure, Microsoft Azure DevOps, Microsoft Power Platform, Microsoft Windows Server & Client, Programing language C# and holds several Microsoft certifications.

He now works as an Azure Solutions Architect and IT trainer at NWORKIT Digital Solutions. In his free time, he actively organizes, participates, volunteers, and speaks in technical community meetings.

I'd like to thank my family, all my friends, and a special Eugénia Azevedo that helped guide me in my decisions and offered encouragement in everything that I do. I'd also like to thank Packt Publishing for the opportunity to review this wonderful book.

Mesut Aladağ is a seasoned Senior Technical Specialist and Cloud Solution Architect (Azure) at Microsoft. With over 25 years of experience, he has architected, deployed, and managed complex cloud solutions for various organizations. Mesut specializes in Azure cloud technologies, enterprise architecture, security, and infrastructure. He has authored multiple books on these topics and holds numerous Microsoft certifications. Mesut has been responsible for architecting, leading, coaching and mentoring the customers and partners end-to-end cloud transformation experience, driving the design, plan and deployment of the workloads into Azure by providing architecture design, deployment guidance, supporting development of the cloud adoption model and providing appropriate recommendations to overcome blockers, identify, onboard, and realize workloads and grow opportunities to accelerate consumption in high potential enterprise customers. Mesut has a proven track record of successfully leading and delivering complex projects, published books, articles, webinars and earned recognition as a Microsoft MVP in multiple areas. He is also holding Microsoft Certified Trainer Regional Lead role. He is also an active Microsoft Certified Trainer. He holds a BSc degree in Computer Science and MSc degree in Computer Engineering.

From his own words: *"I'd like to thank Pack Publishing for including me to contribute to this great work. Practical knowledge is power, and sharing knowledge is the superpower because knowledge continue growing as it is shared."*

Table of Contents

Preface — xxi

1

Managing Microsoft Entra ID Objects — 1

Making the Most Out of This Book – Your Certification and Beyond — 1
Technical Requirements — 3
Microsoft Entra P1 Trial — 4
Microsoft Entra ID — 5
Users, Groups, and Administrative Units — 6
Users — 6
Groups — 7
AUs — 8
Common Microsoft Entra ID Concepts — 9
Microsoft Entra ID versus Active Directory (On-Premises) — 11
AD DS — 11
Administration — 12
Integration — 13
B2C — 13
B2B — 14

Creating Users and Groups — 15
Creating Users in Microsoft Entra ID — 15
Creating Groups in Microsoft Entra ID — 20

Creating Microsoft Entra ID AUs — 24
Managing User and Group Properties — 28
User Account Properties — 28
Microsoft Entra ID group settings — 30

Summary — 32

2

Devices in Microsoft Entra ID — 33

Technical Requirements — 33
Configuring and Managing Devices — 34
Configuring Device Identities — 34
Microsoft Entra Device Registration — 34
Microsoft Entra Join — 35
Microsoft Entra Hybrid Join — 36
Device Settings — 37
Enterprise State Roaming — 39
Managing Device Settings — 40
Device Audit Logs — 42
Licensing — 43
Try/Buy License Products for Microsoft Entra — 45
Assigning a License — 47

Configuring Microsoft Entra Join — 48

Microsoft Entra Join Methods	49	Updating Multiple Users	58
Microsoft Entra Join Management	49	Performing Bulk Creations Using PowerShell	59
Microsoft Entra Join Scenarios	49		
Configuring Microsoft Entra Join	49	**Navigating Guest Accounts**	**61**
		Managing Guest Accounts	62
Performing Bulk Operations	**53**	**Configuring SSPR**	**63**
Performing Bulk Updates Using the Azure Portal	54	Configuring SSPR	64
Downloading a User List	54	**Summary**	**66**
Bulk User Deletion Operations	57		

3

Managing Role-Based Access Control in Azure   67

Technical Requirements	**68**	**Understanding role-based-access-control**	**78**
Understanding Azure Regions	**68**	RBAC Requirements	78
Managing RBAC across Multiple Regions	68	RBAC built-in Roles	79
Managing Azure Subscriptions and Management Hierarchy	**69**	Getting Started with Azure RBAC	79
Billing Profiles	70	Role Definitions	80
Azure Management Hierarchy	70	Scope	82
Core Concepts	71	Role Assignments	83
Key Considerations of the Hierarchy of Management for Enterprise Agreements	72	Example of Role Assignment	84
Relationship Between Microsoft Entra and Subscriptions	73	**Creating a custom RBAC role**	**85**
Why Have Multiple Subscriptions in an Environment?	74	Assigning Access to Resources by Assigning a Custom Role	91
		Confirming the Role Assignment Steps	93
Configuring Management Groups	**74**	**Interpreting Access Assignments**	**95**
Creating a Management Group	76	**Summary**	**98**
		Exam Readiness Drill - Chapters 1-3	**99**
		HOW TO GET STARTED	99

4

Creating and Managing Governance   101

Technical Requirements	**101**	How Does Azure Policy work?	103
Understanding Azure Policies	**102**	Azure Policy versus RBAC	104

Working with Azure Policy	104	**Applying and Managing Tags on Resources**	**125**
Constructing a Policy Definition	106	How Tags Look in Azure	126
Effect Types	107	Tagging Strategy	126
Example Policy Definition	108	Applying a Resource Tag	127
Creating a Policy Definition	109	PowerShell Scripts	129
Creating an Initiative Definition	113	**Summary**	**132**
Assigning a Policy Definition and Initiative	118		
Policy Compliance	123		

5

Managing Governance and Costs 133

Technical Requirements	**133**	Applying a Resource Lock to a Resource Group	153
Managing Resource Groups	**134**	Viewing Resource Locks in Effect	153
Deploying a Resource Group	135	ARM Templates	154
Listing Resource Groups	137	**Managing Costs**	**155**
Deleting a Resource Group	138	Cost Management	155
Migrating or Moving Resource Groups	140	Cost Analysis	155
PowerShell Scripts	144	Scheduled Reports	158
Configuring Resource Locks	**145**	Budgets	160
Permissions Required for Creating or Deleting Locks	145	Example Budget	161
		Modifying an Existing Budget	168
Built-In Azure Roles	146	Cost Alerts	168
Custom RBAC Roles	146	Creating a New Alert	169
Adding a Resource Lock	146	Viewing Alert Details	169
Creating a Read-only Lock	151	Modifying an Existing Alert	170
PowerShell Scripts	153	Advisor Recommendations	171
Applying a Resource Lock to a Resource	153	Reservations	172
		Summary	**173**

6

Understanding Storage Accounts 175

Technical Requirements	**175**	Standard	178
Understanding Azure Storage Accounts	**176**	Premium	178
		Storage Account Types	178
Storage Account Performance Categories	177	Standard GPv2	179
		Premium Block Blobs	182

Premium File Shares	183	ZRS	189
Premium Page Blobs	183	GRS	190
Legacy Storage Account Types	184	GZRS	191
Storage Access Tiers	184	Storage Encryption	192
Hot	185	Need for Encryption and the Value it Brings	192
Cool	185	Difference between Storage Encryption	
Cold	185	on Azure and Infrastructure Encryption	192
Archive	185	Different Encryption Types on a Storage Account	193
Service-Level Agreement for Storage Accounts	185	**Creating and Configuring Storage Accounts**	**195**
Azure Disk Storage	186		
Standard Disk Storage	186	Creating a storage account	195
Premium Disk Storage	186	PowerShell scripts	203
Ultra Disk Storage	187		
Unmanaged versus Managed Disks	188	**Summary**	**204**
Redundancy	188	**Exam Readiness Drill - Chapters 4-6**	**205**
LRS	188	HOW TO GET STARTED	205

7

Copying Data To and From Azure 207

Technical Requirements	**207**	Creating an Azure Files Share	222
Using Azure Data Box (Previously, Import/Export)	**208**	Accessing Your Azure File Shares from the Portal	224
Importing into an Azure Job	208	Connecting an Azure Files Share to Windows Using SMB	226
Exporting from an Azure Job	214	Configuring Azure Blob Storage	229
Installing and Using Azure Storage Explorer	**218**	Configuring Storage Tiers	231
		Azure URL Paths for Storage	235
Installation	219	PowerShell Scripts	236
Configuring Azure Files and Azure Blob Storage	**222**	**Summary**	**237**

8

Securing Storage 239

Technical Requirements	**239**	Public Endpoints	240
Configuring Network Access to Storage Accounts	**240**	Azure Virtual Network (VNet) Integration	241

Configuring Storage Account Network Security	241	Stored Access Policies	258
Private Endpoints	244	Creating a Stored Access Policy	258
Network Routing from Storage Accounts	247	Editing a Storage Access Policy	260
PowerShell Scripts	249	Removing an Existing Storage Access Policy	260
Storage Access Keys	**250**	**Configuring Access and Authentication**	**261**
Managing Access Keys	250	Configuring AD DS Authentication for a Storage Account	262
Rotating Storage Access Keys	251	Configuring Access to Azure Files	278
Working with SAS Tokens	**252**	Assigning Share-Level Permissions	278
Types of SAS	253	Mounting the File Share	279
Forms of SAS	253	Configuring File-Level Permissions	282
Generating SAS Tokens	253	**Summary**	**283**

9

Storage Management and Replication   285

Technical Requirements	**285**	Immutable Storage	292
Copying Data by Using AzCopy	**286**	Storage Account Deletion	293
Downloading and Installing	286	Creating and Configuring an Azure File Sync Instance	293
Copying Data by Using AzCopy	287	Working with Azure File Snapshots	301
Copying Data between Containers Using AzCopy	288	Implementing Azure Storage Redundancy	302
Configuring Storage Replication and Lifecycle Management	**290**	Configuring Blob Object Replication	303
		Configuring Blob Life Cycle Management	304
Storage Replication and Management Services	290	Lifecycle Management Policy Deployed as Code	306
Azure File Sync	290	Deleting a Life Cycle Management Rule	309
Blob Object Replication	291	Configuring Blob Data Protection	310
Blob Life Cycle Management	291	**Summary**	**311**
Blob Data Protection	291	**Exam Readiness Drill - Chapters 7-9**	**312**
Blob Versioning	292	HOW TO GET STARTED	312

10

Azure Resource Manager Templates — 313

Technical Requirements	313	Using VS Code to Create ARM Templates	323
Understanding ARM Templates	314	Modifying an Existing ARM Template	326
Benefits of ARM	315	Deploying an ARM Template – Azure Portal	332
Understanding the ARM Template Structure	316	Deploying an ARM Template – Azure PowerShell	334
Object Types	316	Saving a Deployment as an ARM Template	335
Schema	317	Exporting an ARM Template	337
Content Version	317	Azure QuickStart Templates	340
Parameters	317	Accessing Azure QuickStart Templates	341
Variables	318	Summary	341
Functions	318		
Resources	320		
Outputs	320		
Creating an ARM Template	321		

11

Azure Bicep — 343

Technical Requirements	343	Modules	352
Understanding Azure Bicep	344	Outputs	352
Benefits of Azure Bicep	344	Creating a Bicep Template	353
Comparing Azure Bicep to ARM Templates	345	Modifying an Existing Bicep Template	356
Setting up the Bicep Extension for VS Code and the Bicep CLI	345	Deploying a Bicep Template – Azure PowerShell	356
Understanding the Bicep Template Structure	347	Converting ARM to Bicep	357
Metadata	348	Prerequisites	358
Target Scope	348	Converting an Existing ARM File to Bicep	358
User-Defined Data Types	348	Converting Bicep to ARM	359
User-Defined Functions	349	Prerequisites	359
Parameters	349	Converting an Existing Bicep File to ARM	359
Variables	350	Summary	360
Resources	351		

12

Understanding Virtual Machines — 361

Technical Requirements — 361	VM Security Types — 378
Understanding Azure Disk Storage — 362	Standard — 379
Disk Management Options — 362	Trusted Launch — 379
Disk Performance — 363	Confidential VMs — 380
Disk Caching — 364	VM Images — 380
Calculating Expected Caching Performance — 365	VM Architectures — 381
Disk Types — 367	Hibernation — 381
Ultra Disk — 367	Licensing — 382
Premium SSD — 368	Azure Spot VMs — 382
Premium SSD v2 — 368	Reserved Instances — 383
Standard SSD — 369	Capacity Reservation — 383
Standard HDD — 369	Proximity Placement Groups — 383
Disk Summary Table — 369	**Deploying a VM in Azure** — 384
Disk Redundancy Options — 370	Exercise 12.1 — 384
Understanding Azure VMs — 370	PowerShell Scripts — 390
VM Sizes — 371	**Deploying and Configuring Scale Sets** — 391
Networking — 373	Exercise 12.2 — 391
Network Security Groups — 373	**Summary** — 394
Availability Sets — 373	**Exam Readiness Drill - Chapters 10-12** — 395
Fault Domain versus Update Domain — 374	HOW TO GET STARTED — 395
Availability Zones — 375	
Scale Sets — 376	
Allocation Policy — 377	
Comparing Horizontal and Vertical Scaling — 378	

13

Managing Virtual Machines — 397

Technical Requirements — 398	**Adding Data Disks to VMs** — 401
Managing VM Sizes — 398	Exercise 13.3: Adding Data Disks — 401
Exercise 13.1: Resizing Your VM Using the Azure Portal — 398	**Troubleshooting VM Networking** — 403
Exercise 13.2: Resizing a VM Using the CLI — 400	Exercise 13.4: Troubleshooting VM Networking — 403

Moving VMs between Resource Groups — 405
Exercise 13.5: Moving VMs from One Resource Group to Another — 405

Redeploying VMs — 408
Exercise 13.6: Redeploying VMs — 409
Exercise 13.7: Redeploying a VM from PowerShell — 410

Disk Encryption in Azure — 411

Exercise 13.8: Configuring ADE — 411

Automating Configuration Management — 413

Deploying VM Extensions — 414
Exercise 13.9: Deploying a VM Extension Using the Portal — 414

Configuring and Deploying a VM ARM Template — 416

Summary — 424

14

Creating and Configuring Containers — 427

Technical Requirements — 428
Docker — 428

Introduction to Containers — 429
The Problems Containers Solve — 429
Complexity — 429
Resource Requirements and Costs — 430
Scalability — 430
Portability and Consistency — 430
The Differences between VMs and Containers — 431
Isolation — 432
OS — 432
Deployment — 432
Storage Persistence — 433
Fault Tolerance — 433

Azure Container Instances — 434

Container Groups — 434
Common Scenarios for Using Multi-Container Groups — 435
Resources — 436
Networking — 436
Deployment — 437

Docker Platform — 438
Docker Terminology — 438

Setting Up Docker — 439
Creating Your First Docker Image — 442

Azure Kubernetes Services — 445
Upgrading an AKS Cluster — 447
Node Security Channel Types — 447
Authentication and Authorization — 448
AKS Networking Options — 448
Private Access — 448
Public Access — 449
Network Configuration — 449
Network Policy — 450
Traffic Routing — 451
AKS Security — 451

Creating an Azure Container Registry — 452

Deploying Your First Container Instance — 454

Configuring Container Groups for ACI — 456

Configuring Sizing and Scaling for ACI — 460

Deploying AKS — 462

Configuring Storage for AKS	466	Upgrading an AKS Cluster	472
Configuring Scaling for AKS	469	Summary	473

15

Creating and Configuring App Service — 475

Technical Requirements	475	General settings	494
Understanding Azure App Service and App Service Plans	476	Path mappings	496
		Error pages	496
App Service Plans	477	Authentication Settings	497
Runtime Stacks	477	Identity Settings	500
Operating Systems	478	Backups	501
SKUs/Sizes	478	Certificates	501
Authentication Settings	479	Networking	502
Continuous Deployment	479	CORS	506
Creating an App Service Plan	480	Additional Considerations	507
Creating an App Service Instance	481	Configuring Custom Domain Names	507
PowerShell Scripts	484	Configuring a Backup for an App Service Instance	510
Configuring Scaling	486		
Vertical Scaling	486	Configuring Networking Settings	512
Horizontal Scaling	487	Configuring Deployment Settings	515
PowerShell Scripts	491	Summary	518
Securing Azure App Service	493	Exam Readiness Drill - Chapters 13-15	519
Environment Variables	493		
Configuration settings	494	HOW TO GET STARTED	519

16

Implementing and Managing Virtual Networking — 521

Technical Requirements	521	Configuring a VNet Peer	525
Creating and Configuring Virtual Networks	522	Testing your VNet Peer	528
		Creating Private and Public IP Addresses	531
IP Addressing Overview	522		
Creating a VNet	523	Configuring a Private IP Address	531
VNet Peering	525	Configuring a Public IP Address	532

xvi   Table of Contents

User-defined Routing	533	**Configuring Private Endpoints**	544
Creating a Route Table	534	Creating a Private Endpoint	544
Implementing Subnets	538	Integrating into a VNet	548
Adding a Subnet to a VNet	539	**Configuring Azure DNS**	549
Configuring Endpoints on Subnets	540	Creating an Azure Private DNS Zone	551
Configuring a Service Endpoint	540	Testing Private DNS	552
		Summary	553

17

Securing Access to Virtual Networks 555

Technical requirements	556	Rule Processing Logic	569
Network Security Groups	556	Azure Firewall SKUs	571
Creating an NSG	559	Azure Firewall Basic	571
Associating an NSG with a Subnet	560	Azure Firewall Standard	572
Configuring NSG Rules	561	Azure Firewall Premium	573
Evaluating Effective Security Rules	564	Comparing Firewall SKUs	574
Azure Firewall	567	**Azure Bastion**	576
Traffic Flow Direction	569	**Deploying Azure Bastion and Azure Firewall**	577
Firewall Rules	569	**Summary**	585

18

Configuring Load Balancing 587

Technical Requirements	587	Deciding on the Right Load Balancer Solution	594
Azure Load-Balancing Services	588	**Azure Load Balancer**	594
Regional Services	588	Features and Capabilities	595
Global Services	589	Load-Balancing	595
Multi-Cloud Considerations	589	Port Forwarding	596
Load Balancer Service Options	589	Automatic reconfiguration	596
Non-HTTP(S) Workloads	590	Outbound Connections (SNAT)	596
HTTP(S) Workloads	590	Health Probes	596
SSL Offloading	591	Metrics	597
Path-Based Load-Balancing	591	Security	597
Session Affinity	592	Load Balancer SKUs	597
WAF	593		

Basic	598	Troubleshooting Load Balancing	617
Standard	599	**Azure Application Gateway**	**619**
Gateway	600	Features and Capabilities	619

Configuring an ILB — 601

Creating the VNet	601	**Configuring Azure Application Gateway**	**620**
Creating the VMs	602	Creating an Azure Application Gateway	620
Creating a Load Balancer	603	Deploying Your Web App	625
Creating the Health Probes	606	Testing the Application Gateway	626
Creating Load-Balancing Rules	607	**Azure Front Door**	**627**
Testing the Load Balancer	608	**Summary**	**628**

Configuring a Public Load Balancer — 609

Creating the Public Load Balancer	609	**Exam Readiness Drill - Chapters 16-18**	**629**
Creating the VNet and NSG	612	HOW TO GET STARTED	629
Creating Backend Servers	614		
Testing the Load Balancer	616		

19

Integrating On-Premises Networks with Azure — 631

Technical Requirements	**632**	VPN Server Deployment	640
Azure VPN Gateway	**632**	S2S VPN Configuration	650
Azure VPN Gateway SKUs	633	Verify Connectivity via the Azure Portal	652
Generation 1 VPN SKUs	633	VNet-to-VNet Connections	653
Generation 2 VPN SKUs	634	**Creating and Configuring Azure ExpressRoute**	**654**
Pricing Considerations	634		
Point-to-Site VPN Connections	634	**Azure Virtual WAN**	**656**
Site-to-Site VPN Connections	635	**Configuring Azure Virtual WAN**	**658**
Multi-Site VPN Connections	637	Creating a VPN Site	659
VNet-to-VNet VPN Connections	637	Connecting Your VPN Site to the Hub	660
ExpressRoute	638	Connecting to Your VPN Site	661
Creating and Configuring an Azure VPN Gateway	**639**	**Summary**	**663**

20

Monitoring and Troubleshooting Virtual Networking 665

Technical Requirements	665	Migrate Flow Logs	676
Understanding Network Watcher	666	Diagnostic Logs	676
Monitoring	666	**Configuring Network Watcher**	**677**
Topology	667	Network Resource Monitoring	677
Connection Monitor	667	Installing the Network Watcher Agent	677
Traffic Analytics	671	Enabling Network Watcher	678
Network Diagnostic Tools	671	Monitoring Network Connectivity	680
IP Flow Verify	671	Managing VNet Connectivity	683
NSG Diagnostics	672	Network Topology	683
Next Hop	673	Monitoring On-Premises Connectivity	685
Effective Security Rules	674	Configuring Next Hop	685
VPN Troubleshoot	674	VPN Troubleshoot	687
Packet Capture	674	Troubleshooting External Networking	689
Connection Troubleshoot	674	IP Flow Verify	689
Metrics	675	Using IP Flow Verify	690
Usage + Quotas	675	Effective Security Rules	691
Logs	676	Connection Troubleshoot	692
Flow Logs	676	**Summary**	**694**

21

Monitoring Resources with Azure Monitor 695

Technical Requirements	695	Data Platform	703
Understanding Azure Monitor	696	Metrics	704
Metrics versus Logs	696	Log Analytics	704
What Data Azure Monitor Collects	696	Traces	705
Data Sources	698	Changes	705
Data Collection	699	Consumption	705
Application Instrumentation with the SDK	700	Insights	706
Azure Monitor Agent	701	Application Insights	706
Data Collection Rules	701	Container Insights	708
Automatic Data Collection (Zero Configuration)	701	VM Insights	708
Azure Diagnostic Settings	701	Network Insights	708
Azure Monitor REST API	703	The Activity Log	709
Data Collection Best Practices	703	Alerts	709

Action Groups	709	Triggering an Alert	725
Service Health	710	**Querying Log Analytics**	**727**
Active Events	710	Creating a Log Analytics Workspace	728
History	711	Utilizing Log Search Query Functions	728
Resource Health	712	Querying Logs in Azure Monitor	729
Alerts	712	**Monitoring with Workbooks**	**735**
Working with Metrics and Alerts	**713**	**Configuring Application Insights**	**737**
Creating a VM	713	Creating Your Application	738
Viewing a Metric	714	Creating Your Application Insights Resource	739
Creating a Dashboard	718	Associating Your Web App with Application Insights	740
Creating an Alert	720		
Configuring Diagnostic Settings on Resources	724	**Summary**	**742**

22

Implementing Backup and Recovery Solutions — 743

Technical Requirements	**743**	Restoring a Backup via Azure Backup Center	752
Understanding Azure Backup Vaults	**744**	Recovering from a Disaster with Azure Site Recovery	755
Understanding Azure Recovery Services Vaults	**744**	Configuring and Reviewing Backup Reports	761
Creating a Recovery Services Vault	**745**	**Summary**	**766**
Understanding Backup Policies	**746**	**Exam Readiness Drill - Chapters 19-22**	**767**
Creating and Configuring Backup Policies	**747**	HOW TO GET STARTED	767
Backing Up via Azure Backup Center	**751**		

23

Accessing the Online Practice Resources — 769

Index — 775

Other Books You May Enjoy — 788

Preface

In today's digital landscape, public cloud computing has greatly transformed how organizations operate. It provides scalable resources, reduces infrastructure costs, and offers flexibility in work environments. Azure, Microsoft's primary cloud computing service, is renowned for its robust, integrated cloud environment that supports various computing services. It enables the seamless execution and management of applications across different platforms while optimizing speed, scalability, and security.

With the increasing shift toward cloud solutions, the role of an Azure administrator has become crucial. Proficiency in Azure administration equips professionals with the ability to shape and direct their organizations' technological framework. The Microsoft Azure Administrator (AZ-104) exam is essential for administrators, engineers, and architects seeking to validate their skills in this role. This book is designed to help you pass the AZ-104 exam confidently. It will also provide you with the practical knowledge and tools necessary to excel in your career as an Azure administrator. The guide combines theoretical insights and hands-on labs to help you master Azure's extensive features, laying a strong foundation as you aspire to become an expert in cloud administration.

Who This Book Is For

This book is aimed at both experienced and aspiring cloud administrators, engineers, and architects. It is designed to help those who want to gain a better understanding of the Azure platform and master Azure administrative skills. It is especially useful for those preparing to take the Microsoft Azure Administrator (AZ-104) exam.

What This Book Covers

In this comprehensive guide, you'll learn everything you need to know to become an expert Azure administrator. The content has been divided into 22 chapters, covering all aspects of Azure administration.

Chapter 1, *Managing Microsoft Entra ID Objects*, teaches you about managing Microsoft Entra (formerly Azure AD) objects, including users, groups, and administrative units.

Chapter 2, *Devices in Microsoft Entra ID*, covers device management, bulk operations, guest accounts, and self-service password reset for seamless integration within your organization's infrastructure.

Chapter 3, *Managing Role-Based Access Control in Azure*, teaches you how to master **role-based access control** (**RBAC**) to manage access to resources and data in Azure, including role creation, management, and assignments.

Chapter 4, *Creating and Managing Governance*, guides you through establishing governance with Azure policies and resource tags, setting the foundation for a well-managed organization.

Chapter 5, *Managing Governance and Costs*, takes you through governance-related functions to manage resources, services, and costs in Azure, ensuring effective governance and cost optimization.

Chapter 6, *Understanding Storage Accounts,* teaches you about storage account basics, performance tiers (Standard and Premium), and storage access tiers for optimal data management.

Chapter 7, *Copying Data to and from Azure*, guides you through using Azure Data Box for large-scale data transfer, and Azure Storage Explorer for convenient storage management.

Chapter 8, *Securing Storage*, sheds light on storage security configurations, including network access control, authentication, authorization, and **shared access signature** (**SAS**) tokens.

Chapter 9, *Storage Management and Replication*, illustrates how to manage a blob life cycle, replication options, data protection, versioning, and account deletion for reliable data storage.

Chapter 10, *Azure Resource Manager Templates*, guides you on using **Azure Resource Manager** (**ARM**) templates for **infrastructure as code** (**IaC**), ensuring consistent and repeatable infrastructure deployments.

Chapter 11, *Azure Bicep*, unpacks the newer domain-specific language, Azure Bicep, for IaC and teaches you how to define, deploy, and manage Azure resources efficiently.

Chapter 12, *Understanding Virtual Machines*, covers **virtual machine** (**VM**) basics, including VM storage, disk redundancy, sizes, networking, availability sets, and zones for optimal resource utilization.

Chapter 13, *Managing Virtual Machines*, unpacks how to manage VMs, including resizing, configuring disks, networking, moving between resource groups, redeployment, and disk encryption.

Chapter 14, *Creating and Configuring Containers*, introduces container basics, sizing, scaling, **Azure Container Instances** (**ACI**), **Azure Kubernetes Service** (**AKS**), AKS storage, and scaling options for efficient container management.

Chapter 15, *Creating and Configuring App Services*, shows you how to create and configure App Service instances for web applications, including administrative functions such as configurations, scaling, backups, and networking integrations.

Chapter 16, *Implementing and Managing Virtual Networking*, covers virtual networking, including creating and configuring Azure **virtual networks** (**VNets**), peering networks, and configuring private and public IP addresses, user-defined network routes, subnets, endpoints, and private endpoints.

Chapter 17, *Securing Access to Virtual Networks*, provides you with information on securing access to VNets with **network security groups** (**NSGs**), Azure Bastion, Azure Firewall, security rules, and threat protection services.

Chapter 18, *Configuring Load Balancing*, unpacks load balancing concepts and services such as **high availability** (**HA**), Azure Load Balancer, Application Gateway, and Front Door.

Chapter 19, *Integrating On-Premises Networks with Azure*, covers how to integrate your on-premises networks with Azure VNets using VPN connections, Express Route, **site-to-site** (**S2S**) VPN connections, point-to-site VPN, and Azure Virtual WAN for seamless network connectivity.

Chapter 20, *Monitoring and Troubleshooting Virtual Networking*, guides you through network monitoring and troubleshooting using Network Watcher to monitor virtual networks and external networking.

Chapter 21, *Monitoring Resources with Azure Monitor*, teaches how to use Azure Monitor for resource monitoring, including metrics, alerts, Log Analytics, Application Insights, and troubleshooting skills.

Chapter 22, *Implementing Backup and Recovery Solutions*, explains how to implement and configure backup and recovery solutions using Azure Backup and Recovery Service vaults, including deployment, configuration, backup policies, restore operations, and S2S recovery via Azure Site Recovery.

Online Practice Resources

With this book, you will unlock unlimited access to our online exam-prep platform (*Figure 0.1*). This is your place to practice everything you learn in the book.

> **How to Access These Materials**
> To learn how to access the online resources, refer to *Chapter 23*, *Accessing the Online Practice Resources*, at the end of this book.

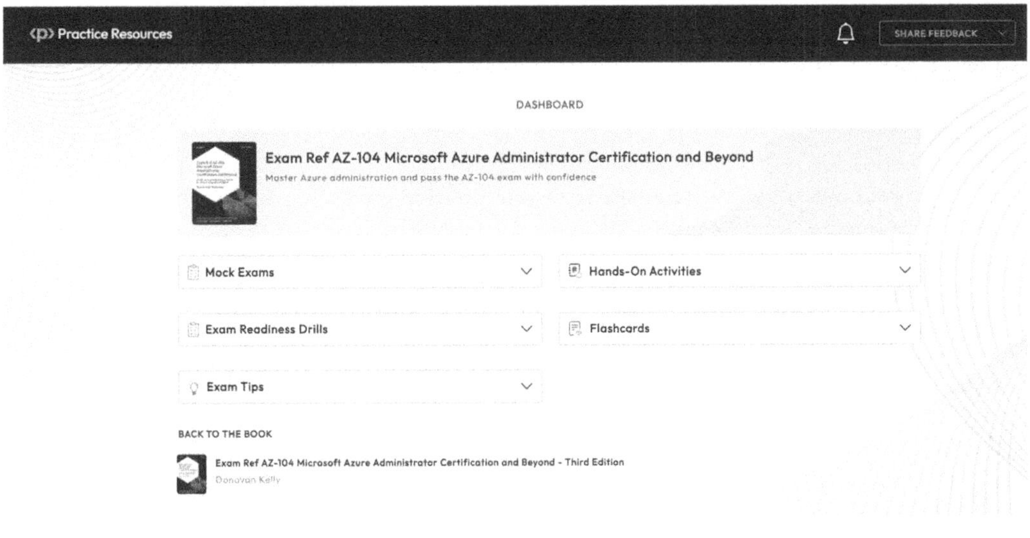

Figure 0.1: Online exam-prep platform on a desktop device

Sharpen your knowledge of AZ-104 concepts with multiple sets of mock exams, interactive flashcards, hands-on activities, and exam tips, accessible from all modern web browsers.

Accessing the Code Files

You can find the complete code files of this book at https://github.com/PacktPublishing/AZ-104-Microsoft-Azure-Administrator-Certification-and-Beyond-3rd-Edition.

Download the Color Images

We also provide a PDF file that has color images of the screenshots/diagrams used in this book. You can download it here: https://packt.link/sGNuI.

Conventions Used

There are several text conventions used throughout this book.

`Code in text`: Indicates code words in text, database table names, folder names, filenames, file extensions, pathnames, dummy URLs, user input, text on screen, and X (formerly Twitter) handles. Here is an example: "The `Unable to connect` response tells the tester that the connection is closed."

Blocks of Code

A block of code is set as follows:

```
# First connect your Azure account credentials
Connect-AzAccount

# Parameters
$ResourceGroup = "AZ104-StorageAccounts"
$StorageAccountName = "az104storageaccountdemo1"
$ContainerName = "testps"
$Context = (Get-AzStorageAccount -ResourceGroupName $ResourceGroup -AccountName $StorageAccountName).Context;

# Create a blob container
New-AzStorageContainer -Name $ContainerName -Context $Context
```

Bold: Indicates a new term or an important word and abbreviations. Here is an example: "These experts (all of whom hold a CISSP certification) gather every three years to review and revise the exam outline during the **job task analysis (JTA)** portion of the certification's life cycle."

> **Tips or important notes**
> Appear like this.

Get in Touch

Feedback from our readers is always welcome.

General feedback: If you have any questions about this book, please mention the book title in the subject of your message and email us at customercare@packt.com.

Errata: Although we have taken every care to ensure the accuracy of our content, mistakes do happen. If you have found a mistake in this book, we would be grateful if you could report this to us. Please visit www.packtpub.com/support/errata and complete the form. We ensure that all valid errata are promptly updated in the GitHub repository at https://packt.link/L3xk9.

Piracy: If you come across any illegal copies of our works in any form on the internet, we would be grateful if you could provide us with the location address or website name. Please contact us at copyright@packt.com with a link to the material.

If you are interested in becoming an author: If there is a topic that you have expertise in and you are interested in either writing or contributing to a book, please visit authors.packtpub.com.

Setting Up Your Environment

As you navigate through the book, you will be required to install some software to participate in all the exercises shared in this book. You will enjoy the process more if you set up your environment before the setup steps for the chapter. In the following sections, you will learn about some of the tools required and how to install them. You will then learn about how to access the code files that will be used for your labs and the code you will use in the rest of the book.

Technical Requirements

The following are the technical requirements for this chapter:

- Access to an Azure subscription with owner or contributor privileges. If you do not have access to one, students can enroll for a free account at `https://azure.microsoft.com/en-us/free/`.

- **PowerShell 5.1** or later installed on a Windows PC or PowerShell Core 6.x where other operating systems are used to practice the labs.

- For Windows users, you will need to install **.NET Framework 4.7.2 or later** using the following link: `https://learn.microsoft.com/en-us/dotnet/framework/install`.

- Where PowerShell is not installed or available, `https://shell.azure.com` can be used as a browser-based shell.

- Installation of the Az PowerShell module, which can be performed by running the following in an administrative PowerShell session:

    ```
    Set-ExecutionPolicy -ExecutionPolicy RemoteSigned -Scope
    CurrentUser
    Install-Module -Name Az -Scope CurrentUser -Repository PSGallery
    -Force
    ```

> **Note**
>
> The `AzureRM` module has been deprecated as of February 29, 2024. If the `AzureRM` module is already installed, remove this before installing the `Az` module, which is the officially supported module. Installation of the `Az` module will fail should you try to run both. To read more details on this and how to migrate from the `AzureRM` module, you can follow this link: `https://learn.microsoft.com/en-us/powershell/azure/migrate-from-azurerm-to-az`.

Accessing the Microsoft Labs

As you go through the labs in this book, you will need to access the provided GitHub repo. This section is a helpful guide on using the GitHub repo content.

The base link for the labs is the following: `https://microsoftlearning.github.io/AZ-104-MicrosoftAzureAdministrator/`. Navigating to this link will bring you to the repository landing page, as illustrated in *Figure 0.2*:

Figure 0.2: The Microsoft Labs GitHub repo

At the top of the page, you can see a link to download all the files required for the courseware. One of the important folders is the `Allfiles` folder, which contains all the lab folders with the relevant files needed for each lab.

You can also see several links, with each going to a unique lab that you can practice. Entering one of these labs will present you with the details of that lab.

To navigate back to the main page of the repo, click the hamburger menu at the top right.

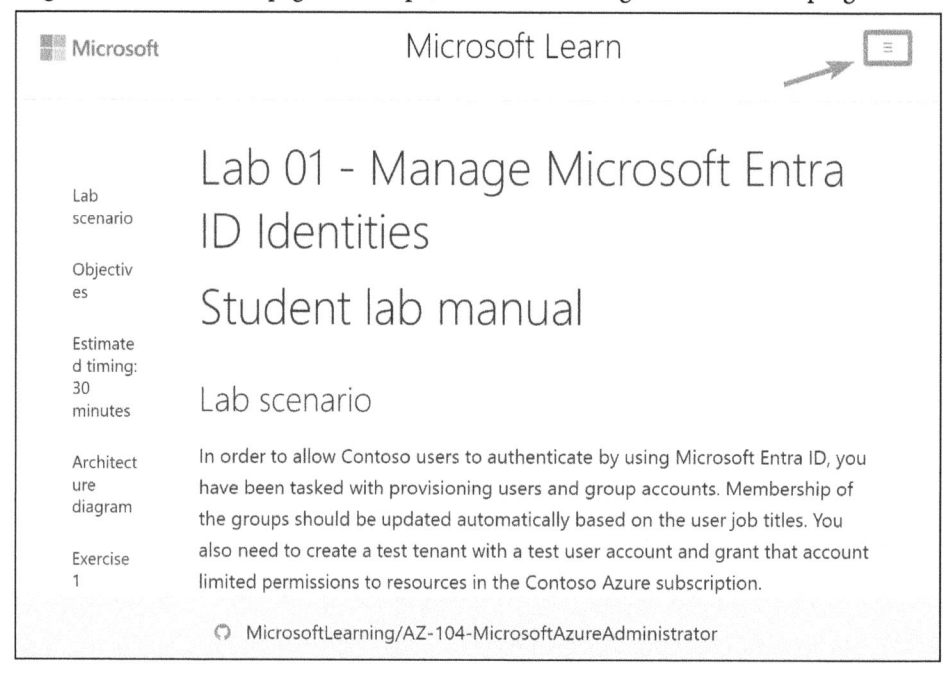

Figure 0.3: The Microsoft Lab GitHub repo home button

> **Note**
> Should you find it challenging to access the Microsoft GitHub repo, we have uploaded the files for the accompanying repo to assist you, which contains the files that are relevant at the time of writing. You can access this repo here: `https://github.com/PacktPublishing/AZ-104-Microsoft-Azure-Administrator-Certification-and-Beyond-3rd-Edition`.

Lab Files

This lab requires some additional files that you will need to download and access. You will use the GitHub repository that is provided in the next section.

> **Note**
> Even though the labs are on GitHub, a GitHub account is not required to access them.

Downloading and Extracting Files for Labs

Follow these steps to download and extract the required files:

1. Navigate to the following URL and download the archive folder (`.zip`): https://github.com/MicrosoftLearning/AZ-104-MicrosoftAzureAdministrator/archive/master.zip.
2. Depending on the browser you are using, you will likely be presented with different versions of the following dialog. Choose a location and save.
3. Right-click the ZIP file you downloaded and click `Extract All...` (on Windows systems):

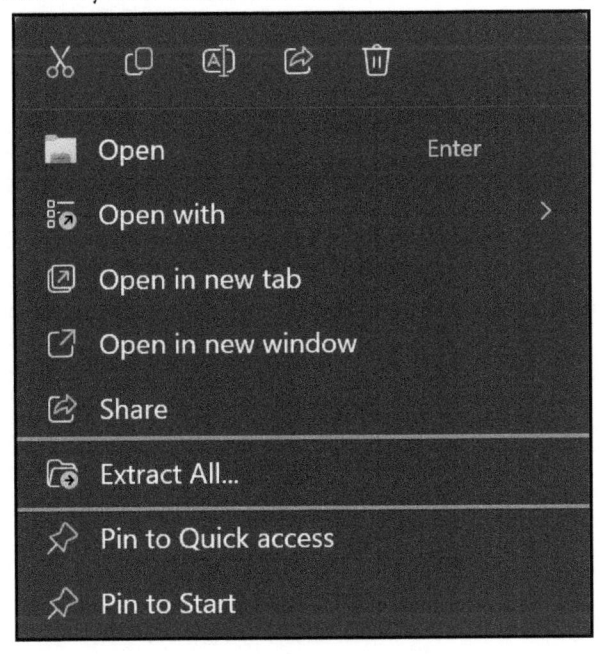

Figure 0.4: Extract All... (ZIP)

4. Navigate to your downloaded folder and follow instructions from labs when you require files that will be in that folder.

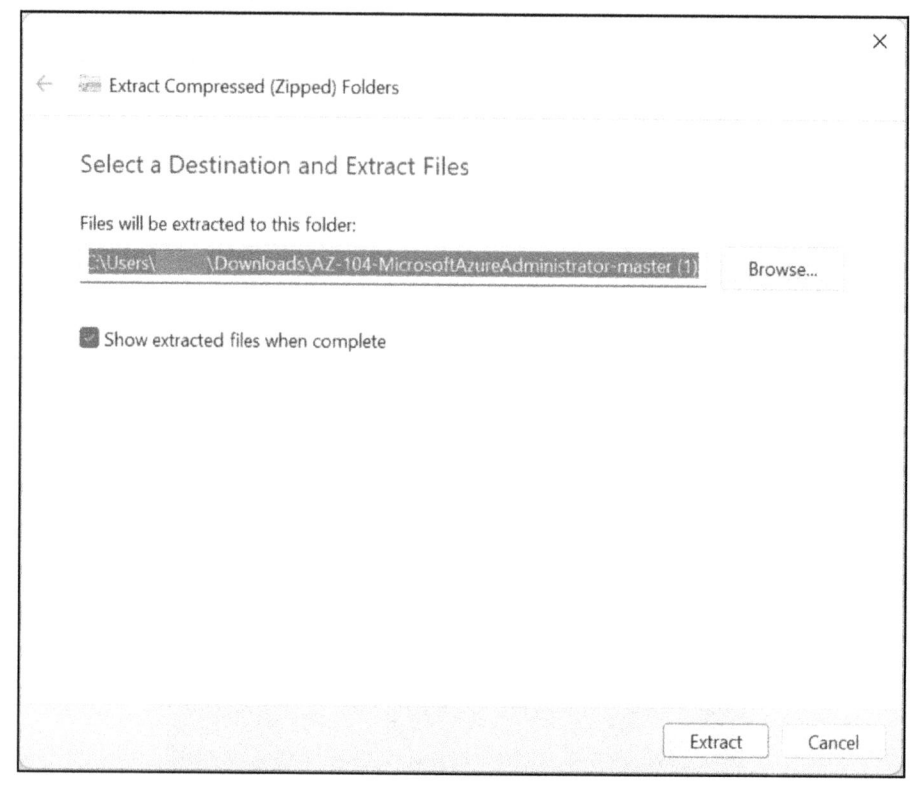

Figure 0.5: Extracting files on Windows 11

You have now downloaded all the files you need to perform the labs later in the chapter.

Share Your Thoughts

Once you've read *Exam Ref AZ-104 Microsoft Azure Administrator Certification and Beyond, Third Edition*, we'd love to hear your thoughts! Scan the QR code below to go straight to the Amazon review page for this book and share your feedback.

`https://packt.link/r/1805122851`

Your review is important to us and the tech community and will help us make sure we're delivering excellent quality content.

Download a free PDF copy of this book

Thanks for purchasing this book!

Do you like to read on the go but are unable to carry your print books everywhere?

Is your eBook purchase not compatible with the device of your choice?

Don't worry, now with every Packt book you get a DRM-free PDF version of that book at no cost.

Read anywhere, any place, on any device. Search, copy, and paste code from your favorite technical books directly into your application.

The perks don't stop there, you can get exclusive access to discounts, newsletters, and great free content in your inbox daily

Follow these simple steps to get the benefits:

1. Scan the QR code or visit the link below

https://packt.link/free-ebook/9781805122852

2. Submit your proof of purchase
3. That's it! We'll send your free PDF and other benefits to your email directly

1
Managing Microsoft Entra ID Objects

This book's first chapter focuses on learning how to manage **Microsoft Entra ID** (previously Azure AD) objects. Microsoft Entra is an identity service that natively integrates into Azure and several other Microsoft products. This chapter will teach you about Microsoft Entra ID and how to create and manage users and groups within it (including user and group properties). Additionally, you will look at Microsoft Entra ID's **Administrative Units** (**AUs**) and discover how to create them, alongside managing device settings and performing bulk user updates.

This chapter will cover the following topics:

- Microsoft Entra ID
- Creating Microsoft Entra ID Users and Groups
- Managing User and Group Properties

Making the Most Out of This Book – Your Certification and Beyond

This book and its accompanying online resources are designed to be a complete preparation tool for your **AZ-104 Exam**.

The book is written in a way that you can apply everything you've learned here even after your certification. The online practice resources that come with this book (*Figure 1.1*) are designed to improve your test-taking skills. They are loaded with timed mock exams, interactive flashcards, hands-on activities, and exam tips to help you work on your exam readiness from now till your test day.

> **Before You Proceed**
>
> To learn how to access these resources, head over to *Chapter 23, Accessing the Online Practice Resources*, at the end of the book.

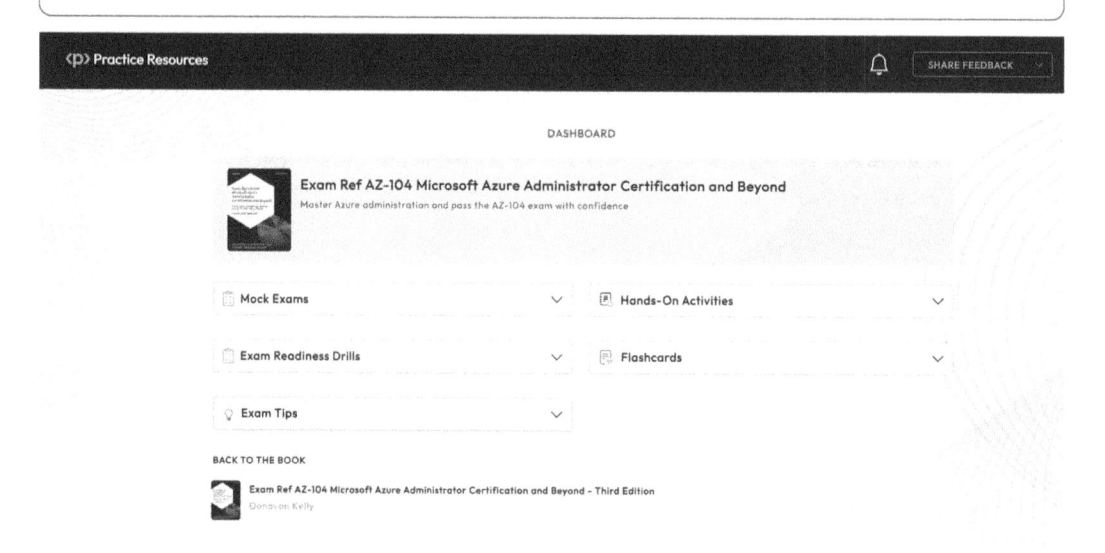

Figure 1.1: Dashboard interface of the online practice resources

Here are some tips on how to make the most out of this book so that you can clear your certification and retain your knowledge beyond your exam:

1. Read each section thoroughly.
2. **Make ample notes**: You can use your favorite online note-taking tool or use a physical notebook. The free online resources also give you access to an online version of this book. Click the BACK TO THE BOOK link from the Dashboard to access the book in **Packt Reader**. You can highlight specific sections of the book there.
3. **Chapter Review Questions**: At the end of this chapter, you'll find a link to review questions for this chapter. These are designed to test your knowledge of the chapter. Aim to score at least **75%** before moving on to the next chapter. You'll find detailed instructions on how to make the most of these questions at the end of this chapter in the *Exam Readiness Drill - Chapter Review Questions* section. That way, you're improving your exam-taking skills after each chapter, rather than at the end.

4. **Flashcards**: After you've gone through the book and scored **75%** more in each of the chapter review questions, start reviewing the online flashcards. They will help you memorize key concepts.
5. **Mock Exams**: Solve the mock exams that come with the book till your exam day. If you get some answers wrong, go back to the book and revisit the concepts you're weak in.
6. **Hands-On Activities**: After completing this book, complete the hands-on activities online to improve your practical experience.
7. **Exam Tips**: Review these from time to time to improve your exam readiness even further.

Technical Requirements

To follow along with the hands-on lessons, you will need access to the following:

- **Microsoft Entra ID** as a global administrator.
- Azure subscription with owner or contributor privileges. If you do not have access to one, students can enroll for a free account: `https://azure.microsoft.com/en-us/free/`.
- **PowerShell 5.1** or later installed on a Windows PC or PowerShell Core 6.x on other operating systems where labs can be practiced.
- For Windows users, you will need to install **.NET Framework 4.7.2** or later using the following link: `https://learn.microsoft.com/en-us/dotnet/framework/install`.
- Note that, occasionally, examples can only be followed on a PC or `https://shell.azure.com` (PowerShell 7.0.6 LTS or later is recommended).
- Install the `Az` PowerShell module, which can be done by running the following in an administrative PowerShell session:

    ```
    Set-ExecutionPolicy -ExecutionPolicy RemoteSigned -Scope
    CurrentUser
    Install-Module -Name Az -Scope CurrentUser -Repository PSGallery
    -Force
    ```

> **Note**
>
> The `AzureRM` module has been deprecated as of February 29, 2024. Should the `AzureRM` module be installed, remove it before the `Az` module is installed, which is the officially supported module. Installation of the `Az` module will fail should you try to run both. To read more details on this and how to migrate from the `AzureRM` module, follow this link: `https://learn.microsoft.com/en-us/powershell/azure/migrate-from-azurerm-to-az`.

Microsoft Entra P1 Trial

A Microsoft Entra P1/Microsoft E3 license is required for some of the sections. Luckily, there is also a free one-month trial for Microsoft Entra ID for Entra ID P1 and P2 at the following URL: https://www.microsoft.com/en-gb/security/business/microsoft-entra-pricing.

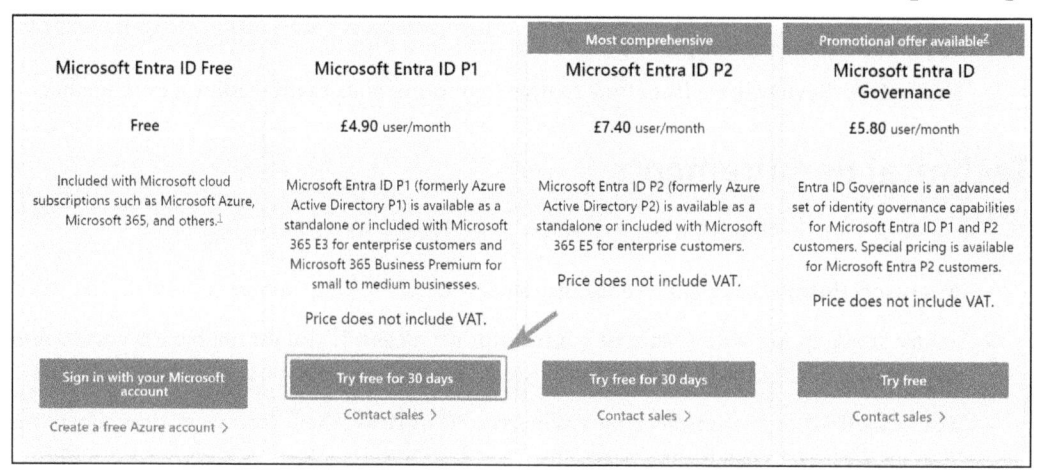

Microsoft Entra ID Free	Microsoft Entra ID P1	Microsoft Entra ID P2 (Most comprehensive)	Microsoft Entra ID Governance (Promotional offer available[2])
Free	£4.90 user/month	£7.40 user/month	£5.80 user/month
Included with Microsoft cloud subscriptions such as Microsoft Azure, Microsoft 365, and others.[1]	Microsoft Entra ID P1 (formerly Azure Active Directory P1) is available as a standalone or included with Microsoft 365 E3 for enterprise customers and Microsoft 365 Business Premium for small to medium businesses. Price does not include VAT.	Microsoft Entra ID P2 (formerly Azure Active Directory P2) is available as a standalone or included with Microsoft 365 E5 for enterprise customers. Price does not include VAT.	Entra ID Governance is an advanced set of identity governance capabilities for Microsoft Entra ID P1 and P2 customers. Special pricing is available for Microsoft Entra P2 customers. Price does not include VAT.
Sign in with your Microsoft account	Try free for 30 days	Try free for 30 days	Try free
Create a free Azure account >	Contact sales >	Contact sales >	Contact sales >

Figure 1.2: Signing up for an Entra trial

For those who want to attempt the exercises using the Microsoft E3 license, visit this URL: https://www.microsoft.com/en-us/security/business/microsoft-entra-pricing.

Navigate to the preceding chosen link and activate the trial.

> **Note**
> Trying to get the trial without being signed into a Microsoft account may cause unexpected behavior, such as the trial notifying you that you are signed into a work account that is managed by your organization. Simply signing in solved the problem for us at the time of writing.

When activating either of the trials, you will be greeted by the following screen:

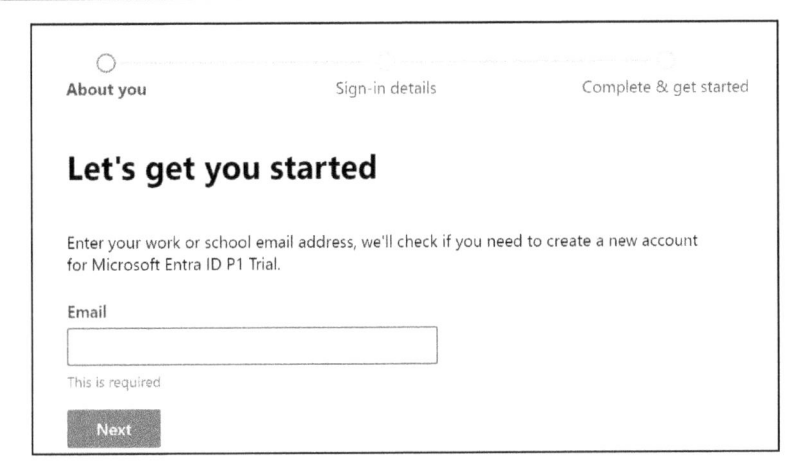

Figure 1.3: Trial signup

Once you have signed up for a trial, you are ready to start with the lessons in this chapter.

Microsoft Entra ID

Microsoft Entra ID, previously named **Azure Active Directory** (**AAD**), is a cloud-based **Identity and Access Management** (**IAM**) service provided by Microsoft and is an integral part of the Azure cloud platform. It allows organizations to manage user accounts and access resources, both on-premises and in the cloud. Microsoft Entra ID provides a centralized location for managing user authentication and authorization across multiple applications, platforms, and devices.

Microsoft Entra ID is designed to integrate with other Microsoft services such as Office 365, Azure, and Dynamics 365, as well as with third-party cloud services and applications. It provides a variety of features for IAM, such as user and group management, application management, device management, identity protection, single sign-on, and multi-factor authentication.

Microsoft Entra ID also provides security and compliance features such as Conditional Access policies, identity protection, threat intelligence, and auditing and reporting capabilities. This makes it a crucial component of many organization's security and compliance strategies.

Next, you will learn a bit more about some of the objects you can find in Microsoft Entra ID.

Users, Groups, and Administrative Units

Microsoft Entra ID is a cloud-based IAM solution that provides a range of features and tools for managing users, groups, and administrative units. Understanding these fundamental concepts is essential for effectively managing user accounts and maintaining control over access to company resources. In the following sections, you will explore what these objects are, and in the sections that follow, you will find exercises on how to effectively utilize them within your organization. The following diagram illustrates some common objects used in Entra ID.

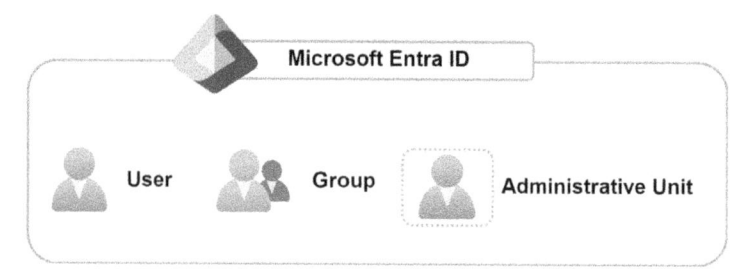

Figure 1.4: Microsoft Entra ID objects

Users

In Microsoft Entra, a user is an identity that is used to authenticate and authorize access to resources in an organization's environment. Users can be employees, contractors, partners, or customers who require access to applications and services that are secured by Microsoft Entra ID. Each user has a unique identity, which is represented by a user account. A user account contains information such as the user's name, email address, and other attributes that are used to identify and manage the user's access to resources. The user account can also be used to assign licenses, roles, and group memberships, determining what resources the user can access and what actions they can perform.

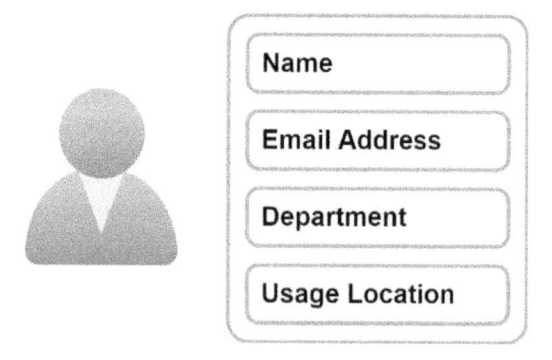

Figure 1.5: Microsoft Entra ID – user properties

Groups

Microsoft Entra groups are a powerful feature within Microsoft's cloud-based IAM service. These groups allow organizations to organize users, devices, and resources into logical units to simplify and streamline access management. The benefits of Microsoft Entra groups include the following:

- **Centralized management**: Easily manage access to resources and permissions for multiple users in one place, reducing administrative overhead
- **Role-Based Access Control (RBAC)**: Assign roles and permissions to groups instead of individual users, enabling efficient and secure access management
- **Dynamic group membership**: Automatically update group membership based on user attributes, ensuring the right users have access to the resources they need
- **Collaboration**: Enhance collaboration by granting access to shared resources, such as Microsoft 365 groups, SharePoint sites, and Teams
- **Reduced security risks**: Minimize the risk of unauthorized access by regularly reviewing and managing group memberships

Microsoft Entra groups serve as an efficient tool for handling users who need identical access levels and permissions for various resources, including restricted applications and services. By organizing users into logical groups, administrators can streamline access control management. Rather than granting special permissions to each user separately, a group can be created to apply the permissions collectively to all its members. For instance, to provide a group of users access to a specific resource, permissions can be assigned to the group, eliminating the need to assign permissions individually.

There are two main group types, as follows:

- **Security groups**: These groups serve the same function as traditional on-premises groups, which is to secure objects within a directory. In this case, it is to secure objects within Microsoft Entra.
- **Microsoft 365 groups**: These groups are used to provide a group of people access to a collection of shared resources that is not limited to Microsoft Entra ID but also includes shared mailboxes, calendars, SharePoint libraries, and other Microsoft 365-related services.

Security groups are used as container units to group users or devices together. There are three main membership types for security groups:

- **Assigned**: This is where you manually assign users to a group
- **Dynamic user**: This is where you can specify parameters to automatically group users – for example, grouping all users who have the same job title
- **Dynamic device**: This is where you can specify parameters to automatically group devices –for example, grouping all devices that have the same operating system version

The following diagram depicts a group structure that contains users:

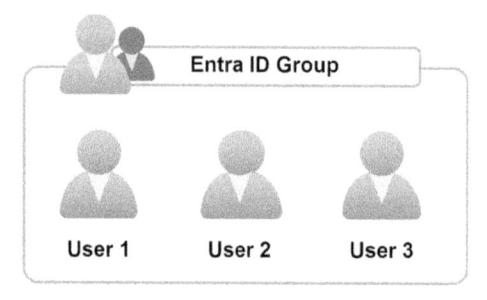

Figure 1.6: Microsoft Entra ID – a group depiction

Next, you will learn what AUs are.

AUs

Microsoft Entra AUs are a feature that allows organizations to group users and resources in logical containers, based on administrative or geographic boundaries. AUs enable you to delegate administrative control over specific subsets of users and resources to different AUs, based on role or location. For example, a global organization can use AUs to delegate control of users and resources to administrators, based on regions or departments. This helps ensure that each AU has control over only the resources it needs, without interfering with other units. AUs provide a simple and effective way to manage the complexity of large organizations and help organizations maintain control over their resources, while reducing administrative overhead.

The following roles can be assigned within an AU:

- Authentication administrator
- Groups administrator
- Help desk administrator
- License administrator
- Password administrator
- User administrator

> **Note**
> Groups can be added to an AU as an object. This means that any user within a group is not automatically part of the AU, and delegated permissions do not transfer to them by being a member of the group.

The easiest way to illustrate this concept is through the following scenario. A company called Fictitious Inc. is a worldwide organization with users across 11 countries. Fictitious Inc. has decided that each country is responsible for its own users from an administrative point of view. That is where AUs come in handy. With AUs, Fictitious Inc. can group users per country and assign administrators that only have control over these users, and it cannot administrate users in other countries.

The following diagram displays a high-level overview of how AUs work in the same tenant across different departments. The following example is based on different regions:

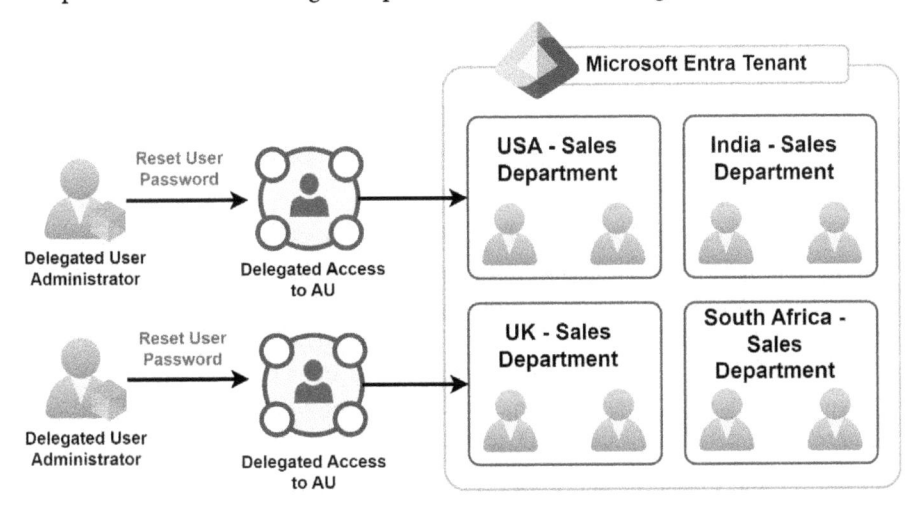

Figure 1.7: An AU overview displaying the separation of users

Now that you are aware of the basic Microsoft Entra ID objects, we will unpack some of the other Microsoft Entra ID concepts you should be familiar with.

Common Microsoft Entra ID Concepts

To fully utilize Microsoft Entra in your organization's setup, it is important to have a clear understanding of the key components and concepts of the service. The following list outlines these components and how they work together to support Microsoft Entra ID features:

- **Identity**: An Azure identity represents an individual or entity that can interact with Azure resources. It is used for authentication, authorization, administration, and auditing purposes, ensuring secure access to resources within an Azure environment. Azure identities can be associated with users, applications, or services.

- **Account**: An account in the context of Microsoft Entra typically refers to a user account. A user account is an individual identity associated with a person within an organization or an external partner. Each account contains a unique username, such as an email address, and is authenticated against the tenant's directory. Accounts are used to grant access to applications, resources, and services within the organization. User accounts can also have different permission levels, allowing the delegation of various administrative tasks, such as managing subscriptions and billing.

- **Microsoft Entra ID account**: An Entra ID account is a specific type of user account in Microsoft Entra that represents a user's identity across various applications and services. Entra ID accounts enable users to access both internal and external resources with **single sign-on** (**SSO**) capabilities, streamlining the login process and reducing the need to remember multiple passwords. These accounts can be managed centrally, allowing for easy control of access permissions and facilitating the enforcement of organizational security policies.

- **Microsoft Entra tenant**: A Microsoft Entra tenant represents a single organization's instance of Microsoft Entra ID, containing all relevant data, such as users, groups, devices, and application registrations. This tenant serves as both an administrative and security boundary, helping the organization manage and restrict access to various resources, applications, and services. Each tenant is identified by a unique ID (tenant ID) and a domain name (e.g., `example.onmicrosoft.com`). It is created when an organization signs up for Azure or other Microsoft cloud services, such as Microsoft 365 or Dynamics 365.

- **Microsoft Entra directory**: While the terms **Microsoft Entra directory** and **Microsoft Entra tenant** are often used interchangeably, the directory is essentially a logical container within a tenant. It organizes and stores resources and objects related to IAM, including users, groups, applications, devices, and other directory objects. In essence, the directory functions like a catalog or database of identities and resources associated with an organization's tenant. Notably, a Microsoft Entra tenant comprises a single directory.

- **Azure subscription**: An Azure subscription is a logical entity used to provision and manage Azure resources. It is associated with an Azure account and provides access to Azure services, based on a specific pricing tier or service agreement. Subscriptions help organizations manage costs, monitor usage, and organize resources by projects, departments, or environments.

The following diagram highlights the relationship between the Microsoft Entra tenant, directory, subscriptions, and resource groups:

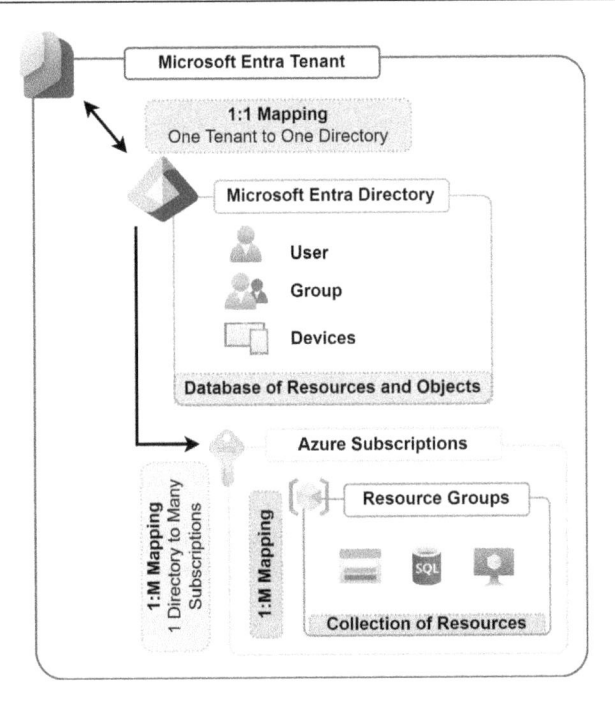

Figure 1.8: The Microsoft Entra ID structure

Now that you understand the core principles behind Microsoft Entra ID concepts and understand what we refer to when these concepts come up, we will move on to investigating another important topic. You will learn about the differences between Microsoft Entra ID and Active Directory.

Microsoft Entra ID versus Active Directory (On-Premises)

In this topic, you will learn about the differences between Microsoft Entra ID and **Active Directory Domain Services** (**AD DS**). We will start by looking at what AD DS is and then explore the key differences between the two services.

AD DS

AD DS is a Windows Server-based service that provides centralized authentication and authorization for Windows-based computers. It is designed to handle a variety of networked resources, such as computers, printers, and applications in a Windows domain. AD DS also offers features such as Group Policy management, domain trust relationships, and directory replication. Some feature comparisons are as follows:

- **Directory services versus identity solution**: AD DS is primarily a directory service designed for on-premises environments, whereas Microsoft Entra ID is a cloud-based full IAM solution that can also be used to manage on-premises resources. Microsoft Entra ID has been optimized for internet-based applications with strong identity management capabilities.

- **Communication protocols**: AD DS uses the Kerberos protocol for authentication, while Microsoft Entra ID supports multiple authentication protocols, including **Security Assertion Markup Language (SAML)**, OAuth, and OpenID Connect, that largely rely on HTTP and HTTPS-based communication.

- **Federation**: Microsoft Entra ID supports federation with other identity providers, enabling users to authenticate using credentials from third-party services, whereas AD DS does not support federation.

- **Structure**: AD DS has a hierarchical structure that consists of domains, trees, forests, OUs, and Group Policy, while Microsoft Entra ID has a flat structure that is organized around tenants.

- **Managed services**: With AD DS, you are responsible for managing the infrastructure and maintaining the servers that host the service. With Microsoft Entra ID, Microsoft manages the infrastructure, and you only need to manage user accounts, groups, and access policies.

Now that you understand the differences between Microsoft Entra ID and AD DS, you will learn about some of the administration activities you may need to perform that the service offers you.

Administration

Microsoft Entra ID provides a wide range of administration functions to manage user accounts and access resources within organizations. With Entra ID, administrators can create, manage, and delete user accounts, assign roles and permissions, manage groups, and register applications. In addition, Microsoft Entra ID offers device management capabilities, identity protection, SSO, and auditing and reporting features. Here are some of the common functions that administrators can expect to use in Entra:

- **User and group management**: Create and manage user accounts, assign roles and permissions, and manage groups to simplify access management

- **Application management**: Register applications in Entra ID and manage their access to user accounts and resources

- **Device management**: Manage devices registered in Entra ID and enforce policies on devices, such as requiring encryption or disabling specific features

- **Identity protection**: Monitor for suspicious activity, set policies to protect user accounts from security threats, and enforce multi-factor authentication

- **SSO**: Enabling SSO allows users to use their current set of credentials in Entra ID to access multiple applications and services

- **Auditing and reporting**: Generate reports on user activity, audit logs, and security events to monitor usage and identify potential security issues

- **Policies**: Control access to resources based on specific conditions or scenarios, using Conditional Access policies

By using Microsoft Entra ID's administration functions, administrators can effectively manage access to resources and enhance security within their organization.

Integration

Integration with Microsoft Entra ID allows organizations to manage access to resources and applications from a centralized platform. Microsoft Entra ID provides a cloud-based IAM solution that offers a range of features to help organizations secure their digital assets. In addition to supporting native integration with Microsoft services, Microsoft Entra ID can also integrate with other identity providers, such as Google and Facebook, to enable social sign-in and identity federation. There are several integration types, including **Business-to-Consumer (B2C)** and **Business-to-Business (B2B)**, that enable organizations to extend their IAM capabilities beyond their traditional boundaries. With AAD, organizations can streamline authentication and authorization to cloud-based applications and resources, making it easier for users to access the resources they need from anywhere, on any device.

B2C

Microsoft Entra ID supports a range of integration types, including B2C, which allows organizations to provide their customers with secure access to applications and resources. **Azure Active Directory B2C (Azure AD B2C)** is a cloud-based IAM service, specifically designed to handle customer-facing applications. It enables organizations to securely manage user identities, authenticate users, and provide SSO capabilities for their applications, websites, and mobile apps. With Azure AD B2C, organizations can provide a seamless customer experience across multiple applications and services, while maintaining control over user access and data. Azure AD B2C can be configured through the Azure portal, and developers can integrate it into their applications using various authentication protocols and libraries. You can read more here: https://learn.microsoft.com/en-us/azure/active-directory-b2c/overview.

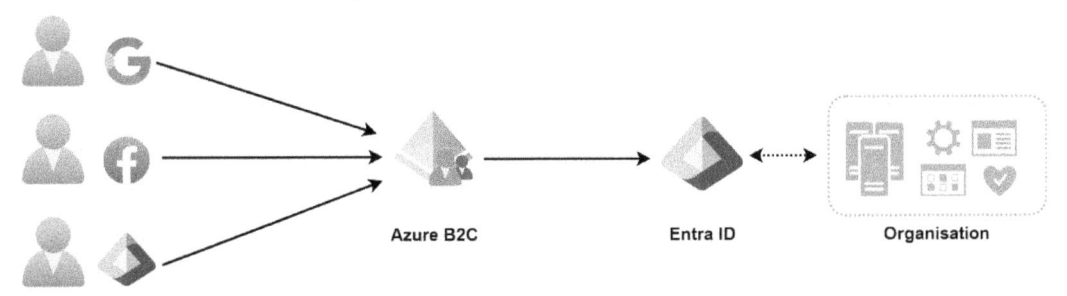

Figure 1.9: External identities – Azure B2C

B2B

Microsoft Entra B2B collaboration is a feature within Microsoft Entra External ID that allows organizations to invite external users to collaborate securely with their organization. This feature enables external users to access an organization's applications and services without compromising the security of its data. Microsoft Entra provides a range of controls for managing collaboration with external users, including customized invitations, self-service sign-up, and access monitoring. With Microsoft Entra B2B, organizations can expand their reach and collaborate effectively with external partners and clients.

> **Note**
>
> To learn more about Microsoft Entra B2B collaboration, visit the Microsoft Learn website for an Azure Entra B2B collaboration overview: `https://learn.microsoft.com/en-us/entra/external-id/what-is-b2b`.

The following diagram illustrates the flow for B2B with external identity integration:

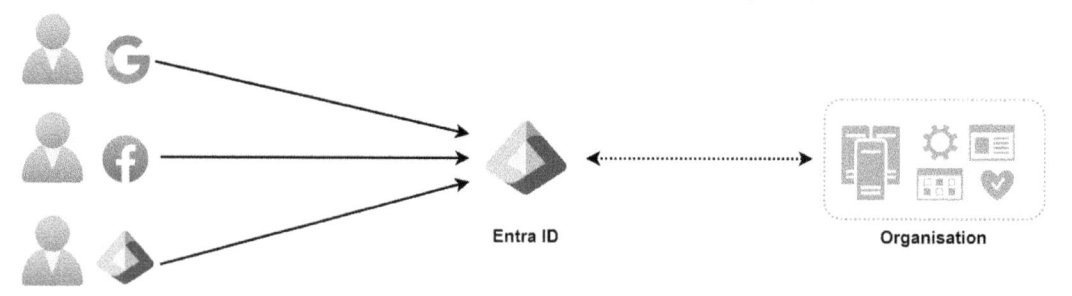

Figure 1.10: External identities – Azure AD B2B

> **Note**
>
> The following website URL provides further details from Microsoft should you want to read about Entra ID in more detail: `https://learn.microsoft.com/en-us/entra/identity/`.
>
> The following URL provides information about the Microsoft Entra name changes from Azure AD, as well as items that are not changing: `https://learn.microsoft.com/en-us/entra/fundamentals/new-name`.

Next, we will dive into some tasks relating to Microsoft Entra ID that you will perform as part of your administrative function.

Creating Users and Groups

Microsoft Entra ID offers a directory and identity management solution within the cloud. It offers traditional username and password identity management, alongside roles and permission management. On top of that, it offers more enterprise-grade solutions, such as **Multi-Factor Authentication** (**MFA**), application monitoring, solution monitoring, and alerting.

Microsoft Entra ID can also be easily integrated with your on-premises Active Directory to create a hybrid infrastructure.

In the section that follows, you will explore the actions involved in creating a Microsoft Entra ID user account object.

Creating Users in Microsoft Entra ID

You will begin by creating a couple of users in your Microsoft Entra ID directory from the Azure portal. To do this, perform the following steps:

1. Navigate to the Azure portal by opening a web browser and browsing to `https://portal.azure.com`.
2. From the left-hand hamburger menu or the main search bar, select `Microsoft Entra ID`.
3. Under the `Manage` context of Microsoft Entra ID from the left-hand menu, click `Users`.
4. From the left menu, click `All users`. Then, select the `+ New user` drop-down option from the top-level menu and click `Create new user`, as follows:

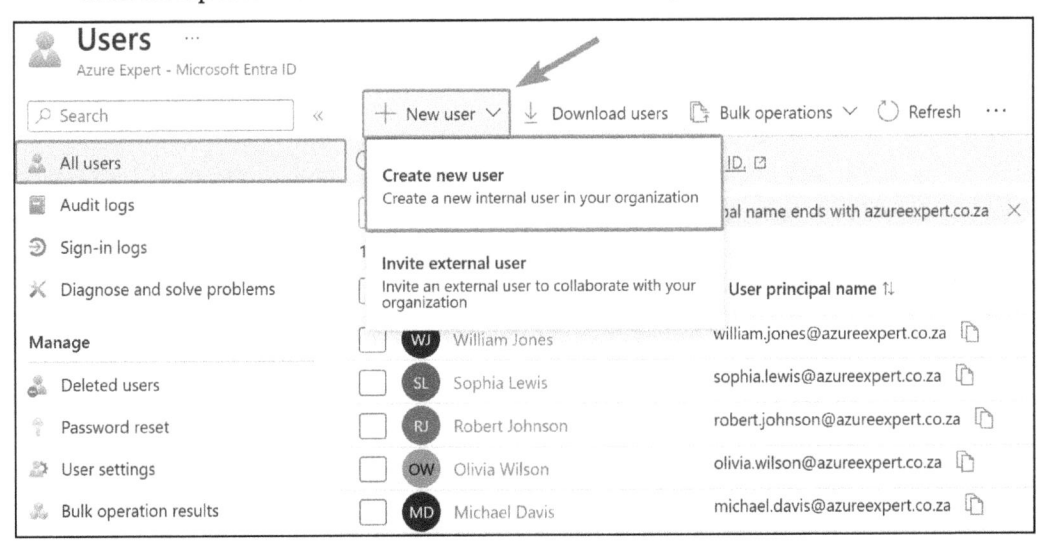

Figure 1.11: The Microsoft Entra ID Users blade

5. You are going to create three users. Add the values that are shown in the following screenshot:

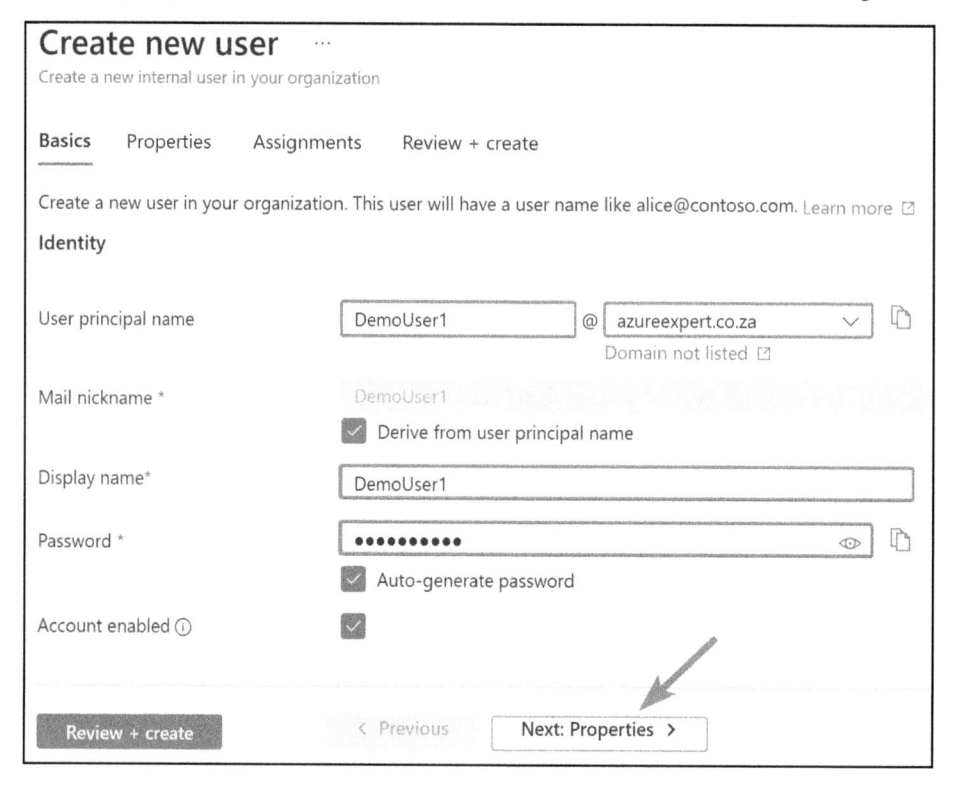

Figure 1.12: Microsoft Entra ID – creating a user identity

- `User principal name`: DemoUser1.
- `Domain suffix`: Select your domain name, which has been configured, and add this to the end of the username. The default is usually an `onmicrosoft.com` domain, but in my case, I have assigned a custom domain name, called `azureexpert.co.za`; you should replace this with your assigned domain name.
- `Mail nickname`: DemoUser1 (derived from the user principal name).
- `Display name`: DemoUser1.
- For the `Password` section, you can choose to either allow Azure to auto-generate the password or create your own.

6. Click `Next: Properties >` at the bottom of the window to start defining the properties of the user account you are creating.

7. Enter the following in the `Identity` section on the `Properties` tab:

- First name: Demo.
- Last name: User1.
- User type: Member. Two options can be chosen from here. Member refers to an association with someone who works within your organization while the guest type does not. There are some fundamental differences between these two options as well, related to permissions that would vary where guest accounts are more restrictive by nature.

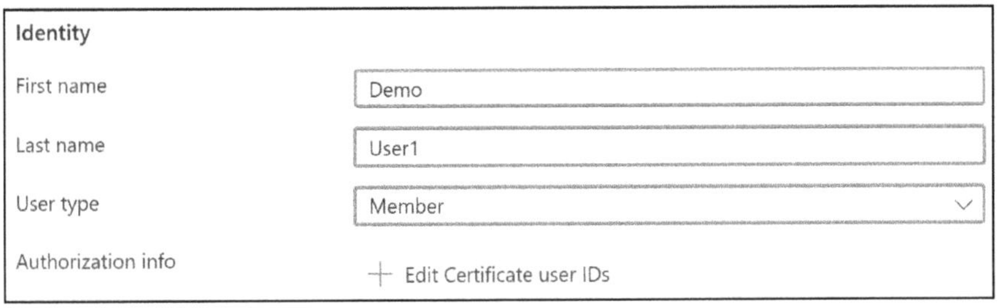

Figure 1.13: Microsoft Entra ID – creating a user identity

8. Enter the following in the Job Information section on the Properties tab:

- Job title: Azure Administrator
- Company name: Azure Expert
- Department: IT
- Employee ID: IT0035 (you can make up what you want here)
- Employee Type: Permanent
- Employee hire date: Sun Jan 01 2023
- Office Location: South Africa

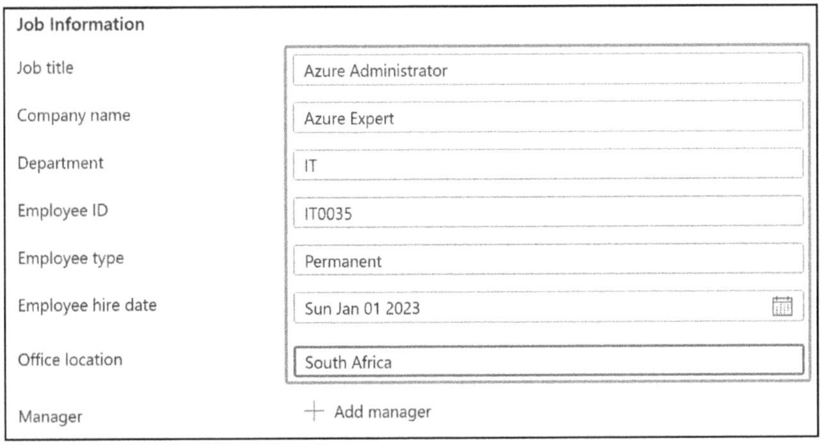

Figure 1.14: Microsoft Entra ID – creating a user – Job Information

Managing Microsoft Entra ID Objects

> **Note**
> The username is the identifier that the user enters to sign into Microsoft Entra ID. In the `First name` section, I have chosen `Demo`, and in the `Last` name section, I have added `User1`. Therefore, the `User` name value, in my case, will be `DemoUser1@azureexpert.co.za`.

9. Enter the following in the `Contact Information` section on the `Properties` tab:

    - `Street address:` 1 Fake Street
    - `City:` Some City
    - `State or province:` This State
    - `ZIP or postal code:` 10101
    - `Country or region:` South Africa
    - `Business phone:` 101010101
    - `Mobile phone:` 10101010111
    - `Email:` demouser1@azureexpert.co.za (replace with your domain name)

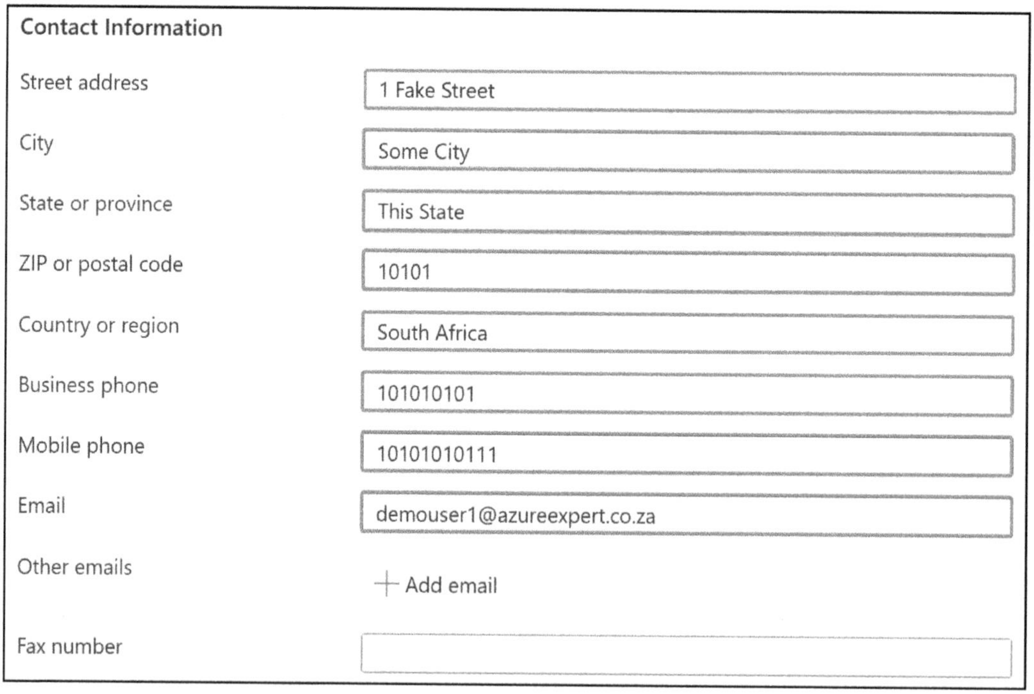

Contact Information	
Street address	1 Fake Street
City	Some City
State or province	This State
ZIP or postal code	10101
Country or region	South Africa
Business phone	101010101
Mobile phone	10101010111
Email	demouser1@azureexpert.co.za
Other emails	+ Add email
Fax number	

Figure 1.15: Microsoft Entra ID – creating a user – Contact Information

10. Enter the following for the `Parental controls` section under the `Properties` tab:
    - `Age group:` Adult
    - `Consent provided for minor:` Not required

Parental controls	
Age group	Adult
Consent provided for minor	Not required

Figure 1.16: Microsoft Entra ID – creating a user – Parental controls

11. Enter the following in the `Settings` section, and then click `Next: Assignments >`:
    - `Usage location:` South Africa

Settings	
Usage location	South Africa

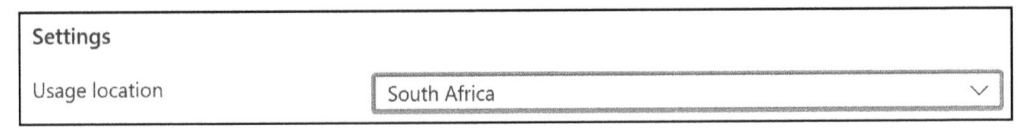

Figure 1.17: Microsoft Entra ID – creating a user – Settings

12. You can leave the `Assignments` section with the default settings for now, meaning that you don't add the created user to any AUs or groups; you will also not assign any roles.

Basics	Properties	**Assignments**	Review + create

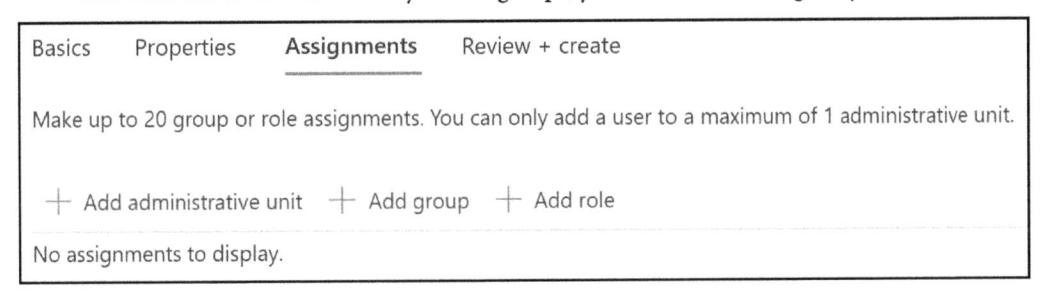

Make up to 20 group or role assignments. You can only add a user to a maximum of 1 administrative unit.

+ Add administrative unit   + Add group   + Add role

No assignments to display.

Figure 1.18: Microsoft Entra ID – creating a user – Assignments

13. At the bottom of the screen, click `Review + create`. Then, click on `Create`.
14. Repeat these steps to create two more users – `DemoUser2` and `DemoUser3`.

Now that you have created users in your Microsoft Entra ID directory, you can add them to a group, which you will do in the next section.

Creating Groups in Microsoft Entra ID

In this exercise, you are going to create a **dynamic** group using the Azure portal that contains **all Azure admins**. The group will automatically add users based on the dynamic query you populate.

To create and manage groups in Microsoft Entra ID in the Azure portal, you need to perform the following steps:

1. Navigate to the Azure portal by opening a web browser and browsing to `https://portal.azure.com`.
2. From the left-hand hamburger menu, select `Microsoft Entra ID`.
3. Under the `Manage` context of the Microsoft Entra ID blade in the left-hand menu, select `Groups`.
4. Select `All groups` from the left management pane, and then select the `New group` option from the top-level menu, as follows:

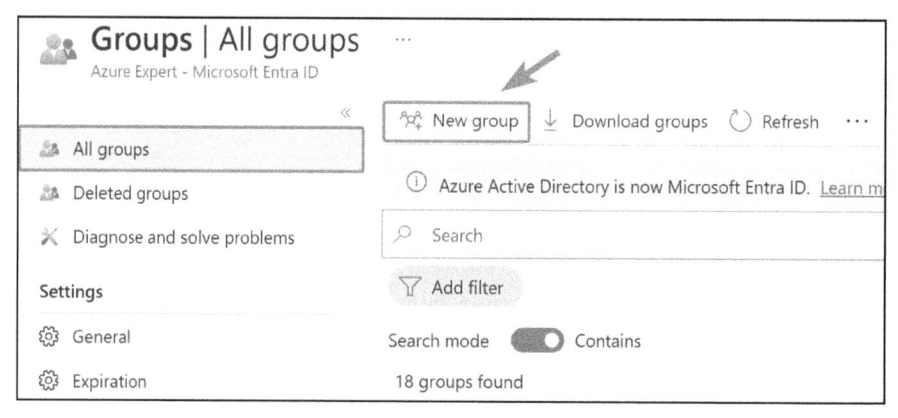

Figure 1.19: Creating a new Microsoft Entra ID group

5. Enter the following values to create the new group:

   - Group type: `Security`
   - Group name: `Azure Admins`
   - Group description: `Dynamic group for all Azure Admins`
   - Microsoft Entra roles can be assigned to the group: `No`
   - Membership type: `Dynamic User`
   - Owners: `No owners selected` (the default value)
   - Dynamic user members: Click `Add dynamic query`

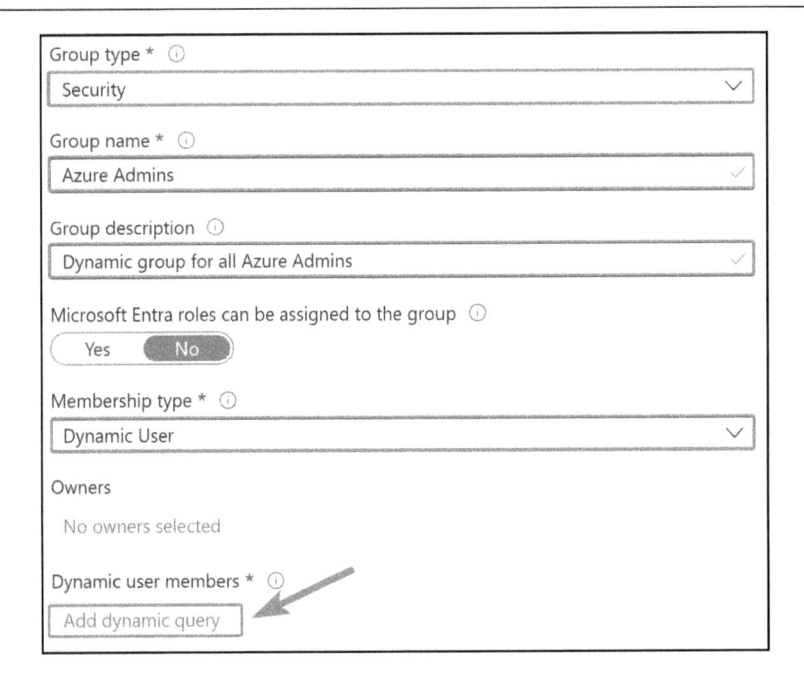

Figure 1.20: Configuring a new group

6. For the Dynamic Query rule, click the Property dropdown and select jobTitle. Click the Operator dropdown and select Equals. Finally, enter Azure Administrator in the Value textbox, and then click Save, as shown in the following screenshot:

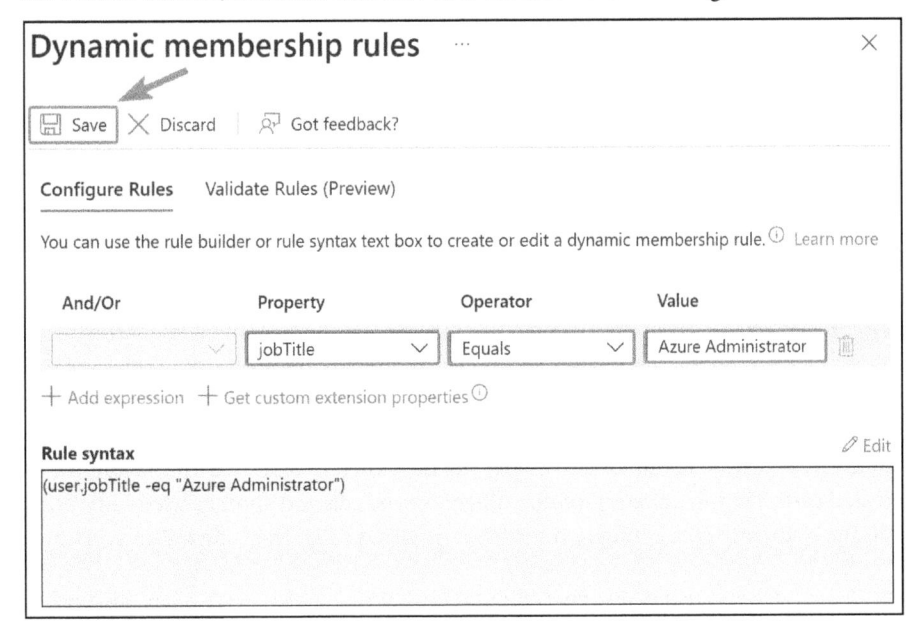

Figure 1.21: A group dynamic query

7. On the New Group blade, click Create.

> **Note**
> Remember that when using dynamic groups, a Microsoft Entra P1 license needs to be assigned to the user.

8. Now that you have created the group, replication takes around five minutes. Refresh the Azure web page and navigate back to the Groups blade from Microsoft Entra ID. Click on the group name (the blue text) for the group you just created to open its properties.

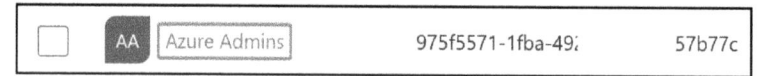

| | AA | Azure Admins | 975f5571-1fba-49; | 57b77c |

Figure 1.22: Opening the Azure Admins group

9. From the left-hand menu pane, under the Manage section, click Members. The users will appear as members of the Azure Admins group that you just created:

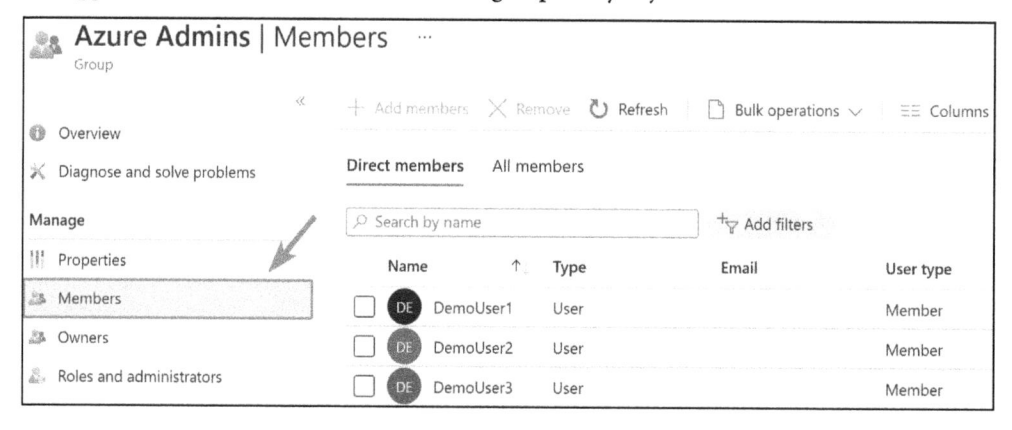

Figure 1.23: The Azure Admins group with dynamically populated users

10. In some circumstances, you may not see your group dynamically adding your users as quickly as expected. You may want to validate the rules you have implemented to confirm that they are set up correctly. To do this, navigate to the Azure Admins group properties screen, as seen in the preceding figure, and click on Dynamic membership rules from the left-hand menu pane under the Manage context menu. Click on the Validate Rules (Preview) tab from the top tab menu for this blade, and then click + Add users to add the users you created earlier in this chapter; for due diligence, you can add another user without the Azure administrator attribute configured for the job title. Then, click Validate.

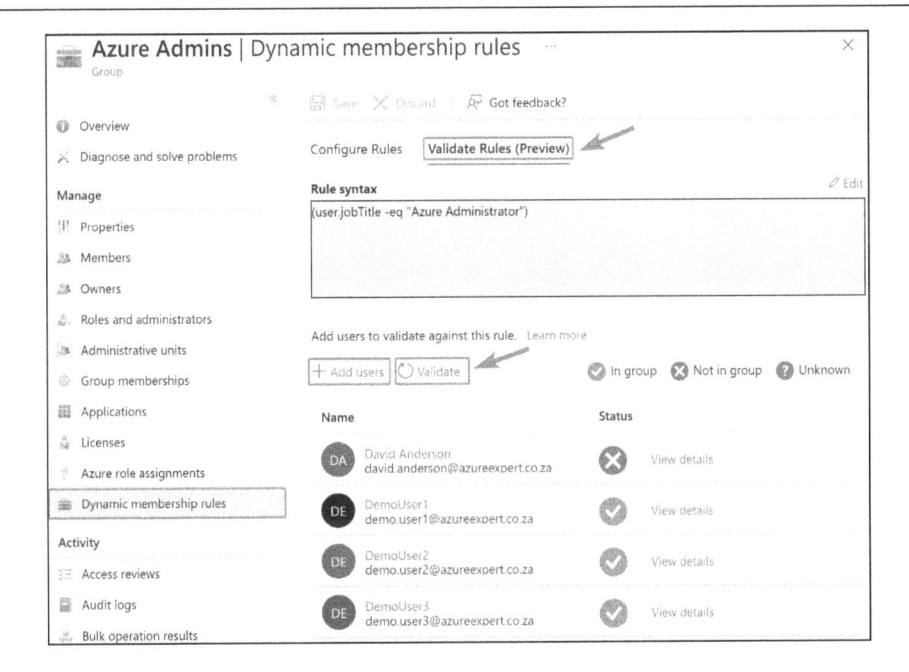

Figure 1.24: Validating the dynamic membership rules

11. Note that the green ticks indicate users who abide by the defined rule and are added to the group, whereas the red crosses indicate users who do not. You have now successfully validated the membership rule you created and confirmed that the logic should work as expected. Note that at the time of writing, this feature is still in preview.

In this section, you explored Microsoft Entra ID users and groups and created a few accounts. You also created a dynamic membership group to include users via dynamic membership rules.

> **Note**
>
> You are encouraged to read further at the following links, which are based on Microsoft Entra ID fundamentals such as adding users, assigning RBAC roles, creating groups, and also creating dynamic groups:
>
> `https://learn.microsoft.com/en-us/entra/fundamentals/add-users`
>
> `https://learn.microsoft.com/en-us/entra/fundamentals/add-custom-domain`
>
> `https://learn.microsoft.com/en-us/entra/fundamentals/how-to-manage-user-profile-info`
>
> `https://learn.microsoft.com/en-us/entra/fundamentals/how-subscriptions-associated-directory`
>
> `https://learn.microsoft.com/en-us/entra/identity/users/groups-create-rule`
>
> `https://learn.microsoft.com/en-us/entra/identity/users/groups-dynamic-membership`

Next, we are going to look at Microsoft Entra ID AUs – specifically, where they can be used and how to create them.

Creating Microsoft Entra ID AUs

Microsoft Entra ID AUs are used in scenarios where granular administrative control is required. AUs enable you to delegate administrative control over specific subsets of users and resources to different administrative units, based on role or location.

AUs have the following prerequisites:

- A **Microsoft Entra ID P1 license** is required for each AU administrator
- A **Microsoft Entra ID Free license** is required for AU members
- A privileged role administrator or global administrator is required for configuration

> **Note**
> AUs can be created via the Azure portal or PowerShell.

Next, you will create an AU via the Azure portal:

1. Navigate to the Azure portal by opening a web browser and browsing to https://portal.azure.com.
2. From the left-hand hamburger menu or the main search bar, select Microsoft Entra ID.
3. Under the Manage settings area from the left-hand menu, select Administrative units, and then click on + Add.

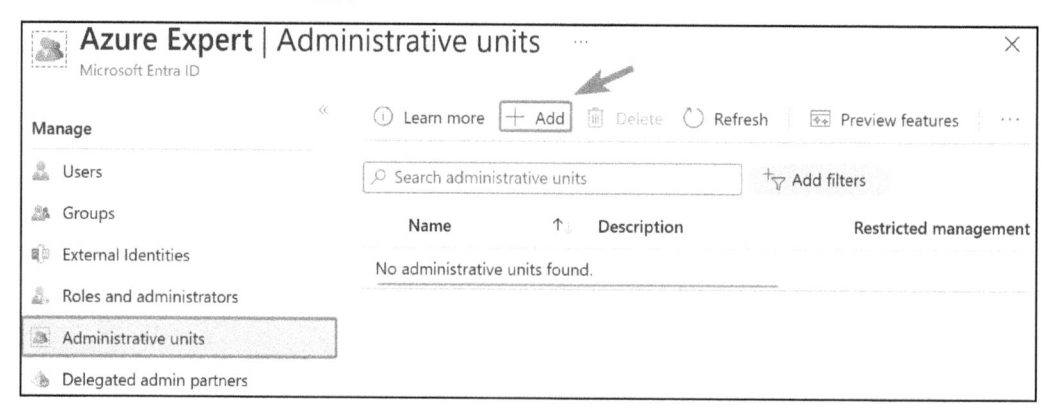

Figure 1.25: The Administrative units management blade

4. Enter a name for the group. For this exercise, you can use `South Africa Users` and select whatever region you prefer. In the `Description` field, it is best practice to add a brief description of what this AU is going to be used for; for this exercise, use the description `All South African Users`, which you can later modify to suit the region you choose. Leave the default setting for `Restricted management administrative unit` to No. You can then click either the `Next: Assign roles >` button at the bottom of the window or the `Assign roles` tab at the top.

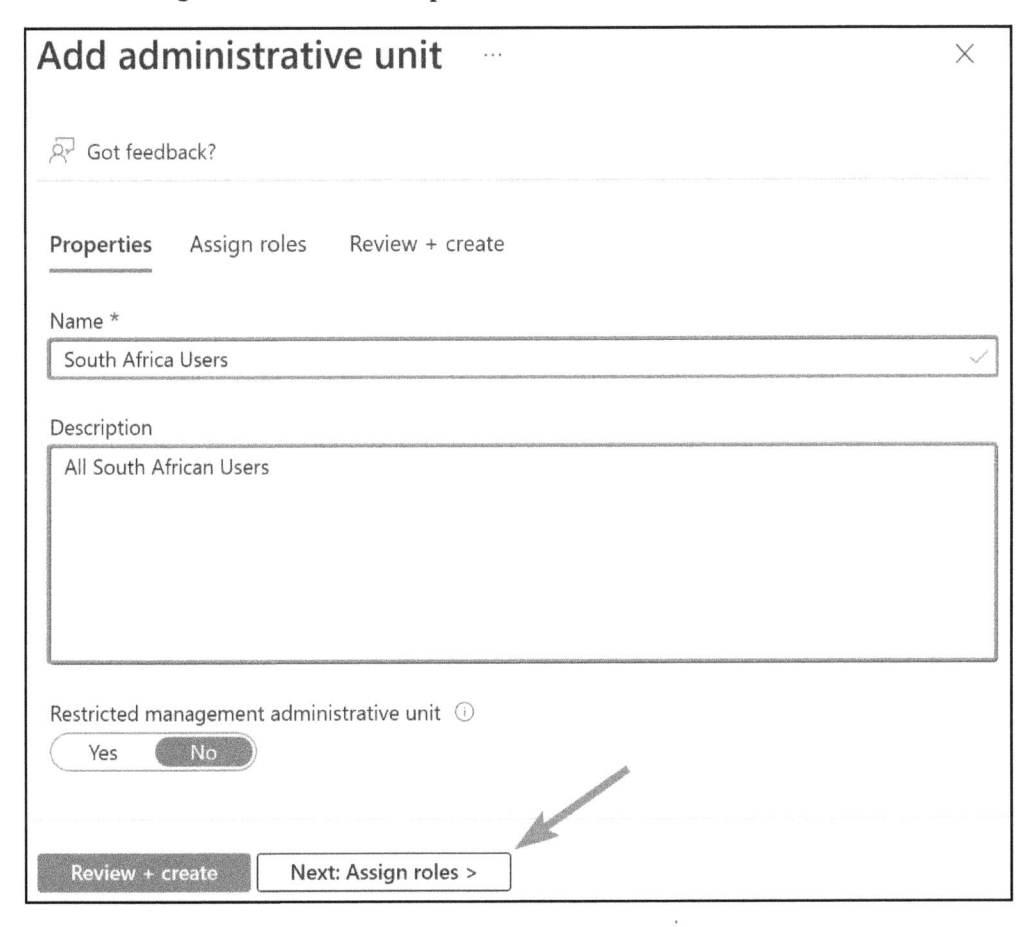

Figure 1.26: The properties blade for an AU

5. Next, on the `Assign roles` tab, select `Password administrator` by clicking the name (the blue text). This will open an `Add assignments` blade on the right of the screen, and you can add users to be part of this role. Select `DemoUser1`, and note that you can add `Demo` to the `Search` bar to filter the users you want to add. Once you have added the users, click Add.

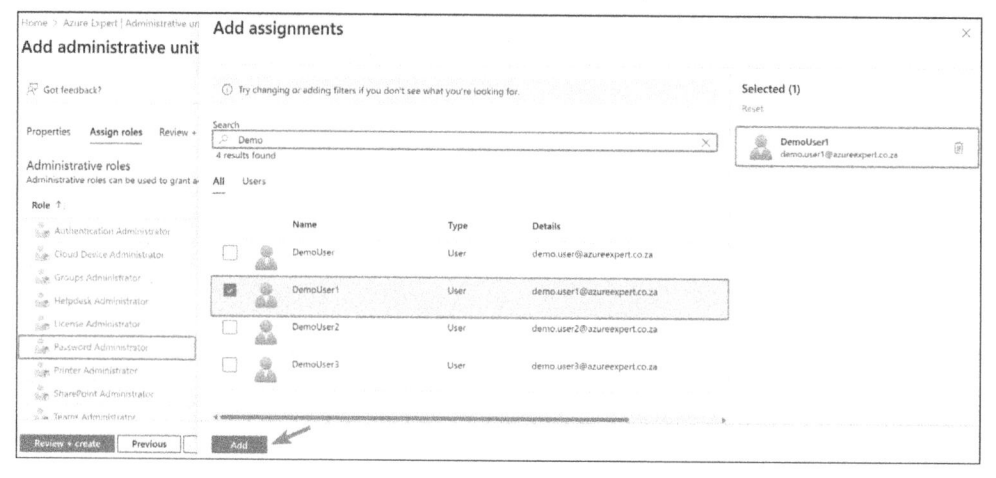

Figure 1.27: AU role assignment

6. Click on `Review + create` and then `Create`.
7. The next step is to add all the users you want `DemoUser1` to manage; in this case, you will add `DemoUser1`, `DemoUser2`, and `DemoUser3`. From the left-hand settings menu on the `Microsoft Entra ID` blade, select `Administrative units` again, and then, select the new administrative unit you just created.
8. From the left menu, under the `Manage` context, click `Users`. On the right-hand side configuration blade, click on `Add member` and select the previously added demo users. Once you're done, click `Select`.

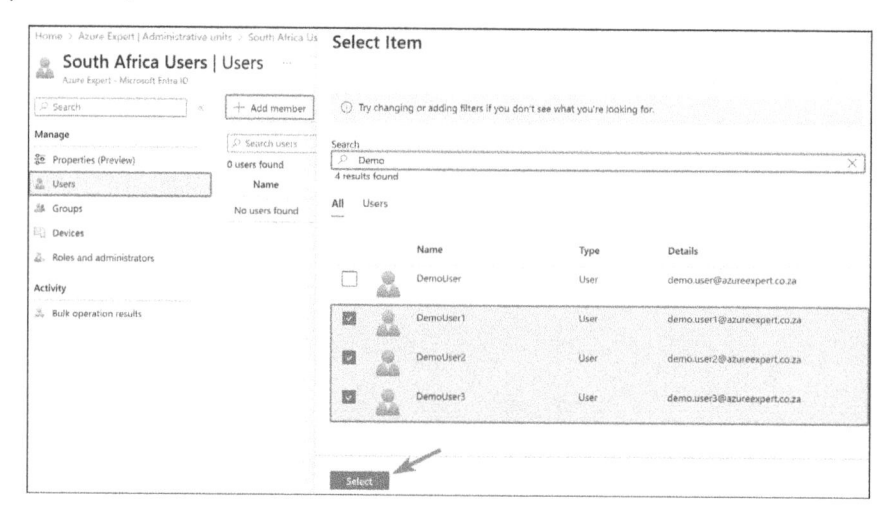

Figure 1.28: Adding users to the AU

9. Now, you will see that all three users have been added to the AU:

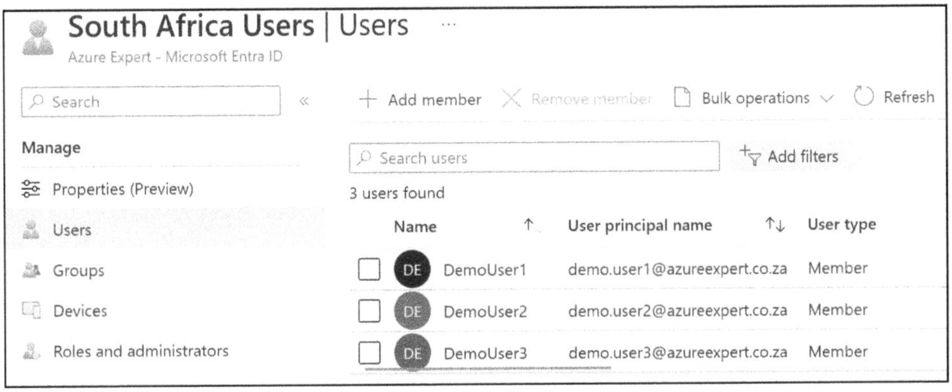

Figure 1.29: Displaying the users for an AU

10. You can now log into Azure with `DemoUser1`, and you should be able to reset the password of `DemoUser2`.

> **Note**
> Remember that you need to assign Microsoft Entra P1 licenses to administrators within AUs.

In this section, you learned what an AU is and how it can be used. Additionally, you walked through the creation of an AU step by step.

> **Note**
> You are encouraged to read further at the following links, which will provide additional information about AU management:
>
> https://learn.microsoft.com/en-us/entra/identity/role-based-access-control/admin-units-manage
>
> https://learn.microsoft.com/en-us/entra/identity/role-based-access-control/admin-units-members-add

Now, let's move on and look at how to manage user and group properties.

Managing User and Group Properties

Part of an Azure administrator's task is to understand what can be done from a user and group perspective within Microsoft Entra ID. In this section, you will explore the properties that can be assigned to users and groups in Microsoft Entra ID. These properties provide valuable information about the users and groups in your organization and can be used for a variety of purposes, such as access control, compliance reporting, and device management. Understanding the different properties available and how to manage them is essential for effective IAM in Microsoft Entra ID.

User Account Properties

Let's look at what you can configure on a user account, which is accessed by navigating to the Users menu from within Microsoft Entra ID. Then, select the corresponding user account by clicking on the display name for the user account you want to manage. The management screen that you are presented with is the User management blade, which contains the following management settings:

- Overview: On the Overview blade, you will find a Properties tab. This is where you can view and modify user details, such as name, job information, and user type.
- Assigned roles: This setting displays all role assignments for a specific account, including eligible, active, or expired assignments.
- Administrative units: This section shows the AUs of which a user is a member.
- Groups: This setting displays the Entra ID groups that a user is part of.
- Applications: This section shows the applications assigned to a user.
- Licenses: This setting displays what licenses are currently assigned to a user account.
- Devices: This section shows the devices associated with a user account, including the join type (e.g., Microsoft Entra-joined).
- Azure role assignments: This setting displays the resources on a subscription level to which an account has access.
- Authentication methods: This setting displays a user's authentication contact information, such as the phone number and email address for MFA. You can also set the account to re-register for MFA or revoke current MFA sessions from this section.
- To modify any properties from the Azure portal for a user account, perform the following steps:

1. Open the Users blade of Microsoft Entra ID and select the user you would like to modify; in this example, you will modify DemoUser3.
2. You will then be presented with the User blade management screen; click Overview on the left-hand menu pane, and then click Edit properties from the Overview pane.

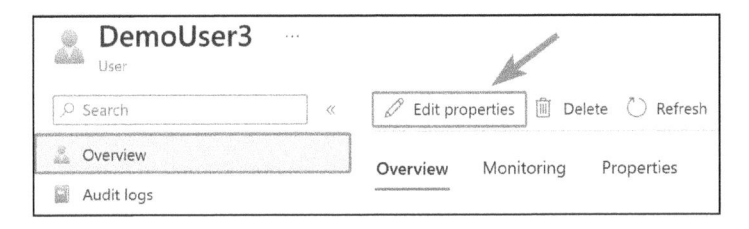

Figure 1.30: Managing users and groups – editing user properties

3. There are several properties you can now modify, organized by category as tabs. Click the desired tab, change the desired properties, and then click `Save` at the bottom of the screen. Note that this section has a default tab selection of `Identity`, next to which is another tab, `All`. The `All` tab allows you to edit all the user properties on one page, or you can select the various categories of properties you would like to edit by selecting the appropriate tab. The following is a screenshot of what these tabs look like.

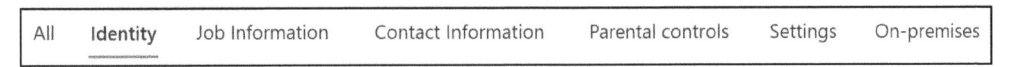

Figure 1.31: Managing users and groups – user property tabs

4. An example of some of the properties you can edit, which pertain to `Job Information`, is shown in the following screenshot.

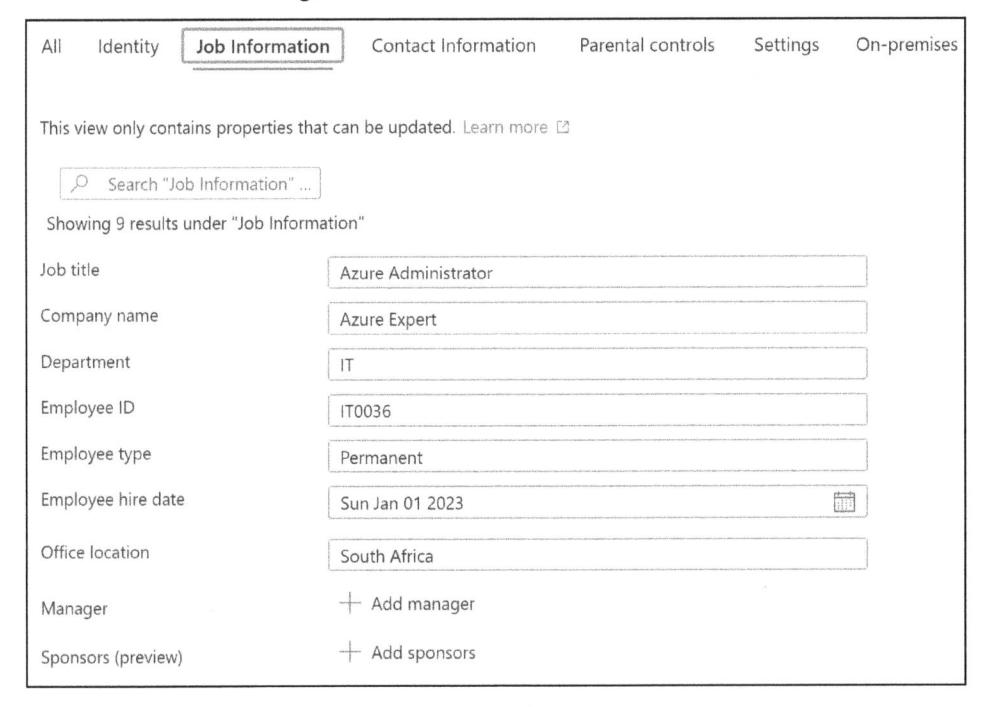

Figure 1.32: Managing users and groups – user properties

Now that we have reviewed the various user properties, we will explore the group settings next.

Microsoft Entra ID group settings

Microsoft Entra ID groups have a range of settings that can be configured to manage group membership and access to resources. In this section, you will explore the different settings available for groups, including membership, ownership, administrative units, applications, and licenses. Understanding these settings is important for managing access to resources and ensuring that groups are configured correctly. You will also provide some additional resources to manage group settings via the command line and explore external user attribute flows. The Group settings management pane is accessed by navigating to the Groups menu from within Microsoft Entra ID. You then select the corresponding group from the All groups management pane that you want to manage. The options under the Group settings management blade are as follows:

- Overview: This displays general information about a group, such as membership type, source directory, object ID, and creation date.
- Properties: This contains the general settings for a group, including group name, description, group type, and membership type.
- Members: This setting displays all of the current members of a group. You can also perform bulk operations related to groups from here.
- Owners: This setting displays the owners of a group who can modify the group and the members within it.
- Administrative units: This setting displays the AUs that a group is part of.
- Group memberships: This setting displays all of the security groups that a group belongs to (the nested grouping).
- Applications: This setting displays the application assignments.
- Licenses: This setting displays the licenses that are assigned to a group, which group members will inherit automatically.
- Azure role assignments: This setting displays the resources of a subscription level to which the group members have access.
- Dynamic membership rules: This setting displays the configuration rules; for dynamic groups, this is where you can change the configuration rules, which will affect the members of a group.
- To modify any properties from the Azure portal for a group, perform the following steps:

1. Open the `Groups` blade under Azure Expert, select `All groups`, and then select the group you would like to modify; in this example, you will modify `Sales`.

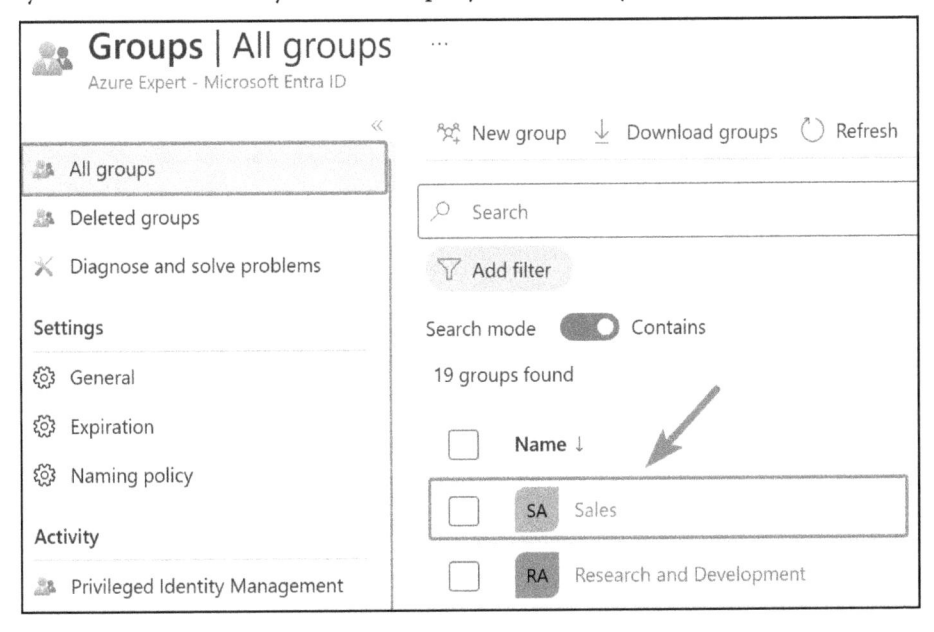

Figure 1.33: Selecting the Sales group

2. You will then be presented with the `Group settings` management blade screen; click `Properties` from the left-hand menu pane.

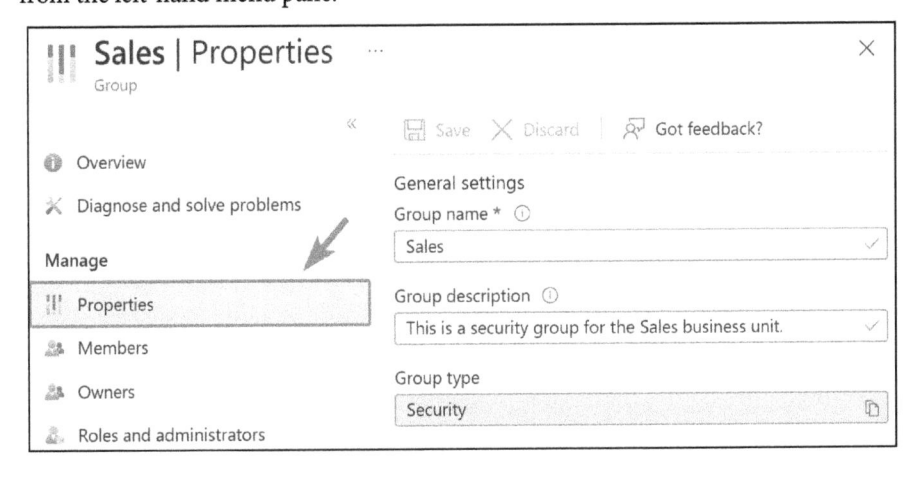

Figure 1.34: Editing group properties

3. There are several settings you can now modify; change the desired settings, and then click Save at the top of the screen.

That brings us to the end of user and group properties. In this section, we looked at all of the different settings for Microsoft Entra ID users and groups and how to configure them.

> **Note**
>
> You are encouraged to read further at the following links, which will provide additional information about managing group settings via the command line and also dive into external user attribute flows:
>
> `https://learn.microsoft.com/en-us/entra/identity/users/groups-settings-v2-cmdlets`
>
> `https://learn.microsoft.com/en-us/entra/external-id/user-flow-add-custom-attributes`

Summary

In this chapter, you learned about Microsoft Entra ID and its purpose, user accounts, groups, administrative units, and licenses. You also learned how to create user accounts via the Azure portal, how to create a dynamic group, and how to add users to that dynamic group. You explored editing user and group properties.

Microsoft Entra ID is an identity management tool that integrates natively with Azure and can be extended into several Microsoft services. It can be used to assign roles and permissions in Azure to your various users, groups, and app registrations.

In the next chapter, you will explore managing devices using Microsoft Entra, as well as how to join or add your devices to Microsoft Entra. You will learn how to perform bulk user operations, how to create and manage guest accounts, and how to enable the configuration options for a self-service password reset.

2
Devices in Microsoft Entra ID

In this chapter, you will delve into Microsoft Entra's functionalities and configurations. As organizations increasingly adopt a digital-first approach, the ability to securely and efficiently manage devices and identities has never been more critical. This chapter is structured to walk you through the essentials of **configuring and managing devices** for seamless integration within your organizational infrastructure. You will learn about **configuring Microsoft Entra Join** to simplify the complexity of integrating devices with Microsoft Entra for enhanced security and user experience. Additionally, you will explore operational agility provided by **performing bulk operations**, essential to managing users and groups at scale. You will learn how to create guest accounts in Microsoft Entra ID. Finally, you will learn about **configuring Self-Service Password Reset (SSPR)**, which is a critical feature that empowers users to reset their own passwords and reduce the administrative burden of password management for IT support.

In this chapter, the following topics will be covered:

- Configuring and Managing Devices
- Configuring Microsoft Entra Join
- Performing Bulk Operations
- Navigating Guest Accounts
- Configuring SSPR

Technical Requirements

To follow along with the hands-on lessons, you will need access to the following:

- **Microsoft Entra ID** as a global administrator.
- Azure subscription with owner or contributor privileges. If you do not have access to one, students can enroll for a free account: https://azure.microsoft.com/en-us/free/.
- **PowerShell 5.1** or later installed on a Windows PC or PowerShell Core 6.x on other operating systems where labs can be practiced.

- For Windows users, you will need to install **.NET Framework 4.7.2** or later using the following link: `https://learn.microsoft.com/en-us/dotnet/framework/install`.

- Note that, occasionally, examples can only be followed from a PC or `https://shell.azure.com` (PowerShell 7.0.6 LTS or later is recommended).

- Install the `Az` PowerShell module, which can be performed by running the following in an administrative PowerShell session:

  ```
  Set-ExecutionPolicy -ExecutionPolicy RemoteSigned -Scope CurrentUser
  Install-Module -Name Az -Scope CurrentUser -Repository PSGallery -Force
  ```

Configuring and Managing Devices

In Microsoft Entra, a device represents any physical or virtual device that is registered with the directory. This can include devices such as laptops, desktops, mobile phones, and tablets. When a device is registered with Microsoft Entra, it can be managed and secured using policies and configurations defined in the directory. By managing devices in Microsoft Entra, IT administrators can ensure that devices accessing corporate resources meet an organization's security and compliance requirements. In the following sections, you will explore device management in more detail and discuss how Microsoft Entra enables device management at scale.

Configuring Device Identities

When it comes to managing your devices through Microsoft Entra, you have several services available to you. You may want to support **Bring Your Own Device** (**BYOD**) scenarios or opt for a more traditional management style through Microsoft Entra joined devices. Joining is the typical approach for larger organizations that have established control and management structures for their IT infrastructure. For this course, you need to only be aware of how to register or join your devices to Microsoft Entra. This topic is worth much more exploration and research before you decide to adopt a certain approach.

Microsoft Entra Device Registration

A Microsoft Entra ID Registered Device is one that is registered within the Microsoft Entra ID directory but not added as a member of an organization:

- The device is then granted access to resources through an attachment to a Microsoft account in Microsoft Entra ID.

- It provides users with a **Single Sign-On** (**SSO**) experience across their devices, including app authentication.

- It enables Conditional Access policy enforcement.

- It is recommended for personally owned devices or devices not used exclusively for business purposes. Personally owned devices are also defined as BYOD, which are devices that can be used for work purposes.

- It offers a streamlined process with minimal administrative overhead.
- The device can be managed through tools such as Microsoft Intune.

The following diagram illustrates a device's connection to Microsoft Entra ID and the relationship flow.

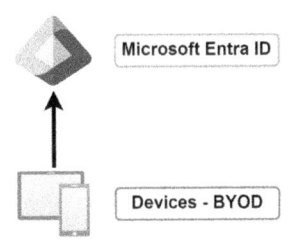

Figure 2.1: Microsoft Entra ID – device registration

For more details, refer to https://learn.microsoft.com/en-us/entra/identity/devices/concept-device-registration.

Microsoft Entra Join

A Microsoft Entra ID joined device is one that is added to an organization's Microsoft Entra ID directory, providing additional benefits and control to the organization:

- It is fully managed by the organization with access to on-premises Active Directory resources. It is, therefore, suitable for dedicated, organization-owned devices that need full access to organizational resources.
- It is explicitly tied to an organizational user account and managed as part of the directory.
- It offers better management capabilities and integration and can use Conditional Access policies.

The following diagram illustrates a device-to-Microsoft Entra ID join connection, demonstrating how the connection is made from the device to Microsoft Entra ID. Entra ID can then form a hybrid connection to an on-premises Active Directory system, with synchronization occurring between the platforms through the Microsoft Entra Connect service.

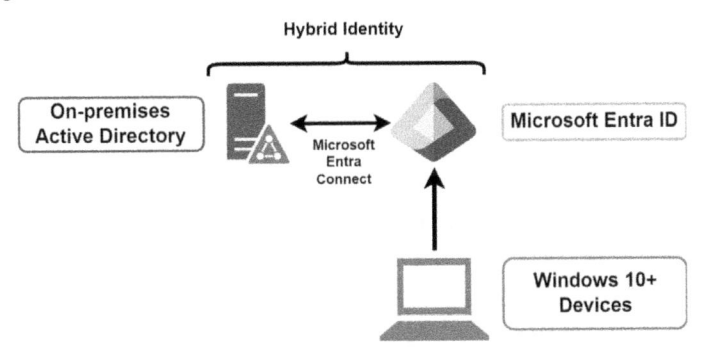

Figure 2.2: Microsoft Entra ID – a device join

For more details, refer to https://learn.microsoft.com/en-us/entra/identity/devices/concept-directory-join.

Microsoft Entra Hybrid Join

A Microsoft Entra ID hybrid joined device is a device that is joined to both the on-premises **Active Directory** (**AD**) and Entra ID, for organizations with a blended infrastructure. It is designed to support Windows 10 and 11 devices:

- It retains the benefits of local on-premises AD while leveraging cloud features, such as enabling the continued use of Group Policy in Entra ID
- It combines cloud authentication with on-premises resources and devices
- It facilitates seamless transitions and secure access to resources in hybrid environments
- It is ideal for organizations that have a mix of cloud and on-premises infrastructure deployments

The following diagram illustrates a device connection to Microsoft Entra ID and the relationship flow for a Microsoft Entra ID hybrid join connection, demonstrating how the connection is made from the device to Microsoft Entra ID as a registration and to an Active Directory for a domain join. Entra ID will then have a hybrid connection to an on-premises Active Directory system, with synchronization occurring between the platforms through the Microsoft Entra Connect service.

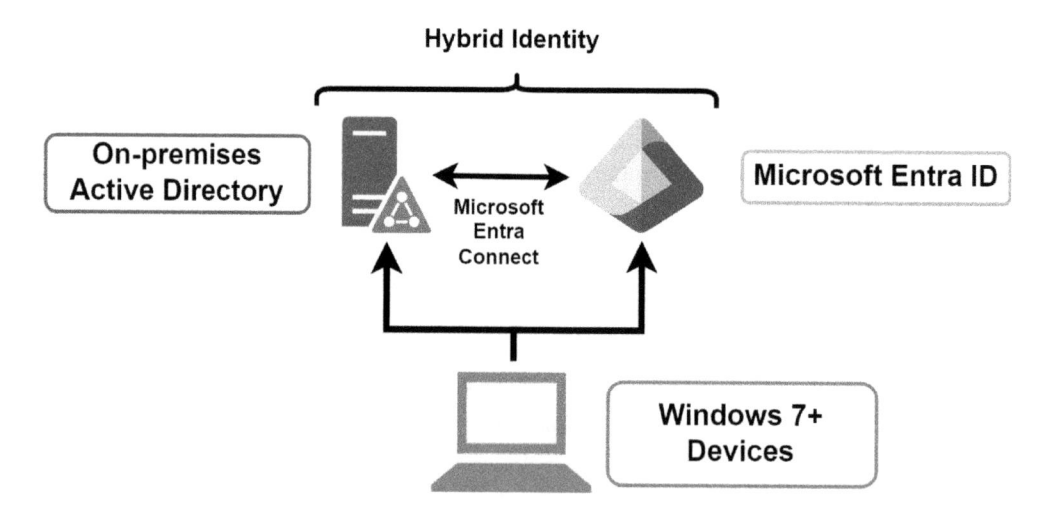

Figure 2.3: Microsoft Entra ID – a device hybrid join

For more details, refer to https://learn.microsoft.com/en-us/entra/identity/devices/concept-hybrid-join.

Next, we will explore what device settings you can manage in Microsoft Entra.

Device Settings

Microsoft Entra enables organizations to ensure that their users access Azure resources from devices that comply with their security and compliance policies. Device management is a crucial component of device-based Conditional Access, where access to corporate resources is restricted only to managed devices.

Device settings can be easily managed from the Azure portal, provided the device is registered or joined to Microsoft Entra. To access `Devices`, you need to select it from the `Manage` context from the left-hand menu under Microsoft Entra ID. On the `Devices` blade, you can select `Device settings` from the left menu. The following device settings are available for configuration in Microsoft Entra ID:

- `Users may join devices to Microsoft Entra`: This setting lets administrators specify which users can join their Windows 10 devices to Entra ID. This setting is only applicable to Microsoft Entra Join on Windows 10. The `Selected` option allows you to specify which members are allowed to join their devices to Entra ID.

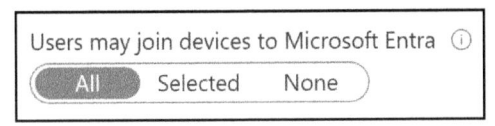

Figure 2.4: Device settings – Users may join devices to Microsoft Entra

- `Users may register their devices with Entra ID`: This setting needs to be configured to allow devices to be registered with Entra ID. There are two options here – `None`, which means that devices are not allowed to register when they are not Microsoft Entra-joined or hybrid Microsoft Entra-joined, and `All`, which means that all devices are allowed to register.

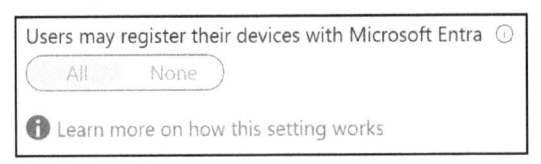

Figure 2.5: Device settings – Users may register their devices with Microsoft Entra

> **Note**
> In order for you to enroll with Microsoft Intune or **Mobile Device Management** (**MDM**) for Microsoft 365, you will be required to register. If you have configured either of these services, the `All` option is selected by default and `None` is not available for selection.

- `Require Multi-Factor Authentication to register or join devices with Microsoft Entra`: This setting adds another layer of security by requiring users to authenticate with **Multi-factor Authentication (MFA)** when registering or joining their devices to Microsoft Entra. Before you can enable this setting, MFA needs to be configured for the users who register their devices.

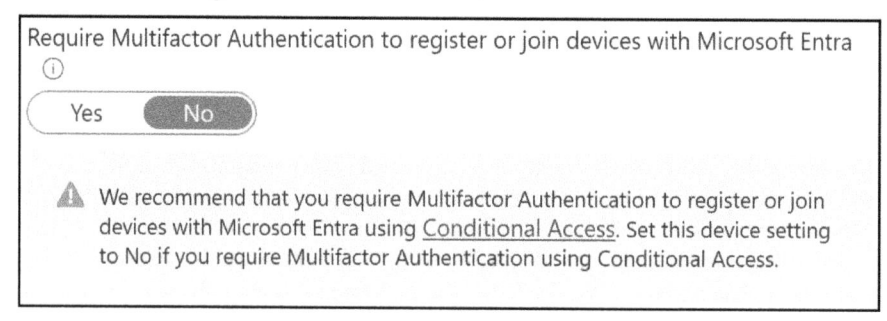

Figure 2.6: Device settings – requiring MFA

- `Maximum number of devices per user`: This setting allows you to select the maximum number of devices that a user can have in Microsoft Entra. Reaching this quota will prevent additional devices from being added until either existing devices are removed or the quota limit is changed.

- `Manage Additional local administrators on all Microsoft Entra joined devices`: This setting allows you to add additional local administrators for Microsoft Entra joined devices. A local administrator is a user who has administrative privileges on a specific device or computer.

Figure 2.7: Device settings – Local administrator settings

- `Enable Microsoft Entra Local Administrator Password Solution (LAPS)`: **Local Administrator Password Solution (LAPS)** is a secure method for managing and retrieving built-in local admin passwords on Windows devices, supporting both Microsoft Entra and Microsoft Entra hybrid join configurations. You can read more about it here: https://learn.microsoft.com/en-gb/entra/identity/devices/howto-manage-local-admin-passwords.

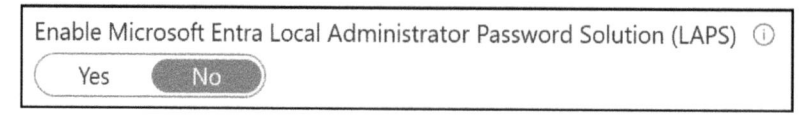

Figure 2.8: Device settings – Microsoft Entra LAPS

- `Restrict users from recovering the BitLocker key(s) for their owned devices`: Restricting users from recovering BitLocker keys for their owned devices is a security measure that prevents non-admin users from accessing their device's BitLocker key(s) for self-service recovery. By setting this restriction to `Yes`, only admin users can retrieve the keys, ensuring an additional layer of security and control over the devices. Conversely, setting it to `No` allows all users to recover their BitLocker key(s), enabling self-service access but potentially reducing security.

Figure 2.9: Device settings – BitLocker key(s)

Enterprise State Roaming

Enterprise State Roaming is a feature in Microsoft Entra ID that allows users to synchronize their application and system settings across their Windows devices. This means that when a user sets up a new Windows device, their familiar settings and preferences will be applied to the new device automatically. This feature is especially useful for organizations that provide employees with multiple Windows devices, or for users who switch between devices frequently. With Enterprise State Roaming, users can have a more seamless and consistent experience across all their Windows devices. The synchronization is achieved through Microsoft Entra ID, and all data is encrypted to ensure security and privacy.

This setting now has its own blade and can be accessed by clicking `Enterprise State Roaming` from the left menu of the `Device` blade, under the `Manage` context.

Selecting `All` will enable all users in your organization to take advantage of this feature, `Selected` allows you to specify users, and `None` will disallow all users from using the feature.

Figure 2.10: Enterprise State Roaming

You can read more about Enterprise State Roaming here: https://learn.microsoft.com/en-us/entra/identity/devices/enterprise-state-roaming-enable.

You now have a basic understanding of what Enterprise State Roaming is and the features and benefits it offers. Next, you will learn about device management settings.

Managing Device Settings

To manage the device settings from the Azure portal, you need to perform the following steps:

1. Navigate to the Azure portal by opening `https://portal.azure.com`.
2. From the left-hand hamburger menu or the main search bar, select `Microsoft Entra ID`.
3. From the left-hand menu, select `Devices` under the `Manage` context, as follows:

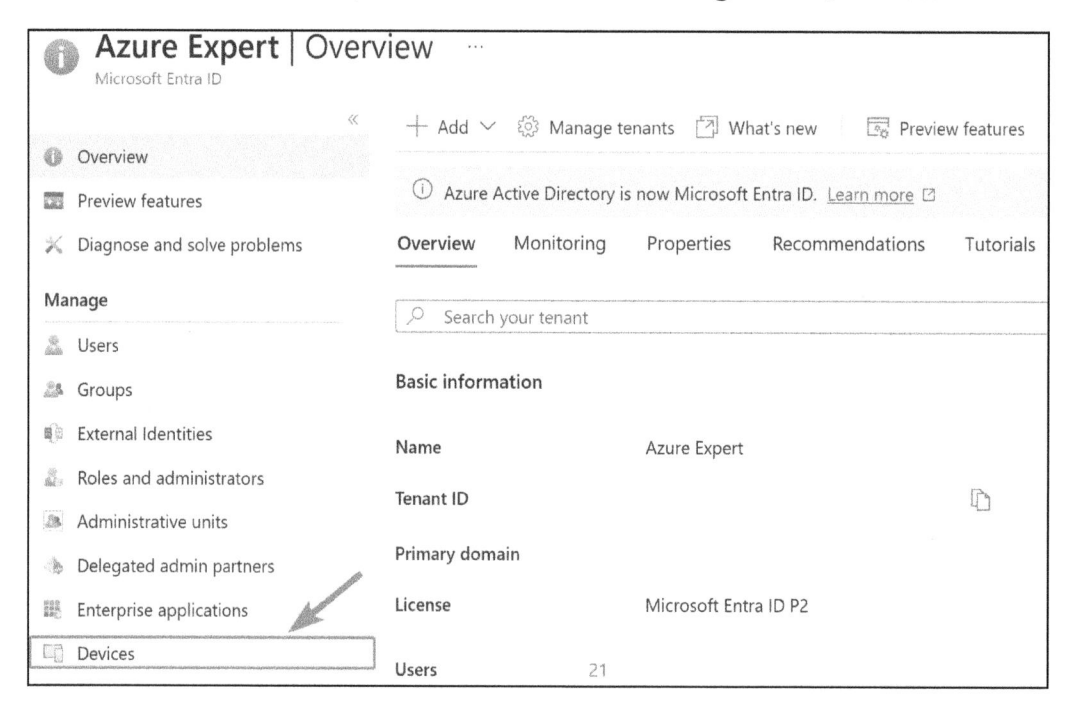

Figure 2.11: The Microsoft Entra ID Devices blade

4. The device management blade will open. Here, you can configure your device management settings, locate your devices, perform device management tasks, and review the device management-related audit logs.
5. To configure the device settings, select `Device settings` from the left-hand menu. From here, you can configure the following settings, which are shown in *Figure 2.12*:

   - `Users may join devices to Microsoft Entra`: `All`
   - `Require Multifactor Authentication to register or join devices with Microsoft Entra`: `No`

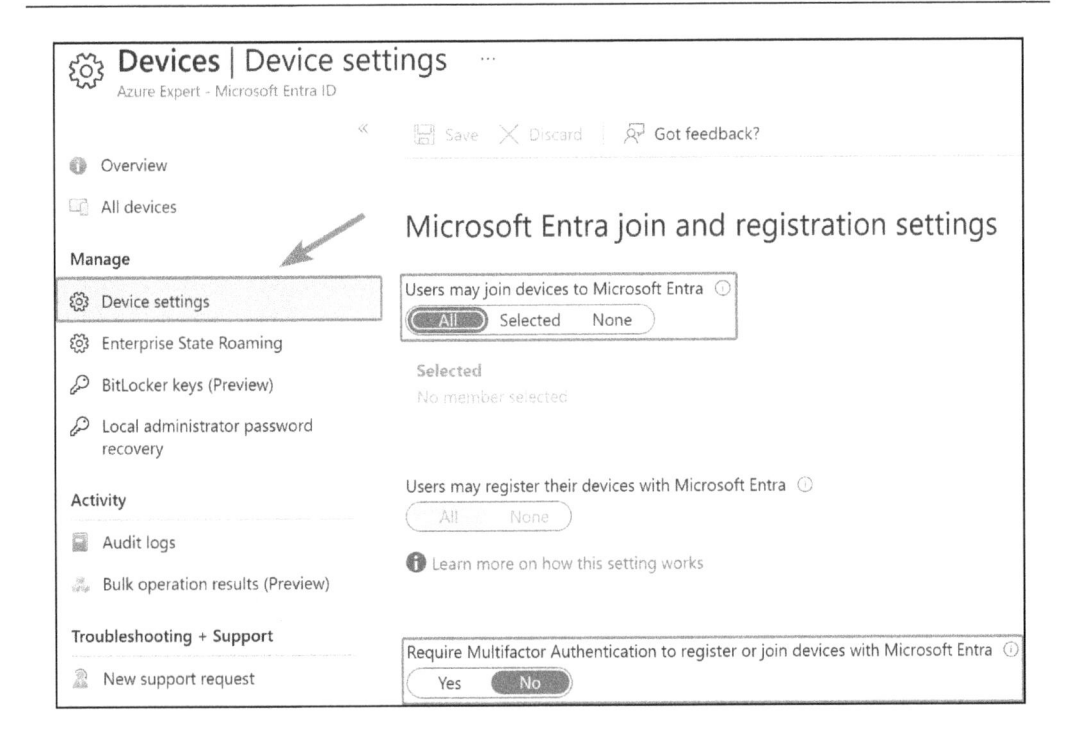

Figure 2.12: Microsoft Entra ID – the Device settings blade

6. To locate your devices, select `All devices` from the left menu. In this pane, you will see all the joined and registered devices, as follows:

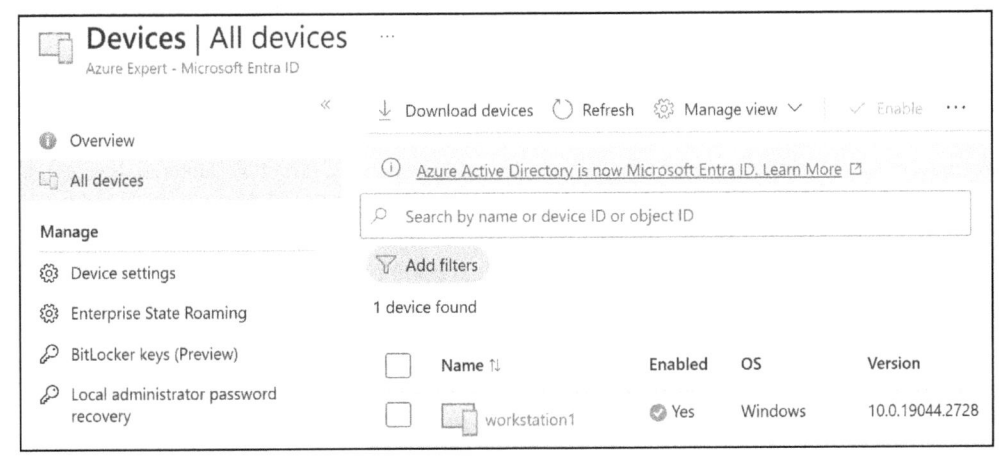

Figure 2.13: Microsoft Entra ID – All devices

7. Additionally, you can select the different devices from the list to get more detailed information about a device. From here, global administrators and cloud device administrators can disable or delete the device:

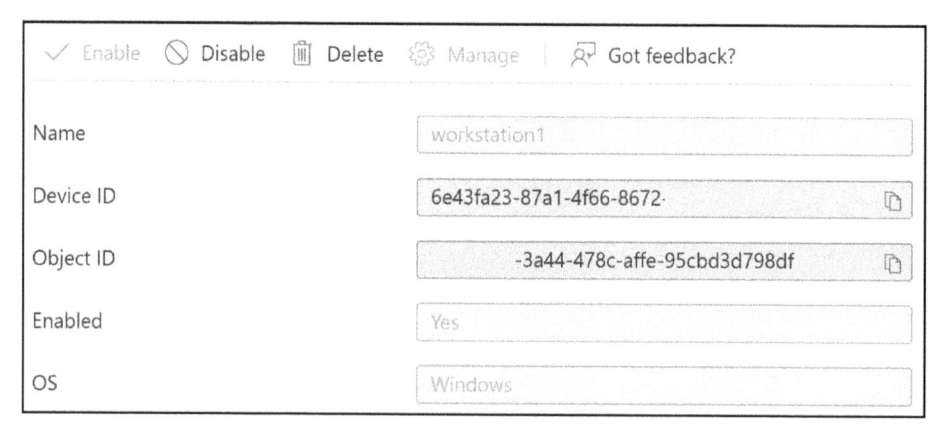

Name	workstation1
Device ID	6e43fa23-87a1-4f66-8672-
Object ID	-3a44-478c-affe-95cbd3d798df
Enabled	Yes
OS	Windows

Figure 2.14: Microsoft Entra ID – workstation 1 details

You now have experience managing a device on Microsoft Entra. The next topic you will learn about is audit logs, under the `Devices` blade.

Device Audit Logs

The audit logs section under `Devices` in Microsoft Entra ID contains a record of all activities related to device management. Audit logs provide detailed information on events and actions performed within the system. These logs offer valuable insights for administrators looking to monitor security, troubleshoot issues, and maintain compliance.

Using device audit logs, administrators can track changes made to device properties, registration and deletion events, and other relevant activities performed by either the users or the system itself. Information stored in the logs typically includes event timestamps, target(s) (affected devices), user details, and the specific category of the activity and actions/changes made during an event. Microsoft Entra offers a user-friendly interface to view and analyze device audit logs, allowing administrators to filter and sort records based on specific criteria, such as event type or date range. This enables you to quickly identify and investigate suspicious activities or potential sources of issues within the device management environment.

By regularly reviewing and analyzing device audit logs, organizations can proactively detect anomalies and maintain regulatory compliance, thus ensuring a secure and efficient device management process within your Microsoft Entra ecosystem. Additionally, the audit logs can be exported to third-party **security information and event management** (**SIEM**) systems for further analysis and correlation with other security events. In this exercise, you will explore how to view audit logs in the Azure portal. Complete the following steps:

1. To view audit logs, navigate to the `Devices` blade from Microsoft Entra ID.
2. From the left menu of the `Devices` blade, under the `Activity` context, select `Audit logs`. This is where you can view and download the different log files for your devices. Additionally, you can create filters to search through the logs, as per the following example:

Figure 2.15: Microsoft Entra ID – the Audit logs blade

This concludes the section on how to manage your device settings via the Azure portal.

> **Note**
>
> You are encouraged to read up further by using the following links:
>
> https://learn.microsoft.com/en-us/entra/identity/devices/manage-device-identities.
>
> https://learn.microsoft.com/en-us/entra/identity/monitoring-health/howto-stream-logs-to-event-hub.
>
> https://learn.microsoft.com/en-us/entra/architecture/security-operations-devices.

In the next section, you will explore the licensing options behind Microsoft Entra.

Licensing

Microsoft Entra offers a range of licensing options to meet your organizational requirements, whether small or large businesses. These licensing options determine which features and functionalities are available to users. Some of the key features of Microsoft Entra include SSO, MFA, and device management. In the following section, you will explore the different pricing plans available for Microsoft Entra and what each plan includes.

Microsoft Entra ID offers the following pricing plans:

- **Microsoft Entra ID Free**: This offers the most basic features, such as support for SSO across Azure, Microsoft 365, and other popular **Software as a Service (SaaS)** applications, Azure **Business-to-Business (B2B)** for external users, support for Microsoft Entra Connect synchronization, self-service password change, user and group management, and standard security reports.

- **Microsoft Entra ID P1**: Previously known as Azure Active Directory P1. In addition to the Free license features, this license offers a service-level agreement, advanced reporting, Conditional Access, Microsoft Entra Connect Health, advanced administration such as dynamic groups, self-service group management, and Microsoft Identity Manager.

- **Microsoft Entra ID P2**: Previously known as Azure Active Directory P2. In addition to the Free and Microsoft Entra ID P1 license features, the Microsoft Entra ID P2 license includes Identity Protection, **Privileged Identity Management (PIM)**, access reviews, and entitlement management.

- **Microsoft Entra ID Governance**: For users of Microsoft Entra ID P1 and P2, Microsoft Entra ID Governance provides a sophisticated suite of identity governance features that can be added at a premium. These capabilities include automated user and group provisioning, HR-driven provisioning, terms of use attestation, basic and advanced access certifications and reviews, basic and advanced entitlement management, life cycle workflows, identity governance dashboard, and PIM.

- **Microsoft Entra Verified ID**: Microsoft Entra Verified ID is a license currently included free within any Microsoft Entra ID subscription, such as Microsoft Entra ID Free. This service enables organizations to verify and issue credentials based on unique identity attributes, granting individuals control over their digital credentials and improving visibility. The benefits of Verified ID include reduced organizational risk, simplified audit processes, and seamless integration for developers to create user-centric serverless applications. Organizations can enable Verified ID for free in the Microsoft Entra admin center.

- **Microsoft Entra Permissions Management**: This is a set of identity governance features tailored for Microsoft Entra ID P1 and P2 subscribers. These capabilities include automated user and group provisioning, HR-driven provisioning, terms of use attestation, basic and advanced access certifications and reviews, basic and advanced entitlement management, life cycle workflows, identity governance dashboard, and PIM.

- **Microsoft Entra Workload ID**: With the standalone Microsoft Entra Workload ID product, organizations can reduce risk exposure from compromised or lost identities or credentials, regulate workload identity access with adaptive policies, and obtain a thorough workload identity health-check view. The monthly pricing for Workload ID is based on the workload identity.

> **Note**
> For a detailed overview of the different Microsoft Entra licenses and all the features that are offered in each plan, refer to `https://www.microsoft.com/en-us/security/business/microsoft-entra-pricing`.

Configuring and Managing Devices   45

Now that you have a basic understanding of what Microsoft Entra ID is and the licensing models involved, you will learn how to implement a license.

Try/Buy License Products for Microsoft Entra

In this exercise, you are going to learn how to try or buy a license that can be associated with your Microsoft Entra instance. To do so, follow the following steps:

1. Navigate to the Azure portal by opening a web browser and browsing to `https://portal.azure.com`.
2. From the left-hand hamburger menu or the main search bar, select `Microsoft Entra ID`.

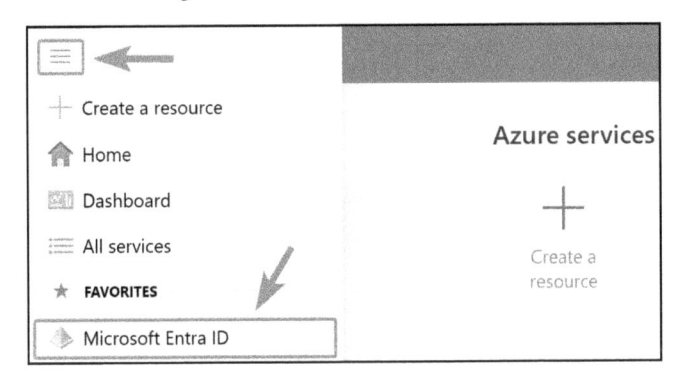

Figure 2.16: Selecting Microsoft Entra ID

3. Click on the `Licenses` setting under the `Manage` context from the left menu.

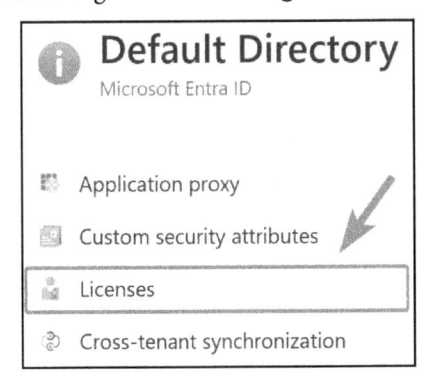

Figure 2.17: Microsoft Entra ID – Licenses

4. From the `Licenses` blade on the left menu, select `All products`, and then click `Try / Buy` from the blade screen that is presented.

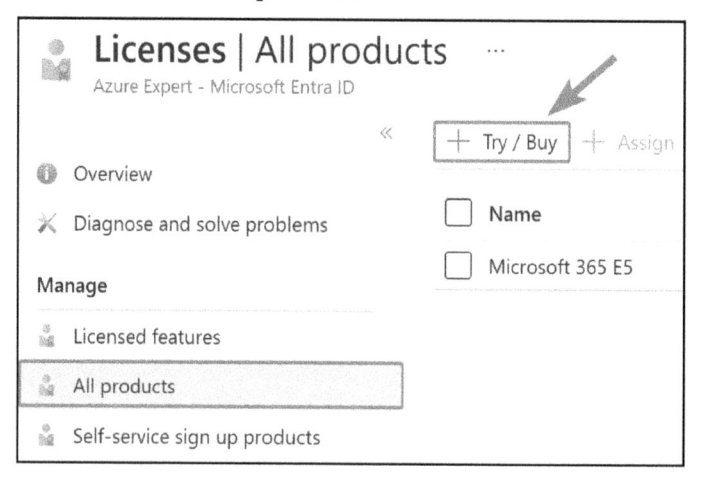

Figure 2.18: Microsoft Entra ID – Licenses | All products

5. An `Activate` pop-up screen will appear. To select a product for trial, you can click the `Free trial` drop-down option and then `Activate` to activate the license for the service offering you want to try, such as the following screenshot for Microsoft Entra ID P2.

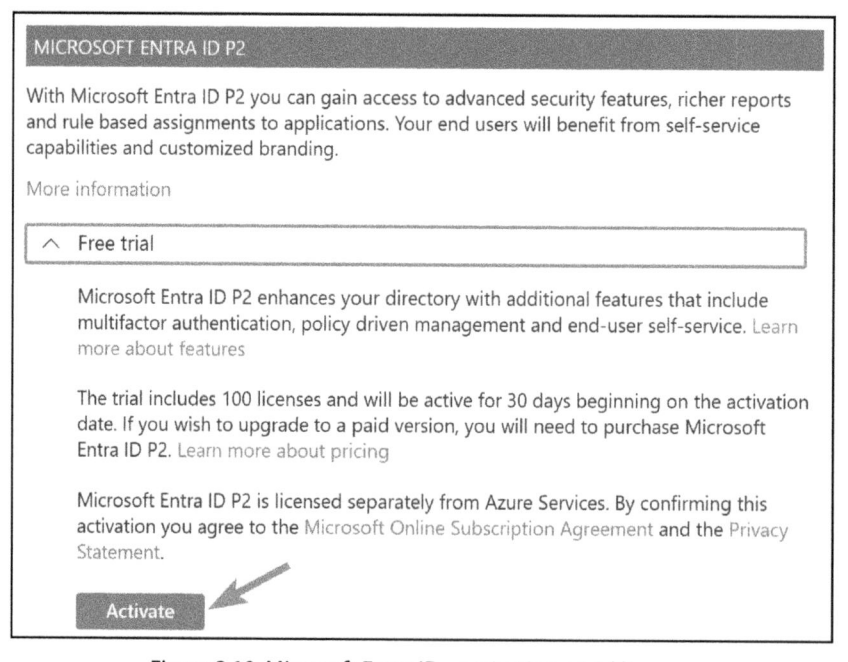

Figure 2.19: Microsoft Entra ID – activating a trial license

You have now seen how to try a licensed product using the Azure portal. Next, you will learn about assigning a license to one of your users or groups.

Assigning a License

In this exercise, you are going to assign an active licensed product to a user to demonstrate the assignment of licenses from within Microsoft Entra ID:

1. Just as you did in the previous exercise, you will navigate back to the `All products` settings screen under the `Licenses` blade.
2. Select the license you are looking to assign; in this instance, we will assign the `Microsoft 365 E5 Developer` license. Then, click `Assign` from the top menu.

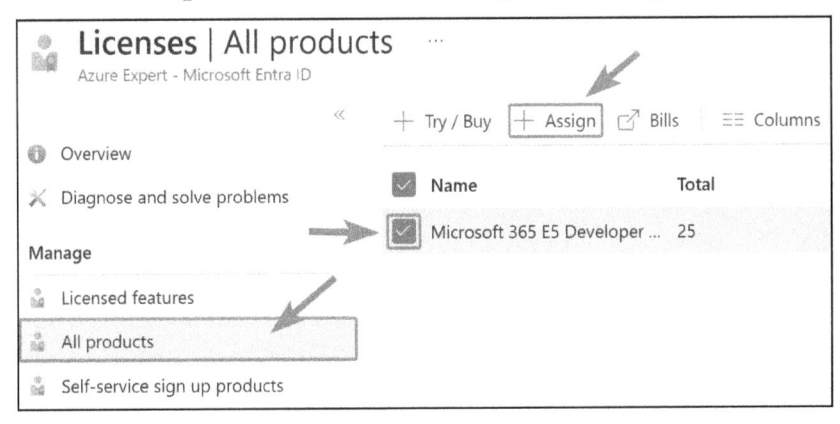

Figure 2.20: Microsoft Entra ID licensing – assigning a license

3. Click `+ Add users and groups`.

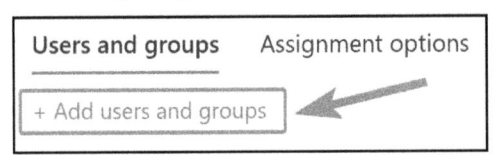

Figure 2.21: Microsoft Entra ID licensing – Add users and groups

4. From the screen that pops up, create a filter to search for the relevant name you are looking for – in this case, `Demo`. Select `DemoUser1` and `DemoUser2`.

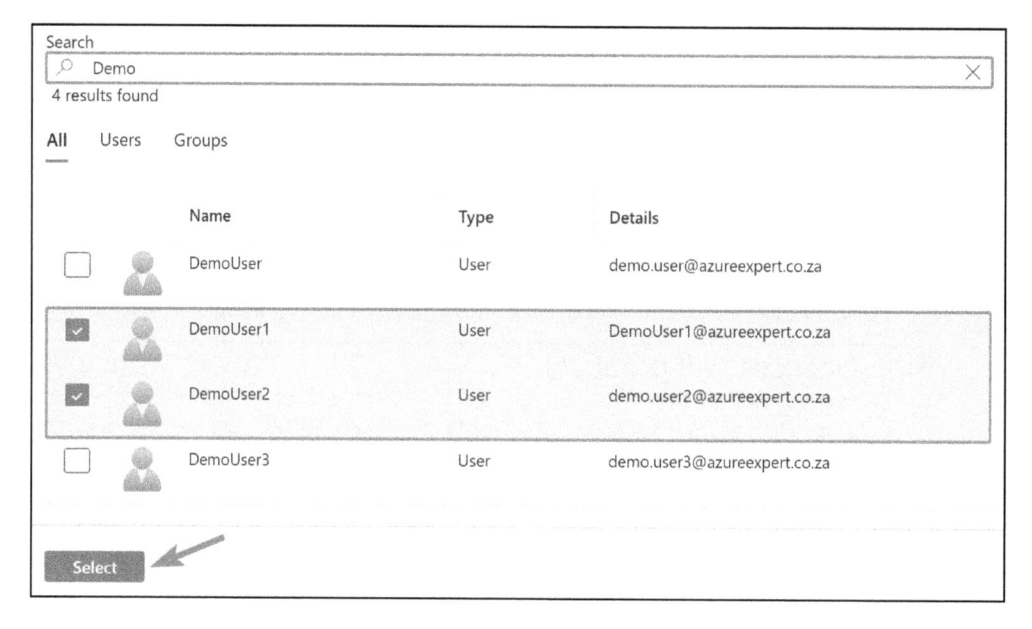

Figure 2.22: Microsoft Entra ID licensing – selecting users

5. Once you have chosen your users, click `Select`.
6. Click `Review + assign`, and then, on the final screen, click `Assign`.

You have now seen how to not only add product licenses but also assign them. Although there are several license types, the basic principles still apply, and the licenses are just as easy to assign. In the next section, we will look at what Microsoft Entra Join is and how to configure it for Windows 10 devices.

Configuring Microsoft Entra Join

With Microsoft Entra Join, you can join devices directly to Microsoft Entra without the need to join your on-premises Active Directory in a hybrid environment. While Microsoft Entra hybrid join with an on-premises Active Directory might still be preferred for some scenarios, Microsoft Entra Join simplifies the process of adding devices and modernizes device management for your organization. This can result in the reduction of device-related IT costs.

Your users may have access to corporate assets through their devices. To protect these corporate assets, you want to control these devices. This allows your administrators to ensure that your users are accessing resources from devices that meet your standards for security and compliance.

Microsoft Entra Join is a good solution when you want to manage devices with a cloud device management solution, when you want to modernize your application infrastructure, when you want to simplify device provisioning for geographically distributed users, and when your company adopts Microsoft 365 as the productivity suite for your users.

Microsoft Entra Join Methods

Microsoft Entra Join can be employed through any of the following methods:

- **Bulk deployment**: This method is used to join large numbers of new Windows devices to Microsoft Entra and Microsoft Intune.
- **Windows Autopilot**: This is a collection of technologies used to preconfigure Windows 10 and later devices so that the devices are ready for productive use. Autopilot can also be used to reset, repurpose, and recover devices.
- **Self-service experience**: This is also referred to as a *first-run experience*, which is mainly used to join a new device to Microsoft Entra.

Microsoft Entra Join Management

When it comes to joining devices to Entra ID, there are two main ways of managing them:

- **MDM only**: This is when the device is managed exclusively by an MDM provider such as **Intune**.
- **Co-management**: This is when the device is managed by an MDM provider and **Microsoft Configuration Manager**.

Microsoft Entra Join Scenarios

When joining a Windows 10 device to Microsoft Entra, there are two scenarios that you need to look at:

- Joining a new Windows 10 or later device via the **Out-of-Box Experience (OOBE)**
- Joining an already configured Windows 10 or later device to Microsoft Entra
- Now that you understand what Microsoft Entra Join is and does, we will take a look at how to configure it.

Configuring Microsoft Entra Join

To follow this exercise, you will require either a virtual machine or a physical machine that has Windows 10 Pro installed and access to the internet.

You will now join an existing Windows 10 device to Microsoft Entra, as follows:

1. On the Windows 10 device, search for `Settings` and open `Accounts`.

2. Select `Access work or school`, and then click `Connect`:

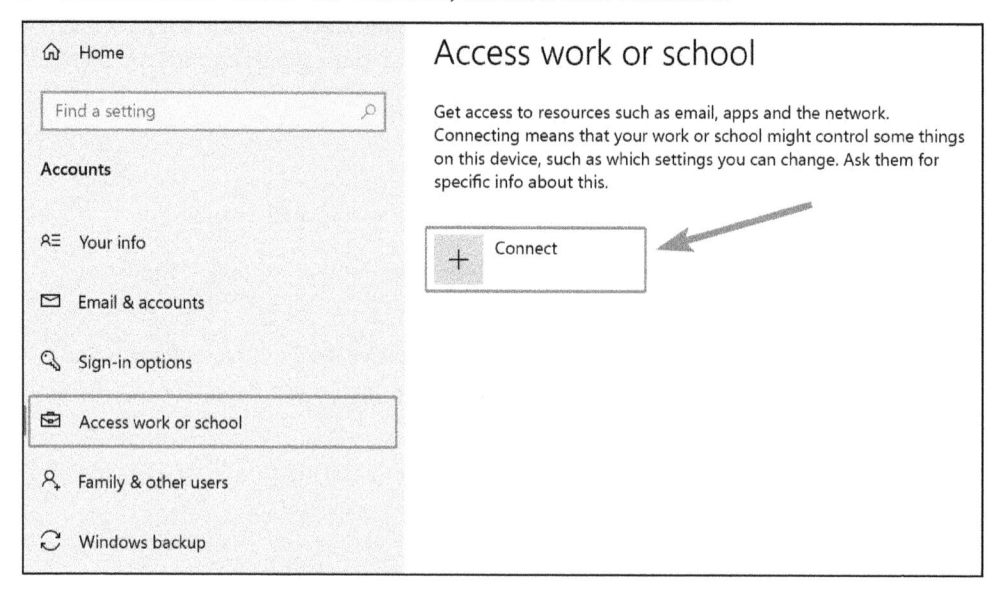

Figure 2.23: The Windows 10 settings menu to add and connect a device

3. Enter the email address of the account you are setting up, and then click on `Join this device to Microsoft Entra ID`.

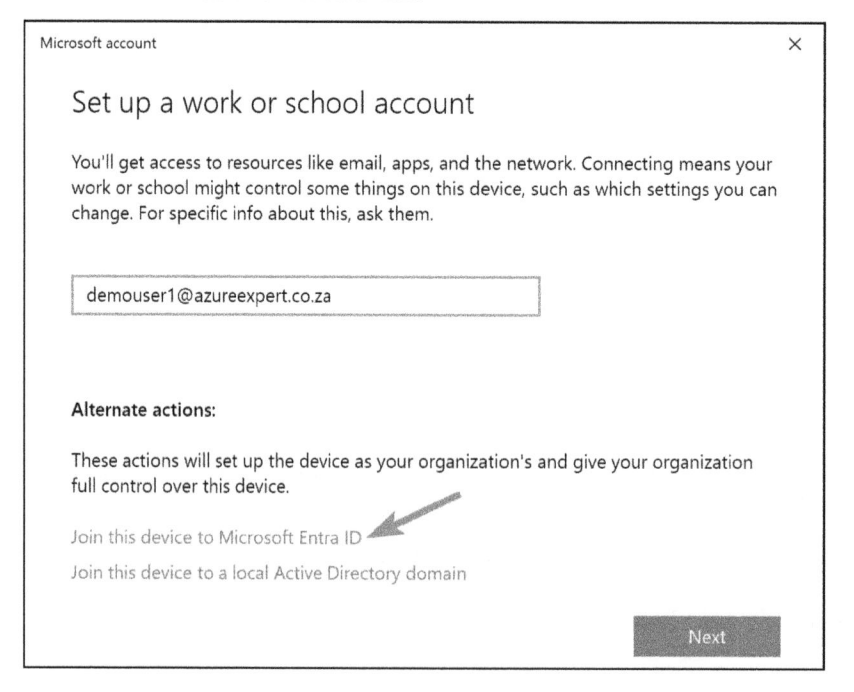

Figure 2.24: Selecting Join this Device to Microsoft Entra ID

4. On the Sign in window that pops up, enter your **user principal name** (**UPN**) (usually the email address of the user account you created earlier in the chapter). For this exercise, use the demouser1 account created previously. Click Next.

Figure 2.25: Signing into Microsoft Entra

5. You will be asked to confirm whether the organization you are joining and the details entered are correct, as per the following screenshot. If so, click Join.

Figure 2.26: Confirming your organization details

6. You will now be joined and momentarily presented with a success screen. Click Done.

> **You're all set!**
>
> This device is connected to Azure Expert.
>
> When you're ready to use this new account, select the Start button, select your current account picture, and then select **'Switch account'**. Sign in using your **DemoUser1@azureexpert.co.za** email and password.

Figure 2.27: A confirmation message for Microsoft Entra Join

7. When you navigate back to the `Access work or school` settings window, you will see that you are now joined to your organization. This will show something similar to the following screenshot with the connected organization. Note that the Entra ID wording will soon change to reflect Microsoft Entra.

> **Access work or school**
>
> Get access to resources like email, apps, and the network. Connecting means your work or school might control some things on this device, such as which settings you can change. For specific info about this, ask them.
>
> + Connect
>
> 💼 Connected to Azure Expert's Azure AD
> Connected by DemoUser1@azureexpert.co.za

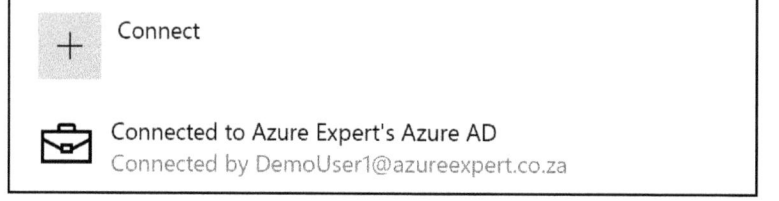

Figure 2.28: Your connected organization on Microsoft Entra

8. Finally, navigate to the Azure portal and the `Devices` blade for Microsoft Entra ID. Select `All devices` from the left menu, and you will then see your newly joined device appear:

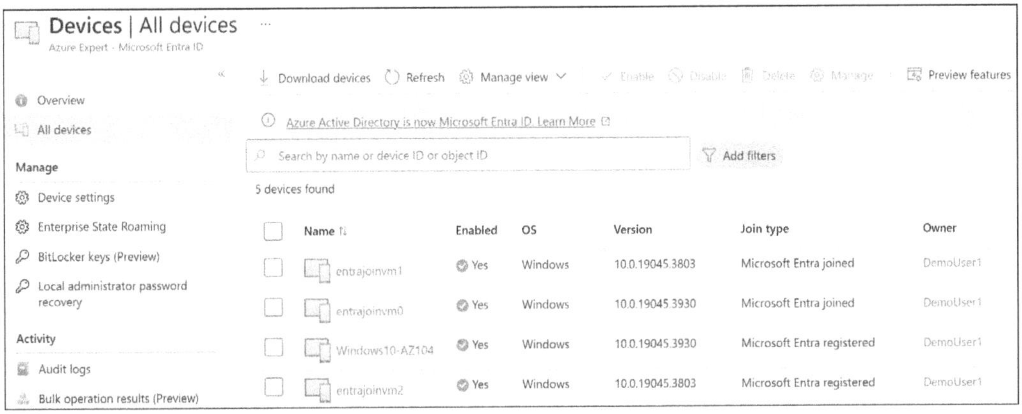

Figure 2.29: Displaying the recently joined Windows 10 devices

That brings an end to this section. You have learned what Microsoft Entra join is and the methods used to enroll, and you have also walked through the steps to manually join a Windows 10 device to Microsoft Entra.

> **Note**
>
> You are encouraged to read further by using the following links, which will provide additional information about Microsoft Entra Join, Windows Autopilot, and bulk device enrollment:
>
> https://learn.microsoft.com/en-us/entra/identity/devices/concept-directory-join
>
> https://learn.microsoft.com/en-us/autopilot/windows-autopilot
>
> https://learn.microsoft.com/en-us/mem/intune/enrollment/windows-bulk-enroll
>
> https://learn.microsoft.com/en-us/entra/identity/devices/device-join-out-of-box

Next, we will look at what bulk operations are and how to perform them.

Performing Bulk Operations

Bulk Microsoft Entra ID operations refer to the ability to perform a single action or update across multiple users, groups, or other objects in Microsoft Entra ID. This can be especially useful for larger organizations with hundreds or thousands of users, where manual updates to each individual object would be time-consuming and inefficient. Bulk operations in Microsoft Entra ID can be performed using PowerShell, Graph API, or other supported methods. Common bulk operations include adding or removing users from groups, updating user attributes, and managing device settings. We will explore more about the bulk operations you can perform and how they work in the following section.

Some of the popular operations you will learn about in this book perform bulk updates, such as the following:

- Bulk user creation
- Bulk user invitation
- Bulk user deletion
- Bulk user downloads

Performing Bulk Updates Using the Azure Portal

Performing bulk user updates is like managing single users (such as internal and guest users). The only property that can't be set for multiple users is resetting a password, which must be done for a single user.

Azure has also improved its bulk user settings by adding a drop-down menu that enables you to perform updates via the downloadable CSV template, which you then re-upload.

Downloading a User List

To download a user list, you can follow the given steps:

1. Navigate to the `Users` overview blade again in Microsoft Entra ID. You should automatically go into the `All users` blade; if not, select that option.
2. Click `Download users` from the top menu.

Figure 2.30: Bulk operations – clicking Download users

3. Enter a desired filename and click `Start`. This will be saved as a `.csv` file, which can be opened in Microsoft Excel if you desire for easy editing. A free version can be used with Microsoft 365 Office online. You can read more about this at this link: https://www.microsoft.com/en-us/microsoft-365/free-office-online-for-the-web. Being a comma-separated file type, where each value is separated by a comma, you can use any text editor, such as Windows Notepad.

Performing Bulk Operations   55

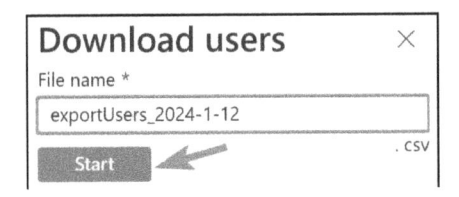

Figure 2.31: Bulk operations – Download users

4. Once complete, the option to download the file will appear. Click the blue text to download.

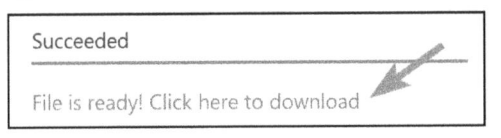

Figure 2.32: Downloading the user's CSV file

When opening the file, if you are presented with what looks like gibberish, you can do the following in Excel to format it neatly for yourself:

1. Click the A column to select all the data:

Figure 2.33: Bulk operations – selecting the A column in Excel

2. Then, select the Data tab from the top menu bar, and then select Text to Columns from the Data Tools context.

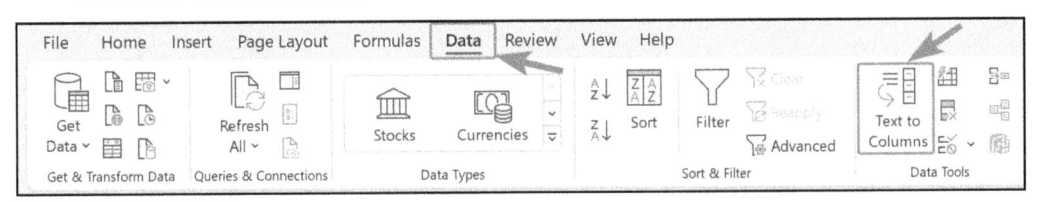

Figure 2.34: Bulk operations – selecting Text to Columns in Excel

3. On the screen that pops up, click `Delimited` and then `Next`.

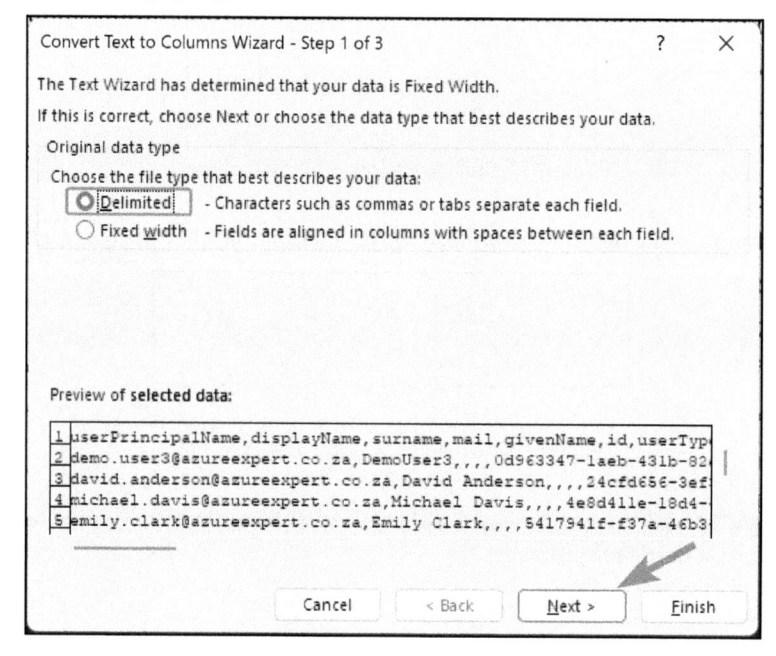

Figure 2.35: Bulk Operations – Delimited in Excel

4. Select `Comma`, and then click `Next >`.

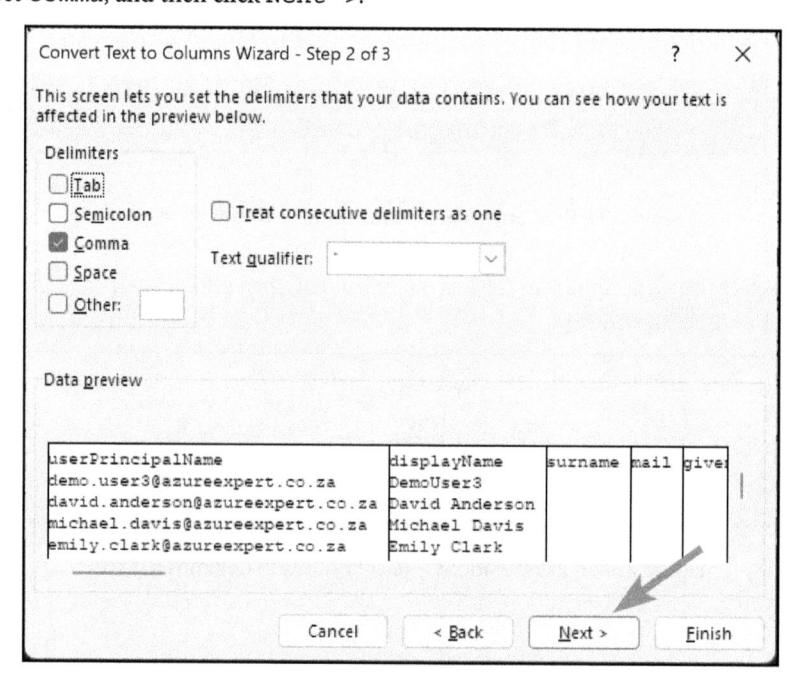

Figure 2.36: Bulk operations – selecting Comma

5. Click General for Column data format, and then click Finish.

Figure 2.37: Bulk Operations – selecting the column data format in Excel

Now, your data will be organized neatly into columns. Next, you will learn how to use this sheet to perform bulk deletion operations in Microsoft Entra ID.

Bulk User Deletion Operations

To demonstrate a bulk deletion, you will select and keep the users you want to retain in the sheet and delete the rows with the remaining users:

1. Navigate back to the Users blade and select All users.
2. Click Bulk operations and then Bulk delete.

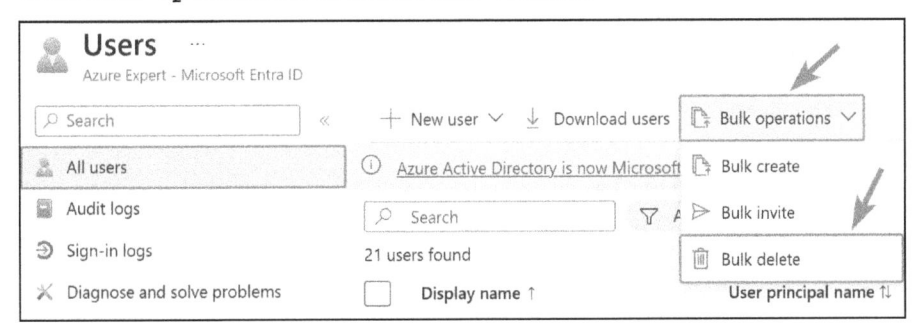

Figure 2.38: Microsoft Entra ID – Bulk delete

3. Click Download.

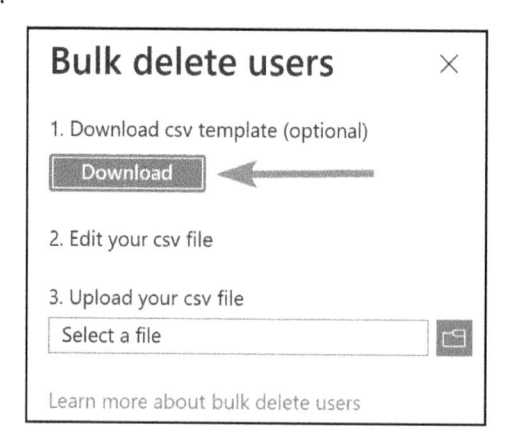

Figure 2.39: Microsoft Entra ID – the bulk delete template

4. Modify the sheet and paste in the user principal name for each user, from row 3 downward. You can copy these users from the sheet you downloaded in the last exercise. Click Save once you are finished and close the Excel sheet.

A
version:v1.0
User name [userPrincipalName] Required
jane.doe@azureexpert.co.za
bob.johnson@azureexpert.co.za

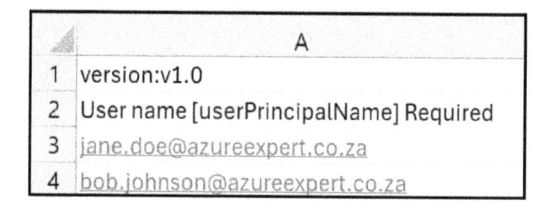

Figure 2.40: Bulk Operations – selecting users to delete in Excel

5. Back in the Azure portal, click the Select a file option from the previous screen. From the open file dialog that pops up, navigate to your file, and then click Open.

6. In the Azure portal, select Yes for the Are you sure you want to perform the delete operation? option, and then click Submit. You will be presented with a success notification once completed successfully.

7. That concludes the bulk user delete operation demonstration. Next, you will briefly explore other possible ways to modify Microsoft Entra ID user accounts.

Updating Multiple Users

You can also update multiple users by selecting them and choosing to delete them, or you can configure MFA for each user from the Azure portal in the Users blade:

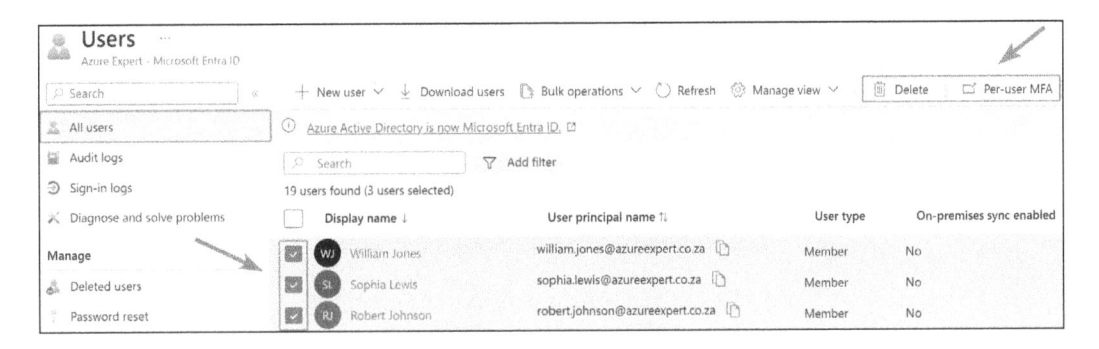

Figure 2.41: An alternative bulk user delete method

This concludes our demonstration of how to perform bulk user deletion operations using the Azure portal. Next, we will take a look at a PowerShell script that I think can help you achieve bulk user creation.

Performing Bulk Creations Using PowerShell

You will now experience running a PowerShell script to enable you to create Microsoft Entra ID users quickly and programmatically in your environment. The following script will create several demo users with a predefined password for you:

1. Start by opening your favorite code editor or notepad; I recommend VS Code, which you can download from here: `https://code.visualstudio.com/download`.

2. Paste the following code and save the file as a `.ps1` file, with whatever name prefix you want. To follow this exercise, it is advised that you save the file in `C:\Scripts` on your computer and name it `Create_AzureAD_Users.ps1`. You will need to populate the `$TenantId` and `$DomainSuffix` details in between the inverted commas on the right.

Create_AzureAD_Users.ps1

```
# Enter the Tenant ID for your Azure AD
$TenantId = ""
# Populate your Domain Suffix
$DomainSuffix = ""
# List of usernames to create
$UserNames = @(
    "John Smith",
    "Jane Doe",
    "Robert Johnson",
```

The complete code is available at `https://packt.link/CEwga`

3. Note the location of your script (e.g., C:\Scripts), and then open PowerShell.
4. Type in cd and the path to your script, and then press the *Enter* key.

Figure 2.42: Changing the directory on PowerShell

5. Now, to run the script, enter .\ and start typing your script name. The .\ notation means that you will look in the path that you are currently in – in my example, C:\Scripts. Click *Enter* once you have your script.

Figure 2.43 – Launching the Create_EntraID_Users script

6. A prompt will pop up, asking you to authenticate; enter your details and sign in.

Figure 2.44: Azure's Sign in prompt

7. Return to the Azure portal and navigate to `Microsoft Entra ID`, and then the `Users` blade. You should see your new users there.

This concludes our demonstration on how to perform bulk user creations using a PowerShell script, helping you to achieve a consistent deployment methodology that can also save you time.

> **Note**
>
> You are encouraged to read further by using the following links, which look at adding bulk users:
>
> `https://learn.microsoft.com/en-us/entra/identity/users/users-bulk-add`
>
> `https://learn.microsoft.com/en-us/entra/identity/users/groups-bulk-import-members`

In the next section, we are going to cover how you can manage guest accounts.

Navigating Guest Accounts

In Microsoft Entra ID, a guest account is a user account that is created in one Microsoft Entra directory, allowing a user from another Microsoft Entra directory, or an external identity provider, to access resources in the first tenant. Guest accounts can be invited to access applications, groups, or resources by users with appropriate permissions in the inviting tenant. This feature enables organizations to collaborate and share resources with external partners, contractors, or customers while maintaining control over their own corporate data. Guest users have limited access to Microsoft Entra ID resources, and their permissions can be managed and revoked by the inviting organization.

You can also add guest accounts in Microsoft Entra ID using Azure AD B2B. Azure AD B2B is a feature on top of Microsoft Entra ID that allows organizations to work safely with external users. External users don't require a Microsoft work or personal account that has been added to an existing Azure AD tenant to be added to Azure B2B.

All sorts of accounts can be added to Azure B2B. You don't have to configure anything in the Azure portal to use B2B; this feature is enabled by default for all Microsoft Entra tenants.

Next, we will explore how to manage guest accounts on Microsoft Entra ID.

Managing Guest Accounts

We can manage guest accounts by performing the following steps:

1. Adding guest accounts to your Microsoft Entra ID directory is similar to adding internal users. When you navigate to the `Users` overview blade, you can choose `+ New user` from the top-level menu and then select `Invite external user`, as follows:

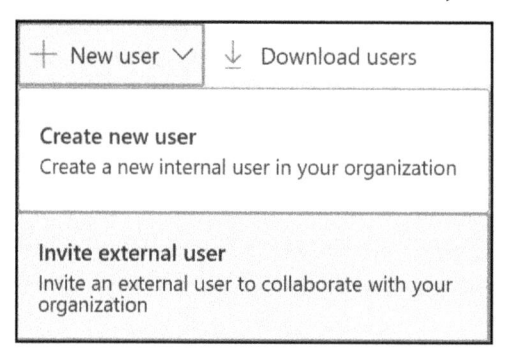

Figure 2.45: Inviting an external user

2. Provide an email address and a personalized message, which is sent to the user's inbox. This personalized message includes a link to log into your tenant.
3. Click `Review + invite` at the bottom of the blade screen, and then click `Invite` to add the user to your Microsoft Entra ID directory and send an invitation to the user's inbox:

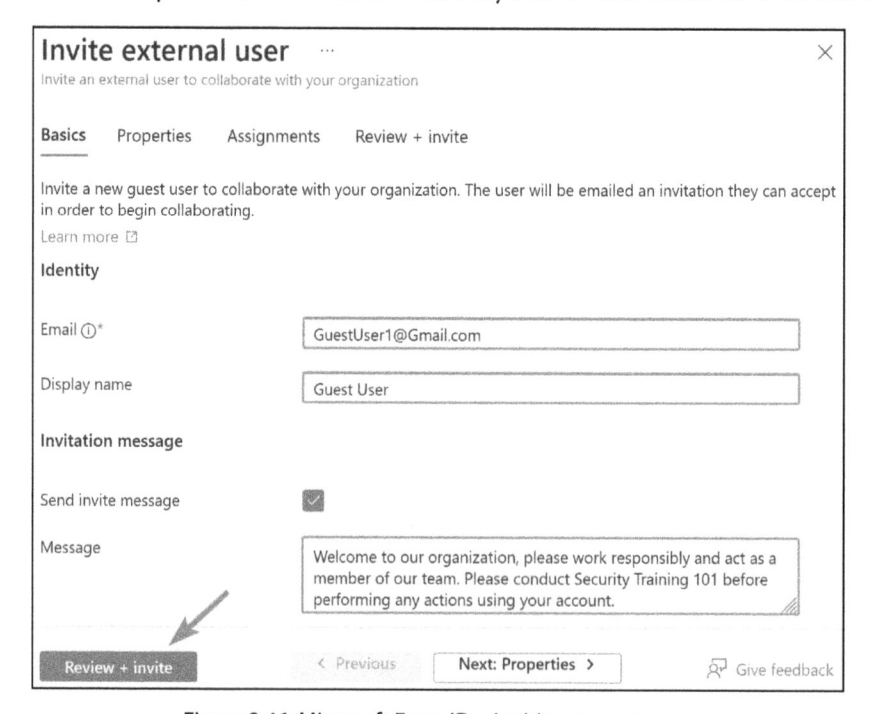

Figure 2.46: Microsoft Entra ID – inviting a guest user

4. To manage external users after creation, you can select them from the `Users` overview blade. They will have a `User type` value, which is named `Guest`. Simply select a user from the list, and you will then be able to manage the settings that are displayed in the top-level menu for the user, as follows:

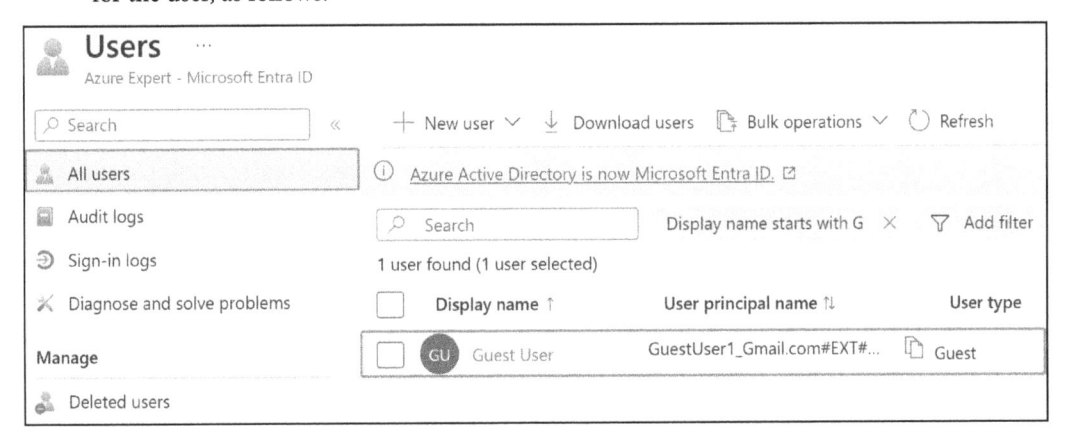

Figure 2.47: A guest user in Microsoft Entra ID

That brings an end to this section. In this short section, we have reviewed guest accounts in Microsoft Entra ID and learned how to configure them.

> **Note**
> You are encouraged to read further by using the following links, which will provide additional information about restricting guest permissions: `https://learn.microsoft.com/en-us/entra/identity/users/users-restrict-guest-permissions`.

In the next section, we will look at **SSPR**.

Configuring SSPR

Microsoft Entra ID SSPR allows users to reset their own passwords without the need to contact IT support or administrators. With SSPR, users can verify their identity using different methods, such as email, text message, or a mobile app notification, and reset their password without any help. This feature is not only convenient for end users but also reduces the workload for IT support, increases security by ensuring that users have strong passwords, and saves time and resources. SSPR is an essential feature for any organization that wants to improve user productivity and reduce IT costs.

There are several things to keep in mind when considering implementing this feature in your organization:

- Firstly, SSPR requires a Microsoft Entra ID account with **Global Administrator** privileges to manage SSPR options. This permission will allow the user to always be able to reset their own passwords, no matter what options are configured.

- Additionally, SSPR uses a **security group** to limit the users who have SSPR privileges, providing an added layer of security to the feature.
- It's important to note that all user accounts in your organization must have a valid license to use SSPR. This means that if your organization has licenses for Office 365 or Microsoft Entra P1 or P2, you can enable SSPR for all users. If not, you must purchase Microsoft Entra P1 licenses to enable SSPR for your users.

Overall, implementing Microsoft Entra ID SSPR can be a useful and convenient tool for both users and IT administrators. However, it's important to carefully consider the requirements and characteristics of this feature before enabling it for your organization.

Next, we will explore how to configure SSPR for your users.

Configuring SSPR

By enabling SSPR for your users, they are able to change their passwords automatically without calling the help desk. This can significantly eliminate the management overhead.

> **Note**
> The Microsoft Entra free-tier license only supports cloud users for SSPR, and only password change is supported, not a password reset.

SSPR can be easily enabled from the Azure portal. To do this, perform the following steps:

1. Navigate to the Azure portal by opening `https://portal.azure.com`.
2. From the left-hand hamburger menu or the main search bar, select `Microsoft Entra ID`.
3. From the left-hand menu under the `Manage` context, select `Password reset`, as follows:

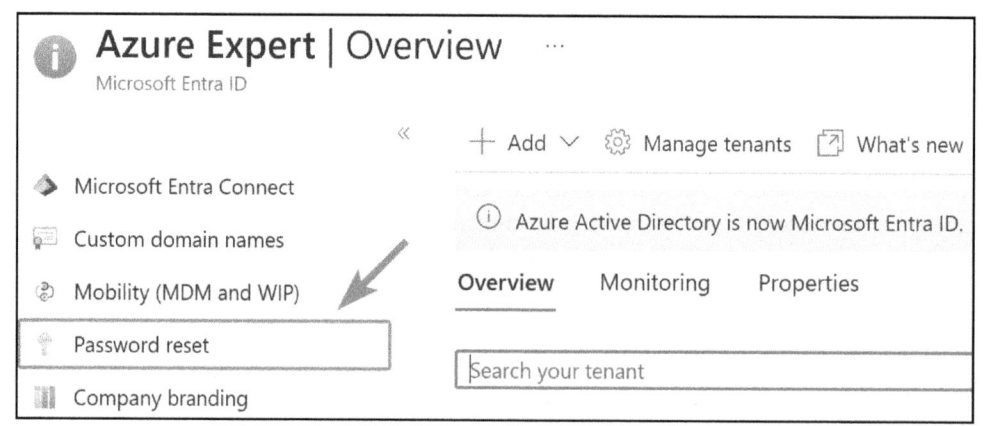

Figure 2.48: The Password reset blade

4. In the `Password reset` blade, you can enable SSPR for all your users by selecting `All`; for selected users and groups, select `Selected`. For this demonstration, enable it for all users, and then click on `Save` in the top-level menu, as follows:

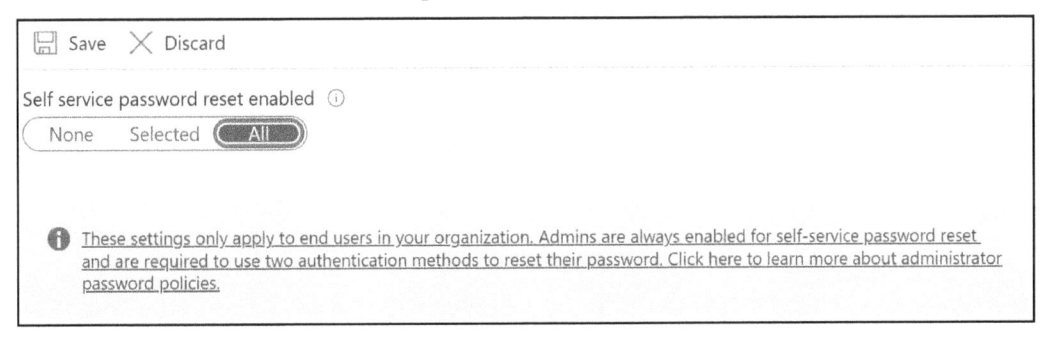

Figure 2.49: SSPR

5. Next, you need to set the different required authentication methods for your users. To do this, under the `Manage` context from the left menu, select `Authentication methods`.

6. In the next blade, you can set the number of authentication methods that are required to reset a password and explore what methods are available for your users, as follows:

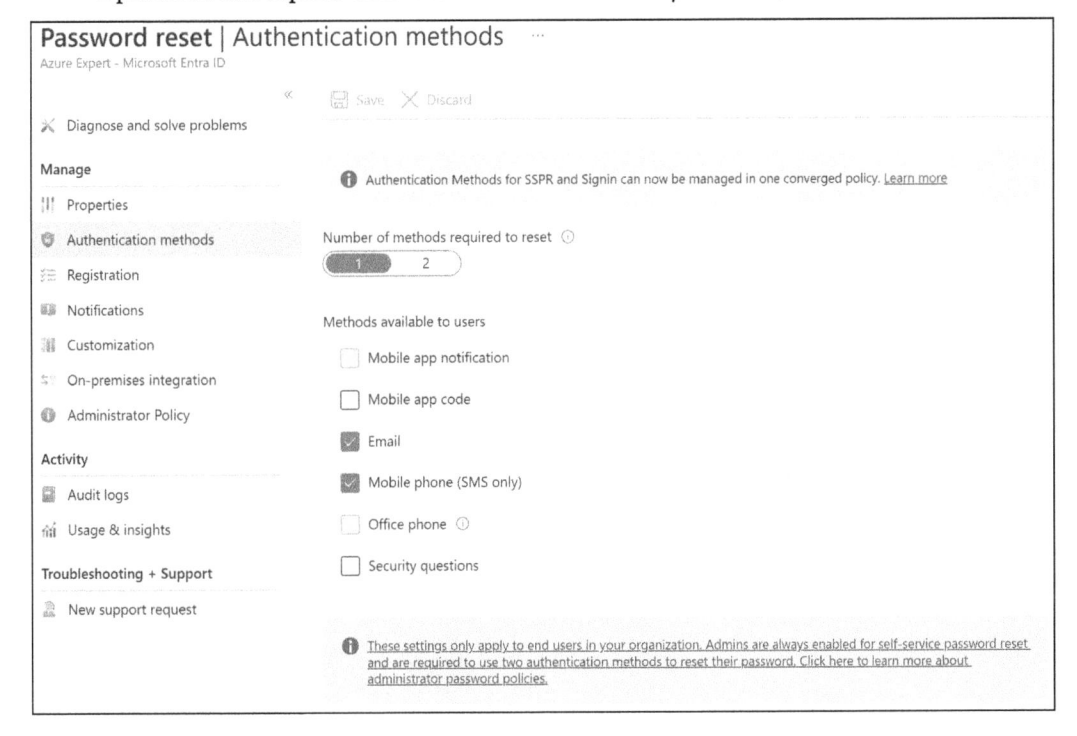

Figure 2.50: Authentication methods for a password reset

7. Make a selection, and then click Save at the top of the screen. If you want to test SSPR after configuration, make sure that you use a user account without administrator privileges.

> **Note**
>
> You are encouraged to read further by using the following links:
>
> https://learn.microsoft.com/en-us/entra/identity/authentication/concept-sspr-howitworks
>
> https://learn.microsoft.com/en-us/entra/identity/authentication/tutorial-enable-sspr

Summary

In this chapter, you learned about configuring and managing devices in Microsoft Entra ID (device identities, device settings, Enterprise State Roaming, device settings, audit logs, and licensing). You learned about the various mechanisms to integrate your devices into Entra ID (device registration, Entra join, and Entra hybrid join). Additionally, you explored different bulk user operations and how to create a guest account from the Azure portal. Finally, you learned how to configure SSPR, which is a feature critical to empower users to reset their own passwords and reduce the administrative burden of password management for IT support.

In the next chapter, you will learn about **Role-Based Access Control** (**RBAC**) and get hands-on with creating custom RBAC roles. Additionally, you will learn how to interpret role assignments.

3
Managing Role-Based Access Control in Azure

In an ever-evolving digital landscape, safeguarding resources and sensitive information is crucial. Microsoft Azure addresses this challenge through **Role-Based Access Control** (**RBAC**), a system that manages access to resources by defining permissions via roles. This chapter delves into the core concepts and functionalities of Azure RBAC, encompassing role creation, management, and assignments. Additionally, you will learn how to distinguish between Azure RBAC and Microsoft Entra ID roles, shedding light on how the former administers access to subscriptions. Lastly, you will examine built-in Azure RBAC roles and their respective use cases. By the chapter's end, you will possess a comprehensive understanding of Azure RBAC and its application in managing access to resources and data within your organization.

In this chapter, you will explore the following topics:

- Understanding Azure regions
- Managing Azure subscriptions and management hierarchy
- Configuring management groups
- Understanding RBAC
- Creating a custom RBAC role
- Interpreting access assignments

> **Note**
> Azure makes use of an additive model when there are overlapping permissions for a specific user: `https://docs.microsoft.com/en-us/azure/role-based-access-control/overview#multiple-role-assignments`.

Technical Requirements

To follow this chapter, you will need access to a Microsoft Entra ID tenant as a global administrator. If you do not have access to one, you can enroll with a free account: `https://azure.microsoft.com/en-us/free/`.

You will also need an Azure subscription on which you have owner permissions with a resource group deployed and a virtual machine of any size that is part of the resource group.

Understanding Azure Regions

An Azure region is a set of data centers deployed within a specific geographic area. Each region is connected to the Azure backbone network and is designed to be highly available and resilient to ensure maximum uptime for your applications and services. When you create resources in Azure, you have the option to select a specific region where those resources will be located.

The region you choose for your resources can have implications for RBAC management. This is because different regions may have different compliance requirements, data residency regulations, and network topologies. For example, some regions may have specific security certifications that may be required for certain types of data, while other regions may have restrictions on data transfer across geographic borders.

When creating roles and role assignments in RBAC, it is important to consider the region where your resources are located, and whether there are any specific access policies or requirements for that region. Some RBAC features, such as resource locks, can only be applied at the resource group or subscription level, and may not be supported across all regions.

Managing RBAC across Multiple Regions

If your organization operates across multiple regions, managing RBAC can become more complex. You may have different teams responsible for managing resources in different regions, each with their own RBAC requirements and policies. Additionally, you may need to ensure compliance with regulations and laws that vary across different regions.

To help manage RBAC across multiple regions, Azure provides several tools and features, such as Azure Policy and Azure Blueprints, that allow you to define and enforce policies and configurations across multiple subscriptions and regions. You can also use Azure Resource Manager templates to automate the deployment of RBAC configurations and resources across multiple regions.

In summary, Azure regions play an important role in RBAC management, and it is important to consider the implications of region selection when creating roles and role assignments. By leveraging Azure's tools and features, you can manage RBAC across multiple regions and ensure compliance with regulations and policies.

Managing Azure Subscriptions and Management Hierarchy

Azure subscriptions are agreements between Microsoft and a customer that grant access to Azure services and resources based on pay-as-you-go or commitment-based payment models. They serve as the primary means for managing resources, services, and costs within Azure. Every subscription has a unique identifier, and customers can maintain multiple subscriptions in a single Azure account.

Azure subscriptions assign various roles to users, thereby enabling them to manage and control resources. Roles such as Owner, Contributor, and Reader offer different levels of access and permissions. Subscriptions also act as boundaries for billing, usage monitoring, and resource quotas.

When implementing a subscription, it is important to make several considerations as to how you plan to use the subscription. While it's out of the scope of this course, it's important for you to be aware of some of the factors behind subscription designs. One of the first things to consider is the environment the subscription will serve, such as production or non-production workloads. Some organizations look to further segment subscriptions by introducing additional workload layers, such as a sandbox environment or the split of non-production workloads into Test, **User Acceptance Testing (UAT)**, Development, and Pre-Production. You will almost certainly, with modern design practices, encounter a form of a hub subscription, which serves as a shared space for workloads that interact across all environments, such as identity systems such as Active Directory. The shared space (hub) subscription would normally house the shared networking, identity, logic systems, and the like to be used between environments. More elaborate designs may be considered depending on the size of the organization and the level of segmentation that is instituted from an Architecture layer, which would see the incorporation of subscriptions related to policy management, provider service management, and identity management. Subscriptions also serve as a great boundary mechanism for governance. Typically, when wanting to understand the full dynamics behind subscription design, you may want to read more around landing zone designs.

Figure 3.1 illustrates the typical hub and spoke model you could expect to encounter in a typical environment. As you can see, all the workload subscriptions (`Production`, `Non-Production`, and `Sandbox`) are connected to the hub subscription.

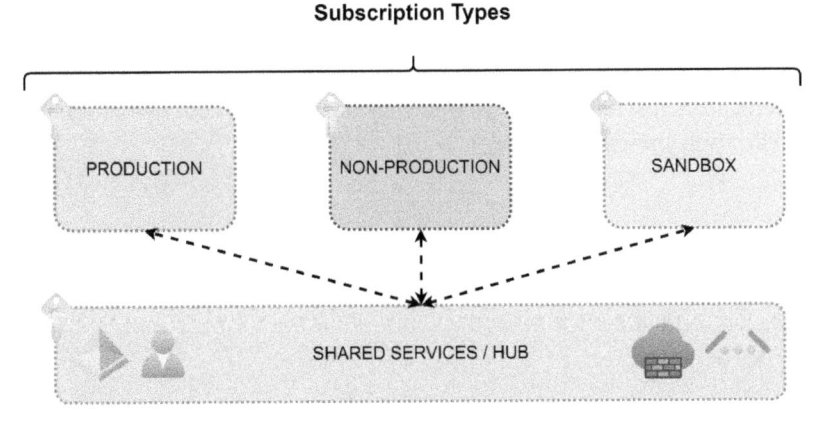

Figure 3.1: Azure subscription types

> **Note**
>
> For more information on subscriptions, please refer to the following URL: `https://learn.microsoft.com/en-us/azure/cloud-adoption-framework/ready/landing-zone/design-area/resource-org-subscriptions`.
>
> For more information on subscriptions in relation to landing zone designs, please refer to the following URL: `https://learn.microsoft.com/en-us/azure/cloud-adoption-framework/ready/landing-zone/design-area/resource-org-subscriptions`.

Billing Profiles

Billing profiles are part of the Azure Cost Management and Billing system, designed to help customers manage and track their Azure spending. A billing profile is a container for invoices, payments, and other billing-related information. It is associated with a specific Azure subscription or set of subscriptions and can be used to organize and consolidate billing information.

Billing profiles include features such as invoice management, payment method management, billing address management, and cost management alerts. Customers can create multiple billing profiles to separate and manage the billing information for different projects, departments, or business units.

> **Note**
>
> Please refer to the following URL to read more about billing profiles: `https://learn.microsoft.com/en-us/microsoft-365/commerce/billing-and-payments/manage-billing-profiles`.

Azure Management Hierarchy

As organizations grow, managing Azure resources can become increasingly complex, especially with multiple departments, teams, or projects. Microsoft has designed a hierarchy of management that enables you to delegate control and assign responsibilities to different levels of your organization.

The Azure management hierarchy is a structured approach to organizing and managing resources within an Azure environment. It enables organizations to delegate control, assign responsibilities, and streamline governance across different levels. Understanding the core concepts and key considerations is essential to effectively present this topic.

Core Concepts

Azure introduces management granularity, allowing you to define permission structures at four primary levels. Deciding on the level of granularity that would be best for you depends on which layer you will assign permissions that transitively flow into the lower corresponding layers. These layers of management are listed here:

- **Management groups**: Management groups provide a way to organize and manage subscriptions efficiently. They allow you to apply consistent policies and access control to multiple subscriptions, which can be particularly beneficial for organizations with complex structures or multiple Azure subscriptions. Management groups can be nested, allowing you to create a hierarchy that reflects your organization's structure and needs.

- **Subscriptions**: Azure subscriptions are agreements between Microsoft and a customer that grant access to Azure services and resources. Subscriptions can be used to manage resources, services, and costs within Azure, and they act as boundaries for billing, usage monitoring, and resource quotas. Subscriptions also allow you to assign user roles, which determine the level of access and permissions users have within the Azure environment.

- **Resource groups**: Resource groups are logical containers for resources deployed within an Azure subscription. They provide a way to organize and manage resources based on their lifecycles and relationships with each other. Resource groups enable you to manage resources collectively, apply consistent policies, and provide access control.

- **Resources**: Resources are individual Azure components, such as virtual machines, storage accounts, and databases. Resources are managed and organized within resource groups and subscriptions.

The hierarchy of management within Azure is defined as per *Figure 3.2* below:

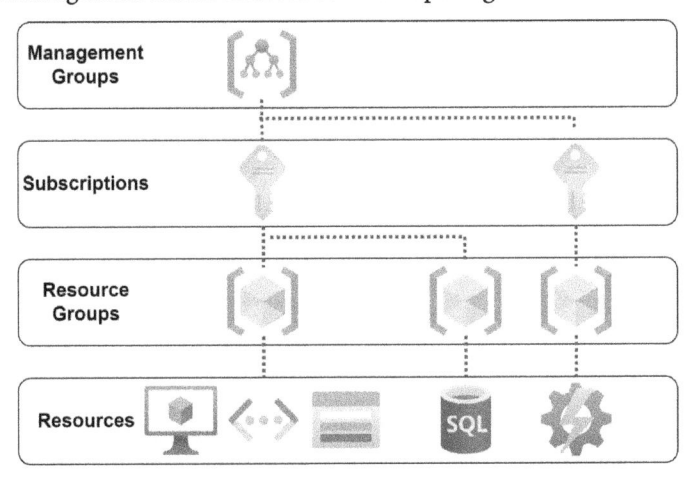

Figure 3.2: Resource management scope

Key Considerations of the Hierarchy of Management for Enterprise Agreements

The Azure **Enterprise Agreement** (**EA**) management hierarchy consists of four main levels:

- **Enterprise**: At the Enterprise level, the organization is identified by its Microsoft Entra tenant, and the layer at which the Azure agreement is defined (e.g., **pay-as-you-go** (**PAYG**), **Cloud Solution Provider** (**CSP**), also identified as an Azure Plan, or EA). This level serves as the identifier for your organization on Azure.

- **Departments**: At the department level, sub-accounts are created for different organizational departments. Departments can be grouped functionally (e.g., IT and finance) or geographically (e.g., North America and Europe). A department owner can be added to manage the budget for the department.

- **Accounts**: Within a department, multiple accounts can be created. Additional owners can be added to manage these accounts. When creating a personal account in Azure, this level serves as the starting point for creating subscriptions, with the Microsoft account used for Azure portal login added as the owner.

- **Subscriptions**: Multiple subscriptions can be created within an account. This level is where billing occurs, and Azure resources are created. Additional subscription owners can be added to manage subscriptions, create resources, and assign users to a subscription. Subscriptions always maintain a trust relationship with a Microsoft Entra instance.

You can see this hierarchy illustrated in the following diagram. Typically, this would align with the different organizational structures you would define for your organization, illustrated by the different variations of hierarchy in the diagram shown in *Figure 3.3*:

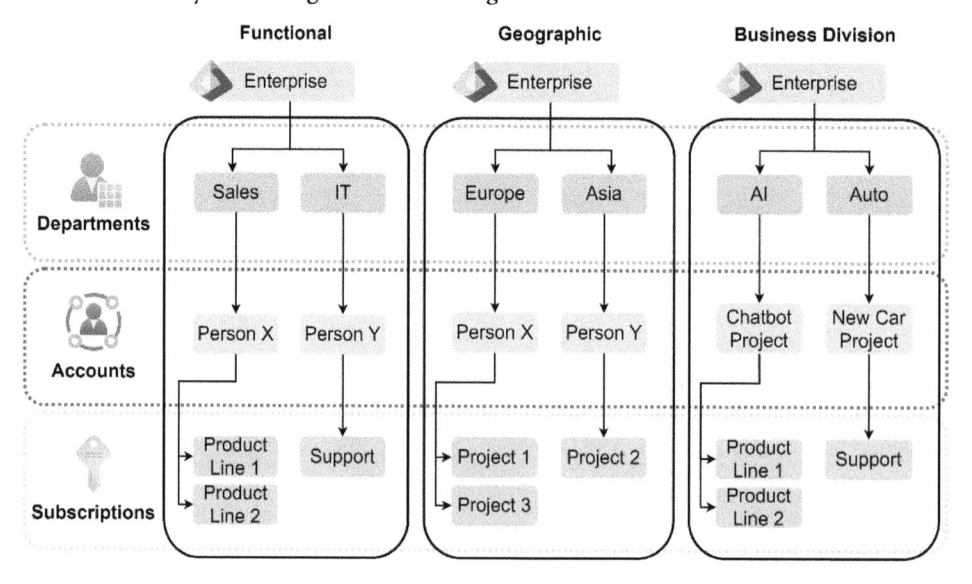

Figure 3.3: Azure management hierarchy

> **Note**
> There are occasions where resource limits might be reached within a subscription, and this may be the criterion for you to create a new one. For resource limits, please refer to the following URL: https://learn.microsoft.com/en-us/azure/azure-resource-manager/management/azure-subscription-service-limits.

While this structure may be unique in this context to the EA subscription, the same principles apply when considering organizational design and governance, which should all be considered when deploying and designing a landing zone. You are encouraged to explore this topic more, where you will learn about types of organizational structures such as **Functional**, **Matrix**, **Multi-divisional**, and **Flatarchy**. There are additional patterns that have been emerging with modern cloud practices but note from these that the pattern should dictate how you manage resource allocation, costs, and more, considering the four levels of management available to Azure.

Relationship Between Microsoft Entra and Subscriptions

Azure subscriptions have trust relationships associated with Microsoft Entra. Through this trust, a subscription enables Microsoft Entra ID to authenticate users, services, and devices.

A Microsoft Entra tenant can have a **1:M (one to many)** relationship with subscriptions (meaning it can be associated with multiple subscriptions), but a subscription can only have a 1:1 relationship with a tenant (meaning one subscription can only be associated with one tenant). You can see an overview of this in the following *Figure 3.4*:

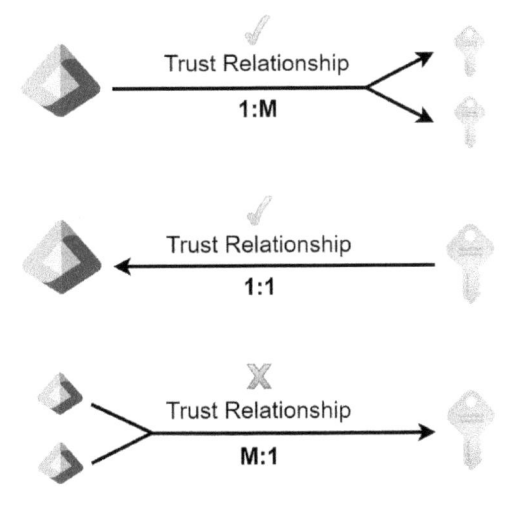

Figure 3.4: Microsoft entra and subscription relationships

You will notice that there are a several relationship types mentioned. For quick reference, they are: `1:M` - one to many, `M:1` - many to one, and `1:1` - one to one.

You have now seen the relationship structure and understand the management hierarchy.

Why Have Multiple Subscriptions in an Environment?

This is part of the organizational strategy when defining Azure, and it's important to understand the segregation of data and resources and how this will be managed perpetually by the business. Some motivations to split out resource groups are separating resources by the following:

- Different **business units** (**BUs**) (Finance/IT/Marketing)
- Different environments (Dev/Test/UAT/PROD)
- Geographic (West Europe/Central US)
- Cost centers (could be the same as BUs or a unique code)

> **Note**
>
> When defining governance around Azure, it's important to define a naming convention that will be applied across multiple layers, including subscriptions. It's recommended to identify a subscription location and purpose in the name—for example, **WE_PROD**. We advise that you carefully consider a landing zone design when contemplating subscriptions. You can read more here: `https://learn.microsoft.com/en-us/azure/cloud-adoption-framework/ready/landing-zone/`.

That brings this section to an end. In this section, you have learned about what subscriptions are, why they are necessary, strategic items to consider, and billing ownership associated with subscriptions.

> **Note**
>
> You are encouraged to read up further by using the following links:
>
> Initial subscription strategy: `https://docs.microsoft.com/en-us/azure/cloud-adoption-framework/ready/azure-best-practices/initial-subscriptions`
>
> Multi-subscription strategy: `https://docs.microsoft.com/en-us/azure/cloud-adoption-framework/ready/azure-best-practices/scale-subscriptions`

Next, you will look at what management groups are and how they assist you with organization and management.

Configuring Management Groups

Azure management groups help you organize your resources and subscriptions and sit above the subscription layer, which allows global governance of the Azure platform.

Subscriptions are organized into containers called **management groups** that allow a transitive flow of common conditions through subscription layers, such as Azure policies and RBAC permissions. This structure should always dictate a form of logical hierarchy structure that should be constructed to allow a flow of permissions or policies as required by the organization.

Generally, aligning to a company organogram can help determine structures to be implemented by discerning the desired outcomes from the management group structure, bearing in mind that this may be policy, permission, and/or governance. To support this decision, logical breakdowns should identify the overall hierarchy to be developed in Azure relating to the management and reporting of services. This is usually defined to be either functional/business divisions or geographical divisions, and a combination of these can be derived based on the desired outcomes.

An example management group structure is presented in *Figure 3.5*:

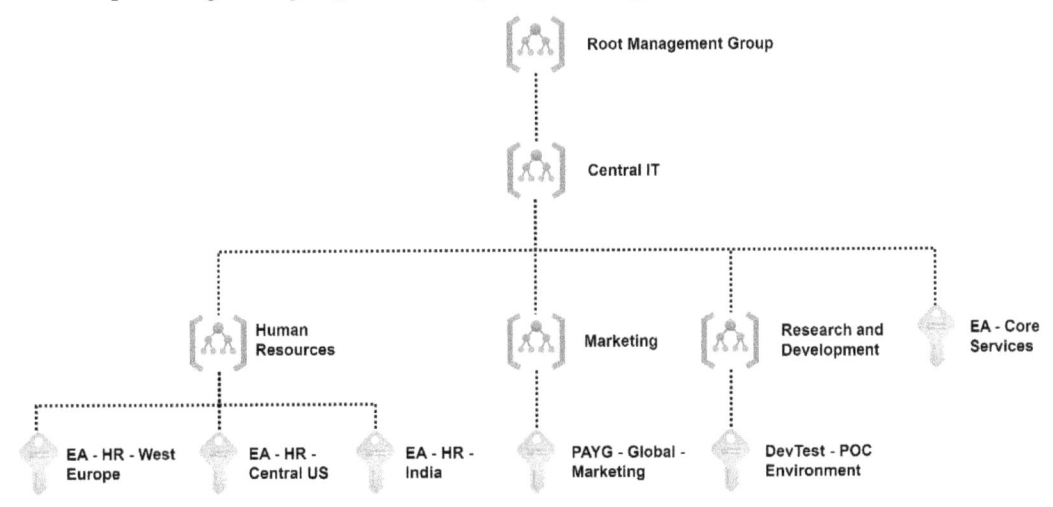

Figure 3.5: Example management group structure

As you can see from this diagram, you have `Root Management Group` at the top of the hierarchy, with `Central IT` defined straight after. In this example, you are assuming that `Central IT` will be able to manage the entire organization, and as such you allow them to have permissions set at the top layer, allowing transitive permission structures for all subscriptions. Next, you can see the split between the various business functions and the associated subscriptions for those departments. Remember that the permission structure could be loosely defined at the subscription layer but is more appropriately defined at the level that allows the most restrictive access and only access to what is required. This structure makes it much easier to apply permissions, policies, and standards at different layers of the organization and will make management much simpler with these structures in place.

Now that you understand the structure of management groups, you will create one.

Creating a Management Group

In the following example, you will create a management group named IT and associate your subscription with this group. Here's what you will do:

1. You will search for management groups in the search bar at the top of the Azure portal and click Management groups when the service is identified, as illustrated in the following *Figure 3.6*:

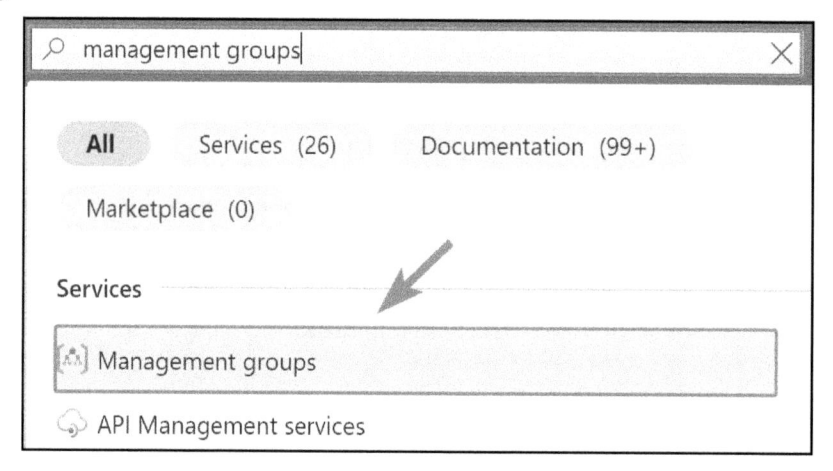

Figure 3.6: Searching for management groups

2. Since you do not have any management groups yet, you will need to enable the feature. Click Start using management groups, as illustrated in the following *Figure 3.7*:

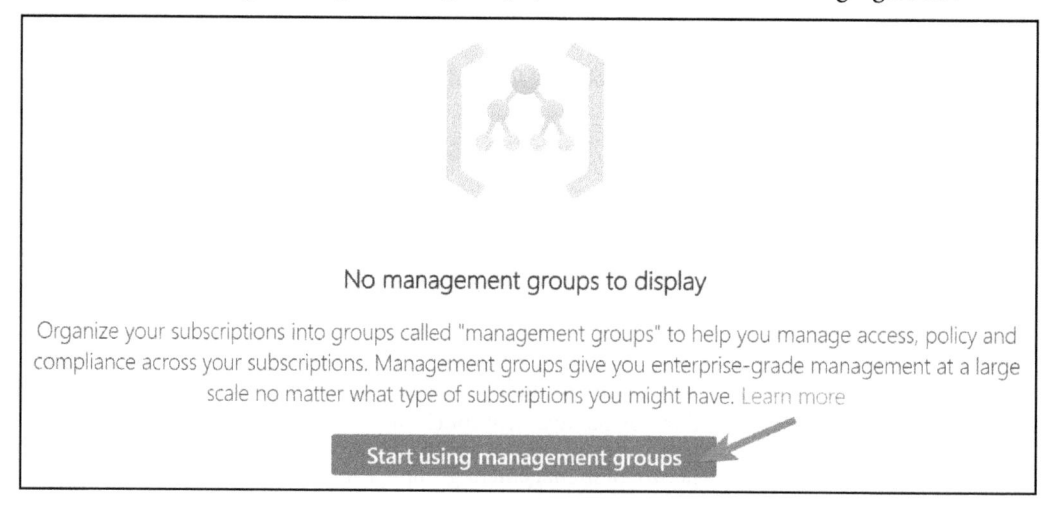

Figure 3.7: Enabling management groups

3. Enter a `Management group ID` and `Management group display name` value and click `Submit`, as illustrated in the following *Figure 3.8*:

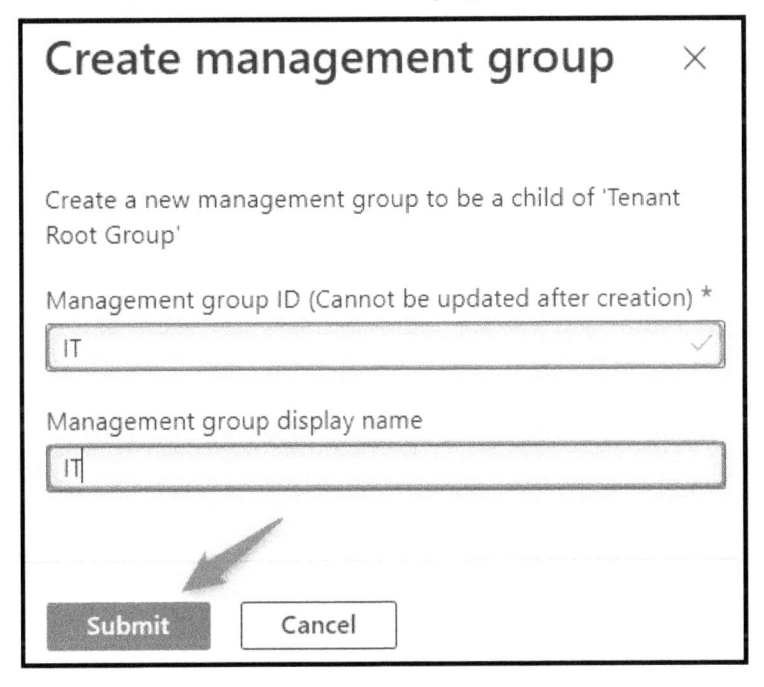

Figure 3.8: Creating a management group

4. A notification will indicate the successful creation of a management group, and you will be presented with the management group overview. Note the `Tenant Root Group` entity in the following screenshot—this is enabled by default on all environments and sits above all management groups and subscriptions.

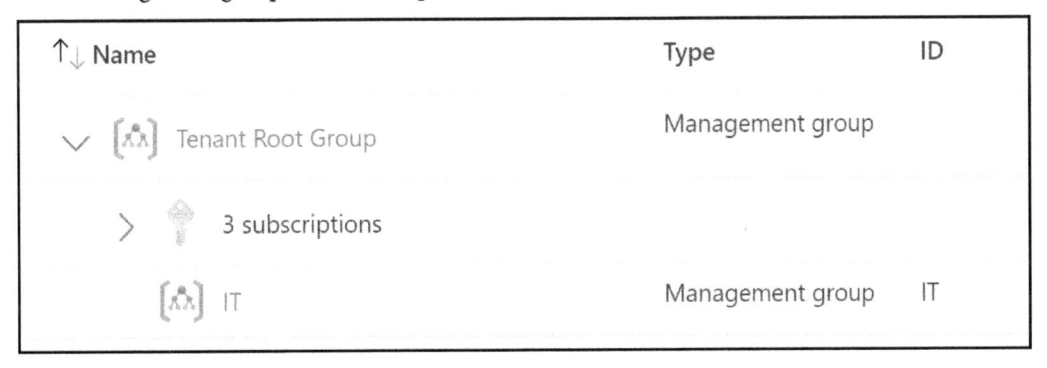

Figure 3.9: Management groups overview

> **Note**
> The first management group in Azure is the **Tenant Root Group**—this is created by default and is the top parent group; all subsequent management groups will fall as child management groups under the root group. Also, the root group cannot be deleted.

You have now created your first management group, and this can be used for better governance and management of Azure.

That brings this section to an end. You have learned what management groups are, how they contribute to organizational structure and management within Azure, and how to create one.

> **Note**
> You are encouraged to read up further by using the following links:
>
> Organizing subscriptions: https://learn.microsoft.com/en-us/azure/cloud-adoption-framework/ready/azure-best-practices/organize-subscriptions
>
> Management groups documentation: https://learn.microsoft.com/en-us/azure/governance/management-groups/

In the next section, you will discover what RBAC is and how it's pertinent to successfully managing your environment when considering access, and how to grant access in the correct way. Remember that RBAC can be used in conjunction with management groups too.

Understanding role-based-access-control

Azure **Role-Based Access Control** (**RBAC**) is a tool that's used to manage access to Azure resources. It provides fine-grained control over who can perform specific actions (such as creating, updating, or deleting resources) on specific resources within an Azure subscription. With Azure RBAC, you can grant permissions to users, groups, and applications, which is defined as the scope, such as a management group, subscription, resource group, or individual resource. This way, you can ensure that users have the necessary permissions to perform their tasks, while preventing them from accessing resources that they do not need.

RBAC Requirements

To use Azure RBAC, you need to have an Azure subscription and a Microsoft Entra tenant. You can then assign roles to users, groups, or applications within the Azure portal or by using Azure PowerShell or the Azure CLI. You can also assign roles to users within your organization or to users in external organizations.

RBAC built-in Roles

Azure RBAC includes built-in roles such as Owner, Contributor, and Reader, as well as custom roles that you can define yourself. There are three predominant roles that you will encounter, one of which is the owner role, which allows the designated administrator to have full access to all resources within the scope that they are associated with. Another similar role is the contributor role, where designated administrators can create and manage all the resources within the applied scope but will be restricted from granting access to others, and finally, the reader role, which grants view-only access to resources within the applied scope.

The following list summarizes these roles, which are the most common built-in roles within Azure:

- **Owner role**: This is the role that includes all permissions related to management; you can read, add, and remove resources. You also have the capability to add and remove other users to and from resources as owners or other roles.
- **Contributor role**: This role has the same permissions as an owner, except you cannot add or remove additional users to and from resources.
- **Reader role**: This role has the ability to view resources but cannot amend, add, or remove users or resources.

> **Note**
> There are multiple built-in roles within Azure, and it is recommended that you have a look at them to learn more: `https://learn.microsoft.com/en-us/azure/role-based-access-control/built-in-roles`.

Getting Started with Azure RBAC

Azure RBAC can help you ensure security and compliance by limiting access to your resources to only those who need it. It can also help you manage costs by preventing users from accidentally deleting or modifying resources they do not need.

RBAC is a general term used for restricting access to users, based on a role. It works on the **Just Enough Access (JEA)** concept, where a specific user/group will be provided the minimum access required to perform their specific job on a specific resource. Custom roles can only be created and updated by a user who has the following role assigned: `Microsoft.Authorization/roleDefinitions/write permissions`.

When it comes to RBAC, it is very important to understand how and where it is applied. Azure RBAC can be applied to the following security principals:

- User
- Group

- Service principal
- Managed identity

The following diagram shows these security principals:

Figure 3.10: Security principals

You now know about some of the basic building blocks related to RBAC. Next, you will explore role definitions, what they are, and how they are used.

Role Definitions

Now that you know what security principals support RBAC, the next step is to have a look at role definitions. In RBAC, access is granted based on the role assigned to a user or a security principal, instead of granting permissions directly to the user. A role definition is a collection of permissions that defines the actions that can be performed on resources in Azure. When a user is assigned a role, they inherit the permissions defined in the role definition.

In Azure, there are built-in roles that provide common sets of permissions, such as owner, contributor, and reader. However, custom roles can also be defined by combining one or more of the available permissions in a role definition. This allows more fine-grained control over access to resources.

When a user is assigned a role, they can perform the actions defined in the role definition. For example, a user assigned the contributor role for a resource group can create, update, and delete resources in that resource group. The role definition determines what actions the user can perform, such as read access, write access, or the deletion of resources.

Overall, RBAC in Azure provides a flexible and scalable way to manage access to resources, allowing organizations to control access to their resources based on roles and permissions.

The following *Figure 3.11* is an example of what a role definition looks like. Observe that the `Contributor` role definition in this example can perform all actions denoted by the `*`, and `NotActions` are items that are explicitly excluded from the role definition. They overwrite the allowed `Actions` that could be performed. To become proficient at creating role definitions, you will need to practice and read a lot more about the various available actions. Then you can carefully consider what actions you are required to perform under the desired role you are creating. You will get to practice later in this chapter.

Figure 3.11: Example role definition

```
Built-in:
  Owner
  Contributor
  Reader
  ...
  Backup Operator
  Security Reader
  Virtual Machine Contributor

Custom:
  App Service Operator
  Log Auditor
```

Contributor Role Definition

```
"Actions" : [
    "*"
],
"NotActions" : [
    "Authorization/*/Delete",
    "Authorization/*/Write",
    "Authorization/elevateAccess/Action"
],
"DataActions": [],
"NotDataActions": [],
"AssignableScopes": [
    "/"
]
```

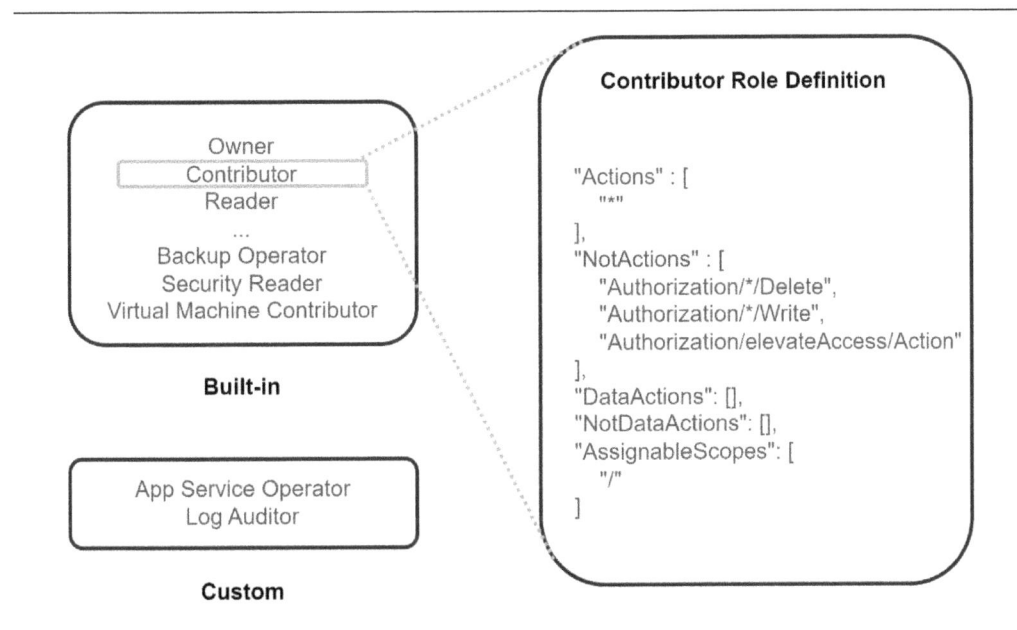

Figure 3.11: Example role definition

A role definition consists of three main elements:

- `Actions`: These are the operations that can be performed on Azure resources, such as read, write, delete, and manage access. Actions are represented in string format, which contains the resource provider and the resource type, like `Microsoft.Storage/storageAccounts/write`.

- `NotActions`: These are the operations that are explicitly denied, even if they are included in the `Actions` section. This is useful for creating custom roles with a limited set of permissions.

- `AssignableScopes`: This defines the scope within which the role definition can be assigned to users, groups, or applications. The scope can be a subscription, resource group, or a specific resource.

Azure provides many built-in role definitions, such as Owner, Contributor, and Reader, that cover common use cases. However, you can also create custom role definitions to meet your specific requirements.

> **Note**
>
> It is highly recommended that you become more familiar with creating custom roles as well as understanding the definitions behind the built-in roles. If you would like to read more, please have a look at this URL, which provides some more insights into the breakdown of this concept: https://learn.microsoft.com/en-us/azure/role-based-access-control/role-definitions.

Now that you have a good understanding of what role definitions are and the various components behind them, you will explore the next important aspect of RBAC – scope.

Scope

The next part of RBAC is scope. **Scope** is the target resource that you need to assign a role to. In Azure, there are four main scope levels that roles can be assigned to:

- Management groups
- Subscriptions
- Resource groups
- Resources

The following *Figure 3.12* displays the main scope levels in Azure:

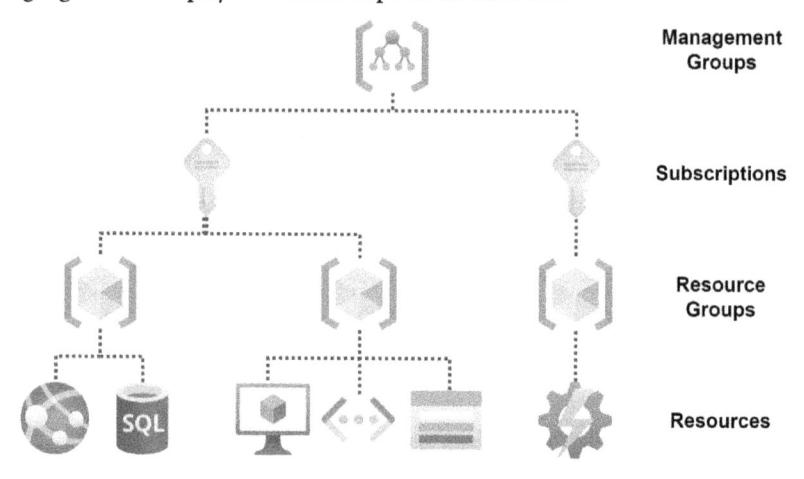

Figure 3.12: Scope levels in Azure

In summary, RBAC consists of three main sections:

- **Security principal**: Selects who is going to have access
- **Role:** Selects what type of access is going to be assigned to the security principal
- **Scope:** Selects the resource that the user and the role will be applied to

Now that you understand built-in RBAC roles within Azure, you will look at custom RBAC roles.

> **Note**
> **Microsoft Entra ID** roles are used to manage the identities within the directory, whereas **RBAC** in this section is used to define permissions for resources that reside within the relevant subscription or management group.

Custom RBAC roles can be created if the built-in RBAC roles do not meet specific requirements. Custom RBAC roles can be created in the following ways:

- The Azure portal
- Azure PowerShell
- The Azure CLI
- The REST API

In this section, you had a look at RBAC in Azure and how it works from a logical perspective.

> **Note**
> You are encouraged to read more by using the following links: https://learn.microsoft.com/en-us/azure/role-based-access-control/built-in-roles
>
> https://learn.microsoft.com/en-us/azure/role-based-access-control/overview

Next, you will explore what role assignments are and how they bring together all that you have built up to now.

Role Assignments

Role assignments are the core component of RBAC that associates a role definition to a user, group, or application in the context of a specific Azure resource or resource group. The role assignment determines what actions the user, group, or application can perform on that resource.

There are several components that form the construct of role assignments that you should be aware of. All three are required to form a role assignment, and therefore it's imperative that you have an understanding of what each component is and what it does:

- **Security Principal**: This represents the identity requesting access to Azure resources. This can be a user, group, or application.
- **Role Definition**: This is a collection of permissions with a unique name that defines the set of actions that can be performed on a resource. Azure provides built-in roles such as Owner, Contributor, and Reader, but you can also create custom roles.
- **Scope**: The scope defines the level at which the role assignment is applicable. It can be at the management group, subscription, resource group, or individual resource level. The role assignment is inherited by all child resources within the scope.

Example of Role Assignment

Suppose you want to grant read-only access to a user named John for a specific resource group in Azure. You can create a role assignment by associating the Reader role definition with the user John and setting the scope to the desired resource group. This way, John will have read-only access to all resources within that resource group. The following *Figure 3.13* is a graphical depiction of the components of the role assignments along with visual representations of the expected types of information required for each component, such as the Security Principal component, where you can see on the right that it could consist of a choice or a variation of users, groups, service principals, and/or managed identities.

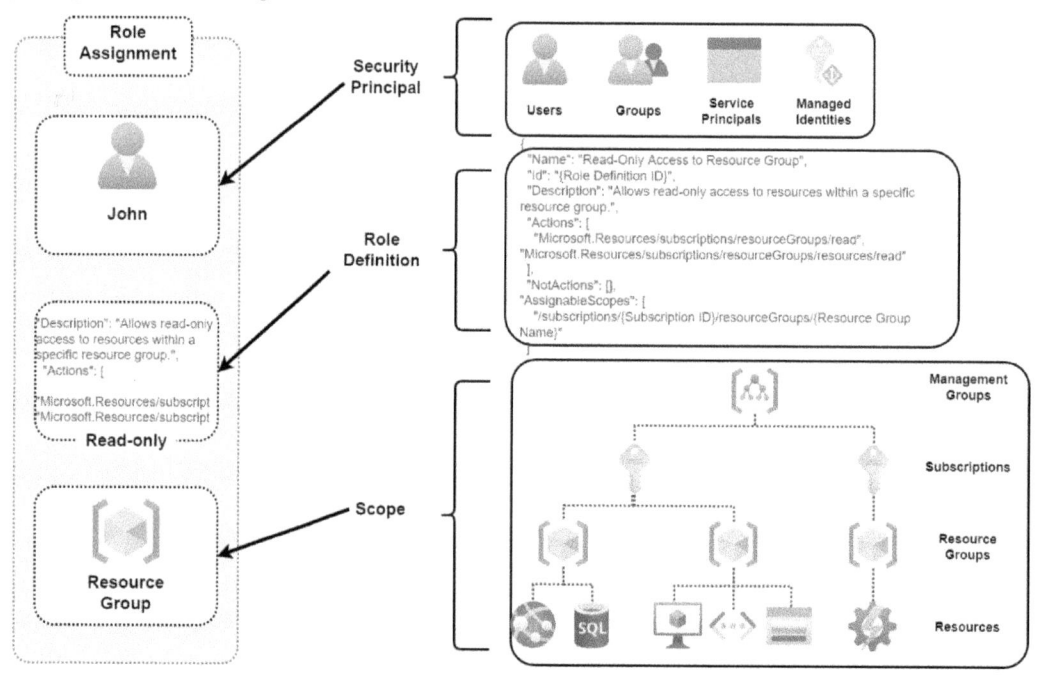

Figure 3.13: Example role assignment

Now that you have the basics of RBAC under your belt and you have a good idea of how it fits into the greater picture of Azure permission management, you will learn how to create a custom role in the next section.

> **Note**
> There is a limit of 5,000 custom RBAC roles per Microsoft Entra organization.

Creating a custom RBAC role

Now that you have become familiar with what roles are and you understand the differences between built-in roles and custom RBAC roles, you will learn how to use the Azure portal to create a custom RBAC role from scratch. For this exercise, you will name your new custom RBAC role `IT Support - Restart VMs only`, which can only restart virtual machines and deny the startup and shutdown of them.

Perform the following steps to begin creating your custom role:

1. Navigate to the Azure portal by opening a web browser and browsing to `https://portal.azure.com`.
2. In the top section search bar, search for and select `Subscriptions`, as shown in the following *Figure 3.14*:

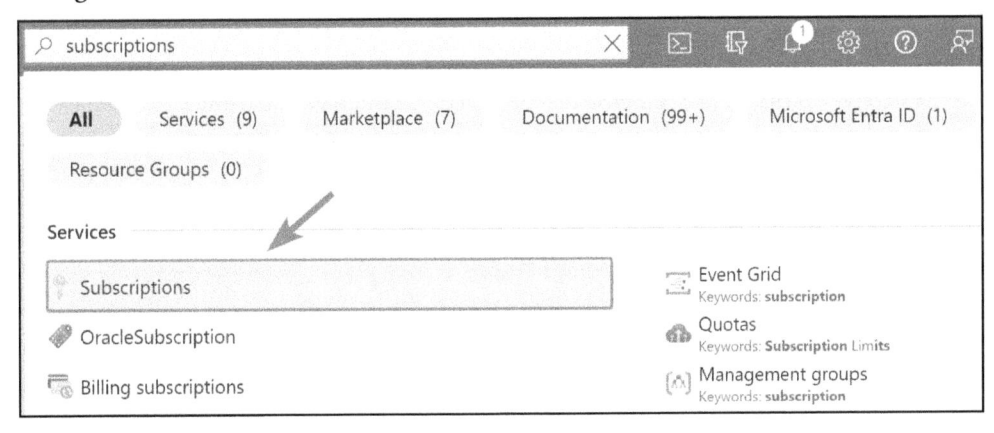

Figure 3.14: The search bar in Azure

3. Select an active subscription; in this case, this will be the `Demo` subscription, as seen in the following *Figure 3.15*:

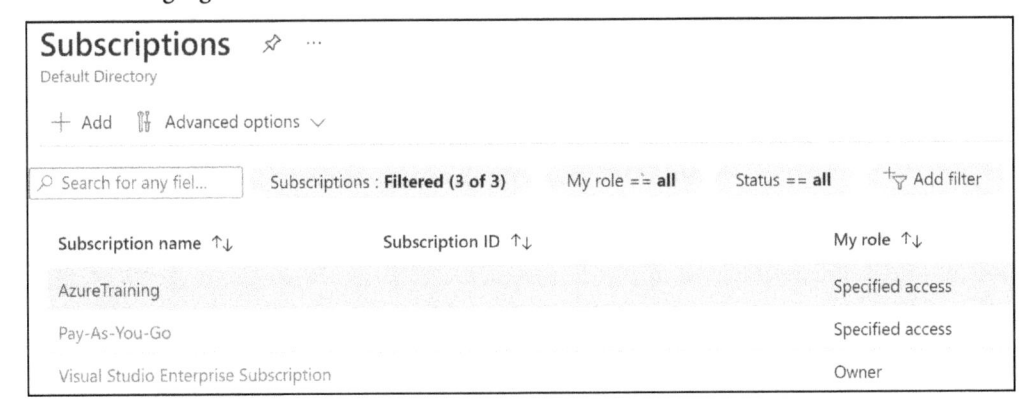

Figure 3.15: All available subscriptions

4. Select Access control (IAM), click on Add, and select Add custom role:

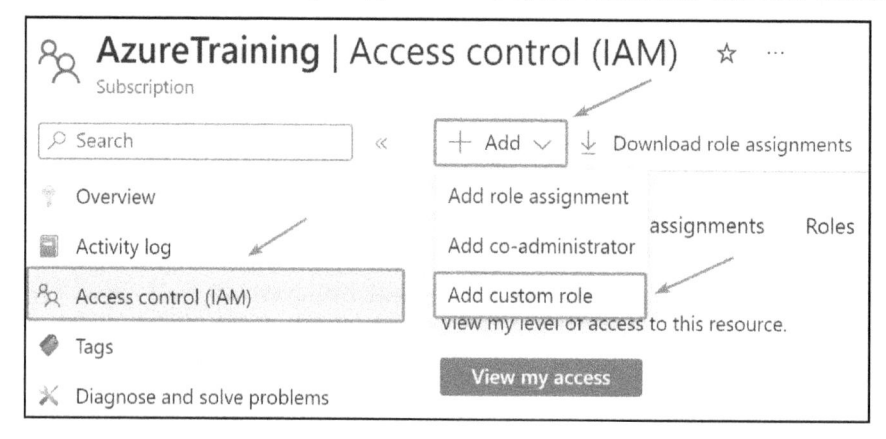

Figure 3.16: The access control (IAM) blade for a selected subscription

5. Next, on the Basics tab, complete the Custom role name and Description fields and select the Start from scratch setting under Baseline permissions. For Custom role name, specify IT support - Restart VMs only; it is also best practice to provide a brief description in the Description field when creating resources in Azure.

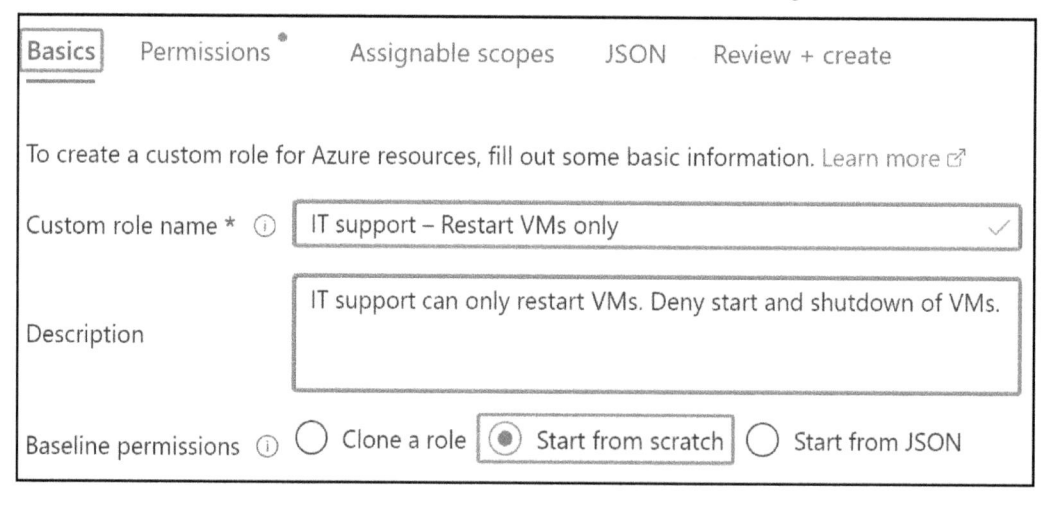

Figure 3.17: The custom role creation blade

6. Next, you need to specify the permissions. Click Next. On the Permissions tab, click on the Add permissions button, and in the search bar that pops up, search for Virtual machines and select Microsoft Compute, as shown in the following *Figure 3.18*:

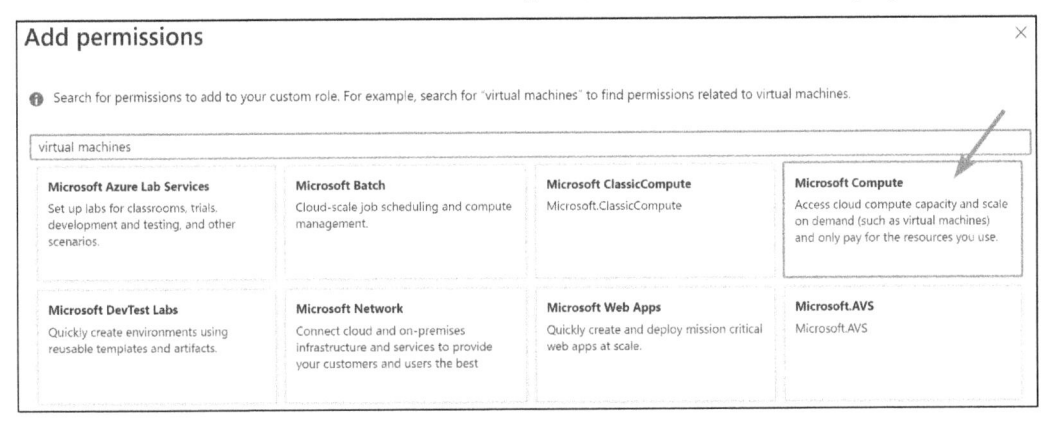

Figure 3.18: Adding permissions to a custom role

7. A new blade will pop up with all the compute permissions. Scroll all the way down to Microsoft.Compute/virtualMachines and select Read: Get Virtual Machine and Other: Restart Virtual Machine, then click Add.

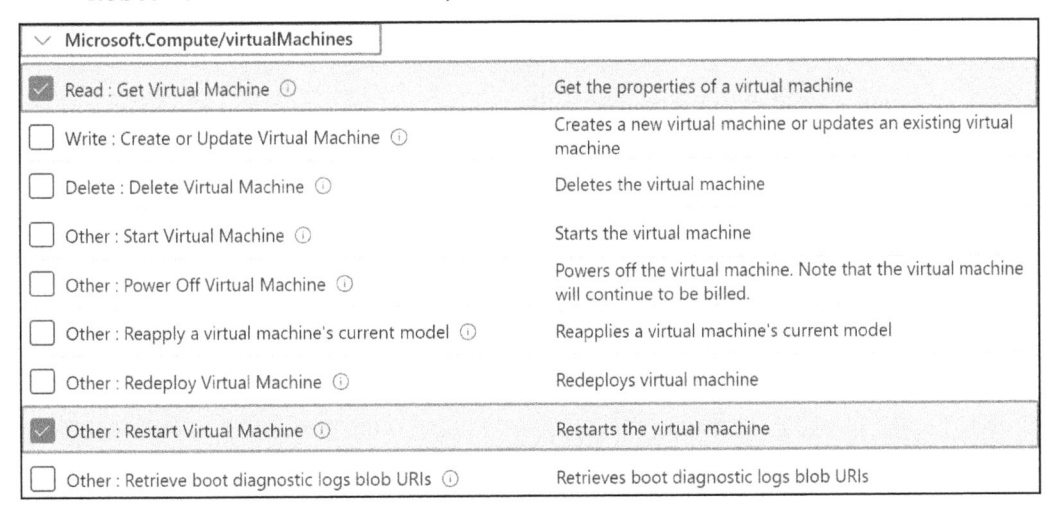

Figure 3.19: The custom role creation permissions available for Microsoft.Compute

8. Next, you need to prevent this role from starting and shutting down virtual machines. Click on the `+ Exclude permissions` button and search for `Virtual machines` again, and then select `Microsoft Compute`, as shown in the following *Figure 3.20*:

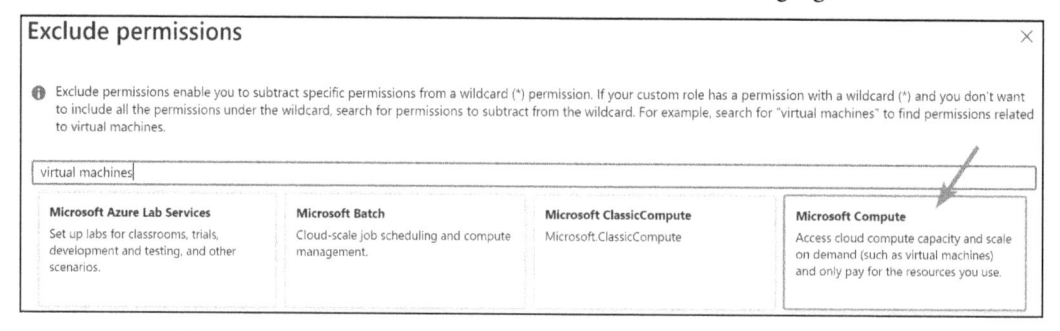

Figure 3.20: Custom role exclusions when searching for virtual machines

9. Go to `Microsoft.Compute/virtualMachines` and select `Other: Start Virtual Machine`, `Other: Power Off Virtual Machine`, and `Other: Deallocate Virtual Machine`, and then click Add:

Figure 3.21: The custom role exclusion list for Microsoft.Compute

10. You will notice that the new role now has the following permission types:

- `Action: Read the Virtual Machine (VM).`
- `Action: Restart the VM.`
- `NotAction: Start the VM.`
- `NotAction: Powers off the VM.`
- As you can see in the following *Figure 3.22*, it contains the `Actions` and `NotActions` specified above:

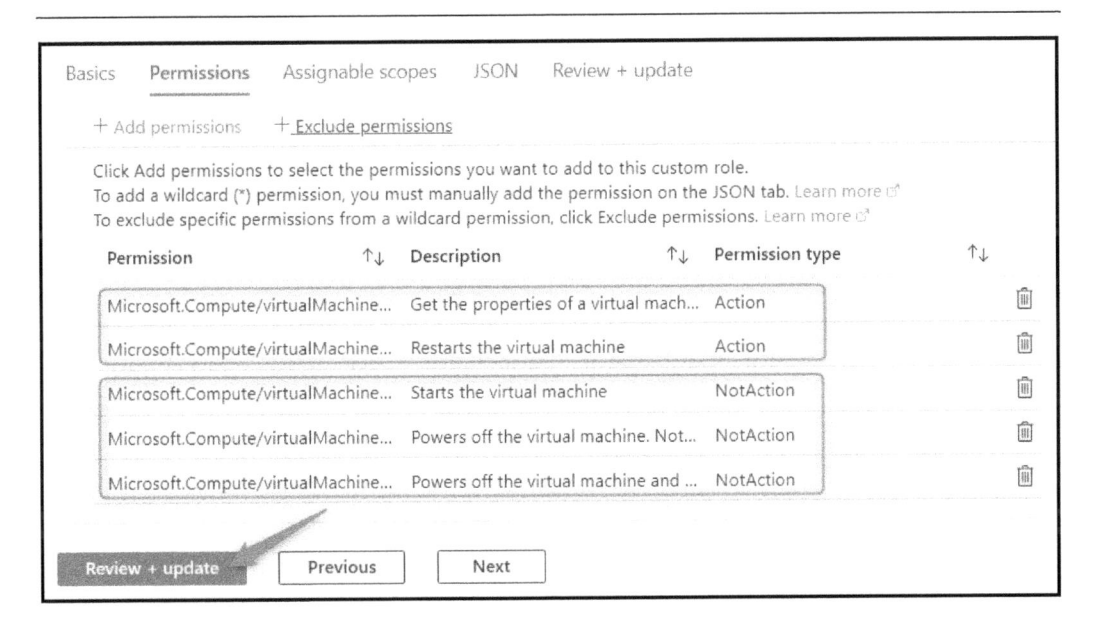

Figure 3.22: A custom role permissions overview displaying Actions and NotActions

11. Click on Next.

> **Note**
>
> Actions are permission actions that are allowed; NotActions are permission actions that are specifically not allowed.

12. Next, you have Assignable scopes, where you can choose where this custom role will be available for assignment. In this scenario, you are going to leave it at the default subscription level that was automatically added and then click on Next:

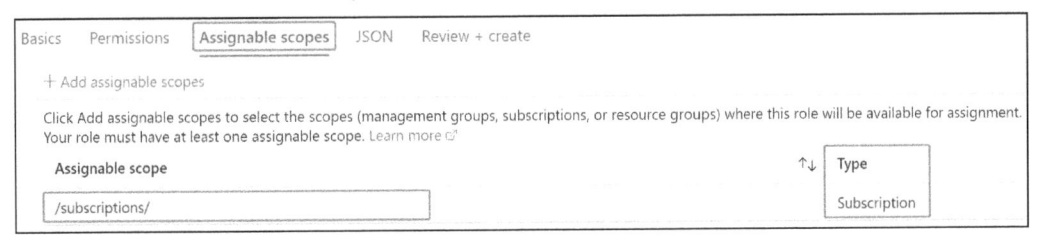

Figure 3.23: The custom role's assignable scopes

13. Next, you have the JSON tab, which shows the permissions for the new role in JSON format; here, you can also download the JSON code. For now, click on Next:

```
{
    "properties": {
        "roleName": "IT support - Restart VMs only",
        "description": "IT support can only restart VMs. Deny start and shutdown of VMs.",
        "assignableScopes": [
            "/subscriptions/"
        ],
        "permissions": [
            {
                "actions": [
                    "Microsoft.Compute/virtualMachines/read",
                    "Microsoft.Compute/virtualMachines/restart/action"
                ],
                "notActions": [
                    "Microsoft.Compute/virtualMachines/start/action",
                    "Microsoft.Compute/virtualMachines/powerOff/action",
                    "Microsoft.Compute/virtualMachines/deallocate/action"
                ],
                "dataActions": [],
                "notDataActions": []
            }
        ]
    }
}
```

Figure 3.24: The custom role's JSON notation

14. The last tab is the Review + create tab, which is a summary of your configuration; click on Create:

Basics

Role name	IT support – Restart VMs only
Role description	IT support can only restart VMs. Deny start and shutdown of VMs.

Permissions

Action	Microsoft.Compute/virtualMachines/read
Action	Microsoft.Compute/virtualMachines/restart/action
NotAction	Microsoft.Compute/virtualMachines/start/action
NotAction	Microsoft.Compute/virtualMachines/powerOff/action
NotAction	Microsoft.Compute/virtualMachines/deallocate/action

Assignable Scopes

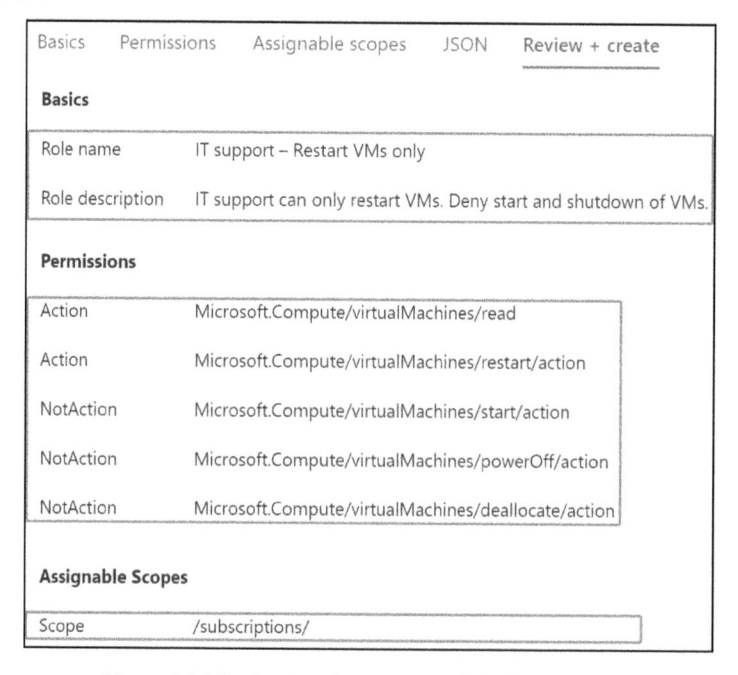

Scope	/subscriptions/

Figure 3.25: Reviewing the custom role before creation

15. A new pop-up window will appear, stating that the new custom role has been created and that you can start assigning the role as soon as replication has taken place, which is usually around 5 minutes or less.

> You have successfully created the custom role "IT support – Restart VMs only". It may take the system a few minutes to display your role everywhere.
>
> **OK**

Figure 3.26: New role notification

In this section, you have created a custom RBAC role via the Azure portal from scratch, which only allows a virtual machine to be restarted and blocks any start or shutdown attempts on a virtual machine.

> **Note**
>
> You are encouraged to read more by using the following links, which go into detail about Microsoft Entra ID custom roles:
>
> `https://learn.microsoft.com/en-us/azure/role-based-access-control/custom-roles`
>
> `https://learn.microsoft.com/en-us/entra/identity/role-based-access-control/custom-create`
>
> Students should be comfortable using the JSON format while creating a custom role.

Assigning Access to Resources by Assigning a Custom Role

The next step is to assign this custom role to a user on a different level. You are going to assign access on the resource group level with an account that has owner permissions at the resource group level:

1. Navigate to the Azure portal by opening a web browser and going to `https://portal.azure.com`.

2. Navigate to your intended subscription as you did in the previous exercise, scroll down the left menu under `Settings`, and select `Resource groups`, which will show all the current resource groups:

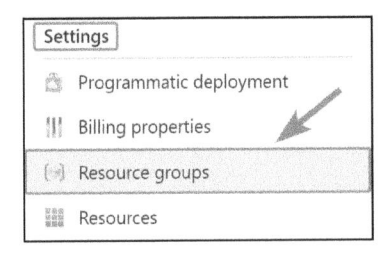

Figure 3.27: Selecting Resource groups from the subscription

3. Select one of your resource groups; if you do not have one yet, you need to create one in any region you want and call it `AZ-104`:

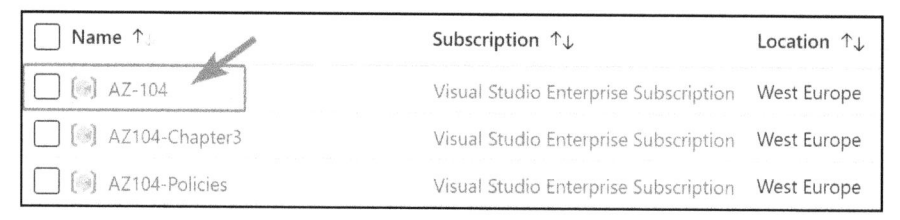

Figure 3.28: Selecting a resource group

4. Next, go to the `Access control (IAM)` section, click on `Add`, and select `Add role assignment`:

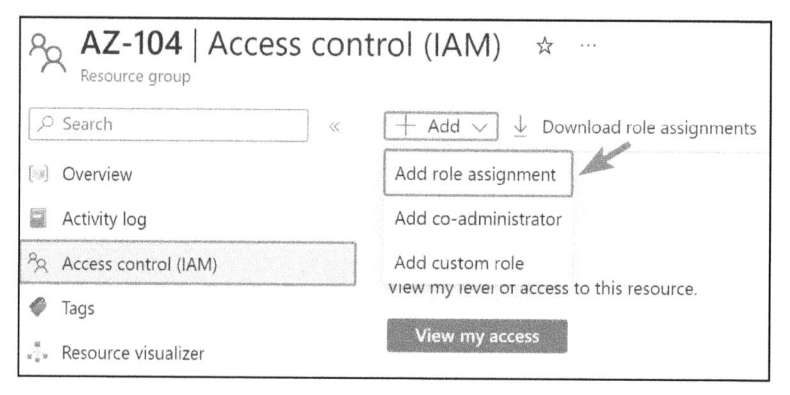

Figure 3.29: The Access control (IAM) setting for the selected resource group

5. A new blade opens; under `Role`, search for the custom role you created called `IT support - Restart VMs only`. Click the role from the results and click `Next` at the bottom of the window.

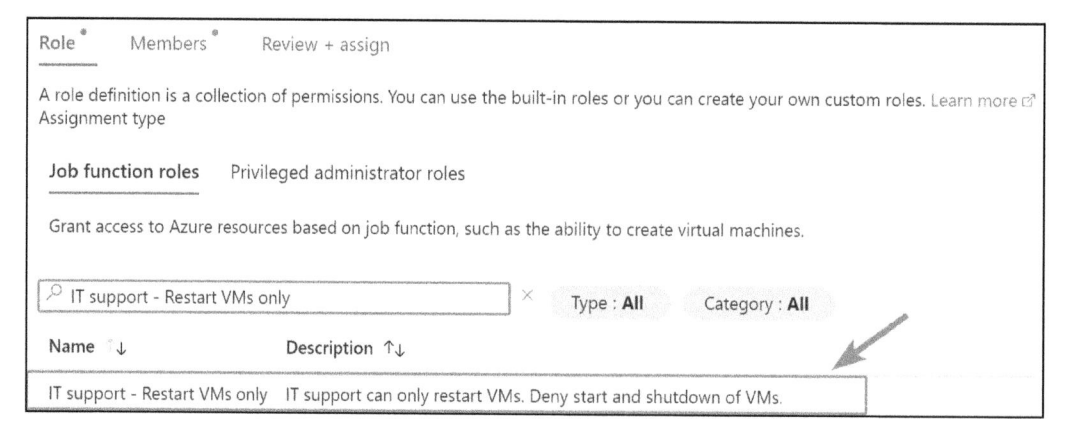

Figure 3.30: Selecting a custom role

6. On the Members tab, select `User, group, or service principal` under `Assign access to`, and then click `+ Select members`.

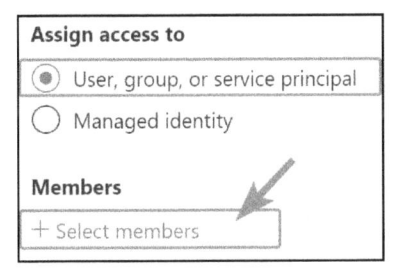

Figure 3.31: Role assignment

7. From the pop-up blade, enter `Demo` in the search bar, then select `DemoUser1`, which you created in *Chapter 1, Managing Microsoft Entra ID Objects*. Click `Select`. Finally, once the pop-up blade closes, click `Review + assign` at the bottom of the screen, then on `Review + assign` to add the role assignment.

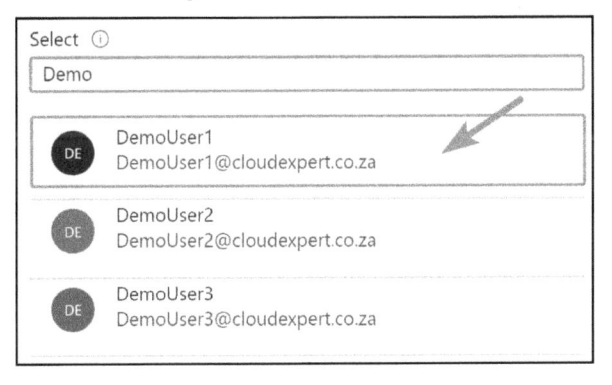

Figure 3.32: Selecting a member

That's it – you have now successfully created and assigned a custom RBAC role to a user named `DemoUser1`. The final step is to validate the role assignment.

Confirming the Role Assignment Steps

Now that you have assigned a role to a user, go ahead and confirm that it's working as expected. For the purpose of this exercise, it is best to have a virtual machine deployed into the resource group that you just assigned permissions to. If you are not sure how to do this, perform the virtual machine creation exercise later in this book and revisit this chapter to complete this exercise:

1. Navigate to the Azure portal by opening a web browser and browsing to `https://portal.azure.com` (you will need to sign in as the user that you assigned your custom role to).

2. Open the left hamburger menu on the main Azure blade and select `All resources`, which will show all the current resource groups:

Figure 3.33: Selecting all resources from the main Azure menu

3. You will be able to see all the resources that are within that subscription based on the scope of the role you created earlier. Have a look at the virtual machine you created. In the following example, it is `prod-vm1`. Click on the name of the virtual machine to open its configuration pane.

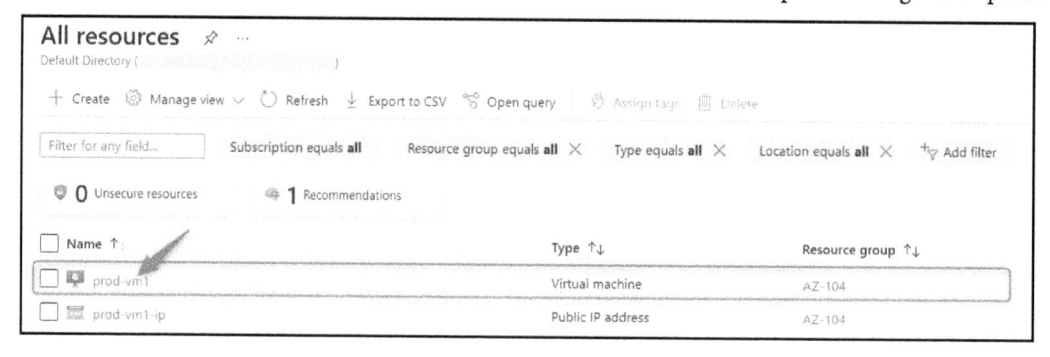

Figure 3.34: Displaying all resources for the resource group

4. To test the permissions, you will try to stop the virtual machine. From the `Overview` blade, click `Stop` at the top of the screen.

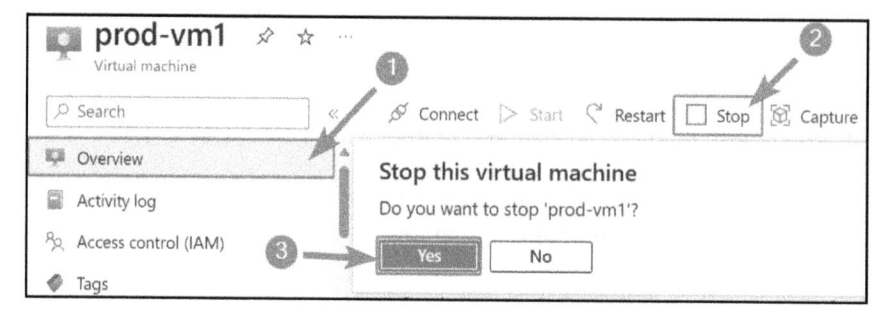

Figure 3.35: Stopping the virtual machine

5. A pop-up error message will say `Failed to stop virtual machine`, and that is how you can confirm your custom RBAC role, which prevents a user from stopping a virtual machine that is working as expected and only allows restarting the virtual machine:

> **Failed to stop virtual machine** ×
>
> Failed to stop the virtual machine 'prod-vm1'. Error: The client 'DemoUser1@cloudexpert.co.za' with object id '███████████████████████' does not have authorization to perform action 'Microsoft.Compute/virtualMachines/deallocate/action' over scope 'AZ-104/providers/Microsoft.Compute/virtualMachines/pro... vm1'>prod-vm1' or the scope is invalid. If access was recently granted, please refresh your credentials.

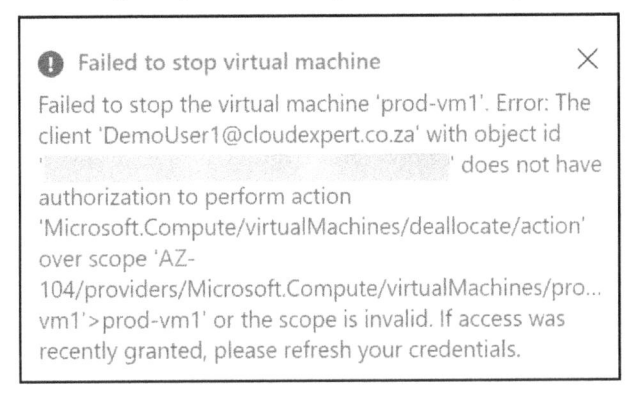

Figure 3.36: Stop virtual machine error

You have just successfully proved that your new role assignment is working. In this section, you looked at how to assign a custom RBAC role via the Azure portal and confirmed that the custom role is applied and working as expected.

> **Note**
>
> You are encouraged to read further by using the following link, which goes into more detail about assigning roles in Azure: `https://learn.microsoft.com/en-us/azure/role-based-access-control/role-assignments-portal`.

Interpreting Access Assignments

There are a few tips when interpreting access assignments. First off, you need to understand the scope of the assignment – that is, is it at the management group, subscription group, resource group, or resource level?

Next, you can have a look at the role rules. In order to do this, you need to do the following:

1. Navigate to the Azure portal by opening a web browser and browsing to `https://portal.azure.com`.
2. Select `Resource groups` from the left menu after clicking the hamburger button. This will show all the current resource groups. Select a resource group in your subscription (in this case, it will be `AZ-104`).

3. Under `Access control (IAM)`, choose `Role assignments` and select a role you want to have a look at in detail. Notice the `IT support - Restart VMs only` assignment you did in the previous exercise.

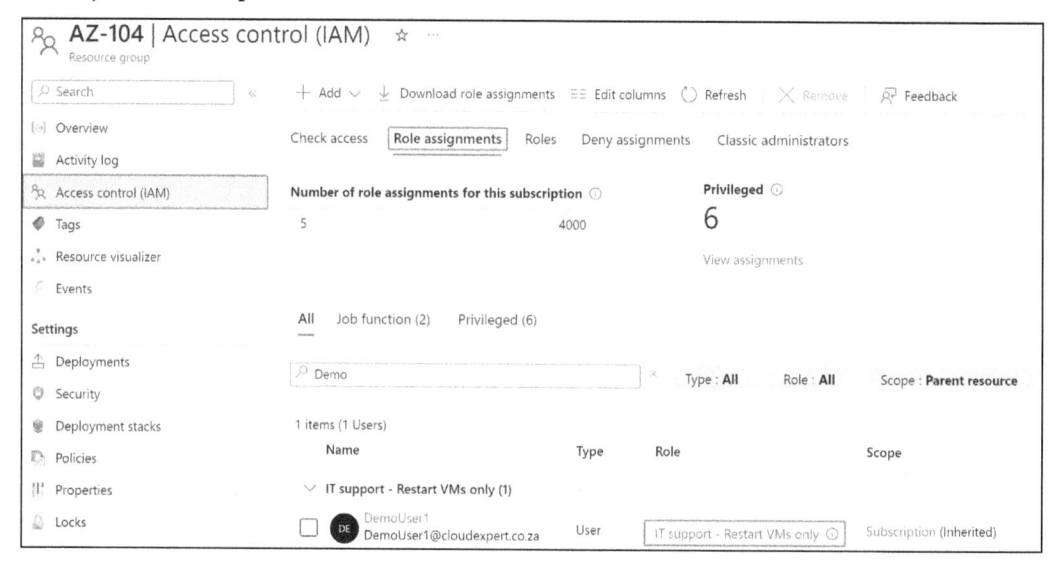

Figure 3.37: The role assignments section on the Access control (IAM) blade

4. For this example, you are going to select the `Contributor` role. Click on the word `Contributor` for the role you are interested in, as shown in the following *Figure 3.38*:

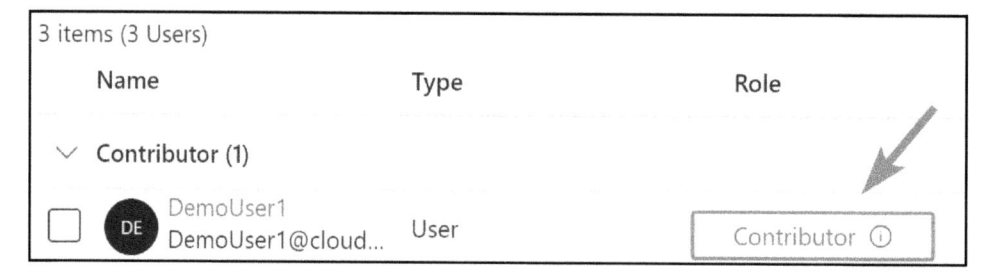

Figure 3.38: The available role assignments

5. Click on the `JSON` tab. From here, you will be able to view what the role has access to and also what actions are not allowed:

```
Permissions   JSON   Assignments

 1  {
 2      "id": "/subscriptions/                              /providers/Microsoft.Authorization
 3      "properties": {
 4          "roleName": "Contributor",
 5          "description": "Grants full access to manage all resources, but does not allow you to as
 6          "assignableScopes": [
 7              "/"
 8          ],
 9          "permissions": [
10              {
11                  "actions": [
12                      "*"
13                  ],
14                  "notActions": [
15                      "Microsoft.Authorization/*/Delete",
16                      "Microsoft.Authorization/*/Write",
17                      "Microsoft.Authorization/elevateAccess/Action",
18                      "Microsoft.Blueprint/blueprintAssignments/write",
19                      "Microsoft.Blueprint/blueprintAssignments/delete",
20                      "Microsoft.Compute/galleries/share/action",
21                      "Microsoft.Purview/consents/write",
22                      "Microsoft.Purview/consents/delete"
23                  ],
```

Figure 3.39: JSON notation of the contributor role

> **Note**
>
> NotActions always take precedence over Action items.

In this section, you learned how to interpret role assignments by viewing the JSON format for a specific role.

> **Note**
>
> You are encouraged to read further by using the following links, which go into more detail about custom RBAC:
>
> https://learn.microsoft.com/en-us/azure/role-based-access-control/custom-roles-template
>
> https://learn.microsoft.com/en-us/azure/role-based-access-control/role-assignments-list-portal
>
> https://learn.microsoft.com/en-us/azure/role-based-access-control/role-definitions

Summary

This chapter provided a comprehensive overview of custom roles, their functionality within Azure, and the various scope levels applicable to RBAC. You observed the process of creating a custom RBAC role designed to grant users the ability to restart a virtual machine without stopping it. Furthermore, you explored the interpretation of RBAC role assignments within the Azure portal and discussed managing subscriptions.

As you progress to the next chapter, you will delve into the concepts behind creating and managing governance within Azure. The core topics covered will be understanding Azure policies and applying, as well as managing, tags on resources. This knowledge will equip you with the tools required to effectively manage resources and maintain control within your Azure environment.

Exam Readiness Drill - Chapters 1-3

Apart from mastering key concepts, strong test-taking skills under time pressure are essential for acing your certification exam. That's why developing these abilities early in your learning journey is critical.

Exam readiness drills, using the free online practice resources provided with this book, help you progressively improve your time management and test-taking skills while reinforcing the key concepts you've learned.

HOW TO GET STARTED

- Open the link or scan the QR code at the bottom of this page
- If you have unlocked the practice resources, already log in to your registered account. If you haven't, follow the instructions in *Chapter 23* and come back to this page.
- Once you log in, click the START button to start a quiz
- We recommend attempting a quiz multiple times till you're able to answer most of the questions correctly and well within the time limit.
- You can use the following practice template to help you plan your attempts :

Attempt	Target	Time Limit
Working On Accuracy		
Attempt 1	40% or more	Till the timer runs out
Attempt 2	60% or more	Till the timer runs out
Attempt 3	75% or more	Till the timer runs out
Working On Timing		
Attempt 4	75% or more	1 minute before time limit
Attempt 5	75% or more	2 minutes before time limit
Attempt 6	75% or more	3 minutes before time limit

The above drill is just an example. Design your drills based on your own goals and make the most out of the online quizzes accompanying this book.

> **First time accessing the online resources?** 🔒
> You'll need to unlock them through a one-time process. **Head to** *Chapter 23* **for instructions**.

Open Quiz

`https://packt.link/az104e3ch1-3`

OR scan this QR code →

4
Creating and Managing Governance

This chapter covers how to establish governance in Azure and create mechanisms for managing it. In this chapter, you will learn how to create Azure policies and why they exist. You will also learn how to apply and manage resource tags. This chapter will assist you in building the skills required to establish a good governance baseline within your organization and understanding the importance of policies and tags in Azure, with the practical application of these skills in the examples. Establishing good governance within an organization is a difficult task due to the many factors of consideration involved in achieving good governance practices. This chapter sets out to guide you in your journey to understanding policies, a mechanism for enforcing governance in Azure, and tagging.

In this chapter, you are going to learn about the following main topics:

- Understanding Azure policies
- Applying and Managing Tags on Resources

Technical Requirements

This chapter has the following requirements for the examples:

- Access to an Azure subscription with owner or contributor privileges. If you do not have access to one, students can enroll for a free account at https://azure.microsoft.com/en-us/free/
- **PowerShell 5.1** or later installed on a Windows PC or PowerShell Core 6.x on other operating systems, to practice the labs.
- Note that examples can only be followed from a PC or https://shell.azure.com (PowerShell 7.0.6 LTS or later is recommended).

- Installation of the Az PowerShell module, which can be performed by running the following in an administrative PowerShell session:

```
Set-ExecutionPolicy -ExecutionPolicy RemoteSigned -Scope
CurrentUser
Install-Module -Name Az -Scope CurrentUser -Repository PSGallery
-Force
```

Understanding Azure Policies

Azure Policy is a mechanism for effecting organizational compliance on the Azure platform. The service allows aggregated views to understand the overall state of an environment, with the ability to view resource-level granularity for compliance. All this can be viewed on the `compliance` dashboard as part of the Policy service. Remediation can be applied automatically and through bulk operations.

The following screenshot gives an overview of Azure Policy service for an organization:

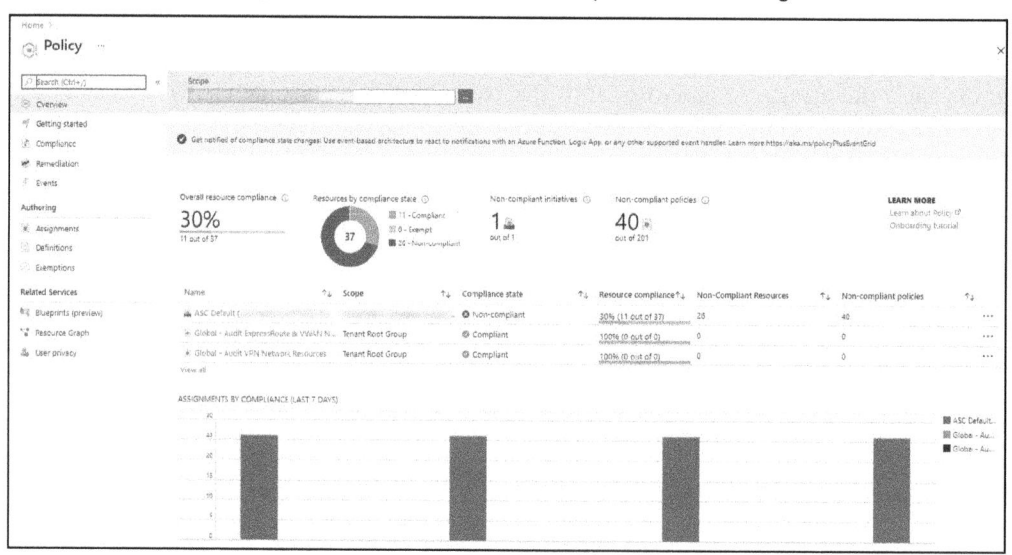

Figure 4.1: Azure Policy example

As you will observe, this is where you will create and manage policies, as well as get an overview of compliance for policies that you have implemented in Azure. Azure Policy enables users to define, implement, and monitor policies for their Azure resources to ensure they meet specific standards and regulations. Azure Policy helps maintain consistency across the entire cloud environment, improve security posture, and achieve greater operational efficiency.

Some key features of Azure Policy include the following bulleted items, which will be explored in more detail in the sections ahead:

- **Policy definition**: Users can create custom policies using Azure Policy definition language (a **JavaScript Object Notation (JSON)**-based format) or choose from a library of built-in policy definitions provided by Azure
- **Policy assignment**: Policies can be assigned to specific resources, resource groups, or entire subscriptions, allowing for granular control over policy enforcement
- **Policy evaluation**: Azure Policy continuously evaluates the assigned policies against the existing resources and identifies any non-compliant resources
- **Remediation**: In certain cases, Azure Policy can automatically remediate non-compliant resources by applying the required changes to bring them into compliance
- **Compliance reporting**: Azure Policy provides comprehensive compliance reporting, enabling users to track the compliance status of their resources and identify any issues that need to be addressed
- **Integration**: Azure Policy can be integrated with Azure DevOps, Azure Security Center, and Azure Monitor to enhance governance, security, and monitoring capabilities across the cloud environment

Overall, Azure Policy is an essential tool for organizations that want to maintain control over their Azure resources, ensuring they adhere to the necessary governance, risk, and compliance requirements.

How Does Azure Policy work?

Azure Policy assesses compliance by comparing resource properties to business rules defined in JSON format. These are known as **policy definitions**.

A **policy initiative** is a grouping of definitions that align with business objectives, such as the secure configuration of **virtual machines (VMs)**. This could contain a policy to assess antivirus compliance and a policy for assessing disk encryption compliance, as well as other policies.

Figure 4.2 gives a high-level overview of how Azure Policy works.

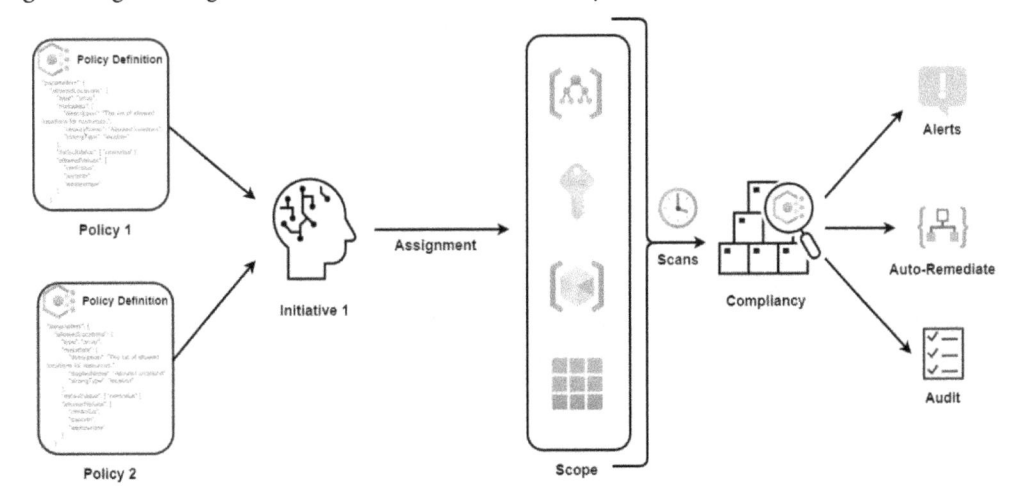

Figure 4.2: Azure Policy visualization

From the preceding figure, you can see how the various components of Azure Policy relate to each other, such as the definition, initiative, and scope of a policy.

Azure Policy resides above the subscription and management group layers, and it can therefore be assigned to various scope levels—an individual resource, resource group, subscription, or management group. This is defined as a **policy assignment** or **scope**.

Azure Policy versus RBAC

Both Azure Policy and **role-based access control** (**RBAC**) contribute to controlling **governance** within Azure. While both create methods of controlling access, there is often confusion between the two. The differences between them are distinguished for clarity, as follows:

- **Azure Policy** focuses on resource properties for existing resources and resources being deployed. Azure Policy is used for the enforcement of governance standards within the Azure platform.
- **RBAC** focuses on user actions at different scopes. RBAC contributes to governance by enforcing permissions at the service principal layer.

Working with Azure Policy

Azure offers predefined built-in policies, as well as an option to create custom policies. The same applies to initiatives, which you will explore in this section.

Some examples of built-in policies are the following:

- **Allowed virtual machine size SKUs**: This policy specifies a set of VM sizes and types that can be deployed in Azure.
- **Allowed locations**: This policy restricts available locations where resources can be deployed.
- **Allowed resource types**: This policy defines a list of resource types that can be deployed. Resource types that are not on the list can't be deployed inside the Azure environment.
- **Not allowed resource types**: This policy prevents certain resource types from being deployed.
- **Require a tag and its value on resources**: This policy enforces a required tag and its value. It does not apply to resource groups.
- Microsoft maintains a repository of policies at the following GitHub link: https://github.com/Azure/azure-policy. This can be handy for starting new policy templates that you want to build and understanding how the native policies are constructed.

If the built-in policies don't meet your desired requirements, you can create a custom policy instead. Custom policies are created in JSON, with the code defining several properties. When creating in the portal, the second part defines policy rules (which are usually just extended in the same JSON file).

The following code is an example of a policy definition:

```
{
    "properties": {
        "displayName": "Deny storage accounts not using only HTTPS",
        "description": "Deny storage accounts not using only HTTPS. Checks
the supportsHttpsTrafficOnly property on StorageAccounts.",
        "mode": "all",
        "parameters": {
            "effectType": {
                "type": "string",
                "defaultValue": "Deny",
                "allowedValues": [
                    "Deny",
                    "Disabled"
                ],
                "metadata": {
                    "displayName": "Effect",
                    "description": "Enable or disable the execution of
the policy"
                }
            }
        },
```

In this part of the code, you can see the policy rule:

```
        "policyRule": {
        "if": {
            "allOf": [
                {
                    "field": "type",
                    "equals": "Microsoft.Storage/storageAccounts"
                },
                {
                    "field":
"Microsoft.Storage/storageAccounts/supportsHttpsTrafficOnly",
                    "notEquals": "true"
                }
            ]
        },
        "then": {
            "effect": "[parameters('effectType')]"
        }
    }
} }
```

As you will notice, the preceding policy assesses Azure storage accounts and identifies whether the configuration for **HyperText Transfer Protocol Secure (HTTPS)**-only communication is set to `true`. Where it does not comply, the configured effect will be enforced based on what is entered for the `parameter` sections.

Constructing a Policy Definition

In the following section, you will explore the structure of a policy definition. The policy definition is what describes how a policy looks and behaves. In order for you to effectively work with policies, it is important that you maintain a core understanding of the components they contain. They are constructed of the following key components:

- **displayName**: This is the display name of the policy file.
- **Description**: This is a descriptor field that allows you to add a small write-up on the desired effect and scope of the policy.
- **Effect**: Several effects can be applied to policies. It's important to note that this is typically for logical evaluation (`if, then`), which belongs to the policy rule. To understand these effects in more detail, please refer to the following Microsoft **Uniform Resource Locator (URL)**: `https://learn.microsoft.com/en-us/azure/governance/policy/concepts/effects`.
- **Category**: This defines the category type of your policy.
- **Location**: This defines the location of the policy to be deployed.
- **ID**: This is the definition **identifier (ID)** of the policy that is created and is enumerated based on the policy name.
- **Type**: This defines the policy type to be implemented and can be a **Built-in**, **Custom**, or **Static** policy type.
- **Mode**: This is used to define whether a policy is scoped toward a resource provider or **Azure Resource Manager (ARM)** property.

The following screenshot depicts a sample Azure policy definition:

Require a tag and its value on resources			
Policy definition			
📋 Assign policy ✏️ Edit definition 📋 Duplicate definition 🗑️ Delete definition			
∧ Essentials			
Name	: Require a tag and its value on resources	Definition location	: --
Description	: Enforces a required tag and its value. Does not apply t...	Definition ID	: /providers/Microsoft.Authorization/policyDefinitions/1...
Available Effects	: Deny	Type	: Built-in
Category	: Tags	Mode	: Indexed

Figure 4.3: Policy definition overview example

Effect Types

Effect types describe the actions to be performed as part of the policy. They are, as described previously, a core component of the policy definition, and it's important to ascertain before constructing a policy what effect would be required. You will need to understand the different effect types to be more effective in creating policies that work in the desired manner to meet your requirements.

The different effect types are described as follows:

- **Append**: This is used to modify existing or new resources by adding additional fields or properties to a resource.
- **Audit**: This is used to flag a resource that is not compliant. It notes the non-compliance but will not restrict the deployment request.
- **AuditIfNotExists**: This is used to identify resources identified within the policy's (or policies') scope that are missing the required properties for the resource type.
- **Deny**: This is used to disallow the deployment of resources that do not meet the policy definition criteria.
- **DeployIfNotExists**: This is used to perform a template deployment when non-compliance is met, as described in the `AuditIfNotExists` policy criteria.
- **Disabled**: This is used to nullify the effect of a policy and is typically used for testing scenarios.
- **Modify**: This is used to modify the properties of resources and will apply to new and existing resources that meet the policy criteria. Resources can be remediated through a remediation task.

Example Policy Definition

The screenshot that follows provides an example of a policy defined to look for key-value pairs (`Tag Name` and `Tag Value`). As you can see in the following screenshot, when the policy assesses resources, if it identifies that the resource does not have the required tag (that is, it is not compliant), it will proceed to reject the creation of a resource due to the `deny` effect in place:

```json
{
    "properties": {
        "displayName": "Require a tag and its value on resources",
        "policyType": "BuiltIn",
        "mode": "Indexed",
        "description": "Enforces a required tag and its value. Does not apply to resource groups.",
        "metadata": {
            "version": "1.0.1",
            "category": "Tags"
        },
        "version": "1.0.1",
        "parameters": {
            "tagName": {
                "type": "String",
                "metadata": {
                    "displayName": "Tag Name",
                    "description": "Name of the tag, such as 'environment'"
                }
            },
            "tagValue": {
                "type": "String",
                "metadata": {
                    "displayName": "Tag Value",
                    "description": "Value of the tag, such as 'production'"
                }
            }
        },
        "policyRule": {
            "if": {
                "not": {
                    "field": "[concat('tags[', parameters('tagName'), ']')]",
                    "equals": "[parameters('tagValue')]"
                }
            },
            "then": {
                "effect": "deny"
            }
        },
        "versions": [
            "1.0.1"
        ]
    },
    "id": "/providers/Microsoft.Authorization/policyDefinitions/1e30110a-5ceb-460c-a204-c1c3969c6d62",
    "type": "Microsoft.Authorization/policyDefinitions",
    "name": "1e30110a-5ceb-460c-a204-c1c3969c6d62"
}
```

Figure 4.4: Policy definition example

The definition accepts inputs (identified as parameters) for the template assignment; these will be accepted in the definition. For example, you may want a tag environment with a `PROD` value. If the assignment doesn't see these tags on a resource, it will reject the creation of the resource. This is specified by the `if` condition, which reads as follows: if the parameter's tag key (`Environment`) and tag value (`PROD`) do not match the resource tag, then deny deployment. You can see this in the following highlighted code:

Understanding Azure Policies 109

```
"policyRule": {
    "if": {
      "not": {
        "field": "[concat('tags[', parameters('tagName'), ']')]",
        "equals": "[parameters('tagValue')]"
      }
    },
    "then": {
      "effect": "deny"
    }
},
```

Creating a Policy Definition

In this section, you will run through the creation of a policy definition. The steps are as follows:

1. Search for `policy` in the portal main search bar and click `Policy` in the returned list, as illustrated in the following screenshot:

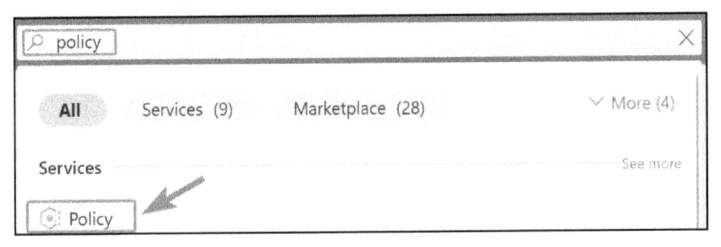

Figure 4.5: Searching for Azure Policy in the search bar

2. Click on the `Definitions` button under the `Authoring` context from the left menu, then click on the `+ Policy definition` button, as illustrated in the following screenshot:

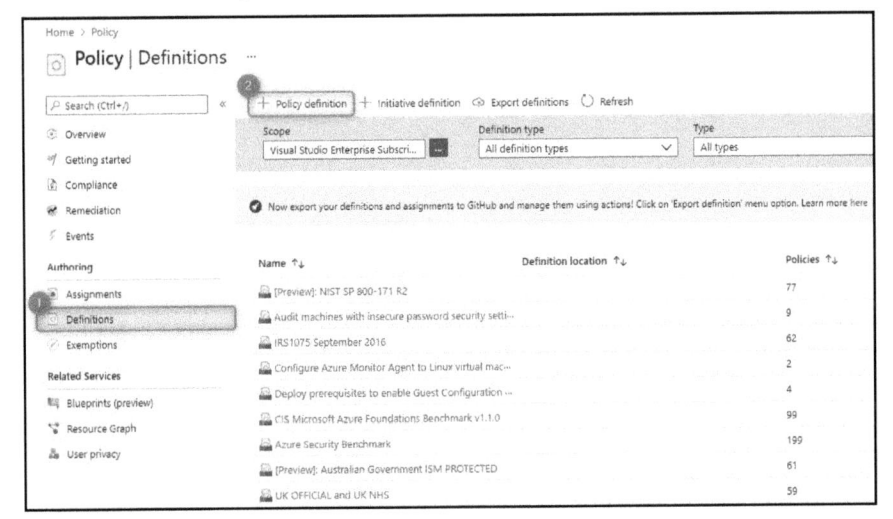

Figure 4.6: Creating a policy definition

3. On the `Policy definition` blade, populate values for the following:

- `Definition location`: This is the subscription to which the policy is to be saved.
- `Name`: This is the policy definition name.
- `Description`: This is a brief description of the policy definition to be created.
- `Category`: This will align with a set of predefined service categories in Azure, such as `App Service`, `Entra ID`, and `Backup`, or a custom category can be created; this can be used for future definition grouping too.
- `POLICY RULE`: This is a rule that determines what the definition will assess, as well as the effect. Policy rules are structured in JSON format and can be created from scratch or by importing from GitHub.

For this example, you will create a policy definition for allowed locations for resources (this is a predefined definition; therefore, the following example is only implemented if additional requirements are needed).

1. Select a definition location by clicking the ellipsis button (...), as illustrated in the following screenshot:

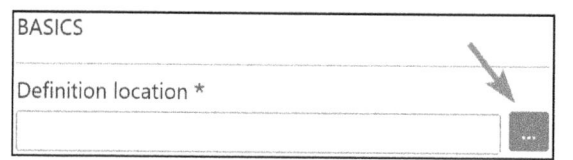

Figure 4.7: Selecting a definition location

2. Select a subscription from the `Subscription` dropdown, which pops up a selection pane. Select your subscription and then click `Select` at the bottom of the pane, as illustrated in the following screenshot:

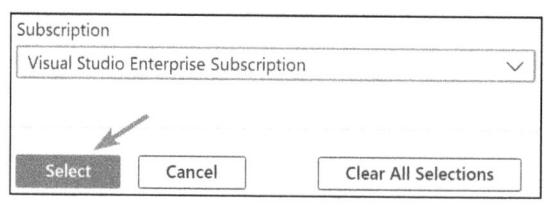

Figure 4.8: Selecting a definition location – Subscription

3. Enter the appropriate details for `Name`, `Description`, and `Category`, as illustrated in the following screenshot:

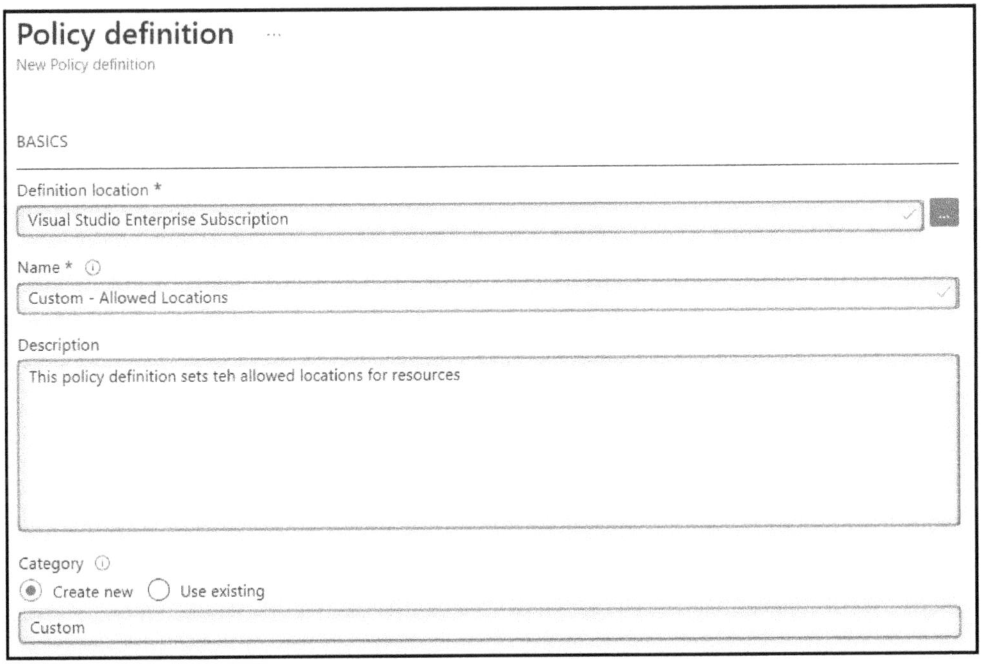

Policy definition
New Policy definition

BASICS

Definition location *

Visual Studio Enterprise Subscription

Name * ⓘ

Custom - Allowed Locations

Description

This policy definition sets teh allowed locations for resources

Category ⓘ
◉ Create new ○ Use existing

Custom

Figure 4.9: Policy definition

Then, enter the appropriate policy rule JSON code, as follows (the following screenshot is the remaining half of the same `Policy definition` page shown previously):

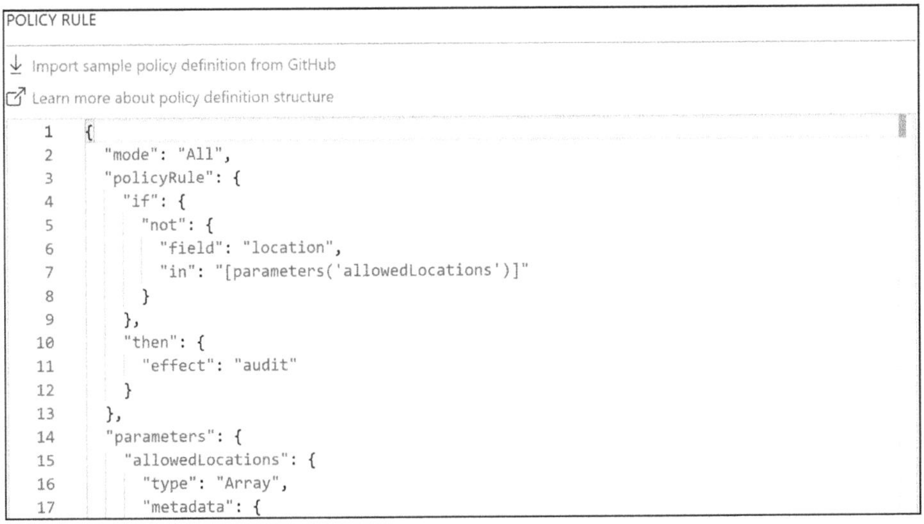

```
POLICY RULE
↓ Import sample policy definition from GitHub
   Learn more about policy definition structure
1  {
2      "mode": "All",
3      "policyRule": {
4          "if": {
5              "not": {
6                  "field": "location",
7                  "in": "[parameters('allowedLocations')]"
8              }
9          },
10         "then": {
11             "effect": "audit"
12         }
13     },
14     "parameters": {
15         "allowedLocations": {
16             "type": "Array",
17             "metadata": {
```

Figure 4.10: Custom policy definition

1. Click Save upon completing the configuration.
2. For those who would like to follow along, the JSON code looks like this:

```
{
  "mode": "All",
  «policyRule": {
    "if": {
      "not": {
        "field": "location",
        «in»: «[parameters(<allowedLocations')]"
      }
    },
    "then": {
      "effect": "deny"
    }
  },
  "parameters": {
    «allowedLocations": {
      "type": "Array",
      "metadata": {
        "description": "The list of allowed locations for resources.",
        «displayName": "Allowed locations",
        «strongType": "location"
      }
    }
  }
}
```

3. You will get a notification to signify that a policy definition has been created successfully, as illustrated in the following screenshot:

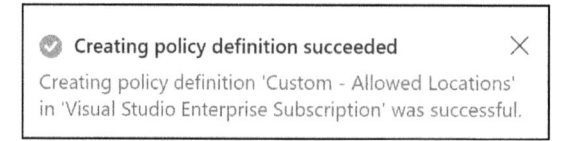

> ✅ **Creating policy definition succeeded**   ✕
> Creating policy definition 'Custom - Allowed Locations' in 'Visual Studio Enterprise Subscription' was successful.

Figure 4.11: Policy definition success notification

4. Return to the `Policy | Definitions` blade. Change the `Category` filter to `Custom` to view the newly created definition, as illustrated in the following screenshot:

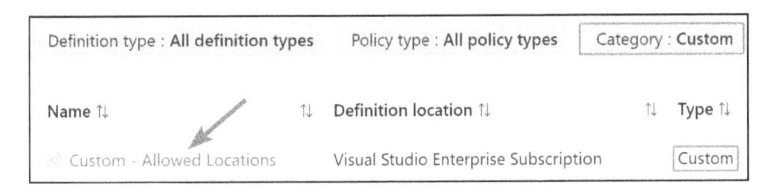

Figure 4.12: Displaying your custom policy definition

Creating an Initiative Definition

In this section, you will create an initiative definition that is used for the grouping of policy definitions that align with business objectives, such as the secure configuration of VMs. The initiative that you will be creating is for grouping policies that define resources allowed for the subscription in Azure. Proceed as follows:

1. To start creating a new policy initiative, from the `Policy | Definitions` blade, select `Initiative definition`, as illustrated in the following screenshot:

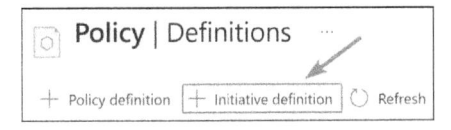

Figure 4.13: Creating a new initiative definition

2. Define the fields on the `Basics` tab, as illustrated in the following screenshot, and click `Next` to continue.

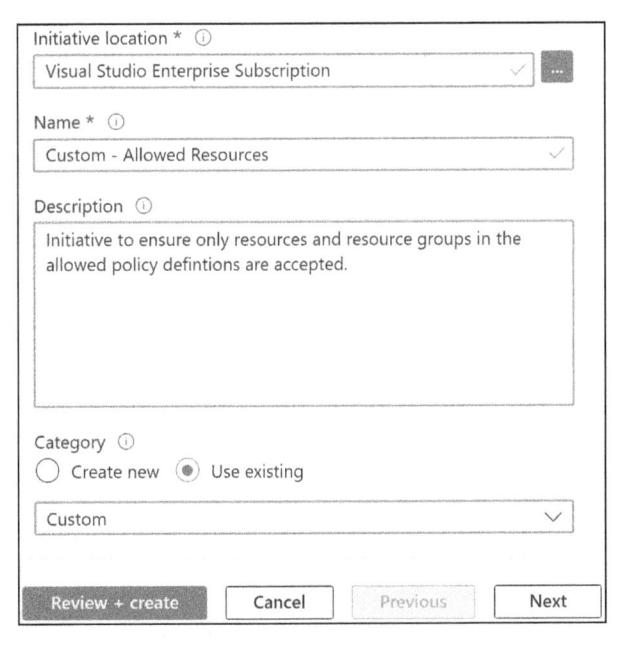

Figure 4.14: The Basics tab on the Initiative definition screen

3. Select `Add policy definition(s)` to be included in the initiative. The following screenshot shows you how to do this:

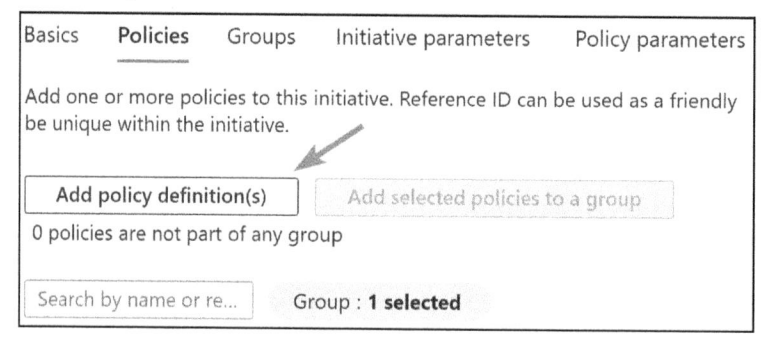

Figure 4.15: The Policies tab on the Initiative definition screen

4. Change the `Type` filter to `Custom` and then select the policy definition(s). Click `Add`. The process is illustrated in the following screenshot:

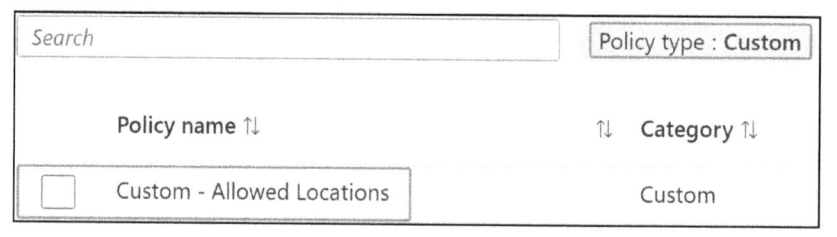

Figure 4.16: Selecting policies for an initiative definition

5. Your screen should now look like the following figure. You may now click `Next` after adding all associated policy definitions.

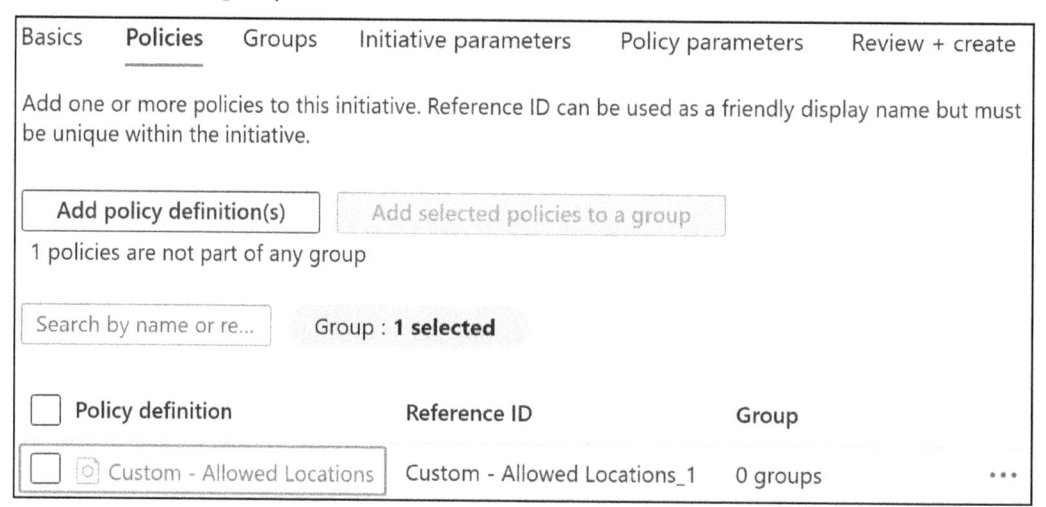

Figure 4.17: Added policies on the Initiative definition screen

6. The `Groups` tab, shown in the following screenshot, allows you to create groups that organize policies within an initiative. Skip this and click `Next`.

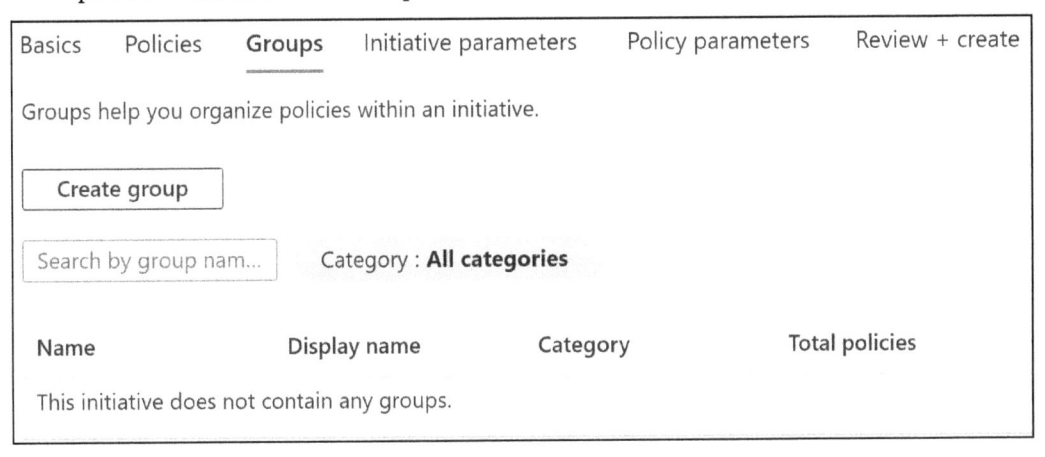

Figure 4.18: The Groups tab on the Initiative definition screen

7. Now, you will configure the `Initiative parameters` setting. Initiative parameters are inputs that align with policy definitions. Remember that `definitions` are a guideline set of rules that are assessed, and `parameters` are the values to assess for. Click `Create initiative parameter`, as illustrated in the following screenshot:

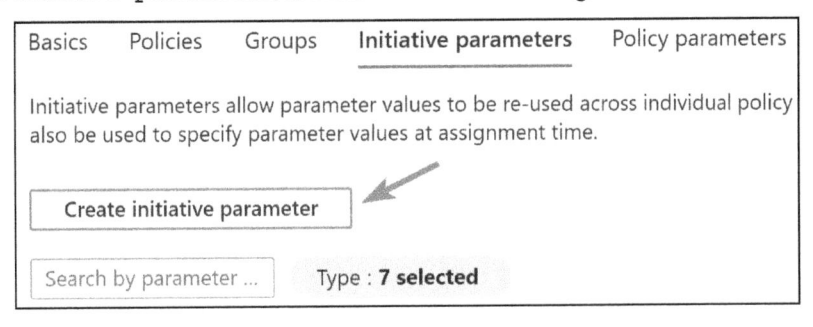

Figure 4.19: The Initiative parameters tab on the Initiative definition screen

8. Complete the respective details for Name, Display name, Description, Type, Allowed Values, and Default Value, as illustrated in the following screenshot. The Portal Review and Strong Type options can be left as the default values. Default Value will serve as a placeholder for parameter values to be assigned to policy definitions in the Policy parameters section. Click Save.

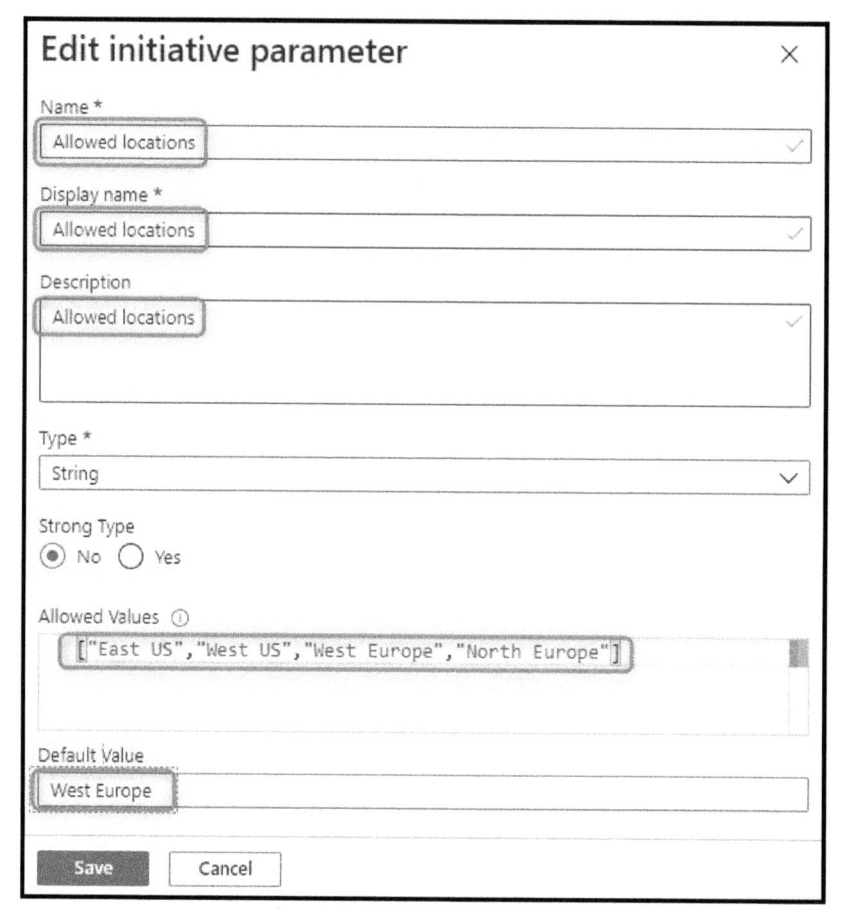

Figure 4.20: Creating an initiative parameter for an initiative definition

9. For this demonstration, go ahead and delete the initiative parameter again, as illustrated here, then click Next at the bottom of the screen.

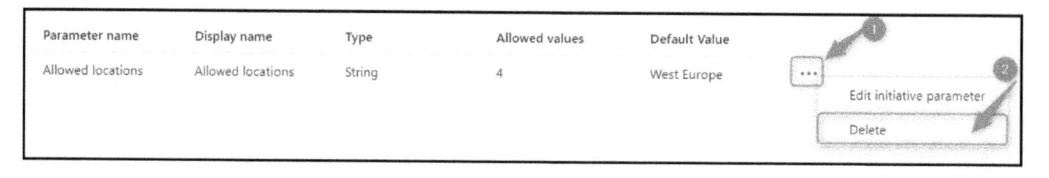

Figure 4.21: Deleting an initiative parameter on an initiative definition

10. On the `Policy parameters` tab, you have the option to select a value for parameters by choosing predefined values where `Value Type` is set to `Set value`, as illustrated in the following screenshot. Where `Use initiative parameter` is chosen, the values become what was defined previously. Change the `Value(s)` selection to `West Europe`.

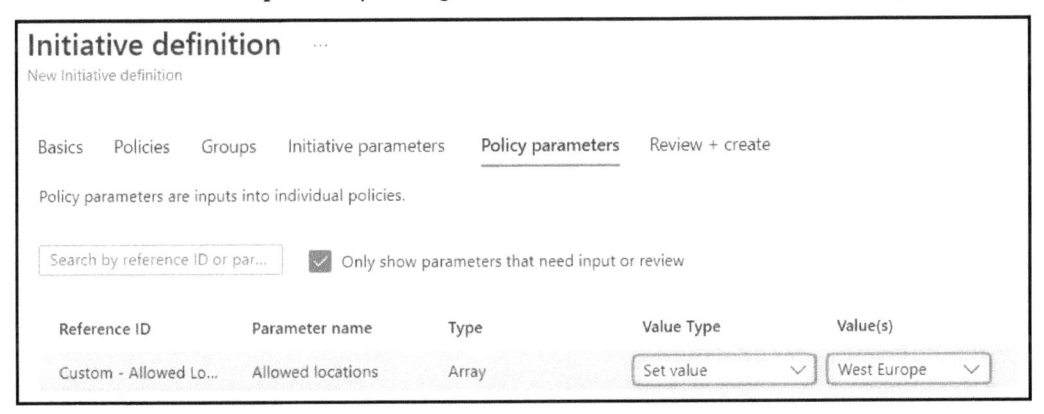

Figure 4.22: Selecting predefined parameters

11. Click `Review + create`.
12. Click `Create` after reviewing the configuration, as illustrated in the following screenshot:

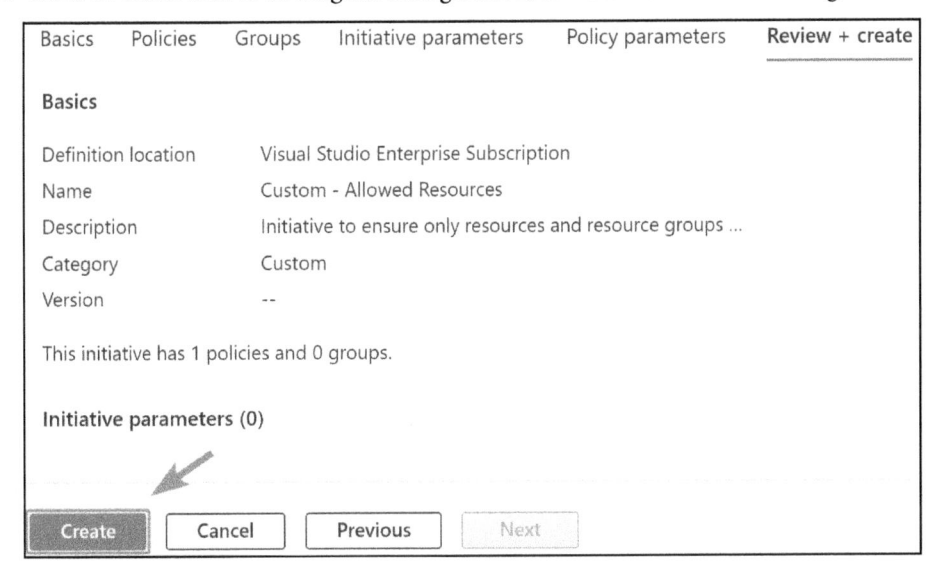

Figure 4.23: The Basics tab on the Initiative definition screen

You will be notified of completion and will now have a new initiative definition.

Assigning a Policy Definition and Initiative

Policy definitions or initiatives now need to be applied to take effect. The next course of action when assigning the policy is to select the scope. Proceed as follows:

1. Return to the `Policy` blade. From the left menu, under the `Authoring` context, click the `Assignments` button. From the top of the blade screen, click `Assign policy`, as illustrated in the following screenshot:

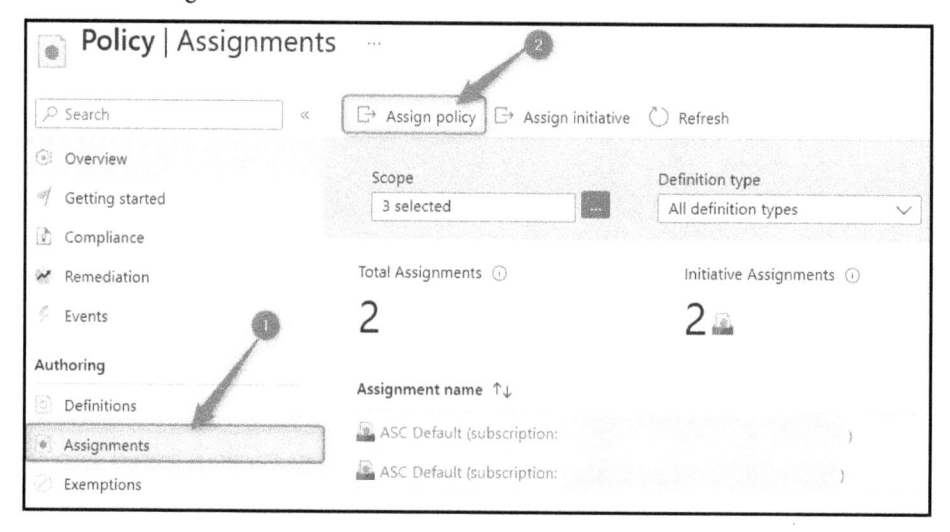

Figure 4.24: Assigning a policy

2. The `Assign policy` blade will come up. On the `Basics` tab, select a scope; this will be your subscription. Then, select a policy definition by clicking the ellipsis button (...), as illustrated in the following screenshot:

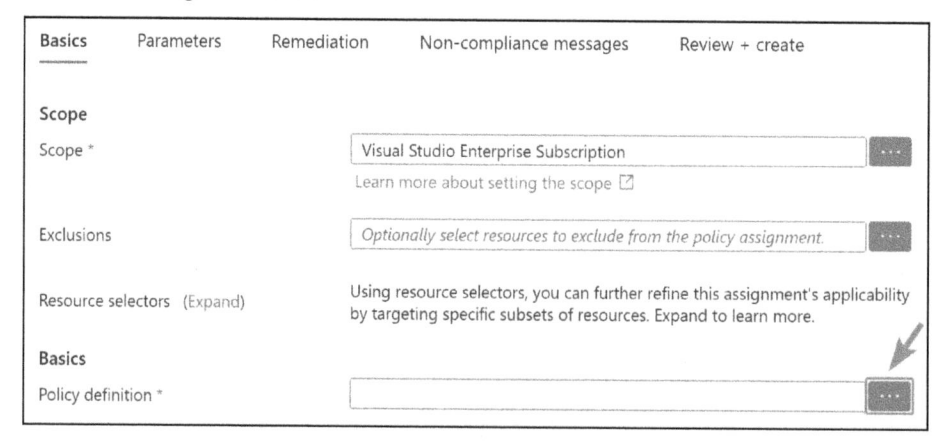

Figure 4.25: Selecting a policy definition

3. Select the desired definition and click Add. For this example, you will select Custom - Allowed Locations. To make it easier to find, you can type it into the search filter, as in the following screenshot:

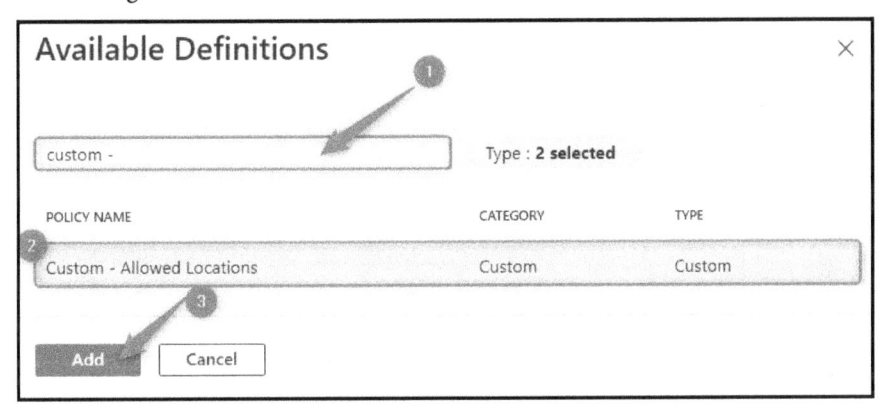

Figure 4.26: Selecting a policy definition for assignment

4. Click Next from the bottom menu of buttons. Then, click Next again to skip the Advanced tab.
5. On the Parameters tab, select a value for Allowed locations. For this example, you will select West Europe, as illustrated in the following screenshot. Click Next.

Figure 4.27: Entering parameters for assigned policies

6. Remediation can be configured on the next tab for non-compliant resources; this is facilitated through the creation of a managed identity that performs remediation tasks related to it. The following screenshot illustrates this in more detail. Click `Next`.

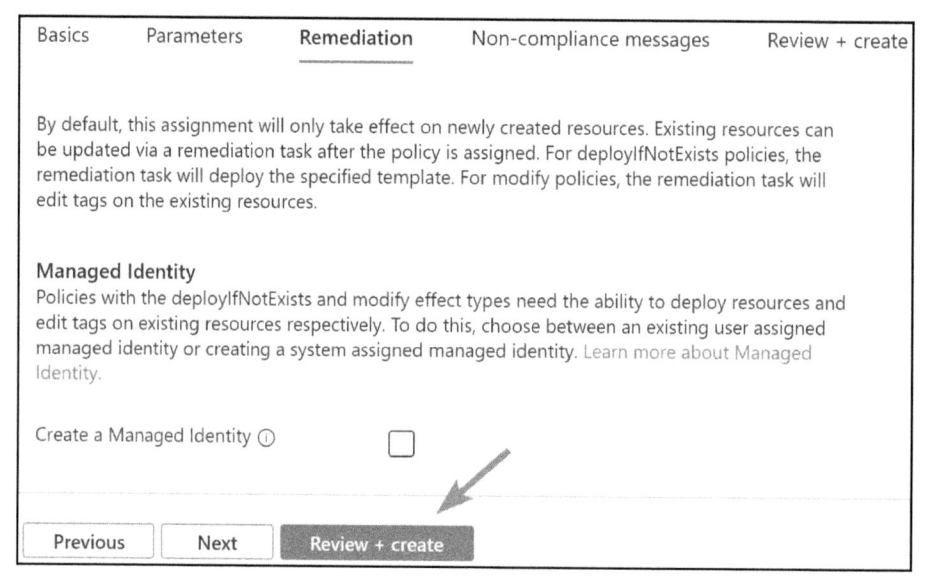

Figure 4.28: Azure Policy – Remediation

> **Note**
> Remediation is only supported for `DeployIfNotExists` and `Modify` effects.

7. Enter a meaningful non-compliance message, as illustrated in the following screenshot, then click `Review + create`.

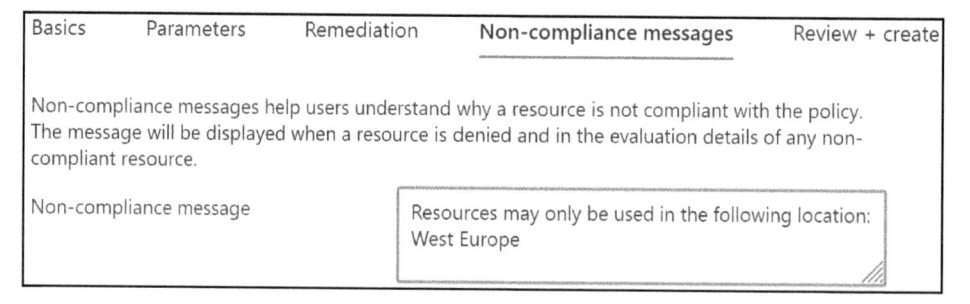

Figure 4.29: Non-compliance message

8. Review the configuration and click `Create`. A notification alert will signify a successful operation, as illustrated here:

Understanding Azure Policies | 121

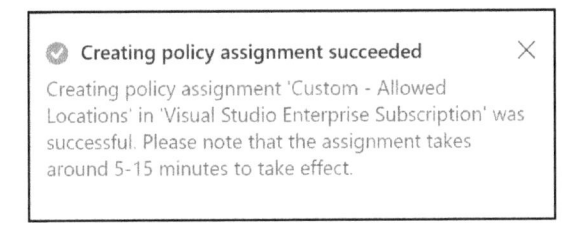

> ✓ **Creating policy assignment succeeded** ✕
>
> Creating policy assignment 'Custom - Allowed Locations' in 'Visual Studio Enterprise Subscription' was successful. Please note that the assignment takes around 5-15 minutes to take effect.

Figure 4.30: Success notification

9. To confirm that your new policy works, you will attempt to deploy a resource that will be denied by the policy. Open any resource group you have, or you can create one to match the exercise named `AZ104-Policies`. From the `Overview` menu, click `Create`. This will open the Marketplace.

Figure 4.31: Creating a resource from the Marketplace

10. You can choose any resource to test; in this example, you will be creating a managed disk. Enter `managed disks` in the Marketplace search bar and select the `Managed Disks` option that comes up. On the screen that follows, click `Create`.

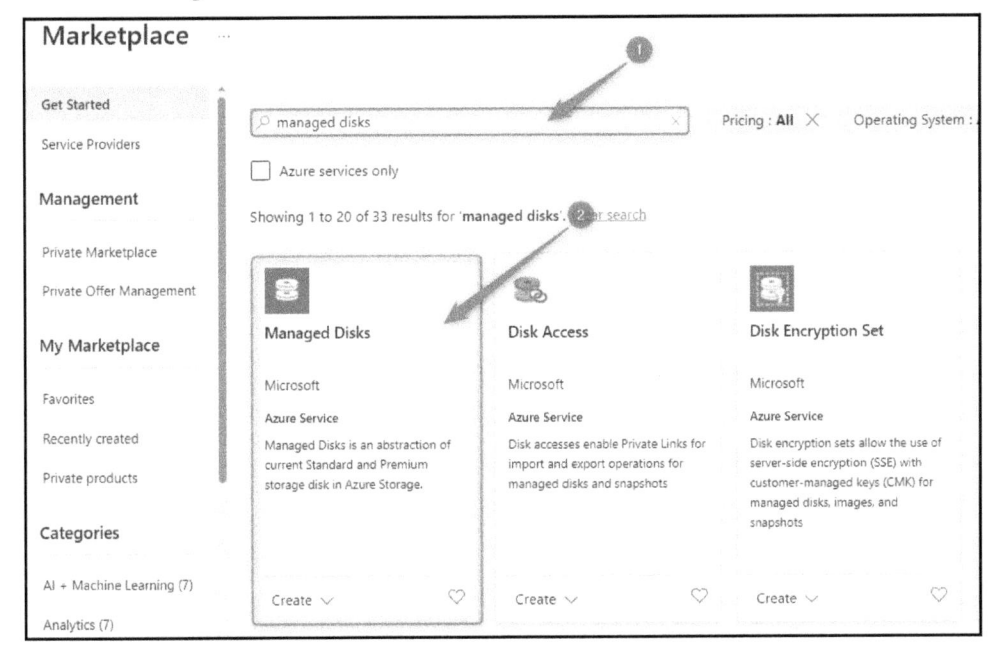

Figure 4.32: Selecting Managed Disks from the Marketplace

122 | Creating and Managing Governance

11. Enter a disk name, such as `testdisk01`, then choose an unsupported region for the `Region` option that you know will conflict with your policy, such as `UK South`. Click `Review + create`. The process is illustrated in the following screenshot:

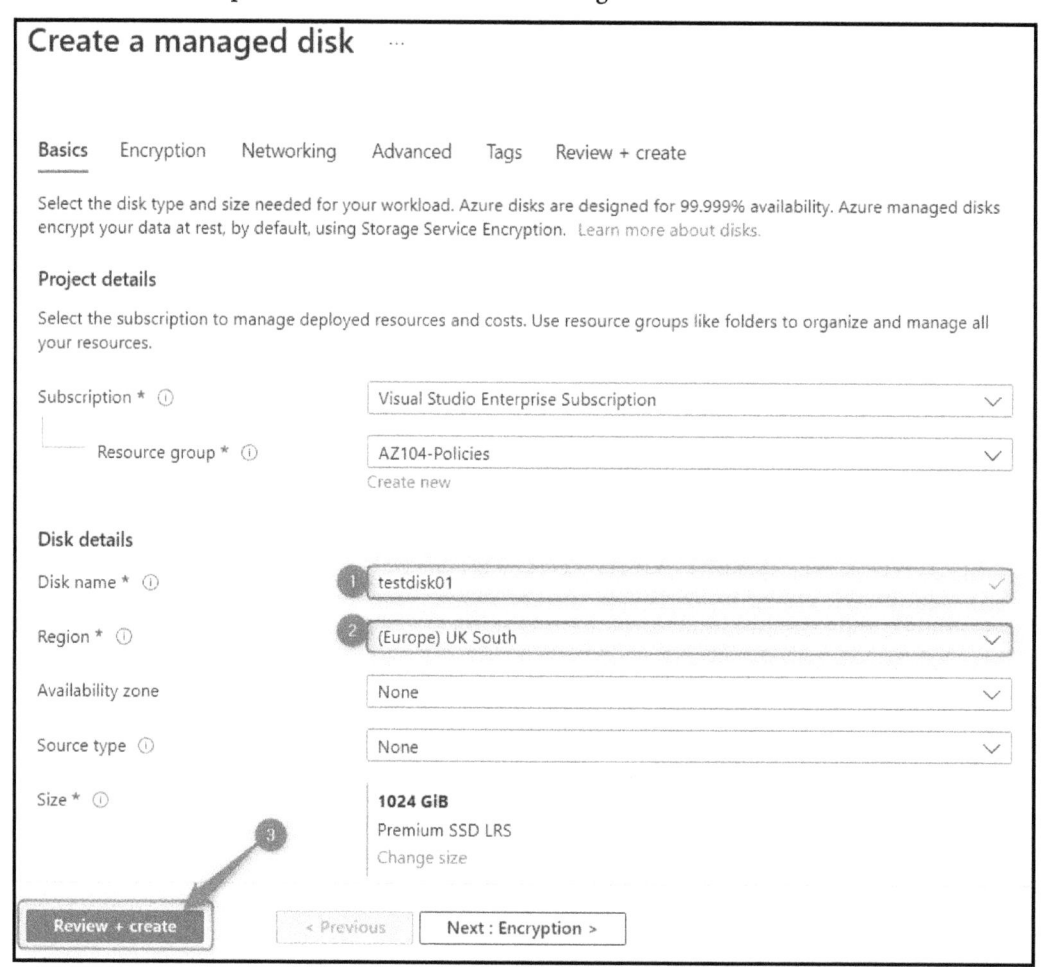

Figure 4.33: Creating a managed disk

12. Notice that validation fails due to policy non-compliance:

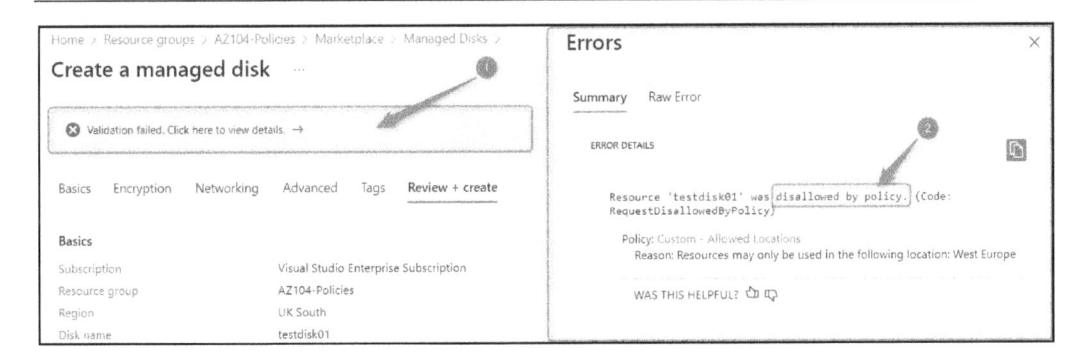

Figure 4.34: Non-compliance failure message

Now that you know how to assign policies and initiatives, you will move on to see where you can view compliance for policies and initiatives.

Policy Compliance

Policy compliance discusses the concept of adherence within Azure to your defined policy. This is ranked as a percentage illustrating the distribution of adherence by `Compliant`, `Exempt`, and `Non-Compliant` compliance states for the defined policies. To view the policy compliance status against assigned definitions, you can select the `Compliance` option from the left menu on the `Policy` blade. Note the compliance on the right-hand side. Compliance is reflected in a percentage (%) form to understand compliance effectiveness. Note that newly applied policies may take several minutes to be applied, as well as for compliance to be reflected. Typically, policies take about 30 minutes to apply, while compliance runs once every 24 hours.

The following screenshot provides an example of policy compliance within an Azure estate:

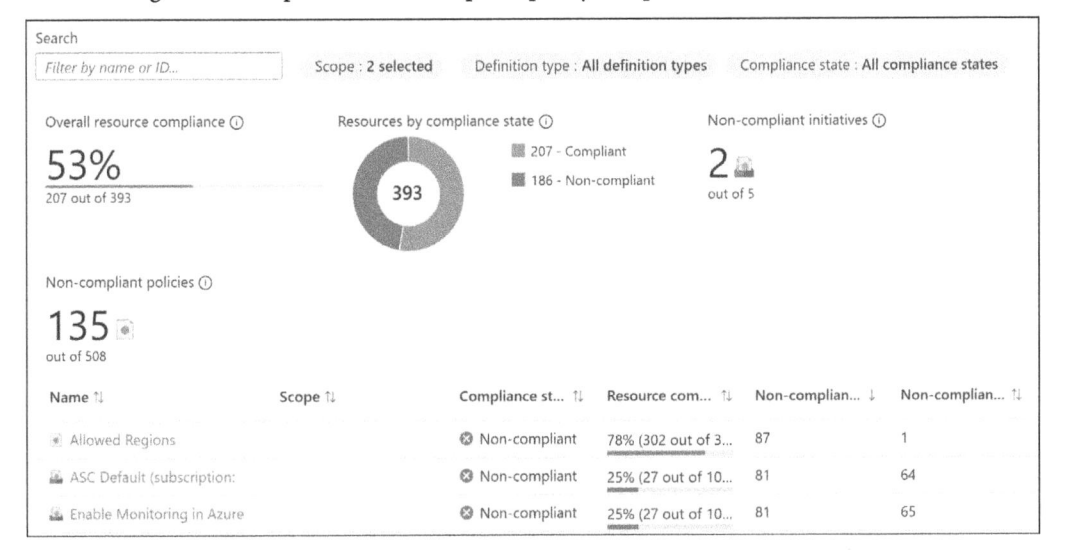

Figure 4.35: Policy compliance overview

Resource compliance describes resource adherence to the defined policies to which they are applicable. Policy compliance can exist in three different states, as outlined here:

- `Compliant`: A resource conforms to defined policy standards.
- `Non-compliant`: A resource does not conform to the required policy standard.
- `Exempt`: A resource has been identified to be exempt from the policy evaluation. This is explicitly defined for an exemption or can't be evaluated. Exempt resources will still be evaluated in the total compliance rating score.

Diving into any of the line items will provide further details; for this example, you will see a dashboard showing policy compliance for the `ASC Default` initiative:

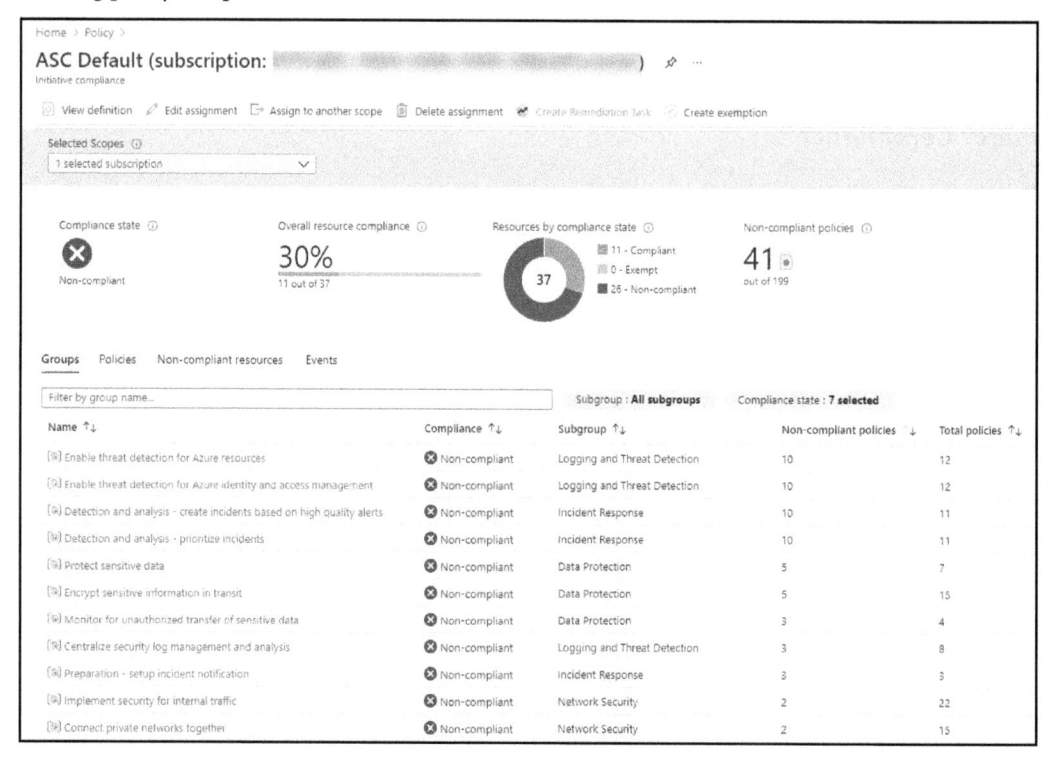

Figure 4.36: Example policy compliance overview

Now that you understand how to view overall compliance within your subscription, you can begin to apply this in your organization and with your customers.

> **Note**
> Policies can be used in conjunction with tags to effect compliance in an organization.

That brings this section to an end. In this section, you have learned what Azure policies are, why they are necessary, and how they work. You also learned how to create a policy definition, how to create a policy initiative, and how to manage and apply policies.

> **Note**
>
> You are encouraged to read up on this further by using the following links:
>
> **Microsoft Azure Policy documentation**: `https://learn.microsoft.com/en-us/azure/governance/policy/`
>
> **Azure Policy definition structure**: `https://learn.microsoft.com/en-us/azure/governance/policy/concepts/definition-structure`
>
> **Built-in Azure policy definitions**: `https://github.com/Azure/azure-policy/tree/master/built-in-policies`
>
> **Community-managed policy repository**: `https://github.com/Azure/Community-Policy`

Applying and Managing Tags on Resources

Tags in Azure are metadata labels that can be assigned to resources, resource groups, and subscriptions to help users organize, categorize, and manage their cloud resources more effectively. Tags are key-value pairs that provide additional information about the resources and can be used for various purposes, such as tracking ownership, managing cost allocation, and enforcing governance policies. Here are some reasons why organizations may want to use tags in Azure:

- **Organization**: Tags help users organize their resources based on specific criteria, such as project, environment, or department. This makes it easier to manage and locate resources within a complex cloud environment.

- **Cost management**: By tagging resources with relevant **cost center**, **project**, or **department** information, organizations can more accurately track and allocate costs associated with their cloud resources.

- **Governance and compliance**: Tags can be used in conjunction with Azure Policy to enforce governance rules and ensure that resources comply with organizational standards. For example, a policy can require that all resources have specific tags assigned, such as **owner** and **expiration date**.

- **Automation**: Tags can be utilized in automation scripts or templates to filter resources based on specific criteria, streamlining operations and management tasks.

- **Reporting and monitoring**: Tags can be used in reporting and monitoring tools, such as Azure Cost Management or Azure Monitor, to create custom dashboards and reports based on specific resource groupings.

In summary, tags in Azure provide a flexible and powerful way to organize, manage, and track cloud resources, enabling organizations to maintain better control over their cloud environment and optimize resource usage, costs, and compliance.

How Tags Look in Azure

In the following screenshot example, you have the following two tags applied to a resource group:

- `Department`, with a value of `IT`
- `Owner`, with a value of `Infrastructure`

You can see the tags here:

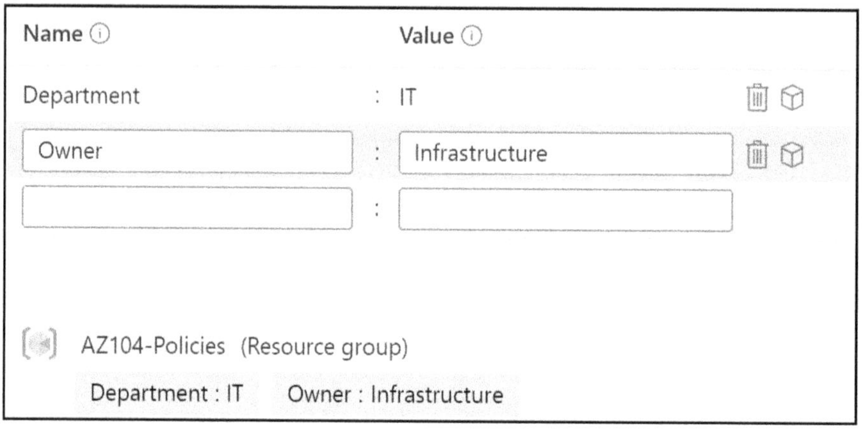

Name		Value		
Department	:	IT	🗑	📦
Owner	:	Infrastructure	🗑	📦
	:			

AZ104-Policies (Resource group)
Department : IT   Owner : Infrastructure

Figure 4.37: Tag example

> **Note**
> Tag names are case-insensitive and tag values are case-sensitive.

Tagging Strategy

A tagging strategy is a structured approach and plan as to how tags will be used within your Azure environment to support your organizational requirements, such as operational support functionality and cost management. When implementing a tagging strategy, it is important to consider the requirements for having tags in place. Tags will assist in presenting value to either business or **information technology** (**IT**)-aligned tagging requirements. The key to implementing a defined tag strategy is consistency, in the application of tags as well as the implementation (especially on the casing). Some important common tag patterns are noted here:

- **Functional**: Classification of resources by defining the functionality the resource(s) introduces to the workload environment. Here are examples of functional tags:

  - **Application name**: Use this to classify a set of resources for an application
  - **Environment**: `DEV/TEST/UAT/STAGING/PROD/DR`

- **Classification**: This tag can be used to describe data classification pertaining to resources. This is particularly valuable for compliance alignment, such as with the **General Data Protection Regulation (GDPR)**. The following is an example of a classification tag:

  - **Confidentiality**: `Private/Public/Restricted`

- **Accounting**: This set of tags is particularly focused on cost governance and the assignment of resource(s) to a billing unit/entity within the organization. The following are examples of accounting tags:

  - **Department**: `Finance/IT/HR/Marketing/Sales`
  - **Region**: `West Europe/Central US`, and so on

- **Partnership**: This set of tags is used to identify people in the organization who can or should be contacted as they contain relevance to the resource. The following are examples of partnership tags:

  - **Owner**: Identify the product owner for the service
  - **Support email**: Identify who to contact when support is needed
  - **Business criticality**: Define how important the resource is to the business (normally a metric value such as `BC1/BC2/BC3`)
  - **SLA objectives**: Define a **service-level agreement (SLA)** tier that would apply to determine the support required for the service (for example, `SLA Tier 1/SLA Tier 2/SLA Tier 3`)

- **Purpose**: This set of tags is reserved for understanding the key deliverable for the application and is aligned with a business objective. Here is an example of a purpose tag:

  - **Purpose**: Describe the application's purpose in a single line. This assists later in troubleshooting by providing a basic understanding of what the application is and what it does.

Applying a Resource Tag

In this example of applying a resource tag, you will open a resource group on the portal, open the tagging section, and apply a tag. The steps are outlined here:

Creating and Managing Governance

1. Open the resource group and select `Tags` from the left menu pane, as illustrated in the following screenshot:

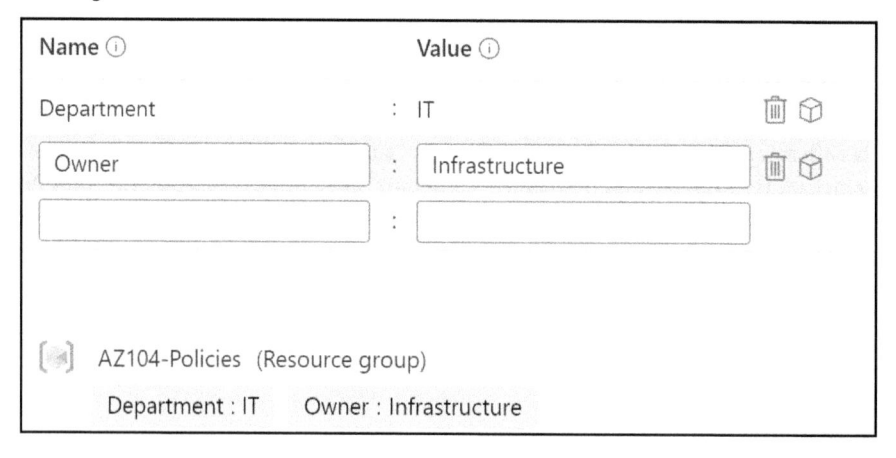

Figure 4.38: Tag example

2. Apply a tag name and value pair (or multiple pairs) and click `Apply`. You will create a new tag named `Purpose` with a value of `Demo`, as illustrated in the following screenshot:

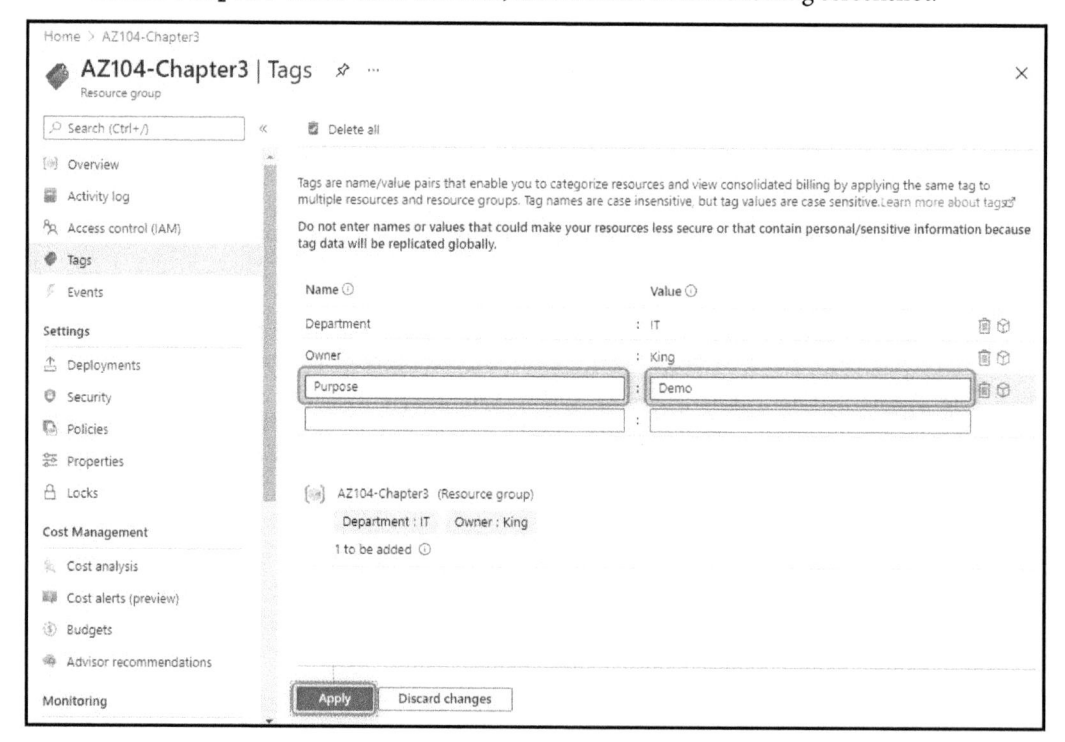

Figure 4.39: Applying a new tag

3. After selecting `Apply`, you will get a notification; notice the changes in the section above the `Apply` button.

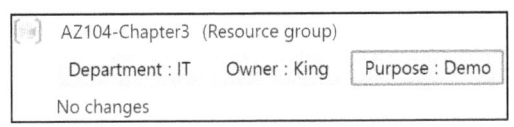

Figure 4.40: Applied tags overview

4. To modify a tag, you simply update the value, as illustrated in the following screenshot, and click `Apply`.

Figure 4.41: Updating a tag

In this exercise, you learned how to apply a resource tag to a resource group. The concept is the same for all types of Azure resources that can be tagged. You should now feel much more comfortable with applying tags in general to resources and resource groups.

Now that you know how to configure and apply tags, you will learn about the PowerShell commands to assist with the management of tags.

PowerShell Scripts

This section introduces PowerShell scripts that can be used for the automation of tag management, as well as for quicker administration times. Please ensure that the Az module is installed, as per the *Technical requirements* section at the beginning of the chapter. To run the scripts, simply run the code in a PowerShell window after authenticating to Azure from PowerShell.

Authenticating to Azure from PowerShell

Paste the following code and then enter your username and password in the prompt:

```
# Enter your Azure Tenant ID
$TenantId = ""
# login to Azure
Connect-AzAccount -TenantId $TenantId
```

Applying a Tag to a Resource Group

The following script creates a new tag named Purpose with a value of Demo in the AZ104-Chapter3 resource group. Simply paste this code into the PowerShell window you authenticated yourself in:

```
$tags = @{"Purpose"="Demo"}
$resourceGroup = Get-AzResourceGroup -Name AZ104-Chapter3
New-AzTag -ResourceId $resourceGroup.ResourceId -tag $tags
```

Applying a Tag to a Resource

Applying a tag to a resource is very similar; in this instance, you will apply the preceding tag to a storage account resource. Tags will be applied to a resource named AZ104Storage. The code is illustrated in the following snippet:

```
$tags = @{"Purpose"="Demo"}
$resource = Get-AzResource -Name AZ104Storage -ResourceGroup AZ104-Chapter3
New-AzTag -ResourceId $resource.id -Tag $tags
```

Updating Tags

Update-AzTag is another very useful command. It allows you to update tags to the $tags variable that is parsed or to merge tags from the $tags variable with existing tags. Merging combines two operations—namely, adding absent tags to the resource or resource group and updating the value key for existing tags.

In the following example, you will add a new tag named Tags with a value of Merge. The result will be two tags on the AZ104-Chapter3 resource group:

```
$tags = @{"Tags"="Merge"}
$resourceGroup = Get-AzResourceGroup -Name AZ104-Chapter3
Update-AzTag -ResourceId $resourceGroup.ResourceId -Tag $tags -Operation Merge
```

The following example will replace the tags and leave the `AZ104-Chapter3` resource group with only the tag for `Purpose`:

```
$tags = @{"Tags"="Merge"}
$resourceGroup = Get-AzResourceGroup -Name AZ104-Chapter3
Update-AzTag -ResourceId $resourceGroup.ResourceId -Tag $tags
-Operation Replace
```

To run multiple tags in the commands, simply add a semicolon (;) between tag pairs, as per the following example:

```
$tags = @{"Tag1"="Value1"; "Tag2"="Value2"}
```

> **Note**
> The `replace` command switch will remove tags that are not present in the `$tags` variable. The `merge` command will amend tags that are present and add any missing tags defined in the `$tags` variable.

This concludes our discussuion on resource tags. In this section, you have learned what resource tags are, why they are necessary, and how they work.

> **Note**
> You are encouraged to read up further by using the following links:
>
> **Microsoft documentation on tags**: https://learn.microsoft.com/en-us/azure/azure-resource-manager/management/tag-resources?tabs=json
>
> **Resource naming and tagging decision guide**: https://learn.microsoft.com/en-us/azure/cloud-adoption-framework/ready/azure-best-practices/resource-naming-and-tagging-decision-guide?toc=%2Fazure%2Fazure-resource-manager%2Fmanagement%2Ftoc.json
>
> **Prescriptive guidance for resource tagging**: https://learn.microsoft.com/en-us/azure/cloud-adoption-framework/govern/guides/complex/prescriptive-guidance#resource-tagging
>
> **Applying tags in PowerShell**: https://learn.microsoft.com/en-us/azure/azure-resource-manager/management/tag-resources?tabs=json#powershell

Summary

In this chapter, you have established how to create and manage governance in Azure using Azure policies and tags. You have learned how to perform administrative actions through the portal and PowerShell. You also know where to look for information pertaining to managing both policies and tags and how to build a strategy for tag governance, and have been provided with further reading sources to improve your application of these new skills. You now have the skills required to implement governance requirements and assist in establishing baselines for governance.

As part of the experience you have gained, you have learned how to define, apply, and manage Azure Policy resources. You have learned the value they offer and how to utilize them within your environments. You have also learned about tags within Azure, how these can be used, and how to apply these to resources within the platform. These are both core skills in enforcing governance in Azure and a good foundation for good operational design for your environments. Please note that while a great starting point, these are only two topics within a vast spectrum of topics that could be considered within governance. When designing effective environments, you will want to design with the principles defined within the Well-Architected Framework, which considers several pillars of design best practices when considering cloud applications.

In the next chapter, you will be expanding upon the skills learned in this chapter and investigating how to manage resources and services available in Azure that support governance objectives and costs within Azure.

> **Note**
>
> Remember to delete the resources you created in this chapter to minimize costs. You can do this with the following command for convenience, which will remove the resource group and all the corresponding resources:
>
> ```
> Remove-AzResourceGroup -Name AZ104-Policies
> Remove-AzResourceGroup -Name AZ104-Chapter4
> ```

5
Managing Governance and Costs

In the previous chapter, you learned about some services that assist you in managing governance in Azure. You learned about Azure policies, why they exist, and the value they provide. You also learned about resource tags and how to apply them. This chapter covers how to manage the resources and services available in Azure that support governance objectives, as well as costs. You will learn about resource groups, resource locks, cost management, budgets, and alerts, all of which play a crucial role in maintaining governance within the Azure platform. You will build confidence in this chapter to do just that and understand how to apply what you have learned to your organization.

In this chapter, you are going to explore the following main topics:

- Managing resource groups
- Configuring resource locks
- Managing costs

Technical Requirements

To follow along with the hands-on material, you will need the following:

- Access to an Azure subscription with owner or contributor privileges. If you do not have access to one, students can enroll for a free account: https://azure.microsoft.com/en-us/free/
- **PowerShell 5.1** or later installed on a Windows PC or PowerShell Core 6.x on other operating systems, to practice the labs.
- Where PowerShell is not installed https://shell.azure.com can be used as a browser-based Azure PowerShell.

- Installation of the Az PowerShell module, which can be performed by running the following in an administrative PowerShell session:

  ```
  Set-ExecutionPolicy -ExecutionPolicy RemoteSigned -Scope
  CurrentUser
  Install-Module -Name Az -Scope CurrentUser -Repository PSGallery
  -Force
  ```

Now, you will dive into the first topic and learn about resource group management.

Managing Resource Groups

Resource groups are logical containers for grouping multiple resources together. Resources can be **virtual machines** (**VMs**), databases, virtual networks, web apps, and so forth. A resource group should group all resources that have a similar or the same life cycle—for instance, all items that are deployed, updated, or deleted with some form of commonality, such as belonging to the same application, service, type, department, or location. In other words, they behave or are viewed as a single entity. Resource groups create a mechanism for logical grouping that enables the order and organization of resources created in Azure.

Some important points to note when defining resource groups are outlined here:

- A resource can only belong to a single resource group at any time.
- Resources can be added and removed from a resource group at any time.
- Resource group metadata (the data describing the resource group and resources) is stored in the region where the resource group is created.
- Resources in a resource group are not bound by the location defined for the resource group and can be deployed into different regions.
- If a resource group's region is unavailable, you cannot update, modify, or delete any resources in the group due to the metadata being unavailable. Resources in other regions will continue to function as expected, even in the resource group.
- Access control actions can be associated with resource groups through **role-based access control** (**RBAC**) roles, Azure Policy, or resource locks.

> **Note**
> Consider a resource group organization strategy when creating resource groups, to identify ownership, billing, location, resource type, department, applications, and access.

In the exercises that follow, you will work through some common operations relating to resource groups, such as deployment and deletion. To get the most out of this book, it is advised that you follow along with the exercises.

Deploying a Resource Group

In this section, you are going to run through an exercise of creating a resource group using the Azure portal. Proceed as follows:

1. In the Azure portal, select the hamburger menu icon from the top left of the Azure portal and click `Resource groups`, as illustrated in the following screenshot:

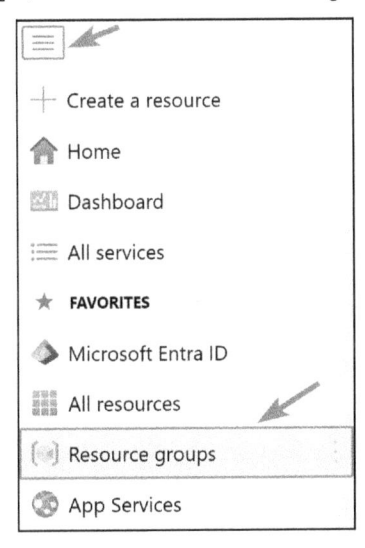

Figure 5.1: Selecting the resource groups option

2. Click + `Create`, as illustrated in the following screenshot:

Figure 5.2: Creating a resource group

136 Managing Governance and Costs

3. Enter a resource group name; this example uses `AZ104-Demo`. Choose a `Region` (location) option and click `Next : Tags >` if you wish to add tags to the resource group. Alternatively, click `Review + create` to jump to the `Review + create` pane. The following figure shows clicking `Review + create`:

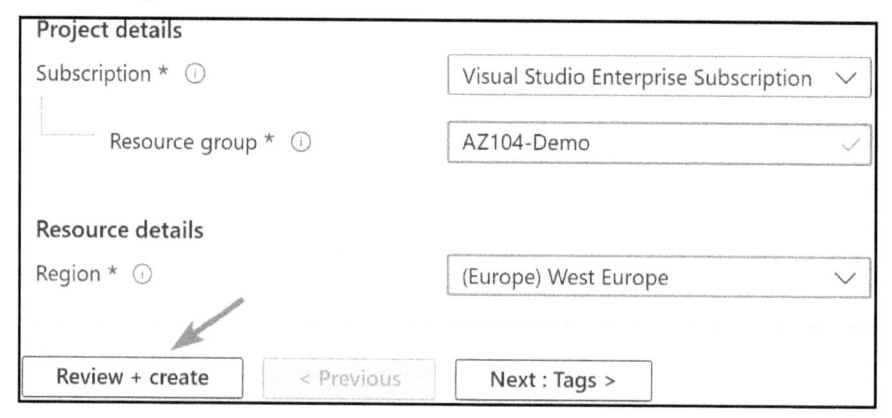

Figure 5.3: The Basics tab – creating a resource group

> **Note**
> Resource group names must be unique per subscription.

4. Upon successful validation, click `Create`, as illustrated in the following screenshot:

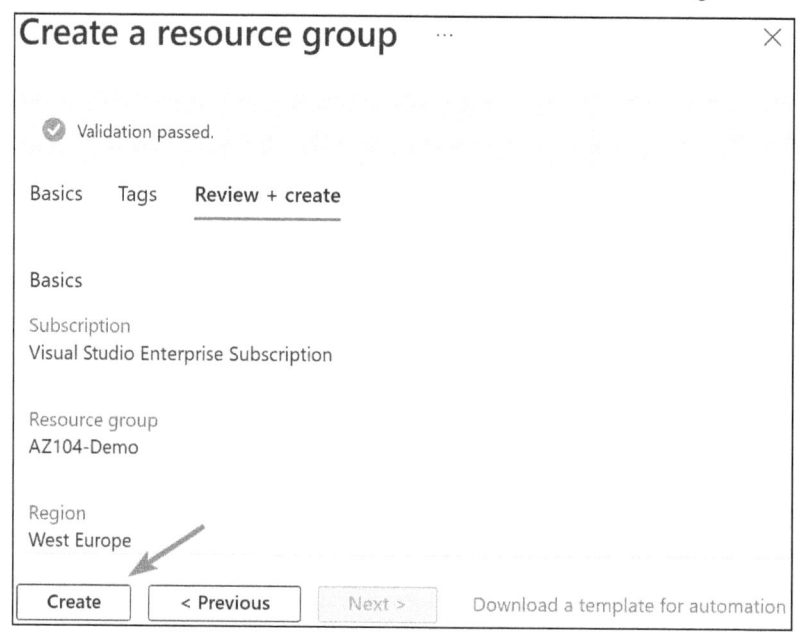

Figure 5.4: The Review + create tab – creating a resource group

5. You will receive a notification to indicate the successful creation of the resource group, as illustrated in the following screenshot:

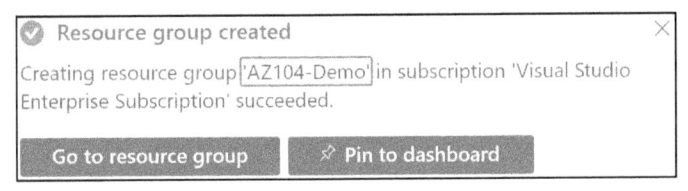

Figure 5.5: Resource group overview

You have now learned how to deploy a resource group through the Azure portal. Although basic, deploying resource groups is a fundamental part of using Azure. Resource groups facilitate resource deployments and the grouping of resources with commonality.

In the next section, you will learn how to view existing resource groups.

Listing Resource Groups

On some occasions, you may want to see which resource groups you have or utilize existing resource groups for future deployments. To do this, you will perform the following steps to view your existing resource groups:

1. In the Azure portal, select the hamburger menu icon and click `Resource groups`, as illustrated in the following screenshot:

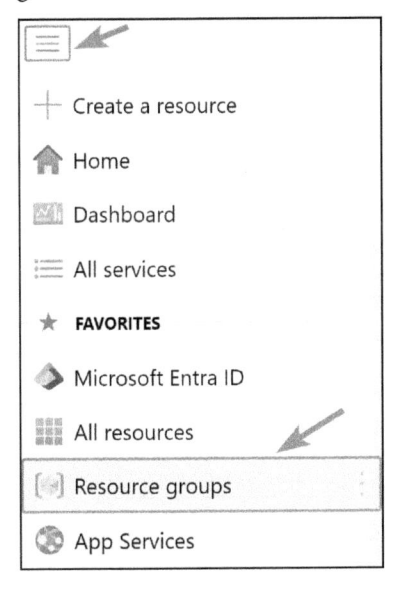

Figure 5.6: Selecting the resource groups option

2. In the following screenshot, notice all the resource groups identified by the `Name`, `Subscription`, and `Location` values:

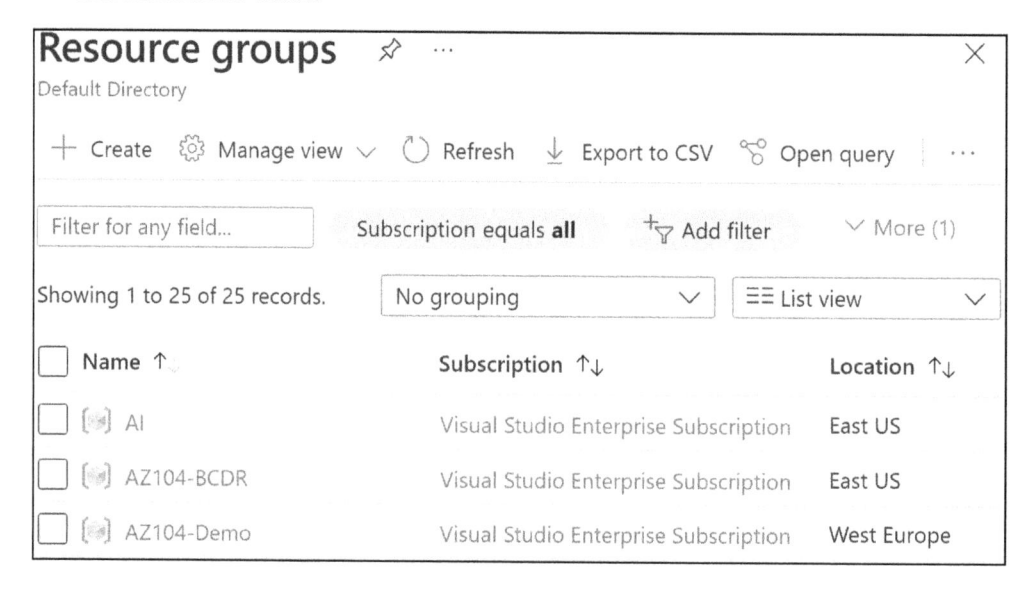

Figure 5.7: Listing resource groups

You now know how to list resource groups that exist within your subscription. Listing resource groups is important for navigating resources in Azure.

In the next section, you will explore the process behind deleting resource groups.

Deleting a Resource Group

To delete a resource group, complete the following steps in the portal:

1. On the `Resource groups` blade, select a resource group to be deleted, as illustrated in the following screenshot:

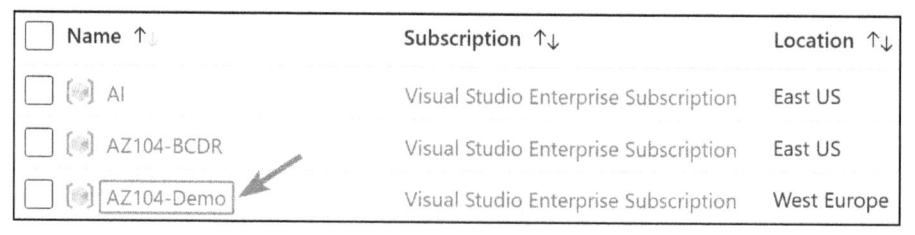

Figure 5.8: Selecting a resource group

> **Note**
> Deleting a resource group is a quick and easy method of deleting all your resources deployed to that group.

2. On the `Overview` blade, click `Delete resource group`.

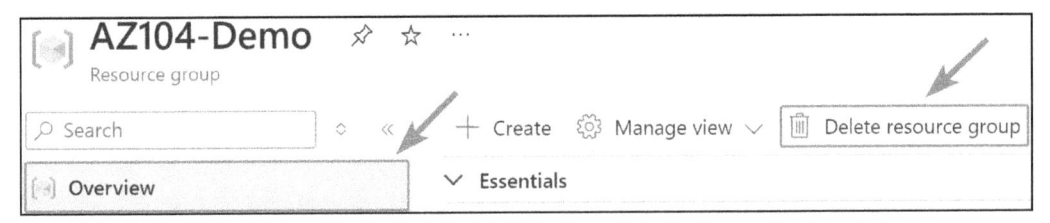

Figure 5.9: Selecting delete resource group

3. A pop-up dialog will appear; enter the resource group name in the `Enter resource group name to confirm deletion` dialog box (for this example, `AZ104-Demo`). Then, click `Delete`. The process is illustrated in the following screenshot:

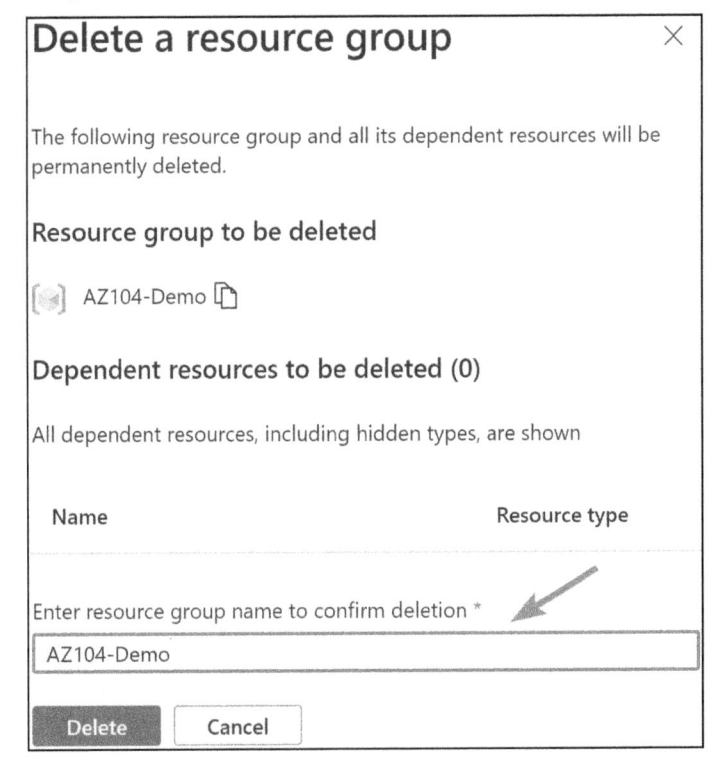

Figure 5.10: Deleting a resource group

4. You will further receive a notification asking you to confirm that you want to delete this resource group and its associated resources. Click `Delete`.

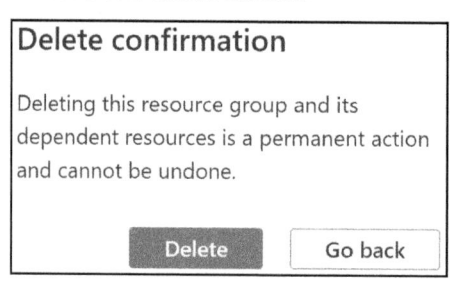

Figure 5.11: Delete confirmation

5. You will receive a notification that the resource group has been successfully deleted, as illustrated in the following screenshot:

Figure 5.12: Resource group deletion notification

You have now learned the process behind deleting resource groups. Deleting resource groups is important when cleaning up your environment and removing unnecessary resources. Also, in situations where you may find yourself needing to delete a collection of resources at once that all reside in a resource group, deleting the resource group can be a very effective method of removing these at all at once.

Next, you will learn about the process behind moving resources in a resource group.

Migrating or Moving Resource Groups

When you start to get more familiar with working with resources on Azure, you may start to find some interesting scenarios that come up with regard to your daily functions. There may be times when you wish to migrate or move resources to another resource group or subscription. The good news is that resources can also be moved to a different resource group and subscription. However, there are limitations to this. When migrating or moving resources, it is important to plan properly. While out of the scope of the exam, an example of the migration of resources from one resource group to another has been included for your benefit. Refer to the following:

1. To begin with, you will need to create two resource groups: one named `ResourceGroupA` and the other `ResourceGroupB`, as in the following screenshot. The resource groups must be in the same subscription.

Managing Resource Groups 141

Figure 5.13: Resource group migration – creation of groups

2. Open `ResourceGroupA` and click `Create` from the `Overview` pane.

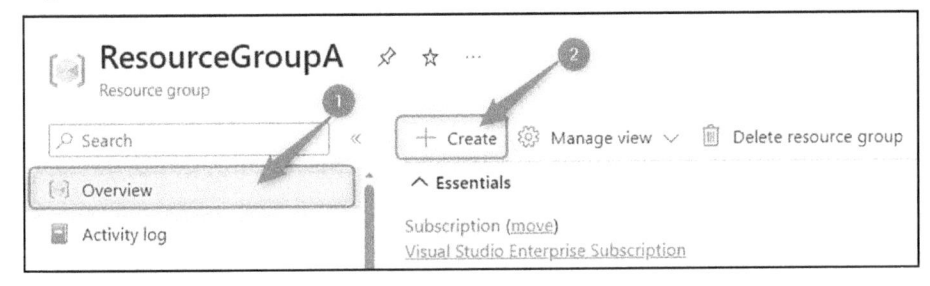

Figure 5.14: Resource group migration – creating a resource

3. We will create a simple resource for this example. Enter `storage account` in the search box, and select the Microsoft `Storage account` option; it should be your first choice.

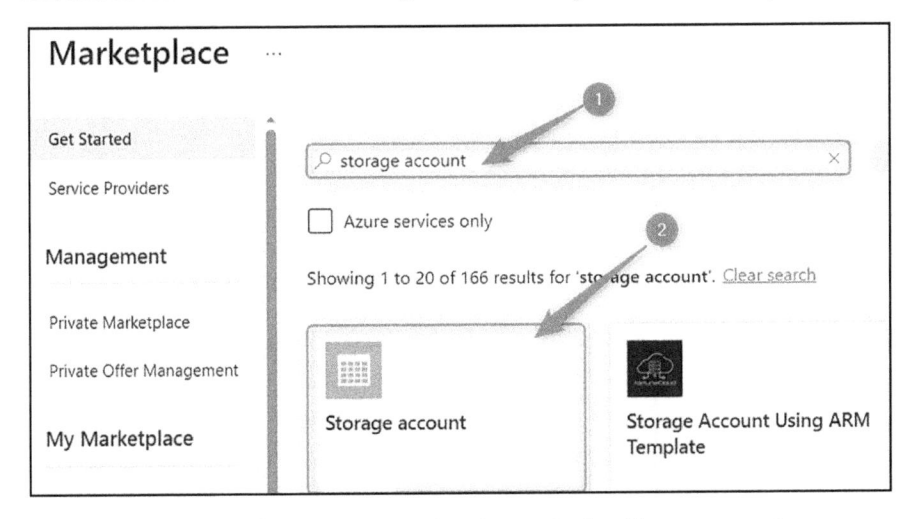

Figure 5.15: Resource group migration – selecting Storage account

4. On the next screen, click `Create`.

5. Select your `Subscription` type, and then select `ResourceGroupA` for `Resource group`. Next, enter a `Storage account name` value; use a name such as `demochapter4[date]` (for example, `demochapter401052023`), which should be random enough to still be a globally unique storage account name. Finally, select `West Europe` for `Region`. This will lead to a complaint due to the policy you implemented previously. This policy can be deleted now. Then, click `Review`.

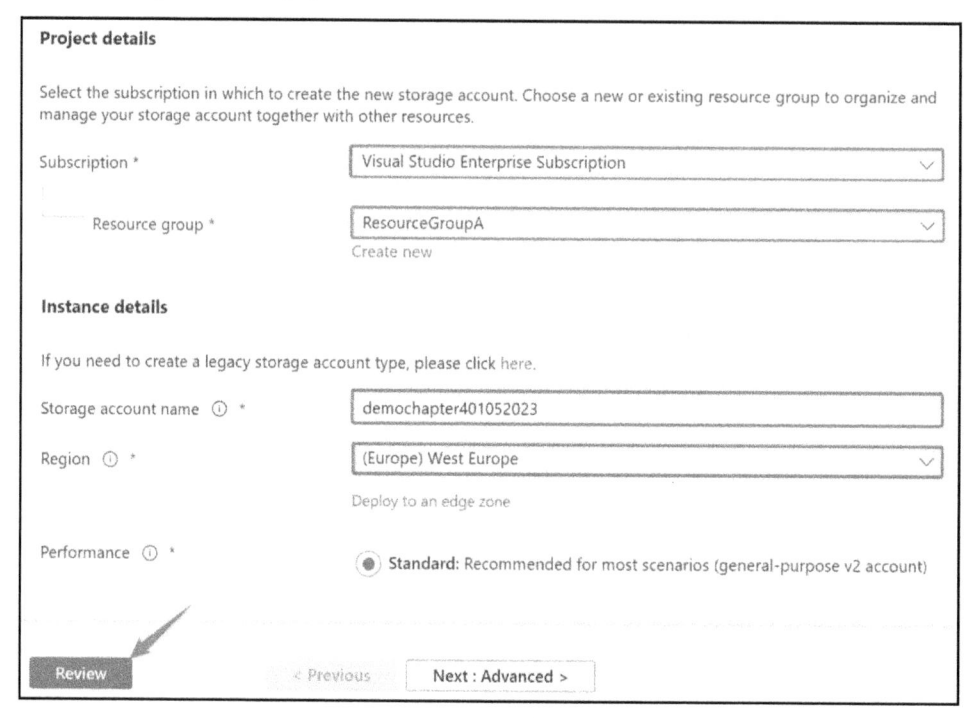

Figure 5.16: Resource group migration – creating a storage account

6. After validation succeeds, click `Create` at the bottom of the screen.
7. Once your deployment has been completed, return to `ResourceGroupA`. From the `Overview` pane, you should notice your resource deployed in the `Resources` list. Select this by clicking the checkbox next to the resource and notice that the `Move` button becomes accessible at the top of the screen. Click `Move` and then the `Move to another resource group` option.

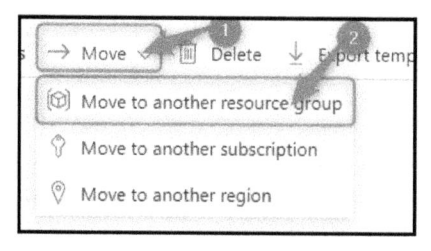

Figure 5.17: Move to another resource group

8. You will be asked to select a `Target` subscription and resource group. For the `Resource group` option, select `ResourceGroupB` and click `Next`. Notice the subscription matches your `ResourceGroupA` subscription.

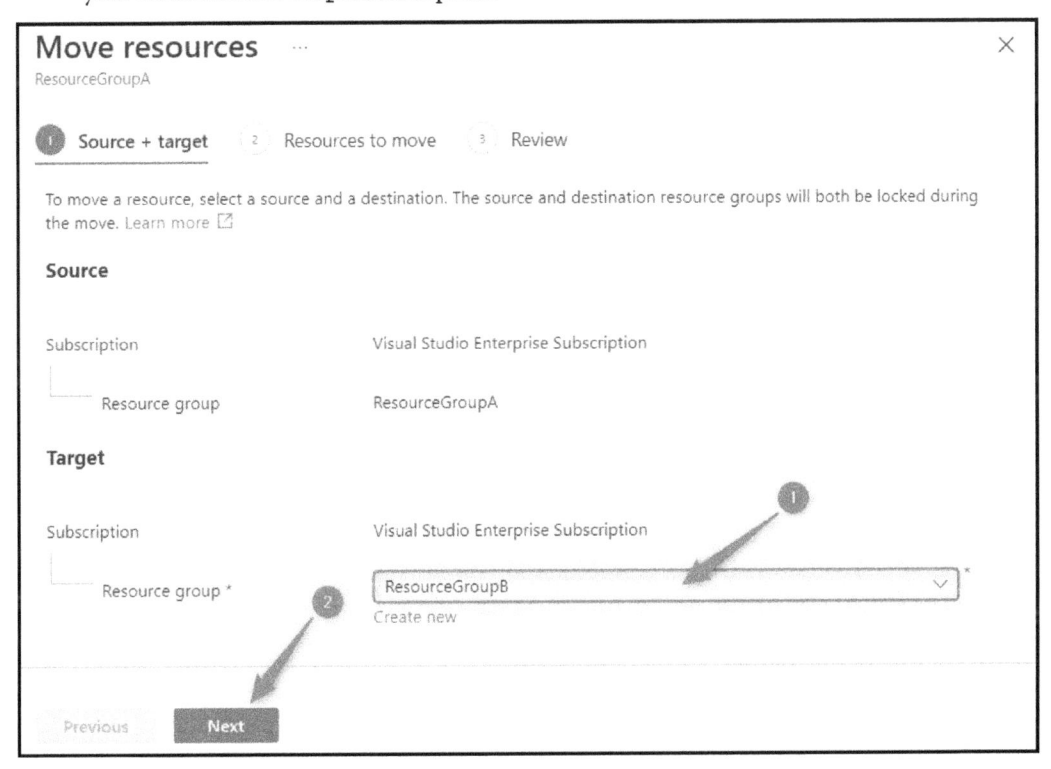

Figure 5.18: Moving resources

9. A validation will be run to confirm whether the resources can be moved. Wait for this validation to complete, which can take a few minutes. When it completes the validation, click `Next` to go to the `Review` phase.

10. At the bottom of the screen, you are asked to click a checkbox that confirms your understanding of the risks behind moving resources. It reads as follows: `I understand that tools and scripts associated with moved resources will not work until I update them to use new resource IDs`. Click this checkbox and then click the `Move` button.

11. You will receive a notification that the move process has started. This can also take several minutes to complete, and you will get a notification to confirm the status of the move. It should be a success for this example. Once complete, give it another minute to show on the portal. You should now see it listed under the `Overview` pane's `Resource` list for `ResourceGroupB`.

You have now experienced a move migration, demonstrating how a resource can be moved from `ResourceGroupA` to `ResourceGroupB`. The process is very similar for moving across subscriptions, too. Although a slightly different operation, you will find the `Move to another region` option from the `Move` menu to be very similar as well, only instead of selecting a resource group, you will select a new region.

One of the great things about the `Move` options available in Azure is that no downtime is incurred on those resources. If you had to move a VM, you would be surprised to note that you would lose no pings to the VM if you ran a continuous ping while moving the resources. This can be very helpful when performing this for your company or customers.

> **Note**
>
> For further reading, refer to the following links that may assist you:
>
> The following URL will assist in considering items before moving: `https://learn.microsoft.com/en-us/azure/azure-resource-manager/management/move-resource-group-and-subscription#checklist-before-moving-resources`
>
> Not all resources support migrations, and the following up-to-date link will provide supported operations by resource type: `https://learn.microsoft.com/en-us/azure/azure-resource-manager/management/move-support-resources`

In the next section, you will look at some PowerShell scripts to accomplish resource group creation tasks.

PowerShell Scripts

This section introduces PowerShell scripts that can be used for the automation of resource group management, as well as for quicker administration times. Please ensure that the Az module is installed, as per the *Technical Requirements* section at the beginning of the chapter. Then, proceed as follows:

1. Create a new empty resource group. Define a location and name for the new resource group to be deployed, as follows:

   ```
   New-AzResourceGroup -Name RG01 -Location "West Europe"
   ```

2. Create another new empty resource group with tags. Define a location, a name, and tags for the resource group, as follows:

   ```
   $tags = @{"Tag1"="Value1"; "Tag2"="Value2"}
   New-AzResourceGroup -Name RG02 -Location "West Europe" -Tag $tags
   ```

That brings this section to an end. In this section, you have learned about what resource groups are, why they are necessary, the metadata and its effects, and how to deploy a resource group both with and without tags.

> **Note**
>
> You are encouraged to read up on this further by using the following links:
>
> Managing resource groups: `https://docs.microsoft.com/en-us/azure/azure-resource-manager/management/manage-resource-groups-portal`
>
> Moving resources to other resource groups or another subscription: `https://docs.microsoft.com/en-us/azure/azure-resource-manager/management/move-resource-group-and-subscription`

Configuring Resource Locks

Azure resource locks are a security feature that helps prevent the accidental modification or deletion of resources in an Azure subscription. These locks can be applied to various resources, such as VMs, storage accounts, and databases. There are two types of resource locks:

ReadOnly: This lock allows you to view the resource but prevents any modifications or deletions. It ensures that the resource remains in its current state and is not accidentally altered. It grants authorized users the read permissions to resources only. This means that they can't **add**, **delete**, or **modify** resources. The effect is similar to the **Reader** role in RBAC.

CanNotDelete: This lock allows you to view and modify the resource but prevents it from being deleted. This is useful for protecting critical resources from accidental deletion.

In summary, locks can be applied to multiple layers (the subscription, resource group, or even at a resource level) and will prevent other administrators from modifying or deleting the resources. You also can apply different types of locks, such as **ReadOnly** and **CanNotDelete**. Restrictions applied through management locks will apply across all users and roles.

> **Note**
>
> When applying locks, it's important to understand that the precedence assigned is based on the most restrictive lock that is inherited.

It is important to note that when applying resource locks, the law of inheritance applies, meaning that all resources inherit the lock from the parent scope. The parent scope will be from the highest level of resources in the Azure hierarchy to the resource level, meaning that you can go from subscription down to resource groups down to resources; the parent will be the level at which the lock is applied.

Permissions Required for Creating or Deleting Locks

Azure provides very granular control over the delegation of permissions within the platform but also comes with predefined roles that cater to the deployment and management of resource locks, as with most resources and services. The following roles are required on the platform; either built-in roles or custom roles can be used as per your preference.

Built-In Azure Roles

If your preference is to use a predefined Azure role, then either of the following will be suitable: **Owner** or **User Access Administrator**

Custom RBAC Roles

If your preference is to define or update a custom role, then the following action permissions are required:

- `Microsoft.Authorization/*`
- `Microsoft.Authorization/locks/*`

Let's move on to adding a resource lock.

Adding a Resource Lock

If you have been following along so far in this book with the previous section and created an `AZ104-Policies` resource group, then please use that for this exercise; alternatively, use any resource group that would suit you.

We will create a resource group, add a delete lock, add a resource, demonstrate the delete lock effect, remove the lock, and apply a read lock to demonstrate the effect. Your user account will require `Owner` or `User Access Administrator` privileges in order to add the lock. The steps are outlined here:

1. Open the resource group, then on the left menu, click on `Locks`, then click `Add`. The process is illustrated in the following screenshot:

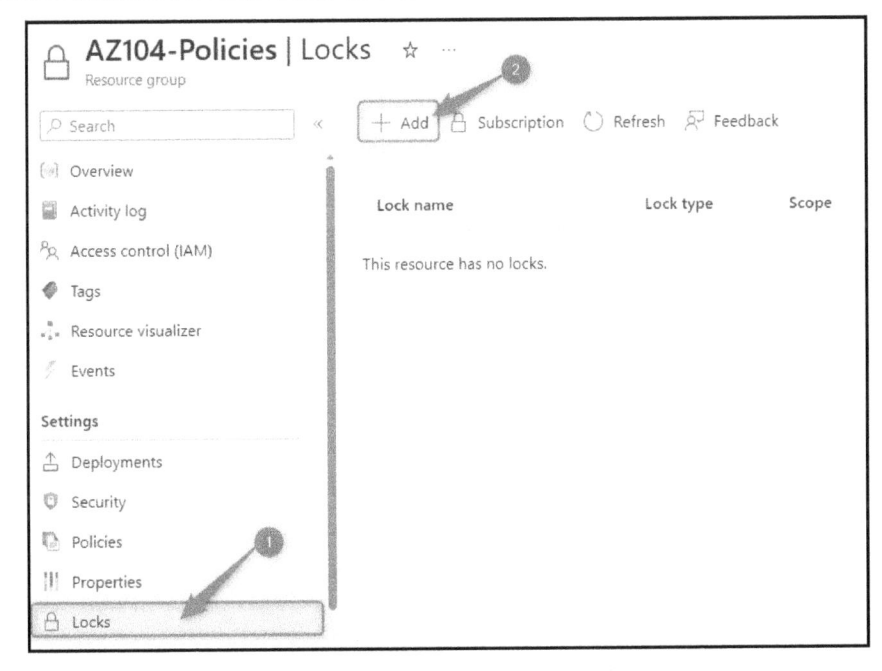

Figure 5.19: Adding a resource lock

2. Enter the corresponding lock details, such as Lock name, Lock type, and Notes values, as illustrated in the following screenshot:

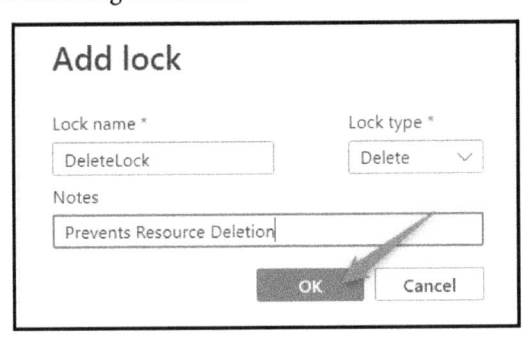

Figure 5.20: Lock details

3. Open the resource group, click Overview on the left menu, and then click Create. The process is illustrated in the following screenshot:

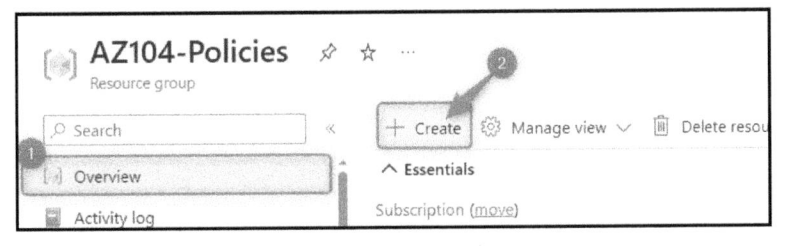

Figure 5.21: Creating a resource from the marketplace

4. You can create any desired resource. For this exercise, you will create a storage account, similar to the previous exercises, as follows. After filling in the relevant details, click `Review`.

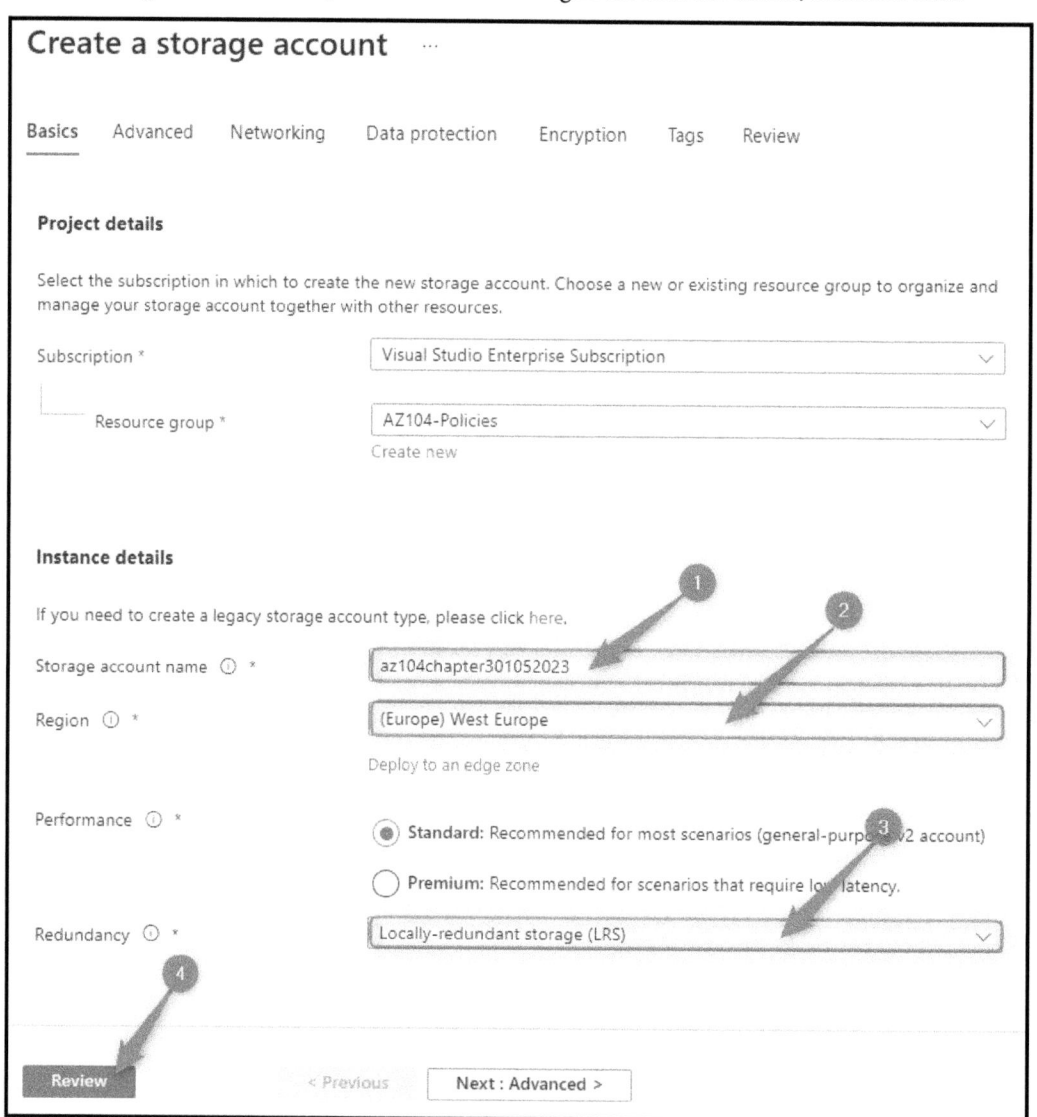

Figure 5.22: Creating a storage account

5. After validation, click `Create`.

6. After the deployment has completed, click `Go to resource`, as illustrated in the following screenshot:

Figure 5.23: Deployment progress screen

7. Now, to demonstrate the resource lock, click on the `Delete` button on the top menu bar, as illustrated in the following screenshot:

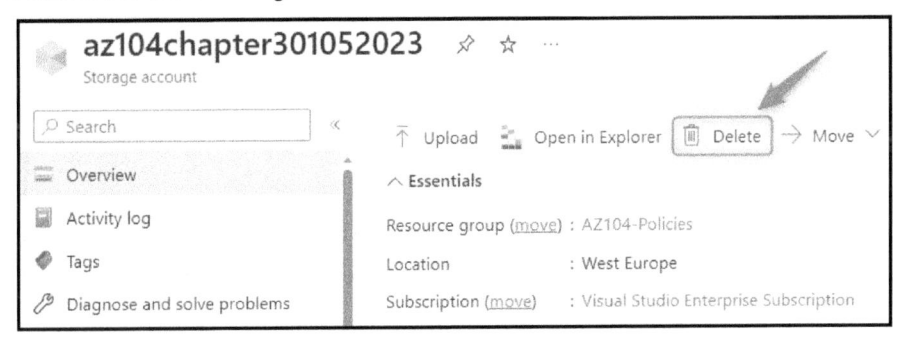

Figure 5.24: Deleting a storage account

> **Note**
> There are times when you may want to delete an individual resource, which can be done as per the preceding step, and you will notice that the process resembles the deletion of a resource group.

8. Notice here the error that follows, indicating that the resource lock you have implemented is working:

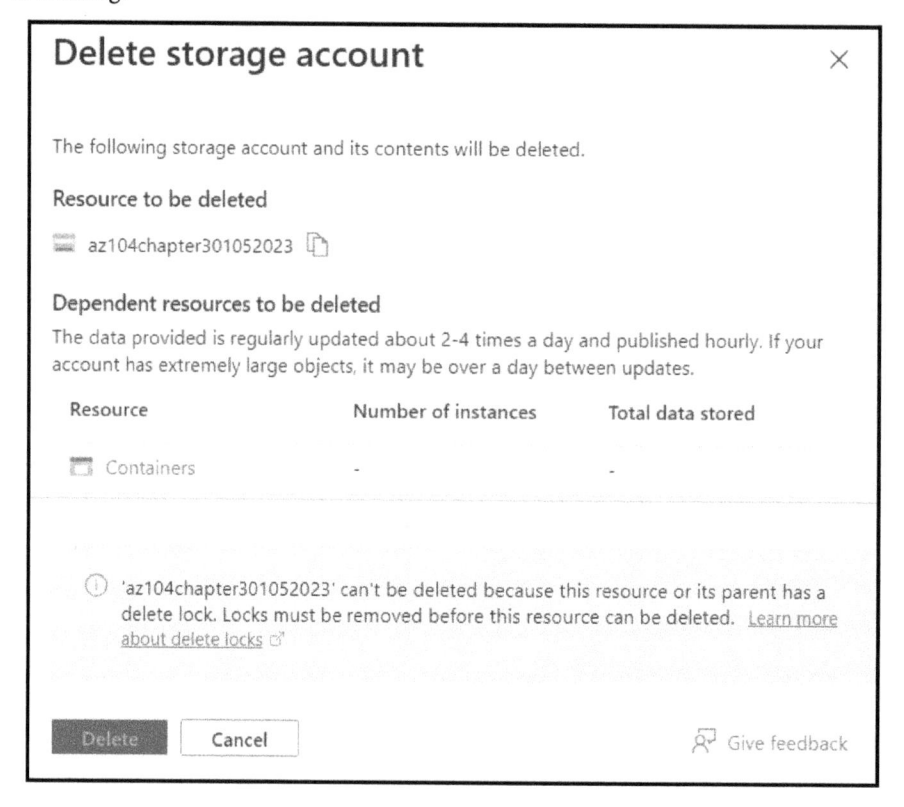

Figure 5.25: Deletion failure from resource lock

9. Go back to the resource group, select `Locks`, and delete the `DeleteLock` lock, as illustrated in the following screenshot:

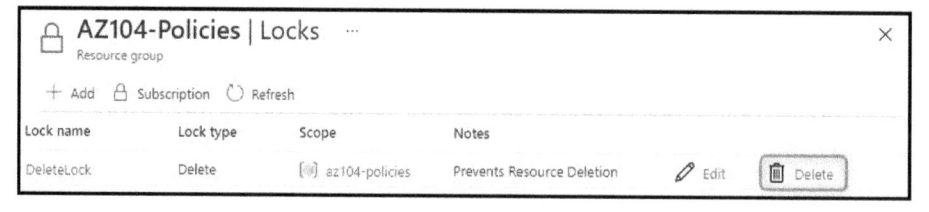

Figure 5.26: Deleting a resource lock

10. Go back to the resource group and attempt a deletion of the resource again. Note that you will need to enter the storage account name, and a confirmation dialog will also come up asking you to confirm deletion. Click `Confirm delete`.

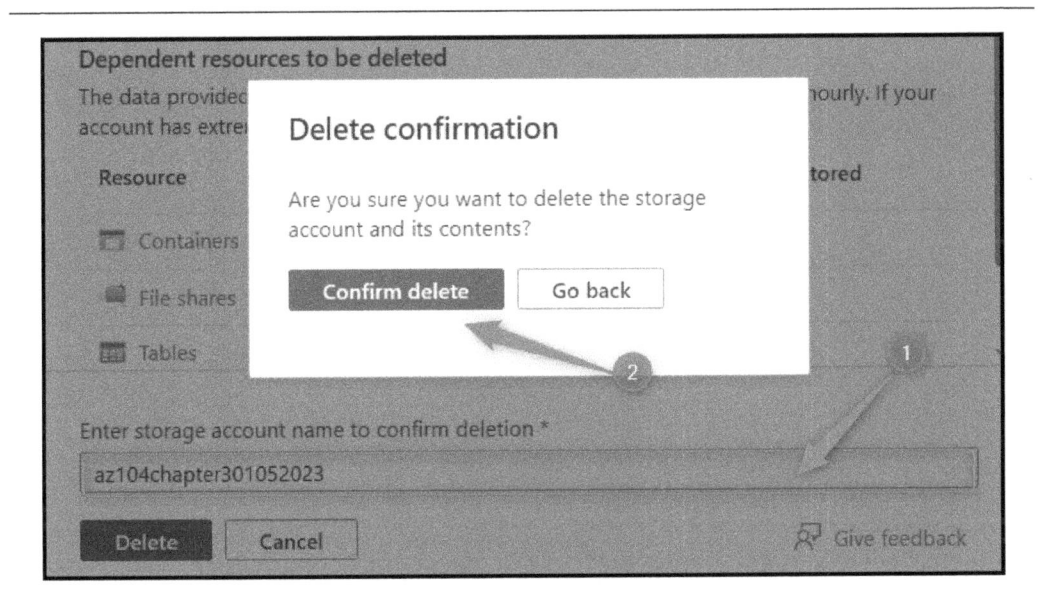

Figure 5.27: Delete confirmation

11. Notice here that you receive a success message this time:

Figure 5.28: Successful deletion notification

You have now seen how to successfully implement a resource lock to prevent the deletion of resources. Next, you will explore how to add a Read-only lock and observe the effects it has.

Creating a Read-only Lock

In this exercise, you will explore the effects of creating a Read-only lock on a resource group. You will continue with the resource group you used in the previous exercise:

1. Open the resource group, then on the left menu, click on `Locks`, then click `Add`. Enter the corresponding lock details, such as the `Lock name`, `Lock type`, and `Notes` values, as illustrated in the following screenshot:

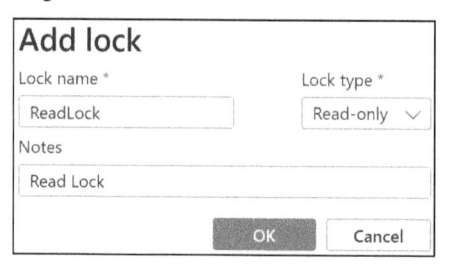

Figure 5.29: Creating a Read-only resource lock

2. Navigate to the resource group `Overview` pane from the left menu, then click `Create`. Attempt to create any resource and notice the validation error, as indicated in the following screenshot; also note that you cannot click `Create`.

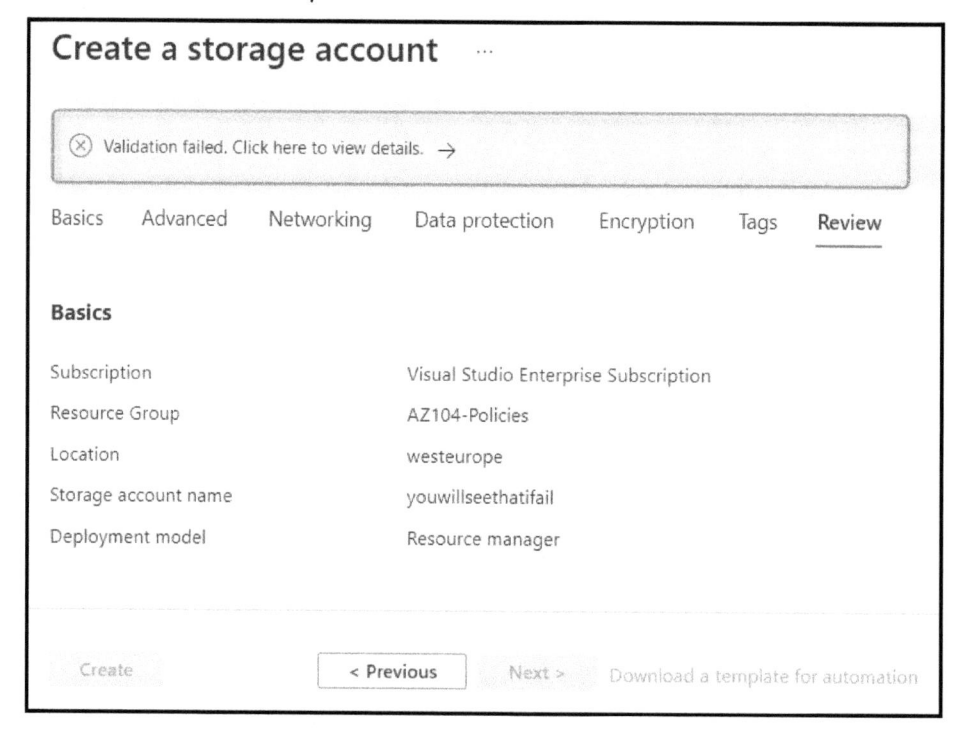

Figure 5.30: Failure to create a resource from a lock

You have now learned how to add a Read-only resource lock and prove that it's working as expected. You should now feel comfortable with applying resource locks after these two exercises. At times, you may find this process cumbersome when you have large environments, and you may want to automate this more or simplify the application process. Next, you will explore PowerShell scripts that should assist with your daily administrative functions.

PowerShell Scripts

This section introduces PowerShell scripts that can be used for the automation of resource lock management, as well as for quicker administration times. Please ensure that the Az module is installed, as per the *Technical Requirements* section at the beginning of the chapter.

Applying a Resource Lock to a Resource

In order to apply a lock to a resource, you will need to provide the name of the resource, its resource type, and its resource group name, as in the following script:

```
New-AzResourceLock -LockLevel CanNotDelete -LockName DontDeleteProd
-ResourceName ProductionWebApp -ResourceType Microsoft.Web/sites
-ResourceGroupName ProdNorthEuropeRG
```

Now, let's try the same for a resource group.

Applying a Resource Lock to a Resource Group

To lock a resource group, provide the name of the resource group and the type of lock to be applied using the following script:

```
New-AzResourceLock -LockName LockDeleteQA -LockLevel CanNotDelete
-ResourceGroupName QualityAssuranceRG
```

This applies the resource lock to the resource group successfully.

Viewing Resource Locks in Effect

To get information about a lock, use the `Get-AzResourceLock` cmdlet. To get all locks in your subscription, use the following command:

```
Get-AzResourceLock
```

> **Exam Tip**
>
> One important exam tip is to always check restrictions to prevent unexpected behaviors, such as locks preventing backup. See the following page for more information on this: https://learn.microsoft.com/en-us/azure/azure-resource-manager/management/lock-resources?tabs=json#considerations-before-applying-locks.

ARM Templates

For automation or simplified administration, you can also make use of **Azure Resource Manager (ARM)** templates for the creation of resource locks. This is just another way to achieve the same goal. Here's how to do this:

- When applying to an individual resource, the `scope` property must be specified
- When applying to a resource group or subscription, the `scope` property can be omitted

The following example **JavaScript Object Notation (JSON)** template code defines a lock at the resource group level:

```
{
  "$schema": "https://schema.management.azure.com/schemas/2019-04-01/deploymentTemplate.json#",
  "contentVersion": "1.0.0.0",
  "parameters": {
  },
  "resources": [
    {
      "type": "Microsoft.Authorization/locks",
      "apiVersion": "2016-09-01",
      "name": "rgLock",
      "properties": {
        "level": "CanNotDelete",
        "notes": "Resource group should not be deleted."
      }
    }
  ]
}
```

> **Note**
> It's advisable to always apply **Delete** locks on resource groups to prevent accidental resource deletion.

That brings this section to an end. In this section, you have learned what resource locks are, why they are necessary, and how they work.

> **Note**
>
> You are encouraged to read up further by using the following link:
>
> Microsoft documentation for resource locks: `https://learn.microsoft.com/en-us/azure/azure-resource-manager/management/lock-resources`?
>
> The following link will provide some references to situations where you might want to apply resource locks within your Azure Blueprints:
>
> Resource locks in Azure Blueprints: `https://learn.microsoft.com/en-us/azure/governance/blueprints/concepts/resource-locking`

Managing Costs

Effective cost management is crucial when utilizing cloud services such as Azure to ensure that you are getting the most value from your investment. With a seemingly endless array of services and resources available, it's essential to keep a close eye on your expenses and optimize your usage. Thankfully, Azure offers various tools and features to assist in managing costs and monitoring resource consumption. These tools enable organizations to gain insights into their spending patterns, optimize resource allocation, and implement budget controls to prevent unexpected costs. By leveraging these capabilities, businesses can maximize the benefits of Azure while maintaining control over their cloud expenditures.

One place to find these tools is **Azure Cost Management + Billing**.

Azure Cost Management + Billing is a suite of tools designed to assist in the analysis, management, and cost optimization of Azure workloads. It assists in the following management tasks relating to costs:

- Billing administration tasks
- Managing billing access
- Reports on cost and usage data
- Configuration of budgets
- Identifying opportunities to optimize costs

Cost Management

Cost management contains many facets and should be considered in its entirety; this includes cost analysis, governance, and reporting. For the purpose of the exam, we will investigate cost analysis and report scheduling.

Cost Analysis

Cost analysis assists in understanding expenditure within Azure. Quick reports are automatically generated to provide insights into current and historical expenditures on the scope chosen. Further to understanding current costs, the utility predicts anticipated forecast expenditure for the month ahead.

Managing Governance and Costs

In the following screenshot, you will notice expenditure on an **area** chart on the top portion of the report that shows accumulative expenditure over the course of the current billing period (this is a filter that can be changed), with some charts below that showing costs by `service name`, `location`, and `resource group name`. It is good to note that Azure also provides insights into the forecasted cost, as you can see for the following subscription.

This will be invaluable in predicting your estimated expenditure.

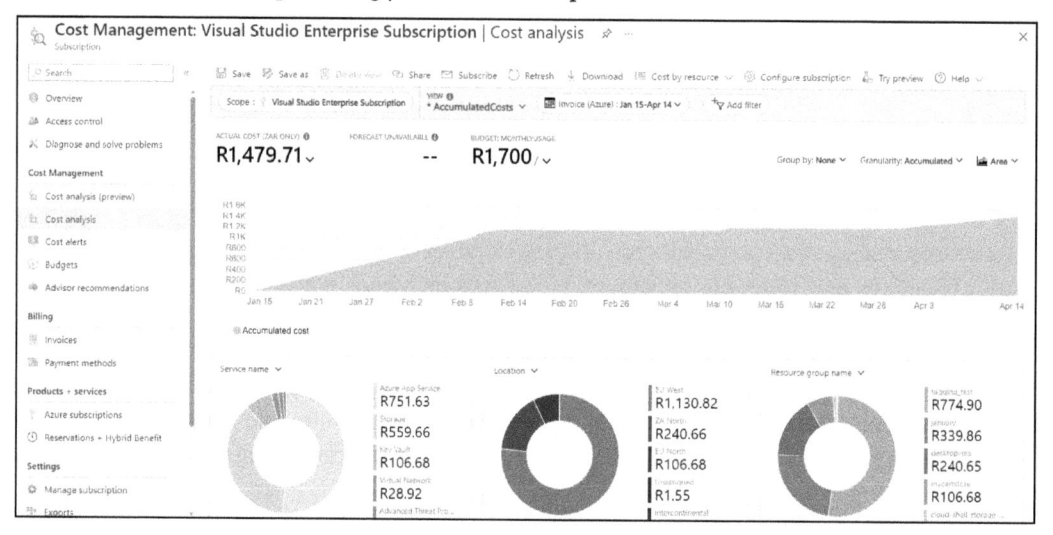

Figure 5.31: Cost analysis

Additional filters can be added and modified depending on the desired preference for viewing costs. The following is an example of setting `Group by` to `Meter category` and `Granularity` to `Monthly` and changing the graph type to `Column (grouped)`.

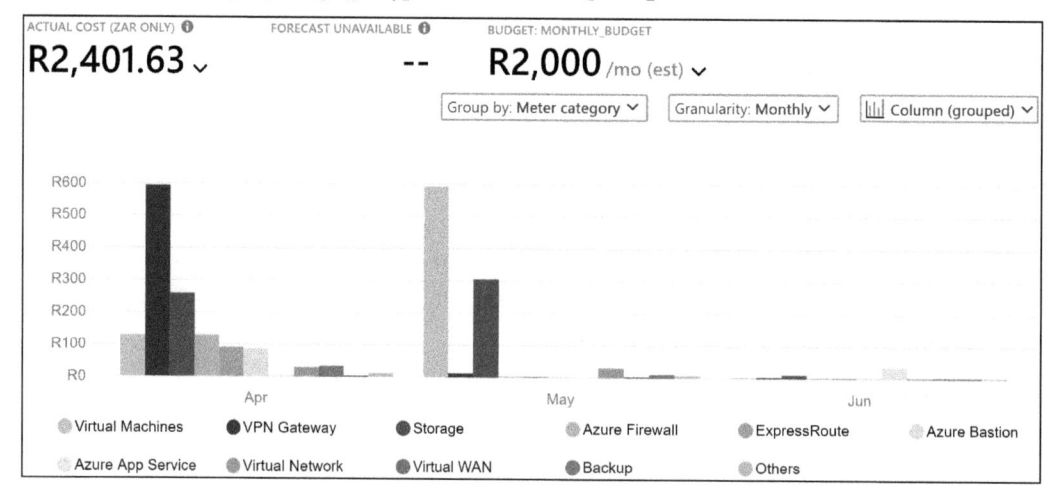

Figure 5.32: Example Cost analysis view modification

Costs can also be exported for viewing in **Portable Network Graphics** (PNG), Excel, and **comma-separated values** (CSV) format by clicking on the `Download` button, as illustrated in the following screenshot:

Figure 5.33: Cost analysis – Download

Select the appropriate `Download` option and click `Download charts`, as illustrated in the following screenshot:

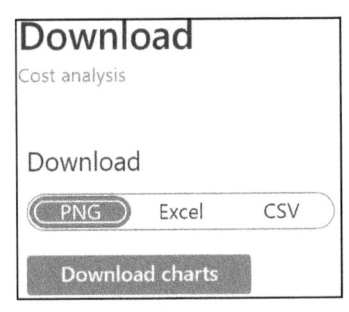

Figure 5.34: Cost analysis – Download options

You are encouraged to play around with the views and try filtering to see how it changes the displayed data; there are many variations of the data that you can construct to support your various requirements.

> **Note**
>
> For more information on working with **Cost analysis**, please visit the following link: https://learn.microsoft.com/en-us/azure/cost-management-billing/costs/quick-acm-cost-analysis.

Now that you have experience working with **Cost analysis** data and exporting the data, you will look at how to schedule required reports from Azure.

Scheduled Reports

Depending on the requirements, scheduled reports can also be created, as illustrated in the following screenshot:

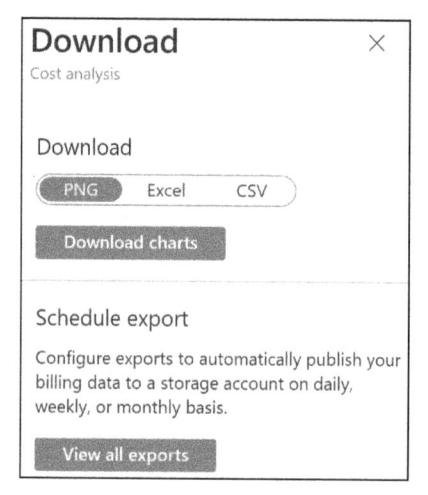

Figure 5.35: Cost analysis – Schedule export

Continuing from the previous exercise, clicking the `View all exports` button shown in the preceding screenshot will bring you to the `Exports` blade, where you can click on `Schedule export`.

Figure 5.36: Schedule export

Click the `Create your own export` card.

Figure 5.37: Create your own export card

Fill in the following details and click the Add button at the bottom of the pane:

- Type of data: Cost and usage details (usage only)
- Export name: MonthlyUsage
- Dataset version: 2019-11-01
- Frequency: Monthly export of last month's costs

Figure 5.38: Scheduled report – export configuration

Enter an export prefix of MonthUsage and click Next >.

Figure 5.39: Scheduled report – Export prefix

Fill in the relevant details for the `Destination` tab and click `Next >`.

Storage type *	Azure blob storage
Destination and storage *	● Use existing ○ Create new When selecting existing storage, trusted Azure service access is allowed.
Subscription *	Visual Studio Enterprise Subscription
Storage account *	csa10032002a42eb069
Container *	monthlyreports
Directory *	monthlyreports
File partitioning	☑

Figure 5.40: Scheduled report – destination configuration

On the screen that follows, click the `Create` button to complete your scheduled report deployment.

You have now seen how to analyze costs, export reporting data, and schedule reports. You will now investigate how to create cost alerts in the following section.

Budgets

In Azure, budgets are an essential component of Cost Management, allowing organizations to set spending limits and monitor their cloud expenses. Budgets in Azure consist of several components that help define and manage the financial constraints of your cloud usage:

- **Scope**: The scope defines the level at which the budget is applied. It can be set at the subscription, resource group, or management group level. By selecting the appropriate scope, you can create budgets for specific projects, departments, or the entire organization.

- **Time frame**: Budgets in Azure can be set for different durations, such as monthly, quarterly, or annually. This allows you to track spending over various periods and align the budget with your financial reporting cycles.

- **Amount**: The amount represents the spending limit for the defined scope and time frame. Once the budget is set, Azure will track the costs incurred within the selected scope and notify you when specific thresholds are reached.
- **Cost filters**: You can apply filters to your budgets based on resource types, locations, services, or tags. This allows you to create more granular budgets that focus on specific areas of your cloud environment.
- **Alert thresholds**: Alert thresholds are percentage values that trigger notifications when your spending reaches a certain level relative to your budget. For example, you can set alerts at 50%, 75%, and 90% of the budget to receive timely updates about your spending progress and take necessary actions to stay within the budget limits.
- **Notification recipients**: Budgets in Azure allow you to specify email recipients for the budget alerts. By adding appropriate stakeholders, you can ensure that the right people are informed about the budget status and any potential cost overruns.

By understanding and leveraging these components, organizations can create effective budgets in Azure that help manage costs, monitor spending, and ensure that their cloud investments stay aligned with financial goals.

Example Budget

In the following example, you will walk through the creation of a budget:

1. Select Budgets from the Cost Management context from the Cost Management service, as illustrated in the following screenshot:

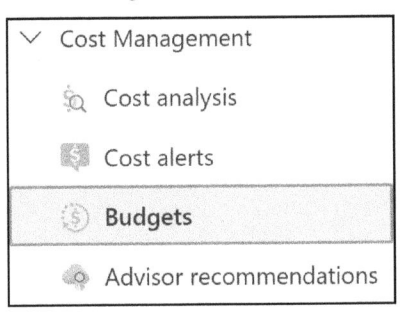

Figure 5.41: Budgets

2. Click + Add to create a new budget. You will now complete the relevant fields, as well as select a scope for the budget. For this exercise, leave your scope as the subscription you used in previous exercises, and don't add any filters.

3. For Name, you can enter `Monthly_Budget`. Leave `Reset period` defined as `Billing month`. You will notice a field for `Creation date`; this specifies the first day on which your budget evaluation begins and the subsequent day to be used for all future evaluations of your budget. Set this to today's date.

4. The `Expiration date` field determines when the budget will stop running, which will be some date you detail in the future; for the exercise, you can set any date you want.

5. Finally, for the `Budget Amount` field, assess the chart information on the right to understand expected costs and predict the budget to be implemented. You will notice the chart shows expected expenditure observed from the months prior as well as forecasting to future months, and looks similar to this:

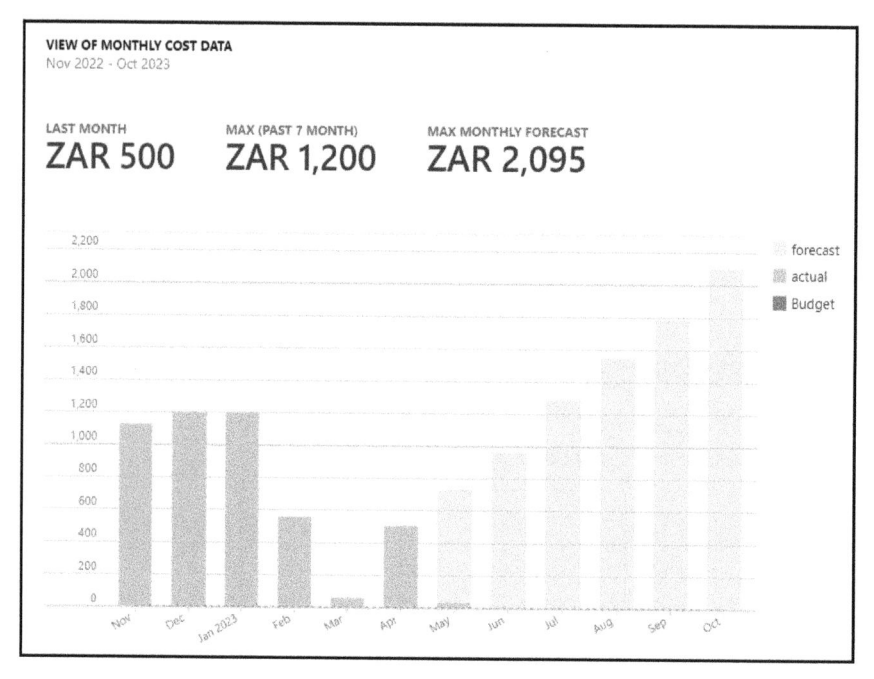

Figure 5.42: Predicted budget costs

6. Enter a value in the `Budget Amount` field and click `Next >`. You will note in the following screenshot that the currency is reflected as ZAR, which is the national currency of South Africa. This will change depending on the region you are billed in.

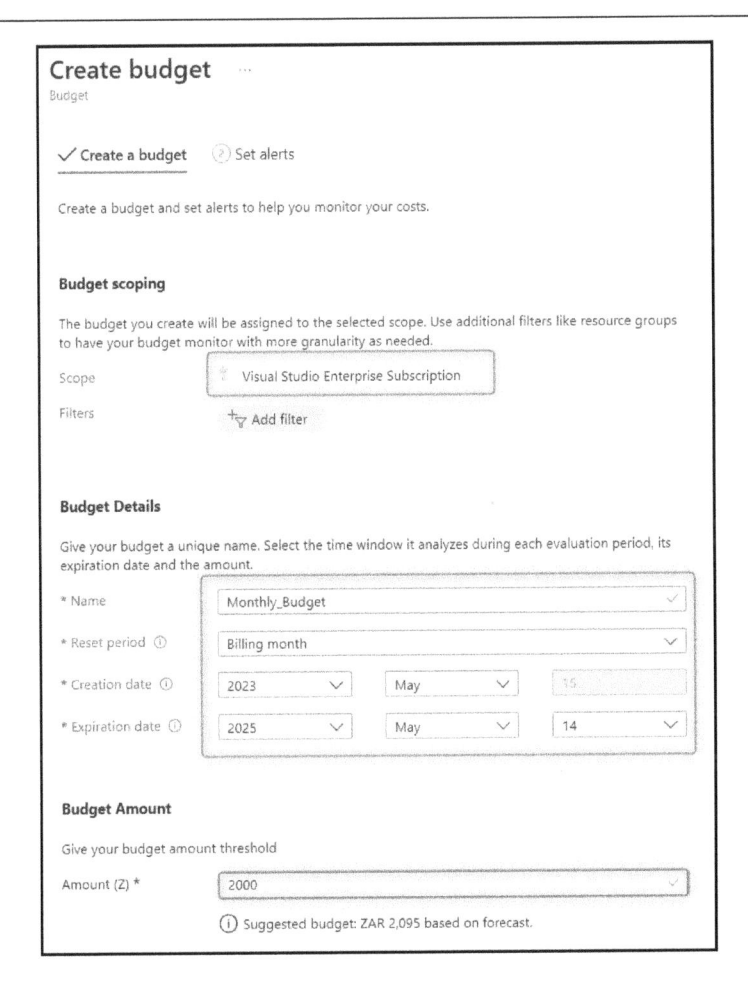

Figure 5.43: Creating a budget

7. Next, you will need to define conditions for an alert to be triggered: for instance, 85% of the defined budget. Notice that in selecting the `Alert conditions` options, you have two different options for `Type`:

- `Actual`: This is the actual amount spent on Azure
- `Forecasted`: This is based on the forecast prediction Azure has made on what it expects your expenditure to be

- You will notice that you need to select an `Action group` option but you haven't defined one of these yet. Click `Manage action group`, which is below the budget configuration.

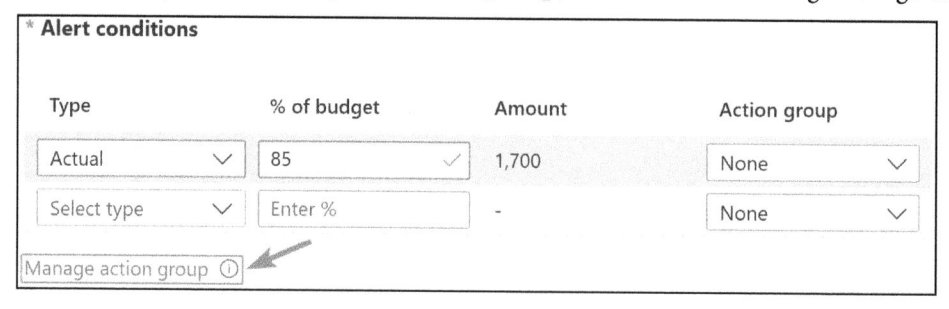

Figure 5.44: Clicking Manage action group

8. You can select an action group for notifications (more intelligent notification management can include **Short Message Service** (**SMS**), **Azure Functions**, and **Azure Logic Apps**), and you can specify an **email** notification. To get started with creating an action group, click the `+ Create` button.

Figure 5.45: Action groups – Create

9. Select your `Subscription`, `Resource group`, and `Region` options under the `Project details` context; use a `Budgets` resource group, as illustrated here:

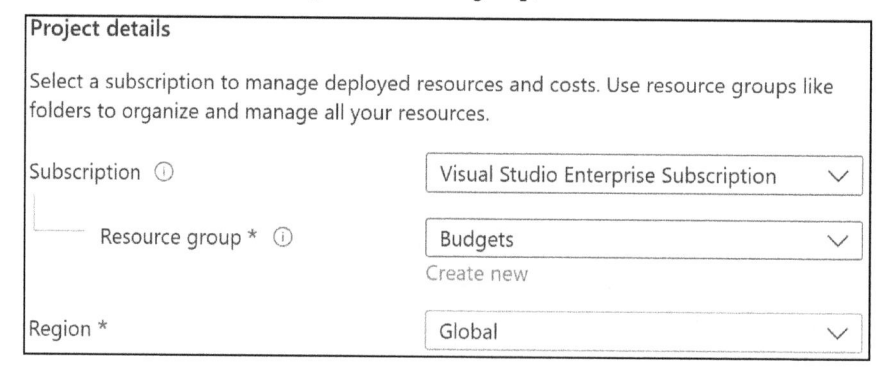

Figure 5.46: Action groups – Project details

10. Enter the following details for `Instance details`: `Action group` name as `Budget-AzureExpert-Monthly` and `Display name` as `Budget-Azure`. Click `Next: Notifications` once completed.

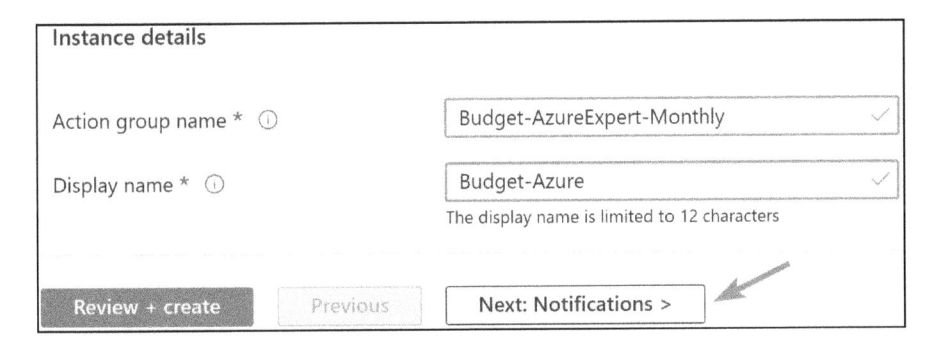

Figure 5.47: Action groups – Instance details

11. Select the notification type of Email/SMS message/Push/Voice, and a pop-up dialog will appear. Click the checkbox next to Email and enter an email address. Click OK at the bottom of the dialog box.

Figure 5.48: Action groups – Email address

12. Enter a Name value of email to administrator. Click Review + create at the bottom of the screen. Then, click Create on the screen that follows.

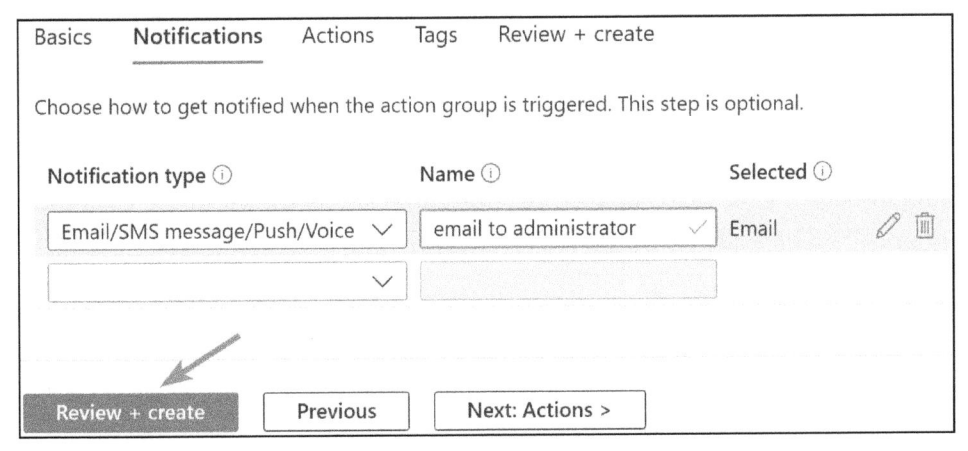

Figure 5.49: Action groups – email name

13. Click the cross on `Action groups` to go back to the original budget's setup blade.

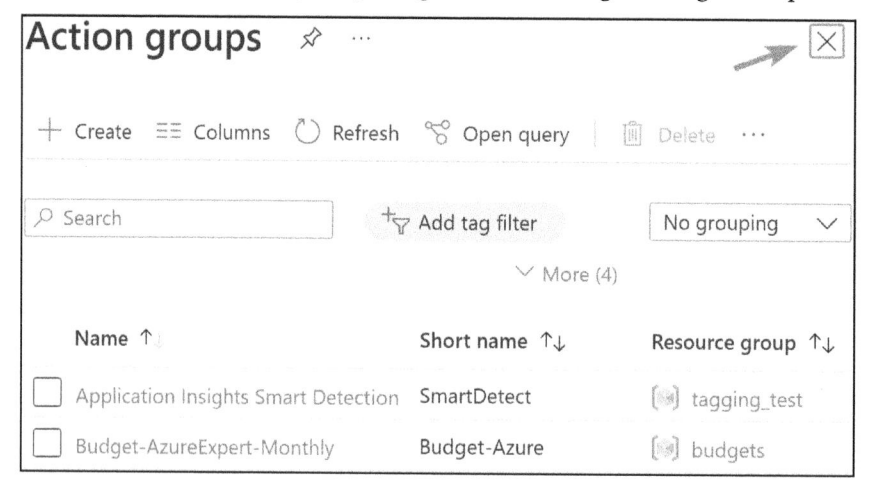

Figure 5.50: Closing Action groups

14. Select the action group from the `Action group` drop-down box, as depicted in the following figure, and then scroll down the page to the next section.

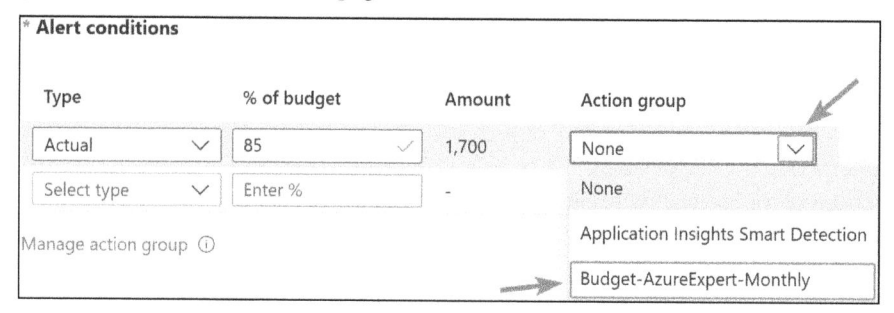

Figure 5.51: Action group – selecting an action group

15. Enter an `Alert recipients` email address, as shown in the example, such as `ihavegoneover@azureexpert.co.za`.

Figure 5.52: Action group – Alert recipients email address

16. Scroll down further, select a language for the notification to be delivered in, and click `Create`. For the `Languages` dropdown, you will select `English (United Kingdom)`. The following screenshot shows the selection as described:

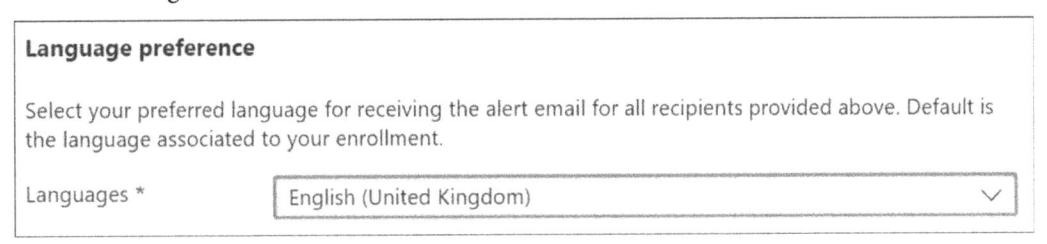

Figure 5.53: Action group – Selecting a language

17. Scrolling down further will show you a chart that highlights previous expenditures in a historical diagram as well as forecasted expenditures based on historical usage. Your budget will be the red line that appears on the chart.

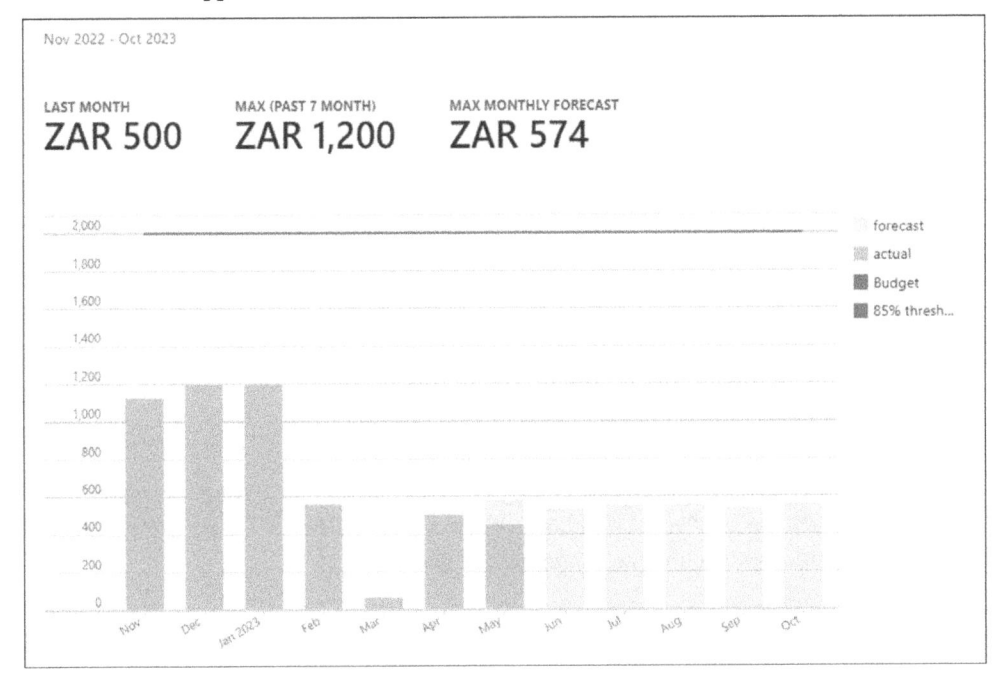

Figure 5.54: Budget – view of monthly cost data

18. Scroll down and click `Create`. Validation will begin, and shortly after, you will be presented with a notification confirming the successful creation of the budget.

Modifying an Existing Budget

To modify an existing budget, perform the following steps:

1. To create a budget, select `Budgets` from the `Cost Management` menu.
2. Click on your budget, and on the following pane, click `Edit budget`, as illustrated in the following screenshot:

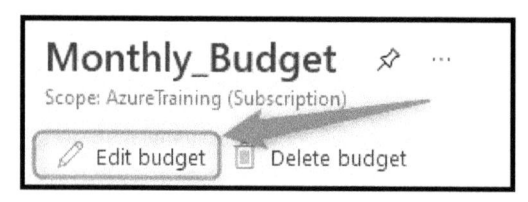

Figure 5.55: Edit budget

3. Modify the values you would like to change; for this example, modify `Amount` to now reflect `1500`, then click `Next >`.

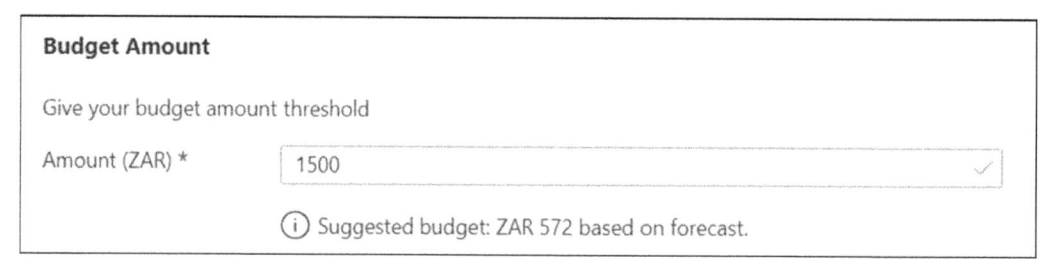

Figure 5.56: Editing Budget Amount

4. Don't modify the alert detail settings. Click `Save`.

You have now learned how to define, apply, and modify budgets in Azure. You are actively encouraged to implement budgets as part of your cost management and governance strategy. In the next section, you will explore Azure Advisor and the recommendations it offers.

Cost Alerts

Cost alerts enable notifications for identified alert trigger points that are configured for an environment. You can create these for resources or resource groups that exceed an expected expenditure or when you are getting close to a threshold. In this exercise, you will view implemented alerts by completing the steps that follow:

1. Select `Cost alerts` from the `Cost Management` menu, as illustrated in the following screenshot:

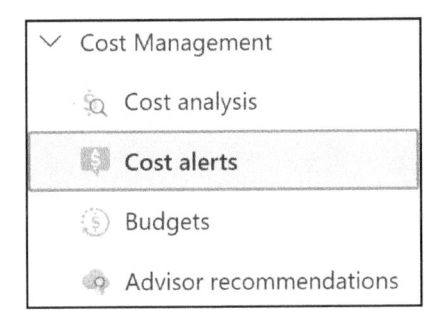

Figure 5.57: Cost alerts

2. Any alerts derived from defined budgets will appear here:

Figure 5.58: Cost alerts – preview

As you can see from the preceding screenshot, you have a single budget alert in your subscription from the budget creation.

Creating a New Alert

The following steps will guide you through creating a new alert:

1. To create an alert notification, you require a budget; you can create another budget in the same way as you did in the previous exercise. To do this, click `Cost alerts` from the `Cost Management` menu under `Cost alerts`. This will be the same screen as shown in *Figure 5.54*
2. You will be presented with the same setup window as the previous budget creation exercise where you are prompted to create a budget, followed by an alert.
3. This is all very similar to what you did previously, and you can see how these two components are so tightly integrated, being different functions of the same operation.

Viewing Alert Details

To view the details of the alert that has been fired, you should remain in the `Cost alerts` blade. Perform the following steps:

1. Click on the alert in question from the `Cost alerts` blade.

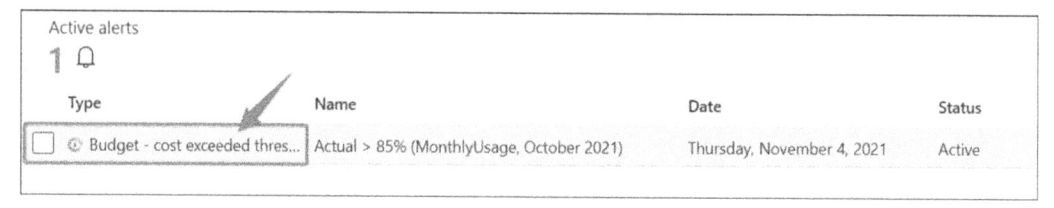

Figure 5.59: Cost alerts – viewing details

2. The details of the alert that has been received are shown below the `alerts` section. Notice from this example how the trigger is identified: in this example, exceeding 85% of the defined budget. Then, to the right of that, you can see the current costs as well as when the alert was sent. There are other details, too, such as the subscription and email.

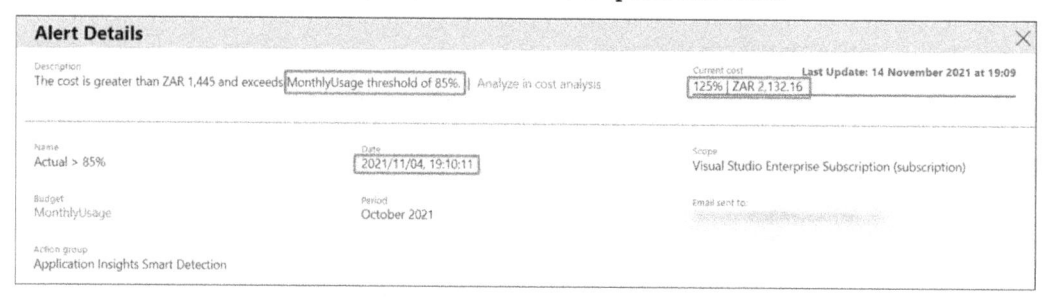

Figure 5.60: Cost alerts – Alert Details

You now know how to view alerts aside from receiving the email. In the next section, you will learn how to modify the defined alerts you have.

Modifying an Existing Alert

To modify an existing alert, you will need to modify the budget settings. To do so, perform the following steps:

1. Navigate to `Budgets` from the left-hand menu under the `Cost Management` context.
2. Select the budget you would like to modify by clicking on the name.
3. Click `Edit budget`.
4. Click `Next >` to go to the `Set alerts` tab.
5. Modify the condition for the alert or add in a new condition. You will add a new condition here as follows:
6. Type: `Forecasted`
7. % of budget: `105`

8. Action group: `Budget-AzureExpert-Monthly`

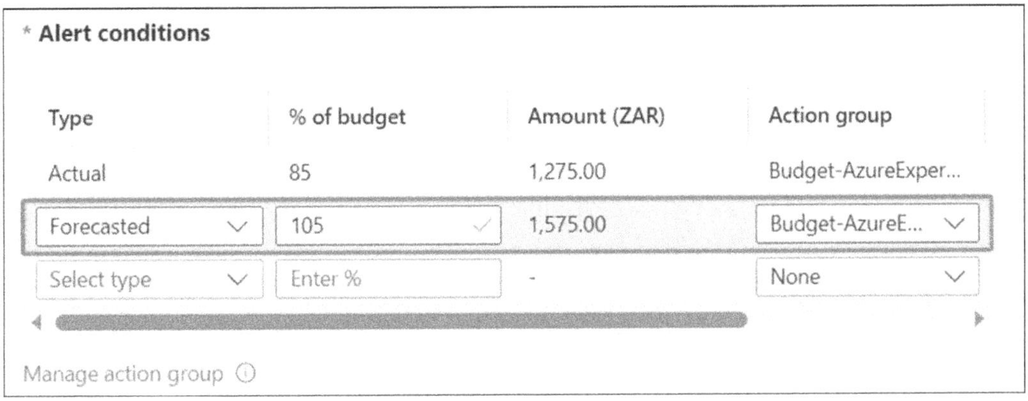

Figure 5.61: Cost alerts – Alert conditions

9. Click `Save`.

You have just successfully modified the alert conditions associated with your budget. Now that you understand budgets and alerts, we highly recommend incorporating this into your cost management and governance strategy. Next, you will explore Azure Advisor.

Advisor Recommendations

Advisor automatically detects cost optimizations that can be implemented within the tenant. While the recommendations are particularly good and will absolutely lead to cost savings, review each item and confirm where costs can be further reduced through an understanding of resources within the Azure environment. **Right-sizing** is critical for managing costs and is highly advised as the first exercise to be conducted before considering **reserved instances** and **capacity**.

You can see some example Advisor recommendations in the following screenshot:

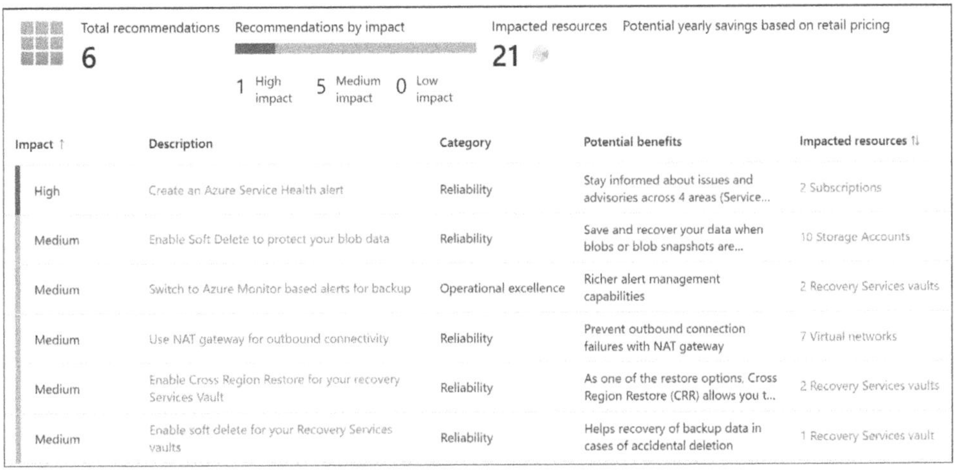

Figure 5.62: Azure Advisor recommendations

It is recommended to consult Azure Advisor regularly to gain insights into the valuable information shared by the platform, especially when considering costs. In later chapters, you will learn how this can be used to expose security, performance, and reliability insights, too.

Reservations

Reservations are a mechanism for saving money on Azure by committing to one-year or three-year plans for resources. Through this, you receive a significant discount from Microsoft, up to 72% compared to pay-as-you-go prices. Reservations must be carefully planned as they are long-term investments and are applied at **stock-keeping unit (SKU)**, **scope**, and sometimes **region** levels. Reservations do offer some form of flexibility (especially when applied to VMs) but are limited in nature, particularly on the same family of VMs where a ratio will be applied when the applicable SKU is not found.

> **Note**
>
> If the organization you are working with has subscribed to an Enterprise Agreement with Microsoft and has subscribed to Software Assurance, cost-savings can be leveraged on VMs by enabling **Azure hybrid benefit** on the **VM properties** page.

That brings this section to an end. In this section, you have learned what subscriptions are, why they are necessary, strategic items to consider, and billing ownership associated with subscriptions.

> **Hands-on activities and Further reading**
>
> Reinforce what you learned in *Chapters 1* through *5* by completing the hands-on activities for these chapters. Open the online practice resources using this link: `https://packt.link/az104dash`. Then, from the `Dashboard`, click `Hands-on Activities` and open the menu `Managing Azure Identities and Governance`.
>
> You are encouraged to read up further by using the following links:
>
> Transfer billing ownership of a subscription: `https://learn.microsoft.com/en-us/azure/cost-management-billing/manage/billing-subscription-transfer`
>
> Cost Management overview: `https://learn.microsoft.com/en-gb/azure/cost-management-billing/cost-management-billing-overview`
>
> Cost Management best practices: `https://learn.microsoft.com/en-gb/azure/cost-management-billing/costs/cost-mgt-best-practices`
>
> Azure reservations: `https://learn.microsoft.com/en-us/azure/cost-management-billing/reservations/save-compute-costs-reservations`

Summary

In this chapter, you learned about resource group management, resource locks, cost management, budgets, and alerts. You have acquired several skills so far in this book to assist you in driving governance within the organization for Azure resources, as well as understanding costs for effective management of the platform.

As a reminder, please delete the resources created in this chapter to prevent incurring unnecessary additional costs. In the next chapter, you will go through some labs relating to this entire first section on managing Azure identities and governance.

> **Note**
>
> Remember to delete the resources you created in this chapter to minimize costs. You can do this with the following commands for convenience that will remove the resource group and all the corresponding resources:
>
> ```
> Remove-AzResourceGroup -Name ResourceGroupA
> Remove-AzResourceGroup -Name ResourceGroupB
> Remove-AzResourceGroup -Name RG01
> Remove-AzResourceGroup -Name RG02
> Remove-AzResourceGroup -Name AZ104-Policies
> Remove-AzResourceGroup -Name Budgets
> ```

6
Understanding Storage Accounts

In this chapter, you will learn about the various aspects to be considered when choosing a storage account in Azure. You will learn about the different performance tiers (Standard and Premium) and explore the different types of storage accounts available in each performance tier. You will then learn about the different storage access tiers available and when to choose each option. You will learn about disk storage, which is the core mechanism for **virtual machines** (**VMs**) (**operating system** (**OS**) and data disks). Another topic you will explore is the varying redundancy options available and how to make the right choice to meet your availability needs. Finally, you will create a storage account using both the Azure portal and a PowerShell script. By the end of the chapter, you will have the skills required to choose the correct storage in Azure and the knowledge to deploy a storage account, which will serve as the foundational block for shared storage, such as Azure Files and Blob Storage.

In this chapter, you are going to learn about the following main topics:

- Understanding Azure Storage Accounts
- Creating and Configuring Storage Accounts

Technical Requirements

To follow along with the hands-on material, you will need the following:

- Access to an Azure subscription with owner or contributor privileges. If you do not have access to one, you can set up a student account for free: https://azure.microsoft.com/en-us/free/.
- **PowerShell 5.1** or later installed on a Windows PC, or PowerShell Core 6.x on other OSs, on a machine where labs can be practiced.

- For Windows users, you will need to install **.NET Framework 4.7.2** or later using the following link: `https://learn.microsoft.com/en-us/dotnet/framework/install`
- Where PowerShell is not installed or available, `https://shell.azure.com` can be used as a browser-based shell.
- Installation of the `Az` PowerShell module, which can be performed by running the following in an administrative PowerShell session:

    ```
    Set-ExecutionPolicy -ExecutionPolicy RemoteSigned -Scope
    CurrentUser
    Install-Module -Name Az -Scope CurrentUser -Repository PSGallery
    -Force
    ```

Understanding Azure Storage Accounts

Azure offers a variety of services that can be utilized for storage; these can vary from database options to messaging systems to files. One of these services for supporting your storage needs is **Azure storage accounts**. Azure has created four core types of services as part of Azure storage accounts: **Blob Storage**, **Azure Files**, **Queue Storage**, and **Tables Storage**. All these services can be consumed from a **Standard general-purpose v2 (Standard GPv2)** storage account, and some can be consumed individually as the Premium variations (such as Azure Files and Blob Storage), where more performance is required. Various types of data—such as files, documents, datasets, blobs, and **virtual hard disks** (**VHDs**)—can be stored in the storage account, and most will be accommodated by the defined structure. The following figure illustrates the different storage services associated with a storage account. It illustrates the storage accounts split by the various performance type categories with the storage account types contained within them. On the right of the figure, you can see a brief list of use cases for each storage service type:

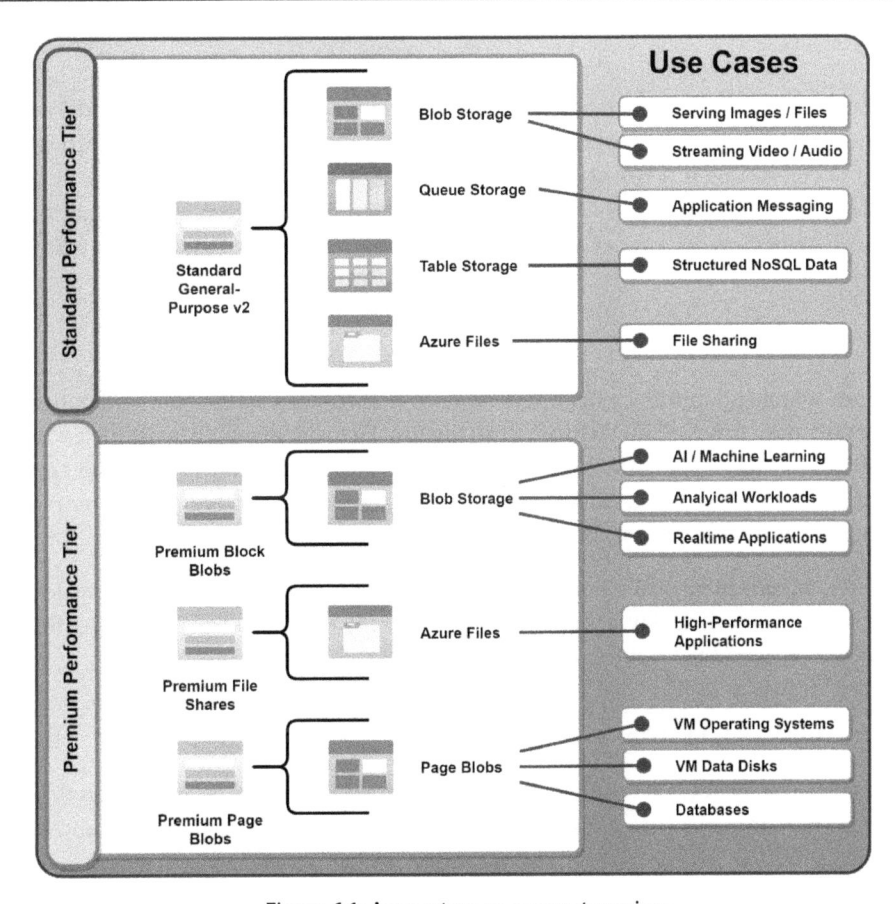

Figure 6.1: Azure storage account services

In this section, you have learned about the types of storage services that are provided within a storage account. In the next section, you will explore the different tiers of storage performance associated with the storage accounts.

Storage Account Performance Categories

Before creating your storage account, it is important to consider the level of performance required for your storage. Azure distinguishes between two performance grades of service by associating the performance categories directly with different grades of hardware that back the offerings. It is important to note that you cannot convert the type you have selected, and if you later discover that it does not meet your requirements, you will then need to redeploy your storage to the preferred grade of performance tier.

Standard

The Standard storage performance tier is backed by spinning magnetic **hard disk drive** (**HDD**) infrastructure, which is the lowest performance grade of hardware storage available through Azure. The benefit of consuming this storage grade is affordability, as you pay a lower price per GB. It is most suitable for storage requirements where you experience low-frequency usage scenarios or large data stores where performance is not as much a concern as the capacity requirement, and you have constrained budgets.

Premium

The Premium storage performance tier offers superior performance to the Standard option, as it is backed by **solid-state drive** (**SSD**) storage infrastructure. You will benefit from low latency and fast throughput by selecting this tier of storage for your storage account. It is most suitable for applications requiring extensive disk I/O operations, such as databases. Premium storage costs more than the Standard tier and is directly proportionate to the performance you require.

As you can see, understanding your storage performance requirements is fundamental to deciding on the type of storage you will deploy to meet your storage needs. Next, you will learn about the various storage account types and the services they offer.

Storage Account Types

Azure Storage currently offers several different types of storage accounts, as detailed in this section. There are various components to consider when choosing the correct type of account, including the following:

- Type of storage account (consider the service required)
- Redundancy
- Intended usage
- Performance
- Replication
- Security
- Limitations

With these considerations in mind, you will explore each of the various storage account types offered by Azure.

Standard GPv2

The **Standard GPv2** storage account is a Standard performance tier account. It supports several services as part of its construct: blobs, queues, tables, and file shares. This is the storage account type recommended for most scenarios due to its versatility in storage services and is the default option. It also supports several storage redundancy options: **locally redundant storage (LRS)**, **geo-redundant storage (GRS)**, **read-access geo-redundant storage (RA-GRS)**, **zone-redundant storage (ZRS)**, **geo-zone-redundant storage (GZRS)**, and **read-access geo-zone-redundant storage (RA-GZRS)**. The following figure illustrates the set of services offered by the storage account:

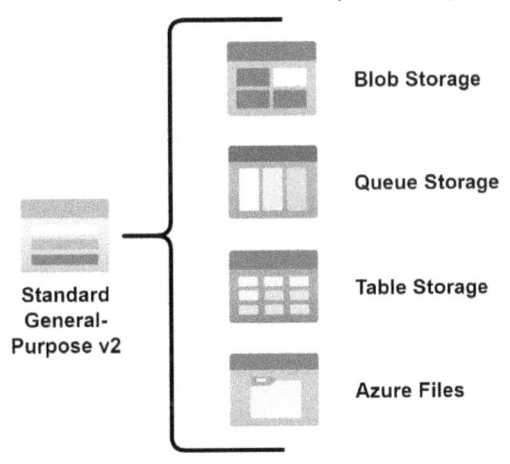

Figure 6.2: Standard General-Purpose v2 storage account

> **Note**
> v1 storage accounts can easily be upgraded to v2; however, be aware that an upgrade is permanent and therefore cannot be rolled back. Read this article for more information: `https://learn.microsoft.com/en-us/azure/storage/common/storage-account-upgrade`. Also, note that you can no longer create a v1 storage account using the Azure portal.

Each of the various services offered by the Standard GPv2 storage account is unpacked in the following sections.

Blob Storage

The storage solution created to cater to object storage in Azure is **Azure Blob Storage**. Blob Storage offers unstructured data storage in the cloud and can store all kinds of data, such as documents, VHDs, images, and audio files. There are three types of blobs that you can create:

- **Page blobs**: Blobs that are used for the storage of disks. These blobs are optimized for read and write operations and stored in 512-byte pages. If you have a VHD that needs to be stored and attached to your VM, you will create a page blob. The maximum size of a page blob is 8 **tebibytes** (TiB).

- **Block blobs**: Basically, these cover all the other types of data that you can store in Azure, such as files and documents. The maximum size of a block is 4,000 **mebibytes** (**MiB**) and the maximum size of a blob is 190.7 TiB.
- **Append blobs**: These blobs are optimized for append operations, basically meaning that data (blocks) is added to the end of a blob. Each block can be of different sizes, up to a maximum of 50,000 blocks. Updating or deleting existing blocks written to the blob is unsupported. Use cases include logging and auditing.

The Blob Storage offering within the Standard GPv2 storage account supports all the preceding blob types. Where more performance is required, consider using the Premium blob offerings.

In addition to the variety of storage services, the Standard GPv2 storage account offers multiple access tiers that consist of hot, cool, cold, and archive storage. These storage tiers will be covered later in this chapter, in the *Storage Access Tiers* section.

Example use cases for Blob Storage include the following:

- Backup and archiving data
- **Disaster recovery** (**DR**) datasets
- Streaming media content (such as audio and video)
- Storing unstructured data

Blob Storage is an in-depth topic that you are recommended to explore in more detail. According to the exam objectives, you will not be tested beyond the basic concepts of Blob Storage and basic management practices (creating and configuring blob containers, adding and removing data, blob life cycle management, and blob versioning). However, reading further will aid you in being more adept at the topic and being able to build more relevant solutions to your requirements.

> **Note**
>
> You can read up further on Blob Storage here, and navigate through the following link: `https://learn.microsoft.com/en-us/azure/storage/blobs/storage-blobs-overview`.

Queue Storage

Azure Queue Storage is a service designed for storing messages in Azure. Messages are used to enable decoupled infrastructure to be able to communicate by sending data for processing. This data is typically consumed in an asynchronous format by the services reading the queue that the messages are stored in. Each queue can be thought of as a line where messages are placed waiting to be processed, with each queue normally relating to a particular topic of message for your services. For instance, imagine you run a website that receives photos, and you frame them on canvases.

You could have two queues for your application, one indicating that a new image has been uploaded to your site and needs to be processed, and another one for purchases that have been made and scheduling an order. The respective components of your application would process these queues independently of each other and systematically through received messages in each respective queue. By decoupling the various components of your application, you can create highly resilient and scalable infrastructure as each layer of the application can be managed independently of each other. When a problem occurs, only the affected part of the application stops working. When you need to scale, you can scale at a granular level (for those components that require scale only).

The following figure illustrates the hypothetical queues discussed previously, with the system containing a storage account sending the messages for the respective systems to their queues:

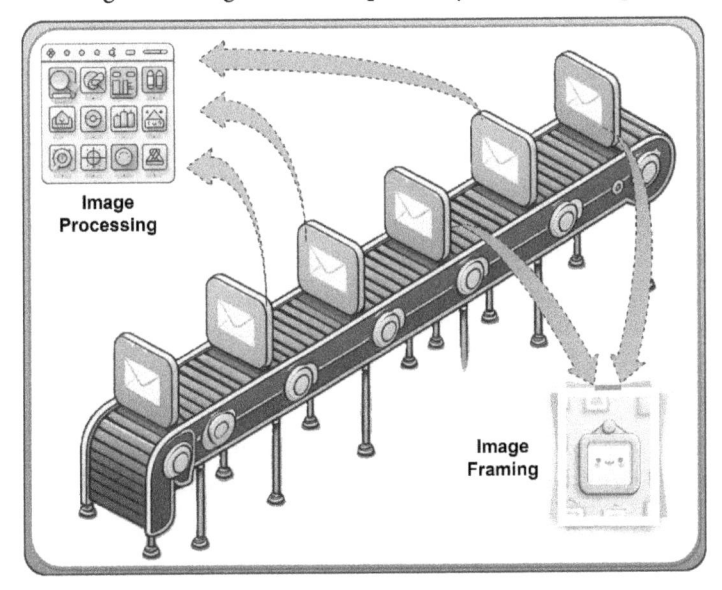

Figure 6.3: Azure Queue Storage

As you have learned, the queue service can be valuable in creating decoupled applications that process asynchronously. Next, you will learn about Table Storage.

Table Storage

Azure Table Storage is a solution designed for the storage of NoSQL data (non-relational structure data). Data is stored in tables, hence the name Table Storage. By design, Table Storage is schemaless and therefore adapted to easy consumption of data into the database as you do not have to specify the data structure before being able to ingest it. It is flexible in structure and can evolve with your application, meeting its changing demands. Table Storage is a cost-effective solution for many basic database needs, such as storing the user data required by your applications.

Table Storage can provide a cost-effective solution offered through a Standard GPv2 storage account for your database needs. Next, you will explore Azure Files.

Azure Files

With **Azure Files**, you can create file shares in the cloud. Using the version of Azure Files available to the Standard GPv2 storage account, you can access your files using the **Server Message Block** (**SMB**) protocol, which is an industry standard that can be used on Linux, Windows, and macOS devices. Azure Files can also be mounted as if they were a local drive on these same devices, and they can be cached for fast access on Windows Server using **Azure File Sync**. File shares can be used across multiple machines, which makes them suitable for storing files or data that are accessed from multiple machines, such as tools for development machines, configuration files, or log data. Azure Files is part of the Azure Storage client libraries and offers an Azure Storage **Representational State Transfer Application Programming Interface** (**REST API**) that can be leveraged by developers in their solutions.

As you have learned, Azure Files is a simple service for sharing data amongst your servers and services. Next, you will explore Premium block blobs.

Premium Block Blobs

Premium storage is used for situations requiring **low latency** and **high performance**. Premium storage performance is enabled through the underlying high-performance hardware associated with the presentation of storage within Azure, such as through SSDs, and provides faster throughput and **input/output operations per second** (**IOPS**) compared to Standard storage, which is backed by hard disks (spinning disks). This storage is typically used for block blobs and append blobs. It supports LRS and ZRS redundancy options.

Premium block blobs leverage Premium Storage to offer high-performance storage for all kinds of files that are stored in block format. Common scenarios where Premium block blobs are used include the following:

- Workloads requiring fast access and functionality, such as e-commerce applications
- Large datasets that are constantly added, manipulated, and analyzed, such as **internet of things** (**IoT**) applications
- **Artificial intelligence** (**AI**) or **machine learning** (**ML**) applications
- Data transformation workloads

> **Note**
>
> Storage is measured in binary units; when translating back to the decimal number system, this does not always reflect as 1 to 1 and depends on the terminology or unit used. For instance, it is common practice to refer to 1 **megabyte** (**MB**) as 1,000 **kilobytes** (**KB**), but it is technically equal to 1,024 KB. To reflect the correct measurement, a standard developed by the **International Electrotechnical Commission** (**IEC**) in 1998 that referred to a binary system of data measurement was created. This standard refers to various derivatives of the decimal data measurement described previously in a format such as MiB and **kibibyte** (**KiB**). This standard portrays a measure of 1 MiB to reflect 1,024 KiB.

Premium block blobs can also be cost-effective in scenarios where you expect a large number of transactions. The storage costs are higher, but transaction costs are lower, which can make all the difference when deciding on the right solution. Next, you will learn about Premium file shares and how they are superior in performance to Standard file shares.

Premium File Shares

Premium storage is used for situations requiring **low latency** and **high performance**. Premium file shares are typically used for workloads requiring enterprise-scale or high-performance applications. The service presents storage in the form of SMB or **Network File System (NFS)** storage. SMB is typically used for Microsoft Windows environments, such as Windows Server, whereas NFS is typically used for Linux-based environments. NFS can only be enabled on Premium file shares. Some differences worth noting when choosing your file-share storage service are IOPS and provisioned storage limitations. GPv2-backed Standard file shares have a limit of 20,000 IOPS and 5 **pebibytes (PiB)** of provisioned storage, while Premium file shares storage offers 100,000 IOPS but only 100 TiB of provisioned storage.

> **Note**
> Blob storage has a flat-file hierarchy, meaning that it does not work as a filesystem, as we are traditionally used to working with, such as on servers and workstations. While containers may appear as folders, they are only logical structures to emulate a filesystem. Bearing this in mind, Blob Storage is not meant to be consumed directly as a shared storage system, such as SMB or NFS, but through technologies such as BlobFuse, direct storage into a blob can be achieved.

As you can see, when you require a high-performance storage-sharing solution, Premium file shares may be a good option to support your needs. In the next section, you will learn about Premium page blobs.

Premium Page Blobs

Premium page blobs are designed for high-performance storage requirements and can offer low-latency access. They are more expensive when compared to Standard storage, which is typically for less demanding storage workloads. This storage is ideal for storing disk-type data for VMs, such as the OS and data disks. It is also recommended for Azure SQL DB persistent storage.

One limitation of Premium page blobs is that they can only use the hot access tier, not the cool or archive tiers. This means that they are not suitable for long-term storage with infrequent access.

> **Note**
> You may want to compare managed disks to Premium page blobs and understand why you would use one over the other. The most summarized way to view this is as follows. Use managed disks when you need simplified management, better resiliency, and integration with Azure fault-tolerance features for VM storage. You should opt for Premium page Blobs when you require direct REST API access, concurrent data access, and the flexibility to create custom storage solutions or scenarios not tied to VMs.

Premium page blobs can be beneficial in supporting your high-performance storage requirements when working with OS-related data and SQL DB persistent storage. In the next section, while it's not an exam requirement, you will learn about the legacy storage account types.

Legacy Storage Account Types

The following list of account types is not recommended by Microsoft, although they are still available for consumption. It is advised that you rather utilize Standard GPv2 storage.

General-Purpose Version 1 (Legacy)

A **general-purpose version 1 (GPv1)** storage account is the oldest type of storage account. It offers storage for page blobs, block blobs, files, queues, and tables, but it is not always the most cost-effective storage account type. It is the only storage account type that can be used for the classic deployment model but does not support the latest features, such as access tiers. This account type is no longer recommended by Microsoft. It is still generally considered the cheapest of storage options but is highly limited compared to GPv2 storage. Although legacy, these accounts can be upgraded to GPv2 storage. However, you should also consider storage costs as they might increase as a result of the change.

Blob Storage

This storage option is the v1 offering of Blob Storage and is now considered legacy. The Blob Storage account offers all the features of StorageV2 accounts, except that it only supports block blobs (and append blobs). Page blobs are not supported. It offers access tiers that consist of hot, cool, cold, and archive storage, just like the GPv2 option. Microsoft recommends using GPv2 storage instead of Standard page blobs, as this is supported without the requirement for limitations. It supports LRS, **Geo-Redundant Storage (GRS)**, and **Read-Access Geo-Redundant Storage (RA-GRS)** redundancy options. This storage account should only be considered where you have legacy requirements, such as the requirement to use the Azure classic deployment model or a version of the Azure Storage REST API that precedes 14 February 2014.

In this section, you learned all about the storage account performance tiers, the various storage account types in Azure, and the benefits and use cases of each. In *Chapter 8, Securing Storage*, you will explore blob management, which includes sections such as blob life cycle management, replication, the Azure File Sync service, versioning, and data protection. In the next section, you will learn about the various storage access tiers for your storage accounts and how each of the individual tiers can add benefit to you.

Storage Access Tiers

Blob storage accounts use access tiers to determine how frequently data is accessed. Based on the chosen access tier, you will get billed accordingly at different rates. Azure offers four storage access tiers: **hot**, **cool**, **cold**, and **archive**. Azure also offers configuration options for blob life cycle management, which you will learn more about in the next chapter.

Hot

The **hot access tier** is most suitable for storing data that is accessed frequently and data that is in active use. For instance, you would store images and style sheets for a website inside the hot access tier. The storage costs for this tier are higher than for the other access tiers, but you pay less to access files. This is the default access tier for storage.

Cool

The **cool access tier** is the most suitable for storing data that is not accessed frequently (less than once in 30 days). Compared with the hot access tier, the cool tier has lower storage costs, but you pay more to access files. This tier is suitable for storing backups and old content that is not viewed often. The cool tier is ideal for data that will be stored for more than 30 days.

Cold

The **cold tier** of storage is similar to the cool tier of storage. Again, the cold tier is cheaper than the cool and hot tiers for storage costs but has comparatively higher access costs. The cold tier is ideal for data that will be stored for more than 90 days.

Archive

The **archive storage tier** is set on the blob level and not on the storage level. It has the lowest costs for storing data and the highest cost for accessing data compared to the hot and cool access tiers. This tier is for data that will remain in the archive for at least 180 days, and it will take several hours of latency before it can be accessed. This tier is most suitable for long-term backups or compliance and archive data. A blob in the archive tier is offline and cannot be read (except for the metadata), copied, overwritten, or modified. Although the blob data remains unreadable in the archive tier, its metadata remains readable. You will need to rehydrate the blob before you can read or alter data within the archive storage. **Rehydrating** is the process of restoring data from the archive data store to an online storage tier.

Service-Level Agreement for Storage Accounts

It is worth considering the **service-level agreement (SLA)** for all services when designing and deploying to Azure. The great news with storage accounts is that you are assured of 99% availability of services.

Choosing a cool tier implies a lower SLA from Microsoft, whereas the hot tier allows better SLAs up to 99.99%.

> **Note**
> Data tiers can be changed between hot and cool; doing so will charge the full Premium at the conversion of the existing storage tier. This charge does not apply to Blob Storage accounts. Costs are incurred as write operation charges when converting from the hot to the cool tier and as read and data retrieval operations when converting from the cold to the hot tier.

In this section, you learned about the various storage access tiers and how the tiers are determined based on the frequency of access you anticipate. Moving through the tiers will result in cost changes relating to the operational usage of your data in the storage account. Knowing how you intend to use your data and the frequency of each transaction type will help you manage costs effectively. Next, you will learn about Azure disk storage, which is typically used for VMs.

Azure Disk Storage

Azure disk storage leverages page Blob Storage to accommodate the required disks on **Infrastructure as a Service (IaaS)** VMs, such as the OS disk. VMs typically have two core disks as part of the standard offering: the OS disk and the temporary disk volume. The temporary disk is used as a short-term storage mechanism that operates at high speeds but is non-persistent in nature and may lose its data when the VM is turned off. Since the temporary disk is unmanaged, it will not be encrypted unless you choose to enable this feature. This temporary storage is intended primarily for use in storing temporary data (such as page files, swap files, or SQL Server `.tempdb` files).

You can choose from four different performance tiers that Azure offers: **Standard HDD (S series)**, **Standard SSD (E series)**, **Premium SSD (P series)**, **Premium SSD v2 (Pv2 series)**, and **Ultra disk storage**. The choice you make ultimately depends on the performance requirements you have for your OS and applications running on your server. You may also consider the SLA requirements of your server, which is better as you decide to go with more Premium storage. Let's review the different options available to you.

Standard Disk Storage

Standard disk storage offers two flavors: a **Standard hard disk drive (HDD)** or **Standard SSD** to store data, and it is the most cost-effective storage tier that you can choose. Standard disk storage can only use **LRS** or **GRS** to support **high availability (HA)** for your data and applications. The Standard HDD disk type is best suited for scenarios that require infrequent access (such as for backups), dev/test workloads, or workloads with non-critical data. While the Standard SSD disk type is best suited for test and development workloads, most web servers and applications do not require fast throughput or high IOPs.

Premium Disk Storage

With Premium disk storage, your data is stored on SSDs. This storage is faster than the Standard SSD range. Not all Azure VM series can use this type of storage. It can only be used with VM **stock-keeping units (SKUS)** that contain an **S** in them, signifying the SSD portion of the VM, such as DS, DSv5, GS, LS, ES, or FS series Azure VMs. It offers high-performance and low-latency disk support. At the time of writing, there are two flavors of Premium SSD: Premium SSD and Premium SSD v2. The difference between the two is that Premium SSD (we will observe as v1) has predefined and dedicated sizes that can be consumed as part of the service, such as selecting 64 GB, 128 GB, and so on, whereas the Premium SSD v2 disks allow you to select any size you prefer, and by allowing you to make performance adjustments without downtime, they also have much lower latency.

Premium SSD v2 disks unfortunately cannot be used as the OS disk and can only be attached to zonal VMs. These disks are best suited to production workloads that require high levels of performance and low latency. One positive impact of choosing this storage on your VMs is that it improves your SLA.

> **Note**
> A great benefit of the Premium SSD v2 storage type is that through the enhancements relating to latency and on-the-fly storage performance adjustments, disk striping requirements could potentially be mitigated.

Ultra Disk Storage

Azure Ultra Disks are a type of managed disk designed to provide extremely high performance and low latency for mission-critical and data-intensive workloads. They are suitable for applications that require consistent sub-millisecond latency and high IOPS and throughput.

The following are key features of Ultra Disks:

- **High performance**: Ultra Disks offer up to 300,000 IOPS and 2,000 MB/s of throughput per disk, making them ideal for workloads that demand high storage performance
- **Low latency**: Ultra Disks provide **sub-millisecond latency**, ensuring a smooth and responsive experience for applications that require real-time data access
- **Flexible configuration**: Ultra Disks allow you to independently configure and scale IOPS, throughput, and capacity, providing granular control to optimize storage performance and costs based on your specific needs
- **Managed disk benefits**: As a type of Managed disk, Ultra disks inherit the benefits of simplified management, better resiliency, and integration with Azure fault-tolerance features, such as availability sets and **availability zones (AZs)**
- **Zone-resilient storage (ZRS)**: Ultra Disks support ZRS, enabling replication across multiple AZs to ensure HA and data durability

Azure Ultra Disks are ideally suited for applications such as large-scale databases, **high-performance computing (HPC)**, big data analytics, and other data-intensive or latency-sensitive workloads that require the highest level of storage performance.

Unmanaged versus Managed Disks

Managed disks are the default disk type in Azure and automatically handle storage account creation for you. With unmanaged disks, which are the traditional legacy disks used for VMs, you need to create a storage account manually, and then select that storage account when you create a VM. When you deploy unmanaged disks, you need to ensure that you cater to limits on the storage account (such as a maximum of 40 disks per Standard storage account) before incurring throttling limitations. With managed disks, this burden is handled for you by Azure. Performance is predictable and more reliable, disks are secure by default, and you have better SLAs. When deploying, you select the disk type and the performance tier (Standard or Premium), and a managed disk is created. It also handles scaling automatically for you and removes limitations, such as IOPS and disk count limits, placed on storage accounts through throttling for unmanaged disks. Managed disks are recommended by Microsoft over unmanaged disks.

> **Note**
>
> As of 13 September 2022, Microsoft has started deprecating unmanaged disks in Azure. The anticipated date for the complete retirement of this service is 30 September 2025. You are advised to strongly consider migration of unmanaged disks to the managed disks offering.

In this section, you have learned about the various disk storage offerings available to you in Azure. You have also learned how each offering has a set of performance specifications linked to each SKU that you can select. Disk storage is primarily used for your VMs as either an OS disk or a data disk for storing files. In the next section, you will learn about various redundancy types and the impact on the number of copies each type offers.

Redundancy

Redundancy refers to the number of copies of data that are available at any time; this supports the failure of copies and ensures the continuity of services dependent on the redundancy option chosen. Regardless of the option, data is replicated three times in a storage account for the primary region. The redundancy options that you should be aware of for the exam are unpacked in more detail in this section.

LRS

This is storage that is copied three times synchronously within a single data center in a chosen region. **LRS** is the cheapest replication option that can be chosen and is not intended for business-critical workloads that require HA or resiliency. Protection is provided against server rack and drive failures; however, the protection is limited against unforeseen disasters that could occur within the data center (such as flooding or fire). For this reason, it is important to explore more durable redundancy options if you cannot afford any risk of loss of your data.

The following screenshot illustrates replication for LRS:

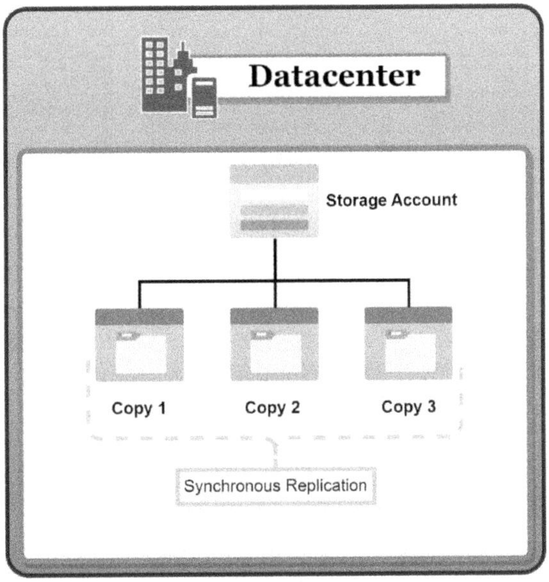

Figure 6.4: LRS replication

You learned about LRS storage replication and how it has been designed to protect against failure within a server rack and drive failures. It is the base offering for storage replication, and you will always have three copies of your data available. Where further protection is required, you are likely to adopt other redundancy offerings, such as the **ZRS** replication offering that protects your data across AZs within a region.

ZRS

ZRS maintains three copies of data are copied synchronously across three Azure AZs for the selected region; this protects against failure at a data center layer. Each AZ is a distinct physical site equipped with its own power, cooling, and networking infrastructure. The ZRS redundancy option is recommended for HA within a single region and can provide reliability of at least 99.9999999999% (12 9s) annually. If a zone becomes unavailable, your data is still accessible, both for read and write operations. This option may also be chosen where data residency requirements apply, such as through a compliance standard that the organization aligns with.

The following screenshot illustrates replication for ZRS:

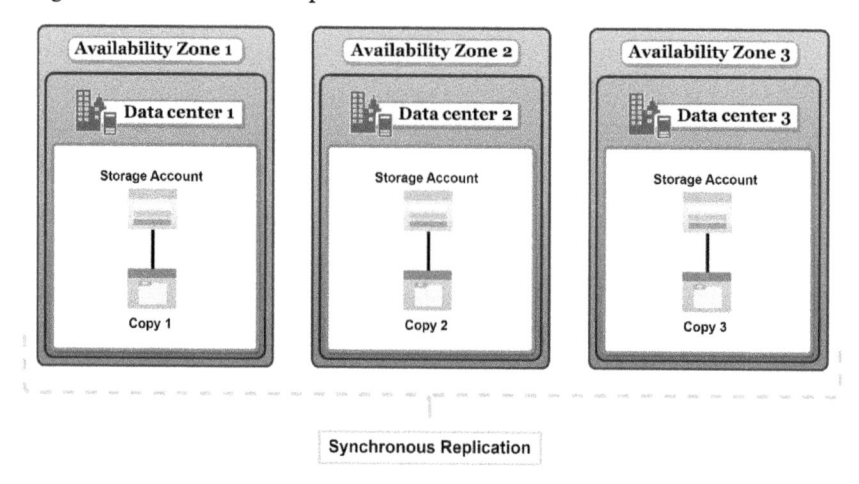

Figure 6.5: ZRS replication

In this section, you learned about ZRS storage replication and how it offers more reliability compared to LRS storage. You learned that ZRS is able to offer enhanced durability to the copies of data it creates across data centers and zones within a single region. This option is suitable for most workloads where a single region of consumption is utilized and for HA scenarios. If, however, you require a solution to protect you against regional failure, you will require a more resilient solution, such as GRS replication, which is discussed next.

GRS

This option is chosen to protect against regional failure while also offering protection within a single data center for each region. Effectively, you get six copies of data (three in each region). Data is copied asynchronously across regions but synchronously within the data center. The following screenshot illustrates replication for GRS:

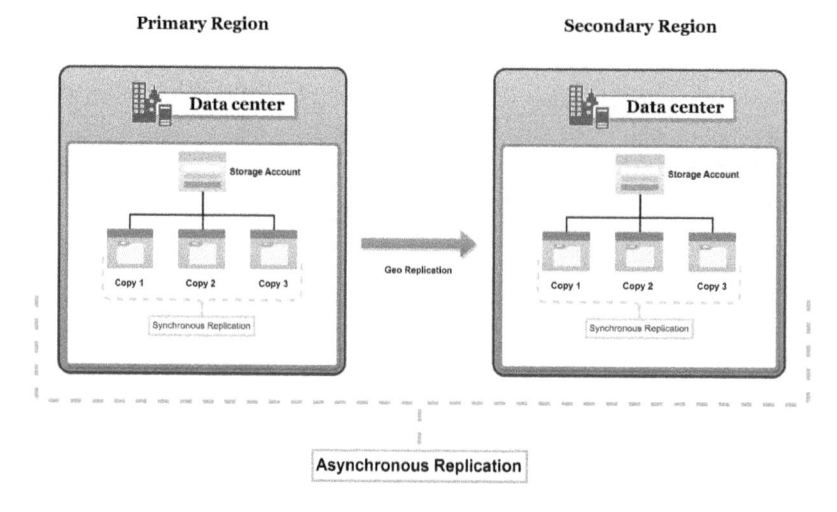

Figure 6.6: GRS replication

It is important to note that data copied to the secondary region is inaccessible for read and write operations unless a failover has been initiated. In the failover state, you can choose to select the secondary region as the new primary region, and you will then have the option to read and write data again. To enable read access to data in the secondary region, you should deploy RA-GRS storage.

In this section, you learned about GRS/RA-GRS storage replication and how it provides a solution for resiliency to protect against regional failures. GRS also maintains six copies of data at all times. When you require the ultimate form of protection against both regional and zonal outages, you will need to explore GZRS replication, which is discussed next.

GZRS

GZRS is chosen to protect against a regional failure while also offering zonal HA and protection within each region. Effectively, you get six copies of data (three in the primary region distributed across AZs, and three distributed within a data center in the secondary region). Data is copied asynchronously across regions but synchronously within the region and data centers. There are two types of GZRS storage, the first being GZRS, where data is replicated but, in the event of a failure, remains inaccessible during the failover process. The second is RA-GZRS, where your data is accessible in the event of a failure in a read-only state in the secondary region during the failover process. You can, however, read and write your data in the new primary region upon completion of the failover for both offerings.

The following screenshot illustrates replication for GZRS/RA-GZRS:

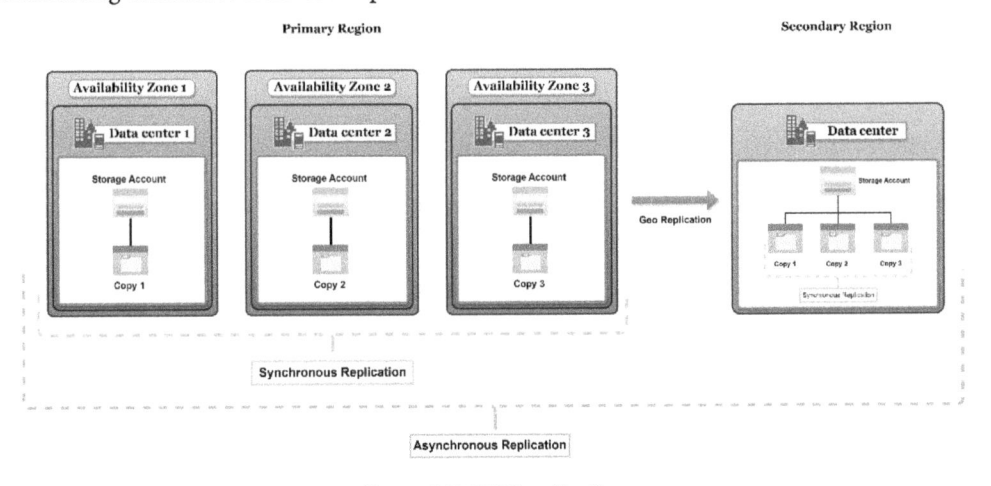

Figure 6.7: GZRS replication

In this section, you learned about GZRS storage replication and how it provides the most robust and resilient offering for your storage. It provides the most value in no-compromise scenarios for data loss and can suffer both regional and zonal failures. You have also learned how the RA-GZRS enhances the offering by enabling read access to data in the secondary region during a failover process. In the next section, you will learn about storage encryption and how it protects your data, as well as the various options available.

> **Note**
> The archive tier of storage does not support ZRS, GZRS, and RA-GZRS redundancy options.

Storage Encryption

Encryption is the process of converting data into a format that is unreadable by unauthorized parties, protecting the confidentiality and integrity of the information. This is done using cryptographic algorithms, which require encryption keys to transform the data into an encrypted form (ciphertext) and back to its original form (plaintext). Encryption plays a crucial role in securing sensitive data from unauthorized access, tampering, or theft.

Need for Encryption and the Value it Brings

Encrypting data is a vital security measure for safeguarding sensitive information and adhering to various regulations and industry norms. Implementing encryption allows you and your organization to do the following:

- Defend confidential data against unauthorized access and potential data breaches
- Uphold privacy and foster trust among parties participating in data transactions
- Meet the requirements of industry-specific rules and standards (such as GDPR, HIPAA, and PCI DSS) that demand data protection measures
- Secure intellectual property, proprietary knowledge, and other valuable data assets
- Preserve the integrity of data by deterring tampering and illegitimate modifications

Azure offers the ability to activate encryption at multiple levels within the platform, such as on the infrastructure layer and the storage layer. You will examine the available options in the following sections.

Difference between Storage Encryption on Azure and Infrastructure Encryption

Azure provides the option to encrypt not only storage on Azure but also the infrastructure. It's important to understand the differences between these, and it is always advised where possible to maintain the highest levels of security possible. Here, you will learn about encryption for the Azure platform and for storage:

- **Storage encryption on Azure**: This refers to encryption services provided by Azure to protect data stored within its storage services, such as Azure Blob Storage, Azure Files, and Azure Disks. Azure provides several encryption options, including **server-side encryption** (**SSE**) using service-managed keys, **customer-managed keys** (**CMK**), or customer-provided keys. Azure Storage uses SSE, which is encryption on the host layer of services within Azure and is used to automatically encrypt data when it is persisted to the cloud. This encryption helps protect your data and meet organizational security and compliance commitments. Azure also supports **client-side encryption**, where data is encrypted before it is sent to Azure Storage. Some key points to note are as follows:

- Azure Storage service-side encryption encrypts data using 256-bit AES encryption, which is FIPS 140-2 compliant.
- Encryption is enabled for all storage accounts and cannot be disabled.
- Data is encrypted regardless of performance tier, access tier, or deployment model.
- There is no additional cost for Azure Storage encryption.

- **Infrastructure encryption**: Infrastructure encryption in Azure storage accounts is an enhanced security feature that offers customers an elevated level of data protection. When this feature is activated, data stored in a storage account undergoes two distinct encryption processes, one at the service level and another at the infrastructure level. This dual encryption approach employs two separate encryption algorithms and keys, ensuring that even in the event of a compromise of one encryption layer, the other layer continues to safeguard the data.

Different Encryption Types on a Storage Account

There are two types of encryption key management available for Azure Storage: **Microsoft-managed keys** (MMK) and **customer-managed keys** (CMK):

- **MMK**: By default, data in a new storage account is encrypted with MMK. These keys are managed and maintained by Microsoft, ensuring that the encryption and decryption of data are handled seamlessly without any additional effort from the user. Microsoft also takes care of key rotation, adhering to compliance requirements.
- **CMK**: Users who prefer to have more control over their encryption keys can opt for CMK. With CMK, you can specify your own key for encryption tasks. These keys are stored in the Azure Key Vault or Azure Key Vault Managed **Hardware Security Module** (HSM) to use for encrypting and decrypting data in Blob Storage and Azure Files. This option allows users to manage and audit key rotation themselves, providing a higher level of control over their data encryption.

Both MMK and CMK offer robust encryption for data in Azure Storage, allowing users to choose the level of control they prefer over their encryption keys.

Azure offers various encryption options for storage accounts:

- **SSE**: Azure automatically encrypts data before it's stored in Azure Storage services and decrypts it when accessed. There are three key management options for SSE:
  - **Service-managed keys**: Azure automatically manages the encryption keys. This is the default option, and it requires no additional configuration.
  - **CMK**: Customers can manage their encryption keys using Azure Key Vault. This provides greater control over key management and rotation.
  - **Customer-provided keys**: Customers can supply their encryption keys for each data transaction. This offers the highest level of control but also requires more management overhead.

- **Client-side encryption**: Data is encrypted by the client application before it's sent to Azure Storage. Decryption also occurs on the client side when the data is accessed. This approach ensures that data is encrypted both in transit and at rest in Azure Storage, and it gives customers full control over the encryption process and key management.

Encryption is a crucial component of securing sensitive data in Azure Storage. Understanding the various encryption options available, such as SSE with service-managed, customer-managed, or customer-provided keys, and client-side encryption, helps organizations choose the appropriate level of control and security for their storage accounts. In the *Creating a Storage Account* exercise, you will learn how to configure a storage account with different encryption options to ensure data protection and compliance with industry standards and regulations.

In this section, you have learned what **storage accounts** are, why they are necessary, and how they work. After learning about the various storage types and configurations available, you are now more prepared for the AZ104 exam.

> **Note**
>
> You are encouraged to read further using the following links to enhance your understanding of the exam-related topics. BlobFuse is not an exam topic but is nonetheless beneficial to your administrative role.
>
> **Storage accounts:** https://learn.microsoft.com/en-us/azure/storage/common/storage-account-overview
>
> **Azure Blob Storage:** https://learn.microsoft.com/en-us/azure/storage/blobs/storage-blobs-introduction
>
> **Blob access tiers:** https://learn.microsoft.com/en-us/azure/storage/blobs/access-tiers-overview
>
> **Understanding block blobs, append blobs, and page blobs:** https://learn.microsoft.com/en-us/rest/api/storageservices/understanding-block-blobs--append-blobs--and-page-blobs
>
> **Blobfuse2:** https://github.com/Azure/azure-storage-fuse
>
> **Rehydrating blob data from the archive tier:** https://learn.microsoft.com/en-us/azure/storage/blobs/archive-rehydrate-overview
>
> **Storage account SLA:** https://azure.microsoft.com/en-us/support/legal/sla/storage
>
> **Storage redundancy:** https://learn.microsoft.com/en-us/azure/storage/common/storage-redundancy

You now understand storage accounts and their configurations, such as the various types of storage, the different access tiers, redundancy types, and encryption options. In the next section, you will experience creating and configuring storage accounts through some hands-on labs.

Creating and Configuring Storage Accounts

You now understand storage accounts and have learned of their many configurations, such as storage types, access tiers, and redundancy options. In the following exercise, you are going to create a storage account in Azure. A storage account needs to be in place before you can upload any data or files to Azure. Complete the activities that follow.

Creating a storage account

For this demonstration, you will first proceed with creating a storage account using the portal. In the exercise that follows this, you will create the equivalent resources' PowerShell code to create this using the Az module. Proceed as follows:

1. Sign in to the Azure portal at `https://portal.azure.com`.
2. Open the `AZ104-StorageAccounts` resource group you will be using for this exercise, click `Overview` on the left menu, and then click `+ Create`.
3. Enter `storage account` in the search bar and click the `Storage account` block result that pops up showing Microsoft as the vendor, as illustrated in the following screenshot:

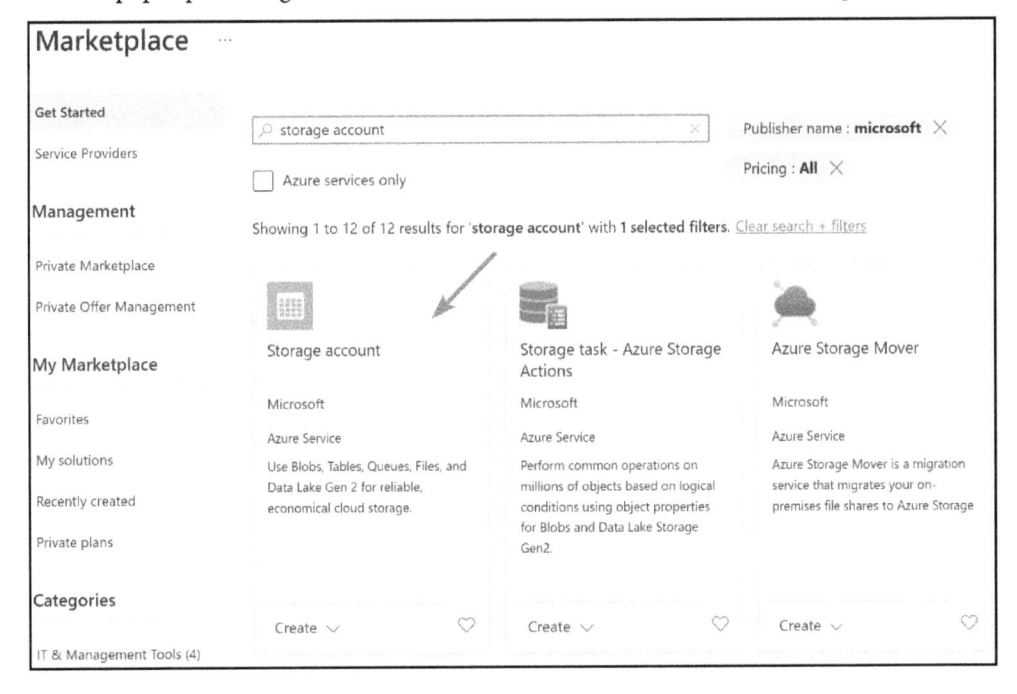

Figure 6.8: Searching for storage account in Marketplace

4. You will be presented with an option to create the storage account; click `Create`, as illustrated in the following screenshot:

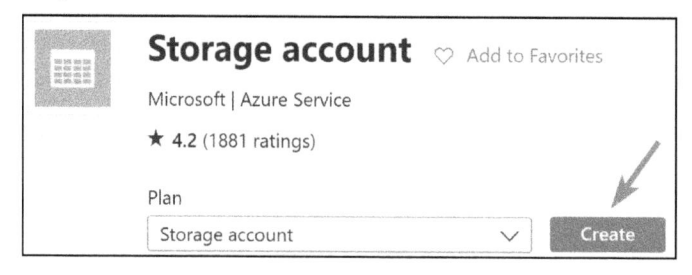

Figure 6.9: Creating a storage account

5. On the following screen, select a resource group where the storage account must be created, enter a globally unique storage account name (limited to a maximum of 24 characters, consisting only of lowercase letters and numbers), and select a region.

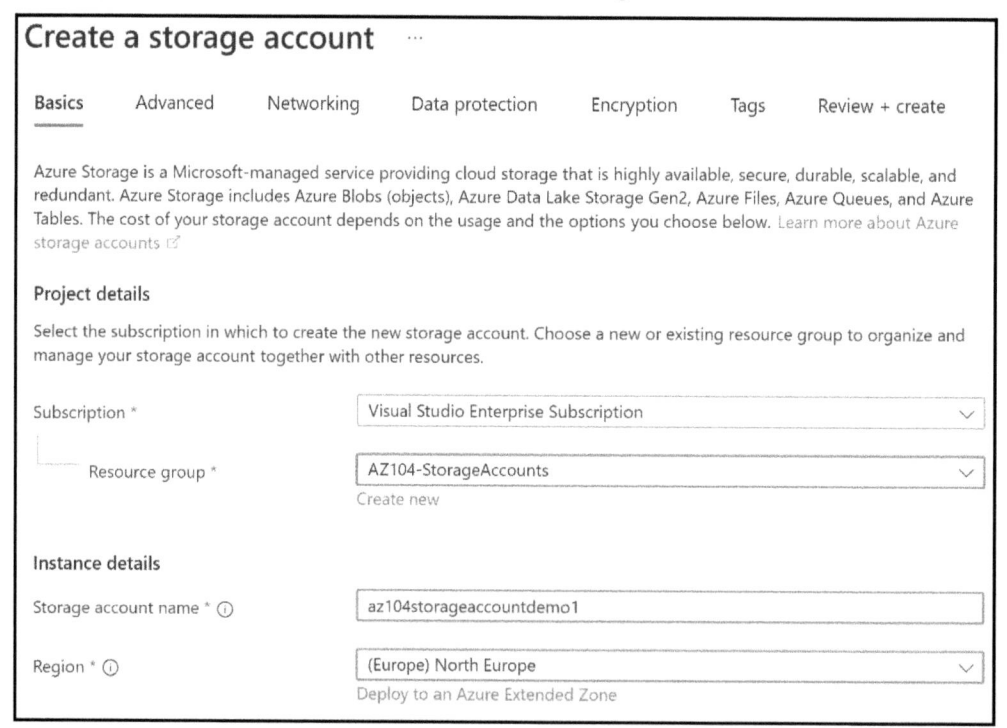

Figure 6.10: Creating a storage account – the Basics tab

6. Scroll down, select a performance tier, and select the desired redundancy for the account. Notice the different redundancy options available. For this exercise, you are going to choose `Locally-redundant storage (LRS)`, as illustrated in the following screenshot:

Creating and Configuring Storage Accounts   197

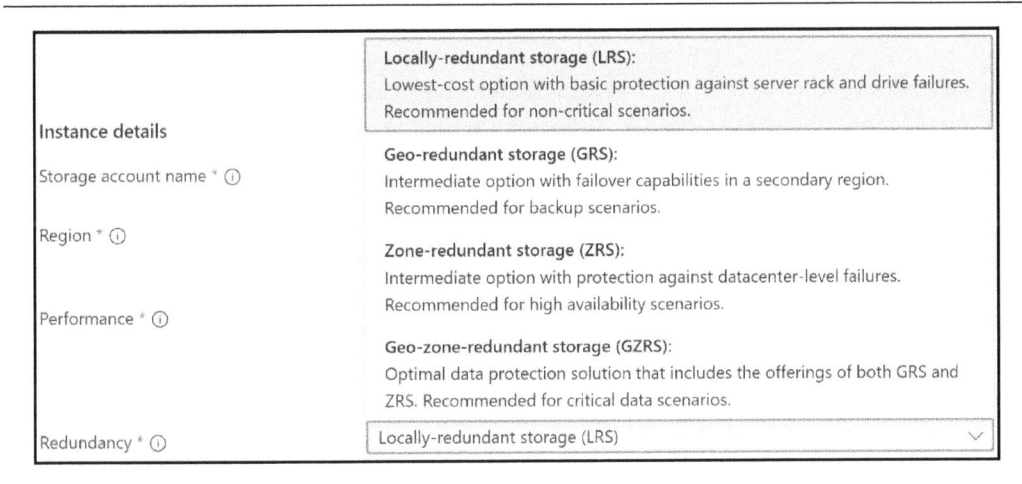

Instance details	**Locally-redundant storage (LRS):** Lowest-cost option with basic protection against server rack and drive failures. Recommended for non-critical scenarios.
Storage account name * ⓘ	**Geo-redundant storage (GRS):** Intermediate option with failover capabilities in a secondary region. Recommended for backup scenarios.
Region * ⓘ	**Zone-redundant storage (ZRS):** Intermediate option with protection against datacenter-level failures. Recommended for high availability scenarios.
Performance * ⓘ	**Geo-zone-redundant storage (GZRS):** Optimal data protection solution that includes the offerings of both GRS and ZRS. Recommended for critical data scenarios.
Redundancy * ⓘ	Locally-redundant storage (LRS)

Figure 6.11: Storage redundancy options

7. Your final options should look as follows; click `Next`.

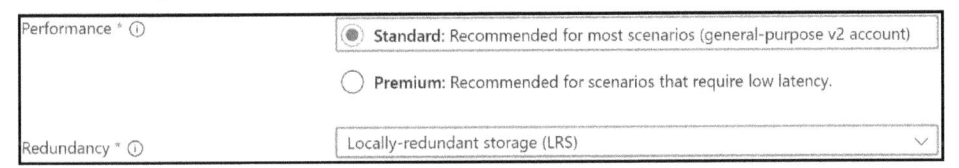

Performance * ⓘ	● **Standard:** Recommended for most scenarios (general-purpose v2 account)
	○ **Premium:** Recommended for scenarios that require low latency.
Redundancy * ⓘ	Locally-redundant storage (LRS)

Figure 6.12: Creating a storage account – the Basics tab – 2

8. For the `Advanced` tab, you will leave the default options enabled. Take note of the `Security` settings on this tab as you will explore security further in the next chapter.

Security

Configure security settings that impact your storage account.

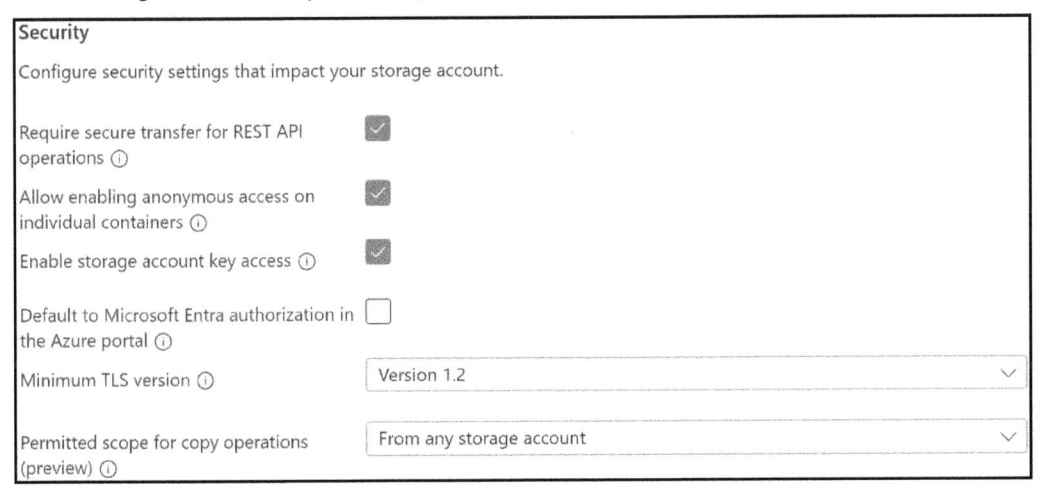

Require secure transfer for REST API operations ⓘ	☑
Allow enabling anonymous access on individual containers ⓘ	☑
Enable storage account key access ⓘ	☑
Default to Microsoft Entra authorization in the Azure portal ⓘ	☐
Minimum TLS version ⓘ	Version 1.2
Permitted scope for copy operations (preview) ⓘ	From any storage account

Figure 6.13: Creating a storage account – the Advanced tab – Security

9. Scroll down and look at the hierarchical namespace and access protocol configurations; these should just be left as their `unchecked` default settings. By selecting `Enable SFTP`, you can enable your storage accounts to be accessible through the **SSH File Transfer Protocol** (**SFTP**) protocol using an SFTP client. This is a secure mechanism for connecting to your storage where the SFTP protocol is desired. The `Enable network file system v3` option enables your storage account to be utilized by the NFS protocol. This protocol enables Linux clients to connect seamlessly to your storage accounts due to the compatibility with the Linux file system and is best suited for high performance and throughput needs.

Figure 6.14: Creating a storage account – the Advanced tab – Access

10. Scroll down further and observe the **Blob storage** and **Azure Files** configuration options; again, leave these as default. Click `Next`, as illustrated in the following screenshot:

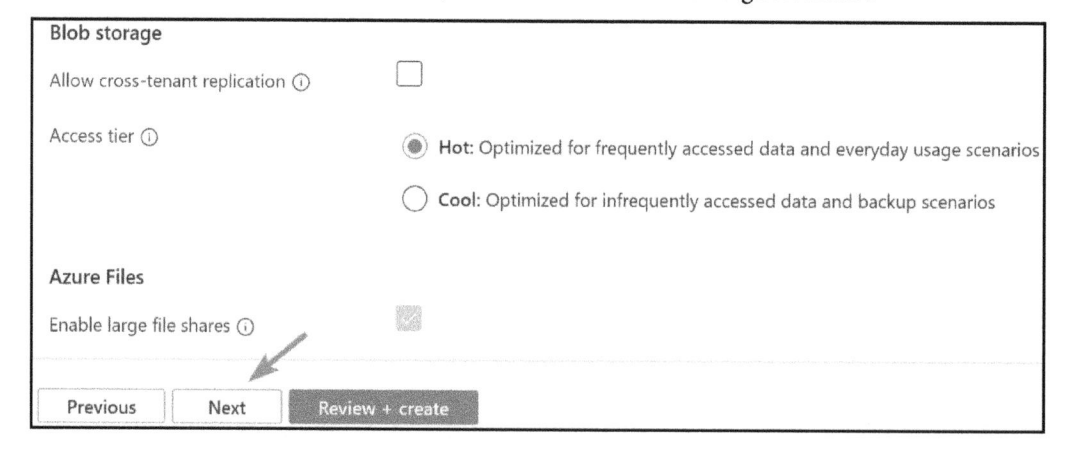

Figure 6.15: Creating a storage account – the Advanced tab – Blobs and Files

11. The configurations on the `Networking` tab will also be addressed in the next chapter but note that the service can be integrated with a VNet using both the public interface on the storage account and the private interface (private endpoint). Leave the default options as illustrated in the following screenshot:

Network connectivity

You can connect to your storage account either publicly, via public IP addresses or service endpoints, or privately, using a private endpoint.

Network access *

- (•) Enable public access from all networks
- ( ) Enable public access from selected virtual networks and IP addresses
- ( ) Disable public access and use private access

ⓘ Enabling public access from all networks might make this resource available publicly. Unless public access is required, we recommend using a more restricted access type. Learn more

Figure 6.16: Creating a storage account – the Networking tab

12. Notice the `Routing preference` setting shown in the following screenshot and click `Next`:

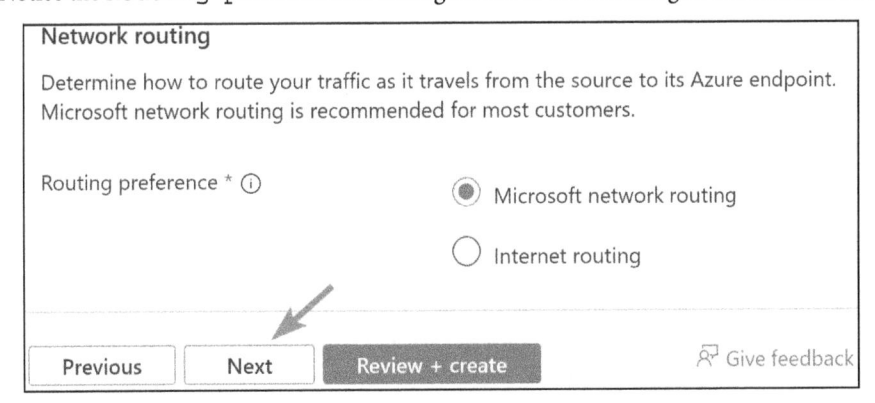

Network routing

Determine how to route your traffic as it travels from the source to its Azure endpoint. Microsoft network routing is recommended for most customers.

Routing preference * ⓘ
- (•) Microsoft network routing
- ( ) Internet routing

[Previous] [Next] [Review + create]   ⁂ Give feedback

Figure 6.17: Creating a storage account – Routing preference

13. The `Data protection` tab exposes controls that are available to you for the recovery of data and is labeled `Recovery`. There are multiple categories of data protection-related items that can be configured. The first section you explore on this tab is `Recovery`. There are several features you can go into here. Leave the default settings as displayed in the screenshot. `Soft delete` acts as a recycling bin for data on the storage account and allows the retrieval of deleted files for a specified period. There is a setting pertaining to the configuration of each of the storage services in the storage account, blobs, containers, and file shares. `Point-in-time` restoration refers to the ability to restore files based on a moment in time within a defined restore point interval.

Understanding Storage Accounts

All these settings are defined in days.

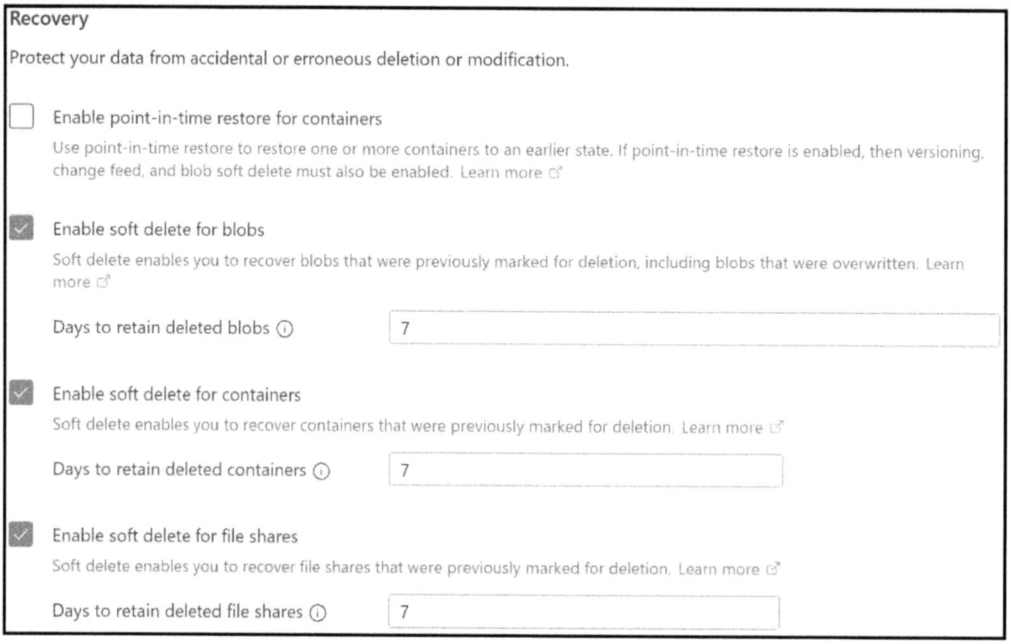

Recovery

Protect your data from accidental or erroneous deletion or modification.

☐ **Enable point-in-time restore for containers**
Use point-in-time restore to restore one or more containers to an earlier state. If point-in-time restore is enabled, then versioning, change feed, and blob soft delete must also be enabled. Learn more

☑ **Enable soft delete for blobs**
Soft delete enables you to recover blobs that were previously marked for deletion, including blobs that were overwritten. Learn more

Days to retain deleted blobs ⓘ | 7

☑ **Enable soft delete for containers**
Soft delete enables you to recover containers that were previously marked for deletion. Learn more

Days to retain deleted containers ⓘ | 7

☑ **Enable soft delete for file shares**
Soft delete enables you to recover file shares that were previously marked for deletion. Learn more

Days to retain deleted file shares ⓘ | 7

Figure 6.18: Creating a storage account – Data Protection – Recovery

14. Scroll down. The next category of items you will learn about are those related to `Tracking`. Here, you have the option to enable versioning, which is used to maintain multiple versions of your blobs and make previous versions accessible to you. For instance, you upload your logo to the blob and, two weeks later, when you update this with a new image, you realize you have made a mistake and want to revert, and even though you overwrote the image on the blob, you can restore the previous version to restore your old logo. The next setting is the blob change feed option, which enables you to set the period you would like to keep logs for. Leave the default configurations for this section, as illustrated in the following screenshot.

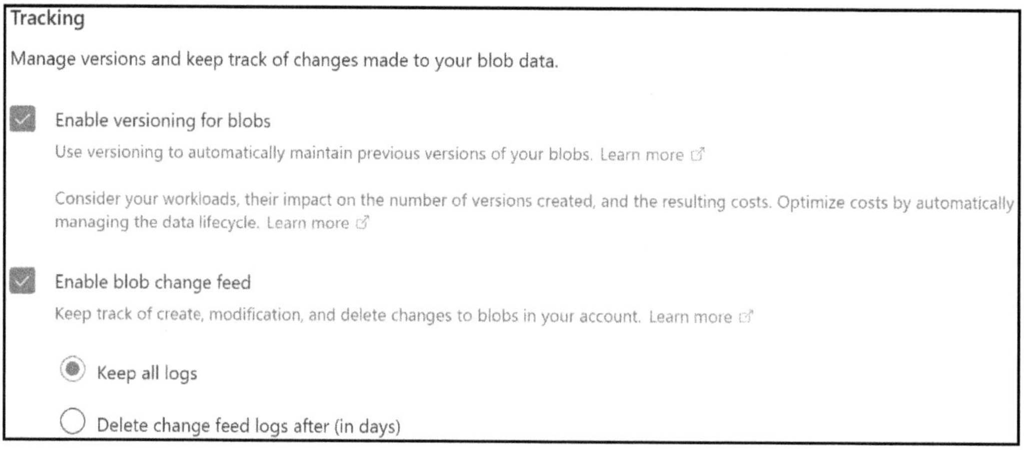

Tracking

Manage versions and keep track of changes made to your blob data.

☑ **Enable versioning for blobs**
Use versioning to automatically maintain previous versions of your blobs. Learn more

Consider your workloads, their impact on the number of versions created, and the resulting costs. Optimize costs by automatically managing the data lifecycle. Learn more

☑ **Enable blob change feed**
Keep track of create, modification, and delete changes to blobs in your account. Learn more

● Keep all logs

○ Delete change feed logs after (in days)

Figure 6.19: Creating a storage account – Data Protection – Tracking

15. Scroll down further to view the last category of controls – `Access control`. This has an option for enabling version-level immutability support. Immutability refers to the storing of data where you have the option to only write once (i.e., does not modify written data). It is often referred to as the principle of **write once read many** (**WORM**). This setting also denies the deletion of data. These policies can be configured at multiple levels, being either time-based or legal hold. **Time-based retention** means that data will be retained for a specified period, after which it is identified as being expired and the data can be deleted but still not modified or overwritten. **Legal hold policies**, on the other hand, refer to the data being stored in an immutable state until such time as the legal hold policy is explicitly cleared. Objects can still be created and read when the policy is in effect but in the same instance, data cannot be modified or deleted. A legal hold is typically used for litigation purposes and is temporarily applied. Applying the setting at this level will enforce the policy for all objects created for the storage account after a policy has been configured on the account level of the storage account. If you do not implement this setting at the account level, you can still have the option to configure it at the container level. Leave the default setting as illustrated in the following figure and click `Next`:

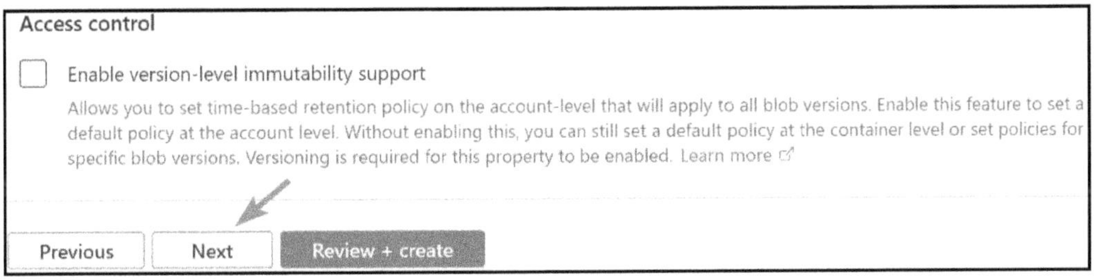

Figure 6.20: Creating a storage account – Data Protection – Access control

> **Note**
> Note that the **point-in-time restoration** option is limited to Blob Storage only. If a container is deleted, data cannot be restored from this operation. Instead, delete individual blobs to prevent complications if you intend to restore them later using this operation.

16. The `Encryption` tab allows you to configure the various encryption settings related to your storage account as discussed in the previous section of this chapter. You will select MMK for this exercise for the `Encryption type` setting. For the next setting, you will select `All service types (blobs, files, tables, and queues)`. This will enable the ability to allow CMK for those services should you desire to enable that later. Finally, check the box next to `Enable infrastructure encryption`.

Understanding Storage Accounts

Click `Review + create`.

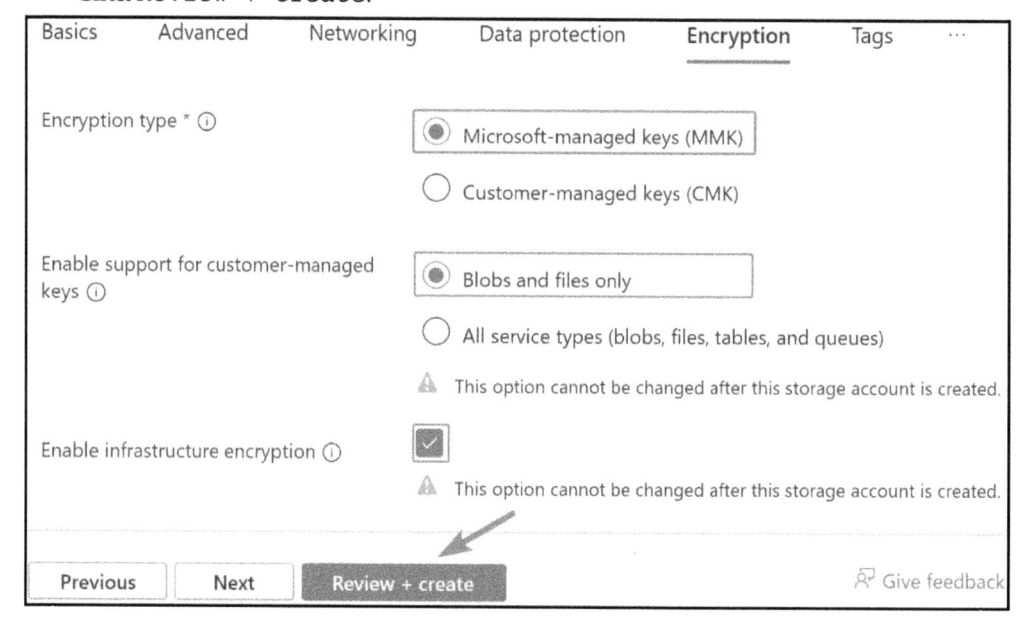

Figure 6.21: Creating a storage account – Encryption

17. Review the options and click `Create`, as illustrated in the following screenshot:

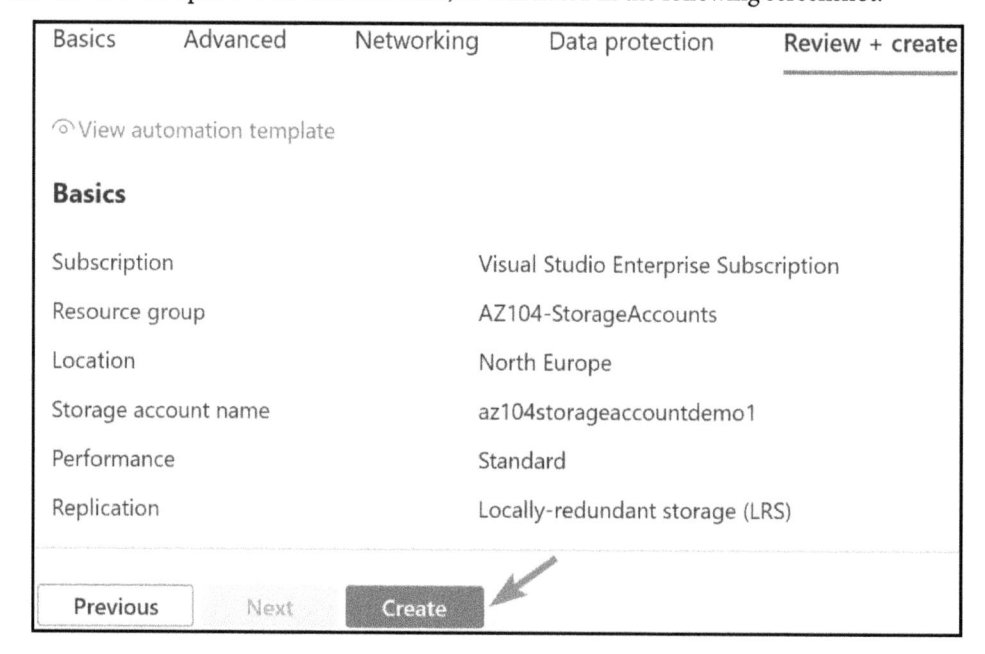

Figure 6.22: Creating a storage account – Review

You have now completed the deployment of a storage account. Next, you will learn how to do the same thing through PowerShell.

PowerShell scripts

Please ensure that the Az module is installed, as per the *Technical Requirements* section at the beginning of the chapter.

The following script will create a new storage account (change the parameters to suit your requirements):

```
# First connect your Azure account credentials to perform
Connect-AzAccount
# Parameters
$ResourceGroup = "AZ104-StorageAccounts"
$Location = "WestEurope"
$StorageAccountName = "az104storageaccountdemo1"
$SkuName = "Standard_LRS"
# Create the Storage Account
New-AzStorageAccount -Name $StorageAccountName -ResourceGroupName $ResourceGroup `
-Location $Location -SkuName $SkuName -AllowBlobPublicAccess $False
```

In this exercise, you created a storage account using PowerShell scripts. The experience gained is particularly useful when employing programmatic management in your environment, especially in large environments requiring the same actions to be performed several times.

> **Note**
>
> You are encouraged to read up further by using the following links:
>
> **Point-in-time restoration for blob storage:** https://learn.microsoft.com/en-gb/azure/storage/blobs/point-in-time-restore-overview
>
> **Soft delete for blobs:** https://learn.microsoft.com/en-gb/azure/storage/blobs/soft-delete-blob-overview
>
> **Data protection overview:** https://learn.microsoft.com/en-gb/azure/storage/blobs/data-protection-overview

After completing the exercises in this section, you now have the ability to create storage accounts using the Azure portal or Azure PowerShell. Storage accounts are versatile storage solutions that can be utilized with your various Azure resources and are great for saving and sharing your data. In the next chapter, you will learn about **Azure Data Box**, which is a tool used for quickly and securely transferring data to or from Azure.

Summary

In this chapter, you have learned about the different types of storage accounts available to Azure (Standard GPv2, Premium block blobs, Premium file shares, and Premium page blobs), the different access tiers (hot, cool, cold, and archive), disk storage options (Standard HDD, Standard SSD, Premium SSD, and Ultra Disk), and the various redundancy options. You have also created a storage account using both the Azure portal and a PowerShell script. You now have the skills required for choosing the correct storage in Azure and knowledge on deploying a storage account, which will serve as the foundational block for shared storage, such as Azure Files and Blob Storage.

In the next chapter, we will expand upon this knowledge, and you will work with Azure Storage Explorer, a convenient and versatile tool for managing Azure Storage. You will also learn how to manage storage through the Azure Storage Explorer tool to create file shares and blob containers and delete them. The next chapter will also explore Azure Data Box, a tool for importing and exporting large volumes of data to and from Azure quickly.

Exam Readiness Drill - Chapters 4-6

Apart from mastering key concepts, strong test-taking skills under time pressure are essential for acing your certification exam. That's why developing these abilities early in your learning journey is critical.

Exam readiness drills, using the free online practice resources provided with this book, help you progressively improve your time management and test-taking skills while reinforcing the key concepts you've learned.

HOW TO GET STARTED

- Open the link or scan the QR code at the bottom of this page
- If you have unlocked the practice resources, already log in to your registered account. If you haven't, follow the instructions in *Chapter 23* and come back to this page.
- Once you log in, click the START button to start a quiz
- We recommend attempting a quiz multiple times till you're able to answer most of the questions correctly and well within the time limit.
- You can use the following practice template to help you plan your attempts :

Attempt	Target	Time Limit
Working On Accuracy		
Attempt 1	40% or more	Till the timer runs out
Attempt 2	60% or more	Till the timer runs out
Attempt 3	75% or more	Till the timer runs out
Working On Timing		
Attempt 4	75% or more	1 minute before time limit
Attempt 5	75% or more	2 minutes before time limit
Attempt 6	75% or more	3 minutes before time limit

The above drill is just an example. Design your drills based on your own goals and make the most out of the online quizzes accompanying this book.

> First time accessing the online resources? 🔒
> You'll need to unlock them through a one-time process. **Head to** *Chapter 23* **for instructions**.

Open Quiz

`https://packt.link/az104e3ch4-6`

OR scan this QR code →

7
Copying Data To and From Azure

In this chapter, you will learn about the Azure Data Box service, which enables you to move large amounts of data quickly into or out of Azure. You will experience working with Azure Storage Explorer, which is a convenient and versatile tool for managing storage in Azure. You will also learn how to manage storage through the Azure Storage Explorer tool, creating file shares and blob containers and deleting them. By the end of the chapter, you will have the skills required to implement and configure storage in Azure, as well as be able to identify the appropriate management tool needed in a given situation.

In this chapter, you are going to learn the following main topics:

- Using Azure Data Box (previously, Import/Export)
- Installing and Using Azure Storage Explorer
- Configuring Azure Files and Azure Blob Storage

Technical Requirements

To follow along with the hands-on material, you will need the following:

- Access to an Azure subscription with owner or contributor privileges. If you do not have access to one, you can set up a student account for free: `https://azure.microsoft.com/en-us/free/`.
- **PowerShell 5.1** or later installed on a Windows PC, or PowerShell Core 6.x on another operating system, on a machine where labs can be practiced from.
- For Windows users, you will need to install **.NET Framework 4.7.2** or later using the following link: `https://learn.microsoft.com/en-us/dotnet/framework/install`
- Where PowerShell is not installed or available, `https://shell.azure.com` can be used as a browser-based shell.

- Installation of the `Az` PowerShell module, which can be performed by running the following in an administrative PowerShell session:

  ```
  Set-ExecutionPolicy -ExecutionPolicy RemoteSigned -Scope
  CurrentUser
  Install-Module -Name Az -Scope CurrentUser -Repository PSGallery
  -Force
  ```

Using Azure Data Box (Previously, Import/Export)

Azure Data Box (previously known as Azure Import/Export) is a service that allows you to import and export data quickly and securely to and from an Azure data center. Imported data is stored either in Azure Blob Storage or Azure Files. The value of the Azure Data Box service is overcoming the limitations experienced in network capacity, time, or costs when transferring data into or out of Azure. By utilizing Azure Data Box, you can transfer large amounts of data quickly into or out of Azure affordably.

To use Azure Data Box, you will need to prepare disk drives that will be shipped to the Azure data center. These disk drives must have BitLocker encryption enabled. Once the volume is encrypted, you can copy your data to the drives before shipment. After encryption, a disk needs to be prepared using the `WAImportExport.exe` tool. By running this tool, a journal file is automatically created in the same folder that you ran the tool. There are two other files created as well – a `.xml` file and a `drive-manifest.xml` file. You will need these files later to create an import/export job. The disk is now ready to be shipped to Azure. Read this Microsoft article for more details: `https://learn.microsoft.com/en-us/azure/import-export/storage-import-export-data-to-files`.

> **Note**
> You may come across Azure Data Box Disk in your studies and find that its offering looks similar to Azure Import/Export. The key difference used to be that Azure Data Box Disk was a service where you import Microsoft-owned devices as part of Azure Data Box, whereas Azure Import/Export supported your own disks, provided they conformed to requirements. This has since changed, and now all are managed through the Azure Data Box service.

Importing into an Azure Job

After disks are shipped to Azure, you can create an import or export job from the Azure portal. The import process flow for Azure import/export looks like this:

Import Job Flow

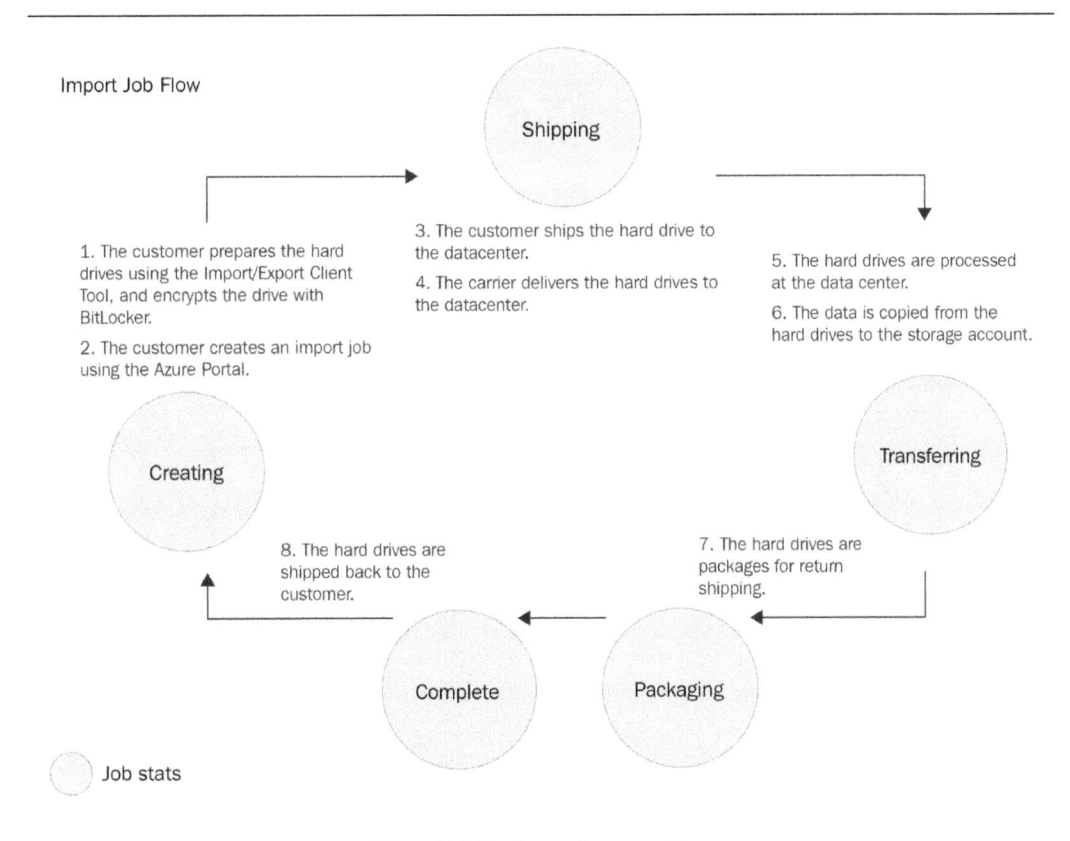

Figure 7.1: The import process flow

Therefore, to import data to Azure using the import/export service, you must take the following steps:

1. Navigate to the Azure portal by opening `https://portal.azure.com`.
2. Enter `Azure Data Box` in the search bar at the top of the portal, and then click `Azure Data Box`, as illustrated in the following screenshot:

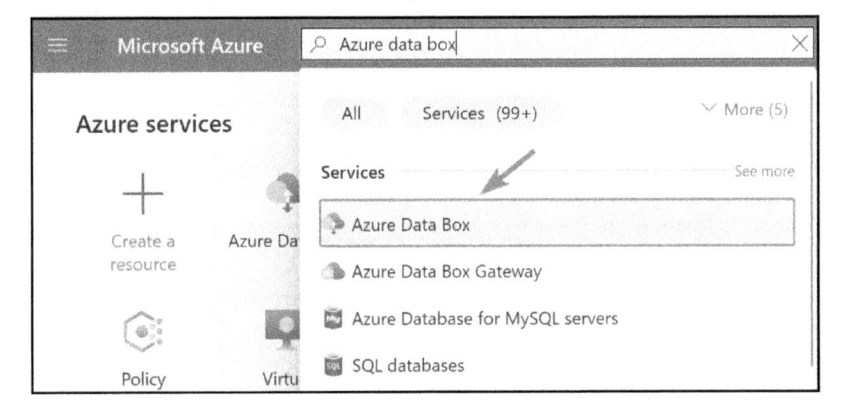

Figure 7.2: Searching for Azure Data Box

3. Click + Create from the top menu, as illustrated in the following screenshot:

Figure 7.3: Creating an Azure Data Box job

4. On the next blade, select Import to Azure for the Transfer type setting, select your Subscription, Resource group, Source country/region, and Destination Azure region, and click Next.

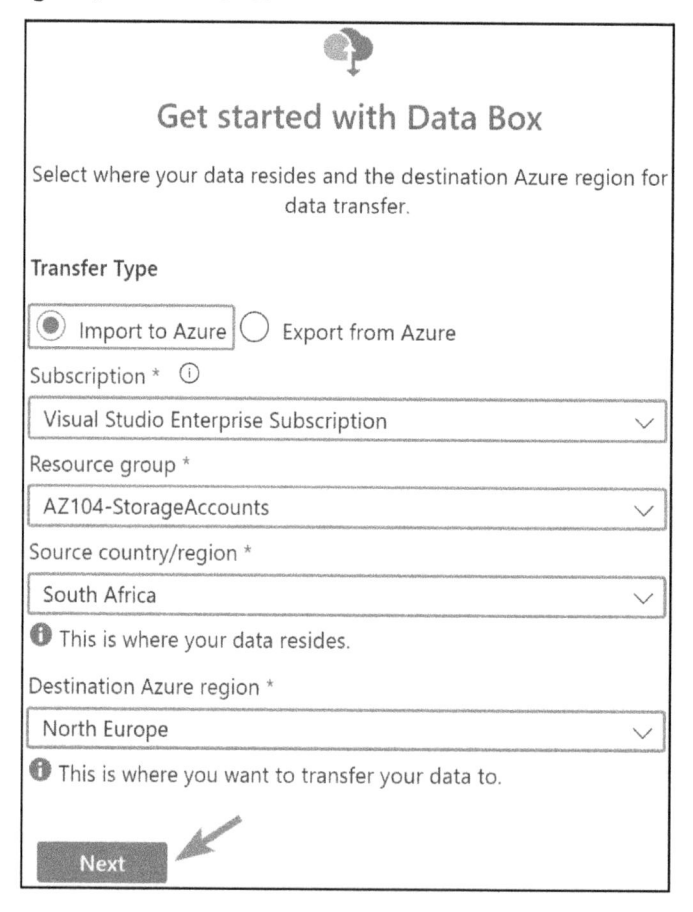

Figure 7.4: Entering the Azure Data Box options

5. Click Select from the Import/Export Job option card.

Using Azure Data Box (Previously, Import/Export) 211

Data Box - Disk
35 TB
Total usable capacity per order
- Up to 5 disks per order
- Available with BitLocker or Hardware Encryption (new)
- Supports Azure Blobs, Files, Managed Disks and ADLS Gen2 accounts
- Copy data to 1 storage account
- USB 3.1/SATA interface

Learn more Device Specifications

Pricing details   Select

Data Box
80 TB
Total usable capacity per order
- 10 day use at no extra cost
- Supports Azure Blobs, Files, Managed Disks and ADLS Gen2 accounts
- Copy data across 10 storage accounts
- 1x1/10 Gbps RJ45, 2x10 Gbps SFP+ interface

Learn more Device Specifications

Pricing details   Select

Data Box - Heavy
800 TB
Total usable capacity per order
- 20 day use at no extra cost
- Supports Azure Blobs, Files, Managed Disks and ADLS Gen2 accounts
- Copy data across 10 storage accounts
- 4x1 Gbps, 4x40 Gbps interface

Learn more Device Specifications

Pricing details   Select

Import/Export Job
1 Tb Onwards
- Send up to 10 disks per order
- Supports SATA/SSD disks. Supported hardware
- Supports Azure Blobs and Files
- Copy data to 1 storage account

Learn more Device Specifications

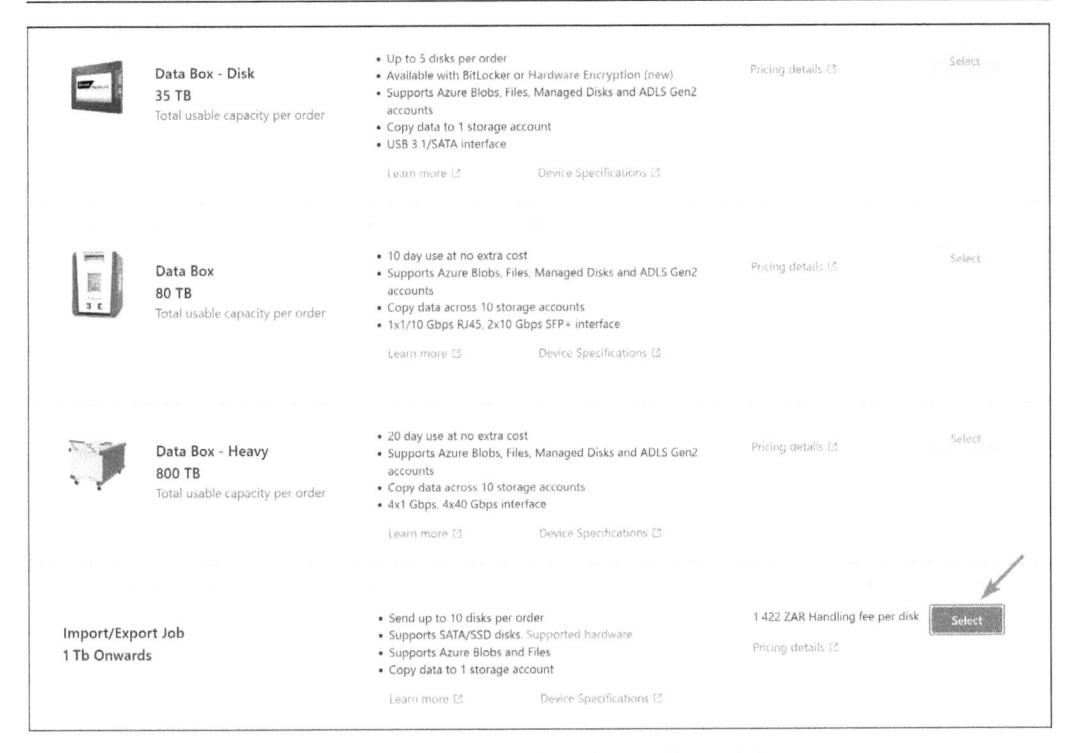

1 422 ZAR Handling fee per disk
Pricing details   **Select**

Figure 7.5: Azure Data Box – Import/Export job

6. Enter `az104labimport` as the `Import job name` value for the import/export Job. Then, click `Next: Job Details >`.

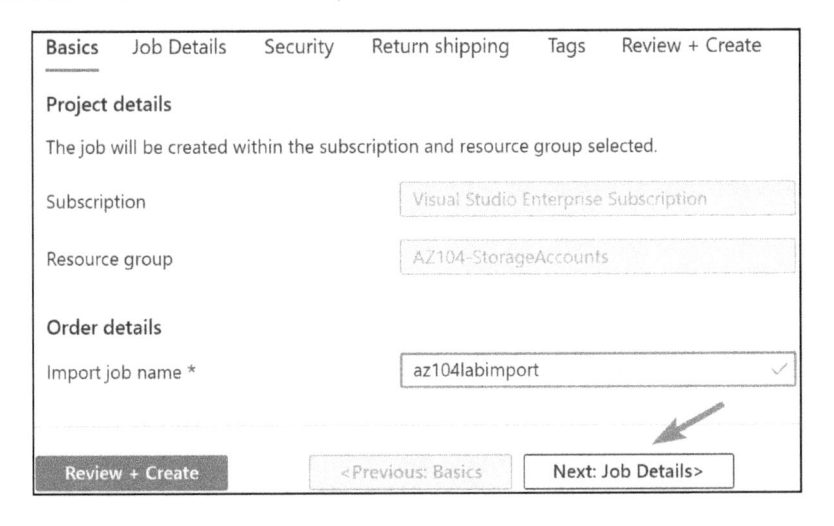

Figure 7.6: Azure Data Box – Basics

7. Select your destination Azure region; if you noticed in the previous settings, this should be set to `North Europe`. Select your storage account, which can be set to the storage account you created earlier – `az104storageaccountdemo1`. Finally, upload your `*.jrn` file for processing. If you do not have a `*.jrn` file yet, you can create one using the WAImportExport tool from this link: `https://aka.ms/waietools`. Then, click `Next: Security>`.

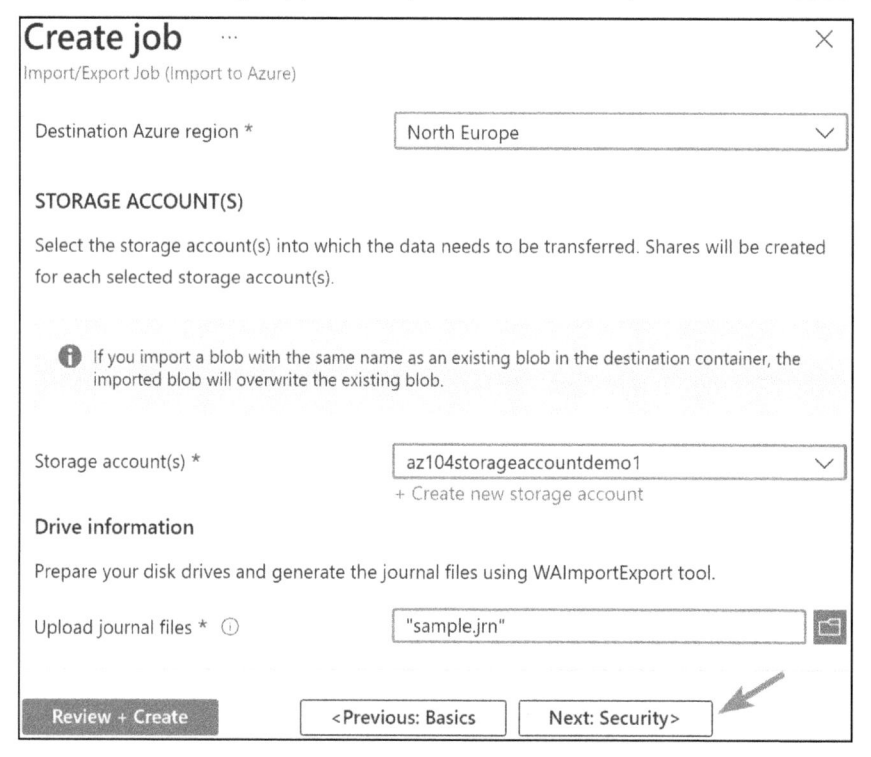

Figure 7.7: Azure Data Box – Job details

8. For `Encryption type`, you can leave the default setting, which is `Microsoft managed key`. Then, click `Next : Return shipping >`.

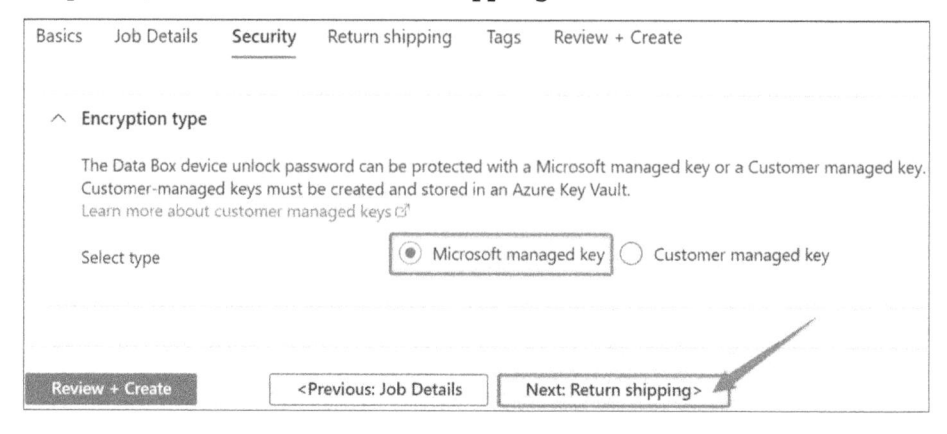

Figure 7.8: Azure Data Box – Security

9. Select your carrier, which at the time of writing is a choice between `UPS`, `DHL`, `FedEx`, `Blue Dart`, and `TNT`. Enter the account number you have with the selected carrier too, and then scroll down the page.

Figure 7.9: Azure Data Box – Carrier details

10. Click `+ Add Address` next to the `Ship to address` section; this will pop up another window where you can fill in the details for your shipping. Then, click `Add shipping address`.

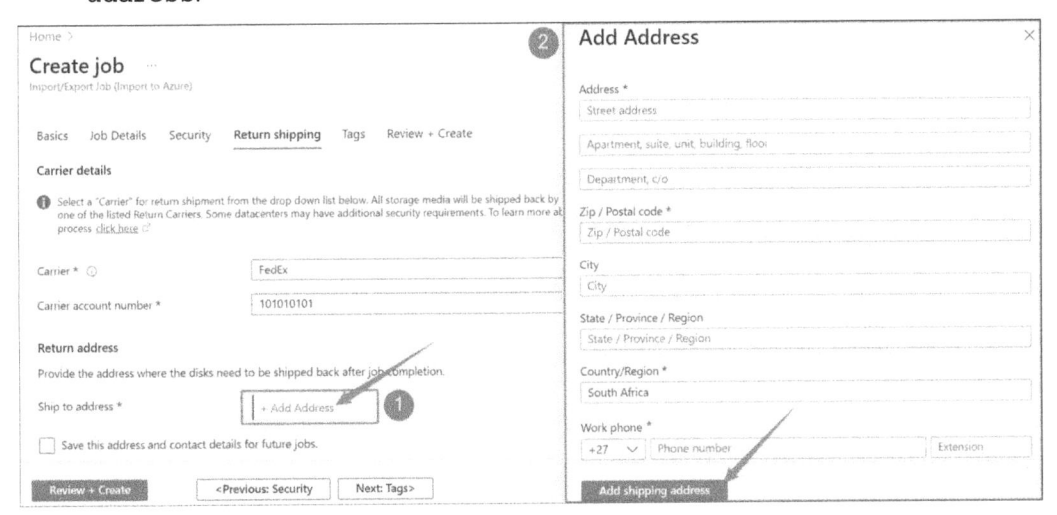

Figure 7.10: Azure Data Box – The shipping address

11. In the `Notification` section, enter an email address. Then, click `Review + Create`.

Figure 7.11: Azure Data Box – Notification

12. Once validation has passed, click the `I acknowledge that all the information provided is correct and agree to the terms and conditions above` checkbox, and then click `Create`.

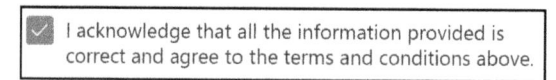

Figure 7.12: Azure Data Box – Acknowledgment

You have completed the import job process. Next, you will review the process to perform an export job from Azure.

Exporting from an Azure Job

Exporting data from Azure is a relatively simple process. It is similar to importing data in the previous exercise, except in the reverse order.

The export process flow for Azure import/export looks like this:

Export Job Flow

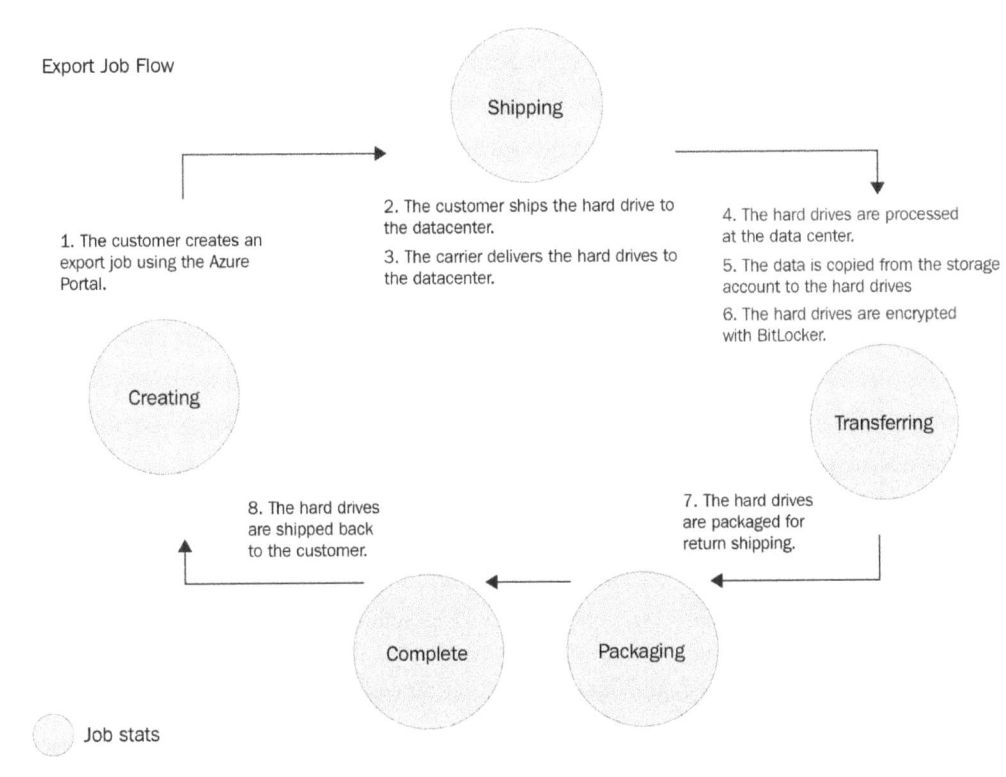

1. The customer creates an export job using the Azure Portal.
2. The customer ships the hard drive to the datacenter.
3. The carrier delivers the hard drives to the datacenter.
4. The hard drives are processed at the data center.
5. The data is copied from the storage account to the hard drives
6. The hard drives are encrypted with BitLocker.
7. The hard drives are packaged for return shipping.
8. The hard drives are shipped back to the customer.

Shipping → Transferring → Packaging → Complete → Creating

Job stats

Figure 7.13: The export process flow

Therefore, you must take the following steps:

1. Navigate to the Azure portal by opening `https://portal.azure.com`.
2. Enter `export` or `Azure Data Box` in the search bar at the top of the portal, and then click `Azure Data Box` from the list of services under the search bar.
3. Click `Create` from the top menu.
4. On the next blade, select `Export from Azure` for the `Transfer type` setting. Select your subscription and resource group.

Then, click Next.

Figure 7.14: Azure Data Box – Export from Azure

5. Select your source Azure region and the destination country/region that you will be using. Then, click Next.

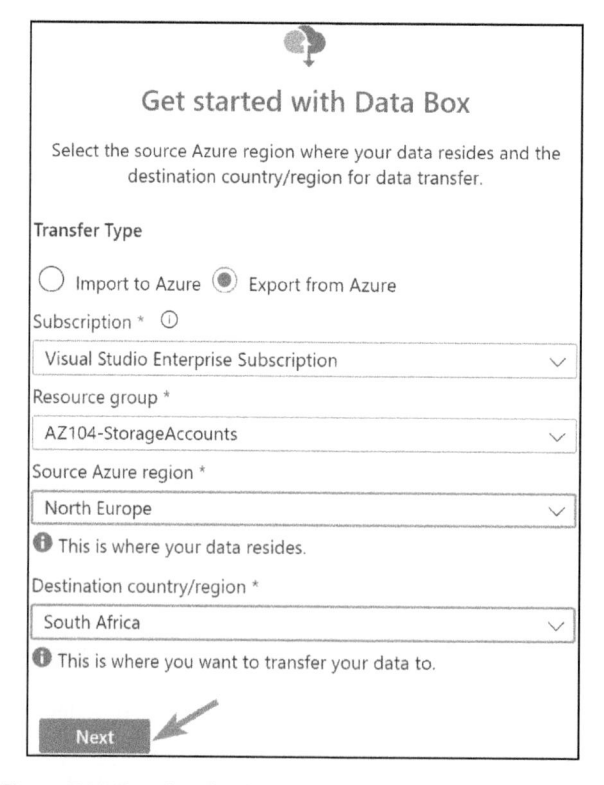

Figure 7.15: Entering the Azure Data Box options for exporting

6. Click `Select` on the `Import/Export Job` option card.

Figure 7.16: Azure Data Box – Import/Export job

7. Enter a Name value for the import/export Job (use `az104labexport`). Then, click `Next: Job Details >`.

8. Select your Source Azure region. As before, this should be set to `North Europe`. Select your storage account, which can be set to the storage account you created earlier – `az104storageaccountdemo1`. Select `All objects` for `Blobs to export`. Then, click `Next: Security>`.

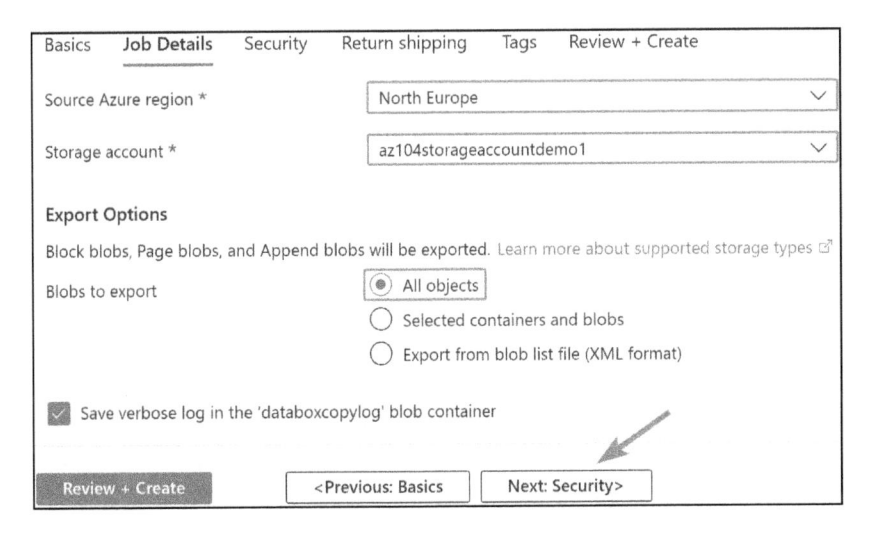

Figure 7.17: Azure Data Box – Job details

9. Leave the default encryption type that is selected, which is `Microsoft managed key`. Then, click `Next: Return shipping >`.

10. Enter the shipping details as you did for the import exercise earlier in the chapter. Then, click `Review + Create`.

11. Once validation has passed, click the `I acknowledge that all the information provided is correct and agree to the terms and conditions above` checkbox, and then click `Create`.

The data will now be exported and shipped to you, which is how you can export data out of Azure.

> **Note**
>
> You are encouraged to read more on this topic by using the following links:
>
> **Importing data to blobs:** `https://learn.microsoft.com/en-us/azure/import-export/storage-import-export-data-to-blobs`
>
> **Importing data to files:** `https://learn.microsoft.com/en-us/azure/import-export/storage-import-export-data-to-files`
>
> **Exporting data from blobs:** `https://learn.microsoft.com/en-us/azure/import-export/storage-import-export-data-from-blobs`

As you have seen, Azure Data Box provides a valuable service in Azure for importing and exporting large amounts of data quickly and securely. When you require this level of service, consider Azure Data Box. In the next section, you will learn about installing and using Azure Storage Explorer.

Installing and Using Azure Storage Explorer

Azure Storage Explorer is a standalone application that can be used to easily work with the different types of data stored in an Azure storage account. There is also an implementation in preview in the Azure portal that allows integrated access to storage accounts. You can upload, download, and manage files, queues, tables, blobs, data lake storage, and Cosmos DB entities using Azure Storage Explorer. Aside from that, you can also use the application to configure and manage **cross-origin resource sharing** (**CORS**) rules for your storage accounts. This application can be used on Windows, Linux, and macOS devices.

> **Note**
>
> CORS is a mechanism that allows the loading of resources from origins dissimilar to the pattern origin. The feature tells a browser whether it should permit the loading of resources when it detects a CORS pattern. This is a frequently used feature of web design and something to be cognizant of.

Installation

To install the Azure Storage Explorer application, perform the following steps:

1. Navigate to `https://azure.microsoft.com/en-us/products/storage/storage-explorer/` to download the application.
2. Once the application has been downloaded, install it. Click `I accept the agreement` and then `Install`. You will need to click `Next` a few times.

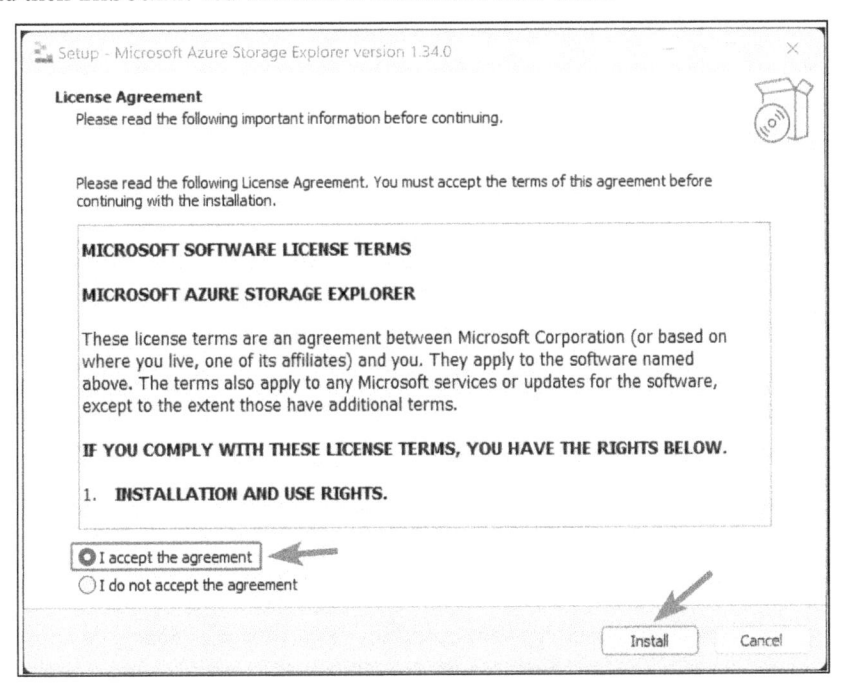

Figure 7.18: Azure Storage Explorer – installation

3. When the application is installed, open it. When you connect for the first time, you will be prompted to choose the type of Azure resource you want to connect to. There are several options to choose from: `Subscription`, `Storage account or service`, `Blob container or directory`, `ADLS Gen2 container or directory`, `File share`, `Queue`, `Table`, or `Local storage emulator`.
4. For this demonstration, you will connect Storage Explorer to the subscription level of Azure, as illustrated in the following screenshot. This will run under the context (i.e., the permissions) for the user credentials you enter.

Click `Subscription`:

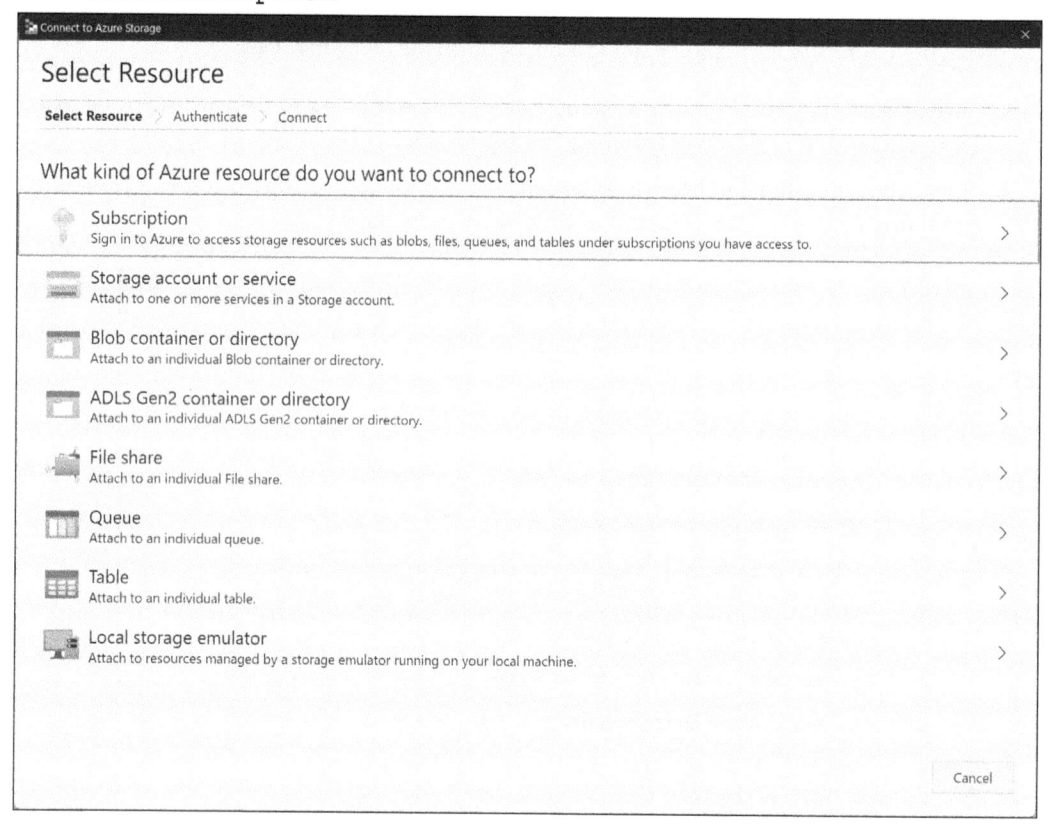

Figure 7.19: Selecting an Azure resource for storage explorer

5. You will see several environments available to choose from; unless you are working in one of the special Azure regions, such as China, Germany, or the **United States** (**US**) government, you can select `Azure`, as shown in the following screenshot. Azure is the default environment for most Azure users. Then, click `Next`:

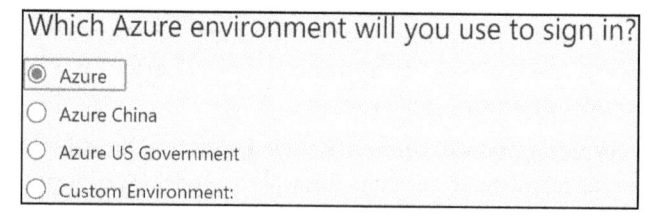

Figure 7.20: Selecting an Azure environment for storage explorer

6. You will be prompted to sign in on the Azure portal, so sign in and click `Next`, as illustrated in the following screenshot:

Installing and Using Azure Storage Explorer | 221

Figure 7.21: Signing into Azure

7. You will be directed to the ACCOUNT MANAGEMENT page, as illustrated in the following screenshot. Click Open Explorer at the bottom of the screen to view your storage information:

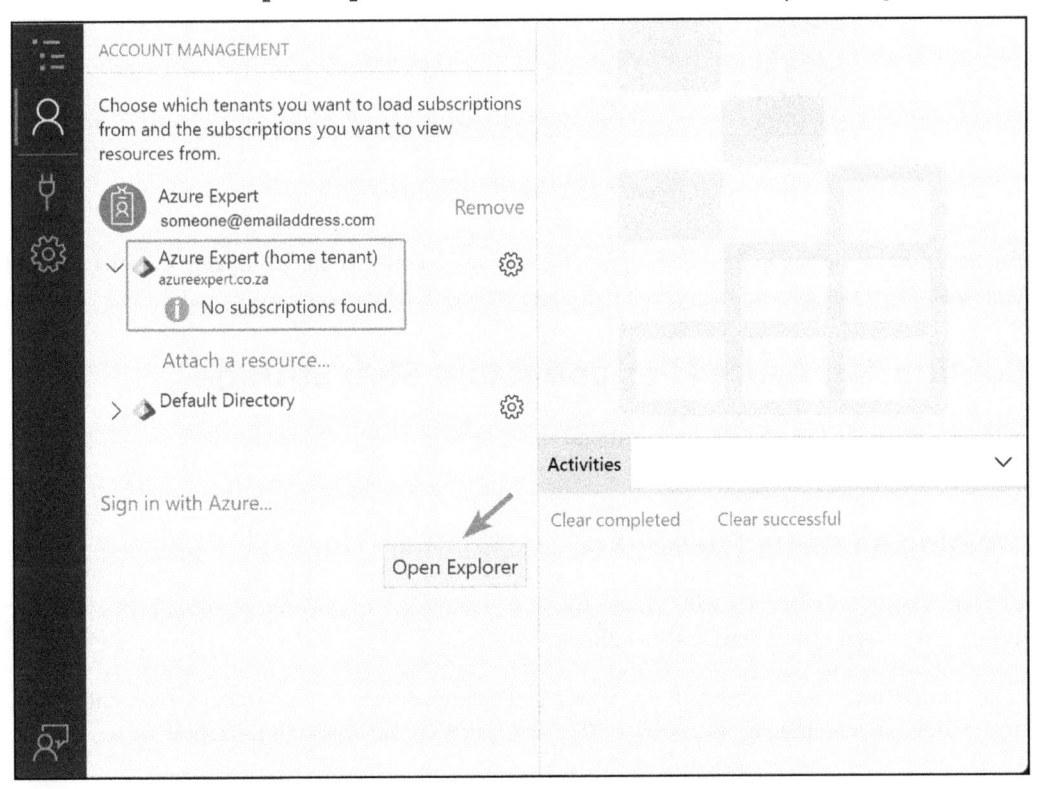

Figure 7.22: Adding an account to storage explorer

> **Note**
>
> Azure Storage Explorer uses your default browser to authenticate you. If you wish to change this and instead sign in with the relevant credentials, you can go to the `Settings` menu, scroll down to `Sign-In`, and change the `Sign In With:` drop-down box to `Integrated Sign-in`.

8. On the EXPLORER menu, take some time to familiarize yourself with the different storage options presented. Expand the subscription you have, expand `Storage Accounts`, and then expand any account that requires you to view its available storage options. Note in the following screenshot the storage types, as discussed earlier in the chapter:

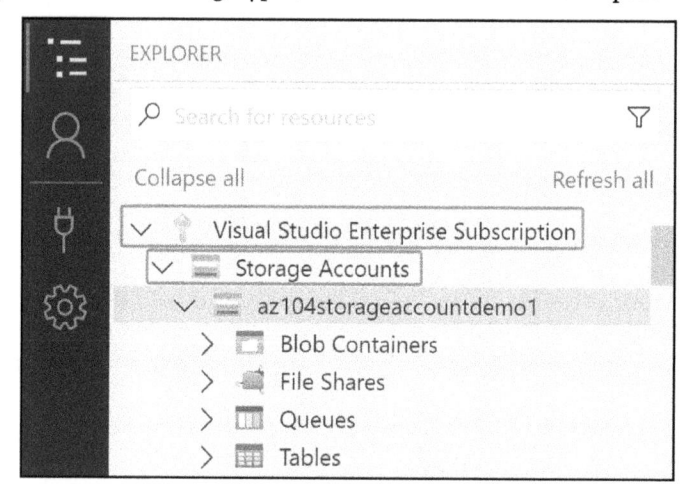

Figure 7.23: Using storage explorer

You have now connected to Azure Storage using Storage Explorer. In the subsequent sections, you will explore storage management using both the Azure Storage Explorer application and the Azure portal.

Configuring Azure Files and Azure Blob Storage

In the following section, you will walk through an example of how to create file shares and blob storage on a storage account.

Creating an Azure Files Share

In the following exercise, you will create a file share named `test` and demonstrate connectivity to this on a Windows system. Proceed as follows:

1. On the EXPLORER screen in Azure Storage Explorer, open a storage account, right-click `File Shares`, and then click `Create File Share`, as illustrated in the following screenshot:

Configuring Azure Files and Azure Blob Storage 223

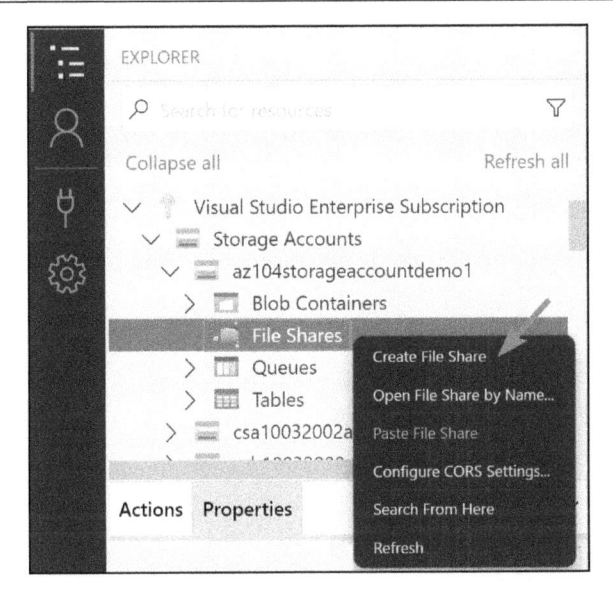

Figure 7.24: Using Storage Explorer – Create file share

2. A folder icon will be propagated at the bottom of `File Shares`; you can type in the name `test`, as illustrated in the following screenshot, and press the `Enter` button on your keyboard:

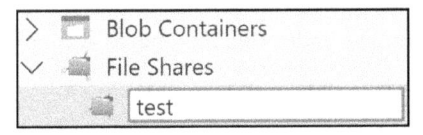

Figure 7.25 – Creating a file share

> **Note**
> Creating a file share on Azure will prompt for a **quota** size. A quota is a limit on the amount of storage that can be consumed. You should always configure this.

3. You now have your folder in `File Shares`, which you will now upload something to. Click the `Upload` button and then `Upload Files...`, as illustrated in the following screenshot:

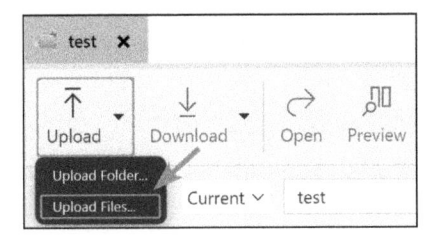

Figure 7.26: Uploading files

4. Select a file by clicking the ellipsis icon (...), and then click `Upload`, as illustrated in the following screenshot:

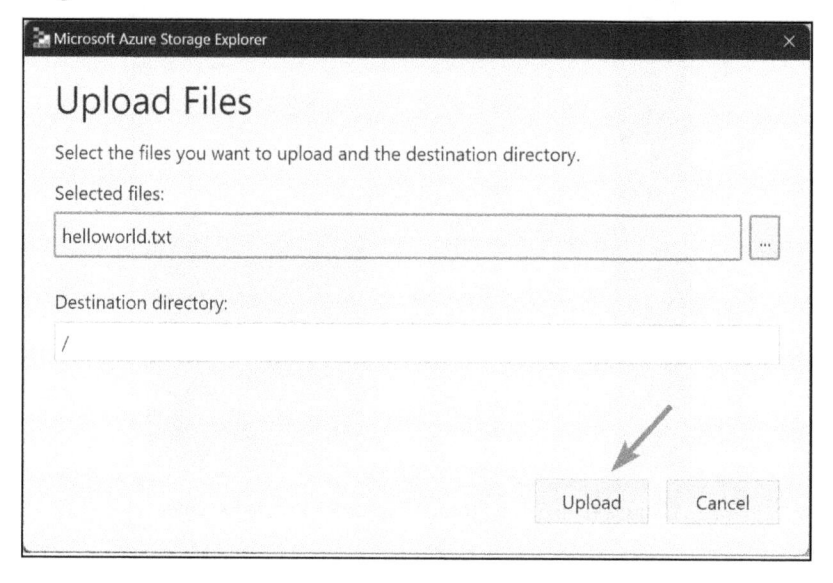

Figure 7.27: Uploading your first file

5. You will see a success message, indicating that the file was uploaded successfully.

> **Note**
> You can also drag and drop files to the Storage Explorer window with your file share open. This may be more convenient than uploading through the preceding dialog.

In this exercise, you have learned how to upload a file to Azure storage through file shares. File shares offer a great mechanism for sharing files using the **Server Message Block** (**SMB**) storage protocol. Working with SMB shares is a common administrative function that you will encounter, and it is widely used in organizations to share information between systems. In the next section, you will learn how to access your storage through the portal.

Accessing Your Azure File Shares from the Portal

In the following example, you will explore how to access your file share and data from the Azure portal. Follow the following steps:

1. Navigate to the Azure portal and select your storage account. Click the `File shares` option on the left menu under `Data storage` and click `test`, as illustrated in the following screenshot:

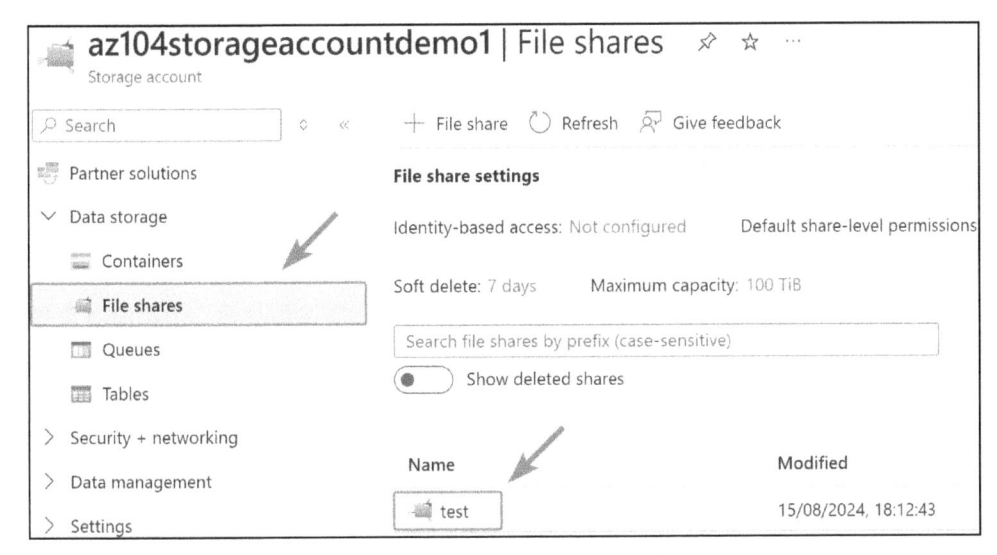

Configuring Azure Files and Azure Blob Storage   225

Figure 7.28: Azure Portal – Viewing the file share

2. Click Browse on the left menu and note the file that you uploaded through Azure Storage Explorer.

Figure 7.29: The Azure portal – Viewing files in the share

3. Another method to navigate files is to use the breadcrumb navigation at the top of the screen. You can navigate back to the respective sections by clicking them; in this example, clicking `az104storageaccountdemo1 | File shares` will take you back to the File shares blade, as illustrated in the following screenshot:

Figure 7.30: The Azure portal – Breadcrumb navigation

In this exercise, you learned how to create a file share and interact efficiently with shares on Azure Files, using Storage Explorer. Storage Explorer simplifies the process of working with Azure storage without requiring you to install or configure additional tools to work with it. With Storage Explorer, you have consistent user experience across devices, even on different operating systems. In the next section, you will learn how to connect an SMB share to a Windows machine.

Connecting an Azure Files Share to Windows Using SMB

You will now learn how to connect an Azure Files share to your Windows machine using the SMB protocol. Follow along with the following steps:

1. In the Azure portal, while in the `File share settings` blade, you can click the ellipsis icon (…) and then `Connect`. Do this now on the `test` folder you made in the previous exercise, as illustrated in the following screenshot:

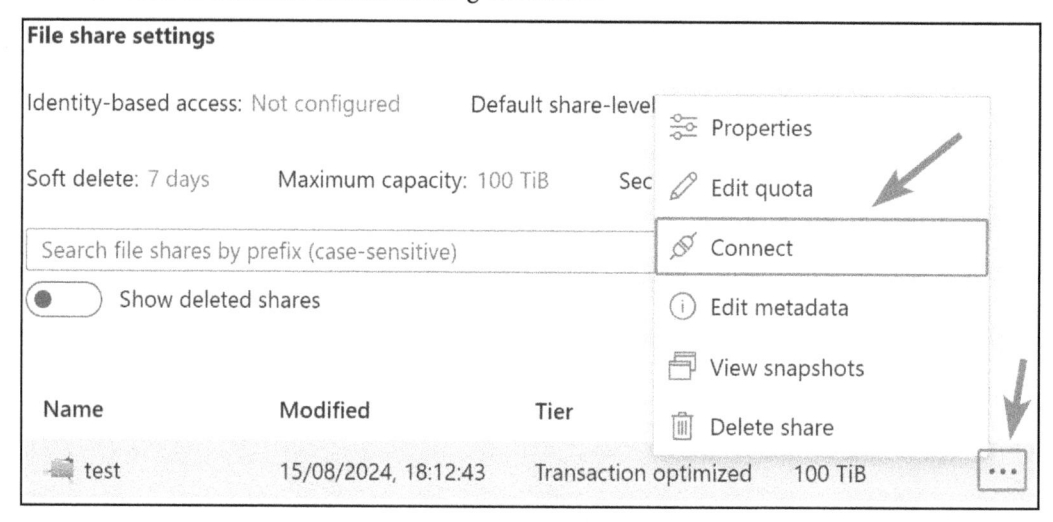

Figure 7.31: Connecting to Azure Files Shares using SMB

2. On the pop-up blade that appears, select a `Drive letter` value; for this exercise, you can leave this as Z. Leave the authentication method as `Storage account key`. Click `Show Script`, and copy then the code in the gray box that appears below the button, as indicated in the following screenshot. Paste this into PowerShell and press `Enter`. Note that this will be, by default, for the Windows operating system.

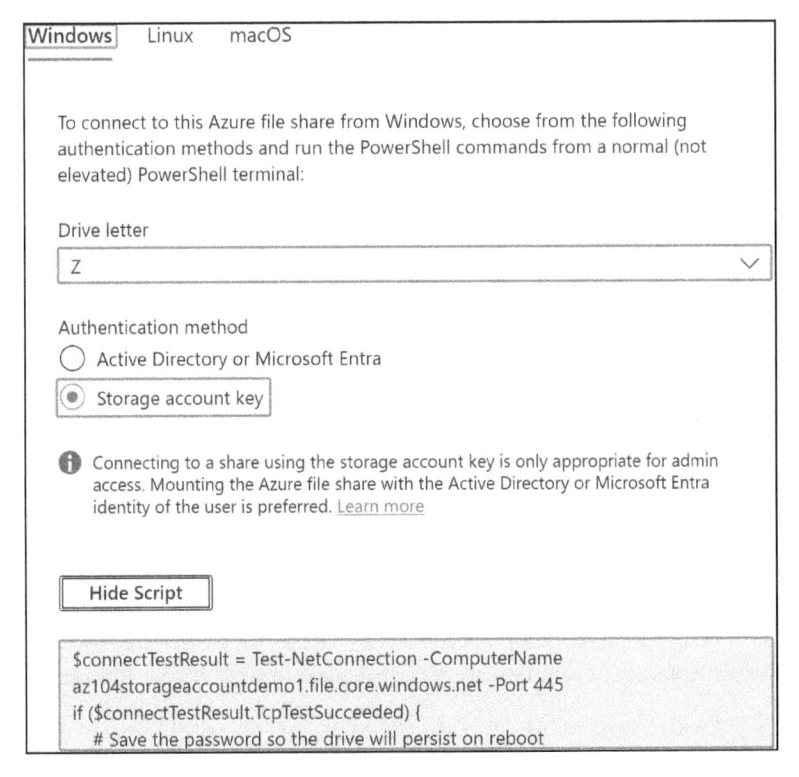

Configuring Azure Files and Azure Blob Storage   227

Figure 7.32: File share – Windows connection script

> **Note**
>
> PowerShell may not allow the running of scripts. You can remove this by setting the execution policy with the following command – `Set-ExecutionPolicy -ExecutionPolicy Unrestricted`. There are other policies that can be applied; visit this URL for more information: https://learn.microsoft.com/en-us/powershell/module/microsoft.powershell.security/set-executionpolicy.

After running this in PowerShell on your Windows computer, note the success message and the new drive, mapping to the Z drive.

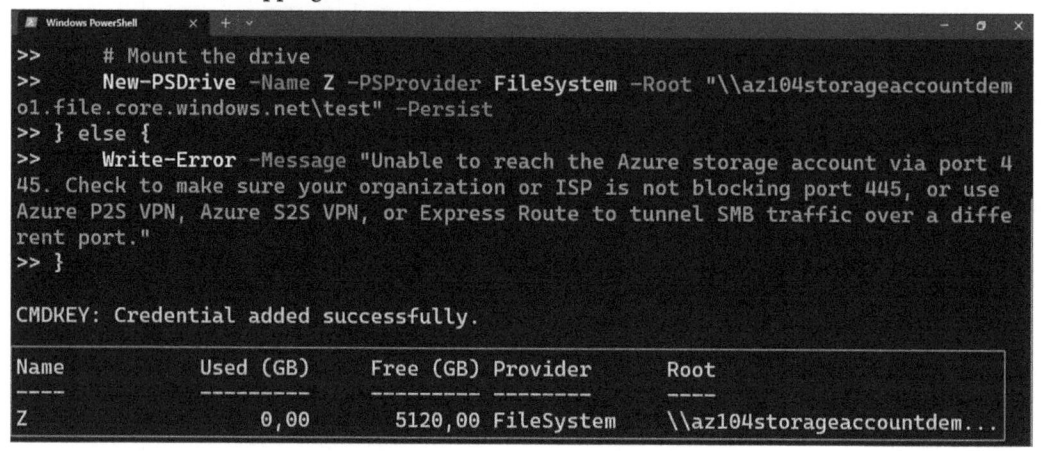

```
>>      # Mount the drive
>>      New-PSDrive -Name Z -PSProvider FileSystem -Root "\\az104storageaccountdem
o1.file.core.windows.net\test" -Persist
>> } else {
>>      Write-Error -Message "Unable to reach the Azure storage account via port 4
45. Check to make sure your organization or ISP is not blocking port 445, or use
Azure P2S VPN, Azure S2S VPN, or Express Route to tunnel SMB traffic over a diffe
rent port."
>> }

CMDKEY: Credential added successfully.

Name            Used (GB)      Free (GB) Provider       Root
----            ---------      --------- --------       ----
Z                    0,00        5120,00 FileSystem     \\az104storageaccountdem...
```

Figure 7.33: File share – Mapping in PowerShell

Note in the preceding screenshot that there is a `-Persist` switch used in the command, and this will persist storage to your operating system, meaning that storage is accessible after reboot.

3. Navigate to the Z:\ drive in the PowerShell window by running `cd z:`, and then press Enter. Type `ls` and press Enter; this will display any files in the current location. Note that you are now connected and can see your uploaded file from the previous exercises.

```
PS C:\Users> cd z:
PS Z:\> ls


    Directory: Z:\


Mode                 LastWriteTime         Length Name
----                 -------------         ------ ----
-a----         2023/08/04     09:27            12 helloworld.txt
```

Figure 7.34: File share – Viewing files in PowerShell

4. Return to Azure Storage Explorer, right-click on the share, and then click `Delete`, as illustrated in the following screenshot. Click `Yes` on the following prompt, and your folder should now be deleted:

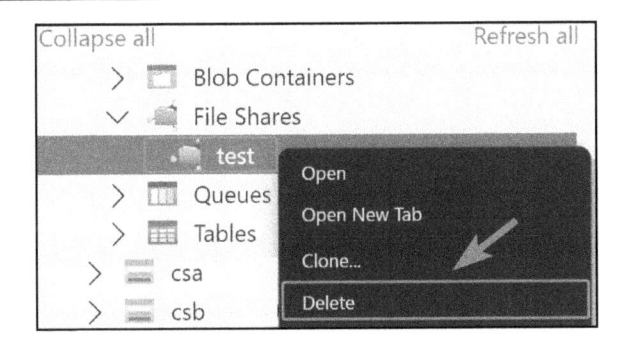

Figure 7.35: Storage Explorer – Deleting a file share

In this exercise, you have learned the following skills pertaining to Azure Files – creating a file share, mapping a file share, uploading and downloading data from a file share, and deleting a file share. Working with file shares is a simple way to share data among several servers and services using the SMB protocol. File shares are organized into a hierarchical structure, similar to most desktop systems, allowing easy navigation and categorization. This makes working with file shares seamless when transitioning from traditional storage mechanisms, such as disks on VMs.

> Note
>
> You may want to mark your file shares as persistent, meaning that after a restart, they will still be there. To achieve this, add the `-persist` switch to your `New-PSDrive` command, as illustrated in *Figure 7.34* as part of *Step 4*.

Configuring Azure Blob Storage

Thanks to Azure Storage Explorer, working with blobs on a storage account is very similar to and just as easy as working on a file share. For this exercise, you will use the Storage Explorer service built into the Azure portal, which has been named `Storage browser`. Since blob storage has no filesystem, it maintains a flat structure; Azure implements logical folders to emulate a filesystem, similar to that of file shares, to make blobs easier to work with. For this exercise, you will create a blob container and upload a file using the portal. Proceed as follows:

1. Navigate to the Azure portal and select the storage account resource you will use for the exercise. From the left menu, select `Storage browser`, and then click on `Blob containers` on the right. Next, click `+ Add container`.

This process is illustrated in the following screenshot:

Figure 7.36: The Azure portal – Creating a blob container

2. Name the container `test`, leave the other settings as their default values, and then click `Create`, as illustrated in the following screenshot:

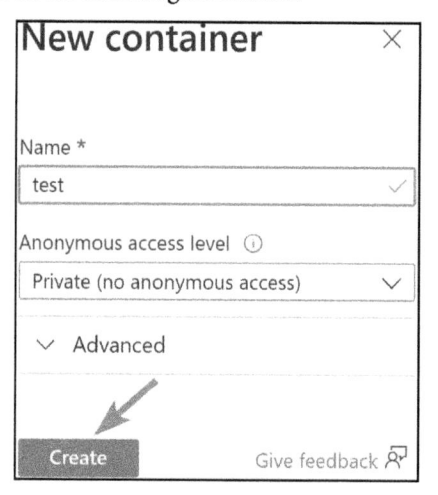

Figure 7.37: A new container

3. You can see in the following screenshot the new container you just created. Click on the new container, and then click `Upload`. From the blade that pops up, click `Browse for files`, select a file, and then click `Upload`:

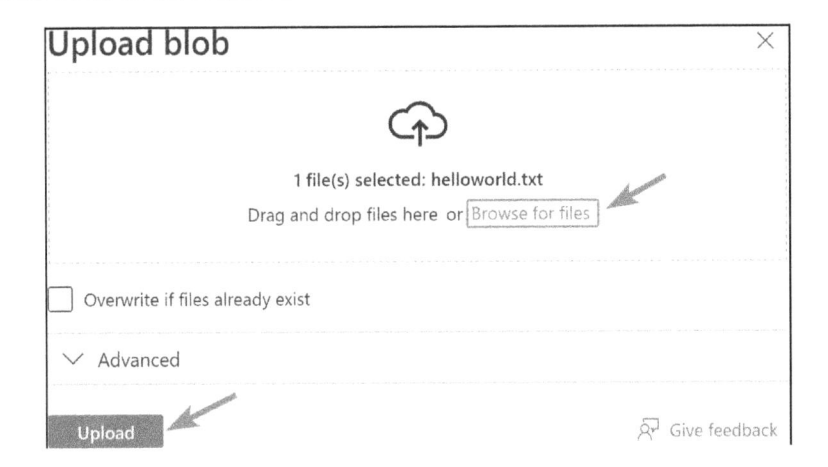

Figure 7.38: Uploading to blob

4. You have now successfully completed an upload and should receive a similar notification, as follows:

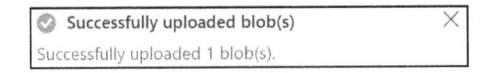

Figure 7.39: Blob upload success notification

In this exercise, you have successfully configured Azure blob storage, which is an effective solution for storing your unstructured data, such as images for a website. In the next section, you will learn how to configure storage tiers.

Configuring Storage Tiers

As mentioned earlier in the chapter, there are four storage tiers available for Azure Blob Storage – namely, **hot**, **cool**, **cold**, and **archive**, which can only be set for blob storage. The storage tier can be configured both during the creation of a storage account – where settings apply to the entire account by default (these will be reflected as inferred) – and at the blob level. Changing blob storage tiers allows more granular control of the performance and reliability characteristics required of each blob, such as in backup-type solutions or for **Disaster Recovery (DR)** scenarios. It is possible to change between tiers at any stage; however, bear in mind that tier changes result in pricing considerations, as the operations incur charges in the changing of tiers. For example, changes from hot to cool or archive, and from cool to archive, will incur write charges (operation and access charges). For changes from archive to cool, cold, or hot, and from cool to hot, read charges will be incurred (operation and access charges).

We will now demonstrate the change of storage from the hot tier to the cool tier in the following activity:

1. Open any storage account on the Azure portal.
2. Upload a file to test your blob storage. For this exercise, you can use the container you created in the previous section.

3. Navigate to your container by selecting `Containers` under `Data storage` for your storage account. Click on your container and then on a folder or file, select the ellipsis icon (…) from the `Overview` section, and click `Change tier` on the pop-up menu, as illustrated in the following screenshot:

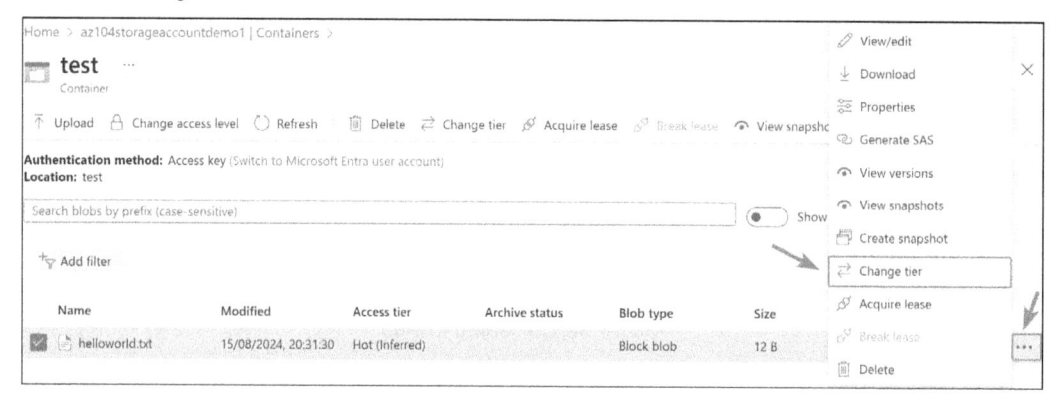

Figure 7.40: Changing the storage access tier

4. Select the desired `Access tier` value and click `Save`. For this exercise, you will select `Cool`, as illustrated in the following screenshot:

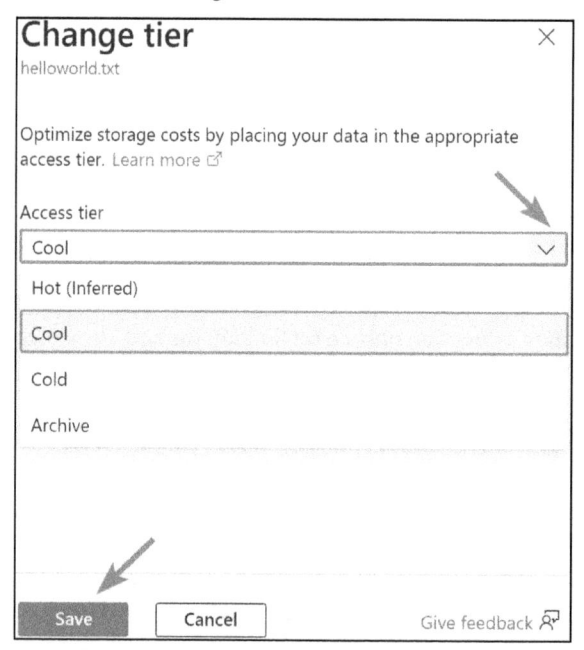

Figure 7.41: Changing the storage access tier to Cool

5. Note in the following screenshot that the change of access tier is now applied to your blob, and it also removes (Inferred) from the tier:

Name	Modified	Access tier
helloworld.txt	15/08/2024, 20:31:30	Cool

Figure 7.42: Storage access tier – Cool

You have completed a storage-tier change in this activity. The same process can be applied to the cold and archive tiers, with the difference being that recovery from the archive tier requires storage to be rehydrated as cold, cool, or hot to be accessible. Changing storage tiers becomes beneficial in cost reduction or performance-improving activities, where the tiers are matched to your desired outcome.

You will now perform an exercise to change storage to the archive tier and restore the archived data, as follows:

1. Select the blob from the previous exercise and proceed to change the storage tier again. This time, select Archive and click Save.
2. Note that if you attempt to access the blob, you will get an informational message noting that the blob is archived. Click X to go to the previous screen, as indicated in the following screenshot:

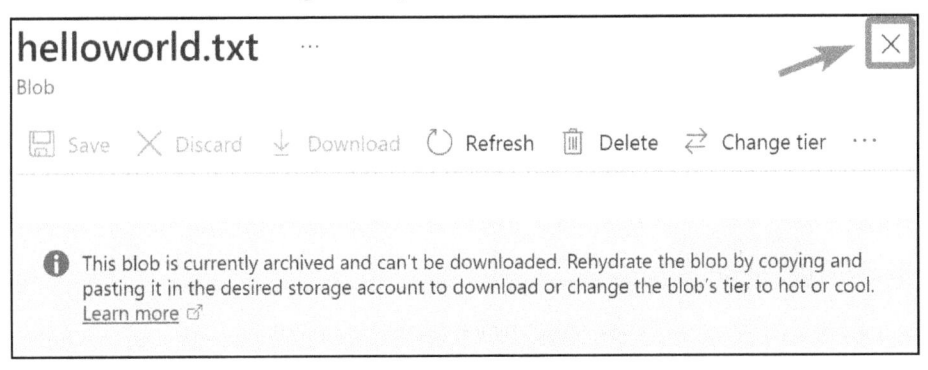

helloworld.txt
Blob

Save   Discard   Download   Refresh   Delete   Change tier

This blob is currently archived and can't be downloaded. Rehydrate the blob by copying and pasting it in the desired storage account to download or change the blob's tier to hot or cool.
Learn more

Figure 7.43: The archive storage tier – An informative message

3. Click `Change tier`, select the `Access tier` value on the pop-up menu, and select a `Rehydrate priority` type. For this demo, use `Hot` and `Standard`, respectively. Note that changing the priority from `Standard` to `High` will incur additional charges and is only required for critical recovery tasks. Click `Save`. The process is illustrated in the following screenshot:

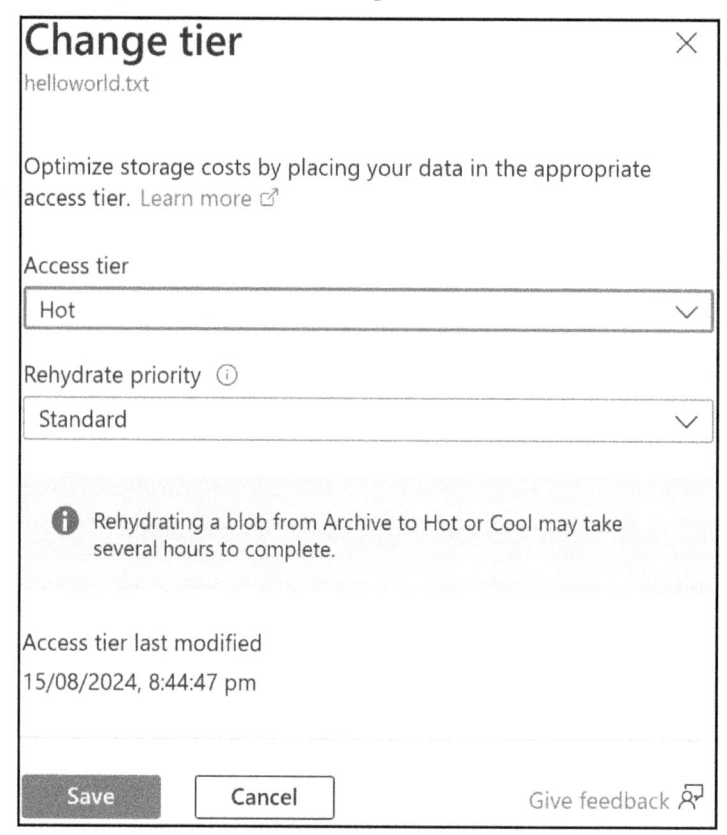

Figure 7.44: Rehydrating archive storage

4. You will need to give this a few hours to rehydrate; Microsoft notes that data can take up to several hours to restore. Once the operation is complete, you will see the `Access tier` type change to the desired tier, as indicated in the following screenshot:

Figure 7.45: Changing a storage tier – A rehydrated blob

You have completed the archive tier change as well as rehydrated data. This marks the end of the section on storage tiers, and you now learn how to manage tiering on blob storage within Azure. As part of the exam objectives, in the next section, you will learn about the **Uniform Resource Locator** (**URL**) construct for storage endpoints.

Azure URL Paths for Storage

The storage services each contain their own endpoint links, relative to the service they provide (such as file or blob), which are labeled as part of the **Fully-qualified Domain Name** (**FQDN**) and begin with the storage account name. You are expected to know the construction of all storage endpoints for the exam. Having this knowledge will also assist you in more easily constructing endpoint FQDNs to connect to your services. These service endpoints can be used through Storage Explorer or programmatically (such as scripts).

The following is a summary of each endpoint by service type:

- **Azure Files**: `https://[storageAccountName].file.core.windows.net`
- **Blob Storage**: `https://[storageAccountName].blob.core.windows.net`
- **Queue Storage**: `https://[storageAccountName].queue.core.windows.net`
- **Table Storage**: `https://[storageAccountName].table.core.windows.net`
- **Data Lake Storage**: `https://[storageAccountName].dfs.core.windows.net`
- **Static website**: `https://[storageAccountName].[zone].web.core.windows.net`

These can also be found on the **Endpoints** menu when browsing the storage account on the portal. There is another set of endpoints that you should be aware of when making use of Azure DNS zone endpoints on the storage account, which are as follows:

- **Azure Files**: `https://[storageAccountName].z[00-50].file.storage.azure.net`
- **Blob Storage**: `https://[storageAccountName].z[00-50].blob.storage.azure.net`
- **Queue Storage**: `https://[storageAccountName].z[00-50].queue.storage.azure.net`
- **Table Storage**: `https://[storageAccountName].z[00-50].table.storage.azure.net`

- **Data Lake Storage**: `https://[storageAccountName].z[00-50].dfs.storage.azure.net`
- **Static website**: `https://[storageAccountName].z[00-50].web.storage.azure.net`

Note the addition of `z[00-50]` in each endpoint, compared to the standard endpoints; this denotes a zone that is automatically selected between 0 and 50 as a double-digit representation, which is why you see `00`.

> **Note**
> At the time of writing, this function is still under preview. It should also be noted that Azure DNS Zone endpoints are only supported for the **Azure Resource Manager** (**ARM**) deployment model.

In this section, you learned about the various URL endpoints for storage accounts, which are useful when accessing endpoints through Storage Explorer or code-driven solutions (such as scripts). In the next section, you will explore two PowerShell scripts – one that creates a blob container in an existing storage account and another that creates a file share in an existing storage account.

PowerShell Scripts

Ensure that the `Az` module is installed, as per the *Technical Requirements* section at the beginning of the chapter.

The following script will create a blob container in an existing storage account (change the parameters to suit your requirements):

```
# First connect your Azure account credentials
Connect-AzAccount

# Parameters
$ResourceGroup = "AZ104-StorageAccounts"
$StorageAccountName = "az104storageaccountdemo1"
$ContainerName = "testps"
$Context = (Get-AzStorageAccount -ResourceGroupName $ResourceGroup
-AccountName $StorageAccountName).Context;

# Create a blob container
New-AzStorageContainer -Name $ContainerName -Context $Context
```

The following script will create a file share in an existing storage account (change the parameters to suit your requirements):

```
# First connect your Azure account credentials
Connect-AzAccount
# Parameters
$ResourceGroup = "AZ104-Chapter6"
$StorageAccountName = "az104chap6acc220072021"
$ShareName= "testfileshare"
$Context = (Get-AzStorageAccount -ResourceGroupName $ResourceGroup
-AccountName $StorageAccountName).Context;
New-AzStorageShare -Name $ShareName -Context $Context
```

You now have some PowerShell scripts to assist you in the daily management of your storage, such as creating file shares and linking servers to the created shares. In this section, you learned how to create and configure file shares and blob storage in Azure, as well as change tiers within Blob Storage.

> **Note**
>
> You are encouraged to read more about this topic by using the following links:
>
> **Storage documentation:** https://learn.microsoft.com/en-us/azure/storage/common/storage-introduction
>
> **Storage API information:** https://learn.microsoft.com/en-us/rest/api/storageservices/
>
> **Storage rehydration:** https://learn.microsoft.com/en-gb/azure/storage/blobs/archive-rehydrate-overview
>
> **Storage access tiers:** https://learn.microsoft.com/en-us/azure/storage/blobs/access-tiers-overview
>
> **Deploying Azure File Sync:** https://learn.microsoft.com/en-us/azure/storage/file-sync/file-sync-deployment-guide

Summary

In this chapter, you learned how to set up file shares and blob storage. You learned how to use Azure Storage Explorer to manage storage accounts. You also explored how to import and export data from Azure using the Azure Data Box service, quickly transferring large amounts of data in and out of Azure. You now have the skills required to implement and configure storage in Azure, as well as identify the appropriate management tool needed for your purposes.

In the next chapter, you will expand upon this knowledge, and you will investigate how to secure storage within Azure, as well as replication and life cycle options for storage.

8

Securing Storage

In the previous chapters, you explored the concept of a storage account, the different options available to you in a storage account, the configuration and management of them, the different tiers available, as well as their associated purposes. You also explored interaction with them and the different types of storage on storage accounts, such as Azure Files. In this chapter, you are going to learn about how to configure network access to storage accounts, how to work with authentication and authorization on storage accounts, and how to copy data. This chapter focuses on one of the most common concepts when it comes to Azure, that is securing storage on the Azure platform. The focus here will be on implementing and managing storage security, such as generating **Shared Access Signature (SAS)** tokens, managing access keys, configuring Azure **Active Directory (AD)** / Entra ID integration, and configuring access to Azure Files.

In this chapter, you are going to cover the following main topics:

- Configuring Network Access to Storage Accounts
- Storage Access Keys
- Working with SAS tokens
- Configuring Access and Authentication

Technical Requirements

To follow along with the hands-on material, you will need the following:

- Azure Storage Explorer must be installed, as discussed in *Chapter 7*, *Copying Data To and From Azure*.
- Access to an Azure subscription with owner or contributor privileges. If you do not have access to one, you can set up a student account for free: https://azure.microsoft.com/en-us/free/.
- **PowerShell 5.1** or later installed on a Windows PC or PowerShell Core 6.x on other operating systems to practice the labs.

- For Windows users, you will need to install **.NET Framework 4.7.2** or later using the following link: `https://learn.microsoft.com/en-us/dotnet/framework/install`.
- Where PowerShell is not installed or available, `https://shell.azure.com` can be used as a browser-based shell.
- Installation of the `Az` PowerShell module, which can be performed by running the following in an administrative PowerShell session:

    ```
    Set-ExecutionPolicy -ExecutionPolicy RemoteSigned -Scope
    CurrentUser
    Install-Module -Name Az -Scope CurrentUser -Repository PSGallery
    -Force
    ```

Configuring Network Access to Storage Accounts

One of the first security concepts you should consider when securing your storage account is to consider how and where your storage account is accessed. You can secure your storage account to a specific set of supported networks, which are granted access by configuring network rules so that only applications that request data over the specific set of networks can access the storage account. When these network rules are effective, the application needs to use proper authorization on the request. This authorization could be through either Entra ID credentials for blobs and queues, a SAS token, or a valid account access key.

In this section, you will explore the various methods of connectivity to your storage. You will learn about how each supports different objectives for your storage and how they introduce security within different boundaries. The first connection type you will explore is public endpoints. This topic explores how your storage is accessed over public network infrastructure (the internet).

Public Endpoints

By default, storage accounts are provisioned with a public endpoint, and thanks to the enhanced control Azure offers, network traffic can be limited to those trusted IP addresses and networks to which you have granted access on Azure. For good security practice, all public access to storage accounts should be set to deny for the public endpoint by default, unless public access is specifically required. The network rules defined for the storage account will apply across all protocols, including **Server Message Block** (**SMB**) and **Representational State Transfer** (**REST**). Therefore, to allow access, an explicit rule will need to be defined. There are additional **exceptions** that can be configured that give you the ability to allow access to Azure services on the trusted services list to the storage account, as well as configuring logging and metric access for any networks (such as for Log Analytics).

Azure Virtual Network (VNet) Integration

There are occasions where you require your traffic to still flow securely from your application whilst allowing certain inbound traffic from over the internet. You may want to explicitly allow only certain VNets within your Azure environment to access this storage account. For instance, imagine that the storage account stored sensitive HR-type data that you wouldn't want employees to see unless granted authorized access. You may, in this scenario, restrict access to IPs within a specific VNet allocated to HR as your first layer of security. This functionality is built into the storage account offering, as mentioned in the *Public Endpoints* section. In the activity that follows, you will explore both restricting public access and VNet access to your storage account.

Configuring Storage Account Network Security

In the following demonstration, you are going to configure network access to the storage account that you created in the previous chapter to restrict network access to a specific network in Azure, as well as allowing your public IP to communicate with the storage account:

1. Navigate to the Azure portal by opening `https://portal.azure.com`.
2. Go to the storage account you created in the previous chapter. If you followed the storage account creation from the last chapter, it should look something like `az104storageaccountdemo1`.
3. On the `Storage account` blade, select `Networking` from the left menu under `Security + networking`.
4. Click `Enabled from selected virtual networks and IP addresses` under `Public network access`. Notice that you have the option to create a new network or choose an existing one. Click `Add new virtual network` under the `Virtual networks` context that has now appeared.

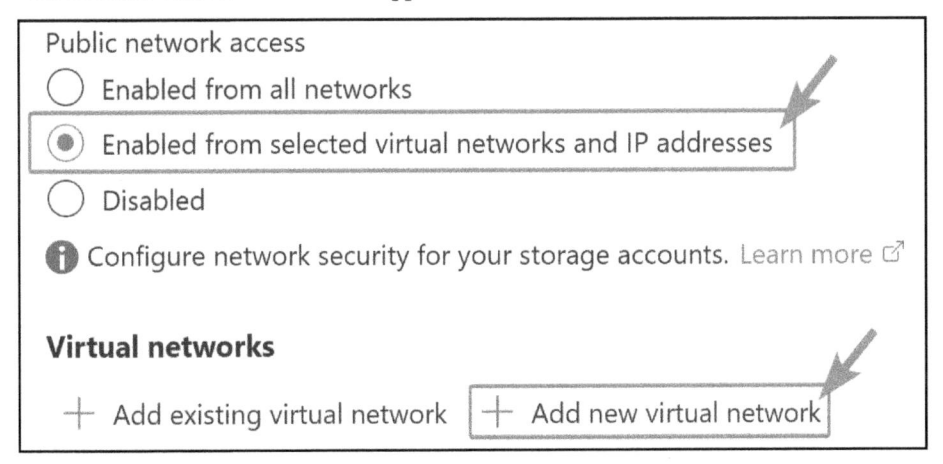

Figure 8.1: Storage accounts – Add a new virtual network

5. Enter information for the `Name` and `Address space` fields, select the `Subscription`, `Resource group`, and `Location` options, and then leave all other settings on their default values. You will need to modify the `Address range` option of the subnet configuration to match the range you have specified for the `Address space` VNet. Click `Create`.

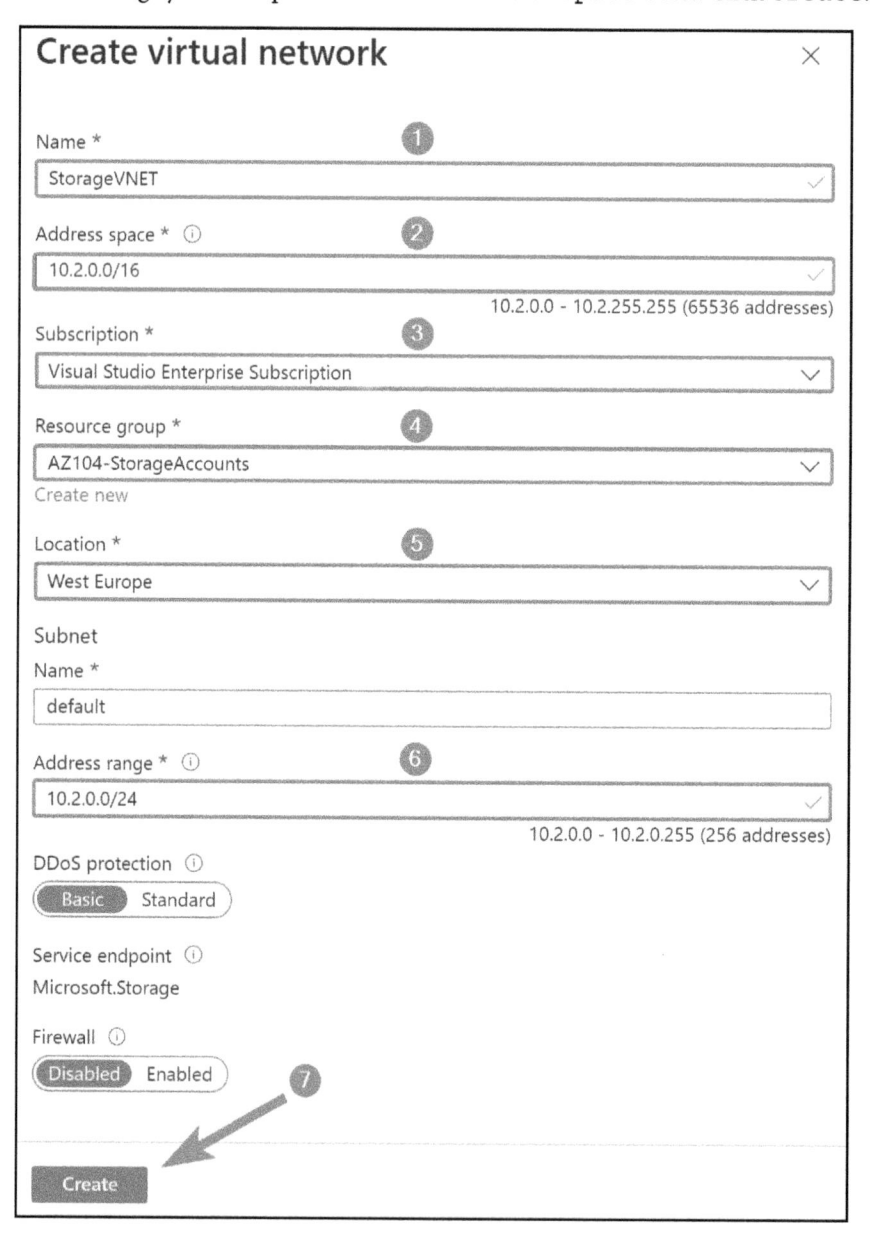

Figure 8.2: Storage accounts – Creating a VNet

> **Note**
> The VNet can be created in a different resource group from your storage account and can even be in a different subscription.

6. Now, scroll down to the `Firewall` section and add the IP addresses or ranges that you would like to specify to add access. For this exercise, you will click the `Add your client IP address` checkbox and then click `Save`.

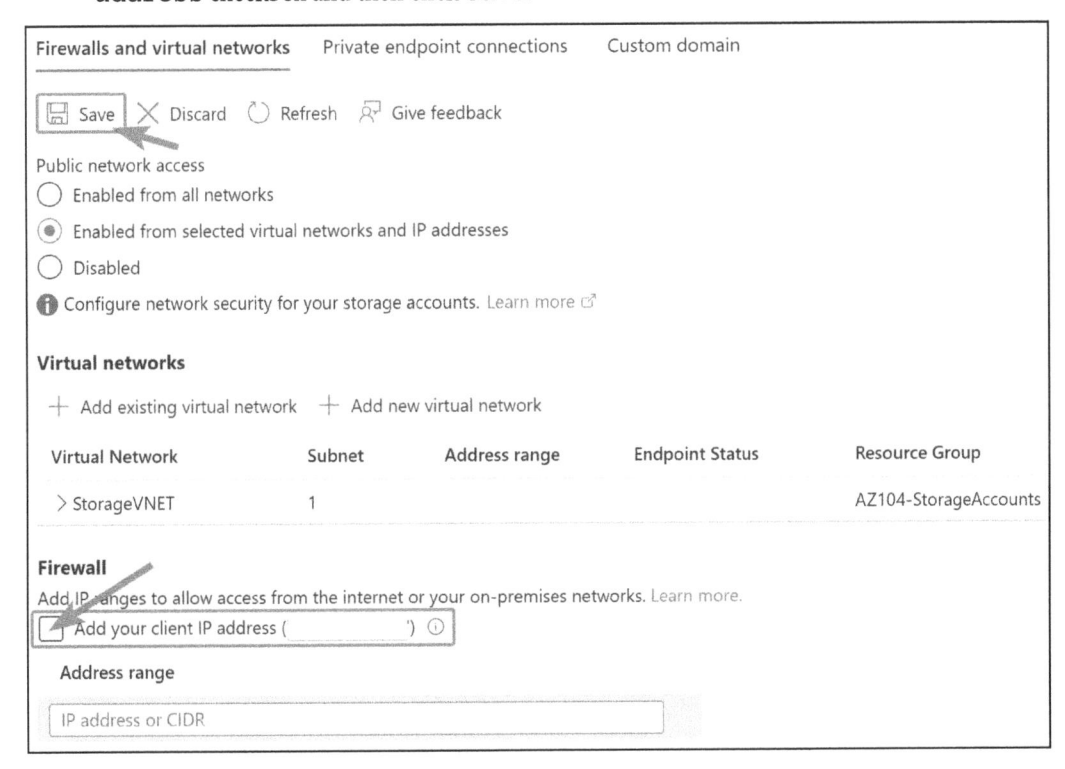

Figure 8.3: Storage accounts – configuring the firewall and VNets

7. You have now locked down access to the specified network and your public IP address. Open `Storage browser` from the left menu for the storage account.

Figure 8.4: Storage browser

8. Open `File shares`, click on any of your folders, and note that it is accessible. You can confirm its functionality by uploading a file to the service.

9. To demonstrate the effect of IP restriction from the firewall configuration, navigate back to the `Networking` blade by clicking `Networking` on the left menu. In the `Firewall` configuration section, click the trash can icon to delete your IP and click `Save`.

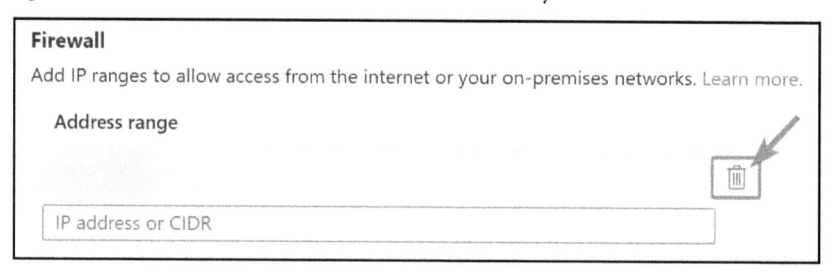

Figure 8.5: Storage accounts – deleting a public IP

10. Now, navigate back to `Storage browser`, click `File shares` once more, and open the share you used previously. Note that you are denied access now.

Figure 8.6: Storage accounts – authorization failure

You have now completed this section on network restrictions on public endpoints. Should you wish to test connectivity with this, you can deploy a **virtual machine** (**VM**) in the same VNet as the storage account and connect to the storage account from inside the VM. In the next section, you will learn about private endpoints.

Private Endpoints

Private endpoints provide a mechanism for Azure Storage accounts to have a private interface for a storage account and can be used to eliminate public access. They provide enhanced security over a public endpoint because they prevent unauthorized access by not being exposed publicly. When implementing a private endpoint, a **network interface card** (**NIC**) is associated with the storage account and will be placed in a VNet. The traffic for the storage account will traverse the VNet with which it is associated. Private endpoints are provided through a service called **Private Link**.

> **Note**
>
> For scenarios requiring advanced security, you should disable all public access to the storage account and enable a private endpoint. All traffic should then be redirected through private network connectivity and ideally through a firewall for inspection and analysis. To further restrict and prevent unauthorized access, you can implement a **network security group** (**NSG**) on the subnet layer (although not always required, it is a double safety mechanism). Remember, when routing traffic, you will require route tables to create custom **user-defined routes** (**UDRs**). This topic will be discussed in *Chapter 16, Implementing and Managing Virtual Networking*.

In the following demonstration, you will attach a private endpoint to a storage account:

1. Navigate to the Azure portal by opening `https://portal.azure.com`.
2. Go to the storage account you created in the previous chapter.
3. On the `Storage account` blade, select `Networking` from the left menu under the `Security + networking` context.
4. On the tab menu bar, select the `Private endpoint connections` tab and click + `Private endpoint`.

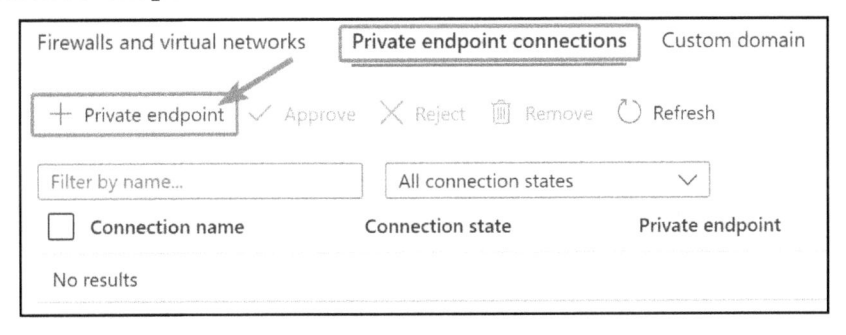

Figure 8.7: Storage accounts – Private endpoint connections

5. On the new blade that opens, on the `Basics` tab, select the `Subscription` and `Resource group` options, enter `az104privateendpoint` for the Name field and `az104privateendpoint-nic` for the `Network Interface` Name field, and select a Region option. Click `Next : Resource >`.

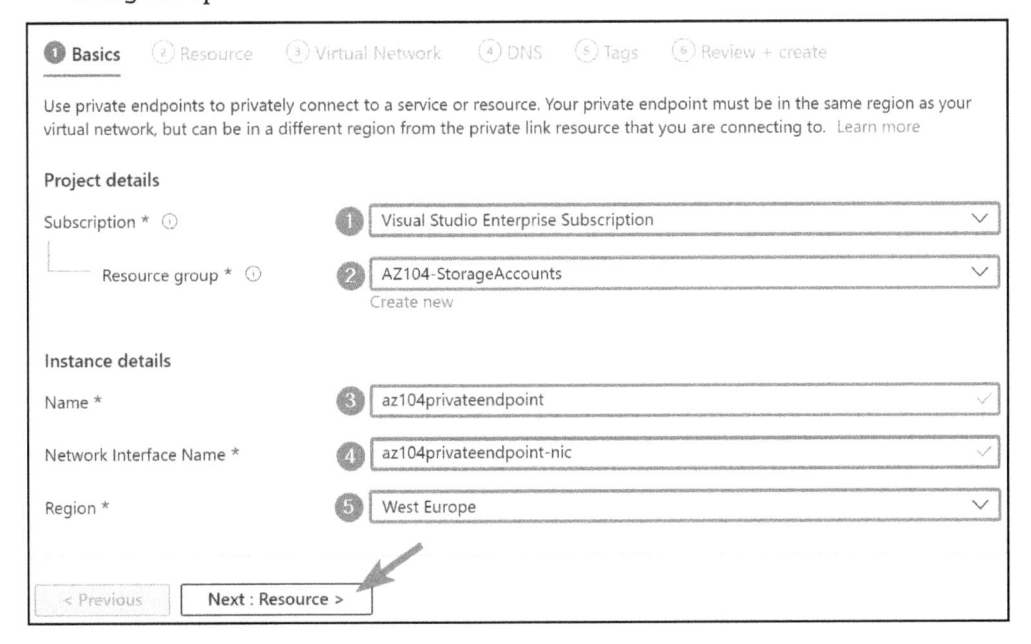

Figure 8.8: Private endpoint connections – the Basics tab

Securing Storage

6. On the `Resource` tab, select the target sub-resource. This will be the type of storage being consumed from the storage account. Select `file`. Click `Next : Virtual Network >`.

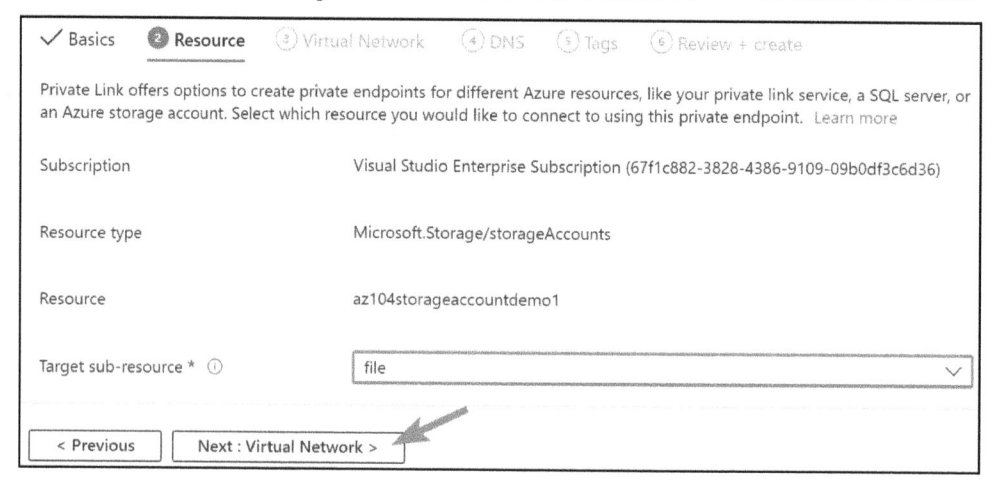

Figure 8.9: Private endpoint connections – the Resource tab

7. On the `Virtual Network` tab, enter all the networking configurations for the private endpoint. Select your `Virtual network` and `Subnet` options. Do not set up `Network policy for private endpoints`; for `Private IP configuration`, you can leave the default option of `Dynamically allocate IP address`. Lastly, you can also skip the `Application security group` setting. Click `Next : DNS >`.

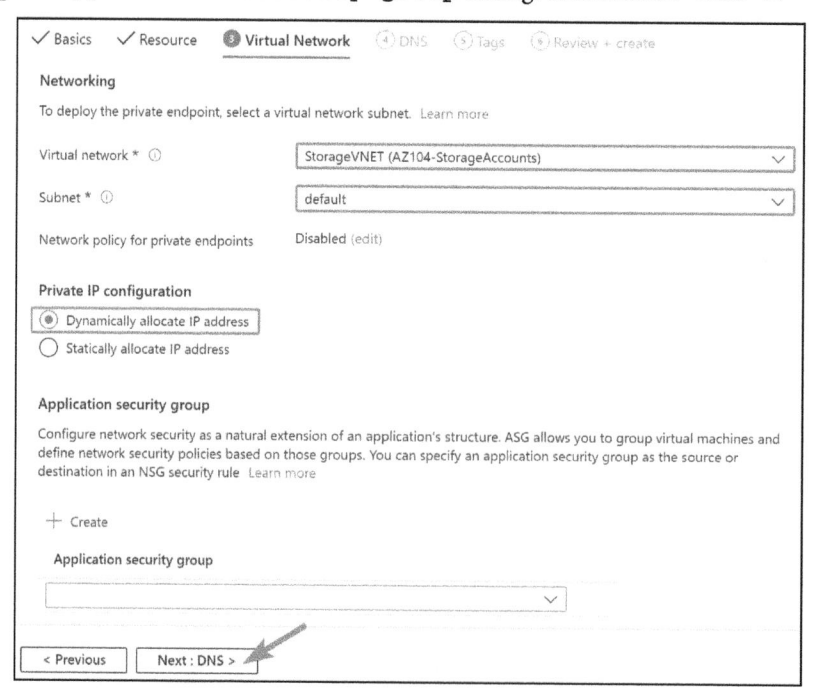

Figure 8.10: Private endpoint connections – the Virtual Network tab

8. For the `Integrate with private DNS zone` option, select No. A private **Domain Name System (DNS)** allows you to create a DNS entry for the private endpoint you are using on the service. This will be hosted within the private DNS zone you provision in Azure. Private DNS in Azure provides a mechanism for managing your own DNS entries hosted by Azure. You will learn about this in *Chapter 16, Implementing and Managing Virtual Networking*. Click `Next: Tags >`.

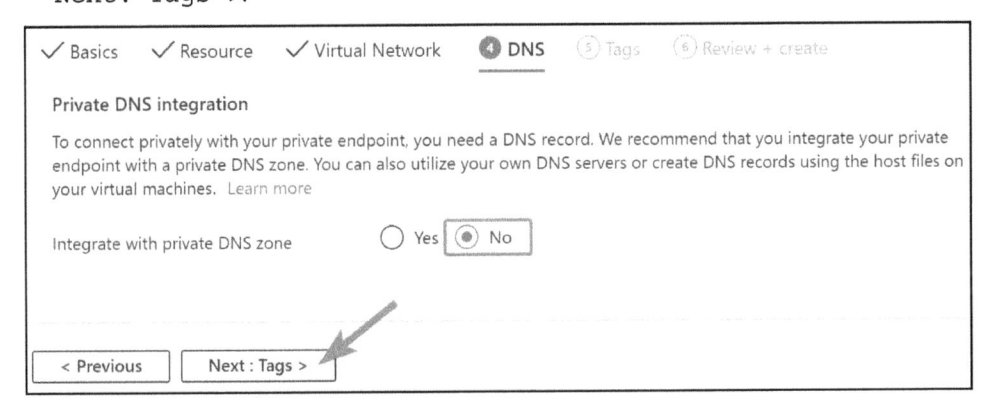

Figure 8.11: Private endpoint connections – DNS

9. Click `Review + create`.
10. Once validation has passed, click `Create`.

You have now successfully deployed a private endpoint. That brings this section to an end. You are encouraged to play with this more in the next chapter, where you can follow along with a lab deployment. You will now learn about network routing on a storage account.

> **Note**
> Note that a private endpoint can also be provisioned on the creation of a storage account.

Network Routing from Storage Accounts

The default network routing preference option chosen for storage accounts and most Azure services will be for the Microsoft network. This is a high-performance, low-latency global connection to all services within Azure and serves as the fastest delivery service to any consumer service or user. This is due to Microsoft configuring several points of presence within their global network. The closest endpoint to a client is always chosen. This option costs slightly more than traversing the internet. If you select `Internet routing`, then traffic will be routed in and out of the storage account outside the Microsoft network.

Securing Storage

The following screenshot shows the setting on the `Firewall and virtual networks` tab of the `Networking` blade for your storage account:

Network Routing

Determine how you would like to route your traffic as it travels from its source to an Azure endpoint. Microsoft routing is recommended for most customers.

Routing preference *
- ◉ Microsoft network routing
- ○ Internet routing

Publish route-specific endpoints
- ☑ Microsoft network routing
- ☐ Internet routing

Figure 8.12: Storage account – routing configuration

You will note there is also an option to publish route-specific endpoints for the storage account. This can be used in scenarios where you might want the default network routing option to be configured for the Microsoft network, while providing internet endpoints or vice versa. These endpoints can be found in the `Endpoints` section of your storage account, as shown in the following screenshot:

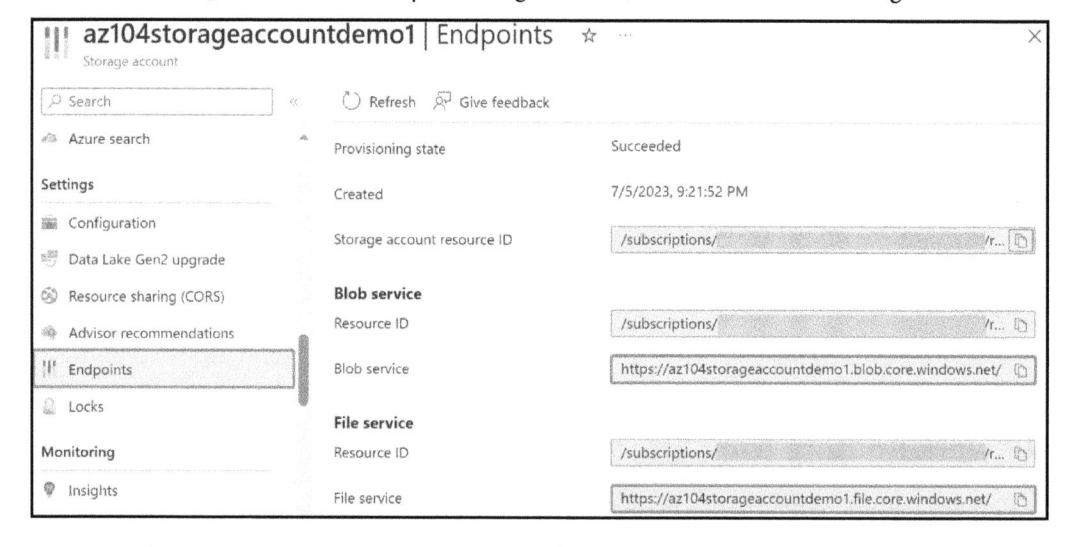

Figure 8.13: Storage account – Endpoints

From this list, you may copy the endpoints that are required. Now that you have briefly observed the configuration options available for network routing on storage accounts. In the next section, you will explore a PowerShell script for configuring a private endpoint on a storage account.

PowerShell Scripts

The following script creates a new private endpoint that is associated with an existing storage account. It is linked to the defined VNet and links to the first subnet within that VNet:

```
# Update the variables below according to your deployment
$storageAccountName = "az104storageaccountdemo1"
$privateEndpointName = "az104privateendpoint"
$resourceGroup = "AZ104-StorageAccounts"
$region = "westeurope"
$vNetName = "StorageVNET"

# Create the Storage Account
$storageAccount = Get-AzStorageAccount -ResourceGroupName
"$resourceGroup" -Name "$storageAccountName"

## Disable private endpoint network policy ##
$vnet = Get-AzVirtualNetwork -ResourceGroupName "$resourceGroup" -Name
"$vNetName"
$vnet.Subnets[0].PrivateEndpointNetworkPolicies="Disabled"
$vnet | Set-AzVirtualNetwork

## Create private endpoint
$privateEndpointConnection = New-AzPrivateLinkServiceConnection -Name
'myPrivateConnection' -PrivateLinkServiceId ($storageAccount.Id)
-GroupId 'file';
New-AzPrivateEndpoint -ResourceGroupName "$resourceGroup" -Name
"$privateEndpointName" -Location "$region" -Subnet ($vnet.Subnets[0])
-PrivateLinkServiceConnection $privateEndpointConnection
```

Once this code has been run, you will have successfully created a private endpoint for your storage account. It will be linked to the VNet and subnet you defined. You can navigate to the private endpoint to discover its private IP address, which will be used for internal communication to the service going forward.

To navigate to the private endpoint, follow these steps:

1. From the storage account, navigate to the `Networking` blade.
2. At the top of the screen, click the `Private endpoint connections` tab.
3. Click the private endpoint name to navigate to its configuration.
4. Click the DNS configuration from the left menu.
5. Note the IP address listed under `Customer Visible FQDNs`; this is your private IP.

That brings an end to this section. You have learned about VNet integration for the storage accounts and the different options available. In the next section, you will explore managing access keys.

> **Note**
>
> You are encouraged to read up further on this topic by reading the following links:
>
> **Configure Azure Storage firewalls and virtual networks:** `https://learn.microsoft.com/en-us/azure/storage/common/storage-network-security`
>
> **Use private endpoints for Azure Storage:** `https://learn.microsoft.com/en-us/azure/storage/common/storage-private-endpoints`
>
> **Private Link resources:** `https://learn.microsoft.com/en-us/azure/private-link/private-endpoint-overview`

Storage Access Keys

Storage access keys are like passwords for your storage account and Azure generates two of these when you provision your account, namely a primary and secondary key. Just like passwords, they need to be changed from time to time to ensure you are not compromised through potential leakage (such as in code files). Whilst this scenario may feel uncommon, it is a very real risk, and for this reason, it is best to change your keys every few months. This practice is referred to as **key rotation**. In the following section, you will run through an example of accessing your keys and how to renew them.

Managing Access Keys

In this demonstration, you will explore how to view access keys as well as how to renew them:

1. Navigate to the Azure portal by opening `https://portal.azure.com`.
2. Go to a storage account.
3. On the left menu for the storage account, click `Access keys` under the `Security + networking` context. You will notice `key1` and `key2`, as well as the last rotated date for each specified.
4. To copy the access keys, a two-step process will be performed. First, click on `Show` next to the relevant key you want to view the key details for.

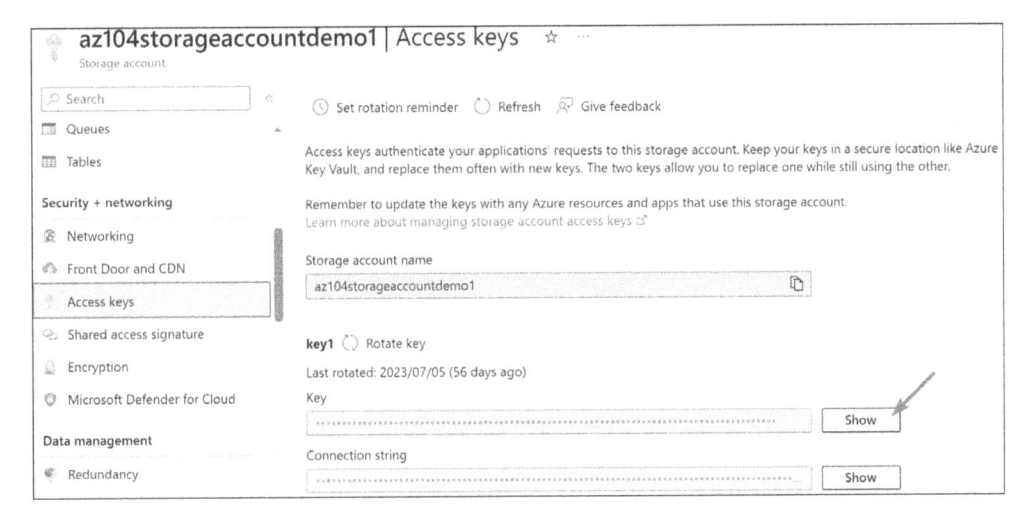

Figure 8.14: Show keys

5. Then, copy the corresponding key for the storage account by clicking the clipboard icon.

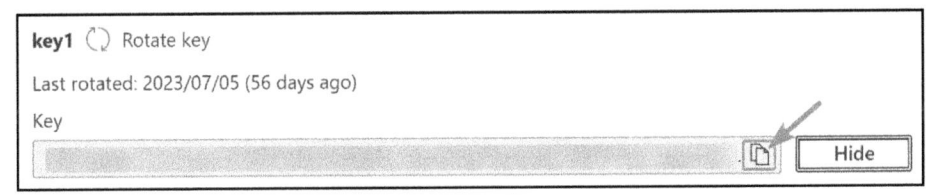

Figure 8.15: Copying an access key

Now that you know how to access the storage access keys, you will learn how to rotate keys in the following exercise.

Rotating Storage Access Keys

In this exercise, you will learn how to rotate storage access keys using the Azure portal:

1. Navigate to the Azure portal by opening `https://portal.azure.com`.
2. Go to a storage account.
3. On the left menu for the storage account, click `Access keys` under the `Security + networking` context. Click `Rotate key` next to `key2`.

Figure 8.16: The Rotate key option

4. A notification will come up to confirm that you want to regenerate the key. Click Yes.

Regenerate access key

The current key will become immediately invalid and is not recoverable. Do you want to regenerate access key 'key2'?

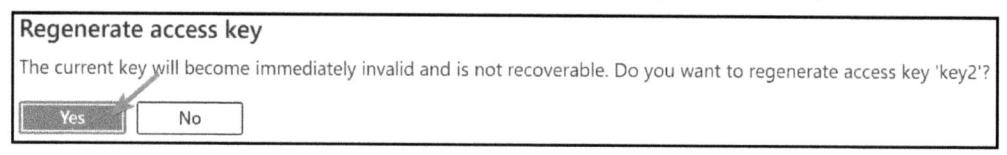

Yes   No

Figure 8.17: Regenerate access key

5. Repeat the process for `key1`.

You have now completed key rotation for a storage account. This ensures unauthorized access is prevented on the storage keys and it is best practice to rotate these keys every **90 days**. As a recommendation, `key2` should be rotated first and updated for any relevant applications and services, then followed by `key1`. This process ensures that the primary key (`key1`) is not directly impacting all business-critical services and causing unnecessary downtime. The rotation process should still be properly planned and maintained through an appropriate change control process within your organization.

> **Note**
>
> As a best practice, keys should be rotated every 90 days to prevent unauthorized exposure to the account. This will also limit the potential attack window for compromised SAS tokens.

In the next section, you will explore SAS tokens.

Working with SAS Tokens

SAS tokens are secure access tokens that provide delegated access to resources on your storage account. The storage service confirms the SAS token is valid in order to grant access. The construct of a SAS token includes the permissions granted on the token, the date validity, and the signing key for the storage account. When creating a SAS token, several items that govern the process of granting access at a granular level need to be considered. They are as follows:

- Resource types that the client might use
- Permissions on the resource types that are required
- The period the SAS key should function for

Types of SAS

There are three types of SAS supported by Azure Storage:

- **User-delegated SAS**: This is a SAS token that is secured by Entra ID credentials.
- **Account SAS**: An account SAS is created and secured using a storage key. The permissions granted can span several services (blob, file, queue, and table), as well as accessing permissions for the chosen services.
- **Service SAS**: A service SAS is identical to an account SAS except that it is limited to a single service. There are limitations to some read, write, and delete operations for a service SAS that the account SAS has higher privileges to allow.

Forms of SAS

SAS tokens can take two forms, as detailed here:

- **Ad hoc SAS**: This SAS token is created as needed where permissions are chosen along with accessible services in alignment with the type of SAS used. The configuration is specified in the SAS URI. This is generally used for scenarios where quick access is required for a temporary period. SAS tokens cannot be managed after being issued. User-delegated SAS and account SAS can only be provisioned as an ad hoc SAS.
- **Service SAS with stored access policy**: This form of SAS token is more secure and enhances the functionality upon that which an ad hoc SAS token delivers. Service SAS tokens can be managed after being issued and are manufactured to comply with policies configured in the stored access policy. SAS tokens can be modified and deleted using a stored access policy.

> **Note**
> Microsoft advises the best security practice is to use Entra ID credentials whenever possible.

Now that you understand the core components of a SAS token, you will explore some exercises for creating and managing SAS tokens.

Generating SAS Tokens

In this demonstration, you will learn how to create a SAS token for sharing access to a storage account:

1. Navigate to the Azure portal by opening https://portal.azure.com.
2. Go to a storage account.

3. On the left menu for the storage account, click `Shared access signature` under the `Security + networking` context. Create a new SAS key by selecting the `Container` and `Service` options on the `Allowed resource types` options list. Change the `Allowed services` option list as desired.

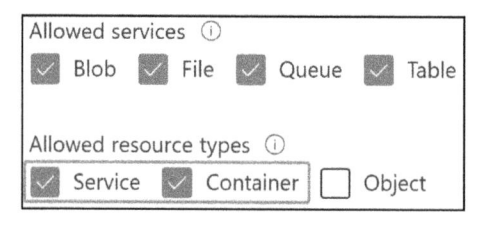

Figure 8.18: SAS permissions

4. Next, select the permissions you would like to grant under `Allowed permissions`.

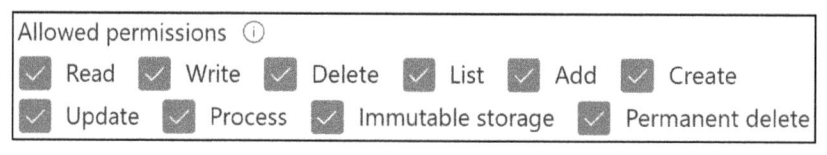

Figure 8.19: SAS – Allowed permissions

5. `Blob versioning permissions` allows you to have multiple copies of files if you need to restore against any changes made. This may be something that causes risk by allowing users to delete versions. For this exercise, you may leave this as `Enabled`. For `Allowed blob index permissions`, you can leave the default configuration too.

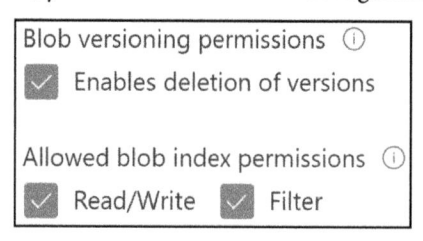

Figure 8.20: SAS blob and index permissions

6. Set the time for `Start` to five minutes before your current time, and `End` to at least two hours from now. Also, select your relevant time zone.

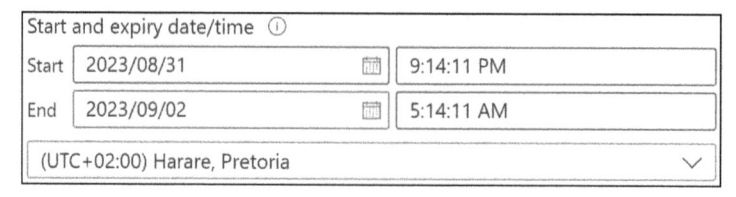

Figure 8.21: SAS Start and expiry date/time

7. For the networking configuration settings, configure the allowed IP address if you would like to restrict access to specific IP addresses. For this exercise, you may leave this blank, meaning that all IP addresses are allowed. For the `Allowed protocols` option, please select `HTTPS only`. Finally, for `Preferred routing tier`, you may leave the default setting, normally being `Basic (default)`.

Figure 8.22: SAS network settings

8. Finally, you can select a `Signing key` option; leave this as the default, but just know that you can choose `key1` or `key2`. Then, click `Generate SAS and connection string`. Copy the connection string – you are only ever presented with this once.

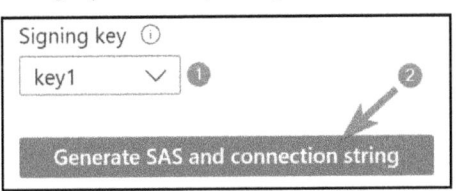

Figure 8.23: SAS signing key

9. Once the SAS and connection strings are generated you can copy the appropriate ones you would like to use. This screen is only shown once, so copy the relevant details. For this exercise, copy the `Connection string` and the `SAS token`.

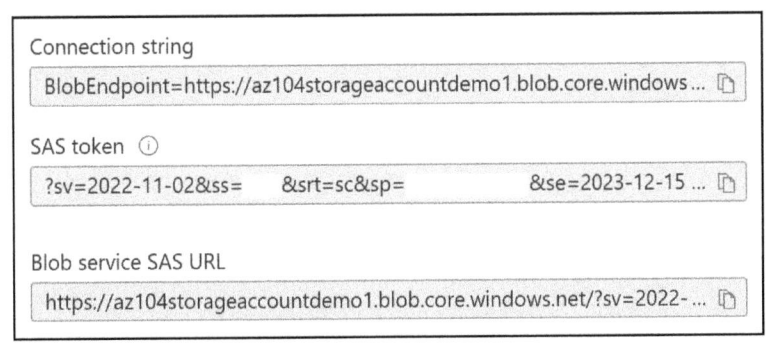

Figure 8.24: SAS URLs and connection string

Securing Storage

10. Open `Microsoft Azure Storage Explorer` from your desktop computer, then click the `Open Connect Dialog` button.

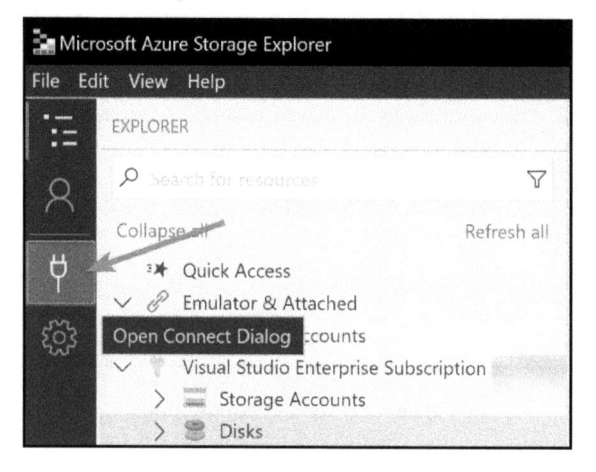

Figure 8.25: Open Connect Dialog

11. Click `Storage account or service`, select `Connection string` as your connection method, and then click `Next`.

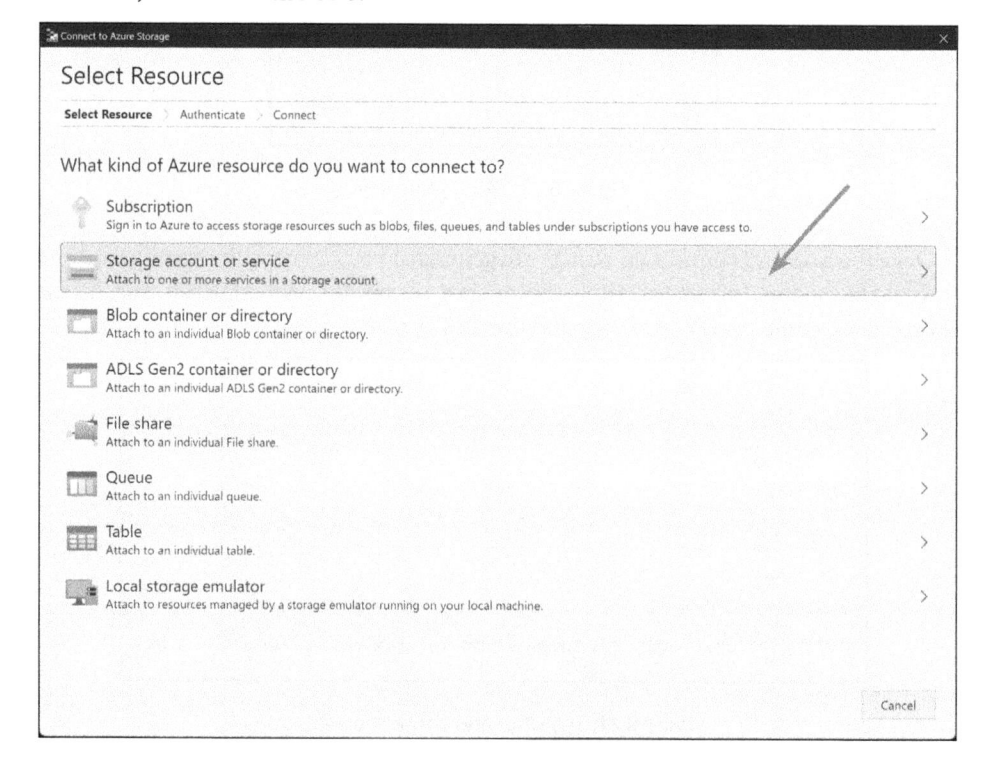

Figure 8.26: Storage Explorer – Storage account or service

12. Paste the connection string you copied earlier into the `Connection string` dialog. Change the `Display name` text if desired, such as `StorageAccountDisplayName`. Click `Next`.

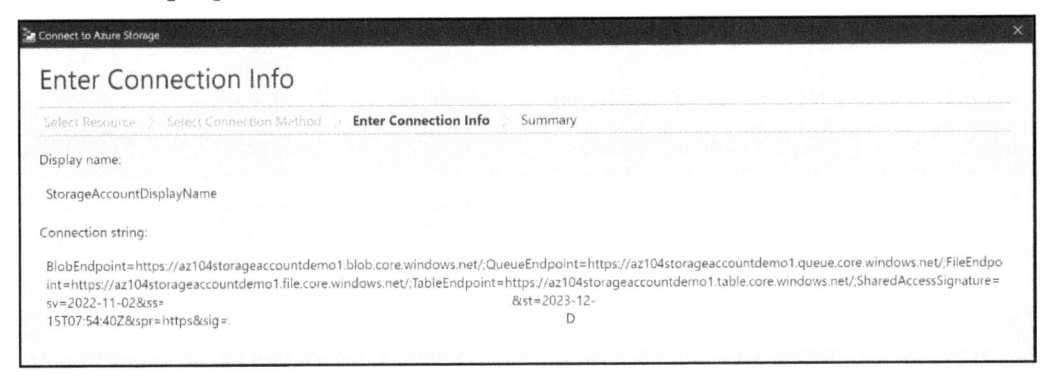

Figure 8.27: Storage Explorer – Connection string

13. You will be presented with a summary page noting all endpoints and other details. Click `Connect`.
14. You will get a success message, as follows:

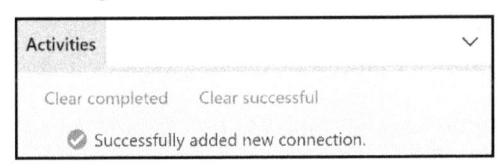

Figure 8.28: Storage Explorer – success message

15. Navigate through the `EXPLORER` view to the `Storage Accounts` section, click the arrow to open all accounts, and notice your storage account connection. To view all the storage items related to your account, click the arrow next to your account, as per the following screenshot.

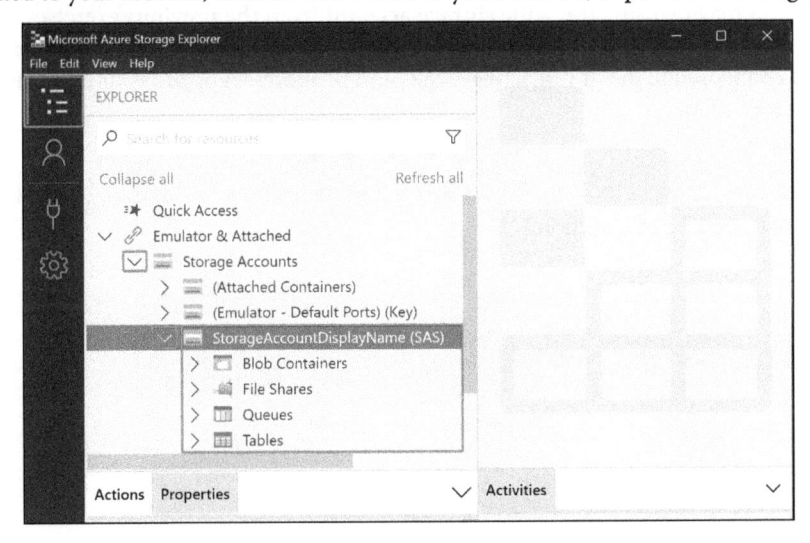

Figure 8.29: Storage Explorer – account navigation

You now know how to generate a SAS token and connect to a storage account using the token. In the next section, you will explore storage access policies and how these enhance the concept of SAS tokens.

> **Note**
> Allowed protocols should be limited to HTTPS on the SAS creation for enhanced security. The SAS start and end time should be limited as far as possible to the necessary time required for access.

Stored Access Policies

A **stored access policy** provides an additional layer of control over SAS by introducing policies for managing the SAS token. SAS tokens can now be configured for a start and expiry time with the ability to edit and revoke access after they have been issued. This added functionality can prove to be tremendously useful when it comes to managing access to your storage accounts in the future using SAS-based access. Without access policies, your provisioned SAS access will be available for the defined period you had at issue time unless you change the signing keys for the storage account.

Creating a Stored Access Policy

The following steps demonstrate the process for creating a storage access policy on a container:

1. Navigate to the Azure portal by opening `https://portal.azure.com`.
2. Navigate to your storage account, click `Containers` on the left-hand menu from under the `Data storage` context, and click on a container. If you don't have one, then create one for this exercise.

> **Note**
> Some of you may be using the same storage account from the previous exercises and may discover that you don't have access to the containers. For this exercise, you can either remove the VNet configuration that is restricting VNets and IP addresses or add your client IP address to the firewall rules.

3. Click `Access policy` from the left menu, and then click `+ Add policy` in the `Stored access policies` section.

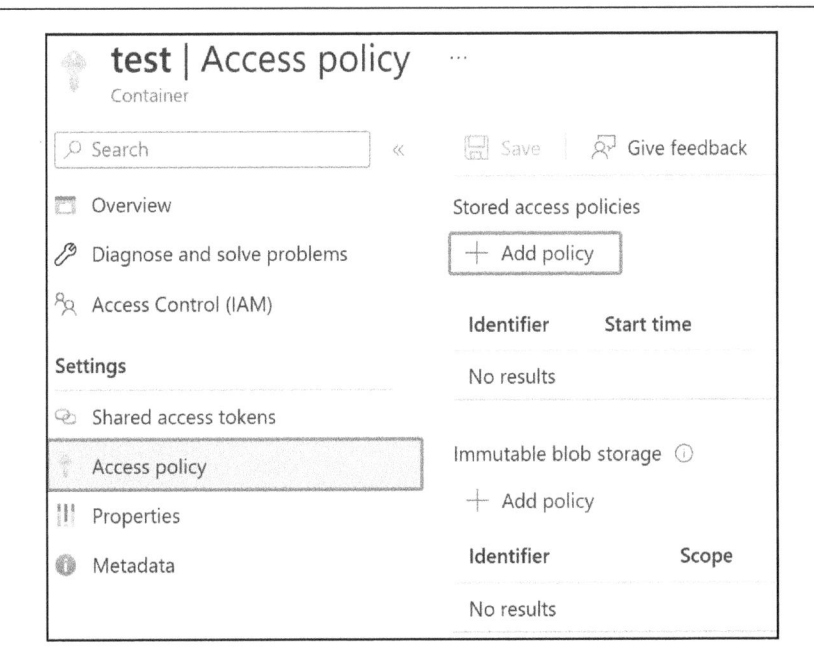

Figure 8.30: Storage account – Access policy

4. Enter a value for the `Identifier` field, which will be representative of the name of the policy and select the desired permissions. For this exercise, you may select the `Read` and `List` permissions. Enter the desired start and expiry date and time values. Click OK. Finally, click `Save` at the top of the screen.

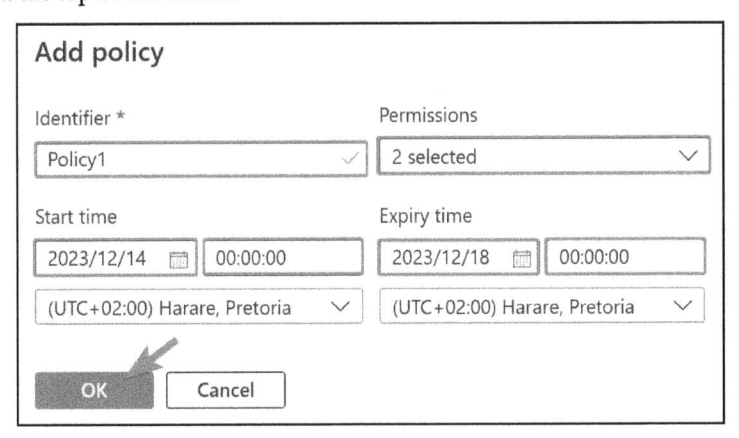

Figure 8.31: Storage account – Add policy

You have now learned how to create a storage access policy. Next, you will learn how to edit an existing policy.

Editing a Storage Access Policy

To edit an existing policy on your storage access, perform the following steps:

1. Navigate to the Azure portal by opening `https://portal.azure.com`.
2. Navigate to your storage account, click `Containers` on the left-hand menu, and click on a container.
3. Click `Access policy` from the left menu under the `Settings` context, and click the ellipsis (...) icon of the identifier that matches the name you gave to the policy you defined in the previous exercise. Click `Edit`.

Identifier	Start time	Expiry time		Permissions	
Policy1	14/12/2023, 12:00:00 am	18/12/2	Edit		...
Immutable blob storage			Delete		

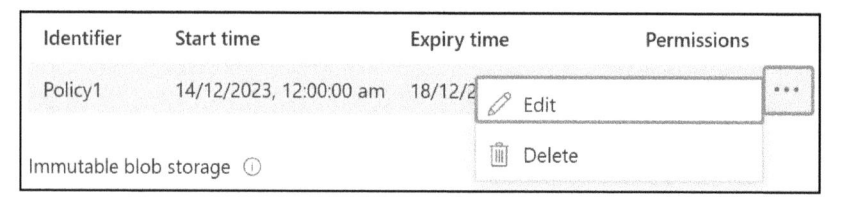

Figure 8.32: Storage account – modifying an existing access policy

4. Note that you may modify the `Identifier`, `Start time`, `Permissions`, and `Expiry time` settings. Update your settings as desired and click OK.

You have now learned how to modify an existing policy. Next, you will learn how to remove a storage access policy.

Removing an Existing Storage Access Policy

Follow the given steps to remove an existing access policy:

1. Navigate to the Azure portal by opening `https://portal.azure.com`.
2. Navigate to your storage account, click `Containers` on the left-hand menu, and click on a container.
3. Click `Access policy` from the left menu under the `Settings` context and click the ellipsis (...) icon of the identifier that matches the name given in the previous step. Click `Delete`.

Identifier	Start time	Expiry time		Permissions	
Policy1	14/12/2023, 12:00:00 am	18/12/2	Edit		...
Immutable blob storage			Delete		

Figure 8.33: Storage account – deleting an access policy

You have now learned how to delete an access policy. That concludes this section, where you have learned what SAS tokens are and how they work. You have also explored storage access policies as well as how these enhance the management of SAS tokens. In the following section, you are provided with additional reading material to learn more if further assistance is required.

> **Note**
>
> You are encouraged to read up further on the topic by using the following links:
>
> **Manage storage account access keys:** https://learn.microsoft.com/en-us/azure/storage/common/storage-account-keys-manage
>
> **Automation of storage access key rotation:** https://learn.microsoft.com/en-us/azure/key-vault/secrets/tutorial-rotation-dual

In this section, you learned about SAS tokens, the different types you get (user delegation SAS, service SAS, and account SAS), the forms they can be consumed in (ad hoc SAS and service SAS with stored access policy), and how to generate them. You also learned about stored access policies and how they provide an additional layer of control over SAS by introducing policies for managing SAS tokens. In the next section, you will learn about the access and authentication features available to storage accounts and configure them on a storage account in an exercise.

Configuring Access and Authentication

In this section, you will explore the various methods of identity-based authentication available to Azure storage accounts. **Authentication** is the function of verifying an identity, typically through a process of verifying some form of credentials (such as username and password, biometrics, or security tokens). By instituting good authentication practices, you can improve security. Integration into Entra ID or AD is important in leveraging existing and known identities into applications and services as opposed to having unknown users potentially accessing your resources.

Azure identities and governance is a core aspect of the AZ104 administrator exam, and it is important to know about the various authentication options available and how to generally configure these settings. After completing the theoretical sections, you will experience setting up **Active Directory Domain Services** (**AD DS**) and integrating this into a file share. The practical exercise is more of a real-world scenario that you will experience and not requisite for passing but it is beneficial in your knowledge and role.

Storage accounts provide several identity-based authentication methods as listed in the following list:

- AD DS, which is your typical on-premises AD environment
- **Microsoft Entra Directory Domain Services (Microsoft Entra DS)**
- Microsoft Entra Kerberos for hybrid identities
- AD Kerberos authentication for Linux clients

All the preceding identity-based authentication options offer the ability to utilize Kerberos authentication. Kerberos authentication is a network protocol designed to provide secure authentication, even on unsecured networks, using cryptographic methods. Kerberos relies on tickets in the authentication process. When joining a storage account to AD, note that it is limited to a single forest. Multiple forest connections will require the configuration of domain trusts, which enables users from different domains to access resources.

Domain trusts are relationships established between two or more domains in a network, allowing users in either domain to access resources from each other. They are designed for sharing resources and enabling collaboration between users in different domains that have established trust with each other. Trusts enable users to authenticate their current credentials without requiring credentials in the other domain.

For the file share to provide authentication capabilities, it will join the respective directory service as a computer account object. There are three primary permissions (authorization) on the SMB share that you should be cognizant of:

- **Storage File Data SMB Share Reader**: This permission grants read access to the SMB share files and directories
- **Storage File Data SMB Share Contributor**: This permission grants read, write, list, and delete access to the SMB share files and directories
- **Storage File Data SMB Elevated Contributor**: This grants contributor access as well as the ability to assign permissions (modify **access control lists** (**ACLs**)) to other SMB share files and directories

In the following sections, you will investigate the steps involved in configuring AD domain-joined Azure file shares and the allocation of permissions to these shares.

> **Note**
> None of the preceding authentication methods support computer accounts being assigned as share-level permissions through **Role-Based Access Control** (**RBAC**) because an identity is required for authentication and computer accounts cannot be synced to Microsoft Entra ID. Also, **Network File System** (**NFS**) shares do not support identity-based authentication.

Configuring AD DS Authentication for a Storage Account

To authenticate through either directory service, several requirements are needed. The following diagram illustrates the requirements for an AD integration:

Configuring Access and Authentication | 263

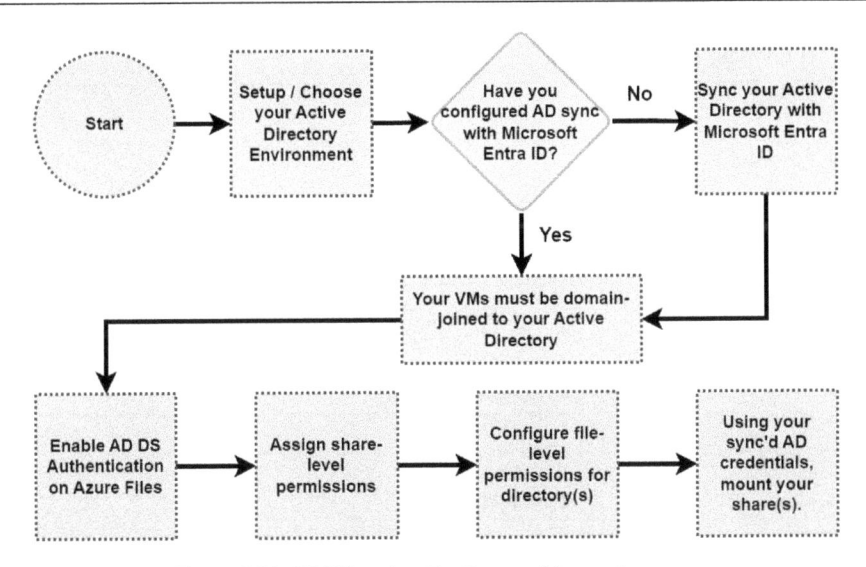

Figure 8.34: AD DS authentication enablement process

You will now follow the process for configuring AD DS authentication on an Azure file share. In the section that follows this, you will explore configuring access to the file share and then mounting the file share. Finally, you will explore how to configure permissions on the share:

1. Create an AD environment. You can run the following quick-start template, which will deploy an AD server in Azure: `https://github.com/Azure/azure-quickstart-templates/tree/master/application-workloads/active-directory/active-directory-new-domain`. Select the `Deploy to Azure` button to initiate a deployment.

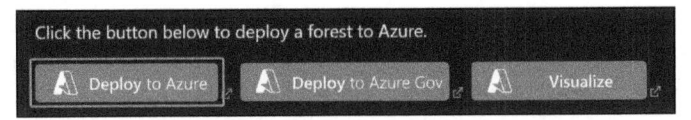

Figure 8.35: Creating a new AD forest in Azure

2. Set up your new AD forest; if you would like guided configurations, you can use the settings as per the following screenshot and leave the remaining settings as default. Please make a note of your admin username and password as they will be required later. Click `Next` and then `Create`.

The deployment takes approximately 30 minutes.

Figure 8.36: New AD forest in Azure – configurations

3. Connect to the VM that you just set up. You haven't learned about working with VMs yet as this will be touched on in *Chapter 10, Azure Resource Manager Templates*, and *Chapter 13, Managing Virtual Machines*, but for now, you can carry on by following the steps. Go to the resource group where you set up your deployment in the previous step, and look for the `virtual machine` resource, which is likely to be named adVM. At the top of the screen, click Connect and then Connect again.

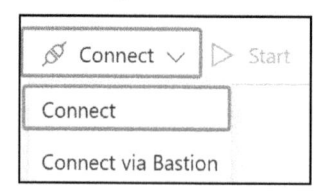

Figure 8.37: Connecting to your AD VM

Configuring Access and Authentication | 265

4. At the top of the screen, click `Connect` using the dropdown and select `Load balancer public IP address` as follows.

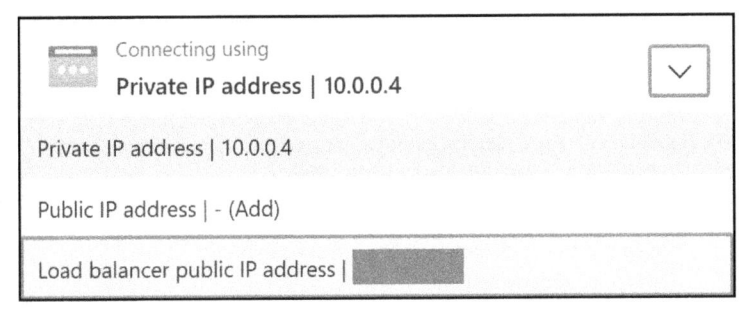

Figure 8.38: Connecting to your AD VM – Connecting using

5. At the bottom of the screen, set the connection method to `RDP file`. Then, click `Download RDP file` and save the connection `.rdp` file.

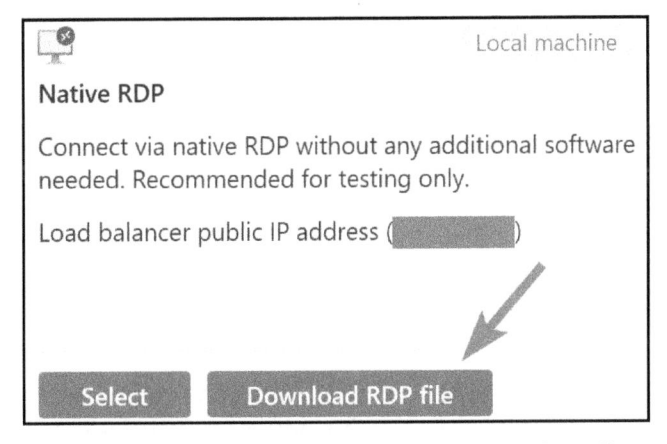

Figure 8.39: Connecting to your AD VM – Download RDP file

6. Open the RDP file you just downloaded, and it will show a prompt asking if you want to connect. Click `Connect`. Paste in the password you used earlier and click `OK`. You may be prompted by another screen that mentions the identity of the remote computer cannot be verified;

click `Yes` on this screen.

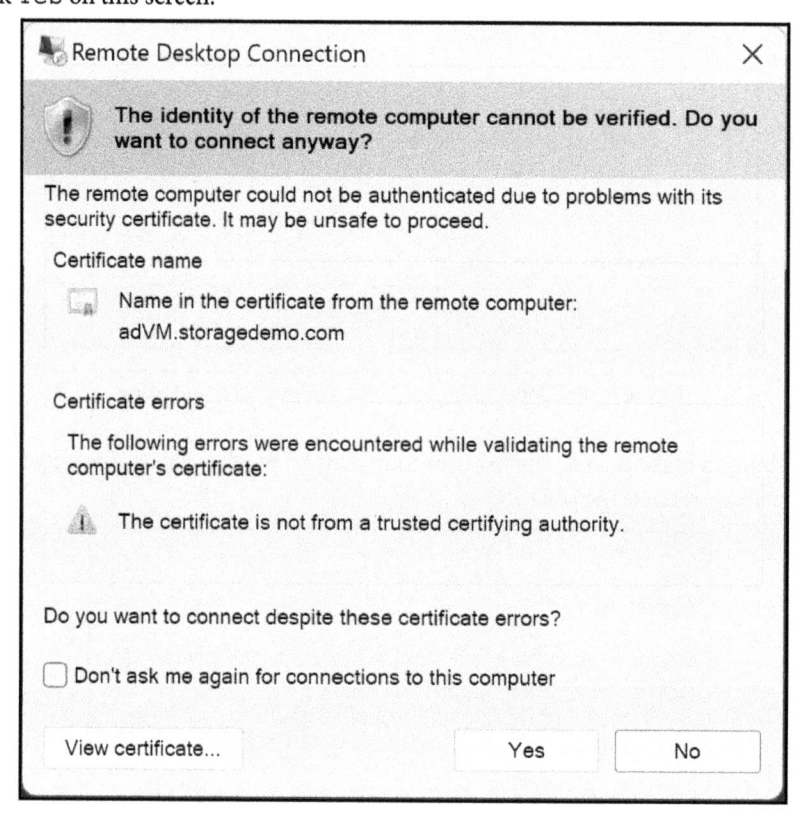

Figure 8.40: Connecting to your AD VM – certificate warning

7. Now that you are in your VM, you will see that it is very similar to working on your desktop computer. This is a server installation so there will be some windows you are not familiar with, but don't worry about those for now.

> **Note**
> Microsoft has recently gone through a name change of the services previously referred to as Azure AD; they are now named Microsoft Entra. Some of the product name changes are Azure AD becoming Microsoft Entra ID, Azure MFA becoming Entra MFA, and so on. To read more about it, you can refer to the following link: `https://learn.microsoft.com/en-us/entra/fundamentals/new-name`.

8. Download and set up Microsoft Entra Connect and sync AD with Entra ID. You can follow this link for instructions on setting it up, which will guide you through the express settings installation: `https://learn.microsoft.com/en-us/entra/identity/hybrid/connect/how-to-connect-install-express`. You can use the following settings if you are unsure what to configure:

A. Click on I agree to the license terms and privacy notice on the first screen and then click Continue.

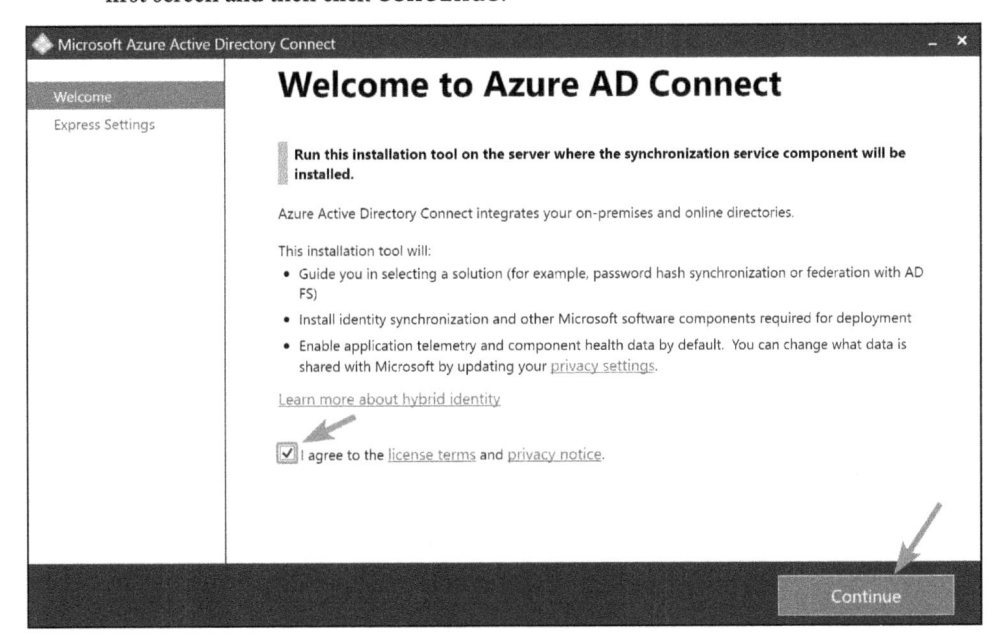

Figure 8.41: Entra Connect setup – license terms

B. Then, click Use express settings on the next screen.

9. You will be prompted for USERNAME and PASSWORD. These will be the credentials you set up when you created your Azure tenant and likely the same credentials you are using for the exercises in this book. Then, click Next. Here is an example:

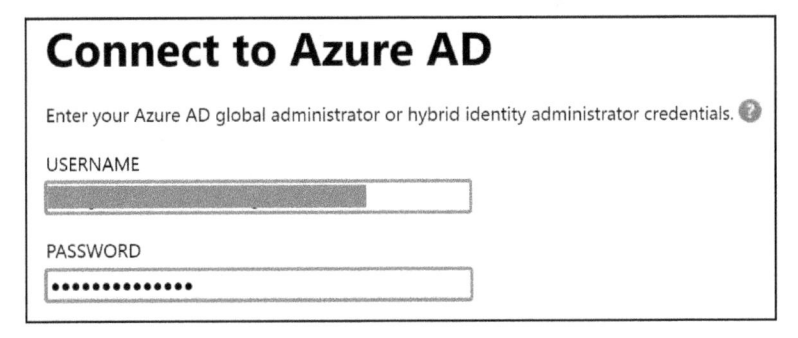

Figure 8.42: Entra Connect setup – USERNAME and PASSWORD

A. You will likely be presented with this screen as you try to connect. Click Add and then Add on the subsequent screen that follows. Then, click Close. Repeat this for all addresses that are shown. Eventually, when all the addresses are added, close that top window and attempt to verify your credentials again from the Entra Connect setup windows.

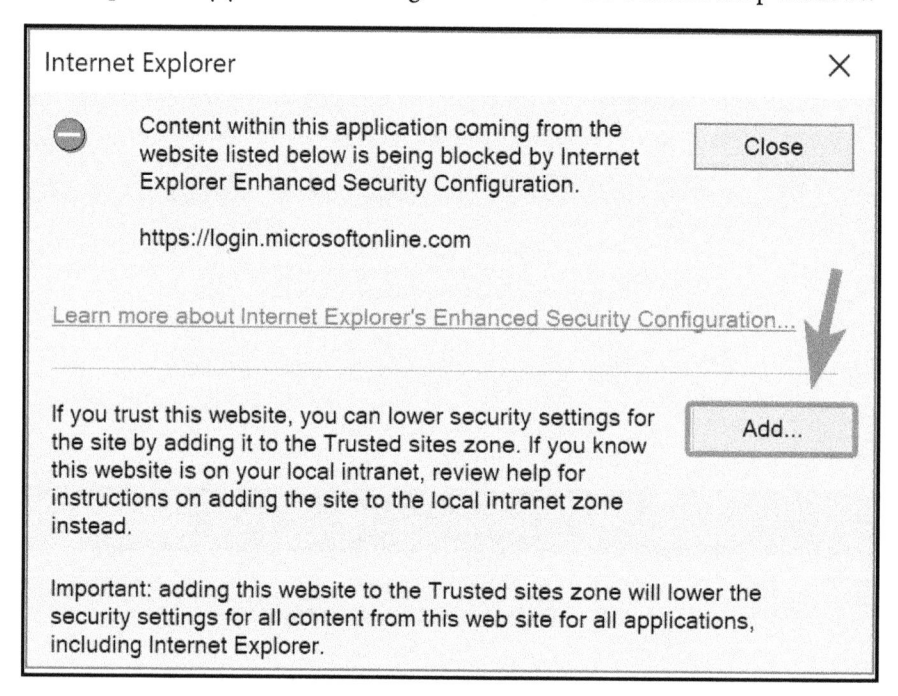

Figure 8.43: Entra Connect setup – browser configuration

B. Enter the email address you use for your Azure tenant as well as your password when prompted for it. Then, click Sign in.

C. You will then be prompted to fill out the USERNAME and PASSWORD fields for AD DS. These will be the credentials you created earlier in the AD deployment on Azure. If you were following along with the settings used in this exercise, then your username will be storagedemoadmin@storagedemo.com. Click Next.

Figure 8.44: Entra Connect setup – AD DS USERNAME and PASSWORD

D. Click the checkbox for `Continue without matching all UPN suffixes to verified domains` and then click `Next`.

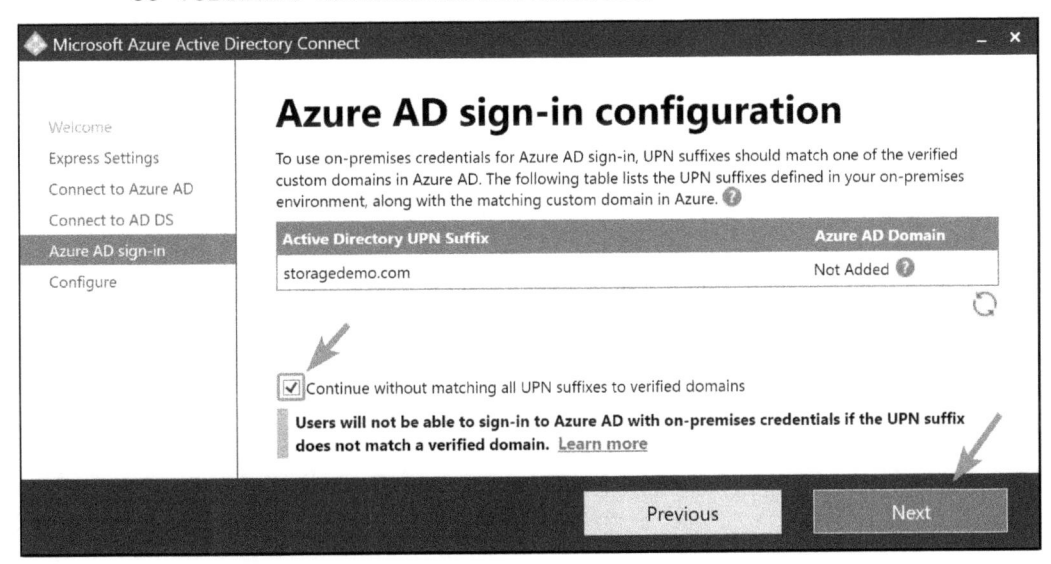

Figure 8.45: Entra Connect setup – Azure AD sign-in configuration

E. On the final screen, click `Install` and ensure the checkbox is ticked for `Start the synchronization process when configuration completes`.

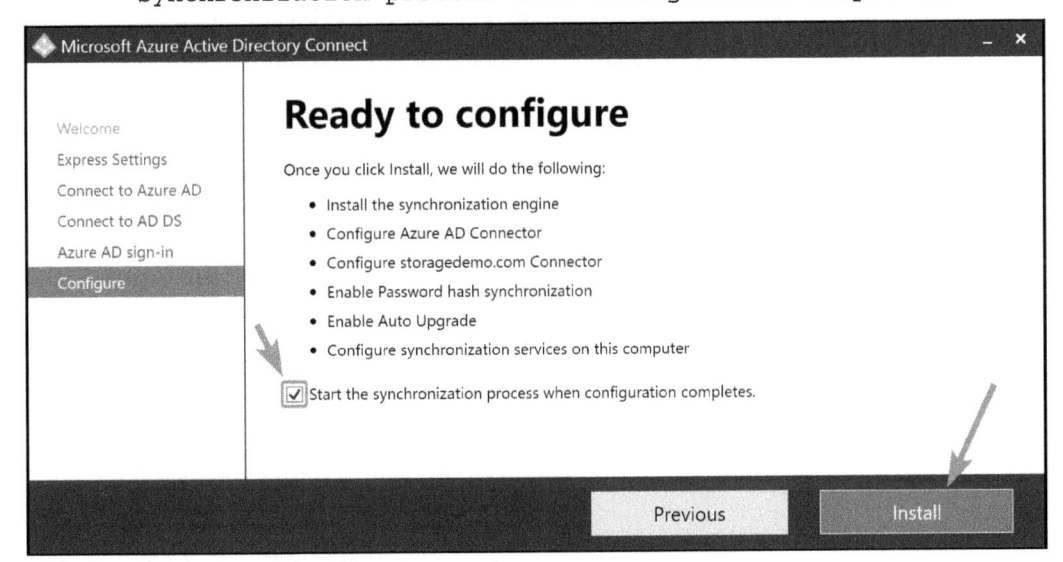

Figure 8.46: Entra Connect setup – Install

F. The configuration will run for a short period, normally less than 10 minutes. Once it's complete, click `Exit`.

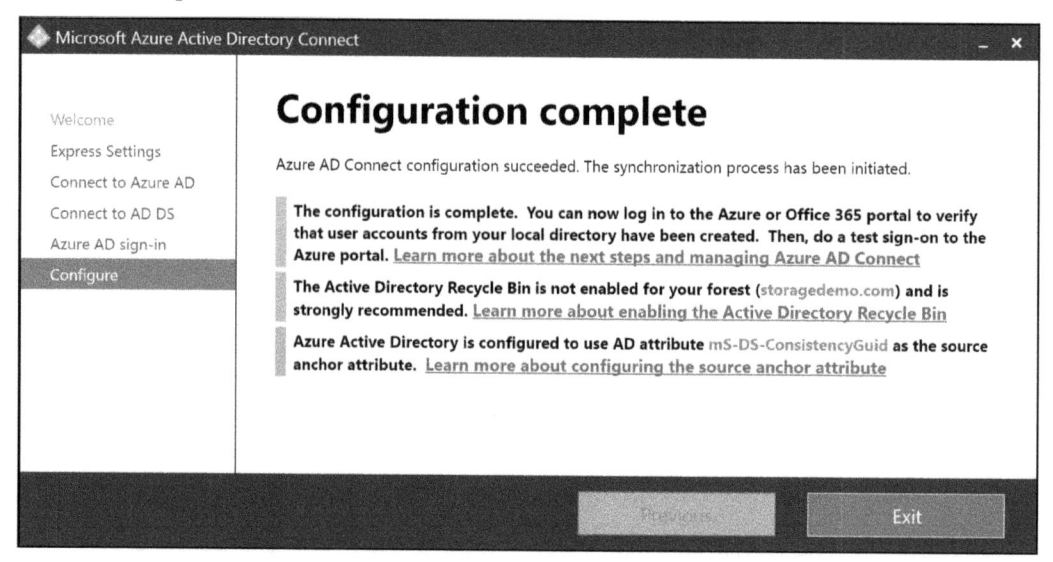

Figure 8.47: Entra Connect setup – Configuration complete

10. Deploy a test VM that is joined to the same network as adVM. You can refer to *Chapter 10*, *Azure Resource Manager Templates*, or *Chapter 13*, *Managing Virtual Machines*, for VM deployment details if you are interested, or you can follow along using the **Azure Resource Manager** (**ARM**) template in the GitHub repository for this chapter, found here: https://github.com/PacktPublishing/AZ-104-Microsoft-Azure-Administrator-Certification-and-Beyond-3rd-Edition/tree/main.

11. Following the template, it will domain-join your VM to the domain that includes the AD domain controller server you configured earlier. Your settings should look as shown in *Figure 8.48*. If you have been following the prescribed configurations, use the same username and password combination for your domain credentials as the credentials from the previous exercises:

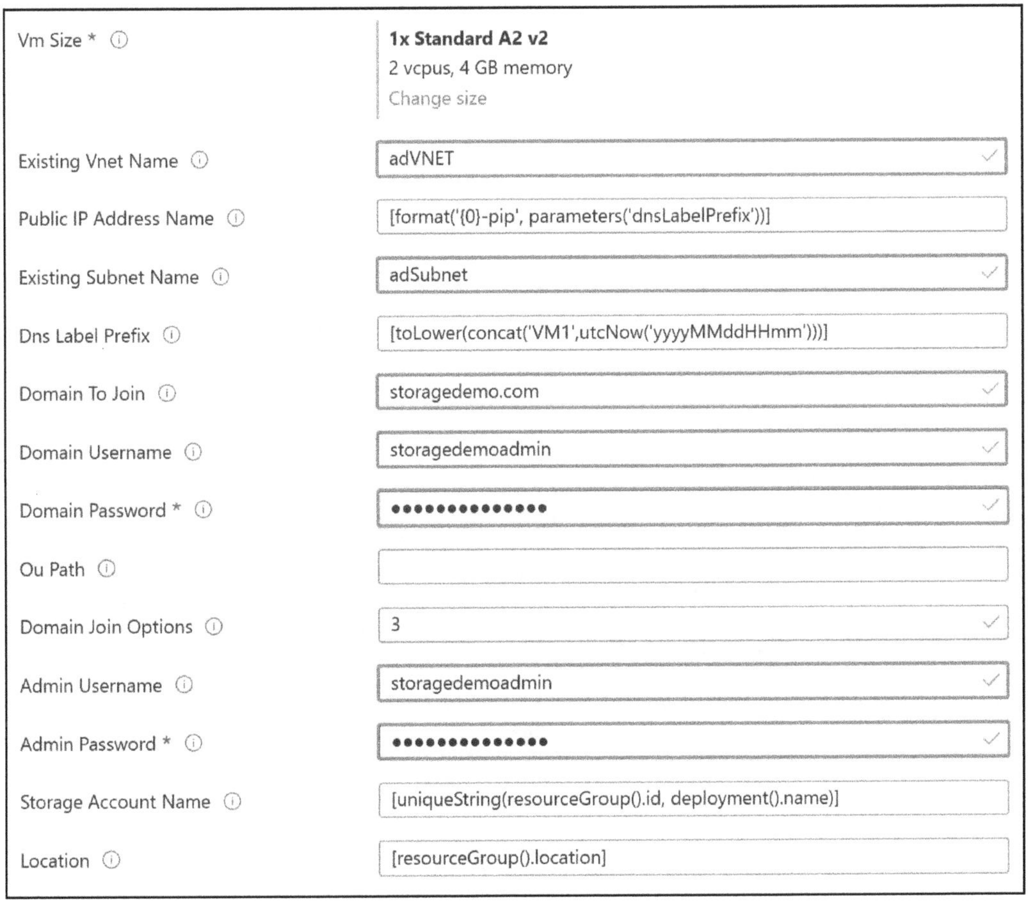

Vm Size * ⓘ	**1x Standard A2 v2** 2 vcpus, 4 GB memory Change size
Existing Vnet Name ⓘ	adVNET
Public IP Address Name ⓘ	[format('{0}-pip', parameters('dnsLabelPrefix'))]
Existing Subnet Name ⓘ	adSubnet
Dns Label Prefix ⓘ	[toLower(concat('VM1',utcNow('yyyyMMddHHmm')))]
Domain To Join ⓘ	storagedemo.com
Domain Username ⓘ	storagedemoadmin
Domain Password * ⓘ	●●●●●●●●●●●●●●
Ou Path ⓘ	
Domain Join Options ⓘ	3
Admin Username ⓘ	storagedemoadmin
Admin Password * ⓘ	●●●●●●●●●●●●●●
Storage Account Name ⓘ	[uniqueString(resourceGroup().id, deployment().name)]
Location ⓘ	[resourceGroup().location]

Figure 8.48: Domain-joined VM template deployment

12. Click `Review + create` and then click `Create` to deploy the template.
13. Set up an Azure Storage account (limit the account name to 15 characters) and set up an Azure file share.
14. Connect to your new VM remotely using RDP by following the same steps you used previously to connect to a VM.
15. Open PowerShell on the remote server under the administrator context (right-click PowerShell and click `Run as Administrator`). Execute the following commands (you can respond `Yes` or `Yes to All` with any of the prompts):

    ```
    Set-ExecutionPolicy -ExecutionPolicy Unrestricted
    Install-Module AZ
    Connect-AzAccount
    ```

16. Download the following module for configuring AD DS authentication: `https://github.com/Azure-Samples/azure-files-samples/releases/tag/v0.2.8`. At the time of writing, this was version 0.2.8. Click `AzFileHybrid.zip` to download the `.zip` file.

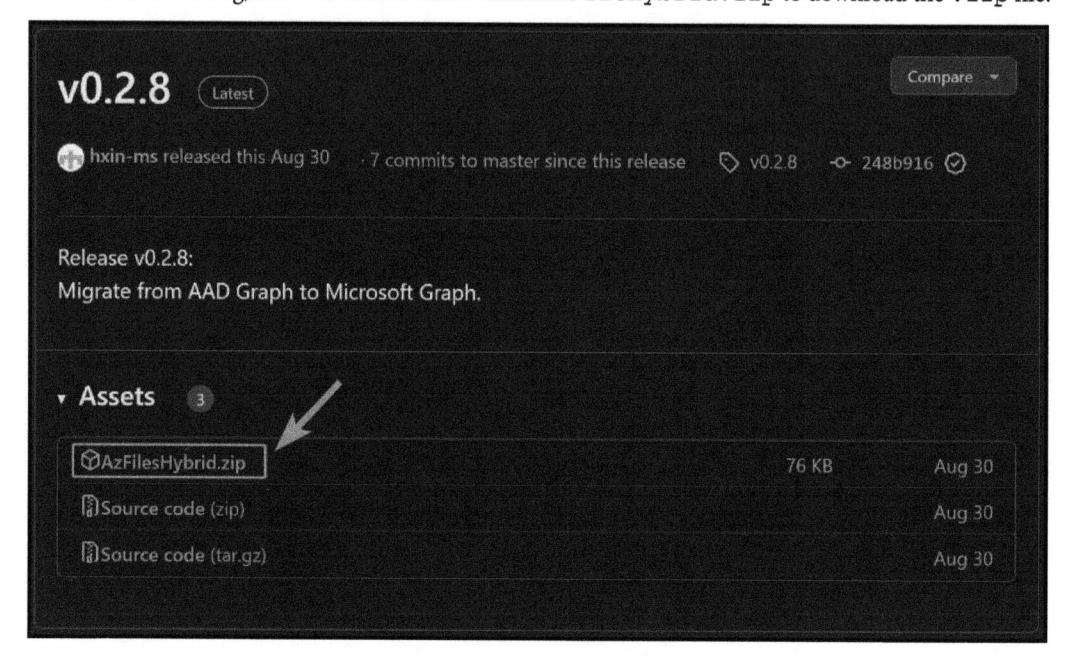

Figure 8.49: Downloading the Azure Files repository

17. Extract the files from the `.zip` file and copy the files to your VM. Right-click the `CopyToPSPath` file and click `Run with PowerShell`. Close PowerShell and relaunch it with administrative credentials again.

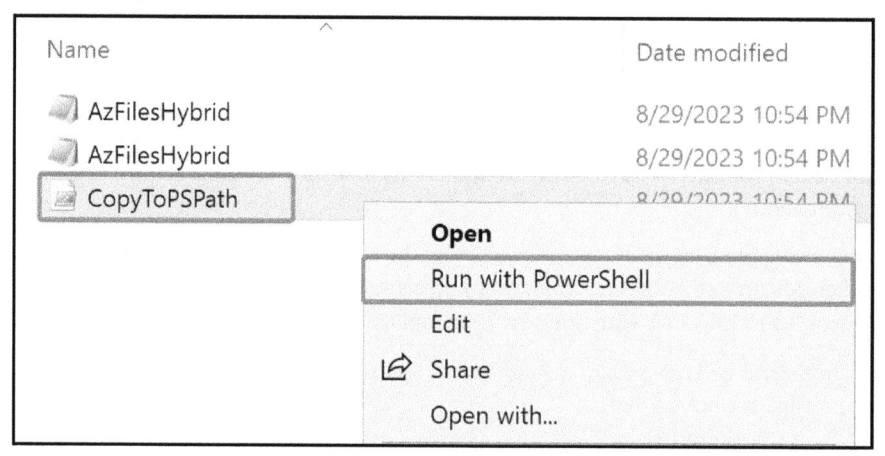

Figure 8.50: Running CopyToPSPath

> **Note**
> Should you receive an error for updating any module, such as the `PowerShellGet` module, you can run the following command to force an update. The module name can be changed accordingly:
>
> `get-module | Where-Object{$_.name -like "*PowerShellGet*"} | Update-module`

18. Enable AD DS authentication on the file share by running the following PowerShell script and changing the domain name to what you configured on AD. This must be run on the AD-joined machine you just created. Note that when you try `Connect-AzAccount`, you will need to approve the connections again just like adVM:

    ```
    # Import the required modules for working with Azure Files
    Import-Module -name AZFilesHybrid;

    # Variables
    $ResourceGroupName = "AZ104-StorageAccounts"
    $StorageAccountName = "somefileshare16122023"
    $Domain = "storagedemo.com"

    # Connect your Azure account to the script (# out the 1 you dont need)
    Connect-AzAccount;
    #Connect-AzAccount -tenantId "[tenantID]" # Use this if you are connected to multiple Azure / Microsoft Entra ID tenants

    # Select your desired subscription if required
    # Select-AzSubscription -subscriptionId "[subscriptionId]"

    # Join your storage account to your AD for authentication
    Join-AzStorageAccountForAuth -ResourceGroupName "$ResourceGroupName" -StorageAccountName "$StorageAccountName" -Domain "$Domain"
    ```

19. You will be presented with the following prompt; reply with A.

```
Set password on AD object somefileshdszbx$ for somefileshare16122023
to value of kerb2.
This action will change the password for the indicated AD object
from kerb1 to kerb2. This is intended to be a two-stage process:
rotate from kerb1 to kerb2 (kerb2 will be regenerated on the storage
 account before being set), wait several hours, and then rotate back
 to kerb1 (this cmdlet will likewise regenerate kerb1).
[Y] Yes  [A] Yes to All  [N] No  [L] No to All  [S] Suspend
[?] Help (default is "Y"): A
```

Figure 8.51: Running Join-AzStorageAccountForAuth

20. Your Azure file share should now be joined to your on-premises server environment.

> **Note**
>
> For some people, their Azure accounts are linked to multiple Azure AD / Entra ID tenants. Where this is the case, you need to specify the **Tenant ID** you are connecting to when running the `Connect-AzAccount` command, such as `Connect-AzAccount -tenantid "xxxxxxxxxxxx"`.
>
> You may also have multiple subscriptions, in which event you also need to run the following command in conjunction with your tenant connection: `Select-AzSubscription -SubscriptionId "[subscriptionid]"`; replace `[subscriptionid]` with the desired subscription ID you are connecting to.

21. Create a new AD user named `storageuser1`. You can do this by logging into your AD server, opening the `Windows Administrative Tools` folder from the Start menu (Windows icon), and selecting `Active Directory Users and Computers`.

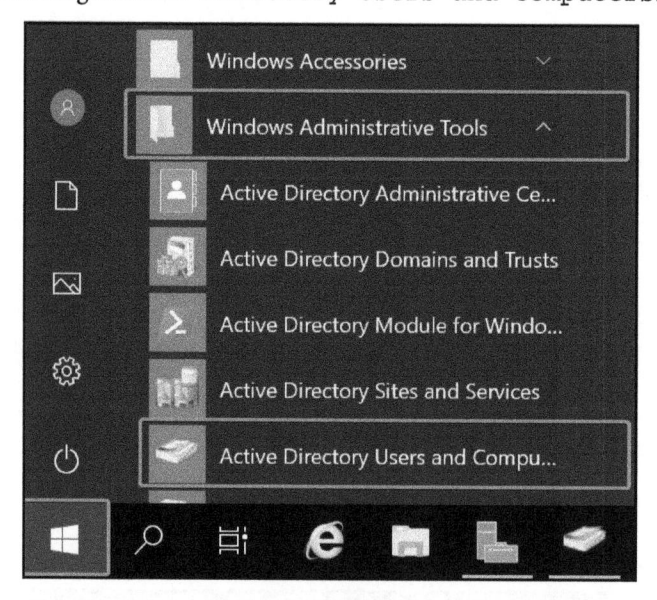

Figure 8.52: Launching Active Directory Users and Computers

22. Right-click the `Users` **Organizational Unit (OU)** from the main navigation pane on the left, hover over `New`, and click `User`.

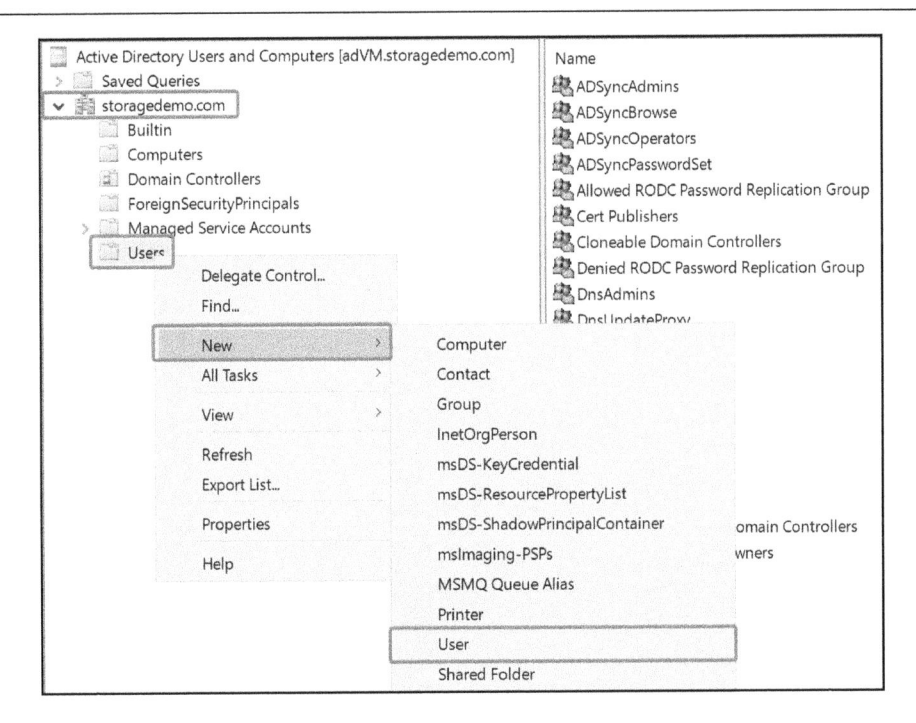

Figure 8.53: Creating a new AD user

23. Complete the New Object - User dialog as follows and click Next.

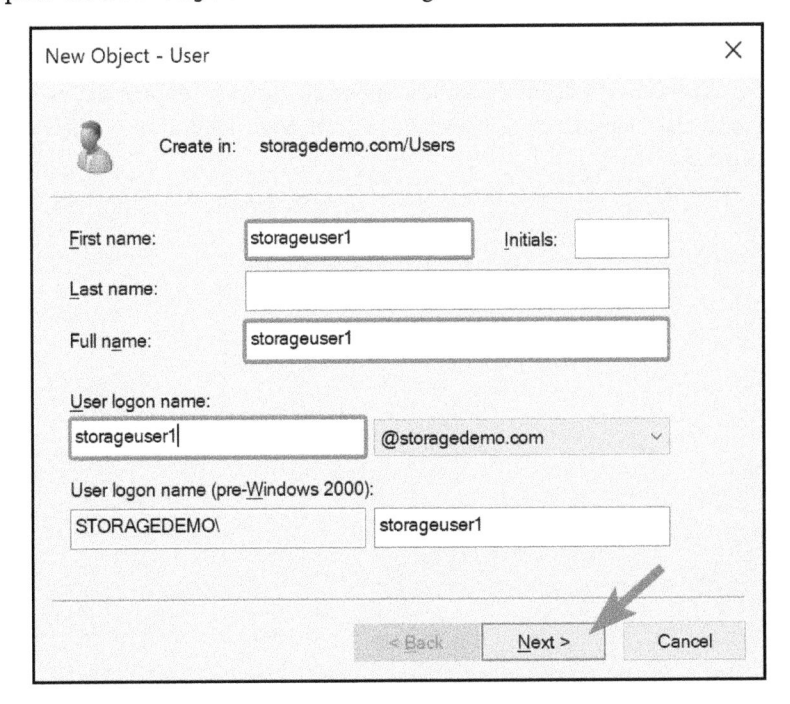

Figure 8.54: New user – name and login details

24. Enter a password and the same password in the `Confirm` text input boxes and ensure all checkboxes are unticked.

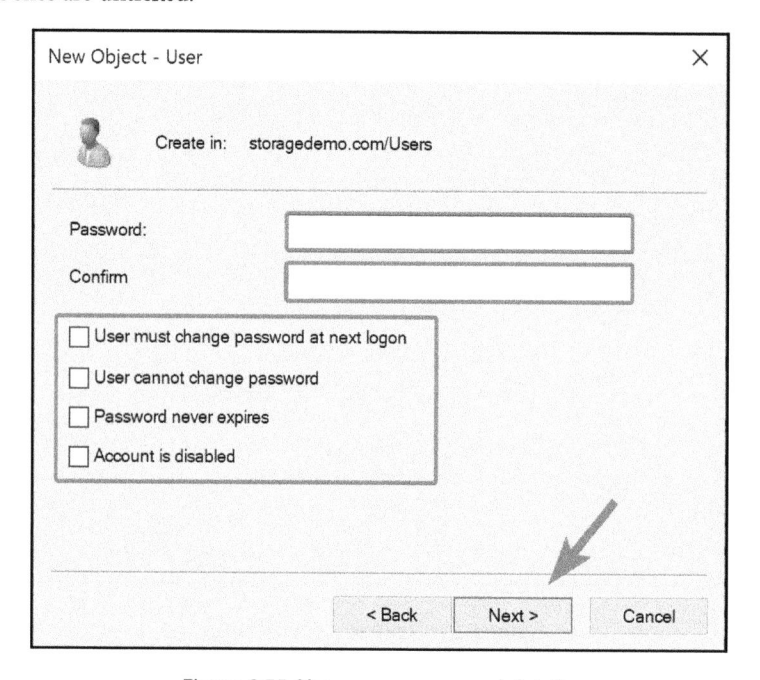

Figure 8.55: New user – password details

25. Click `Finish`.
26. Double-click your newly created user account in the `Users` OU. You will be presented with a dialog with many tabs. Click the `Member Of` tab and click `Add...` to add it to the `Domain Admins` group.

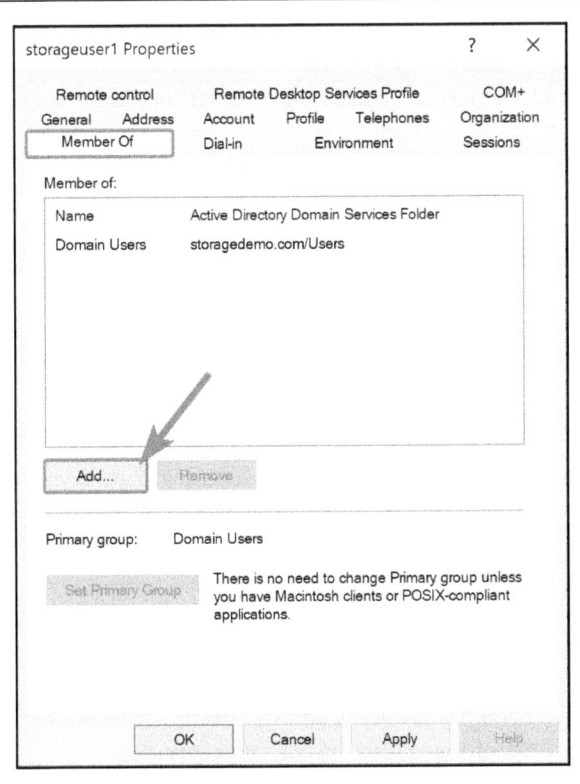

Figure 8.56: AD user – Add to AD group

27. Enter `Domain Admins`, click `Check Names`, and finally, click OK.

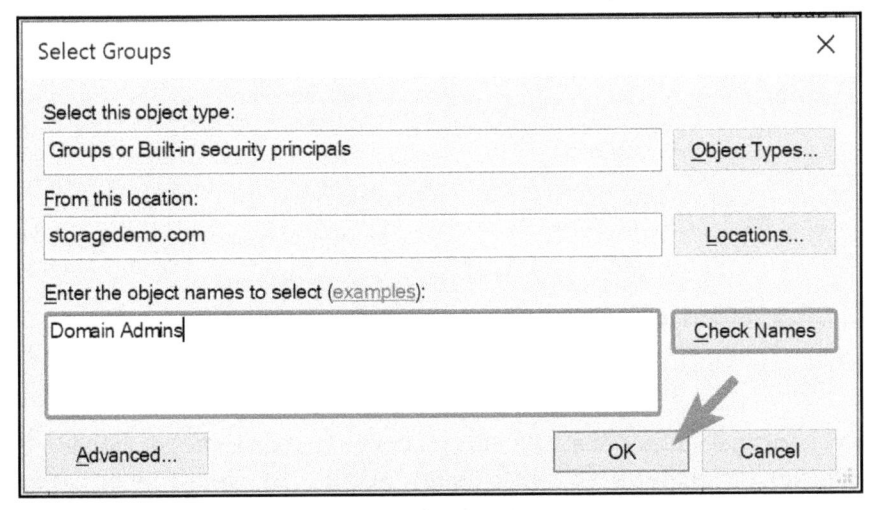

Figure 8.57: AD user – Selecting an AD group

28. Click `Apply` and then `OK`.
29. Your user account has now been created and is ready for use for the next exercise.

In the next section, you will explore assigning share-level and file-level permissions, as well as mounting an SMB share on a Windows machine.

Configuring Access to Azure Files

In the following section, you will explore assigning share and file permissions on the AD-joined storage from the previous exercise, as well as mounting the share and exploring how to validate the security.

Assigning Share-Level Permissions

In this section, you will explore the steps involved in assigning share-level permissions:

1. Navigate to the Azure portal by opening `https://portal.azure.com`.
2. Go to the storage account from the previous exercise.
3. Click on `File shares` on the left menu under the `Data storage` context.
4. Create a file share, name it `shared`, and disable backup.
5. Click the new share you just created, and then on the left menu, click `Access Control (IAM)`. Click `+ Add` and then `Add role assignment`.

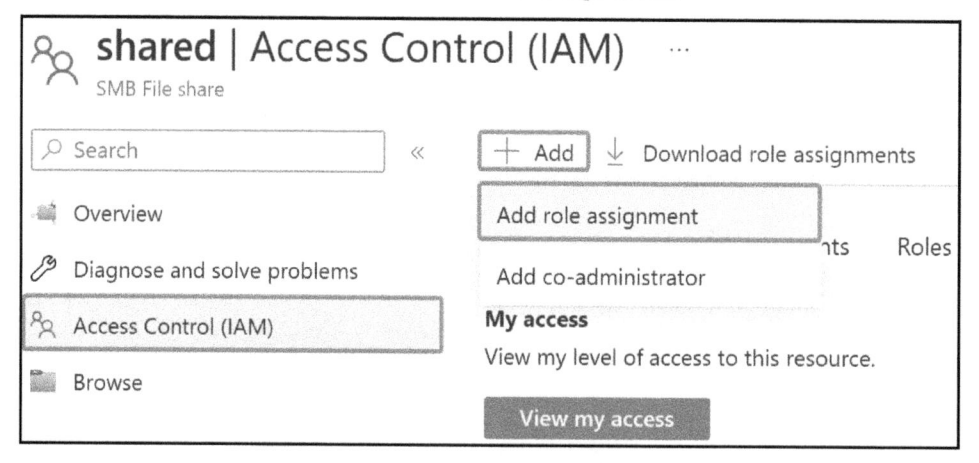

Figure 8.58: Adding SMB permissions

6. Select `Storage File Data SMB Share Contributor` for `Role`, and under `Members`, ensure `Assign access to` is set to `User, group, or service principal`; then, click `+ Select members`, search for the appropriate user account (`storageuser1`) you created on AD, and then click `Select`.
7. Click `Review + assign` and then click `Review + assign` again.

You have just added contributor permissions for a user to your SMB share on Azure. This same process can be applied to the other SMB roles if desired. In the next section, you will experience mounting a file share using your AD credentials on a Windows VM. You will then explore how to access the files it contains.

Mounting the File Share

In this section, you will perform the steps involved in mounting an Azure file share on the test VM with AD credentials. It should be noted that port 445 will need to be open on the Windows server and SMB 3.x enabled (they should be open by default). Follow these steps:

1. Navigate to the Azure portal by opening https://portal.azure.com.
2. Go to the storage account from the previous exercise.
3. Click on File shares on the left menu under the Data storage context.
4. Click the share you used in the previous exercise, and on the left menu, click Overview, and then click Connect on the top menu of the Overview blade.
5. Select a Drive letter (the default is Z) option and set Authentication method to Active Directory or Microsoft Entra. Click Show Script.
6. Copy the generated script at the bottom of the page. For this, you have three options that you can choose from to map your SMB file share:

    A. **Option 1**: Use the same account on your test VM that you are logged in with using the following modified script that you downloaded or copied from the Azure portal from the previous step. Change the parameters, such as your storage account name, username, and password. You will be prompted for your credentials, which must match username@yourdomain.com (e.g., storageuser1@storagedemo.com) and the password you provided for the account when you created it:

    ```
    # Create your User Credentials
    $username = "storageuser1"
    # Set up the default password for the users - this will be
    changed on first login
    $Password = "updatewithyourpassword"
    $Password = ConvertTo-SecureString -AsPlainText -Force $Password
    $Credential = New-Object System.Management.Automation.
    PSCredential ($username, $Password)

    # Connect your Share
    $credential = Get-Credential;
    $storageAccountName = "somefileshare16122023";
    $fileshare = "shared";
    $connectTestResult = Test-NetConnection -ComputerName
    "$($storageAccountName).file.core.windows.net" -Port 445
    ```

```
if ($connectTestResult.TcpTestSucceeded) {
    # Mount the drive
    New-PSDrive -Name Z -PSProvider FileSystem -Root
"\\$storageAccountName.file.core.windows.net\$fileshare"
-Persist -Credential $credential
} else {
    Write-Error -Message "Unable to reach the Azure storage
account via port 445. Check to make sure your organization or
ISP is not blocking port 445, or use Azure P2S VPN, Azure S2S
VPN, or Express Route to tunnel SMB traffic over a different
port."
}
```

When executing this script, you will be greeted with a credential request window like the following figure and you will enter the credentials mentioned in the preceding script. Click OK when done. This will then continue mapping the SMB share with the provided credentials from the window.

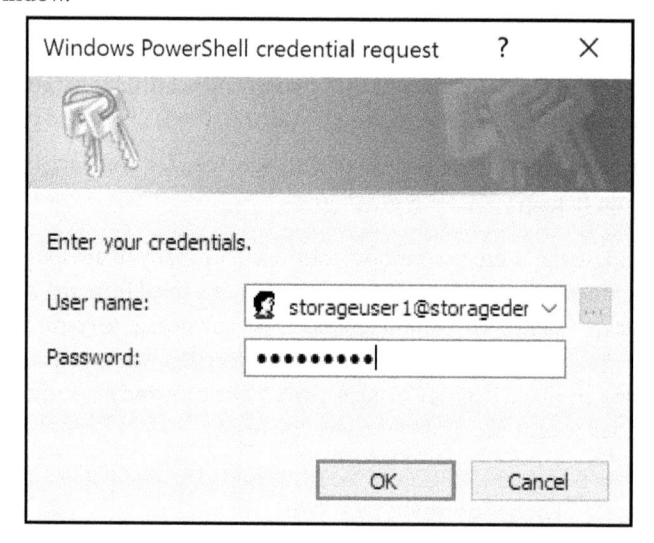

Figure 8.59: Entering SMB credentials

B. **Option 2**: Navigate to your test VM and log in with the user account you added to the SMB share (this must be an on-premises account). Open PowerShell, paste your script directly from Azure into the PowerShell window, and hit `Enter`. This will map the share as a PSDrive.

C. **Option 3**: To have this mapped in Windows File Explorer, you could also map the network path you have from the share, such as `\\storageaccountname.file.core.windows.net\shared`.

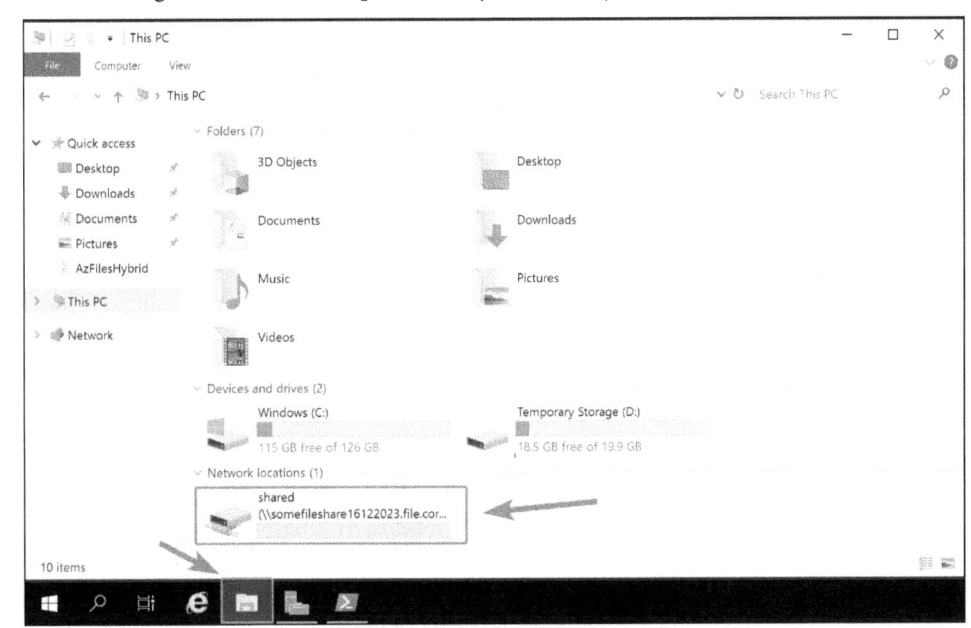

7. Now, navigate to Windows Explorer, and you can see your new shared drive attached.

Figure 8.60: Navigating your Azure file share

8. **Additional**: Log on to your AD server and attempt the same connection under your administrator account. Note that you get an `Access is denied` message. This is because you haven't assigned SMB permissions to this user.

In this exercise, you mounted the SMB share for your Azure Files storage, which enables you to utilize the storage in your operating system in the same way you would locally attached storage. If you follow *Step 8*, you will have noticed the effect placed on the share-using permissions when you have not been granted the appropriate permissions. In the next section, you will learn about the effects of file-level permissions.

Configuring File-Level Permissions

In this section, you will look at the steps involved in assigning file-level permissions:

1. Create a new user on AD and assign this user the `Storage File Data SMB Share Contributor` permissions for the share from the previous exercise. The synchronization can take some time to replicate to Azure.

2. Navigate to your test VM and paste some files into your shared folder. Notice that you have permission to do so. Right-click one of the files and click `Properties`. On the window that pops up, click `Security`.

3. Click `Edit...`. Notice that your user has full permission.

4. Click `Add...`, type in the new username, click the `Check Names` button, and then click OK. Click `Apply`.

    You get an error stating that you don't have permission. This is because you need to assign the `Storage File Data SMB Share Elevated Contributor` role to the first user account you created (`storageuser1`) to modify ACL permissions. Add the `Storage File Data SMB Share Reader` role to the new user account you created. Wait about 15 to 30 minutes or force the AD Connect agent to sync and repeat the security operation after assigning permissions, and you will now complete the operation successfully.

> **Note**
> You may find that you will have to restart your server during the preceding operations due to some hanging, and you are no longer seeing a mapping on the share to `storagedemo.com`. If you find yourself in this situation, please rerun the PowerShell script to add the drive to your server.

5. Navigate to the AD server and mount the SMB share using the new user credentials. Note that you may need to wait for synchronization to complete before this works as expected. Notice that you can view the file but cannot edit or add any new files to the share.

6. You can play around with changing settings, completely removing read permissions on the files, and confirming the other users indeed cannot read this.

In this section, you learned how to configure file-level ACLs for Azure Storage shares. This concludes the section for Entra ID authentication and integration for access to Azure file shares. Next, you are provided additional reading material should you wish to learn more.

> **Note**
>
> You are encouraged to read up further on this topic by using the following links:
>
> **Enabling AD DS authentication:** https://learn.microsoft.com/en-us/azure/storage/files/storage-files-identity-auth-active-directory-enable
>
> **Automation of storage access key rotation:** https://learn.microsoft.com/en-us/azure/key-vault/secrets/tutorial-rotation-dual?tabs=azure-cli
>
> **How to mount an SMB file share on Windows:** https://learn.microsoft.com/en-us/azure/storage/files/storage-how-to-use-files-windows
>
> **Configuring file-level permissions:** https://learn.microsoft.com/en-us/azure/storage/files/storage-files-identity-ad-ds-configure-permissions
>
> After learning about how to mount a file share, you are going to want to experience managing your storage by adding or even removing files to become more familiar with the service. You know how to perform this process using both Windows and Azure Storage Explorer; however, there is a utility for Azure, AzCopy, that is also beneficial for working with storage. AzCopy is a command-line utility for copying files and data. It works for both copying data to and from your storage accounts. The tool is also beneficial in programmatic scenarios for copying data to and from storage accounts.

Summary

In this chapter, you learned how to manage the security of storage within Azure by integrating storage with VNets, using private endpoints, working with SAS tokens, and configuring access and authentication. You now have the skills to securely implement Azure Storage. Having the ability to safeguard against undesired actions, unauthorized access, and potential security breaches is paramount to securing your organization.

In the next chapter, you will have the opportunity to put these skills into practice through hands-on labs, which will reinforce your understanding of storage management concepts.

> **Note**
>
> Remember to delete the resources you created in this chapter to minimize costs. You can do this with the following command for convenience; these will remove the resource group and all the corresponding resources:
>
> `Remove-AzResourceGroup -Name AZ104-StorageAccounts`

9
Storage Management and Replication

In previous chapters, you explored the concept of storage account security. You learned about configuring network access to your storage accounts to restrict access to known and wanted networks only. You explored storage keys and how they can be used when generating **Shared Access Signature** (**SAS**) tokens for granting secure access to your storage for a predefined window of access. You then learned about stored access policies and how they extend the concepts of SAS tokens, as you can create a policy that can be modified and deleted after being shared, giving you more control over shared permissions. Finally, you explored access and authentication for your storage account. In this chapter, you will learn about the storage replication options available to you in Azure and understand the management of a blob's lifecycle. You will learn about the Azure File Sync service (used for caching copies of Azure file shares), blob object replication, blob lifecycle management (moving data between tiers for improved performance or cost efficiency), blob data protection, blob versioning, and storage account deletion.

In this chapter, you are going to cover the following main topics:

- Copying Data by using AzCopy
- Configuring Storage Replication and Lifecycle Management

Technical Requirements

To follow along with the hands-on material, you will need the following:

- Azure Storage Explorer, which is installed as shown in *Chapter 7, Copying Data To and from Azure*.
- Access to an Azure subscription with owner or contributor privileges. If you do not have access to one, you can set up a student account for free: https://azure.microsoft.com/en-us/free/.
- **PowerShell 5.1** or later installed on a Windows PC, or PowerShell Core 6.x if you're using another operating system.
- **.NET Framework 4.7.2** or later, which can be installed using the following link: https://learn.microsoft.com/en-us/dotnet/framework/install.

- If PowerShell is not installed or available, `https://shell.azure.com` can be used as a browser-based shell.
- The Az PowerShell module, which can be installed by running the following in an administrative PowerShell session:

  ```
  Set-ExecutionPolicy -ExecutionPolicy RemoteSigned -Scope CurrentUser
  Install-Module -Name Az -Scope CurrentUser -Repository PSGallery -Force
  ```

Copying Data by Using AzCopy

AzCopy is a utility that can be used for copying files to and from Azure Storage accounts through a command-line-based utility. Authentication for the tool can be conducted using either an Active Directory account or a SAS token from storage. The tool provides many other functions but is primarily designed for file copying. It can also be used for monitoring and managing various other copy jobs. Some of the other features are its delete capability, its sync functionality for replicating storage from one location to another, and even the ability to make containers and file shares. A couple of use cases for `AzCopy` are replicating data from one storage account to another as a means of backup and migrating from one environment to another (such as development to production). You might also need to process data from the storage account on your local machine or server; `AzCopy` will enable you to copy files for local processing.

The AzCopy commands are structured in the following format: `azcopy [command] [source] [destination] [flags]`.

In the activity that follows, you will learn how to install the `AzCopy` tool, and then in the subsequent exercises, you will learn how to copy data using it.

Downloading and Installing

You can download `AzCopy` from here: `https://docs.microsoft.com/en-us/azure/storage/common/storage-use-azcopy-v10`.

In this exercise, you will copy data to your Azure Blob Storage using a SAS token:

1. Download and install the relevant `AzCopy` installer from the preceding link.
2. Extract the files from the archive you downloaded and place them in a location that suits you, such as `C:\AzCopy`.
3. Launch PowerShell, navigate to the folder using the `cd` command, and press *Enter*.

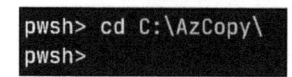

```
pwsh> cd C:\AzCopy\
pwsh>
```

Figure 9.1: Changing directory in PowerShell

You now have a copy of AzCopy on your machine ready to work with.

Copying Data by Using AzCopy

In this demonstration, you will copy data using the `AzCopy` utility and SAS tokens. This exercise can also be conducted using Entra ID credentials. Follow these steps to complete the exercise:

1. Identify a file you would like to copy to the Azure storage account and note the path. For simplicity, place it in the same path as `AzCopy`.
2. Navigate to the Azure portal by opening `https://portal.azure.com`.
3. Select a storage account and create two containers in the storage account, one named `azcopysource` and the other named `azcopydestination`. These can be named anything you like in later implementations.
4. On the left menu for the storage account, click `Shared access signature` under the `Security + networking` context. Create a new SAS key by selecting the `Container` option from the `Allowed resource types` list.

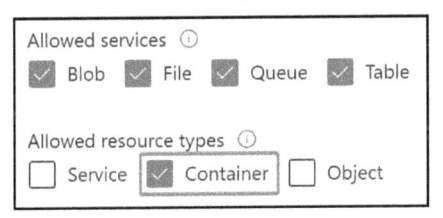

Figure 9.2: SAS resource type

5. Set `Allowed permissions` to enabled (ticked). Some of the permissions you may not be familiar with are `Immutable storage` (data storage that imposes a restriction whereby once data is written, no alterations or deletions to the data can be made within a predefined period of time) and `Permanent delete` (whereby you can delete a snapshot or blob version permanently, even before the retention period's predefined end date) options. `Immutable storage` is typically instituted for governance and compliance reasons, as well as data security. The `Permanent delete` option is a high-risk permission and should be handled with care to prevent accidental permanent deletion.
6. Your allowed permissions should match those in the following figure:

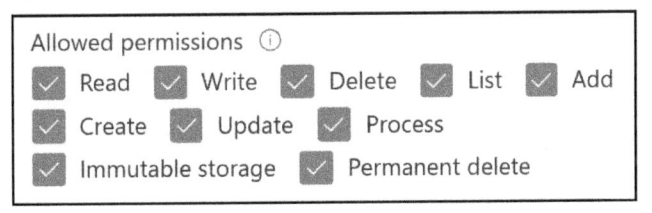

Figure 9.3: SAS allowed permissions

7. Set the time for `Start` to `5 minutes before your current time` and click `Generate SAS and connection string`. Copy the SAS token – remember that you are only ever presented with this once.

8. Copy the filename for the file identified in *Step 1* and insert this name in the following script. The following script will copy the file you enter in `SourceFilePath` to the blob container you specified with `StorageAccountName` and `ContainerName`:

```
# Change all Variables Below
$SourceFilePath = "C:\AzCopy\MyFile.txt"
$StorageAccountName = "az104storageaccountdemo1"
$ContainerName = "azcopydestination"
$SASToken = "?sv=xxxxxxxxxxxxxxxxxxxxxxxxxxxxxxxxxxxxxxxxxxxxxx%3D"
# Run AzCopy Command
./azcopy.exe copy "$SourceFilePath" "https://$StorageAccountName.blob.core.windows.net/$($ContainerName)$SASToken"
```

9. The script can either be saved as a PowerShell script file (`*.ps1`) and called in PowerShell, or you can copy and paste your edited script code into PowerShell and press *Enter* for it to run.

Now that you have seen `AzCopy` in action, you will complete the same task of copying files from a source container on a storage account to a destination container in the same storage account.

Copying Data between Containers Using AzCopy

You will now perform a similar copy task to the previous section, except this time, you will be copying data from a source container in a storage account to a destination container in the same storage account. Note that this technique can also be used across storage accounts as the principle is the same. Follow these steps:

1. Navigate to the Azure portal by opening `https://portal.azure.com`.

2. Select a storage account and create two containers on the storage account, one named `azcopysource` and the other named `azcopydestination`. These can be any name you choose should you want to implement this again later for other environments; just remember to update these names in your copy script.

3. Upload a file to the `azcopysource` container.

4. In the left menu for the storage account, click `Containers` under the `Data storage` context, then click on the `azcopysource` container. Click `Shared access tokens` under the `Settings` context in the left menu. Create a new container-level SAS by setting `Signing method` to `Account key`, `Signing key` to `Key 1` or `Key 2`, `Permissions` to `Read` and `List`, and `Start` to 5 minutes before your current time. Then, click `Generate SAS token and URL`.

5. Copy the SAS token – remember you are only ever presented with this once. Perform the same operation for the destination container. This time, set the `Shared access tokens` permissions to `Read`, `Add`, `Create`, `Write`, `Delete`, and `List`.

6. The following script will copy the files from the `source` container, `azcopysource`, to the `destination` container, `azcopydestination`. Note the extra switches (flags) used by the following script. `-overwrite=ifsourcenewer` performs the operation of overwriting files on the destination if the source files are new. The `--recursive` flag recursively copies data from the source container and subsequent folders in any filesystem you copy from, essentially copying all the files and folders it finds:

```
# Change all Variables Below
$StorageAccountName = "az104storageaccountdemo1"
$SrcContainerName = "azcopysource"
$DestContainerName = "azcopydestination"
$SourceSASToken = "sp=rxxxxxxxxxxxxxxxxxxxxxxxxxxxxxx%3D"
$DestSASToken = "sp=rxxxxxxxxxxxxxxxxxxxxxxxxxxxxxx%3D"
# Run AzCopy Command
./azcopy.exe copy "https://$StorageAccountName.blob.
core.windows.net/$($SrcContainerName)?$SourceSASToken"
"https://$StorageAccountName.blob.core.windows.
net/$($DestContainerName)?$DestSASToken"
--overwrite=ifsourcenewer --recursive
```

7. After running the preceding script, you will notice text like this appearing, indicating that a file copy operation has been completed:

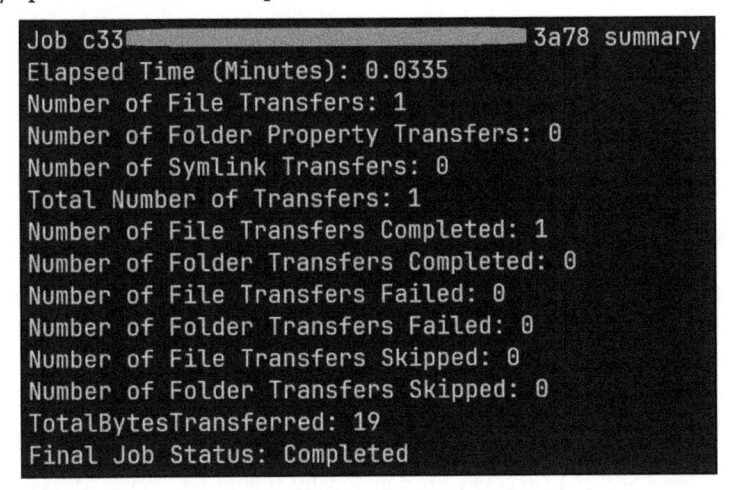

```
Job c33█████████████████████████3a78 summary
Elapsed Time (Minutes): 0.0335
Number of File Transfers: 1
Number of Folder Property Transfers: 0
Number of Symlink Transfers: 0
Total Number of Transfers: 1
Number of File Transfers Completed: 1
Number of Folder Transfers Completed: 0
Number of File Transfers Failed: 0
Number of Folder Transfers Failed: 0
Number of File Transfers Skipped: 0
Number of Folder Transfers Skipped: 0
TotalBytesTransferred: 19
Final Job Status: Completed
```

Figure 9.4: AzCopy Script Run

You have just learned how to copy data between containers using `AzCopy`, which brings this section to an end, where you have learned what `AzCopy` is, how to download it, how it works, and also how to copy data between different containers. In the next section, you will learn about storage replication and lifecycle management.

> **Note**
>
> You are encouraged to read up further on the topic by using the following links:
>
> **AzCopy documentation:** https://learn.microsoft.com/en-us/azure/storage/common/storage-use-azcopy-v10
>
> **Authorizing to AzCopy using Azure AD/Microsoft Entra ID:** https://learn.microsoft.com/en-us/azure/storage/common/storage-use-azcopy-authorize-azure-active-directory

Configuring Storage Replication and Lifecycle Management

In this section, you will explore the various storage replication and lifecycle management features available to you in Azure. Storage replication involves copying data from a source to a destination, typically to ensure that it remains accessible in the event of a failure or disaster. Lifecycle management refers to the management of an object from its creation to its retirement or disposal. These features enable the efficient use of your storage resources through policies that move blob data to different access tiers in accordance with your predefined rules. For example, you can configure a policy to move data not accessed within the last 90 days to cool storage and then transfer it back to the hot tier for enhanced performance when it is required again.

As part of the storage replication and management services section to follow, you will learn about topics such as the Azure File Sync service, blob object replication, blob lifecycle management, blob data protection, blob versioning, immutable storage, and storage account deletion.

Storage Replication and Management Services

The following section will explore the various storage replication services available for Azure Storage.

Azure File Sync

Azure File Sync enables you to synchronize your organization's file shares (on-premises or similar) with Azure Files, providing a local cache of your data for faster access and improved performance. This allows you to enjoy the flexibility, compatibility, and performance of your local file shares (such as an on-premises file server) but also store a copy of all the data within the file share in Azure.

The service offers versatility when it comes to connectivity, as it allows you to use any protocol that's available on Windows Server to access your data locally, including **Server Message Block** (**SMB**), **Network File System** (**NFS**), and **File Transfer Protocol over TLS** (**FTPS**).

The Azure File Sync service also enables disaster recovery for your data, protecting you from unforeseen outages in your synced environments that are replicated with Azure Files. Should any synced sites go down, you can recover your data from Azure by building a new server and reestablishing the sync without the loss of existing data in Azure Files. You can also directly access Azure Files storage. In addition, you can leverage Azure Storage redundancy to maintain multiple copies of your data. This means you can change to **zone-redundant storage** (**ZRS**) or **geo-redundant storage** (**GRS**) to prevent data loss at various layers. For an added layer of protection, you should consider Azure Backup for the recovery of data modifications (such as unintentional overwrites) and prevention of data loss.

Blob Object Replication

Blob object replication provides the capability within Azure to replicate blob objects based on replication rules. The copy will run asynchronously between source and destination containers across two different storage accounts. Several rules can be configured for your desired outcome. Note that for replication to be enabled, blob versioning needs to be enabled. Blob object replication is similar to the exercise you completed earlier using `AzCopy` on the copy side of the replication. The replication for the storage account is conducted automatically once it's enabled and uses a special technique for detecting changes.

Blob Life Cycle Management

This is a capability available for GPv2 storage accounts, Blob Storage accounts, and Azure Data Lake Storage. It allows the management of the blob lifecycle through rule-based policies. Data can be automatically transitioned to cooler and cheaper tiers using this functionality. Data can also, in accordance with policies, be expired and deleted. The following actions can be applied to blobs based on the requirements, automated data tiering, blob snapshots, blob versioning, and blob deletion. Multiple rules can be created and can also be applied to a subset of blobs and containers through filters such as name prefixes. If multiple rules are created, you will need to apply the rules in order of tier temperature, moving from hot to cool, then from cool to cold, then to archive, and then to deletion. Pricing for blob lifecycle management is based upon tier operational charges, but the service itself is free, and delete operations are also free. It should be noted that this is a great feature to assist in the optimization of your overall storage account costs by automatically transitioning between tiers.

Blob Data Protection

Blob data protection is a mechanism that assists with the recovery of data in the event of data being deleted or overwritten. The implementation of data protection is a proactive measure to secure data before an incident occurs. Azure Storage provides the capability of protecting data from being deleted or modified, as well as the restoration of data that has been deleted or modified. **Soft delete for containers or blobs** enables you to restore data based on a chosen period for retaining deleted data; the default configuration is seven days. When you restore a container, the blobs, as well as the versions and snapshots, are restored.

Blob Versioning

Blob versioning enables a blob to maintain several versions of an object, which can be used for restoring blob data as the version captures the current state of the blob upon being created or modified. This operation is run automatically when blob versioning is enabled. Blob versioning is a powerful feature as it enables you to restore data if it has been modified or deleted. There are several use cases where this may be useful to you:

- **Data recovery**: Restore data to a previous version if it has been deleted or modified. This is particularly useful for the restoration of accidentally deleted data.
- **Compliance**: With blob versioning, a history of all changes is maintained, which is crucial for audit trails and meeting any compliance requirements you may need to adhere to, such as a rule where data cannot be deleted for seven years. You can also see who made changes and when.
- **Application development**: While developing applications, many changes can happen to code files. A version history will allow the recovery of any data that it stores.
- **Data anaylsis**: Historical data can be beneficial for data analysts looking to analyze trends and make comparisons of metrics over time.
- **Backup and restore**: Blob versioning can act as an additional layer of backup and remove the need for solely relying on traditional backup solutions.

In the next section, you will learn how immutable storage provides additional benefits by enhancing your compliance and preventing changes to data.

Immutable Storage

Immutable storage, often referred to as **Write Once, Read Many** (**WORM**), can be configured on Blob Storage. This is often used to protect data from accidental deletion or overwrites. Often, there is a legal requirement to manage data in this manner. It is always advised that you understand your organization's governance requirements regarding data to ensure you comply with them.

Immutable storage can be configured with two types of policies:

- **Time-based retention policies**: Data objects are managed against a time policy for the duration that the active policy data follows WORM, but after the expiration of this, *data may be deleted but not overwritten*.
- **Legal hold policies**: Data is held in a WORM state until the legal hold policy is explicitly cleared. This is often for *litigation requirements*.

> **Note**
> Container soft delete can only restore the entire container with all the contents, not individual blobs. To achieve blob-level recovery capability, soft delete for blobs should be enabled.

Storage Account Deletion

There are circumstances when you may delete a storage account and, after deletion, realize that you need to recover the data. In these instances, the storage account can potentially be recovered, provided the account was deleted fewer than 14 days ago and the following requirements are also met:

- The storage account was created using the ARM model
- A storage account with the same name has not been provisioned since the deletion of the storage account in question
- The user performing the recovery has the appropriate permissions

> **Note**
> You can read more about this process of recovery here: `https://learn.microsoft.com/en-us/azure/storage/common/storage-account-recover`.

Next, you will explore the creation and configuration of an Azure File Sync instance.

Creating and Configuring an Azure File Sync Instance

In the next demonstration, you are going to configure Azure File Sync. You will need the following to be in place to follow this demonstration; if you have not deleted the resources from the previous chapter, you can use them for the requirements of this chapter:

- **Windows Server**: You may use Windows Server 2012 R2, 2016, 2019, or 2022. Make sure that you enable **Remote Desktop (RDP)** on the server.
- **A storage account**: You will create a storage account in one of the supported regions for Azure File Sync. The following website can be referenced for the available regions: `https://azure.microsoft.com/en-gb/explore/global-infrastructure/products-by-region/?products=storage`. Please note that either the storage account must allow public network access from all networks, or the server IP and the storage account service must be added for secure access.
- **An Azure file share**: This must be provisioned in the storage account.

> **Note**
> Opening the RDP port for a VM during its creation is covered later in the book. This can be configured upon VM creation in Azure. You can also do the exercises in previous chapters where you set up an RDP session.

You can begin the creation of the Azure File Sync instance in Azure once the preceding resources have been created for the exercise. Following this, you can move on to the installation of Azure File Sync on Windows Server. To create an Azure File Sync instance in Azure, follow these steps:

1. Navigate to the Azure portal by opening `https://portal.azure.com`.
2. From the left hamburger menu, click `+ Create a resource`.

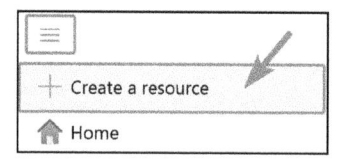

Figure 9.5: Creating a resource

3. In the search box, type `Azure File Sync` and press *Enter* on your keyboard. Click `Azure File Sync` from the search results. Then, click *Create*.

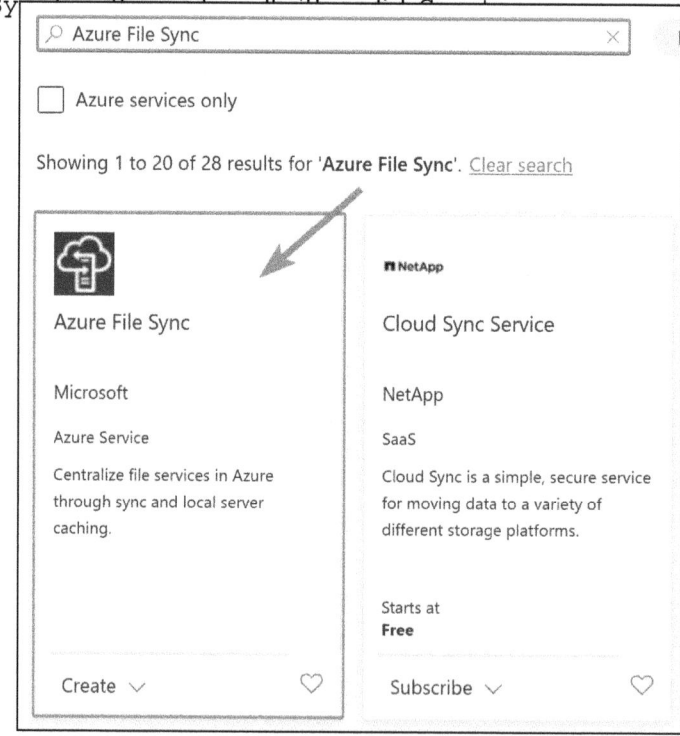

Figure 9.6: Searching for Azure File Sync

4. Set `Subscription` and `Resource group`. The resource group should be the same as the one where the storage account resides that you created for this exercise. Define `Storage sync service name`, and then select the same region as the storage account region.

Configuring Storage Replication and Lifecycle Management | 295

After entering the values, click `Review + Create`. Then, click `Create`.

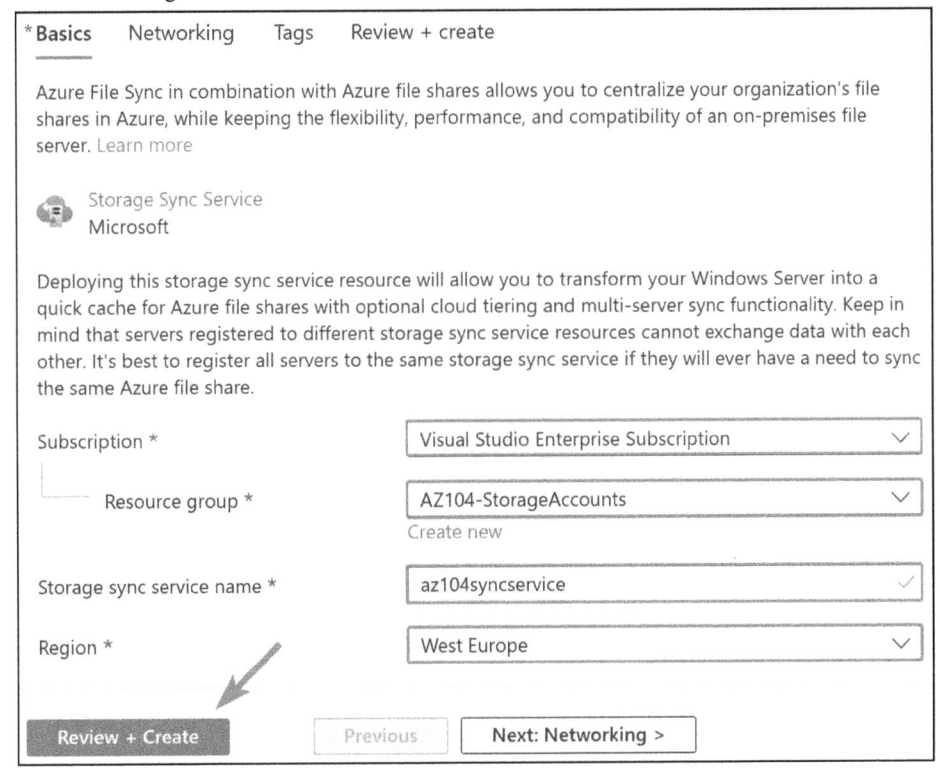

Figure 9.7: Deploying Azure File Sync

5. After deployment, open the Storage Sync Service resource. From the left menu, select `Sync groups` and click `+ Sync group` in the top menu of the blade.

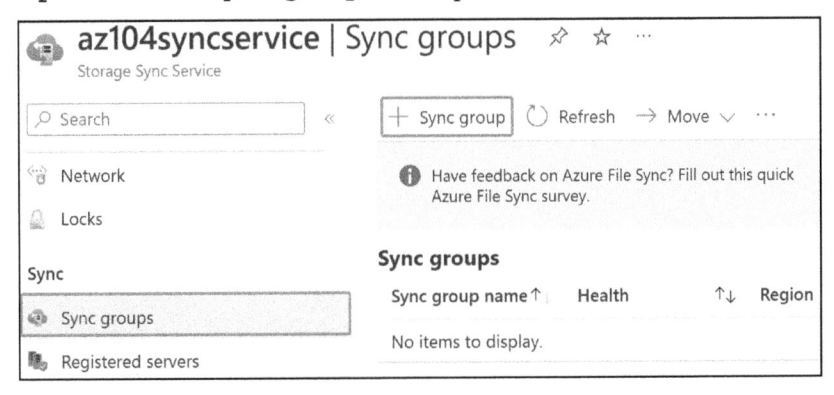

Figure 9.8: Creating an Azure File Sync group

6. Fill in `Sync group name`, configure `Subscription`, set `Storage account`, and choose the Azure file share you created at the beginning of this section. Click `Create`.

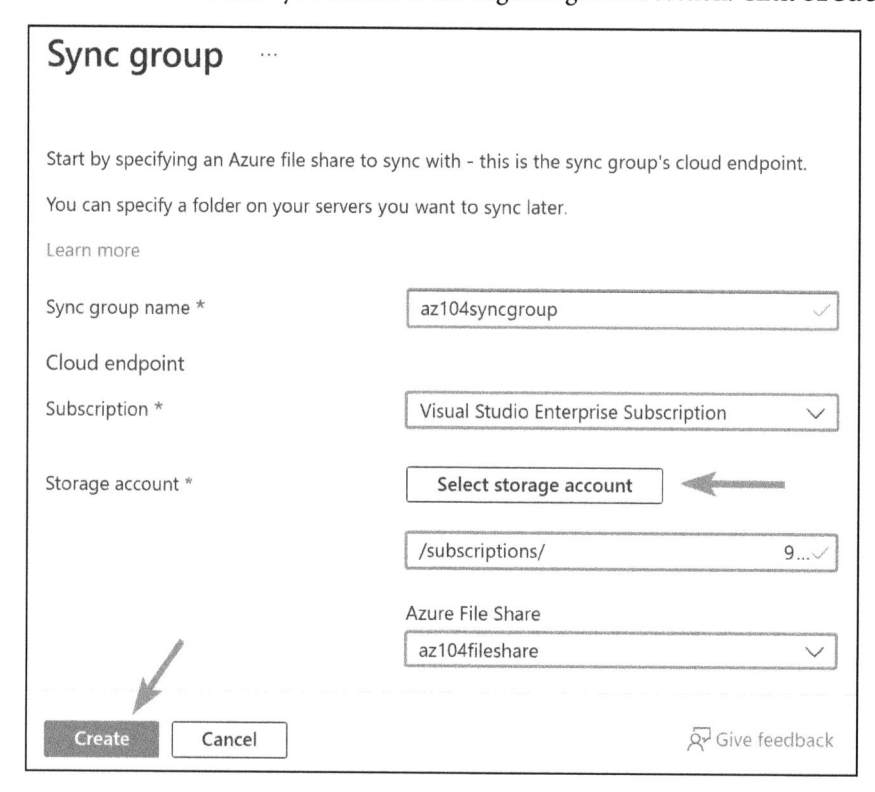

Figure 9.9: Deploying an Azure File Sync group

7. RDP to one of your Windows Server instances and log in. You should first disable `Internet Explorer Enhanced Security Configuration`. To do this, open `Server Manager` and select `Local Server` from the left menu. Click `IE Enhanced Security Configuration`. Disable it for administrators, then click `OK`.

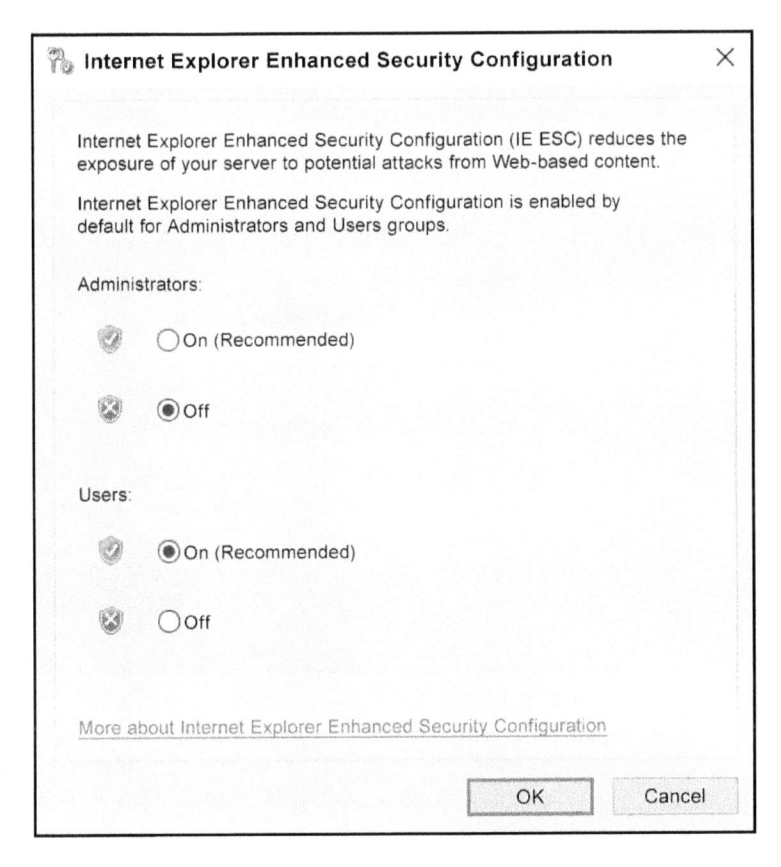

Figure 9.10: Disabling IE Enhanced Security Configuration

8. Download the Azure File Sync agent from the following website and select the appropriate downloader: https://www.microsoft.com/en-us/download/details.aspx?id=57159.

9. Install the agent on the server (choose the appropriate one for your server version). On the first screen, click Next, then check the box for I accept the terms in the License Agreement. Keep the default path to install the agent and click Next.

10. On the next screen, select Use the existing proxy settings configured on the server, and click Next.

11. Select Use Microsoft Update and click Next. On the following screen, click Install.

12. Once the installation is complete, click Finish to exit the setup wizard.

13. The Server Registration tool will start to run. This is where you can register the server. You need to sign in by clicking the Sign in button (leave the Azure environment as AzureCloud and leave the default settings).

14. Choose the Azure subscription, resource group, and Storage Sync Service instance, then click `Register`.

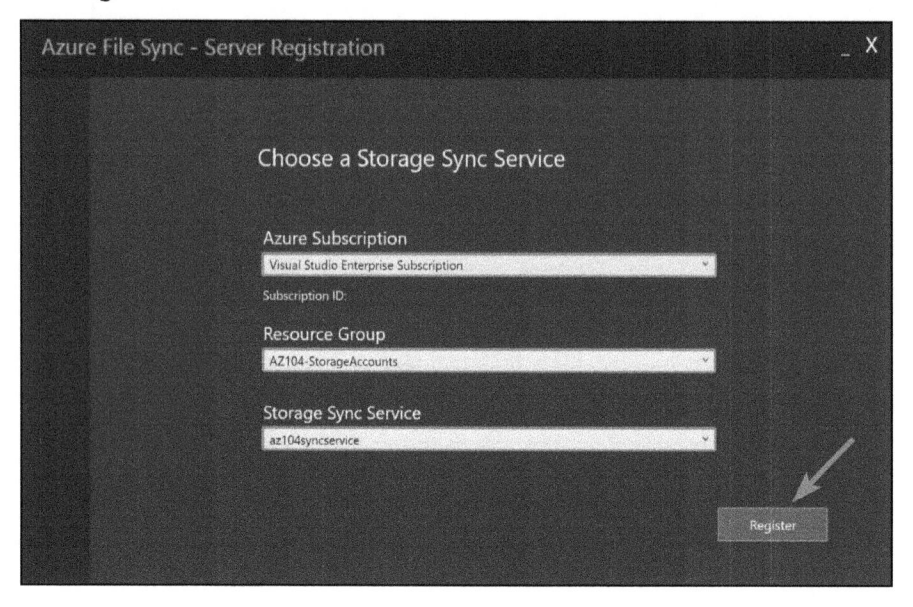

Figure 9.11: Azure File Sync – Server Registration

15. A trust relationship will be established once the registration is complete. This will establish trust between the on-premises server and Storage Sync Service in Azure. Click `Close`.

16. Next, return to the Azure portal. Navigate to Storage Sync Service again and select the sync group that you created earlier. Within the sync group settings blade, under the `Server endpoints` context, click `+ Add server endpoint`.

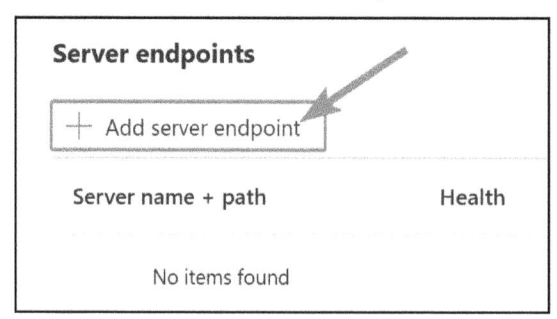

Figure 9.12: Azure File Sync – adding a server endpoint

17. Select the registered server and provide the following path: `D:\Data`. Keep `Cloud Tiering` as `Disabled`.

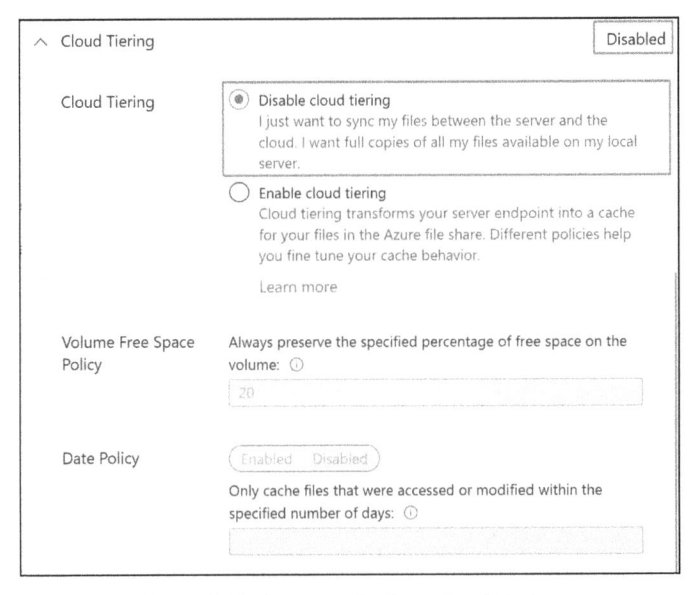

Configuring Storage Replication and Lifecycle Management

Figure 9.13: Server endpoint – cloud tiering

18. Leave `Initial Upload` configured as the `merge` option, with the `Initial download` configuration set to `Download the namespace first`. Click `Create`.

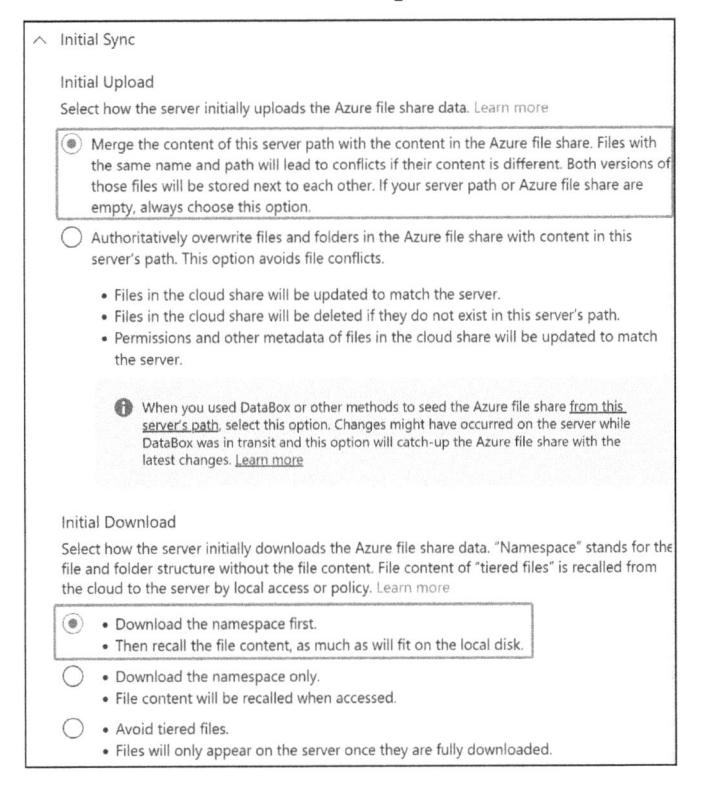

Figure 9.14: Server endpoint – initial sync

19. It will take about 15 minutes for the endpoint to be created. Once it has been created, return to the VM where you installed the sync agent and open the D: drive. You will see that there is a folder added named Data. As you can see from the following screenshot, you can now copy files to the Data folder:

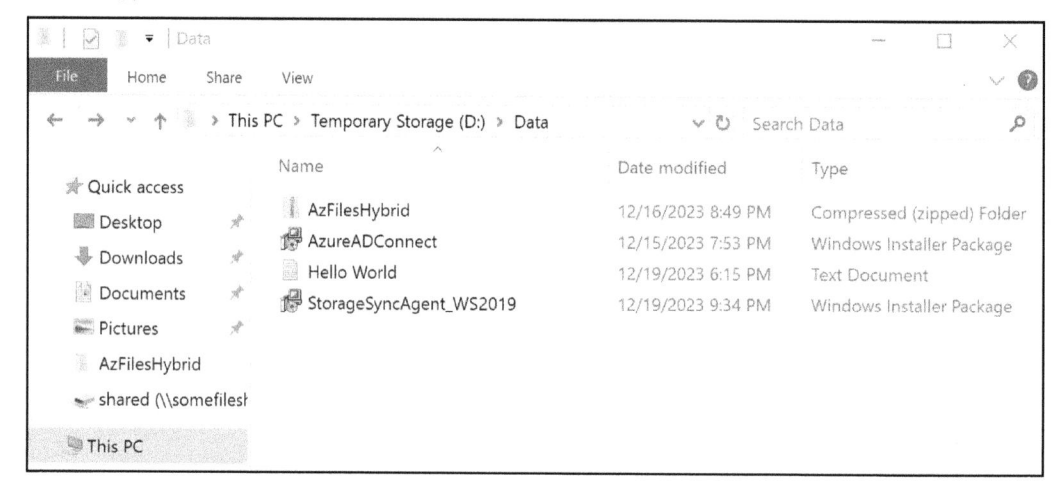

Figure 9.15: Azure File Sync – Data folder

20. Navigate back to the file share in Azure. You will see that all the files are synced to the storage account, as shown in the following screenshot:

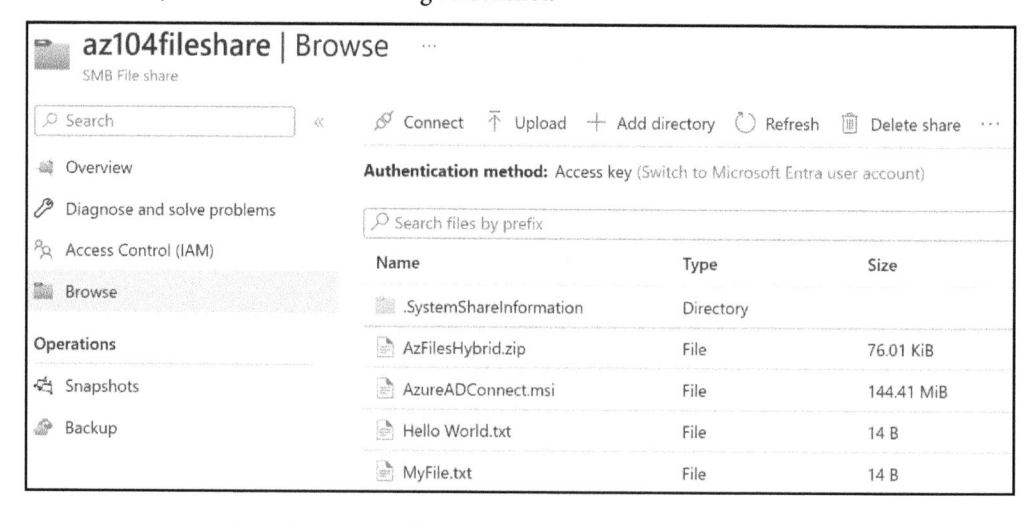

Figure 9.16: Azure File Sync – synced files in Azure file storage

This concludes the section about Azure file storage and the Azure File Sync service. Next, you are going to explore snapshots for Azure Files.

Working with Azure File Snapshots

File snapshots are point-in-time, read-only copies of data as found in Azure file shares. These snapshots enable you to restore previous versions of files, protecting against data corruption and unwanted changes or deletions and providing backup functionality. A couple of examples of where this might be useful are recovering data from accidental deletions and reverting to previous versions of a file (such as a development version) if previous iterations of a file are needed.

There are several benefits of snapshots:

- Protection against data corruption
- Protection against unwanted changes or deletions
- Backup functionality
- Incremental data storage nature (only data that has changed since the last snapshot will be added to your current storage usage)

In this exercise, you are going to create a snapshot of an Azure file share:

1. Navigate to the Azure portal by opening `https://portal.azure.com`.
2. Select a storage account with an Azure file share.

Navigate into the file share and, in the left-hand menu under the `Operations` context, click `Snapshots`.

Click `+ Add snapshot` to create a snapshot. Enter any comment and click OK.

You have now learned how to create a snapshot of your Azure file share. Next, you will explore opening your snapshot to browse the files it contains. Follow these steps to open snapshots of your file share:

1. Navigate to the Azure portal by opening `https://portal.azure.com`.
2. Select the storage account from the previous exercise.
3. Navigate into the file share and, in the left-hand menu under the `Operations` context, click `Snapshots`.
4. Click on the snapshots to open the next blade, which contains all the files at that point in time.
5. Selecting any file will present a properties window that will allow you to download the specific file.

You have now learned how to download specific files from a snapshot in your Azure file shares. In the next section, you are going to look at Azure Storage redundancy.

Implementing Azure Storage Redundancy

In the previous chapter, you learned about the different replication options available in Azure, including **locally redundant storage (LRS)**, **zone-redundant storage (ZRS)**, **geo-redundant storage (GRS)**, and **geo-zone-redundant storage (GZRS)**. In this section, you will explore changing the replication strategy chosen for a deployed storage account. Follow these steps to implement Azure Storage replication:

1. Navigate to the Azure portal by opening `https://portal.azure.com`.
2. Select a storage account to configure.
3. In the `Storage account` blade, navigate to the left menu, then under `Data management`, click on `Redundancy`. Note the option to be able to change redundancy and the visual map of the storage locations.
4. Click on the `Redundancy` drop-down menu, then select the appropriate option and click `Save` at the top of the screen.

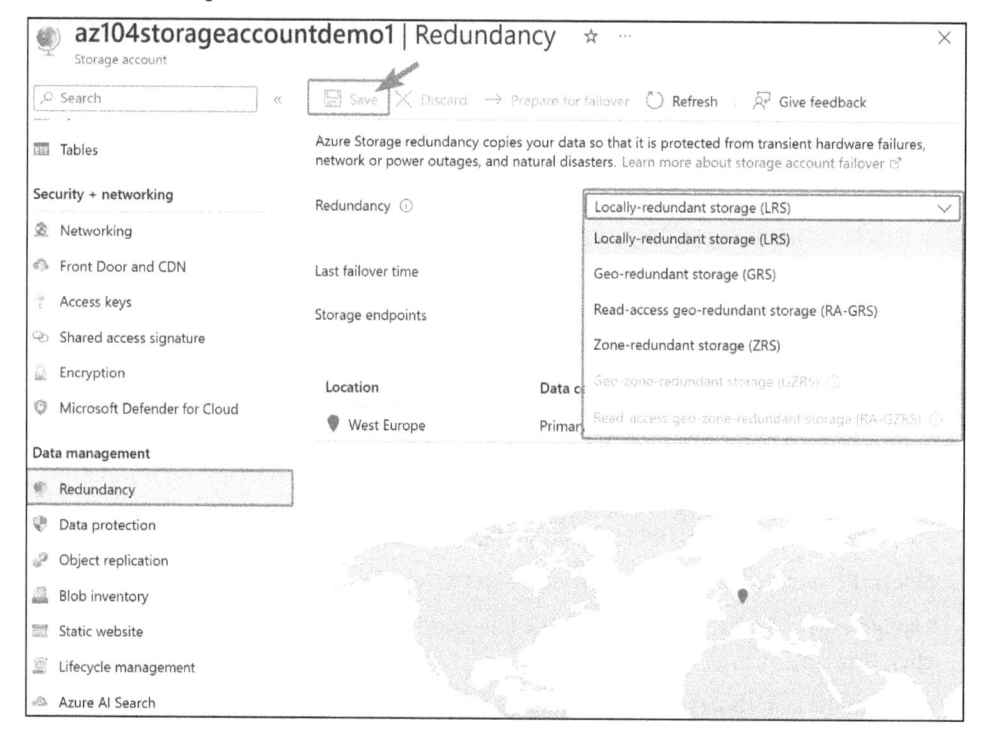

Figure 9.17: Storage account redundancy configuration

In this exercise, you completed the configuration of the replication type for a storage account, which is beneficial when planning the required redundancy for your storage. This is particularly useful when considering geographically dispersed redundancy. In the next section, you will look at configuration blob object replication.

> **Note**
>
> For enhanced security, it is advised that the `Secure transfer required` and `Allow Blob anonymous access` options in the `Configuration` blade for a storage account are configured to `Enabled`. Also, `Minimum TLS version` should be set to `TLS 1.2`.

Configuring Blob Object Replication

In the following demonstration, you will learn how to configure blob object replication. To follow along, you will require two storage accounts:

1. Navigate to the Azure portal by opening `https://portal.azure.com`.
2. Go to a storage account, then in the left menu, under `Data management`, click `Object replication`. Click `+ Create replication rules` in the top menu.

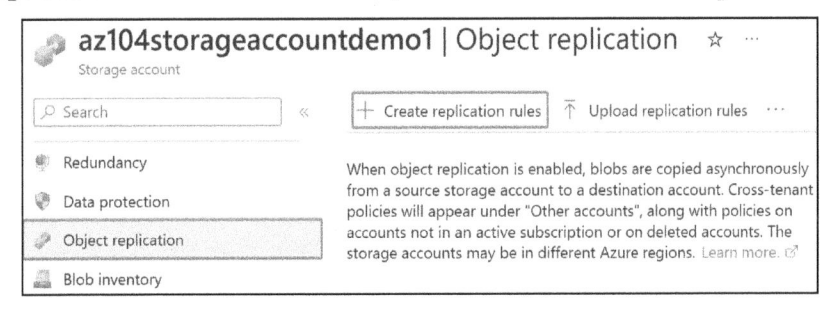

Figure 9.18: Object replication – Create replication rules

3. Select the destination storage account; you can create a new one if you don't have one yet and then return to this step. Next, choose source and destination containers. Click add under `Filters`.

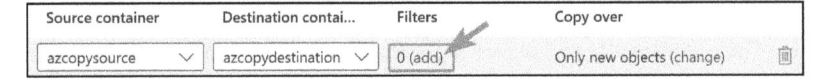

Figure 9.19: Object replication – Filters

4. On the screen that pops up, enter `Azure` for `Prefix match` and click `Save`. This will be used to filter all items, such as folders and blobs, that match the prefix entered.

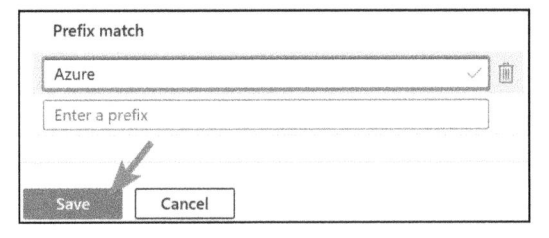

Figure 9.20: Object replication – Prefix match

5. Under the `Copy over` context, click `change`.

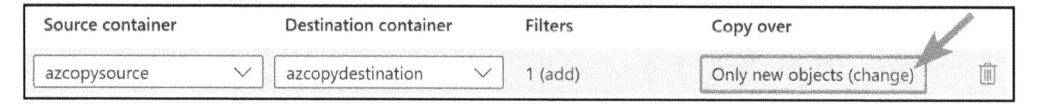

Figure 9.21: Object replication – copy over rules

6. On the subsequent screen, select `Everything`. Click `Save`. Then, click `Create`.

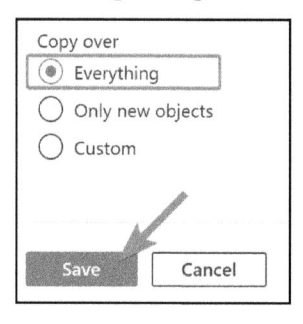

Figure 9.22 – Copy over rules

7. Navigate to your source storage account and then the source container. Upload some items that have names starting with "Azure." You can even make some files up.

8. Wait five minutes and then navigate to your destination container and notice that the files copied across are now in your destination container too, matching the implemented rule(s).

You have now completed the configuration of blob object replication and have seen it in action. In the next section, you will explore blob lifecycle management.

> **Note**
> While it may be tempting to view object replication as a backup mechanism, this should not be relied upon as a backup service. There are differences in SLAs, for instance, and errors will be replicated too. Also, remember that data is copied asynchronously, which means there is a delay before the changes appear in the destination copy.

Configuring Blob Life Cycle Management

The following exercise will demonstrate the configuration of blob lifecycle management:

1. Navigate to the Azure portal by opening `https://portal.azure.com`.
2. Go to a storage account and create a container named `demo`.

3. In the left menu, under `Data management` for the storage account, click `Lifecycle Management`. Click `+ Add a rule` in the top menu.

4. Enter `HotToCoolTiering` as `Rule name` and change `Rule scope` to `Limit blobs with filters`. You can leave `Blob type` as `Block blobs` and `Blob subtype` as `Base blobs`. Click Next.

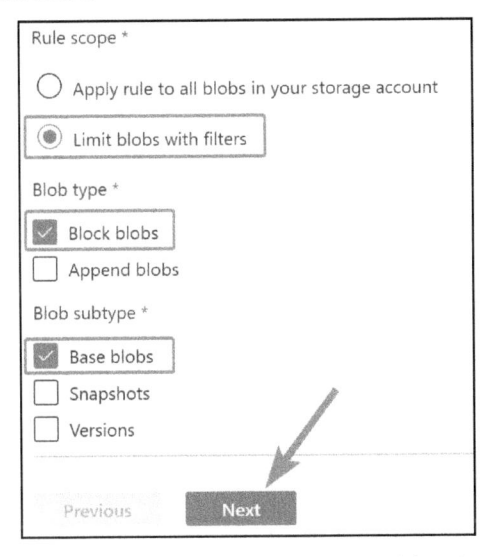

Figure 9.23: Lifecycle management – add a rule

5. You will note that the `Base blobs` tab will present a conditional statement (`if..then`) for the blobs. Based on a time interval, an automated action can be performed. Set the first condition parameter for `Base blobs were to Last modified`. For the `More than (days ago)` field, enter 1. For the `Then` field, change the drop-down option to `Move to cool storage`. Note that to apply multiple actions for a rule, you can click `+ Add conditions`. Please click this now. The condition you have just configured basically applies as follows: for blobs that are more than one day old, automatically move them to cool storage.

6. For the next conditional block, enter 1 in the `More than (days ago)` field, and select `Delete the blob` for the Then dropdown. Click Next. The condition you have just configured will delete blobs that are more than two days old. For example, if a blob is already two days old, saying it is a further one day older means it will be deleted three days after it was last modified. To summarize how the rule works, blobs that are more than one day old will be moved to cold storage for archival purposes, and blobs that remain in cold storage for another day (i.e., become two or more days old) are then deleted.

7. The `Filter set` tab allows you to define a blob prefix for filtering a subset of blobs. In the `Blob prefix` field, enter `demo/pic`. Click `Add`.

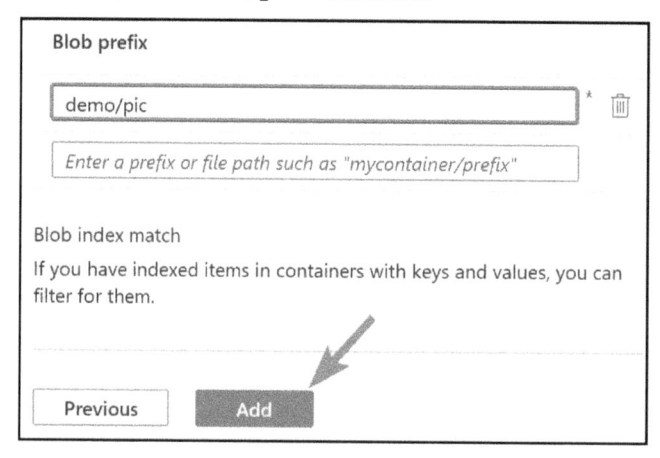

Figure 9.24: Lifecycle management – filter set

In this exercise, you created your first lifecycle management rule for transitioning your blobs to cool storage for archival and then deleting where the age exceeds two days or more. Next, you will explore how to implement a lifecycle management policy using JSON code.

Lifecycle Management Policy Deployed as Code

At times, it may be desired to implement your policy as code, especially where the reuse of policies is applicable. This approach drives better consistency and reduces the likelihood of errors. In the following exercise, you will deploy a lifecycle management policy using code. You will configure a policy to move blobs starting with the word `log` in the `files` container to the **cool tier** if they have not been accessed for **three or more days**. Complete the steps that follow:

1. Navigate to the Azure portal by opening `https://portal.azure.com`.
2. Go to a storage account and create a container named `demo2`.
3. In the left menu, under `Data management` at the storage account level, click `Lifecycle Management`. Click `Code View`.

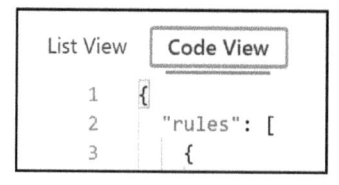

Figure 9.25: Code View

4. Modify the following JSON code to suit your deployment. The current code *moves any blob to the cold tier where the period since the last modification is more than three days*. The filter part will ensure that the code is designed to run only against your `files` container where files start with `log`:

```json
{
    "rules": [
      {
        "enabled": true,
        "name": "move-to-cool",
        "type": "Lifecycle",
        "definition": {
          "actions": {
            «baseBlob": {
              «tierToCool": {
                «daysAfterModificationGreaterThan": 1
              }
            }
          },
          "filters": {
            «blobTypes": [
              «blockBlob"
            ],
            «prefixMatch": [
              "files/log"
            ]
          }
        }
      }
    ]
}
```

5. Copy the modified code in the preceding code block into the `Code View` section in the Azure portal and click `Save`.

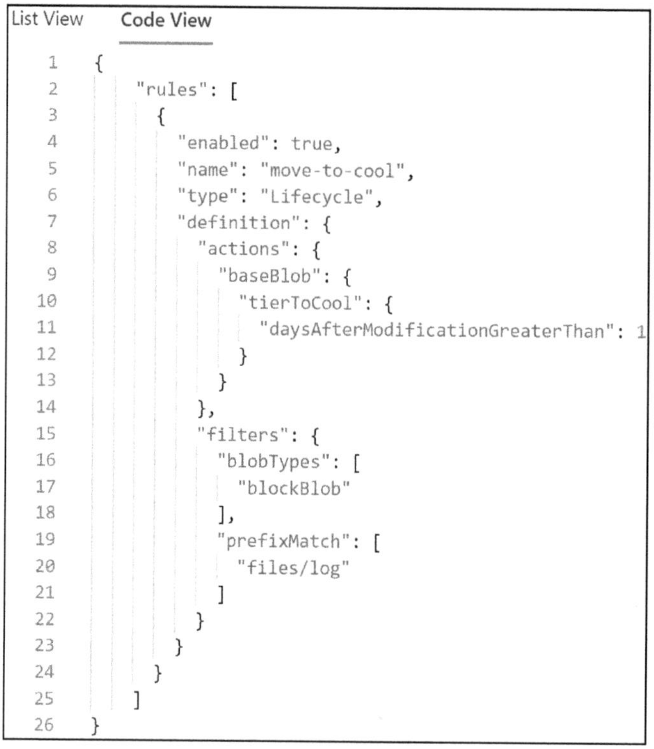

```
List View    Code View
1    {
2        "rules": [
3            {
4                "enabled": true,
5                "name": "move-to-cool",
6                "type": "Lifecycle",
7                "definition": {
8                    "actions": {
9                        "baseBlob": {
10                           "tierToCool": {
11                               "daysAfterModificationGreaterThan": 1
12                           }
13                       }
14                   },
15                   "filters": {
16                       "blobTypes": [
17                           "blockBlob"
18                       ],
19                       "prefixMatch": [
20                           "files/log"
21                       ]
22                   }
23               }
24           }
25       ]
26   }
```

Figure 9.26: Blob life cycle management – Code View

6. Go back to `List View` and notice that the rule has been modified to reflect the new name and will of course adopt the new settings that you have implemented.

In this exercise, you learned how to configure a lifecycle management policy using JSON code. The rule moves blobs starting with the keyword `log` to cool-tier storage if they have not been accessed for three or more days. This feature is useful in either reducing costs for infrequently accessed data or for improving performance on certain data. In the next section, you will explore the ability to disable and delete a rule.

Deleting a Life Cycle Management Rule

You might want to delete a lifecycle management rule when it is no longer needed, such as in a scenario where the log files you are gathering are all being moved to the cold tier and you are receiving complaints about slow access to the log data. You might decide that you no longer wish to have this rule in place and therefore plan to delete it. The following steps will guide you through the process of deleting a rule:

1. Open a storage account with a lifecycle management rule configured and click the **Lifecycle management** button in the storage account menu.
2. Hover over the rule you would like to modify and note that a checkbox appears to the left of it. Click this.

Name	Status	Blob type
move-to-cool	Enabled	Block

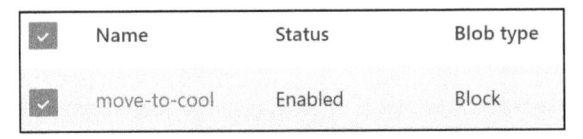

Figure 9.27: Selecting a rule

3. Note that the top menu bar now provides the option to disable or delete the rule. Disabling will stop the rule from applying until enabled again and deleting will remove the rule permanently. Click `Delete`.

Figure 9.28: Deleting a rule

That brings an end to the blob lifecycle management section. In the next section, you will explore blob data protection.

> **Note**
> Automated data tiering moves blobs to cooler tiers or deletes them. Associated actions within a single rule must follow a transitive implementation from hotter tiers to cooler tiers. This feature can be an asset in managing and optimizing storage costs.

Configuring Blob Data Protection

In the following exercise, you will explore configuring soft delete options as part of the data protection options available to you:

1. Navigate to the Azure portal by opening `https://portal.azure.com`.
2. Go to a storage account. In the left menu, under the `Data management` context, click `Data protection`. Select the options under the `Recovery` context for `Enable soft delete for blobs` and `Enable soft delete for containers`.

    Set both periods to 7 days and click `Save`.

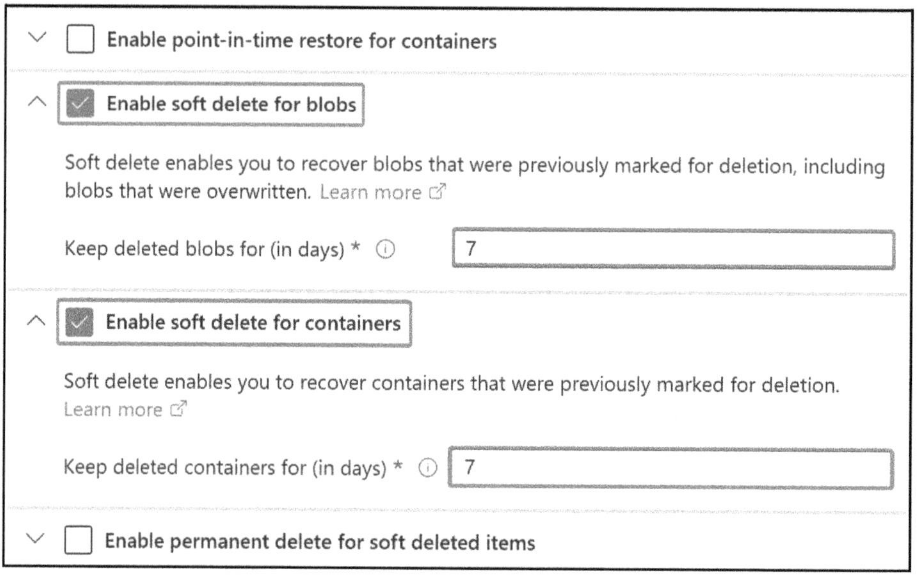

Figure 9.29: Blob data protection

3. You will receive a success notification indicating that the setting has taken effect.

You now know how to configure blob data protection settings on your storage accounts. Now you will be provided with additional reading material for the configuration of storage replication and lifecycle management.

> **Hands-on activities and Further reading**
>
> Reinforce what you learned in *Chapters 6* through *9* by completing the hands-on activities for these chapters. Open the online practice resources using this link: `https://packt.link/az104dash`. Then, from the Dashboard, click `Hands-on Activities` and open the menu `Implementing and Managing Storage`
>
> You are encouraged to read up further on the topic by using the following links:
>
> **Azure File Sync:** `https://learn.microsoft.com/en-us/azure/storage/file-sync/file-sync-introduction`
>
> **Configuring object replication:** `https://learn.microsoft.com/en-gb/azure/storage/blobs/object-replication-configure`
>
> **Blob versioning:** `https://learn.microsoft.com/en-gb/azure/storage/blobs/versioning-overview`
>
> **Blob lifecycle management:** `https://learn.microsoft.com/en-us/azure/storage/blobs/lifecycle-management-overview`
>
> **Blob data protection overview:** `https://learn.microsoft.com/en-us/azure/storage/blobs/data-protection-overview`

Summary

In this chapter, you learned how to use the `AzCopy` tool for copying data, and about the various storage replication options and blob lifecycle management. You explored topics relating to Azure File Sync (used to create caches of your Azure files) for increased localized performance. You learned about blob object replication (used to copy data between storage accounts and regions), blob lifecycle management (used to move data between storage tiers for enhanced performance or storage cost optimization), blob data protection, blob versioning, immutable storage (used for protecting against modifications and accidental deletion of data needed for adherence to compliance), and storage account deletion. You now have the skills to configure storage replication and blob lifecycle management. You also know how to utilize the `AzCopy` tool to copy files using code.

> **Note**
>
> Remember to delete the resources you created in this chapter to minimize costs. You can do this with the following command, which will remove the resource group and all the corresponding resources: `Remove-AzResourceGroup -Name AZ104-StorageAccounts`

Exam Readiness Drill - Chapters 7-9

Apart from mastering key concepts, strong test-taking skills under time pressure are essential for acing your certification exam. That's why developing these abilities early in your learning journey is critical.

Exam readiness drills, using the free online practice resources provided with this book, help you progressively improve your time management and test-taking skills while reinforcing the key concepts you've learned.

HOW TO GET STARTED

- Open the link or scan the QR code at the bottom of this page
- If you have unlocked the practice resources, already log in to your registered account. If you haven't, follow the instructions in *Chapter 23* and come back to this page.
- Once you log in, click the START button to start a quiz
- We recommend attempting a quiz multiple times till you're able to answer most of the questions correctly and well within the time limit.
- You can use the following practice template to help you plan your attempts :

Attempt	Target	Time Limit
Working On Accuracy		
Attempt 1	40% or more	Till the timer runs out
Attempt 2	60% or more	Till the timer runs out
Attempt 3	75% or more	Till the timer runs out
Working On Timing		
Attempt 4	75% or more	1 minute before time limit
Attempt 5	75% or more	2 minutes before time limit
Attempt 6	75% or more	3 minutes before time limit

The above drill is just an example. Design your drills based on your own goals and make the most out of the online quizzes accompanying this book.

First time accessing the online resources? 🔒
You'll need to unlock them through a one-time process. **Head to** *Chapter 23* **for instructions.**

Open Quiz

https://packt.link/az104e3ch7-9

OR scan this QR code →

10
Azure Resource Manager Templates

In this chapter, you will delve into Azure **infrastructure as code** (**IaC**) using **Azure Resource Manager** (**ARM**) templates. IaC involves using code and automation to provision and manage infrastructure instead of relying on manual methods. This technique ensures that infrastructure components are deployed consistently and can be repeated reliably. You will gain an essential understanding of and hands-on experience with this powerful tool to define, deploy, and manage Azure resources in a consistent, manageable, and repeatable structure. You will learn about key concepts and practical examples to help you confidently author, modify, and deploy Azure resources using ARM templates. By the end of this chapter, you'll be well equipped with the knowledge and skills needed to manage Azure resources and infrastructure efficiently and effectively.

In this chapter, you will learn about the following topics:

- Understanding ARM templates
- Benefits of ARM
- Understanding the ARM template structure
- Creating an ARM template
- Modifying an existing ARM template
- Exporting an ARM template
- Azure QuickStart Templates

Technical Requirements

This chapter has the following technical requirements:

- To follow along with the hands-on lessons, you will need access to **Microsoft Entra ID** as a global administrator.
- You will need access to an Azure subscription with owner or contributor privileges. If you do not have access to one, students can enroll for a free account: https://azure.microsoft.com/en-us/free/.

- **PowerShell 5.1** or later must be installed on a Windows PC, or PowerShell Core 6.x on other operating systems where labs can be practiced from.

- Windows users need to install **.NET Framework 4.7.2** or later using the following link: https://learn.microsoft.com/en-us/dotnet/framework/install.

- Where PowerShell is not installed or available, https://shell.azure.com can be used as a browser-based shell.

- Installation of the Az PowerShell module, which can be performed by running the following in an administrative PowerShell session:

    ```
    Set-ExecutionPolicy -ExecutionPolicy RemoteSigned -Scope
    CurrentUser
    Install-Module -Name Az -Scope CurrentUser -Repository PSGallery
    -Force
    ```

Understanding ARM Templates

ARM templates are used to define infrastructure that needs to be deployed in Azure, which is also often referred to as **IaC**. One of the benefits of ARM templates is the ability to deploy resources rapidly via code with a level of consistency as opposed to deploying resources via the Azure portal, which is prone to errors and might introduce misconfigurations when repeating tasks. It is also useful to view deployment history.

ARM templates make use of the **JavaScript Object Notation (JSON)** format to define resources. To deploy ARM templates, there are two JSON files of importance:

- **Template file**: This is the main file and has sections to define parameters, variables, user-defined functions, resources, and outputs

- **Parameters file**: This file can be standalone or linked to the template file, which is usually done when there are many parameters used in complex deployments

Figure 10.1 shows how the ARM template structure looks when empty. Notice that each area has an opening and closing brace, { }; this is how JSON objects are defined as starting and ending in their description:

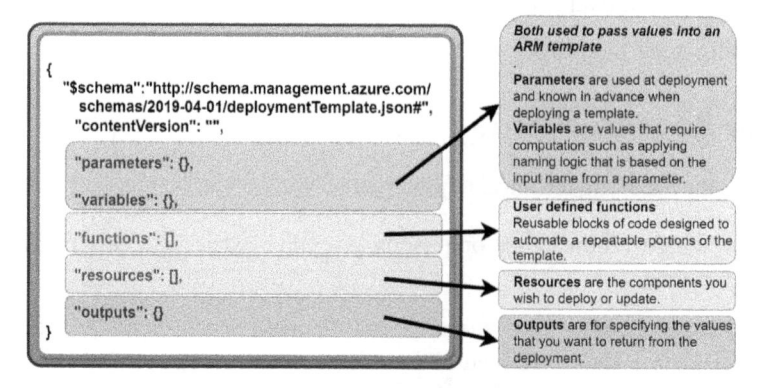

Figure 10.1: ARM structure

> **Note**
> As of version 2.0 of the ARM language, `resources` are declared as `"resources": {}`. There is also the introduction of a new section called `definitions` that sits above `parameters` in the structure definition. Read more about the enhancements to the ARM language with version 2.0 here: https://learn.microsoft.com/en-us/azure/azure-resource-manager/templates/syntax#languageversion-2-0.

The next few sections will be pivotal in building the foundations of your knowledge around ARM template deployments and potentially your exposure to IaC.

Understanding ARM is important to be able to answer the IaC-related questions you can expect in your exam, where you will be tested on being able to write the correct code or spot syntax errors. First, you will learn about the benefits of ARM and then move on to the structure and eventually into the deployment of ARM templates.

Benefits of ARM

There may be situations where you would like to rapidly deploy infrastructure in a consistent and automated manner. ARM is a great tool for enabling this capability as well as several other benefits, as listed here, which are sure to pique your interest:

- **Consistency**: ARM templates ensure that deployments are consistent and repeatable across different environments (development, testing, and production) and subscriptions, reducing the chances of configuration drift. Your deployments are standardized because they are predefined in a template file, and as a result, risk is reduced too.

- **Declarative**: With ARM templates, you define the desired end state of your infrastructure using JSON. This declarative approach focuses on what resources you require, rather than specifying the sequence in which they need to be created or deployed.

- **Idempotence**: ARM templates are idempotent, meaning you can run them multiple times, and the result will be the same desired state. This feature ensures consistent deployments, making it seamless to maintain, update, or recreate your infrastructure.

- **Modularity**: ARM supports linked and nested templates, enabling you to modularize your deployments. This modularity allows you to separate the components of your infrastructure into reusable chunks, making it easier to maintain and manage complex environments.

- **Resource dependency management**: ARM templates can automatically manage dependencies between resources, ensuring that resources are created in the correct sequence. You can also explicitly define dependencies if needed.

- **Versioning**: Using source control systems, such as Git, you can version control your ARM templates. Versioning helps you maintain an organized, trackable history of your IaC and easily roll back to previous versions if needed.

- **Validation**: Before deployment, you can validate your ARM templates for syntax and structural accuracy, as well as verify whether they fulfill resource constraints. This validation helps prevent errors during the actual deployment process.

Now that you have a basic understanding of the value that ARM templates provide, you will learn about the structure of ARM templates in the next section.

Understanding the ARM Template Structure

As you have seen in the previous section, there are several constructs as part of the ARM template structure. This section serves to help you in understanding the components more deeply. The most important items have been expanded on. First, you will need to understand the different object types, which are like classifications for the type of data they contain, that are used by the variables and parameters that you require in your templates. They also reference repeatable parts of your code, which are stored as functions. Next, you will explore the schema, which describes the structure of your template, and then you will learn about the content version that stores the versioning information of your template. You will learn about parameters, which are inputs that the consumer of your template enters at deployment time. Variables are the next component and are essentially the same as parameters other than where they are defined in the template; they are not inputs from the user but can be used for storing information to be used in your template or for performing calculations that are run at deployment time. The `resources` component will be for defining the actual Azure resources you wish to deploy in Azure along with their configurations; these configurations can reference the data stored in your variables and parameters and also leverage functions for performing calculations. Finally, the last component you will explore will be the `outputs` component, which is used to display information relevant to you, post the ARM deployment you execute. The components are described in the following subsections.

Object Types

ARM templates are constructed with various object types, which are essentially building blocks that help describe and organize the desired Azure infrastructure. These are also referred to as variable types, in that they describe the data that they store. To put it in simpler terms, think of these object types as different types of building blocks that you can use to build your desired infrastructure. In the list that follows, you will explore the main object types and their purposes:

- **String**: Strings represent text, such as **names**, **descriptions**, or **messages**. They are often used to label resources, define parameter input values, or set configuration settings.
- **Number**: Numbers refer to **numerical values** used for various purposes, such as defining the size of a **virtual machine** (**VM**), setting capacity limits, or specifying the number of instances of a resource.
- **Boolean**: Booleans represent **true or false** values for binary choices, such as **enabling or disabling** a feature of a resource.

- **Array**: Arrays are used to store a list of items of the same data type, such as strings, numbers, or other objects. They help organize multiple values under a single variable or output. Imagine an array as a container holding a group of bricks with the same color or shape, making it easier to store and access them as needed.
- **Object**: Objects are collections of key-value pairs, where each key (property) is associated with a value. These values can be of any data type, such as strings, numbers, or even other objects. Objects are used to describe the configuration and settings of resources in an ARM template. Think of an object as a building block with multiple attributes, such as color, size, and shape, which define its appearance and functionality.
- **Resource functions**: Resource functions are **built-in functions** provided by ARM templates to perform various tasks and return values. Examples include retrieving values of existing resources, performing operations on strings or numbers, or encoding values.

These object types, when combined and used together, allow you to create ARM templates that accurately describe and deploy your desired Azure infrastructure. Next, you will explore the various components of the ARM template structure. For most of the components, notice they end with , ; this signifies there is a property to follow.

Schema

The $schema element defines the JSON schema that ARM templates follow. It ensures the structure of the template follows the expected format. Consider the following example:

```
"$schema": "https://schema.management.azure.com/schemas/2019-04-01/deploymentTemplate.json#",
```

Content Version

The contentVersion element is used to represent the current version of the template. It's a string value that helps track and differentiate the iterations of your template. The default version is shown as an example here:

```
"contentVersion": "1.0.0.0",
```

Parameters

The parameters section is an optional component that allows you to define input values to customize the deployment. These values can be entered at deployment time. Parameters give you flexibility when deploying to different environments and conditions.

The following example shows a parameter block that you could expect to see in a template. Notice that `storageAccountName` has several properties as part of it, with `type` being `string` and `metadata` further having a property of `description`. The `storageAccountName` parameter starts with `:`, then `{`, and finally, after the closing brace of the `metadata` property, it has `}`, signifying the object has been described fully now. The comma after the closing brace signifies that there will be another parameter object below it:

```
"parameters": {
  "storageAccountName": {
    "type": "string",
    "metadata": {
        "description": "Enter a unique storage account     name."
    }
  },
    ... {delete this line, it represents all subsequent parameters
 that you want to define until complete}
  },
```

You may find that you only have a single parameter and therefore the comma can be removed after the closing brace, signifying there are no further objects to follow. This same principle applies to all JSON templates and is part of JSON notation.

Variables

The `variables` section is used to store intermediary values derived from parameters or hardcoded constants used across the template. Variables simplify resource property definitions and improve template readability.

An example variable is defined here where `storageAccountType` is predefined as `Standard_LRS` and is not offered as a parameter input:

```
"variables": {
  "storageAccountType": "Standard_LRS"
},
```

Functions

User-defined functions have a unique namespace and are defined within the `functions` section of the ARM template. User-defined functions are custom functions created within an ARM template to perform specific operations or calculations that the creator of the template desires. They help reduce complexity, improve reusability, and enhance the maintainability of ARM templates. User-defined functions are particularly useful when you need to perform recurrent operations or calculations throughout your template, streamlining the process and making the code more efficient.

This section is different from the other components, such as parameters, variables, resources, and outputs, in that it leverages some of the component types seen previously and also performs calculations and returns a value when called. A user-defined function consists of a name, parameters, and a return value. This value may include other functions, parameter references, expressions, or resource properties.

Here's a basic example of an ARM template with a user-defined function that returns the **fully qualified domain name (FQDN)** of a storage account:

```
    "functions": [
      {
        "namespace": "myFunctions",
        "members": {
          "createFQDN": {
            "parameters": [
              {
                "name": "accountName",
                "type": "string"
              },
              {
                "name": "environmentZone",
                "type": "string"
              }
            ],
            "output": {
              "type": "string",
              "value": "[concat(parameters('accountName'), '.blob.', parameters('environmentZone'), '.azure.com')]"
            }
          }
        }
      }
    ],
```

In this example, a user-defined function called `createFQDN` expects two input parameters, `accountName` and `environmentZone`. It concatenates these parameters with the `.blob.azure.com` string to form the FQDN of a storage account.

To use this user-defined function, you can reference it in your `resources` or `variables` section using the following syntax:

```
"[myFunctions.createFQDN('mystorageaccount', 'core.windows.net')]"
```

This section may seem quite advanced right now and it's highly recommended to become very familiar with the other ARM components before attempting to understand the content of this section. The preceding referencing syntax is also confusing where you have not yet learned how to reference variables or parameters in an ARM template. Come back to this section when you are ready to experiment with functions.

Resources

The `resources` section is the core component of an ARM template. It defines the Azure resources you want to create, update, or delete in the deployment. Each resource has its specific properties and configuration settings.

The following is an example of a storage account resource. Notice the various properties that are defined for the resource; this is different for each resource type:

```
"resources": [
  {
    "type": "Microsoft.Storage/storageAccounts",
    "apiVersion": "2021-04-01",
    "tags": {
      "displayName": "storageaccount1"
    },
    "name": "[parameters('storageAccountName')]",
    "location": "[resourceGroup().location]",
    "sku": {
      "name": "[variables('storageAccountType')]"
    },
    "kind": "StorageV2"
  }
],
```

Notice that there is a new property that you haven't seen: the `tag` property. Tags are great for creating metadata about the resources that you deploy. They are constructed of a set of key-value pairs that describe the resources in any way you wish to describe them. This will come in handy when considering cost and operational management.

Outputs

The `outputs` section is optional and is used to return values resulting from the deployment. These values can be used in other processes, templates, or scripts to chain deployments or gather information. You can have multiple outputs defined as part of your template as desired on completion of the template.

The following example snippet outputs `storageAccountConnectionString`. Notice the use of the built-in function called `concat`; this function is responsible for joining strings together for a single string output, such as `concat('Hello ','world')`, which will output `Hello world`. Outputs are optional and something you will want to use more as you become more comfortable with working with ARM templates:

```
"outputs": {
  "storageAccountConnectionString": {
    "type": "string",
```

```
      "value":
 "[concat('DefaultEndpointsProtocol=https;AccountName=',
 parameters('storageAccountName'), ';AccountKey=',
 listKeys(resourceId('Microsoft.Storage/storageAccounts',
 parameters('storageAccountName')), '2019-06-01').keys[0].value)]"
    }
  }
}
```

These components define the overall structure of an ARM template and help manage the deployment of resources within an Azure environment. You now understand the structure of ARM templates and the constructs of the various components. Next, you will put your skills to the test and create your first ARM template.

> **Note**
>
> You can download Microsoft's **Visual Studio Code (VS Code)** application and the ARM tools required for free to view and edit ARM templates. If you haven't installed VS Code already, download and install it from the official website: `https://code.visualstudio.com`.
>
> The VS Code ARM extension can be downloaded here: `https://marketplace.visualstudio.com/items?itemName=msazurermtools.azurerm-vscode-tools`

Creating an ARM Template

ARM templates are JSON-formatted files that describe your desired Azure infrastructure. To create an ARM template, you can perform the following steps:

1. Using a text editor of your choice, begin by creating a blank JSON file and specify the JSON schema to ensure your template follows the expected format. If you do not have a preferred editor, VS Code can be a great choice, which is detailed in the next section. This tool can be hugely beneficial to editing ARM template files. The default schema you can use is `https://schema.management.azure.com/schemas/2019-04-01/deploymentTemplate.json#`.

2. Define the content version of the template. It is typically written in a `1.0.0.0` semantic versioning format. This can be left as the default when you are unsure.

3. Optionally, include input parameters for customizing deployments, such as resource names, locations, or configuration settings. For simplification in the creation process, it is better to create a template file and move backward to create parameters based on the ARM template structure and requirements for adjustment.

4. Defining variables simplifies your template by minimizing resource property repetition and enhancing readability. This is also optional, and when starting with ARM, you may want to leave this until you feel very comfortable working with ARM templates to prevent unnecessary confusion and troubleshooting that may occur when trying this for the first time.

5. Define the resources you want to deploy, specifying their type, API version, name, location, and associated properties. Ensure that you consider dependencies too. These should be added for your resource deployments; it is recommended to run as a second pass after your template is defined, and then outline dependencies required for each resource.
6. Optionally, add output values to return information about the resources deployed, such as connection strings or endpoints. This is typically when you want to receive information about the deployment post-deployment.
7. Save the JSON file with a `.json` extension and deploy it using the Azure portal, Azure PowerShell, Azure CLI, or other tools.

The following example template creates a **storage account** and returns (outputs) its **connection string**. It takes two parameters as input: the storage account name and the storage account type. This deployment is a common task you are likely to encounter when creating for users in your organization requiring storage accounts.

This is also helpful for the exam in understanding what a deployment would look like and its structure.

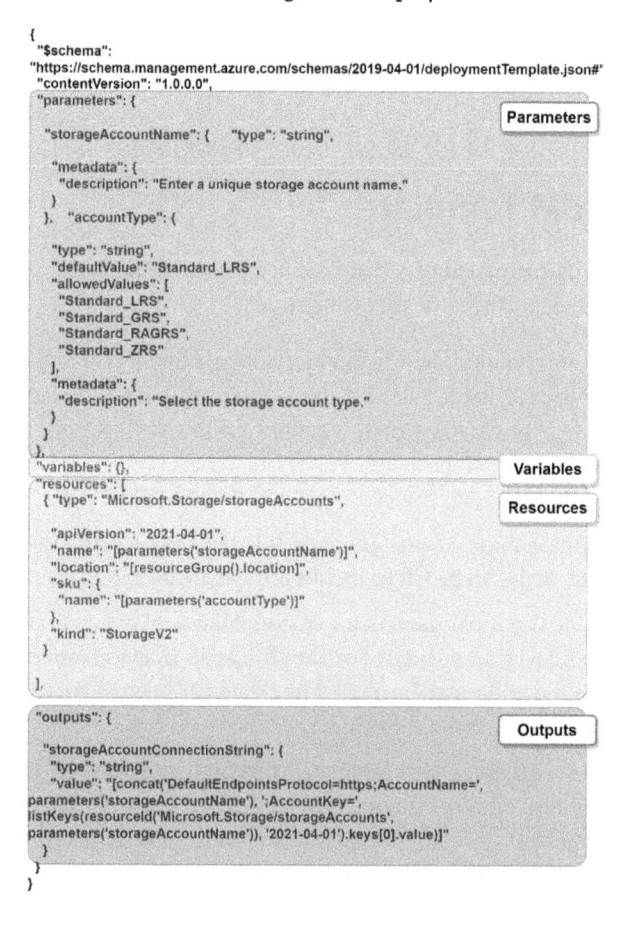

```
{
  "$schema": "https://schema.management.azure.com/schemas/2019-04-01/deploymentTemplate.json#",
  "contentVersion": "1.0.0.0",
  "parameters": {
    "storageAccountName": { "type": "string",
      "metadata": {
        "description": "Enter a unique storage account name."
      }
    }, "accountType": {
      "type": "string",
      "defaultValue": "Standard_LRS",
      "allowedValues": [
        "Standard_LRS",
        "Standard_GRS",
        "Standard_RAGRS",
        "Standard_ZRS"
      ],
      "metadata": {
        "description": "Select the storage account type."
      }
    }
  },
  "variables": {},
  "resources": [
    { "type": "Microsoft.Storage/storageAccounts",
      "apiVersion": "2021-04-01",
      "name": "[parameters('storageAccountName')]",
      "location": "[resourceGroup().location]",
      "sku": {
        "name": "[parameters('accountType')]"
      },
      "kind": "StorageV2"
    }
  ],
  "outputs": {
    "storageAccountConnectionString": {
      "type": "string",
      "value": "[concat('DefaultEndpointsProtocol=https;AccountName=', parameters('storageAccountName'), ';AccountKey=', listKeys(resourceId('Microsoft.Storage/storageAccounts', parameters('storageAccountName')), '2021-04-01').keys[0].value)]"
    }
  }
}
```

Figure 10.2: Storage account ARM template

Using VS Code to Create ARM Templates

To create an ARM template in VS Code, follow these steps:

1. Install VS Code. If you haven't installed VS Code already, download and install it from the official website: `https://code.visualstudio.com`.

2. Install the ARM Tools extension by launching VS Code and opening the `Extensions` view by clicking on the extensions icon in the Activity Bar on the left side of the window. Search for `Azure Resource Manager` in the marketplace search bar and click on `Azure Resource Manager (ARM) Tools` by Microsoft; on the following screen, click `Install`.

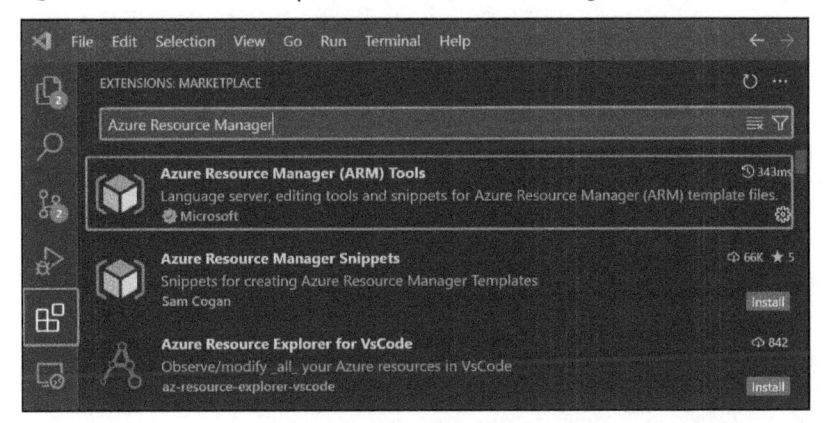

Figure 10.3: The Azure Resource Manager (ARM) Tools extension

This extension provides syntax highlighting, linting, IntelliSense support, and code snippets for ARM templates, making it easier to create and edit templates in VS Code.

3. Next, you will create a new JSON file to use for your template. Click on `File` and then `New File` from the VS Code top menu, or press *Ctrl + N* (Windows) or *cmd + N* (macOS) to create a new file. Save it using the `.json` file extension by clicking `File`, then `Save As...`, and choose any name you desire followed by `.json`, such as `armTemplate1.json`.

4. To add the ARM template skeleton, start typing `arm` in your JSON file, and you will see an autocomplete suggestion for the ARM template skeleton. Select the `arm!` suggestion. If you notice an error in VS Code mentioning it running in restricted mode, the ARM extension will be disabled and unable to run.

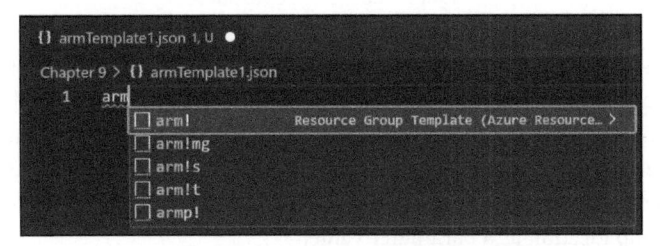

Figure 10.4: ARM template skeleton generation

5. This will generate the basic structure of an ARM template, including `$schema`, `contentVersion`, `parameters`, `functions`, `variables`, `resources`, and `outputs`.

```
armTemplate1.json
Chapter 9 > armTemplate1.json
1  {
2      "$schema": "https://schema.management.azure.com/schemas/2019-04-01/deploymentTemplate.json#",
3      "contentVersion": "1.0.0.0",
4      "parameters": {},
5      "functions": [],
6      "variables": {},
7      "resources": [],
8      "outputs": {}
9  }
```

Figure 10.5: ARM template skeleton

6. Customize your ARM template by filling in the `parameters`, `variables`, `resources`, and `outputs` sections according to your desired Azure infrastructure. For this example, you will create a storage account. Inside the square braces next to `resources` (indicating an array of resources), press *Enter* to separate these braces. You will be automatically positioned on the next line; type `arm-storage` and select `arm-storage` from the IntelliSense dialog that pops up.

```
"resources": [
    arm-storage
],
"outputs": {}
    arm-storage                Storage Account (Azure Resource Manager T...
    arm-storage-blob-container
    arm-cosmos-tablestorage-table
    arm-automanage-custom-profile
    arm-container-registry
    arm-app-security-group
    arm-automanage-bp-prod-assignment
    arm-cosmos-gremlin-database
    arm-app-insights
    arm-log-analytics-workspace
    arm-automanage-bp-devtest-assignment
    arm-automanage-custom-assignment
```

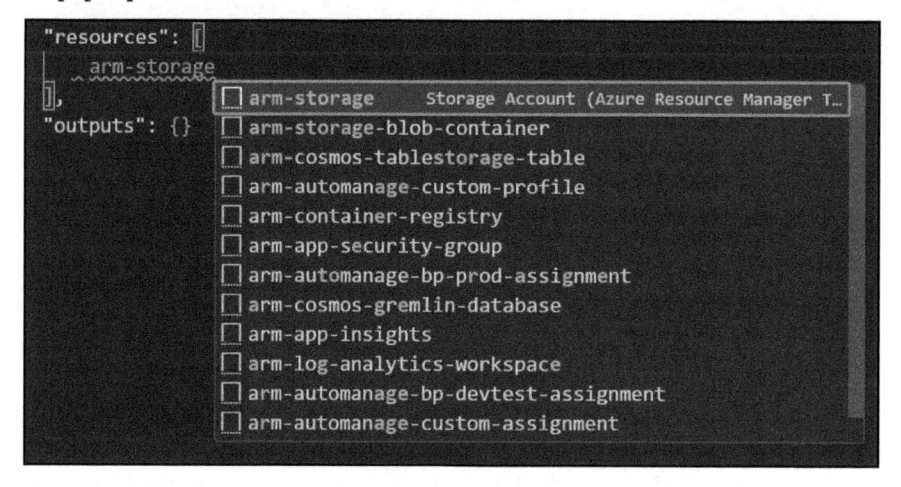

Figure 10.6: Storage resource

7. This will automatically populate the resource code for the ARM template for the storage account. Notice the following code that is generated. All the highlighted items are great for parameters. Notice that the `location` value has some strange-looking text in square brackets: `[resourceGroup().location]`. This is a built-in ARM function; the square brackets indicate that you want to use some kind of ARM resource lookup. This function uses the resource group location as a parameter value.

```
"resources": [
    {
        "name": "storageaccount1",
        "type": "Microsoft.Storage/storageAccounts",
        "apiVersion": "2023-01-01",
        "tags": {
            "displayName": "storageaccount1"
        },
        "location": "[resourceGroup().location]",
        "kind": "StorageV2",
        "sku": {
            "name": "Premium_LRS",
            "tier": "Premium"
        }
    }
],
```

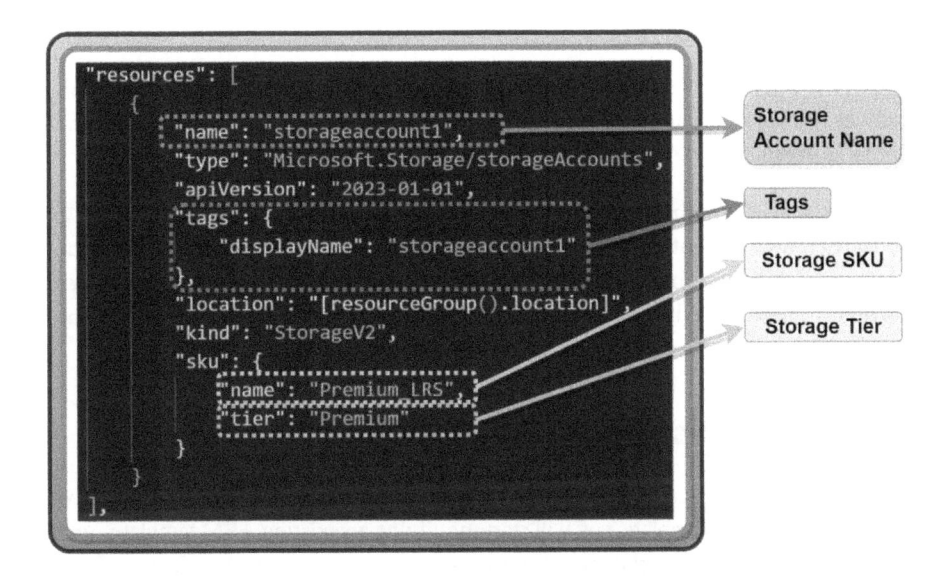

Figure 10.7: Storage resource code

8. Save your changes to the ARM template by selecting File and then Save from the top menu, or by pressing *Ctrl + S* (Windows) or *cmd + S* (macOS).

9. Navigate to the parameters section of the ARM template and press *Enter* between the { } braces. Insert the following code:

```
"parameters": {
    "storageAccountName": {
        "type": "string",
        "metadata": {
            "description": "Enter a unique storage account name."
        }
    }
},
```

10. Now, go to the resources section of the code that you wrote before. Here, you are going to change name and displayName to "[parameters('storageAccountName')]".

```
"name": "[parameters('storageAccountName')]",
"type": "Microsoft.Storage/storageAccounts",
"apiVersion": "2023-01-01",
"tags": {
    "displayName": "[parameters('storageAccountName')]"
},
```

Figure 10.8: Using parameters

11. Save the template again.
12. To deploy the ARM template, use the Azure portal, Azure PowerShell, Azure CLI, or other tools as per your preference. Deployment will be covered later in the chapter in the *Deploying an ARM Template – Azure Portal* section.

You have now experienced the creation of an ARM template both with and without VS Code. You have also learned how to configure parameters and use these in the template. In the exam, you will be tested on your ability to understand, troubleshoot, and remediate templates, likely in a multiple-choice format, so understanding the syntax is key. In the next section, you will modify an existing ARM template.

Modifying an Existing ARM Template

Now that you understand at a high level what ARM templates are used for and you have worked through creating your own template, you will start modifying an existing ARM template. You are going to modify an existing ARM template that is used to create a resource group. Your goal is to modify the template to deploy the resource group in North Europe instead of West Europe.

First, have a look at the template file, located in the GitHub repository for this chapter; the filename is `Modifying_Existing_Template.json`:

1. The first thing you should notice is the schema. This looks somewhat different from the previous template you made; the scope is designed for a subscription level and, therefore, uses the subscription-level schema, whereas the previous deployment was focused on a resource group-level deployment. You can see this in *Figure 10.9*:

```
"$schema": "https://schema.management.azure.com/schemas/2018-05-01/subscriptionDeploymentTemplate.json#",
```

Figure 10.9: Subscription deployment template

2. You will notice that some parameters have been defined for the resource groups (`resourceGroups`) and resource tags (`resourceTags`). This is important for the `resources` section that you will see next. The type for the `resourceGroups` parameter is `array`; this is populated as an object of two values, `name` and `location`, which you will see in the parameter file later in *Figure 10.17*. The other parameter is `resourceTags`, which is of the `object` type; there will be one or more entries as key-value pairs for the tags. Notice that this one contains `defaultValue`; this is for populating a `Function` tag should no tags be defined at the deployment stage.

3. Notice that there is a single resource declared, the resource group, and note that this is only deployed at a subscription level as this is where resource groups reside. Effectively, your scope is different from a normal resource group deployment.

4. Next, notice that there are several property values already declared that point to parameters. These parameters reference the ones you saw in the `parameters` section. They are called through the `[]` braces, indicating there is a calculated value or function. Next, the `parameter` value is called, and the specific parameter name is referenced.

```
"resources": [
    {
        "name": "[parameters('resourceGroups')[copyIndex('rgCopy')].name]",
        "type": "Microsoft.Resources/resourceGroups",
        "apiVersion": "2022-09-01",
        "location": "[parameters('resourceGroups')[copyIndex('rgCopy')].location]",
        "dependsOn": [],
        "tags": "[parameters('resourceTags')]",
        "copy": {
            "name": "rgCopy",
            "count": "[length(parameters('resourceGroups'))]"
        }
    }
],
```

Figure 10.10: Resource group ARM

5. As part of the resource declaration, there is a reference to an array object. You need to understand how arrays are referenced as memory before you continue to the next function that will be shared. Arrays store groups of items, as mentioned previously, and they also start with 0 as the first space. So, by referencing an object, such as `parameters('resourceGroups')[0]`, you are referencing the first item in the array. *Figure 10.11* shares a visual representation of an array of three value types similar to the `resourceGroups` array parameter:

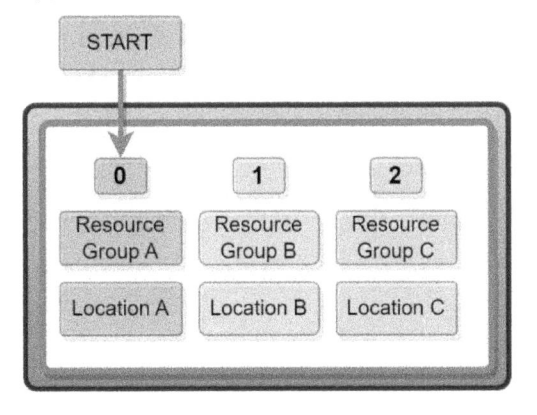

Figure 10.11: Array representation

6. Another important component of the resource group resource defined previously is the `copy` function. This is a built-in function available to ARM templates with the purpose of creating multiple instances of the same resource type defined. It iterates through the items of the `resourceGroups` parameter in this example by making use of another function length that determines the number of objects in the `resourceGroups` array parameter.

```
"copy": {
    "name": "rgCopy",
    "count": "[length(parameters('resourceGroups'))]"
}
```

Figure 10.12: The copy and length functions

7. When looking back at the `name` and `location` properties of the resource, you will notice that it references index for the `copy` function named `rgCopy` for the item in the array of the `resourceGroups` parameter; then, it specifies the `name` or `location` property. As copy iterates from 0 by 1 to the final count of the array length, it will put that number as the `index` value in the name, thereby creating each array item as a new resource group when deployed.

```
"name": "[parameters('resourceGroups')[copyIndex('rgCopy')].name]",
"type": "Microsoft.Resources/resourceGroups",
"apiVersion": "2022-09-01",
"location": "[parameters('resourceGroups')[copyIndex('rgCopy')].location]",
```

Figure 10.13: name and location for resource group

8. Your full JSON template should look like the following screenshot. The gray text between *lines 3 and 4* is a note from the VS Code system about where it is possible to link a parameter file to the template for review of the inputted values. This is not an issue at all; rather, it is an extended feature and benefit of working with ARM in VS Code.

```
1  {
2      "$schema": "https://schema.management.azure.com/schemas/2018-05-01/
       subscriptionDeploymentTemplate.json#",
3      "contentVersion": "1.0.0.0",
       Select or create a parameter file to enable full validation...
4      "parameters": {
5          "resourceGroups": {
6              "type": "array",
7              "metadata": {
8                  "description": "Name and location"
9              }
10         },
11         "resourceTags": {
12             "type": "object",
13             "metadata": {
14                 "description": "Tags to be applied"
15             },
16             "defaultValue": {
17                 "Function": "To learn how to edit a template"
18             }
19         }
20     },
21     "functions": [],
22     "variables": {},
23     "resources": [
24         {
25             "name": "[parameters('resourceGroups')[copyIndex('rgCopy')].name]",
26             "type": "Microsoft.Resources/resourceGroups",
27             "apiVersion": "2022-09-01",
28             "location": "[parameters('resourceGroups')[copyIndex('rgCopy')].location]",
29             "dependsOn": [],
30             "tags": "[parameters('resourceTags')]",
31             "copy": {
32                 "name": "rgCopy",
33                 "count": "[length(parameters('resourceGroups'))]"
34             }
35         }
36     ],
37     "outputs": {}
38  }
```

Figure 10.14: Resource group ARM template

Now that you have your template ready, you will work on the corresponding parameter file for this template. Follow these steps to create and edit your parameter file:

1. Right-click anywhere on the template code section, and from the pop-up menu, click `Select/Create Parameter File...`.

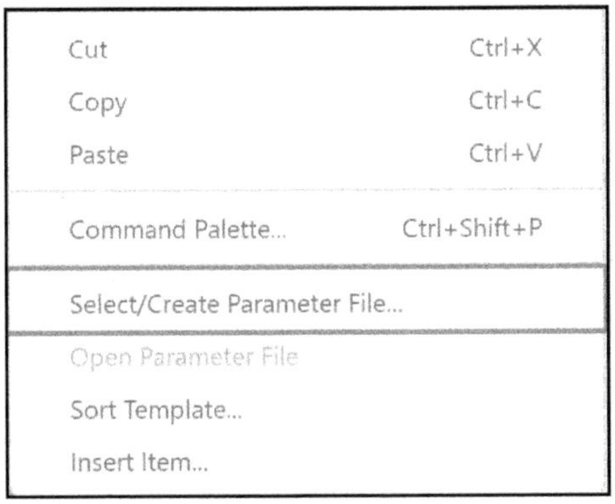

Figure 10.15: Select/Create Parameter File…

2. From the list of options that appear at the top of the window, select New....

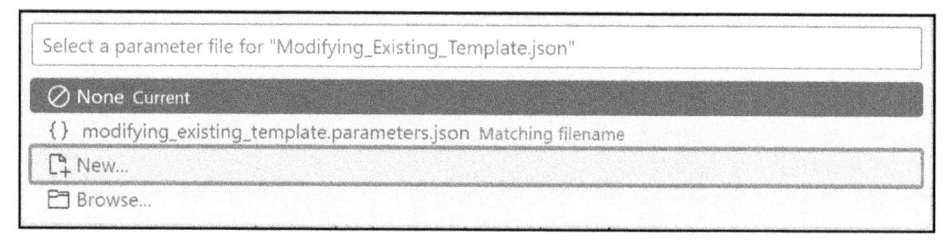

```
Select a parameter file for "Modifying_Existing_Template.json"
⊘ None  Current
{ } modifying_existing_template.parameters.json  Matching filename
   New...
   Browse...
```

Figure 10.16: Selecting a new parameter file

3. From the next set of options that appears, select `All parameters`. This will populate a new parameter file with all the parameters that are required for your template. You will be prompted to give a name and then press `Save`. Your file should look as follows:

```
 1  {
 2      "$schema": "https://schema.management.azure.com/schemas/2019-04-01/
        deploymentParameters.json#",
 3      "contentVersion": "1.0.0.0",
 4      "parameters": {
 5          "resourceGroups": {
 6              "value": [
 7                  // TODO: Fill in parameter value
 8              ]
 9          },
10          "resourceTags": {
11              "value": {
12                  "Function": "To learn how to edit a template"
13              }
14          }
15      }
16  }
```

Figure 10.17: New parameter file

4. Note you will need to fill in values for both parameters and that the `resourceTags` parameter has been prepopulated for you based on the default value observed in the ARM template. Note there are two resource groups; this is to demonstrate the deployment of multiple resource groups using your defined template. The resource groups have been defined by both their name and location. The `resourceTags` parameter is optional thanks to the default value populated in the ARM template and the parameter values do not have to match. The resource tags contain key-value pairs for the tags you would like to assign to your resources. In this example, you are going to create three values: `Environment`, `Managed By`, and `Function`. Save your file once you have completed editing it.

The following figure is what your ARM template file should look like after making all the changes:

```
1  {
2      "$schema": "https://schema.management.azure.com/schemas/2019-04-01/deploymentParameters.json#",
3      "contentVersion": "1.0.0.0",
4      "parameters": {
5          "resourceGroups": {
6              "value": [
7                  {
8                      "name": "ResourceGroupA",
9                      "location": "westeurope"
10                 },
11                 {
12                     "name": "ResourceGroupB",
13                     "location": "westeurope"
14                 }
15             ]
16         },
17         "resourceTags": {
18             "value": {
19                 "Environment": "Production",
20                 "Managed By": "Azure Support L3",
21                 "Function": "To learn how to edit a template"
22             }
23         }
24     }
25 }
```

Figure 10.18: Completed resource group parameter file

Now that you understand the two templates in more detail, you will need to modify the template to demonstrate your capability in editing an existing defined template. You will need to change the location of the resource groups for the deployment prior to deploying them. You only need to change the parameters file to change the deployment region. To do this, you will modify the parameters template file you just created and change the location from `westeurope` to `northeurope`.

The following screenshot shows the change made under the `location` parameter:

```
"resourceGroups": {
    "value": [
        {
            "name": "ResourceGroupA",
            "location": "northeurope"
        },
        {
            "name": "ResourceGroupB",
            "location": "northeurope"
        }
    ]
},
```

Figure 10.19: Modifying location from westeurope to northeurope

In this section, you explored modifying an existing ARM template and how to change the resource location via the parameter template. Being able to leverage parameter files enables you to consistently deploy your infrastructure and have baseline templates with different deployment values, making it a lot more extensible and repeatable in different use cases. These skills are important for both the exam and in your daily administrative roles for Azure.

> **Note**
>
> You are encouraged to read up on the topic of ARM templates further by using the following links:
>
> `https://learn.microsoft.com/en-us/azure/azure-resource-manager/templates/overview`
>
> `https://learn.microsoft.com/en-us/azure/azure-resource-manager/templates/deployment-tutorial-local-template`

Now that you have understood how ARM templates work and how to modify a template and corresponding parameter file, you will explore how to deploy it in the next section.

Deploying an ARM Template – Azure Portal

In the previous section, you modified an existing ARM template, which created two resource groups with tags. Now that you have both ARM templates (the main **template** file and the parameters file), you will experience the deployment of this template.

You will begin by deploying the ARM templates via the Azure portal through the following steps:

1. Navigate to the Azure portal by opening a web browser and going to `https://portal.azure.com`.

2. In the top search bar, enter `deploy a custom template` and select `Deploy a custom template` from the search results:

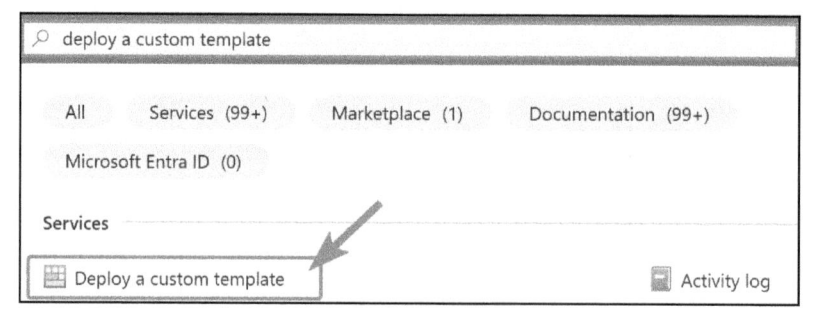

Figure 10.20: Deploy a custom template

3. Next, click `Build your own template in the editor`.

Figure 10.21: Build your own template in the editor

4. Paste in your ARM template code on the Edit template screen and click Save at the bottom of the screen.

5. You will now be directed to the Custom deployment blade. Click Edit parameters.

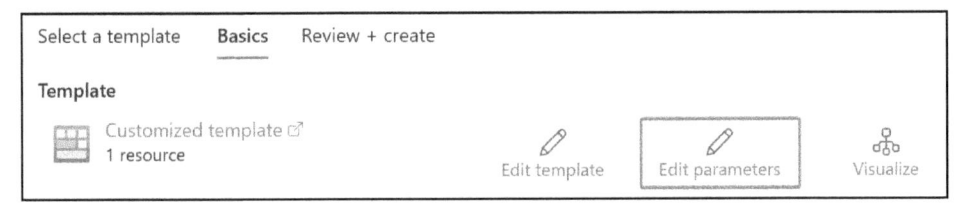

Figure 10.22: Edit parameters

6. Paste in your code for the parameter file and click Save at the bottom of the screen.

7. You are now ready to deploy; your screen should look like the following. Click Review + create.

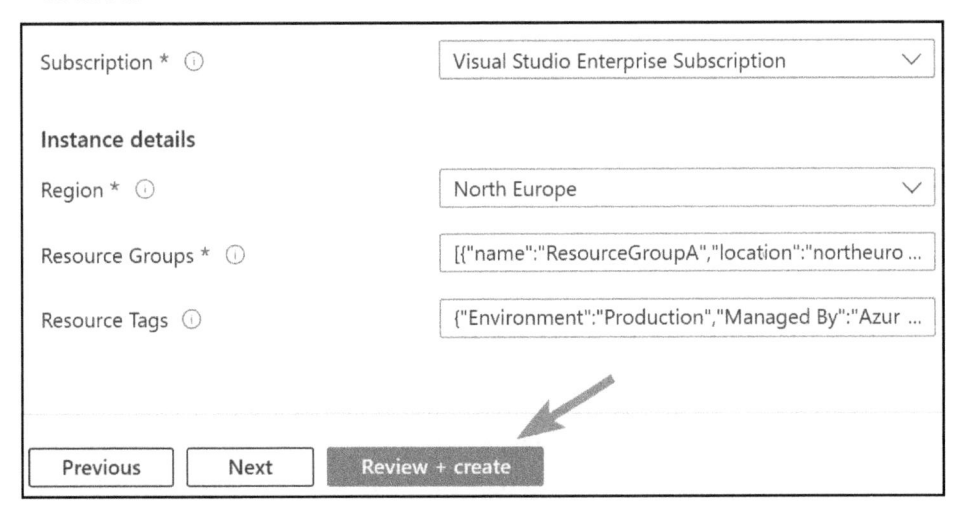

Figure 10.23: Deploying your ARM template

8. Click Create. Your deployment will now initiate. Once it's complete, you can navigate to *Resource Groups* and confirm your resource groups exist and are in North Europe.

You have successfully deployed a custom ARM template with a parameters file via the Azure portal. In the next section, you are going to look at how to deploy a template using Azure PowerShell.

Deploying an ARM Template – Azure PowerShell

In the previous section, you deployed an existing ARM template using the Azure portal, which created two resource groups with tags. In this section, you will deploy the same templates using Azure PowerShell:

1. Copy the template from the *Creating an ARM Template* section and save it as `azuredeploy.json`.
2. Create a parameter file for the template and save it as `azuredeploy.parameters.json`.
3. Populate the parameter file and ensure that you are choosing a unique name for the storage account. Adding in the date string as part of the account name generally helps to ensure a unique name, for example, `teststorageaccount291223`.
4. Open your PowerShell terminal and run the following code to navigate to the folder where you saved your files; change the path to match your directory:

   ```
   cd c:\jsontemplatesfolder\
   ```

5. In your PowerShell terminal, run the following code to start deployment:

   ```
   New-AzResourceGroupDeployment -ResourceGroupName ResourceGroupA
   -TemplateFile ./azuredeploy.json -TemplateParameterFile ./
   azuredeploy.parameters.json
   ```

6. Once the script has finished running, your deployment will be complete.

Notice that the outputs display the storage account connection string.

> **Note**
> You can read more here: https://learn.microsoft.com/en-us/azure/azure-resource-manager/templates/quickstart-create-templates-use-visual-studio-code?tabs=PowerShell#deploy-the-template.

You have just completed a deployment of an ARM template using Azure PowerShell. You can now deploy ARM templates via PowerShell and the Azure portal. These skills are important to have so that you aren't limited to either option. Being equipped for both the portal and PowerShell is important as it gives you more extensive capabilities to support your daily role, and you are likely to be tested on both in the exam.

Next, you will learn how to save a deployment in ARM template format to automate future deployments and minimize the effort involved in creating a base ARM template.

Saving a Deployment as an ARM Template

Now that you know how to deploy resources from custom ARM templates, you will learn another method of creating ARM templates by saving a deployment to an ARM template via the Azure portal. Complete the steps that follow:

1. Navigate to the Azure portal by opening a web browser and going to `https://portal.azure.com`.

2. Navigate to your resource group and click + `Create` at the top of the overview pane to initiate a new deployment.

3. From the `Marketplace` blade, enter the type of resource you would like to deploy or navigate through the marketplace to find the resource type you desire. For this exercise, select `storage account`.

4. Click `Create` on the resource screen.

5. Run through the resource deployment screens until you get to the review screen. For this exercise, you can configure it as per the following settings:

    - Resource group: `ResourceGroupA`
    - Storage account name: `teststorage2[date]` (e.g., `teststorage23012223`):
    - Region: `North Europe`
    - Performance: `Standard`
    - Redundancy: `Locally-redundant storage (LRS):`
    - Leave all other settings as their default values

6. Click `Review` to go to the `Review` tab.

7. At the bottom of the screen, there is a hyperlink to download a template for automation; click the text.

Figure 10.24: Download a template for automation

8. Notice that you are taken to a `Template` blade, where the ARM code is displayed on the screen. At the top of the screen is a `Download` button to download the template; click that button.

Figure 10.25: Download the template

9. This will initiate a download prompt where you can save the archive file for the template, which will include both your ARM template and parameter files. Save this as any name you like and extract the files.

10. When you extract the files, you will see one named `template.json` and the other named `parameters.json`.

11. Open both files in VS Code.

12. Notice that almost every property for a storage account has been populated into the `parameters` section of the ARM template. Now, this will look a lot more comprehensive than the storage account template you created earlier. The beauty of ARM templates is that you do not have to define every single property to successfully deploy them. This is just more comprehensive and gives the option for configuration. You can modify the parameters file with the values you desire for your deployment.

13. To see how your parameters adhere to the requirements of the template parameters, right-click your template file and click `Select/Create Parameter File...` from the pop-up menu.

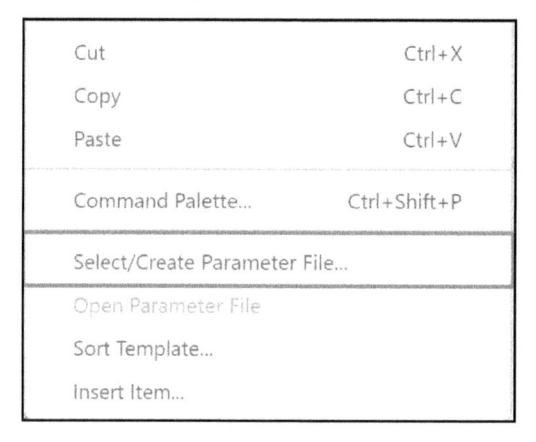

Figure 10.26: Select/Create Parameter File…

14. Select `parameters.json` from the list of options at the top of the screen.

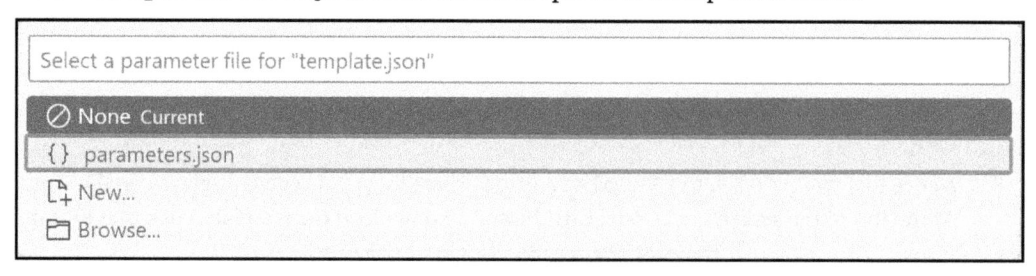

Figure 10.27: Selecting the parameters file

15. Notice that your parameter values will now show above your parameter declarations in your template file. They are the rows that start with `Value:`.

```
"parameters": {
    Value: "northeurope"
    "location": {
        "type": "string"
    },
    Value: "teststorage2301223"
    "storageAccountName": {
        "type": "string"
    },
    Value: "Standard_LRS"
    "accountType": {
        "type": "string"
    },
```

Figure 10.28: Template value preview

16. You can deploy your template as before on the portal.

You have now learned how to extract deployments from the Azure portal and use these for creating your ARM templates and parameter files. This can be extremely helpful in starting your IaC automation templates, and for complex deployments, this will help group your deployment resources together. You should be comfortable at this point with creating, editing, and deploying ARM templates; the more you practice, the better you will get. Next, you will learn about how to export existing deployments on Azure to an ARM template.

Exporting an ARM Template

Now that you have experienced working with ARM templates in many forms, from creating them from scratch to saving deployments you initiate in the Azure portal, you will explore another method of generating ARM templates from the Azure portal. Complete the following steps to export an ARM template from a resource group:

1. Navigate to the Azure portal by opening a web browser and going to `https://portal.azure.com`.
2. Navigate to your resource groups. You can do this by selecting `Resource groups` from the left hamburger menu in the portal or by searching `Resource groups` from the main search bar at the top of the screen.

3. Once in the `Resource groups` blade, select a desired resource group. If you have been following along until now, you can select your `ResourceGroupA` resource group by clicking on its name.

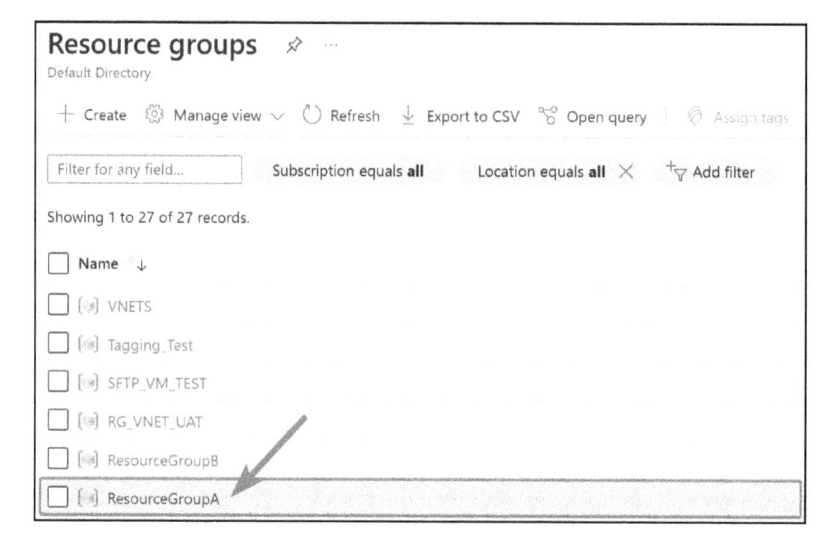

Figure 10.29: Selecting ResourceGroupA

4. Scroll down the left menu to the `Automation` context and click `Export template`.

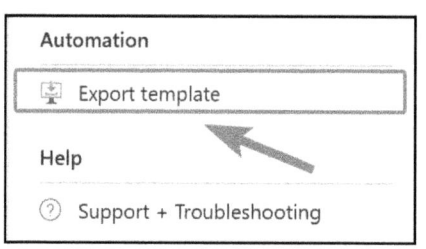

Figure 10.30: Export template

5. You will notice the `Template` blade closely resembles the one from the previous exercise. Click `Download` at the top of the screen and the ARM template and parameter file will download, which can then be used to redeploy resources and amended to create custom resources:

Figure 10.31: Downloading the ARM templates for existing resources

6. One final item you may wish to explore is the `Visualize template` option. This is great when you want to see a graphic expressing the deployment you are working on. Click this button at the top of the screen.

Figure 10.32: Visualize template

7. There is not much to see in `Resource visualizer` right now as you only have a single resource deployed, but when you have multiple resources deployed, this can be a handy tool. Note that it has buttons for scrolling, zooming in and out, and even an `Export` button that allows you to export an image file.

Figure 10.33: Resource visualizer

In this section, you explored how to export all existing resources within a resource group to an ARM template via the Azure portal. This skill is important as it can reduce the administrative effort and time in creating ARM templates by creating a template based on existing working infrastructure.

> **Note**
>
> You are encouraged to read up on the topic of ARM templates further by using the following links:
>
> `https://learn.microsoft.com/en-us/azure/azure-resource-manager/templates/export-template-portal`
>
> `https://learn.microsoft.com/en-us/azure/azure-resource-manager/templates/export-template-cli`
>
> `https://learn.microsoft.com/en-us/azure/azure-resource-managezr/templates/export-template-powershell`

As you start working with ARM templates more, you will find new methods to become more efficient with them and leverage them more in your daily role. An important concept to note is that you can not only save a deployment from a resource group, but you can export a single resource to an ARM template as well.

In the next section, you are going to investigate Microsoft's repository for some ARM templates that assist in rapid deployments.

Azure QuickStart Templates

Azure QuickStart Templates offers many advantages, such as quicker deployments, community resources for easier learning, and alignment to best practices, and they cover a broad range of scenarios.

Azure QuickStart Templates is a repository of pre-built, customizable ARM templates that streamline the deployment of resources on Azure. They are designed to help users deploy various types of infrastructure and applications quickly and easily. Microsoft and the Azure community contribute and maintain these templates, ensuring that they are up to date and adhere to best practices.

The following are some key advantages of utilizing Azure QuickStart Templates:

- **Rapid deployment**: QuickStart templates speed up the process of deploying resources and configurations in Azure, reducing the time it would take to create ARM templates from scratch.

- **Learning resource**: These templates serve as an excellent learning resource for those new to Azure or ARM templates. By inspecting and modifying the templates, users can acquire hands-on knowledge of how to create and manage their ARM templates.

- **Best practices**: The QuickStart templates are developed following Azure best practices, ensuring that your infrastructure deployments are optimized, secure, and reliable.

- **Customizable**: Although the templates are pre-built, they're designed to be easily customizable to suit specific use cases and requirements, ultimately saving time and effort when adapting them to your environment.

- **Wide variety**: The QuickStart Templates repository contains templates for various Azure resources, such as VMs, storage accounts, web apps, container registries, and so on. This variety allows you to deploy a diverse set of solutions.

Accessing Azure QuickStart Templates

You can access and browse Azure QuickStart Templates in Microsoft's GitHub repository: `https://github.com/Azure/azure-quickstart-templates`. The templates can also be downloaded and used in deployments directly or modified to suit requirements before deployment.

As of the time of writing, there is a catalog for these templates available here: `https://learn.microsoft.com/en-us/samples/browse/?expanded=azure&products=azure-resource-manager`.

Once you find a suitable template, you can deploy it directly to your Azure subscription using the Azure portal, PowerShell, Azure CLI, or other deployment tools.

You have now learned an extensive amount of information about ARM templates, including how to create them, modify them, export them from Azure, and even deploy them.

Summary

In this chapter, you have gained a comprehensive understanding of ARM templates. You learned the benefits of ARM templates, such as consistency, repeatability, and ease of deployment. Additionally, you explored the structure of ARM templates and worked on creating, modifying, and deploying resources using these templates. With VS Code, you experienced an efficient way to author and manage ARM templates, leveraging the power of built-in tools and extensions. Furthermore, you learned how to save deployments as ARM templates and export templates for reuse and sharing. This chapter has equipped you with the essential knowledge and skills to manage and deploy Azure resources using ARM templates effectively.

These foundational concepts will accelerate your journey into automated, code-driven infrastructure deployments. This will make you a more effective administrator and provide you with the confidence and knowledge you will require for the test topics in this exam area.

In the next chapter, you will explore another IaC tool called Azure Bicep. This domain-specific language streamlines your IaC deployments through its modularized approach. It adapts the concepts of ARM templates and simplifies their readability. You can convert ARM templates to the Bicep format and vice versa.

11
Azure Bicep

In this chapter, you will delve further into Azure **infrastructure as code** (**IaC**), exploring the newer **domain-specific language** (**DSL**), **Azure Bicep**. IaC involves using code and automation to provision and manage infrastructure instead of relying on manual methods. This technique ensures that infrastructure components are deployed consistently and can be repeated reliably. You will gain essential understanding and hands-on experience with Azure Bicep to define, deploy, and manage Azure resources in a consistent, manageable, and repeatable manner. You will cover key concepts and practical examples to help you confidently author, modify, and deploy Azure resources. By the end of this chapter, you'll be well equipped with the knowledge and skills needed to effectively manage Azure resources and infrastructure with efficiency and ease using either Azure Bicep or **Azure Resource Manager** (**ARM**) templates.

In this chapter, you will learn about the following topics:

- Understanding Azure Bicep
- Understanding the Bicep Template Structure
- Creating a Bicep Template
- Modifying an Existing Bicep Template
- Deploying a Bicep template – Azure PowerShell
- Converting ARM to Bicep
- Converting Bicep to ARM

Technical Requirements

To follow along with the hands-on lessons, you will need the following:

- Access to **Microsoft Entra ID** as a global administrator.
- Access to an Azure subscription with owner or contributor privileges. If you do not have access to one, students can enroll for a free account: `https://azure.microsoft.com/en-us/free/`
- **PowerShell 5.1** or later installed on a Windows PC or PowerShell Core 6.x on other operating systems where labs can be practiced.

- For Windows users, you will need to install **.Net Framework 4.7.2** or later using the following link: `https://learn.microsoft.com/en-us/dotnet/framework/install`.
- Where PowerShell is not installed or available, `https://shell.azure.com` can be used as a browser-based shell.
- Installation of the `Az` PowerShell module, which can be performed by running the following in an administrative PowerShell session:

    ```
    Set-ExecutionPolicy -ExecutionPolicy RemoteSigned -Scope
    CurrentUser
    Install-Module -Name Az -Scope CurrentUser -Repository PSGallery
    -Force
    ```

Understanding Azure Bicep

Azure Bicep is a DSL for deploying and managing Azure resources using declarative syntax. It's an open source language that aims to simplify the IaC experience when working with Azure. Bicep is a higher-level abstraction over ARM templates, and Bicep files (`.bicep`) are automatically compiled into ARM templates when deployed.

Bicep is the next evolution of IaC from Microsoft and is an Azure-native deployment language that enhances template creation and management activities. You are likely to see some questions come up in the exam around Bicep, and it is important for you to have a basic working knowledge of the language, be able to interpret templates, and understand the core syntax. You will dive a bit deeper in this section into the benefits of Bicep and how it differ from ARM templates, as well as understanding how to work with Bicep files.

Benefits of Azure Bicep

Having now worked with Azure ARM templates, your interest has likely peaked at what IaC can do for you. Bicep takes the same benefits of ARM and simplifies working with IaC on Azure. There are several benefits to using Bicep, such as simplified syntax, your files becoming more human-readable and easier to work with, the reusability of your files increasing through modules, native integration with ARM, and the capability for Bicep to easily convert IaC templates (Bicep files can easily be converted into ARM templates and vice versa). There is also a strong, active community involved in Bicep development. The benefits are expanded on more here:

- **Simplified syntax**: Bicep offers a more concise and readable syntax compared to JSON-based ARM templates, making it easier to create and modify Azure infrastructure code. The same template in Bicep can be about half the size of an ARM template.
- **Strong type-checking**: Bicep integrates with development tools, such as **Visual Studio Code (VS Code)**, providing efficient type-checking, autocompletion, and syntax highlighting. This feature enhances productivity and reduces errors while writing code. **Type-checking** is a process in programming languages and development tools that verifies the data types of variables, functions, and expressions.

It helps ensure that the operations and interactions between variables and data structures are valid according to the predefined rules of the language. Type-checking minimizes the risk of runtime errors due to type-related mismatches or inconsistencies. In the context of Azure Bicep, type-checking during code-writing helps ensure that the right data types are used for resource properties, parameter values, and variables, thereby reducing the likelihood of deployment errors.

- **Modules**: Bicep supports creating reusable modules, **improving maintainability and consistency** across different environments and projects. Modules in Azure Bicep are **reusable pieces of code** that can be used to encapsulate a set of related Azure resources or configurations. Modules allow you to create modular, organized, and maintainable infrastructure code by separating different components of your infrastructure into smaller, manageable units. You can create and deploy your own custom modules or use the modules shared by the community.
- **Native integration with ARM**: Since Bicep files are translated into ARM templates, they are **fully compatible with ARM**. Existing ARM templates can also be easily decompiled into Bicep files using the Bicep CLI.
- **Growing ecosystem**: Bicep benefits from a thriving community, and the language is continually evolving with new features and enhancements to improve the user experience.

Comparing Azure Bicep to ARM Templates

The primary distinction between Azure Bicep and ARM templates is that Bicep is a higher-level language specifically designed for managing Azure infrastructure, while ARM templates are a JSON-based method to achieve the same goal. Although Bicep intends to advance beyond ARM templates, it's essential to note that Bicep is built on top of ARM and compiles down to ARM templates upon deployment.

Here's how Bicep could be seen as an improvement and, in some cases, a potential successor to ARM templates:

- Bicep offers a simpler, more human-readable language that is easier to learn and edit
- It integrates seamlessly with development tools, providing a modern and efficient development experience
- It fosters code reusability and modularization, making it easier to maintain and manage infrastructure code

Despite these advantages, ARM templates are still widely used, and given that Bicep uses the ARM backbone, they're not being phased out. Choosing between Bicep and ARM depends on factors such as developer background, use case, and preference.

Setting up the Bicep Extension for VS Code and the Bicep CLI

To start working with Bicep, you will need to have a code editor, and VS Code, introduced previously, will be a great editor for you to start utilizing for Bicep and ARM templates. To install the Bicep extension, follow these steps:

1. Open VS Code and click on the extensions icon in the Activity Bar on the side of the window. Search for `Bicep` in the marketplace search bar and click on the `Bicep` option by Microsoft; on the following screen, click `Install`.

Figure 11.1: Installing the Bicep extension

2. Once installed, click the cog wheel to manage settings on the Bicep extension tab, then click `Extension Settings`.

Figure 11.2: Bicep Extension Settings

3. You can select the settings you want; for this exercise, enable `Bicep: Decompile on Paste` and leave all settings as the default configuration. Once finished, you can close the `Settings` and `Extension: Bicep` tabs.

You are now ready to start editing Bicep files in VS Code. You now need to install the Bicep CLI to deploy Bicep templates from your machine. Follow these steps to install Bicep tools with `winget`. Please note that `winget` requires the App Installer to be up to date and that can be done from the Windows Store or https://apps.microsoft.com/detail/9nblggh4nns1:

1. Open a PowerShell window.
2. Paste the following code and press *Enter*. The installation takes approximately five minutes.

   ```
   winget install -e --id Microsoft.Bicep
   ```

3. Restart your PowerShell window so it will be active in your session.
4. If you want to confirm Bicep has been installed, you can run the following command and press *Enter*; as long as you get a version back, you are set up:

   ```
   bicep --version
   ```

You are now all set up to work with Bicep files. In the next section, you will learn about the Bicep template structure before diving into the creation of your first template.

Understanding the Bicep Template Structure

Before you start working on your Bicep templates, you need to understand the structure, which is very similar to ARM as it's been built on top of the ARM syntax and designed to be largely interchangeable. There are noticeable syntax differences, and the same key components have been highlighted as was done in the ARM section, with the addition of a new component being the module.

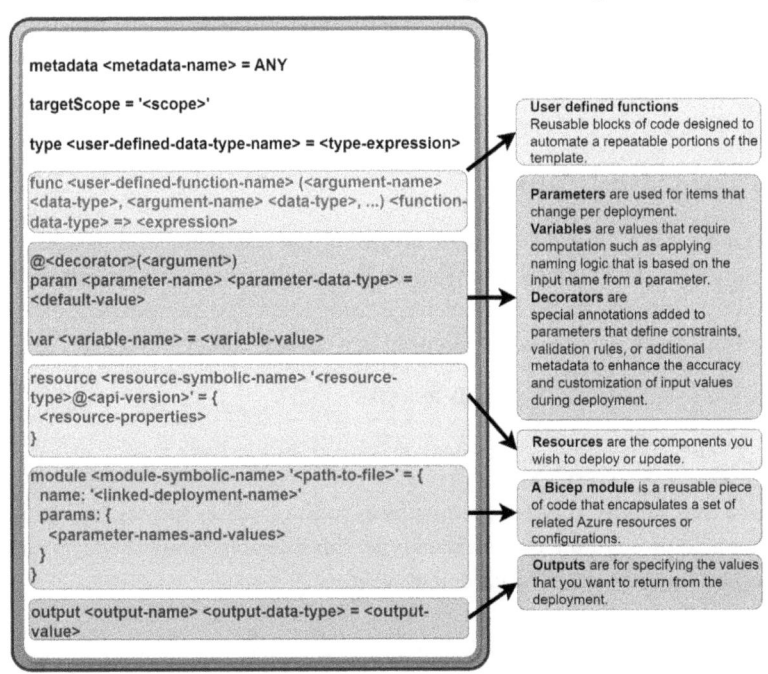

Figure 11.3: Bicep template structure

Since you already have an understanding of the structure behind ARM templates, it will be better to review the Bicep components by drawing comparisons to the ARM templates so you can see the differences in code where applicable. This will be done in the sections that follow.

Metadata

Metadata in Bicep refers to additional descriptive information added to parameters or resource properties to provide better context, clarification, or usage instructions for users deploying the template.

An example of a description of a template for deploying a storage account is as follows:

```
metadata description = 'Creates a storage account'
```

Target Scope

Target scope in Bicep defines the desired management level at which a deployment template is executed. It can be set to `resourceGroup`, `subscription`, `managementGroup`, or `tenant`. The target scope helps you control templates and manage resources more effectively. You do not need to set the target scope, as the default value is `resourceGroup`, and not setting this value will assume the default.

An example of setting the scope to the subscription layer would be the following:

```
targetScope = 'subscription'
```

> **Note**
> You are encouraged to read more about target scopes for subscriptions here: https://learn.microsoft.com/en-us/azure/azure-resource-manager/bicep/deploy-to-subscription.

User-Defined Data Types

User-defined data types in Bicep allow you to create custom data types for organizing and validating input parameters. They facilitate code reusability and consistency across parameters with similar requirements. User-defined data types are defined using the `type` keyword and can include one or multiple properties. The types are then referenced in a `param` call.

The syntax for a user-defined data type is as follows:

```
type <user-defined-data-type-name> = <type-expression>
```

An example of a user-defined data type would be as follows, where the configuration for a storage account is populated through the custom data type; this example shows the `type` declaration and then the corresponding `param` call with default values:

```
type storageSecuritySettings = {
  Tls: string
```

```
    Https: bool
    PublicAccess: bool
  }
  param storageProperties storageSecuritySettings = {
    Tls: 'TLS1_2'
    Https: true
    PublicAccess: false
  }
```

You are unlikely to be tested on this component for the exam; however, awareness is key to maintaining your skills in Bicep. For more information on this topic, you are encouraged to read more here: https://learn.microsoft.com/en-us/azure/azure-resource-manager/bicep/user-defined-data-types.

User-Defined Functions

User-defined functions are custom functions created within a Bicep file to perform specific operations or calculations, enhancing the maintainability, reusability, and simplicity of the Bicep code. These are separate from the built-in Bicep functions available. These are typically used for complex expressions that you use frequently.

At the time of writing, this feature is still under preview and requires **Bicep CLI version 0.20.X** and the experimental feature to be enabled in the `bicepconfig.json` settings file. This will not be covered in this book and you are encouraged to read more here: https://learn.microsoft.com/en-us/azure/azure-resource-manager/bicep/user-defined-functions.

Parameters

Parameters are user-supplied input values used to customize the Bicep deployments, providing desired resource names, locations, or configuration settings. They offer flexibility and adaptability in the template across various use cases and environments. Furthermore, you can apply **optional decorators** to parameters, such as `@minLength`, `@maxLength`, and `@allowed`, to enforce constraints and validation rules. **Decorators** are special annotations added to parameters that define constraints, validation rules, or additional metadata to enhance the accuracy and customization of input values during deployment.

The syntax for a parameter is as follows:

```
param <parameter-name> <parameter-data-type> = <default-value>
```

Referring back to the example of a storage account deployment, a parameter could be defined as follows:

```
param storageAccountName string
```

To further constrain this now, you could then add a minimum and maximum length using the decorators, as in the following example:

```
@minLength(5)
@maxLength(15)
param storageAccountName string
```

> **Note**
> You are encouraged to read more about parameters here: https://learn.microsoft.com/en-us/azure/azure-resource-manager/bicep/parameters.

Variables

Variables store intermediate values and expressions that are reusable across the Bicep file, promoting readability, centralizing configuration values, and reducing repetitions.

The syntax for variables is as follows:

```
var <variable-name> = <variable-value>
```

You can define some more advanced logic in variables, such as the following example, where the environment type chosen will determine the storage account configuration to be used:

```
@allowed([
  'dev'
  'prod'
])
param environmentName string = 'dev'
var storageSettings = {
  dev: {
    sku: 'Standard_LRS'
    location: 'westus'
  }
  prod: {
    sku: 'Premium_ZRS'
    location: 'northeurope'
  }
}

resource storageaccount 'Microsoft.Storage/storageAccounts@2023-01-01' = {
  name: storageAccountName
  location: storageSettings[environmentName].location
```

```
  kind: 'StorageV2'
  sku: {
    name: storageSettings[environmentName].sku
  }
  properties: {
    minimumTlsVersion: storageProperties.Tls
    supportsHttpsTrafficOnly: storageProperties.Https
    allowBlobPublicAccess: storageProperties.PublicAccess
  }
}
```

> **Note**
>
> You are encouraged to read more about variables here: https://learn.microsoft.com/en-us/azure/azure-resource-manager/bicep/variables.

Resources

In Bicep, **resources** denote the Azure services created, updated, or deleted. Each resource is declared with its type, name, properties, and version. They have **optional decorators**, such as `@description`, to provide additional metadata or information.

The syntax for resources is as follows:

```
resource <symbolic-name> '<full-type-name>@<api-version>' = {
  <resource-properties>
}
```

The `symbolic-name` reference is an identifier for your resource in the template and not the actual resource name; it allows for a reference to the resource through the template.

The following example is a storage account resource:

```
resource storageAccount 'Microsoft.Storage/storageAccounts@2021-04-01' = {
  name: storageAccountName
  location: location
  sku: {
    name: accountType
  }
  kind: 'StorageV2'
}
```

> **Note**
>
> You are encouraged to read more about resources here: https://learn.microsoft.com/en-us/azure/azure-resource-manager/bicep/resource-declaration.

Modules

Modules in Bicep are reusable code components that encapsulate a collection of related Azure resources or configurations. They improve code reusability and maintainability and simplify complex deployments. Modules, like resources, can have decorators to provide descriptions as metadata. These are Bicep or ARM JSON files deployed from another Bicep file, and because of this, you can attain reusability from your templates in later deployments.

The syntax for a module is as follows:

```
module <symbolic-name> '<path-to-file>' = {
  name: '<linked-deployment-name>'
  params: {
    <parameter-names-and-values>
  }
}
```

An example of referencing a storage account deployment file would be the following example, where the referenced file contains your organization's hardened standard storage account configurations:

```
module hardenedStorageAccount '../hardenedStorageAccount.bicep' = {
  name: 'hardenedStorage'
  params: {
    storageAccountName: 'supersecret0416'
    environmentName: 'prod'
  }
}
```

> **Note**
>
> You are encouraged to read more about modules here: https://learn.microsoft.com/en-us/azure/azure-resource-manager/bicep/modules.

Outputs

Outputs are optional values returned from a Bicep deployment that deliver additional information about deployed resources, such as endpoints or connection strings. They can be consumed in other processes, scripts, or templates.

The syntax for an output is as follows:

```
output <name> <data-type or type-expression> = <value>
```

An example output from a storage account deployment where we want to know the configuration applied may be the following user-defined data type shared in the example for that section:

```
output storageConfiguration storageSecuritySettings =
storageProperties
```

You are encouraged to read more about outputs here: https://learn.microsoft.com/en-us/azure/azure-resource-manager/bicep/outputs.

You have now learned about the syntax of the various components in a Bicep file and should be feeling a lot more comfortable with the general format of the files. Bicep files are useful in creating modernized IaC where you can leverage these files for repeatable, consistent, and automated deployments. Now that you understand the basic structure of a Bicep template, you are ready to start creating your first Bicep template. You will do this in the next section.

Creating a Bicep Template

You are now ready to start working on your first Bicep template. For this exercise, you will create a storage account using Bicep, which you can compare to working on ARM:

1. Open VS Code.
2. Create a new file named `Storage_Account_Bicep.bicep`.
3. Paste in the code from your previous ARM storage account template, and it will automatically convert your code to Bicep. Your code should resemble the following:

   ```
   @description('Enter a unique storage account name.')
   param storageAccountName string
   param location string = resourceGroup().location

   @description('Select the storage account type.')
   @allowed([
     'Standard_LRS'
     'Standard_GRS'
     'Standard_RAGRS'
     'Standard_ZRS'
   ])
   param accountType string = 'Standard_LRS'

   resource storageAccount 'Microsoft.Storage/storageAccounts@2021-04-01' = {
     name: storageAccountName
     location: location
     sku: {
       name: accountType
   ```

```
    }
    kind: 'StorageV2'
}

output storageAccountConnectionString string = 
DefaultEndpointsProtocol=https;AccountName=
${storageAccountName};
AccountKey=${listKeys(storageAccount.id, '2021-04-01').
keys[0].value}'
```

4. Whilst this will be a fully functioning Bicep file, you are going to recreate this somewhat from scratch. Delete all the code now.

5. On the first line of your file, start typing `storage`; IntelliSense will pop up with a suggestion as follows; click this:

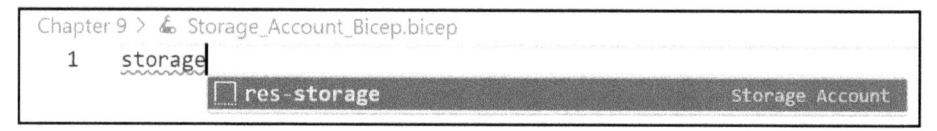

Figure 11.4: IntelliSense storage resource

6. Your storage resource has been predefined for you. You will now change the API to the latest version available. Delete everything to the right of the @ symbol, including @. Type in @ and select the latest-date API version from the pop-up list.

Figure 11.5: Changing the API version

7. Next, click before the word `resource` and hit *Enter* a few times to create some spaces. On *line 1*, you can enter the following:

```
metadata description = 'Creates storage account'
```

8. You will want to create a parameter for the storage account name; this has a maximum length limit of 24 characters. For this example, though, you want to restrict this to using a *minimum* of 5 characters in the name and a *maximum* of 15 characters. Type in the following code on *lines 3* to *5*:

    ```
    @minLength(5)
    @maxLength(15)
    param storageAccountName string
    ```

9. You would now like to have the storage **Stock Keeping Units (SKU)** parameter; enter the following on *lines 7* to *13*. This defines the allowed SKUs and sets the default value to Standard_LRS:

    ```
    @description('Select the storage account type.')
    @allowed([
      'Standard_LRS'
      'Standard_GRS'
      'Standard_ZRS'
      'Premium_LRS'
    ])
    param storageSKU string = 'Standard_LRS'
    ```

10. Next, you would like to set the default location to be the same as the resource group you are deploying to. Insert the following code on *line 16*:

    ```
    param location string = resourceGroup().location
    ```

11. With all your parameters now in place, you will modify your resource defined on *lines 18* to *25*. It should reflect the following:

    ```
    resource storageaccount 'Microsoft.Storage/storageAccounts@2023-01-01' = {
      name: storageAccountName
      location: location
      kind: 'StorageV2'
      sku: {
        name: storageSKU
      }
    }
    ```

12. You can save this, and your template file is now ready for deployment. Note how this compares to the file you made in *Chapter 10, Azure Resource Manager Templates*.

You have learned what Bicep files are, the structure of a Bicep template, and finally, you have created your own Bicep template. You should now be feeling much more comfortable working with Bicep files and can see the similarity to ARM templates. Next, you will modify your template to change some options.

Modifying an Existing Bicep Template

In the previous section, you created a Bicep template for a storage account that closely resembles the ARM storage account template you created previously. You realize that you forgot to add a description for the storage account name and would like to add that now, as well as adding an output from the template. Follow these steps to update your existing template from the previous section:

1. Open VS Code.
2. Open your `Storage_Account_Bicep.bicep` file.
3. Insert a new line above *line 3* and add the following code:

   ```
   @description('Enter a unique storage account name between 5 and 15 characters in length.')
   ```

4. *Lines 3* to *6* should look as follows:

   ```
   3   @description('Enter a unique storage account name between 5 and 15 characters in length.')
   4   @minLength(5)
   5   @maxLength(15)
   6   param storageAccountName string
   ```

   Figure 11.6: Storage account name parameter

5. On *lines 28* and *29*, add the following code to output the name of your storage account and the SKU chosen:

   ```
   output name string = storageAccountName
   output sku string = storageSKU
   ```

You have just successfully modified your Bicep template and are now ready to deploy it to Azure. You will do this in the next section.

Deploying a Bicep Template – Azure PowerShell

You built a Bicep template for deploying storage accounts in the previous section. You will now deploy the storage account to `ResouceGroupA`, which you created earlier. To do this, follow these steps:

1. Open your PowerShell terminal and run the following code to navigate to the folder where you saved your files; change the path to match your directory:

   ```
   cd c:\biceptemplatesfolder\
   ```

2. You are going to choose a name for your storage account name that is unique, such as `teststor3012231`. Then, in your PowerShell terminal, run the following code to start deployment:

   ```
   New-AzResourceGroupDeployment -ResourceGroupName ResourceGroupA
   -TemplateFile ./Storage_Account_Bicep.bicep -storageAccountName
   "teststor0312231"
   ```

3. Once the script has finished running, your deployment will be complete. Notice that there are outputs that resemble the configurations we are expecting to see.

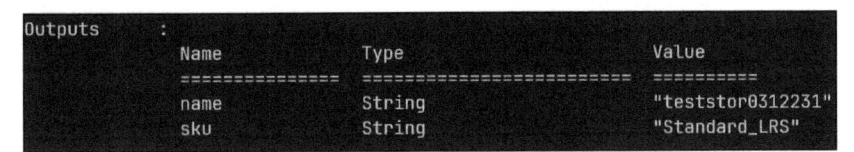

```
Outputs         :
                  Name              Type                          Value
                  ================  ============================  ==========
                  name              String                        "teststor0312231"
                  sku               String                        "Standard_LRS"
```

Figure 11.7: Storage account deployment outputs

In this exercise, you learned how to deploy Bicep templates using Azure PowerShell. You should now have an understanding of both creating and deploying Bicep templates. You now know how to leverage Bicep for your Azure deployments. As you can see, the steps to deploy are not complicated and there is no requirement to pass a parameter file in for deployment, although it is also possible.

It is also possible to deploy a Bicep file from VS Code directly.

> **Note**
>
> You are encouraged to read more about Bicep through the following URLs:
>
> **You can learn more about Bicep here**: https://learn.microsoft.com/en-us/azure/azure-resource-manager/bicep/overview
>
> **You can read more about Bicep deployments here**: https://learn.microsoft.com/en-us/azure/azure-resource-manager/bicep/deploy-powershell

In the next section, you will learn how to convert an ARM template to a Bicep template.

Converting ARM to Bicep

You have become familiar with both ARM and Bicep templates and may find yourself wanting to now reuse your existing ARM templates as Bicep templates. The following section will outline the steps involved in converting your template using the VS Code extension for Bicep, as detailed earlier in the chapter.

Prerequisites

There are a couple of items you need in place to be able to convert ARM to Bicep:

- Installation of the Bicep extension on VS Code.
- Configuration of the Bicep extension as described earlier in the chapter to allow for the automatic conversion of JSON to Bicep. You must ensure the setting for `Decompile On Paste` is enabled as per *Figure 11.8*:

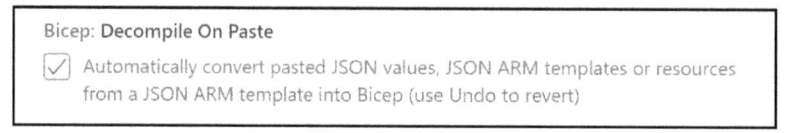

> Bicep: Decompile On Paste
> ☑ Automatically convert pasted JSON values, JSON ARM templates or resources from a JSON ARM template into Bicep (use Undo to revert)

Figure 11.8: The Decompile On Paste setting

Converting an Existing ARM File to Bicep

To convert your ARM file, you should follow these steps:

1. Open VS Code.
2. Create a new Bicep file and save it.
3. Open your existing ARM template, select all the code, and copy it to your new Bicep file.
4. This should automatically convert your ARM to Bicep code for you simply, just as you saw in the previous section when creating a Bicep template.

You now know how to convert your ARM templates to Bicep format and can bring in your existing templates to Bicep. Converting existing ARM template files can assist you in leveraging existing ARM assets that you would like in Bicep format, which makes the files easier to use and read. It will save you a lot of time and effort in having to rewrite your existing IaC ARM templates to Bicep. Another handy tool you can use is the Bicep CLI for converting templates, and you can read more about that here: `https://learn.microsoft.com/en-us/azure/azure-resource-manager/bicep/decompile`.

In the next section, you will learn how to convert your Bicep templates to ARM again.

Converting Bicep to ARM

In the previous section, you learned how to convert your ARM templates to Bicep. In this section, you are going to learn how to do the reverse operation, demonstrating the simplicity of converting between formats. Note that this is not a perfect solution and, at times, some information is not converted successfully or as expected.

Prerequisites

Before converting, there are a couple of items you need to have in place:

- Installation of the Bicep CLI as described in the *Setting Up the Bicep Extension for VS Code* section and the *Bicep CLI* section of this chapter.
- A Bicep template ready for conversion to ARM.

Converting an Existing Bicep File to ARM

To convert your Bicep file, you should follow these steps:

1. Open your PowerShell terminal and run the following code to navigate to the folder where you saved your files; change the path to match your directory:

    ```
    cd c:\biceptemplatesfolder\
    ```

2. Run the following command; you will use your Bicep template from the previous exercise for this exercise:

    ```
    bicep build .\Storage_Account_Bicep.bicep
    ```

3. A new file will be generated in the same path labeled `Storage_Account_Bicep.json`.

You have now successfully converted from Bicep back to ARM. This enables you to be more versatile when working with the file type of your choice for IaC templates. Should you prefer ARM templates, you can leverage Bicep to convert existing files to ARM format. This can also be handy for sharing files with others who are unfamiliar with the Bicep format. You should now feel comfortable working with any IaC format.

Summary

In this chapter, you gained a comprehensive understanding of the Azure Bicep language. You have learned about the benefits of Bicep templates, such as consistency, repeatability, and ease of deployment. Additionally, you explored the structure of Bicep templates and worked on creating, modifying, and deploying resources using the language. With VS Code, you experienced an efficient way to author and manage Bicep templates, leveraging the power of built-in tools and extensions. These foundational concepts will accelerate your journey into automated, code-driven infrastructure deployments. This will make you a more effective administrator and also provide you with the confidence and knowledge you will require for the test topics in this area of the exam.

Furthermore, you learned how to save deployments and export templates for reuse and sharing. You also gained valuable insights into Azure Bicep, an improved DSL that streamlines the IaC experience, and learned how to create and modify Bicep templates. Finally, you acquired skills for interconverting ARM and Bicep templates, allowing you to leverage the best aspects of both languages for your infrastructure needs. Altogether, this chapter has equipped you with the essential knowledge and skills to effectively manage and deploy Azure resources using Azure Bicep.

In the next chapter, you will cover how to configure virtual machines.

> **Note**
> Remember to delete the resources you created in this chapter to minimize costs. You can do this with the following commands; these will remove the resource group and all the corresponding resources: `Remove-AzResourceGroup -Name ResourceGroupA`

12
Understanding Virtual Machines

In the previous chapter, you learned about automating deployments using ARM templates, a good way to standardize and simplify deployments.

In this chapter, you will learn all about **Azure Virtual Machines** (**VMs**). You will learn about VM storage (the various disk types available and their configurations), disk redundancy (planning for resiliency in the number of failures you can sustain), VM sizes (the different types of VMs you can consume), networking, availability sets and zones (how they assist in planning against failures), different VM security types (choosing the level of security to apply to your VM deployment), and the various scaling options available. You will also experience deploying and provisioning VMs. As part of this topic, you will learn why VMs are the cornerstone of running applications and, subsequently, the services they assist in delivering, such as web apps. Each section has instructions and guidance on how to apply the skills you have learned.

In this chapter, you are going to explore the following main topics:

- Understanding Azure Disk Storage
- Understanding Azure VMs
- Deploying a VM in Azure
- Deploying and Configuring Scale Sets

Technical Requirements

This chapter has the following requirements:

- Access to an Azure subscription with owner or contributor privileges. If you do not have access to one, students can enroll for a free account here: `https://azure.microsoft.com/en-us/free/`.

- **PowerShell 5.1** or later installed on a Windows PC or PowerShell Core 6.x or other operating systems on which labs can be practiced.

- For Windows users, you will need to install **.NET Framework 4.7.2** or later using the following link: https://learn.microsoft.com/en-us/dotnet/framework/install.

- Note that, occasionally, examples can only be followed from a PC or https://shell.azure.com (PowerShell 7.0.6 LTS or later is recommended).

- Where PowerShell is not installed or available, https://shell.azure.com can be used as a browser-based shell.

- Installation of the Az PowerShell module, which can be performed by running the following in an administrative PowerShell session:

    ```
    Set-ExecutionPolicy -ExecutionPolicy RemoteSigned -Scope
    CurrentUser
    Install-Module -Name Az -Scope CurrentUser -Repository PSGallery
    -Force
    ```

Understanding Azure Disk Storage

Azure disks provide block-level storage primarily intended for VMs (such as an application server you may deploy with Windows Server 2022). They present varying levels of performance on Azure depending on your requirements and choice of **Stock-Keeping Unit** (**SKU**). Azure disks are designed to support both Windows and Linux operating systems in standalone or clustered deployments.

Disk Management Options

Azure offers the ability to either manage disks yourself (with you taking on the administrative burden) or subscribe to a managed disk option (where you don't need to be involved in the complexity of managing your storage for scale). As of 30 January 2024, you can no longer provision unmanaged disks, as the functionality of managed disks has replaced and enhanced the capabilities of the offering.

The two Azure disk management options are described here:

- **Unmanaged disks**: These disks are managed by the user. This management configuration requires the allocation of the disk to a storage account. Allocating disks to storage accounts is vital to ensure their reliability. Factors such as storage space available on the storage account and storage account type are necessary for managing these disk types. Disk costs for this service are calculated based on the data consumed on the disk. Since this type of disk is discontinued, you are highly encouraged to migrate any unmanaged disks to managed disks.

- **Managed disks**: The Azure platform automatically manages where the disk is stored, how it scales, and how it delivers the intended performance. Managed disks also come with higher **Service-Level Agreements** (**SLAs**) than unmanaged disks. Disk costs for this service are calculated at the size of the provisioned disk, regardless of the data consumed. Managed disks are recommended by Microsoft over unmanaged disks and are designed for 99.999% availability. With this functionality, you can sustain loss/issues on one or two replicas, therefore ensuring high durability levels of 99.999999999% or more. As of 30 January 2024, this is not your only option for disks for your VM deployments.

> **Note**
> As of 30 January 2024, you cannot create new unmanaged disks. Unmanaged disks are intended to be discontinued by 30 September 2025. You are advised to migrate to managed disks as soon as possible.

Disk Performance

When selecting the correct disk type for your workload's purpose, consider the reliability and performance requirements. For instance, you would select a high-performance disk for your production SQL-type workloads and a lower-performance disk for your dev/test workloads.

Factors that should be taken into consideration include the following:

- **IOPS**: **Input/Output Operations per Second** (**IOPS**) refers to a performance measurement for storage that describes the count of operations performed per second.
- **Throughput**: Disk throughput describes the speed at which data can be transferred through a disk. Throughput is typically calculated as *IOPS x I/O Size = Disk Throughput* and is measured in **Megabytes per Second** (**MBps**).
- **Reliability**: Azure offers better SLAs based on the disk type chosen in conjunction with a VM.
- **Latency**: Latency refers to the length of time it takes for a disk to process a request received and send a response. It will limit the effective performance of disks, and therefore, it is pertinent to use disks with lower latency for high-performance workloads. The effect of latency on a disk can be expressed through the following example. If a disk can offer 2,500 IOPS as the maximum performance but has 10 ms latency, it will only be able to deliver 250 IOPS, which will potentially be highly restrictive. The impact of high latency will significantly decrease the performance of the disk as a result.
- **Premium storage**: This provides consistently lower latency than other Azure storage options and is advised when considering high-performance workloads.

Deciding between the various storage options can be challenging. The following decision tree can help when trying to select the right type for your requirements. Keep in mind that as performance increases, so does the cost of the disks.

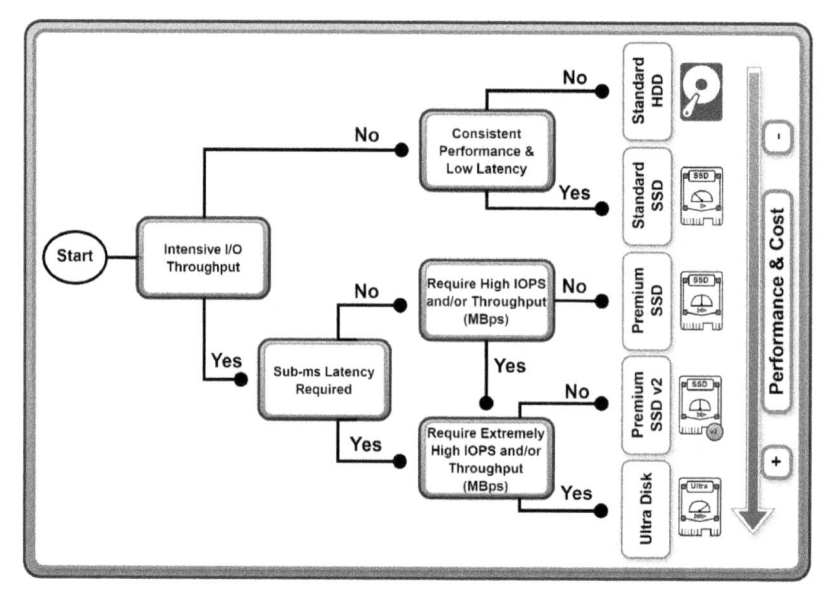

Figure 12.1: Azure disk decision tree

Now that you understand the various factors that impact disk performance, you will learn about disk caching and its effect on performance.

Disk Caching

Caching refers to temporary storage utilized as a copy of data from a connected disk to provide faster read and write performance than traditional permanent storage. This is done by loading disk components that are read or written frequently (therefore, representing repeatable patterns) to the cache storage. Data needs to be predictable to benefit from caching, meaning it follows a known pattern of access (such as frequently accessed data). Data is only loaded into the cache storage from the connected disk when it has been read or written at least once.

Write caching is used to speed up data writes by persisting storage in a lazy write fashion. This means data written is stored on the cache and the app considers this data to be saved to the persistent disk, but the cache waits for an opportunity to write the data to the disk as it becomes available. This presents a risk of data loss if the system is shut down unexpectedly, as the cached data may have not been written to the disk.

`Host caching` can be enabled on your VMs and can be configured per disk (both OS and data disks). The default configuration for the **Operating System** (**OS**) disk is set to `Read/write`. The default setting for data disks is `Read-only` mode, as you can see in the following figure:

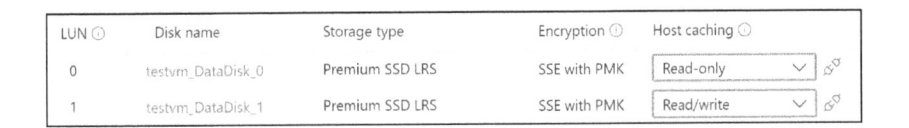

LUN	Disk name	Storage type	Encryption	Host caching
0	testvm_DataDisk_0	Premium SSD LRS	SSE with PMK	Read-only
1	testvm_DataDisk_1	Premium SSD LRS	SSE with PMK	Read/write

Figure 12.2: Disk cache configuration on a VM

The following caching modes can be selected depending on your requirements:

- **Read-only**: When you expect workloads to predominantly perform repeatable read operations. Data retrieval performance is enhanced as data is read from the cache.
- **Read/write**: When you have workloads where you expect to perform a balance of repeatable or predictable read and write operations.
- **None**: If your workload does not follow either of these patterns, then it is best to set host caching to None.

> **Note**
> Caching provides little or no value for random I/O, and where data is dispersed across the disk, it can even reduce performance. Therefore, carefully consider the impact on your storage and VM performance before enabling caching.

You now understand the different types of caching available. You will explore how to calculate the impact on performance by implementing the different caches available.

Calculating Expected Caching Performance

When configuring your VM to take advantage of disk caching, you should consider the type of operations mentioned in the preceding sections, and whether your workloads will benefit from caching. Set the disks that will provide caching to the appropriate caching option. Each VM SKU has its unique limit on the performance cap applied to the VM. One of the advantages to the disk performance on the VM is that by enabling caching and setting some disks to not be cached, you can potentially exceed the performance limits of VM storage.

Let's look at an example of this.

Imagine you have a **Standard_D16as_v4** VM SKU provisioned with 8 data disks. This VM has the following performance limits:

- **Cached IOPS**: 32,000
- **Uncached IOPS**: 25,600
- 8 x P40 data disks that can achieve 7,500 IOPS each

Some items to note are the following:

- Four of the P40 data disks are attached in Read-only cache mode and the others are set to None
- Although the VM SKU can have 32 data disks, only 8 data disks were used and attached for the example

An application that is installed makes a request for 65,000 IOPS to the VM, 5,000 to the OS disk, and 30,000 to each of the data disk arrays. The following transactions occur on the disks:

- The OS disk offers 2,000 IOPS
- The 4 data disks that are cached offer a collective 30,000 IOPS
- The 4 data disks that are not cached offer a collective 30,000 IOPS

Since the VM limit imposes an uncached limit of 25,600 IOPS, this is the maximum delivered by the uncached disks. The cached disks are combined with the performance of the OS disk for a collective total of 32,000 IOPS. Since this is the limit imposed on the SKU, this performance metric is maxed out too. Using the cache effectively in this example, the VM is able to achieve a total of 57,600 IOPS, which far exceeds either of the single limits imposed on the VM. This is illustrated in the following diagram:

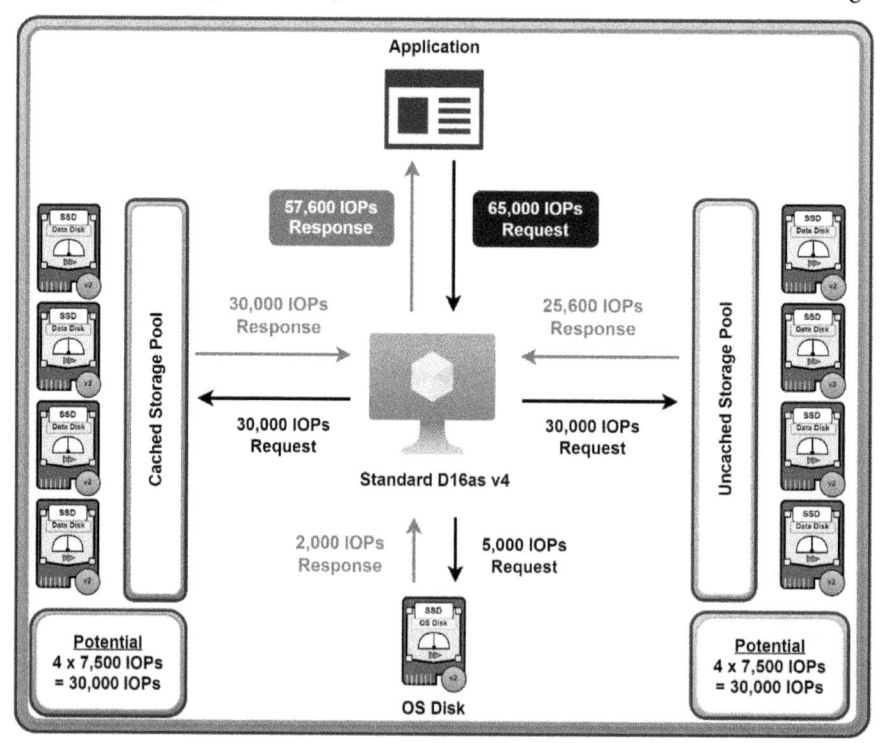

Figure 12.3: Cache calculations

As you can see in the preceding diagram, by carefully analyzing disk caching, significant performance improvements can be achieved. Also note that when the cache does not contain the requested data (for instance, on a read) then the cache limit is used for the request as well as the non-cache limit. So, if a 5,000 IOPS request was pushed to the cached disks that can deliver 30,000 IOPS, then 5,000 IOPS will be taken from the 30,000 in the cache limit, leaving the total of cached IOPS to be 25,000 IOPS and then the subsequent total for the uncached IOPS limit to be 25,600 – 5,000, which leaves a total of 20,600 IOPS remaining.

> **Note**
> Take note that changing the cache setting on the disks will cause an interruption to the disk on the VM. In the event that the cache setting is modified on a data disk, it is detached and reattached again, but when the setting is modified for the OS disk, it will cause the VM to be restarted.

Now that you understand the impact of caching on disks and VMs, you will explore the different types/SKUs of disks available to you within Azure.

Disk Types

Azure currently offers five disk types to meet specific customer scenarios based on the level of performance required. The performance offered also directly correlates with the physical storage hardware type that backs the service offering, such as Premium SSDs being backed by physical SSD storage. The following list of disk types is offered by Azure:

- Ultra Disk
- Premium SSD
- Premium SSD v2
- Standard SSD
- Standard HDD

Ultra Disk

Azure's highest-performance SSD storage is **Ultra Disk**, and this option is ideal for scenarios where you need fast access to your data, such as I/O-intensive or high-throughput workloads. Ultra Disks offer flexibility in dynamically changing the throughput and IOPS performance of your disks without requiring a restart of your VM. Examples of workloads where you might want high I/O are SAP HANA and forensic applications. If you have highly transactional SQL workloads that require more performance than Premium SSD disks, this is a good option. Ultra Disks can only be used as data disks and not OS drives. The maximum throughput of Ultra Disks is 10,000 MBps per disk and is provisioned at 256 KiB/s per provisioned IOPS. Maximum IOPS performance per disk is limited to 400,000 IOPS per disk, and 300 IOPS per GiB of provisioned storage. The maximum size of the disk that can be deployed is 65,536 GiB (64 TiB). These disks are designed to achieve sub-millisecond latencies, which are beneficial for high-performance storage requiring workloads such as SQL databases.

There are, however, several limitations to the service, such as these disks not being able to be used for the OS, not supporting availability sets, and VMs with Ultra Disks not being supported by Azure Site Recovery. These limitations, which are changing with the service, should be reviewed before you utilize them in your workloads.

> **Note**
>
> Ultra Disk resize operations can take up to an hour to take effect, and a maximum of 4 resize operations can be performed during a 24-hour period. To review any of the limitations of Ultra Disk, please visit the following link: https://learn.microsoft.com/en-us/azure/virtual-machines/disks-types.

Premium SSD

Premium SSD is a high-performance storage option for Azure VMs and Azure Files. This storage is best suited for production workloads (for example, enterprise applications such as SAP). It is backed by SSD storage offering low latency and high performance at a better price point than Ultra Disks. If you are looking to offer the best SLAs for your VMs, this is the storage type you should select. This is also best for most SQL-based workloads. Premium SSDs are available only to Azure VMs that are compatible with Premium storage (generally, VM SKUs ending with an "s") and can be attached as either OS or data disks.

Premium SSD v2

Microsoft has launched a newer tier of Premium SSD disks called **Premium SSD v2**. These offer high performance both on the IOPs and throughput layers. These disks are highly customizable to the requirements you have of the storage where small disks can be provisioned with high IOPs or throughput to meet your scaling needs. They are suitable for a wide variety of workloads, for instance, database servers, analytics, and even gaming servers. These disks have several limitations that will impact your architecture and require careful consideration before being incorporated into your workloads. These disks unfortunately cannot be used as OS disks, they only support zonal VMs, and they are only available to certain regions. There are other limitations that you should inquire about before deploying this disk type. Due to their flexible design, they do not have dedicated sizes, which can be very useful for maintaining cost efficiency for your applications alongside the high-performance requirements you have.

> **Note**
>
> You are encouraged to read up on the limitations of the Premium SSD v2 disk before implementation as the list is likely to change over time. To read more, follow this link: https://learn.microsoft.com/en-us/azure/virtual-machines/disks-types#premium-ssd-v2.

Standard SSD

Azure **Standard SSDs** provide a cost-effective solution for workloads that need consistent performance at lower IOPS levels. This is one of the best choices for non-production workloads such as dev/test workloads. This is best suited for web servers, low IOPS application servers, lightly used or under-used enterprise applications, and dev/test workloads. Standard SSDs provide better availability, consistency, reliability, and latency than regular **Hard Disk Drives** (**HDDs**), although the performance is remarkably similar. Standard SSDs are available on all Azure VMs and can be attached as either OS or data disks.

Standard HDD

The Azure **Standard HDD** storage option offers excellent value and consistent performance at a more affordable price point than the other three types of Azure disks. It can only use **Locally Redundant Storage** (**LRS**) for your data and applications. HDD storage is most suitable when you do not have high-performance requirements and you can tolerate variable performance, and it is ideal for test or lab environments.

Disk Summary Table

The following table displays key differences between the disk types available to you:

	Standard HDD	Standard SSD	Premium SSD	Premium SSD v2	Ultra Disk
Disk Tech	HDD	SSD	SSD	SSD	SSD
Max Disk Size	32 TiB	32 TiB	32 TiB	65 TiB	65 TiB
Max Disk Throughput	500 MBps	750 MBps	900 MBps	1,200 MBps	10,000 MBps
Max IOPs	2,000 IOPs	6,000 IOPs	20,000 IOPs	80,000 IOPs	400,000 IOPs
Can Be Used as an OS Disk?	Yes	Yes	Yes	No	No

Table 12.1: Azure disks compared

> **Note**
> Azure VM SLAs on a single instance that have Premium SSD disks attached go up to 99.9% compared to 99.5% for a Standard SSD and 95% for a Standard HDD. Because of this, it is advised to utilize Premium SSD disks on production or critical VMS in Azure.

In the next section, you will explore what disk redundancy is and its options.

Disk Redundancy Options

Redundancy refers to the number of copies of your disk that are available at any time. This supports the failure of copies and ensures the continuity of services depending on the redundancy option chosen. Regardless of the option, data is replicated three times in a storage account for the primary region.

In *Chapter 6, Understanding Storage Accounts*, you learned about the various redundancy options available in Azure, and the way replication occurs between data centers. You are encouraged to revise this material.

For managed disks, Azure offers two options: LRS and **Zone-Redundant Storage** (**ZRS**). ZRS provides higher availability than LRS, as you learned previously. The ZRS option is only supported for Premium SSD disks (excluding the Premium SSD v2 variant) and Standard SSD disks. It is also only available for limited regions. Interestingly, the LRS option offers better write latency than ZRS disks due to the synchronous nature of how it writes data.

Understanding Azure VMs

A VM is a logical configuration of resources to emulate a machine that runs similarly to a normal computer. The difference is that you can leverage a set of pooled resources, such as memory, CPU, and storage, to create customized VMs. Typically, a physical machine is limited by its physical specifications and is designed to run a single machine. Through virtualization, though, you can carve up the resources to create several machines according to the limits of your physical resources. By being able to leverage a hyperscale hypervisor such as Azure, you benefit from being able to leverage the nearly unlimited resources that Microsoft builds into its data centers to allow massive scale. You essentially need to identify the number and size of resources you need and select an appropriate VM that matches your requirements.

You can run both Windows VMs as well as Linux VMs in Azure. VMs come in all sorts of sizes and a variety of prices, ranging from VMs with a small amount of memory and processing power for general purposes to large VMs that can be used for **Graphics Processing Unit** (**GPU**)-intensive and high-performance computing workloads. To create a VM, you can choose from several predefined images. There are images available for OSs such as Windows Server or Linux, as well as predefined applications, such as SQL Server images and complete farms, which consist of multiple VMs that can be deployed at once. An example of a farm is a three-tier SharePoint farm. VMs can be created and managed either from the Azure portal, PowerShell, or the CLI, and they come in the following series and sizes.

VM Sizes

As of 21 August 2024, the following VM series and sizes are available in Azure:

Type	Series	Description
General purpose	Av2, Bsv2, Basv2, Bpsv2, Dpsv6, Dplsv6, Dpdsv6, Dpldsv6, Dalsv6, Daldsv6, Dpsv5, Dpdsv5, Dplsv5, Dpldsv5, Dlsv5, Dldsv5, Dv5, Dsv5, Ddv5, Ddsv5, Dasv5, Dadsv5, DCasv5, DCadsv5, DCas_cc_v5, DCads_cc_v5, DCesv5, DCedsv5, DCsv3, DCdsv3 Including previous generation variants of the A, B, D, and DC families of VMs.	These VMs are best suited to small and medium-sized workloads, typically databases and web servers with low to medium traffic. They have a balanced CPU-to-memory ratio that is ideal for testing and development scenarios, too. Typically, the ratio of CPU to memory is 1:4 or 1:3.5.
Compute-optimized	Fasv6, Falsv6, Fsv2, FX Including previous generation variants of the F families of VMs.	These VMs are best suited to CPU-intensive workloads such as application servers, web servers with medium traffic, and network appliances for nodes in batch processing. They have a high CPU-to-memory ratio. Typically, the ratio of CPU to memory is 1:2.
Memory-optimized	Epsv6, Epdsv6, Easv6, Eadsv6, Ev5, Esv5, Edv5, Edsv5, Easv5, Eadsv5, Epsv5, Epdsv5, Ebsv5, Ebdsv5, ECasv5, ECadsv5, ECas_cc_v5, ECads_cc_v5, ECesv5, ECedsv5, Msv3, Mdsv3, Mv2, Msv2, Mdsv2 Including previous generation variants of the E and other memory-optimized families of VMs.	These VMs are best suited to deployments requiring more memory, such as relational database servers, medium to large caches, and in-memory analytics. They have a high memory-to-CPU ratio. Typically, the ratio of CPU to memory is 1:8.

Type	Series	Description
Storage-optimized	Lsv3, Lasv3 Including previous generation variants of the L families of VMs.	These VMs are best suited to high storage requirement scenarios or high-performance storage. They have high disk throughput.
GPU	NC, NCads_H100_v5, NCCads_H100_v5, NCv2, NCv3, NCasT4_v3, NC_A100_v4, ND_MI300X_v5, ND_H100_v5, NDm_A100_v4, ND_A100_v4, NGads V620, NV, NVv3, NVv4, NVadsA10_v5 Including previous generation variants of the NV families of VMs.	These VMs are best suited to graphically demanding deployments such as heavy graphic rendering and video editing, deep learning applications, and machine learning model training. These VMs are available with single or multiple GPUs.
Field Programmable Gate Array (FPGA)	NP	These VMs are designed for very compute-heavy processing tasks such as machine learning and analytics.
High performance compute	HB, HBv2, HBv3, HBv4, HC, HX	These VMs are best suited to batch processing or high-compute, demanding deployments. They are the fastest VMs available and offer the most powerful CPUs with optional high-throughput network interfaces (Remote Direct Memory Access (RDMA)).

Table 12.2: Azure VM sizes

VM series are updated constantly. New series, types, and sizes are added and removed frequently.

> **Note**
>
> To stay up to date with these changes, you can refer to the following site: `https://learn.microsoft.com/en-us/azure/virtual-machines/sizes`.

Networking

VMs on Azure have a plethora of networking options available to them, as you will see further in the chapter when you deploy a VM. The **Virtual Network** (**VNet**) and subnet can be created on the creation of a VM. Alternatively, you can join an existing subnet on a VNet you have created. Networking can be controlled through a basic five-tuple network firewalling service named Network Security Groups.

Network Security Groups

When deploying resources on VNets within Azure, it is recommended from a security point of view to only allow the required traffic to your resource. One of the solutions on the Azure platform for traffic filtering is **Network Security Groups** (**NSGs**). Traffic filtering is the activity of allowing or denying traffic based on a set of predefined rules, helping to control inbound and outbound traffic to and from your Azure resources. NSGs act as a basic five-tuple firewall service for network-connected resources. These can be either applied at a subnet layer or a **Network Interface Card** (**NIC**) layer in Azure. NICs are typically associated directly with VMs but could also be from services that have a private endpoint attached. NSG rules are the configurations for the traffic filtering patterns and are defined by the following components: **source**, **destination**, **port**, **protocol**, and **action** (deny or allow). Each rule is given a priority, and the lower the number of priorities, the higher the precedence. The first rule matched on the traffic will be the rule that is chosen and followed. The more specific the rule, the higher the precedence it takes when being evaluated by the NSG in the processing of the rules. For example, if you have a rule for inbound internet traffic to your VM and you specify the VM IP address in the rule, it will precede a more generic rule for a whole network range that could contain IP addresses for several VMs.

You can use NSGs to restrict who can access services, from which source (such as an IP address), and to which hosts (normally the destination). You can also choose to associate a single NSG with a NIC and/or subnet. The same NSG can be applied several times in that it can be associated with several NICs and subnets. For VM deployments, you will likely open port 3389 (RDP – Windows) or 22 (SSH – Linux) for VM access or management, but carefully consider the source addresses you allow. As a rule of thumb, issue access to known IPs only from within your organization for the source address. This prevents access from unwanted sources, including other regions, and is an easy way to better secure access to your services. For enhanced security, you should also consider a service such as Bastion or another jump-box service.

Availability Sets

Availability sets are a feature in Azure designed to enable high availability and increase the reliability of VMs. It does this by grouping VMs logically by spreading them across fault and update domains. On the backend, VMs are essentially being split across isolated hardware nodes. Several scenarios can have an impact on the availability of your Azure VMs. These are as follows:

- **Unplanned hardware maintenance event**: When hardware is about to fail, Azure fires an unplanned hardware maintenance event. **Live migration** technology is used, which predicts failure and then moves the VM, the network connections, memory, and storage to different physical machines, without disconnecting the client. When your VM is moved, the performance is reduced for a short time because the VM is paused for 30 seconds. Network connections, memory, and open files are still preserved.

- **Unexpected downtime**: Should a VM go down due to a hardware or physical infrastructure failure, Azure will attempt to restore the VM to another healthy host. There is a risk of temporary downtime when this event occurs.

- **Planned hardware maintenance event**: This type of event is a periodic update from Microsoft in Azure to improve the platform. Most of these updates do not have a significant impact on the uptime of VMs, but some of them may require a reboot or restart.

To provide redundancy during these types of events, you can group two or more VMs in an availability set. By leveraging availability sets, VMs are distributed across multiple isolated hardware nodes in a cluster within a single region. This way, Azure can ensure that during an event or failure, only a subset of your VMs is impacted and your overall solution will remain operational and available. To meet the 99.95% Azure **Service-Level Agreement** (**SLA**) during outages and other failures, Microsoft advises that two or more VMs be deployed within an availability set. There are no costs associated with availability sets themselves; however, be mindful that there are costs associated with the underlying resources such as the VMs and disks.

> **Note**
> VMs can only be assigned to an availability set during initial deployment.

Fault Domain versus Update Domain

When you place your VMs in an availability set, Azure guarantees they will be spread across fault and update domains. By default, Azure will assign three fault domains and five update domains (which can be increased to a maximum of 20) to the availability set.

Fault domains in Azure are designed to protect against hardware failures by maintaining services in other fault domains and isolating problems to the problem fault domain. It does this by grouping hardware with its own power source and network switch. Update domains facilitate planned maintenance by spreading VMs across domains and updating them systematically to prevent downtime. Update domains enable continuity of services during maintenance windows by grouping VMs and underlying hardware into domains that can be updated and rebooted simultaneously. This, in turn, minimizes the impact on your VM environment.

When spreading your VMs over fault domains, your VMs sit over three different racks in the Azure data center. In the case of an event or failure of the underlying platform, only one rack gets affected, and the other VMs remain accessible, as depicted here:

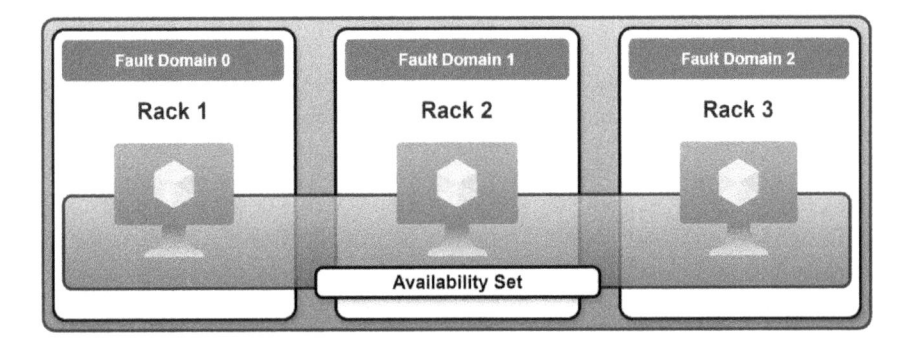

Figure 12.4: VMs spread across fault domains

Update domains are useful in the case of an OS or host update. When you spread your VMs across multiple update domains, one domain will be updated and rebooted while the others remain accessible, as depicted in the following diagram:

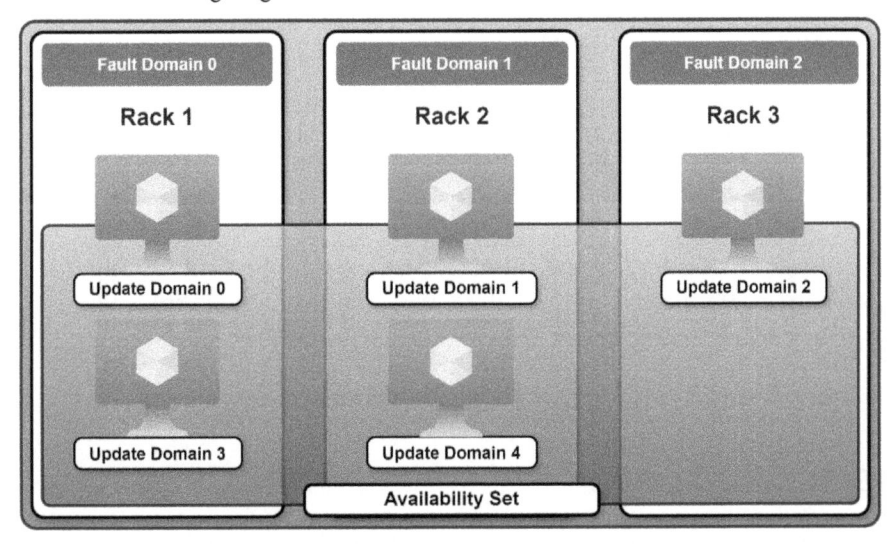

Figure 12.5: VMs spread across update and fault domains

Availability Zones

Availability zones in Azure are designed to protect your applications and data from data center failures by distributing resources across multiple isolated regions. They do this by leveraging different regional zones to handle faults and updates. The service is designed to have other zones maintain regional services and support high availability, especially where outages are experienced. Therefore, the service's efficient management of faults and updates increases its resiliency capability. Availability zones will span physical data centers, whereas availability sets are designed to provide data center resiliency.

Updates in availability zones are handled by a single zone receiving updates at a time. This minimizes the downtime associated with updates and enables continuity of your highly available workloads that span multiple zones. The different regions will have different counts of zones ranging between 0 and 3 zones for the region.

The following figure depicts an availability zone operating across update and fault domains. Note that the fault domain and update domain numbers do not necessarily align, and the figure is for illustration only.

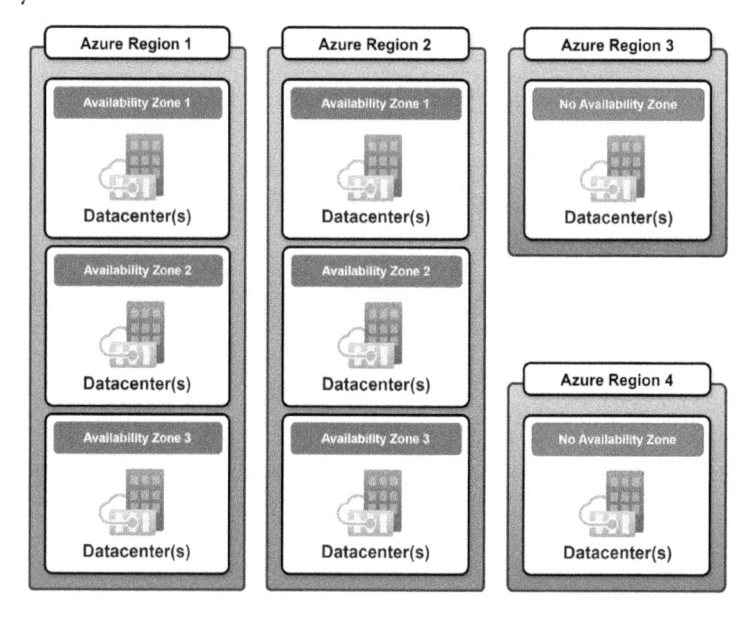

Figure 12.6: Availability zones

Scale Sets

VM scale sets are used to deploy multiple VMs at once without the need for manual actions or scripts. You can then manage them all at once from a single place. VM scale sets are typically used to build large-scale infrastructures, where keeping all your VMs in sync is key. Azure handles the maintenance of VMs, including keeping them in sync. VM scale sets are spread across fault domains using availability zones under the hood. VMs inside a scale set achieve resiliency by enabling high availability through scale compared to availability sets that enable high availability through distribution across fault and update domains. **Autoscale** is a feature on scale that sets to scale automatically and is enabled by default to accommodate scaling requirements for automatically distributing VMs across fault and update domains.

You can, however, manually add or remove VM instances to the scale set yourself instead of using Autoscale. When creating a scale set, a few artifacts are created for you automatically. Alongside the number of VMs you specified being added to the scale set, **Azure Load Balancer**, **Azure Autoscale**, a VNet, and a public IP address are added as well. All these components collectively enable the scalability functionality offered by scale sets. They are illustrated in the following figure:

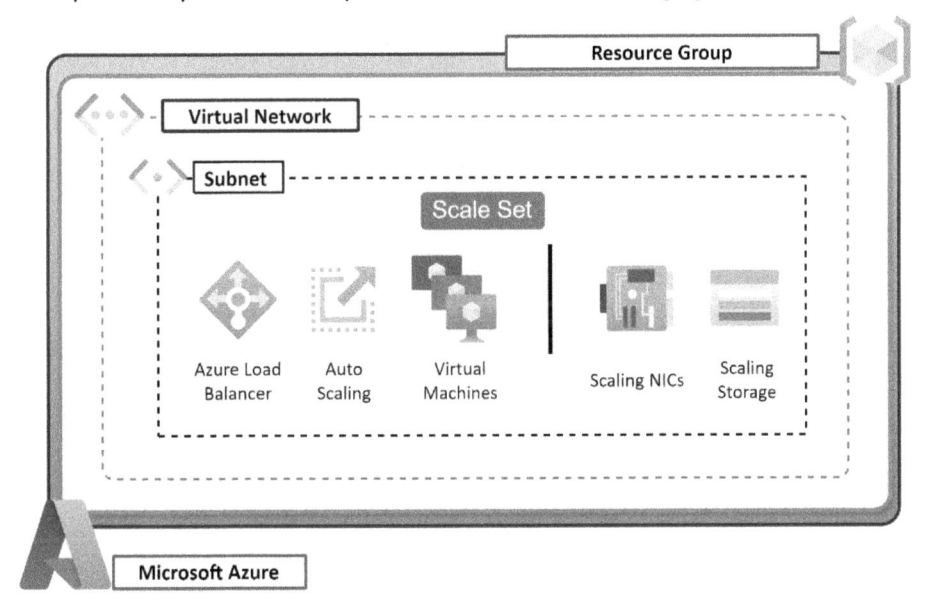

Figure 12.7: VM scale sets

Allocation Policy

There are two different variations for scale sets regarding how nodes are spread within them. Spreading occurs across fault domains with two configurations:

- **Max spreading**: This will spread VM nodes across as many fault domains as are available
- **Fixed spreading**: This configuration is designed where five fault domains are available; VM nodes will be spread equally across all available fault domains

> **Note**
> Where less than five fault domains are available, the `fixed spreading` option will be disabled.

Comparing Horizontal and Vertical Scaling

When discussing scaling, you can quickly get confused by the terminology if you are not aware of the different types of scaling that are typically used. You will frequently hear the terms vertical and horizontal scaling in the industry.

Vertical scaling refers to reallocating resources for your services, such as resizing a VM by adding resources (scaling up) and removing resources (scaling down). An example of this is illustrated in the following figure when changing from the VM SKU of a D2s VM to a D4s VM.

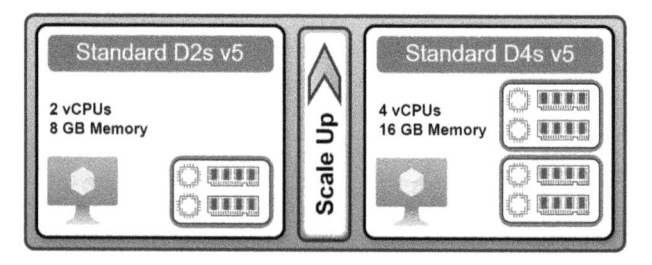

Figure 12.8: Vertical scaling

Horizontal scaling refers to scaling resources by increasing (scaling out) and decreasing (scaling in) the number of instances. In the following figure, one node is scaled out to four nodes.

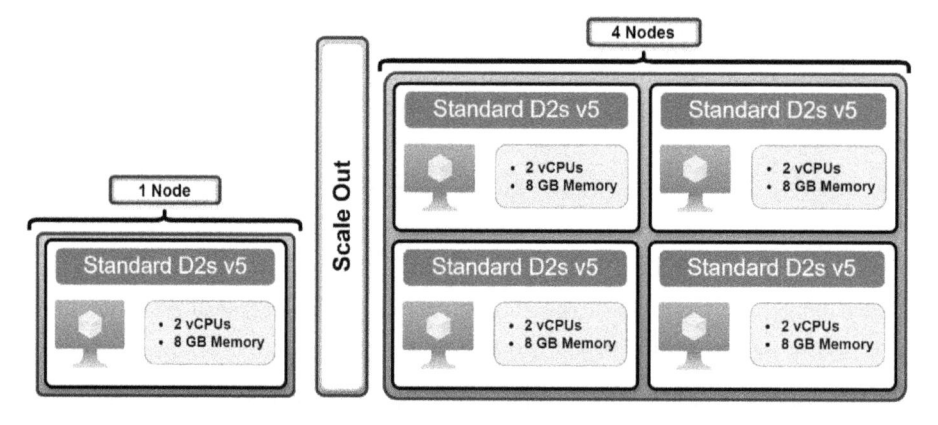

Figure 12.9: Horizontal scaling

VM Security Types

With the introduction of Generation 2 VMs, Azure has introduced functionality for enhanced security on the VM hosting layer. Standard has the most relaxed security settings, and confidential is the most secure.

There are three options to select from:

- Standard
- Trusted Launch VMs
- Confidential VMs

Each is a default configuration type aligned to the security settings you can apply to your VM on a hosting layer. Next are the three types of security defaults.

Standard

Standard is defined as the configuration on Azure with the most basic security settings. These are the default deployment options for VMs where the following settings have not been enabled for enhanced security:

- Secure Boot
- **Virtualized Trusted Platform Module (vTPM)**
- Integrity monitoring

Trusted Launch

Trusted Launch is the default selection for all new VMs created in Azure and applies to Generation 2 VMs and newer. It is designed to protect you from modern, sophisticated attacks by adding additional layers of security, such as verified boot loaders and OS kernels. The core security features implemented are as follows:

- **Secure Boot**: This feature prevents malware-based rootkits and boot kits from being installed by restricting booting to signed drivers and OSs only. It is implemented at the platform layer into the firmware and, as of the time of writing, supports several Windows and Linux OSs.

- **vTPM**: With this configuration, you may use a virtualized trusted platform in your VMs to act as a separate safe vault for measurements and keys. TPM2.0 compliance is maintained via vTPM. Trusted Launch conducts cloud-based remote attestation using the vTPM by measuring the entire boot chain of your VM (system, drivers, OS, and UEFI). Your VM is cryptographically verified for a successful boot, to which failure will trigger an alarm through Microsoft Defender for Cloud.

- **Virtualization-Based Security (VBS)**: VBS is a technology that enhances the security of a VM through virtualization features on the hypervisor layer to protect sensitive parts of the OS.

- **Microsoft Defender for Cloud integration**: Through Microsoft Defender for Cloud, you can regularly assess the configuration status of your VMs by surfacing recommendations such as enabling Secure Boot, vTPM, the installation of the guest attestation extension, boot integrity monitoring, as well as enabling several alerts for your VM.

Using all these technologies together can reduce the opportunity for attacks and prevent compromise through vulnerabilities and exploits.

You can read more about Trusted Launch VMs here: https://learn.microsoft.com/en-gb/azure/virtual-machines/trusted-launch.

Confidential VMs

Utilizing the confidential VM configuration can further enhance the security of your VM. It improves upon the security of Trusted Launch VMs by including a hardware-based trusted execution environment. This is done by encrypting data in memory with hardware-based isolation between the VMs, hypervisor, and host management code.

These types of VMs also offer a new type of enhanced disk encryption scheme, which is an optional feature. The scheme securely links the disk encryption keys to the VM's **Trusted Platform Module** (**TPM**), ensuring that only the VM can access the encrypted contents on the disk. Encryption keys are bound to the TPM of the VM you are securing, ensuring that the disk that is being protected is only accessible by that VM.

> **Note**
>
> When **Secure Encryption Virtualization – Secure nested Paging** (**SEV-SNP**) is configured on the VM, if any critical settings are detected as missing or compromised, the Azure Attestation tests will fail, preventing the VM from booting. You can read more about Azure Attestation here: https://learn.microsoft.com/en-us/azure/attestation/overview.
>
> If you would like to know more about confidential VMs, you can read more about them here: https://learn.microsoft.com/en-us/azure/confidential-computing/confidential-vm-overview.

You have learned about the various factors that comprise VM configurations, such as **availability sets** and **scale sets**. Next, you will explore the process of deploying a VM in Azure.

VM Images

Azure VM images, applicable to all VM types, are generally what you observe as the OS due to their labeling. Images are a copy of a full VM containing both data and OS disks where defined. In most cases, it contains the OS disk only, and the name is often derived from the OS version you intend to install, such as `Win2022AzureEdition` (Microsoft Windows Server 2022 Azure Edition). You can consume various image types, both from the marketplace and custom images that you can create such as a **Red Hat Enterprise Linux** (**RHEL**) image with your organization's libraries preloaded. VM images provide a versatile solution for your organization to preconfigure approved images for use in your standardized VM deployments.

If you would like to read more about images, you can do so here: https://learn.microsoft.com/en-us/azure/virtual-machines/shared-image-galleries.

VM Architectures

As with physical infrastructure, virtualized infrastructure also contains different architectures pertaining to the underlying CPU architecture found on the physical hosts in Azure. When you provision a VM, you have the choice of what processor architecture you would like to deploy.

Currently, there are two options available in Azure: **x64** and **Arm64**. Both architecture types are 64-bit CPU architectures. The x64 architecture supports your standard CPU architecture types found in most modern computers and servers (such as those manufactured by Intel and AMD).

The Arm64 architecture type is a new variation developed for mobile processors based on 64-bit architecture and designed to deliver enhanced performance-to-power ratios. It is based on the **Reduced Instruction Set Computer** (**RISC**) architecture, whereas x64 is based on the **Instruction Set Architecture** (**ISA**). Therefore, x64 is backward compatible with x86 (32-bit) instruction sets as it is based on the same architecture standard.

The best way to compare the processors is to understand that x64 is designed for high performance, which comes with a high-power draw, while Arm64 is designed for efficiency, providing high levels of performance using the least power possible. x64 is generally much more powerful than Arm64 in terms of raw processing power.

> **Note**
> Currently, only Linux OSs support the Arm64-based CPUs.

Hibernation

Hibernation is a feature for VMs that allows you to suspend the current state of your memory contents and store it to disk. When invoked in Azure, it will issue an instruction to the OS to suspect operations and store memory to disk for restoration later. The VM will then proceed to be deallocated, thereby reducing costs significantly.

Since the disk contains all the memory contents, when a restore is invoked, the VM is powered back on and the data from the disk is transferred back into memory to restore operations.

This can be a very helpful feature for saving costs across your estate. You are cautioned to obviously consider this with careful planning.

Licensing

When using a VM, there is often a cost associated with the running of the OS that is chosen, known as licensing costs. Some OSs come with a zero cost while most, especially for business scenarios, incur a cost. Depending on the model of consumption for Azure (e.g., **Pay as You Go (PAYG)**, **Enterprise Agreement (EA)**, **Managed Service Provider (MSP)**, **Cloud Service Provider (CSP)**), you will have slightly different costs applied.

If you are an enterprise client, you may take advantage of Software Assurance as a licensing feature, which enables you to take advantage of the Hybrid Benefit, which reduces the cost of the OS component for a VM to zero.

Another consideration to have when it comes to licensing is to consider whether the correct license model for your requirements has been consumed. For instance, there are special developer environments that come with reduced charges for workloads (such as the Azure Plan for DevTest subscriptions type).

Azure Spot VMs

Azure offers the ability to buy unused computing capacity for significantly reduced costs. This provides a great mechanism for test or development workloads that can handle interruptions at a very low cost. The limitation is that if Azure needs the capacity again, it will evict the Azure Spot VMs depending on your configuration. The sizes available are completely dependent on the current capacity used within Azure. They will be influenced by factors such as region and the time of day.

When configuring Spot instances, you define an **eviction policy** based on **capacity** and the **maximum price** you are willing to pay for the VM. You will also select the action to be taken upon eviction, either to **deallocate** or to **delete**.

When the VM is deployed, the following rules will apply:

- **Max price is set to >= the current price**: The VM will be deployed if capacity and quota are available.

- **Max price is set to <= the current price**: The VM will be evicted, and you will be given 30 seconds' notice.

- **The max price option is set to -1**: The VM will not be evicted due to pricing reasons. You will pay the amount of the standard VM charges, and it will not exceed those costs.

- **Changing the max price**: Before you can change the max price on a VM, the VM will need to be deallocated, and you will need to define your new max price to apply.

Some limitations apply Spot instances, such as VMs cannot be migrated, there are no offered SLAs, and there are no high availability guarantees.

The following subscription types provide support for Spot instances: **EA**, **Pay as You Go (003P)**, **Sponsored (0036P and 0136P)**, and **CSP**.

Reserved Instances

Azure Reserved VM Instances offer a significant opportunity to save when you commit to paying for compute resources upfront for a predefined period, which is either a 1-year or 3-year commitment. Savings can be up 72% compared to PAYG costs. There is a penalty for exiting the agreement early as the opportunity for savings is based on Azure being able to predictably sell the compute power available as part of the hypervisor platform; they account for amortizing costs of hardware and pass this predicted cost of aging hardware to you as a benefit for committing to the agreed period. This is great for workloads that do not change frequently and are expected to remain the same for long periods of time.

Capacity Reservation

Capacity reservation is a mechanism available to you in Azure reserve compute at standard PAYG rates. You can define the duration of the reservation, and you have full control over it. However, it is limited to a single VM size, a single location, and the specified quantity that is defined at deployment. Capacity reservation depends on the available quota to your subscription quota and availability to Azure.

This mechanism ensures you have available compute within Azure. It will be dedicated to you until you delete the capacity reservation. With this in mind, understand that you are eligible for the associated costs of the VMs allocated to the capacity reservation, whether or not they are used, so be sure to delete the reservation if this is no longer required.

> **Note**
> Read more about them here: `https://learn.microsoft.com/en-us/azure/virtual-machines/capacity-reservation-overview`.

Proximity Placement Groups

Proximity placement groups are for placing Azure resources physically close to each other within the same data center. While there are multiple mechanisms for reducing latency in Azure, this is the best option when you require low latency and high performance as part of your requirements. Azure regions allow workloads to be geographically close to each other, and availability zones are even closer by spanning data centers. Proximity placement groups take the win by being positioned within the same data center.

There are many considerations when exploring proximity placement groups; read this link for more details: `https://learn.microsoft.com/en-us/azure/virtual-machines/co-location`.

Deploying a VM in Azure

In the previous chapter, you learned about the deployment of a VM through ARM templates. In this section, you will briefly explore the manual deployment of a VM using the Azure portal.

Exercise 12.1

This exercise will guide you through manually deploying a VM using the Azure portal:

1. Sign in to the Azure portal: `https://portal.azure.com`.
2. Open the resource group you will be using for this exercise, click `Overview` on the left menu, then click `Create` from the top menu options.
3. Click `Compute` on the left menu under `Categories`, enter `virtual machine` in the top search bar, then click the `Virtual machine` card from the results:

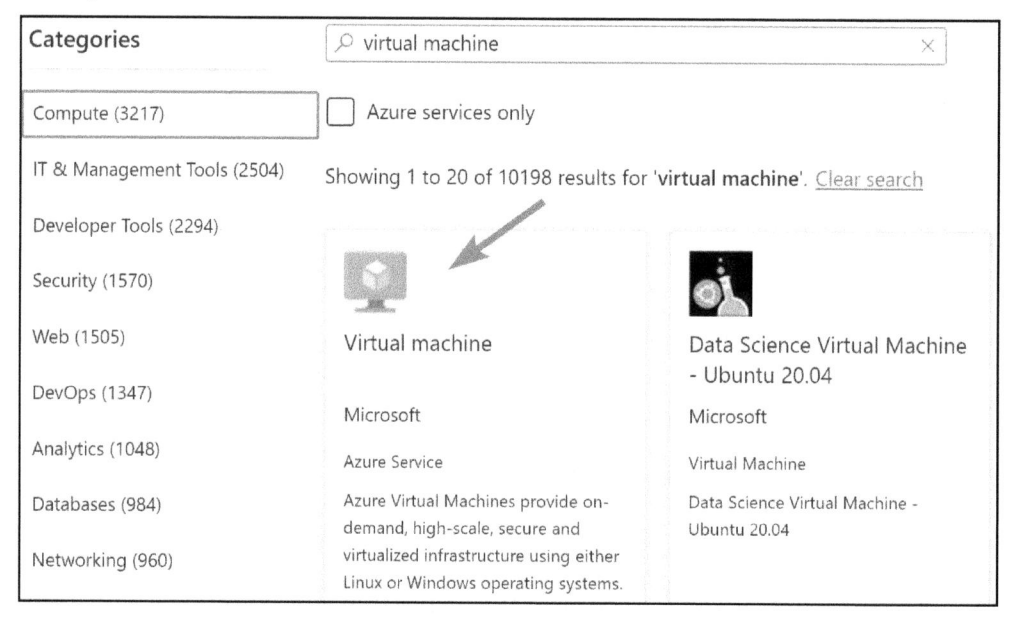

Figure 12.10: Creating a VM resource

4. Click `Create` on the screen that follows.
5. On the `Basics` tab, select options for `Subscription` and `Resource group`.

Project details

Select the subscription to manage deployed resources and costs. Use resource groups like folders to organize and manage all your resources.

Subscription *: Visual Studio Enterprise Subscription

Resource group *: AZ104-VirtualMachines
Create new

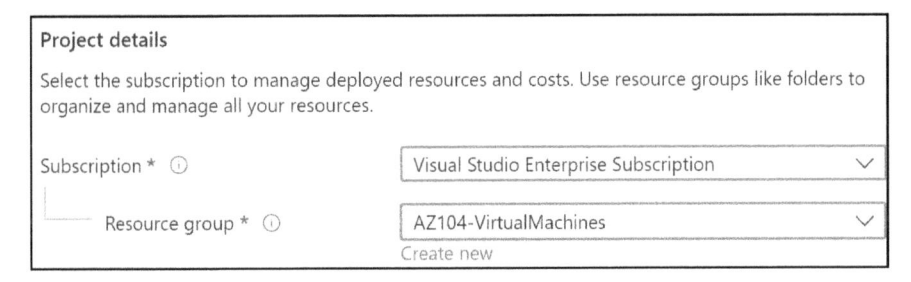

Figure 12.11: Creating a VM – Project details

6. Enter the following for your `Instance details` settings:

   - `Virtual machine name`: Enter any name that is limited to 15 characters
   - `Region`: Select any region from the drop-down menu
   - `Availability options`: `No infrastructure redundancy required`
   - `Security type`: `Trusted launch virtual machines`
   - `Image`: `Windows Server 2019 Datacenter - x64 Gen2`
   - `VM architecture`: `x64`
   - `Run with Azure Spot discount`: Choose as appropriate for you
   - `Size`: `Standard_D2ds_v5`
   - `Enable Hibernation (preview)`: Leave unchecked

Instance details

Virtual machine name *	demovm01
Region *	(Europe) North Europe
Availability options	No infrastructure redundancy required
Security type	Trusted launch virtual machines
	Configure security features
Image *	Windows Server 2019 Datacenter - x64 Gen2
	See all images | Configure VM generation
VM architecture	○ Arm64
	⦿ x64
	ⓘ Arm64 is not supported with the selected image.
Run with Azure Spot discount	☐
Size *	Standard_D2ds_v5 - 2 vcpus, 8 GiB memory (ZAR 1,635.40/month)
	See all sizes
Enable Hibernation (preview)	☐
	ⓘ To enable Hibernation, you must register your subscription. Learn more

Figure 12.12: Creating a VM – Instance details

7. In the `Administrator account` section, fill in the `Username` and `Password` fields.

Figure 12.13: Creating a VM – Administrator account

8. Click `Allow selected ports` for the `Public inbound ports` option, and choose `RDP (3389)` for the `Select inbound ports` dropdown.

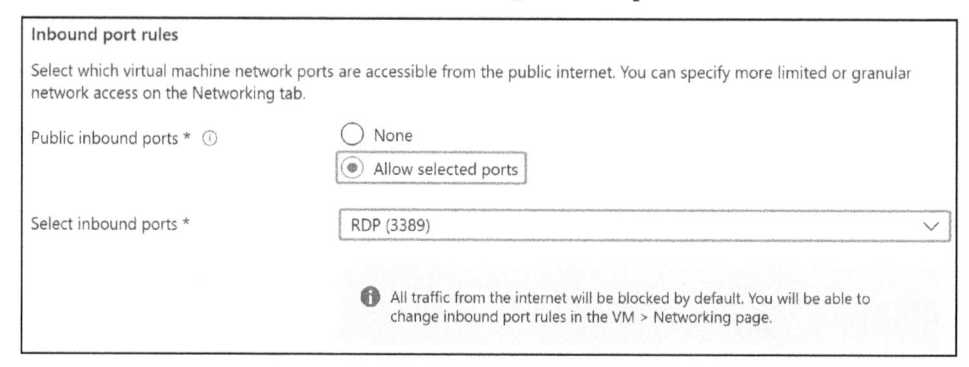

Figure 12.14: Creating a VM – Inbound port rules

9. Finally, for the `Licensing` section, you can leave the checkbox unticked for the `Would you like to use an existing Windows Server license?` option. Click on `Next : Disks >`.

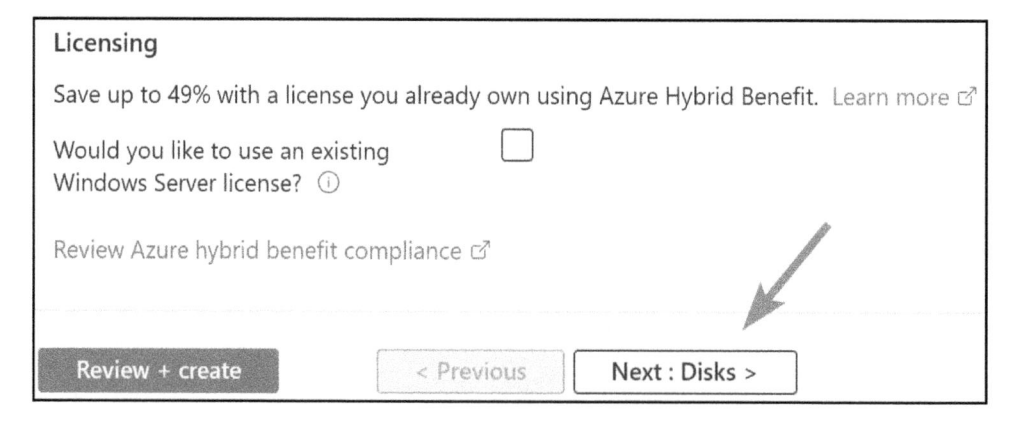

Figure 12.15: Creating a VM – Licensing

10. You are unlikely to have the option to enable `Encryption at host` unless you have registered this for your subscription. Leave this unchecked.

Figure 12.16: Creating a VM – VM disk encryption

11. Configure your `OS disk` options as per the following settings:

    - `OS disk size:` Image default (127 GiB)
    - `OS disk type:` Premium SSD (locally-redundant storage)
    - `Delete with VM:` Checked
    - `Key management:` Platform-managed key
    - `Enable Ultra Disk compatibility:` Unchecked

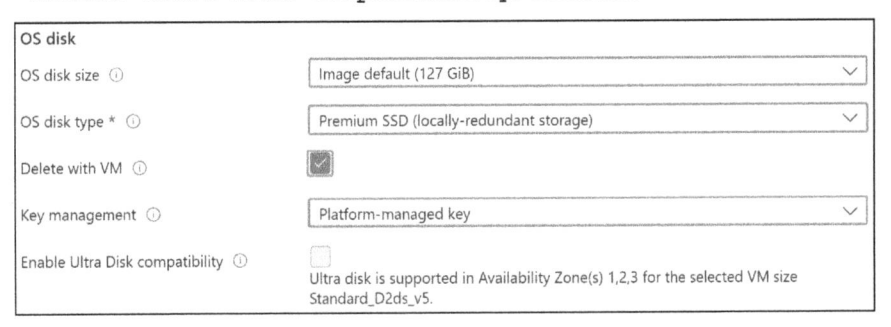

Figure 12.17: Creating a VM – OS disk

12. You will not add any data disks for this VM. Scroll to the bottom of the page to the `Advanced` expanded section. Note the options available for VMs, such as `Use managed disks` and `Ephemeral OS disk`. Click `Next : Networking >`.

Figure 12.18: Creating a VM – Advanced options

13. You have the option to create a new VNet and subnet (the default option) or to join an existing network and subnet. A public IP is not required, but leave the default, where it will create one for this demonstration. Select `Basic` for `NIC network security group`. Ensure that the inbound ports selected are set to `RDP (3389)` as you configured on the `Basics` tab. Enable both checkboxes for `Delete public IP and NIC when VM is deleted` and `Enable accelerated networking`. Click `Next : Management >`.

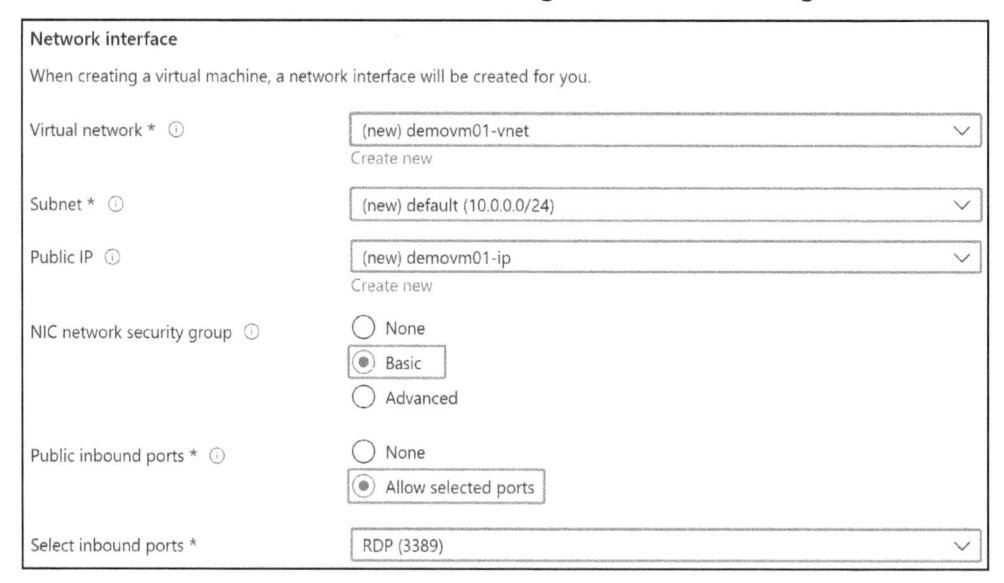

Figure 12.19: Creating a VM – Network interface

14. Note the various options available to you on this tab and click `Next : Monitoring >`.
15. On the `Monitoring` tab, configure as per the following:

    - `Enable recommended alert rules`: Leave unchecked
    - `Boot diagnostics`: `Enable with managed storage account (recommended)`
    - `Enable OS guest diagnostics`: Leave unchecked
    - `Enable application health monitoring`: Leave unchecked

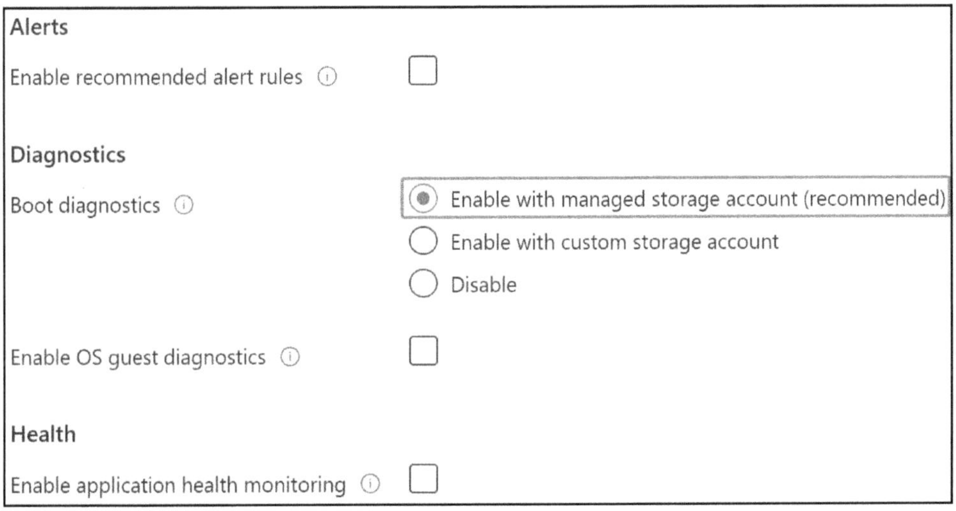

Figure 12.20: Creating a VM – Monitoring

16. Click `Next : Advanced >`.
17. Note that on the `Advanced` tab that you can configure `Extensions`, `VM applications`, and `Custom data` (used for passing scripts or configuration files into a provisioning VM), as well as select a dedicated host group and proximity placement group. There are several other settings, such as performance (NVMe) and capacity reservations, that you can configure on this tab. Click on `Review + create`.
18. After validation has been completed and passed, click `Create`.

    - You have now completed the deployment of a VM on Azure. You will have noticed there are several different configurations for a VM that you can deploy. Spend some time reviewing them to become more comfortable.

PowerShell Scripts

Please ensure that the Az module is installed as per the *Technical Requirements* section at the beginning of the chapter. In the next demonstration, you are going to create two Windows Server VMs from PowerShell and place them in an availability set. To do so, you will perform the following steps:

```
# Parameters
$ResourceGroup = "AZ104-VirtualMachines"
$Location = "WestEurope"
$SubscriptionId = "xxxxxxx"
$AvailabilitySetName = "VMAvailabilitySet"
$VirtualNetworkName = "VMVnet"
$SubnetName = "VMSubnet"
```
→ Input Parameters

```
# First connect your Azure account using your credentials
Connect-AzAccount

# If necessary, select the right subscription as follows
Select-AzSubscription -SubscriptionId $SubscriptionId
```
→ Connect to Azure and Select a Subscription

```
# Create a resource group for the Availability Set as follows
New-AzResourceGroup -Name "$ResourceGroup" -Location "$Location"
```

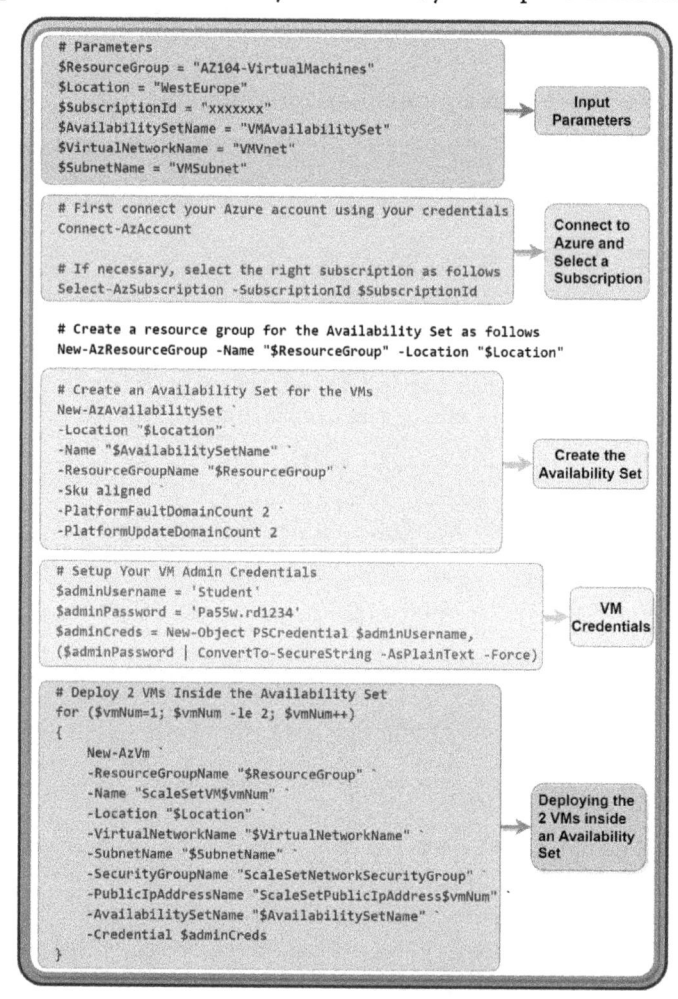

```
# Create an Availability Set for the VMs
New-AzAvailabilitySet `
-Location "$Location" `
-Name "$AvailabilitySetName" `
-ResourceGroupName "$ResourceGroup" `
-Sku aligned `
-PlatformFaultDomainCount 2 `
-PlatformUpdateDomainCount 2
```
→ Create the Availability Set

```
# Setup Your VM Admin Credentials
$adminUsername = 'Student'
$adminPassword = 'Pa55w.rd1234'
$adminCreds = New-Object PSCredential $adminUsername,
($adminPassword | ConvertTo-SecureString -AsPlainText -Force)
```
→ VM Credentials

```
# Deploy 2 VMs Inside the Availability Set
for ($vmNum=1; $vmNum -le 2; $vmNum++)
{
    New-AzVm `
    -ResourceGroupName "$ResourceGroup" `
    -Name "ScaleSetVM$vmNum" `
    -Location "$Location" `
    -VirtualNetworkName "$VirtualNetworkName" `
    -SubnetName "$SubnetName" `
    -SecurityGroupName "ScaleSetNetworkSecurityGroup" `
    -PublicIpAddressName "ScaleSetPublicIpAddress$vmNum" `
    -AvailabilitySetName "$AvailabilitySetName" `
    -Credential $adminCreds
}
```
→ Deploying the 2 VMs inside an Availability Set

Figure 12.21: Deploying Two VMs – PowerShell script

> **Note**
> Change the parameters of the script to suit your requirements.

In these last two demonstrations, you have created a VM using the Azure portal and deployed two VMs inside an availability set using PowerShell. In the next section, you will cover deploying scale sets.

Deploying and Configuring Scale Sets

Scale sets are beneficial for deploying horizontally scalable workloads, meaning that you can increase and decrease the number of assigned VM instances to the scale set to meet your resource requirements. This works particularly well for websites, especially when you consider special events such as holiday periods when usage is expected to peak sporadically. Having scale sets can enable you to provision resources to meet the increasing demand at the time of the sale and, conversely, reduce the instances when the sale is over, all without risking downtime.

In the following exercise, you will experience creating a VM scale set in Azure.

Exercise 12.2

To create a VM scale set from the Azure portal, take the following steps:

1. Navigate to the Azure portal by opening `https://portal.azure.com/home`.
2. Click on `Create a resource` and type `Scale Set` in the search bar. Select `Virtual machine scale set` from the set of Azure services returned.
3. On the next screen, click on `Create`.
4. On the `Basics` tab, select your `Subscription` and `Resource group` options.

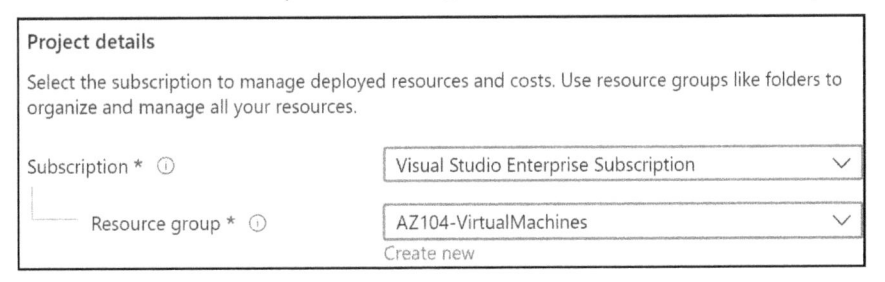

Figure 12.22: Creating a Scale Set – Project details

5. Enter the following for `Scale set details`:

   - `Virtual machine scale set name`: Enter a name up to 15 characters long
   - `Region`: East US
   - `Availability zone`: Zones 1

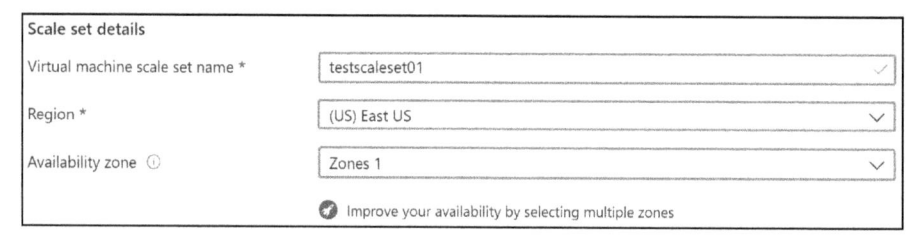

   Figure 12.23: Creating a Scale Set – Scale set details

6. For `Orchestration`, configure as follows:

   - `Orchestration mode`: Flexible
   - `Security type`: Standard

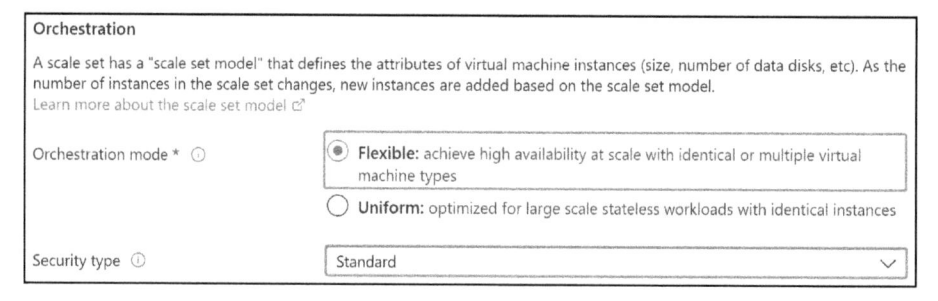

   Figure 12.24: Creating a Scale Set – Orchestration

7. Select the following for `Instance details`:

   - `Image`: Windows Server 2019 Datacenter - x64 Gen2
   - `VM architecture`: x64
   - `Run with Azure Spot discount`: Unchecked
   - `Size`: Standard_D2s_v5
   - `Enable Hibernation (preview)`: Unchecked

Instance details	
Image * ⓘ	🪟 Windows Server 2019 Datacenter - x64 Gen2 ⌄
	See all images | Configure VM generation
	ⓘ This image is compatible with additional security features. Click here to swap to the Trusted launch security type.
VM architecture ⓘ	○ Arm64
	⦿ x64
	ⓘ Arm64 is not supported with the selected image.
Run with Azure Spot discount ⓘ	☐
Size * ⓘ	Standard_D2s_v5 - 2 vcpus, 8 GiB memory (ZAR 1,246.02/month) ⌄
	See all sizes
Enable Hibernation (preview) ⓘ	☐

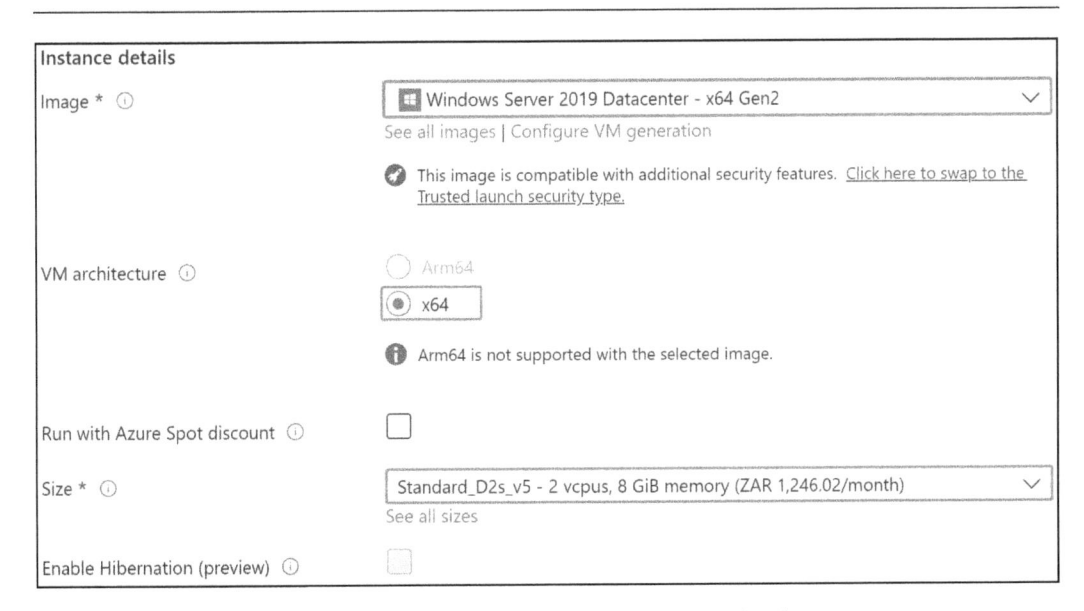

Figure 12.25: Creating a Scale Set – Instance details

8. For the `Administrator account` section, fill in the `Username` and `Password` fields.

9. Finally, for the `Licensing` section, you can leave the checkbox unticked for the `Would you like to use an existing Windows Server license?` option. Click on `Next : Spot >`.

10. Notice the various options available to you; these are only enabled when you select `Azure Spot discount` from the `Basics` tab. Click `Next : Disks >`.

11. Leave all settings as the default configuration.

12. Click the `Scaling` tab at the top of the configuration screen, skipping `Networking`.

13. On the `Scaling` tab, you can configure the `Autoscale` settings for your scale set. You can configure settings such as `Initial instance count` and `Scaling policy`. Configure the following settings:

    - `Initial instance count`: 2
    - `Scaling policy`: Custom
    - Leave all other settings as the default values.

14. Click `Review + create` at the bottom of the screen. This will skip several settings, which you are encouraged to review.

15. Click `Create`.

In this exercise, you covered how to deploy a VM scale set in an availability zone, which is for creating resilient workloads that can suffer data center failure. In the next section, you will explore the summary of all that you have learned in this chapter.

Summary

In this chapter, you covered Azure VMs, how to configure them, and the various management functions, including components such as networking, high-availability configurations, and changing the VM host. As part of this topic, you explored the various types of Azure disks that exist, how they can be added to a VM, and how you can encrypt them.

You have now attained the skills required for managing VMs within the Azure environment and should be able to provision, scale, and manage them confidently. You have also learned different deployment methods to assist you with consistent delivery on the platform while ensuring fewer mistakes and faster deployment times than doing this manually, using PowerShell or the cloud CLI. Alongside these skills, you also learned about the various storage options, how to best scope the storage required, and how to implement storage as needed. Finally, you also learned about VM extensions and how to add them to a VM.

In the next chapter, you will explore the various management tasks you should be familiar with regarding VMs. You will explore common tasks such as resizing VMs, configuring disks and networking, moving VMs between resource groups, VM redeployment, and disk encryption. You will also explore a VM ARM deployment template.

Exam Readiness Drill - Chapters 10-12

Apart from mastering key concepts, strong test-taking skills under time pressure are essential for acing your certification exam. That's why developing these abilities early in your learning journey is critical.

Exam readiness drills, using the free online practice resources provided with this book, help you progressively improve your time management and test-taking skills while reinforcing the key concepts you've learned.

HOW TO GET STARTED

- Open the link or scan the QR code at the bottom of this page
- If you have unlocked the practice resources, already log in to your registered account. If you haven't, follow the instructions in *Chapter 23* and come back to this page.
- Once you log in, click the START button to start a quiz
- We recommend attempting a quiz multiple times till you're able to answer most of the questions correctly and well within the time limit.
- You can use the following practice template to help you plan your attempts :

Attempt	Target	Time Limit
Working On Accuracy		
Attempt 1	40% or more	Till the timer runs out
Attempt 2	60% or more	Till the timer runs out
Attempt 3	75% or more	Till the timer runs out
Working On Timing		
Attempt 4	75% or more	1 minute before time limit
Attempt 5	75% or more	2 minutes before time limit
Attempt 6	75% or more	3 minutes before time limit

The above drill is just an example. Design your drills based on your own goals and make the most out of the online quizzes accompanying this book.

> First time accessing the online resources? 🔒
> You'll need to unlock them through a one-time process. **Head to** *Chapter 23* **for instructions**.

Open Quiz

`https://packt.link/az104e3ch10-12`

OR scan this QR code →

13
Managing Virtual Machines

In the previous chapter, you learned about VM concepts, understanding what VMs are and the related services they comprise (such as disks and network interface cards), as well as the various components they interact with, such as **Network Security Groups** (**NSGs**) and **Virtual Networks** (**VNets**).

VMs are a foundational resource for servicing your applications and services due to their versatile nature of enabling application consumption and interaction. In this chapter, you will explore **Azure VM management tasks**. Management will relate to almost any activity you perform on the VM in Azure, such as ensuring sufficient resources are always available for required tasks. Management tasks are a core part of administering VMs, and to be successful in the exam and your role, you will need to be familiar with the concepts and have practiced these activities.

Some topics you will explore will be resizing VMs, configuring disks and networking, moving VMs between resource groups, VM redeployment, and disk encryption. You will also explore a VM ARM deployment template.

In this chapter, you are going to explore the following main topics:

- Managing VM Sizes
- Adding Data Disks to VMs
- Troubleshooting VM Networking
- Moving VMs between Resource Groups
- Redeploying VMs
- Disk Encryption in Azure
- Automating Configuration Management
- Deploying VM Extensions
- Configuring and Deploying a VM ARM Template

Technical Requirements

This chapter has the following requirements for the exercises:

- Access to an Azure subscription with owner or contributor privileges. If you do not have access to one, students can enroll for a free account here: https://azure.microsoft.com/en-us/free/.

- **PowerShell 5.1** or later installed on a Windows PC or PowerShell Core 6.x on other operating systems to practice the labs.

- For Windows users, you will need to install **.NET Framework 4.7.2** or later using the following link: https://learn.microsoft.com/en-us/dotnet/framework/install.

- Note that, occasionally, examples can only be followed from a PC or https://shell.azure.com (PowerShell 7.0.6 LTS or later is recommended).

- Where PowerShell is not installed or available, https://shell.azure.com can be used as a browser-based shell.

- Installation of the Az PowerShell module, which can be performed by running the following in an administrative PowerShell session:

    ```
    Set-ExecutionPolicy -ExecutionPolicy RemoteSigned -Scope
    CurrentUser
    Install-Module -Name Az -Scope CurrentUser -Repository PSGallery
    -Force
    ```

Managing VM Sizes

When you want to add or remove resources to your VM, you will look at the VM size option in Azure. After creating your VM, you can manage and change the sizes of Windows and Linux VMs from the Azure portal, PowerShell, and the Azure CLI. This is known as vertical scaling (scaling up and down). Vertical scaling refers to increasing or decreasing resources (CPU and memory) by changing VM SKU sizes in response to different workloads.

In this section, you will learn how to resize your VM using the Azure portal and CLI.

Exercise 13.1: Resizing Your VM Using the Azure Portal

In the following demonstration, you will explore how to change the VM size of your VM:

1. Sign in to the Azure portal: https://portal.azure.com/home.
2. Navigate to a VM you created in the previous exercise. On the left menu, under the Availability + scale context, click the Size option:

Availability + scale
🖳 Size
🗔 Availability + scaling

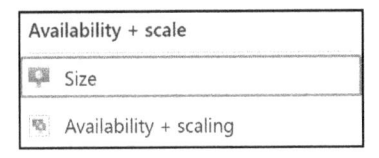

Figure 13.1: VM size setting

3. You will be presented with several `VM Size` options to choose from. You will also note that there is a filter bar above the VMs that allows you to view them against the configuration you choose. Click `vCPUs : All`, select 2, and click OK. You will see the SKU options for changing VM size:

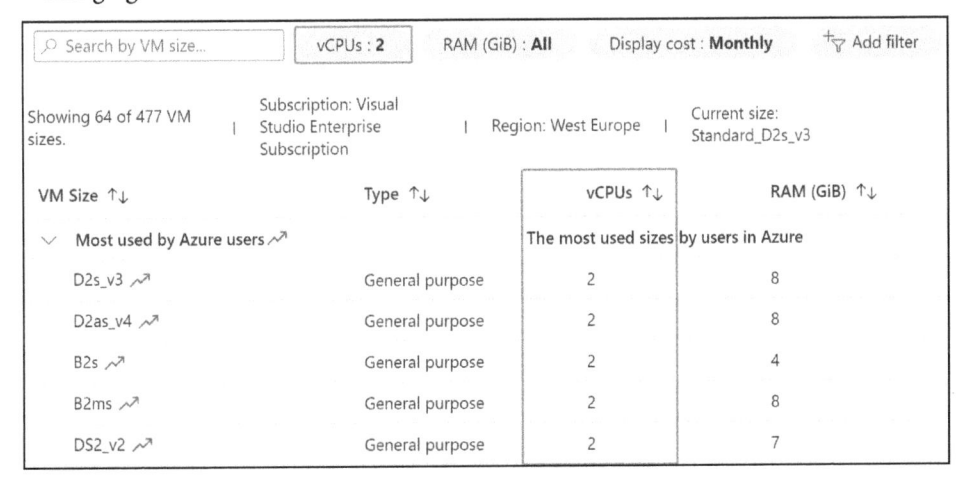

VM Size ↑↓	Type ↑↓	vCPUs ↑↓	RAM (GiB) ↑↓
∨ Most used by Azure users ↗		The most used sizes by users in Azure	
D2s_v3 ↗	General purpose	2	8
D2as_v4 ↗	General purpose	2	8
B2s ↗	General purpose	2	4
B2ms ↗	General purpose	2	8
DS2_v2 ↗	General purpose	2	7

Search by VM size... | vCPUs : 2 | RAM (GiB) : **All** | Display cost : **Monthly** | Add filter

Showing 64 of 477 VM sizes. | Subscription: Visual Studio Enterprise Subscription | Region: West Europe | Current size: Standard_D2s_v3

Figure 13.2: VM size filter

4. Click the `Cost/month` column button. You will notice this changes the sorting for the list. The default sorting is smallest to largest. Clicking this button again will reverse the order:

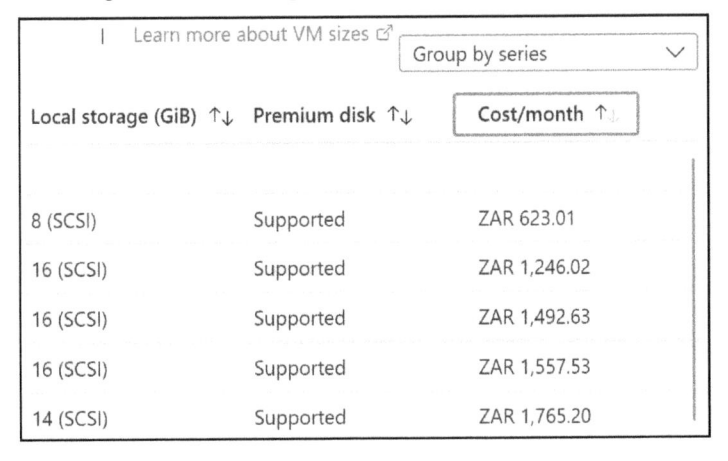

Local storage (GiB) ↑↓	Premium disk ↑↓	Cost/month ↑
8 (SCSI)	Supported	ZAR 623.01
16 (SCSI)	Supported	ZAR 1,246.02
16 (SCSI)	Supported	ZAR 1,492.63
16 (SCSI)	Supported	ZAR 1,557.53
14 (SCSI)	Supported	ZAR 1,765.20

Learn more about VM sizes | Group by series

Figure 13.3: VM size selection sorting

5. Click any SKU and click `Resize`.

In this exercise, you resized your VM, which is a common exercise in scaling your compute to meet your changing resource requirements. In the next section, you will explore performing the same activity using the Azure CLI.

> **Note**
>
> VM sizes that contain an "s" at the end of the size component typically support Premium SSD storage, for example, **D2s_v3**.

Now that you have seen how to resize a VM using the Azure portal, you will explore how to perform this action through the CLI.

Exercise 13.2: Resizing a VM Using the CLI

You can also resize your VM using the **Command-Line Interface (CLI)**. The CLI is a command-line tool that enables you to manage Azure resources and services through simple instructions. You can run CLI scripts from Azure Cloud Shell or your local filesystem. You can use Azure Cloud Shell for PowerShell scripts and commands as well. In this exercise, you are going to resize the VM from Azure Cloud Shell using the CLI by completing the following steps:

1. Navigate to the Azure portal by opening `https://portal.azure.com/home`.
2. Open Azure Cloud Shell by clicking the following menu item in the top-right menu in the Azure portal:

Figure 13.4: Opening Azure Cloud Shell

3. Make sure that the `Bash` shell is selected:

Figure 13.5: Bash Cloud Shell

4. Enter the following line of code to list the different available machine sizes for your region:

```
az vm list-vm-resize-options --resource-group AZ104-
VirtualMachines --name ScaleSetVM1 --output table
```

5. To resize your VM to a different size, enter the following line of code. If the size is not available, you can replace the required VM size with one that is available for your subscription or region:

```
az vm resize --resource-group AZ104-VirtualMachines --name
ScaleSetVM1 --size Standard_DS3_v2
```

You have now resized your VM using the Azure portal and the CLI. In the next section, you are going to work on adding data disks to a VM.

Adding Data Disks to VMs

At some point, you will require additional storage for your VMs. One option to introduce storage is to attach a data disk to your VM, which will serve as locally attached storage. In the exercise that follows, you will gain hands-on experience adding disks to your VMs.

Exercise 13.3: Adding Data Disks

In the following exercise, you will explore adding data disks to a VM in Azure:

1. Sign in to the Azure portal: `https://portal.azure.com/home`.
2. Create a new managed disk in Azure, set the resource group and subscription to the one you used in the previous exercise, and configure the `Disk details` options as follows:

   - `Disk name:` `scalesetvm1_datadisk2`
   - `Region:` Same as the VM
   - `Availability zone:` `No infrastructure redundancy required`
   - `Source type:` `None`
   - `Size:` `32 GiB`

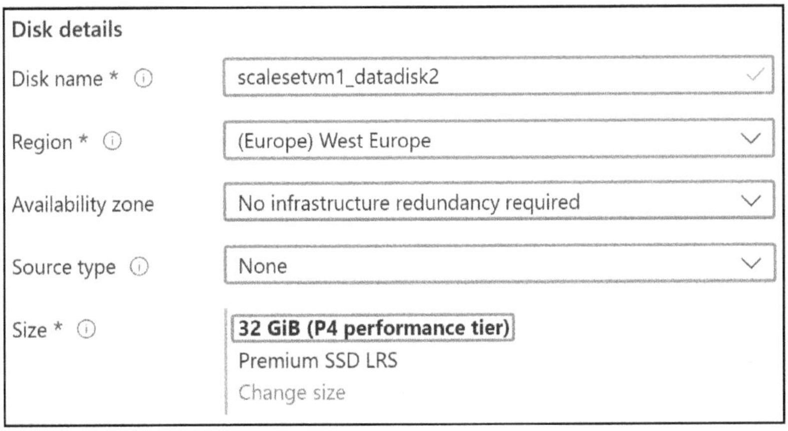

Figure 13.6: Managed disk – Disk details

3. Click `Next : Encryption >`. Configure the following setting:

   - `Key Management:` `Platform-managed key`

4. Click `Next : Networking >`.
5. Leave the default settings and click `Next : Advanced >`.
6. Notice all the settings available and the options for sharing the disk or configuring bursting. Click `Review + create`.
7. Click `Create`.
8. Once deployment has been successfully completed, navigate to the VM you created in the previous exercise. On the left menu, under `Settings`, click `Disks`.
9. This page will display all disks attached to the VM. Notice the OS disk deployed and attached to the VM. In the `Data disks` section, you will see the options to create a new disk or attach existing storage. Click `Create and attach a new disk`, then configure it as follows:

   - `LUN:` 0
   - `Disk name:` `scalesetvm1_datadisk1`
   - `Storage type:` `Standard HDD`
   - `Size (GiB):` 32
   - `Encryption:` `Platform-managed key`
   - `Host caching:` `Read-only`

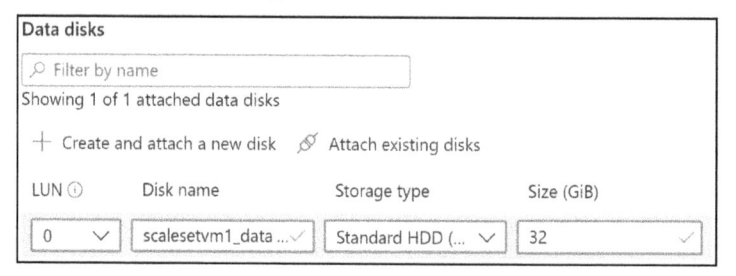

Figure 13.7: VM – Creating and attaching a data disk

10. Next, click `Attach existing disks`, select the disk you made in *step 2*, and assign it to LUN 1 as follows:

Figure 13.8: VM – Attaching an existing data disk

11. At the bottom of the blade, click the `Apply` button.

You have now learned how to create and attach a data disk to a VM, as well as how to attach an existing data disk. In the next section, you will explore the network options available for Azure.

Troubleshooting VM Networking

Networking services can be tricky, especially when communicating between multiple VMs. Many factors can influence traffic reaching its intended destination, such as route tables with custom routes, NSGs, firewalls, and open ports within the operating system. The exercise in this section assists you in uncovering how to test connectivity between two VMs within a network and understanding the impact of resources such as an NSG on the routing of traffic between your VMs.

Exercise 13.4: Troubleshooting VM Networking

In this exercise, you will assess the connectivity of two VMs within a network, join two VMs onto the same subnet within a VNet, and prove they can communicate. You will then configure an NSG on both the NIC and subnet layers and demonstrate the net effect of an NSG across both layers. Finally, you will connect the VMs to another subnet and demonstrate communication between the VMs. Follow these steps:

1. Sign in to the Azure portal: `https://portal.azure.com`.

2. Navigate to one of the VMs you created in the previous exercise. On the left menu, under `Networking`, click `Network settings`.

3. Note the network interface name, virtual network, and subnet assigned to the NIC. Also note the private IP address:

```
Network interface / IP configuration
ScaleSetVM1 (primary) / ScaleSetVM1 (primary)

∧ Essentials

Network interface          : ScaleSetVM1
Virtual network / subnet   : VMVnet / VMSubnet
Public IP address          : ScaleSetPublicIpAddress1
Private IP address         : 192.168.1.4
```

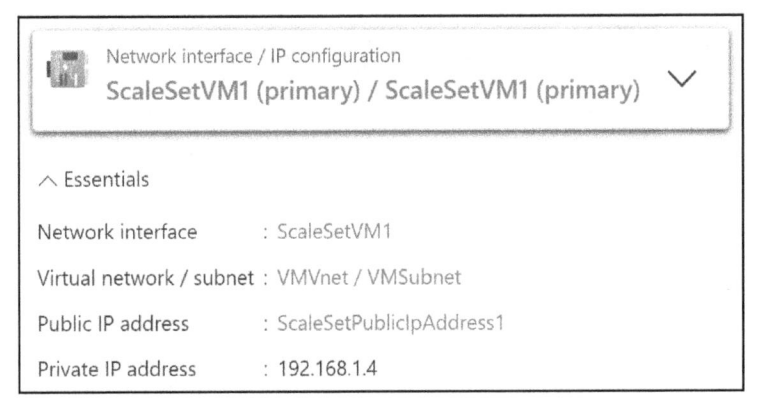

Figure 13.9: Network interface configuration settings

4. From the left menu, click `Connect`. Click `Download RDP file` from the options on the blade. Open the file that downloads.

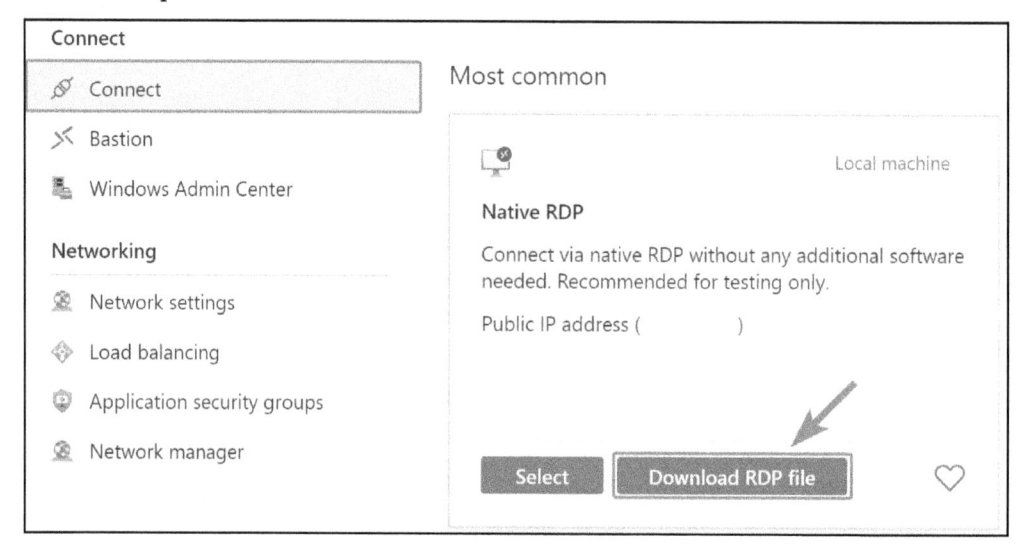

Figure 13.10: Connecting to your VM

5. On the screen that shows up, your username should be `Student`; enter the password and click OK.

Figure 13.11: Remoting to a VM

6. You have just created a remote desktop connection to your VM.

7. Navigate to Azure and find the private IP address of the second VM in your scale set.
8. Going back to the VM you just remoted into, click the Start button and type PowerShell. Click the PowerShell option that comes up on the search pane.
9. In PowerShell, enter the following command, adjusting the private IP address to match the IP address you noted in *step 7*:

    ```
    test-netconnection 192.168.1.5 -Port 3389
    ```

10. You should note a successful connection.

> **Note**
>
> Management ports, port 22 – SSH (Linux) and port 3389 – RDP (Windows), should always be restricted and preferably not exposed to the internet. If exposed to the internet, access should be restricted to specific known IP addresses.

Moving VMs between Resource Groups

You may deploy your VM resources to a resource group only to move them at a later date. You might have done this because of changing internal organizational policies and your resource group name not adhering to the convention. The solution may be to create a new resource group with the correct convention for you to move your VM into. In this section, you will explore the tasks involved in moving your VMs across resource groups.

Exercise 13.5: Moving VMs from One Resource Group to Another

In this exercise, you will move (migrate) a VM from one resource group to another. In order to initiate the move, you will first need to validate the readiness for the move:

1. Open the Azure portal and create a new resource group named AZ104-VirtualMachines-Migration.
2. Navigate to the resource group where your scale set VM is saved.
3. Select the Overview option on the left menu and select all resources in the AZ104-VirtualMachines resource group.

Managing Virtual Machines

Click Move:

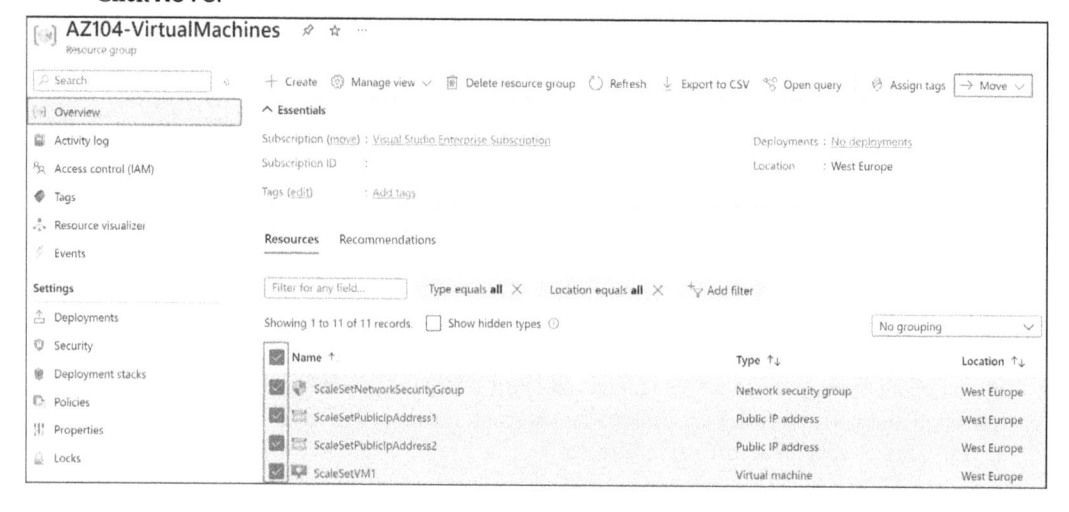

Figure 13.12: Selecting Azure VM resources

4. Select the `Move to another resource group` option:

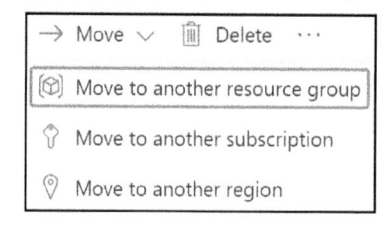

Figure 13.13: Move to another resource group

5. Select the target resource group you created in *Step 1* and click `Next`:

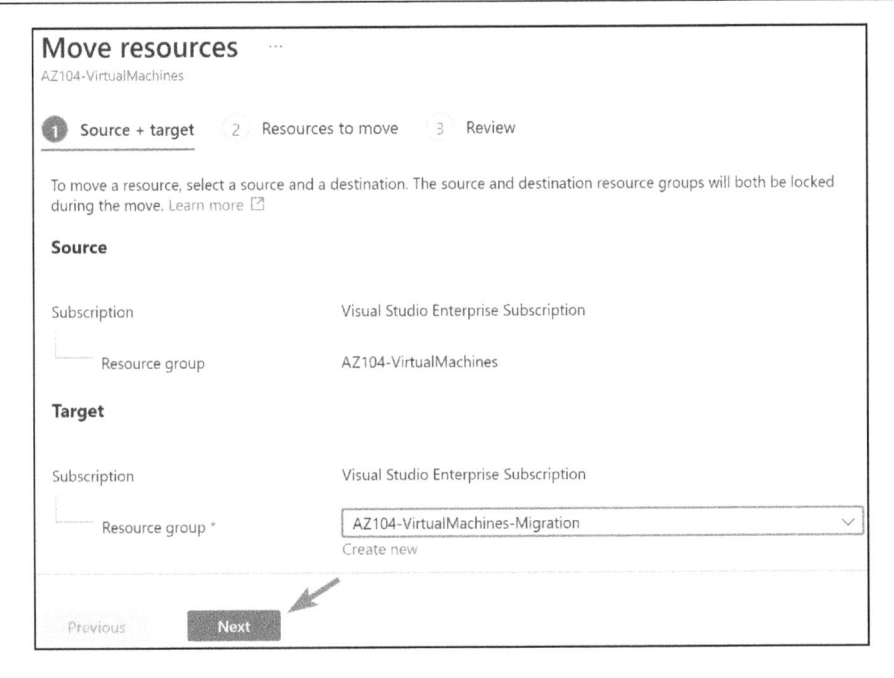

Figure 13.14: Moving Azure Resources – Source + target

6. Wait for the validation to complete that confirms the resources can be migrated:

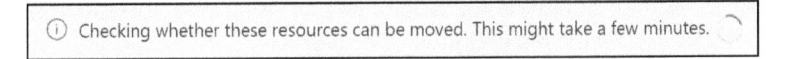

Figure 13.15: Resource Migration Validation Message

7. Once validation has been completed successfully, click Next:

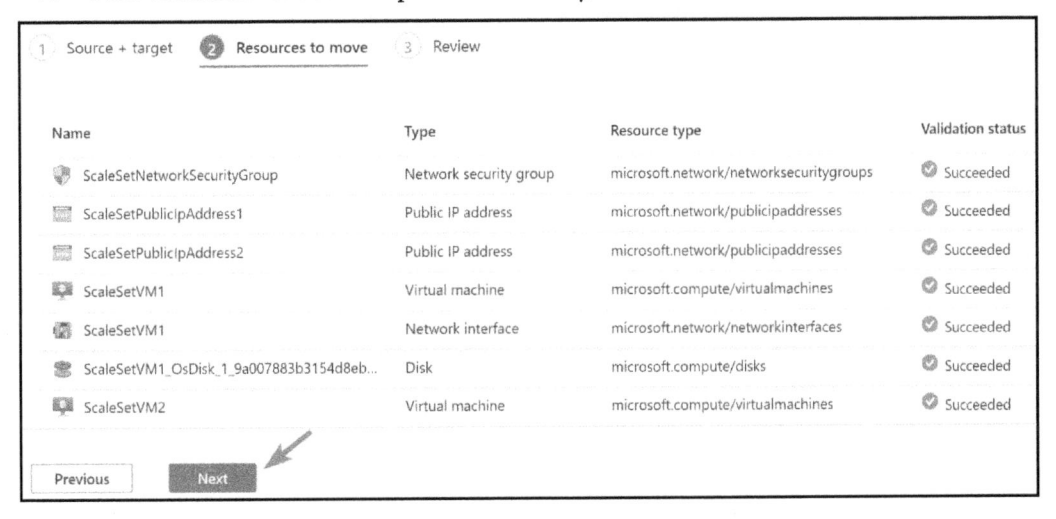

Figure 13.16: Moving Azure Resources – Resources to move

8. Click the checkbox and click Move.

9. The move will take several minutes to complete. Once complete, you will receive a notification informing you of the success status:

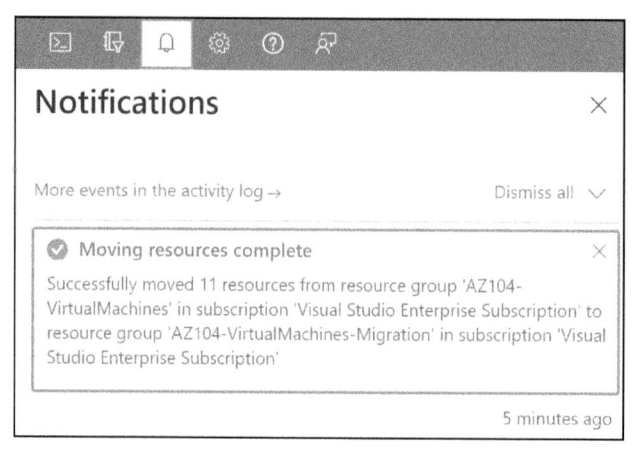

Figure 13.17: Move success notification

> **Note**
>
> You may be tempted to think that migrating a resource from one resource group to another would change its location, but this is not the case. You will remember that resources can reside in a different location from the resource group. Furthermore, a resource location cannot, at the time of writing, be changed and will require redeployment for the desired location.

In this exercise, you completed the migration of resources across resource groups. This process is almost identical in behavior to the activities you need to carry out to move resources across subscriptions. In the next section, you will learn about redeploying VMs.

Redeploying VMs

There might be occasions when you experience some difficulties in working with VMs and identify that certain services are not functioning as expected, such as **remote desktop connections** using the **Remote Desktop Protocol** (**RDP**) or other types of services. In these circumstances, you may find that redeploying a VM will help. The redeployment will result in your VM moving to a new node within the Azure infrastructure. This will also result in the VM shutting down during the move and restarting on the new node. All your configurations and associated resources will still be retained.

> **Note**
>
> When you redeploy a VM, take note that the dynamic IP address assigned to your VM will be updated, and your temporary disk data will be lost.

In the following exercises, you will explore redeploying your VMs through the Azure portal and through PowerShell.

Exercise 13.6: Redeploying VMs

In this exercise, you will redeploy your VM using the Azure portal by completing the following steps:

1. Navigate to the VM that you wish to redeploy.
2. On the left menu pane, near the bottom, click on the `Redeploy + reapply` option, under the `Help` context:

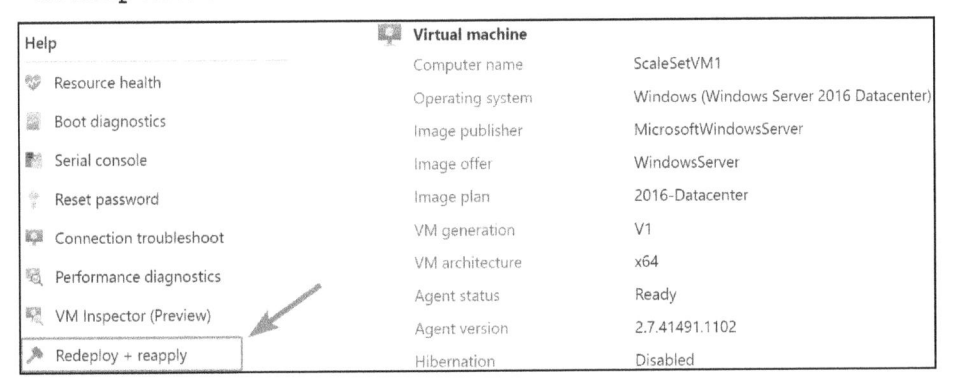

Figure 13.18: Redeploy + reapply

3. Click the `Redeploy` button:

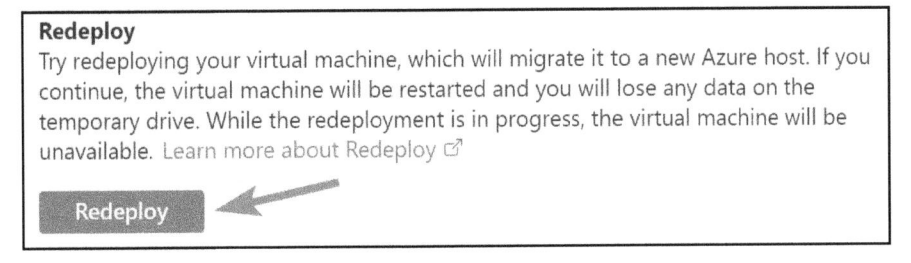

Figure 13.19: Redeploy

4. You will see a notification that the process has started:

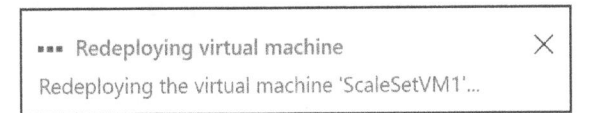

Figure 13.20: Redeploy notification

5. After a few minutes, you will receive a success message signifying successful reallocation for the server:

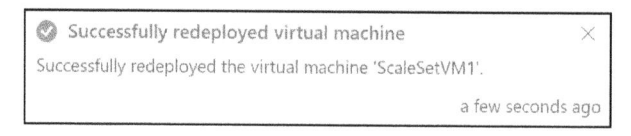

Figure 13.21: Redeployment success notification

In this exercise, you redeployed a VM using the Azure portal, which is useful when you experience difficulties with your VM features not functioning as you expect. In the next exercise, you will explore redeploying a VM using PowerShell.

Exercise 13.7: Redeploying a VM from PowerShell

The Azure PowerShell module is a tool designed for working with Azure resources such as deploying Azure VMs. In this exercise, you are going to redeploy a VM, similar to the previous exercise but through PowerShell this time.

To redeploy a VM from PowerShell, you will perform the following steps:

1. Navigate to the Azure portal by opening `https://portal.azure.com`.
2. Open Azure Cloud Shell again by clicking the following menu item in the top-right menu in the Azure portal:

Figure 13.22: Top navigation bar

3. Make sure that, this time, `PowerShell` is selected.

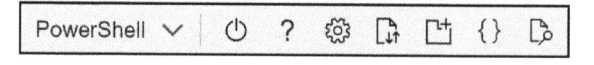

Figure 13.23: PowerShell

4. Add the following line of code to redeploy the VM:

```
Set-AzVM -Redeploy -ResourceGroupName "Az104-VirtualMachines-Migration" -Name "ScaleSetVM1"
```

You have now redeployed a VM using PowerShell. You have completed the VM redeployment topic. Next, you will explore what Azure disk encryption is and how to configure it.

Disk Encryption in Azure

Encrypting Azure disks ensures that unattended and unauthorized access to the disks is prevented by encrypting the data. This can be done at both the infrastructure level, through **Server-Side Encryption (SSE)**, and at the **Operating System (OS)** level, through **Azure Disk Encryption (ADE)**.

SSE is a technology used to encrypt your persisted cloud data, also referred to as encryption at host. SSE protects your data stored in the cloud by encrypting it.

ADE provides a mechanism to safeguard and protect your data. It is zone resilient just like Azure VMs. In Windows OS, the encryption is done through **BitLocker** with the option to store the encrypting key in Key Vault. It is the same for Linux, with the utility for encryption being **DM-Crypt**.

In the following exercise, you are going to explore how to encrypt an Azure Windows VM.

Exercise 13.8: Configuring ADE

You will now walk through the steps involved in activating ADE. This will be performed on a Windows VM:

1. Navigate to your VM in the Azure portal and select the `Disks` option on the left-hand menu. Click on `Additional settings`:

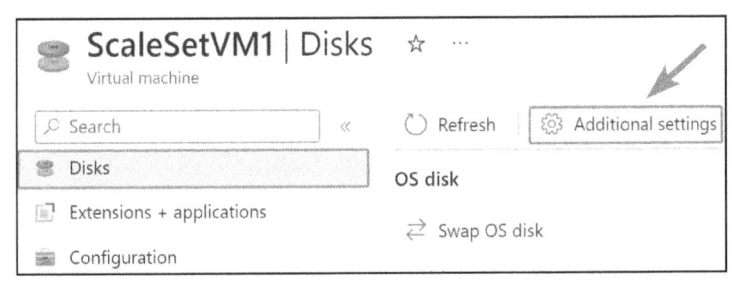

Figure 13.24: Additional settings

2. For the `Disks to encrypt` dropdown, select `OS and data disks`. Click `Create new` in the `Key vault` section:

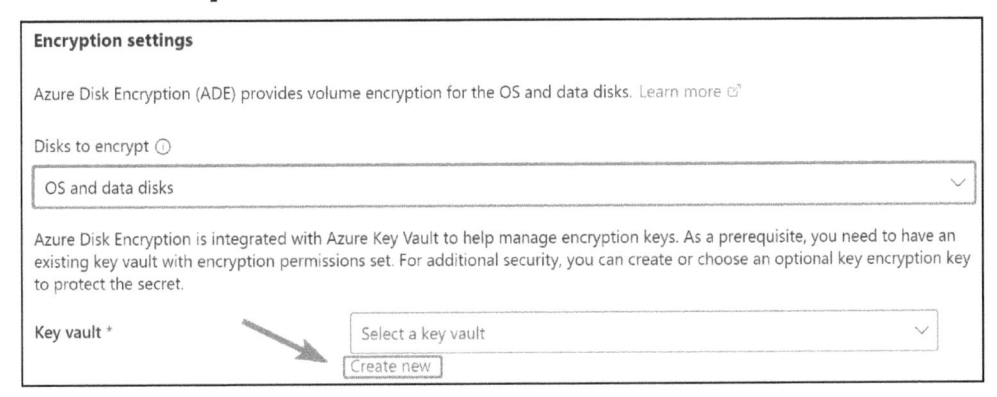

Figure 13.25: Discs to Encrypt

3. Enter a name in the `Key vault name` field and click `Next`.

4. Select the checkboxes next to both the `Azure Virtual Machines for deployment` and `Azure Disk Encryption for volume encryption` options.

Resource access

☑ Azure Virtual Machines for deployment
☐ Azure Resource Manager for template deployment
☑ Azure Disk Encryption for volume encryption

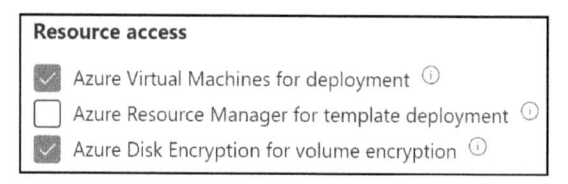

Figure 13.26: Encryption resource access

5. Click `Review + create`.
6. Click `Create`.
7. Once completed, you will be taken back to the `Disk settings` blade. Note your new key vault is selected. You will now need to create a new key by clicking `Create new` for the `Key` setting. Enter a name such as `diskencrypt`.

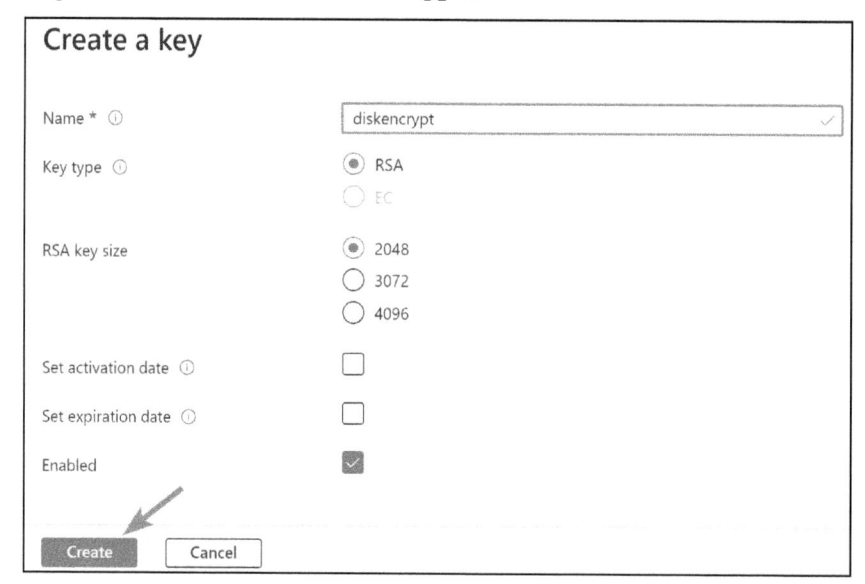

Create a key

Name *	diskencrypt
Key type	● RSA
	○ EC
RSA key size	● 2048
	○ 3072
	○ 4096
Set activation date	☐
Set expiration date	☐
Enabled	☑

[**Create**] [Cancel]

Figure 13.27: Disk encryption key

8. Once your key is created, you can click Save on the Disk settings blade.
9. After a few minutes, note that your disk is now encrypted:

Disk name	Storage type	Size (GiB)	Max IOPS	Encryption
ScaleSetVM1_OsDisk_1_9a007	Premium SSD LRS	127	500	SSE with PMK & ADE

Figure 13.28: Disks overview

You have now completed the disk encryption exercise and understand how to perform this operation within Azure. In the next section, you will explore the reliability and availability options available to you in Azure.

Automating Configuration Management

There are different ways to automate the creation and configuration of your infrastructure in Azure. One such way is to codify your Azure deployments through **Infrastructure as Code** (**IaC**). IaC allows you to specify the desired state of your resources using files, which can be deployed by a language of choice without manual intervention. You therefore can be concerned only with the resource configurations. Native Azure tools that you can use for IaC deployments are ARM templates or Azure Bicep. Another popular third-party tool for IaC is Terraform (made by HashiCorp). You could also use code or Azure Automation, PowerShell scripts, and more.

When different Azure resources are deployed, there are some tools that you can use to manage the configuration of the resources. For example, when you want to automate the configuration of your VMs, Azure provides the following tools:

- **Chef**: Chef is a third-party solution that offers a DevOps automation platform for Linux, Windows, and macOS devices. It can be used for virtual and physical server configurations. It requires an agent to be installed on the VMs or servers that connects to the Chef server to check whether there are available updates and other configurations for the machines. You can use the Chef Automate platform to package and deploy applications as well.

- **Puppet**: Puppet is another third-party solution that has similar capabilities to Chef. You can enable support for Puppet when you create a VM from the Azure portal automatically. You can add it as an extension when you create a new VM that installs the Puppet agent and connects to the master server. Although the Puppet agent supports Windows and Linux, the Puppet VM extension on Azure is supported on the Linux OS only.

- **Desired State Configuration (DSC):** DSC is the process of forcing a configuration on a system. It uses configuration files that consist of PowerShell scripts. These scripts are responsible for doing the required configurations for the system and for ensuring that these systems stay in sync. So, for example, when you have created a DSC file to configure IIS on a Windows server and it is removed by an administrator, the DSC file will reinstall and configure IIS again. This can be used in conjunction with Azure Automation for enhanced reporting.

- **Custom Script Extension:** You can configure software installation tasks and various post-deployment, configuration, and management tasks using Custom Script Extension. Scripts can be downloaded from Azure Storage or GitHub, or provided to the Azure portal at extension runtime, and are executed on the VMs. You can integrate Custom Script Extension with ARM templates, and you can run the extensions using PowerShell, the CLI, the VM REST API, and the Azure portal.

Deploying VM Extensions

VM extensions are applications that you can install as part of the script or post-deployment. For example, you could add antimalware applications to a VM. VM extensions can be configured for existing and future deployments.

Exercise 13.9: Deploying a VM Extension Using the Portal

In this exercise, you are going to configure the **Microsoft Antimalware** extension for an existing Windows VM:

1. Navigate to the Azure portal by opening a web browser and going to `https://portal.azure.com`.
2. Navigate to one of your scale-set VMs.
3. Under the `Settings` tab for the VM, select `Extensions + applications` and click on `Add` on the next page.
4. Now, scroll down and select the `Microsoft Antimalware` extension, click on the card, then click `Next`.

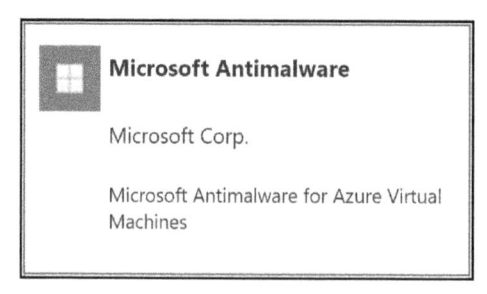

Figure 13.29: Microsoft Antimalware extension

5. You can choose the antimalware settings for your VM; for this scenario, you are going to leave them at the default settings and click `Review + create`:

Figure 13.30: Microsoft Antimalware settings

6. Click `Create`.
7. Once the extension has successfully been deployed, it will show along with other extensions configured for the VM:

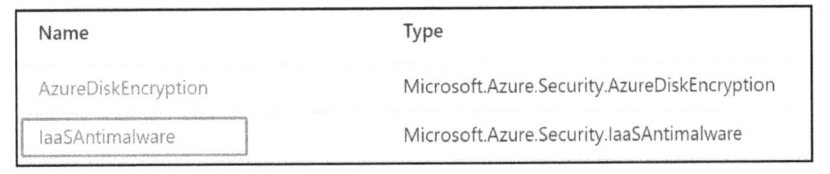

Name	Type
AzureDiskEncryption	Microsoft.Azure.Security.AzureDiskEncryption
IaaSAntimalware	Microsoft.Azure.Security.IaaSAntimalware

Figure 13.31: Successfully deployed Microsoft Antimalware extension

> **Note**
> You can only add VM extensions if the VM is running.

In this section, you learned how to deploy VM extensions via the Azure portal. In the next section, you will explore an ARM template for deploying a VM. You will explore the various configurations as part of the template and enter these customized configurations through a parameter file.

> **Note**
>
> You are encouraged to read more by visiting `https://learn.microsoft.com/en-us/azure/virtual-machines/extensions/overview`.

Configuring and Deploying a VM ARM Template

Deploying IaC is an efficient strategy for consistent deployments. A particularly useful example is deploying VM infrastructure with an ARM template to minimize mistakes and ensure a standardized configuration. In this exercise, you will deploy a few resources that will include **Virtual Hard Disks** (**VHDs**). Your VM will contain both an **OS** and a **data disk**.

You are going to deploy the following resources with your ARM template:

- Windows Server 2019
- VNet
- **Network Security Group** (**NSG**)

> **Note**
>
> Microsoft has several ARM templates available on GitHub to help get you started: `https://github.com/Azure/azure-quickstart-templates`.

The following ARM template can be used to deploy the resources. The script is long and, therefore, has been split up into sections to explain what the ARM code does. To use the following script, you can download the complete template from the GitHub repo for this book: `https://packt.link/Xo9Yw`.

The following code section indicates the schema version and relevant details:

```
{
    "$schema": "https://schema.management.azure.com/schemas/2019-04-01/deploymentTemplate.json#",
    "contentVersion": "1.0.0.0",
```

The following code section indicates the start of the `parameters` section within the main template file, which will be overwritten with values from the `parameters` file. The following snippet includes the admin username for the VM as well as the password that is required in secure string format:

```
"parameters": {
        "adminUsername": {
        "type": "string",
        "metadata": {
            "description": "Username for the Virtual Machine."
```

```
        }
    },
    "adminPassword": {
    "type": "secureString",
    "minLength": 12,
    "metadata": {
        "description": "Password for the Virtual Machine."
    }
    },
```

The following code section indicates the DNS name for the public IP address of the VM as well as the definition of the public IP address:

```
"dnsLabelPrefix": {
        "type": "string",
        "defaultValue": "[toLower(format('{0}-{1}',
parameters('vmName'), uniqueString(resourceGroup().id,
parameters('vmName'))))]",
        "metadata": {
            "description": "Unique DNS Name for the Public IP used to
access the Virtual Machine."
        }
    },
    "publicIpName": {
        "type": "string",
        "defaultValue": "myPublicIP",
        "metadata": {
            "description": "Name for the Public IP used to access the
Virtual Machine."
        }
    },
```

The following code section indicates that the public IP address is going to use the dynamic type, which means it will change when the VM is restarted. The public IP address will be configured for the Basic SKU by default:

```
"publicIPAllocationMethod": {
        "type": "string",
        "defaultValue": "Dynamic",
        "allowedValues": [
            "Dynamic",
            "Static"
        ],
        "metadata": {
            "description": "Allocation method for the Public IP used
```

```
            to access the Virtual Machine."
        }
        },
        "publicIpSku": {
        "type": "string",
        "defaultValue": "Basic",
        "allowedValues": [
            "Basic",
            "Standard"
        ],
        "metadata": {
            "description": "SKU for the Public IP used to access the
Virtual Machine."
        }
        },
```

The following code section indicates the different allowed values to choose from when choosing an OS; this will be in the form of a drop-down list within the Azure portal:

```
"OSVersion": {
        "type": "string",
        "defaultValue": "2019-Datacenter",
        "allowedValues": [
            "2008-R2-SP1",
            "2012-Datacenter",
            "2012-R2-Datacenter",
            "2016-Nano-Server",
            "2016-Datacenter-with-Containers",
            "2016-Datacenter",
            "2019-Datacenter",
            "2019-Datacenter-Core",
            "2019-Datacenter-Core-smalldisk",
            "2019-Datacenter-Core-with-Containers",
            "2019-Datacenter-Core-with-Containers-smalldisk",
            "2019-Datacenter-smalldisk",
            "2019-Datacenter-with-Containers",
            "2019-Datacenter-with-Containers-smalldisk"
        ],
        "metadata": {
            "description": "The Windows version for the VM. This will
pick a fully patched image of this given Windows version."
        }
        },
```

The following code section indicates the VM SKU, which will, in this case, be a `Standard_D2_V3` VM with the name `simple-vm`:

```
"vmSize": {
        "type": "string",
        "defaultValue": "Standard_D2_v3",
        "metadata": {
            "description": "Size of the virtual machine."
        }
    },
    "location": {
    "type": "string",
    "defaultValue": "[resourceGroup().location]",
    "metadata": {
        "description": "Location for all resources."
    }
    },
    "vmName": {
    "type": "string",
    "defaultValue": "simple-vm",
    "metadata": {
        "description": "Name of the virtual machine."
    }
    }
},
```

The following code section indicates the variables for the virtual network called `MyVNET` with an address range of `10.0.0.0/16`, a subnet with a range of `10.0.0.0/24`, and a default NSG:

```
"variables": {
        "storageAccountName": "[format('bootdiags{0}', uniqueString(resourceGroup().id))]",
        "nicName": "myVMNic",
        "addressPrefix": "10.0.0.0/16",
        "subnetName": "Subnet",
        "subnetPrefix": "10.0.0.0/24",
        "virtualNetworkName": "MyVNET",
        "networkSecurityGroupName": "default-NSG"
    },
```

The following code section indicates the creation of a `Standard_LRS` storage account and the public IP address:

```
"resources": [
    {
    "type": "Microsoft.Storage/storageAccounts",
    "apiVersion": "2021-04-01",
    "name": "[variables('storageAccountName')]",
    "location": "[parameters('location')]",
    "sku": {
        "name": "Standard_LRS"
    },
    "kind": "Storage"
    },
    {
    "type": "Microsoft.Network/publicIPAddresses",
    "apiVersion": "2021-02-01",
    "name": "[parameters('publicIpName')]",
    "location": "[parameters('location')]",
    "sku": {
        "name": "[parameters('publicIpSku')]"
    },
        "properties": {
        "publicIPAllocationMethod":
"[parameters('publicIPAllocationMethod')]",
        "dnsSettings": {
        "domainNameLabel": "[parameters('dnsLabelPrefix')]"
        }
    }
    },
```

The following code section indicates the creation of the NSG with a basic inbound rule that will allow RDP on port `3389` from any source address. It is a security risk to do this with production VMs; it is recommended to rather use VPN access and local IP ranges instead:

```
    {
        "type": "Microsoft.Network/networkSecurityGroups",
        "apiVersion": "2021-02-01",
        "name": "[variables('networkSecurityGroupName')]",
        "location": "[parameters('location')]",
        "properties": {
            "securityRules": [
            {
                "name": "default-allow-3389",
```

```json
            "properties": {
                "priority": 1000,
                "access": "Allow",
                "direction": "Inbound",
                "destinationPortRange": "3389",
                "protocol": "Tcp",
                "sourcePortRange": "*",
                "sourceAddressPrefix": "*",
                "destinationAddressPrefix": "*"
            }
        }
        ]
    }
},
```

The following code section defines the creation of the VNet based on the variables. It is important to note that there is a `dependsOn` field, which means that to create the resources, it requires another resource to be created first – the NSG:

```json
{
        "type": "Microsoft.Network/virtualNetworks",
        "apiVersion": "2021-02-01",
        "name": "[variables('virtualNetworkName')]",
        "location": "[parameters('location')]",
        "properties": {
            "addressSpace": {
            "addressPrefixes": [
                "[variables('addressPrefix')]"
            ]
            }
        }
},
{
        "type": "Microsoft.Network/virtualNetworks/subnets",
        "apiVersion": "2021-02-01",
        "name": "[format('{0}/{1}', variables('virtualNetworkName'), variables('subnetName'))]",
        "properties": {
            "addressPrefix": "[variables('subnetPrefix')]",
            "networkSecurityGroup": {
            "id": "[resourceId('Microsoft.Network/networkSecurityGroups', variables('networkSecurityGroupName'))]"
            }
        },
```

```
            "dependsOn": [
                "[resourceId('Microsoft.Network/networkSecurityGroups',
    variables('networkSecurityGroupName'))]",
                "[resourceId('Microsoft.Network/virtualNetworks',
    variables('virtualNetworkName'))]"
            ]
        },
```

The following code section defines the configuration of the VM **Network Interface Card** (**NIC**) with the variable values:

```
    {
        "type": "Microsoft.Network/networkInterfaces",
        "apiVersion": "2021-02-01",
        "name": "[variables('nicName')]",
        "location": "[parameters('location')]",
        "properties": {
            "ipConfigurations": [
                {
                    "name": "ipconfig1",
                    "properties": {
                    "privateIPAllocationMethod": "Dynamic",
                    "publicIPAddress": {
                        "id": "[resourceId('Microsoft.Network/
    publicIPAddresses', parameters('publicIpName'))]"
                    },
                    "subnet": {
                        "id": "[resourceId('Microsoft.Network/
    virtualNetworks/subnets', variables('virtualNetworkName'),
    variables('subnetName'))]"
                    }
                }
            }
            ]
        },
            "dependsOn": [
                "[resourceId('Microsoft.Network/publicIPAddresses',
    parameters('publicIpName'))]",
                "[resourceId('Microsoft.Network/virtualNetworks/subnets',
    variables('virtualNetworkName'), variables('subnetName'))]"
            ]
        },
```

The following code section indicates the creation of the VM based on the variables declared in this script, which include `vmSize`, `computerName`, `adminUsername`, and `adminPassword`:

ARM_Vhd_Template_Deployment.json

```
{
"type": "Microsoft.Compute/virtualMachines",
"apiVersion": "2021-03-01",
"name": "[parameters('vmName')]",
"location": "[parameters('location')]",
"properties": {
    "hardwareProfile": {
    "vmSize": "[parameters('vmSize')]"
    },
    "osProfile": {
    "computerName": "[parameters('vmName')]",
    "adminUsername": "[parameters('adminUsername')]",
    "adminPassword": "[parameters('adminPassword')]"
    },
```

The complete code is available at https://packt.link/WuEbA

The following code is the final section of the ARM template and will output the **Fully-qualified Domain Name** (**FQDN**) for the public IP resource:

```
"outputs": {
   "hostname": {
      "type": "string",
      "value": "[reference(resourceId('Microsoft.Network/publicIPAddresses', parameters('publicIpName'))).dnsSettings.fqdn]"
   }
  }
}
```

The following is the accompanying `parameters` file for the ARM template. Note that the parameters for the following are configured:

- Admin username
- Admin password
- DNS label prefix
- Public IP name
- Public IP allocation method
- Public IP SKU
- OS version
- VM size (SKU)
- Location
- VM name

In this section, you had a look at a VM ARM deployment template and `parameters` file that configured several resources including a virtual hard disk for the OS and an additional data disk.

> **Note**
>
> You are encouraged to read up further by using the following links based on Azure ARM templates:
>
> `https://learn.microsoft.com/en-us/training/modules/deploy-vms-from-vhd-templates/`
>
> `https://learn.microsoft.com/en-us/azure/virtual-machines/using-managed-disks-template-deployments`

Summary

In this chapter, you covered Azure VM management tasks, learned how to configure VMS, and learned about the various management functions, including components such as networking, high-availability configurations, and changing the VM host.

You have now attained the skills required for the management of VMs within the Azure environment and should be able to confidently provision, scale, and manage these going forward. You learned different methods of deployment to assist you with consistent delivery on the platform while ensuring fewer mistakes and faster deployment times than doing this manually, using PowerShell or the CLI. You also learned about VM extensions and how to add these to a VM. Finally, you explored a VM ARM template and learned how to configure various settings for a VM deployment.

In the next chapter, you will explore Azure containers and how to configure and manage them.

> **Note**
>
> Remember to delete the resources you created in this chapter to minimize costs. You can do this with the following command for convenience, which will remove the resource group and all the corresponding resources:
>
> `Remove-AzResourceGroup -Name AZ104-VirtualMachines`
>
> `Remove-AzResourceGroup -Name AZ104-VirtualMachines-Migration`

14
Creating and Configuring Containers

Containers introduce a paradigm that allows you to package applications and their dependencies together into a single, portable unit, known as a container. These containers include everything required to run the application and ensure consistent performance regardless of the hosting environment. They offer some key benefits such as portability, consistency, efficiency, scalability, isolation, and speed. Containers have also become a fundamental part of modern application deployment, enabling faster, more reliable, and more efficient workloads.

In this chapter, some of the topics to look forward to include the following: configuring the sizing and scaling of containers, working with **Azure Container Instances** (**ACI**), and working with **Azure Kubernetes Service** (**AKS**), including AKS storage, scaling AKS, and the networking side of AKS. You will explore what containers are and the difference between containers and **virtual machines** (**VMs**). You will also examine use cases for containers. Lastly, you will learn how to manage and orchestrate container deployments within Azure. By the end of this chapter, you should understand the core principles of working with containers and be confident in being able to administer them on Azure.

This chapter will cover the following main topics:

- Introduction to containers
- Core concepts of containers
- Container groups
- Docker platform
- Azure Kubernetes Service
- Creating an Azure container registry
- Deploying your first Azure container instance
- Configuring container groups for ACI
- Configuring sizing and scaling for ACI

- Deploying AKS
- Configuring storage for AKS
- Configuring scaling for AKS
- Upgrading an AKS cluster

Technical Requirements

This chapter uses the following tools for the examples:

- Access to an Azure subscription with owner or contributor privileges. If you do not have access to one, you can create a student account, which is free, at either https://azure.microsoft.com/en-us/free/
- **PowerShell 5.1** or later installed on a Windows PC or PowerShell Core 6.x on other operating systems, to practice the labs.
- Where PowerShell is not installed or available, https://shell.azure.com can be used as a browser-based shell.
- Installation of the Az PowerShell module, which can be performed by running the following in an administrative PowerShell session:

    ```
    Set-ExecutionPolicy -ExecutionPolicy RemoteSigned -Scope
    CurrentUser
    Install-Module -Name Az -Scope CurrentUser -Repository PSGallery
    -Force
    ```

Docker

For this chapter, you are going to configure Docker so that you can see your containers running locally. Follow these steps to configure Docker:

1. Sign up on Docker Hub at the following URL: https://hub.docker.com/subscription?plan=free.
2. Click the Sign Up link at the bottom of the screen, and follow the steps to complete the sign-up.
3. Next, proceed to download the Docker application, as follows:

    - For Windows, use the following link and select the appropriate installer: https://docs.docker.com/desktop/install/win
    - ows-install/.
    - For Linux, use the following link and select the appropriate installer: https://docs.docker.com/desktop/install/linux-install/.
    - For macOS, use the following link and select the appropriate installer: https://docs.docker.com/desktop/install/mac-install/.

Docker is required for the completion of the exercises in this chapter. Once you have installed the application, you are ready to continue.

Introduction to Containers

Businesses are constantly looking for newer and quicker ways to deploy applications and keep businesses running. These requirements need software development and support teams to find solutions for saving money and time. Adopting an approach of using containers for rapid deployments leaves more time for software deployment and reduces time spent on creating and configuring environments.

Containers are specialized packages of software that bundle application software with associated configuration files, libraries, and dependencies that are required to enable an application to run. Containers also contain the kernel for an **Operating System (OS)** and don't require the entire OS, which allows for larger-scale deployments than VMs could achieve using the same resources. The reason for this is that the OS consumes resources, such as storage, memory, and processing power. In the previous chapter, you learned how VMs abstract the hardware layer in their composition, meaning that they are created by utilizing existing physical hardware resources and logically dividing them. When deploying a VM, you will still need to specify the type of OS you require—this is typically Windows or Linux. Containers, by association, abstract the OS layer, meaning the host machine (VM or physical) assigns resources to the OS and then further subdivides resources specific to the containers being hosted. Since the OS overhead is removed from the subsequent container deployments, it is more efficient with resource utilization and requires fewer resources for running the container.

The exact kernel version won't be required to make the container work, as the kernel will be packaged in your container, and you just need to concern yourself with the application code, libraries, and dependencies to get your application to work. Using this approach allows easy scaling, and only a single OS is consumed on the host of the containers, as opposed to within each container as a VM does for the OS type, such as Windows or Linux. Being lightweight, containers are easier to manage and much faster to deploy and scale. They introduce a standardized and repeatable mechanism for packaging, managing, and deploying applications.

The Problems Containers Solve

Containers solve several problems in modern computing, and these have been split into key topical areas for easy comprehension.

Complexity

Before containers, the challenge was writing applications for various systems with different versions of dependencies that the developers couldn't control. This leads to several issues that make solutions very difficult to manage, such as applications breaking due to different versions of the packages and OS.

Another example that illustrates the complexity of non-consistency is with enterprise environments, where, typically, servers and client machines are managed through Active Directory Group Policy. If it does not apply the same policies to all devices running your application, then the configuration can be different from the intended design and not run as expected. With containers, you can standardize the deployment with dependencies and enable a consistent experience for all users.

Resource Requirements and Costs

As mentioned previously, containers require significantly fewer system resources to deliver services due to the reduced footprint of running containers compared to VMs. This factor not only reduces the number of required resources but also the associated costs for running containers.

Scalability

Containers are by their very nature designed for massive scale. They can easily be scaled out horizontally (adding instances) to meet your specific requirements and back in again when fewer resources are required. The applications that run on them subsequently benefit from this feature too, allowing them to meet scaling demands on the application. Due to the decoupled nature of containers (where applications are typically split into the frontend, middleware, and backend layers), scalability extends to all layers configured within the application. This, in turn, also enables resilience at each layer and allows the portion of the application that requires scale to adapt appropriately. This prevents wasting resources for unnecessary compute allocated to the parts of the application that don't need them.

Portability and Consistency

Another valuable area of consideration is that containers are not limited to your local machine and can run on most of the major hyperscalers, including Azure. This makes containers more ubiquitous, allowing you to place them where they add the most benefit and introduce new functionality, such as hybrid and multi-cloud scaling. Configurations are not specific to the environment you create anymore, and you can be assured that what you deploy in a container in your environment will work in other environments, too.

Azure container instances allow you to run containers in Azure without the requirement to deploy a container host or VM.

> **Note**
>
> Windows container hosts can run both Windows and Linux containers; conversely, Linux can only run Linux containers to date. Running Linux containers on Windows will require Hyper-V services and using a system called LinuxKit (essentially a Linux VM). When deploying to ACI, however, it is important to select the correct OS for your requirement, as Linux containers run on the Linux OS and Windows containers run on the Windows OS.

Before diving into working with containers, you will explore some of the core concepts related to them to enhance your understanding. The most effective method is to compare containers to virtualized hardware because you already have an understanding of the latter. While they are similar, they are distinctly different, which you will explore next.

The Differences between VMs and Containers

Hardware virtualization has enabled the possibility of running multiple isolated OS instances at the same time on physical hardware. Containers abstract the OS by virtualizing it, and this enables several applications to be run using the same OS while still being isolated from each other. VMs, on the other hand, contain the entire OS and files and, essentially, only abstract the hardware layer, whereas containers abstract the OS layer and contain your application files as well as configuration files and dependencies. Containers are much smaller in size and utilize fewer resources.

A hypervisor is the software, firmware, and hardware that enables VMs to be created and run. It is the layer that resides between the physical hardware and the software-implemented VM. New machines have virtualization instruction sets built into the processes and specialized hardware to enable VMs to run just as well as physical hardware and leverage physical hardware resources as native services.

Figure 14.1 depicts the relationship between VMs and containers. It shows the hypervisor layer present on the host for VM systems compared to the configuration of containers that run the container engine on top of the OS. Containers are a more lightweight deployment of applications:

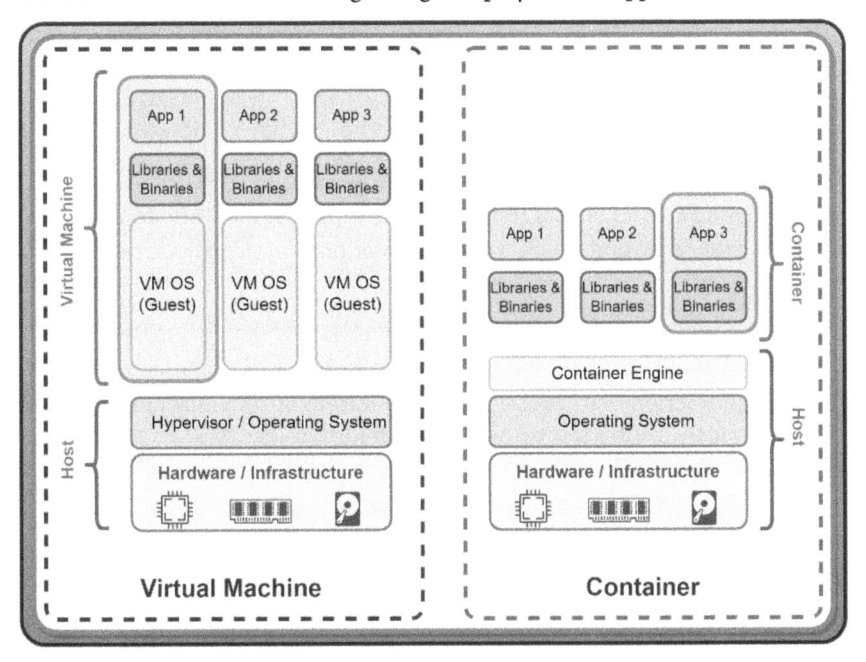

Figure 14.1: VMs infrastructure compared to containers

It should be noted that hypervisors are formed at different levels of integration from systems. As you will note in *Figure 14.1*, there is a hypervisor layer present just above the hardware/infrastructure layer—this is referred to as a type 1 hypervisor (also known as a bare-metal hypervisor) as it has direct access to hardware. There is another type of hypervisor, referred to as type 2 (also known as a host OS hypervisor); this runs much like an application within the OS, and this is the technology that Docker uses.

It can become confusing to distinguish between containers and VMs, so to help you better understand their differences, some key concepts have been identified, as outlined next.

Isolation

VMs provide the most comprehensive and secure isolation solution such that not only are all VMs isolated from each other but also the host OSs are isolated from each other. This is the best mechanism for security when you have shared infrastructure and are looking to isolate applications or services from competing companies that are on the same server or cluster. **Containers**, in comparison to VMs, provide a much more lightweight isolation mechanism. They don't provide as strong a security boundary from the host and other containers as a VM does.

> **Note**
> When choosing a solution that requires the most secure method of isolation, it is best to go with VMs, especially when considering the host as an attack vector.

OS

VMs run the entire OS, including the kernel. This is a more resource-intensive approach as the OS requires system resources such as memory, **central processing unit** (**CPU**), and storage. Containers, in comparison, require far fewer system resources to run applications. They do this by only running the customized user-mode portion of OSs, which contains only services that are essential for running your application.

> **Note**
> When choosing a solution that requires better utilization of system resources, you can't go wrong with containers. Your resources will go much further than with a VM.

Deployment

VMs are deployed using some form of a hypervisor. With Windows systems, they can be deployed and managed by **Windows Admin Center**, **Hyper-V Manager**, and **System Center Virtual Machine Manager** (**SCVMM**). PowerShell can also be used with the relevant Hyper-V modules enabled.

Containers are deployed using Docker through the command line for single instances, and for multiple containers, it is advised that an orchestrator service such as AKS is used.

> **Note**
> On Azure, Docker is predominantly used for containers and AKS for container orchestration.

Storage Persistence

VM storage is very easy to scale and maintain in Azure. You simply add or scale up disks as required, which you learned about in the previous chapter. This storage is persistent as it doesn't disappear if disconnected or if the VM shuts down. Another mechanism of providing persistent storage is through **Server Message Block (SMB)** shares. Containers, in comparison, have the option of leveraging Azure disks for local storage on a single-node deployment and configuring SMB shares for multiple nodes or servers.

> **Note**
> Identify whether storage requires persistence and find the mechanism that best suits your requirements. For shared storage, SMB shares make a lot of sense, but several other mechanisms can be used to achieve the same result. These are beyond the scope of this book, however, and you are still encouraged to explore and find what works for you.

Fault Tolerance

VMs can fail over to another server in a cluster when configured for fault tolerance. The resultant effect, however, is that the VM's OS will be restarted on the new hosting server, which can potentially add significant time to restore services. Containers, in comparison, can quickly recover instances. The orchestrator recreates the container on another cluster node when it detects a failed cluster node.

> **Note**
> Catering to fault tolerance is always advised, especially when dealing with production workloads. You need to understand the caveats of each system and be able to plan accordingly. Containers, being more lightweight, are more resistant to failures and more readily restored.

Having understood the comparison, you are now ready to examine the advantages that containers hold over VMs and physical machines, as follows:

- Due to better resource utilization, containers can achieve better workload density.
- They standardize deployments and simplify the application testing process.
- Application deployment is quicker and more streamlined. It is also more standardized, making it more consistent and reliable.
- The speed and flexibility in developing application code are improved, as well as sharing.

You should now understand the key differences between containers and VMs as well as be able to identify scenarios that best suit either deployment. In the next section, you will explore ACI and how it allows the easy deployment of containers to the Azure platform.

Azure Container Instances

ACI is a container hosting service that provides a fast and easy method for running containers in Azure. Using this solution will enable you to deploy containers without needing to manage any VMs or underlying infrastructure and hosting services. ACI provides a great solution for applications that can run in isolated containers. There are several benefits to working with containers on Azure, as outlined here:

- **Fast startup times**: Azure containers are designed to be able to start in seconds.
- **Public connectivity**: Azure containers have been designed to enable direct exposure to the internet by associating with a public **Internet Protocol** (**IP**) address that also allows the association of a **fully qualified domain name** (**FQDN**), which is a user-friendly name for finding the public IP address associated with a container instance. This name can be referenced through a public **Domain Name System** (**DNS**) and is associated with the public IP.
- **Security**: Azure container applications apply hypervisor-level security that enables container applications to be isolated as they would be in a VM.
- **Elasticity**: Azure container nodes are designed to be dynamically scaled to meet the resource demands required for an application.
- **Storage persistence**: Azure containers enable storage persistence through Azure file shares by allowing them to be directly mounted. Without this, storage is only ephemeral.
- **Various OSs**: ACI can schedule containers for both Windows and Linux systems. Simply select the OS type you need when you create your container groups.
- **Co-scheduled groups**: Azure containers are designed to support the sharing of host machine resources through multi-container groups on the same host.
- **Virtual network (VNet) deployment**: Azure containers are designed to allow integration into Azure VNets.

You just learned what ACI is and the several benefits it can offer. Next, you will learn about container groups and how they group together container instances. You will also learn what to consider when designing and deploying container groups.

Container Groups

Container groups contain a set of containers that share their life cycle, resources, network configuration, and storage resources, essentially grouping them. Containers within a container group are scheduled together on the same host (the server on which these run) and in ACI, which is the top-level resource. Container groups can consist of one or more containers.

Figure 14.2 shows an example container group that contains two containers scheduled on the same host. The container group exposes port 80 as the default configuration on a single public IP (an IP accessible from the internet) and has a public DNS label associated with it. The container group also contains two different storage accounts, each of which is associated with one of the containers. Of the two containers, one container exposes port 80 while the other exposes port 1433. On private ports, as illustrated in the following diagram, *private* refers to ports, IP, or DNS being restricted to access within the local network only:

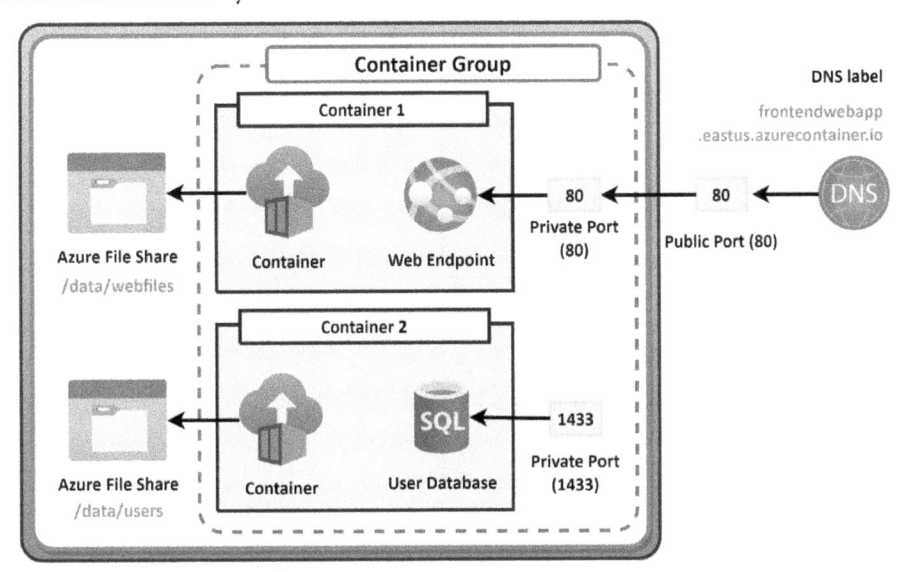

Figure 14.2: Example container group

You now have a basic understanding of what a container group is. Next, you will explore some common scenarios for using multi-container groups.

Common Scenarios for Using Multi-Container Groups

There are several scenarios where multi-container groups prove beneficial, such as when you define a frontend and backend for your container groups. Tasks may be divided into an application container and a logging or monitoring container; these perform two separate functions but are complementary to the end service delivery of the application. Images can be deployed and managed by different teams within your organization.

Some other scenarios include the following:

- An application container and a database container. The application container(s) may deliver the end application, while the database container commits data to a service location.
- A web application service deployed to a container within the group and another container for managing source control.

Resources

Container groups are allocated resources by ACI by adding resource requests for all instances in a container group, such as CPUs, memory, and even **Graphics Processing Units (GPUs)**. For example, if you have two container instances in a container group and each instance requires 2 CPUs and 4 **gigabytes (GB)** of memory, the container group will then be allocated 4 CPUs and 8 GB of memory, as depicted in *Figure 14.3*:

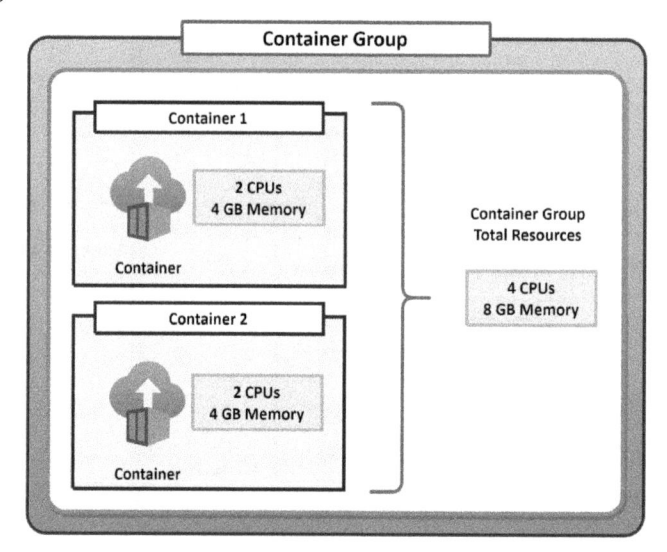

Figure 14.3: Container group resource allocation

The next section will take you through the networking components of the ACI service.

Networking

Containers within a container group can share a public-facing IP address with an associated DNS label. This label is referred to as an FQDN, which is a user-friendly name for finding an IP associated with your web application. The container group exposes ports on the public IP address to enable external clients to reach a container.

The exposed public ports must also be enabled on the container level, which doesn't always need to be publicly accessible and can be limited internally, too. When the container group is deleted, the associated public IP and FQDN will be removed too.

> **Note**
> All containers within a group share a port namespace, and because of this, port mapping isn't supported.

An example to help you understand the concept better is provided here: suppose you have a container group deployment that contains one frontend server and one backend server. The frontend server requires access over port 443 (**HyperText Transfer Protocol Secure**, or **HTTPS**) on a public IP, and the container serving the web endpoint must be exposed on port 443 as well. The backend server communicates over port 8080 and will be limited to local communication. You can see a depiction of this in *Figure 14.4*:

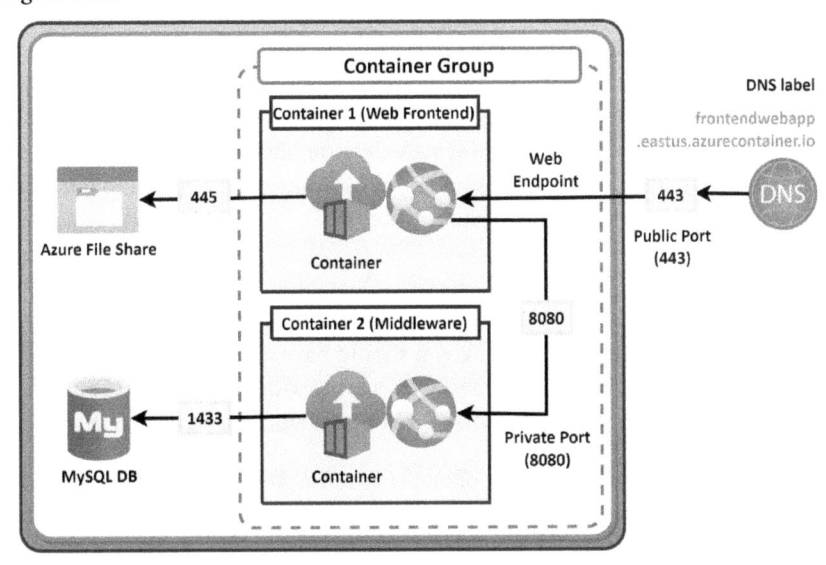

Figure 14.4: Example container group frontend and backend

You now know more about how some networking components work for container groups. Next, you will explore different methods of container group deployment.

Deployment

There are two primary methods of deployment for a multi-container group: an **Azure Resource Manager** (**ARM**) template or a **YAML Ain't Markup Language** (**YAML**) file. In *Chapter 13, Managing Virtual Machines*, you explored the deployment of VM resources using an ARM template; this section serves as an extension of that information. The beauty of ARM deployment is that it allows additional resources to be deployed alongside container instances, such as Azure file shares. YAML files, on the other hand, are designed for supporting container instance deployments within a container group only. These are designed as an alternative to ARM templates for container deployments due to them being more concise in their nature and structure.

Now that you understand more about container groups, in the next section, you will explore Docker, which is one of the platforms that enable containerization. Docker is one of the most popular platforms and is well integrated into Azure.

Docker Platform

Docker is one of the most popular platforms that enables developers to host their applications within containers. It can be run on either Windows, Linux, or macOS and ensures standardized software deployment. The beauty of containers is that they allow local development on a container platform (such as Docker) that can be easily redeployed for sharing and distribution across other platforms that support containers, such as Azure. The container will run as expected since all the package components are bundled into the Docker image you deploy. A Docker image is a lightweight, standalone, and executable package that includes everything needed to run a piece of software, including code, runtime, libraries, environment variables, and configuration files. Docker acts as the container host as well as a tool for building containers. When containers are deployed through ACI, Docker allows them to be scaled easily. You will need to learn the terminology associated with Docker to understand how to work with the tool, which you will explore next.

Docker Terminology

When working with Docker and containers, you should have an understanding of the associated terminology. This will help you become comfortable working with containers and performing actions such as creating, building, and testing containers. The terms are presented as follows:

- **Container**: This refers to an instance of one of your Docker images. As mentioned previously, containers are specialized packages of software that bundle application software with associated configuration files, libraries, and dependencies that are required to enable an application to run. In Docker, this consists of the Docker image, the execution environment, and your standard set of instructions. The platform enables you to create multiple instances of a container using the same image, which is important to remember when you want to scale your application.

- **Container image**: This refers to all the dependencies and information packaged together that are required to create a container. These include frameworks, as well as configurations for deployment and executions that a container runtime uses. An image is typically created from multiple base images stacked on top of each other to form the container's filesystem. An image is immutable once it has been created.

- **Docker Registry**: This is the repository provided by the Docker platform for storing various image files. Azure has another solution, **Azure Container Registry**, which is the solution you will use in this chapter.

- **Build**: This is the action of building your container. The build will be based on the container image and will be constructed based on the information provided by the Dockerfile. The build also includes any other necessary files, such as your application files, which will be included in the container image.

- **Pull**: This refers to the action of downloading a container image from one of your container registries.

- **Push**: This refers to the action of uploading a container image to one of your container registries.
- **Dockerfile**: This defines instructions for building your image. It is stored as a text file. The first line in a Dockerfile structure is used to identify the base image needed, while the rest of the file contains the associated build actions for your image.

The Docker platform is structured as shown in *Figure 14.5*. You will notice the container registry comprises Azure Container Registry, Docker Hub, or another container registry, the Docker Engine components, and the containers. *Figure 14.5* will help you understand the relationship between these components:

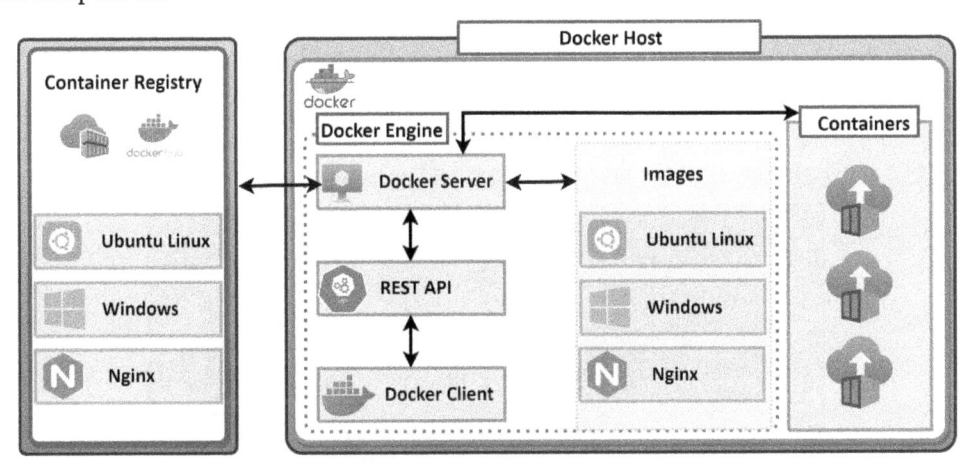

Figure 14.5: Docker components

Having understood more about the Docker platform and its various components that work together to enable your solution, you are now ready to set up Docker.

Setting Up Docker

For this exercise, you are going to configure Docker so that you can see your first container in action. Proceed as follows:

1. Sign up on Docker Hub at the following URL: https://hub.docker.com/subscription?plan=free.
2. Next, proceed to download the Docker Desktop application and install it:
   - For Windows, use the following link and select the appropriate installer: https://docs.docker.com/desktop/install/windows-install/
   - For Linux, use the following link and select the appropriate installer: https://docs.docker.com/desktop/install/linux-install/

- For macOS, use the following link and select the appropriate installer: `https://hub.docker.com/editions/community/docker-ce-desktop-mac`

  For the remainder of the exercise, it will be assumed you are running Docker from a Windows machine; if not, then please adjust the exercise to meet your requirements. After installing the Docker application, you may be required to restart your machine.

3. After installation, you may want to update the **Windows Subsystem for Linux 2** (**WSL 2**) package. Run the following link and restart your machine: `https://aka.ms/wsl2kernel`. This installer will install the latest version of WSL.

4. Once Docker is set up, run the following command for your first Docker image. Launch an administrative PowerShell session for this and add the following command, then press *Enter*:

   ```
   docker run -d -p 80:80 docker/getting-started
   ```

Figure 14.6 shows the output of the preceding command:

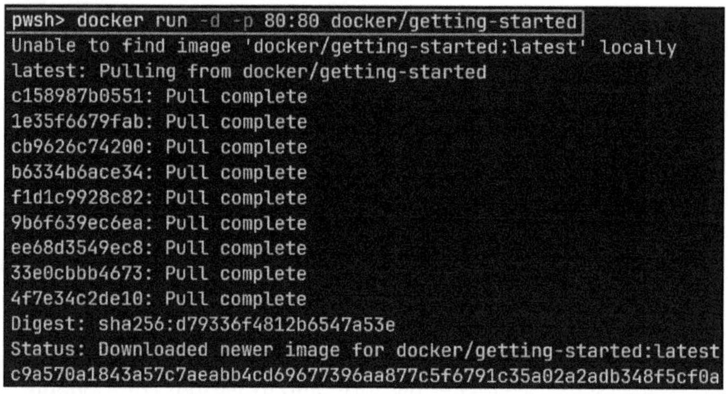

```
pwsh> docker run -d -p 80:80 docker/getting-started
Unable to find image 'docker/getting-started:latest' locally
latest: Pulling from docker/getting-started
c158987b0551: Pull complete
1e35f6679fab: Pull complete
cb9626c74200: Pull complete
b6334b6ace34: Pull complete
f1d1c9928c82: Pull complete
9b6f639ec6ea: Pull complete
ee68d3549ec8: Pull complete
33e0cbbb4673: Pull complete
4f7e34c2de10: Pull complete
Digest: sha256:d79336f4812b6547a53e
Status: Downloaded newer image for docker/getting-started:latest
c9a570a1843a57c7aeabb4cd69677396aa877c5f6791c35a02a2adb348f5cf0a
```

Figure 14.6: First Docker container

Note that this command runs a `pull` command for a `docker/getting-started` image.

> **Note**
>
> If you are one of the users who faces an issue when running the previous command, try running the following command to fix Docker: `cd "C:\Program Files\Docker\Docker`. Then, press *Enter* and add the following code: `./DockerCli.exe -SwitchDaemon`. Following this, press *Enter*.

After running this command, you may open the Docker Desktop application, and if you click the **Containers/Apps** icon on the left menu, you will notice an image on the right, as shown in *Figure 14.7*. A name is randomly generated each time you create a container unless you specify otherwise:

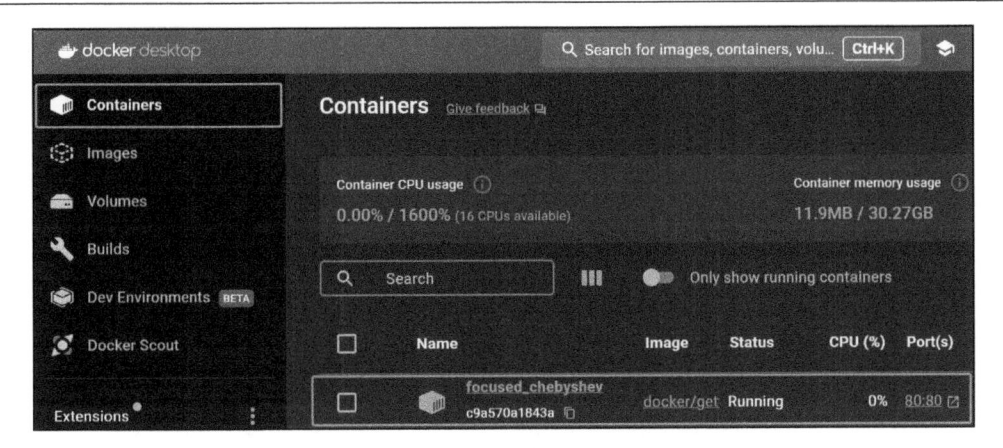

Figure 14.7: First Docker container – Docker Desktop

You will note that the container is running on port 80, which means the application is accessible as a web application locally. To access this, launch a browser and navigate to the following URL: http://127.0.0.1. You will see a success message, along with guidance on other exercises you can follow, as shown in *Figure 14.8*. You are encouraged to carry out these exercises and learn more:

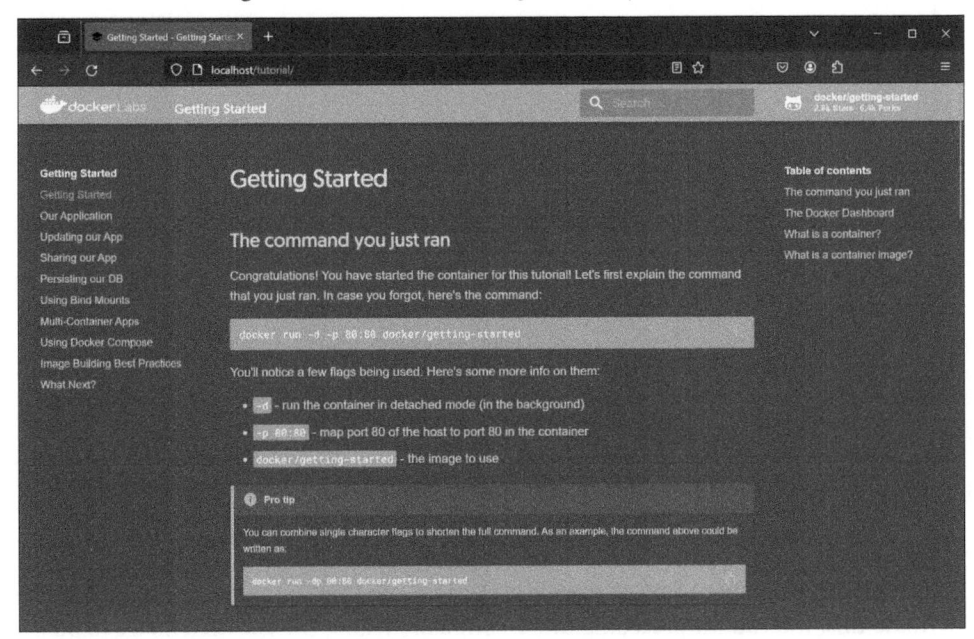

Figure 14.8: Using your Docker container

Now that you have successfully installed Docker and run your first container from a pre-compiled image, you will explore the creation of your first image and publish it to Docker Hub.

Creating Your First Docker Image

For this exercise, you will need to first sign in to Docker Hub. Then, follow the next steps:

1. Once signed in, click on the `Repositories` button on the top menu bar, as shown in *Figure 14.9*:

Figure 14.9: Repositories button

2. Click `Create repository` (the button is at the top right of the page).
3. Enter a name and description for this repository, then click `Create`. Note that you may select whether your repository is public or private, too. For this repository, leave it as `Public`, as shown in *Figure 14.10*:

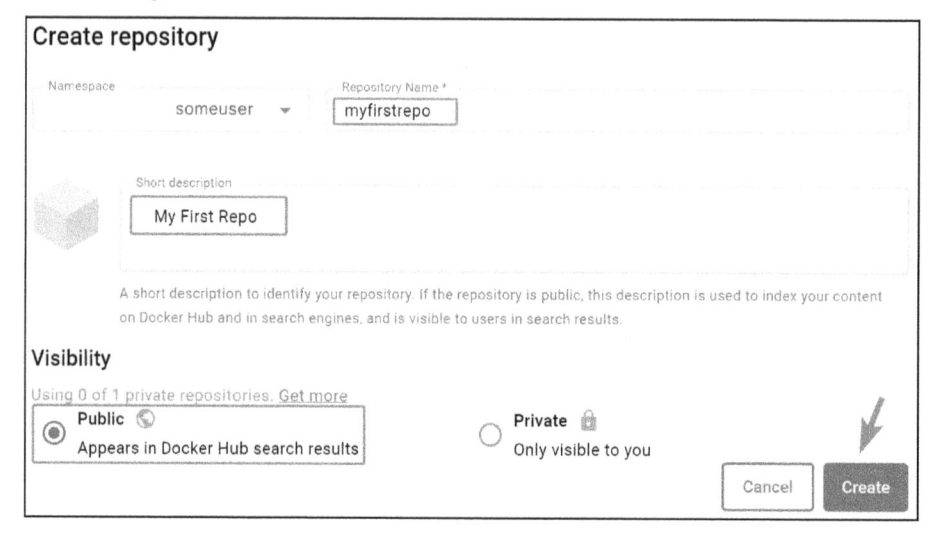

Figure 14.10: Creating your first repository

4. Return to your PowerShell window and paste the following command into it:

```
docker pull mcr.microsoft.com/azuredocs/aci-helloworld
```

For this demonstration, you will download the `aci-helloworld` image made by Microsoft. To do this, you run the preceding `pull` command telling Docker what image to pull. Your terminal should look like the following figure when you run it:

Figure 14.11: Pull of the aci-helloworld image

5. Now that your image is downloaded, run the following command to list your Docker images on your system and press *Enter*:

    docker images

    The following figure shows the output from the command when you run it:

    ```
    pwsh> docker images
    REPOSITORY                                      TAG        IMAGE ID
    docker/welcome-to-docker                        latest     c1f619b6477e
    docker/getting-started                          latest     3e4394f6b72f
    mcr.microsoft.com/azuredocs/aci-helloworld      latest     7367f3256b41
    ```

    Figure 14.12: Listing all local Docker images

    This command lists all images on your local system and may be different from the preceding figure but very similar.

6. Now, you will list all running containers on your system using the following command: docker ps. Then, press *Enter*. You will notice the container you ran from earlier in the PowerShell window. Note the name and proceed by running the following command: docker stop [container name]. Then, press *Enter*. To confirm the container has been stopped, run docker ps, then press *Enter*. The process is shown in the following screenshot:

    ```
    pwsh> docker ps
    CONTAINER ID   IMAGE                    COMMAND                 CREATED          STATUS          PORTS                  NAMES
    c9a570a1843a   docker/getting-started   "/docker-entrypoint..."  42 minutes ago   Up 42 minutes   0.0.0.0:80->80/tcp    focused_chebyshev
    pwsh> docker stop focused_chebyshev
    focused_chebyshev
    pwsh> docker ps
    CONTAINER ID   IMAGE   COMMAND   CREATED   STATUS   PORTS   NAMES
    ```

    Figure 14.13: Using PowerShell to manage Docker containers

7. Now, you have downloaded the image to be used. The image will run on the local port 80 and expose port 80 for connecting back to the container. Note your image name from earlier. You can run the following command to confirm that you have downloaded the image:

    docker images

    The output of this command will be like the following screenshot, where you will notice the image that you wanted to download from *Step 4*:

    ```
    pwsh> docker images
    REPOSITORY                                      TAG
    docker/welcome-to-docker                        latest
    docker/getting-started                          latest
    mcr.microsoft.com/azuredocs/aci-helloworld      latest
    ```

    Figure 14.14: Listing Docker images

8. The command will be constructed as follows, after which you can run `docker ps` again:

   ```
   docker run -d -p 80:80 mcr.microsoft.com/azuredocs/
   aci-helloworld
   ```

   The following screenshot shows the output of the preceding command:

   ```
   pwsh> docker run -d -p 80:80 mcr.microsoft.com/azuredocs/aci-helloworld
   7d8154da130653c7e92608e2744ae198102                          31245d0f45393
   pwsh> docker ps
   CONTAINER ID    IMAGE                                            COMMAND
    NAMES
   7d8154da1306   mcr.microsoft.com/azuredocs/aci-helloworld   "/bin/sh -c
   ```

   Figure 14.15: Your second container

9. To access this container, launch your browser and navigate to the following URL: `http://127.0.0.1`. You will see a welcome message, as shown in *Figure 14.16*. This message denotes that the application is working:

   Figure 14.16: Running ACI

10. You will now push the image to your repository based on the repository name you gave earlier. First, tag your image for Docker to understand which image file to push. Run the following command in PowerShell and press *Enter*:

    ```
    docker tag mcr.microsoft.com/azuredocs/aci-helloworld [docker
    hub username]/myfirstrepo
    ```

11. Run `docker images` and note your newly tagged image, as shown in *Figure 14.17*:

    ```
    pwsh> docker images
    REPOSITORY                                        TAG
    docker/welcome-to-docker                          latest
    docker/getting-started                            latest
    mcr.microsoft.com/azuredocs/aci-helloworld        latest
              someuser/myfirstrepo                    latest
    ```

    Figure 14.17: Tagging a Docker image

12. Now, log in to Docker using the `docker login` command. You will now push an image to your Docker repository. The easiest way to push the image is to follow the `push` command on the page where you created your repository earlier:

    ```
    docker push [docker hub username]/myfirstrepo
    ```

13. The command on the web page will look like the following figure, but in your own repository, `someuser` will be replaced with your name:

Figure 14.18: The docker push command

Notice that when you push without a tag, the **latest** tag is automatically assigned.

You have now successfully pulled and pushed an image from and to Docker Hub. In the next section, you will explore deploying an Azure container instance and using Azure as the host instead of Docker for your images.

Azure Kubernetes Services

Kubernetes is designed as a management and orchestration service to assist with managing containers and creating a mechanism for scale. AKS is a serverless implementation of the Kubernetes service and minimizes the management of the Kubernetes cluster for you. The service is designed so that you only take care of the agent nodes. Azure builds upon Kubernetes by enhancing some of its default implementations to enable functions, such as the following:

- **Identity and Access Management (IAM)**: Identity is integrated into **Microsoft Entra ID**, making the sign-on experience more seamless and easier to integrate. Management through Entra ID roles can also be done either with user accounts or the system identity.

- **Integrated logging and monitoring**: You can monitor your containers through native Azure tools through the Azure Monitor service and view data relating to the health and performance of your containers.

- **Clusters and nodes**: AKS creates new abilities such as creating accessibility in your AKS clusters for running mixed OSs and integrating GPUs.

- **Azure VNet integration**: Enable private networking natively to Azure networks, **network security groups (NSGs)**, and even network policies. You can also configure SSL termination when integrating with Azure Key Vault.

- **Persistent storage**: Azure overcomes the ephemeral-based storage native to containers by enabling easy integration of persistent storage mechanisms such as Azure file shares.

- **Autoscaling**: This function enables the autoscaling of Pods and clusters.
- **Image support**: AKS enables multiple image repositories such as the Docker Hub repository or Azure Container Registry for private repository storage of your images.

AKS also offers health monitoring and the coordination of upgrades. As part of the service, master nodes are not billed for and are included for free, but all agent nodes are billed for. The service constitutes master nodes, node pools, Pods, networks, and storage. It's important to grasp how all these components function together as well as what they are.

The AKS components are as follows:

- **Control plane**: The control plane component of the service contains all the functions that allow you to administer your containers within AKS, as well as the master node, which is the orchestrator service within AKS
- **Node pools**: Node pools are essentially your VM infrastructure and are used to provide resources for your Pods and, by association, containers for the service
- **Pods**: Pods are your collections of containers within AKS where containers are grouped into their respective functions or applications

Figure 14.19 illustrates the relationship between the various components showing the control plane being a core segment of the AKS cluster that is used for managing the master node and containers. You can also see the Pods above the node pools, indicating that they consume resources from the node pool:

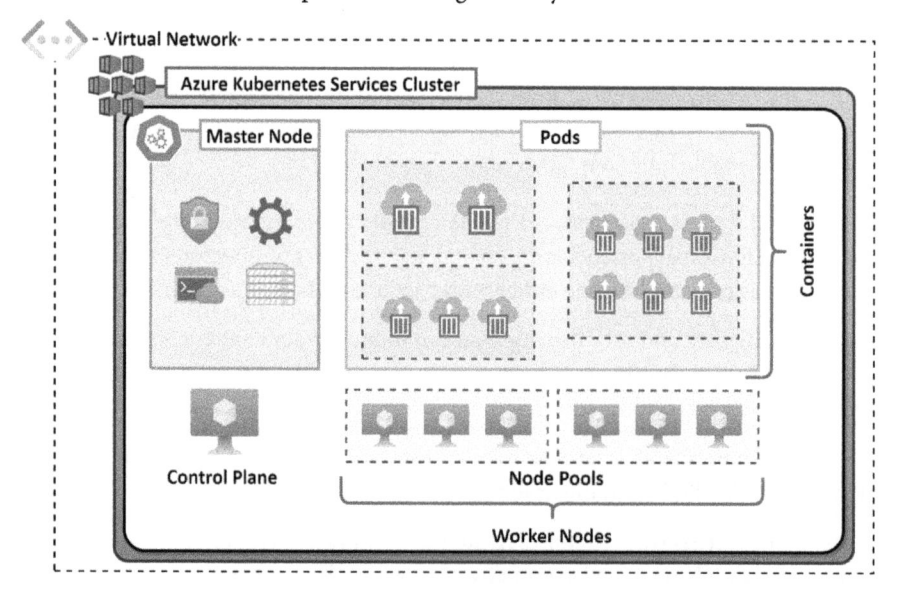

Figure 14.19: AKS structure

Now that you are more familiar with containers and the orchestration tools that you can use, such as AKS, you will dive into some exercises to give you some hands-on experience of working with these services.

Upgrading an AKS Cluster

You can either automatically upgrade your AKS clusters or manually manage upgrades yourself. As part of your upgrade decisions, you can decide whether you would like to upgrade both the node pools and control plane or the control plane only. Automatic upgrades allow you to choose different channels that best match your requirements. These are listed as follows:

- **None**: Used for disabling auto upgrading.
- **Patch**: The cluster is automatically updated to the latest support patch version.
- **Stable**: The cluster is automatically updated to the latest stable version.
- **Rapid**: The cluster is automatically updated to the latest N-2 minor version.
- **Node-image**: The cluster is automatically updated to the latest version available. This does not automatically upgrade the Kubernetes version, though.

> **Note**
> Note that when upgrading your AKS clusters, you will upgrade to a supported patch version for your cluster and one version at a time where more than one version upgrade exists.

Node Security Channel Types

Node security channel types for AKS refer to the mechanisms for automatically updating and securing the OS of nodes to ensure they have the latest security patches and updates. The following options can be chosen for this configuration and are related to the timing of the upgrades to be performed:

- **None**: Updates are your responsibility and will need to be manually applied.
- **Unmanaged**: Your nodes receive updates through the OS built-in patching solution only. Be aware that your nodes will initially not have OS updates applied as a result.
- **Node Image**: Updates are applied weekly with a patched **Virtual Hard Disk** (**VHD**) preconfigured with all the fixes for bugs and other security issues to be applied. This option is disruptive, meaning that the node will restart and be offline for the duration of the update.
- **Security Patch**: At the time of writing, this option is in preview and has to be enabled through a feature flag before it can be used. It also has additional costs associated with it, such as incurring costs on the VHD image, while the **Node Image** option does not. This option enables updates labeled as security-only updates. Like the **Node Image** option, it can be disruptive.

Authentication and Authorization

When considering authentication and authorization, it is first important to understand the difference between these concepts. Authentication is the act of verifying a user (principal) and authorization is the process of evaluating what the user (principal) has access to.

Kubernetes has three configurations related to authentication and authorization that you can select from; the different configurations are discussed in more detail and are based on the responsible service in each configuration for authentication and authorization:

- **Local accounts with Kubernetes Role-Based Access Control (RBAC)**: This is the default option when building AKS clusters on Azure. These are basic accounts created within the Kubernetes cluster. Kubernetes provides a method of managing access control through internal RBAC within the cluster and access is based on the user identity. Authentication and authorization are conducted through Kubernetes.

- **Azure AD authentication with Kubernetes RBAC**: This option leverages Entra ID for identity within the Kubernetes cluster. The label will likely change to reflect Entra ID in the coming months. This option uses Entra ID for authentication and Kubernetes RBAC for authorization.

- **Azure AD authentication with Azure RBAC**: The final option uses Entra ID for both authentication and authorization. Entra ID role assignments will be used for authorization. This is the preferred method for authentication and authorization. The label for Azure AD will change to Entra ID in the coming months of launching this book.

You now know about the various authentication and authorization options available to AKS, and how to choose the one to meet your requirements. In the next section, you will explore the various networking components and services available to you for use on your containers through AKS.

AKS Networking Options

Configuring the networking options for AKS can feel overwhelming at first due to the breadth of understanding required for a holistic implementation. It is important to have a thorough understanding of all the options available to you and the configurations for each one to know when and how to use features. The options are discussed next.

Private Access

There is only one option for private access achievable directly through AKS, which is to enable a private cluster. A private cluster restricts all access for your worker nodes to API-level access and blocks inbound connections from outside of your AKS cluster network, enhancing isolation and security for your environment. While enabling a private cluster is the primary method for achieving private access in AKS, you can further enhance privacy by leveraging the extensibility of the Azure platform through its integrations with AKS, incorporating NSGs, Azure Firewall, private endpoints, **Virtual Private Network** (**VPN**), ExpressRoute connections, and jump box connections.

Public Access

This option is similar to a private configuration, but it allows specific IP ranges to access the API server. By restricting access to a limited set of IP ranges, security can be enhanced over public networks, which reduces the potential for unauthorized access and compromise. This approach provides a balance between accessibility and security, ensuring that only trusted IP addresses can interact with your AKS cluster's API server.

The following components are used in conjunction with the public access configuration to enhance security over public networks:

- **IP whitelisting**: This specifies which IP ranges are allowed to access the API server, which helps in controlling and monitoring access.
- **Azure Firewall and NSGs**: These can be used in conjunction with IP whitelisting to further refine and secure access to your AKS cluster.
- **Use cases**: Clearly define the use cases for which you intend your application to be consumed. Use them to maintain a high level of security in your AKS deployment by catering to the required specific use cases.
- **Monitoring and logging**: Monitoring and logging can assist in tracking access attempts and detecting any suspicious activity, which provides an additional layer of security. This results in improved security over public networks by limiting the potential for compromise by restricting to limited IP ranges.

Network Configuration

There are two options for your AKS environment when selecting the network configuration for your containers:

- **kubenet**: A VNet for the cluster whereby Pods are allocated an IP address, and containers have **network address translation** (**NAT**) connections over the shared Pod IP. This is the most basic networking service for AKS. With kubenet, an IP address is allocated from an Azure VNet to the nodes for a Pod. The Pods receive an IP address from an internal network that is deployed in a logically different address space from the VNet. Connections to these Pods are then performed through NAT connections that allow Pods to communicate to resources on the Azure VNet. This approach reduces the number of IP addresses required for your solution but disables the ability to directly connect to your containers.

- **Azure Container Networking Interface (Azure CNI):** Enables Pods to be directly connected to a VNet. In association, this allows containers to have an IP mapped to them directly, removing the need for a NAT connection. This is a more advanced implementation networking service for AKS. However, without careful planning, you may exhaust your IP allocation on the subnet you are connecting to. Typically, you need to rebuild your AKS cluster in a bigger subnet to remediate this problem, which is not ideal. However, Azure CNI solves this problem through dynamic IP allocation, as this feature allows the Azure CNI service to allocate Pod IPs from a different subnet to the one hosting the AKS cluster.

Regardless of the solution you choose, external traffic is still conducted over a NAT connection to nodes within AKS from a public IP interface. You also have the option to connect your own VNet when setting up the AKS networking using one of your existing Azure VNets.

Network Policy

This is used to manage traffic flow between Pods in an AKS cluster. By default, all traffic is allowed, and by utilizing a network policy, you enable the mechanism to manage this traffic using **Linux IPTables** or Linux **Berkeley Packet Filter (BPF)**. This is done by configuring the AKS cluster with a network policy enabled at creation time. Two implementations for IPTables can be followed: **Calico** and **Azure network policies**. Calico is an open source solution provided by Tigera, whereas Azure has its own implementation of the same type of technology. Both services are fully compliant with the Kubernetes specification. **Cilium**, on the other hand, only supports Linux and enforces traffic to use the BPF technology, which is considered more efficient than IPTables. Cilium is also the preferred network policy engine according to Microsoft. The choice of network policy provider can only be chosen during the creation of the AKS cluster and can't be changed thereafter. Therefore, it is pivotal that you understand the differences between the solutions before making your choice.

The key differences between the solutions are presented in *Table 14.1*:

Supported Platforms	• Calico supports both Linux and Windows Server 2019 and 2022 • Azure network policy supports Linux and Windows Server 2022 (in preview) • Cilium supports Linux only
Supported Networking Options	• Calico supports Azure CNI and kubenet • Azure network policy supports Azure CNI only • Cilium supports Azure CNI only
Support Options	• All network policy engines are supported by Azure engineering and support
Kubernetes Specification Compliance	• All network policy engines support all the policy types for Kubernetes

Table 14.1: Features by network policy engine

Traffic Routing

Traffic routing refers to the concept of managing how traffic flows to and from your applications running in your Kubernetes cluster. Traffic routing comprises the load balancing and application routing configurations available to your AKS cluster. You will learn more about these configurations next.

Load Balancer

Load balancing refers to the concept of distributing traffic across multiple endpoints to prevent any single endpoint from becoming overwhelmed with incoming traffic. It also enables continuity of services as it exposes a single frontend endpoint that services the backend endpoints you are connecting to. Should any of the backend endpoints go down, the connecting user would be none the wiser as the next endpoint would continue communication flows, and there is no perceived loss of service to the end user. The AKS cluster can be deployed using both a **Standard SKU** and a **Basic SKU** load balancer. A Standard SKU enforces traffic securely, restricts traffic by default, and requires explicit allow rules to enable traffic flow. The default option is **Standard** and is the recommended choice unless there is a specific reason for **Basic**, such as your organization only allowing private IP access. The Basic SKU can be deployed using the Azure **command-line interface** (**CLI**), PowerShell, or an ARM template.

Application Routing

Application routing is the process of directing incoming network traffic to the appropriate application or service using an ingress controller to your applications based on predefined rules. The solution deploys two components, one being an **ExternalDNS controller** component, which creates DNS host A records for the cluster DNS zone, and the second resource being an **ingress controller** component, which is responsible for routing ingress traffic to application endpoints.

More about this aspect can be found here: https://learn.microsoft.com/en-us/azure/aks/app-routing?tabs=default%2Cdeploy-app-default.

You now understand the core network concepts related to AKS, how to configure private and public access, and how to leverage network policy. You have also learned how to control traffic routing for your AKS applications. Next, you will explore the topic of security within AKS.

AKS Security

When configuring your network for AKS, you should consider the security components that also impact your design and management decisions. There are a couple of aspects to consider that can improve the security of your containers:

- **Enabling a private cluster**: For enhanced security, you can enable a private cluster. This ensures that traffic between your **application programming interface** (**API**) server and node pools is conducted over private network paths only. When configured, the control plane (API server) runs within the AKS-managed Azure subscription while your AKS cluster runs in your own subscription. This separation is key. Communication will then occur over a private endpoint (private link) from your AKS cluster to the private link service for the AKS VNet.

- **Setting authorized IP ranges**: Authorized IP ranges are ranges that you use to access your AKS cluster. This can be specified as a single IP, a list of IP addresses, or a range of IP addresses in **classless inter-domain routing (CIDR)** notation.

You have completed the theoretical component of containers, exploring what they are, their use cases, and how they differ from VMs. You have also learned about Docker, an engine for running containers and creating images. You have explored the various solutions available to Azure for running containers and learned about the AKS orchestration tool and its various components and configurations. In the next section, you will gain hands-on experience in working with a container registry, which is used for storing your container images.

Creating an Azure Container Registry

In this exercise, you are going to create a registry in Azure Container Registry. As mentioned previously, this is very similar to Docker Hub but is native to Azure. Follow these steps:

1. Sign in to the Azure portal at `https://portal.azure.com`.
2. Open or create the resource group you will be using for this exercise; you can use `AZ104-Containers`. Click `Overview` on the left menu, then click `Create`.
3. In the top search bar, type `container registry`, and click the `Container Registry` option that appears. Then, click `Create`, as shown in *Figure 14.20*:

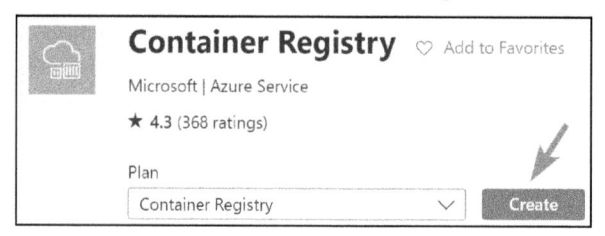

Figure 14.20: Creating a container registry

4. Give it a unique `Registry name` and select the appropriate `Location` entry. Leave the `Pricing plan` value as `Standard` for this exercise. Click `Review + create`. The configurations are shown in the following screenshot:

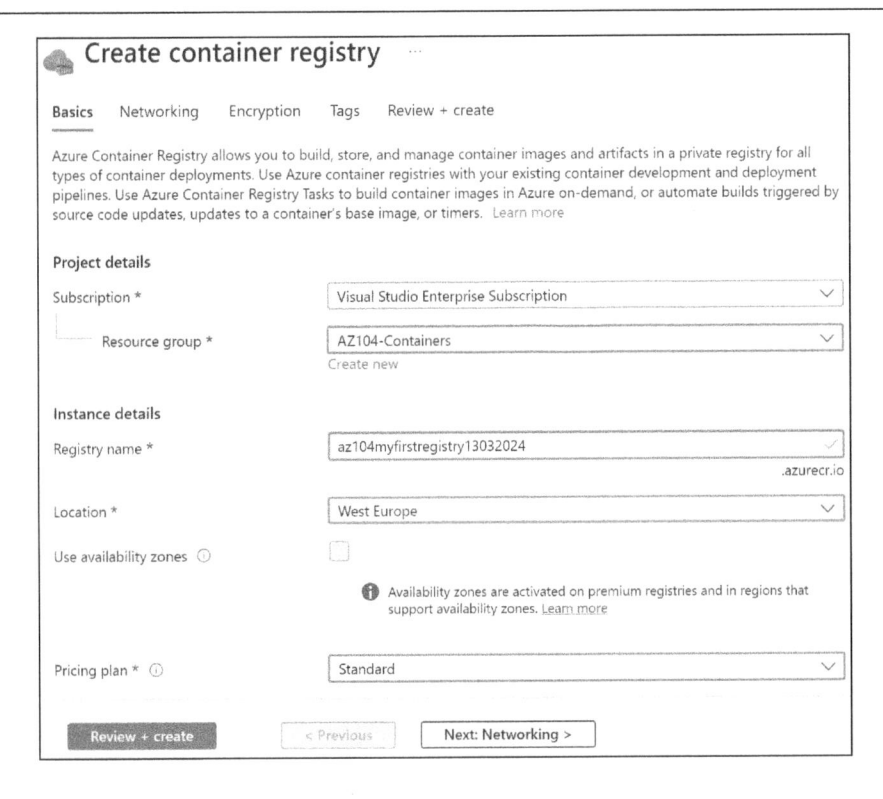

Figure 14.21: Creating an Azure container registry

5. Next, click `Create`.
6. After the deployment has succeeded, navigate to the resource. Click on `Access keys` on the left-hand menu under the `Settings` context. Then, on the right screen, click the checkbox next to `Admin user`, and note your username and password. This will enable you to connect to the registry using Docker. The process is shown in the following screenshot:

Registry name	az104myfirstregistry13032024	
Login server	az104myfirstregistry13032024.azurecr.io	
Admin user ⓘ	✓	
Username	az104myfirstregistry13032024	
Name	Password	Regenerate
password	somepassword	↻
password2	somepassword	↻

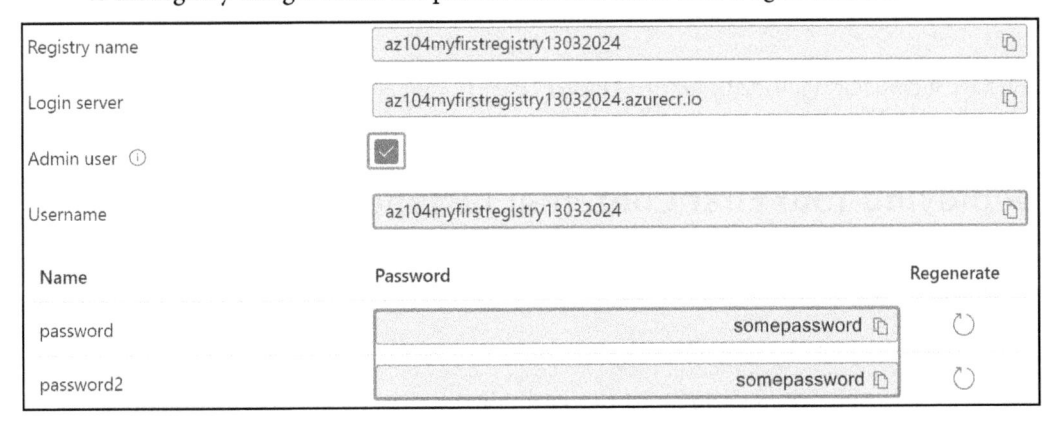

Figure 14.22: Container registry access keys

7. In PowerShell, type the following command and press *Enter*:

   ```
   docker login [yourregistryname].azurecr.io
   ```

   For your username and password, enter the username and password you just copied from the portal, as shown in the following screenshot:

   ```
   pwsh> docker login az104myfirstregistry13032024.azurecr.io
   Username: az104myfirstregistry13032024
   Password:

   Login Succeeded
   ```

   Figure 14.23: The docker login command

8. You will now tag the image you used previously for your container registry using the following command:

   ```
   docker tag mcr.microsoft.com/azuredocs/aci-helloworld [your registry name].azurecr.io/myimages/containerdemo:latest
   ```

9. You will then run the following `push` command to push your container to the registry:

   ```
   docker push [your registry name].azurecr.io/myimages/containerdemo:latest
   ```

10. In the Azure portal, if you navigate to `Repositories` on the menu on the left, you will now notice that your image has been uploaded to the registry, as shown in the following screenshot:

Repositories ↑↓	Cache Rule
myimages/containerdemo	

    Figure 14.24: Listing Azure container images

You have successfully uploaded your first Docker image to your container registry. Now that you have the basics under your belt, you will explore deploying your first container instance in the next section.

Deploying Your First Container Instance

For this exercise, you will create a container group and then deploy a container instance to the group with the following steps:

1. Sign in to the Azure portal at `https://portal.azure.com`.
2. Open the resource group you will be using for this exercise, click `Overview` on the left menu, then click `Create`.

3. From the menu bar on the left, scroll down and click `Containers`, then click `Container Instances` from the right screen options that display. If you are not seeing this, you can also search for container instances. Click `Create`.

4. Select your resource group. Enter the following container details and click `Next: Networking >`:

   - `Container name`: Enter any name that is limited to 63 characters
   - `Region`: Select any region from the drop-down menu
   - `Availability zones`: None
   - SKU: Standard
   - `Image source`: Azure Container Registry – notice that you can connect to other registry types too
   - `Registry`: az104myfirstregistry13032024 – select the registry you created in the previous exercise.
   - `Image`: myimages/containerdemo
   - `Image tag`: latest
   - `Size`: Leave the default value

Container details	
Container name *	myfirstcontainerinstance
Region *	(Europe) West Europe
Availability zones (Preview)	None
SKU	Standard
Image source *	○ Quickstart images ◉ Azure Container Registry ○ Other registry
Run with Azure Spot discount	☐
Registry *	az104myfirstregistry13032024
	ⓘ If you do not see your Azure Container Registry, ensure you have been assigned the Reader Role for the Azure Container Registry or select an Azure Container Registry in a different subscription. Learn more
Image *	myimages/containerdemo
Image tag *	latest
OS type	Linux
Size *	1 vcpu, 1.5 GiB memory, 0 gpus Change size

Figure 14.25: Creating a container instance

5. For this exercise, select `Public` as your `Networking type` value, and create a unique `DNS name label` value for your container, then leave the `Ports` configuration as it is. Just note that you are exposing port `80` (HTTP) traffic to the internet for access to this container. Click `Next: Advanced >`. The process is shown in the following screenshot:

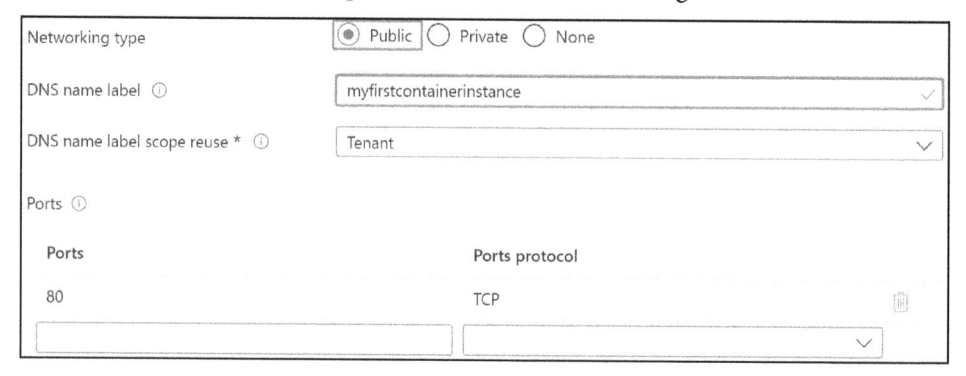

Figure 14.26: Container instance – networking

6. On the `Advanced` tab, configure the `Restart policy` field for your container. Leave the default option, which should be `On failure`. You could configure `Environment variables` values if you choose. Click `Review + create`.

7. Click `Create`.

8. Once your resource has been deployed, connect to it on the DNS name label you configured previously.

Now, you know how to deploy a container instance within Azure and are ready to start your journey on containers. In the next exercise, you will explore creating your first container group.

Configuring Container Groups for ACI

For this exercise, you are going to configure an Azure container group using an ARM template and Azure Cloud Shell using the following steps:

1. Sign in to the Azure portal at `https://portal.azure.com`.

2. From the top menu bar, click the `Cloud Shell` icon, as shown in the following screenshot:

Figure 14.27: Azure management icons

3. Type `code azuredeploy.json` and press *Enter*. For better readability of your shell, you may resize the screen, as shown, by using the highlighted button in the following screenshot:

Configuring Container Groups for ACI | 457

[Figure 14.28: Azure Cloud Shell]

4. Alternatively, you could also select the `Open a new session` icon, which will open a shell in a new browser tab. You can see the icon for this in the following screenshot:

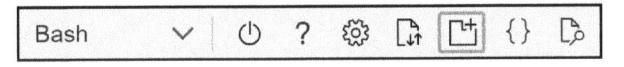

Figure 14.29: Azure Cloud Shell – new session

5. The following code snippet contains the ARM template code for deploying your container instances. The script is long and, therefore, has been split up into sections to explain what the ARM code does. To use the following script, you can download the complete template from the GitHub repo for this book: `https://packt.link/4Fy46`.

Use the `AzureContainerGroup.json` file, which contains the text in the figures that follow, to copy the contents:

```
{
  "$schema": "https://schema.management.azure.com/schemas/2019-04-01/deploymentTemplate.json#",
  "contentVersion": "1.0.0.0",
  "parameters": {
    "containerGroupName": {
      "type": "string",
      "defaultValue": "myfirstcontainergroup",
      "metadata": {
        "description": "My First Container Group"
      }
    }
  },
  "variables": {
    "container1name": "aci-tutorial-app",
    "container1image": "mcr.microsoft.com/azuredocs/aci-helloworld:latest",
    "container2name": "aci-tutorial-sidecar",
    "container2image": "mcr.microsoft.com/azuredocs/aci-tutorial-sidecar"
  },
```

Figure 14.30: Container group ARM – part 1

6. The following is the continuation of the preceding ARM code that contains the resources and output sections:

```json
"resources": [
  {
    "name": "[parameters('containerGroupName')]",
    "type": "Microsoft.ContainerInstance/containerGroups",
    "apiVersion": "2019-12-01",
    "location": "[resourceGroup().location]",
    "properties": {
      "containers": [
        {
          "name": "[variables('container1name')]",
          "properties": {
            "image": "[variables('container1image')]",
            "resources": {
              "requests": {
                "cpu": 1,
                "memoryInGb": 1.5
              }
            },
            "ports": [
              {
                "port": 80
              },
              {
                "port": 8080
              }
            ]
          }
        },
        {
          "name": "[variables('container2name')]",
          "properties": {
            "image": "[variables('container2image')]",
            "resources": {
              "requests": {
                "cpu": 1,
                "memoryInGb": 1.5
              }
            }
          }
        }
      ],
      "osType": "Linux",
      "ipAddress": {
        "type": "Public",
        "ports": [
          {
            "protocol": "tcp",
            "port": 80
          },
          {
            "protocol": "tcp",
            "port": 8080
          }
        ]
      }
    }
  }
```

(Resources)

Figure 14.31: Container group ARM – part 2

7. Paste the ARM template code into the code editor screen.
8. After pasting into the code screen, you can press *Ctrl + S* or right-click and click Save. Then, right-click the screen again and click Quit:

Figure 14.32: Azure Cloud Shell – Visual Studio Code (VS Code)

9. Now, type in the following code to deploy the ARM template and press *Enter*:

```
az deployment group create --resource-group AZ104-Containers
--template-file azuredeploy.json
```

10. Once your deployment is complete, close the Cloud Shell window by clicking the cross on the top-right bar.
11. Navigate to the resource group where you deployed your container group. Open the container group resource by clicking on it. On the Overview pane, note the public IP address and that you have two containers. Copy the IP address to your browser, and connect to the site served by your container group:

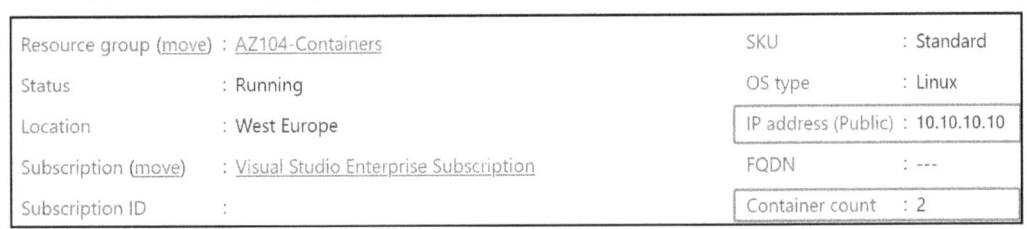

Resource group (move)	: AZ104-Containers	SKU	: Standard
Status	: Running	OS type	: Linux
Location	: West Europe	IP address (Public)	: 10.10.10.10
Subscription (move)	: Visual Studio Enterprise Subscription	FQDN	: ---
Subscription ID	:	Container count	: 2

Figure 14.33: Container group public IP

12. Back in the Azure portal, click on the `Containers` menu option on the pane on the left and note your two containers are deployed to the container group, as shown in the following screenshot:

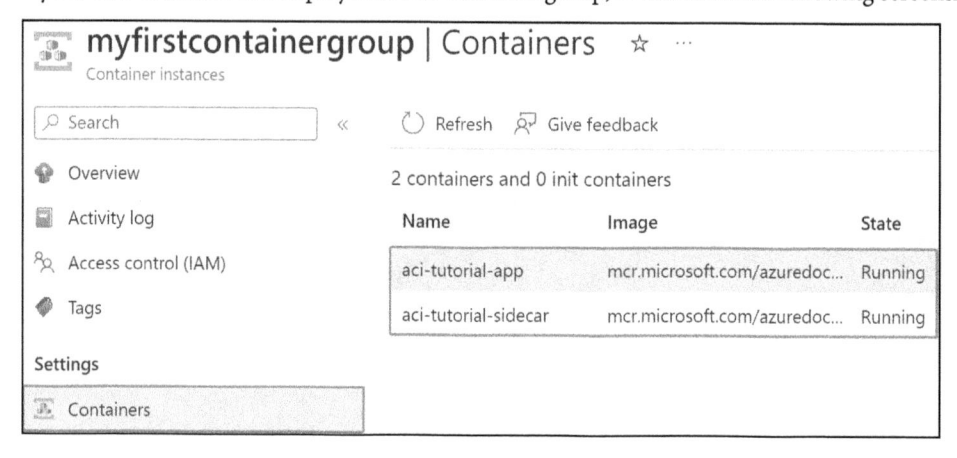

Figure 14.34: myfirstcontainergroup – Containers

You have just successfully deployed your first container group in Azure. In the next section, you will explore how to manage the sizing and scaling of your deployed container instances.

Configuring Sizing and Scaling for ACI

Azure container instances cannot be resized after deployment; you will notice there are no options to do so in the Azure portal. The only way to resize a container instance is to redeploy the solution as per the required size. If you are looking to scale horizontally (multiple instances), you can achieve this through the container group or by deploying several instances. To configure sizing for your container instance, you will recall that on the instance setup, there is a `Change size` option, as shown in the following screenshot:

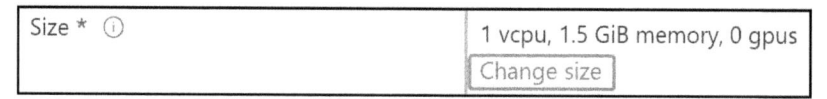

Figure 14.35: ACI – Size

The following screen will pop up for you to configure the desired size for your container instance:

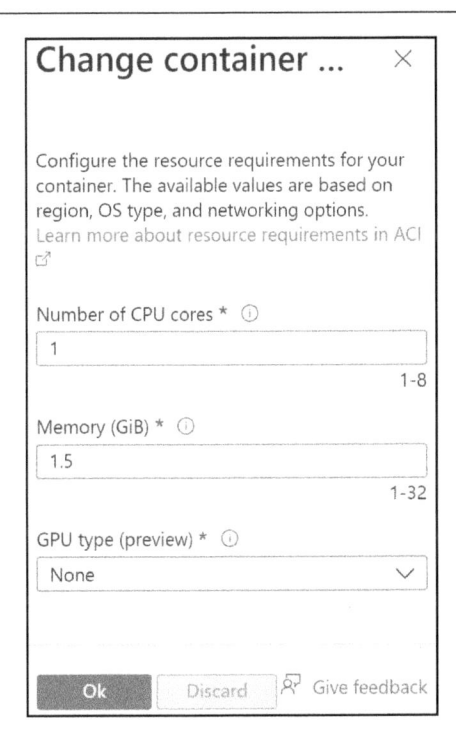

Figure 14.36: ACI – size options

Follow these steps to deploy a new container instance to experience changing sizes:

1. Create a new container instance. When you get to `Size`, click `Change size`.
2. Enter the following details:

   - `Number of CPU cores`: 3
   - `Memory`: 2 GiB
   - `GPU type`: V100
   - `GPU count`: 1

   Note that GPUs are only available to some regions, and at the time of writing, this is still a preview feature. Only the `V100` option is available. The GPU selected enables further options for selecting the number of GPUs you would like from 1, 2, or 4, as shown in the following screenshot:

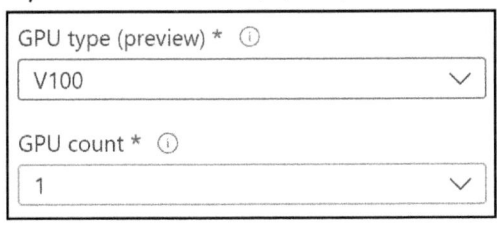

Figure 14.37: ACI – GPU options

> **Note**
>
> 1 **gibibyte (GiB)** = 1,024 **mebibytes (MiB)**, and 1 GB = 1,000 **megabytes (MB)**. Most people refer to MB or GB, and due to easy conversions and the internet industry, the conversion is often defined as 1,000 MB in 1 GB. Computers work on a binary number system, meaning that all numbers are calculated from a base of 2. Therefore, 1 GiB is defined as 2^10 MiB, which is 1,024.

You now know about the sizing available for container instances, so in the next section, you will explore how Kubernetes can assist in the management of your containers.

Deploying AKS

This exercise will help you gain familiarity with AKS. You will deploy your first AKS instance, and then with the corresponding exercises, you will explore the different management components for your instance. Proceed as follows:

1. Sign in to the Azure portal at `https://portal.azure.com`.
2. Open the resource group you will be using for this exercise, click `Overview` on the left menu, then click `Create` from the top menu.
3. Search for `Azure Kubernetes Service` and click the card. Click `Create` on the screen that follows:

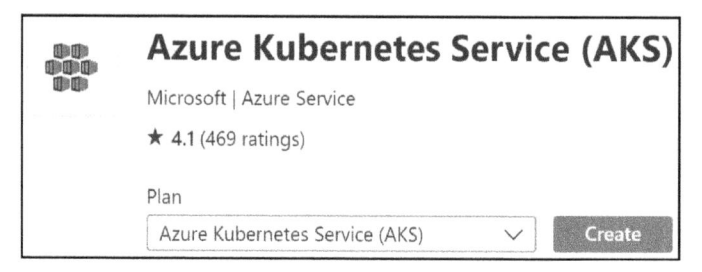

Figure 14.38: Creating an AKS service

4. Select your resource group.
5. Enter the following cluster detail items:
   - `Kubernetes cluster name:` `myfirstakscluster`.
   - `Region:` Select any region.
   - `Availability zones:` `None`.
   - `AKS pricing tier:` `Standard`.

- **Kubernetes version**: Select the `default` version (`1.27.9` at the time of writing).
- **Automatic upgrade**: `Disabled`.
- **Node security channel type**: `None`.
- **Authentication and Authorization**: `Azure AD authentication with Azure RBAC`. This will be used by AKS for managing the infrastructure related to the service. Selecting this will enable you to manage permissions for users on the service based on their group membership within Microsoft Entra ID. Note that the Azure AD naming should change to Entra ID.

6. Click **Next**. The configuration is shown in the following screenshot:

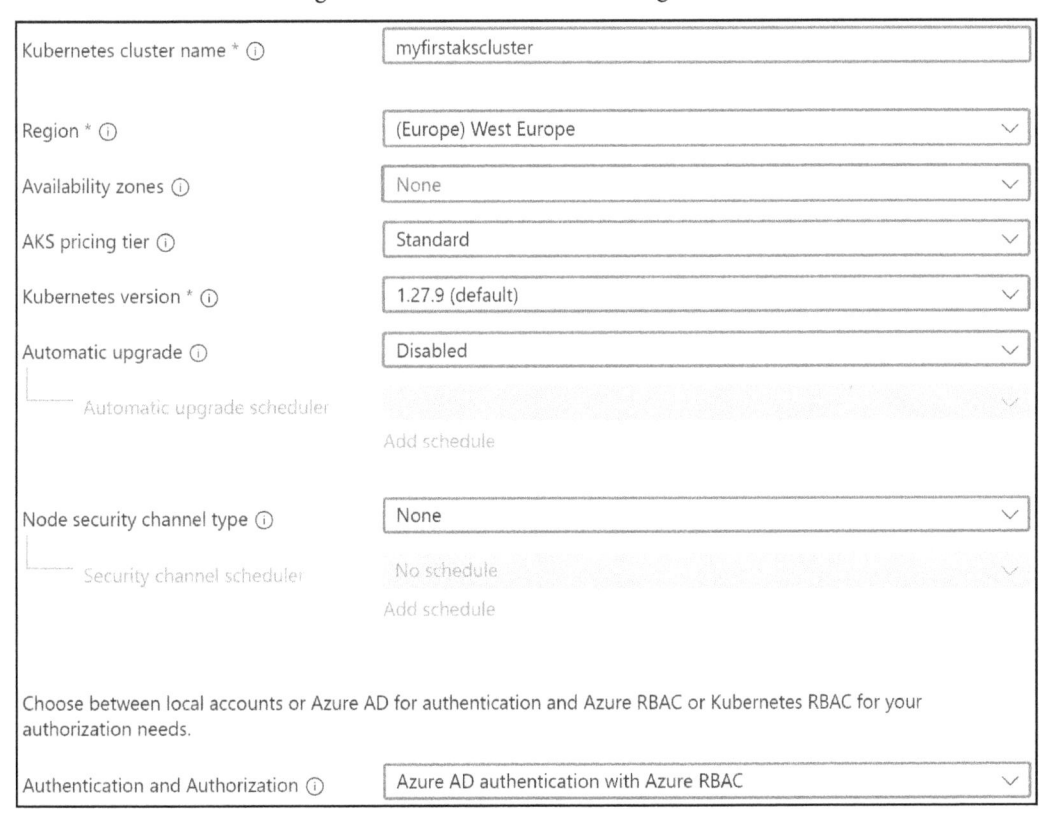

Figure 14.39: Creating a Kubernetes cluster

7. You will notice a `node pools` section that should contain a preconfigured pool for you, the `agent pool`. Click the name of the pool and it will take you to an additional configuration screen. You will be presented with configurations for `Node pool name`, `Mode`, `OS SKU`, `Node size`, and so on. Scroll down the page and note that you can configure scaling; you can select the **scale method**, which can be either **Manual** or **Autoscale**. **Manual** means that you would like to modify the scale count yourself whenever you would like to change the count of nodes for your pool, whereas **Autoscale** will allow you to scale automatically based on a scaling rule. When configuring **Autoscale**, you can select a minimum and maximum node count that the autoscaling function can scale between. As you can see, there is a lot of room for scaling with this service. Click either `Update` or `Cancel` to close the screen:

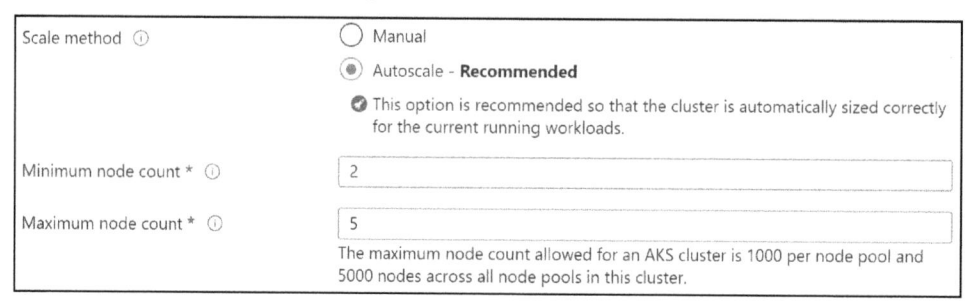

Figure 14.40: Updating a node pool

8. On the `Node pools` tab, you will note you can add additional pools that can also be configured to scale in the same fashion as the existing pools. You also have the `Enable virtual nodes` option, which enables you to scale your containers beyond your VM specified in the previous steps and scale to use ACI as additional nodes when AKS needs to scale out. The last option on this tab is the configuration of `Node pool OS disk encryption`. Leave all options as their default values. Click `Next`.

9. For the `Networking` section, leave most of the settings as their default configuration. Select the following configurations and click `Next`:

   - `Network configuration: Kubenet`
   - `DNS name prefix: myfirstakscluster-dns` (you will need to change this to an available DNS prefix)
   - `Network policy: Calico`

Deploying AKS | 465

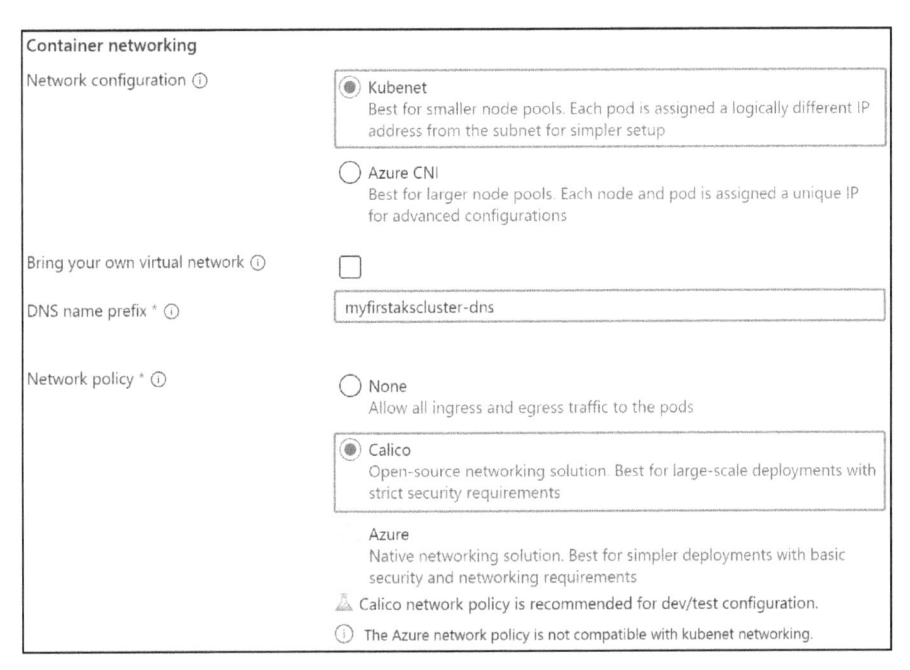

Container networking	
Network configuration ⓘ	● Kubenet Best for smaller node pools. Each pod is assigned a logically different IP address from the subnet for simpler setup ○ Azure CNI Best for larger node pools. Each node and pod is assigned a unique IP for advanced configurations
Bring your own virtual network ⓘ	☐
DNS name prefix * ⓘ	myfirstakscluster-dns
Network policy * ⓘ	○ None Allow all ingress and egress traffic to the pods ● Calico Open-source networking solution. Best for large-scale deployments with strict security requirements Azure Native networking solution. Best for simpler deployments with basic security and networking requirements ⚠ Calico network policy is recommended for dev/test configuration. ⓘ The Azure network policy is not compatible with kubenet networking.

Figure 14.41: Creating a Kubernetes cluster – the Networking tab

10. On the `Integrations` tab, note the option to select a container registry. Select the registry that you previously deployed. Note that you have the option to deploy a new registry directly from this creation dialog. Leave all other settings as default and click `Next`:

Azure Container Registry	
Connect your cluster to an Azure Container Registry to enable seamless deployments from a private image registry. Learn more ⧉	
Container registry	az104myfirstregistry13032024 ⌄ Create new

Figure 14.42: Selecting an Azure Container Registry

11. You will notice several options for monitoring your containers and a quick setting for enabling alerts. Observe all the options and click `Review + create`.
12. Click `Create`.

You have just successfully deployed your first Kubernetes cluster and you now know how to deploy and manage containers at scale in a standardized manner. Next, you will learn how to configure persistent storage for Kubernetes.

Configuring Storage for AKS

AKS enables different storage options for containers. You can leverage either local (non-persistent) storage or shared storage (persistent storage) for your containers through AKS. For persistent storage options, you can leverage Azure managed disks, which primarily focus on premium storage solutions, such as for fast **input/output** (**I/O**) operations, as you learned in *Chapter 6, Understanding Storage Accounts*. Azure file shares is another option and is the default storage mechanism for enabling persistent storage on containers. These are typically cheaper to deploy and provide decent levels of performance for most workloads. For better performance, premium file shares can be used. Azure file shares are also great for sharing data between containers and other services, whereas a managed disk is restricted to a single Pod but is easier to deploy. Another new option is Azure Blob storage.

The following diagram illustrates the different storage options available:

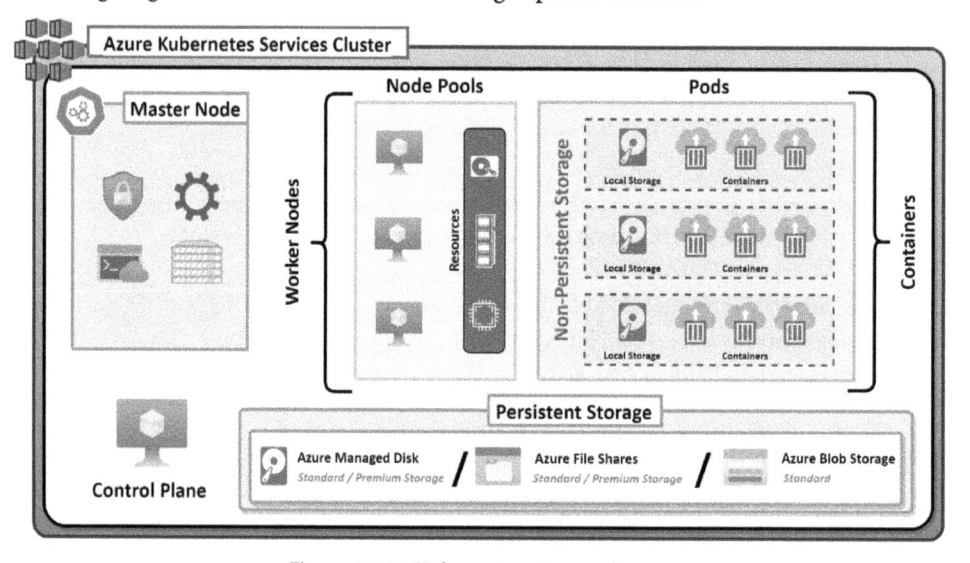

Figure 14.43: Kubernetes storage layers

In this exercise, you will configure shared storage using Azure file shares in your AKS cluster. Proceed as follows:

1. Sign in to the Azure portal at `https://portal.azure.com`.
2. Create a storage account and a file share named `fileshare01`. Once they have been created, note the primary storage account key.
3. Launch Azure Cloud Shell, change the environment to PowerShell from Bash, and run the following commands. Replace the resource group name with your resource group name and the AKS cluster name for the Name field. If it prompts you to import the Kubernetes config, enter y:

   ```
   Import-AzAksCredential -ResourceGroupName AZ104-Containers -Name myfirstakscluster
   ```

4. Modify the following script with your storage account name and storage account key, then paste or type it into Cloud Shell and press *Enter*:

   ```
   kubectl create secret generic azure-secret --from-literal=azures
   torageaccountname=storageaccountname --from-literal=azurestorage
   accountkey=storageaccountkey
   ```

5. You will be prompted to sign in on a web browser with a code presented on the screen for authentication. Complete this.

6. Navigate to the AKS cluster you created in the previous section. Click on `Storage` from the left menu, then ensure you are on the `Persistent volume claims` tab, as shown in the following screenshot:

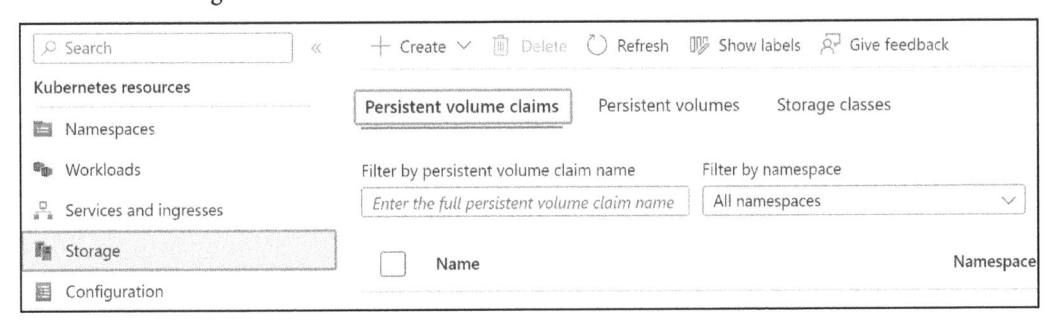

Figure 14.44: Adding a persistent volume claim

7. Click `Create` and then click `Apply a YAML`, as shown here:

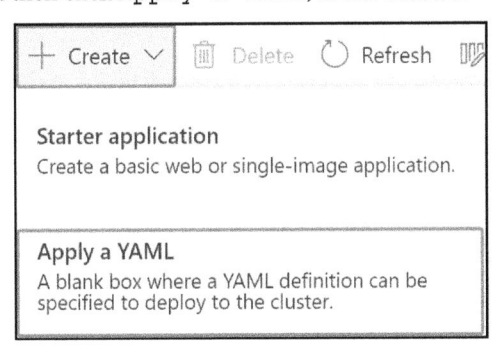

Figure 14.45: Apply a YAML

8. Open AKS - Storage - YAML.yaml file from the GitHub repo: https://packt.link/TbEYG. Then, paste or type the YAML contents into the window:

```yaml
apiVersion: v1
kind: PersistentVolume
metadata:
  name: azurefile
spec:
  capacity:
    storage: 5Gi
  accessModes:
    - ReadWriteMany
  azureFile:
    secretName: azure-secret
    shareName: fileshare01
    readOnly: false
  mountOptions:
  - dir_mode=0777
  - file_mode=0777
  - uid=1000
  - gid=1000
  - mfsymlinks
  - nobrl
```

9. Click Add.
10. Click `Create` and `Apply a YAML` again.
11. Open AKS - PersistentVolumeClaim.yaml file from the GitHub repo: https://packt.link/ifww5. Then, paste or type the YAML contents into the window. Click Add to create a persistent volume claim.

```yaml
apiVersion: v1
kind: PersistentVolumeClaim
metadata:
  name: azurefile
spec:
  accessModes:
    - ReadWriteMany
  storageClassName: ""
  resources:
    requests:
      storage: 5Gi
```

12. You now have a persistent volume claim. Click on the `Persistent volume claims` tab, as shown in the following screenshot:

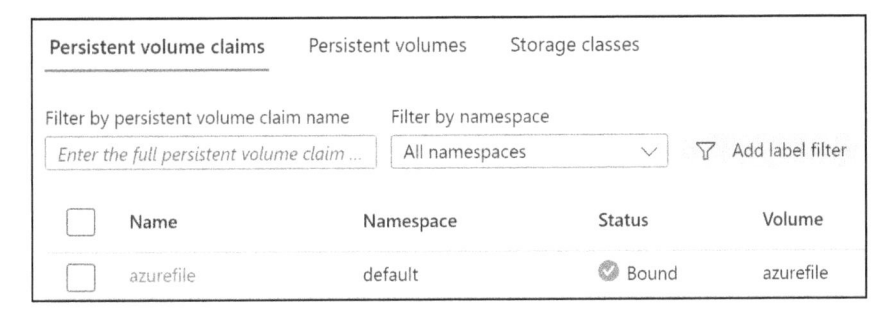

Figure 14.46: The Persistent volume claims tab

13. Note your persistent volumes by clicking on the `Persistent volumes` tab, as shown in the following screenshot:

Figure 14.47: The Persistent volumes tab

You have successfully added persistent storage to your AKS cluster. You now know the tasks involved in achieving this goal. In the next section, you will explore AKS scaling.

Configuring Scaling for AKS

You may have noted in the previous exercises that there was no option to automatically scale and resize containers. The only way to change this is to redeploy your container instances and groups. With Kubernetes, this dynamic changes as you can change the scale settings before and after your deployment, and these settings can be configured to scale manually or automatically. In the following exercise, you will run through changing the autoscale settings of your AKS cluster. Follow these steps:

1. Sign in to the Azure portal at `https://portal.azure.com`.

2. Navigate to the AKS cluster you created in the previous section. On the left menu, select the `Node pools` option and click on your deployed `agentpool` node pool, as shown in the following screenshot:

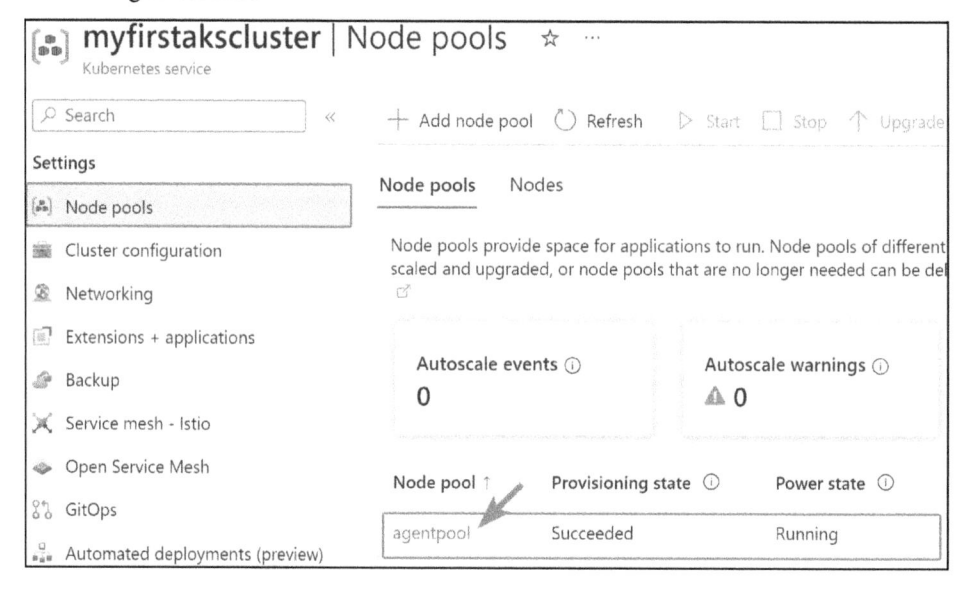

Figure 14.48: Configuring a Kubernetes cluster – Node pools

3. Select the `Overview` pane and you will be presented with the option to change your pool scale settings. Click `Scale node pool`, as shown in the following screenshot:

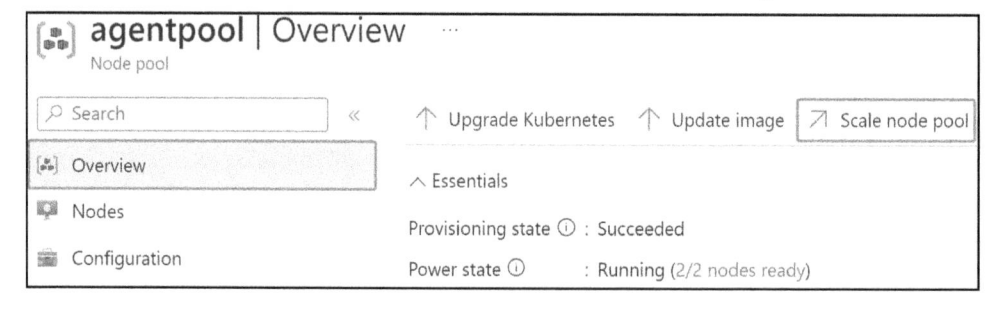

Figure 14.49: Configuring a Kubernetes cluster – Overview

4. To change the automatic scale option, set the `Scale method` type to `Autoscale`, enter a value for your minimum and maximum node count, and then click `Apply`. The process is shown in the following screenshot:

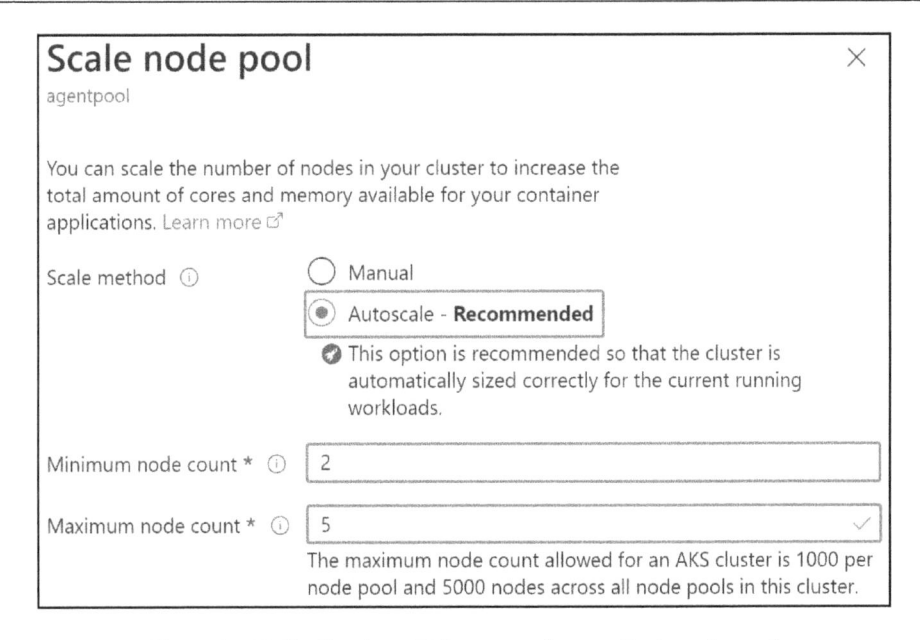

Figure 14.50: Configuring a Kubernetes cluster – Scale node pool

5. For the manual scale option, set the Scale method type to Manual, enter a Node count value (this will be the number of nodes you want to run), and click Apply. The process is shown in the following screenshot:

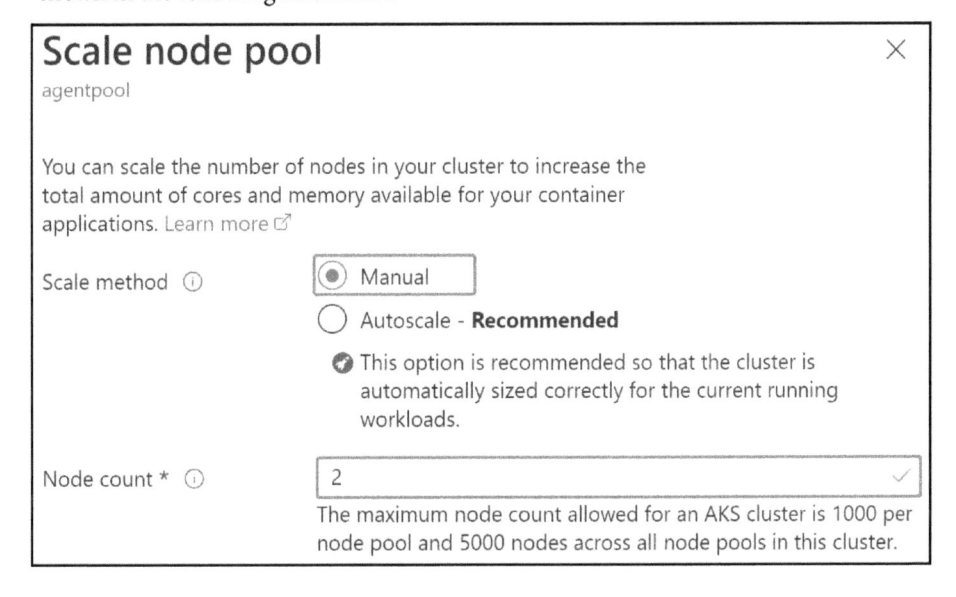

Figure 14.51: Configuring a Kubernetes cluster – Manual scale

6. After applying the settings, you will notice your agent pool goes into an Updating state.

You now know how to scale your agent pools within AKS and can feel confident about managing this aspect. If you would like to change the VM size for the agent pool, you will need to redeploy the pool. In the next section, you will experience upgrading your AKS cluster.

Upgrading an AKS Cluster

You have the choice to automatically upgrade your AKS clusters or to manually manage upgrades yourself. As part of your upgrade decisions, you can decide whether you would like to upgrade both the node pools and control plane or the control plane only. Automatic upgrades provide different channels that best apply to your requirements; these are listed as follows:

- **None**: Used for disabling auto upgrading
- **Patch**: Used to update the cluster automatically to the latest support patch version
- **Stable**: Used to update the cluster automatically to the latest stable version
- **Rapid**: Used to update the cluster automatically to the latest N-2 minor version
- **Node-image**: Used to update the cluster automatically to the latest version available

> **Note**
> When upgrading your AKS clusters, you will upgrade to a supported patch version for your cluster, one version at a time where more than one version upgrade exists.

Use the following steps to upgrade your cluster:

1. Sign in to the Azure portal at `https://portal.azure.com`.
2. Navigate to the AKS cluster you created previously in the chapter. On the left menu, select the `Cluster configuration` option. On the right side of the screen, click `Upgrade version` next to the Kubernetes version configuration, as shown in the following screenshot:

Upgrade

You can upgrade your cluster to a newer version of Kubernetes or configure automatic upgrade settings. If you upgrade your cluster, you can choose whether to upgrade only the control plane or to also upgrade all node pools. To upgrade individual node pools, go to the 'Node pools' menu item instead.

Learn more about upgrading your AKS cluster
View the Kubernetes changelog
View the AKS changelog

Kubernetes version	1.27.9
	Automatic upgrade type: Disabled
	Upgrade version
AKS pricing tier	Standard

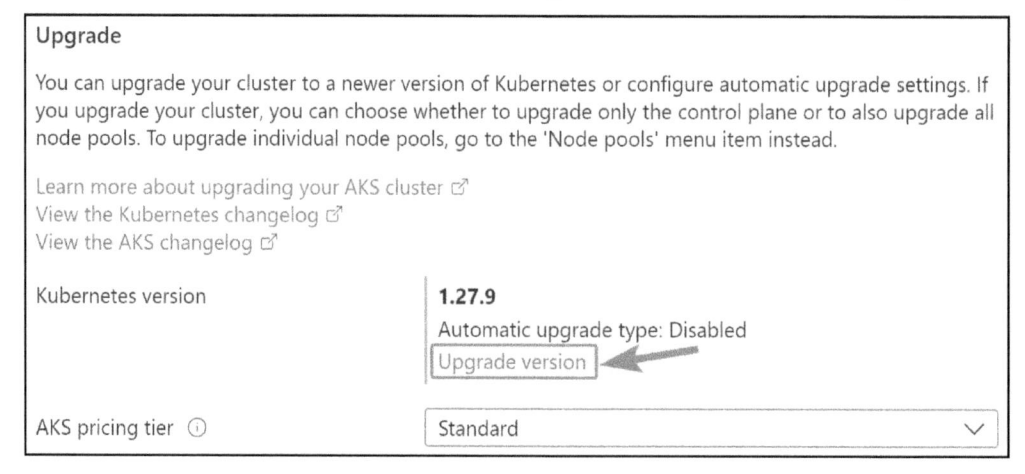

Figure 14.52: Kubernetes version upgrade

3. Select your desired Kubernetes version and select an `Upgrade scope` type, then click `Save`. The process is shown in the following screenshot:

Automatic upgrade	Disabled
Kubernetes version	1.28.3
Upgrade scope	● Upgrade control plane + all node pools ○ Upgrade control plane only
Force upgrade	☐

Figure 14.53: Upgrading the version of Kubernetes

You have just successfully upgraded your Kubernetes version and gone through the various automated options also available to do this.

Summary

In this chapter, you learned what containers are and how you deploy and manage them. You learned about Docker, the limitations of Docker, and container deployments. You examined how to extend default container services through orchestration tools such as Kubernetes, which greatly enhance the way you manage and scale containers. As part of your learning, you reviewed how to work with ACI, how to attach persistent storage to containers using AKS, how to enhance the security around containers, and the various networking options available to you as part of AKS. You also gained hands-on experience working with deployments and administrative tasks such as creating an Azure container registry, deploying Azure container instances, and creating and configuring Azure container groups.

You should now feel confident in the administration of containers within Azure, the methods of deployment, and how to orchestrate and manage these. These skills will not only benefit you in the exam but also in daily administration activities involving containers on Azure. This is a modern skill that is in big demand within the industry, and you are encouraged to grow in this space if you want to accelerate your career opportunities.

In the next chapter, you will dive into Azure App Service, what this is, how to configure and deploy it, and become confident using it.

> **Note**
> Remember to delete the resources you created in this chapter to minimize costs.
>
> Remove the resource group and all the corresponding resources with the following:
>
> `Remove-AzResourceGroup -Name AZ104-Containers -Force`

15
Creating and Configuring App Service

This chapter focuses on how to create and configure App Service instances in Azure. You will explore what Azure App Service is, its relevance, and why you should consider using it. You will also learn about the administrative functions that you need to perform concerning App Service, such as configurations, scaling, backups, and networking integrations. After reading this chapter, you should be confident in how to administer these services and how to present solutions when needed.

In this chapter, you are going to learn about the following main topics:

- Understanding Azure App Service and App Service plans
- Creating an App Service plan
- Creating an App Service instance
- Configuring Scaling
- Securing Azure App Service
- Configuring Custom Domain Names
- Configuring a Backup for an App Service Instance
- Configuring Network Settings
- Configuring Deployment Settings

Technical Requirements

This chapter uses the following tools for the examples:

- Access to an Azure subscription with owner or contributor privileges. If you do not have access to one, students can enroll for a free account: https://azure.microsoft.com/en-us/free/
- **PowerShell 5.1** or later installed on a Windows PC or PowerShell Core 6.x where other **operating systems (OSs)** are used to practice labs.

- Where PowerShell is not installed or available, `https://shell.azure.com` can be used as a browser-based shell.

- Installation of the `Az` PowerShell module, which can be performed by running the following in an administrative PowerShell session:

    ```
    Set-ExecutionPolicy -ExecutionPolicy RemoteSigned -Scope CurrentUser
    Install-Module -Name Az -Scope CurrentUser -Repository PSGallery -Force
    ```

Understanding Azure App Service and App Service Plans

When discussing Azure App Service and understanding what it is, compared to traditional servers, it's important to understand the relationship between **Infrastructure as a Service (IaaS)**, **Platform as a Service (PaaS)**, **Software as a Service (SaaS)**, and serverless (such as **Function as a Service (FaaS)**). As you move through the different service offerings, you have different layers of responsibility that you manage. IaaS, PaaS, SaaS, and serverless are cloud-based services and fit well into the Azure platform, as Microsoft has developed some great ways to manage the services you deploy. This also allows you to choose the level of control you would like to adopt. There are limitations to each model, which is a broad topic, but understanding these limitations at a core level will help you succeed in your Azure journey. The following diagram illustrates the management relationships between the cloud-based services:

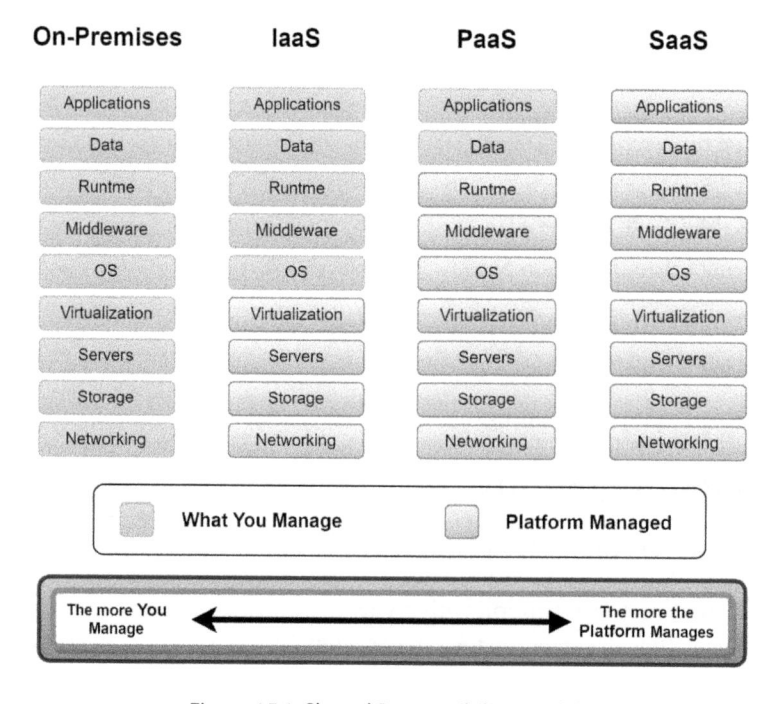

Figure 15.1: Shared Responsibility Model

As you can see in *Figure 15.1*, the closer you get to SaaS, the fewer components you are required to manage and, subsequently, can manage. Finally, the serverless component can be a little confusing as it falls between the PaaS and SaaS layers; you can only manage your code and, ideally, split your code into single repeatable components called functions. Serverless components are also classified as **microservices** since the services are broken down into their most basic forms. Here, you define the functions you need to run your code; you can deploy the code and forget about which server it runs on. This approach leads to more in-depth and complex discussions that are beyond the scope of this book. For now, you just need to understand that this exists and that in Azure, it is often referred to as FaaS. Now that you understand the relationship between these services and what you manage, you can classify Azure App Service. Since it falls into the PaaS category, you must only worry about how you manage your application and its data. You also have the choice of securing your application using controls that have been exposed to Azure. The rest is taken care of by the platform itself.

App Service Plans

To run your applications, you must deploy and configure your server infrastructure appropriately to suit your applications. For example, your applications may require the Windows OS and .NET Framework. To accommodate these configurations, Azure has App Service plans. This is a server that's related to your application deployments, where you can choose an OS, the number of nodes in your cluster, server-related security configurations, and operations. It also allows you to run several applications against a server with the chosen specifications for memory and CPU resources and only scales as per your requirements or budget. Azure App Service is a PaaS offering for hosting web applications, REST APIs, and backend services for mobile applications. An App Service instance always runs in an App Service plan, which defines the compute resources and runtime platform for a web app to run in a certain region.

> **Note**
> Although Azure Functions falls into the serverless category, when assigned to an App Service plan, it becomes PaaS since it is linked to a server. This increases what you can manage on the service and allows better control over some settings, for example, security features.

Runtime Stacks

Runtime stacks are the programming languages, frameworks, and tools used for running your applications. These can be viewed as the collective set of technologies used for running and developing your applications.

There are several varieties on offer for Azure App Service:

- .NET (both as base variations and as ASP.NET)
- Java
- Node.js
- PHP
- Python

Operating Systems

App Service is a PaaS offering on Azure where the OS and application stack are managed and updated for you by Azure. You only need to manage your application and data. Just as with VMs, you have the option to choose the type of OS you require for your applications. You can choose between Linux and Windows for your application, but you do not have the option to select the version or flavor of your OS for your App Service instance.

SKUs/Sizes

Several **stock-keeping units** (**SKUs**) and sizes for your App Service plan are available. The SKU refers to the specific configuration of a service. The greater the SKU, the more resources are allocated and available for your App Service instance assigned to the plan. Just as with all other services you have consumed to date, there are different tiers of pricing offering different features and availability requirements. App Service plans can be broken down as follows:

SKU Family	Plan Description	SLA
Free (F Series)	This plan is free and is intended for trials and learning about services. It is not supported for production workloads.	None
Shared (D Series)	This plan is shared among other users, reduces the cost of services, and is intended for trials and learning about services. It is not supported for production workloads.	None
Basic (B Series)	This plan is designed to support low-traffic workloads for up to 3 instances. Some features are excluded such as autoscale and traffic management.	Yes
Standard (S Series)	This plan is designed to support production workloads for up to 10 instances.	Yes

SKU Family	Plan Description	SLA
Premium (P Series)	This plan is designed to support production workloads for up to 30 instances. This service offers high levels of reliability, performance, and scale. It utilizes faster storage, memory, and processing power compared to the standard series. All features are available for the service tier. The Premium v3 pricing tier introduces faster processing coupled with SSD storage with larger memory-to-CPU ratios than you get from the Standard-tier offering. Consider whether the possibility exists for your workloads, through the enhanced performance from this SKU, to reduce the number of instances you require. This could reduce costs more than existing SKUs you may have.	Yes
Isolated (I Series)	This series supports production workloads that are mission-critical and is designed to support high-security-related functions as well as allow for high performance to be achieved. Workloads are isolated to a private and dedicated environment in Azure. The service can scale up to 100 instances and just like the Premium series, it offers enhanced performance levels. All features are available for the service tier.	Yes

Table 15.1: App Service plan SKUs

Authentication Settings

When selecting how your application plans to authenticate, you are presented with the option to enable or disable basic authentication only on setup. Azure App Service can communicate with several identity providers through a federated identity. Providers such as Microsoft Identity, Facebook, Google, and OpenID are supported. To leverage those authentications, you need to disable the basic authentication option. Basic authentication refers to a username and password combination that is local to the service only and not integrated with an identity provider.

Continuous Deployment

Continuous Deployment (**CD**) refers to a strategy for releasing code changes to an application automatically based on prerequisite tests you configure for the deployment. It streamlines your code deployment by reducing time through automation. Common to most modern development strategies, you will find references to **Continuous Integration/Continuous Deployment** (**CI/CD**), which is typically delivered through a pipeline-driven service. As of the time of writing, the section on deployment of your App Service instance includes GitHub, Bitbucket, Azure Repos, and local Git deployment integrations.

Now that you understand more about Azure App Service and App Service plans, let's dive into some exercises where you will work with these later. In the next section, you will deploy an App Service plan and dive into the available configuration options.

Creating an App Service Plan

In this exercise, you will be creating an App Service plan for Azure. This will act as the server configuration for hosting your Azure web applications and function applications. Follow these steps to do so:

1. Sign in to the Azure portal at `https://portal.azure.com`.
2. Create a new resource group to use for this exercise named `AZ104-AppServices`.
3. Once created, navigate to the new resource group, click `Overview` via the left menu, and click `Create`.
4. Type `app service plan` in the Marketplace search bar and click the `App Service Plan` card.
5. On the next screen, click `Create`, as shown in the following figure:

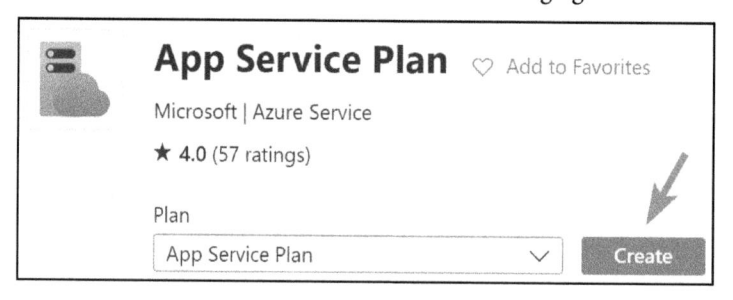

Figure 15.2: App Service Plan – Create

6. Enter the following details for the `App Service Plan details` section:
7. `Name`: `myappserviceplan`
8. `Operating System`: `Windows`
9. `Region`: Any region that suits your preference

Figure 15.3: App Service Plan details

10. For the `Pricing plan` dropdown, select `Standard S1`.

Pricing Tier	
App Service plan pricing tier determines the location, features, cost and compute resources associated with your app. Learn more ↗	
Pricing plan	Standard S1 (100 total ACU, 1.75 GB memory, 1 vCPU) ⌄ Explore pricing plans

Figure 15.4: Pricing Tier

11. You will note the final component for configuration on the page relates to zone redundancy. This option will be grayed out since it is only available for Premium v2 and v3. Click `Review + create`, then click `Create`.

With that, you have configured your first App Service plan and are ready to host your first application on the service. In the next section, you will learn how to create an App Service instance in your newly deployed App Service plan.

Creating an App Service Instance

In this exercise, you will deploy your first web application in Azure using the Azure Web Apps service. Follow these steps:

1. Sign in to the Azure portal at `https://portal.azure.com`.

2. Open the resource group from the previous exercise. Click `Overview` via the left menu and click `Create`.

3. From the left menu bar, click `Web`, then click the `Web App` card, as shown in the following figure:

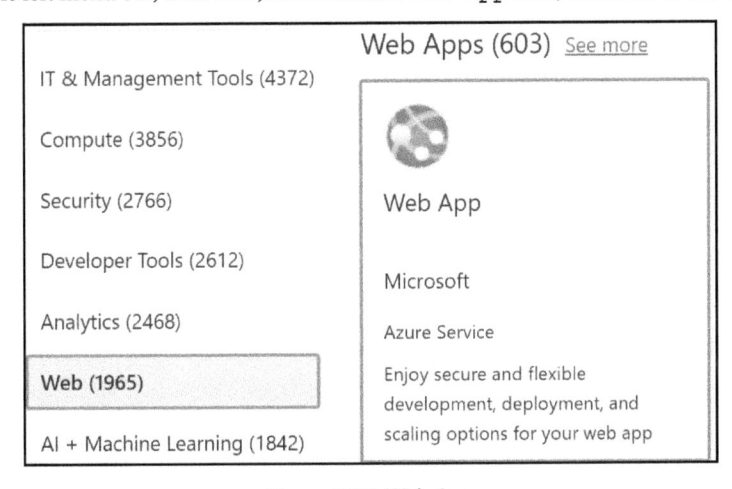

	Web Apps (603) See more
IT & Management Tools (4372)	
Compute (3856)	
Security (2766)	**Web App**
Developer Tools (2612)	Microsoft
Analytics (2468)	Azure Service
Web (1965)	Enjoy secure and flexible development, deployment, and scaling options for your web app
AI + Machine Learning (1842)	

Figure 15.5: Web App

4. Click `Create`.

5. Enter the following under `Instance Details`:

   - `Name`: `myfirstwebapp[date]`.

   - `Publish`: `Code`. This is the type of deployment that you will use. Note that you could also select `Docker Container`.

   - `Runtime stack: .NET 8 (LTS)`. This is for selecting the language your application is written in.

   - `Operating System`: `Windows`. Note how this matches the OS for the App Service plan created earlier. When creating an App Service instance, you need to have an App Service plan that meets the OS requirements of your App Service instance.

   - `Region`: Select the same region you use for your App Service plan.

Instance Details	
Name *	myfirstwebapp200324 ✓
	.azurewebsites.net
Publish *	● Code ○ Docker Container ○ Static Web App
Runtime stack *	.NET 8 (LTS)
Operating System *	○ Linux ● Windows
Region *	West Europe

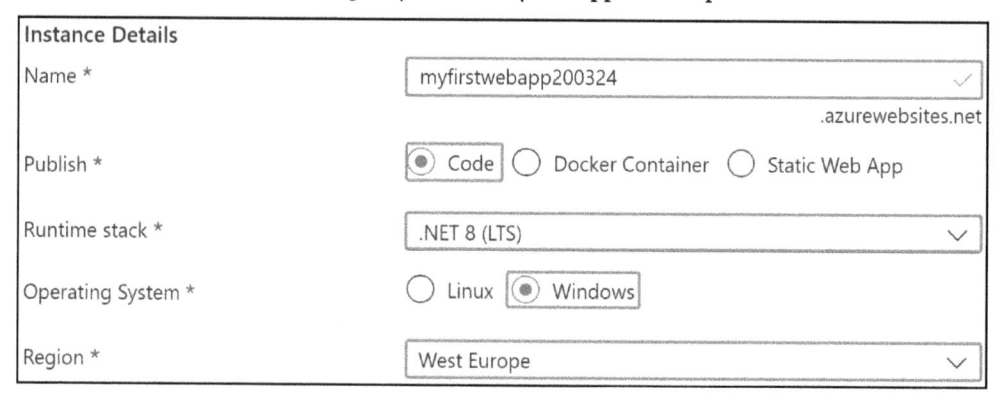

Figure 15.6: Instance Details

6. Finally, select an option for `Windows Plan` – this will be the App Service plan you created previously. Notice how the region that your App Service instance is in is displayed in brackets next to the words `Windows Plan`, which is helpful in selecting a suitable App Service plan. Also note that when you select a plan, it automatically configures your SKU and size, which will match what you chose for your App Service plan. You will see later that you have the option to create your App Service plan directly in the `Deployment` menu too. Click `Next : Database >`.

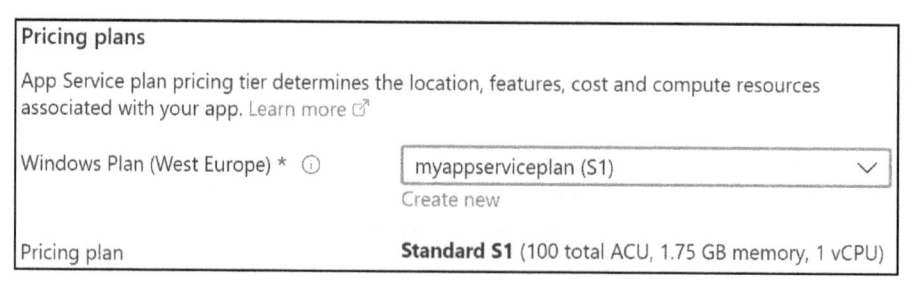

Pricing plans	
App Service plan pricing tier determines the location, features, cost and compute resources associated with your app. Learn more ⧉	
Windows Plan (West Europe) * ⓘ	myappserviceplan (S1)
	Create new
Pricing plan	**Standard S1** (100 total ACU, 1.75 GB memory, 1 vCPU)

Figure 15.7: Pricing plan

7. The `Database` tab has the option to create a database that will be linked to your App Service instance. Note that it requires a new App Service plan, but when utilized will assist in not only creating your database resource but also the **Virtual Network** (**VNet**) and any related networking resources to support the database connection. Click `Next: Deployment >`.

8. Next, you have the option to enable `Continuous deployment`. You won't be configuring this setting in this exercise. Click `Next : Networking >`:

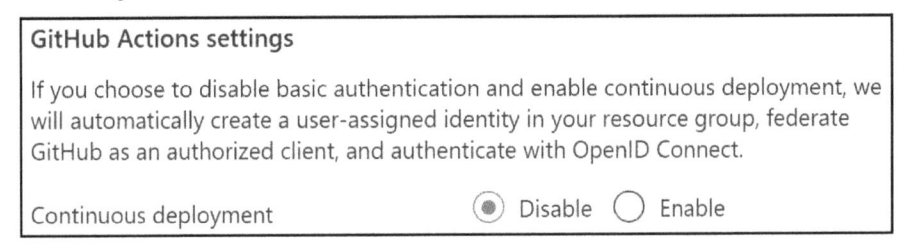

Figure 15.8: Continuous deployment

9. Observe the settings for `Networking`. Leave the settings as the default configuration. Note that you can enable or disable public access and you can integrate into an Azure VNet with the network injection option. Click `Next : Monitoring >`.

Figure 15.9: Networking

10. On the `Monitoring` tab, you will have the option to deploy `Application Insights` for your application. Note that you can either create a new Application Insights deployment through this blade or create it as part of the deployment. For this exercise, you will select No for `Enable Application Insights`.

Figure 15.10: Application Insights

11. Click `Review + create`, then `Create`.

12. Navigate to your application, click on `Overview` via the left-hand menu, and note the URL (`Default domain`) for your application. This blue text is clickable; you can either click on this or copy it into your browser to navigate to your application to confirm that it's working:

Resource group (move)	Default domain
AZ104-AppServices	myfirstwebapp200324.azurewebsites.net
Status	App Service Plan
Running	myappserviceplan (S1: 1)

Figure 15.11: Web app – Overview

13. You will be presented with a screen similar to the following for your application. Congratulations – you have successfully deployed your application using the Azure portal!

Figure 15.12: Running a web app

Now that you know how to deploy a web application using the Azure portal, let's learn how to do the same using PowerShell. This time, you will be deploying a web application within a Linux App Service plan.

PowerShell Scripts

Please ensure that the `Az` module is installed, as per the *Technical Requirements* section at the beginning of this chapter.

Here, you are going to create an App Service plan and Web Apps service via PowerShell. To do so, run the following code in PowerShell.

> **Note**
> Change the parameters to suit your requirements.

The following figure displays the code you will use to create your App Service plan. Note the top section that highlights the area for input parameters. You will configure these with your specific settings for running in the script to follow. Next, your subscription will be selected, and you will be required to update your subscription ID string by replacing the `"xxxxxxx"` placeholder. The final area of consideration when running this code is to observe the code responsible for deploying the App Service plan, which will act as your logical server, hosting your App Service instances, followed by your App Service deployment.

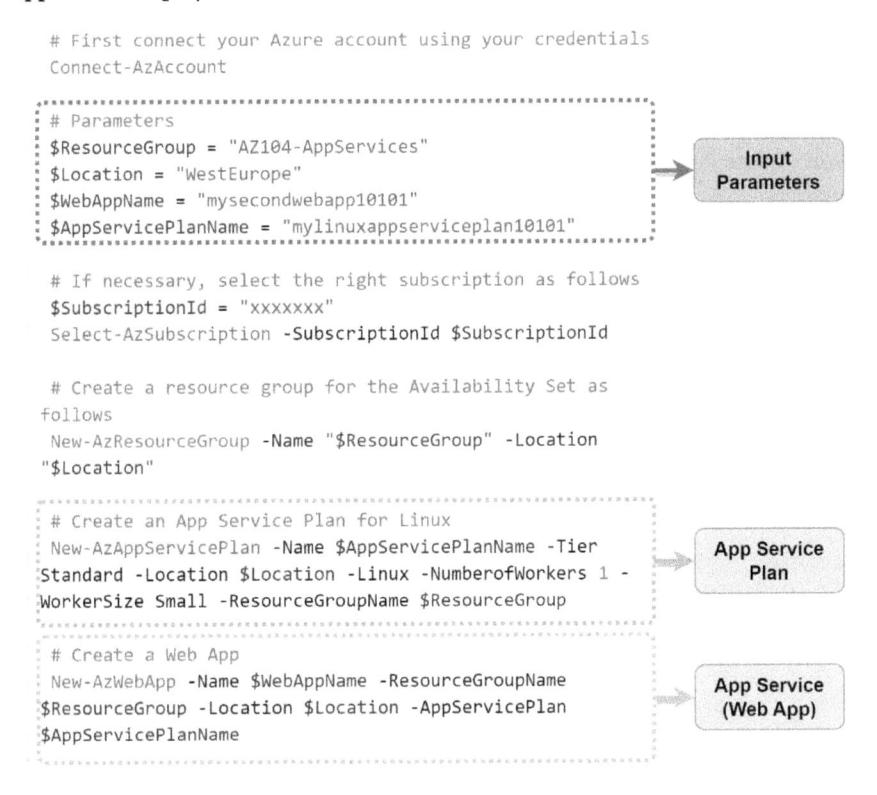

```
# First connect your Azure account using your credentials
Connect-AzAccount

# Parameters
$ResourceGroup = "AZ104-AppServices"
$Location = "WestEurope"
$WebAppName = "mysecondwebapp10101"
$AppServicePlanName = "mylinuxappserviceplan10101"

# If necessary, select the right subscription as follows
$SubscriptionId = "xxxxxxx"
Select-AzSubscription -SubscriptionId $SubscriptionId

# Create a resource group for the Availability Set as follows
 New-AzResourceGroup -Name "$ResourceGroup" -Location "$Location"

# Create an App Service Plan for Linux
New-AzAppServicePlan -Name $AppServicePlanName -Tier Standard -Location $Location -Linux -NumberofWorkers 1 -WorkerSize Small -ResourceGroupName $ResourceGroup

# Create a Web App
New-AzWebApp -Name $WebAppName -ResourceGroupName $ResourceGroup -Location $Location -AppServicePlan $AppServicePlanName
```

Figure 15.13: PowerShell – web app deployment

After running the script in *Figure 15.13*, you will now have a new App Service plan named `mylinuxappserviceplan10101` with an attached web app named `mysecondwebapp10101` in your `AZ104-AppServices` resource group.

Just as you did previously, you can browse to the web application's URL and see the same screen you did previously. With that, you have just completed your first few web application deployments to Azure using the Web Apps service. You should now feel confident in deploying web applications when required in Azure, either through the portal or via PowerShell. Next, you will learn how to scale your applications.

Configuring Scaling

In this exercise, you will configure the scaling settings for the App Service plan you created previously. Recall that there are two different types of scaling options you can choose from. Horizontal scaling (**Scale out** in the application menu) refers to the number of App Service instances that have been deployed, while vertical scaling (**Scale up** in the application menu) refers to the size of the App Service plan hosting the Web App service. VM refers to the App Service plan. As you may recall, you have the option to choose an SKU and size when you deploy, which refers to the specifications for the App Service plan that you would like to have.

Vertical Scaling

First, you will explore the **Scale up** functionality:

1. Navigate to the App Service plan you worked on in the previous exercise.
2. From the left menu, under the `Settings` context, click `Scale up (App Service plan)`.
3. You will be presented with a screen containing different SKU sizes that you can choose from. The list is further categorized by the family type of the SKUs, such as dev/test and production. Note that you can change views between `Hardware view` and `Feature view`.
4. For this exercise, under the `Dev/Test` category, select `Basic B1` and click `Select` at the bottom of the screen.

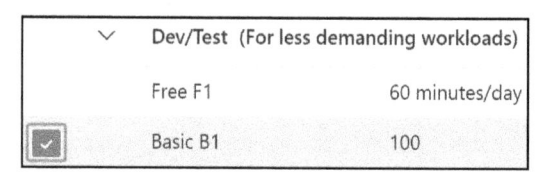

Dev/Test (For less demanding workloads)	
Free F1	60 minutes/day
Basic B1	100

Figure 15.14: Scale up

You have just scaled down your application from the **S1 SKU** to the **B1 SKU**, which shows how easy it is to change its size. Note that the **application will restart upon being resized**. You have now learned how to scale your applications vertically through changing SKUs, which changes the number of resources available to an instance in your application. This is very important for meeting the resource requirements of the applications you intend to run in your environment.

For the next exercise, you will need to resize the application back to the **Premium v3 P0V3** SKU, which can be found under the **Production** SKUs.

Horizontal Scaling

Now, you will learn how to **scale out** horizontally:

1. Navigate to the App Service plan you worked on in the previous exercise.
2. From the left menu, click `Scale out (App Service plan)`.
3. When selecting the `Scale out method` option, note that you can choose either `Manual` or `Rules Based`. Here, it would be best to manually scale since you are working on dev/test workloads, but for production workloads, you should choose the `Rules Based` or `Automatic` option. Change `Instance count` to 2 and click `Save`:

Scale out method	● Manual Maintain a constant instance count for your application
	Automatic (preview) Platform managed scale up and down based on traffic Automatic scaling requires a Premium v2 or Premium v3 App Service Plan. Upgrade your App Service Plan to enable this feature. See recommended pricing plan
	○ Rules Based User defined rules to scale on a schedule or based on any app metric
Instance count	──O─────────────────────────── 2

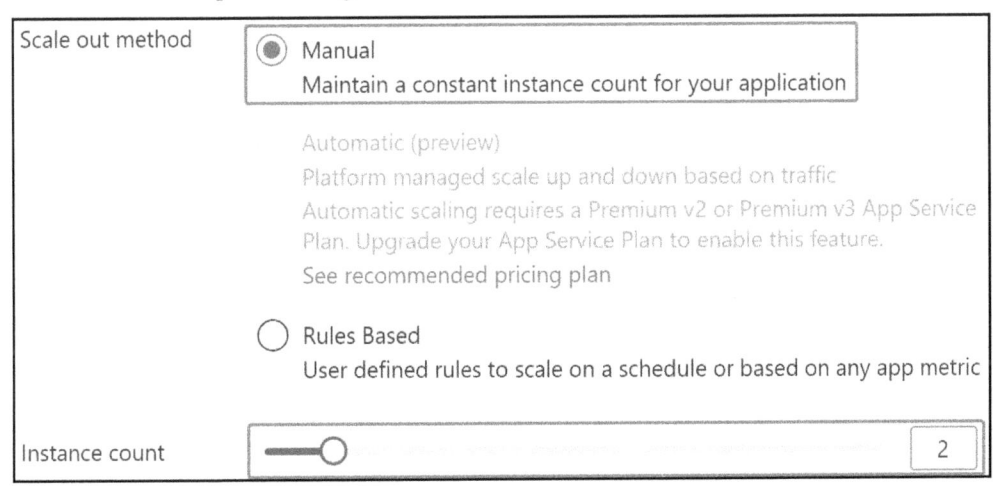

Figure 15.15: Manual scaling

4. Now, go back to the `Scale out (App Service plan)` setting screen, and change the setting to `Rules Based`. At the bottom of the selection options will be a red warning label – click `Manage rules based scaling`.

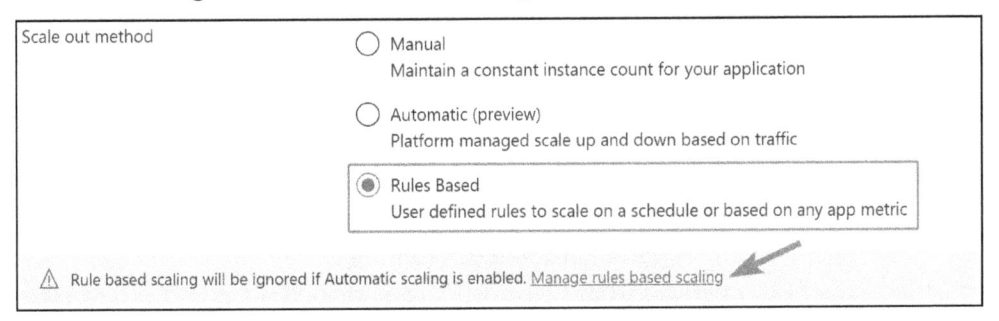

Scale out method	○ Manual Maintain a constant instance count for your application
	○ Automatic (preview) Platform managed scale up and down based on traffic
	● Rules Based User defined rules to scale on a schedule or based on any app metric
⚠ Rule based scaling will be ignored if Automatic scaling is enabled. Manage rules based scaling	

Figure 15.16: Manage rules based scaling

5. Click `Custom autoscale`. Enter a name for the `Autoscale setting name` field and select your resource group.

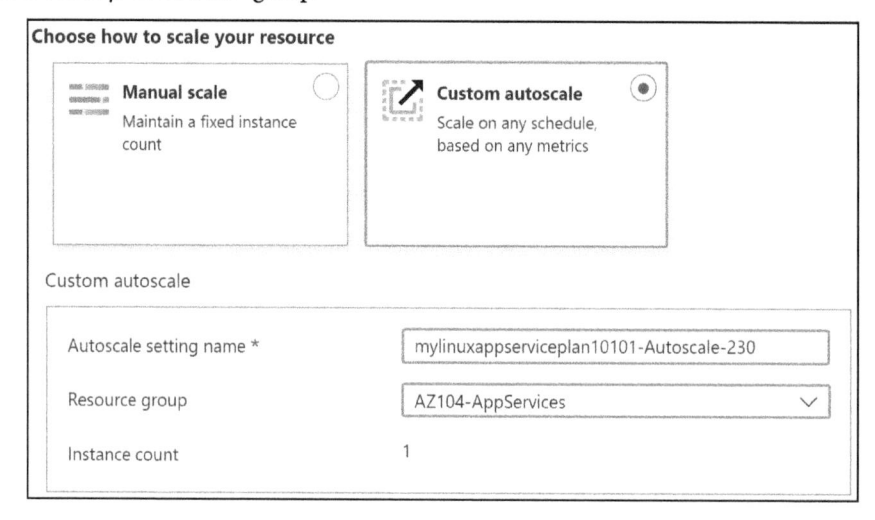

Figure 15.17: Custom autoscale

6. For the `Default` scale condition, you will create the first one using `Scale based on a metric` for `Scale mode`. Set `Instance limits` to 1 for `Minimum`, 2 for `Maximum`, and 1 for `Default`. Click `Add a rule` in the `Rules` section.

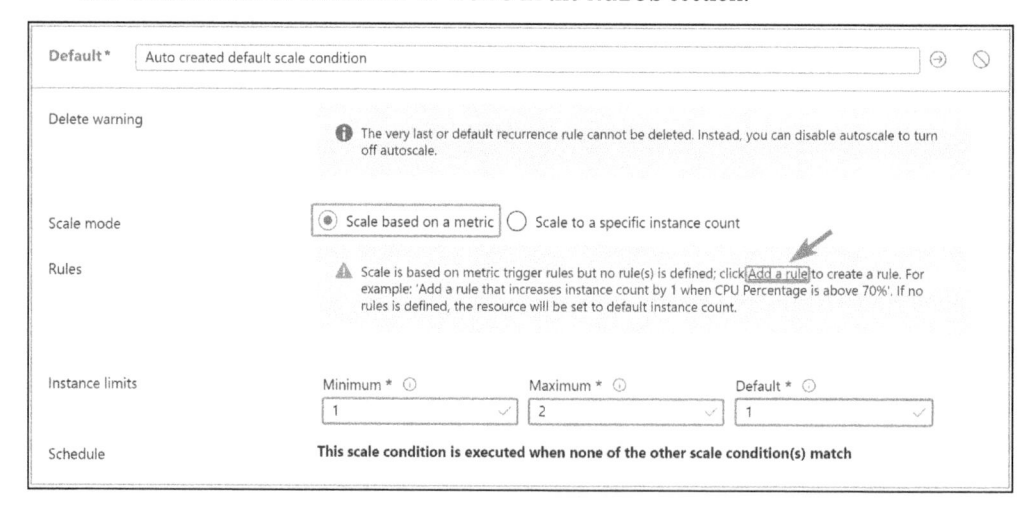

Figure 15.18: Scale condition setup

7. For the `Criteria` section, configure the following settings:

    - `Metric namespace`: `App service plans standard metrics`
    - `Metric name`: `CPU Percentage`

- `Instance Operator:` =
- `Dimension Values:` All values
- `Operator:` Greater than
- `Metric threshold to trigger scale action:` 70
- `Duration (minutes):` 10
- `Time grain (minutes):` 1
- `Time grain statistic:` Average
- `Time aggregation:` Average

Note the timeline chart, which indicates the average CPU percentage that you have experienced over time, with the average also written below it. In this case, it is 3.78 %:

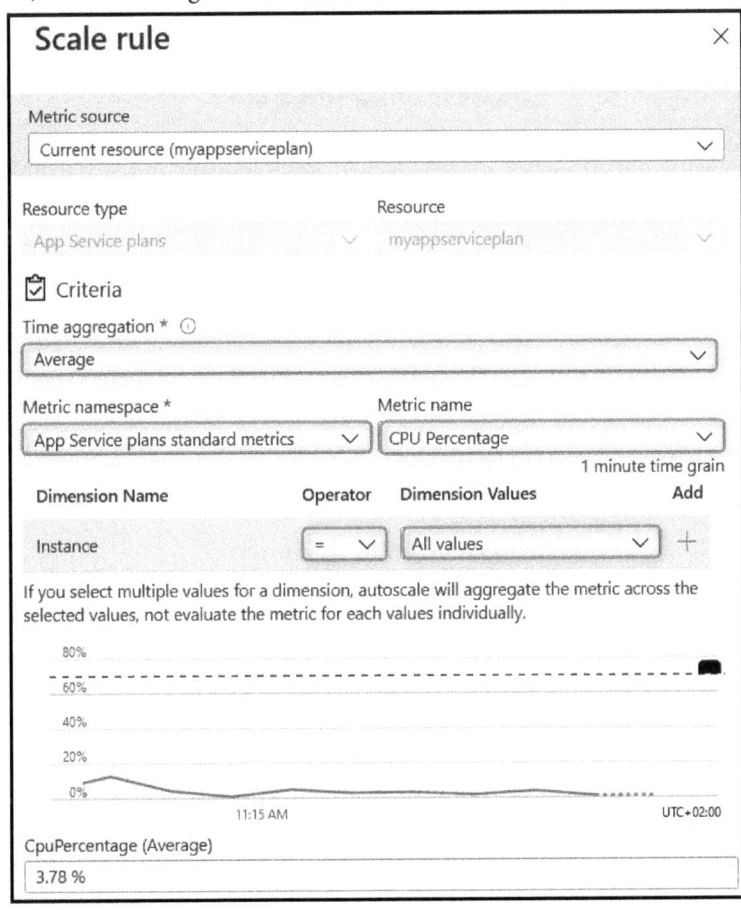

Figure 15.19: Scale rule

The preceding setup defines a rule that states that when the CPU average percentage goes above 70% usage for more than 10 minutes, it will trigger an action.

8. For the `Action` section, set `Operation` to `Increase count by`, `Cool down (minutes)` to 5, and `instance count` to 1. This will increase the instance count of the running web applications by 1 when the criteria configured in *Step 7* have been identified. Once triggered, a cooldown period will occur, where no further actions can be performed until the cooldown window has elapsed. In this case, it is `5 minutes`. If the criteria for scaling are observed again after this cooldown period, then the action will be triggered again. Click Add:

Action

Operation *	Cool down (minutes) *
Increase count by	5
instance count *	
1	

Figure 15.20: Scale rule action

9. You have just configured a rule for scaling your application out in terms of its instance count, but what if you would like the application to scale back in when you don't need as many instances anymore? You would need to configure a new scale condition to trigger the scale-in action you would like to be performed. Click `+ Add a rule` below the `Scale out` rule you just created:

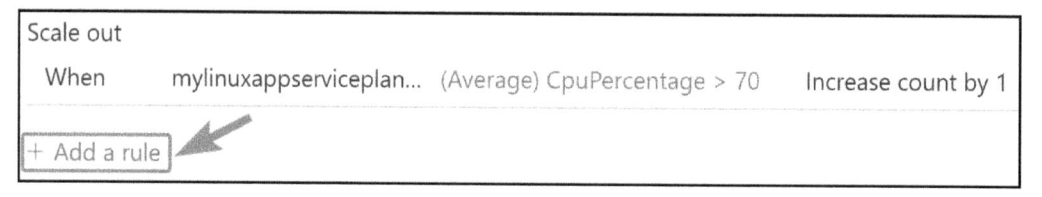

Scale out

When   mylinuxappserviceplan... (Average) CpuPercentage > 70   Increase count by 1

+ Add a rule

Figure 15.21: Add scale-in rule

10. Leave all the defaults the same for this rule and configure the following settings:

    - `Operator: Less than`
    - `Metric threshold to trigger scale action: 30`
    - `Duration (minutes): 10`

    This will define a rule that states that when the CPU average percentage reaches less than 30% usage over 10 minutes, it will trigger an action.

11. For the Action section, set Operation to Decrease count by, Cool down (minutes) to 5, and instance count to 1. This will decrease the instance count of the running web applications by 1 when the criteria that you configured in *Step 10* have been identified. Once triggered, there will be a cooldown period where no further actions can be performed until the cooldown window has elapsed. In this case, it is 5 minutes. If the criteria for scaling are observed again after this cooldown period, then the action will be triggered again. Click Add.

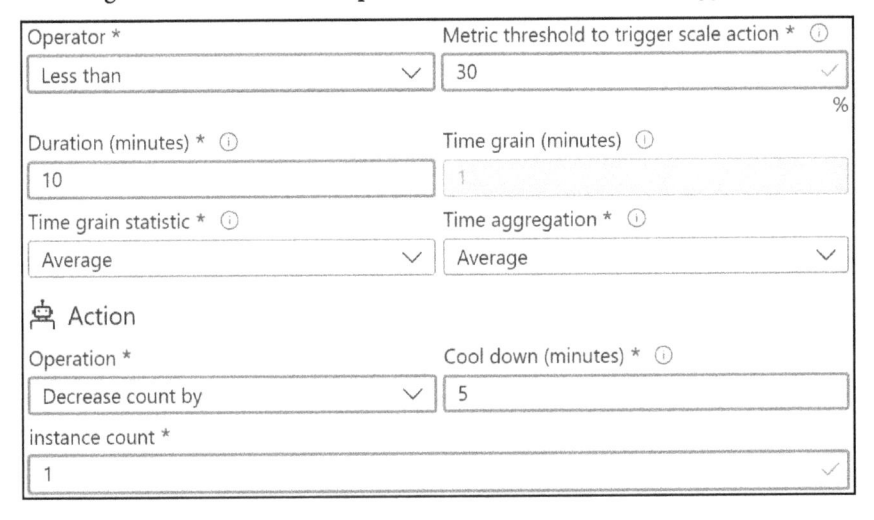

Figure 15.22: Scale-in rule

12. Click Save.
13. Lastly, you will try the Automatic scale-out method. Go back to the Scale out (App Service plan) setting blade. Click Automatic for Scale out method. For the section that opens up below, set Maximum burst as 1, Always ready instances as 1, and Enforce scale out limit as disabled. Click Save.

Now that you have configured your autoscale rules using the Azure portal, you will learn how to use PowerShell to do the same.

PowerShell Scripts

You have experienced scaling your web applications through the Azure portal and will now learn how to perform autoscale activities through PowerShell. This skill is very relevant in your daily role of Azure administration where you may desire efficiency in your role, which can be attained by automating activities. This also leads to fewer mistakes as it is a code-driven solution. These skills are also relevant to the AZ-104 exam as you will potentially need to demonstrate knowledge through the application of skills in correctly answering presented questions on the topic. These skills come through experience in using PowerShell for various activities, such as creating autoscaling configurations. In the following exercise, you are going to create an App Service plan and Web Apps service via PowerShell.

> **Note**
> Change the parameters to suit your requirements.

You will execute the following PowerShell code to create an autoscale rule for your `mysecondwebapp10101` application. The first part of the code presents the input parameters, which can be modified according to your preferences and used as variables for the remaining parts of the script. Next, your subscription will be selected, and you will be required to update your subscription ID string by replacing the `"xxxxxxx"` placeholder. You then come to the autoscale rule that will be created, and finally, the last part of the script will assign the autoscale rule to your `mysecondwebapp10101` application. Once you have made the modifications required to the script, copy and paste this into PowerShell to execute the code.

```powershell
# Parameters
$ResourceGroup = "AZ104-AppServices"
$Location = "WestEurope"
$WebAppName = "mysecondwebapp10101"
$AppServicePlanName = "mylinuxappserviceplan10101"
```
→ **Input Parameters**

```powershell
# If necessary, select the right subscription as follows
$SubscriptionId = "xxxxxxx"
Select-AzSubscription -SubscriptionId $SubscriptionId

# Retrieve the App Service Plan for Linux
$AppServicePlan = Get-AzAppServicePlan -Name $AppServicePlanName `
-ResourceGroupName $ResourceGroup
```
→ **Autoscale Rule**

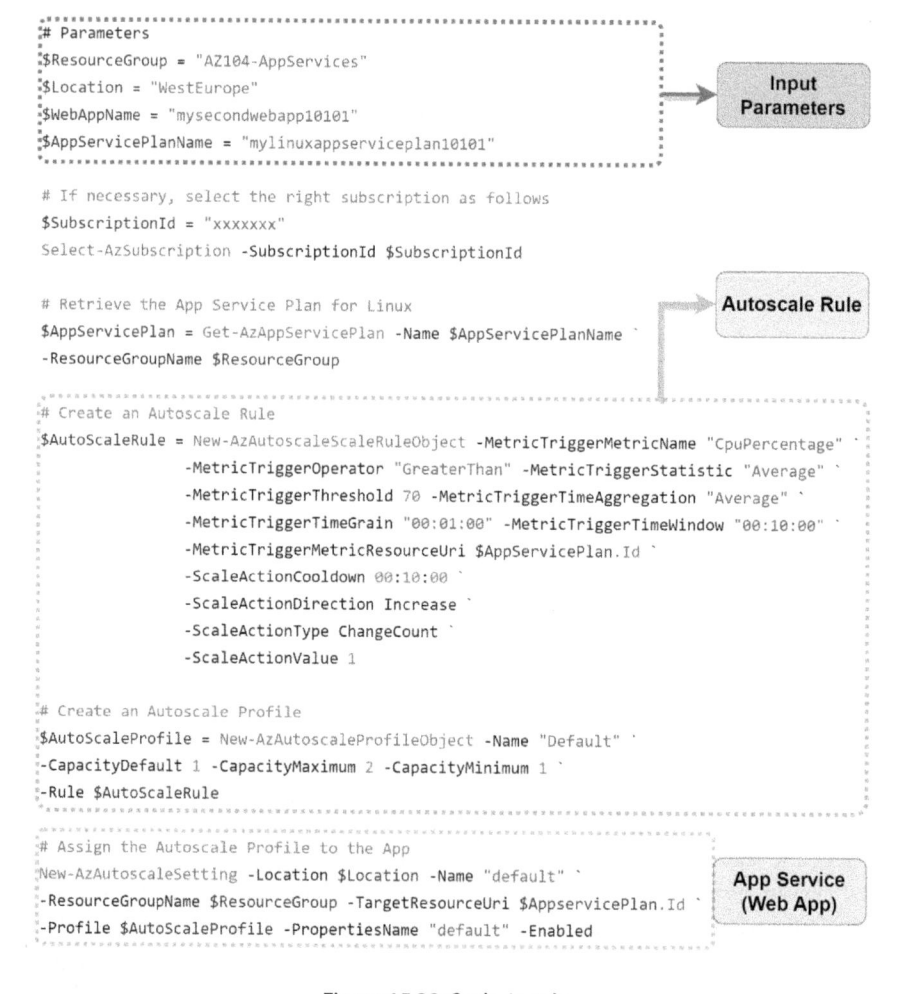

```powershell
# Create an Autoscale Rule
$AutoScaleRule = New-AzAutoscaleScaleRuleObject -MetricTriggerMetricName "CpuPercentage" `
        -MetricTriggerOperator "GreaterThan" -MetricTriggerStatistic "Average" `
        -MetricTriggerThreshold 70 -MetricTriggerTimeAggregation "Average" `
        -MetricTriggerTimeGrain "00:01:00" -MetricTriggerTimeWindow "00:10:00" `
        -MetricTriggerMetricResourceUri $AppServicePlan.Id `
        -ScaleActionCooldown 00:10:00 `
        -ScaleActionDirection Increase `
        -ScaleActionType ChangeCount `
        -ScaleActionValue 1

# Create an Autoscale Profile
$AutoScaleProfile = New-AzAutoscaleProfileObject -Name "Default" `
-CapacityDefault 1 -CapacityMaximum 2 -CapacityMinimum 1 `
-Rule $AutoScaleRule
```

```powershell
# Assign the Autoscale Profile to the App
New-AzAutoscaleSetting -Location $Location -Name "default" `
-ResourceGroupName $ResourceGroup -TargetResourceUri $AppservicePlan.Id `
-Profile $AutoScaleProfile -PropertiesName "default" -Enabled
```
→ **App Service (Web App)**

Figure 15.23: Scale-in rule

After running the code in *Figure 15.23*, you have configured an autoscaling rule for your `mysecondwebapp10101` application. This rule will automatically scale out when the **CPU usage percentage** value on the application exceeds **70%** as an **average** measure over a period of **1 minute** within the last 10 minutes. After an autoscaling trigger has been activated, a cool-down period of 10 minutes will apply before further increases are effected. The App Service instance has been configured for a **maximum of 2 instances**, which will prevent scaling beyond 2 instances and protect you against over-expenditure. You should now understand how to scale your applications via Azure App Service. You have learned how to perform manual scaling, as well as autoscaling, using the Azure portal and PowerShell. Autoscaling allows you to manage your applications and accommodate varying workload requirements. Next, you will learn about the security configurations that you can use to secure your application.

Securing Azure App Service

There are several mechanisms you can use to enhance the security of your application on Azure. As part of the AZ-104 exam, you will explore the configuration options that are native to the web application directly. However, note that for real-world implementations, you should investigate additional measures for enhancing the security of your applications, such as employing a firewall – especially a web application firewall – for your web-based applications. These services provide traffic that's in line with your application and scan for disallowed or heuristic behavior.

In this exercise, you will look at various native application configurations that can be used to increase the security level of your App Service instances. This has been broken up into several sections as part of a single exercise to help you understand the segmentation of settings better and make it easier to reference later.

Environment Variables

This section contains settings related to parsing in environment variables and connection string data to your applications. They are obfuscated from the code and therefore more secure by design in how they are presented to your applications. They are presented at the App Service layer in alignment with the separation of roles and responsibilities in management. Developers focus on the code and operational support and management roles manage the infrastructure components such as the App Service instance.

You will explore where to configure both settings by following these steps:

1. Navigate to the App Service instance you worked on in the previous exercise.
2. From the left menu, under the `Settings` context, click `Environment variables`. The first tab you will be greeted by is called `App settings`. Application settings are variables that are presented securely to your application, but they can be configured externally to the application code. This enhances security by obfuscating secret information such as passwords from code and prevents developers without the requisite RBAC permissions on the Azure portal for the App Service resource from seeing sensitive data, such as secrets that may be stored under `App settings`.

The other item that can be configured is `Connection strings`, as shown in the following figure:

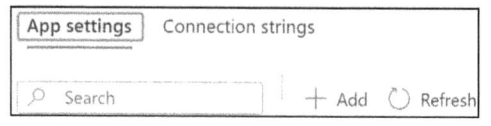

Figure 15.24: App settings

Configuration settings

This section contains the collection of settings related to your App Service instance presented through several tabs related to the category of settings. It contains settings related to your application stack settings, platform settings, certificates, path mappings, and error pages. The various components will be discussed in more detail next.

General settings

The first tab is `General settings`. Here, you will want to configure several settings to enhance the security of your application. Not all the best-practice settings will be chosen for this exercise as the intention is to explore some of the potential options available to you in a practical example. Follow these steps:

1. Navigate to the App Service instance you worked on in the previous exercise.
2. From the left menu, under the `Settings` context, click `Configuration`.
3. Configure the following settings:

    - `SCM Basic Auth Publishing Credentials`: `On`. **The best-practice option is off with more secure deployment methods utilized.**
    - `FTP Basic Auth Publishing Credentials`: `On`. **The best-practice option is off with more secure deployment methods utilized.**

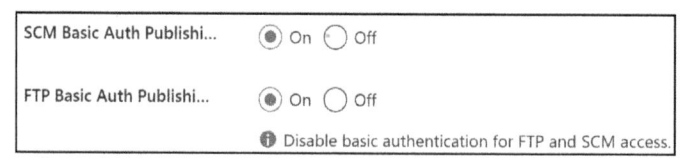

    Figure 15.25: Application settings – basic authentication

    - `FTP state`: `FTPS only`. Ensure **File Transfer Protocol** (**FTP**) traffic is conducted securely if it's allowed by your organizational policies. FTP is a technology that enables file transfer operations for your systems. It is commonly used by developers to upload code to the system; an alternative, as explored previously, is to use a source code repository such as Git. The most secure option is to disallow all FTP-based traffic as prevention is better than a cure. However, since many applications require developers to be able to upload their code, changing the FTP transfer protocol that's being used is the next best option.

Setting traffic to FTPS only ensures that the FTP traffic is conducted over an HTTPS tunnel, meaning that all the data is encrypted. So, even if it is intercepted, it is less likely to be compromised. Set this to **FTPS only** for this exercise.

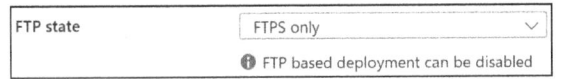

Figure 15.26: FTP state

- `HTTPS Only`: On. Enabling this setting ensures that all connections and traffic to your application are encrypted. This setting protects against any unsecured HTTP-related requests. HTTP traffic allows compromises to occur and should always be configured to forward all HTTP requests to HTTPS. HTTP communicates in clear text, so any credentials or sensitive information that's sent would be visible to anyone who could intercept the traffic, which is highly insecure. The following screenshot shows the **HTTPS Only** setting:

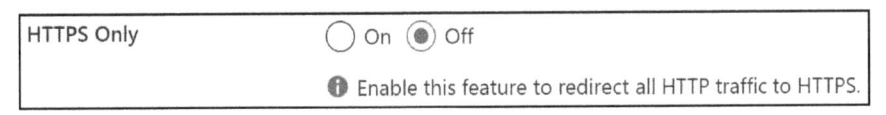

Figure 15.27: HTTPS Only

- `Minimum Inbound TLS Version`: 1.2. Compromises have been identified on prior TLS versions and it's best to be on the highest version possible. **Transport Layer Security (TLS)** is the cryptographic protocol that is used for communication encryption over IP and is particularly used in securing HTTPS communication. The following screenshot shows the setting for configuring the minimum inbound TLS version:

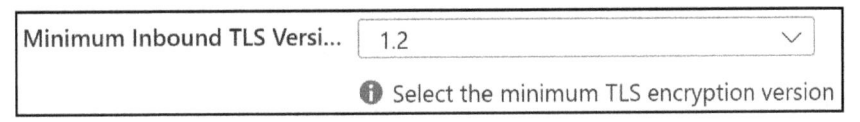

Figure 15.28: Minimum Inbound TLS Version

- `Minimum Inbound TLS Cipher`: `TLS_ECDHE_ECDSA_WITH_AES_256_GCM_SHA384`. A cipher is the translation table of your secret message code, meaning that if you had, for instance, agreed that wherever your secret message contained A, your cipher would show that A represents H, R represents E, and T represents L, and Y represents O; then a ciphertext message such as ARTTY would be deciphered as HELLO. There are many variations of ciphers to choose from and the deciding factor on complexity lies in the decryption time, so the preceding example of the most secure cipher you can choose at the time of writing will be slower when accessing your application.

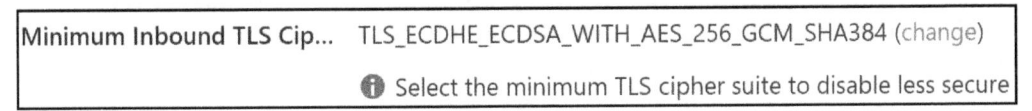

Figure 15.29: Minimum Inbound TLS Cipher

- `End-to-end TLS encryption: Off`. The most secure option is to enable this. When set to **Off**, the option will enable TLS encryption to the frontend of the web services only (i.e., the web page being accessed over the internet). For internal TLS encryption between your workers and the frontend (intra-cluster), you would change this option to **On**. The trade-off, of course, is performance as with most security settings. At the time of writing, this feature is only available for Linux.

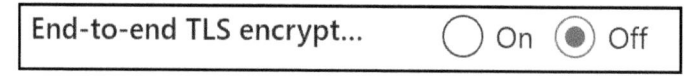

Figure 15.30: End-to-end TLS encryption

- `Incoming client certificates: Ignore`. The most secure option is to require client certificates; however, this does involve some more administration and will go beyond the effort of configuring the website for working client connections. Establishing a connection would require a client certificate to be installed on the host that is connecting to your web application for authentication.

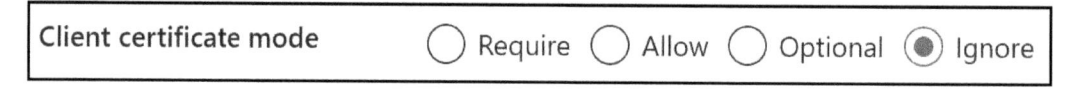

Figure 15.31: Incoming client certificates

4. Click `Save` at the top of the screen:

Figure 15.32: Configuration settings – Save

Note that after clicking `Save`, you will be warned that the application needs to be restarted. Click `Continue` to do so.

Path mappings

The next tab that can be configured in the **Configuration** menu is **Path mappings**. This is beyond the scope of this book and won't be explored here. Just understand that through this mapping functionality, you can link your Azure Files or Blob containers to your App Service instance and make the storage available.

Error pages

The last tab in the **Configuration** menu is **Error pages**. This deals with customized error pages you may like to present to the users of your application by the error code number. At the time of writing, this feature is still under preview and allows for pages for 403, 502, and 503 errors only. This feature is only available to App Service instances that make use of a Premium SKU at a minimum.

Authentication Settings

The next set of security settings you will explore is related to authentication:

1. From the left menu, click `Authentication`. This blade contains the configuration settings related to authentication, the type of identity provider service that's being used, and the authentication flow. To explore the available configurations, click `Add identity provider`, as shown in the following figure:

Figure 15.33: Add an identity provider

2. At the time of writing, you can choose from several identity providers – that is, Microsoft, Apple, Facebook, GitHub, Google, Twitter/X, and OpenID Connect. Select `Microsoft` as per the following screenshot. Then select `Workforce configuration (current tenant)`.

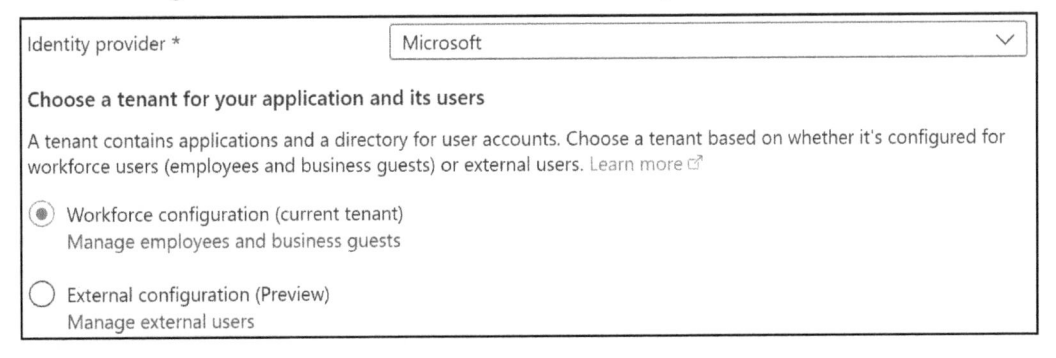

Figure 15.34: Select Microsoft as an identity provider

3. Below the `Identity provider` settings, you will see a section to configure the application registration (`App registration`). This can be used to assign permissions and will configure a service principal account in Entra ID called an app registration. For this exercise, select `Create new app registration` and assign a name. Next, for `Supported account types`, select `Current tenant - Single tenant`.

App registration type *	● Create new app registration
	○ Pick an existing app registration in this directory
	○ Provide the details of an existing app registration
Name * ⓘ	mysecondwebapp10101
Supported account types *	● Current tenant - Single tenant
	○ Any Microsoft Entra directory - Multi-tenant
	○ Any Microsoft Entra directory & personal Microsoft accounts
	○ Personal Microsoft accounts only

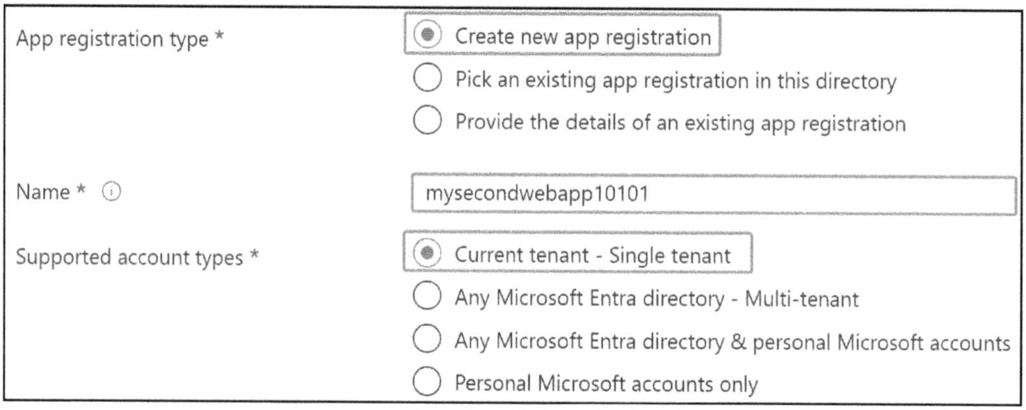

Figure 15.35: App registration

As you can see, there are several options for supported account types for your application. Depending on how and where your application is used, this will dictate the configuration that best suits your security requirements. For instance, if you are looking to deliver an internal application such as something that lists the mobile numbers of employees within your organization so that you can contact someone urgently (where sharing this information is disallowed publicly), then you would want to restrict public access (that is, anyone external to your organization). Using your identity provider will help you determine whether they have an account with your organization or not. In such cases, you can select `Current tenant - Single tenant`. `Any Microsoft Entra ID directory - Multi-tenant` will allow you to accept user logins from any other Microsoft Entra ID directory. The next option, `Any Microsoft Entra ID directory & personal Microsoft accounts`, opens access to public accounts too, where personal accounts can be used. Finally, `Personal Microsoft accounts only` removes access from other Entra ID accounts and limits this to personal Microsoft accounts. This is typically used for gaming services, where you want to allow friends to connect but you also want to restrict business accounts from accessing the service. As you can see, the most secure option is `Current tenant - Single tenant`.

4. The `Additional checks` section allows you to be more restrictive with the level of control you will grant for your application. The more restrictive, the more secure—in practice. However, you may also need to weigh up practicality considerations. For instance, you cannot restrict the application use to one user when it's intended for the entire organization. You can leave this at the default settings for this exercise.

Client application requirement *	◉ Allow requests only from this application itself
	○ Allow requests from specific client applications
	○ Allow requests from any application (Not recommended)
Identity requirement *	◉ Allow requests from any identity
	○ Allow requests from specific identities
Tenant requirement *	◉ Allow requests only from the issuer tenant (5b0e3813-06bb-4766-97ea-77f05fbbf65c)
	○ Allow requests from specific tenants
	○ Use default restrictions based on issuer

Figure 15.36: Additional checks

5. At the bottom of the screen, you can configure `App Service authentication settings`. Configure the following settings:

   - `Restrict access`: Require authentication
   - `Unauthenticated requests`: HTTP 302 Found redirect: recommended for websites
   - `Redirect to`: Microsoft (this will be preconfigured for you)
   - `Token store`: Enabled (default setting)

6. To explain the settings you have configured, **Restrict access** is where you can force authentication to be conducted before access is granted to your application. **Unauthenticated access** allows users to log in anonymously. You can choose what kind of error handling you would like to deliver upon detection of anonymous/unauthenticated connection attempts by configuring the `Unauthenticated requests` setting. Here you can select the returned error, such as delivering an `HTTP 401 Unauthorized` error message.

Restrict access *	◉ Require authentication
	○ Allow unauthenticated access
Unauthenticated requests *	◉ HTTP 302 Found redirect: recommended for websites
	○ HTTP 401 Unauthorized: recommended for APIs
	○ HTTP 403 Forbidden
	○ HTTP 404 Not found
Redirect to	Microsoft
Token store ⓘ	✓

Figure 15.37: App Service authentication settings

7. Click `Next : Permissions >`.

8. The `Permissions` blade relates to the permissions options you would like to grant. The default option is `User.Read`, which allows the application to read the user's profile. These permissions can be modified as needed to deliver the required information to your application. The user will be prompted to approve these permissions when they access the application and are authenticated. They will need to consent to this permission request if they wish to access the application. Click `Add`.

Identity Settings

The next collection of settings you will explore relates to identity. You will be presented with two tabs – **System assigned** and **User assigned**. Here, you can choose which deployment configuration you would like to use. **System assigned** allows you to create a managed identity whose life cycle is controlled and managed by Azure. A managed identity allows you to grant RBAC permissions to the application as if it were a user, which gives you better control over resources and prevents user management issues such as abuse of privileges or mistakes being made. Enabling this setting increases the security of your application and prevents credentials from being injected directly into code, which would allow account and system compromise to occur. **User assigned** is managed manually but can be configured more granularly to control the specific RBAC permissions you would like to grant to the application. Follow the steps to explore the various identity settings available to you on an App Service instance:

1. Click `Identity` from the left menu for the application.

2. On the `System assigned` tab, click `On` under the `Status` option, then click `Save`:

Figure 15.38: System assigned identity

3. You will be presented with a confirmation dialog informing you that you will create a new app registration and that it will be used for permission management. Click `Yes`.

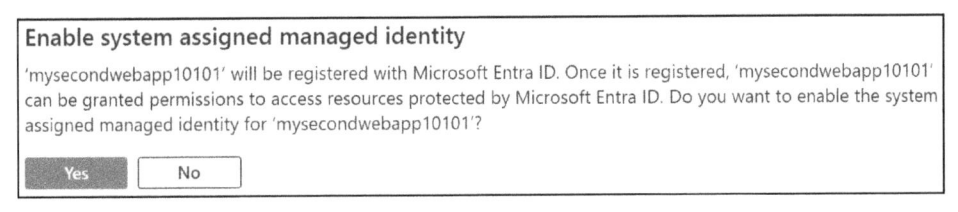

Figure 15.39: Enable system assigned managed identity

4. After clicking Save, you will see a new configuration option, where you can configure the Azure RBAC permissions for your application:

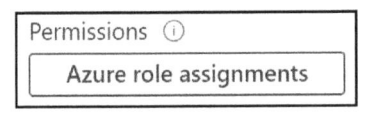

Figure 15.40: Azure role assignments

Backups

You can also consider using backups and **disaster recovery** (**DR**) for your applications. How do backups relate to security? If your application becomes compromised and you need to perform restoration tasks, without backups, you will potentially lose all your critical data. Therefore, anything that could cause the application to go offline or become inaccessible could compromise the security of the application. The same is true for DR; if you can't restore an active instance of the application, its security could potentially be considered as compromised as potential usage of the application will be restricted, potentially as part of an attack, which could lead to several other issues for an organization and a loss of revenue.

Certificates

The role of certificates in your application is to facilitate encryption, such as when using HTTPS on your web applications.

An interesting note is that Microsoft provides a free certificate for your App Service instance on Azure, with some limitations on use and deployment. This can save a lot of money especially when considering web applications. This free certificate is designed to be a turn-key solution for securing your custom DNS address in your App Service instance. The benefit of using this service is that it is automatically managed and renewed for you as part of the App Service instance, removing the administrative burden on you. When the certificate is renewed, so too are the bindings associated with it.

Networking

Networking is an interesting topic for your applications and can result in many sleepless nights if it's not planned and managed correctly. The rule of thumb for hardening your network is to secure your perimeters and isolate traffic via perimeters, as well as by adopting the **Zero Trust model** (where you don't trust any application or service that doesn't intend to communicate with the application). It should only be public-facing if your application requires public access. You will also want to consider a **Web Application Firewall (WAF)** and a **firewall** service for public traffic, as well as something internal. Azure provides several options for privatizing traffic for your application and it's important to understand your traffic flow when you're considering your implementation.

To explore the settings related to networking security for your App Service instance, complete the following steps:

1. Click on the `Networking` option from the left menu of the application.
2. The first item you will want to configure is `access restriction`, which applies to inbound traffic. To access this, click the blue text next to `Public network access`:

Figure 15.41: Public network access

3. You will be presented with the `Access restrictions` blade. This will act as a whitelist or blacklist for your traffic, depending on how you configure your rules. As the most secure option, you should restrict all traffic except for your allowed rules. The options for `Public network access` are as follows:

   - `Enabled from all networks`: This option allows access from anywhere including from public networks (internet) to your application.
   - `Enabled from select virtual networks and IP addresses`: This option allows you to be more selective with the networks that are allowed to connect to your application, and you can be specific on the IP addresses allowed as well. This is the second most secure option.
   - `Disabled`: This option completely removes public access to your web application and is the most secure.

   For this exercise, select `Enabled from all networks`.

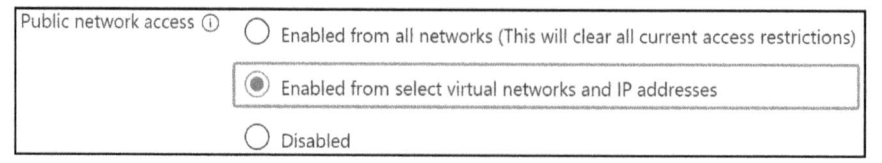

Figure 15.42: Public network access setting

4. Next is the `Site access and rules` section. Here, you will configure the rules for connecting to your site. The first choice is deciding what action to take when your rules are not matched. The more secure option is `Deny` and that is what you will use for this exercise. Click `+ Add` to start adding your first rule.

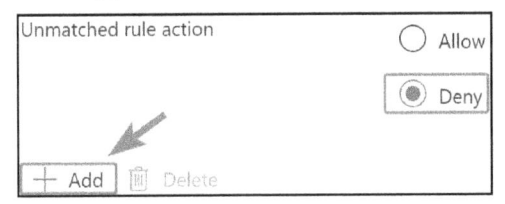

Figure 15.43: Unmatched rule action

5. Enter the following into the `Add rule configuration` blade that shows up:

   - Name: `myfirstrule`.
   - Action: `Allow`.
   - Priority: `300`.
   - Type: `IPv4`.
   - `IP Address Block`: Place your IPv4 address here with a `/32` suffix. You can obtain your address from Google by searching `whatsmyip` or going to a site such as `whatsmyip.com` to find your IP.

6. Click `Add rule`. When entering a range, you can enter it in CIDR notation, with a single IP being `/32` for CIDR. Enter an IP address. IPv6 works in the same fashion except for IPv6 addresses or ranges. Note that the rule with an IP range of `/32` specifies that it is that specific IP address that will be allowed to access the application. The following screenshot shows the settings you will configure for this section:

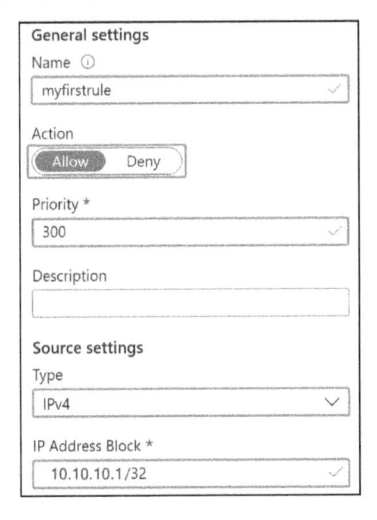

Figure 15.44: First rule

7. You will notice that you can configure your restriction rules for two different sites, designated by each tab. The first is the public endpoint for your application labeled as `Main site`, while the second is identified as `Advanced tool site`. If you click the second tab, note that it contains its own set of rules and there is a checkbox option to allow it to use the main site's rules too. This `Advanced tool site` has an endpoint suffix of `scm.azurewebsites.net`, which is used for the Kudu console and web deployments. The `Virtual Network` source option allows you to select a network that you have configured previously to allow traffic through. Click `Save` at the top of the screen.

8. The next configuration for inbound traffic is `App assigned address`. Clicking this option will take you to the `Custom domains` blade. This will be configured in the next step. This is another method of enhancing security as the domain can be configured to something that is trusted by your organization or users. It will confirm that you are using certificate delivery to enhance the security of your application.

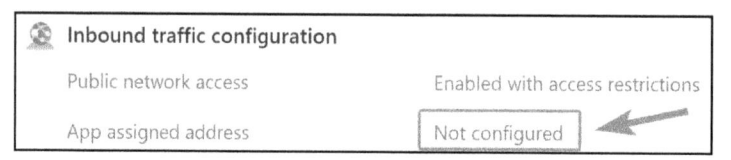

Figure 15.45: App assigned address

9. The last inbound configuration option is **Private endpoints**. Selecting this allows you to completely remove all public access to your application. Your application will be assigned an NIC with a private IP from the associated VNet and subnet you connect it to. To enable public access for this configuration, you would need some form of **network address translation** (**NAT**) configuration to reach your application. This can be achieved by deploying an **application gateway**, using **Azure Front Door**, or using your firewall service to translate traffic from one of its public IP addresses to your application over the private endpoint. This is a great way to secure traffic to your application, but as you can see, it can quickly cause complications. This setting will force you to consider how the other components of your application communicate with each other and the outside world. You won't be configuring a private endpoint in this exercise.

10. For outbound communication, you can configure **Virtual network integration**, which will associate your application with a designated subnet. Note that to assign a web app to a subnet, it will need to assume delegated access for the subnet. This means that it can manage the DHCP deployment for the subnet and will be responsible for IP assignment on the subnet. Furthermore, it restricts what can access the subnet and limits you to which subnet can be used for what service as only a single service can have delegated administration. Note that this is for outbound communication only and will not protect inbound communication. The subnet should also be allowed to communicate with the relevant services within Azure. Click the blue text next to `Virtual network integration`:

Figure 15.46: Virtual network integration

11. Click Add virtual network integration.

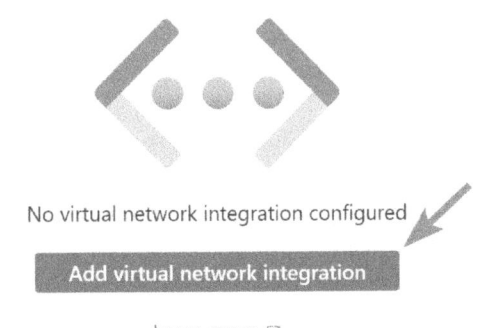

Figure 15.47: Adding a virtual network integration

12. You can also select an appropriate option from the Virtual Network dropdown, which will give you the option to either create a new subnet or use an existing one. Use whichever best suits this demo and click Connect. If you do not have a pre-configured VNet for this exercise, then you can always revisit it after reading *Chapter 16, Implementing and Managing Virtual Networking*.

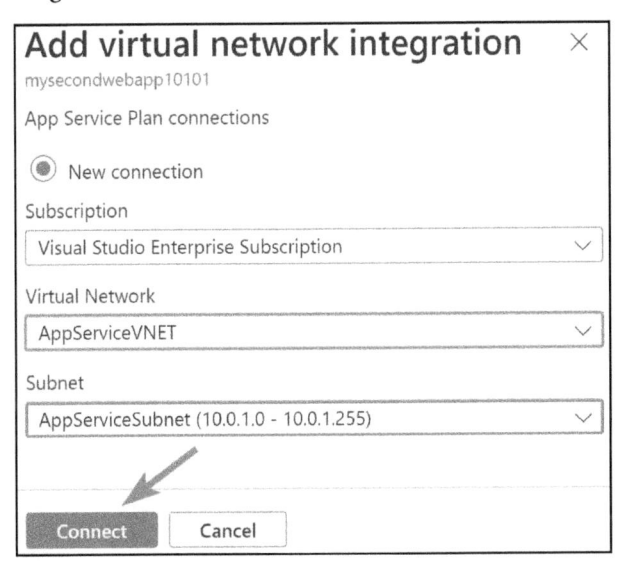

Figure 15.48: Connecting a VNet integration

13. Note that your application is now connected to the VNet and subnet you selected. Note the address details as well. Traffic from your application can now be controlled for outbound traffic using **user-defined routes (UDRs)** on the network. You can also associate NSGs and a NAT gateway:

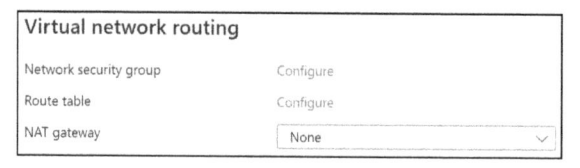

Figure 15.49: Virtual network routing

14. The last configuration item for outbound traffic is `Hybrid connections`. This feature is a service that enables endpoint connectivity for your application and provides a connection solution where you don't have direct access paths to your on-premises environments or other environments from Azure. It enables a mechanism for TCP communication that's mapped to a port number for that corresponding system or service. Each hybrid connection is associated with a single host and port, which enhances security as it's easier to manage and correlate the traffic.

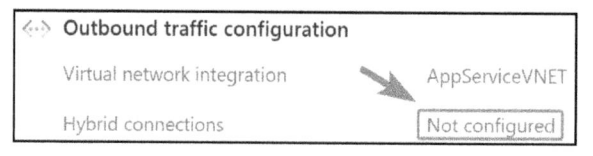

Figure 15.50: Hybrid connections

CORS

The final security configuration item to be aware of is the `CORS` option under **API context** on the left menu. CORS should be disabled unless it's required as it exposes more vulnerabilities to your application, especially when it's not managed correctly.

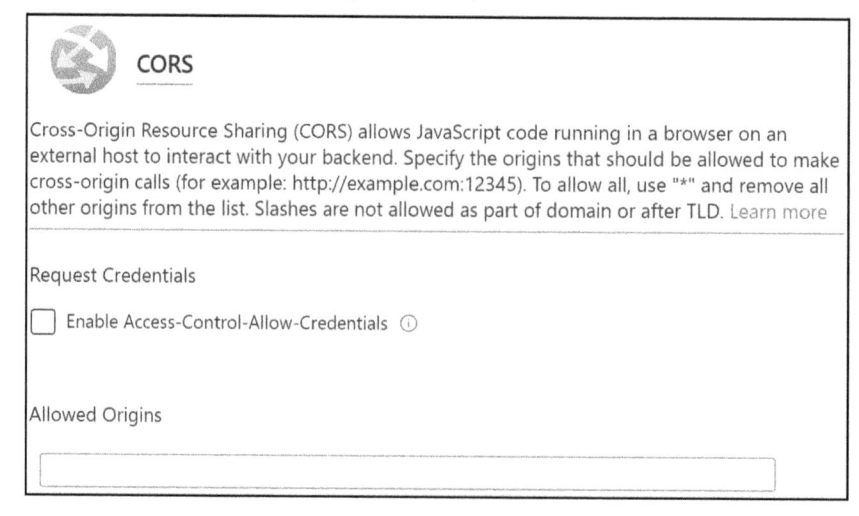

Figure 15.51: CORS

Additional Considerations

As you have seen, there are a variety of options for securing your App Service instances on Azure. A security-in-depth approach should be adopted, and you need to consider it in terms of multiple layers from identity to networking to code management. While you have seen most configurable items available directly from Azure, there are some others you should be aware of when implementing your workloads, such as the following:

- Azure Front Door
- Azure Application Gateway with WAF
- Network virtual appliance/Azure Firewall (either native or third-party firewall)
- Vulnerability scanning
- GitOps

Now that you have reviewed the different security settings, you should feel more familiar with the controls that are available and when to use them. It's especially important to understand the configurations that are relative to traffic flow. In the next section, you will learn how to configure custom domain names.

Configuring Custom Domain Names

Custom domains allow you to connect to your web application using the public DNS name that you have chosen for your application. To do this, you need to own the respective domain and prove that you have authority over it. Your custom domain could be, for example, www.yourapp.com. There are several providers for purchasing a domain, though this is outside the scope of this book. For suggestions on getting started, you could buy directly from Microsoft, which also leverages GoDaddy. To configure a custom domain, follow these steps:

1. Navigate to the App Service instance you worked on in the previous exercises.
2. From the left menu, under the `Settings` context, click `Custom domains`. From the blade that appears, click `+ Add custom domain`.
3. Select the following configurations:
   - `Domain provider:` `All other domain services`. Any domain not procured through Azure will be specified under this option.
   - `TLS/SSL certificate:` `App Service Managed Certificate`. You also have the option to add a certificate later, which can be an externally purchased certificate or you can take advantage of the Azure-generated certificate, with one free at a time offered per App Service instance on the platform.

- `TLS/SSL type: SNI SSL`. **Server Name Indication Secure Sockets Layer (SNI SSL)** is used to verify multiple domains, even through multiple certificates when required on the same IP address. In other words, this allows multiple domains to exist behind a single IP address. IP-based SSL refers to the domain being bound to a specific IP address. On Azure, IP-based SSL incurs a cost whereas SNI SSL does not.
- `Domain: yourapp.com`. This must be changed to whatever custom domain entry you require. If you do not have a domain then consider renting one for a year or just following the exercises in the book.
- `Hostname record type: CNAME`. There are two types of records you can deploy to verify domain ownership: CNAME or `A record` (or `Host A`).

The configurations of each are specified here:

Type	Host	Value
CNAME	`[sub domain]` or `[sub domain].[domain]` E.g.: `www` or `www.[sub domain]`	Azure App Service FQDN E.g.: `[appname].azurewebsites.net`
TXT	`Asuid.[sub domain]` or `[asuid.www.[sub domain]` Eg: `asuid.www` or `asuid.www.[sub domain]`	Custom domain verification. See Figure 15.52.

Table 15.2: Hostname record types

1. You will be presented with a section labeled `Domain validation`. Copy the value of each and note the host record.

Type	Host	Value
CNAME	mysecondwebapp10101	mysecondwebapp10101.azurewebsites.net
TXT	asuid.mysecondwebapp10101	625A956EC25C69FB14837299E326AB10EDF250344D1AABB45DFEB1A4E17C0B79

Figure 15.52: Domain validation

2. Create new records for your domain and follow the preceding table for guidance.
3. Back on the `Add custom domain` screen, click `Validate` at the bottom of the window. Note that sometimes, it can take a while before validation is successful.

Configuring Custom Domain Names

Domain validation

To validate your domain ownership, copy the hostname records below and enter them with your domain provider. Learn more

↓ Export to CSV

Type	Host	Value	Status
CNAME	mysecondwebapp10101	mysecondwebapp10101.azurewebsites.net	
TXT	asuid.mysecondwebapp10101	625A956EC25C69FB14837299E326	

ⓘ App Service Managed Certificate only supports alphanumeric, dash, and period characters. If you need to use special characters for your custom domain, select "Add certificate later" and secure it with another trusted certificate.

[**Validate**] [Add] [Cancel]

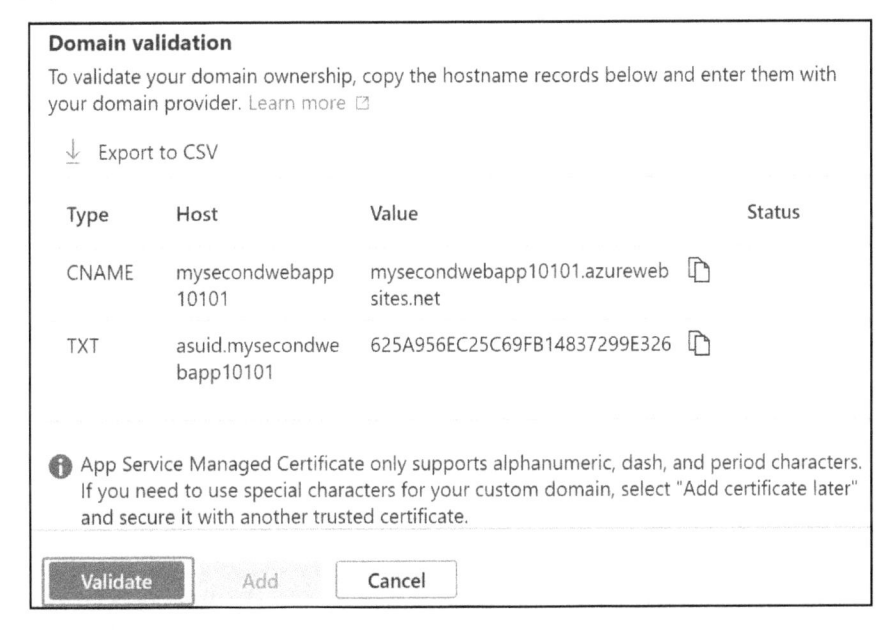

Figure 15.53: Domain validation records

> **Note**
>
> You can also map custom domains using **A** records or a wildcard (*) **CNAME** record. Go to https://learn.microsoft.com/en-us/azure/app-service/app-service-web-tutorial-custom-domain for more details.

4. Once completed, click the Add button.

Type	Host	Value	Status
CNAME	mysecondwebapp10101	mysecondwebapp10101.azurewebsites.net	✓
TXT	asuid.mysecondwebapp10101	625A956EC25C69FB14837299E326	✓

✓ Validation passed. Select **Add** to finish up.

ⓘ App Service Managed Certificate only supports alphanumeric, dash, and period characters. If you need to use special characters for your custom domain, select "Add certificate later" and secure it with another trusted certificate.

[Validate] [**Add**] [Cancel]

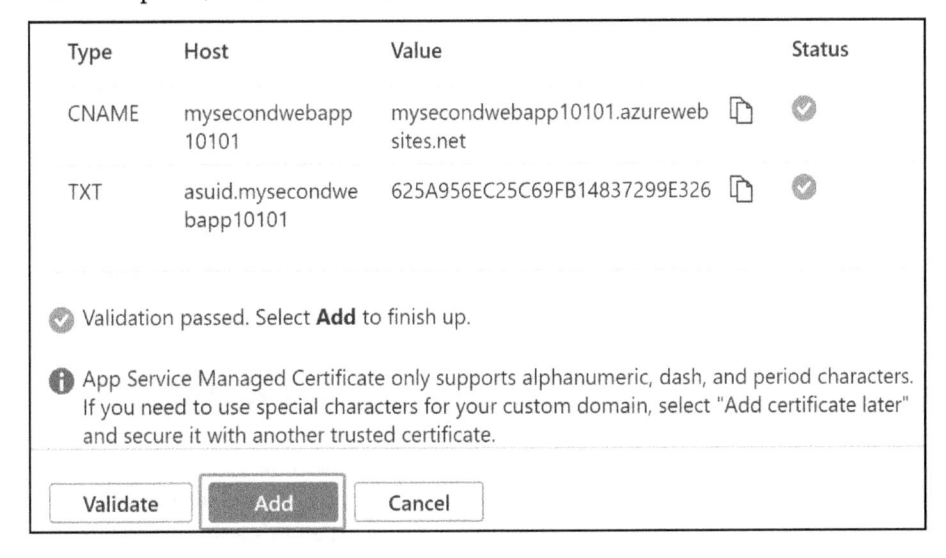

Figure 15.54: Validated domain records

5. The following screenshot shows an example of the TXT and CNAME records that you may have created with your domain host (all the providers have slightly different configurations):

Figure 15.55: TXT and CNAME records

6. With that, your custom domain has been added. Azure will automatically generate a certificate for you. Azure allows one certificate per web app to be generated by the platform for your custom domain. This can save you a lot of money as, typically, you will need to procure a certificate from a third-party vendor. Your certificate will be valid for six months once it's been created.

7. DNS propagation can take up to 48 hours to occur, though sometimes, this can happen within minutes, depending on whether your DNS was used and the **Time to Live** (**TTL**) setting has been configured. You should now be able to browse your web app using the custom domain you configured. Note that you can connect using HTTPS and get a valid certificate check:

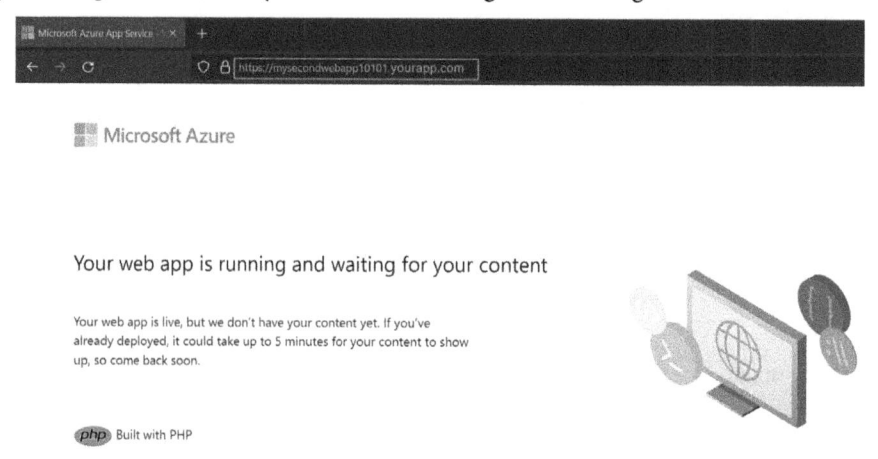

Figure 12.56: Browsing to your custom domain

You now know how to configure a custom domain for your web app within Azure, as well as how to generate a valid certificate using the platform for a certified secure HTTPS connection. Typically, this is done for production-based applications that are exposed to the internet and it is a common administrative duty for those that work in organizations that utilize many web applications. In the next section, you will learn how to configure backups for your applications.

Configuring a Backup for an App Service Instance

Your application is running well, but you're concerned that if something fails or data is lost, you won't be able to restore your application. You decide that backing it up is a good idea and start to explore different ways to back up your application. Thankfully, Azure makes this a simple process, where you just need to think about what your backup strategy needs to look like and then configure the service accordingly.

Remember that using a backup is different from performing DR in that DR restores operational services, whereas backups enable point-in-time restorations of data to recover from loss or accidental deletion. Azure automatically enables backups to be run every hour for new App Service instances. You may want to customize the schedule. Follow these steps to configure a custom backup schedule for your application:

1. Navigate to the App Service instance you worked on in the previous exercises.
2. From the left menu, under `Settings`, click `Backups`. From the blade that appears, click `Configure custom backups` at the top of the screen.
3. You will need a storage account to store your backups. Since you haven't pre-created an account, you will create it as part of this exercise. Click the `Create new` button by `Storage account:`

Figure 15.57: Create a storage account

4. Configure your storage account details and click `Create`.
5. Next, you will need a container. Currently, this doesn't exist since you just created a new storage account. Click `Create new` by `Container`.
6. Name the container `backups` and click `Create`.
7. For backups, you have the option to specify whether to use an automated schedule or you would like to manually back up as and when needed. Preferably, you would opt for an automated schedule that prevents mistakes from occurring, such as forgetting to back up. Click `Set schedule`.
8. Configure your backup so that it runs `every day` at a `set time` from the date you would like this to start. In this example, I have set this to `2024/03/23` at `7:00:00` am. Set your `Retention` period (in days) to `60` and set `Keep at least one backup`. Click `Next : Advanced >`.

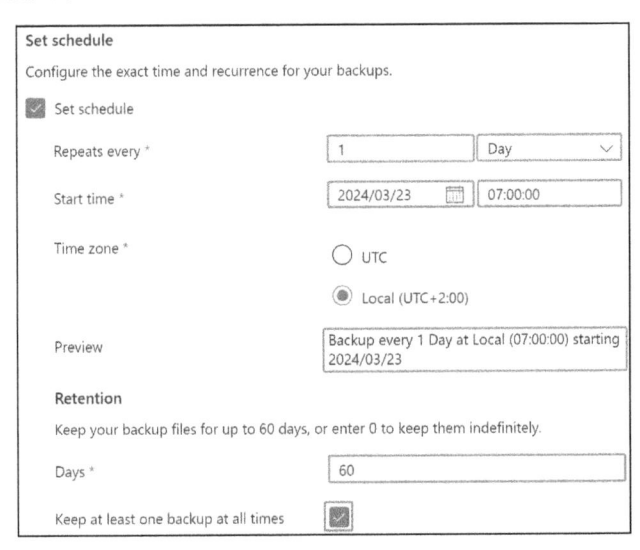

Figure 15.58: Backup schedule

9. Note that you also have the option to configure a backup for your database. You won't configure this for this exercise. Click `Configure`.

10. You will see that your first custom backup has run, and you may also see other backups from the automatic backup schedule.

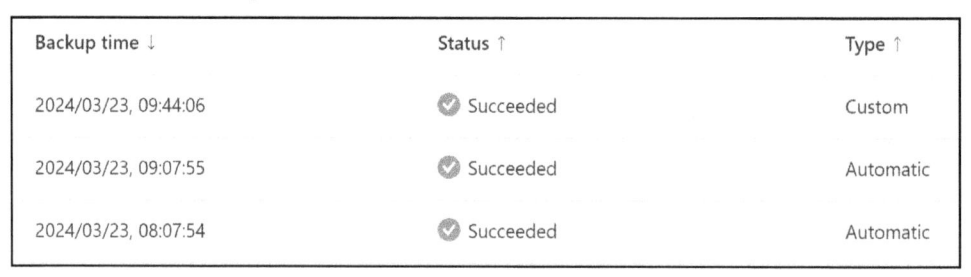

Backup time ↓	Status ↑	Type ↑
2024/03/23, 09:44:06	✓ Succeeded	Custom
2024/03/23, 09:07:55	✓ Succeeded	Automatic
2024/03/23, 08:07:54	✓ Succeeded	Automatic

Figure 15.59: Backup overview

11. Look at the options at the top of the screen and notice you have an option for `Backup Now` as well as a `Restore` button; the first, `Backup Now`, is for manually initiating a backup to be performed, while the other, `Restore`, allows you to recover data when required:

Figure 15.60: Backup and restore

You now understand how to back up your Azure App Service instance and should feel confident in configuring this going forward. In the next section, you will learn about the various network settings. Since you covered some of the available networking configurations in the previous sections, we will predominantly focus on how to configure a private endpoint.

Configuring Networking Settings

You learned how to perform VNet integration in the *Securing an App Service Instance* section. In this section, you will learn how to configure a private endpoint for your App Service instance. Complete the steps that follow:

1. Navigate to the App Service instance you worked on in the previous exercises.

2. From the left menu, under `Settings`, click `Scale up (App Service plan)`. On the blade that appears, ensure that you have chosen a `Premium V2` or `Premium V3 SKU` to continue with this exercise. Click `Select`.

3. From the left menu, under `Settings`, click `Networking`. From the blade that appears, click the blue text by `Private endpoints`.

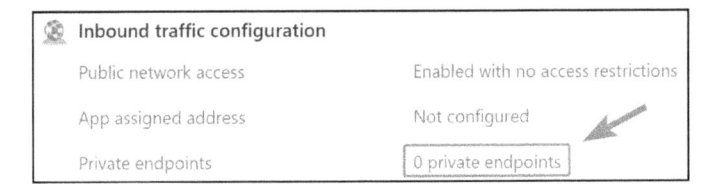

Figure 15.61: Private endpoints

4. Click Add, then Express.

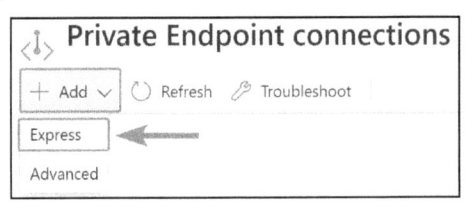

Figure 15.62: Add private endpoint connections

5. Enter a name, ensure that you have the right subscription selected, and select the correct VNet your private endpoint will be connecting to. Then, select a subnet you would like to connect to. Finally, select Yes for Integrate with private DNS zone. This last feature allows Azure to create a **Fully Qualified Domain Name** (**FQDN**) in your private zone for your private endpoint that can be reached by your resources. If you select No, then you will need to ensure that your DNS zone is maintained by another DNS service, such as Active Directory (on-premises version) and configured on your VNet for DNS lookup queries to forward to your DNS server(s). Click OK.

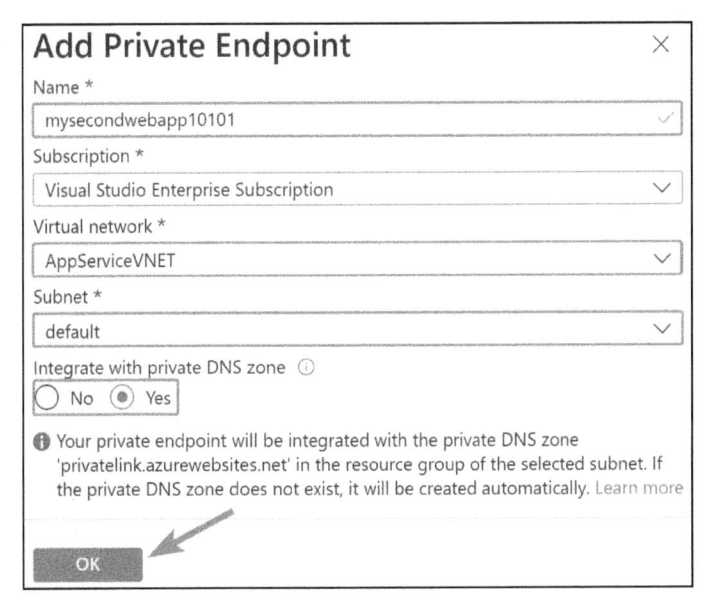

Figure 15.63: Add Private Endpoint

6. On the `Private Endpoint connections` screen, which you will see after deploying your resource, click on the new endpoint you have created. Click the name of your private endpoint (where the text is highlighted in blue) to open the `Private endpoint` blade:

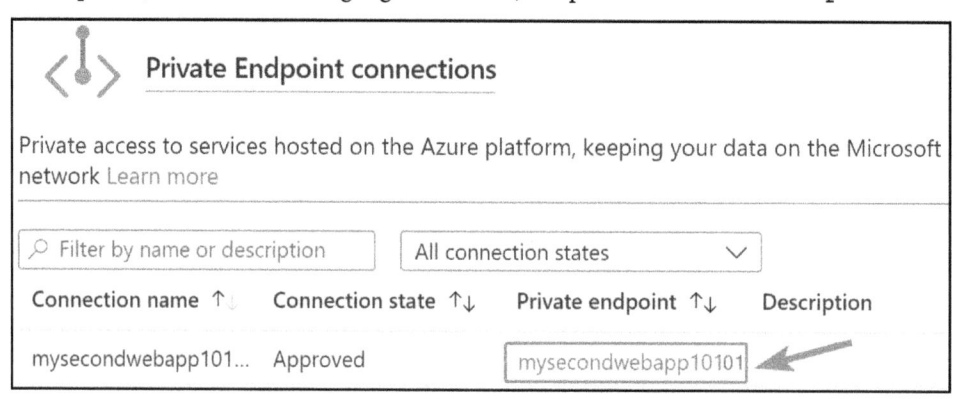

Figure 15.64: Private Endpoint connections

7. From the left menu, under the `Settings` context, click `DNS configuration`. From the blade that appears, scroll down to `Customer Visible FQDNs` and note the FQDN names associated with your service. Note that these are now associated with a private IP that belongs to the subnet you selected previously:

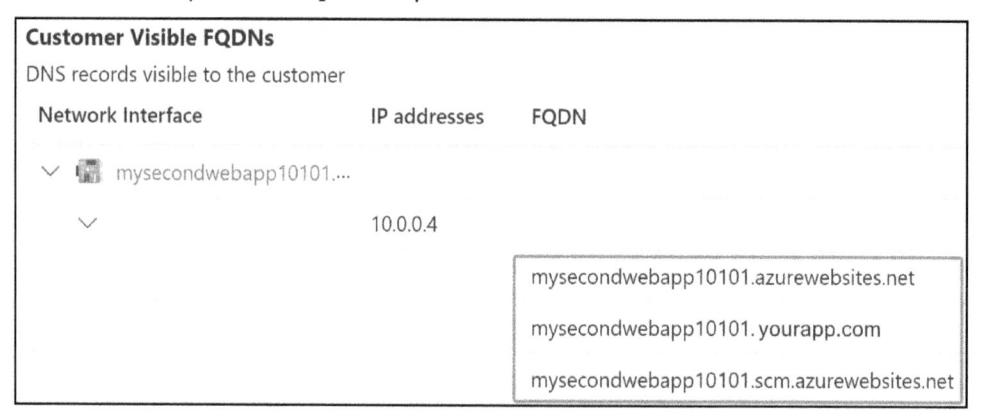

Figure 15.65: Customer Visible FQDNs

8. Scrolling down further, you will see `Custom DNS records`. Note that the **FQDN** variable that's been assigned is very much the same as the website FQDN you have for `azurewebsites.net`, except it also contains `privatelink` as a prefix. So, you now have an FQDN of `[app name].privatelink.azurewebsites.net`. This is also associated with the private IP you saw previously. Note that if you were to perform an `nslookup` command on the preceding FQDNs, you would get a public IP address for your service:

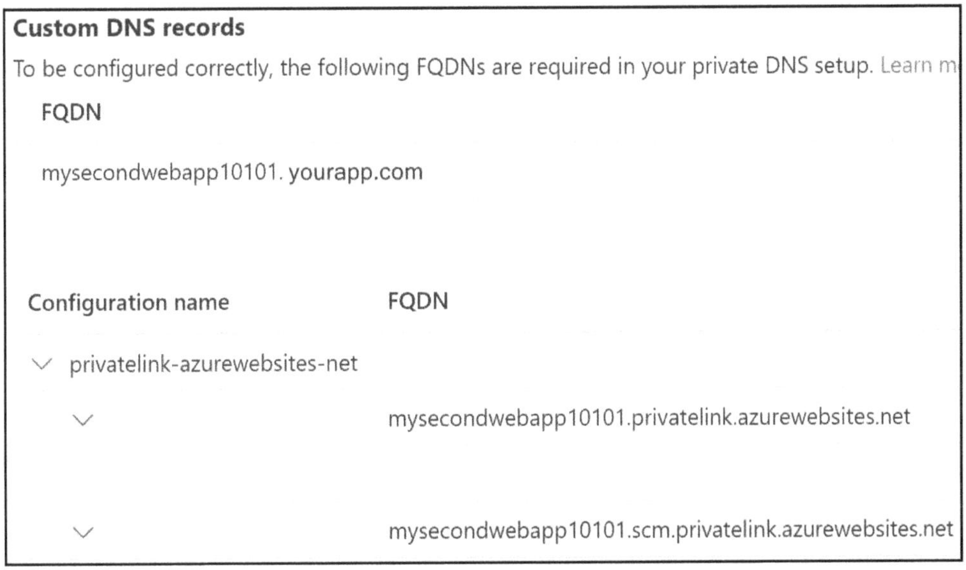

Custom DNS records

To be configured correctly, the following FQDNs are required in your private DNS setup. Learn m

FQDN

mysecondwebapp10101. yourapp.com

Configuration name   **FQDN**

∨ privatelink-azurewebsites-net

   ∨   mysecondwebapp10101.privatelink.azurewebsites.net

   ∨   mysecondwebapp10101.scm.privatelink.azurewebsites.net

Figure 15.66: Custom DNS records

9. Attempting to access your site now will deliver an error since public access is now revoked.

> **Note**
> If you have applied DNS to the VNet you are associating with and have configured a private DNS zone, you will need to ensure that your DNS servers have been configured to forward lookup to Azure for the private endpoint namespace related to your service. You can find alternative details about configuring the on-premises DNS solution to forward DNS traffic to Azure DNS in the following article: `https://learn.microsoft.com/en-us/azure/private-link/private-endpoint-dns-integration`

With that, you have just configured a private endpoint and should feel confident in deploying one. You are also aware of some of the DNS complexities you should look out for to ensure you can resolve the host correctly with your resources.

Configuring Deployment Settings

There are several deployment settings related to your App Service instance that you should be aware of. Deployment settings allow you to upload your code or manage source control and deployment slots.

Deployment slots are logical segmentations of your application that can pertain to different environments and versions. Let's say you have an application that is running in production mode (meaning it's live and operational), and you want to work on some new code updates to introduce new features to the next version of your application. Typically, you would work on this in a test environment and deploy it accordingly to the production environment, once you felt that adequate testing had been performed before deploying anything to production.

Well, deployment slots provide a solution that allows you to deploy code to these slots to test the different functions and features of your applications, as well as code updates. You can run your primary deployment slot as the native application and deploy additional slots, such as test, staging, and pre-production, that can be used for your new code. You have the option to swap deployment slots and revert at any time. The transition period is quick and enables a different paradigm in app management. You can, for instance, switch to the another slot and find that your application is not connecting to the required services and is slow. In this case, you can quickly flip back to the original code you had before any changes were made.

Let's look at a brief configuration of a deployment slot before proceeding to the next part of this section:

1. Navigate to the App Service plan you worked on in the previous exercises.
2. From the left menu, under `Deployment`, click `Deployment slots`.
3. From the top of the blade, click `+ Add Slot`.
4. Enter a name – in this case, `TEST` – and leave `Clone settings from` set to `Do no clone settings`. Click Add, then `Close`:

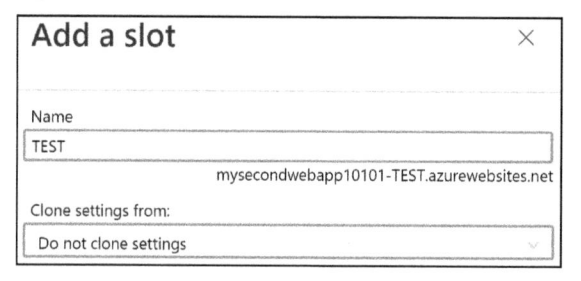

Figure 15.67: Add a deployment slot

5. The name you chose previously will form part of the FQDN for the deployment slot so that it can be accessed as a normal application, as shown in the preceding screenshot.
6. Click `Swap` and set your source as the new deployment slot you just created, and `Target` as the current slot. Click `Swap`, then `Close`.

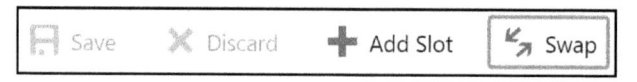

Figure 15.68: Swap

Now that you know about deployment slots, let's explore Deployment Center:

1. Navigate to the App Service instance you worked on in the previous exercises.
2. From the left menu, under `Deployment`, click `Deployment Center`.

3. Click the `Settings` tab. Here, you have the option to deploy code from a CI/CD tool from the `Source` drop-down menu. At the time of writing, the available options are `GitHub`, `Bitbucket`, `Local Git`, and `Azure Repos`. You also have the option to push from an external Git resource. Once you have chosen your `Source` tool, you must authorize your account and click `Save` at the top of the screen.

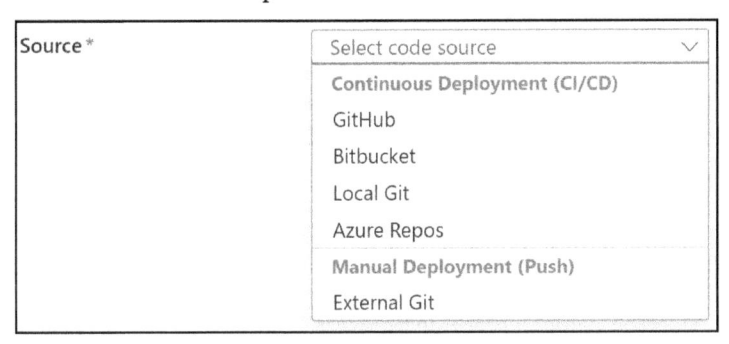

Figure 15.69: Deployment source

4. Click the `FTPS credentials` tab and note the `FTPS endpoint` value. `Application scope` contains automatically generated `FTPS Username` and `Password` values that are unique to your application and deployment slot. You can use this to connect to your FTPS endpoint. You can also define a user scope and create a username and password:

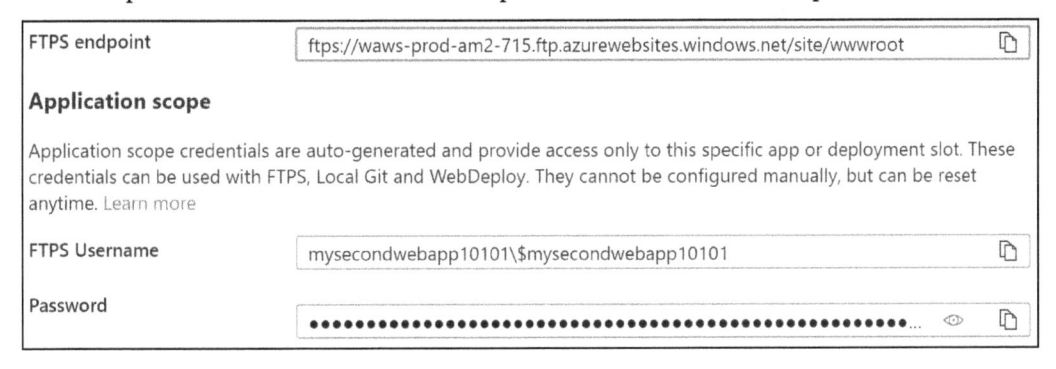

Figure 15.70: Deployment Center – FTPS credentials

With that, you have learned about the deployment settings that are available to you for your App Service instances. You should now feel comfortable navigating this aspect of Azure App Service as you know where to integrate CI/CD and where to find your FTPS credentials so that you can modify your application code.

> **Hands-on activities**
>
> Reinforce what you learned in *Chapters 10* through *15* by completing the hands-on activities for these chapters. Open the online practice resources using this link: `https://packt.link/az104dash`. Then, from the `Dashboard`, click `Hands-on Activities` and open the menu `Deploying and Managing Azure Compute Resources`

Summary

In this chapter, you learned about Azure App Service, the role of App Service plans and why they are essential to your App Service instance, and how to deploy an application, including how to manage its settings and configurations and how to secure it. Then, you explored various networking configurations for your application and the considerations you need to have when configuring these settings. You should now feel confident working with applications on Azure using App Service.

> **Note**
>
> Remember to delete the resources that you created in this chapter to minimize costs.

Exam Readiness Drill - Chapters 13-15

Apart from mastering key concepts, strong test-taking skills under time pressure are essential for acing your certification exam. That's why developing these abilities early in your learning journey is critical.

Exam readiness drills, using the free online practice resources provided with this book, help you progressively improve your time management and test-taking skills while reinforcing the key concepts you've learned.

HOW TO GET STARTED

- Open the link or scan the QR code at the bottom of this page
- If you have unlocked the practice resources, already log in to your registered account. If you haven't, follow the instructions in *Chapter 23* and come back to this page.
- Once you log in, click the START button to start a quiz
- We recommend attempting a quiz multiple times till you're able to answer most of the questions correctly and well within the time limit.
- You can use the following practice template to help you plan your attempts :

Attempt	Target	Time Limit
Working On Accuracy		
Attempt 1	40% or more	Till the timer runs out
Attempt 2	60% or more	Till the timer runs out
Attempt 3	75% or more	Till the timer runs out
Working On Timing		
Attempt 4	75% or more	1 minute before time limit
Attempt 5	75% or more	2 minutes before time limit
Attempt 6	75% or more	3 minutes before time limit

The above drill is just an example. Design your drills based on your own goals and make the most out of the online quizzes accompanying this book.

> First time accessing the online resources? 🔒
> You'll need to unlock them through a one-time process. **Head to** *Chapter 23* **for instructions**.

Open Quiz

`https://packt.link/az104e3ch13-15`

OR scan this QR code →

16
Implementing and Managing Virtual Networking

This chapter is the start of the exam objective called *Configure and Manage Virtual Networking*, which has an exam weighting of 20–30% of the overall exam.

In this chapter, you are going to experience implementing and managing virtual networking. This includes how to create and configure **Virtual Networks** (**VNets**), peer networks with each other, configure private and public IP addresses, create user-defined network routes, implement subnets, create endpoints on subnets, configure private endpoints, and finally, configure Azure DNS, including custom DNS settings and private or public DNS zones. This chapter is very important, as networking is often referred to as the cornerstone of **Infrastructure as a Service** (**IaaS**) and of all services in modern infrastructure design.

In brief, the following topics will be covered in this chapter:

- Creating and configuring virtual networks, including peering
- Configuring private and public IP addresses
- Configuring user-defined network routes
- Implementing subnets
- Configuring endpoints on subnets
- Configuring private endpoints
- Configuring Azure DNS, including custom DNS settings and private or public DNS zones

Technical Requirements

This chapter uses the following tools for the examples:

- Access to an Azure subscription with owner or contributor privileges. If you do not have access to one, students can enroll for a free account: https://azure.microsoft.com/en-us/free/.

- **PowerShell 5.1** or later installed on a Windows PC or PowerShell Core 6.x on other operating systems, to practice the labs.
- Note that, occasionally, examples can only be followed from a PC or https://shell.azure.com (PowerShell 7.0.6 LTS or later is recommended).
- Installation of the Az PowerShell module, which can be performed by running the following in an administrative PowerShell session:

```
Set-ExecutionPolicy -ExecutionPolicy RemoteSigned -Scope CurrentUser
Install-Module -Name Az -Scope CurrentUser -Repository PSGallery -Force
```

Creating and Configuring Virtual Networks

In this section, you are going to learn how to create and configure VNets and the peering of these networks. You will start with an overview of VNets and IP addressing and explore how it works within Azure.

Before you dive into how to configure VNets, take a moment to understand what VNets are and what their purpose is. A VNet in Azure is a representation of your network in the cloud that is used to connect resources such as **Virtual Machines** (**VMs**) and other services to each other.

Unlike traditional networks, which make use of physical cables, switches, and routers to connect resources, VNets are completely software-defined. VNets have isolated IP ranges, and resources placed inside a VNet do not talk to the resources in other VNets by default. To allow resources in two different VNets to talk to each other, you would need to connect the VNets using VNet peering.

> **Note**
> All resources deployed to a VNet must reside in the same region as the VNet.

IP Addressing Overview

Azure supports both private and public IP addresses. Private IP addresses are assigned within the VNet in order to communicate with other resources within it and cannot be accessed via the internet by design. Public IP addresses are internet-facing by design and can be assigned to a VM or other resources, such as VPN gateways and load balancers.

Both private and public IP addresses can be configured to be dynamic or static. Dynamic IP addresses change when the host or resource is restarted, whereas static IP addresses do not change even if the resources are restarted.

Dynamic IP addresses are automatically assigned by an Azure DHCP service based on the subnet range. When a VM is deallocated (stopped), the dynamic IP address is released back into the pool of IP addresses that can be assigned to other resources again. By default, private IP addresses are dynamic but can be changed to static via the Azure portal, PowerShell, and the Azure **Command-Line Interface** (**CLI**) when needed.

Static public IP addresses are random public IP addresses that do not change after being assigned to a resource. Unlike a dynamic IP address that changes when a resource is restarted, the static IP address is reserved and persisted. Public IPs are usually assigned to internet-facing resources such as VPN Gateway, Azure Firewall, Azure Bastion, Application Gateway, Azure Load Balancer, and, in some instances, VMs.

Creating a VNet

Now that you have covered the basic networking components, you will learn how to configure a VNet via PowerShell.

The following script will connect you to your Azure tenant and subscription, then you will create a new resource group named `az104-vnets`, followed by the deployment of a VNet:

Copy and paste the code into PowerShell. You can obtain it from the exercise files here: https://packt.link/KRur7.

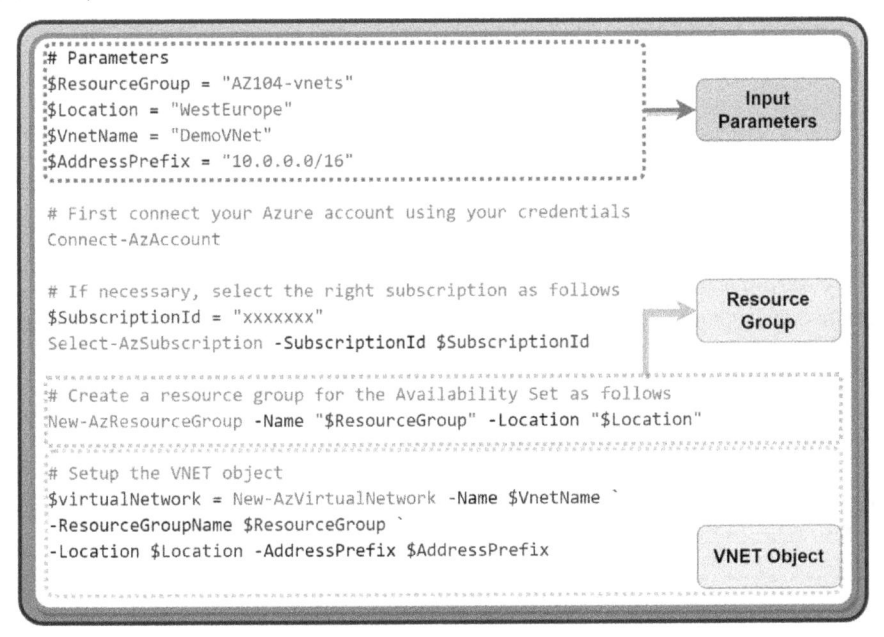

```
# Parameters
$ResourceGroup = "AZ104-vnets"
$Location = "WestEurope"
$VnetName = "DemoVNet"
$AddressPrefix = "10.0.0.0/16"

# First connect your Azure account using your credentials
Connect-AzAccount

# If necessary, select the right subscription as follows
$SubscriptionId = "xxxxxxx"
Select-AzSubscription -SubscriptionId $SubscriptionId

# Create a resource group for the Availability Set as follows
New-AzResourceGroup -Name "$ResourceGroup" -Location "$Location"

# Setup the VNET object
$virtualNetwork = New-AzVirtualNetwork -Name $VnetName `
-ResourceGroupName $ResourceGroup `
-Location $Location -AddressPrefix $AddressPrefix
```

Figure 16.1: Creating a new VNet

1. Next, you will need to configure a subnet range within the VNet and apply the changes to the VNet with the last line of code:

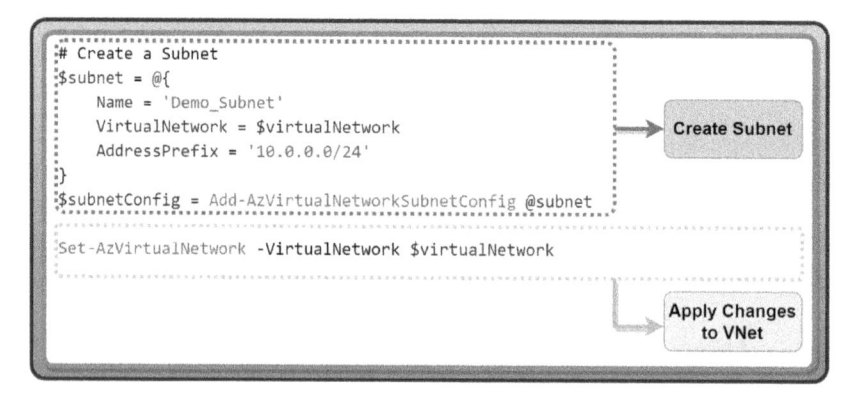

```
# Create a Subnet
$subnet = @{
    Name = 'Demo_Subnet'
    VirtualNetwork = $virtualNetwork
    AddressPrefix = '10.0.0.0/24'
}
$subnetConfig = Add-AzVirtualNetworkSubnetConfig @subnet

Set-AzVirtualNetwork -VirtualNetwork $virtualNetwork
```

→ Create Subnet

→ Apply Changes to VNet

Figure 16.2: Adding a subnet

2. Verify in the Azure portal that the new VNet and subnet have been created:

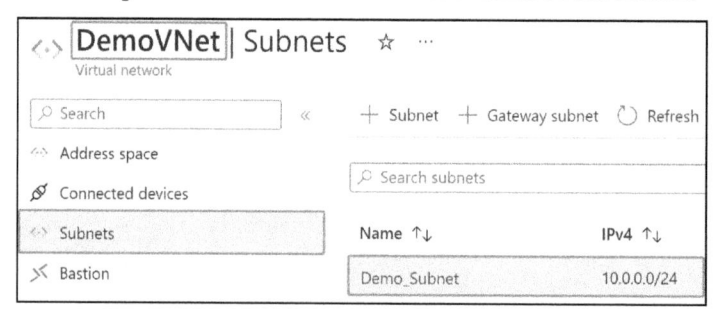

Figure 16.3: Your VNet in the Azure portal

In this exercise, you learned about creating a VNet in Azure using PowerShell. This is a frequent administrative task you are likely to encounter, and you have learned a programmatic method of creating networks that makes your VNet creation more consistent and less error-prone.

> **Note**
> If you are getting an error stating that scripts are disabled on your system, you can use the following PowerShell command to resolve it: `set-executionpolicy unrestricted -Scope CurrentUser`.

VNet Peering

One of the exam objectives is to gain the ability to configure VNet peering. VNet peering is when two or more VNets are linked with each other so that traffic can be sent from one network to another. There are two types of VNet peering:

- **VNet peering**: Connects VNets within the same region. There is a cost associated with inbound and outbound data transfers for VNet peering.

- **Global VNet peering**: Connects VNets across different regions. This is more costly than VNet peering within the same region.

When utilizing VNet peering, you benefit from networks working in conjunction with each other seamlessly as a logically spanned network with low latency and high bandwidth.

There are a few additional VNet peering configurations that you should be aware of. For the following list, assume the VNet you are configuring peering on is named S_VNET:

- **Allow the peered virtual network to access 'S_VNET'**: Allows communication from a peered network to S_VNET. This automatically adds the remote VNet address space to be included as a part of the VNET service tags.

- **Allow the peered virtual network to receive forwarded traffic from 'S_VNet'**: Allows traffic forwarded by a VNet appliance in a VNet that did not originate from S_VNET to flow via VNet peering to the peered VNet.

- **Allow gateway or route server in the peered virtual network to forward traffic to 'S_VNET'**: This is relevant when sending traffic from a VNet gateway deployed to the peered VNet to S_VNET.

- **Enable the peered virtual network to use 'S_VNET's' remote gateway or route server**: Should S_VNET contain a remote gateway or route server, you can select this option to forward traffic from your gateway in S_VNET to your peered network.

- Now that you understand the various configuration items available for VNet peering, you will learn how to configure a VNet peer in the next exercise.

Configuring a VNet Peer

To configure VNet peering, follow these steps. You will first need to create another VNet using the following PowerShell code:

1. In PowerShell, paste the following code and run it to create another VNet in the same resource group as the previous VNet you created earlier:

```powershell
# First connect your Azure account using your credentials
Connect-AzAccount

# Setup the VNET object
$vnet = @{
    Name = 'DemoVNet_2'
    ResourceGroupName = 'AZ104-vnets'
    Location = 'WestEurope'
    AddressPrefix = '192.168.0.0/24'
}
$virtualNetwork = New-AzVirtualNetwork @vnet

# Create a Subnet
$subnet = @{
    Name = 'Demo_Subnet'
    VirtualNetwork = $virtualNetwork
    AddressPrefix = '192.168.0.0/24'
}
$subnetConfig = Add-AzVirtualNetworkSubnetConfig @subnet

# Apply VNet Configurations
Set-AzVirtualNetwork -VirtualNetwork $virtualNetwork
```

Figure 16.4: Deploying a second VNet

2. Sign in to the Azure portal, navigate to the resource group, and confirm that you now see that two networks exist:

Name ↑↓	Type ↑↓	Location ↑↓
DemoVNet	Virtual network	West Europe
DemoVNet_2	Virtual network	West Europe

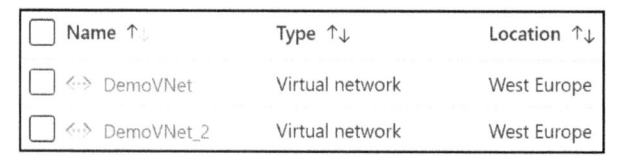

Figure 16.5: Your VNets for peering

3. Next, select `DemoVNet`.
4. From the `Settings` pane on the left, click `Peerings`. Click + Add at the top of the screen:

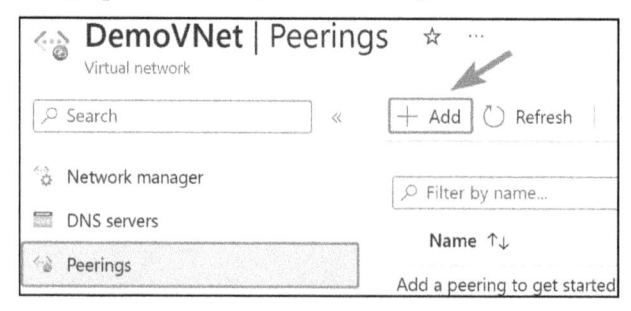

Figure 16.6: Configuring VNet peering

5. Next, configure the peering link name under `This virtual network`: `DemoVNet_to_DemoVNet2`.

- Check `Allow 'DemoVNet' to access the peered virtual network` to allow traffic to flow from `DemoVNet` to the peered VNet, `DemoVNet2`.

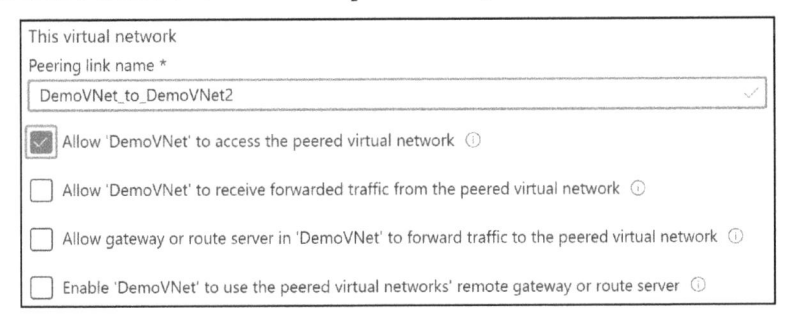

Figure 16.7: This virtual network

6. For `Remote virtual network`, configure the settings as follows and click `Add`:

    - `Peering link name`: `DemoVNet2_to_DemoVNet`
    - `Virtual network deployment model`: `Resource manager`
    - `Virtual network`: `DemoVNet_2`
    - Check `Allow 'DemoVNet_2' to access 'DemoVNet'` to allow traffic to flow from `DemoVNet_2` to the peered VNet, `DemoVNet`.

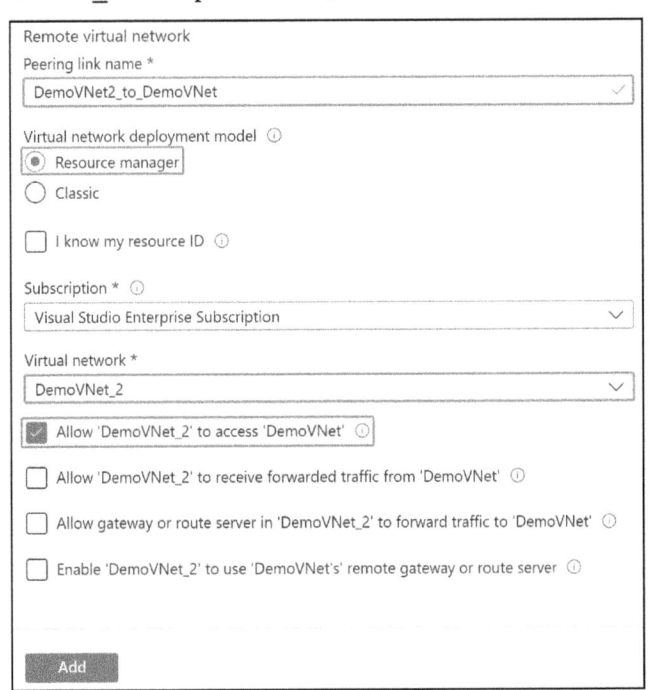

Figure 16.8: Remote virtual network

7. Give the peering status a few minutes to enforce the peering. The final peering status will show as `Connected`:

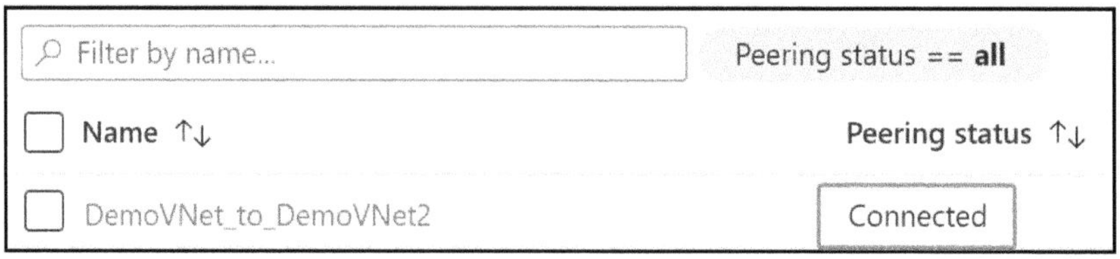

Figure 16.9: Successfully configured peering

In this exercise, you learned how to create a peer between two Azure VNets, `DemoVNet` and `DemoVNet_2`. You also learned how to configure traffic to be allowed to flow in the various directions between the source and remote networks across the peer. This is a valuable skill to have in your daily administrative tasks as this is a common networking scenario on Azure, especially when observing hub-and-spoke topologies.

In the next exercise, you will learn how to test that your VNet peer is operating as expected by sending traffic across the peer.

Testing your VNet Peer

Now test your VNet peer so that you can see the peering in action. Typically, the two networks in Azure would be isolated from each other and communication would not reach other networks without peering. To test the peer, you are going to deploy two VMs, one in each of the networks you have created, and test sending traffic from a VM in the `DemoVNet` network to the `DemoVNet_2` network. The code for this exercise can be found here: `https://packt.link/KRur7`.

The steps to test the VNet peer you created for your `DemoVNet` and `DemoVNet_2` networks are as follows:

Deploy the VMs using the following PowerShell code (VNetTest.ps1):

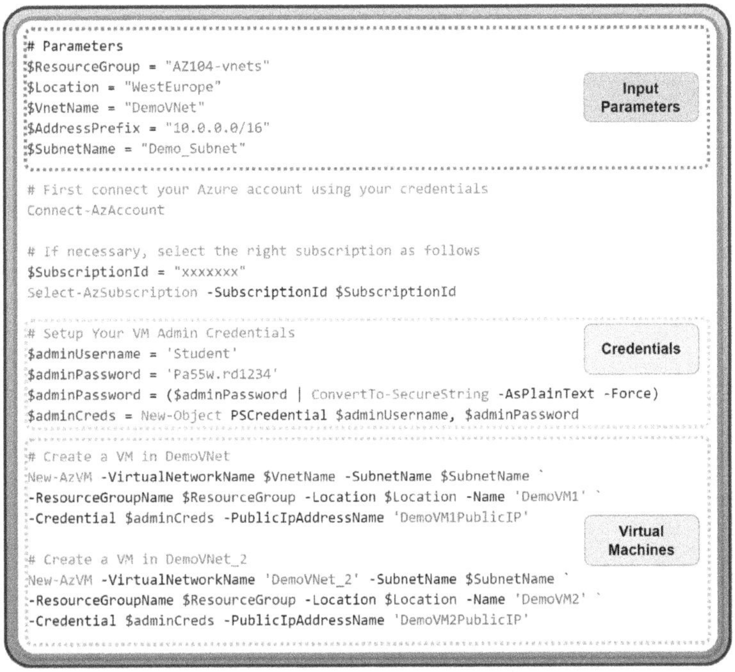

```
# Parameters
$ResourceGroup = "AZ104-vnets"
$Location = "WestEurope"
$VnetName = "DemoVNet"
$AddressPrefix = "10.0.0.0/16"
$SubnetName = "Demo_Subnet"

# First connect your Azure account using your credentials
Connect-AzAccount

# If necessary, select the right subscription as follows
$SubscriptionId = "xxxxxxx"
Select-AzSubscription -SubscriptionId $SubscriptionId

# Setup Your VM Admin Credentials
$adminUsername = 'Student'
$adminPassword = 'Pa55w.rd1234'
$adminPassword = ($adminPassword | ConvertTo-SecureString -AsPlainText -Force)
$adminCreds = New-Object PSCredential $adminUsername, $adminPassword

# Create a VM in DemoVNet
New-AzVM -VirtualNetworkName $VnetName -SubnetName $SubnetName `
-ResourceGroupName $ResourceGroup -Location $Location -Name 'DemoVM1' `
-Credential $adminCreds -PublicIpAddressName 'DemoVM1PublicIP'

# Create a VM in DemoVNet_2
New-AzVM -VirtualNetworkName 'DemoVNet_2' -SubnetName $SubnetName `
-ResourceGroupName $ResourceGroup -Location $Location -Name 'DemoVM2' `
-Credential $adminCreds -PublicIpAddressName 'DemoVM2PublicIP'
```

Figure 16.10: Deploy testing VMs

Log in (RDP) to `DemoVM1` using the preceding credentials and launch a PowerShell terminal. In PowerShell, run the following code to confirm connectivity from `DemoVM1` to `DemoVM2`. It uses the port for RDP connections, so no further configurations are required to enable the test. Should your test fail, please ensure that the private IP address for `DemoVM2` is correct in your code:

```
Test-NetConnection -ComputerName "192.168.0.4" -Port 3389
```

Note the successful connection indicated by the returned message, which should look similar to this:

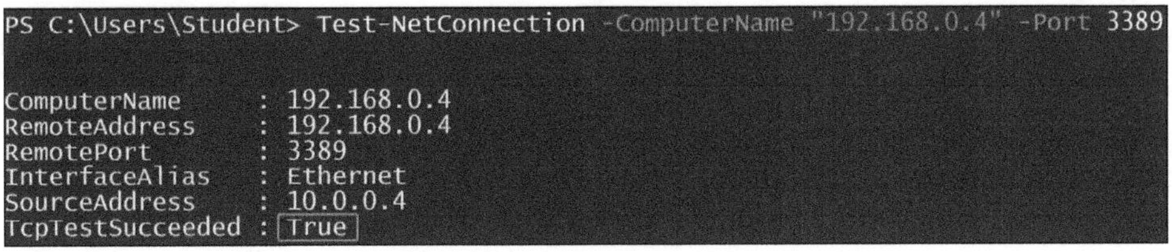

```
PS C:\Users\Student> Test-NetConnection -ComputerName "192.168.0.4" -Port 3389

ComputerName      : 192.168.0.4
RemoteAddress     : 192.168.0.4
RemotePort        : 3389
InterfaceAlias    : Ethernet
SourceAddress     : 10.0.0.4
TcpTestSucceeded  : True
```

Figure 16.11: Testing VNet peer

You have just successfully proved a connection between the VMs across different networks and subnets. This proves connectivity across the VNet peer. The following diagram illustrates the test scenario you have just conducted:

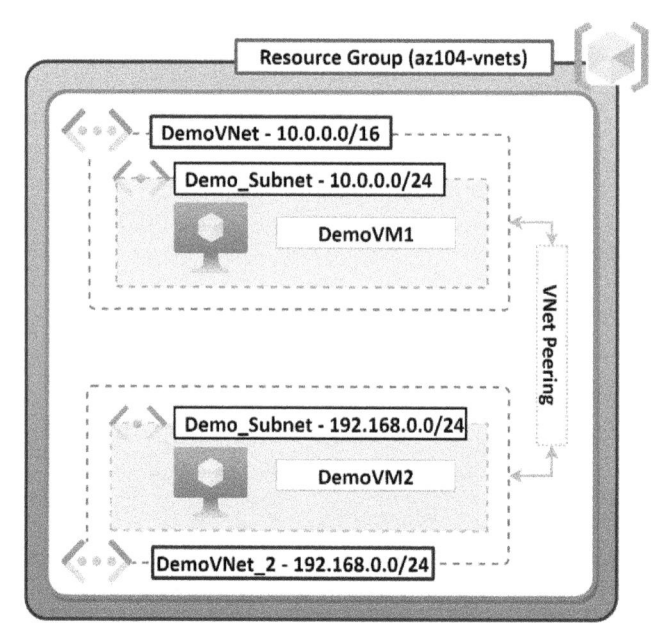

Figure 16.12: VNet peer scenario

In this section, you explored configuring a VNet in Azure as well as how to create a VNet and subnet via PowerShell. You also had a look at how to configure VNet peering between two VNets. Finally, you wrapped up testing the VNet peering you created to demonstrate it works as expected.

> **Note**
>
> You are encouraged to read up on Azure virtual networking and VNet peering further by using the following links:
>
> https://learn.microsoft.com/en-us/azure/virtual-network/quick-create-powershell
>
> https://learn.microsoft.com/en-us/azure/virtual-network/manage-virtual-network
>
> https://learn.microsoft.com/en-us/azure/virtual-network/virtual-network-peering-overview

Creating Private and Public IP Addresses

In the previous section, you had a brief look at IP addressing, such as public and private IP addressing and static and dynamic IP addresses. This section focuses on how to configure private and public IP addresses.

Configuring a Private IP Address

First, you will look at how to configure a private IP address for a VM from dynamic to static via the Azure portal. In order to do this, you are going to reference the VM you created in the previous exercise:

1. Navigate to the Azure portal by opening a web browser and navigating to `https://portal.azure.com`.

2. Navigate to one of your VMs from the previous exercise. From the left menu, under the `Networking` context, select `Network settings`.

3. Click the `Network interface` name (blue text):

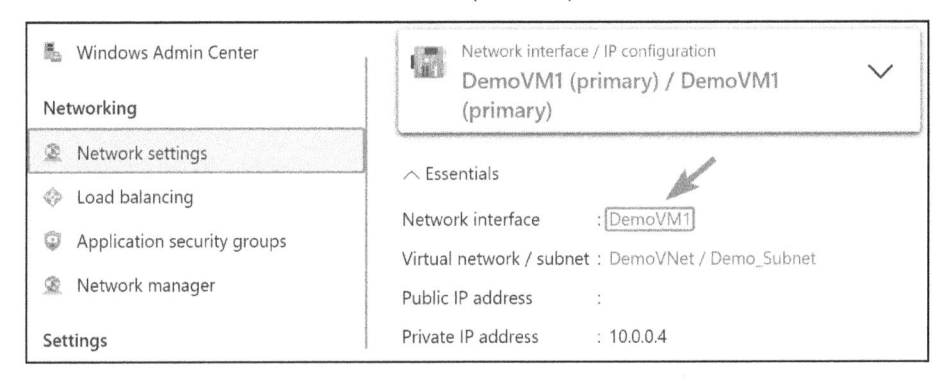

Figure 16.13: Select the NIC for the VM

4. From the left menu, click on `IP configurations` and click on the name of the IP configuration.

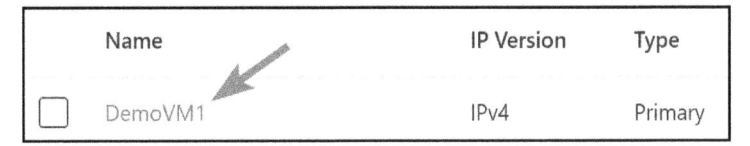

Figure 16.14: Select the IP configuration

5. On the blade window that pops up, select Static as the Allocation configuration for the private IP. Change Private IP address to 10.0.0.5 then click Save.

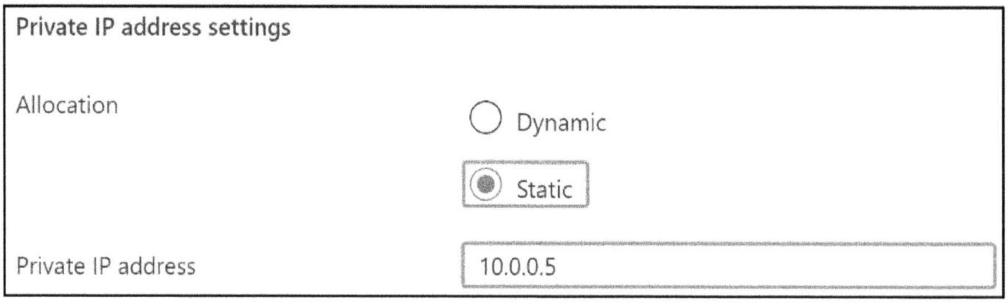

Private IP address settings	
Allocation	◯ Dynamic ⦿ Static
Private IP address	10.0.0.5

Figure 16.15: Changing to static IP allocation

In this exercise, you have learned how to configure a static private IP address. This is an important skill to have when requiring an IP that doesn't change its address.

Configuring a Public IP Address

Next, you are going to create a public IP address via PowerShell. The following implementation will only create a public IP resource that can be allocated to other resources such as VMs after deployment:

1. In PowerShell, run the following commands to connect to Azure and create your public IP resource in West Europe as a standard SKU. CreateaPublicIP.ps1 in the chapter's GitHub repo.

2. Deploy a SQL server and database using the following code in PowerShell. ConfiguringaServiceEndpoint.ps1 in the chapter's GitHub repo.

```powershell
# First connect your Azure account using your credentials
Connect-AzAccount

# Create the public IP address
$ip = @{
    Name = 'myStandardPublicIP'
    ResourceGroupName = 'AZ104-vnets'
    Location = 'WestEurope'
    Sku = 'Standard'
    AllocationMethod = 'Static'
    IpAddressVersion = 'IPv4'
    Zone = 1,2,3
}

New-AzPublicIpAddress @ip
```

Public IP Configuration Settings

Create the Public IP Resource

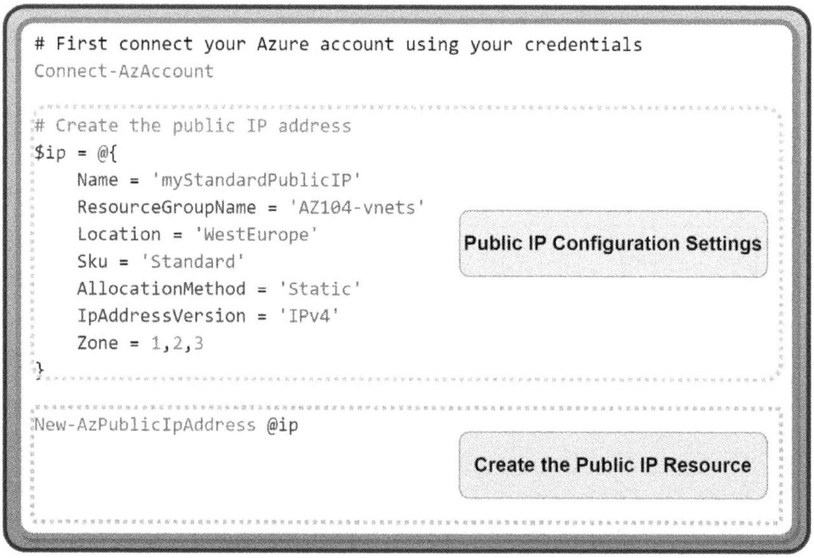

Figure 16.16: Creating a public IP resource

> **Note**
>
> The convention observed previously with the @ symbol represents what is called a splat notation in PowerShell. The configuration settings are switches that are normally used in the command that references the splatted variable. This assists in simplifying the command process into something more readable. The configuration items will directly correlate with the switch name used in the command. If you would like to read more, you can check out this page: `https://learn.microsoft.com/en-us/powershell/module/microsoft.powershell.core/about/about_splatting`.

3. Next, verify that the public IP address has been created in the Azure portal by navigating to your resource group and confirming you can see a `Public IP address` resource named `myStandardPublicIP`.

Name ↓	Type ↑↓	Location ↑↓
myStandardPublicIP	Public IP address	West Europe
DemoVNet_2	Virtual network	West Europe
DemoVNet	Virtual network	West Europe

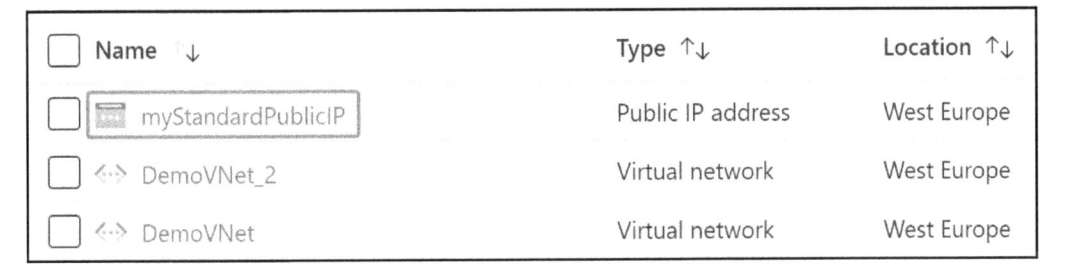

Figure 16.17: Verifying your public IP address resource

It is that simple to create a public IP address via PowerShell. Once the IP address has been created, it is ready to be assigned to a resource such as a VM or other types of resources that support pre-created public IP addresses.

Next, you are going to learn about user-defined routing.

User-defined Routing

By default, Azure automatically creates system routes and assigns them to the different subnets within a VNet. The system routes help guide the network traffic to reach the intended destination, such as another VM in the same subnet or VNet, or even to reach other resources outside of the existing VNet you are in. These routes cannot be removed but can be overridden by custom routes known as **User-Defined Routes (UDRs)** that will enable you to have more control over the next hop of your traffic. These are commonly used in environments that have a hub-and-spoke topology for the networking layer. The next hop for known resources may be to a **Network Virtual Appliance (NVA)** such as a third-party firewall solution that also controls routing between networks. This can force all traffic to be interrogated by the firewall before being directed to the approach location. UDR rules are based on the most granular (i.e., most specific) rules being applied first, so in the event of multiple applicable rules being identified for your traffic, the most specific will always win in precedence. UDRs have a *next-hop* setting that points to the next destination from a routing perspective so that traffic can be sent to the correct destination.

There are three main next-hop types for system routes:

- **VNet**: This routes traffic between address ranges within the address space of a VNet. For each address range defined in the VNet, Azure will create an individual route for each range. It will also automatically enable traffic to route between subnets through the system route table entries.
- **Internet**: This routes traffic specified by the address prefix to the internet; the default route is **0.0.0.0/0**, which means anything that does not have a defined route is by default routed to the internet. For any native Azure service, Azure will route the traffic over the Azure network backbone, preventing traffic from flowing over the internet.
- **None**: Traffic routed to a next-hop type as **none** is dropped.

UDRs are created through a route table if you want to create custom routes. When working with UDRs, it is important to note that they support the preceding routing types as well as the following:

- **VNet gateway**: This is used to route traffic to a VNet gateway
- **Virtual appliance**: A virtual appliance is a VM that usually acts as a firewall
- The relationship between a UDR and a route table is such that a route table contains all applicable routes to be applied to a VNet. System routes, as mentioned, will be automatically propagated where custom routes (UDRs) will be appended to the known list of routes in the route table. Azure automatically creates default system routes for the following address prefixes: `10.0.0.0/8`, `172.16.0.0/12`, and `192.168.0.0/16`, all of which are reserved for private use, as well as `100.64.0.0/10`. Next, you will create a route table.

Creating a Route Table

To experience working with route tables and UDRs, you are going to create a route table resource. You will specify the next hop of the route to route to the internet. Complete the steps to create a UDR via the Azure portal to forward all traffic to a VNet gateway:

1. Navigate to the Azure portal by opening a web browser and navigating to `https://portal.azure.com`.
2. Select `Create a resource`. Search for `Route table` and click on the `Route table` card that appears.
3. Click `Create`.

Figure 16.18: Creating a route table

4. Enter the following settings and click `Review + create`, then click `Create`:
   - `Resource group:` AZ104-vnets
   - `Region:` West Europe
   - `Name:` myFirstRouteTable
   - `Propagate gateway routes:` Yes

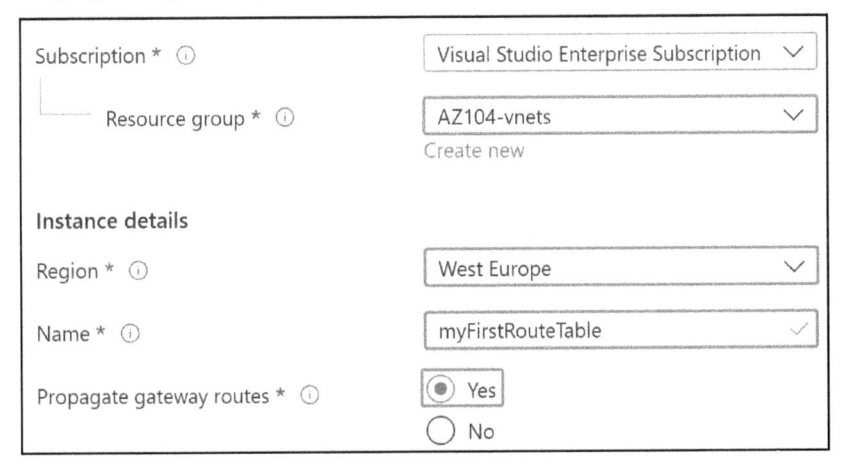

Figure 16.19: Route table configurations

5. Now that the route table has been created, navigate to it on the Azure portal.
6. From the left menu, under the `Settings` context, select `Routes`.
7. Click `+ Add` at the top of the screen.

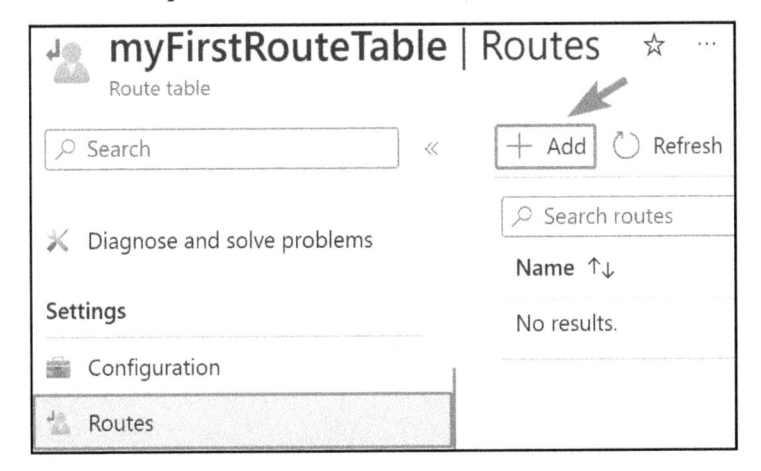

Figure 16.20: Adding a new route

8. In the blade that comes up, enter the following and click Add:

    - Route name: DemoRoute.

    - Destination type: IP Addresses. Note that there are two types of destinations that you could select from, either IP Addresses or Service Tag. The IP Addresses selection is more obvious as you can enter a specific IP or range of IP addresses as a destination. The Service Tag option is more specific to Azure-related services, and you can select a service type from this option (normally accompanied by a region) that denotes the tag for the service, which would have a preconfigured IP range associated with the service.

    - Destination IP addresses/CIDR ranges: 108.177.119.113/32.

    - Next hop type: Internet.

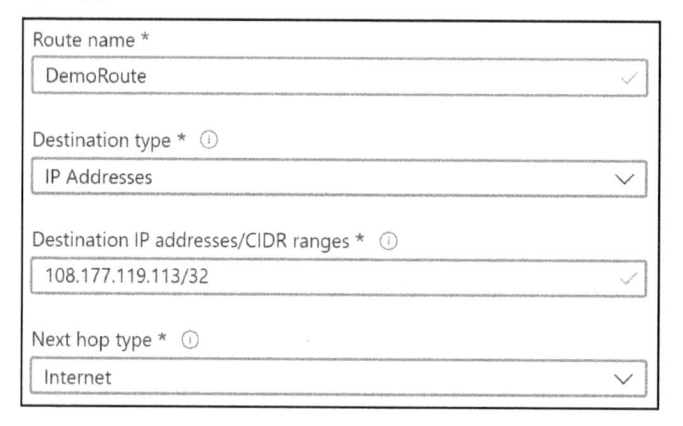

    Figure 16.21: DemoRoute configuration settings

9. You should now be able to verify that there is a new route showing up under Routes:

Name	Address prefix	Next hop type
DemoRoute	108.177.119.113/32	Internet

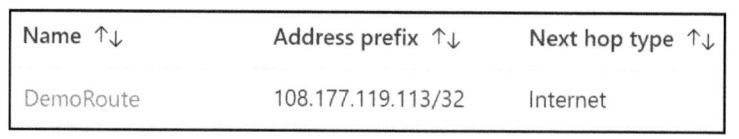

    Figure 16.22: Your new route

10. You will need to associate your new route table with a subnet to have it working. Click the Subnets option from the left menu and click + Associate.

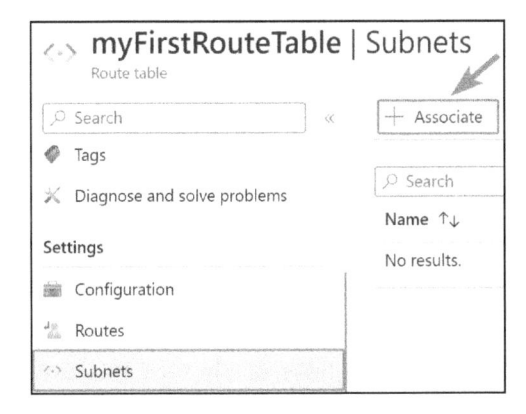

Figure 16.23: Associating to a subnet

11. Select DemoVNet and Demo_Subnet for the network configurations. Click OK.

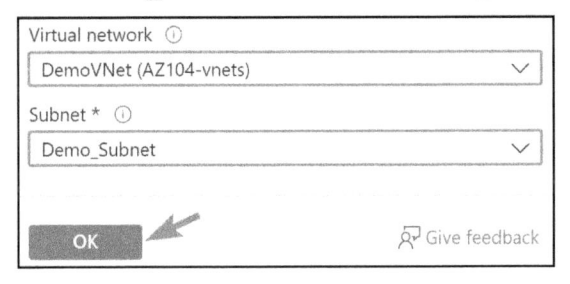

Figure 16.24: Associate network settings

12. Log in to DemoVM1, which was created earlier. Attempt the same connectivity command as before in PowerShell, except this time to a Google server on port 443:

    `Test-NetConnection -ComputerName "108.177.119.113" -Port 443`

13. You should receive a success notice indicating that your custom route works.

You have created your own route table and UDR too. You have now experienced a level of traffic control/management in Azure and should be comfortable with basic routing configurations.

> **Note**
>
> You are encouraged to read up further on Azure UDRs by visiting the following link: https://learn.microsoft.com/en-us/azure/virtual-network/virtual-networks-udr-overview.

Next, you are going to explore more configurations by implementing subnets.

Implementing Subnets

Inside a VNet, subnets allow you to segment your IP address ranges in which to place your resources. Resources in a single subnet get an IP address from the subnet IP address range. Resources in subnets within the same VNet can talk to each other. A VNet can have one or more subnets. Traffic can be filtered between subnets via either **Network Security Groups (NSGs)** or **UDRs**. It is also important to know that Azure reserves five IP addresses within each subnet that cannot be used. The reason for this is that these IPs are reserved for the network address, the Azure default gateway, Azure DNS, and the network broadcast address. An example of this is the following.

Say there is a `10.1.1.0/24` subnet; the following addresses are reserved:

- `10.1.1.0`: This is reserved for the network address
- `10.1.1.1`: This is reserved for the default gateway
- `10.1.1.2` and `10.1.1.3`: These are reserved by Azure to map DNS IPs to the VNet space
- `10.1.1.255`: This is reserved as a broadcast address

> **Note**
> Subnets can be added, removed, or modified. Provided no resources still exist within the subnet, it can be deleted. If you are looking to make modifications to the subnet address range, you can do so as long as no resources are attached to the subnet.

Subnets within a VNet can be managed via the following platform-native methods:

- **The Azure portal**: This is done by signing in to `https://portal.azure.com`
- **PowerShell**: This is done by authenticating to your Azure tenant and making changes via the CLI
- **The Azure CLI**: This is done by authenticating to your Azure tenant and making changes via the CLI
- **A REST API**: This is done by authenticating to your Azure tenant and using the `PUT` command
- **Azure Bicep** or **Azure ARM**: These tools will allow you to leverage infrastructure as code to manage networks
- **Azure Cloud Shell**: This is a shell service that is accessed through the browser as a web page that is globally accessible

> **Note**
> Subnet address ranges cannot overlap one another.

You have learned about the conceptual component of how a subnet functions and can be modified in Azure. In the next exercise, you will add a subnet to a VNet in Azure.

Adding a Subnet to a VNet

Now you can go ahead and add a subnet to an existing VNet via the Azure portal using the following steps:

1. Navigate to the Azure portal by opening a web browser and navigating to `https://portal.azure.com`.
2. Browse to `DemoVNet`, which you made previously, and click `Subnets` from the left menu under the `Settings` context. Click `+ Subnet`.

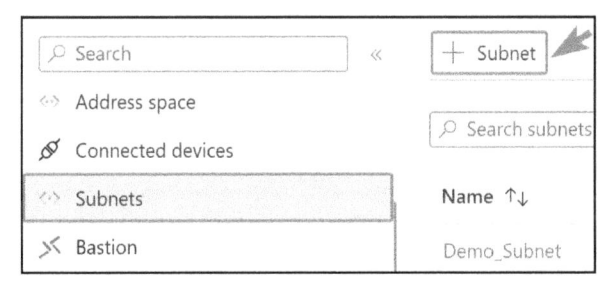

Figure 16.25: Adding a subnet

3. Enter the following and click `Save`:

   - Name: `Demo_Subnet2`
   - `Subnet address range: 10.0.1.0/24`
   - Leave the rest of the settings as the default values

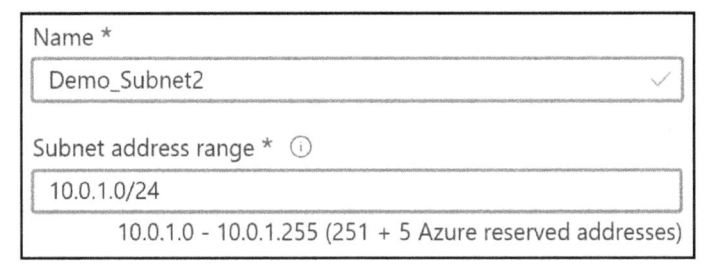

Figure 16.26: Demo_Subnet2 configuration

4. The new subnet will show up under the `Subnets` section once created:

Name ↑↓	IPv4 ↑↓
Demo_Subnet	10.0.0.0/24
Demo_Subnet2	10.0.1.0/24

Figure 16.27: New Demo_Subnet2

In this short section, you looked at subnetting in Azure and learned how to create additional subnets via the Azure portal. In the next section, you are going to look at configuring endpoints on subnets.

Configuring Endpoints on Subnets

Endpoints, also referred to as **service endpoints**, allow secure and direct connectivity to Azure services over the Azure backbone network. Endpoints allow you to secure the traffic between your VNets, including subnets, and critical Azure resources such as Key Vault and SQL databases. Service endpoints allow private IP addresses in a VNet to be routed over the Azure backbone without requiring a dedicated public IP address.

Service endpoints are only supported on a limited number of Azure services.

Here are some of the key benefits of using service endpoints:

- **Improved security for Azure service resources**: Routing of traffic to Azure services *to* and *from* the VNet. Subnets are routed through the Azure network without the need to make use of dedicated public IP addresses.

- **Optimal routing for Azure service traffic from your VNet**: Optimized routing that keeps traffic on the Azure backbone network, allowing you to still audit and monitor outbound internet-facing traffic.

- **Ease of configuration and management**: Less work is required as there are no more public IP addresses required to manage via the firewall and no **Network Address Translation (NAT)** or gateway devices to configure and manage.

Now that you understand more about the components involved in configuring endpoints on subnets, you will configure this in the next exercise.

Configuring a Service Endpoint

In this exercise, you will first deploy a SQL server and a database resource, and then configure a SQL service endpoint on a subnet via the Azure portal:

1. Sign in to the Azure portal at `https://portal.azure.com`.
2. Deploy a SQL server and database using the following code in PowerShell.

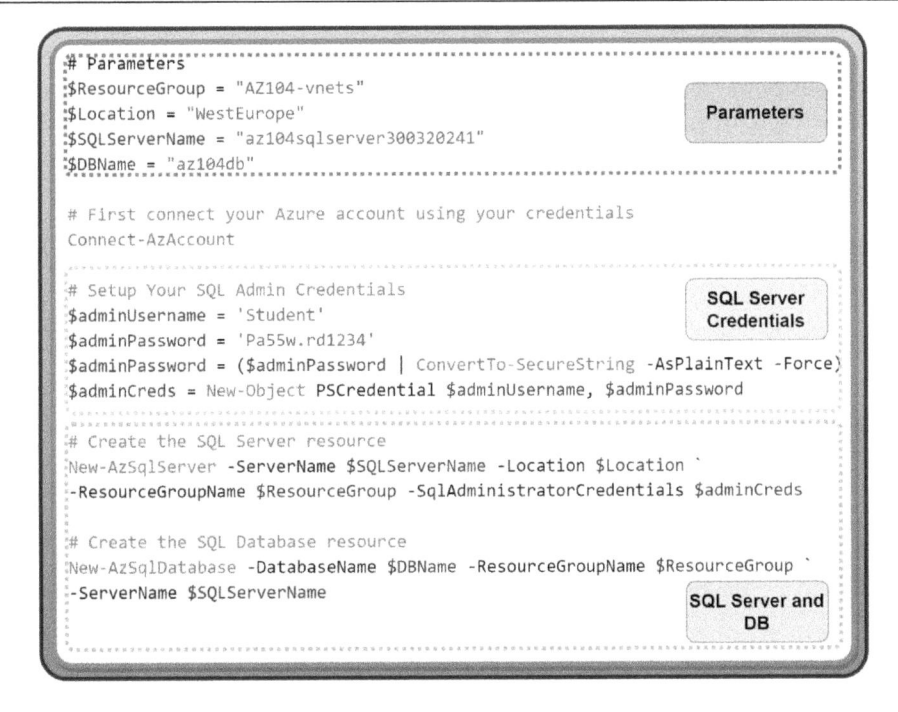

```powershell
# Parameters
$ResourceGroup = "AZ104-vnets"
$Location = "WestEurope"
$SQLServerName = "az104sqlserver300320241"
$DBName = "az104db"

# First connect your Azure account using your credentials
Connect-AzAccount

# Setup Your SQL Admin Credentials
$adminUsername = 'Student'
$adminPassword = 'Pa55w.rd1234'
$adminPassword = ($adminPassword | ConvertTo-SecureString -AsPlainText -Force)
$adminCreds = New-Object PSCredential $adminUsername, $adminPassword

# Create the SQL Server resource
New-AzSqlServer -ServerName $SQLServerName -Location $Location `
-ResourceGroupName $ResourceGroup -SqlAdministratorCredentials $adminCreds

# Create the SQL Database resource
New-AzSqlDatabase -DatabaseName $DBName -ResourceGroupName $ResourceGroup `
-ServerName $SQLServerName
```

Figure 16.28: Creating a SQL server and database

3. You will now create a new subnet for your SQL services. Navigate to your `DemoVNet` resource and click Subnets from the left menu.
4. Click + Subnet from the top menu.
5. Configure the subnet with the following and click Save:
   - Name: SQL_Subnet
   - Subnet address range: 10.0.2.0/24
   - SERVICE ENDPOINTS: Select Microsoft.Sql under Services

SERVICE ENDPOINTS

Create service endpoint policies to allow traffic to specific azure resources from your virtual network over service endpoints. Learn more

Services ⓘ
Microsoft.Sql

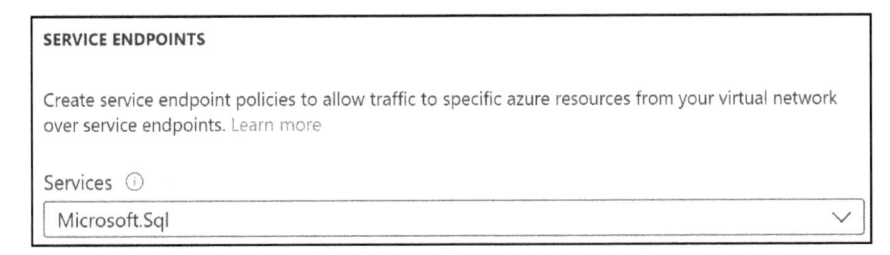

Figure 16.29: Enabling SQL service on subnet

6. For the next section, you will require a VNet in the same region as your SQL Server instance. West Europe was not allowing SQL servers at the time of writing, so another region was used and the respective resources were created in the same region to complete the exercise. Navigate to your SQL Server resource. From the left menu, under `Security`, select `Networking`:

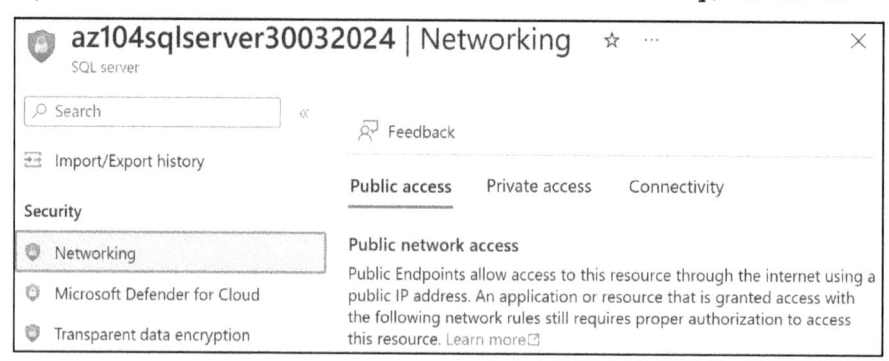

Figure 16.30: Navigating to the SQL Server Networking option

7. Ensure that for `Public network access`, `Selected networks` is chosen. Under `Virtual networks`, click the `+ Add a virtual network rule` button:

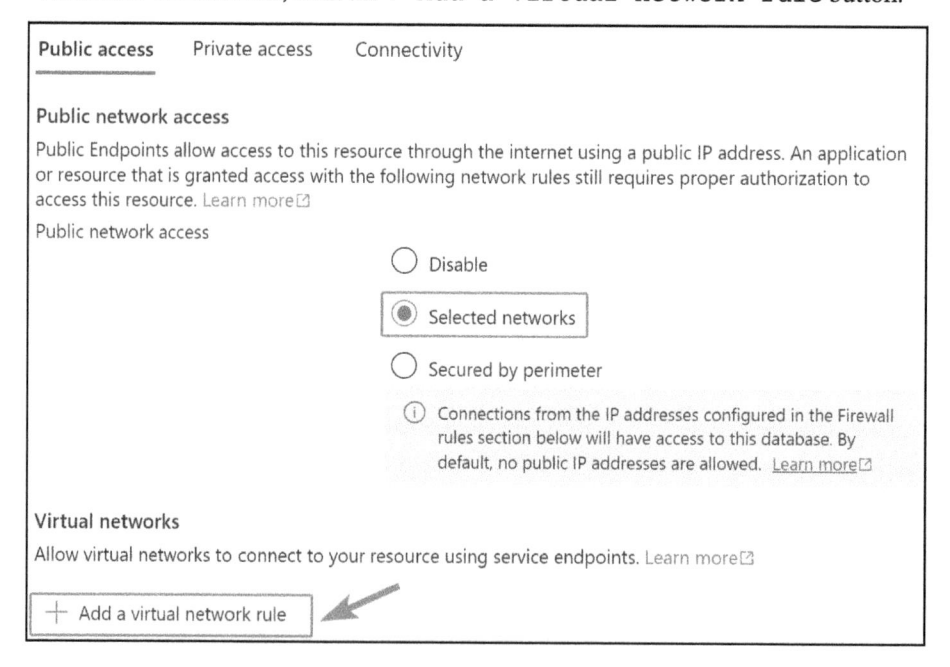

Figure 16.31: Selecting a virtual network

8. You will now select the VNet and subnet to be linked to the SQL server that is allowed access to the service. This is why the service endpoint you created earlier is important. Create the network rule with the following configurations and click OK:

   - Name: `SQLTrafficRule`
   - Virtual network: `DemoVNet`
   - Subnet name / Address prefix: `SQL_Subnet / 10.0.2.0/24`

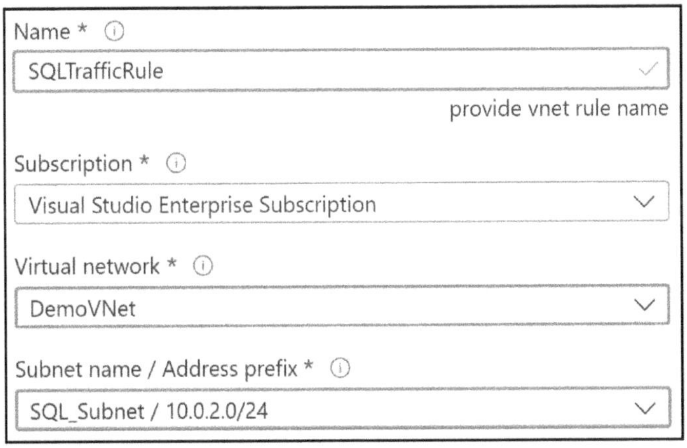

Figure 16.32: SQLTrafficRule

You have just successfully integrated your subnet into the SQL Server list. This is a more secure approach to networking as it limits the accessible layers for the SQL Server resource, meaning that it is more restrictive. Notice that you have not enabled any public IP addresses yet, so administration for your server resource can only occur over the subnet you just integrated.

In this section, you explored service endpoints – what they are, and how to configure them, more specifically for an SQL service with a specific subnet. This same pattern applies to any other service endpoint you would like to integrate with.

> **Note**
> You are encouraged to read up on Azure service endpoints by visiting the following link: `https://learn.microsoft.com/en-us/azure/virtual-network/virtual-network-service-endpoints-overview`.

Configuring Private Endpoints

Azure Private Link enables you to access **Platform as a Service** (**PaaS**) services such as Azure Storage and SQL databases, and Azure-hosted services over a **private endpoint** in your own VNet.

Much like service endpoints, private endpoints allow traffic between a VNet and a service to travel through the Microsoft backbone network. This way, exposing your service over the internet is no longer required.

A key difference between service endpoints and private endpoints is that service endpoints connect to Azure/Microsoft services over their backbone while the PaaS resources are still outside of the VNet and require additional integration to interact with the VNet. To be routed as such, a network interface will be attached to the PaaS service as private endpoints, and this will allow the resources to interact directly with your VNet. It is important to understand that private endpoints keep all the traffic within your VNet.

Creating a Private Endpoint

For this exercise, you will integrate Azure App Service with both a VNet and a private endpoint. The difference between the two is that the private endpoint provides a private inbound connection to the application and the VNet integration provides private outbound connections. So, it is important when considering your services that you account for the direction of the flow of your traffic:

1. Run the following PowerShell code, also found in the GitHub repo for the chapter, to create an App Service instance in your `AZ104-vnets` resource group. CreatingaPrivateEndpoint. ps1 in the chapter's GitHub repo.

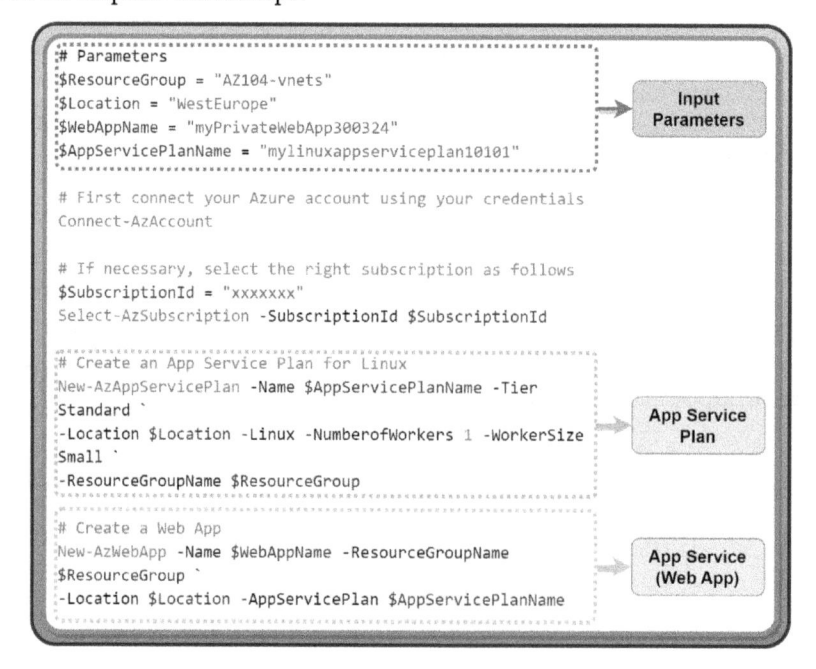

```
# Parameters
$ResourceGroup = "AZ104-vnets"
$Location = "WestEurope"
$WebAppName = "myPrivateWebApp300324"
$AppServicePlanName = "mylinuxappserviceplan10101"

# First connect your Azure account using your credentials
Connect-AzAccount

# If necessary, select the right subscription as follows
$SubscriptionId = "xxxxxxx"
Select-AzSubscription -SubscriptionId $SubscriptionId

# Create an App Service Plan for Linux
New-AzAppServicePlan -Name $AppServicePlanName -Tier Standard `
-Location $Location -Linux -NumberofWorkers 1 -WorkerSize Small `
-ResourceGroupName $ResourceGroup

# Create a Web App
New-AzWebApp -Name $WebAppName -ResourceGroupName $ResourceGroup `
-Location $Location -AppServicePlan $AppServicePlanName
```

Figure 16.33: App Service for private endpoint exercise

Configuring Private Endpoints | 545

> **Note**
> You may notice the following character in the PowerShell scripts: `` ` ``. This character allows the code to continue on the next line and is used for the readability of the code.

2. You will now create a new subnet for App Service. Navigate to your `DemoVNet` resource and click `Subnets` from the left menu.
3. Click `+ Subnet` from the top menu.
4. Configure the subnet with the following and click `Save`:

   - Name: `AppService_Subnet`
   - Subnet address range: `10.0.3.0/24`
   - Delegate subnet to a service: Select `Microsoft.Web/serverFarms`

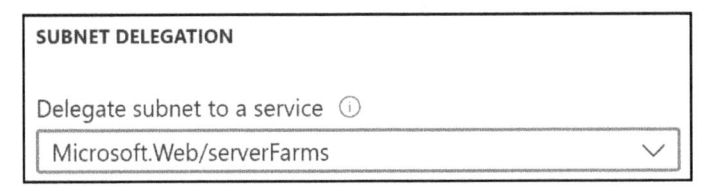

Figure 16.34: Subnet delegation

5. In the Azure portal, navigate to your `AZ104-vnets` resource group. From the top menu, click `Create`.
6. Search for `private link` and click on the `Private Link` card.
7. Click `Create`.

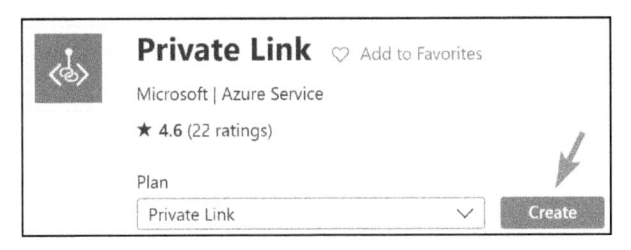

Figure 16.35: Create a private link

8. On the `Overview` pane, click on `Create private endpoint`:

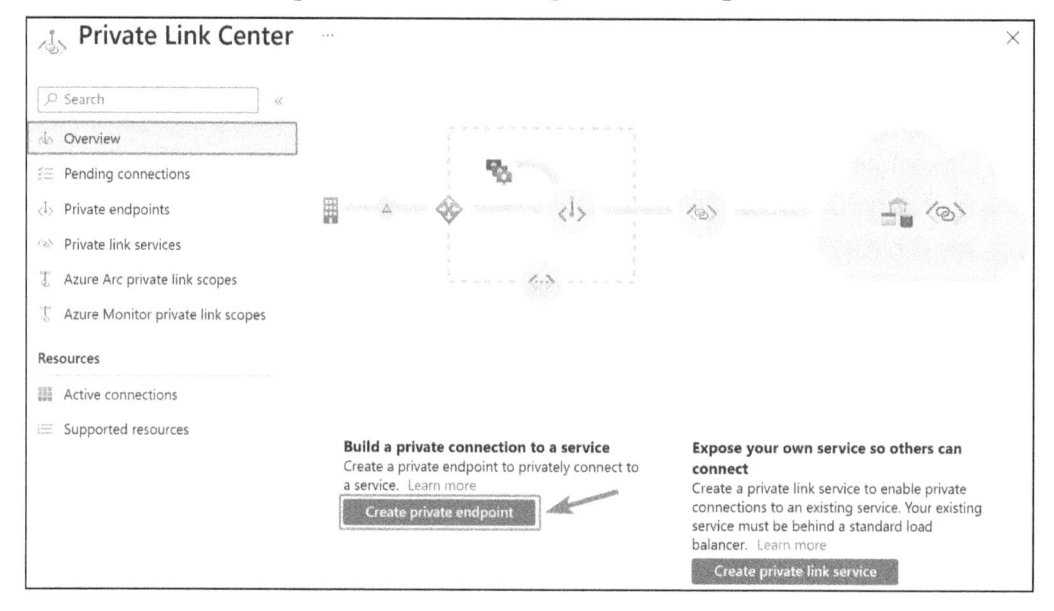

Figure 16.36: Creating a private endpoint

9. On the `Basic` tab, enter the following and click `Next : Resource >`:

   - Resource group: `AZ104-vnets`
   - Name: `DemoPrivateLink`
   - Network Interface Name: `DemoPrivateLink-nic`
   - Region: `West Europe`

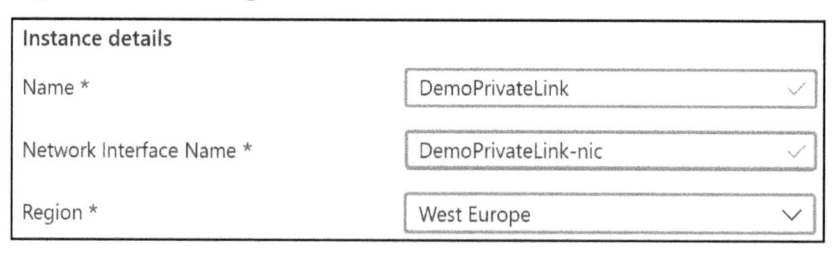

Figure 16.37: Instance details

10. Enter the following configurations for the `Resource` tab and click `Next : Virtual Network >`:

    - Connection method: `Connect to an Azure resource in my directory.`
    - Resource type: `Microsoft.Web/sites`

- Resource: `myPrivateWebApp300324`
- Target sub-resource: `sites`

Figure 16.38: Resource configuration

11. On the `Virtual Network` tab, enter the following and click `Next : DNS >`:

    - Virtual network: `DemoVNet`
    - Subnet: `Demo_Subnet`
    - Private IP configuration: `Dynamically allocate IP address`

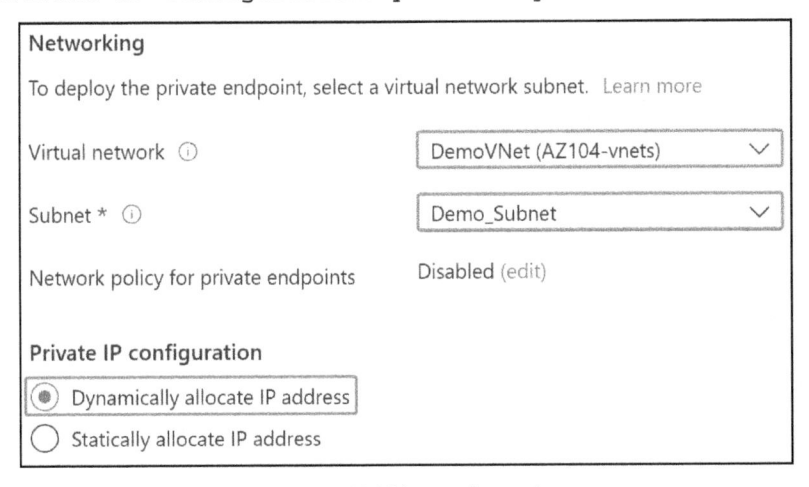

Figure 16.39: VNet configuration

12. The DNS tab will provide you with the option to integrate with your Private DNS zone should you have one. Leave this option as `No` for this exercise and click `Next : Tags >`.
13. You can choose to create some tags and then click `Next : Review + create`.
14. After the review process has been completed, click `Create`.

15. Once the private endpoint has been created successfully, you can verify it by navigating to the resource and confirming that `Connection status` shows as `Approved` in the `Overview` pane.

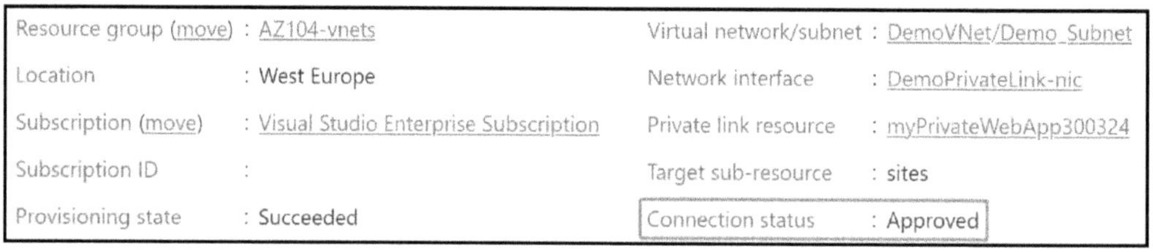

Resource group (move)	: AZ104-vnets	Virtual network/subnet	: DemoVNet/Demo_Subnet
Location	: West Europe	Network interface	: DemoPrivateLink-nic
Subscription (move)	: Visual Studio Enterprise Subscription	Private link resource	: myPrivateWebApp300324
Subscription ID	:	Target sub-resource	: sites
Provisioning state	: Succeeded	Connection status	: Approved

Figure 16.40: Verifying the private endpoint connection

> **Note**
>
> You are encouraged to read up further on Azure private endpoints by visiting the following links:
>
> `https://learn.microsoft.com/en-us/azure/private-link/private-link-overview`
>
> `https://learn.microsoft.com/en-us/azure/private-link/create-private-endpoint-portal`
>
> `https://learn.microsoft.com/en-us/azure/private-link/private-endpoint-dns`

In this section, you learned about private endpoints, how they differ from service endpoints, and how to configure private endpoints for App Service.

Integrating into a VNet

As mentioned previously, the private endpoint you just created is great for securing inbound communication to your application, and the other part of the traffic stream is to consider outbound communication, which will be done through VNet integration. To achieve VNet integration, you can follow these steps:

1. Navigate to your App Service resource.
2. From the left menu, click on `Networking` under the `Settings` context.
3. On the right pane, click the blue text next to `Virtual network integration`:

Configuring Azure DNS

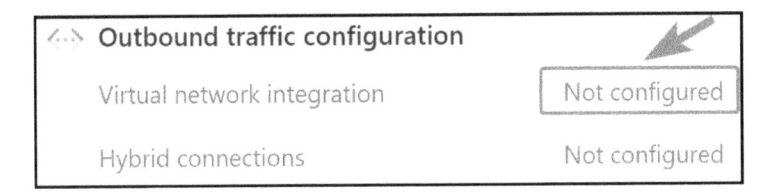

Figure 16.41: Virtual network integration

4. Click `Add virtual network integration`.
5. Select `DemoVNet` and `AppService_Subnet` for the configuration and click `Connect`.

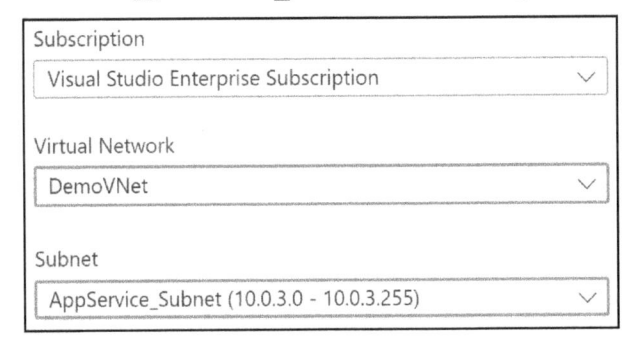

Figure 16.42: Adding a virtual network

You have just configured VNet integration for App Service. Your application now has secure inbound and outbound connections. You can further start to combine this with NSGs and firewall services to further improve upon the network-level security of your application.

In the next section, you will learn about Azure DNS, the role it plays, and how to configure it.

Configuring Azure DNS

Azure DNS is a hosting service for DNS domains where the name resolution is done via the Microsoft Azure infrastructure. It is important to note that you cannot buy domains via Azure DNS. However, you can delegate permissions to Azure DNS for record management.

There is also a feature called Azure Private DNS that provides a reliable and secure DNS service for VNets. When using private DNS zones, you can use a custom domain name instead of using the default domain names provided by Azure. One of the main reasons for using Azure Private DNS is that the domain names in the VNet will be resolved without having to configure a custom DNS on the VNet. A Private DNS zone is a reference to a domain or DNS namespace, such as demo.com, that can be used to resolve DNS names within your environment, the same way you would a custom domain.

The following is a high-level overview of how Azure Private DNS works:

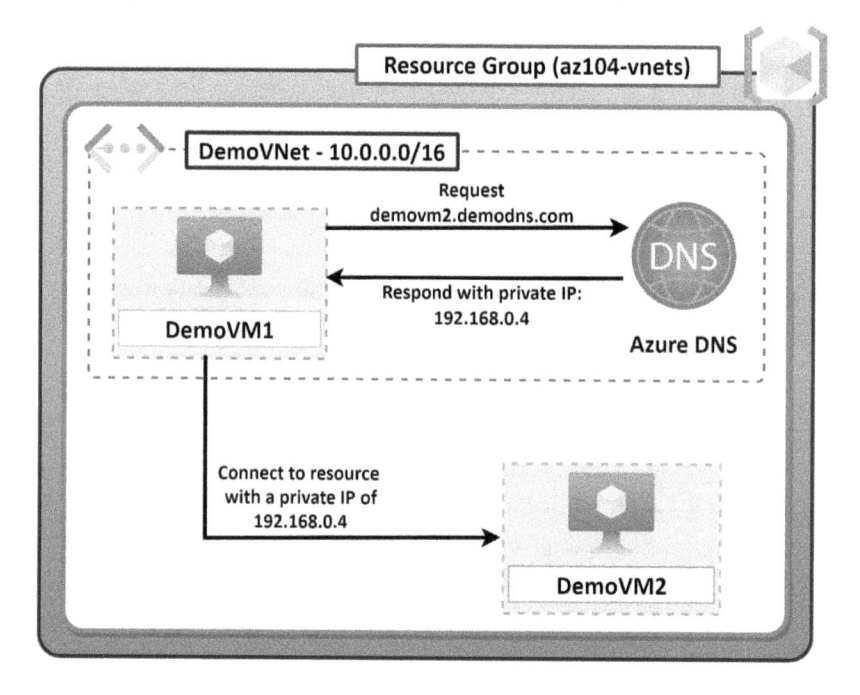

Figure 16.43: Azure Private DNS

> **Note**
> Azure DNS does not support **Domain Name System Security Extensions (DNSSEC)**.

The following are some of the benefits of using Azure Private DNS:

- **Removes the need for custom DNS solutions**: DNS zones can be managed via native Azure infrastructure, which simplifies DNS configuration since complex custom DNS solutions are no longer required

- **Supports common DNS record types**: Azure DNS supports the following records – **A**, **AAAA**, **CNAME**, **MX**, **PTR**, **SOA**, **SRV**, and **TXT**

- **Automatic hostname record management**: Azure automatically maintains hostname records for VMs within a VNet

- **Hostname resolution between VNets**: Azure is able to resolve hostnames on other Vnets, allowing VNets to resolve each other

- **Familiar tools and user experience**: You can use the following to update DNS records – the Azure portal, PowerShell, the Azure CLI, ARM templates, and a REST API

- **Split-horizon DNS support**: The creation of DNS zones with the same name that resolves to different IPs within a VNet and the internet
- **Availability**: DNS private zones are available across all Azure regions and the Azure public cloud
- You have conceptually learned about Azure DNS and the various record types that it supports. You will experience working with a Private DNS zone in the next exercise.

Creating an Azure Private DNS Zone

In this exercise, you will configure Azure Private DNS via PowerShell. The DNS zone will be linked to both the `DemoVNet` and `DemoVNet_2` VNets that you created at the beginning of the chapter. After creating the Private DNS zone, you will also test it to confirm its operation.

Follow along with these steps:

1. You will need to install the Azure Private DNS module using the following command in PowerShell:

    ```
    Install-Module -Name Az.PrivateDns -force
    ```

2. Run the following PowerShell code once the module has been installed, which can be found here: https://packt.link/FOp45.

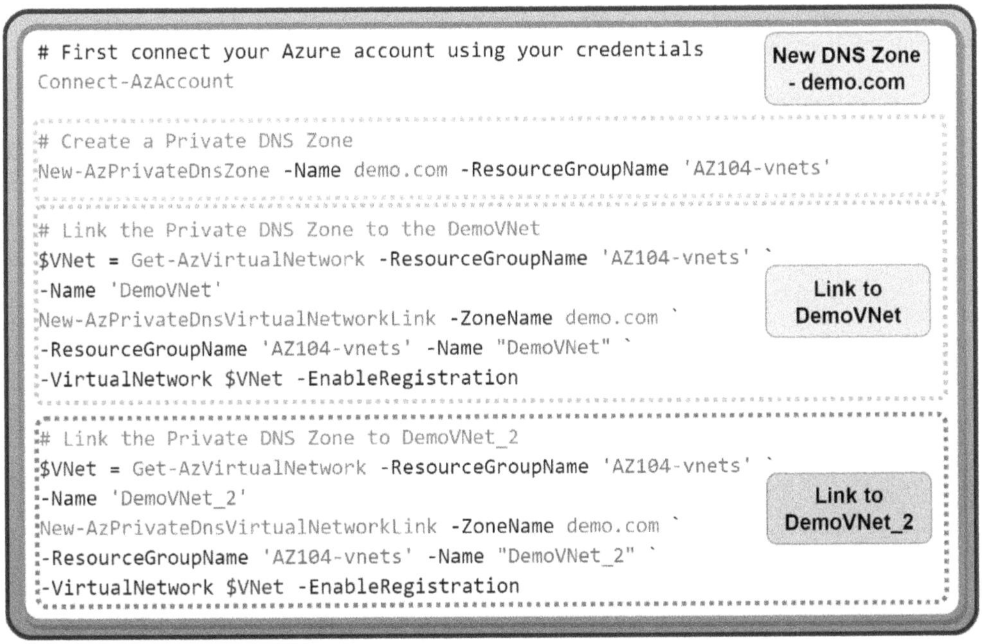

```
# First connect your Azure account using your credentials
Connect-AzAccount

# Create a Private DNS Zone
New-AzPrivateDnsZone -Name demo.com -ResourceGroupName 'AZ104-vnets'

# Link the Private DNS Zone to the DemoVNet
$VNet = Get-AzVirtualNetwork -ResourceGroupName 'AZ104-vnets' `
-Name 'DemoVNet'
New-AzPrivateDnsVirtualNetworkLink -ZoneName demo.com `
-ResourceGroupName 'AZ104-vnets' -Name "DemoVNet" `
-VirtualNetwork $VNet -EnableRegistration

# Link the Private DNS Zone to DemoVNet_2
$VNet = Get-AzVirtualNetwork -ResourceGroupName 'AZ104-vnets' `
-Name 'DemoVNet_2'
New-AzPrivateDnsVirtualNetworkLink -ZoneName demo.com `
-ResourceGroupName 'AZ104-vnets' -Name "DemoVNet_2" `
-VirtualNetwork $VNet -EnableRegistration
```

Annotations: New DNS Zone - demo.com; Link to DemoVNet; Link to DemoVNet_2

Figure 16.44: Configuring a Private DNS zone

3. Lastly, you need to confirm that your DNS zone has been created successfully. To do this, use the following PowerShell command:

```
Get-AzPrivateDnsZone -ResourceGroupName 'AZ104-vnets'
```

4. The output of the command is shown in the following screenshot:

```
pwsh> Get-AzPrivateDnsZone -ResourceGroupName 'AZ104-vnets'


Name              : demo.com
ResourceId        : /subscriptions/                                  /resourceGroups
                    /az104-vnets/providers/Microsoft.Network/privateDnsZones/demo.com
ResourceGroupName : az104-vnets
```

Figure 16.45: Verifying the Private DNS zone has been created successfully

In this exercise, you created a Private DNS zone using PowerShell and linked it to your `DemoVNet` and `DemoVNet_2` network resources. In the following exercise, you will learn how to test that the Private DNS zone works as expected.

Testing Private DNS

For this exercise, you are going to explore the Private DNS entries registered for the zone you created in the previous exercise, and then you are going to remote into one of the VMs you created to test the resolution of the newly instituted Private DNS zone into your VNet. Follow these steps:

1. Navigate to the Azure portal at `https://portal.azure.com`.
2. Open the `AZ104-vnets` resource group and look for the `demo.com` Private DNS zone resource. Click the name of the resource to open its configuration screen.
3. Note that on the `Overview` screen, you can see two entries: `demovm1` and `demovm2`.

Name	Type	TTL	Value
@	SOA	3600	Email: azureprivatedns-host.microsoft.com Host: azureprivatedns.net Refresh: 3600 Retry: 300 Expire: 2419200 Minimum TTL: 10 Serial number: 1
demovm1	A	10	10.0.0.5
demovm2	A	10	192.168.0.4

Figure 16.46: Private DNS zone entries

4. Remote connect (RDP) to DemoVM1.

5. From DemoVM1, launch PowerShell and run the following command:

   ```
   nslookup demovm2.demo.com
   ```

6. Note how this is resolved, and you should see an address of `192.168.0.4` received, indicating that your new Private DNS zone is working and operational. Now your VMs can use names for resolution, and you no longer need to be aware of IP addresses that are allocated.

```
Non-authoritative answer:
Name:    demovm2.demo.com
Address:  192.168.0.4
```

Figure 16.47: Configuring a Private DNS zone

In this section, you learned what Azure DNS is and the difference between Azure DNS and Azure Private DNS. You also learned how to configure a private DNS zone, link it to an existing VNet, and verify that it has been created successfully.

> **Note**
>
> You are encouraged to read up further on Azure DNS by using the following links:
>
> https://learn.microsoft.com/en-us/azure/dns/dns-overview
>
> https://learn.microsoft.com/en-us/azure/dns/private-dns-overview

Summary

In this chapter, you learned how to create VNets, including VNet peering, and how to configure private and public IP addresses and UDRs. You also experienced subnetting in Azure and learned how to configure endpoints and private endpoints for VNets. Lastly, you learned about Azure DNS and how it works and configured a custom private DNS zone, linking it to an existing VNet via PowerShell.

You have gained the following skills after reading this chapter and following along with the hands-on demos: virtual networking, custom routing in Azure, securing resources via endpoints and private endpoints, and configuring Azure DNS.

In the next chapter, you will learn how to secure access to VNets.

> **Note**
>
> Remember to delete the resources you created in this chapter to minimize costs.

17
Securing Access to Virtual Networks

This chapter focuses on securing access to virtual networks. You will explore topics such as **Network Security Groups** (**NSGs**), which introduce traffic filtering capabilities into your network, **Azure Bastion**, which enables jump-box-like services for remotely and securely administering your Azure workloads, and **Azure Firewall**, an advanced threat protection service for filtering and managing network traffic and scanning for threats. Collectively, these concepts will enable you to complete the AZ104 exam and explore additional topics that extend beyond the exam, such as Azure Firewall, to equip you as an Azure administrator to better fulfill your daily responsibilities on the platform.

You will learn how to create security rules and associate an NSG with a subnet or network interface. You will also learn how to effectively evaluate security rules, which is important when determining the net effect of your applied rules. Furthermore, you will gain hands-on deployment experience with Azure Firewall and Azure Bastion, which are core services to many organizations in establishing network security. These are key skills to have as an Azure administrator, as you are likely to face deployments in your administrative role. These are also important concepts to grasp to ensure you have the experience you need to secure a network and deploy network security components. By exploring the various topics in this chapter and completing the exercises, you will become more familiar with the various services that you need to know about in order to pass the AZ104 Azure administrator exam.

In this chapter, you will learn about the following main topics:

- Network Security Groups
- Azure Firewall
- Azure Bastion
- Deploying Azure Bastion and Azure Firewall

Technical requirements

You will need the following tools for the exercises in this chapter:

- Access to an Azure subscription with owner or contributor privileges. If you do not have access to one, you can set up a student account for free: https://azure.microsoft.com/en-us/free/.

- **PowerShell 5.1** or later installed on a Windows PC, or PowerShell Core 6.x if another operating system is being used.

- For Windows users, you will need to install **.NET Framework 4.7.2** or later using the following link: https://learn.microsoft.com/en-us/dotnet/framework/install

- Where PowerShell is not installed or available, https://shell.azure.com can be used as a browser-based shell.

- The Az PowerShell module needs to be installed, which can be done by running the following in an administrative PowerShell session:

    ```
    Set-ExecutionPolicy -ExecutionPolicy RemoteSigned -Scope
    CurrentUser
    Install-Module -Name Az -Scope CurrentUser -Repository PSGallery
    -Force
    ```

Network Security Groups

When deploying resources on virtual networks within Azure, it is recommended from a security point of view to only allow the required traffic to your resource. One of the solutions on the Azure platform for traffic filtering is NSGs. Traffic filtering is the activity of allowing or denying traffic based on a set of predefined rules, helping to control inbound and outbound traffic to and from your Azure resources. NSGs act as a basic five-tuple firewall service for network-connected resources. These can be either applied at the subnet layer or **Network Interface Card** (**NIC**) layer in Azure. NICs are typically associated directly with VMs but can also be from services with a private endpoint attached. NSG rules are the configurations for traffic filtering patterns and are defined by the following components: **source**, **destination**, **port**, **protocol**, and **action** (deny or allow).

Each rule is given a priority, and the lower the priority number, the higher the precedence. The first rule matched on the traffic will be the rule that is chosen and followed. The more specific the rule, the higher the precedence it takes when being evaluated by the NSG in the processing of the rules. For example, if you have a rule for inbound internet traffic to your VM and you specify the VM IP in the rule, it will precede a more generic rule for a whole network range that could contain IPs for several VMs. You can use NSGs to restrict who can access services, whether it's access from certain sources (such as an IP address) or to certain hosts (normally the destination). You can also choose to associate a single NSG with an NIC and/or subnet.

The same NSG can be applied several times in that it can be associated with several NICs and subnets. For VM deployments, you will likely open port 3389 (RDP – Windows) or 22 (SSH – Linux) for VM access or management, but carefully consider the source addresses you allow. As a rule of thumb, you should issue access to known IPs only from within your organization for the source address. This prevents access from unwanted sources, including other regions, and is an easy way to better secure access to your services.

NSG rules are evaluated by priority using the following five-tuple information:

- **Source**: The source is where the traffic will be originating from. It can be set to **any**, **IP address**, **IP address range**, **service tag**, or **application security group**.

    Each of the source types is explained in more detail in the following list:

    - **Any**: Any source will be accepted in the rule.
    - **IP address**: Specify a single IP address as the source address.
    - **IP address range**: This is a range of IP addresses specified in a CIDR format such as 10.0.0.0/24 (which would mean IPs between 10.0.0.1 to 10.0.0.254 would be accepted as a source).
    - **Service tag**: Service tags represent predefined identifiers for a collection of IP addresses, such as those for the internet. Any source traffic identified with the particular Azure service tag matched in the rule will be accepted for the rule.
    - **Application security group**: An application security group is a collection of VMs for the purpose of allowing you to define network security policies at scale. The collection of VMs within the application security group will be assessed by the application security group they reside in.

- **Destination**: This will be the destination receiving the traffic, which can be set to **any**, **IP address**, **IP address range**, **service tag**, or an **application security group**.

    Each of the destination types is explained in more detail in the following list:

    - **Any**: Any destination will be accepted in the rule.
    - **IP address**: Specify a single IP address as the destination address.
    - **IP address range**: This is a range of IP addresses specified in a CIDR format such as 10.0.0.0/24 (which would mean IPs between 10.0.0.1 to 10.0.0.254 would be accepted as a source).
    - **Service tag**: Service tags represent predefined identifiers for a collection of IP addresses, such as those for the internet. Any source traffic identified with the particular Azure service tag matched in the rule will be accepted for the rule.
    - **Application security group**: An application security group is a collection of VMs for the purpose of allowing you to define network security policies at scale. The collection of VMs within the application security group will be assessed by the application security group they reside in.

- **Source port**: This is the port(s) from where the traffic is originating, which can be a single port, such as port 80, or multiple ports, such as 80 and 443.

- **Destination port**: This is the port(s) that the traffic is destined for, which can be a single port, such as port 80, or multiple ports, such as 80 and 443.

- **Protocol**: The protocol can be set to **TCP**, **UDP**, **ICMP**, or **any** protocol.

Based on the preceding configuration, the NSG rule can be configured to either block or allow traffic.

> **Note**
> For an NSG rule to apply to traffic, the traffic must meet all the defined rule criteria. All rules will be processed in order and the first applicable rule will be applied to the traffic.

The following diagram illustrates the construct of an NSG rule, showing the various options you can select from for each configuration item:

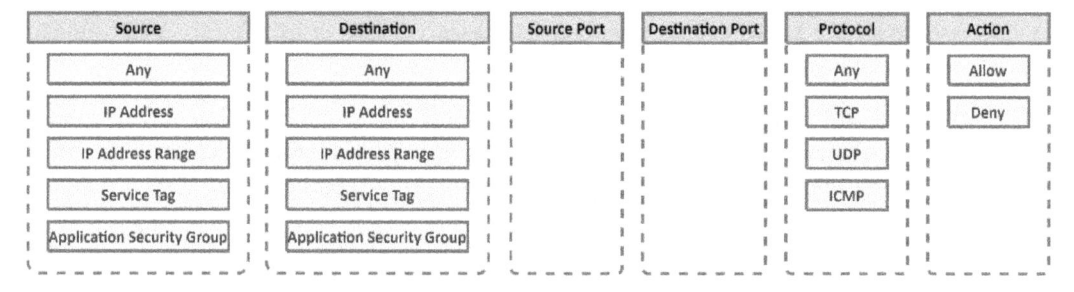

Figure 17.1: NSG rule construct

The following diagram illustrates a real-world example of creating an **allow** rule for accessing a web frontend. It involves a source VM with the IP address 150.0.0.30 connecting to another VM hosting the web service on port 443, with the IP address 10.0.0.50.

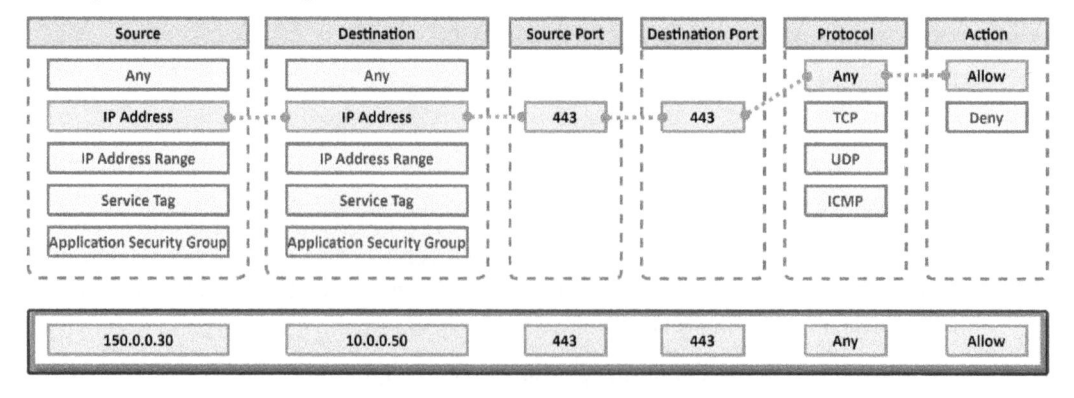

Figure 17.2: NSG rule example

You now understand what an NSG is and how to configure the rules that are so pivotal to the service. In the following exercise, you will create an NSG.

Creating an NSG

In this exercise, you are going to learn how to create an NSG via the Azure portal and associate it with an existing subnet. This will be used for filtering traffic and ensuring that you control the inbound traffic flow by blocking **Remote Desktop Protocol (RDP)** traffic, using one rule. You will then configure another rule to allow the RDP traffic in, using a rule that precedes the first and allows traffic through. This is relevant to real-world scenarios where you want to prevent undesired traffic from reaching your Azure services. Complete the exercise by performing the following steps:

1. Navigate to the Azure portal by opening a web browser and visiting `https://portal.azure.com`.
2. Enter `network security group` into the top search bar. From the search results, click `Network security groups`.
3. Click `Create` from the top menu bar.
4. On the `Create network security group` page, select the `AZ104-vnetsecurity` resource group and enter the name for your NSG instance as `DemoNSG`.

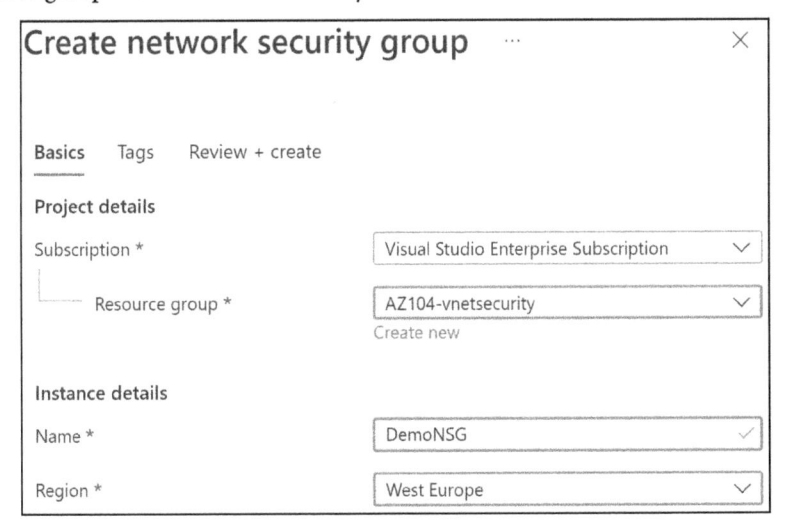

Figure 17.3: Creating a new VNet

5. Click `Review + create` and then `Create`.

> **Note**
> NSGs can be associated with a subnet or at the NIC level.

Associating an NSG with a Subnet

Now that you have successfully created your NSG, you are going to assign it to the subnet level for a specific **virtual network** (**VNet**). This is beneficial for scenarios where you want to create rules that apply to a whole subnet that has a range of IP addresses associated with it. To do this, perform the following steps:

1. Create a new VNet with the following configuration:
   - Resource group: AZ104-vnetsecurity.
   - Virtual network name: DemoVNet.
   - Region: Choose one that best suits you.
   - IP address space: 10.0.0.0/16.
   - Subnet name: default.
   - Subnet IP address range: 10.0.0.0/24.

2. Navigate to the newly created NSG from the previous exercise and click on the overview page.

3. Under Settings on the NSG page, select Subnets from the left menu. On the blade that appears, click on + Associate:

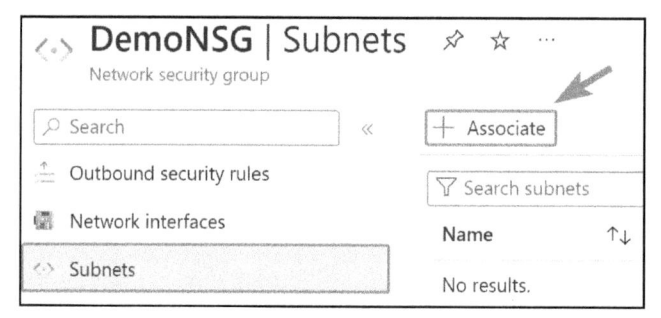

Figure 17.4: The Subnets blade

4. Next, select the DemoVNet and the default subnet and click OK.

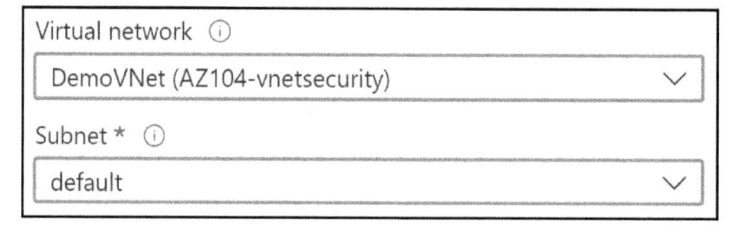

Figure 17.5: Associating to a VNet and subnet

In this demonstration, you assigned an NSG to a subnet. This is predominantly how NSGs are used, and you are now familiar with associating them with subnets, which is particularly useful for applying rules to an IP range.

In the next section, you will learn how to configure NSG rules.

Configuring NSG Rules

Now that you have associated an NSG, using its default rules, with a subnet, you will create a new NSG rule that will deny **RDP** traffic from the internet to the subnet(s) your NSG is associated with. You would typically create this rule as part of a well-managed environment to prevent unauthorized administrative access to your VMs. RDP is the primary protocol for remotely interacting with a VM and is therefore the most likely interface to be exploited. It is advisable that this is blocked publicly where possible or at least restricted to specific IP addresses. Complete the steps in the following exercise:

1. Navigate to the Azure portal by opening a web browser and visiting `https://portal.azure.com`.

2. Create a new VM in the `AZ104-vnetsecurity` resource group, with the name `DemoVM1` and in the `default` subnet within `DemoVNet`. You can use the code from *Chapter 13, Managing Virtual Networks* provided in the GitHub repository for the book (`NSGVM.ps1`): `https://packt.link/coYhx`. Note that the NIC of the VM will be associated with the **DemoNSG** NSG when deploying.

3. Use RDP to connect to the newly created VM and confirm it is accessible.

4. Next, you will configure the inbound rules of your NSG to block RDP traffic to your subnet. Click the hamburger menu button in the top-left corner of your Azure portal and click `All resources`.

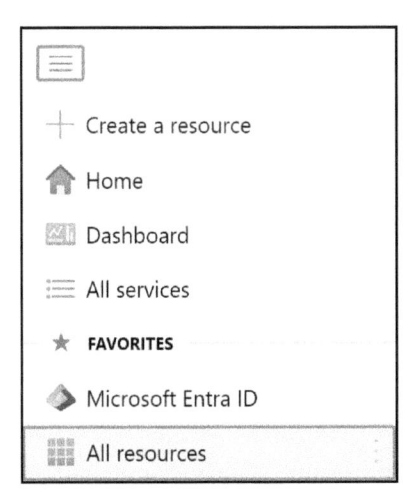

Figure 17.6: Associating to a VNet and subnet

5. Type network security group into the filter bar and press Enter. Select the NSG you created earlier – DemoNSG:

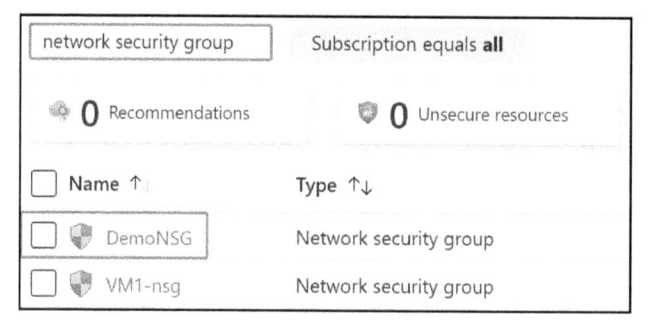

Figure 17.7: Selecting DemoNSG

6. From the menu on the left under the Settings option, select Inbound security rules. Click Add at the top of the screen.

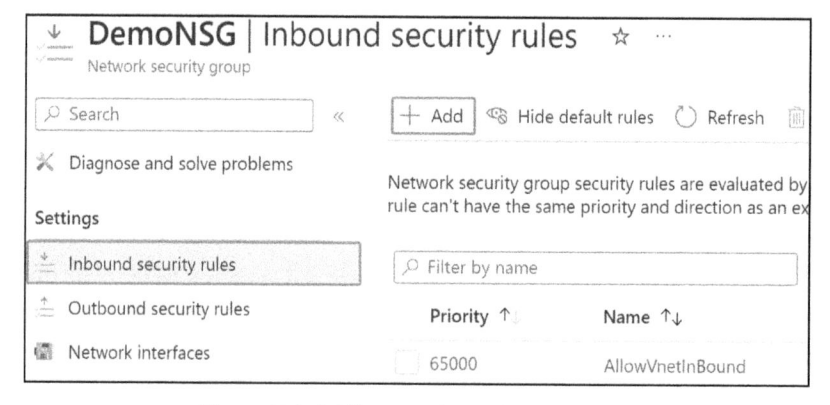

Figure 17.8: Adding an inbound security rule

7. When the blade pops up for adding the new inbound rule, configure it as follows and click Add:

- Source: Service Tag.
- Source service tag: Internet.
- Source port ranges: *.
- Destination: Any.
- Service: RDP.
- Action: Deny.
- Priority: 100.
- Name: DenyTagRDPInbound.

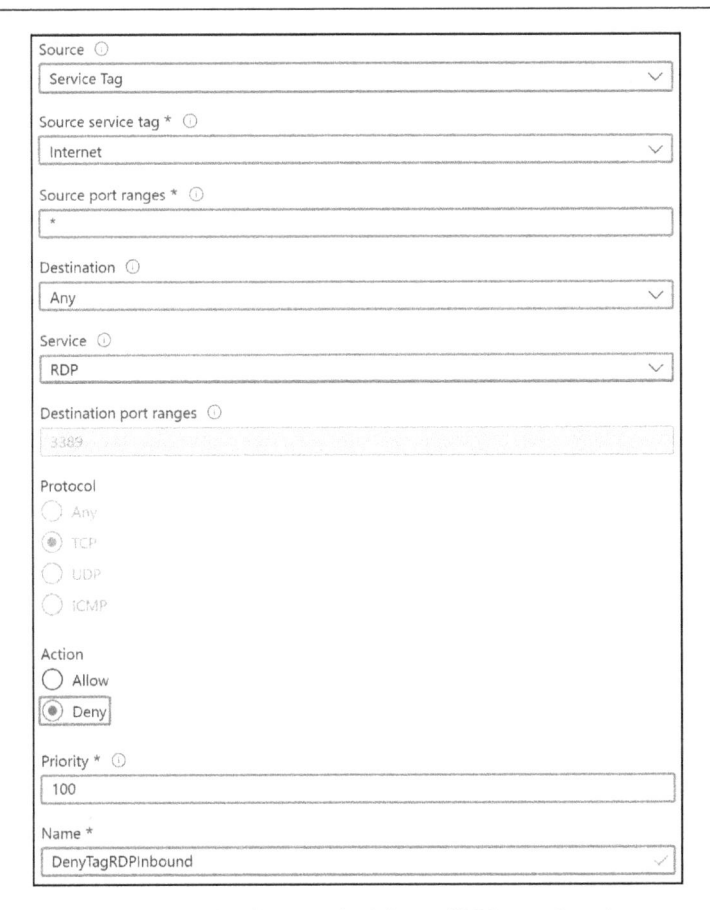

Figure 17.9: Configuring the inbound RDP security rule

Once added, allow the rule two minutes to take effect before moving to the next step.

8. The final step is to verify that the RDP session is disallowed to any VM within the subnet via the internet. You can verify this by attempting to connect to the DemoVM1 instance you made previously. You should be presented with an error message similar to the following, indicating a failure to connect. Receiving a message like this means you have successfully configured a **Deny** rule on your NSG.

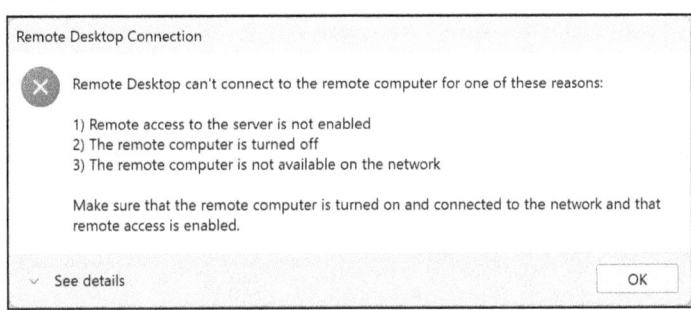

Figure 17.10: RDP connection error

This concludes the exercise for configuring an NSG rule. You also learned a method of testing whether newly created rules are working as expected.

> **Note**
>
> You are encouraged to read up further on NSGs by using the following links, which will further enhance your understanding:
>
> https://learn.microsoft.com/en-us/azure/virtual-network/network-security-groups-overview
>
> https://learn.microsoft.com/en-us/azure/virtual-network/tutorial-filter-network-traffic

In the next section, you are going to look at how to evaluate effective NSG rules.

Evaluating Effective Security Rules

When you create an NSG, there are some default inbound and outbound security rules created for you automatically, as you will have noticed in the previous exercise. The default rules are low-priority rules and are designed to be processed last by default. You can also add custom rules, as you just learned. You can create both inbound and outbound security rules. NSG rules follow priority, with the lowest priority number taking precedence over the next rule.

The following is a screenshot of NSG inbound rules that show two RDP rules – one to allow RDP and one to deny RDP. The RDP rule with the lowest priority number takes precedence, meaning that the `AllowTagRDPInbound` rule will take effect before the `DenyTagRDPInbound` rule.

Priority	Name	Port
100	AllowTagRDPInbound	3389
110	DenyTagRDPInbound	3389
65000	AllowVnetInBound	Any
65001	AllowAzureLoadBalancerInBound	Any

Figure 17.11: Inbound NSG rules for RDP

If there are too many NSG rules to manually review, or multiple NSGs associated with a resource, and you are unsure of which rules are taking precedence, it is a good idea to use a built-in tool in Azure called **Network Watcher**. You can use this tool to evaluate the flow of traffic by using the `IP flow verify` blade of the tool. To utilize Network Watcher, you will need to evaluate an NIC that is associated with an NSG.

To learn how to use the `Effective security rules` tool that is a part of the Network Watcher service, follow these steps:

1. Navigate to the `DemoNSG` network security group you created previously.
2. Change the priority of the `DenyTagRDPInbound` rule you created to `110`, and create a new `AllowTagRDPInbound` rule by creating the same rule as the previous exercise and changing the action to `Allow` and the priority to `100`, as in the previous screenshot.
3. Once completed, click on `Effective security rules` from the left menu under the `Help` option.
4. On the blade that is presented, select your `DemoVM1` VM and the `DemoVM1` network interface.

Scope	Network security group (DemoNSG)
Virtual machine	DemoVM1
Network interface	DemoVM1

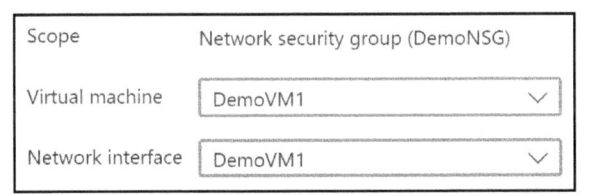

Figure 17.12: Effective security rules

5. Below the selection section, you will see a list of NSGs that are applied to the NIC. Click `DemoNSG` to expand the set of associated rules it contains.

DemoNSG

Inbound rules

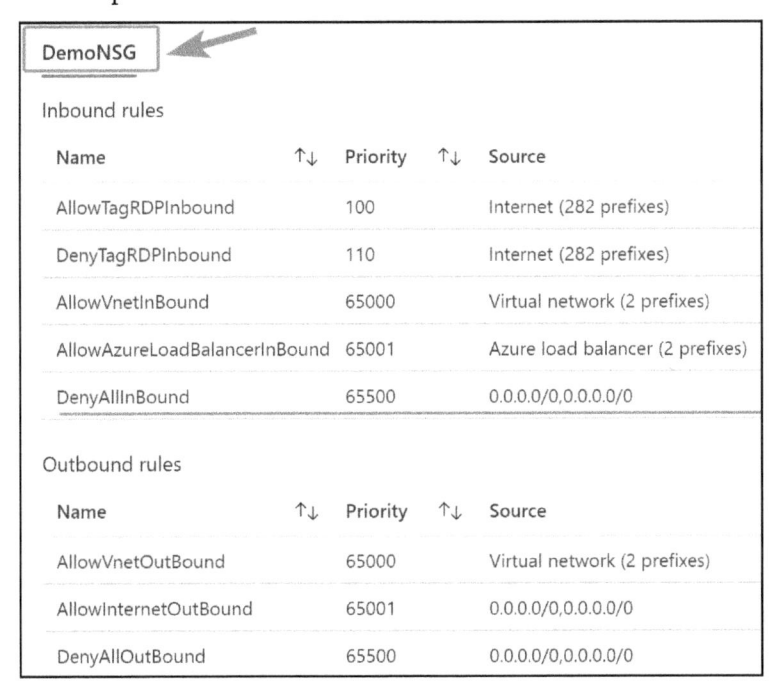

Name	Priority	Source
AllowTagRDPInbound	100	Internet (282 prefixes)
DenyTagRDPInbound	110	Internet (282 prefixes)
AllowVnetInBound	65000	Virtual network (2 prefixes)
AllowAzureLoadBalancerInBound	65001	Azure load balancer (2 prefixes)
DenyAllInBound	65500	0.0.0.0/0,0.0.0.0/0

Outbound rules

Name	Priority	Source
AllowVnetOutBound	65000	Virtual network (2 prefixes)
AllowInternetOutBound	65001	0.0.0.0/0,0.0.0.0/0
DenyAllOutBound	65500	0.0.0.0/0,0.0.0.0/0

Figure 17.13: Expanding the effective DemoNSG rules

You have just evaluated effective security rules under an NSG resource. You now know another mechanism for determining the effective rules that are in place.

For the next exercise, you will perform the same activity through the Network Watcher blade in the portal using the following steps:

1. Search for Network Watcher in the top search bar.
2. Click IP flow verify from the left menu under Network diagnostic tools.
3. Select DemoVM1 as the VM and network interface.

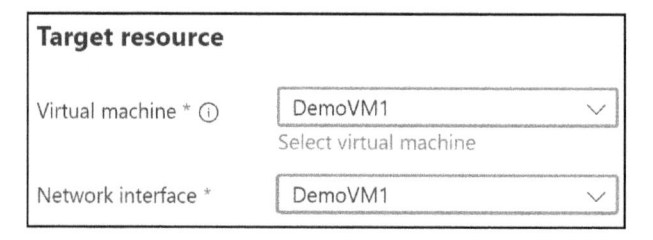

Figure 17.14: Target resource

4. Then select TCP as the protocol and Inbound as the direction.

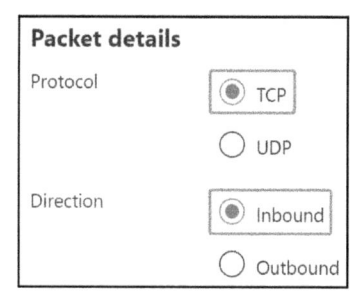

Figure 17.15: Packet details

5. Finally, set the local port as 3389, enter your public IP address for the remote IP address, and enter 3389 for the remote port.

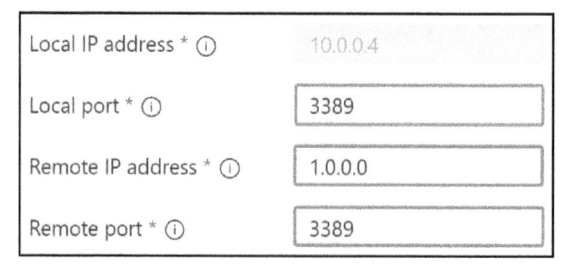

Figure 17.16: Local and remote IP and ports

6. Click `Verify IP flow`. You will receive a result window, which should look similar to this:

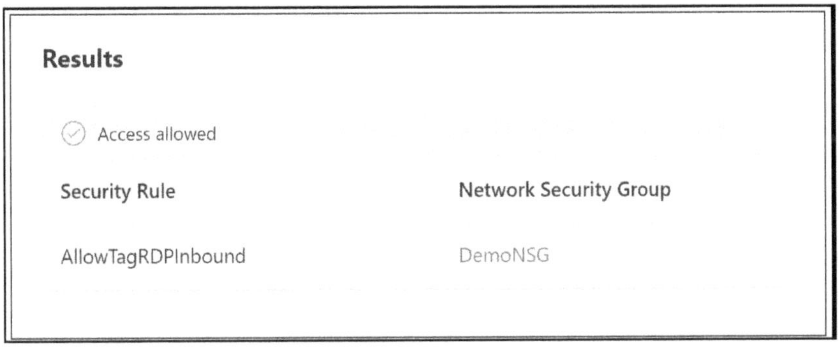

Results

✓ Access allowed

Security Rule	Network Security Group
AllowTagRDPInbound	DemoNSG

Figure 17.17: Verify IP flow

As you just learned, you can verify that RDP traffic will be allowed into your subnet for a VM. You have learned a new method for confirming that your NSG rules are working as expected. In this section, you learned about NSGs and rules. You learned the purpose of NSGs, how to create them, and how to assign them to your subnets. You also learned how rule precedence works and explored some advanced troubleshooting tools that you can use in Azure to verify the flow of traffic. Next, you will learn about Azure firewalls and how they scan and filter traffic to protect your Azure resources.

> **Note**
> More information on discerning effective security rules can be found here: `https://learn.microsoft.com/en-us/azure/network-watcher/network-watcher-overview`.

Azure Firewall

A firewall is a network security service that acts as a gatekeeper, allowing only authorized traffic to flow based on certain configured rules and policies. Firewalls are designed to protect your networked resources from threats. Azure Firewall is an Azure-native firewall offering. All **stock keeping units (SKUs)** offered are stateful firewalls and are designed for scale. When it comes to network security in Azure, NSGs are considered a basic-level firewall. However, sometimes a solution is required that has more granular control over traffic, or a smarter firewall with more functionality is required; this is where Azure Firewall is recommended. Some of the scenarios of more granular control would be application-level filtering, threat intelligence, **intrusion detection and prevention (IDPS)**, and centralized managed functionality. A good example of where you might want to use Azure Firewall is to protect your database workload with a requirement for inspection and advanced threat protection. By routing your traffic through Azure Firewall, you can ensure that only legitimate and authorized requests reach your database systems. It should be used in conjunction with NSGs for additional traffic filtering and access control.

The Azure Firewall service utilizes a service layer named **Firewall Policy**, which contains rule collection groups, rule collections, and rules that determine the configuration of your service. Firewall Policy is designed in a hierarchical structure to enable the centralized management of the network traffic rules contained by the firewall. Firewall Policy is the top-level resource and contains the collective set of components required for traffic management within Azure Firewall. The rule component is used to define the specific criteria you require for how traffic should be handled, such as whether traffic to your SQL database is allowed. Rules are aggregated into rule collections, which are introduced to enable the grouping and prioritization of rules. Rule collections are typically for the grouping of rules aligned to a particular category of management that the rules relate to, such as a set of rules for ensuring storage security. These rule collections are further grouped together into a rule collection group. This may relate to a broader category of protection that the rule collections fit into, such as alignment to a security framework such as the **National Institute of Standards and Technology (NIST)** framework. Firewall Policy encompasses all these components in a hierarchical way to enable structured management that scales within the Azure Firewall service.

The following diagram depicts the relationship just described:

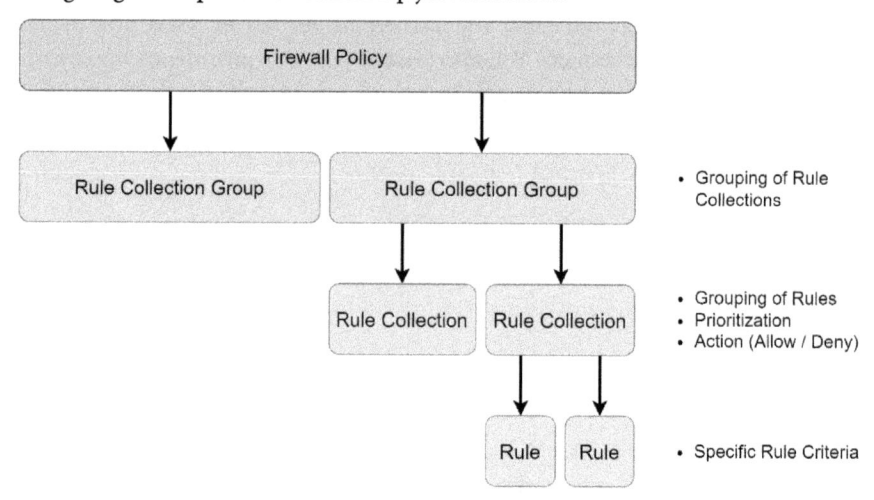

Figure 17.18: Azure Firewall Policy rulesets

You will now learn about the impact of traffic flow direction on design.

Traffic Flow Direction

Traffic flow direction is a general networking concept that is introduced here in the context of Azure Firewall, as it is regularly referenced in firewalling due to the consideration of security boundaries. Traffic flow direction considers which way traffic is flowing and how it impacts the decisions you make in traffic management. The direction of traffic can influence many design considerations, such as the level of security you require. Traffic flow direction also introduces some new terminology that you should be aware of when it comes to networking:

- **East-west traffic**: This refers to internal traffic between your workload environments. For instance, this can be the traffic between your servers and services. An example of internal traffic is your web frontend server pulling data (such as user information) from your database.
- **North-south traffic**: This refers to traffic that is inbound (ingress) and outbound (egress) from and to the internet, a corporate network, or any other network outside of the scope of your control. It is referenced as such due to the breaching of perimeter boundaries by the traffic. An example of North-South traffic is an external user connecting to your website over the internet.

Understanding the context of traffic flow direction will assist you in deciding the requirements for traffic management, where internal traffic (East-West traffic) rules are typically handled with more relaxed security policies, and more stringent security controls are applied to traffic entering and exiting your environment via the internet (North-South traffic). By adopting these thought patterns, you can more effectively design your firewall rules to meet your organization's security requirements.

Firewall Rules

Azure Firewall has three main rule types that can be configured as part of the service:

- **Destination Network Address Translation (DNAT) rule**: This is used to translate the firewall's public IP address and port to a private IP address and port behind the firewall.
- **Network rule**: This has the same rules as NSGs but has additional features such as being able to create rules based on **fully qualified domain names** (**FQDNs**) instead of just using IP addresses. This is for both North-South and East-West traffic.
- **Application rule**: This is used to allow or deny traffic based on specific applications that are based on FQDNs. This is for outbound and East-West traffic only.

Rule Processing Logic

Rules determine how traffic will be filtered and managed through your Azure Firewall instance. They are processed according to the following logic structure: first by service construct and then by priority determined within the rule collection groups. There are default rule collection groups defined within the Azure Firewall service with predefined priorities associated with them. Should you need to change the priority of processing, you can create custom rule collection groups with different priorities.

The following diagram shows how rules in Azure Firewall are processed based on rule type, the top being the highest precedence in the order of processing:

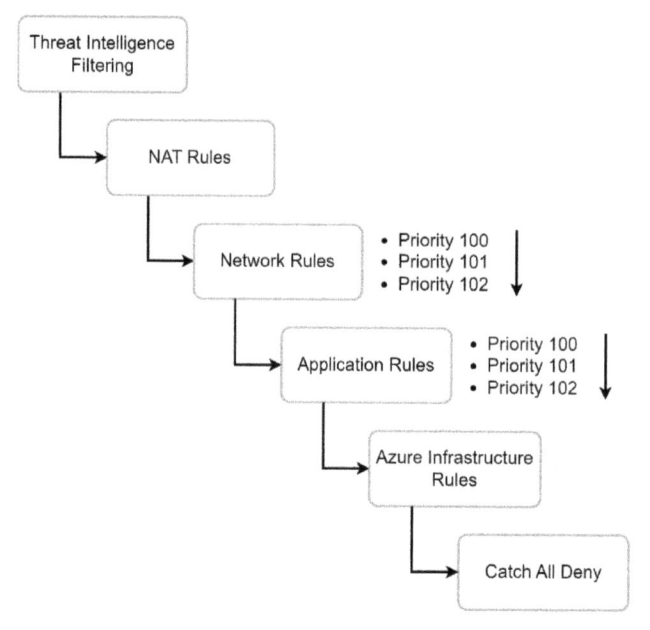

Figure 17.19: Azure Firewall rule processing

An example of how this works in practice is to imagine you have configured an Azure Firewall with two rule collections: Allow HTTP Traffic and Deny Malicious Traffic. The Allow HTTP Traffic rule collection is configured with a priority of 100, and the other rule with a priority of 200. Suppose then that a user attempts to connect to your HTTP website. The first rule to be processed will be the Allow HTTP Traffic rule, which will match the traffic for connecting to the website, since it has the lowest number for the priority. It will be processed first and traffic will be allowed, even though the Deny Malicious Traffic rule collection may explicitly deny access for the user. In this scenario, the security measures in place will be circumvented unintentionally due to the processing order of firewall rules. It is important to understand rule processing within Azure Firewall for correct configurations and troubleshooting scenarios, to ensure security measures are not circumvented unintentionally.

> **Note**
>
> Remember, network rules are processed before application rules. Also, note that NAT rules are prioritized before network rules.

Azure Firewall SKUs

Azure Firewall offers three different SKUs based on the features you require of your firewalling services. As you move up through the tiers in terms of features, the SKUs naturally become more costly. These are categorized as follows:

- **Azure Firewall Basic**: This SKU is designed to provide foundational security services for small and medium-sized customers with throughput needs of less than 250 Mbps.
- **Azure Firewall Standard**: This SKU offers robust security features, including Layer 3 to Layer 7 traffic filtering, web content filtering, DNS proxy, custom DNS, and threat-intelligence-based filtering, making it suitable for medium and large customers requiring enhanced protection.
- **Azure Firewall Premium**: This SKU is designed for highly regulated organizations with high levels of security requirements. It builds upon the same capabilities of the Standard SKU with the addition of **Transport Layer Security** (TLS) inspection, IDPS protection, and URL filtering.

You will now learn about each of the variations of the firewall SKUs in more detail.

Azure Firewall Basic

The Azure Firewall Basic offering is intended for smaller deployments or small to medium-sized businesses. It offers the most foundational security services you would require of the firewall and is much more affordable than the other SKUs.

However, it has a few limitations to be aware of, such as the service scale being limited to two VM instances on the backend and throughput being limited to 250 Mbps. The following figure depicts the set of features available through the Azure Firewall Basic SKU. You will notice it is set up in a hub-and-spoke network configuration; in this particular instance, network connectivity is facilitated through Azure vWAN, but this could also be through standard Azure VNets.

The diagram illustrates that all traffic in the environment is flowing through Azure Firewall, including between on-premises and Azure.

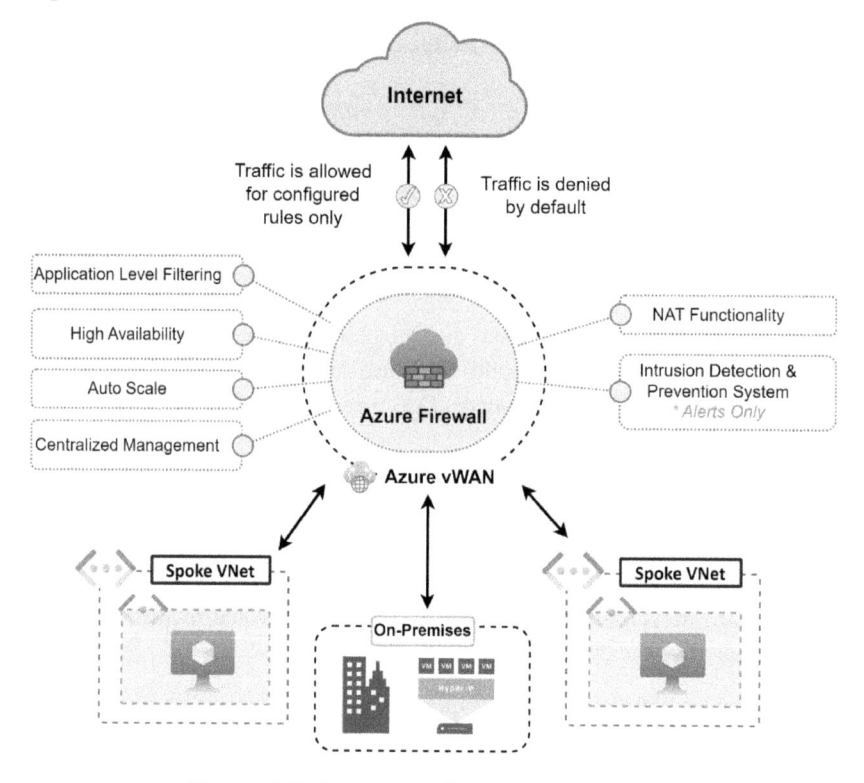

Figure 17.20: Azure Firewall Basic SKU capabilities

Azure Firewall Standard

This provides OSI Layer three to OSI Layer seven filtering, based on threat intelligence feeds directly from Microsoft. This enables Microsoft to feed Azure Firewall intelligence on known malicious IP addresses and domains to block threats from accessing the resources behind the firewall.

Notable feature additions are web content filtering, DNS proxy, custom DNS, and threat-intelligence-based filtering. The following diagram illustrates the key features of the Standard SKU of Azure Firewall in the same configuration as the Basic SKU.

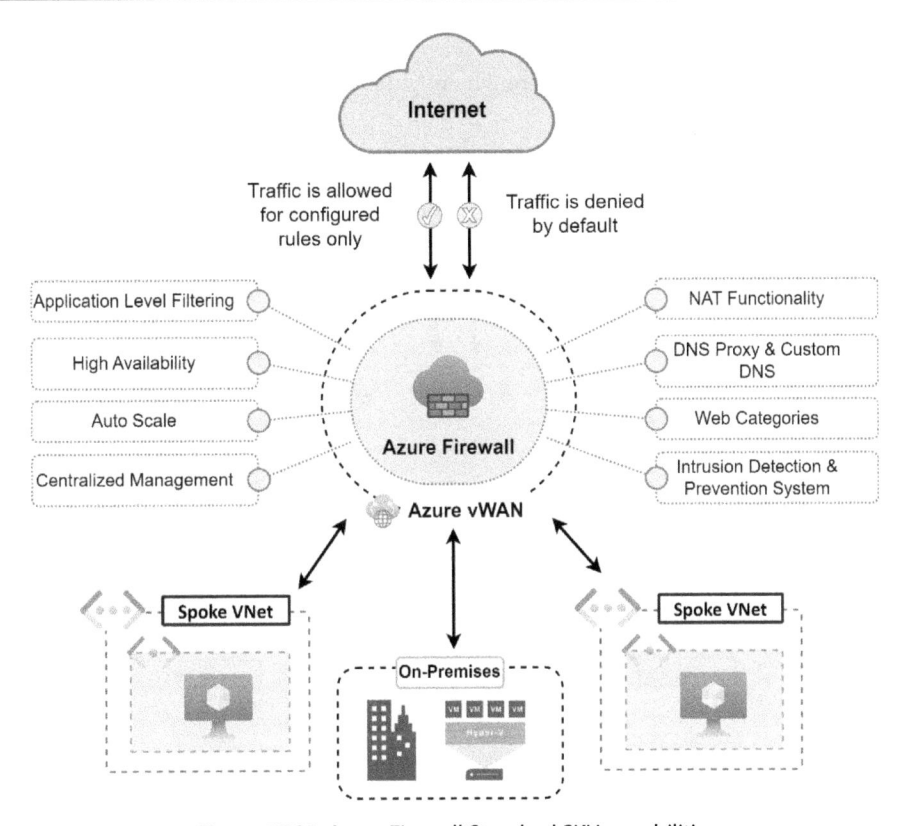

Figure 17.21: Azure Firewall Standard SKU capabilities

The Standard SKU is more beneficial for your organization when security requirements increase and more features are required. This is the most commonly used Azure Firewall SKU, as it meets most organizational needs. As security becomes more of a driving factor, you might want to start to explore the Premium SKU discussed next.

Azure Firewall Premium

The Azure Firewall Premium SKU offers the same features as the Standard SKU and additionally TLS inspection, IDPS protection, and URL filtering. This SKU is best for organizations that are highly regulated, such as financial and healthcare institutions. For financial institutions, Azure Firewall complies with strict security standards such as the **Payment Card Industry Data Security Standard (PCI DSS)**, which provides peace of mind, particularly with stringent security needs. This SKU supports the TLS inspection of traffic to prevent malware and viruses from spreading across a network. URL filtering enables rules for an entire URL to allow or deny a user access to websites by categories, such as gambling sites and social media.

The following diagram illustrates the key features offered by the Azure Firewall Premium SKU, depicted in a hub-and-spoke topology facilitated through an Azure vWAN:

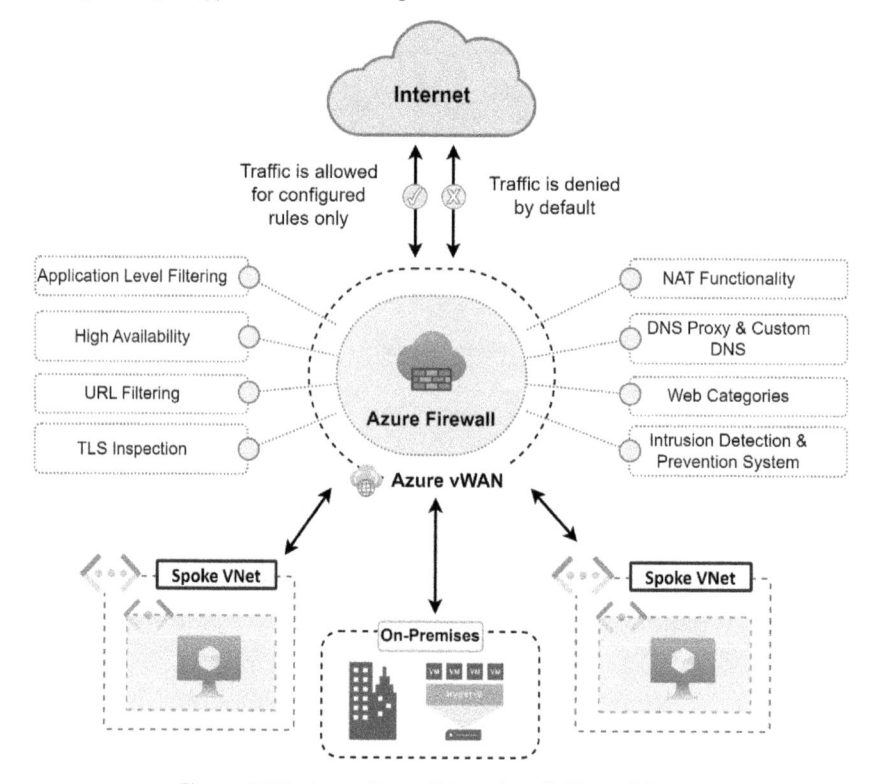

Figure 17.22: Azure Firewall Premium SKU capabilities

Comparing Firewall SKUs

It can be tricky to choose the right SKU for your Azure Firewall resource. The following *Table 17.1* is provided to guide you through the common features available for the various SKUs. The features you require will determine the correct SKU for your purposes.

	Common to All SKUs	Additional Feature(s)	Basic	Standard	Premium
L3-L7 Filtering	<ul><li>Application-level FQDN filtering</li><li>Stateful firewall (five tuple rules)</li><li>NAT functionality (SNAT and DNAT)</li></ul>	Network-level FQDN filtering		✓	✓

	Common to All SKUs	Additional Feature(s)	Basic	Standard	Premium
Reliability and Performance	• Availability Zones • High availability	Auto scaling	✓ Up to 250 MBps	✓ Up to 30 Gbps	✓ Up to 100 Gbps
		Fat flow support		✓ 1 Gbps	✓ 10 Gbps
Management	• Centralized management • Policy analytics		✓	✓	✓
Integration	• Full logging • SIEM integration • Service and FQDN tags • Easy DevOps integration	Web content filtering		✓	✓
		DNS proxy and custom DNS		✓	✓
Advanced Threat Protection	• Threat-intelligence-based filtering		Alerts only	✓	✓
		Inbound TLS termination			✓
		Outbound TLS termination			✓
		Fully managed IDPS			✓
		URL filtering			✓

Table 17.1: Comparing Firewall SKUs

> **Note**
> Azure Firewall Manager can be used to centrally manage Azure firewalls across multiple subscriptions.

You have just learned about Azure Firewall and the various features it offers. Alternatively, you should consider third-party **Network Virtual Appliances** (**NVAs**) that offer firewalling services. They are particularly applicable if your organization already makes use of a firewall vendor, or if you have vendor NVA and firewall skills within your organization already. NVAs are not within the scope of the AZ104 exam but may be used within your organization.

> **Note**
>
> You are encouraged to read further using the following links to enhance your understanding of the exam-related topics:
>
> `https://learn.microsoft.com/en-us/azure/firewall/policy-rule-sets`
>
> `https://learn.microsoft.com/en-us/azure/firewall/choose-firewall-sku`

Azure Bastion

Traditionally, there were two main ways to connect to VMs in the cloud. The first was to assign a static public IP address and connect to VMs via RDP or **Secure Shell** (**SSH**). This was later replaced by removing the public IP address and using a **Virtual Private Network** (**VPN**) to securely connect to the server via RDP or SSH. More secure practices incorporate a jump-box server for connecting to clients. This acts as a proxy server that facilitates your connection to services and VMs as opposed to connecting directly to them, as it adds an additional layer of security. The Azure Bastion service enables you to connect to a VM by using your browser and the Azure portal instead of using other technologies such as VPNs. Bastion is a **platform-as-a-service** (**PaaS**) tool that acts as a jump-box-type service that you provision inside your VNet in Azure. A jump-box service is an intermediary connection point between a user's device and a remote system such as a server, with the primary purpose of providing a secure and controlled environment for accessing remote systems and preventing unauthorized access. Bastion provides secure connectivity on management ports such as RDP and SSH. The following are some key benefits of using Azure Bastion:

- **An RDP and/or SSH directly in the Azure portal**: An RDP or SSH session can take place via the browser. This is a more secure mechanism of connectivity and enables more versatile access to your internal Azure systems.

- **Remote sessions via TLS**: Bastion uses an HTML5-based web client that is streamed to the device, connecting to it via TLS on port 443 for enhanced security purposes.

- **No public IP address required on a VM**: Bastion will open an RDP/SSH connection to a VM by using a private IP address, meaning no public IP address is required.

- **No additional firewall rules required**: There are no additional complex NSG rules required for this solution to work; just allow Bastion to access the required VMs.

- **Reduced attack surface**: VMs are better protected as there are no public IP addresses assigned to them, which means external malicious users cannot port-scan a VM to detect weaknesses in it.
- **Protection against zero-day exploits**: Azure maintains Bastion for you and keeps it hardened to ensure platform protection, which minuses the risk of exploitable vulnerabilities due to it having the latest security patches and improvements applied. Another way that it protects against zero-day exploits is that it provides secure connectivity (RDP or SSH) to your VMs without exposing them to the internet, therefore limiting the attack surface of your VMs.

The following figure shows how Azure Bastion works. You will note that the user can enter through the web interface of the Azure portal and connect to the private IPs of VMs sitting within the same VNet as Azure Bastion, or a peered VNet, even if they are operating on disparate subnets. This is a great option for securely connecting to your resources.

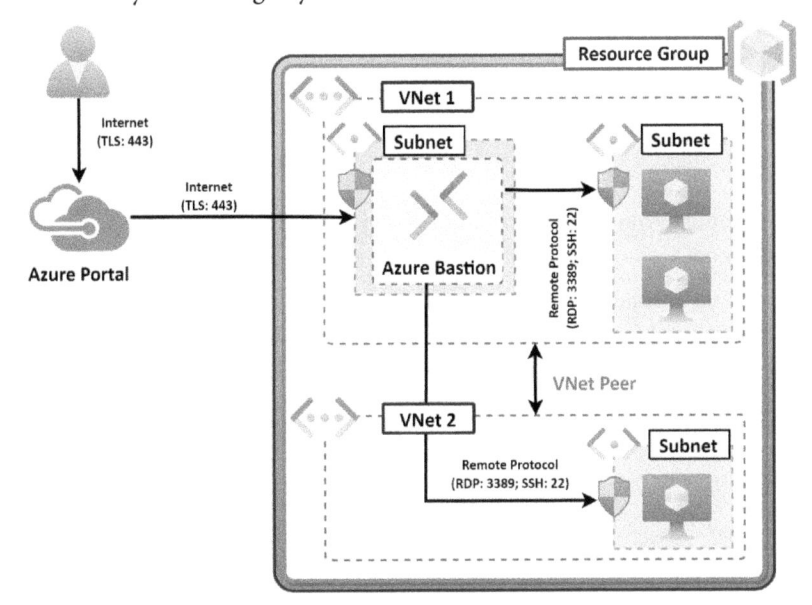

Figure 17.23: How Azure Bastion works

Now that you understand what Azure Bastion is and how it works, you are ready to practice deploying it in the next exercise.

Deploying Azure Bastion and Azure Firewall

Now that you have a better understanding of Azure Firewall and Azure Bastion, you will run through an exercise to do the following via PowerShell:

1. Create a new VNet with a VM.
2. Deploy an Azure firewall.

3. Create a default route within the firewall.
4. Configure an application rule to allow access to www.google.com.
5. Configure a network rule to allow access to external **Domain Name System** (**DNS**) servers.
6. Test the firewall rules.

The code can be found here: https://packt.link/I12Yo.

To achieve the preceding objectives, follow these steps:

1. First, connect to the Azure tenant using the following PowerShell command, followed by selecting your subscription (if you have more than one):

    ```
    # First connect your Azure account using your credentials
    Connect-AzAccount

    # If necessary, select the right subscription as follows
    $SubscriptionId = "xxxxxxx"
    Select-AzSubscription -SubscriptionId $SubscriptionId
    ```

2. For this exercise, you will deploy all further resources to the AZ104-vnetsecurity resource group.

3. Next, create the two subnets in DemoVNet: a Bastion subnet and a Firewall subnet. The default subnet will be used for your VM. Use the following PowerShell code.

    ```
    # Parameters
    $ResourceGroup = "AZ104-vnetsecurity"
    $Location = "WestEurope"
    $VnetName = "DemoVNet"
    $SubnetName = "default"

    # Get VNet Resource
    $VirtualNetwork = Get-AzVirtualNetwork -ResourceGroupName $ResourceGroup `
    -Name $VnetName

    # Create 2 Subnets for this exercise in DemoVNet
    Add-AzVirtualNetworkSubnetConfig -Name 'AzureBastionSubnet' `
    -AddressPrefix '10.0.1.0/27' -VirtualNetwork $VirtualNetwork
    Add-AzVirtualNetworkSubnetConfig -Name 'AzureFirewallSubnet' `
    -AddressPrefix '10.0.1.64/26' -VirtualNetwork $VirtualNetwork
    Set-AzVirtualNetwork -VirtualNetwork $VirtualNetwork
    ```

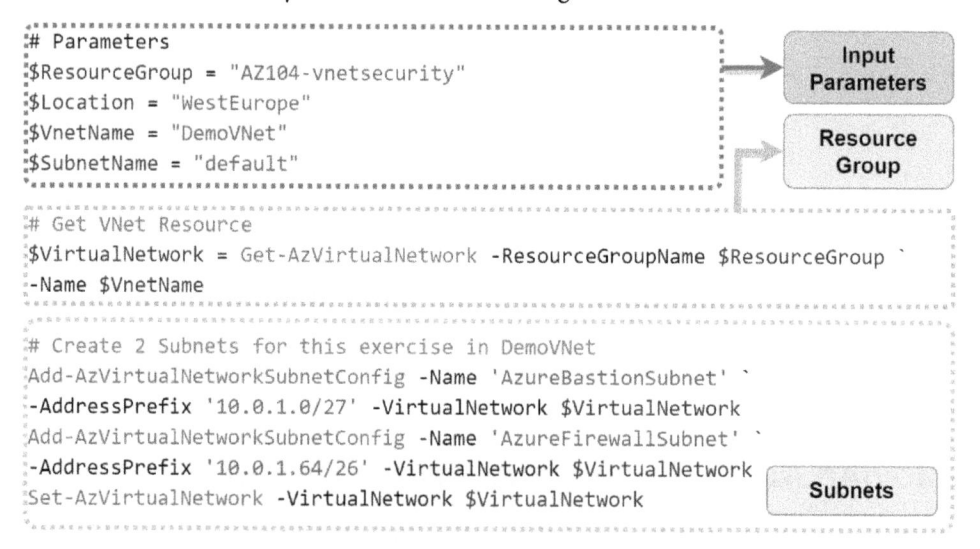

Figure 17.24: Creating subnets

4. Confirm that you see the created subnets in Azure under `DemoVNet` as shown in the following screenshot:

Name ↑↓	IPv4 ↑↓	IPv6 ↑↓	Available IPs ↑↓
default	10.0.0.0/24	-	250
AzureFirewallSubnet	10.0.1.64/26	-	59
AzureBastionSubnet	10.0.1.0/27	-	25

Figure 17.25: New subnets

5. Next, create a public IP address for the Bastion service and deploy the Bastion service:

```
# Create a Public IP for Bastion
$PublicIp = New-AzPublicIpAddress -ResourceGroupName $ResourceGroup `
-Location $Location -Name 'Bastion-pip' -AllocationMethod static -Sku
standard


# Create the Bastion Host
$VirtualNetwork = Get-AzVirtualNetwork -ResourceGroupName $ResourceGroup
-Name $VnetName
New-AzBastion -ResourceGroupName $ResourceGroup -Name 'Bastion-01' `
-PublicIpAddress $PublicIp -VirtualNetwork $VirtualNetwork
```

6. Confirm that you see the public IP address and Bastion in Azure as shown in the following screenshot:

Name ↑	Type ↑↓	Location ↑↓
Bastion-01	Bastion	West Europe
Bastion-pip	Public IP address	West Europe
DemoNSG	Network security group	West Europe

Figure 17.26: Bastion resources in Azure

7. Next, deploy the firewall along with a public IP address using the following PowerShell code:

```
# Create a Public IP for the Azure Firewall
$FWpip = New-AzPublicIpAddress -ResourceGroupName $ResourceGroup `

-Location $Location -Name 'Firewall-pip' -AllocationMethod
static `
-Sku standard


# Create the Azure Firewall
```

```
$Firewall = New-AzFirewall -ResourceGroupName $ResourceGroup `
-Location $Location -Name 'Firewall-01' -VirtualNetwork $VirtualNetwork `
-PublicIpAddress $FWpip
```

8. Confirm that the newly created firewall is present on the Azure portal as shown in the following screenshot:

Name ↓	Type ↑↓	Location ↑↓
☐ Firewall-pip	Public IP address	West Europe
☐ Firewall-01	Firewall	West Europe
☐ DemoVNet	Virtual network	West Europe

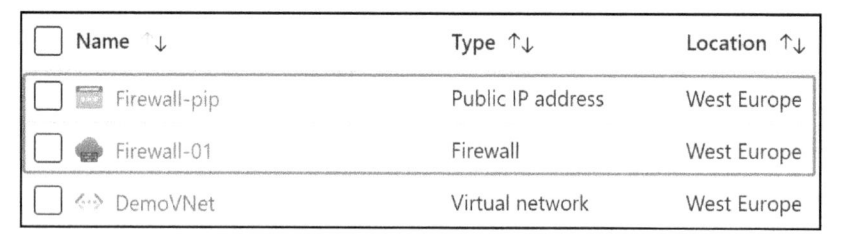

Figure 17.27: Azure Firewall resources

9. Next, configure a default route on the firewall along with a route table, and associate the route table with your `default` subnet:

DeployingAzureBastion.ps1

```
# Create a Route Table
$RouteTable = New-AzRouteTable `
  -Name Firewall-RT `
  -ResourceGroupName $ResourceGroup `
  -Location $Location `
  -DisableBgpRoutePropagation

# Get the Firewall Private IP Address
$FWPrivateIP = $Firewall.IpConfigurations.privateipaddress

# Create a Route
Add-AzRouteConfig `
```

The complete code is available at `https://packt.link/vDcQE`

10. With the preceding code, you have created a new route table with a route named `DemoRoute` and associated it with the `default` subnet. Navigating back to Azure, you should see your route table resource:

Name ↓	Type ↑↓	Location ↑↓
☐ Firewall-RT	Route table	West Europe
☐ Firewall-pip	Public IP address	West Europe

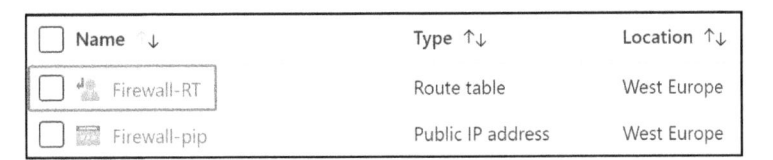

Figure 17.28: Route table resource

11. Next, create an application rule for the firewall to allow outbound access to www.google.com:

```
# Create an Application Rule on the Firewall
$AppRule1 = New-AzFirewallApplicationRule -Name Allow-Google `
-SourceAddress 10.0.0.0/24 -Protocol http, https -TargetFqdn
www.google.com
$AppRuleCollection = New-AzFirewallApplicationRuleCollection `
-Name App-Coll01 -Priority 200 -ActionType Allow -Rule $AppRule1
$Firewall.ApplicationRuleCollections.Add($AppRuleCollection)
Set-AzFirewall -AzureFirewall $Firewall
```

12. The code you just ran created a new Azure Firewall application rule to allow outbound access to Google. To confirm this through the Azure portal, navigate to your Firewall resource. From the menu on the left, click `Rules` under the `Settings` option. On the right side of the screen, click `Application rule collection`. You should see a single collection named `App-Coll01`; click on this name to show the rules under the collection.

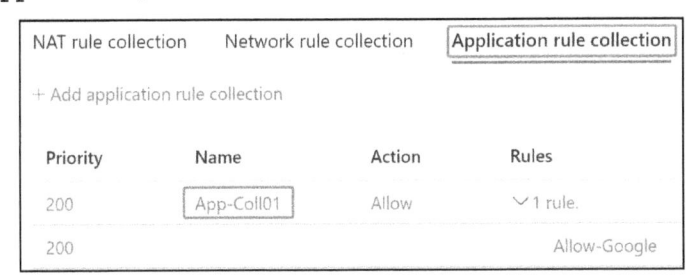

NAT rule collection	Network rule collection	**Application rule collection**	
+ Add application rule collection			
Priority	Name	Action	Rules
200	App-Coll01	Allow	⌄ 1 rule.
200			Allow-Google

Figure 17.29: Application rule collection

On the screen that appears, you will see the `Target FQDNs` section, which should contain your `Allow-Google` rule:

name	Source type	Source	Protocol:Port	Target FQDNs
Allow-Google	IP address	10.0.0.0/24	Http:80,Https:443	www.google.com

Figure 17.30: The application rule

13. Next, configure a network rule for the firewall to allow outbound access to 8.8.8.8 on UDP port 53, which is for DNS resolution:

    ```
    # DNS Resolution Network Rule
    $DNSRule1 = New-AzFirewallNetworkRule -Name "Allow-GoogleDNS"
    -Protocol UDP `
    -SourceAddress 10.0.0.0/24 -DestinationAddress 8.8.8.8
    -DestinationPort 53
    $NetRuleCollection = New-AzFirewallNetworkRuleCollection -Name
    GoogleDNS `
    -Priority 201 -Rule $DNSRule1 -ActionType "Allow"
    $Firewall.NetworkRuleCollections.Add($NetRuleCollection)
    Set-AzFirewall -AzureFirewall $Firewall
    ```

    The section of code you just ran created an Azure Firewall application rule to allow outbound access to Google's DNS server, which is 8.8.8.8 for DNS resolution, as shown in the following screenshot:

Priority	Name	Action	Rules
200	GoogleDNS	Allow	∨ 1 rule.
200			Allow-GoogleDNS

    Figure 17.31: Network rule collection

14. Finally, change the DNS server address for DemoVM1 to 8.8.8.8 to align with the firewall rule for DNS; this will allow the VM to query Google DNS servers for resolution, and because of the configuration you just performed on the firewall, you should be able to communicate with 8.8.8.8.

    ```
    # Set the DNS Target on DemoVM1 Nic to 8.8.8.8
    $NIC = Get-AzNetworkInterface -Name DemoVM1 -ResourceGroupName
    $ResourceGroup
    $NIC.DnsSettings.DnsServers.Add("8.8.8.8")
    $NIC | Set-AzNetworkInterface
    ```

Now that you have completed all the required configurations, you will test whether the VM and firewall rules work as expected. To test this, perform the following steps:

1. Navigate to DemoVM1 on the Azure portal. On the Overview page, select Connect and choose Connect via Bastion:

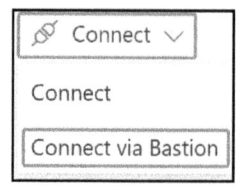

Figure 17.32: Connect to the VM using Bastion

2. The `Bastion` blade will appear. Enter the VM credentials; leave `Authentication Type` as `VM Password`. Click `Connect`:

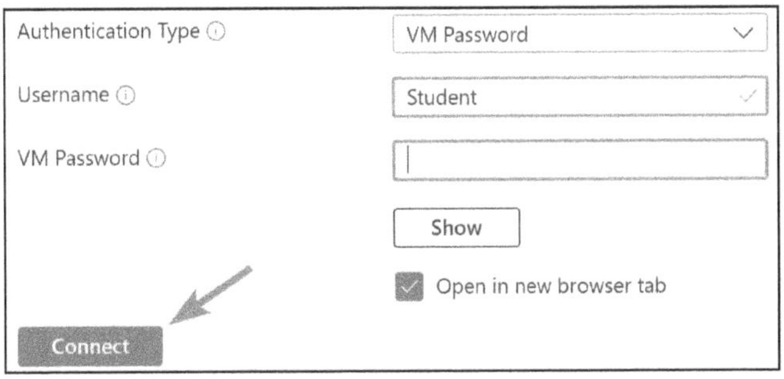

Figure 17.33: Connecting through Bastion

3. Ensure that the new tab that should open is not being blocked by your browser. When the VM loads, open up PowerShell on the VM and enter the following commands:

   ```
   nslookup www.google.com
   nslookup www.microsoft.com
   ```

   Both commands should return answers, as the DNS queries are allowed through the firewall. You will note that it queries 8.8.8.8 as you configured previously:

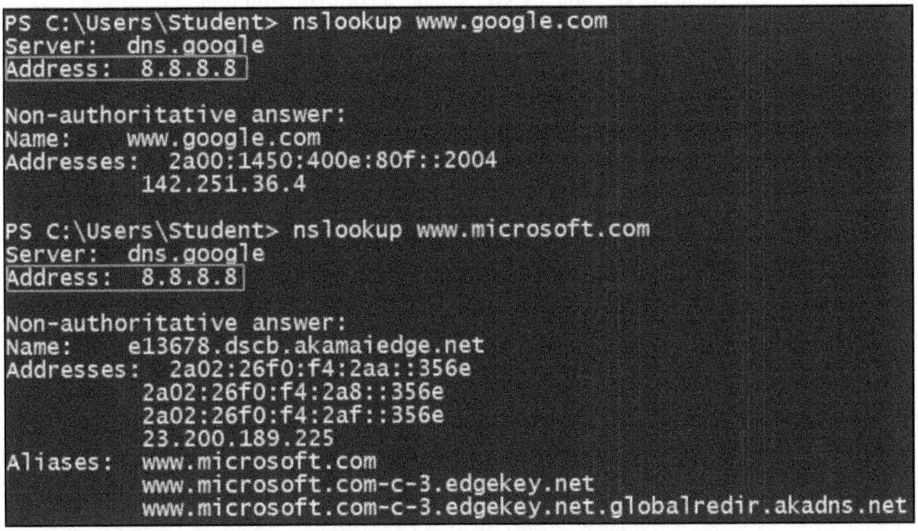

Figure 17.34: Testing DNS resolution

4. Next, you will want to confirm that you can browse only to www.google.com and not any other sites. To do this, run the following command in PowerShell:

   ```
   Invoke-WebRequest -Uri https://www.google.com
   ```

   The preceding command will request the www.google.com website via the PowerShell command-line interface (CLI). You may be prompted by a popup to add the site to a trusted sites zone before the completion of the command; click Add if you see this window. You will receive a 200 status code and an OK description, signifying a successful connection:

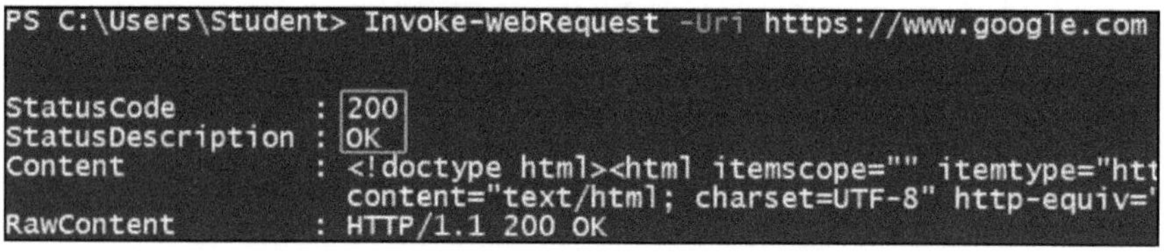

   Figure 17.35: Connection traffic to www.google.com

5. Finally, confirm that you are not able to visit any other FQDNs, such as www.microsoft.com. To test this, run the following command in PowerShell:

   ```
   Invoke-WebRequest -Uri https://www.microsoft.com
   ```

   As shown in the following screenshot, you will get a confirmation that you cannot resolve www.microsoft.com based on the Azure Firewall configuration rules, which is the expected behavior:

   Figure 17.36: Traffic is denied to www.microsoft.com

To summarize this demo section, you have learned how to configure Azure Bastion along with an Azure firewall. You learned to allow DNS requests, such as requests to 8.8.8.8, and how to allow only www.google.com while blocking all other sites. You also learned how to connect to your VM using Bastion and how to test that your firewall configurations are working as expected.

> **Note**
>
> You are encouraged to read further on Azure Bastion and Azure Firewall by using the following links:
>
> https://learn.microsoft.com/en-us/azure/firewall/overview.
>
> https://learn.microsoft.com/en-us/azure/firewall/threat-intel
>
> https://learn.microsoft.com/en-us/azure/firewall/policy-rule-sets
>
> https://learn.microsoft.com/en-us/azure/bastion/bastion-overview.

Summary

In this chapter, you learned about NSGs, what they are and how to use them, how to create new rules, and how to associate NSGs with a subnet. You also learned how to evaluate NSG rules based on priority. Lastly, you learned about Azure Firewall and Azure Bastion, what they do, and how to configure them via a hands-on demo.

You now know how to secure VNets via an NSG and how to secure resources by using Azure Bastion and Azure Firewall. In the next chapter, you will learn about the various load balancing services available in Azure, how to configure load balancing by using Azure Application Gateway and internal and external load balancers, and finally, how to troubleshoot load balancing.

> **Note**
> Remember to delete the resources you created in this chapter to minimize costs. You can do this with the following command, which will conveniently remove the resource group and all the corresponding resources: `Remove-AzResourceGroup -Name AZ104-vnetsecurity`

18
Configuring Load Balancing

In the previous chapter, you learned about network security and explored topics such as **Network Security Groups** (**NSGs**), Azure Firewall, and Azure Bastion. This chapter focuses on Azure public and internal load-balancing by using Azure Load Balancer, Azure Application Gateway, and Azure Front Door to provide **High Availability** (**HA**) for backend computing resources, such as Azure virtual machines, or managed **Platform as a Service** (**PaaS**) services, such as App Service, Azure Kubernetes, and Container Apps. You will also learn how to create health probes for your load balancers and configure load-balancing rules. You will then learn how to troubleshoot these load- balancing services. Finally, you will touch on Azure Front Door services for global load-balancing capabilities. The skills you will gain in this chapter are relevant to the exam and your daily role as an Azure administrator, particularly when building solutions for critical workloads such as websites that can't go down.

In this chapter, you are going to learn about the following main topics:

- Azure Load-Balancing Services
- Azure Load Balancer
- Configuring an Internal Load Balancer
- Configuring a Public Load Balancer
- Azure Application Gateway
- Configuring Azure Application Gateway
- Azure Front Door
- Configuring Azure Front Door

Technical Requirements

In this chapter, you will need access to the following tools:

- Access to an Azure subscription with owner or contributor privileges. If you do not have access to one, students can enroll for a free account: https://azure.microsoft.com/en-us/free/.

- **PowerShell 5.1** or later installed on a Windows PC, or PowerShell Core 6.x on other operating systems, to practice the labs.
- For Windows users, you will need to install **.NET Framework 4.7.2** or later using the following link: https://learn.microsoft.com/en-us/dotnet/framework/install.
- Where PowerShell is not installed or available, https://shell.azure.com can be used as a browser-based shell.
- Installation of the Az PowerShell module, which can be performed by running the following in an administrative PowerShell session:

    ```
    Set-ExecutionPolicy -ExecutionPolicy RemoteSigned -Scope
    CurrentUser
    Install-Module -Name Az -Scope CurrentUser -Repository PSGallery
    -Force
    ```

Azure Load-Balancing Services

Load-balancing refers to the concept of distributing traffic across multiple endpoints to prevent any single endpoint from becoming overwhelmed with incoming traffic. It also enables the continuity of services by exposing a single frontend endpoint that services the backend endpoints you connect to. Should any of the backend endpoints go down, the connecting user would be none the wiser, as the next endpoint would continue communication flows, and there would be no perceived loss of service to the end user.

Azure offers several services for load-balancing. Microsoft views these services as being defined into two distinct categories, web-based workloads defined by HTTP/HTTPS traffic, such as any website or application, and non-web-based workloads and applications, such as some VM-related service (e.g., analytics servers). Load-balancing is further divided into regional and global delivery for both web and non-web workloads.

Regional Services

Regional services are designed to distribute traffic within Azure **Virtual Networks** (**VNets**) and services within a **single** region. For example, you may want to distribute traffic among several web servers in the East US region; you would then utilize regional services to facilitate this, and you would choose the Azure Application Gateway to support this requirement since it is a web-based service. Where you are distributing among non-HTTP(S) workloads (such as an accounting application hosted on several servers), you then leverage Azure Load Balancer to distribute traffic among the servers.

Global Services

Global services are designed to distribute traffic across different regions. They can also be used to extend your application services beyond the Azure cloud into other clouds (such as AWS and GCP) or on-premises environments (such as your organization's data centers and offices). They also include features for better system performance on a global scale by creating distributed workloads that can cater to specific regional requirements (such as delivering a website closer to the region you are connecting from for faster web page loading performance). In some cases, you may service a primary region (such as the West US) and offer more compute resources to that region for the best experience, with other regions waiting on standby in case of errors (such as East US), maintaining continuity if there is a failure but with substantially fewer resources to reduce costs. Typically, these would be used for deployments spanning **multiple** regions. Often, this technology is used to facilitate high-availability environments in active-active (i.e., having standby compute readily available in an active state) or active-passive (i.e., having standby compute available in a non-active state) configurations across regions.

To further enhance redundancy, regional and global load-balancing services are combined by connecting globally load-balanced endpoints with regionally load-balanced endpoints, offering recovery from multiple points of failure at any part of the chain.

Multi-Cloud Considerations

Many organizations have adopted modern computing principles known as hybrid cloud, multi-cloud, or a combination of both (multi-hybrid cloud). These principles are formed from several base theories concerning vendor lock-in (being stuck with a particular vendor due to your configurations and agreements), redundancy objectives (scaling across clouds so that if either cloud platform should fail, you can still retain continuity of services), and cost factors (being that whichever vendor platform offers the best cost for your suitable purposes when needed will be chosen). There may be other factors influencing this move decision, and being aware of the capability to leverage multiple clouds alongside understanding your organizational strategic objectives can assist you in your service considerations, accommodating various types of endpoints and environments.

Load Balancer Service Options

When considering the service to use for your load-balancing requirements, you should first consider the type of workload you are dealing with. The two load balancing options are non-HTTP(S) and HTTP(S) based workloads.

Non-HTTP(S) Workloads

Non-HTTP(S) workloads are workloads that are not intended to deliver applications or services through web-based protocols. This could be backend servers such as databases for your web pages or game servers. When deciding on the service you need to choose, you first need to decide on your global requirements (region or multi-region) and where the service is being delivered over the internet.

Azure provides two load balancer services, catered to network traffic that is not HTTP(S)-related, meaning that they are not intended for web-related workloads. These are frequently used to distribute traffic between VMs and containers:

- Azure Load Balancer (a regional and global service)
- Traffic Manager (a global service)
- The Azure Load Balancer offering is intended for workloads that are not internet-facing (i.e., servicing internal traffic) and, normally, for routing traffic securely over your organizational networks (such as an Azure VNet). It can be used for backend database servers – for instance, behind your web application.
- Conversely, Traffic Manager is intended for internet-facing applications and services, such as an accounting or HR-based system that you may use within your organization. Being DNS-based, Traffic Manager load balances traffic to your public-facing applications through DNS routing.

> **Note**
> Azure has launched a cross-region (global) load balancer that enables you to load-balance across regions and not just a single region; you can read more about the service here: `https://learn.microsoft.com/en-us/azure/load-balancer/cross-region-overview`.

HTTP(S) Workloads

HTTP(S) workloads are web-based workloads, such as any typical web application that you may run (e.g., a basic HTML or WordPress web page, or even something more advanced that is delivered through web-based protocols). In addition to the preceding non-HTTP(S) load balancing services (Azure Load Balancer and Traffic Manager), there are currently two services that can be deployed to cater to web-based HTTP(S) type traffic, and they are delivered as Layer 7 load balancers.

The services that can be used for HTTP(S) web-based load-balancing are as follows:

- Application Gateway (a regional service)
- Azure Front Door (a global service)

These services offer **Secure Sockets Layer** (**SSL**) offloading, path-based load-balancing, and session affinity configuration settings. You can also choose to enable the web application firewall feature, which scans the traffic received by your applications and assesses it for anomalous behavior, particularly focusing on web applications.

The Azure Application Gateway service is designed as a regional Layer 7 load-balancing service to connect to your web applications. It offers integrating **Web Application Firewall** (**WAF**) capabilities to better secure your websites and SSL offloading to reduce compute overhead on your web-based services.

The Azure Front Door service is also designed as a Layer 7 load-balancing service but with a global load-balancing capability. It shares many features with Application Gateway and additionally caters to your geographically dispersed workloads.

Next, we will explore the features available in Application Gateway and Front Door and also learn about their purposes.

SSL Offloading

SSL is the technology that enables encrypted communication between your browser and web application service. This is now being replaced by a new technology called **Transport Layer Security** (**TLS**). One of the benefits of both Application Gateway and Azure Front Door is that they provide SSL offloading or TLS termination that effectively transfers the decryption function to the implemented load-balancing service. This provides several benefits to your application infrastructure – namely, better performance and utilization of your backend services. This termination functionality also enables the load balancer to interrogate traffic to provide more intelligent management features, such as routing and header management.

> **Note**
> TLS termination is very compute-intensive and can significantly degrade the performance of your web applications. Offloading this to a load-balancing service such as Application Gateway can greatly improve your application's performance and redistribute the previously used CPU cycles to other compute-intensive tasks.

Path-Based Load-Balancing

Both Azure Front Door and Application Gateway support URL path-based routing. This feature enables you to split traffic based on your URL path. Traffic can be divided and separated to route to different backend pools by matching your path-based rules. You may choose, for instance, to serve other content types through separate backend server pools. An example would be where you may want to deliver images from a slower storage set, as they are not required for instant consumption, whereas your videos may be designed for live streaming. The delivery of both these resource types requires different sets of resources and configurations; if you enabled path-based routing, you could look for the /image portion of your URL and route those images to the image backend pool, and likewise for your videos. This enables a much more controlled and dynamic management flow for your applications.

The following diagram illustrates the splitting concept:

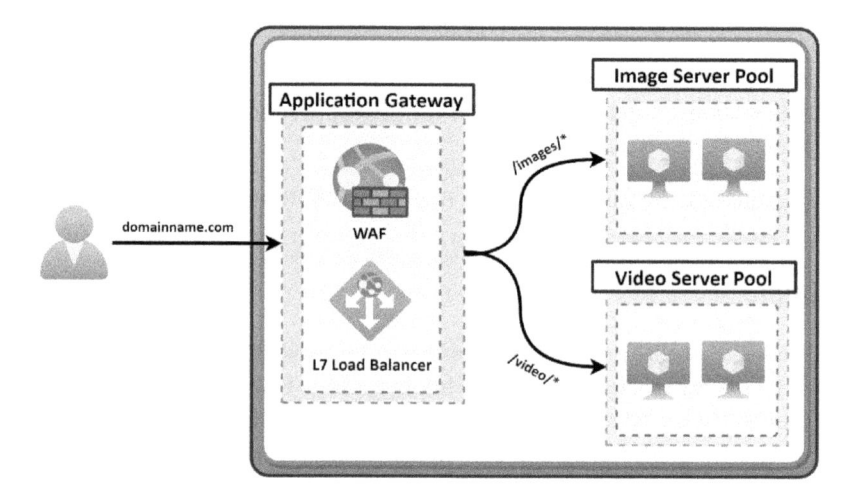

Figure 18.1: URL path-based routing

As you can see in *Figure 18.1*, traffic is routed based on its source URL type. The conventions for this are defined relative to the root path on the server, with / representing the root path. In the figure, if your website domain is domain.com, the /images/* pattern would be the equivalent of domain.com/images/. The wildcard (*) represents any character after the path as part of the search term.

> **Note**
> Note that the URL pattern cannot include # or ? as its character. Each pattern must start with a / character.

Session Affinity

Session affinity refers to the capability to maintain communication between the same source and destination systems for the duration of the established communication window. For example, if **user1** is directed to **server1** through a load-balancing service, it would follow that all subsequent communication from **user1** to the load-balancing service will be routed directly to **server1**. Session affinity ensures consistency in the communication path, preventing traffic from being distributed across multiple servers (such as **server2** or **server3**). Enable this where your applications require session integrity.

WAF

A WAF is a specialized firewall service designed to protect web-based traffic from vulnerabilities and exploits. In Azure, the WAF services offered are based on the **Core Rule Set (CRS)** developed by the **Open Web Application Security Project (OWASP)**. The CRS serves as a foundational set of rules for WAFs to identify and mitigate common web application vulnerabilities and exploits. It is designed to protect against a broad spectrum of threats, such as SQL injection, **Cross-Site Scripting (XSS)**, and HTTP protocol violations.

The Azure WAF service is a cloud-native WAF that is easy to implement and requires no modification of your application code to be functional. It will work in accordance with your traffic. All alerts raised will be logged into the WAF log, which is integrated into Azure Monitor. You can customize rules based on your requirements and against several sites served by the Application Gateway.

There are several protections that the service offers, including the following:

- Protection against HTTP protocol violations and anomalies
- SQL injection attacks
- **XSS** attacks
- Geo traffic filtering (allowing/blocking regions from accessing your applications)
- **Distributed Denial of Service (DDOS)** and bot attacks

The following figure illustrates the WAF service in action. Note on the left of the diagram that the traffic is attempting to come in through the Application Gateway; only valid requests are permitted by the WAF service. The Application Gateway then routes the relevant traffic to the backend services delivering the web application:

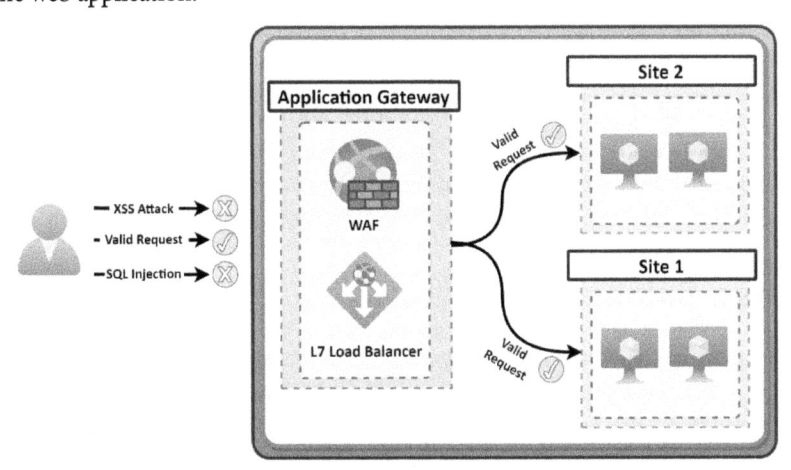

Figure 18.2: WAF request handling

Deciding on the Right Load Balancer Solution

As you have seen previously, several considerations must be made in determining the correct service for your requirements. The following diagram is a decision tree that will help you make the right decision, based on your service requirements.

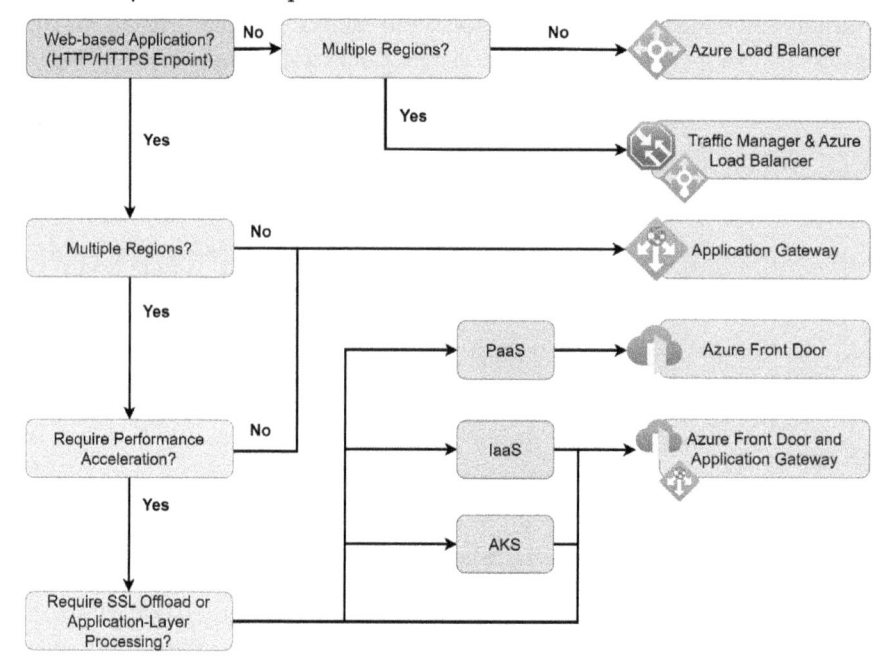

Figure 18.3: The load balancing decision tree

You may have noticed that, at times, combinations of services are available to enhance the offering of each of the basic services. Using the decision tree can help you not only determine the correct solution to choose going forward but also verify that the service you use is appropriate for what you need to deliver.

Now that you understand more about the load-balancing services available in Azure and how to choose between them, we will explore each of them in more detail and explore their configurations.

Azure Load Balancer

Azure Load Balancer is a load balancer that operates at the transport layer (Layer 4 in the OSI network reference stack). Azure Load Balancer supports the **Transmission Control Protocol** (**TCP**) and **User Datagram Protocol** (**UDP**), and it can be used to load-balance traffic to your applications and is generally used in scenarios where you want to enable HA.

The concept of HA refers to the ability of your applications or services to sustain some form of downtime; should you sustain a loss of a workload or node, your load balancer will redirect traffic to the remaining available and functional workloads or nodes.

Load balancers provide scalability by sharing the load of the traffic among several responding servers, which also creates resiliency, as traffic is not dependent on a single node to respond. Azure load balancers also provide high throughput and low latency, and they can scale up to millions of flows. They support various inbound and outbound scenarios as well.

The Azure Load Balancer service can be used for the following:

- **Public load balancer**: Incoming internet traffic is load-balanced to VMs and scale sets.
- **Internal load balancer (ILB)**: Traffic can be load-balanced across VMs and scale sets inside a virtual network. You can also use Azure Load Balancer in a hybrid scenario, reaching a load balancer inside an on-premises network.
- **Port forwarding**: You can forward traffic to specific ports on specific VMs, using inbound **network address translation (NAT)** rules.
- **Outbound connectivity**: You can also provide outbound connectivity for VMs inside a virtual network, using Azure Load Balancer as a public load balancer.

> **Note**
> Whenever you hear a reference to HA or scalability, you should immediately start to question whether a load balancer should be implemented; in many scenarios, this will be one of the resources you will need in your toolset.

You now understand the fundamentals of load balancing and have learned about the Azure Load Balancer service, which offers versatility in meeting your load-balancing requirements. In the following topics, we will explore some of the features and capabilities that Azure Load Balancer provides.

Features and Capabilities

Azure Load Balancer offers several features and capabilities as part of its service, such as load-balancing, port forwarding, automatic reconfiguration, health probes, and outbound **Source Network Address Translation (SNAT)** connections. We will now look into these features in more detail in the following sections.

Load-Balancing

Traffic can be distributed, using rules, from the frontend of the load balancer to a backend pool (such as traffic from the internet connecting to backend web servers). By default, Azure Load Balancer uses a **five-tuple hash**, composed of the source IP address, source port, destination IP address, destination ports, and the IP protocol number, to map flows to the available servers in the backend pool.

Port Forwarding

Inbound **Network Address Translation** (**NAT**) rules can be created to forward traffic from a specific port of a frontend IP address of a load balancer to a specific port of a backend instance inside an Azure VNet. Therefore, the same hash-based distribution is used with load-balancing. This can be used for the **Remote Desktop Protocol** (**RDP**) and **Secure Shell** (**SSH**) sessions for VMs inside a VNet. You can associate several internal endpoints with various ports on the same frontend IP address (NAT). The VMs can be remotely administered using the frontend IP address. This way, an additional jump box is not needed. For example, consider a scenario where you have two servers set up for RDP, and both use port 3389. You have a single public IP address. You want to remotely manage both servers, so you can set up inbound NAT rules to direct incoming internet traffic to the respective backend servers. You achieve this by forwarding port 3389 traffic to **server1** and port 3390 traffic to **server2**, connecting to the backend servers on port 3389 as needed.

Automatic reconfiguration

The load balancer automatically reconfigures itself when instances are scaled out or in. When VMs are added or removed from the backend pool, the load balancer does not need to perform additional operations. For example, imagine you are hosting a game website with two servers on the backend. You are running a sale, and you have much more traffic than anticipated. You decided to add two additional servers to the backend pool to cater to the increased traffic. The load balancer service will automatically reconfigure itself once you add the servers to the backend pool to ensure that they all deliver the website service, enabling more visitors to connect to your website.

Outbound Connections (SNAT)

SNAT is the process of automatically translating outbound connections to the public frontend IP address of the load balancer. When used on ILBs, a rule must be configured to allow outbound internet access. In order to better understand this feature, imagine that you have some database servers that you want to protect by preventing internet users from connecting to the databases. You place these servers behind a load balancer and only assign private IPs to the VMs. However, you still want these servers to be able to connect to the internet. They can do so through a technology called SNAT, which allows private IPs to communicate with external services by translating the private IP address to the public IP address of the load balancer.

Health Probes

Azure Load Balancer uses health probes to determine the health of a VM in the backend pool. When the load balancer detects a probe that fails to respond, placing the VM in an unhealthy state, the load balancer stops sending new connections to the unhealthy VM instance. Different health probes are provided for HTTP, HTTPS, and TCP endpoints. To put this into perspective, imagine you operate an online retail website where you sell various products. It's crucial to maintain website traffic to ensure steady revenue, especially during the secure credit card payment process. You employ health probes on your load balancer to identify when a server fails to respond to HTTP(S) requests. When the load balancer detects any unhealthy servers, it stops directing traffic to those services to ensure a consistent and reliable user experience. This guarantees that users always receive a response from healthy servers.

Metrics

Detailed metrics are provided through the Azure Monitor service, which allows you to explore performance and health metrics at multiple layers and dimensions. There is also a preconfigured dashboard with **Azure Load Balancer Insights** that has several helpful visualizations to manage your resources. When running a website (such as a retail website), you would use metrics to analyze the percentage utilization of your processor and memory. If you notice high levels of CPU usage for extended periods, you may consider adding more workloads (horizontal scaling). These metrics can also be used to create visualizations showing usage over time, which is helpful to analyze peak usage periods. Additionally, you can automate actions to be executed when thresholds are exceeded, such as automatically adding or removing instances to meet demand.

Security

The standard **Stock-Keeping Unit (SKU)** was designed with security first and adopts a zero-trust network security model. The standard public IP SKU requires explicit rules to permit traffic to your environment and services and, therefore, substantially improves security over the basic services that open access to the internet as a default configuration. For example, you might want to open a web port on your server to provide an API for other services to securely communicate over the internet. Therefore, you should limit access to specific known IP addresses to prevent unauthorized access. Internally, you can also open additional ports, such as administrative ports available locally within your VNets. With the standard SKU design, only explicitly allowed traffic rules will permit traffic. This approach will protect you from accidentally exposing your internal administrative ports, thereby providing enhanced security. Load balancers offer additional security benefits, such as protection against **DDOS attacks**. These attacks occur when malicious actors target multiple endpoints to disrupt the operation of your services.

> **Note**
> When you configure an HTTPS health probe, you will require a certificate to perform the probe assessment.

Now that you understand the main features and capabilities of Azure load balancers, you will explore the different **SKUs** available in Azure and their differences.

Load Balancer SKUs

Azure Load Balancer comes with three different SKU options – Basic, Standard, and Gateway. They differ in price, features, and delivery of the service.

Basic

The basic load balancer SKU is suitable for small-scale applications that do not require HA configurations and do not span across availability zones. By default, this solution is insecure, as it adopts an "allow all unless denied" approach. This SKU is best for test workloads or non-critical applications that do not require a **service-level agreement** (**SLA**) or high levels of security. Examples of these workloads may include development and test applications, informational websites that are not critical to daily operations, or a database of fun activities for year-end team building.

The basic load balancer is free to use and has the following capabilities:

- **Backend pool size**: The Basic tier supports up to 300 instances inside a backend pool and a single availability set
- **Backend type**: The backend type for the basic load balancer is NIC-based
- **Health probes**: The basic load balancer supports both TCP and HTTP
- **Diagnostics**: Diagnostics for the basic load balancer include support for Azure Log Analytics (for a public load balancer only), a backend pool health count, and an SNAT exhaustion alert
- **Default security**: The basic load balancer is open by default, and NSGs are optional
- **Management operations**: The management operations for the basic load balancer typically take between 60 to 90 seconds or above
- **Multiple frontends**: The basic load balancer supports multiple frontends but only for inbound traffic

The Basic SKU has the following limitations in the Azure Load Balancer service that the Standard SKU doesn't:

- **Availability zones**: Availability zones are not available in the Basic SKU
- **Outbound rules**: Outbound rules are not available in the Basic SKU
- **HA ports:** HA ports are not available in the Basic SKU
- **TCP Resets on idle**: The TCP Resets on idle feature is not available in the Basic SKU
- **SLA**: An SLA is not available for the Basic SKU
- **Global VNet peering support**: Global VNet is not supported in the basic SKU
- **NAT Gateway support**: NAT Gateway is not supported in the Basic SKU
- **Private link support**: Private link support is not available in the Basic SKU
- **Cross-region load balancing**: Cross-region load-balancing is not supported in the Basic SKU
- **Diagnostics**: Diagnostics are not supported in the Basic SKU

Now that we know what Basic SKU does and does not offer, we will explore Standard SKU's offerings.

Standard

The Standard tier of Azure Load Balancer carries a cost. The charge is based on the number of rules and the data that is associated with a resource and processed, both inbound and outbound. The Standard SKU is ideal for scaling workloads that require high performance and low latency. It can handle workloads needing HA and can scale securely with a security-centered approach. This SKU is backed by an SLA for load-balancing services, which is particularly important for critical workloads. An example of where you might use this is a time capture server for an organization positioned behind a Standard SKU load balancer, ensuring secure access to an application and the ability to scale seamlessly as demand fluctuates and instances are added to or removed from the backend.

This SKU is designed to be secure by default and has the following capabilities:

- **Backend pool size**: The Standard tier supports up to 5,000 instances inside a backend pool.
- **Backend type**: IP-based and NIC-based.
- **Health probes**: TCP, HTTP, and HTTPS.
- **Availability zones**: Support for zone-redundant and zonal frontends for inbound and outbound connections and cross-zone load-balancing.
- **Outbound connections**: Multiple frontends can be used per load-balancing rule opt-out. Pool-based outbound NAT can be explicitly defined using outbound rules. Outbound scenarios must be explicitly created to use outbound connectivity for the VM, VM scale set, or availability set. VNet service endpoints can be reached without defining outbound connectivity. Public IP addresses and PaaS that are not available using VNet service endpoints must be reached with outbound connectivity. It is recommended that you use Private Link for all PaaS services and bypass SNAT.
- **Outbound rules**: Outbound NAT configuration needs to be defined using public IP addresses, public IP prefixes, or both. You can configure the outbound idle timeout as well as custom SNAT port allocation.
- **Diagnostics**: Azure Load Balancer has support for Azure Monitor, with features including health probe status, outbound connection health (successful SNAT and failed flows), multidimensional metrics, and active data-plane measurements.
- **HA ports**: HA ports for the ILB only.
- **Default Security**: These are secure by default. Unless ILBs are whitelisted by an NSG, the endpoints are closed to inbound flows by default. Public IP addresses and load balancer endpoints are secured as well.
- **TCP Resets on idle**: This can be enabled on the idle timeout on any rule.
- **Multiple frontends**: For inbound and outbound connections.
- **Management operations**: < 30 seconds for most operations.

- **SLA**: 99.99% for a data path with two healthy VMs.
- **Global VNet peering support**: Supported for standard ILBs.
- **NAT Gateway support**: Supported for public load balancers and ILBs.
- **Private link support**: Supported only for standard ILBs.
- **Cross-region load-balancing**: Supported for public load balancers.

As you can see, there are some distinct differences between the two types of load balancers, such as the initial approach to traffic handling, the Basic SKU allowing all unless denied, and conversely, the Standard SKU blocking all traffic unless explicitly allowed. Other key differences are the SLAs, cross-region support, backend pool size, diagnostic capability, and Private Link support. It's important to understand these differences before deploying any solution, such as factoring in desired features, costs, scalability and performance requirements, the level of diagnostics and monitoring required, and your desired level of security. Another critical consideration is that changing SKUs will require redeployment. Remember to explicitly define NSG rules to allow traffic to flow through the Standard SKU load balancer.

Another important feature of the Standard SKU is the option to have multiple frontends, which enables you to control traffic to multiple firewalls and services and helps you better manage it. Be mindful that the Basic SKU does not offer an SLA, which is critical to production environments to ensure that you have conducted due diligence.

Gateway

The Gateway load balancer SKU allows for the transparent insertion and management of **Network Virtual Appliances** (**NVAs**) and introduces scaling functionality without making network complexities visible. It can also be used to improve the performance of NVAs. The Gateway load balancer SKU can also maintain flow symmetry and sticky sessions to specific instances in the backend pool. It provides additional functionality by allowing the easy addition of NVAs. This service also enables you to scale and chain applications over regions and subscriptions. This SKU can also be used in combination with the Standard SKU, and the value of the service is the ability to route traffic to an NVA before reaching your applications.

Imagine you have a company, OrionTech, that hosts its applications across multiple regions in Azure for geographical redundancy and closer proximity to your users. However, ensuring secure and efficient traffic flow between these regions and your users while also maintaining HA is a challenge. You run an NVA with firewalling in your environment to protect your workloads. You decide to utilize the Gateway load balancer SKU to insert NVAs seamlessly into the data pathway, enhancing security measures across your Azure-hosted applications. By using the Gateway load balancer SKU, you are able to ensure HA and maintain user session integrity across multiple regions. You achieved your goal of boosting the security and performance of OrionTech's applications while seamlessly accommodating traffic spikes.

Gateway SKU can be beneficial for many advanced network functionality scenarios, such as the aforementioned inline firewalling capability, advanced packet analysis, intrusion detection and prevention scenarios, traffic mirroring, and DDoS protection. For more information, read the following article: `https://learn.microsoft.com/en-us/azure/load-balancer/gateway-overview`.

> **Note**
> The basic load balancer SKU is set to retire on September 30, 2025.

You now understand the different SKUs for Azure Load Balancer. Next, we will explore the different features available to the service and complete an exercise to configure an ILB.

Configuring an ILB

The following sets of exercises will guide you through the process of creating and configuring a load balancer from the Azure portal. You are going to learn to route internal traffic with a Basic load balancer to spread incoming requests among multiple VMs. For this demonstration, you are going to create a load balancer, backend servers, and network resources at the `Basic` pricing tier.

Creating the VNet

First, you will create a VNet, backend servers, and a test VM. The VNet is required for the VMs to have a network range space to join and for there to be IPs to route the traffic from the ILB to. Complete the following steps to deploy your VNet:

1. Navigate to the Azure portal by opening `https://portal.azure.com`.
2. Create a new resource group for this exercise, named `AZ104-InternalLoadBalancer`.
3. Create a new VNet with the following configurations, using the PowerShell code:
   - `Name`: `LoadBalancerVNet`
   - `Region`: A region of your choice (choose the same region for all subsequent resources in this chapter)
   - `IPv4 address space`: `172.16.0.0/16`
   - `Subnet name`: `BackendSubnet`
   - `Subnet address range`: `172.16.0.0/24`

The following PowerShell code will assist with your VNet deployment:

```
# First connect your Azure account using your credentials
Connect-AzAccount

# If necessary, select the right subscription as follows
$SubscriptionId = "xxxxxxx"
Select-AzSubscription -SubscriptionId $SubscriptionId

# Parameters
$ResourceGroup = "AZ104-InternalLoadBalancer"
$Location = "WestEurope"
$VirtualNetworkName = "LoadBalancerVNet"
$SubnetName = "BackendSubnet"

# Create a Virtual Network
New-AzVirtualNetwork -Name "$VirtualNetworkName"
-ResourceGroupName "$ResourceGroup" `
-Location "$Location" -AddressPrefix "172.16.0.0/16" -Subnet
$SubnetName `
-SubnetPrefix "172.16.0.0/24"
```

Creating the VMs

You must ensure that the AZ module is installed as per the *Technical Requirements* section at the beginning of the chapter.

In this exercise, you will create three Windows Server VMs in an availability set using PowerShell. These VMs will reside in `BackendSubnet` and be the endpoints receiving traffic from the load balancer. The code can be found here: https://packt.link/Sb4Yw.

You can change the parameters to suit your requirements:

```
# First connect your Azure account using your credentials
Connect-AzAccount

# If necessary, select the right subscription as follows
$SubscriptionId = "xxxxxxx"
Select-AzSubscription -SubscriptionId $SubscriptionId

# Parameters
$ResourceGroup = "AZ104-InternalLoadBalancer"
$Location = "WestEurope"
$AvailabilitySetName = "LBAvailabilitySet"
$VirtualNetworkName = "LoadBalancerVNet"
```

```
$SubnetName = "BackendSubnet"

# Create an Availability Set for the VMs
New-AzAvailabilitySet -Location "$Location" -Name
"$AvailabilitySetName" -ResourceGroupName "$ResourceGroup" -Sku
Aligned -PlatformFaultDomainCount 2 -PlatformUpdateDomainCount 2

# Setup Your VM Admin Credentials
$adminUsername = 'Student'
$adminPassword = 'Pa55w.rd1234'
$adminCreds = New-Object PSCredential $adminUsername, ($adminPassword
| ConvertTo-SecureString -AsPlainText -Force)

# Deploy 2 VMs Inside the Availability Set and a Test VM
for ($vmNum=1; $vmNum -le 3; $vmNum++){
    if ($vmNum -eq 3){$vmName = "TestVM"} # Test VM
    else{$vmName = "BackendVM$vmNum"}
    New-AzVm -ResourceGroupName "$ResourceGroup" -Name
"$vmName" -Location "$Location" -VirtualNetworkName
"$VirtualNetworkName" -SubnetName "$SubnetName" -SecurityGroupName
"PacktNetworkSecurityGroup" -PublicIpAddressName "$($vmName)
PublicIpAddress" -AvailabilitySetName "$AvailabilitySetName"
-Credential $adminCreds -OpenPorts 3389 -Size "Standard_DS1_v2"
-PublicIpSku Standard
}
```

Now that your VMs are deployed, you will work on the load balancer next.

Creating a Load Balancer

In this exercise, you will create a load balancer using the Azure portal. This load balancer will be used to distribute traffic to the backend VMs and demonstrate that load balancing is working. Complete the steps as follows:

1. Navigate to the Azure portal by opening `https://portal.azure.com`.

2. Open the `AZ104-InternalLoadBalancer` resource group you created, click `Overview` on the left menu, and then click `Create`.

3. Click `Networking` on the left menu under the `Categories` section, and then click `Load Balancer` on the right blade screen.

4. Click Create on the Load Balancer card.

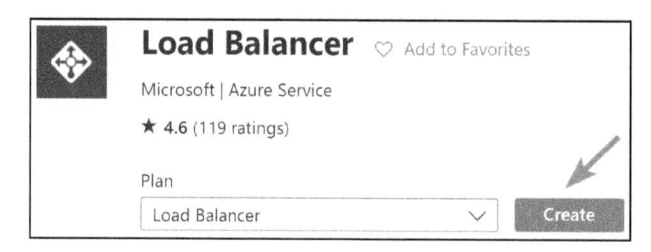

Figure 18.4: Load Balancer

5. Enter AZ104-InternalLoadBalancer for Resource group, InternalLoad Balancer for Name, and West Europe for Region, and then set SKU to Standard, Type to Internal, and finally, Tier to Regional. Click Next : Frontend IP configuration >:

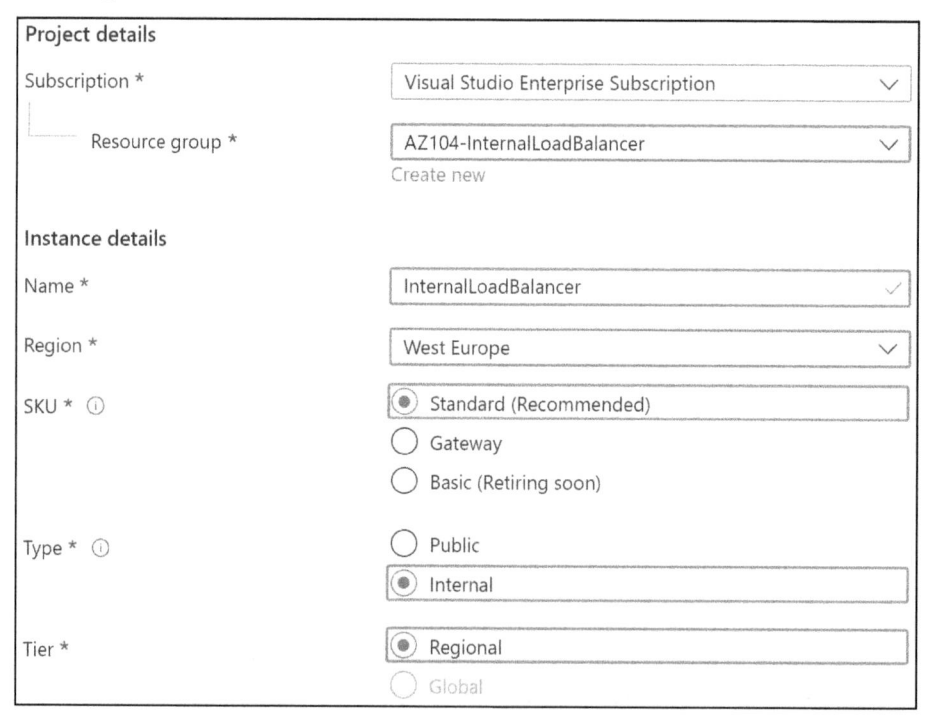

Figure 18.5: The load balancer – Project details

6. Click + Add a frontend IP configuration. This will prompt you to add the details for the IP configuration.

7. Enter `FrontendIP` as Name, select `LoadBalancerVNet` as `Virtual network`, and for Subnet, select `BackendSubnet`. Set `Assignment` to `Dynamic` and `Availability zone` to `No Zone`. Click Save:

Add frontend IP configuration
InternalLoadBalancer

Name *	FrontendIP
IP version	● IPv4 ○ IPv6
Virtual network *	LoadBalancerVNet (AZ104-InternalLoadBal...
Subnet *	BackendSubnet (192.168.1.0/24)
Assignment	● Dynamic ○ Static
Availability zone *	No Zone

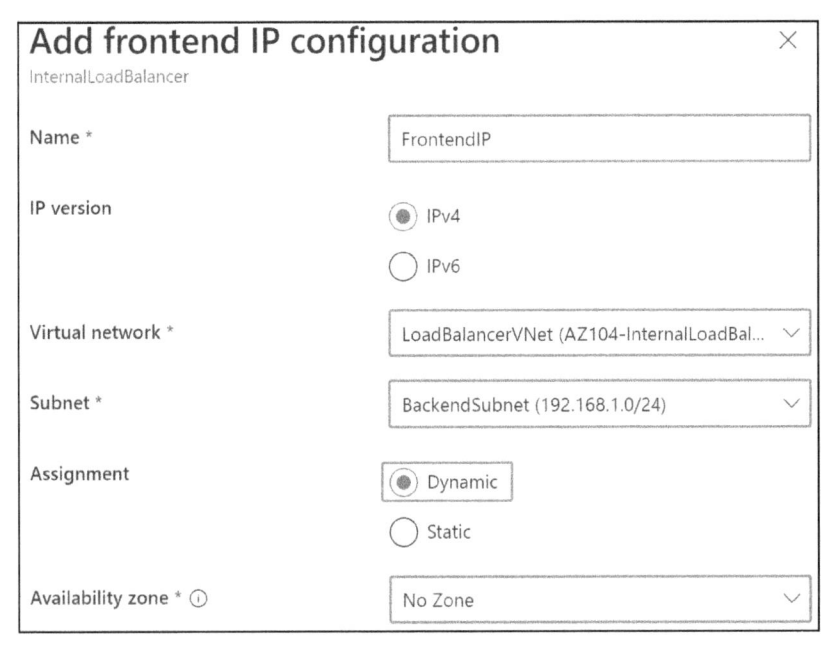

Figure 18.6: The load balancer – the frontend IP

8. Click `Next : Backend pools >`.
9. Click `+ Add a backend pool`.
10. Enter `BackendPool` for Name and set `Backend Pool Configuration` to NIC. Click `+ Add` under `IP configurations`.
11. On the pop-up screen, select `BackendVM1` and `BackendVM2`, and then click Add.

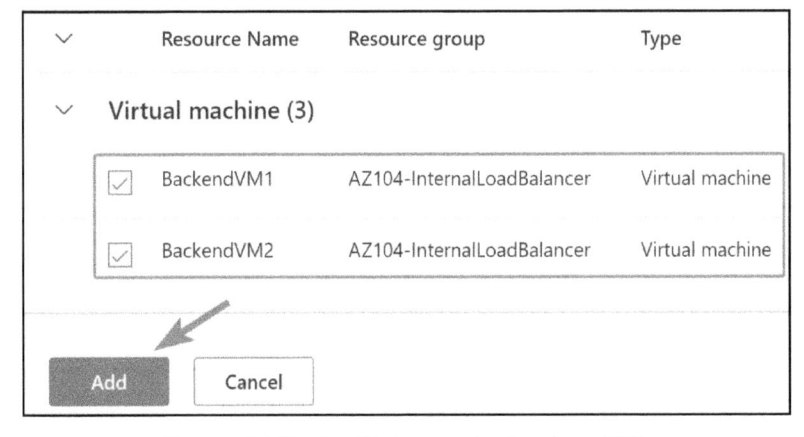

	Resource Name	Resource group	Type
∨	Virtual machine (3)		
☑	BackendVM1	AZ104-InternalLoadBalancer	Virtual machine
☑	BackendVM2	AZ104-InternalLoadBalancer	Virtual machine

[Add] [Cancel]

Figure 18.7: The load balancer – backend pool VMs

12. Click `Save`.
13. Click `Review + create`, and then click `Create`.

You now have the load balancer resource configured with a frontend IP address. You have also configured your backend pool in accordance with the deployment, consisting of `BackendVM1` and `BackendVM2`. You will now need a mechanism for load-balancing traffic between your VMs and a method to detect the health of the services on the VMs. This is where health probes come in.

In the next exercise, you will configure the health probes for your load balancer before we move on to investigating rules to distribute traffic to the VMs.

Creating the Health Probes

The next step is to create a health probe for the load balancer, which is used by the load balancer to monitor the status of the VM. The probe will dynamically add or remove VMs from the load balancer rotation, based on the response to the health checks that are performed by the health probe. The load balancer will only serve requests to healthy backend VMs, and the probe will be configured to assess the health of the backend VMs, using the HTTP protocol on port `80`.

To create a health probe, follow these steps:

1. Open your load balancer resource.
2. Under `Settings` in the left menu, select `Health probes`, and then select `Add`.
3. Enter `BackendHealthProbe` for Name, set `Protocol` to `HTTP`, `Port` to `80`, `Path` to `/`, and `Interval` to 5 (this is the number of seconds between probe attempts), and then click `Save`:

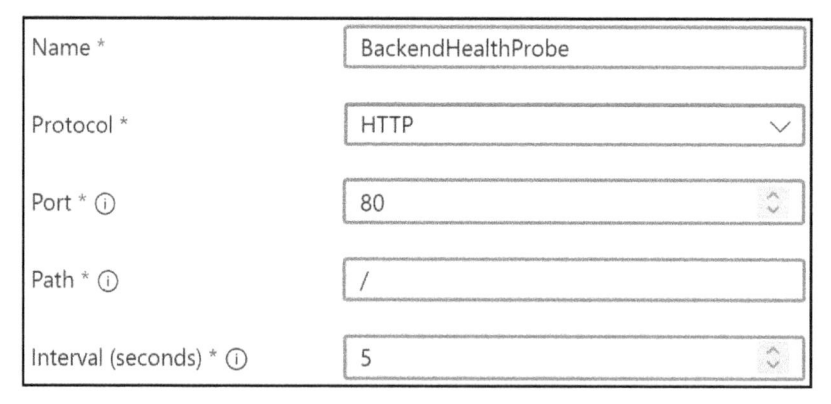

Name *	BackendHealthProbe
Protocol *	HTTP
Port *	80
Path *	/
Interval (seconds) *	5

Figure 18.8: Adding a health probe

Now that you have deployed your health probe for the load balancer, you will work on creating your first load balancing rule.

Creating Load-Balancing Rules

Azure load balancers distribute network or application traffic across multiple servers in the backend pool (such as traffic from the internet connecting to backend web servers) to enhance responsiveness and availability, using rules. Load-balancing rules define how traffic (TCP or UDP) is distributed to the VMs inside the backend pool. When you create a new rule, you define the frontend IP configuration for incoming traffic, the backend IP pool that receives the traffic, and the required source and destination ports. The rule that you are going to create will listen to port 80 on the frontend. The rule then sends the network traffic to the backend pool, also on port 80.

To create the rule, follow these steps:

1. Open the load balancer resource.
2. Under Settings, select Load balancing rules, and then click Add:
3. On the pop-up blade, enter WebTrafficRule for Name, set IP Version to IPv4, select FrontendIP for Frontend IP Address, select BackendPool for Backend pool, set Protocol to TCP, Port to 80, and Backend port to 80, select BackendHealthProbe (HTTP:80) for Health probe, and leave all the other settings as default. Click Save:

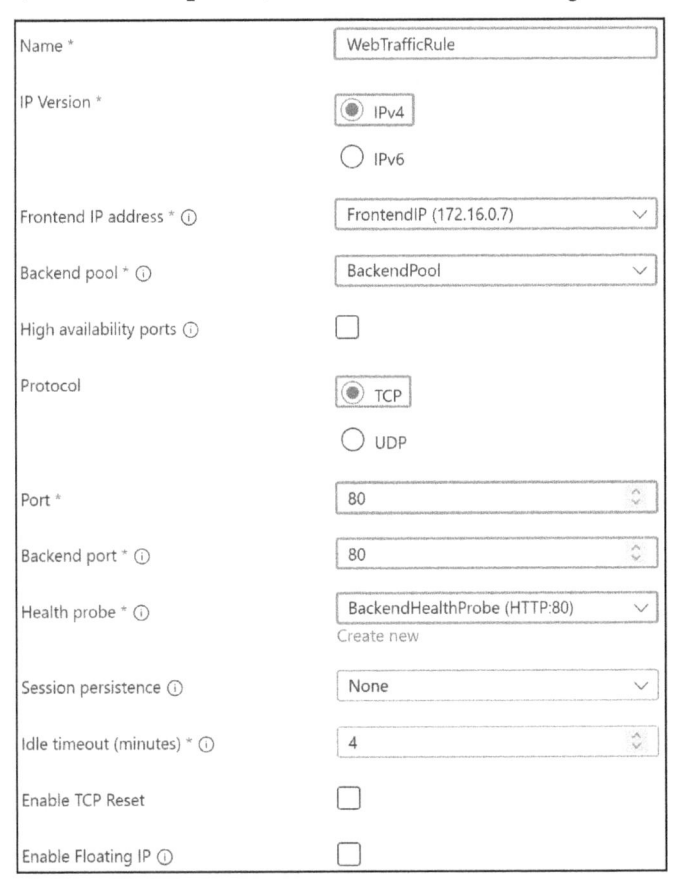

Figure 18.9: Adding a load-balancing rule

Now that your load balancer is all configured, you are ready to start testing it to confirm that it works as expected. Next, you will learn how to test your load balancer.

Testing the Load Balancer

To test the VMs properly, you are going to install **Internet Information Services** (**IIS**) on the `BackendVM1` and `BackendVM2` VMs, using PowerShell. Then, you can use `TestVM` to test the load balancer by calling its private IP address. First, you will need to obtain the private IP address of the load balancer. Follow these steps:

1. Open the load balancer resource.
2. Under `Settings`, select `Frontend IP configuration`, and then copy the private IP address, as follows:

Figure 18.10: Identifying your private IP

3. Now, you need to connect to the `BackendVM1` and `BackendVM2` VMs using an RDP session on the public IPs, installing IIS and a testing web page on it. Connect to both the VMs, open the PowerShell console, and paste and run the following PowerShell script:

```
# Install IIS
Install-WindowsFeature -name Web-Server -IncludeManagementTools
# Remove the default htm file
remove-item C:\inetpub\wwwroot\iisstart.htm
#Add custom htm file
Add-Content -Path "C:\inetpub\wwwroot\iisstart.htm" -Value $("Hello World from " + $env:computername)
```

> **Note**
> Instead of connecting to each VM and configuring IIS services, you can also use an Azure Automation Workbook or Azure VM PowerShell Script Extension.

4. Next, connect to the `TestVM` VM, using RDP as well, open a browser session (such as Internet Explorer), and navigate to the private IP address of the load balancer obtained from *Step 2*. Refresh the browser a couple of times to see the load balancer distributing the requests over the two VMs, as shown in *Figure 18.11*:

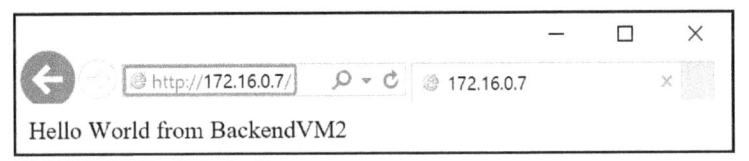

> http://172.16.0.7/   172.16.0.7
> Hello World from BackendVM2

Figure 18.11: Testing the load balancer

You have now successfully deployed your first ILB within Azure, and you now understand how load-balancing is used to distribute access to workloads as needed, as well as how the Azure Load Balancer service caters to HA requirements for inaccessible workloads. You have also learned that ILBs are for traffic that is private or inside your VNets and restricted from public access, and public load balancers are used to load balance public-facing workloads. Next, we will delve into the configuration of a public load balancer.

Configuring a Public Load Balancer

A public load balancer is used to load-balance incoming internet connections to backend servers associated with it. In the next set of exercises, we will work toward creating a publicly accessible web server environment that enables you to access your servers over a public IP, using a public load balancer. In this section, you are going to create a public load balancer using the Azure **Command-Line Interface** (**CLI**). You can copy the code snippets in Azure Cloud Shell, which is accessible from the Azure portal. The full script for creating the public load balancer can be downloaded from GitHub as well, using the following link: `https://packt.link/yDPcr`.

Creating the Public Load Balancer

To create the public load balancer, a series of steps need to be taken. In the upcoming exercises, you will create the public load balancer with all the necessary components:

1. Navigate to the Azure portal by opening `https://portal.azure.com`.
2. Click the `Azure CLI` icon at the top right of the Azure portal to open an Azure CLI instance:

Figure 18.12: Opening the Azure CLI

3. When asked for an environment, you can select either PowerShell or Bash.

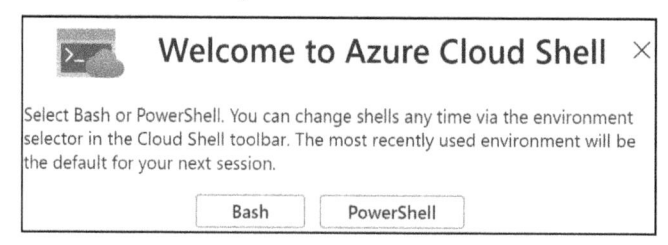

Figure 18.13: Selecting Bash or PowerShell

4. If you have never used the CLI before, you will be required to set up storage for it. Follow the prompts on the screen to configure your container on a storage account. Select Mount storage account and your storage account subscription, as shown in the following figure, and then click Apply:

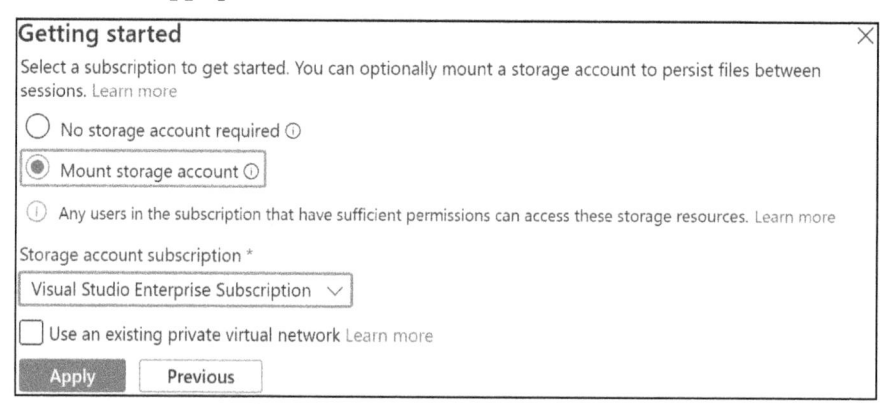

Figure 18.14: Mounting a storage account for the CLI

5. Choose the We will create a storage account for you option, and then click Next.

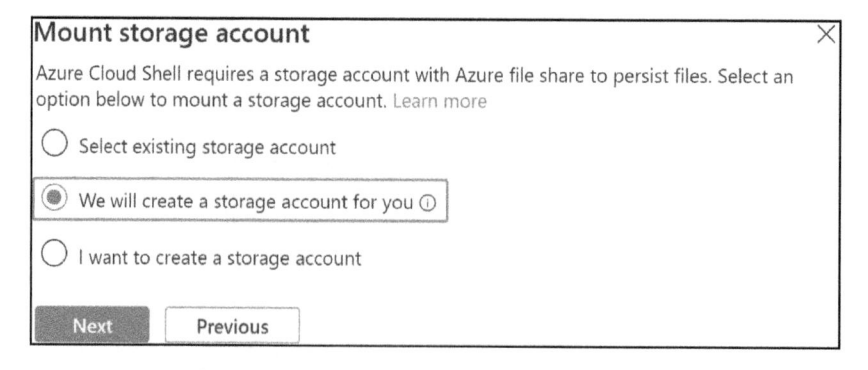

Figure 18.15: The Mount storage account options

The deployment will run and mount your storage.

6. If you decided on Bash, enter the following, which will open PowerShell in the Bash terminal, and then press *Enter*:

   ```
   pwsh
   ```

   > **Note**
   > Note that when using PowerShell within Bash, you cannot define variables in the Linux Bash format.

7. You can reuse the resource group from the previous exercise and adjust it for the remaining exercise steps. Run the command as follows, using `AZ104-PublicLoadBalancer` as an example resource group name:

   ```
   # Create a Resource Group
   az group create --name AZ104-PublicLoadBalancer --location westeurope
   ```

   > **Note**
   > When pasting into the CLI, you will have to right-click and paste; you cannot use keyboard shortcuts such as *Ctrl + V* or *Cmd + V*.

8. Next, you are going to configure a public IP address for the load balancer to access it from the internet. A standard load balancer only supports standard public IP addresses. Use the following code for this:

   ```
   # Create a Public IP Address
   az network public-ip create --resource-group AZ104-PublicLoadBalancer --name PLBPublicIP --sku standard
   ```

9. Now, you are going to create the load balancer and the components, including a frontend IP pool, a backend IP pool, a health probe, and a load balancer rule. To create the load balancer, add the following code:

   ```
   # Create the Load Balancer
   az network lb create `
       --resource-group AZ104-PublicLoadBalancer `
       --name PublicLoadBalancer `
       --sku standard `
       --public-ip-address PLBPublicIP `
       --frontend-ip-name PLBFrontEnd `
       --backend-pool-name PLBBackEndPool
   ```

   > **Note**
   > The ` (tilde) symbol in your Azure CLI commands allows you to split your commands and run them on the next line for more readable code.

10. The health probe checks all VM instances to define whether they are healthy enough to send network traffic to them. VM instances that are unhealthy are blocked from receiving traffic from the load balancer pool until the probe check determines that they are healthy again. To create a health probe to detect the health of your backend VMs serving HTTP web content, add the following code:

```
# Create the Health Probe
az network lb probe create `
    --resource-group AZ104-PublicLoadBalancer `
    --lb-name PublicLoadBalancer `
    --name PLBHealthProbe `
    --protocol http `
    --port 80 `
    --path /
```

11. The load balancer rule defines the frontend IP configuration for the incoming traffic and the backend IP pool to receive the traffic, together with the required source and destination ports. To create the load balancing rule, run the following:

```
# Create the Load Balancer Rule
az network lb rule create `
    --resource-group AZ104-PublicLoadBalancer `
    --lb-name PublicLoadBalancer `
    --name PLBHTTPRule `
    --protocol tcp `
    --frontend-port 80 `
    --backend-port 80 `
    --frontend-ip-name PLBFrontEnd `
    --backend-pool-name PLBBackEndPool `
    --probe-name PLBHealthProbe
```

Now that your load balancer is deployed, you are ready to move on to the deployment of the VNet.

Creating the VNet and NSG

To create your VMs and send traffic to them, you will require a VNet. You will also want to allow or deny traffic for your VMs over a network using an NSG. In this exercise, you will create a rule on your NSG for inbound traffic for HTTP (port 80) traffic to reach your VMs from any source. Since your load balancer is a Standard SKU, you will require an explicit allow rule on your NSG for traffic to flow to your backend VMs. The following steps will guide you through the creation of your VNet and NSG:

1. Create a VNet to deploy VMs into by running the following code:

```
# Create a Virtual Network
az network vnet create `
    --resource-group AZ104-PublicLoadBalancer `
```

```
    --location westeurope `
    --name PLBVnet `
    --subnet-name PLBSubnet
```

2. Next, you will create an NSG to define the inbound connections to the VNet, as follows:

```
# Create an NSG
az network nsg create `
    --resource-group AZ104-PublicLoadBalancer `
    --name PLBNetworkSecurityGroup
```

Creating an NSG is a requirement for a standard load balancer to ensure that the VMs in the backend have NICs placed in an NSG. For standard IPs or resource SKUs in Azure, an NSG defines which traffic is allowed or not. The default configuration for NSGs is to disallow all traffic (that is, the NSG is configured for whitelisting).

3. To allow inbound connections through port 80, create an NSG rule, as follows:

```
# Create a Network Security Group Rule
az network nsg rule create `
    --resource-group AZ104-PublicLoadBalancer `
    --nsg-name PLBNetworkSecurityGroup `
    --name PLBNetworkSecurityGroupRuleHTTP `
    --protocol tcp `
    --direction inbound `
    --source-address-prefix <*> `
    --source-port-range <*> `
    --destination-address-prefix <*> `
    --destination-port-range 80 `
    --access allow `
    --priority 200
```

4. You will require two network interfaces to be created and associated with the NSG, as well as a public IP address for the two VMs you will create in the next exercise. To create the NICs, run the following code:

```
# Create NICs
for ($i = 1; $i -le 2; $i++){
    az network nic create `
        --resource-group AZ104-PublicLoadBalancer `
        --name PLBVMNic$i `
        --vnet-name PLBVnet `
        --subnet PLBSubnet `
        --network-security-group PLBNetworkSecurityGroup `
        --lb-name PublicLoadBalancer `
        --lb-address-pools PLBBackEndPool
}
```

Creating Backend Servers

Now, you need to set up the backend pool of servers, which is a group of VMs in this exercise, to service your load-balanced requests. When you add or remove instances to your backend pool, the load balancer automatically reconfigures to accommodate the adjusted configuration. In this exercise. you are going to create two VMs that will be used as backend servers for the load balancer. You are also going to install NGINX (which is an open source, high-performance HTTP server and reverse proxy) on them to test the load balancer:

1. To create two VMs with NGINX installed on them and a `Hello World Node.js` app on the Linux VMs, create a file called `cloud-init.txt` and paste the following `cloud-init` configuration into it. This configuration installs all the required packages, creates the *Hello World* app, and then starts the app. To create the `cloud-init.txt` file, paste the following line:

   ```
   nano cloud-init.txt
   ```

2. Paste the following configuration code. The `package_upgrade: true` line means that any existing packages will first be upgraded before installing new ones, such as `nginx`. The list of items under `packages:` are the packages to be installed and run on your VM. These packages configure your VM as a web server with the JavaScript runtime environment on Linux:

   ```
   #cloud-config
   package_upgrade: true
   packages:
       - nginx
       - nodejs
       - npm
   ```

3. The next part sets up your web server. Key components to note are `path`, which specifies the path where your web files can be found and delivered from (server block); `listen`, which specifies the ports to list on (`80` = HTTP and `443` = HTTPS); and the `proxy_pass` directive, which is used to specify the URL and port of your web server (in this case, `http://localhost:3000`). Paste the following code into the editor:

   ```
   write_files:
   - owner: www-data:www-data
   - path: /etc/nginx/sites-available/default
   defer: true
   content: |
   server {
      listen 80;
      listen 443 ssl;
      ssl_certificate /etc/nginx/ssl/mycert.cert;
   ```

```
        ssl_certificate_key /etc/nginx/ssl/mycert.prv;
        location / {
           proxy_pass http://localhost:3000;
           proxy_http_version 1.1;
           proxy_set_header Upgrade $http_upgrade;
           proxy_set_header Connection keep-alive;
           proxy_set_header Host $host;
           proxy_cache_bypass $http_upgrade;
        }
     }
```

4. The next part of the code creates the application; paste this into the editor too. This application is configured to return `Hello World from host` with its hostname on execution. It will run on port 3000.

```
- owner: azureuser:azureuser
- path: /home/azureuser/myapp/index.js
  defer: true
  content: |
    var express = require('express')
    var app = express()
    var os = require('os');
    app.get('/', function (req, res) {
    res.send('Hello World from host ' + os.hostname() + '!')
    })
    app.listen(3000, function () {
    console.log('Hello world app listening on port 3000!')
    })
```

5. The final part that you paste is to run the app. It will install all the required npm packages and then run the `index.js` code. Paste it into your editor under the other code you already have:

```
runcmd:
  - secretsname=$(find /var/lib/waagent/ -name "*.prv" | cut -c
-57)
  - mkdir /etc/nginx/ssl
  - cp $secretsname.crt /etc/nginx/ssl/mycert.cert
  - cp $secretsname.prv /etc/nginx/ssl/mycert.prv
  - service nginx restart
  - cd "/home/azureuser/myapp"
  - npm init
  - npm install express -y
  - nodejs index.js
```

6. With the preceding blocks of code, you have created the `cloud-init.txt` file for your VMs. Save the file in the editor by pressing *Ctrl + X*. Then, press *Y* and *Enter* on your keyboard; this will save and exit the editor.

7. Now, you can continue to create the two VMs and apply the configuration on them, as follows:

```
# Create 2 Virtual Machines
for ($i = 1; $i -le 2; $i++) {
    az vm create `
        --resource-group AZ104-PublicLoadBalancer `
        --name PLBVM$i `
        --nics PLBVMNic$i `
        --image Ubuntu2204 `
        --admin-username azureuser `
        --generate-ssh-keys `
        --custom-data cloud-init.txt `
        --no-wait
}
```

Now that your backend servers are in place, they are ready to be used. You will now run them through some testing to confirm that everything operates as expected. Give your servers about 5 to 10 minutes to provision before moving to the next step.

Testing the Load Balancer

To test the load balancer, you need to obtain its public IP address and paste this into a browser window. Wait for the VMs to be fully provisioned and running. You can check this in the Azure portal:

1. To obtain the public IP address, run the following code in the Azure CLI:

```
#Obtain a public IP address
az network public-ip show `
    --resource-group AZ104-PublicLoadBalancer `
    --name PLBPublicIP `
    --query [ipAddress] `
    --output tsv
```

2. Paste the output of this line of code into your browser window, which creates the connection URL in the following pattern – `http://[IP Address]`. This can be run on any browser, as follows:

Figure 18.16: Testing the public load balancer

You have now successfully connected to your web application through the public load balancer. You should now feel confident working with public load balancers and understand the distinction between public load balancers and internal load balancers. Next, we will explore some basic troubleshooting that you can perform on a load balancer.

Troubleshooting Load Balancing

At times, you may have problems with your deployed load-balancing service and resources (such as some servers in an unhealthy state due to conflicting packages). You may be required to troubleshoot and ascertain the root cause of the issue(s) and identify how to rectify them.

For this exercise, you will work with the resources you deployed in the previous section:

1. Navigate to your load balancer on the Azure portal. Under Settings from the left menu, click Health probes.
2. Click on your health probe and change the port from 80 to 800. This is done to put your VM into an unhealthy state according to the load balancers, as the probe will look for running HTTP services on port 800 and fail. Click Save.
3. Navigate to the URL you connected to earlier (http://[IP Address]). You should see a failed connection, as shown in the following figure, or you may just not get any connection:

Figure 18.17: A connection error

4. Change the probe port back to 80, and you will now receive a success message again:

Figure 18.18: Connection success

5. Navigate to your NSG, PLBNetworkSecurityGroup, and click Inbound security rules under Settings from the left menu. Click Add.

6. Configure the following, and then click Add:

   - Source: Any
   - Source port ranges: *
   - Destination: Any
   - Service: Custom
   - Destination port ranges: *
   - Protocol: Any
   - Action: Deny
   - Priority: 100
   - Name: Port_80_Block

7. Wait two minutes. Attempt to connect to your load balancer again, and you will again receive an error message.

8. Navigate back to your PublicLoadBalancer resource and click Insights under the Monitoring context from the left menu. You will get a visual indicator that signifies a connectivity issue to the backend VMs. You can expect to see a screen similar to the following, which will lead you to look for components that may be blocking connectivity from the probe.

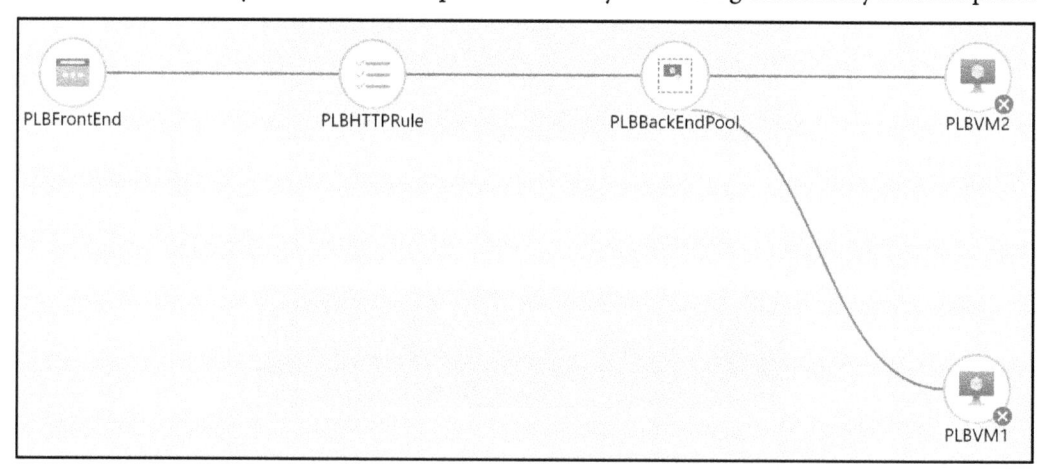

Figure 18.19: Monitoring connections

In this exercise, you looked at how to troubleshoot some common problems that you might face with your load-balancing configuration. You now know where to look for the settings, and you should feel comfortable troubleshooting the connectivity of load balancers. In the next section, you will learn about Azure Application Gateway.

Azure Application Gateway

Azure Application Gateway is a load balancing service that operates as a Layer 7 load balancer, which means it is capable of interrogating the source request and directing its destination based on a path. Splitting destinations by path is a common function for web-based load-balancing scenarios where resource delivery can be split into different pools and SKU types, which we learned about earlier in the chapter.

Azure Application Gateway is designed to balance the **regional** load of **web-based** services. One of the features of the service is the ability to enable WAF features that are designed to protect your web application workloads against exploits and vulnerabilities (such as a SQL injection attack). Another main benefit of the service is the ability to enable SSL offloading, which can improve the performance of your web services, as the strain is removed from them and is delivered by the application gateway directly.

Features and Capabilities

The Application Gateway service offers several features, such as the following:

- **Multiple-site hosting**: This enables several sites to be hosted behind your application gateway, up to 100 websites. Each of these can be associated with its own backend pool. Sites can be directed based on URL, such as `sitea.com` and `siteb.com`, as well as subdomains, such as `images.sitea.com` and `videos.sitea.com`.

- **Redirection**: You can enable the automatic redirection of HTTP-based traffic to HTTPS. Alongside this, you have granular control that allows redirects to occur for a whole site, as well as for path-based redirection and applying HTTPS enforcement for only certain paths of your site. You can also redirect to any other site that may be external to your Azure sites.

- **Auto-scale**: The service is capable of auto-scaling, depending on requirements.

- **Zone-redundancy**: The service also has zone-redundancy options available to it, making it more resilient.

- **Session affinity**: There are occasions when you require traffic to flow to the same server for a connection with a client. The service relies on cookies to provide session affinity.

- **WebSocket and HTTP/2 traffic**: Application Gateway has native support for the WebSocket and HTTP/2 protocols. Configuration is simple, and you can choose to either enable or disable the feature as required.

- **Connection draining**: When you are planning for service outages or unplanned failures, you can enable a more graceful removal of services by disabling new requests to specified servers that are to be removed from a backend pool.

- **Custom error pages**: In the event of an error, you can deliver custom error pages that can contain your own branding and styles.

- **Rewrite HTTP headers and URLs:** You can rewrite HTTP headers, which allows you to pass additional information in your requests and responses between the client and server. This enables you to improve your security and governance posture within your application. When rewriting URLs, you can rewrite the hostname, path, and querying string for your request, based on the conditions you configure.

> **Note**
> The **Standard v2** SKU of Application Gateway requires the use of a static **Virtual IP (VIP)**.

Now that you know about some of the important capabilities and features available to the Application Gateway service, you will learn how to configure it.

Configuring Azure Application Gateway

Azure Application Gateway is a load-balancing service for your web-based (HTTP or HTTPS) workloads that operates at the Layer 7 OSI level. In addition, it offers the capability to protect against exploits and threats and has SSL offloading capability. In the set of exercises that follow, you will see how to create an Azure application gateway, deploy a web app behind the gateway, and finally, test the application gateway.

Creating an Azure Application Gateway

To create an Azure application gateway, follow these steps:

1. Navigate to the Azure portal by opening `https://portal.azure.com`.
2. Create a new resource group for this exercise, named `AZ104-ApplicationGateway`.
3. Create a VNet with the following values:
   - `Subscription`: Select a subscription
   - `Resource group`: `AZ104-ApplicationGateway`
   - `Name`: `ApplicationGatewayVNET_`
   - `Region`: `West Europe`
   - `Address range`: `10.1.0.0/16`
   - `Subnet name`: `Default`
   - `Subnet Address range`: `10.1.0.0/24`

4. Open the newly created resource group, click Overview on the left menu, and then click Create.
5. Type application gateway in the search bar and click Application Gateway card from the search results:

Figure 18.20: Creating an application gateway

6. Click Create.
7. Enter the following values for the Basics tab, and then click Next : Frontends >:

- Subscription: Select a subscription
- Resource group: AZ104-ApplicationGateway
- Name: ApplicationGateway
- Region: West Europe
- Tier: Standard V2
- Enable autoscaling: Yes
- Minimum instance count: 0
- Maximum instance count: 2
- Availability zone: Zones 1
- HTTP2: Enabled
- Virtual network: ApplicationGatewayVNET

- Subnet: `default (10.1.0.0/24)`

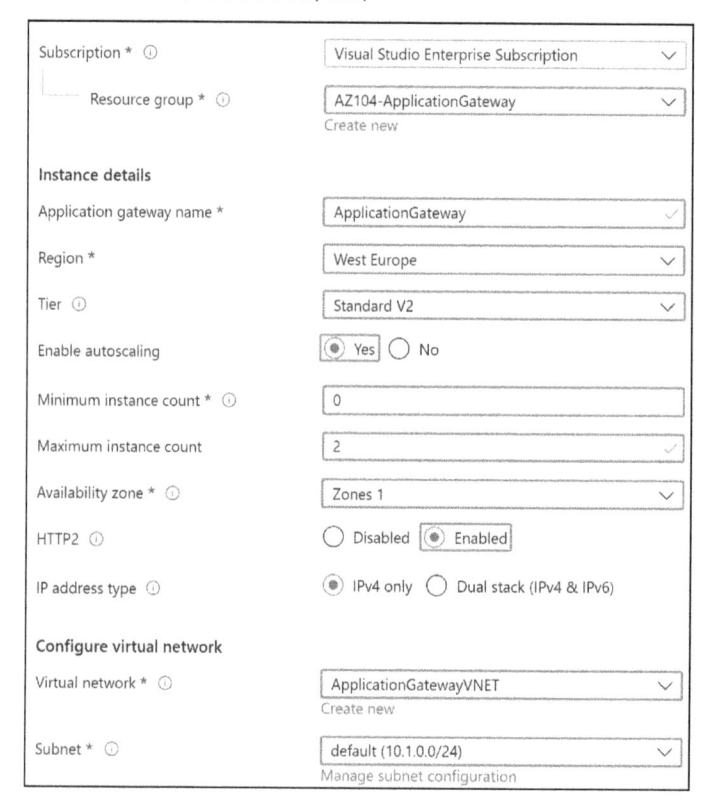

Figure 18.21: Application Gateway – the Basics tab

8. Enter the following values for the `Frontends` tab, and then click `Next : Backends >`:

    - `Frontend IP address type`: Public
    - `Public IP address`: Add new (name this as something unique)

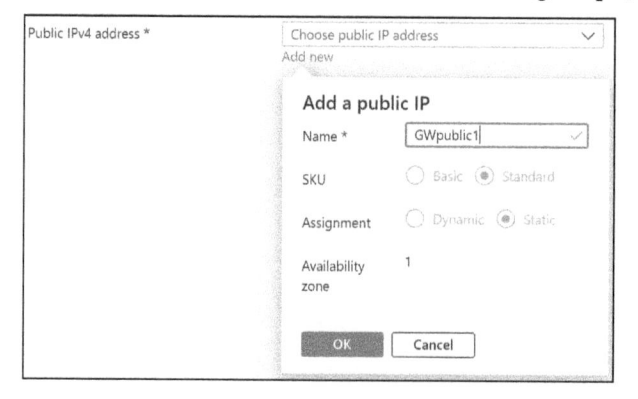

Figure 18.22: Application Gateway – the Frontends tab

9. Click `Add a backend pool`. In the pop-up blade, enter the following and click `Add`:

   - Name: `backendpool`
   - `Add backend pool without targets`: Yes

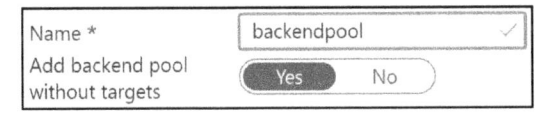

   Figure 18.23: Application Gateway – adding a backend pool

10. Click `Next : Configuration >`.
11. Note that your configuration screen lists your frontend and backend pools. The routing rules are the magic connectors between these linking public IPs and your backend resources. Click `Add a routing rule`. In the pop-up blade, enter the following:

    - Rule name: `webtraffic`
    - Priority: 100

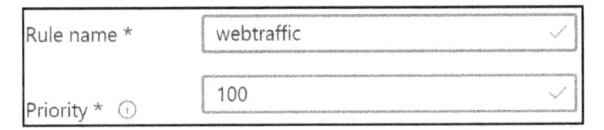

    Figure 18.24: Adding a routing rule

12. Enter the following configurations for the `Listener` tab:

    - Listener name: `webtrafficlistener`
    - Frontend IP: `Public IPv4`
    - Protocol: `HTTP`
    - Port: 80
    - Listener type: `Basic`
    - Custom error pages: Leave as default

    Figure 18.25: Application Gateway – the Listener tab

The rule you are configuring will listen for HTTP traffic on port 80 through the public IP you created. The `Basic` listener type forwards all traffic from any frontend IP to a backend pool, and the `Multi site` option will listen on the domain and redirect according to the specified prefix given for the routing rule. Click the `Backend targets` tab.

13. Enter the following and click `Add`:

    - `Target type`: `Backend pool`.
    - `Backend target`: Select `backendpool` in the dropdown.
    - `Backend settings`: Click `Add new`. Then, enter `httpset1` for `Backend settings name`, `HTTP` for `Backend protocol`, and `80` for `Backend port`.

Backend settings name *	httpset1
Backend protocol	● HTTP ○ HTTPS
Backend port *	80

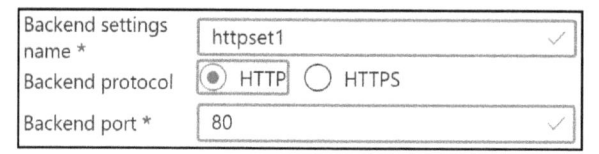

    Figure 18.26: Application Gateway – the backend settings

    - Leave the `Additional settings` section as default. Scroll down, and in the `Host name` section, click `Yes` for `Override with new host name` and select `Pick host name from backend target`. You can leave the rest as default:

    Host name

    By default, the Application Gateway sends the same HTTP host header to the backend as it receives from the client. If your backend application/service requires a specific host value, you can override it using this setting.

    Override with new host name: **Yes** | No

    ⓘ If the backend service is a multi-tenant Azure service such as App Services, Functions, or Portal Apps, we recommend using Custom domain method, instead of overriding the hostname. Using override host name with default domains (azurewebsites.net, azuremicroservices.io, etc.) is good only for the basic tests and operations.

    Host name override:
    ● Pick host name from backend target
    ○ Override with specific domain name
    Yes | No

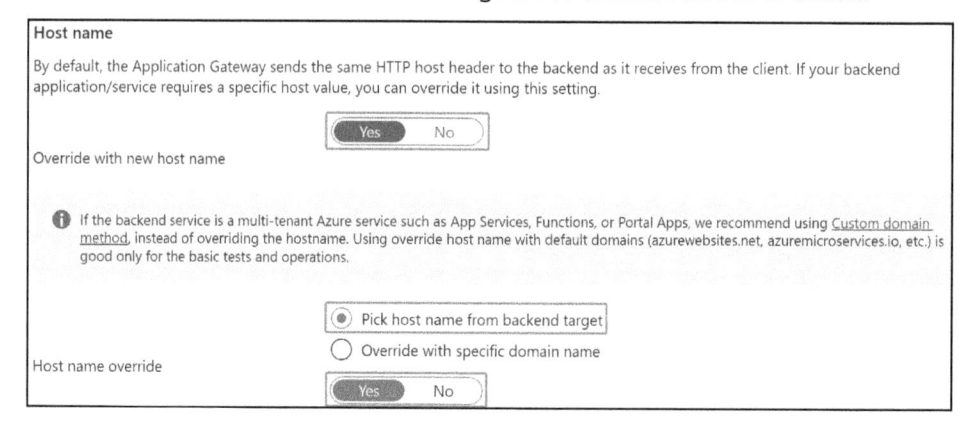

    Figure 18.27: Application Gateway – the HTTP settings

14. Click `Add` and then `Add` again.
15. Click `Next : Tags >` and then `Next : Review + create >`. Finally, click `Create`.

Now that your application gateway is deployed, you will need to deploy an application on the backend to test the service.

Deploying Your Web App

You will need at least one application on the backend of your application gateway for the public IP address you created to route through to the application. We will deploy that app now by following these steps:

1. Open the Azure CLI and select PowerShell or open `pwsh`, as you did in the public load balancer exercise.

2. Run the following command, replacing the name with a unique name of your choice and the resource group with the one you created previously:

   ```
   New-AzWebApp -name "azwebapp12341234" -ResourceGroupName "AZ104-
   ApplicationGateway" -Location "westeurope"
   ```

3. Open your Application Gateway resource and click `Backend pools` on the left navigation menu under the `Settings` context. Click on your backend pool.

4. Drop down the `Target type` selector and change it to `IP address or FQDN`, and then set `Target` to the web app you just created followed by `.azurewebsites.net` (for example, `azwebapp12341234.azurewebsites.net`). Click `Save`.

Figure 18.28: Editing a backend pool

5. Now, go to `Health probes` on the left menu under `Settings`, and if no probes exist, click `Add`; otherwise, skip to the next section.

6. Enter the following details and click `Test`. If a health probe has already been created, then skip to the note below the settings:

   - Name: httpprobe
   - Protocol: HTTP
   - Pick host name from backend settings: Yes
   - Pick port from backend settings: Yes
   - Path: /
   - Backend settings: httpset1
   - Leave all other settings as default

7. After a successful validation, click Add:

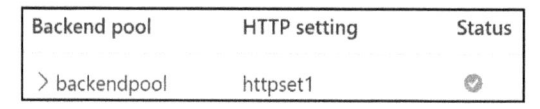

Backend pool	HTTP setting	Status
> backendpool	httpset1	✓

Figure 18.29: A health probe test

You have now successfully configured your web app and added it to the application gateway. You are now ready to test it, which you will do next.

Testing the Application Gateway

Now that your application gateway is configured, it is ready to test. To do this, perform the following steps:

1. Paste the frontend public IP address from the previous section for your application gateway into your web browser. You should see a web page of sorts; this will validate your connection.
2. Navigate back to your web application and click on Overview in the left pane.
3. Click Stop at the top of the page:

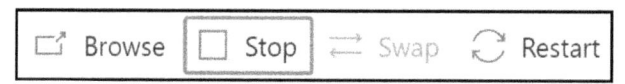

Figure 18.30: Stopping a web app

Note that when you navigate to the public IP of your application gateway, you get an error message, as expected.

Figure 18.31: A web app connection error

4. Wait about five minutes, and then navigate back to your application gateway service and click on `Backend Health` under the `Monitoring` context.
5. You will get an unhealthy message, indicating an issue on the backend:

Server (backend pool)	Status	Port (Backend setting)
azwebapp12341234.azurewebsites.net (bac...	Unhealthy	80 (httpset1)

Figure 18.32: An unhealthy backend message

Do not delete your resources yet, as these will be used in the next chapter.

In this exercise, you created and tested an application gateway that you created for your web application. You configured the application to work through the service and proved you could connect successfully to your application. You then turned off your web application to see how the Application Gateway detects errors on your services and handles them. Now that you understand how to deploy Azure Application Gateway and have seen the merits it brings to regional load-balancing for services, as well as how to troubleshoot when issues occur, you should feel comfortable working with application gateways. Next, you will learn about Azure Front Door.

Azure Front Door

Azure Front Door is another load-balancing service that also operates as a Layer 7 load balancer, much like Azure Application Gateway. The service is very similar (load-balancing, SSL offloading, path-based routing, fast failover, etc.), except that it is designed for the **global** delivery of services as opposed to **regional**. The service can also enable WAF services and is designed for web-based workloads. The Azure Front Door service is Microsoft's variation of a **Content Delivery Network** (**CDN**), with caching capabilities designed to enable high-performance and consistent connectivity over Microsoft's networks for your application. One of the benefits of the Front Door service is its ability to offer different traffic-routing methods:

- **Latency**: This is designed for faster connections to your services by routing requests to the backends that have the lowest latency. This means that services located closer to where you are connecting globally will be faster and, therefore, respond quicker.
- **Priority**: You can assume that there is a primary delivery backend pool for your service with a backup (secondary) backend pool when the primary pool fails.
- **Weighted**: This option is for when you have several backend pools and want to distribute traffic in a weighted fashion, by assigning requests to backend pools in a ratio-type proportion.

- **Session affinity**: This is where the user of your service is required to connect to the same server.

Front Door offers several features (many similar to Application Gateway), such as the following:

- URL path-based routing
- Multiple website hosting
- Session affinity
- SSL offloading
- Health probes
- Custom domains
- WAF
- URL redirect
- URL rewrite
- IPv6 connectivity
- HTTP/2 protocol

You can see that Azure Front Door offers Layer 7 global-level load-balancing services. The service is designed to provide high-performance network traffic (leveraging caching) with secure connectivity to your web-based applications.

Summary

In this chapter, we covered various load-balancing services available on the Azure platform and how they bring HA to workloads, both regionally and globally. We also explored how services such as Azure Application Gateway and Front Door enhance these services by analyzing application layer requests, splitting them across service areas and resources. Finally, you saw how to deploy an internal and public load balancer and an application gateway. In the next chapter, you will learn about integrating on-premises networks with Azure.

Exam Readiness Drill - Chapters 16-18

Apart from mastering key concepts, strong test-taking skills under time pressure are essential for acing your certification exam. That's why developing these abilities early in your learning journey is critical.

Exam readiness drills, using the free online practice resources provided with this book, help you progressively improve your time management and test-taking skills while reinforcing the key concepts you've learned.

HOW TO GET STARTED

- Open the link or scan the QR code at the bottom of this page
- If you have unlocked the practice resources, already log in to your registered account. If you haven't, follow the instructions in *Chapter 23* and come back to this page.
- Once you log in, click the START button to start a quiz
- We recommend attempting a quiz multiple times till you're able to answer most of the questions correctly and well within the time limit.
- You can use the following practice template to help you plan your attempts :

Attempt	Target	Time Limit
Working On Accuracy		
Attempt 1	40% or more	Till the timer runs out
Attempt 2	60% or more	Till the timer runs out
Attempt 3	75% or more	Till the timer runs out
Working On Timing		
Attempt 4	75% or more	1 minute before time limit
Attempt 5	75% or more	2 minutes before time limit
Attempt 6	75% or more	3 minutes before time limit

The above drill is just an example. Design your drills based on your own goals and make the most out of the online quizzes accompanying this book.

> First time accessing the online resources? 🔒
> You'll need to unlock them through a one-time process. **Head to** *Chapter 23* **for instructions**.

Open Quiz

`https://packt.link/az104e3ch16-18`

OR scan this QR code →

19
Integrating On-Premises Networks with Azure

In the previous chapter, you explored load-balancing services in Azure and explored the configuration of services such as Azure Load Balancer and Application Gateway. This chapter builds on this foundation by guiding you through the process of integrating your on-premises network with an Azure **Virtual Network** (**VNet**). In this chapter, you are going to focus on **Virtual Private Network** (**VPN**) connections, which can be used to connect from other environments, such as on-premises, to Azure and other clouds using **Site-to-Site** (**S2S**) VPN connections and from roaming devices using **Point-to-Site** (**P2S**) VPN. These VPN connections provide secure encrypted pathways to access your Azure environment over the public internet, which is important for protecting your private data. You will also learn about **ExpressRoute** (**ER**), which is another technology for connecting your on-premises environment to Azure through a dedicated circuit private to your organization to enable secure pathways back to Azure. You will develop skills in creating an Azure VPN gateway and configuring an S2S VPN using an on-premises server and Azure VPN Gateway. At the end of the chapter, you will explore Azure Virtual WAN and the network management capabilities this service offers, automatically connecting your networks in Azure and removing the complexity of transitive routing configuration.

In this chapter, you are going to learn about the following main topics:

- Azure VPN Gateway
- Creating and Configuring an Azure VPN Gateway
- Creating and Configuring Azure ExpressRoute
- Azure Virtual WAN
- Configuring Azure Virtual WAN

Technical Requirements

To follow along with the hands-on material, you will need the following:

- Access to an Azure subscription with owner or contributor privileges. If you do not have access to one, students can enroll for a free account: https://azure.microsoft.com/en-us/free/.

- **PowerShell 5.1** or later installed on a Windows PC, or PowerShell Core 6.x on other operating systems, to practice the labs.

- Windows users will need to install **.NET Framework 4.7.2** or later using the following link: https://learn.microsoft.com/en-us/dotnet/framework/install.

- Where PowerShell is not installed or available, https://shell.azure.com can be used as a browser-based shell.

- Installation of the Az PowerShell module, which can be performed by running the following in an administrative PowerShell session:

    ```
    Set-ExecutionPolicy -ExecutionPolicy RemoteSigned -Scope
    CurrentUser
    Install-Module -Name Az -Scope CurrentUser -Repository PSGallery
    -Force
    ```

Azure VPN Gateway

Azure VPN Gateway is a service that enables you to build private and secure pathways for encrypted communication by creating VPN tunnels or ER connections. It facilitates the transfer of data between an Azure VNet and other networks (such as on-premises locations and other cloud providers such as AWS and GCP) over the public internet. This gateway's versatility extends beyond on-premises connections, allowing secure encrypted traffic exchange between different Azure VNets and Microsoft's own network infrastructure too.

A VNet can host only one VPN gateway for managing secure connections. However, you have the flexibility to establish multiple connections to that single VPN gateway. When creating multiple connections, all the VPN tunnels will share the available gateway bandwidth.

There are three types of VPN connections you can have:

- S2S VPN connections
- P2S VPN connections
- VNet-to-VNet VPN connections

The VPN gateway relies on a specific subnet created for the VPN connection and will need to be created either with or before the deployment. The gateway services and routing table are automatically created with the service, and it is not possible to configure them manually. In the following section, you will explore the **Stock-Keeping Units** (**SKUs**) of VPN gateways that are available in Azure.

Azure VPN Gateway SKUs

Azure VPN Gateway offers several pricing tiers, mainly categorized as follows:

- **Basic**: The most basic offering with limitations of the service.
- **VpnGw1 to VpnGw5**: There are several tiers of the standard SKUs that incrementally increase the levels of the offering, such as the maximum number of connections included and the bandwidth. This option now includes the BGP services as well as IKEv2 OpenVPN connections.
- **VpnGw1AZ to VpnGw5AZ**: There is also the option for an **Availability Zone (AZ)** variation of each gateway SKU, except for Basic, denoted with a suffix of **AZ**, for example, **VpnGw4AZ**. They offer similar specifications to the non-AZ variants available, mentioned previously, with the inclusion of the deployment for zone redundancy (AZs).

Further to the SKUs, there are generation 1 and 2 offerings available. The following tables highlight the differences between SKUs.

Generation 1 VPN SKUs

All SKUs support P2S connections. All SKUs, except for the Basic SKU, support OpenVPN and BGP connections. The following *Table 19.1* highlights the limits for the respective generation 1 SKUs. Also note the zone-redundant variants, denoted with **AZ** in the SKU name, which offer zone redundancy.

SKU	S2S Tunnels	Aggregate Throughput	Zone Redundant	VMs Supported in VNet
Basic	10	100 Mbps	No	200
VpnGw1	30	650 Mbps	No	450
VpnGw2	30	1 Gbps	No	1,300
VpnGw3	30	1.25 Gbps	No	4,000
VpnGw1AZ	30	650 Mbps	Yes	1,000
VpnGw2AZ	30	1 Gbps	Yes	2,000
VpnGw3AZ	30	1.25 Gbps	Yes	5,000

Table 19.1: Generation 1 VPN SKUs

The table presented in this and the following subsection for the various VPN SKUs is a limited set of comparison items with the most relevant details to assist you in choosing the right SKU for your needs. Also, note that all SKUs include limits of up to 128 P2S SSTP connections and various P2S IKEv2/OpenVPN connections.

Generation 2 VPN SKUs

All SKUs support P2S connections. All SKUs support OpenVPN and BGP connections. The following Table 19.2 highlights the limits for the respective generation 2 SKUs. Also note the zone-redundant variants, denoted with an **AZ** in the SKU name, which offer zone redundancy.

SKU1	S2S Tunnels	Aggregate Throughput	Zone Redundant	VMs Supported in VNet
VpnGw2	30	1.25 Gbps	No	685
VpnGw3	30	2.5 Gbps	No	2,240
VpnGw4	100	5 Gbps	No	5,300
VpnGw5	100	10 Gbps	No	6,700
VpnGw2AZ	30	1.25 Gbps	Yes	2,000
VpnGw3AZ	30	2.5 Gbps	Yes	3,300
VpnGw4AZ	100	5 Gbps	Yes	4,400
VpnGw5AZ	100	10 Gbps	Yes	9,000

Table 19.2: Generation 2 VPN SKUs

> **Note**
>
> All gateway SKUs include up to 128 **P2S SSTP** connections and various limits (250 to 10,000) for the **P2S IKEv2/OpenVPN** connections.

Pricing Considerations

When selecting this service and the appropriate SKU, be aware that there are two predominant cost factors you must consider: the costs of the service itself and the associated network traffic costs (mostly egress data costs). The data egress transfer costs are based on the source and destination of the service, and the first 100 GB of egress internet traffic carries no charge.

For better redundancy (high-availability) options, selecting the AZ variant is better, but understand that it costs significantly more than the standard SKU. This would be desirable for customers and workloads where constant connectivity is essential to operations and downtime would be costly. Next, you will learn about S2S VPN connections.

Point-to-Site VPN Connections

A P2S VPN gateway connection creates a secure connection between an individual client (computer, server, tablet, or even a mobile phone) to your VNet over the internet. It is useful for people working from any remote location to their office (such as from their home or a hotel). A PS2 VPN is also the best solution if you only have a few clients to connect to a VNet.

A P2S connection does not require an on-premises, public-facing IP address as S2S VPN connections do. You can use P2S connections together with S2S connections over the same VPN gateway. You need to ensure that the configuration requirements for both connections are compatible to use both connection types over the same gateway. P2S VPN supports the OpenVPN protocol (VPN protocol based on TLS/SSL), **Secure Socket Tunneling Protocol** (**SSTP**) (protocol based on TLS), and IKEv2 VPN (protocol based on IPsec VPN). OpenVPN is suited to all Android, iOS, Windows, Linux, and Mac devices depending on the versions. SSTP supports Windows 8.1 and later. IKEv2 VPN supports macOS 10.11 and later.

The following diagram shows a P2S VPN connection from an on-premises environment to Azure:

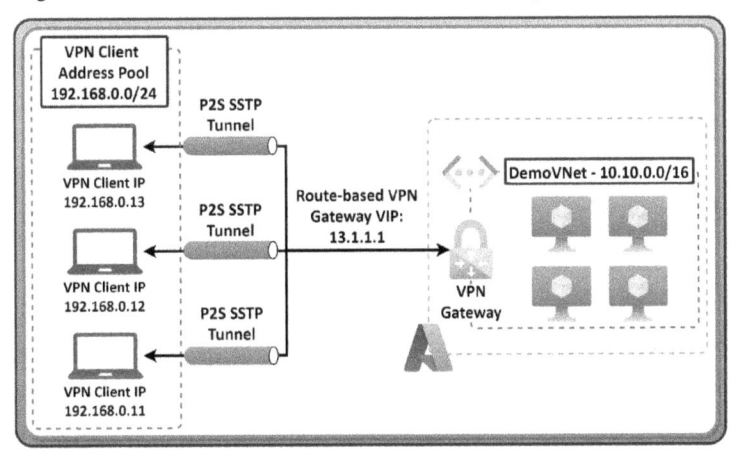

Figure 19.1: P2S VPN tunnel

In the next section, you will learn about S2S VPN connections.

Site-to-Site VPN Connections

A S2S VPN gateway connection establishes a secure tunnel between two separate networks, utilizing the IPsec/IKE (IKEv1 or IKEv2) protocol for encryption. **Internet Protocol Security** (**IPsec**) and **Internet Key Exchange** (**IKE**) are protocols used for the secure encryption and authentication of data transmitted over a network, ensuring the confidentiality, integrity, and authenticity of communication between two endpoints. These S2S connections can be used for hybrid configurations and cross-premises configurations.

They are designed to create a secure connection between a location (with a public IP) and your VNet over the internet. The location can be an office or even another VPN gateway in Azure. Once the S2S VPN connection is established, all devices at the connected location can communicate with resources in Azure using the same VPN connection.

An S2S connection requires a compatible VPN device to connect to, typically an on-premises appliance or device that has a publicly routable IP address assigned to it. It should not be located behind a NAT, as the service requires a public IP to connect to. S2S connections are designed to be persistent (remain continually established) and always on; this is not required, of course, but it is important to understand the intended design.

The VPN gateway is enabled to cater to redundancy requirements, facilitating active-standby and active-active configurations. The active-standby configuration is the default and is used to overcome any unplanned disruptions of service or even planned maintenance that impacts the primary node of the service by activating the secondary node in the event of any detected outages. The active-active configuration establishes a VPN tunnel with both the primary and secondary nodes of the VPN gateway, with each instance getting its own unique public IP and tunnel. In this configuration, both tunnels are used simultaneously for traffic to increase throughput and availability.

> **Note**
>
> For more information about the compatible validated VPN devices defined in partnership with VPN device manufacturers, refer to the following documentation: `https://learn.microsoft.com/en-us/azure/vpn-gateway/vpn-gateway-about-vpn-devices#devicetable`.

The following diagram shows an S2S VPN connection from an on-premises environment to Azure:

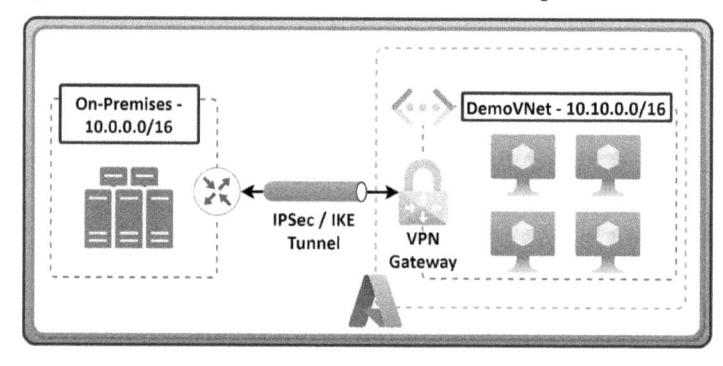

Figure 19.2: S2S VPN tunnel

You have learned about P2S so far and how this enables VPN connectivity from remote locations from a variety of device types. You have also learned about S2S VPN connecting an endpoint to Azure through a VPN gateway. This S2S connection enables multiple devices to connect to Azure and vice versa through the configured link. In the next section, you will learn about multi-site VPNs, which is a feature of S2S that enables multiple sites to connect to Azure through the same VPN gateway.

Multi-Site VPN Connections

A multi-site VPN connection is a variation of the S2S connection. You use this type of connection to connect to multiple on-premises sites from your VNet gateway. Multi-site connections are required to use a route-based VPN-type gateway. Since a VNet can only have one VPN gateway, all connections routed through this gateway will share the available bandwidth. This means that if multiple devices or applications send or receive data, the overall speed experienced by each might fluctuate depending on the total traffic.

The following diagram shows a multi-site VPN connection from an on-premises environment to Azure:

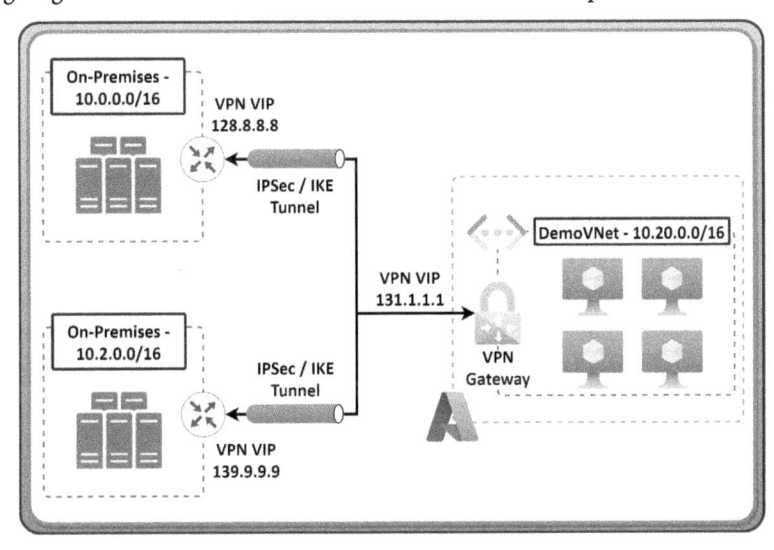

Figure 19.3: Multi-site VPN tunnels

In the next section, you will learn about VNet-to-VNet connections that are used to interconnect Azure VNets, including between regions, for secure and performant network traffic over Microsoft network infrastructure.

VNet-to-VNet VPN Connections

Azure VNet-to-VNet VPN connections directly link two or more separate Azure VNets as if they were part of a single network. This configuration prevents traffic traversing linked VNets from going over the public internet. Azure ensures that sensitive data remains protected (particularly beneficial in highly regulated industries such as financial services and banking) by keeping traffic encrypted between VNets. You don't require dedicated hardware or complex configurations to set up VNet-to-VNet connections, and since traffic does not go through the public internet, there are no egress costs, which can result in cost savings. Connections benefit from the internal Microsoft backbone infrastructure with lower latency because the traffic is routed through the most efficient path within Azure's global network.

The following diagram shows a VNet-to-VNet VPN connection between two VNets in Azure with an established IPsec tunnel:

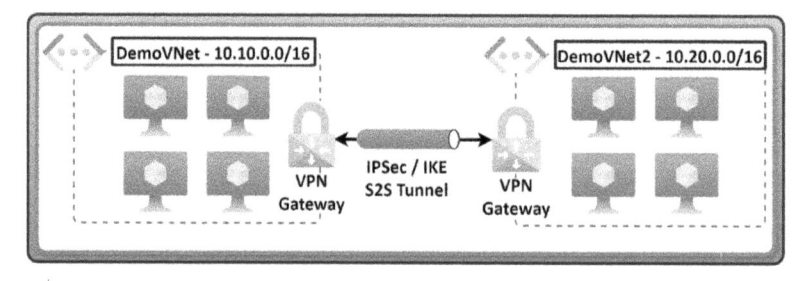

Figure 19.4: VNet-to-VNet VPN tunnels

In the next section, you are going to learn about ER.

ExpressRoute

ER is a layer 3 connectivity service that connects your private on-premises environments through a connectivity provider to Azure. ER connections do not go over the public internet; rather, they use a dedicated high-bandwidth network to connect your environments to Azure. Compared to most public internet-based connections, these connections offer reliable, low-latency, high-bandwidth secure connections. You can use it to extend your on-premises networks to Azure and Office 365. Connections can be made from an any-to-any (IP VPN) network, a virtual cross-connection at a co-location facility, and a point-to-point Ethernet network connection. BGP routes traffic between your on-premises environment and Azure through the ER circuit, which passes through two **Microsoft Enterprise Edge (MSEE)** routers offered by your link provider. The ER circuit requires you to provide two BGP connections through your connectivity provider to facilitate the redundancy on ER.

ER uses a VNet gateway, which is configured with a gateway type of ER instead of a VPN. By default, the traffic is not encrypted, but you can create a solution that encrypts the traffic over the ER circuit.

The following diagram shows an ER connection from an on-premises environment to Azure:

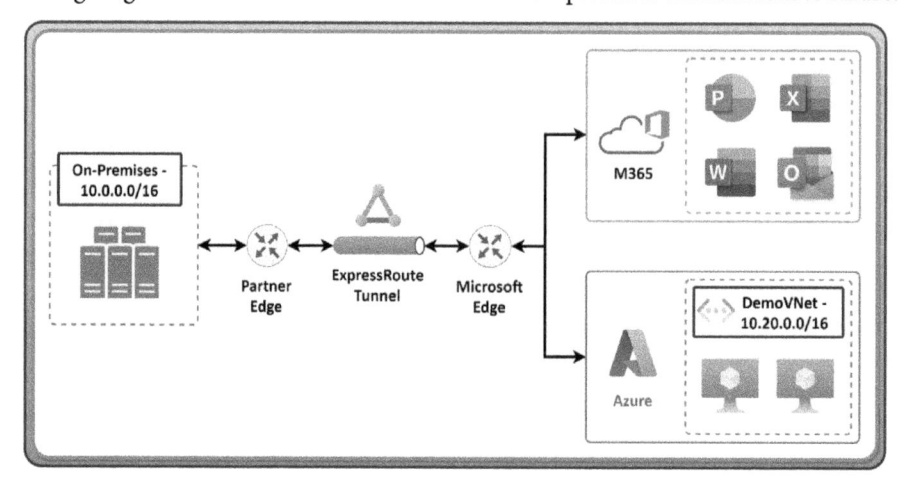

Figure 19.5: ER VPN tunnel

Now that you have learned about the different types of connectivity options, such as the various VPN and ER connections available, you are going to create and configure an Azure VPN gateway.

Creating and Configuring an Azure VPN Gateway

In the upcoming sections, you are going to configure an Azure VPN gateway, configure an S2S VPN, and verify the connectivity between Azure and the on-premises environment.

You are going to use Windows Server 2019 with the **Routing and Remote Access Service** (**RRAS**) enabled to serve as the compatible VPN device that is installed on the on-premises environment. To create a VPN gateway, you can perform the following steps to follow along with the example:

1. Create a new resource group named `AZ104-VPNGateway`.
2. Click `+ Create` on the `Overview` screen for the resource group.
3. Type `vpn gateway` in the search bar and press the *Enter/Return* key. Click `Virtual network gateway` from the options that are returned.
4. Click `Create` on the screen that follows.

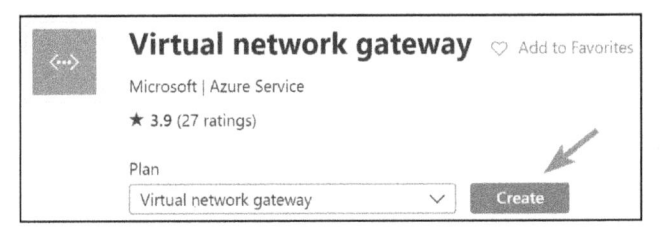

Figure 19.6: Choosing a VPN gateway

5. Enter the following for the `Basics` tab, and click `Review + create`:

    - `Subscription`: Select your Azure subscription
    - `Name`: `az104gateway`
    - `Region`: `North Europe` (or select what you prefer)
    - `Gateway type`: VPN
    - `SKU`: VpnGw1
    - `Generation`: Generation2
    - `Virtual network`: Create a new one named `az104gatewayvnet` with an address range of `10.0.0.0/16` and a default subnet range of `10.0.0.0/24`
    - `Gateway subnet address range`: `10.0.1.0/24`
    - `Public IP address`: Create new

- Public IP address name: `az104gatewayip`
- Enable active-active mode: Disabled
- Configure BGP: Disabled

6. Click `Create`. The creation of the resource takes about 45 to 60 minutes, so it is a good time to grab some coffee and reflect on your learnings so far.

In this exercise, you deployed a VPN gateway. This device will be used for establishing a S2S VPN tunnel in Azure with your VPN server. Configuring a VPN gateway is vital to establishing VPN tunnels (for connecting your roaming and site devices) to Azure outside of using other third-party services. Next, you will explore the creation of an S2S VPN connection using the VPN Gateway service. First, you will need a VM to function as the VPN server.

VPN Server Deployment

This exercise will see you create a test server to prove your VPN functionality. This server will be deployed into the same resource group as the VPN you deployed previously. To deploy your VPN test server, you will need to perform the following steps:

1. Navigate to your VPN resource group.
2. Click + `Create` on the `Overview` screen for the resource group.
3. Type `custom deployment` in the search bar and select `Template deployment (deploy using custom templates)` from the options that are returned.
4. Click `Create`.
5. Click `Build your own template in the editor`:

> Build your own template in the editor

Figure 19.7: Build your own template in the editor

6. Paste the following code, found at the following GitHub URL: `https://packt.link/DV8kU`. Then, click `Save`:

VPN-TestServer.json

```
{
    "$schema": "https://schema.management.azure.com/schemas/2019-04-01/deploymentTemplate.json#",
    "contentVersion": "1.0.0.0",
    "parameters": {
        "vmName": { "type": "string", "defaultValue":
```

```
        "az104vpnserver" },
            "adminUsername": { "type": "string", "defaultValue": 
"Student" },
            "adminPassword": { "type": "securestring", 
"defaultValue": "Pa55w.rd1234" },
            "windowsOSVersion": { "type": "string", "defaultValue": 
"2019-Datacenter" },
            "vmSize": { "type": "string", "defaultValue": "Standard_
D2s_v4" },
            "resourceTags": { "type": "object", "defaultValue": { 
"Application": "AZ104 VPN Gateway" } },
            "vnetName": { "type": "string", "defaultValue": 
"vpnvnet" },
```

The complete code can be found at https://packt.link/TK9ea

7. Notice all your values are prepopulated; click Review + create.
8. Click Create.
9. Log in to your server using a **Remote Desktop Connection** (**RDC**). Use the following credentials:

   - Username: Student
   - Password: Pa55w.rd1234

10. On the Server Manager window that appears, with the default view being the Dashboard menu, click Add roles and features:

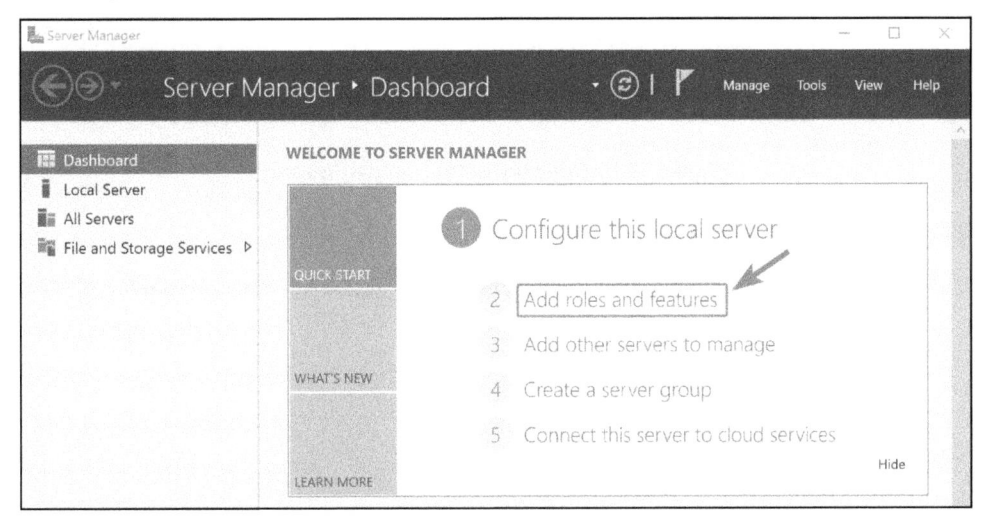

Figure 19.8: Add roles and features

11. On the Add roles and features wizard, click Next.
12. Select Role-based or feature-based installation. Click Next.
13. Click Next again.
14. Select Remote Access and click Next:

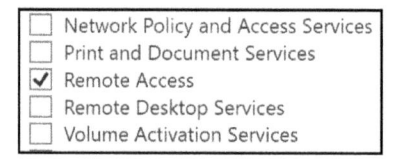

Figure 19.9: Remote Access feature

15. On the Features and Remote Access pages, click Next.
16. For Role Services, select Direct Access and VPN (RAS). Then, click Add Features on the pop-up window that appears. Click Next.
17. Click Next until you get to the confirmation screen and click Install.
18. Before closing the wizard, click Open the Getting Started Wizard:

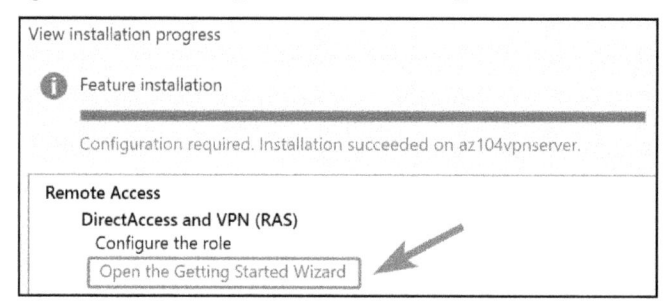

Figure 19.10: Open the Getting Started Wizard

19. On the wizard screen, click Deploy VPN only.
20. Right-click on the Windows Start button and click Computer Management:

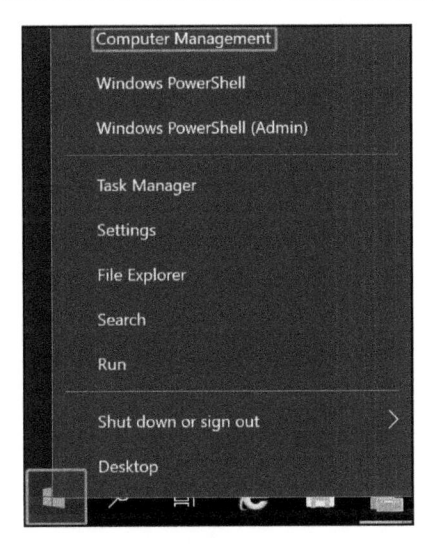

Figure 19.11: Right-click on Start

21. Click on `Device Manager`, then click on `Action` on the top menu, and click `Add legacy hardware`:

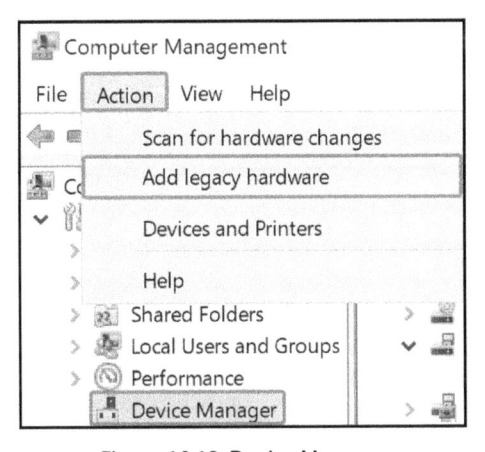

Figure 19.12: Device Manager

22. On the wizard, click `Next`. Then click `Install the hardware that I manually select from a list (Advanced)` on the subsequent screen. Click `Next`:

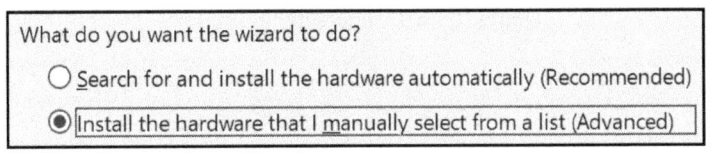

Figure 19.13: Installing hardware

23. Scroll down to select `Network adapters` and click `Next`.
24. Select `Microsoft` under `Manufacturer`, and then `Microsoft KM-TEST Loopback Adapter` under `Model`:

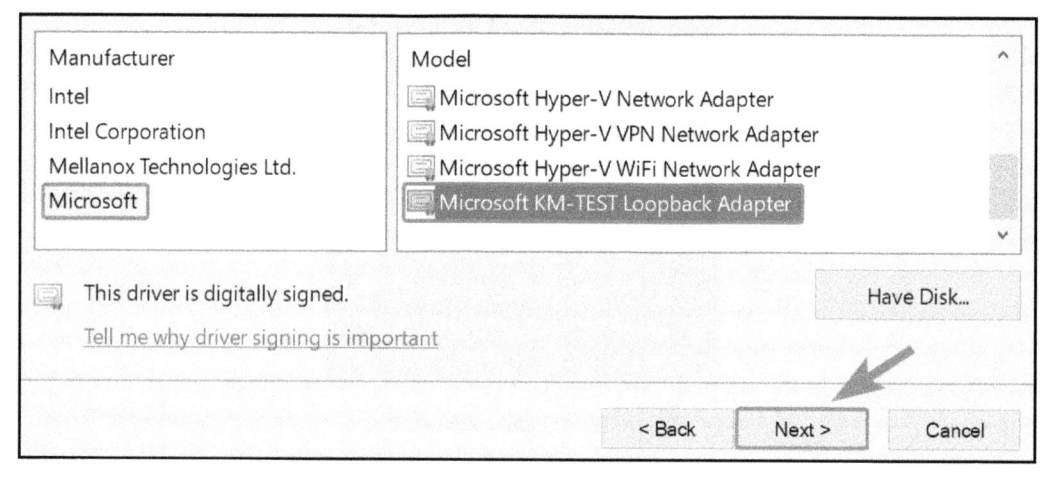

Figure 19.14: Adding a loopback adapter

25. Click `Next`, then click `Finish` on the screens that follow. Close the `Computer Management` window.
26. On the `Routing and Remote Access` window, right-click on your server and click `Configure and Enable Routing and Remote Access` on the pop-up window:

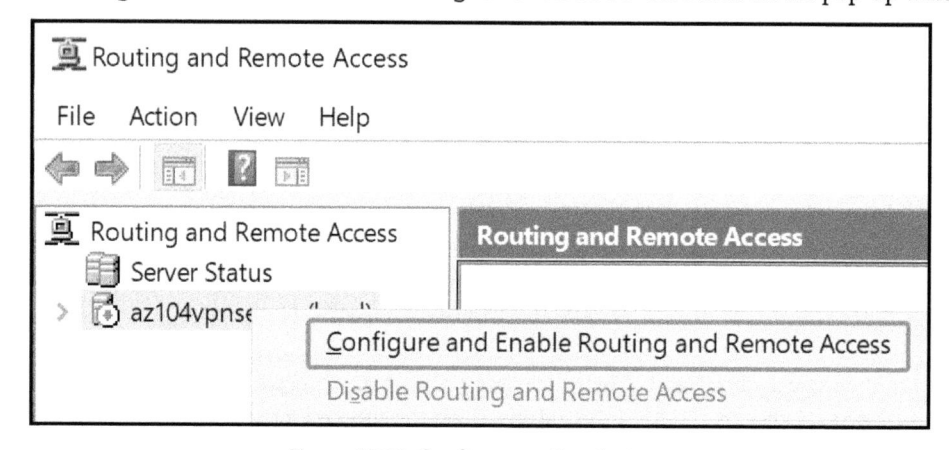

Figure 19.15: Configure routing feature

27. On the next wizard, click Next. Select the Virtual private network (VPN) access and NAT option. Click Next:

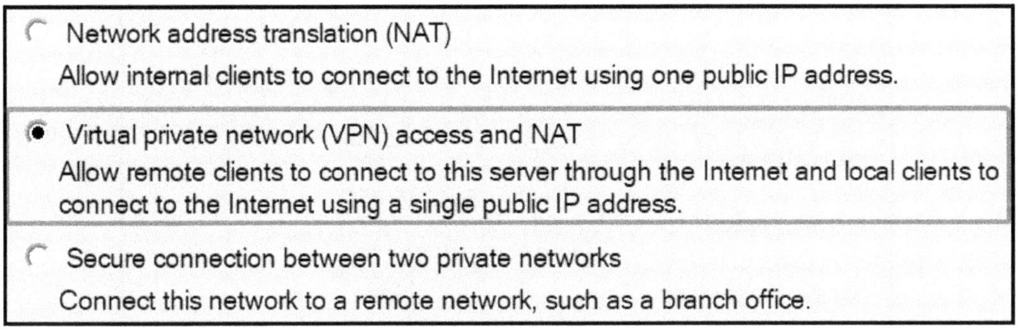

> ○ Network address translation (NAT)
> Allow internal clients to connect to the Internet using one public IP address.
>
> ● Virtual private network (VPN) access and NAT
> Allow remote clients to connect to this server through the Internet and local clients to connect to the Internet using a single public IP address.
>
> ○ Secure connection between two private networks
> Connect this network to a remote network, such as a branch office.

Figure 19.16: VPN and NAT

28. Select the Ethernet interface (which will show the 99.0.0.0 range next to it). Click Next:

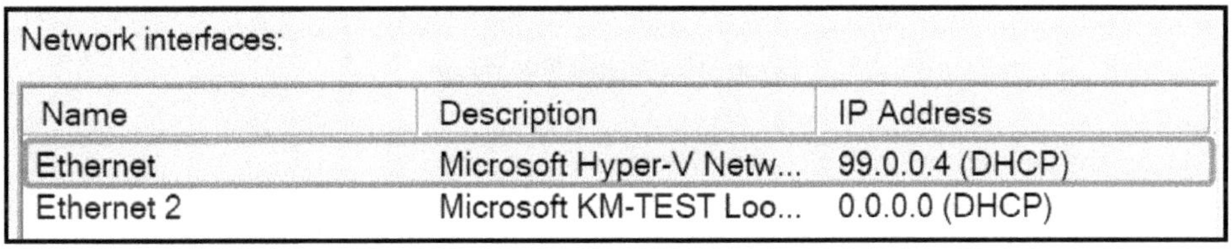

Network interfaces:

Name	Description	IP Address
Ethernet	Microsoft Hyper-V Netw...	99.0.0.4 (DHCP)
Ethernet 2	Microsoft KM-TEST Loo...	0.0.0.0 (DHCP)

Figure 19.17: Ethernet interface

29. For IP Address Assignment, select From a specified range of addresses. Click Next:

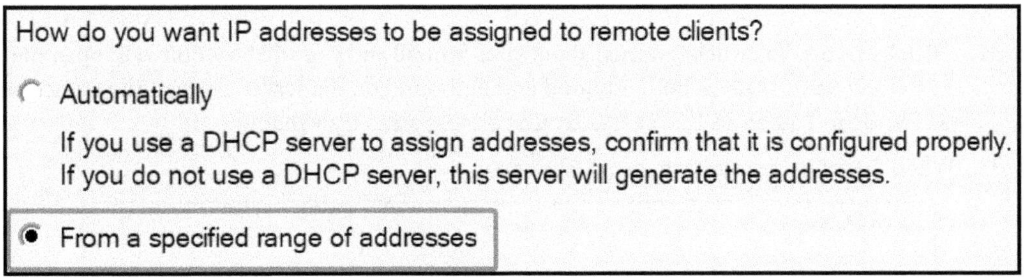

> How do you want IP addresses to be assigned to remote clients?
>
> ○ Automatically
> If you use a DHCP server to assign addresses, confirm that it is configured properly. If you do not use a DHCP server, this server will generate the addresses.
>
> ● From a specified range of addresses

Figure 19.18: IP assignment on VPN

30. Click New.... Specify the following and click OK. Click Next:

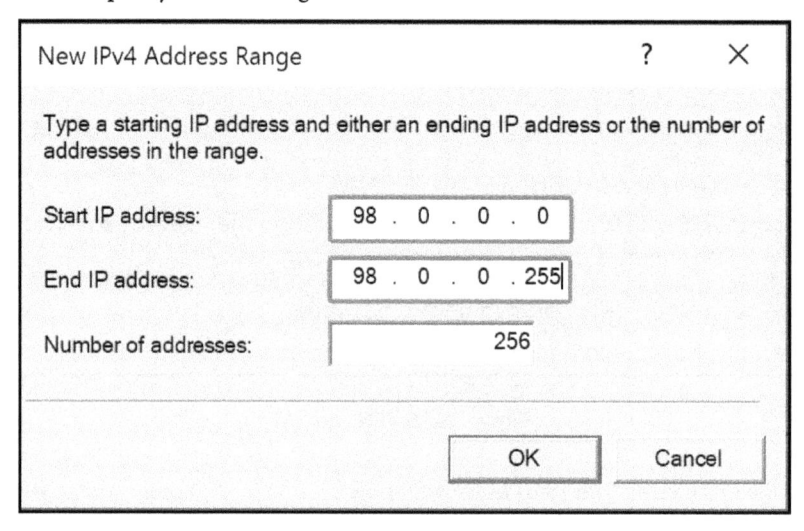

Figure 19.19: New IPv4 range

31. Leave the next selection as No and click Next:

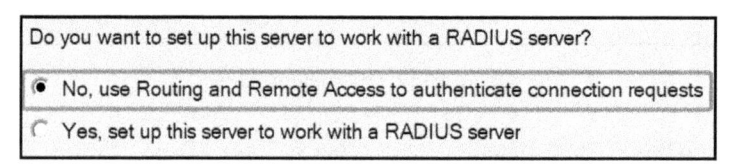

Figure 19.20: RADIUS server configuration

32. Click `Finish`. You will be warned about your firewall and you will be required to open ports `4500` and `500` `UDP` on both inbound and outbound on the server through the `Windows Defender Firewall with Advanced Security` window.

33. When the following screen pops up, click OK:

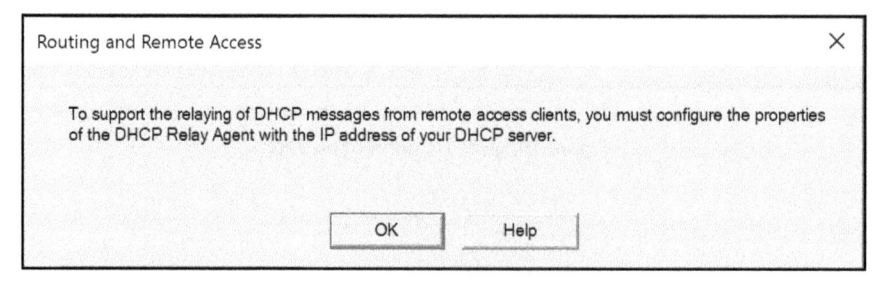

Figure 19.21: DHCP option

34. Click the Start button and then `Windows Security`:

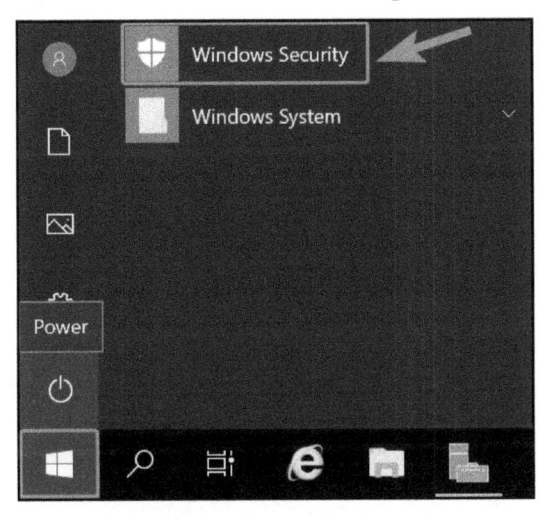

Figure 19.22: Windows Security

35. Click `Firewall & network protection` on the left, then click `Advanced settings` on the right:

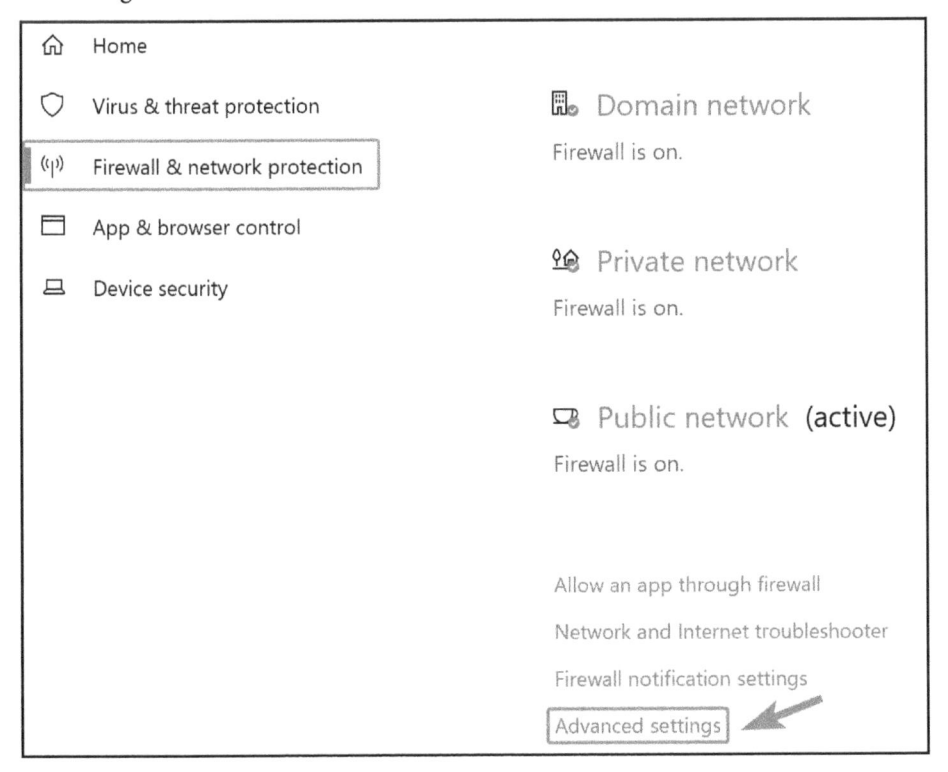

Figure 19.23: Firewall and network protection

36. Click `Inbound Rules` on the left and then `New Rule...` on the right:

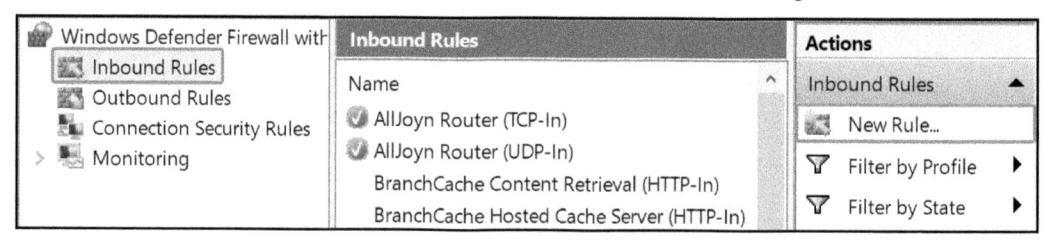

Figure 19.24: New inbound rule

37. Select `Port` and click `Next`.
38. You can configure the rule as UDP, ports `4500` and `500`, and click `Next`:

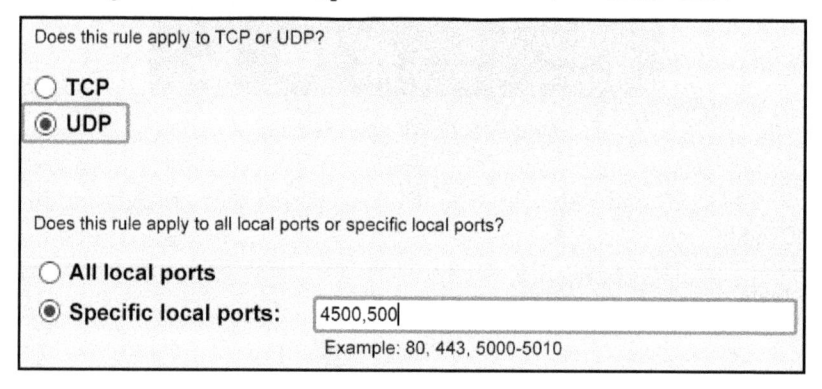

Figure 19.25: UDP rule

39. Click `Allow the connection` and then click `Next`.
40. Click `Next` again, leaving `Domain`, `Private`, and `Public` selected.
41. Enter `VPNGW-inbound` for Name. Click `Finish`.
42. Repeat the process for outbound, changing the name to `VPNGW-outbound`, and ensure that you select `Allow the connection`.
43. Navigate back to the `Routing and Remote Access` window. Right-click on `Network Interfaces` and click `New Demand-dial Interface...`:

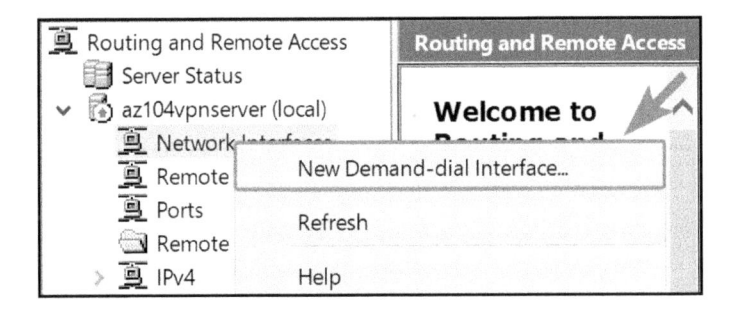

Figure 19.26: New Demand-dial Interface...

44. Click Next, then change the name to Azure VPN, and click Next.
45. Select Connect using virtual private network (VPN) and click Next.
46. Select IKEv2 and click Next.
47. Enter the IP address of the VPN gateway from Azure. Click Next on this and the next screen.
48. Click Add, then enter the following and click OK (if your VNet associated with the VPN gateway is a /16 range, then your subnet is 255.255.0.0; if it is a /24 range, then it is 255.255.255.0). Click Next:

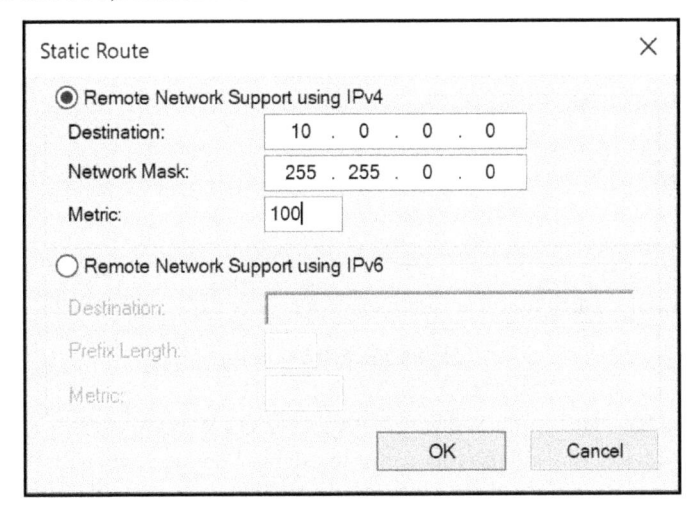

Figure 19.27: Static route

49. Click Next, then Finish.
50. Click on Network Interfaces.
51. Right-click Azure VPN and click Properties.

52. Click the `Security` tab and then click `Use preshared key for authentication`. Generate a key you would like to use as a secret for the S2S connection, such as `Pa55w.rd1234`, and paste it into the `Key` field. Then, click `OK`:

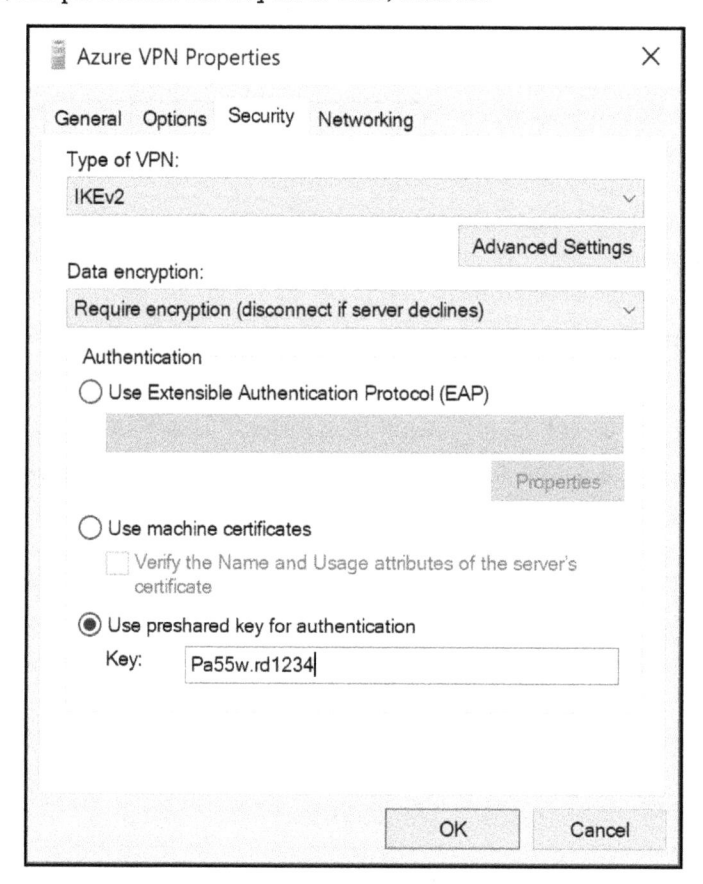

Figure 19.28: IKEv2 key

In this exercise, you have just configured your VPN server as a Windows Server RRAS to emulate an on-premises VPN device. You will use this server to establish connectivity with the VPN gateway in Azure. In the next exercise, you will configure Azure VPN Gateway to establish an S2S connection back to your VPN server.

S2S VPN Configuration

To configure an S2S VPN tunnel using Azure VPN Gateway, you will use Windows Server with RRAS features installed, which you configured in the previous exercise. This will work as the equivalent of an on-premises appliance that would typically run a persistent connection with the VPN gateway. An S2S tunnel is typically designed to be persistent and through a router appliance of sorts:

1. Navigate to your VPN resource group.
2. Click + Create on the Overview screen for the resource group.
3. Type local network gateway in the search bar and press *Enter/Return*. Click Local network gateway from the options that are returned.
4. On the card that is returned, click Create.

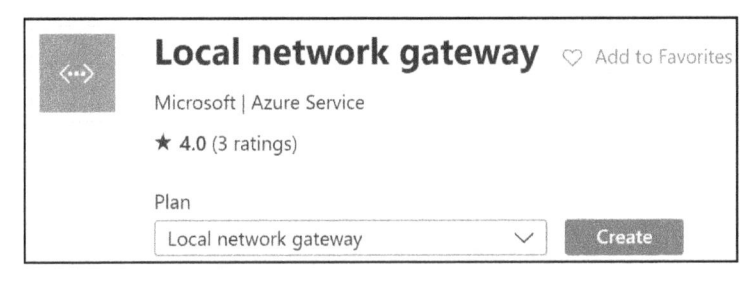

Figure 19.29: Create a local network gateway

5. Enter the following for the Basics tab and click Review + create:
   - Subscription: Select your Azure subscription
   - Resource Group: AZ104-VPNGateway
   - Region: North Europe (or select what you prefer)
   - Name: VPNServer
   - Endpoint: IP address
   - IP address: Enter the public IP address of the VM you spun up in the previous exercise
   - Address Space(s): 99.0.0.0/24
6. Click Create.
7. Navigate to the VPN gateway you deployed earlier in the chapter.
8. Click on Connections under the Settings context from the left menu.
9. Click Add.
10. Enter the following for the Basics tab and click Next: Settings >:
    - Subscription: Select your Azure subscription
    - Resource Group: AZ104-VPNGateway
    - Connection type: Site-to-site (IPsec)
    - Name: AzuretoVM
    - Region: North Europe

11. On the `Settings` tab, enter the following and click `Review + create`.
    - `Virtual network gateway`: The gateway you configured earlier
    - `Local network gateway`: VPNServer
    - `IKE protocol`: IKEv2
    - Leave all other settings as the defaults
12. After validation completes, click `Create`.
13. Navigate back to your VPN gateway and click `Connections` on the left menu.
14. Click on the new connection you created. If it's not there, hit `Refresh` and select your connection.
15. Click on `Authentication` from the left menu.
16. For the `Shared key (PSK)` field, enter the key you used, `Pa55w.rd1234`.
17. Click `Save`.
18. Now that you have configured the S2S components, go back to your VPN server and navigate to the `Routing and Remote Access` window.
19. Click `Network Interfaces`, then right-click on your Azure VPN interface and click `Connect`. If all is configured correctly, you should successfully connect:

| Ethernet | Dedicated | Enabled | Connected |
| Azure VPN | Demand-dial | Enabled | Connected |

Figure 19.30: RRAS VPN connection

In this exercise, you have configured your S2S VPN tunnel between your Windows VPN server and Azure VPN Gateway. This is an important part of experiencing how to configure an S2S VPN tunnel using an emulated VPN device by using Windows RRAS. Configuring this on some form of firewall (which is the most likely scenario) will be a very similar exercise. In the next section, you will test the VPN tunnel.

Verify Connectivity via the Azure Portal

You are now ready to confirm the connectivity of the VPN tunnel. You have seen connectivity from the server side showing successful and will confirm this on the Azure portal too. To perform the exercise, follow these steps:

1. Navigate to your VPN Gateway resource on the Azure portal.

2. Click `Connections` under the `Settings` context from the left menu. Note the connection on the right-hand side of the screen; a status of `Connected` shows that the tunnel has been successfully established. If the view does not update, there is also a `Refresh` button at the top of the page:

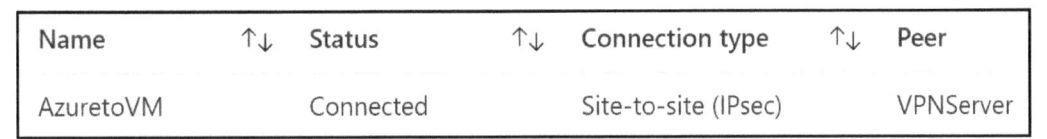

Name	↑↓	Status	↑↓	Connection type	↑↓	Peer
AzuretoVM		Connected		Site-to-site (IPsec)		VPNServer

Figure 19.31: S2S connected in Azure

You have successfully established an S2S VPN connection between a VPN gateway in Azure and a VM. Typically, you would establish connectivity with a routing appliance, but since Windows Server can act as a VPN server too, this also worked. In the next section, you will explore VNet-to-VNet connectivity.

VNet-to-VNet Connections

Configuring a VNet-to-VNet connection is a straightforward method for connecting VNets in Azure. This connection is designed to establish private tunnel connectivity between Azure VNets in different regions and subscriptions. Connecting a VNet to another VNet is similar to creating an S2S IPSec connection to an on-premises environment. Both the connection types use Azure VPN Gateway. The VPN gateway provides a secure encrypted tunnel through IPsec/IKE between the VNets, which otherwise communicate similarly. The difference is in the way the local network gateway is configured.

VNet-to-VNet connections offer a streamlined approach compared to S2S connections. When establishing a VNet-to-VNet link, the system automatically generates and configures the local network gateway address space. Additionally, any updates to the address space in one VNet automatically propagate to the other, ensuring seamless routing. This streamlined process makes VNet-to-VNet connections faster and easier to set up.

> **Note**
> To create a VNet-to-VNet connection from the Azure portal, you can refer to the following tutorial: `https://learn.microsoft.com/en-us/azure/vpn-gateway/vpn-gateway-howto-vnet-vnet-resource-manager-portal`.

Creating and Configuring Azure ExpressRoute

In the following exercise, you will explore the creation of an ER circuit. You will only emulate the deployment as it typically includes involvement from a provider with a corresponding circuit configuration at the edge to join Azure:

1. Create a resource group named `AZ104-ExpressRoute` in `North Europe`.
2. Click in the search bar at the top of the Azure screen and type `express route`; select `ExpressRoute circuits` from the options that appear:

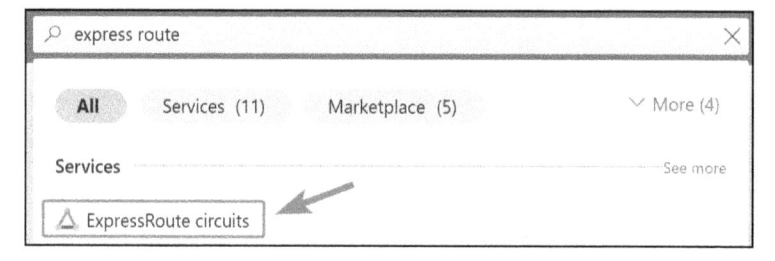

Figure 19.32: Deploying an ER circuit

3. Click `+ Create`. Enter the following and click `Review + create`:

    - `Subscription`: Select your Azure subscription
    - `Resource Group`: `AZ104-ExpressRoute`
    - `Region`: `North Europe` (or select what you prefer)
    - `Circuit Name`: `az104expressroute`
    - `Port type`: `Provider`
    - `Provider`: Select a provider
    - `Peering location`: Select a location
    - `Bandwidth`: `200Mbps`
    - `SKU`: `Standard`
    - `Billing model`: `Metered`

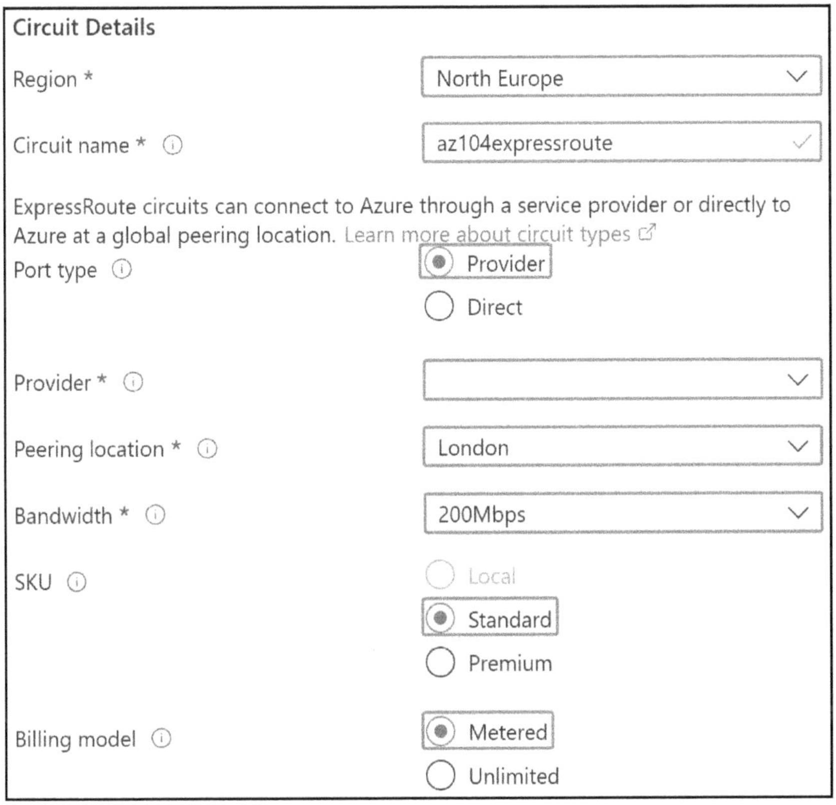

Circuit Details

Region *	North Europe
Circuit name *	az104expressroute

ExpressRoute circuits can connect to Azure through a service provider or directly to Azure at a global peering location. Learn more about circuit types

Port type	● Provider ○ Direct
Provider *	
Peering location *	London
Bandwidth *	200Mbps
SKU	○ Local ● Standard ○ Premium
Billing model	● Metered ○ Unlimited

Figure 19.33: ER circuit deployment configuration

4. Click `Review + create` and then `Create`.

You have just completed the first half of an ER deployment for Azure.

To complete setting up an ER circuit connection, you will need to contact your ER provider and confirm the circuit numbers as part of your deployment. You will provide them with the service key associated with the circuit you have deployed in Azure.

> **Note**
>
> For additional reading and guidance on the deployment steps, you can read these articles:
>
> ER overview: `https://learn.microsoft.com/en-us/azure/expressroute/expressroute-introduction`
>
> Create and modify an ER circuit: `https://learn.microsoft.com/en-us/azure/expressroute/expressroute-howto-circuit-portal-resource-manager`

Now that you understand how to configure an ER circuit, you can feel confident with starting the deployment in your organization. Next, you will learn about Azure Virtual WAN.

Azure Virtual WAN

Azure Virtual WAN provides a mechanism for a managed hub-and-spoke network within Azure. It consolidates all your endpoint connection types into a single service that simplifies the management of your complex networks and enables transitive network functionality.

The following diagram shows an illustration of the various interconnections that may be employed in a typical environment:

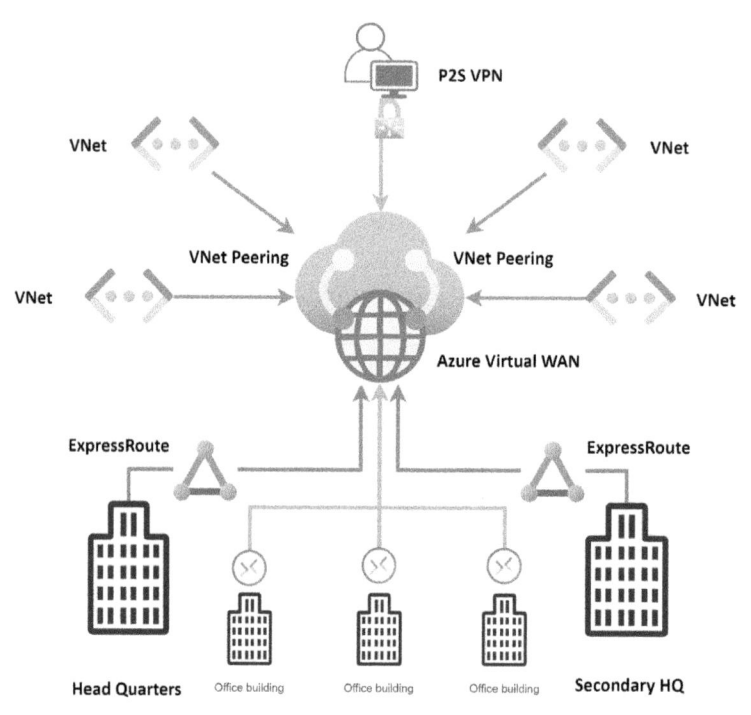

Figure 19.34: Azure Virtual WAN illustration

As illustrated in the diagram in *Figure 19.34*, you can have various connection types, such as ER, S2S connections, P2S connections, and even VNet peering. All the traffic flow configurations are managed through Azure Virtual WAN, which will also configure your transitive network flows, eliminating the need for an additional **Network Virtual Appliance** (**NVA**). The deployment of Virtual WAN also allows for the deployment of a firewall in the solution, allowing you to secure traffic natively through your hub-and-spoke model.

There are two SKUs that you can purchase as part of the Virtual WAN service. Note that in the following comparison *Table 19.3* the Standard SKU caters to significantly more features available to the SKU over Basic:

Basic SKU	Standard SKU
• Basic hub type • S2S VPN connections	• Standard hub type • S2S VPN connections • P2S VPN connections • VNet-to-VNet connections (including Transit Hub) • Azure Firewall • Virtual WAN NVA • ER (ER-to-ER connections are only supported through ER Global Reach)

Table 19.3: Azure Virtual WAN SKUs compared

Effectively, Virtual WAN intends to act as a head-end for your network, being the primary routing service for all your interconnections required. You can read more about Azure Virtual WAN at the following URL: `https://learn.microsoft.com/en-us/azure/virtual-wan/upgrade-virtual-wan`.

> **Note**
> While you can upgrade from the Basic to Standard SKU, you cannot downgrade from Standard to Basic. This is important in deciding your direction for implementation and upgrading.

Now that you understand Virtual WAN, you will see an example of service deployment next.

Configuring Azure Virtual WAN

In this exercise, you will create and configure an Azure Virtual WAN instance and create a virtual hub. Perform the following steps:

1. Create a new resource group named `AZ104-VirtualWAN`.
2. Click `+ Create` on the `Overview` screen for the resource group.
3. Click `Networking` on the left menu, then select `Virtual WAN` from the options returned.
4. Click `Create`.

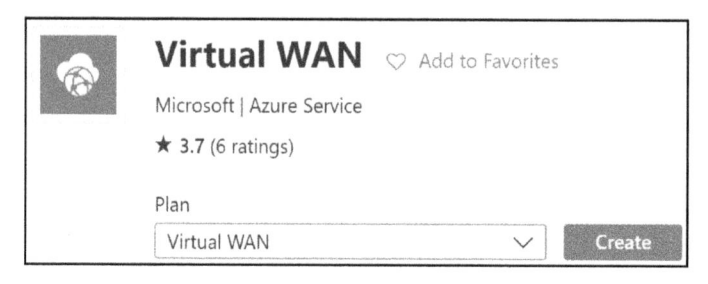

Figure 19.35: Virtual WAN

5. Enter the following and then click `Review + create`:

   - `Subscription`: Select your Azure subscription
   - `Resource group`: `AZ104- VirtualWAN`
   - `Resource group location`: `North Europe` (or select what you prefer)
   - `Name`: `az104virtualwan`
   - `Type`: `Standard`

6. Click `Create`.
7. Navigate to your Virtual WAN and click `Hubs` under the `Connectivity` context.
8. Click `+ New Hub`.
9. Enter the following details on the `Basics` tab and click `Next : Site to site >`:

   - `Region`: `North Europe` (or select what you prefer)
   - `Name`: `vwanhub`
   - `Hub private address space`: `110.0.0.0/24`
   - `Virtual hub capacity`: `2 Routing Infrastructure Units`
   - `Hub routing preference`: `VPN`

Virtual Hub Details	
Region *	North Europe
Name *	vwanhub
Hub private address space *	110.0.0.0/24
Virtual hub capacity *	2 Routing Infrastructure Units
Hub routing preference *	VPN

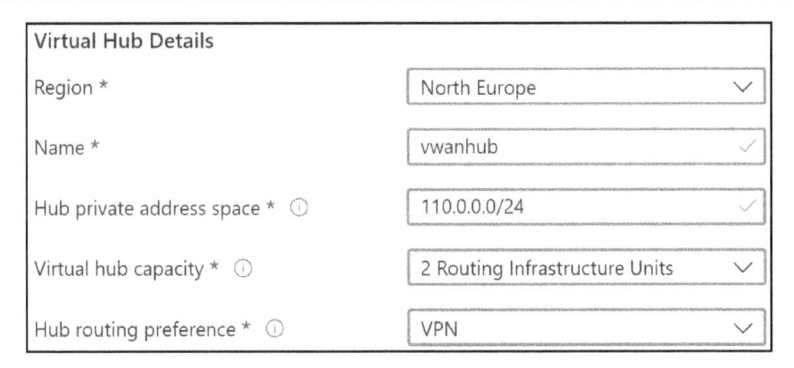

Figure 19.36: Virtual hub details

10. Select Yes for Do you want to create a Site to site (VPN gateway)?

Do you want to create a Site to site (VPN gateway)?	Yes	No

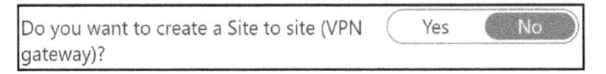

Figure 19.37: S2S settings

11. Click Review + create, then click Create.

The deployment will take approximately five minutes to complete.

You have just completed your Virtual WAN deployment and created a hub site; you will create a VPN site in the next exercise.

Creating a VPN Site

In this exercise, you will create your first VPN site for Virtual WAN:

1. Navigate to your Virtual WAN and click VPN sites under the Connectivity context in the left menu.
2. Click + Create site.
3. Enter the following details and click Next : Links >:
   - Region: North Europe (or select what you prefer)
   - Name: Windows_RRAS
   - Device Vendor: Windows RRAS
   - Private address space: 99.0.0.0/24

4. Enter the following details. Here, `Link Speed` refers to the speed in MBps of the line, and `Link IP address/FQDN` is the VPN server/NVA device that you are connecting to:

   - `Link Name: rraslink`
   - `Link Speed: 50`
   - `Link provider name: rras server`
   - `Link IP address/FQDN`: Public IP of your VPN VM

5. Click `Next : Review + create >` and then click `Create`.

In this exercise, you have created your VPN site, which will be used to establish connectivity to your VPN gateway in Azure. This server represents a router in your organization and, therefore, a site too. You will need to connect this to the hub next.

Connecting Your VPN Site to the Hub

Now that your site is configured, you will need to connect to your VPN connection using your VPN server:

1. Navigate to your Virtual WAN and click `Hubs` under the `Connectivity` context.
2. Click on vwanhub from the options on the right.
3. In the `Virtual Hub` blade, click `VPN (Site to site)` under the `Connectivity` context in the left menu.
4. Click `Create VPN gateway`.
5. Select `1 scale unit: 500 Mbps x 2` for `Gateway scale units` and `Microsoft network` for `Routing preference`, then click `Create`. Note that this operation can take up to 30 minutes to complete.
6. Once created, clear the filter for VPN sites by clicking the X.

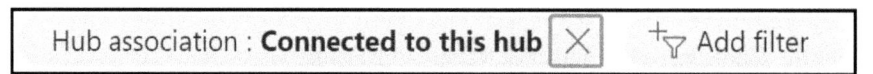

Figure 19.38: Clearing the filter

7. Now, select your VPN site and click `Connect VPN sites`:

Figure 19.39: Associate VPN site

8. Fill in `Pre-shared key (PSK)`, `Pa55w.rd1234`, and leave all the other settings as default values. Click `Connect`.

9. You will see `Connection Provisioning status` stating `Succeeded`:

Site name	Location	Cloud provider	Link	Connection Provisioning status
Windows_RRAS	northeurope		> 1 link	Succeeded

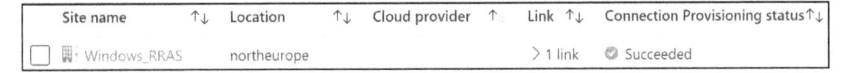

Figure 19.40: Connection Provisioning status

In this exercise, you configured a VPN site connection. Your VPN server is now ready to establish a new tunnel. This is an essential aspect of establishing VPN site connectivity.

Connecting to Your VPN Site

Now that your site is connected to the hub, you can connect to this using your VPN server:

1. Log on to the VPN server you provisioned for the *Creating and Configuring an Azure VPN Gateway* exercise. Navigate to `Routing and Remote Access` and create a new demand-dial interface.

2. Click `Next`, then enter the name `Azure VWAN VPN`, and click `Next`.

3. Select `Connect using virtual private network (VPN)` and click `Next`.

4. Select `IKEv2` and click `Next`.

5. Navigate to your Virtual WAN on the Azure portal and click `Hubs` under the `Connectivity` context. Select `vwanhub` and click `VPN (Site to site)` under `Connectivity` from the left menu.

6. Click on the text next to `Gateway scale units`:

Gateway configuration
1 scale unit - 500 Mbps x 2 (View/Configure)

Figure 19.41: Gateway scale units

7. Note the public IP address under `VPN Gateway Instance 0`:

VPN Gateway Instance 0

Public IP Address   52.23

Figure 19.42: Public IP address

8. Enter this IP address of the VPN gateway from Azure in the `Demand-Dial Interface` wizard on RRAS. Click `Next` on this and the next screen.

9. Click Add, then enter the following and click OK. If your VNet associated with the VPN gateway is in a /16 range, then your subnet is 255.255.0.0; if it is in a /24 range, then it is 255.255.255.0. Click Next:

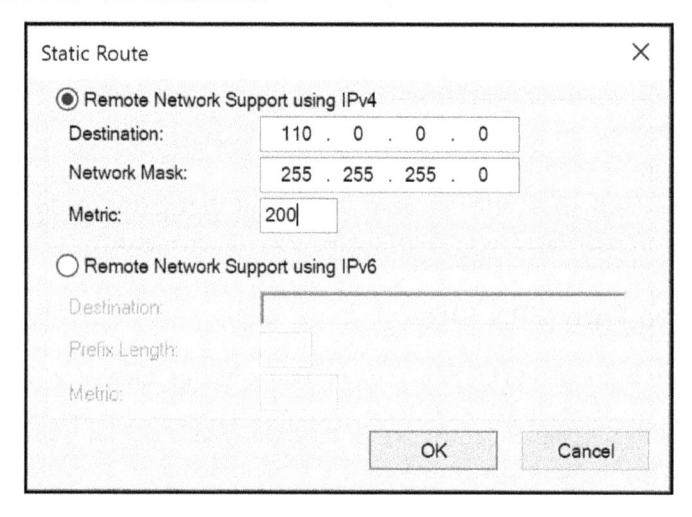

Figure 19.43: Static route

10. Click Next, then Finish.
11. Click Network Interfaces, right-click Azure VWAN VPN, and click Properties.
12. Click the Security tab and then click Use preshared key for authentication. Use the key you generated earlier, Pa55w.rd1234, paste it into the Key field, and click OK.
13. Right-click on your Azure VWAN VPN interface and click Connect. If all is configured correctly, you should successfully connect:

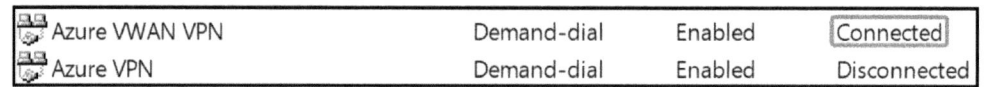

Azure VWAN VPN	Demand-dial	Enabled	Connected
Azure VPN	Demand-dial	Enabled	Disconnected

Figure 19.44: RRAS VPN connection

In this exercise, you have seen how to connect an S2S VPN to Azure Virtual WAN and Azure VPN Gateway. You should feel confident with implementing the basic network structures you need within your Azure environments.

Summary

In this chapter, you learned about the various services for connecting on-premises networks to Azure, connecting Azure networks in different regions or subscriptions through Azure VPN Gateway, ER, and the Azure Virtual WAN service. You learned about the various types of VPN connections available, their differences, and when to choose each offering. You also experienced the configuration of several VPN types and Azure Virtual WAN. You should feel comfortable with connecting your networks to Azure and what services to use. In the next chapter, you will learn in detail about monitoring and troubleshooting for Azure networks.

> **Note**
>
> Remember to delete the resources you created in this chapter to minimize costs. You can do this with the following commands for convenience, which will remove the resource group and all the corresponding resources:
>
> ```
> Remove-AzResourceGroup -Name AZ104-VPNGateway
> Remove-AzResourceGroup -Name AZ104-ExpressRoute
> Remove-AzResourceGroup -Name AZ104-VirtualWAN
> ```

20
Monitoring and Troubleshooting Virtual Networking

This chapter focuses on monitoring and troubleshooting network connectivity. In this chapter, you are going to focus on how you can monitor your virtual networks using Network Watcher. You will learn how to manage your virtual network connectivity and how you can monitor and troubleshoot on-premises connectivity, as well as use Network Watcher. You will finish this chapter by learning how to troubleshoot external networking.

In this chapter, you are going to learn the following main topics:

- Understanding Network Watcher
- Configuring Network Watcher

Technical Requirements

This chapter uses the following tools for the examples:

- Access to an Azure subscription with owner or contributor privileges. If you do not have access to one, you can enroll for a free account: https://azure.microsoft.com/en-us/free/.
- **PowerShell 5.1** or later installed on a PC with Windows installed, or PowerShell Core 6.x if you use another operating system, on a machine where labs can be practiced from.
- For Windows users, you will need to install **.NET Framework 4.7.2** or later.
- Where PowerShell is not installed or available, Azure Cloud Shell (https://shell.azure.com) can be used as a browser-based shell.

- Installation of the AZ PowerShell module, which can be performed by running the following in an administrative PowerShell session:

  ```
  Set-ExecutionPolicy -ExecutionPolicy RemoteSigned -Scope
  CurrentUser
  Install-Module -Name Az -Scope CurrentUser -Repository PSGallery
  -Force
  ```

Understanding Network Watcher

Azure Network Watcher acts as a comprehensive network monitoring suite within Azure. It equips users with a toolbox to diagnose, monitor, and visualize network performance metrics and logs. This powerful toolkit extends its reach to various resources within an Azure virtual network, including application gateway traffic, load balancers, and even ExpressRoute circuits.

Azure Network Watcher offers the following capabilities through the included set of diagnostic tools:

- Monitoring
- Network diagnostics tools
- Flow logs
- Traffic analytics

Network Watcher will be automatically enabled for a subscription and is created when a new virtual network is created or updated. There is no charge to enable the Network Watcher service inside a subscription; however, there is a cost to utilizing the tools and services that Network Watcher provides, such as network log data, and charges per Network Watcher check, Connection monitor test, and network analytics.

> **Note**
> To make use of Network Watcher, you will require the appropriate **Role-Based Access Control (RBAC)** role permissions, such as Contributor, Owner, or Network Contributor.

Monitoring

Monitoring provides tools that are useful to monitor your network traffic, as well as create visibility of your Azure **Virtual Network** (**VNet**) resources and how they communicate with each other. The following figure depicts the tools available in the `Monitoring` context in the `Network Watcher` blade:

Monitoring
Topology
Connection monitor

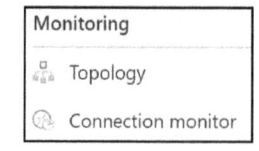

Figure 20.1: Network Watcher – Monitoring tools

Each of these tools is described in more detail in the following subsections.

Topology

The `topology` tool enables you to visually and interactively understand the interconnections and relationships between resources and how they are configured to communicate with each other within a VNet, through a visualization of the network configuration. This can be a great high-level overview of the VNet that you work with. The service works across regions, subscriptions, and resource groups, being able to combine network data across all configurations in Azure into a single tool. The following example is a snippet of what you can expect:

Figure 20.2: An example topology

Connection Monitor

This is a cloud-based hybrid network monitoring solution that can monitor the communication between **Virtual Machines** (**VMs**) and endpoints. An endpoint can be another VM, a URL, an IPv4 or IPv6 address, or a **Fully Qualified Domain Name** (**FQDN**). The network communication is monitored at regular intervals and information about latency, network topology changes, and the reachability between a VM and the endpoint is collected. If an endpoint becomes unreachable, Network Watcher will inform the user about the error. The reason for this could be a problem with the memory or CPU of a VM, a security rule for the VM, or the hop type of a custom route.

The following is a sample of the interface that you will see for the Connection Monitor service:

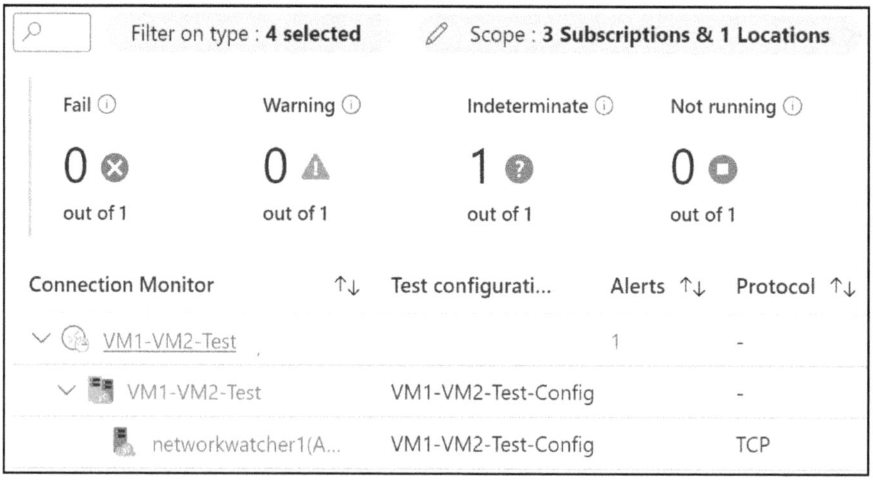

Figure 20.3: Connection Monitor

Scenarios for Using Connection Monitor

There are several scenarios that Connection monitor supports. Knowing where you can use Connection monitor is important in determining whether it's fit for purpose:

- **Multi-tier application monitoring**: Ensure seamless communication between your frontend web server (VM or scale set) and the database server within a multi-tier application hosted on Azure.

- **Cross-regional performance analysis**: Compare network latency between VMs/scale sets in different Azure regions (e.g., East US versus Central US) to identify potential performance bottlenecks.

- **Global office connectivity assessment**: Analyze latency variations for Microsoft 365 access between users in geographically dispersed locations.

- **Hybrid application performance optimization**: Monitor and compare connection speeds between your on-premises environment and an Azure storage account endpoint accessed by your hybrid application.

- **On-premises to Azure connectivity verification**: Validate the health and responsiveness of network connections between your on-premises infrastructure and the Azure VMs/scale sets hosting your cloud application.

- **Multi-tier application reachability (Azure/non-Azure)**: Evaluate the connection stability between individual or multiple instances within an Azure VM scale set and your multi-tier application, whether hosted entirely on Azure or across different platforms.

The Benefits of Connection Monitor

Knowing how Connection monitor adds value to your daily role is as important as using the tool itself. You can benefit from the service, such as leveraging comprehensive insights for enhanced visibility with faster alerting. You may have other tools that can facilitate the same requirements you have; however, if you want a cloud-native solution, it is a great tool to assist you in troubleshooting and monitoring your connections to and from Azure:

- **Streamlined monitoring**: Provides a unified interface for monitoring connectivity across Azure and hybrid environments
- **Comprehensive insights**: Analyzes network performance across regions, workspaces, and various locations
- **Enhanced visibility**: Offers increased monitoring frequency for detailed network performance evaluation
- **Faster alerting**: Enables quicker identification and notification of connectivity issues in hybrid deployments
- **Protocol versatility**: Supports monitoring based on HTTP, TCP, and ICMP protocols for diverse use cases
- **Rich data integration**: Integrates with Azure Monitor Metrics and Log Analytics for both Azure and non-Azure environments, facilitating comprehensive data analysis

Network Performance Monitor

Network Performance Monitor (NPM) is a hybrid network monitoring solution that provides insights into the performance of your network. It can monitor network connectivity for on-premises and cloud networks and between various points in your network infrastructure. It can detect issues such as routing errors and blackholing. The monitoring solution is stored inside Azure Log Analytics.

NPM can create alerts and notifications when network performance errors appear, and it can localize the source of a problem to a specific network device or segment.

It offers the following capabilities:

- **Performance monitor**: A performance monitor can monitor the network connectivity across cloud deployments and on-premises locations. It can also monitor connectivity between multiple data centers, branch offices, multi-tier applications, and microservices.
- **Service connectivity monitor**: You can identify the network bottlenecks inside a network infrastructure and detect the exact locations of the issues in the network. You can also monitor connectivity between users and services.
- **ExpressRoute monitor**: You can monitor the ExpressRoute connection between the on-premises locations and Azure.

Latency problems are also monitored. Connection monitor will provide the average, minimum, and maximum latency observed over time. The monitoring solution is capable of monitoring network performance between various points in the network infrastructure, and it can generate alerts and notifications.

> **Note**
>
> As of July 1, 2021, this has been considered a legacy service; you can no longer add new tests to an existing workspace, nor can you create new workspaces in NPM. You should now use the new Azure Connection monitor instead and are advised to migrate any tests you had configured in NPM to this.

Azure Connection Monitor Components

When evaluating Connection monitor, there are several components to be aware of, as listed here, along with a diagram to help you understand their relationships:

Endpoints: These define the starting or ending points for connectivity checks. They can be various resources, including Azure VMs, scale sets, on-premises machines with agents installed, web addresses (URLs), or specific IP addresses.

Test configurations: These define the specific protocol used for a test (e.g., HTTP, TCP, or ICMP). Based on the chosen protocol, you can configure details such as port numbers, acceptable latency thresholds, test frequency, and other relevant settings.

Test groups: These act as containers to organize your monitoring setup. Each group can include a combination of source and destination endpoints along with their corresponding test configurations. A single Connection monitor resource can hold multiple test groups for better organization.

Tests: These are the most granular units within the monitoring process. Each test represents a combination of a source endpoint, a destination endpoint, and a specific test configuration. The results of these individual tests provide detailed insights, including success/failure rates and **round-trip time** (**RTT**) measurements. The following diagram illustrates the relationship between the components of Connection monitor:

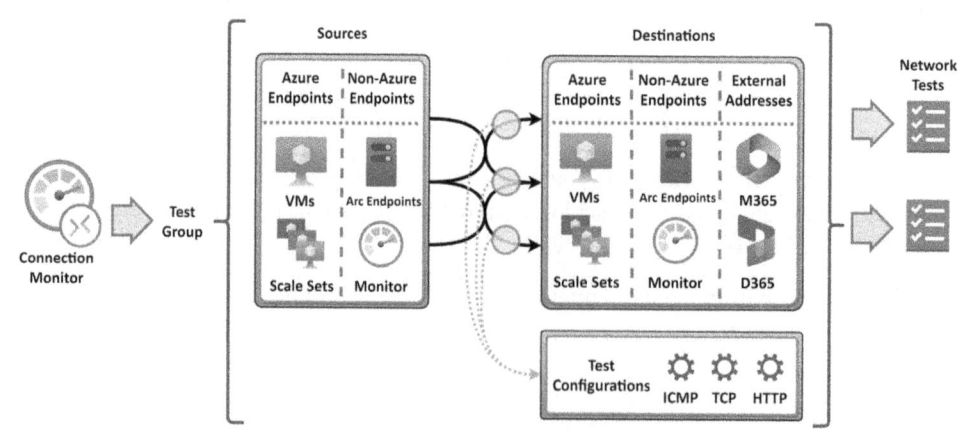

Figure 20.4: Connection monitor components

Traffic Analytics

Traffic analytics is a service designed to surface user and application activity on your networks. It is a cloud-based and native solution that can provide rich visualization of data that is written to the **Network Security Group** (**NSG**) or VNet flow logs. Some of the capabilities it offers are as follows:

- Visualization of networking activity among your various Azure subscriptions
- Highlighting misconfigurations in your network
- Enabling you to better secure your network by assisting you in identifying threat vectors in your network
- Helping you to improve your network environment by understanding traffic patterns in your network and assisting in making your network deployment more efficient, assessing criteria such as performance and capacity

Network Diagnostic Tools

There are several network diagnostic and visualization tools presented to you in Network Watcher. You can, for instance, diagnose network traffic filtering for VMs, determine the next hop of your traffic on route to an intended destination, or even identify why a VM is unable to communicate with other resources because of a security rule.

Using Azure Network Watcher, you can diagnose outbound connections from a VM. You can also diagnose problems with an Azure VNet gateway and connections, capture packets traveling to and from a VM, view security rules for a network interface, and determine relative latencies between Azure regions and internet service providers.

The following network diagnostic tools will be unpacked further shortly – IP flow verify, NSG diagnostics, next hop, effective security rules, VPN troubleshoot, packet capture, and connection troubleshoot.

IP Flow Verify

The **IP flow verify** tool tests the communication between two endpoints and informs you whether the connection has succeeded or failed. This tool is used to assess traffic flow from the internet and on-premises environments to a destination virtual machine in Azure. An IP flow can tell you which security rule allowed or denied the connection and communication. To use IP flow verify, you specify the source (local) and target resource (Azure VM) that you are connecting to and from. You also select the target and source IPv4 addresses and ports.

In addition, you enter the corresponding packet information, such as your protocol, the **transmission control protocol** (**TCP**) or **user datagram protocol** (**UDP**), and the direction of the traffic flow (Inbound/Outbound):

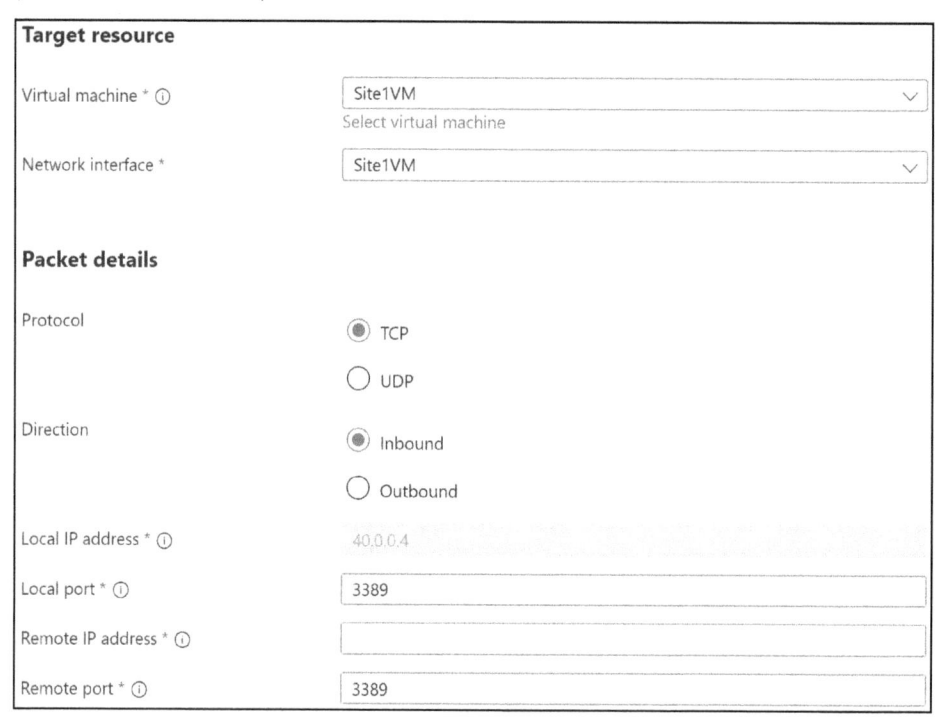

Figure 20.5: Network Watcher – IP flow verify

NSG Diagnostics

This tool enables you to identify the net effect of applied **NSG** rules, as well as identify all NSGs that will be used to control and monitor network traffic. The output will expose the resultant approval (allow/deny) for the identified flow, along with a list of rules processed. To run an **NSG diagnostic**, you again specify your source and destination. The source can be an IPv4 address or a **Classless Inter-Domain Routing** (**CIDR**) range, or it can be a service tag, where the destination specified is an IP address only. You also choose your port for the destination and specify your traffic protocol (TCP/UDP/**Internet Control Message Protocol** (**ICMP**)/any) and direction. The NSG result will look like the following:

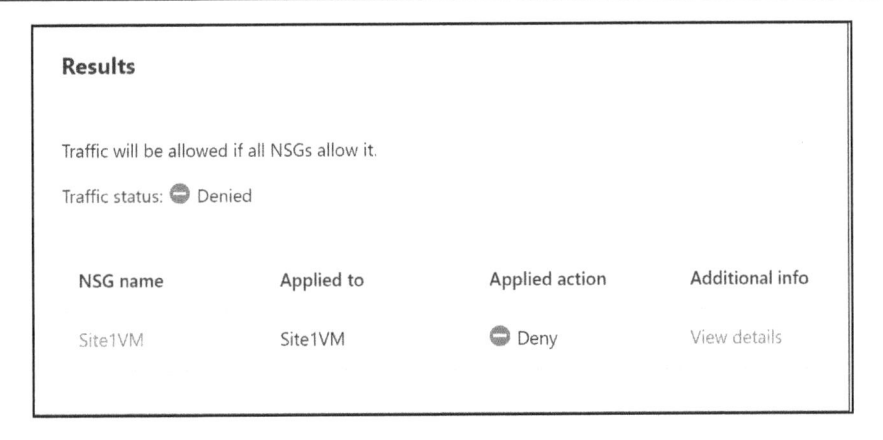

Results			
Traffic will be allowed if all NSGs allow it.			
Traffic status: Denied			
NSG name	Applied to	Applied action	Additional info
Site1VM	Site1VM	Deny	View details

Figure 20.6: Network Watcher – NSG diagnostics

Next Hop

Network Watcher can also diagnose network routing problems from a VM. When a VNet is created, there are several default outbound routes created for that VNet as well. Outbound traffic from all resources that are deployed in a VNet is routed based on Azure's default routes. In cases where you want to override the default routing rules or create additional rules through something such as a route table, the **Next hop** tool can be used to identify the next hop of the IP flow for communication between the different routes. When the communication fails, you can then change, add, or remove a route to resolve the problem.

The following figure shows the output to assess the next hop between two VMs in Azure. In this example, the next hop is the VNet peer. Note that it also shows you the route table that the source IP uses.

Result

Next hop type
VirtualNetworkPeering

IP address
-

Route table ID
System Route

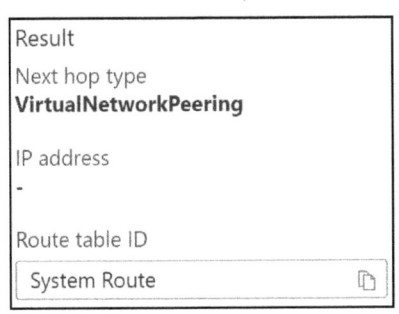

Figure 20.7: Network Watcher – next hop

Effective Security Rules

The **effective security rules** tool is used to determine the overall effective security rules applied to your VM and will combine all relevant NSG rules to display the net rule effect. This can be extremely helpful when assessing why your traffic is blocked and where you have several NSGs. The following figure shows a typical output after running the tool:

Site1VM							
Inbound rules							
Name	Priority	Source	Source Ports	Destination	Destination Ports	Protocol	Access
Site1VM3389	1000	0.0.0.0/0,0.0.0.0/0	0-65535	0.0.0.0/0,0.0.0.0/0	3389-3389	TCP	Allow
Site1VM5985	1001	0.0.0.0/0,0.0.0.0/0	0-65535	0.0.0.0/0,0.0.0.0/0	5985-5985	TCP	Allow
AllowVnetInBound	65000	Virtual network (3 prefixes)	0-65535	Virtual network (3 prefixes)	0-65535	All	Allow
AllowAzureLoadBalancerInBound	65001	Azure load balancer (2 prefixes)	0-65535	0.0.0.0/0,0.0.0.0/0	0-65535	All	Allow
DenyAllInBound	65500	0.0.0.0/0,0.0.0.0/0	0-65535	0.0.0.0/0,0.0.0.0/0	0-65535	All	Deny
Outbound rules							
Name	Priority	Source	Source Ports	Destination	Destination Ports	Protocol	Access
AllowVnetOutBound	65000	Virtual network (3 prefixes)	0-65535	Virtual network (3 prefixes)	0-65535	All	Allow
AllowInternetOutBound	65001	0.0.0.0/0,0.0.0.0/0	0-65535	Internet (282 prefixes)	0-65535	All	Allow
DenyAllOutBound	65500	0.0.0.0/0,0.0.0.0/0	0-65535	0.0.0.0/0,0.0.0.0/0	0-65535	All	Deny

Figure 20.8: Network Watcher – effective security rules

VPN Troubleshoot

The **VPN troubleshoot** tool is used to diagnose issues between your VNet gateways and connection endpoints that require troubleshooting. The tool does this through running checks on your gateways and connections. Multiple gateways and connections can be troubleshot at the same time. You also have the advantage of utilizing the tool through the Azure portal, Azure PowerShell, the Azure CLI, or even a REST API.

Packet Capture

The **packet capture** feature in Network Watcher allows you to capture packets for traffic related to your VM, being both inbound and outbound from the VM. The capture enables you to have more visibility of your network traffic, garnering key insights such as intrusion detection traffic, network statistics, and other network-related communications and traffic. This is enabled as a VM extension, called `AzureNetworkWatcherExtension`, using the Network Watcher agent for VMs. This extension saves you from running your own VM-hosted packet capture utilities to achieve the same results. The tool provides the flexibility to save packet captures to your local disk or blob storage. Utilization of the tool is also flexible in that it can be accessed through the Azure portal, Azure PowerShell, the Azure CLI, or even a REST API.

Connection Troubleshoot

This tool enables you to assess several source types (VMs, VM scale sets, Application Gateway, or Bastion host) against a destination VM, URI, FQDN, or IP address. The protocol to be used (TCP/ICMP) and source and destination ports can be selected.

The tool aims to reduce the time required to identify connectivity issues and assist with determining the root cause. There are four types of diagnostic tests that can be run using this tool – connectivity, NSG diagnostic, next hop, and port scanner.

You have now seen the comprehensive suite of diagnostic tools available to you through the Network Watcher service. Being able to understand when to use each tool and how it will benefit you, as well as the limitations of each tool, is important. It is important for the exam that you understand how to use each tool and what the configuration will look like. In the next section, you will learn about the Metrics category of the Network Watcher service, which contains the usage and quota configurations.

Metrics

The **Metrics** category contains usage and quota data. This configuration section of the Network Watcher service is used to show the available quota remaining of the various service items, such VNets and custom IP prefixes by region, allowing for requests to adjust the available quotas.

Usage + Quotas

The **Usage + quotas** feature within Network Watcher offers a centralized view of your deployed network resources within a specific Azure subscription and region. This view provides two key sets of information:

Current usage: This section summarizes the actual resource consumption for each network resource you have deployed

Corresponding limits: This section displays the predefined quotas or limitations associated with each network resource type

This tool provides an easy mechanism to gain visibility of your usage against each quota, as well as providing the ability to request a quota increase for additional consumption of services. The following diagram displays an example of the quotas, with the name, region, subscription, and current usage for each quota name type:

Quota name	Region	Subscription	Current Usage ↓		
Usage at or near quota (3)					
Network Watchers	North Europe	AzureTraining	▬▬▬▬▬▬▬ 100%	1 of 1
Network Watchers	South Africa North	AzureTraining	▬▬▬▬▬▬▬ 100%	1 of 1
Network Watchers	West Europe	AzureTraining	▬▬▬▬▬▬▬ 100%	1 of 1
No usage (Showing 97 of 1889)					
Virtual Networks	Australia Central	AzureTraining	▬▬▬▬▬▬▬ 0%	0 of 1
Custom Ip Prefixes	Australia Central	AzureTraining	▬▬▬▬▬▬▬ 0%	0 of 5

Figure 20.9: Network Watcher – Usage + Quotas

Next, you will learn about the **Logs** section in Network Watcher. You will also learn about the types of logs that are collected and the value of them.

Logs

The **Logs** category contains several logging tools that are useful for investigating usage and troubleshooting. These logs can be analyzed and consumed from many tools, such as the traffic analytics feature and Power BI. Some of the types of logs you can find within this service are NSG flow logs that track traffic flowing through NSGs and whether they were allowed or denied, VNet flow logs that contain data such as source, destination, and port information, migrate flow logs that allow you to migrate your NSG flow logs to VNet flow logs, and diagnostic logs that contain diagnostic logging information related to your resources.

These various log service types will be unpacked in more detail next.

Flow Logs

There are two types of logs that you can record under **Flow logs**:

- **NSG flow logs**: NSGs are responsible for allowing or denying the inbound and outbound traffic to a network interface in a VM. NSG flow logs are a utility to assist you in knowing your expected network configurations, such as open ports and intended network behavior. It also assists you in identifying irregularities in your network configurations, such as sudden changes in network traffic. The NSG flow logs feature can log IP information flowing through an NSG, such as the port, protocol, whether traffic is allowed or denied, the source, and the destination IP address. The NSG flow logs feature is where you configure the logging of your network traffic flows for Azure. Log data is stored in Azure Storage for consumption from **security information and event management** (**SIEM**) solution and visualization tools.

- **VNet flow logs**: VNet flow logs enable you to collect IP-related data for your VNets and operate at layer 4 on the OSI model. Captured traffic records the source, destination, direction, port, flow state, flow encryption, and throughput information.

Migrate Flow Logs

This menu gives you the option to migrate your NSG flow logs to VNet flow logs. You may want to do this to simplify the monitoring of your network traffic.

Diagnostic Logs

This setting allows you to configure the diagnostic logging settings for your resources; it will record NSG events and rule counts as `NetworkSecurityGroupEvent` and `NetworkSecurityGroupRuleCounter`. The logs can be stored in a variety of locations, such as Log Analytics, Event Hubs, or an Azure storage account.

> **Note**
> Network Watcher is a regional service, which means that you need to deploy it for each region where you require the service.

In the following sections, we will see Network Watcher in action.

Configuring Network Watcher

Now that you understand what Network Watcher is, you will learn how to configure and use the various components available to the service. You will navigate through different scenarios and the ways the tools can assist you in a troubleshooting scenario.

Network Resource Monitoring

In this demonstration, you are going to monitor the network on two Windows Server 2016 data center VMs. You will create the VMs inside one VNet. You can then use these VMs for monitoring. Before you can monitor the network using network resource monitoring, you will need to install the Network Watcher agent on the two VMs. After that, you are going to inspect the network traffic.

Installing the Network Watcher Agent

You will set up two VMs, labeled NetworkWatcher1 and NetworkWatcher2. To install the Network Watcher agent on a VM in Azure, follow these steps:

1. Navigate to the Azure portal by opening https://portal.azure.com/.
2. Run the PowerShell script found in this repo, named ConfiguringNetworkWatcher.ps1: https://packt.link/sHhOx. It will create the following resources:

   - A resource group named AZ104-NetworkWatcher
   - Two new VMs, NetworkWatcher1 and NetworkWatcher2
   - A virtual network, NetworkWatcherVnet
   - A network security group, NetworkWatcherSecurityGroup

3. Once deployed, navigate to your NetworkWatcher1 VM resource on Azure.
4. Click Extensions + applications under the Settings context on the left menu, and then click the Add button:

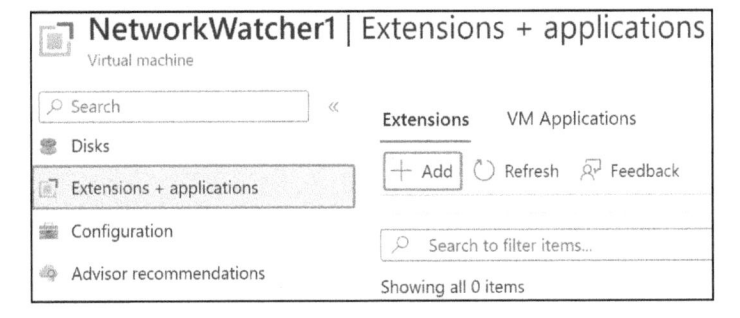

Figure 20.10: Adding a VM extension

5. Type `network watcher` in the search box, click the `Network Watcher Agent for Windows` icon, and then click `Next`:

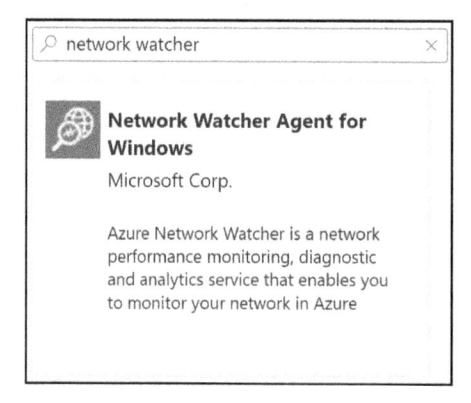

Figure 20.11: Adding the Network Watcher Agent

6. Click `Review + create` on the screen that follows, and then click `Create`.
7. Repeat these steps for the `NetworkWatcher2` VM.

Now that Network Watcher Agent for Windows is installed on all the VMs, you can enable Network Watcher for a specific region.

Enabling Network Watcher

To enable Network Watcher in a specific region, follow these steps:

1. Navigate to the Azure portal by opening `https://portal.azure.com/`.
2. Click the hamburger menu in the top-left corner of the Azure home screen. Select `All services`:

Figure 20.12: Selecting All services

3. Type `network watcher` in the search bar, and then select `Network Watcher` from the list of returned services.

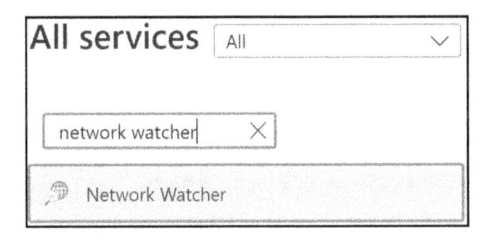

Figure 20.13: Selecting Network Watcher

4. On the Network Watcher `Overview` page, note that the Network Watcher service with the `Subscription` and `Location` details match the VM you deployed earlier. If you ran the script, this should be `West Europe`.

Figure 20.14: Selecting your Network Watcher

> **Note**
> Note that upon deploying your first VNet in an Azure region, Azure will automatically create the associated `NetworkWatcher_<region>` resource.

5. If Network Watcher is not already deployed for your region, click + `Create` at the top of the screen. Select `Subscription` and `Region`, and then click `Add`:

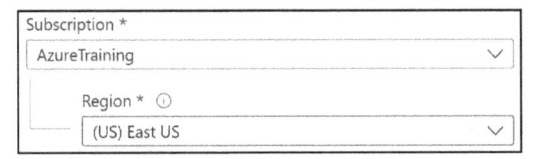

Figure 20.15: Enabling a new Network Watcher region

Now that Network Watcher is enabled, you can start monitoring the network resources; you will experience this in the next activity.

Monitoring Network Connectivity

Network monitoring can be used to monitor connection reachability, latency, and network topology changes. To do this, you need to set up a Connection monitor instance.

Perform the following steps to do so:

1. With the `Network Watcher` blade still open, in the `Monitoring` section of the left menu, select `Connection monitor`. Click `+ Create`.

2. You are going to use the monitor resource to test the connectivity between the `NetworkWatcher1` and `NetworkWatcher2` VMs. Enter the following values for the `Basics` tab, and then click `Next: Test groups >>`:

   - `Connection Monitor Name`: `NetworkWatcher1-NetworkWatcher2`.
   - `Subscription`: Select the subscription where the VMs are deployed
   - `Region`: `West Europe`.

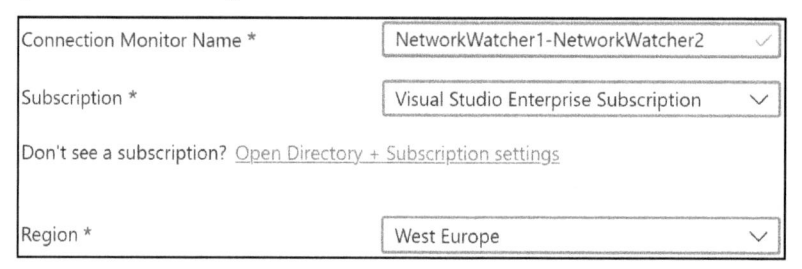

Figure 20.16: Creating a Connection monitor – the basics

3. Type `NetworkWatcher1-NetworkWatcher2` in the `Test group name` field, and then click `Add sources`:

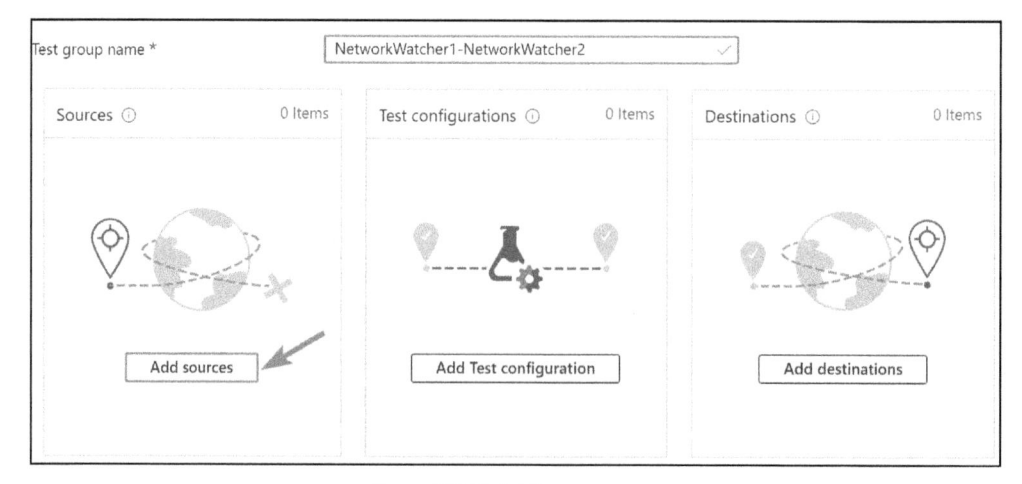

Figure 20.17: Adding a source

4. On the `Add Sources` blade, select your `NetworkWatcher1` VM by expanding `NetworkWatcherVnet` and then the subnet. Click `Add endpoints` at the bottom of the screen:

Name		IP
∨ NetworkWatcherVnet		
∨ NetworkWatcherSubnet		192.168.1.0/24
☑ NetworkWatcher1		Any
☐ NetworkWatcher2		Any

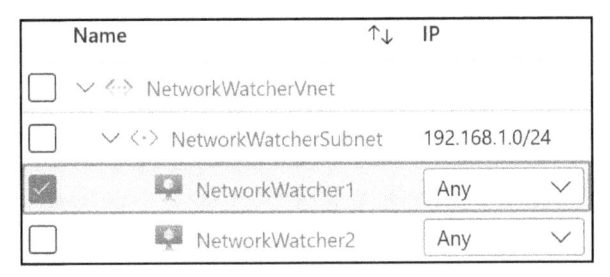

Figure 20.18: Adding a Connection Monitor Source

5. Do the same for `Add destinations`, this time selecting `NetworkWatcher2`. Click `Add endpoints` at the bottom of the screen:

Name		IP
∨ NetworkWatcherVnet		
☑ ∨ NetworkWatcherSubnet		192.168.1.0/24
☐ NetworkWatcher1		Any
☑ NetworkWatcher2		Any

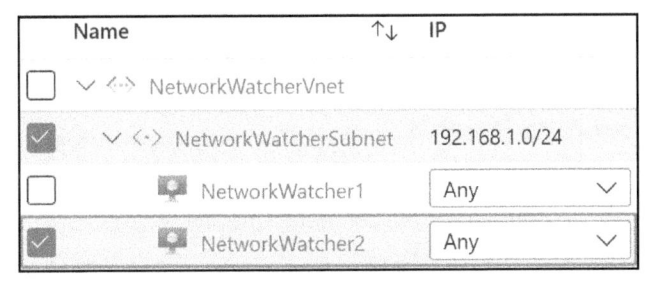

Figure 20.19: Adding a Connection monitor destination

6. Click `Add Test configuration`, and then enter the following into the blade. Click the `Add Test configuration` button at the bottom when done:

- `Test configuration name:` `NetworkWatcher1-NetworkWatcher2-Cfg`
- `Protocol:` TCP
- `Destination port:` 3389
- Check the `Listen on port` checkbox
- `Test Frequency:` `Every 30 seconds`
- `Checks failed (%):` 5

- Round trip time (ms):100

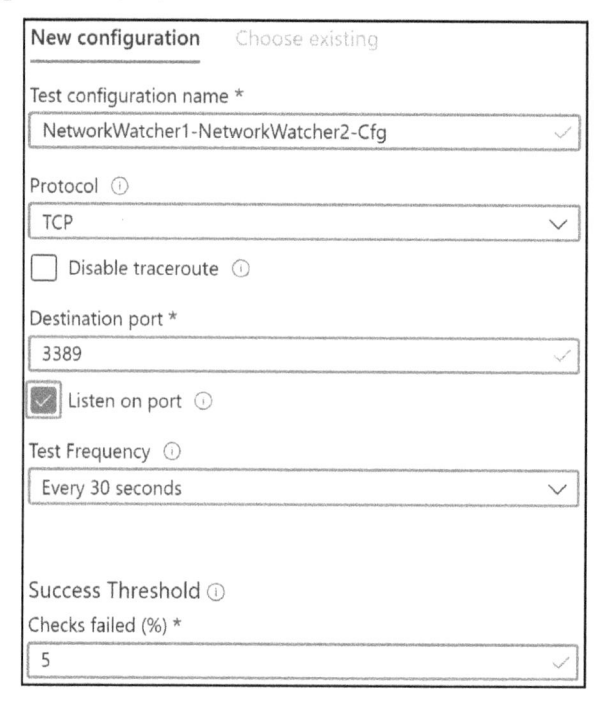

Figure 20.20: The Connection monitor settings

7. Click `Add Test Group`.
8. Click `Next: Workspace >>`.
9. Leave the `Default` setting, which will create a workspace for you automatically.
10. Click `Next : Create alert >>`. Create an alert by clicking the `Create alert` checkbox at the top of the screen. Click `Select action group` near the bottom of the page. You can create an action group by entering your email address and clicking `Create action group`, or by selecting an existing one. Click `Done`.
11. Click `Review + Create`, and then click `Create`.
12. Navigate back to `Network Watcher` and then to the `Connection monitor` screen. You will notice after a few minutes that the connection is good and gets a pass:

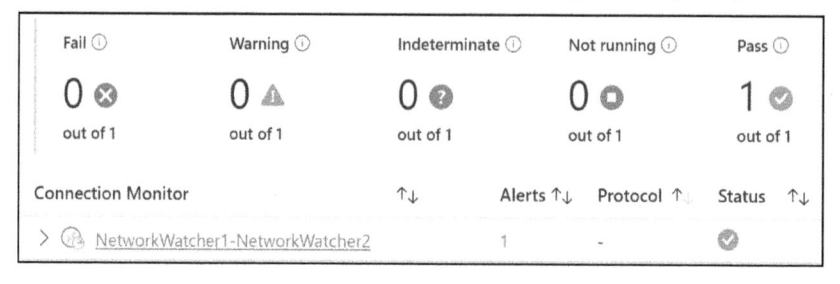

Figure 20.21: A Connection monitor overview

You are now able to monitor network connectivity. In the next section, you will look at how to manage connectivity.

Managing VNet Connectivity

The Network Watcher monitoring capability offers the facility to monitor your networked environments in Azure, the Connection monitor, and the topology tools. The topology tool provides a visualization that can be interacted with, showing the relationships between networked resources across subscriptions and resource groups on a geographical map, with the regions highlighted. Expanding any region will allow you to dive into the subsequent networked layers for more granular detail on your network configuration, enabling you to dive into multiple levels of information. In the upcoming section, you are going to explore the topology tool, discover how to navigate through it, and expose information at multiple layers that will be relevant to you in understanding your environments and assisting in any troubleshooting activities you may encounter. The skills you will gain are important to the exam objectives you will be tested on when it comes to troubleshooting networks.

Network Topology

The topology tool, which is part of the Network Watcher service in the Azure portal, displays an overview of the VNets inside an Azure subscription and a resource group. To view the network topology section, follow these steps:

1. Navigate to the Azure portal by opening `https://portal.azure.com/`.
2. Navigate to `Network Watcher`.
3. Under the `Monitoring` context on the left menu, select `Topology`.
4. Change the filters to view your specific deployments. You can display all resource types for this exercise. To change the filters, click the blue bubbles and change the settings as required.

Figure 20.22: Topology filters

5. You will navigate through the relevant layers. For instance, on the `West Europe` location, click the + icon to expand and view the next level of view.

Figure 20.23: The expansion icon

6. The next screen should present a layer of VNets; expand the `Virtual Networks` option. Then, expand the `NetworkWatcherVnet`.
7. Finally, expand the `NetworkWatcherSubnet`.
8. You will notice all the connected devices in the subnet. If you carefully trace the links from the VM to the various components, you should be able to trace a path from the `network interface`, through the `IP configuration`, to the `public IP`. Also, notice the network interfaces connected to the `NetworkWatcherSecurityGroup` NSG. Your view should resemble the following figure, where the red lines highlight the connections for you:

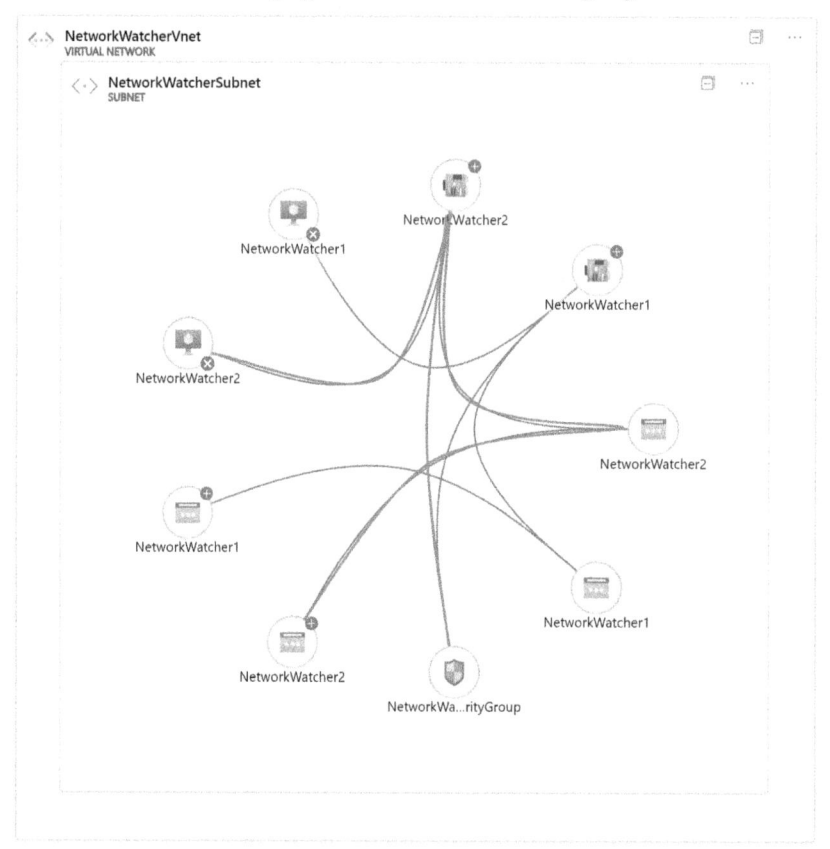

Figure 20.24: Network Watcher – a topology diagram

9. You can also drill down into all the components of the network, such as the **network interface cards** (**NIC**), VMs, and IP address, by clicking on the items in the topology. This will take you to the settings of the different resources. Note that you can download the topology to an **Scalable Vector Graphics** (**SVG**) image file as well, by clicking the `Download topology` button in the top menu:

Figure 20.25: Downloading the network topology

You can see how useful this tool can be in diagnosing some network-related issues, by learning about the components internal to the specific network and subnet you are investigating and understanding the connection between the various components. For instance, this could highlight some NSGs associated with the **Network Interface Cards (NICs)** that you might not have been aware of, if you experienced dropped network traffic for a connection that you expected to work. Another example could be the troubleshooting of connections between two VMs, and through this view, you may discover that one of the VMs is not in the expected subnet; this view could highlight the variations in the expected configurations, as well as allow you to quickly explore the configuration settings of the various components while troubleshooting. Besides monitoring the networks in Azure, you can also monitor the on-premises resource connectivity. We will explore this in the next section.

Monitoring On-Premises Connectivity

You can monitor your on-premises connectivity using Network Watcher as well. It offers three different features for this, Connection monitor, next hop, and VPN troubleshoot, which, just like the other features, are accessible from the Azure portal. These features help ascertain the correct functionality of your on-premises connections to Azure and troubleshoot connectivity issues, which are an important part of your daily administrative roles in an operational support capacity and are also part of the exam objectives that you will be tested on – namely, your ability to troubleshoot networks. In the exercise that follows, you will learn how to configure the next hop for your traffic, which allows you to control the routing points for your traffic. Typically, this is used to reroute your traffic from default paths to a new intended destination – for example, if you introduced a network virtual appliance firewall, traffic could be forced to route through that firewall before going to the next destination. You will then learn in the exercise, after configuring the next hop, how to troubleshoot a VPN connection as well as how to determine the health of the service.

Configuring Next Hop

You can use the next hop feature to specify a source and destination IPv4 address. The communication between these addresses is then evaluated, and you will be informed about what type of next hop is used to route the traffic. When you experience a routing error or problem, you can add, change, or remove a route to resolve this.

> **Note**
> If you do not see your resource group as one of the options in the drop-down selection, give it a few seconds, and then it should show up as an option.

To see this in action, you need to take the following steps:

1. Navigate to the Azure portal by opening `https://portal.azure.com/`.
2. Navigate to the `Network Watcher` service.
3. From the left menu, click `Next hop` under `Network diagnostic tools`.
4. In the Settings blade, add the following values:

   - `Resource group`: `AZ104-NetworkWatcher`
   - `Virtual machine`: `networkwatcher1`
   - `Network interface`: This is selected automatically
   - `Source IP address`: This is selected automatically as well
   - `Destination IP address`: `13.107.21.200` (a Bing server IP address)

5. Click `Next hop`.
6. You will see the following result. In this case, there is no next hop because the connection goes straight to the internet; therefore, it shows `Next hop type` as `Internet`:

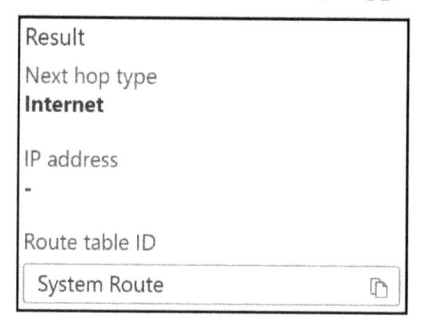

Result
Next hop type **Internet**
IP address -
Route table ID
System Route

Figure 20.26: The next hop result – Internet

7. If you change the destination IP address to one of the IP addresses of the other VMs, which in this case is `192.168.1.5`, you will see the following result:

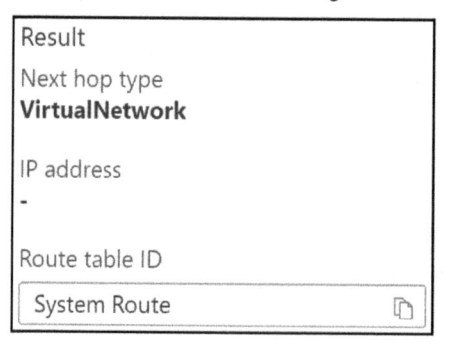

Result
Next hop type **VirtualNetwork**
IP address -
Route table ID
System Route

Figure 20.27: The next hop result – VirtualNetwork

You have just evaluated the next hop within the Azure network fabric and learned how your traffic will flow. The presented hops should align with your expectations for the next hop of traffic, such as **Internet** for a public-facing endpoint such as Bing and **VirtualNetwork** for Azure VNet connections. You now know how to identify whether your traffic flows along the intended path to its destination. This tool will help you identify potential initial network flow issues in the future and save you time. In the next section, you are going to learn how to troubleshoot a VPN connection.

VPN Troubleshoot

For the VPN troubleshoot tool demonstration, you are going to create a VPN connection, just as you did in the previous chapter. Run the following PowerShell script, which will configure a VPN gateway into your `NetworkWatcherVPNVnet` and link to your public IP address of `NetworkWatcher1` VM. Note that the VM will not have the VPN configuration, and to achieve this, do as you did in *Chapter 19, Integrating On-Premises Networks with Azure*. Here is the GitHub code repo: `https://packt.link/24UZD`.

You can diagnose the VPN connection by taking the following steps:

1. Once you have deployed the preceding VPN gateway, waiting 30 minutes for the deployment to complete, navigate to the `Network Watcher` service.
2. Select `VPN troubleshoot` from under `Network diagnostics tools` on the left menu.
3. Select your subscription and resource group, and then notice your list of VPN gateway resources, similar to the following screenshot:

Checkbox	Name ↑↓	Troubleshooting... ↑↓	Resource status ↑↓
☐	NetworkWatcherVPN	Not started	Succeeded

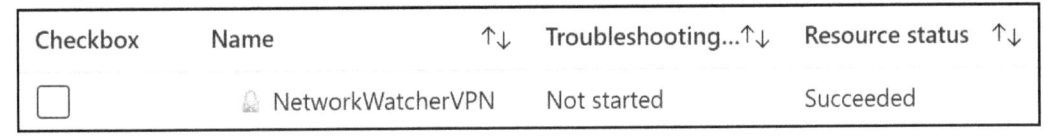

Figure 20.28: VPN troubleshoot

4. Now, since your VPN tunnel has not been established, you will expect a failure to demonstrate a real-world scenario that you could experience. You can start the troubleshooting diagnostic by selecting the checkbox next to your corresponding gateway. You also need to select or create a storage account to store the diagnostic information.

After selecting the checkbox for `NetworkWatcherVPN`, you can start the troubleshooting process by clicking `Start troubleshooting` in the top menu, as shown in the following screenshot:

Figure 20.29: VPN troubleshoot – Start troubleshooting

5. This will start the troubleshooting process, and you should see a failure, since the S2S tunnel has not been established yet:

Figure 20.30: VPN troubleshoot – a failure message

6. Configure the `NetworkWatcher1` VM to establish the VPN tunnel, as you did in *Chapter 19, Integrating On-Premises Networks with Azure*. Start by adding the **Microsoft KM-TEST Loopback Adapter**, and then configure the VPN as you did before, changing the starting IP address to `192.168.1.10` and the end IP address to `192.168.1.50`. Set up the Azure VPN range as follows:

7. `Destination: 40.0.0.0`
8. `Network Mask: 255.255.0.0`
9. `Metric: 100`
10. Establish the connection and rerun the troubleshooting exercise, as you did in *Step 5*. This time, you should notice a `Healthy` status message.

Figure 20.31: VPN troubleshoot – a Healthy status

11. Should you find yourself having an issue with your VPN in the future, you can also click on the `Action` tab in the `Details` section to see the recommendations:

Status	Action
	Resetting the VPN gateway
	If you are having problems with the VPN gateway, try resetting the VPN gateway. Learn more.
	Contact support
	If you are experiencing problems you believe are caused by Azure, contact support.

Figure 20.32: VPN troubleshoot – Action

You have learned how to troubleshoot a VPN connection and have seen what a healthy connection will look like in the tool. These are helpful skills when you need to figure out why you have a connection problem and how to resolve any connectivity-related issues on your VPN connection. Your VPN connection is typically used to connect on-premises work environments to Azure, so a broken connection will likely result in disrupted service delivery. You may well find yourself in a position to remediate this for your organization, and you are now equipped with the knowledge and experience of how to do so; you will also be tested on this knowledge in the exam. Bear in mind that you can also manage external networking using Azure Network Watcher, which we will explore in the next section.

Troubleshooting External Networking

Azure Network Watcher offers three features for monitoring and troubleshooting external networking. The features are IP flow verify, effective security rules, and connection troubleshoot, all three of which are covered in the next sections.

IP Flow Verify

With IP flow verify, you can detect whether a package is allowed or denied to or from the network interface of a VM. Included in this information are the protocol, the local and remote IP addresses, the direction, and the local and remote ports. When a packet is denied, the name of the routing rule that denies the packet is returned. You can use this to diagnose connectivity issues between the on-premises environment and the internet. You can basically choose any source or IP address to verify the connectivity.

To run the IP flow verify tool, you must enable an instance of Network Watcher in the region where you plan to run the tool. This is the same as the demonstration covered in the *Enabling Network Watcher* section earlier in this chapter, where you enabled Network Watcher for a particular region.

Using IP Flow Verify

In this exercise, you are going to use IP flow verify to test the connection between the two VMs that you created earlier in the chapter. Perform the following steps:

1. Navigate to the Network Watcher resource in Azure.
2. From the left menu, under the `Network diagnostic tools` context, select `IP flow verify`.
3. On the `Settings` page, add the following settings:
   - `Virtual machine:` `NetworkWatcher1`
   - `Network interface:` `NetworkWatcher1`
   - `Protocol:` `TCP`
   - `Direction:` `Outbound`
   - `Local IP address:` This is filled in automatically
   - `Local port:` `60000`
   - `Remote IP address:` `13.107.21.200` (a Bing server IP address)
   - `Remote port:` `80`
4. Click `Verify IP flow` and note the successful result. The request is executed, and the result it will return is that access is allowed because of the `AllowInternetOutBound` security rule, as shown in the following screenshot:

```
Results

✓ Access allowed


Security Rule

AllowInternetOutBound
```

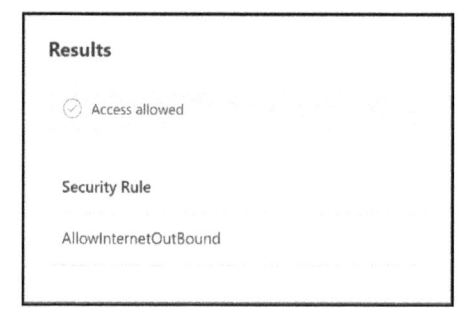

Figure 20.33: The IP flow verify test

5. Repeat the actions up to *Step 3* again, and this time, make the following changes:
   - `Direction:` `Inbound`
6. This will result in the following, which is denied because of the `DenyAllInBound` rule:

```
                    Results

                    ⊗ Access denied


                    Security Rule

                    DenyAllInBound
```

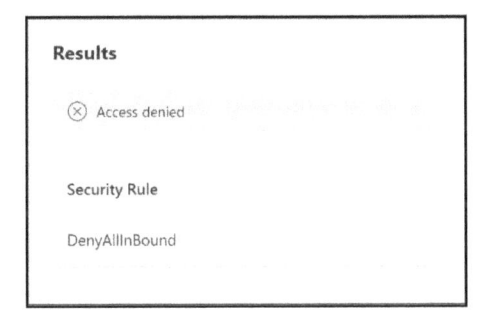

Figure 20.34: The IP flow verify Access denied message

You have learned how to use IP flow verify to test the connection between two VMs, both inbound and outbound. Next, you will learn about the effective security rules tool.

Effective Security Rules

The effective security rules feature displays all the security rules that are applied to the network interface and the subnet where the network interface is allocated. It then aggregates both. This will give you a complete overview of all the rules that are applied to a network interface, and it will enable you to change, add, or remove rules. You need to select the right subscription, the resource group, and the VM to get an overview of the applied security rules, as shown in the following screenshot:

NetworkWatcherSecurityGroup

Inbound rules

Name	Priority	Source	Source Ports
NetworkWatcherSecurityGroup...	1000	0.0.0.0/0,0.0.0.0/0	0-65535
AllowVnetInBound	65000	Virtual network (2 prefixes)	0-65535
AllowAzureLoadBalancerInBound	65001	Azure load balancer (2 prefixes)	0-65535
DenyAllInBound	65500	0.0.0.0/0,0.0.0.0/0	0-65535

Outbound rules

Name	Priority	Source	Source Ports
AllowVnetOutBound	65000	Virtual network (2 prefixes)	0-65535
AllowInternetOutBound	65001	0.0.0.0/0,0.0.0.0/0	0-65535
DenyAllOutBound	65500	0.0.0.0/0,0.0.0.0/0	0-65535

Figure 20.35: Network Watcher – effective security rules

You have now seen an overview of the security rules that are applied to the network interface. In the next section, you are going to learn about the connection troubleshoot tool.

Connection Troubleshoot

The Azure Network Watcher connection troubleshoot tool enables you to troubleshoot network performance and connectivity issues in Azure. It provides visualization of the hop-by-hop path from source to destination, identifying issues that can potentially impact your network performance and connectivity. Azure Network Watcher connection troubleshoot provides the following features and insights:

- A graphical topology view from your source to your destination
- It checks the connectivity between the source (VM) and the destination (VM, URI, FQDN, or IP) address
- It offers hop-by-hop latency
- It can identify configuration issues that impact reachability
- It provides all possible hop-by-hop paths from the source to the destination
- It checks latency (such as minimum, maximum, and average latency) between the source and the destination
- The number of packets dropped during the connection troubleshooting check

> **Note**
>
> Connection troubleshoot requires that the source VM has the `AzureNetworkWatcherExtension` VM extension installed. To install the extension on a Windows VM, you can refer to `https://learn.microsoft.com/en-us/azure/virtual-machines/extensions/network-watcher-windows`, and for a Linux VM, you can refer to `https://learn.microsoft.com/en-us/azure/virtual-machines/extensions/network-watcher-linux`.

To check network connectivity using connection troubleshoot, you can take the following steps:

1. Navigate to the `Network Watcher` service.
2. Click `Connection troubleshoot` under the `Network diagnostic tools` context in the left menu.
3. Enter the following for `Source`:
   - `Source type`: Virtual machine
   - `Virtual machine`: NetworkWatcher1

4. For `Destination`, enter the following:

   - `Destination type:` Specify manually
   - `URI, FQDN, or IP address:` www.microsoft.com

5. Enter the following for `Probe settings`:

   - `Preferred IP version:` Both.
   - `Protocol:` TCP.
   - `Destination port:` 80.
   - `Source port:` 80.

6. Finally, for the diagnostic tests, leave the default configuration.

7. Click `Run diagnostics tests`. The agent will automatically be installed on the source machine when you click the `Check` button if it is not installed already.

8. Note the success message:

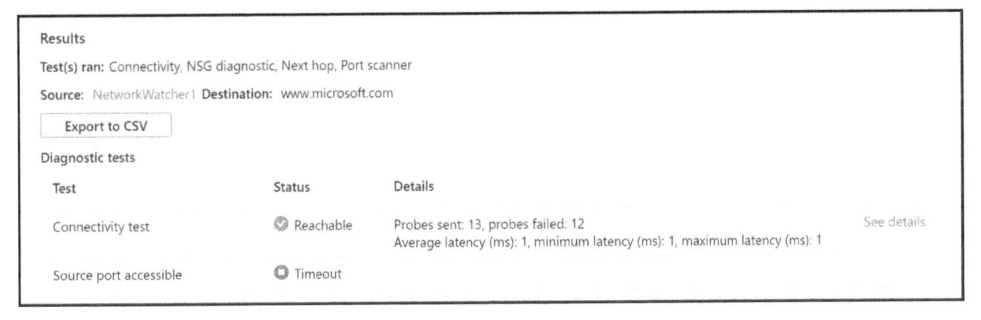

Results			
Test(s) ran: Connectivity, NSG diagnostic, Next hop, Port scanner			
Source: NetworkWatcher1 Destination: www.microsoft.com			
Export to CSV			
Diagnostic tests			
Test	Status	Details	
Connectivity test	Reachable	Probes sent: 13, probes failed: 12 Average latency (ms): 1, minimum latency (ms): 1, maximum latency (ms): 1	See details
Source port accessible	Timeout		

Figure 20.36: Connection troubleshoot – success

9. Repeat the preceding steps – this time, setting `Destination` to a VM and selecting the `NetworkWatcher2` VM. Set the `Destination port` to 22. Click `Run diagnostics tests`.

10. Note the failure message you receive. It includes several assessed components in the results, such as next hop and inbound NSG diagnostic and outbound NSG diagnostic results, and it ultimately identifies a failure in the connectivity test. You can explore more details too, such as in the outbound NSG diagnostic section and the connectivity test, which will show you some ascertained findings specific to the conducted test.

The failure was to be expected, since you hadn't opened port 22 as a service on the Windows box, as this port is typically related to the SSH service and is the default on Linux but not Windows:

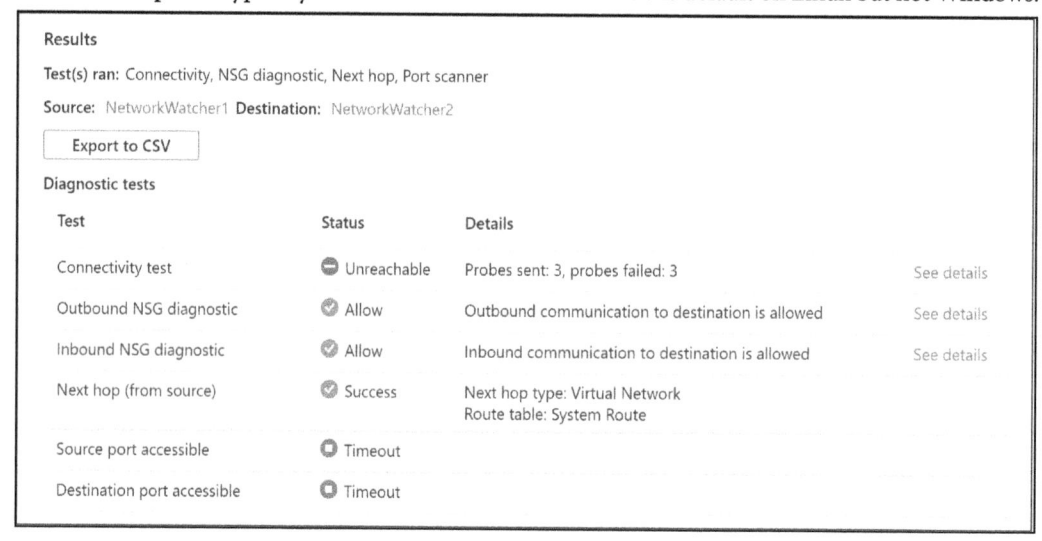

Test	Status	Details	
Connectivity test	Unreachable	Probes sent: 3, probes failed: 3	See details
Outbound NSG diagnostic	Allow	Outbound communication to destination is allowed	See details
Inbound NSG diagnostic	Allow	Inbound communication to destination is allowed	See details
Next hop (from source)	Success	Next hop type: Virtual Network Route table: System Route	
Source port accessible	Timeout		
Destination port accessible	Timeout		

Results
Test(s) ran: Connectivity, NSG diagnostic, Next hop, Port scanner
Source: NetworkWatcher1 Destination: NetworkWatcher2
Export to CSV
Diagnostic tests

Figure 20.37: Connection troubleshoot – an error message

You have now learned how to check an outbound connection from a VM using connection troubleshoot and seen both a success and failure message from the system.

> **Hands-on activities**
>
> Reinforce what you learned in *Chapters 16* through *20* by completing the hands-on activities for these chapters. Open the online practice resources using this link: `https://packt.link/az104dash`.

Summary

In this chapter, you studied the fifth part of the **Configuring and Managing Virtual Networking** objective by covering how to monitor and troubleshoot your network traffic in Azure Network Watcher. You also learned how to monitor and troubleshoot on-premises and external network connectivity using Network Watcher. You should now be able to implement network infrastructure components within Azure and monitor and manage those services. You should be comfortable in distinguishing between the assorted services available in Azure, as well as in identifying which tools you should use to troubleshoot issues on your networks using Network Watcher.

> **Note**
>
> Remember to delete the resources you created in this chapter to minimize costs. For convenience, you can do this with the following commands that will remove the resource group and all the corresponding resources: `Remove-AzResourceGroup -Name AZ104-NetworkWatcher`

21
Monitoring Resources with Azure Monitor

In the previous chapter, you explored monitoring and troubleshooting network connectivity. In this chapter, you are going to focus on how you can monitor the rest of your Azure estate. You will explore the Azure Monitor service and learn about the various functionalities that the service contains, such as metrics, alerts, Log Analytics, and Application Insights. You will also gain hands-on experience in working with several of the components of Monitor and become more confident in troubleshooting and monitoring your applications.

The chapter will start with a description of each of the services contained within Azure Monitor, which is a very comprehensive offering on the Azure platform. Following this, you will get an opportunity to work through some examples of using the various aspects of the service that you are most likely to encounter in your daily role and that will likely be present in the exam.

In this chapter, you are going to learn about the following main topics:

- Understanding Azure Monitor
- Working with Metrics and Alerts
- Querying Log Analytics
- Monitoring with Workbooks
- Configuring Application Insights

Technical Requirements

This chapter requires you to have the following tools for the examples:

- Access to an Azure subscription with owner or contributor privileges. If you do not have access to one, students can enroll for a free account: https://azure.microsoft.com/en-us/free/.
- **PowerShell 5.1** or later installed on a Windows PC or PowerShell Core 6.x on other operating systems, to practice the labs.

- For Windows users, you will need to install **.NET Framework 4.7.2 or later**.
- Where PowerShell is not installed or available, `https://shell.azure.com` can be used as a browser-based shell.
- Installation of the `Az` PowerShell module, which can be performed by running the following in an administrative PowerShell session:

    ```
    Set-ExecutionPolicy -ExecutionPolicy RemoteSigned -Scope
    CurrentUser
    Install-Module -Name Az -Scope CurrentUser -Repository PSGallery
    -Force
    ```

Understanding Azure Monitor

Azure Monitor provides comprehensive and centralized logging, monitoring, and analysis services within Azure. It can be used for both your cloud and on-premises resources and acts as your central hub for monitoring within the Azure portal. The service creates insights that help you to analyze the health, performance, and overall effectiveness of your infrastructure, as well as assist you with troubleshooting issues (such as potential issues impacting your applications and any dependent resources).

Metrics versus Logs

The data collected by Azure Monitor falls into two main categories – metrics and logs:

- **Metrics**: Numerical values that represent a system's state at a specific point in time and are great for near real-time monitoring.
- **Logs**: Records of events, traces, and performance data. Logs can be combined from different sources for in-depth analysis and consumption.

The data in Azure Monitor is stored in a common data platform that enables analysis and visualization of data and the ability to act on the identified data.

What Data Azure Monitor Collects

Azure Monitor supports data collection from a variety of Azure resources, offering the ability to collect the data relevant to your requirements, such as application monitoring data or guest OS monitoring data, which collect performance data such as CPU utilization and memory usage. Some of the metrics and logs that Azure Monitor provides are as follows:

- **Application monitoring data**: Collects data regarding your applications' and code's functionality and performance and is platform-agnostic
- **Guest OS monitoring data**: Provides insights into the OS and operates in both cloud and on-premises environments

- **Azure resource monitoring data**: Gives you in-depth information on how your Azure services are performing
- **Azure subscription monitoring data**: Tracks the health and management of your subscription, plus data about Azure itself
- **Azure tenant monitoring data**: Focuses on data on tenant-level activities and services, such as Microsoft Entra ID

The various data sources, collection mechanisms, data platforms for storing data, and services that consume the collected data are depicted in the following diagram:

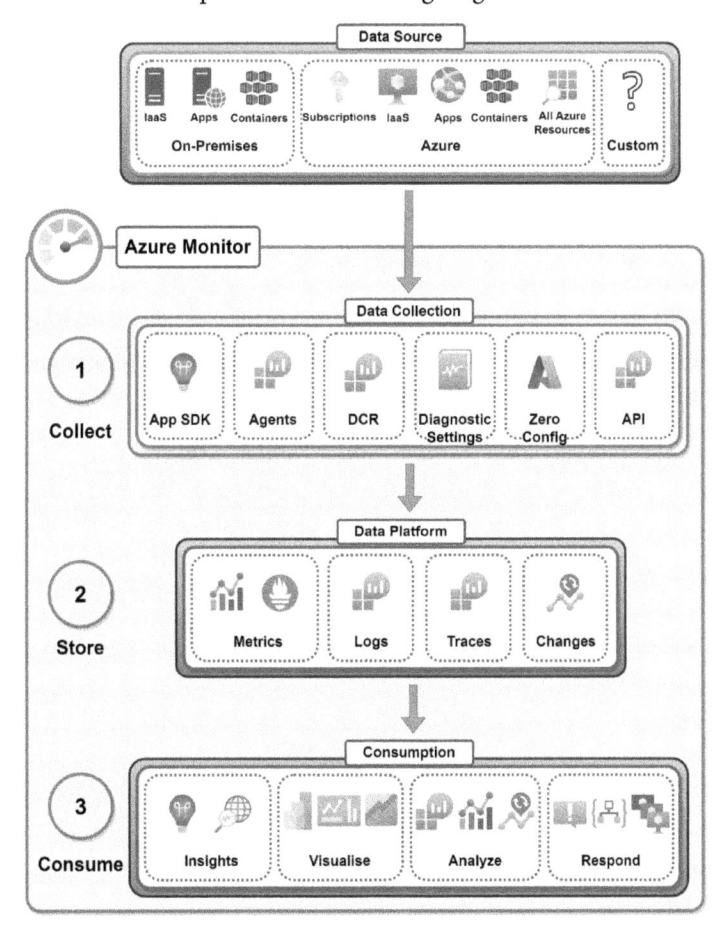

Figure 21.1: Azure Monitor

As you can see from the previous diagram, there are multiple facets to be aware of within Azure Monitor since it is a layered and comprehensive monitoring solution. You need to be aware of the data you are looking to collect (which is the data source), the tool that will be used to collect the data (such as the app **software development kit** (**SDK**) or agents), the platform where you can store the data for consumption later (which is referred to as the data platform), and finally, how you intend on consuming the data (such as through automated alerts, remediation activities, and visualizations such as dashboards).

You will also notice that each layer contains a variety of options from which you can choose, which makes the service more versatile. The value you derive from the system is based on your monitoring and management requirements, and Azure Monitor should be able to cater to nearly all of them.

As you have learned, Azure Monitor's function is not limited to data collection but also becomes the central platform for the following:

- Gaining **insights** into your applications and resources
- Being able to **visualize** your environment and how it is performing
- Being able to **analyze** your data and environments
- Creating a mechanism to **respond** and act against identified issues and triggers
- Allowing **automation** of your environment and creating an integration point between other tools and services that are not limited to Azure

In the coming sections, you will learn about the phases of data within Azure Monitor, starting with data sources. You will then move systematically through the stages of data management that are within the platform, namely, data collection, data platform, and consumption of the data. After learning about these concepts, you will then move on to practical exercises utilizing the various functions that the service offers at a high level to give you first-hand exposure to and experience with the service.

The next section will explore the various data sources from which you can collect data.

Data Sources

Data sources refer to the places you intend to collect your data from and are the prerequisite to Azure Monitor activity. These can be sources within Azure, such as the following:

- Applications and workloads
- Resources within Azure
- OS data
- Subscription and tenant data
- You can also collect data from sources outside of Azure, such as the following:

- Apps and workloads on-premises or in other cloud platforms
- OS data
- Custom source data (this can be across any service)
- This is best summarized in the following table, which shows the sources supported:

Service	Azure	On-Premises	Other Clouds
IaaS Workloads	✓	✓	✓
Operating System	✓	✓	✓
Applications	✓	✓	✓
Containers	✓	✓	✓
Azure Resources	✓		
Azure Subscriptions	✓		
Azure Tenant	✓		
Custom Sources	✓	✓	✓

Table 21.1: Supported Azure Monitor data sources

- In the preceding table, you will notice that the Azure platform has the best support and that data from any platform can also be consumed by the service. The mechanism for collection will change depending on the source of the data and its nature; the first step is understanding that this is possible.

Data Collection

Azure Monitor provides several options for collecting data from your Azure resources, applications, and on-premises environments. This flexibility is essential to accommodate diverse monitoring requirements. For instance, you might need to collect detailed performance metrics from **virtual machines** (**VMs**), while for application logs, a simpler agent-based approach might suffice.

This section will cover the different data collection methods available in Azure Monitor, starting with the following diagram, which illustrates the core data flow within Azure Monitor:

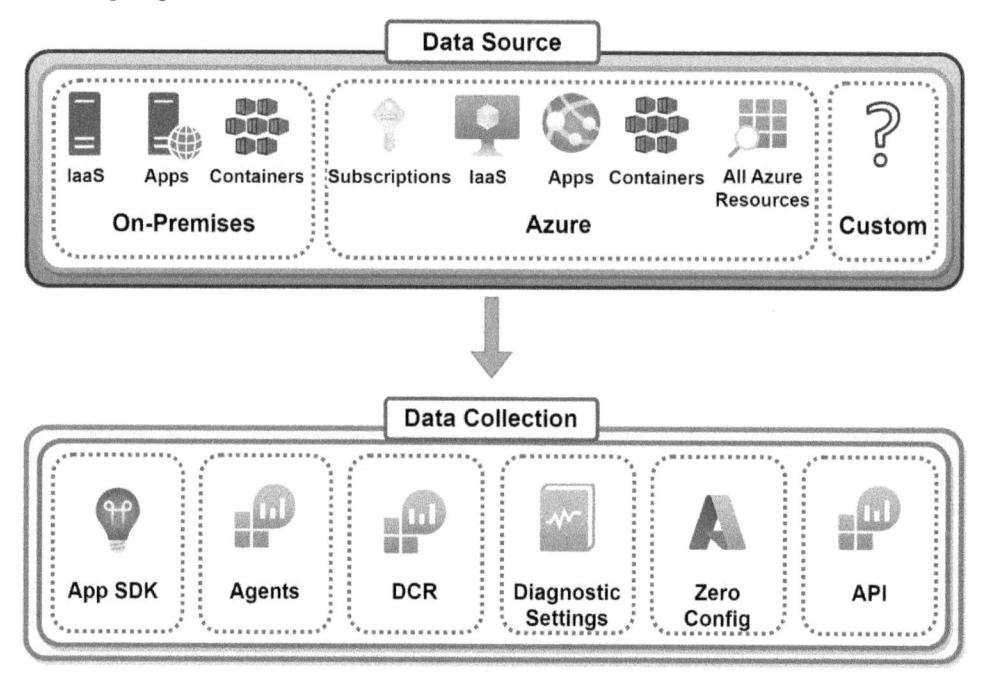

Figure 21.2: Azure Monitor – data source and collection

After reviewing *Figure 21.2*, you will understand the flow of data from the data source to the collection service, and you will better understand the relationship between them. You will explore the various collection services and tools available in this section, starting with the application instrumentation with the SDK for integration with Application Insights.

Application Instrumentation with the SDK

An SDK is a collection of software tools, libraries, and documentation that assists developers in building applications and services specific to a particular platform, such as Azure Application Insights. Each SDK is tailored to a specific programming language, and using it often aligns with development best practices.

When instrumenting applications for Azure Monitor, there are two mechanisms for ingesting data:

- **Auto-instrumentation**: This method utilizes an agent that is installed directly on the Azure resource when selecting a resource for instrumentation
- **Application Insights**: The second method involves manually embedding the Application Insights instrumentation directly into your application code for integration into Application Insights

Azure Monitor Agent

The Azure Monitor agent acts as your monitoring helper for VMs and containers. It's a small piece of software that lives on your VM and gathers essential performance and log data, sending everything back to Azure Monitor for analysis. Some benefits of using the agent include the following:

- **Centralized collection**: Gather data from your OS, various applications, and other sources into one unified platform, Azure Monitor
- **Cross-platform**: Works on both Windows and Linux machines
- **Easy-going**: Designed for simple deployment and management

Data Collection Rules

Data collection rules (**DCRs**) specify the rules by which data should be collected. They define the specific data types to be collected (including logs, performance counters, and custom sources) and the destination storage service (Log Analytics workspaces or Azure Storage accounts) for this data. Finally, any required filtering or transformations to be applied are also configured through DCRs. The crux of DCRs is that they serve as the configuration point in determining how the data at the source should be refined and collected into the destination storage within Azure.

Automatic Data Collection (Zero Configuration)

Azure Monitor automatically collects certain Azure platform metrics with zero config (without requiring manual configuration), capturing this data as metric telemetry. Metric telemetry in Azure Monitor refers to the collection and analysis of numerical data points that represent the performance and health of your application and resources. Some of the types of metrics collected are compute metrics (such as data on CPU usage, disk read and write operations, and data received and sent over the network), storage metrics (such as data on capacity, transactions, and latency), database metrics (such as data on DTU consumption, query performance, and connections), network metrics (such as data transfer details, packet loss, and latency), and application metrics (such as request rates, response times, and error rates).

Azure Diagnostic Settings

Azure diagnostic settings provide a mechanism for collecting data from your Azure resources and sending it to different destinations. The type of data that can be collected ranges from auditing data, such as platform logs, metrics, and analytical data, to troubleshooting information. You can also configure diagnostic settings for each specific resource type, such as VMs or storage accounts.

There are several types of data that can be collected through diagnostic settings:

- **Activity logs**: These are insights into the operations related to resources within your account and are based on subscription-level events. Typically, data related to creation, update, or deletion operations are collected for Azure Resource Manager operational data and Service Health events.
- **Resource logs**: These are resource-level operational events that are collected and specific to each resource type. They are also referred to as **diagnostic logs** and can vary widely by service. Examples include the following:
- **VM**: Performance counters, event logs, crash dumps, and so on
- **App services**: HTTP logs, error logs, diagnostic logs, and so on
- **SQL databases**: Audit logs, query performance insights, and so on
- **Network security group**: Information about network security group events and rule counters
- **Metrics**: Metrics describe an aspect of a system at a particular point in time and are displayed as numerical values such as CPU percentage utilization or available memory. These are logged as time-interval sets of data.
- **Audit logs**: These are a subset of the resource logs that are collected and are specific to each resource with an interpretation of the required minimal set of data for auditing a resource. This may not align with your requirements.
- **Guest OS diagnostics**: If enabled, you can collect metrics and logs from the OS of a VM. This includes performance metrics, application logs, system logs, and so on.

Azure diagnostic settings have four different types of destinations for storage of your collected data to select from as of the time of writing:

- Azure Monitor Logs
- Event Hubs
- Azure Storage
- Azure Monitor Partner solutions
- For specific resources, Azure provides a schema for the logs that can be collected, which defines the structure of the data you can expect in each type of log. This can be very useful for understanding the data you're working with and for setting up proper monitoring and alerting based on that data.

> **Note**
> It is important to note that not all Azure services support all diagnostic settings, and the available logs may vary from one service to another. You should always refer to Microsoft's documentation on supported services.

Azure Monitor REST API

The Azure Monitor REST API provides a programmatic method of interacting with Azure Monitor and uploading data to the service. This is typically used for customized data relating to the application being monitored. The use of the API is encouraged where automation can be adopted.

Data Collection Best Practices

When collecting data in Azure Monitor, it is important to follow best practices to ensure that your data is accurate, complete, and easily accessible.

Some of the best practices you should follow are as follows:

- Use consistent naming conventions for your data sources and logs
- Ensure that your data is properly formatted and structured
- Regularly review and update your data collection configurations

Data Platform

Azure Monitor's data platform serves as the bedrock for its comprehensive monitoring capabilities. It functions as a secure and scalable data store, ingesting various forms of telemetry data generated by your Azure resources and potentially on-premises environments. This data encompasses metrics, logs, and traces, offering a complete picture of your system's health. The platform leverages this stored data to fuel the **consumption** services within Azure Monitor. These consumption services then unlock functionalities such as data analysis, visualization, generation of insights, and automated responses to events. By providing a robust data storage foundation, the platform paves the way for powerful monitoring capabilities within Azure Monitor.

The following figure illustrates the data platform services available to Azure Monitor:

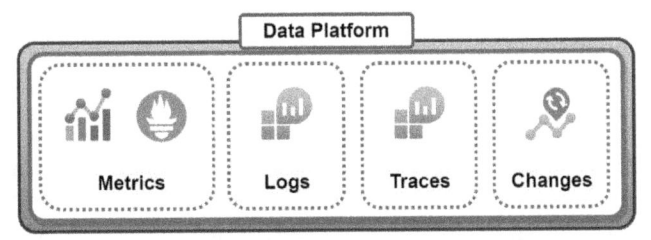

Figure 21.3: Azure Monitor – data platform

As you can see in the preceding figure, there are several data platform services available. You will explore each of these services in more detail as follows, understanding what data each is designed to hold so that you know which platform to choose to support your requirements.

Metrics

Metrics are time-series data that represent the behavior and performance of Azure resources. They provide numerical values for various parameters, such as CPU usage, memory usage, latency, and throughput, to help you understand resource utilization and health.

Metrics can support near-real-time scenarios with some data, including **CPU** and **memory** performance data over time, **disk throughput**, **input/output operations per second** (**IOPS**), and **network performance**.

Metrics collected in Azure Monitor can be defined as platform-native collected data and Prometheus (third-party service) collected data. The metrics can be best viewed and split as follows:

- **Native Azure metrics**:
- **Platform metrics**: These metrics are automatically collected from Azure resources directly and carry zero costs.
- **Log-based metrics**: These metrics are collected through Azure resource logs for deeper insights into resource behavior.
- **Custom metrics**: These metrics are defined and collected through the Azure Monitor service through the various data collection utilities, such as Azure Monitor agents and the REST API. Customized metrics not covered by Azure Monitor are collected through this mechanism.
- **Prometheus metrics**: In addition to the preceding, Azure Monitor integrates with Prometheus, a popular open source monitoring system, to collect from Kubernetes environments such as **Azure Kubernetes Service** (**AKS**). These Prometheus metrics can then be visualized and analyzed using tools such as Grafana, another popular open source tool for analytics and monitoring.
- As part of the service, Azure Monitor also provides a Metrics Explorer tool for visualizing and analyzing metrics, and it allows you to create alerts based on metric thresholds for proactively monitoring your resources. The retention period for metric data depends on the Azure Monitor pricing tier you choose.

Log Analytics

Azure Log Analytics is a service that collects telemetry data from various Azure, on-premises, edge, and even other cloud resources. The service allows you to collect, store, and analyze log data from a variety of sources, including custom applications. The data that is collected is then stored in a Log Analytics workspace for consumption through the **Kusto Query Language** (**KQL**). KQL is a flexible query language that enables you to create custom queries to filter, aggregate, and transform log data. With this powerful query language, you can consume the data in a variety of ways, including through queries that resemble SQL-like query responses, with the ability to create visualizations. The views of the data that you create through the service can also be saved as dashboards for use later or even exported into other systems for further analysis and reporting. Beyond the power of reporting and troubleshooting within the service, it provides a lot of power to you as an administrator to extend into alerts and automation. By integrating into other Azure services, such as Azure Monitor and Azure Sentinel, you can enhance your overall monitoring and security capabilities.

Traces

Traces are detailed diagnostic logs in the Application Insights service that capture the flow of execution within your application. They record each step of how your application handles requests or operations. Each trace corresponds to a specific unit of work, such as a web request or function call, and includes information such as operation name, ID, timestamps, and individual events.

Traces are invaluable for troubleshooting and debugging, helping you find issues in your code, such as performance bottlenecks, errors, and exceptions. You can also view performance information relating to your application and areas where you can optimize for improvement. Additionally, distributed tracing enables you to track requests as they flow across multiple components.

Traces are collected through your Application Insights SDK with the automatic option to collect data directly from Azure services or through instrumentation into your code.

Changes

Azure Change Analysis is a feature of Azure Monitor that captures information regarding any modifications that happen to your Azure resources and applications and stores this in Azure Graph. This service can assist you in detecting any changes to configurations, properties, and states of your resources. Some of the changes tracked are creation, deletion, update, and configuration changes. All these tracked changes can assist you in troubleshooting the root cause behind issues you may encounter in Azure.

Change Analysis offers several benefits, including the following:

- Increased visibility of changes and their effects on your environments
- Reduced time to repair issues by identifying the root cause more quickly
- The ability to consume and analyze change data in more meaningful ways to gain deeper insights into your environment

There are several limitations to the service that you should be aware of, such as, at the time of writing, only Windows is supported on VMs, and only limited resources are currently supported through the service. In the next section, you will explore the next layer of Azure Monitor, which is the consumption layer. This is where you choose how to use your collected data and what to do with it, such as creating dashboards.

Consumption

The consumption layer of Azure Monitor encompasses the tools and mechanisms for accessing and utilizing the collected monitoring data.

These capabilities are organized into four main pillars:

- **Insights**: Contains tools for identifying patterns and trends in your data
- **Visualize**: Dashboards and charts for visual representation of data

- **Analysis**: Querying and manipulating data for deeper insights
- **Response**: Automated actions or alerts against triggers in your data
- This is depicted in the following diagram:

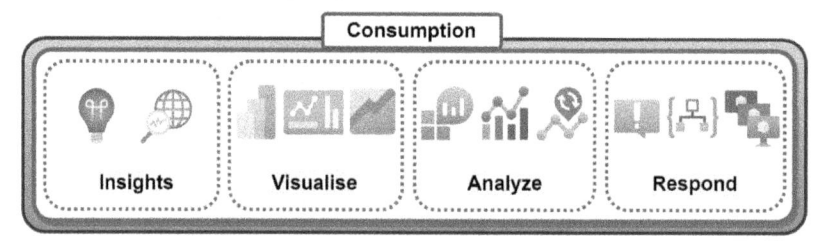

Figure 21.4: Azure Monitor – consumption tools

- As you can see, there are many options available to you for the consumption of your monitored data and a variety of ways you can transform the data into more meaningful applications, such as creating specialized dashboards and automated responses. Each of the consumption pillars is broken down into more detail in the following section.

Insights

Monitor creates a view of relevant monitoring details specific to your resources and uses intelligence to extract value from collected data, such as performance, health, and availability data. These views are compartmentalized into resource-specific insight views, such as Application Insights, VM insights, and Container insights. You will learn about the various insights that you can take advantage of from Azure Monitor as follows.

Application Insights

Application Insights is a telemetry tool used for monitoring and troubleshooting your applications using an instrumentation package (SDK). Your applications don't have to be hosted in Azure to make use of the service, but applications hosted in Azure can more easily consume the service through the click of a button that allows the service to be automatically configured as part of your application. Data collected in Application Insights can be consumed by several other complementary services, such as alerts and **Power BI**. This allows you to build valuable actionable solutions around your application data, as well as create visibility into how your application performs and where problems can occur.

As you can see from the following diagram, you need to consider your data at multiple stages, from instrumentation to the endpoint where your data will be sent, to storage, and then, finally, the consumption layer (**Experiences**):

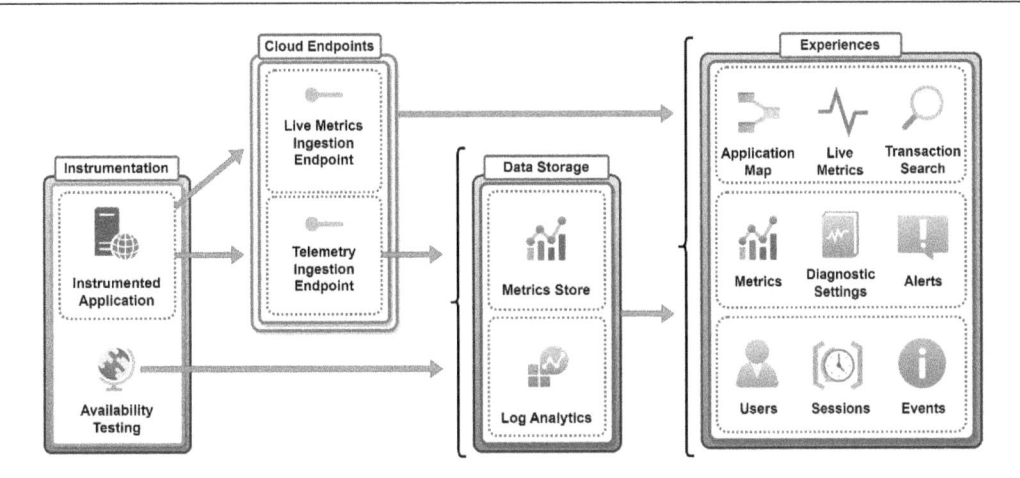

Figure 21.5: An Application Insights overview

The service also has the ability to build an application map, showing components you need to be aware of as part of your service as well as allowing you to triage failures:

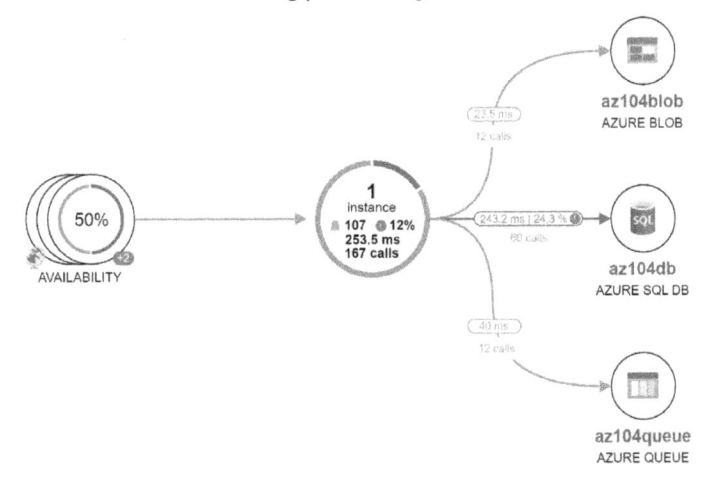

Figure 21.6: Example application map depiction

As you can see, this service can prove invaluable to you and your organization by quickly garnering insights about your applications.

> **Note**
> Azure Monitor now integrates the capabilities of Log Analytics and Application Insights into its service. You can also keep using Log Analytics and Application Insights independently.

Container Insights

This feature is designed specifically for monitoring Kubernetes clusters, whether deployed on AKS or Azure Arc-enabled Kubernetes clusters. It collects and analyzes container logs from your cluster and its components. Container insights offer pre-built dashboards and Prometheus alert rules for analyzing data and setting up notifications, along with the ability to collect and analyze metrics from your cluster.

VM Insights

VM insights provide insight data specifically around your VMs. The utility assists in creating an inventory of your existing VMs as well as initiating a baseline monitoring functionality. There are predefined workbooks that are created through this service that enable easier insights and management of your VM resources. The data is constructed using some of the previously reviewed metric data that is expressed in an easily consumable service.

Network Insights

Just as with the other insights provided through the service, network insights are tailored toward giving you quick visual and diagnostic information about your network-related resources. The insights have been designed to give you rich data about your resources to enable you to better manage your network-related resources. There are several useful tools as part of this service, such as the Topology tool, network health and metrics, connectivity monitor, alerts, traffic views, and even a diagnostic toolkit. The following figure illustrates an example network topology visualization:

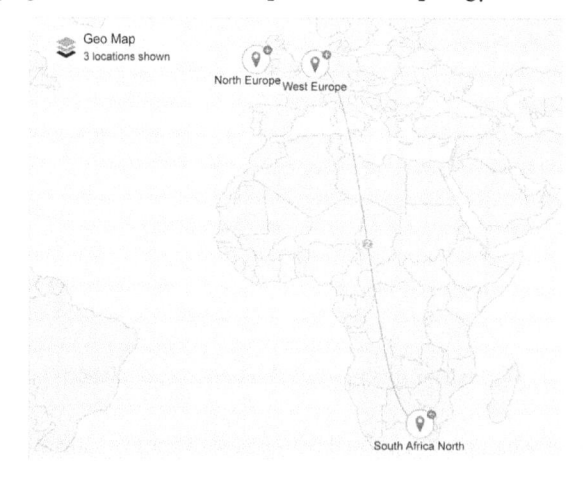

Figure 21.7: Example network topology

As you can see, there are rich insights available to you on the Azure platform. Knowing when and how to leverage the insights will be a key part of your success in your administration role. You have now learned the importance of the different phases of data management in the Azure Monitor service. Next, you will learn about the Activity Log and the functionality it delivers.

The Activity Log

The Activity Log is used to track health data and configuration changes within Azure, such as the deployment of resources to a resource group, or the modification of resources, such as adding tags. It is focused on the subscription level for monitoring.

The following screenshot shows an example view of events in the Activity Log:

Operation name	Status	Time	Time stamp	Subscription
> ⓘ Delete Storage Account	Succeeded	15 hours ago	Tue Apr 30 2024...	AzureTraining
> ⓘ List Storage Account Keys	Succeeded	15 hours ago	Tue Apr 30 2024...	AzureTraining
> ⓘ Check Backup Status for Vault	Failed	15 hours ago	Tue Apr 30 2024...	AzureTraining
> ⓘ List Storage Account Keys	Succeeded	15 hours ago	Tue Apr 30 2024...	AzureTraining
> ⓘ Delete Connection Monitor	Succeeded	5 days ago	Fri Apr 26 2024 ...	AzureTraining
> ⓘ Delete Storage Sync Services	Succeeded	a week ago	Mon Apr 22 202...	AzureTraining

Figure 21.8: The Activity Log

As you can see from the preceding figure, the Activity Log displays several types of operations performed, such as the deletion of a storage account and the listing of storage account keys. The Activity Log contains the following information: **Operation name**, **Status**, **Time**, **Time stamp**, **Subscription**, and **Event initiated by** details. Next, you will learn about alerts.

Alerts

Azure alerts are a feature in Azure Monitor that lets you know of critical events or conditions in your environment based on preconfigured trigger points. These trigger points are typically based on metrics collected from your resources and can also incorporate log data and other sources. When an alert is triggered, the associated action group defines the response, which can include email notifications, SMS messages, webhook calls, ITSM integrations, or automated actions using Azure Functions, Logic Apps, or runbooks.

Azure Monitor offers different types of alerts, including metric alerts (based on numerical thresholds), log alerts (based on search queries), and Activity Log alerts (based on Azure resource events).

Later in this chapter, you will experience creating an alert with an action group and learn more about the purpose and functionality alerts and action groups provide.

Action Groups

Action groups are used to define your notification preferences within Azure. These will be used to send emails, SMS messages, or even voice calls to alert you to something. These are consumed by a resource, such as an alert, that will initiate the notification.

These also provide the option to have an action triggered from the service, such as one of the following **action types**:

- Azure Automation runbook
- Azure Functions
- ITSM
- Logic Apps
- Secure Webhook
- Webhook

These actions make the service particularly powerful, as it can be used for environment automation, such as configuring a logic app to notify users with particular configuration details and initiating a custom script against an application that initiates a workflow. The variation of possibilities is endless and enables you to perform significantly more powerful management tasks and flows. Your focus becomes more geared toward innovating and driving new solutions as opposed to remediation activities.

Now that you have learned about action groups, you will learn about Service Health, which explores the health statistics of the Azure platform.

Service Health

Service Health displays the Azure platform service health statistics; if there are currently any issues that are affecting your resources within your tenant, they will be reflected here. You will now explore the various components of reporting under the Service Health feature in more detail, such as the views for active events, historical events, resource health, and alerts.

Active Events

The **Active Events** section under Service Health contains the list of events that are still active and relevant to your Azure platform. It contains several categories of events that you need to be aware of and monitor.

The following categories of events exist under **Active Events** on the platform:

- **Service issues**: This section notifies you of issues on the Azure platform that you need to be aware of and that may be impacting expected service delivery from the platform.
- **Planned maintenance**: This refers to platform maintenance that is planned and expected to be carried out; it will highlight the affected services as well as the planned work involved. All planned maintenance will contain dates so that your team can plan for outages and disruptions in services.
- **Health advisories**: All platform-related health advisories will appear here.

- **Security advisories**: Platform-related security advisories will show up here; note that these are not resource-related notifications but, rather, platform-related ones.

History

This service also contains Service Health history up to a maximum period of three months.

The events are sortable and filterable depending on your requirements. Events on this screen contain the following types of data: `issue name`, `tracking ID`, `event type`, `services`, `regions`, `start time`, `last update`, and `scope`. The following screenshot shows a sample of advisories that appear in Azure:

Issue name	Tracking ID	Event type	Services
Action required: Update firewall configurati...	B_ZH-HCZ	Health Advisory	Logic Apps
End of Routine Planned Maintenance for Ap...	RS62-RZG	Planned Maintenance	App Service
Post Incident Review (PIR) - Network connec...	VT60-RPZ	Service Issue	Network Infrastructure

Figure 21.9: Service Health

Clicking an entry gives some details about the issue. There are some helpful components to assist you in managing the event. For instance, you can download the details as a PDF; you can also track the issue on your mobile by scanning a QR code. The details contained on the screen offer a plethora of information, such as `Tracking ID`, `Shareable link`, `Impact service(s)`, `Impacted region(s)`, `Status`, `Health Event Type`, `Start` and `End time`, and `Last update`.

The following figure shows an example Service Health event:

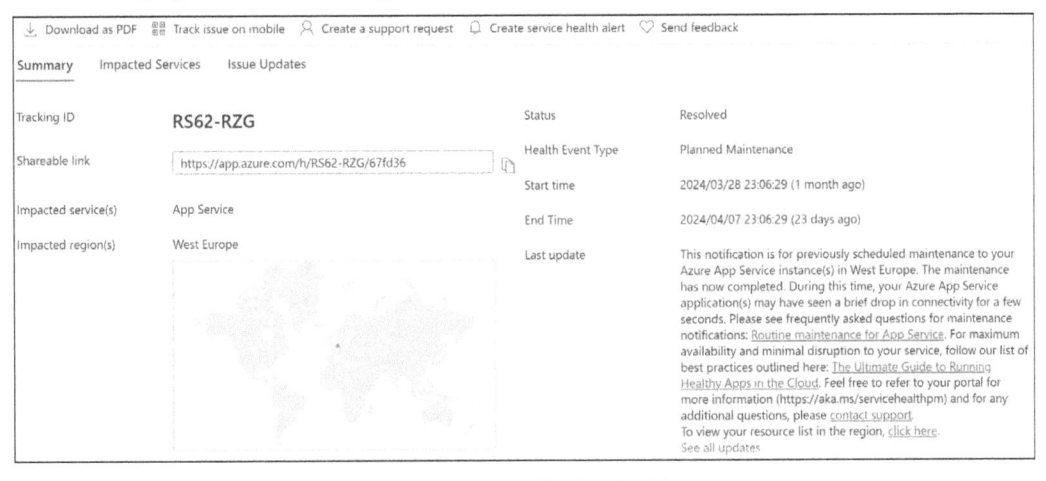

Figure 21.10: Example Service Health event

This part of the service can be a handy feature when needing to report back to the business on issues on the platform or build root cause analysis reports.

Resource Health

The `Resource Health` section enables you to view health details for your selected subscription and resource type within Azure. The following screenshot shows an example of how this may look for a storage account:

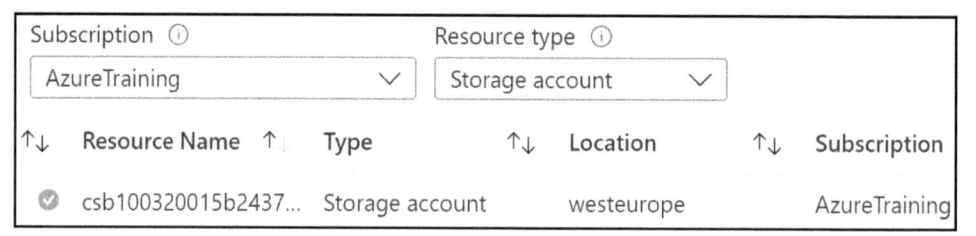

Subscription		Resource type			
AzureTraining	⌄	Storage account	⌄		
Resource Name ↑↓	Type ↑↓		Location ↑↓		Subscription
✓ csb100320015b2437...	Storage account		westeurope		AzureTraining

Figure 21.11: Example Resource Health screen

This tool is again very helpful when troubleshooting services and wanting to understand whether there are platform-level issues that you may be experiencing.

Alerts

The last section, **Alerts**, under Service Health is for any detected health events. You are alerted to any events of importance to you on the platform, which can be configured to alert you based on various criteria being fulfilled, such as the Service Health class (service issues, planned maintenance, health advisories, and security advisories), and the affected platform components (subscription, service, and region). When the conditions for configured health alerts are met, they will be displayed under the **Health Alerts** tab for review. This is a very effective mechanism for alerting you of any relevant health notifications and enabling you to more proactively manage the Azure platform.

> **Note**
>
> You are encouraged to read more on the topic of Azure Monitor as there is a lot to it.
>
> The following link contains a wealth of information that you are encouraged to explore: `https://learn.microsoft.com/en-us/azure/azure-monitor/overview`.
>
> The following link will help you in getting started with using Azure Monitor: `https://learn.microsoft.com/en-us/azure/azure-monitor/getting-started`.

Next, you will see how to create metrics and alerts within Monitor.

Working with Metrics and Alerts

There are several ways to consume and analyze alerts and metrics across Azure Monitor. You can do this directly from the Monitor service as well as from the associated resource blade. In the upcoming exercises, you will set up a VM, then configure a metric view with two charts, analyze them, and create a dashboard. You will also configure an alert rule to fire off an email when CPU usage percentage has been observed to exceed 80% usage over 5 minutes. Finally, you will synthetically push your VM to trigger the alert to experience the completed flow and prove a successful configuration.

The following diagram illustrates the full exercise you will embark on:

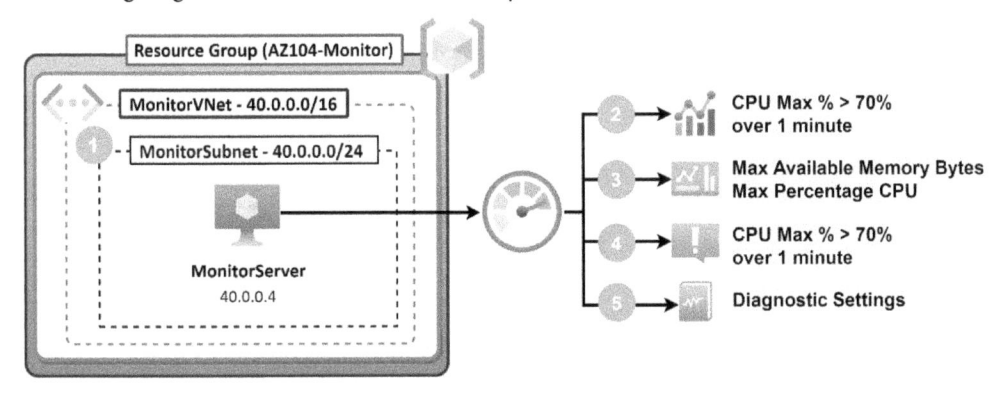

Figure 21.12: Analyzing metrics exercise diagram

In order to follow along, complete the steps in the following sections.

Creating a VM

For this part of the exercise, you will be deploying a new VM to monitor against. Run the script labeled as `Analyzing_Metrics_Exercise.ps1` from the following GitHub repository: https://packt.link/zDNCB.

Now that your VM is deployed, you can proceed to configure a metric monitor.

Viewing a Metric

To display the metrics for the various Azure resources, you will create a view in Azure Monitor. Perform the following steps to create a view of CPU usage:

1. In the top search bar for Azure, type `Monitor` and click `Monitor` from the options that appear:

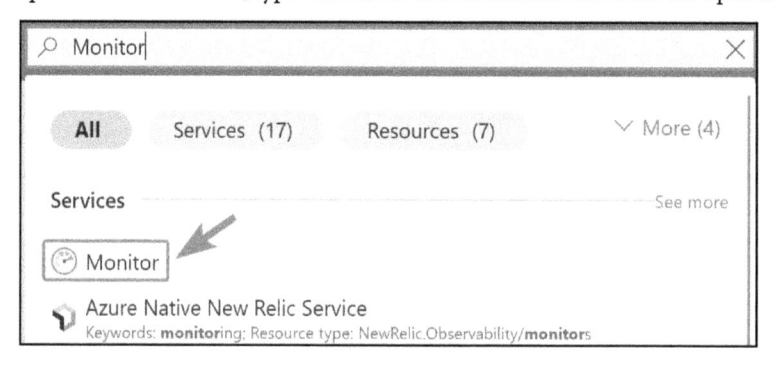

Figure 21.13: Searching for Monitor

2. You will be presented with the `Overview` screen. There are several components categorized in accordance with the function they serve, that is, `Insights` and `Detection, triage, and diagnosis`.

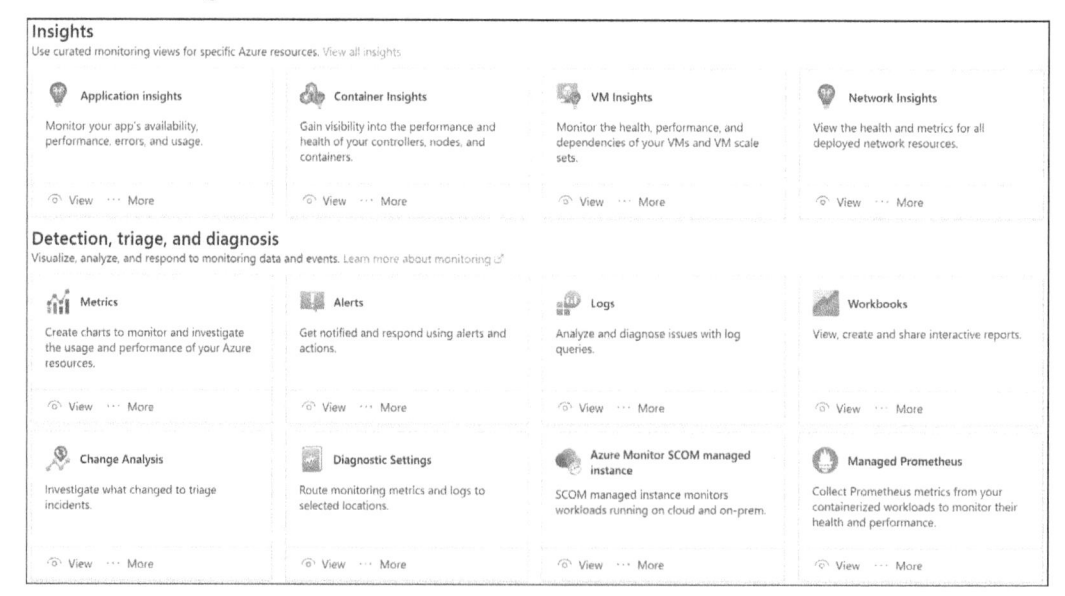

Figure 21.14: Monitor – Overview

3. First, you are going to look at metrics. Click Metrics on the left-hand menu or click View on the Metrics card from the Overview blade.

4. You will be prompted to select a scope; select your Subscription, Resource types, and Location preferences from the filter bar. Then, expand the scope results screen below until you see your server, click the checkbox next to the VM, and click Apply at the bottom of the screen. The details to fill in will be as follows:

   - Subscription: Select your Azure subscription
   - Resource Group: AZ104-Monitor
   - Resource types: Virtual machines
   - Locations: West Europe

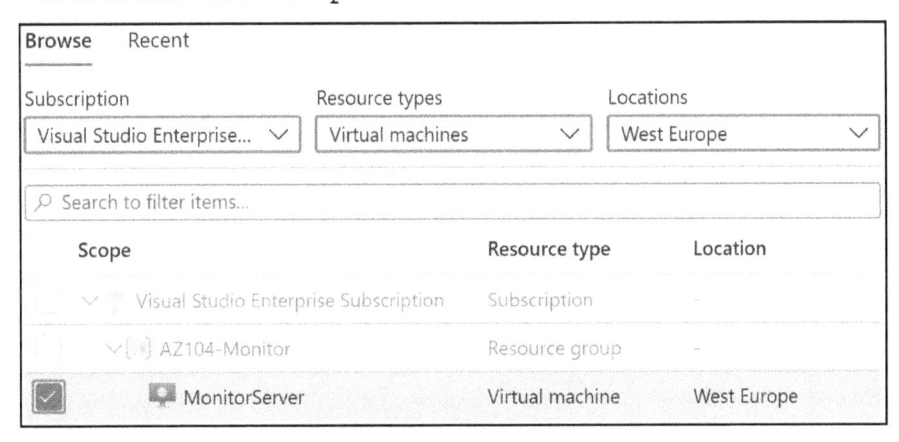

Figure 21.15: Metrics scope

5. On the Scope bar at the top of the screen, select Percentage CPU from the Metric dropdown and Max from the Aggregation dropdown:

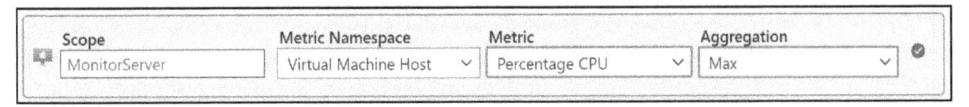

Figure 21.16: Monitor – selecting Metric and Aggregation

6. Since your VM hasn't been running for that long, you will change the time period that the chart is displaying. Click the time bar at the top right of your `Metrics` blade, select `Last hour` from the `Time range` options, and then click `Apply`:

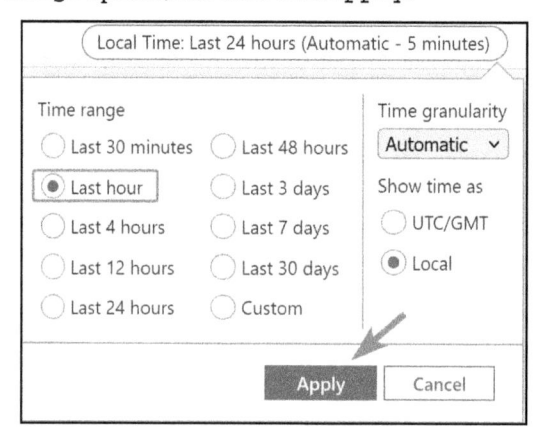

Figure 21.17: Setting the time period

7. Note how you can see your maximum CPU percentage usage over time. As a point of interest, you can load several charts to a single Monitor page, for instance, monitoring available memory bytes on your VM:

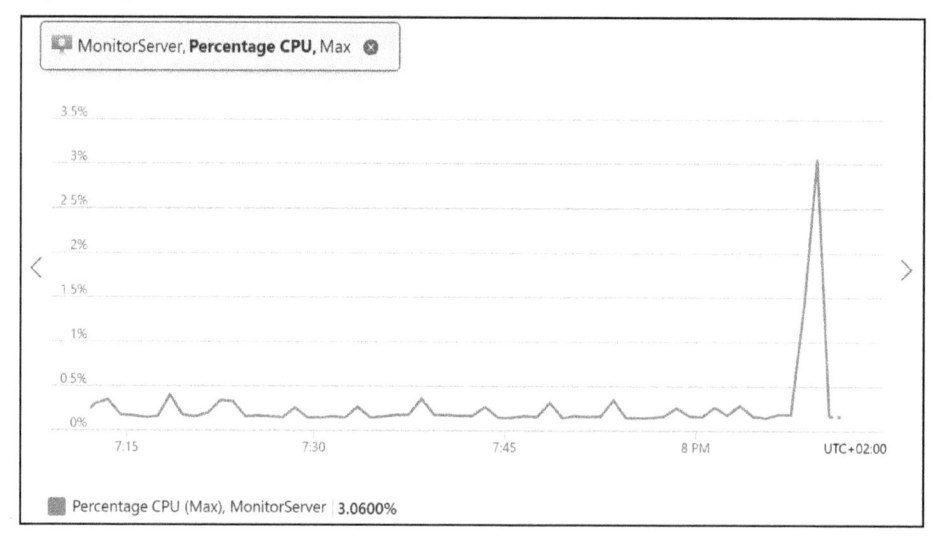

Figure 21.18: Monitor – CPU usage over time

8. Next, you will look at adding another chart; click + `New chart` at the top of the screen:

Figure 21.19: New chart

9. Set the following: Scope to MonitorServer, Metric Namespace to Virtual Machine Host, Metric to Available Memory Bytes, and finally, Aggregation to Max. Azure monitors the available memory as opposed to memory usage, which can be calculated in reverse as total memory minus available memory. This measure is more apt, as you can determine what percentage of memory is left before you trigger an alert that something is wrong on your VM, for instance:

Figure 21.20: New chart – Available Memory Bytes

10. You should have a chart similar to the following:

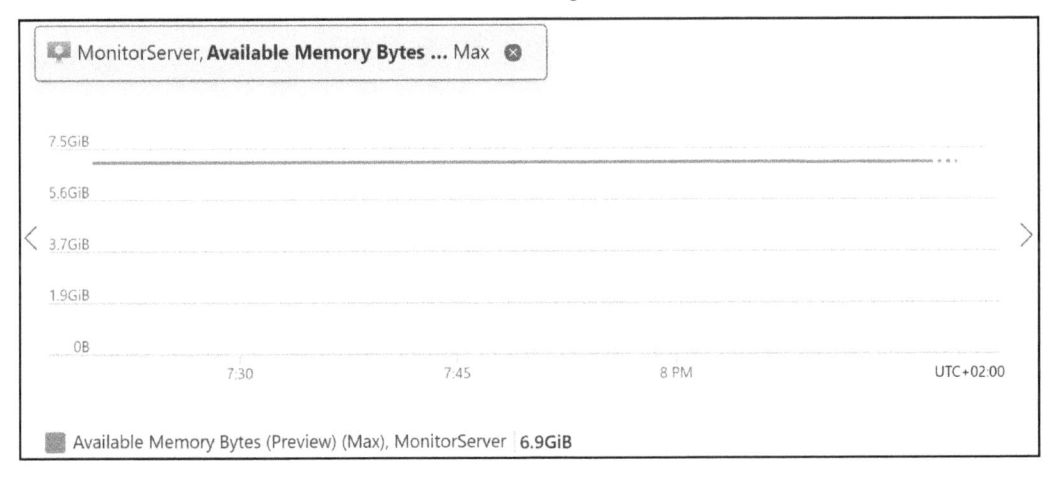

Figure 21.21: Available memory bytes over time

> **Note**
> Take some time to look at the different metrics that you can choose from. This may be a part of the exam questions.

You have now experienced working with metrics and adding them to different charts for monitoring in Azure. Next, you will create a dashboard with these charts. Keep your Metrics screen from this exercise open to continue with the next exercise.

Creating a Dashboard

Azure provides the capability of building dashboards and allows you to build some quick insights for your resources. Follow these steps to build your first dashboard:

1. Using the charts from the previous exercise, click on the `Save to dashboard` dropdown and click `Pin to dashboard`:

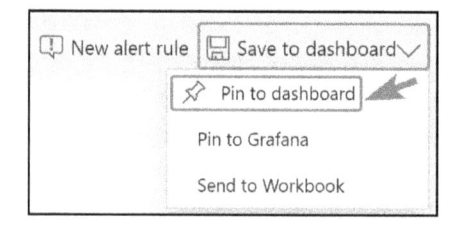

    Figure 21.22: Monitor – Pin to dashboard

2. Since you have not created a dashboard yet, you will create a new one when saving. Click `Create new`, enter the following details, and click `Create and pin`:

    - Type: `Private`
    - Dashboard name: `MyFirstDashboard`

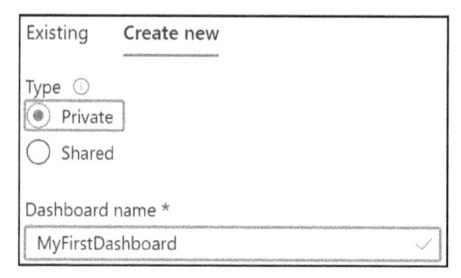

    Figure 21.23: Creating a dashboard

3. Perform the `Pin to dashboard` action on the second chart, this time selecting `Existing` and choosing your dashboard from the previous step. Then, click `Pin`:

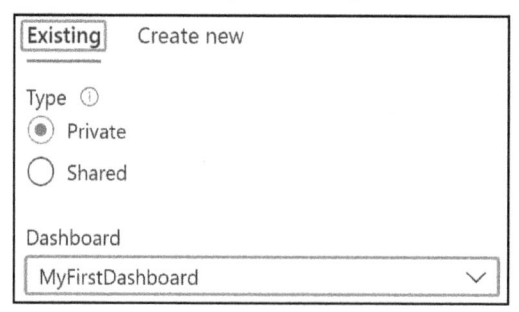

    Figure 21.24: Pinning to an existing dashboard

4. Click the hamburger menu at the top left of the Azure portal:

Figure 21.25: The hamburger menu

5. Click Dashboard from the menu:

Figure 21.26: Dashboard

6. Click the dropdown at the top of the screen to select your dashboard, and select the one you created in the previous steps:

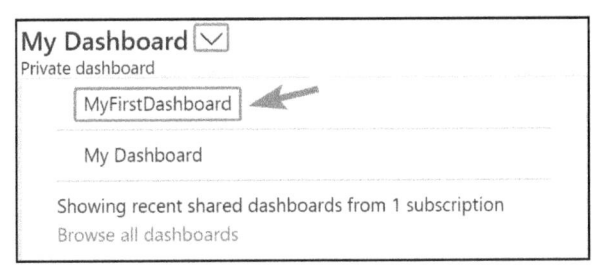

Figure 21.27: Selecting your dashboard

7. Click Edit at the top of the screen to modify your dashboard view:

Figure 21.28: Dashboard – Edit

8. Drag the two charts to be next to each other; each of these is called a tile. Note that you can attach several tiles to the dashboard. Once you are happy with the dashboard design, click `Save`:

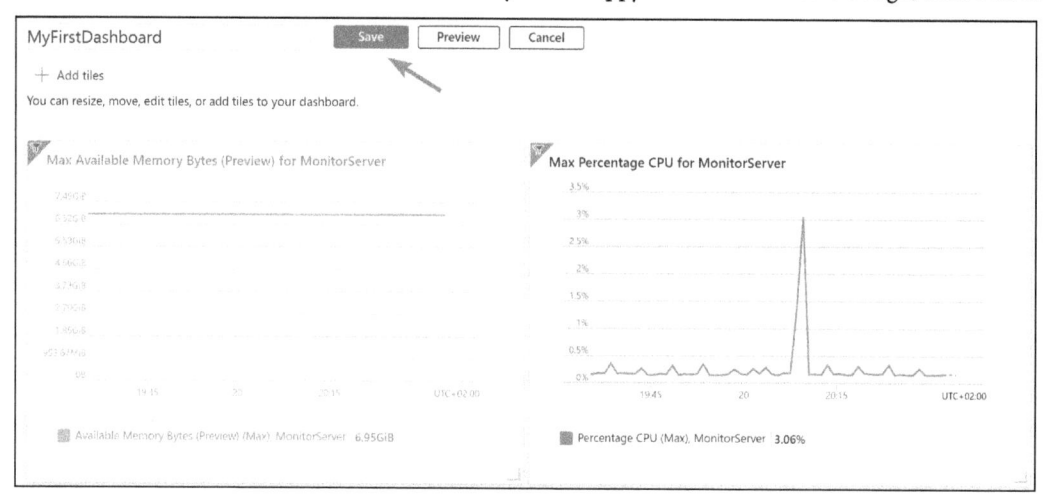

Figure 21.29: Customizing your dashboard

> **Note**
> Metrics are also available directly from the Azure resource blades. So, for instance, if you have a VM, go to the VM resource by selecting it. Then, from the left-hand menu, under `Monitoring`, you can select `Metrics`.

You now have your first dashboard set up and configured and have a convenient way to dive into the relevant insights that you need across a resource or several resources and metrics. In the next section, you are going to look at how to set up and analyze alerts in Azure Monitor.

Creating an Alert

You will create an alert in this exercise to notify you when your CPU usage exceeds 70%. To create the alert rule, perform the following steps:

1. Navigate to the `Monitor` service blade.
2. From the left-hand menu, select `Alerts`.
3. Click `+ Create` and then click `Alert rule`:

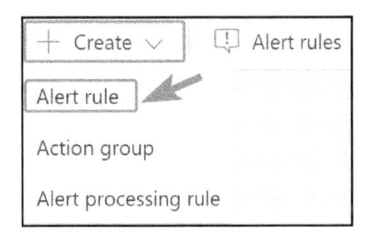

Figure 21.30: Creating an alert rule

4. You will be prompted to select a resource on the right of the screen. Select the subscription where your VM from the previous exercises resides and select `Virtual machines` from the `Filter by Resource type` dropdown. Select your `MonitorServer` VM from the list and then click `Apply` at the bottom of the screen:

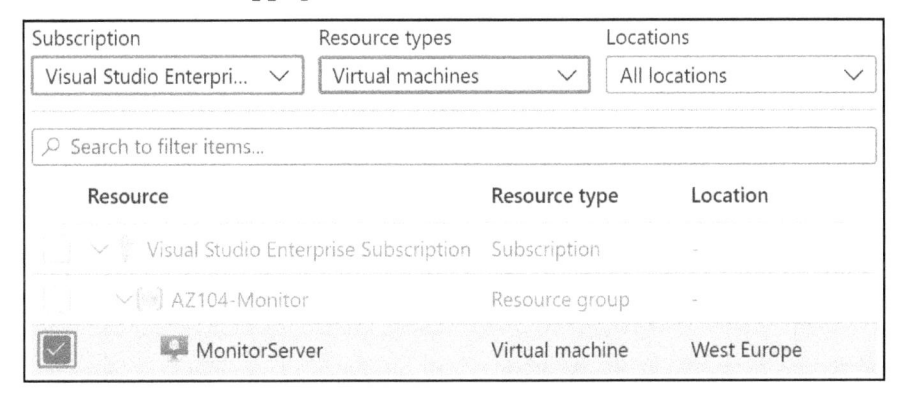

Figure 21.31: Selecting a resource for the alert rule

5. Click `Next: Condition >`.

6. You will now configure the condition that will trigger the alert. On the right-hand side, you will be prompted to configure a signal, which is what alerts you to a condition being met and is the precursor to triggering the alert. Click the dropdown and select `Percentage CPU` from the options.

7. Configure the `Alert logic` section as follows and click `Done`:

    - `Threshold`: Static
    - `Aggregation type`: Average
    - `Operator`: Greater than

- Threshold value: 80

Figure 21.32: Alert logic

8. Then, configure the When to evaluate section as follows:

   - Check every: 1 minute
   - Loopback period: 5 minutes

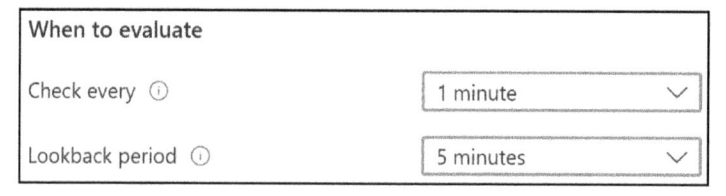

Figure 21.33: When to evaluate

9. Your condition has been configured to assess your CPU usage percentage when it exceeds 70% over a period of 1 minute. The Check every option will run the evaluation check to the frequency you configure, and Loopback period assesses the period past to the interval before the current time, for example, from five minutes ago to now. Notice the Preview metric window at the bottom of the page. This shows you what the metric you are assessing looked like over the past six hours. Click Next: Actions >.

10. To receive an alert, you will need to have an action group configured, of which you currently have none. Choose Use quick actions from the Select actions list.

11. Configure the following settings on the right screen and click Save:

    - Action group name: emailme
    - Display name: emailme

- `Actions: Email` – enter your email address here

Figure 21.34: Action group quick actions

12. Note that you can configure several types of actions, such as firing off a logic app or function; this can be really powerful, especially where you need to adopt an automated remediation strategy.
13. Click `Next : Details >`.
14. For `Alert rule details`, enter the following, then click `Review + create`:
    - `Severity: 3 - Informational`
    - `Alert rule name: highcpu`

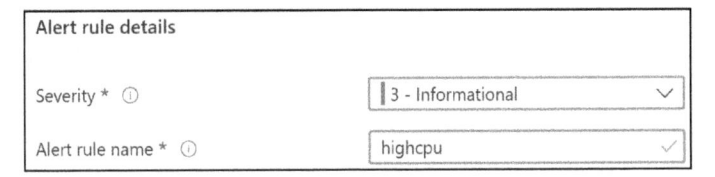

Figure 21.35: Alert rule details

15. Click `Create`.

You have now created an alert and an action group that will alert you via email when the CPU goes over 70% over a period of 5 minutes and is checked every minute. In the next section, you are going to configure diagnostic settings on resources.

Configuring Diagnostic Settings on Resources

For this exercise, you will create a storage account resource and configure diagnostic settings for your VM to link to the storage account.

Perform the following steps to enable diagnostic settings on your VM:

1. Run the following PowerShell command to create a storage account for diagnostic settings. Note that if the storage account name is not available, you can adjust it as necessary as this must be globally unique:

   ```
   # Parameters
   $ResourceGroup = "AZ104-Monitor"
   $Location = "WestEurope"
   $StorageAccountName = "monitorserverdiagnostics"

   New-AzStorageAccount -ResourceGroupName $ResourceGroup -Location $Location -Name $StorageAccountName -SkuName Standard_LRS
   ```

2. Navigate to the VM you created previously in the Azure portal.
3. Ensure that the VM is in a running state, then from the left-hand menu, click `Diagnostic settings` under the `Monitoring` context.
4. The `Diagnostic settings` blade will open up. You will need to select a storage account where the metrics can be stored. Select the one you just created.
5. Click on the `Enable guest-level monitoring` button to update the diagnostic settings for the VM.
6. When the settings are updated, you can navigate through the tabs to view the various configuration settings.
7. Next, navigate to `Metrics` in the `Monitoring` section for your VM on the left menu.
8. Change the metric namespace to `Guest (classic)` and note that you have new metrics available under the `Metric` dropdown after enabling diagnostic logging. You can analyze them in the same way that you did earlier in this chapter, as you can see in the following screenshot:

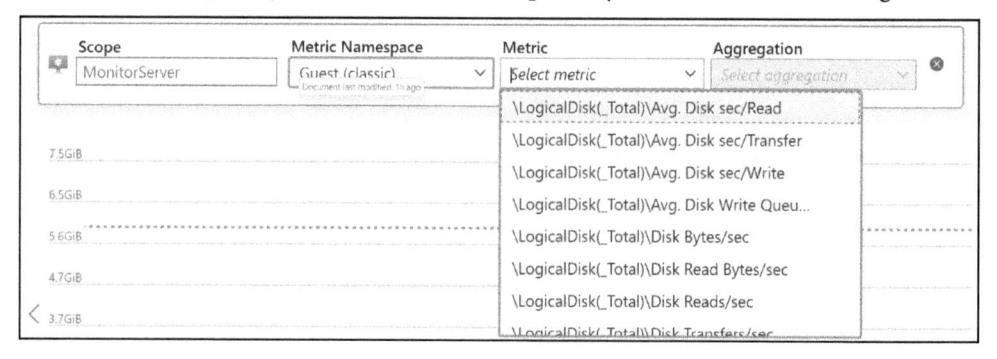

Figure 21.36: Guest metrics

Now that you have configured diagnostic settings, it is time to move on to the last part of this exercise. You will trigger the alert you made earlier for your VM to see how it works.

Triggering an Alert

In this exercise, you will explore a method to push the CPU usage up high enough on your VM to trigger the alert you configured previously:

1. Log on to your Monitor VM using `Remote Desktop Protocol (RDP)`.
2. You will need to disable `IE Enhanced Security Configuration`. From the Server Manager window, you can click `Local Server` on the left-hand menu.
3. Click `On` next to `IE Enhanced Security Configuration`. Change all the settings to `Off` and click OK.

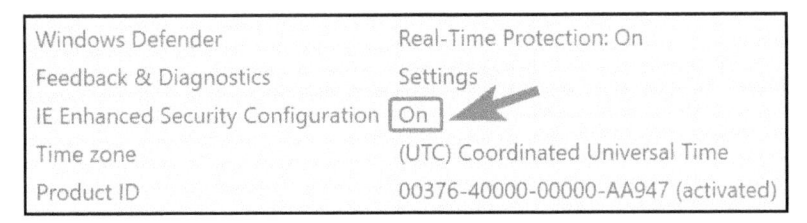

Figure 21.37: IE Enhanced Security Configuration

4. Open your web browser and download Cinebench using the following URL: `https://geeks3d.com/dl/get/10211`.
5. Navigate to the Downloads folder once the download is complete. Right-click the `CinebenchR23.zip` file and click `Extract All…`.

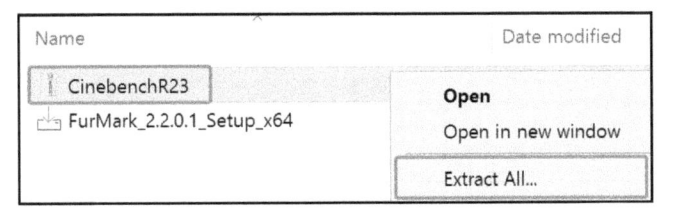

Figure 21.38: Extracting CinebenchR23

6. Click `Extract` on the screen that follows.
7. Launch Cinebench by double-clicking the `Cinebench` application file.
8. Accept the software license agreement.

9. At the top of the screen, click Start:

Figure 21.39: Starting the benchmark

10. The benchmark will start running and stressing the CPU.
11. If you open Task Manager, note that the CPU is now sitting at 100%:

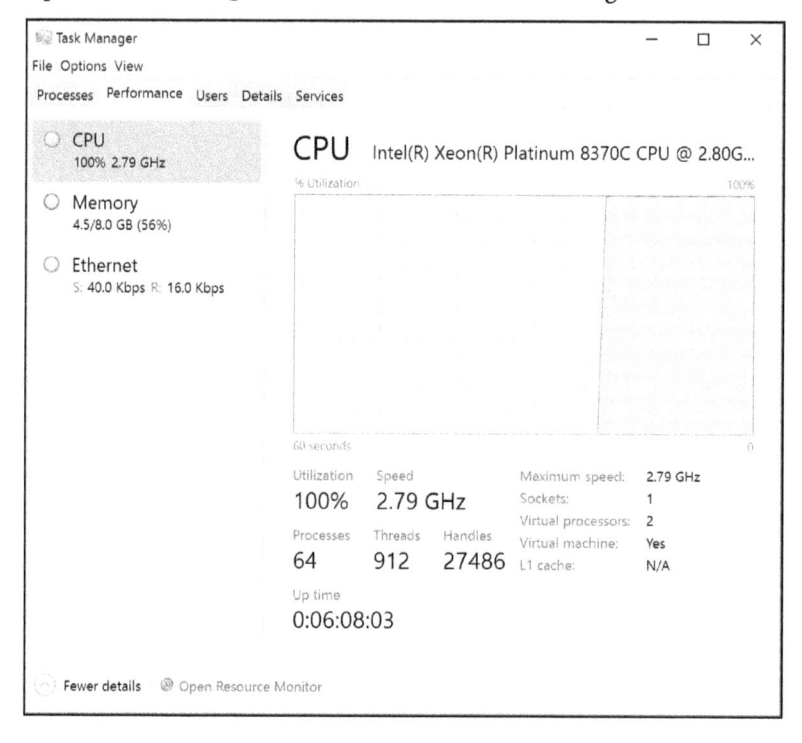

Figure 21.40: Task Manager

12. You will need to leave this running for a few minutes for Azure Monitor to register the detected CPU usage changes.
13. Navigate to the dashboard you created earlier, set the time interval to Past 30 minutes, and note that the CPU is showing as near 100% on the graph:

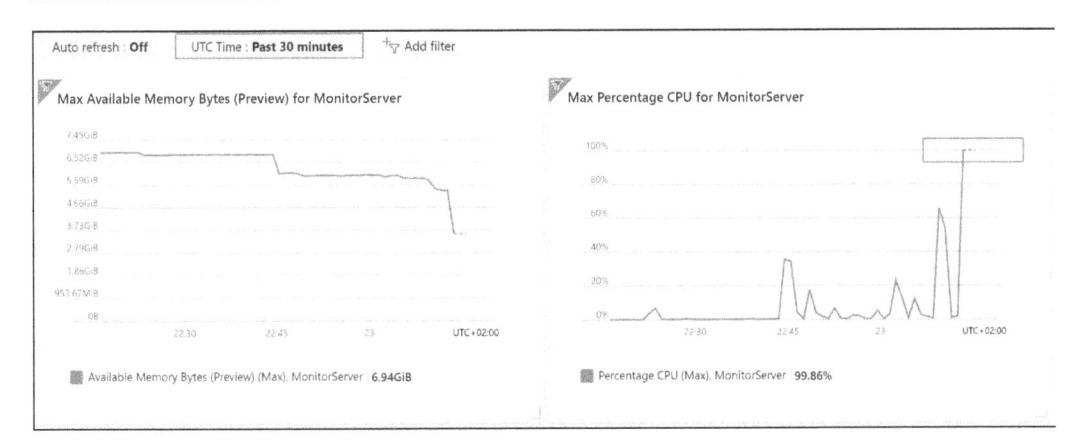

Figure 21.41: Dashboard showing high CPU usage

14. Check your email after 5 to 10 minutes. An alert should now be present to notify you of the detected issue.
15. You can also navigate to the Monitor service on Azure and click `Alerts` on the left menu. The blade that is presented should show an alert named `highcpu`.

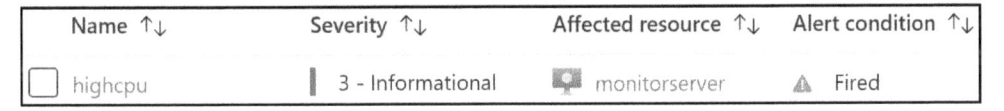

Name ↑↓	Severity ↑↓	Affected resource ↑↓	Alert condition ↑↓
highcpu	3 - Informational	monitorserver	Fired

Figure 21.42: highcpu alert

You have successfully created some metric monitors in this section, explored how to add them to a dashboard, created an alert to be triggered should a metric anomaly be detected, and finally, explored what happens when an alert is triggered. You should now feel comfortable configuring metrics in Azure Monitor.

In the next section, you will learn how to query the Log Analytics service.

Querying Log Analytics

It can be useful to explore your logs in Log Analytics. Being able to query Log Analytics requires an understanding of KQL. You will learn some basic queries in this exercise to understand how the system works. To get started, you will need a Log Analytics workspace, which you will create next.

Creating a Log Analytics Workspace

Before you can display, monitor, and query logs from Azure Monitor, you need to create a Log Analytics workspace for storing your logging data. To create a workspace, perform the following steps:

1. Navigate to the Azure portal by clicking on `https://portal.azure.com`.
2. Navigate to your `AZ104-Monitor` resource group.
3. Click `+ Create` to create a new resource.
4. Type `log analytics` in the search box and click the `Log Analytics Workspace` card when it shows.
5. Click `Create`.

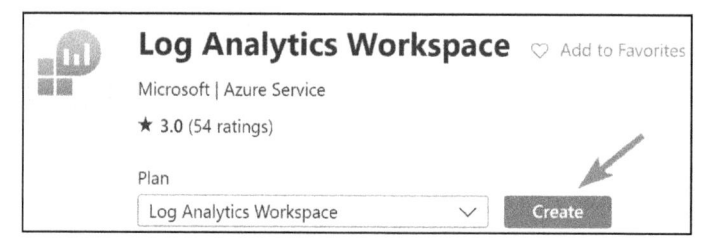

Figure 21.43: Log Analytics Workspace

6. Enter the following values on the `Basics` tab:

- `Subscription`: Select your Azure subscription
- `Resource group`: `AZ104-Monitor`
- `Name`: `az104loganalytics`
- `Region`: `West Europe` (or select what you prefer)

7. Click `Review + create` and then `Create`.

Now that you have created a Log Analytics workspace, you can use it inside Azure Monitor to create some queries to retrieve data. You will do this in the next section.

Utilizing Log Search Query Functions

Azure Monitor has the features and capabilities that Log Analytics offers integrated into the service. Using KQL, you can analyze your data in meaningful ways and extract the information relevant to you. In order to retrieve information, you will need to run a query regardless of whether this will be used for alerts or dashboards. The data can be consumed through the Azure portal, Azure Monitor API, or even an alert, as well as a few others.

The following list provides an overview of some of the different ways data can be consumed from Azure Monitor:

- **Portal**: From the Azure portal, an interactive analysis of log data can be performed. In there, you can create and edit queries and analyze the results in a variety of formats and visualizations.
- **Dashboards**: Dashboards can be used to visually represent your data results from a saved query that can be shared with others too.
- **Workbooks**: By using workbooks in Azure Monitor, you can create custom views of your data. This data is provided by queries as well.
- **Insights**: There is a wealth of information behind the various insight capabilities in Azure Monitor.
- **Alerts**: Alert rules are also made up of queries.
- **Data export**: This is where you can export data configured for a storage account or Event Grid. Using an M query, you can also export data to Excel or Power BI, also created with queries. The query defines the data to export.
- **Azure Monitor Logs API**: The API creates an interface that is easily accessible to any REST API client for retrieving data from the service. The request requires the KQL query to be included in the API call.
- **PowerShell**: You can use the `Invoke-AzOperationalInsightsQuery` command in Azure PowerShell for log data retrieval using your KQL queries. These can also be run through Azure Automation runbooks.

In the following section, you are going to create some queries to retrieve data from the logs in Azure Monitor.

Querying Logs in Azure Monitor

In this exercise, you will run a query against the insight logs relating to VM data. You will then experiment with methods of displaying your result data visually. Perform the following steps:

1. Navigate to the `Azure Monitor` service on the Azure portal. You will be directed to the `Overview` pane.
2. From the left menu, select `Logs`.
3. You may be presented with a tutorial pop-up screen, which you can close, or you can consume the content as you desiroe. All subsequent logins will present a query screen, allowing you to quickly perform common queries easily.
4. For this demo, you will use an environment Microsoft created to allow you to query data in a prepopulated system where there is likely more data than what your current environment may have.

5. Navigate to `https://portal.azure.com/#blade/Microsoft_Azure_Monitoring_Logs/DemoLogsBlade`, which is similar to your Logs query space from *Step 2*.

6. Note that the middle of the screen contains an area that you can type in – this is where you create your queries, the bottom of which is the results area where your query results and graphics will be displayed. On the left pane, note several collapsed data menus; these represent data sources that can be queried from Log Analytics:

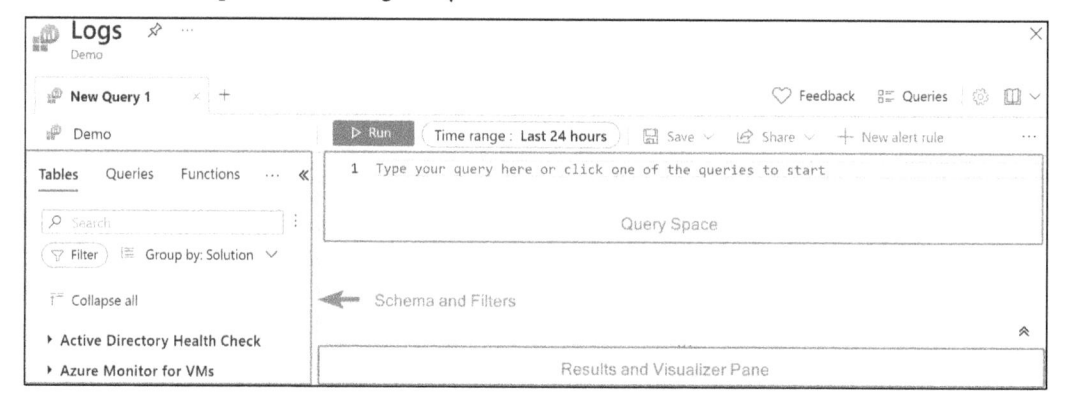

Figure 21.44: The Log Analytics query window

7. You will now select a data source to be queried. In this example, you will use `Azure Monitor for VMs`. Click on the arrow next to `Azure Monitor for VMs` to expand the collection and select `InsightsMetrics`. Hover over the heading and a pop-up window will appear. Click `Use in editor`:

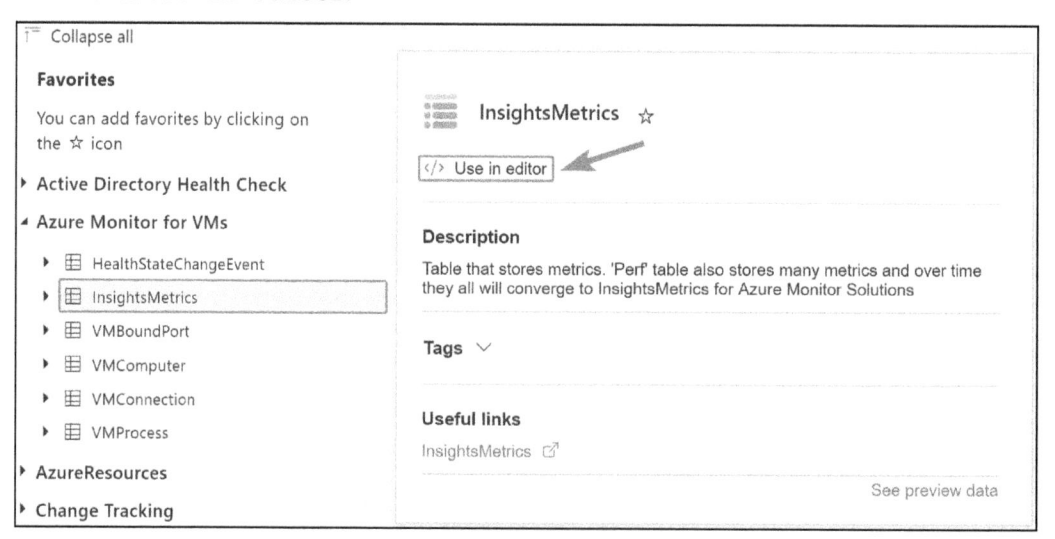

Figure 21.45: Selecting a data source

8. Note that on your query pane, it has initiated a query that is labeled as your data source collection. For future queries, you can type the data source collection as opposed to selecting as you did in the previous step.

9. Click the Run button to generate results that are stored in that table. Note that the data has headings that you can explore as you scroll through the results section. By default, the time period of the query is set to `Last 24 hours`. Some of the headings (columns) may be hidden from the `Results` view:

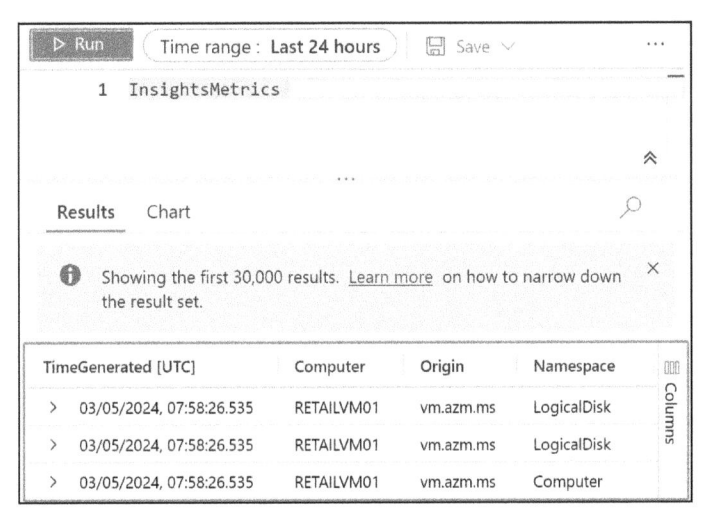

Figure 21.46: Example query

10. Open the collection source on the left pane to see the various data types associated with each row along with their heading name. Notice that each information type is denoted by a symbol representing the type of data it stores and a name giving insight into what you can expect in the data – for instance, `SourceSystem`, which is of the `string` type, meaning text, and you would expect to see the source system name contained in this variable. The information is generally returned as columns in the query results. See the following example snippet of some of the data types stored under the `InsightsMetrics` data source:

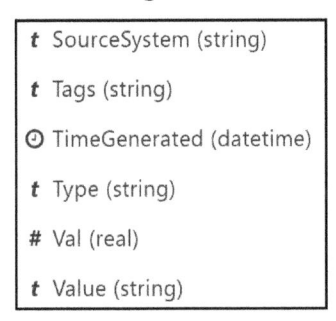

Figure 21.47: InsightsMetrics data

11. Now that you know the types of information you can find, you may want to filter your data further and start to extract some relevant information. For instance, you can return an aggregated table of the computer(s) associated with the record(s) in your table by running the following command:

    ```
    InsightsMetrics | summarize by Computer
    ```

    The result of the command will be output similar to what is displayed in the following screenshot:

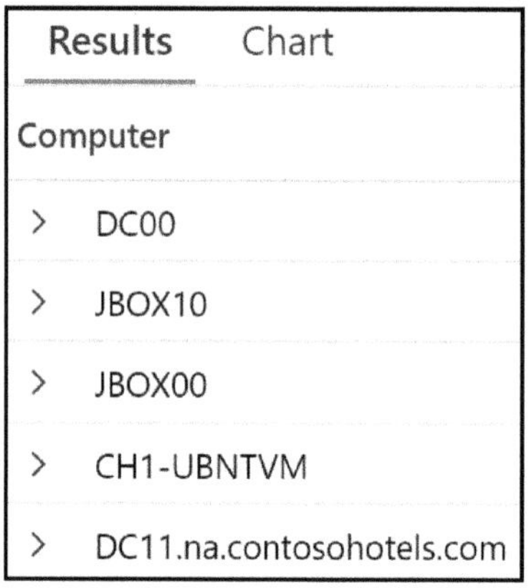

Results	Chart
Computer	
> DC00	
> JBOX10	
> JBOX00	
> CH1-UBNTVM	
> DC11.na.contosohotels.com	

    Figure 21.48: Sample query results

12. You can add a second column by modifying the query accordingly. This time, you will expect to see a computer name several times, as the unique returned value is a combination of the computer and the `TimeGenerated` column. You can read the query as "From the `InsightsMetrics` data source, summarize all the results by the computer and the time the information was generated for each piece of written information":

    ```
    InsightsMetrics | summarize by Computer, TimeGenerated
    ```

13. Next, try a different query that will show the count of each type of alert detected organized by the alert name:

    ```
    Alert | summarize count() by AlertName
    ```

    This will produce output similar to the following:

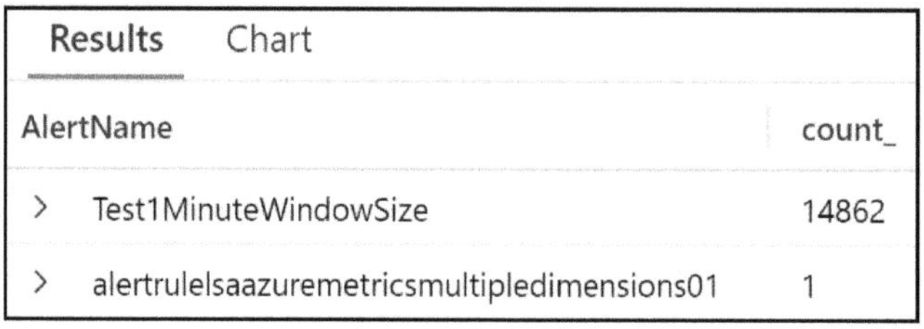

Results	Chart	
AlertName		count_
> Test1MinuteWindowSize		14862
> alertruleIsaazuremetricsmultipledimensions01		1

    Figure 21.49: Alert results query

14. Your default time range is still set to 24 hours. You can manually modify this by clicking the filter next to the Run button and choosing an appropriate time range to query for, or you can modify your query directly:

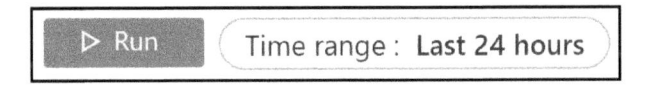

Figure 21.50: Time range filter

15. You can also modify the time in the query:

    ```
    Alert | where TimeGenerated > ago(2d) | summarize count() by
    AlertName
    ```

16. You may want to visually understand the information you are querying and choose to display this as an example as a bar chart. If the data that you want to visualize is reporting on the count of each alert type you had in a week, you can do this with the following command:

    ```
    Alert | where TimeGenerated > ago(7d) | summarize count() by
    AlertName | render barchart
    ```

    This will produce a visual output, defined as a bar chart, similar to the following:

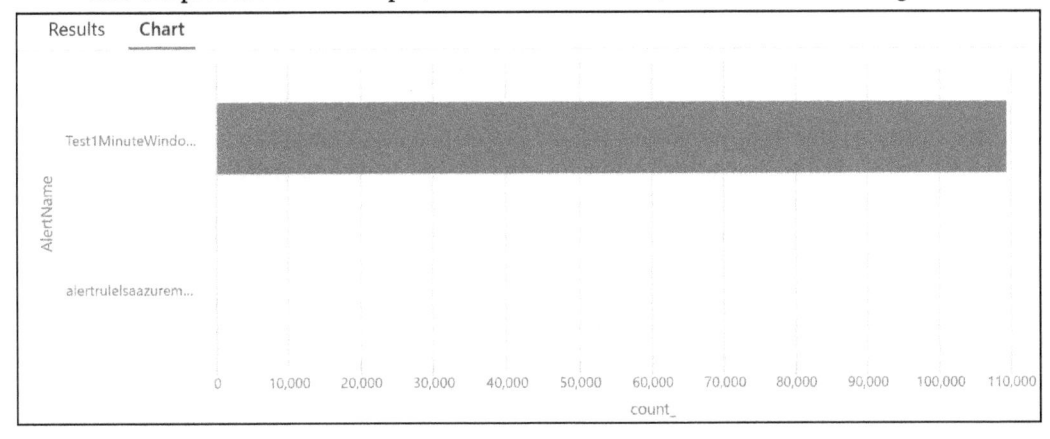

Figure 21.51: Example bar chart

There are many types of charts that you can render from your data, such as stacked bar and column charts, unstacked column and bar charts, 100% stacked column and bar charts, line charts, and scatter diagrams.

17. When you run large queries, you will likely have many lines of data that can become difficult to sift and read through, so you may want to aggregate your results into something discernable, such as grouping results into predefined periods of time. This is called aggregating into `buckets/bins`. Modify the query accordingly to see the alert data collected into one-day buckets, showing the number of alerts received per day for the last seven days:

```
Alert | where TimeGenerated > ago(7d) | summarize count() by
bin(TimeGenerated,1d) | render columnchart
```

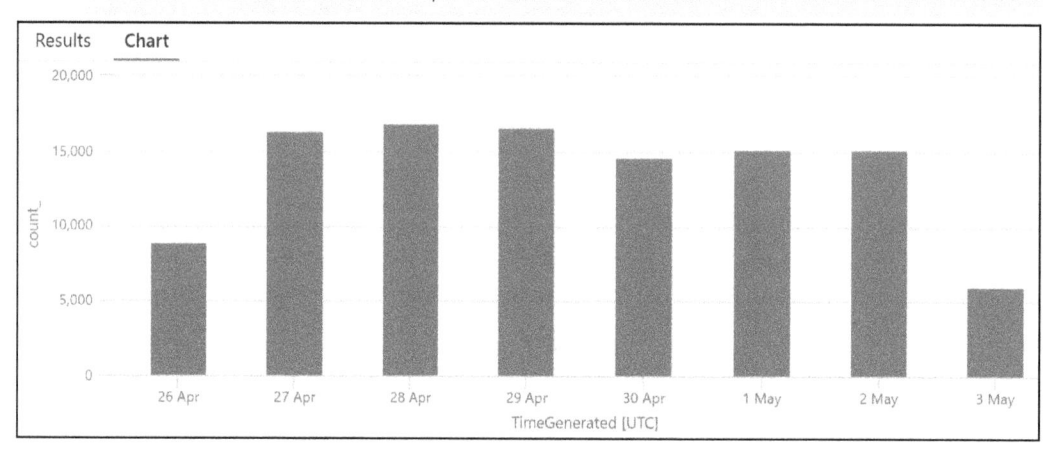

Figure 21.52: Example binning and column chart

You have just seen some basic queries that you can perform in Log Analytics and can now understand the power behind what you can achieve using these queries. Remember that the result of these queries can be visualizations, notifications, and even automated actions as a result of data. You are encouraged to practice and learn more about this resource not just for the exam but also to enhance the way you perform in your role for your organization and customers. You have now gained some valuable skills in navigating the basics of Log Analytics and should feel comfortable in explaining what a query is intended to do and predicting the outcomes of queries, as well as building your own. For some more examples, you can explore this URL: https://learn.microsoft.com/en-us/azure/data-explorer/kusto/query/tutorials/learn-common-operators.

> **Note**
>
> A detailed overview and tutorial on how to get started with KQL are beyond the scope of this book. If you want to find out more about this language, you can also refer to https://learn.microsoft.com/en-us/azure/data-explorer/kusto/query/.

Next, you will see how to work with a workbook to display some visualizations of data relating to a VM. Workbooks are a helpful tool in your daily management of resources.

Monitoring with Workbooks

Azure Monitor is great at exposing the details of your running resources and enabling you to create meaningful views of your data. One of the tools that assist with this is workbooks. In this exercise, you will create a workbook for your VM and visual CPU usage. Follow these steps to continue:

1. Navigate to your BCDRVM1 resource.
2. On the left menu pane, under the Monitoring context, click Workbooks.
3. You will notice that your VM needs to be onboarded to Azure Monitors for VM. Click the Onboard button.

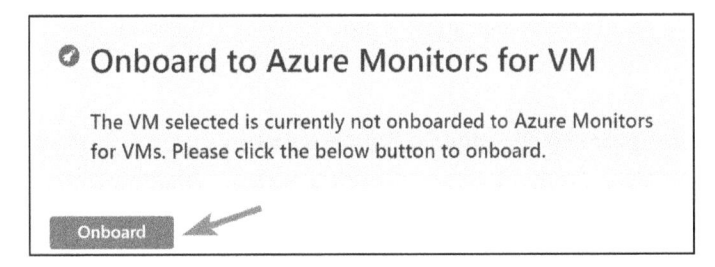

Figure 21.53: Onboard to Azure Monitors for VM

4. If you are presented with another screen to activate monitoring, click the Enable button.
5. On the Monitoring Configuration window that appears, click Create new under the Data collection rule option.
6. Configure your rule as follows:
   - Data collection rule name: WorkbookDCR
   - Enable guest performance: Checked
   - Enable processes and dependencies (Map): Checked
   - Subscription: Select your subscription
   - Log Analytics workspace: Select an existing workspace or create a new one
7. Once completed, navigate back to the Workbooks blade for the VM.
8. Click the + New button at the top of the blade.

9. You will be presented with the workbook editor screen. Click the + Add button to add your first visualization to the workbook.

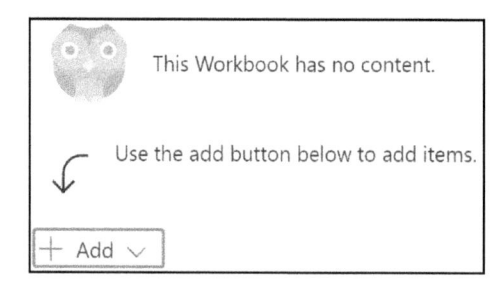

Figure 21.54: Adding a visualization to a workbook

10. Click Add metric.
11. Leave the settings as default and then click Add metric.

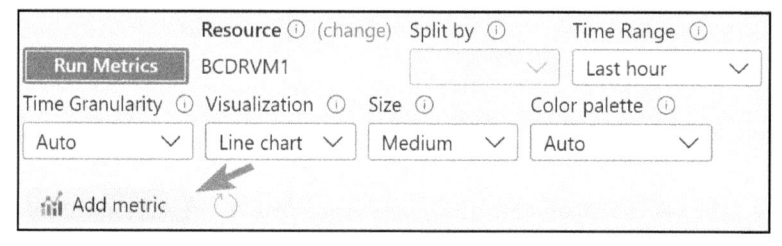

Figure 21.55: Adding a metric

12. Configure the metric settings as follows and click Save:

    - Namespace: Virtual Machine Host
    - Metric: Percentage CPU
    - Aggregation: Max

Figure 21.56: Configuring the metric settings – Percentage CPU

1. Click the `Run Metrics` button at the top of the workbook.
2. You should now see a visualization showing your maximum CPU percentage utilization observed from your VM.

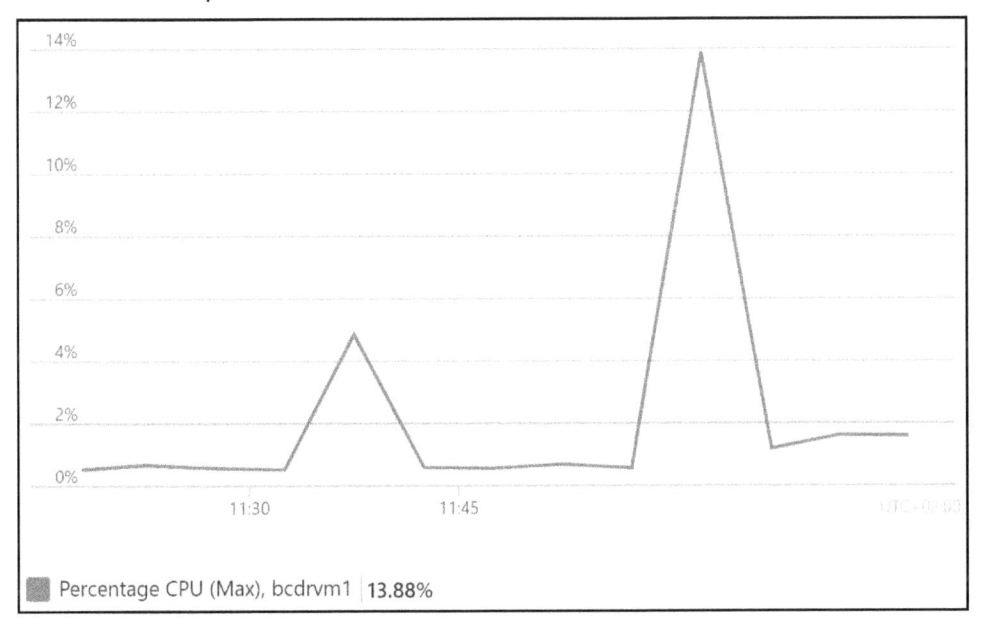

Figure 21.57: Max CPU percentage visualization

3. You can add multiple charts and queries to your workspace. Once done, you must remember to save your workbook.

You should now feel comfortable creating workbooks for your environment. Next, you will learn about Application Insights and the value it brings to your applications.

Configuring Application Insights

As mentioned previously, Application Insights is a telemetry tool used for monitoring and troubleshooting your applications. In this exercise, you will now deploy Application Insights and connect it to your application for monitoring telemetry. You will create a new web application service that will be associated with the Application Insights resource, deploy Application Insights, and then link this to the application.

Creating Your Application

You will deploy an application for monitoring; this application will be built from a GitHub repository and will take several minutes to provision after the code has run:

1. Navigate to the Azure portal by clicking on `https://portal.azure.com`.
2. Click the Azure CLI icon at the top right of the Azure portal to open an Azure CLI instance:

Figure 21.58: Opening the Azure CLI

3. If you have never used the CLI before, you will be required to set up storage for this. Follow the prompts on the screen to configure your container on a storage account.
4. When asked for the environment, you can select `PowerShell`. If you prefer to use `Bash`, then enter the following, which will open PowerShell in the Bash terminal, and press *Enter*:

   ```
   pwsh
   ```

5. Download the following file: `https://packt.link/CsgZZ`.
6. Paste the following into PowerShell and press *Enter*:

   ```
   # Parameters
   $ResourceGroup = "AZ104-Monitor"
   $Location = "WestEurope"
   $AppServicePlanName = "mylinuxappserviceplan10101"
   $webappname="mywebapp$(Get-Random)"

   # Create an App Service Plan for Linux
   New-AzAppServicePlan -Name $AppServicePlanName -Tier Free
   -Location $Location -Linux -ResourceGroupName $ResourceGroup

   # Create a Web App
   New-AzWebApp -Name $WebAppName -ResourceGroupName $ResourceGroup
   -Location $Location -AppServicePlan $AppServicePlanName

   # Publish the Web Files to the Website
   Publish-AzWebApp -Name $WebAppName -ResourceGroupName
   $ResourceGroup -ArchivePath "C:\webfiles\testwebsite.zip"
   ```

7. Navigate to your web application, copy the frontend name, and connect to view your web application.

Now that your application is ready, you will set up Application Insights for the application and view some metrics.

Creating Your Application Insights Resource

You will now create your Application Insights resource using the following steps:

1. Navigate to your `AZ104-Monitor` resource group on the Azure portal.
2. Click `+ Create`.
3. Type `application insights` into the search bar and click the `Application Insights` card that appears.
4. Click `Create` and then enter the following details on the `Basics` tab:
   - `Subscription`: Select your Azure subscription
   - `Resource Group`: `AZ104-Monitor`
   - `Name`: `az104monitorappinsights`
   - `Region`: `West Europe` (or select what you prefer)
   - `Log Analytics Workspace`: `az104loganalytics`

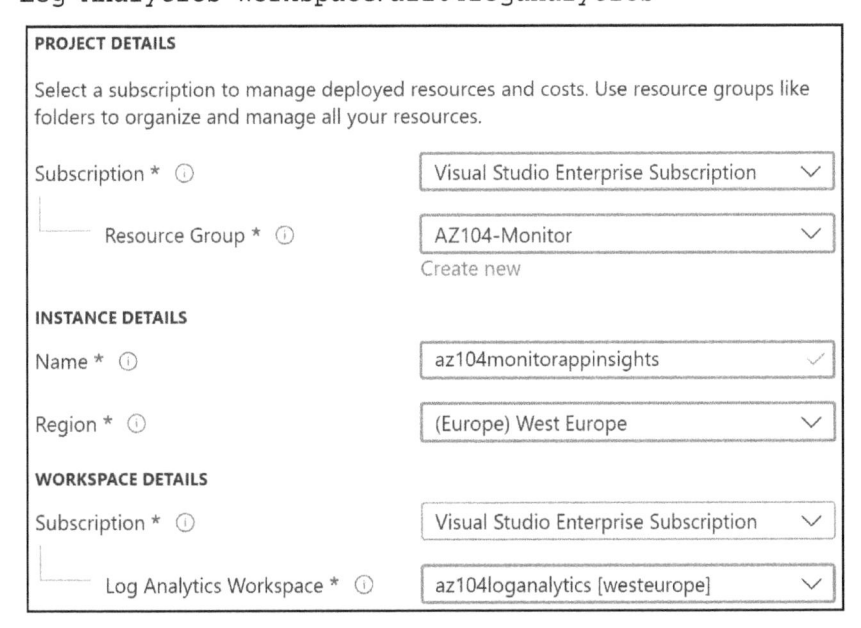

Figure 21.59: Application Insights deployment

5. Click `Review + create`.
6. Click `Create`.

You are ready to now integrate Application Insights with your application.

Associating Your Web App with Application Insights

Now that your Application Insights resource is set up and ready, you can link it to your application. Perform the following steps to do so:

1. Navigate to the web app you created earlier.
2. Expand the `Settings` context and click `Application Insights`.
3. Since the application is deployed in Azure, you can easily activate Application Insights for your web app with a few clicks. Click on `Turn on Application Insights`:

Figure 21.60: Turn on Application Insights

4. Select `Enable` on the `Application Insights` section and scroll down.

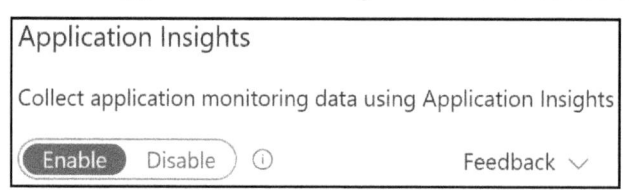

Figure 21.61: Enable Application Insights

5. Then, click `Select existing resource`, select `az104monitorappinsights`, and click `Apply`:

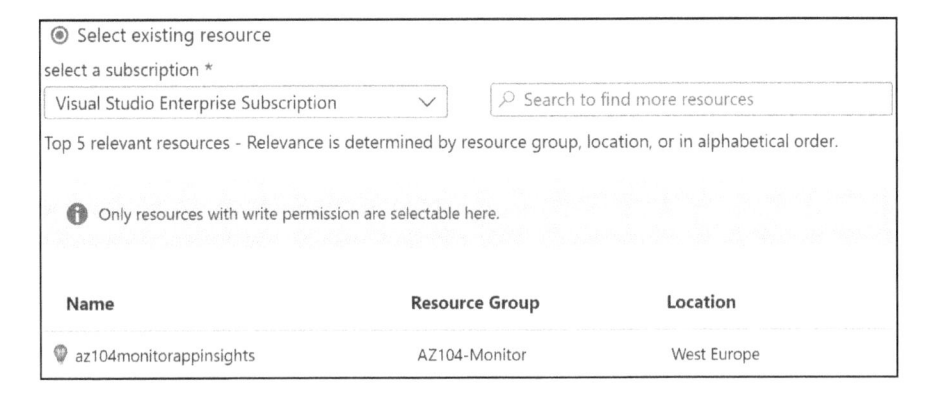

Figure 21.62: Selecting your Application Insights resource

6. A prompt will appear, notifying you that your application will be restarted as an effect of applying the change. Click Yes:

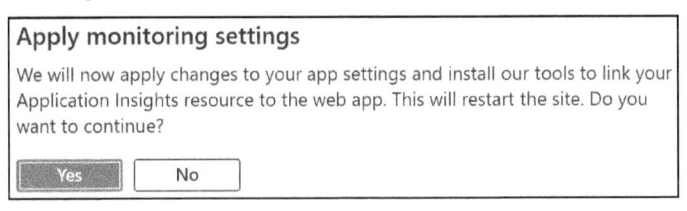

Figure 21.63: Apply monitoring settings

You have now enabled Application Insights for your web app. Some applications do not support the automated integration method and will require a manual configuration of your code for Application Insights. Be aware of how to apply it and when automatic integration is not supported, then explore the instrumentation settings available. You should now feel comfortable with deploying this service and enabling it for your Azure App Service instance.

> **Note**
>
> You are encouraged to read more on the topics presented in this chapter.
>
> Azure workbooks: https://learn.microsoft.com/en-gb/azure/azure-monitor/visualize/workbooks-overview
>
> Azure Monitor: https://learn.microsoft.com/en-gb/azure/azure-monitor/overview
>
> Application Insights: https://learn.microsoft.com/en-us/azure/azure-monitor/app/app-insights-overview
>
> Azure Service Health: https://learn.microsoft.com/en-gb/azure/service-health/overview

Summary

In this chapter, you have learned about Azure Monitor and the various capabilities it offers. You have explored the various features of this service offering as well as investigated the configuration of some of the components. You have learned how to use metrics to monitor your Azure resources and alerts to get notified when you trigger the alerts configured for your Azure resources. You used Azure Log Analytics and created queries to retrieve valuable data from the logs. You also learned how to change the representation of that data to display it as a graphical output of your data. You should now be able to build and monitor resources in Azure, along with configuring alert notifications based on events that occur within your environment.

In the next chapter, you will learn about backup and recovery. You will explore the services offered within Azure and how to configure these to become confident in managing backup and recovery from within Azure.

> **Note**
> Remember to delete the resources you created in this chapter to minimize costs. You can do this with the following command for convenience, which will remove the resource group and all the corresponding resources:
> ```
> Remove-AzResourceGroup -Name AZ104-Monitor
> ```

22
Implementing Backup and Recovery Solutions

This chapter focuses on how to implement and configure backup and recovery solutions. You will learn about **Azure Backup** and **Recovery Services vaults**. This will involve learning how to deploy a **Recovery Services vault**, how to configure **backup policies**, how restore operations work, and how to perform site-to-site recovery via **Azure Site Recovery**. The last part of this chapter will focus on how to configure backup reports. These skills are especially important as they fall into **business as usual** (**BAU**) tasks for almost every organization and are key skills to have going forward.

In this chapter, you will cover the following topics:

- Understanding Azure Backup Vaults
- Understanding Azure Recovery Services Vaults
- Creating a Recovery Services Vault
- Understanding Backup Policies
- Creating and Configuring Backup Policies
- Backing Up via Azure Backup Center
- Restoring a Backup via Azure Backup Center
- Recovering from a Disaster with Azure Site Recovery
- Configuring and Reviewing Backup Reports

Technical Requirements

This chapter uses the following tools for the examples:

- Access to an Azure subscription with owner or contributor privileges. If you do not have access to one, students can enroll for a free account: `https://azure.microsoft.com/en-us/free/`.

- **PowerShell 5.1** or later installed on a PC with Windows or PowerShell Core 6.x where other operating systems are used, on a machine where labs can be practiced from.
- Note that, occasionally, examples can only be followed from a PC or `https://shell.azure.com` (PowerShell 7.0.6 LTS or later is recommended).
- Installation of the `Az` PowerShell module can be performed by running the following in an administrative PowerShell session:

```
Set-ExecutionPolicy -ExecutionPolicy RemoteSigned -Scope
CurrentUser
Install-Module -Name Az -Scope CurrentUser -Repository PSGallery
-Force
```

Understanding Azure Backup Vaults

The Azure Backup vault is a facility provided by Azure for creating backup data. It supports several types of services, such as VMs in Azure and on-premises and Azure file shares. **SQL** and **SAP HANA** applications installed on Azure VMs can also be backed up using vaults. On-premises workload backups are facilitated through the following tools:

- The Azure Backup agent
- Azure Backup Server
- System Center **Data Protection Manager** (**DPM**)
- Azure Backup vaults also extend Azure Recovery Services vaults for the storage of backed-up data. The difference between a Backup vault and a Recovery Services vault is that a Backup vault is limited to backups whereas a Recovery Services vault, which you will read about in the next section, also supports **disaster recovery** (**DR**).

Understanding Azure Recovery Services Vaults

An Azure Recovery Services vault is a native service within Azure that supports the recoverability of services within your Azure environment. It stores information such as copies of data (backups) and enables DR of services (Site Recovery) or replication of VMs to Azure for migration purposes (Site Recovery).

A Recovery Services vault enables you to perform the following:

- **Azure Backup**: Azure Backup can be used to back up a plethora of services across Azure, Azure Stack, and on-premises. Services that can be backed up in Azure include VMs, Azure file shares, managed disks, Azure Database for PostgreSQL, Azure Blob Storage, and Azure Kubernetes Service. These backups include SQL Server and SAP HANA database applications installed on Azure VMs. For on-premises, the following services are supported: VMs, client operating systems (Windows 10 and 11), Windows Server (2012 and up), files and folders, Hyper-V, SQL Server, Microsoft SharePoint, and Microsoft Exchange. This list will likely change as the service matures so it is important to review this list periodically.

- **Site Recovery**: Site Recovery is used for DR. When resources become unavailable, Site Recovery can enable the restoration of services. This can be in a specific region within Azure, or even another data center located elsewhere, such as an on-premises environment.

Here are some of the key benefits of using Recovery Services vaults:

- **Security**: Security is provided as part of the service to help protect cloud backups to ensure they can be safely recovered.
- **Hybrid**: A Recovery Services vault enables Azure Backup to support cloud and on-premises workloads.
- **Permissions**: **Role-Based Access Control** (**RBAC**) permissions are supported to delegate the correct level of permissions to administrators or backup owners.
- **Soft delete**: This is a feature that protects backups or backup data from being deleted by accident or maliciously. The data will be retained for 14 days after deletion to ensure there's no data loss.
- **Cross-region restore**: You can enable the functionality to restore to a secondary region without waiting for a disaster state. This is also an excellent feature for conducting audits of your environments, removing the potentially disrupted nature of audits.
- **Data isolation**: Your data is protected from accidental or malicious damage due to the way it is isolated from your other environments and direct access being removed from users and guests.

Creating a Recovery Services Vault

In this exercise, you will learn how to create a Recovery Services vault using PowerShell. Complete the steps that follow to deploy your Recovery Services vault:

1. Run the code in the following GitHub repo to deploy your resource group and your Recovery Services vault: `https://packt.link/G0e8j`.
2. Next, you are going to set the redundancy level on your vault to georedundant storage with the following command (this is included in the preceding script):

    ```
    $vault1 = Get-AzRecoveryServicesVault -Name $VaultName
    Set-AzRecoveryServicesBackupProperty -Vault $vault1 `
    -BackupStorageRedundancy GeoRedundant
    ```

3. The next step is to confirm that the new vault has been created. Navigate to your `AZ104-BCDR` resource group in the Azure portal.

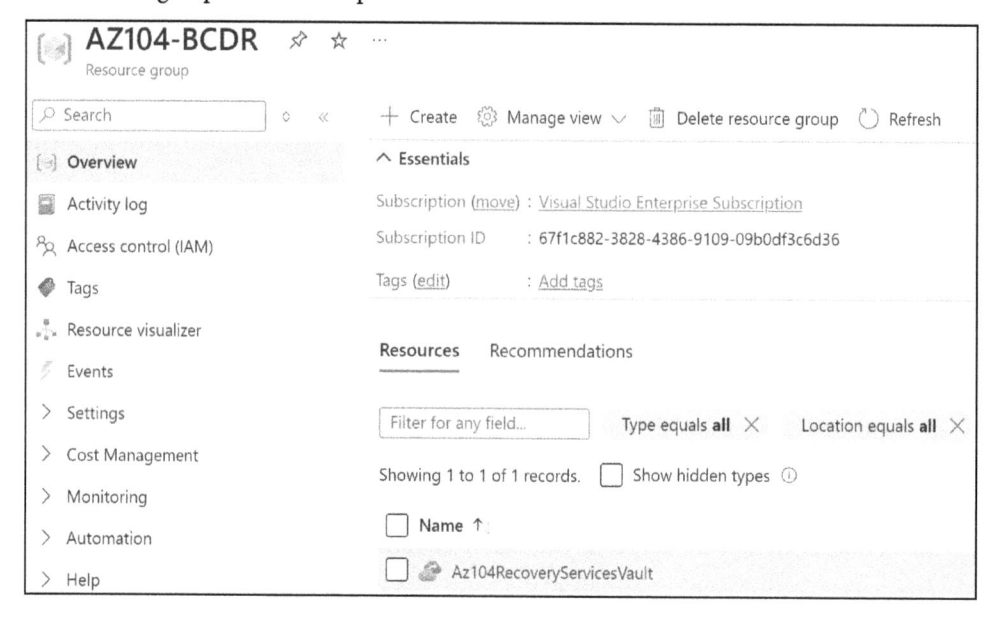

Figure 22.1: Newly created Recovery Services vault

With that, you have successfully created a new Recovery Services vault within Azure via PowerShell. In the next section, you are going to take this a step further and learn about Azure Backup and how to configure a backup policy.

Understanding Backup Policies

The Azure Backup service is used to back up resources and data in Azure through an intuitive, easy-to-use interface that can cost-effectively save your important data. This can be used for both Azure, Azure Stack, and on-premises workloads. Your on-premises backup solution can also be extended to the cloud in conjunction with Azure Backup. Azure Backup can also create backups for VMs, files, folders, applications, workloads, system states, and volumes. Azure Backup consists of the following features and capabilities:

- **Back up on-premises resources to Azure**: Azure Backup offers short- and long-term backup solutions. This can be a replacement for tape and off-site backups.

- **Back up Azure VMs**: Azure Backup offers independent and isolated backups. These backups are stored in a Recovery Services vault. This vault has built-in management for recovery points.

- **Automatic scaling**: You can get unlimited scale without maintenance overheads. Alerts can be set for delivering information about events.

- **Unlimited data transfer**: There is no limit to the amount of inbound and outbound traffic that can be transferred during the backup process. However, if you use the Azure import/export service to import substantial amounts of data, then a cost will be associated with inbound data.
- **Data encryption**: Data can be encrypted using an encryption passphrase. This is stored locally and is then needed to restore the data.
- **Short- and long-term retention**: Recovery Services is where backups are stored and it provides short- and long-term backups. Azure doesn't limit the time or length that data can be stored in a Recovery Services vault.
- **Multiple storage options**: Azure Backup offers three types of replication – **locally redundant storage** (**LRS**), where your data is replicated three times by creating three copies of the data within the same region, **zone redundant storage** (**ZRS**), where a copy of data is replicated across availability zones in a region, and **geo-redundant storage** (**GRS**), which is the default option, where the data is replicated to a secondary region.

> **Note**
> GRS is configured by default and is the Microsoft-recommended storage option in Azure due to its resilience in being able to survive a regional outage.

You need to answer two questions when configuring a backup:

- **Where is your workload running?** (Azure, Azure Stack Hub, Azure Stack HCI, or on-premises)
- **What do you want to back up?** (VMs, files and folders, Microsoft SQL Server, Microsoft SharePoint, Microsoft Exchange, Hyper-V VMs, etc.)

Microsoft has added an experience for administrators to create and manage backups called **Backup center**. With Backup center, you can view Recovery Services vaults, backup instances, and backup policies at scale.

Now that you know about the fundamentals of Azure Backup, it is time to enroll a VM into Azure Backup and create a backup policy.

Creating and Configuring Backup Policies

In this exercise, you will deploy an Azure VM to your `AZ104-BCDR` resource group. You will then configure a backup policy for the VM. Complete the steps that follow to complete this exercise:

1. Start by deploying two VMs using the PowerShell script named `Creating_VMs.ps1` in the following GitHub repo: `https://packt.link/oCGBN`.

2. Navigate to the Azure portal by opening a web browser and going to `https://portal.azure.com`.

3. Browse to your `AZ104-BCDR` resource group and select the Recovery Services vault (`Az104RecoveryServicesVault`).

4. On the `Overview` blade, click `+ Backup`.

Figure 22.2: Configuring Azure Backup

5. Next, select `Azure` as the workload type and choose `Virtual machine`. Then, click `Backup`:

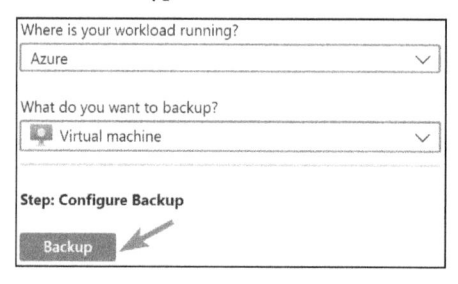

Figure 22.3: Selecting Azure Backup workloads

6. You will be presented with a choice of `Policy sub type` options – enhanced or standard. Note the difference between them. For this exercise, you will create your own new policy instead of using the default backup policy. Select `Standard` for `Policy sub type`.

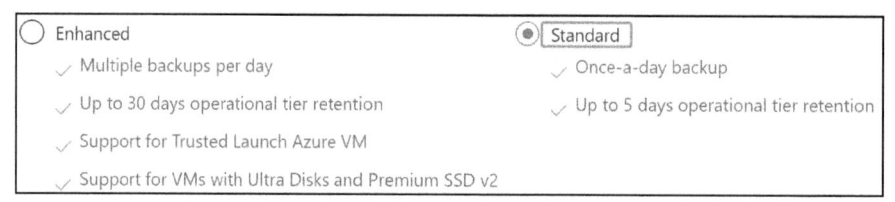

Figure 22.4: Selecting a policy sub type

7. For `Backup policy`, click `Create a new policy` and enter the following:
   - `Policy name: AzureVMBackup`
   - `Backup schedule:`
     - `Frequency: Daily`
     - `Time: 08:00`
     - `Timezone: (UTC) Coordinated Universal Time`
   - `Instant restore: 2 Day(s)`

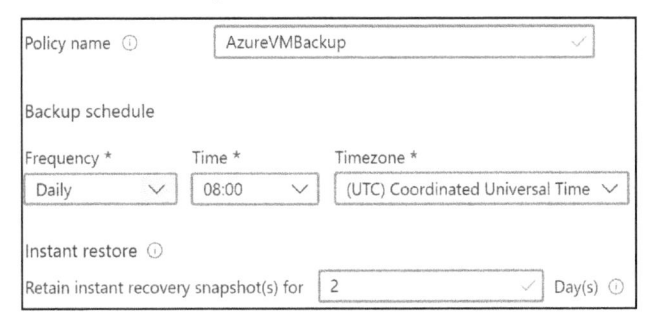

Figure 22.5: Policy settings

8. Scroll down and enter the following for the `Retention range` section:
   - `Retention range: 30 Day(s).`
   - Leave the rest of the settings as not configured

Figure 22.6: Backup retention

9. Scroll down and note at the bottom of the pane that there is an option to enter an `Azure Backup Resource Group` name. It has a notation that also shows n, referring to the number, and then a suffix (a portion that follows the number). Leave this blank and you will inherit the default naming convention of `AzureBackupRG_eastus_1`. Click OK.

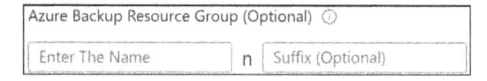

Figure 22.7: Azure Backup Resource Group

10. Back on the `Configure backup` blade, scroll to the bottom and click `Add` under the `Virtual Machines` section.
11. The `Select virtual machines` blade will appear. Select BCDRVM1 from the list of VMs that appear, as per *Figure 22.8*, and click OK.

Virtual machine name	Resource Group
☑ BCDRVM1	az104-bcdr
☐ BCDRVM2	az104-bcdr

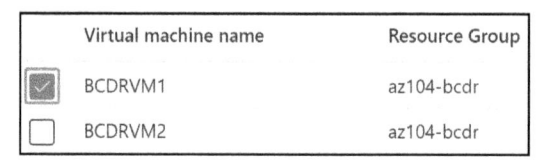

Figure 22.8: Selecting a VM for the backup policy

12. Click on `Enable Backup`.
13. Navigate back to the `AZ104RecoveryServicesVault` resource.
14. On the left menu, expand `Protected items`, and click `Backup items`.
15. You will note a summary of the count of items protected with one `Azure Virtual Machine` showing. Click on the blue text.

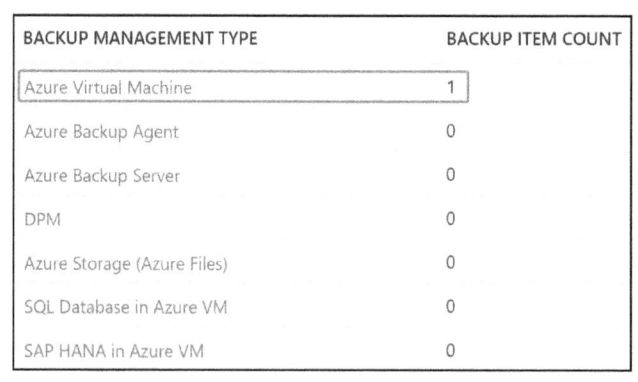

BACKUP MANAGEMENT TYPE	BACKUP ITEM COUNT
Azure Virtual Machine	1
Azure Backup Agent	0
Azure Backup Server	0
DPM	0
Azure Storage (Azure Files)	0
SQL Database in Azure VM	0
SAP HANA in Azure VM	0

Figure 22.9: Summary of protected items

16. You will see that the VM has been enrolled in Azure Backup and that the last backup status will show as pending. After a while, the backup policy will trigger automatically:

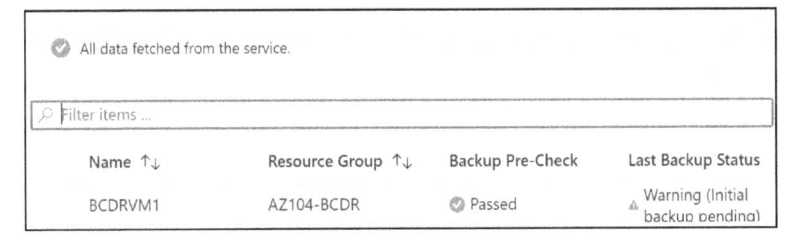

Figure 22.10: Virtual machine successfully enrolled

With that, you have successfully created an Azure Backup policy for your VMs that will run daily, and have created a backup of your BCDRVM1 resource by assigning it to the policy.

Backing Up via Azure Backup Center

Azure Backup center provides a single pane of glass that serves as a unified tool for all backup-related operations and is designed for scale. It supports the governance, operation, monitoring, and analysis of backups. The service can also support monitoring and management facilities for Azure Site Recovery.

You are now ready to perform a backup operation. In this exercise, you will learn how to back up your workloads on demand.

Follow these steps to initiate an on-demand backup:

1. In the Azure portal, search for and select Backup center from the top search bar:

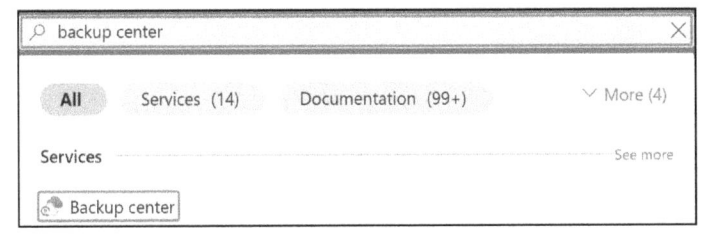

Figure 22.11: Selecting Backup center

2. Under the Manage context on the left menu, select Backup instances. On the right pane, select the BCDRVM1 resource by clicking on it.

3. Select Backup now. This will kick off a backup immediately, regardless of any backup policy. It will ask you for how long you want to retain the backup and kick off the backup. Leave it as the default and click OK.

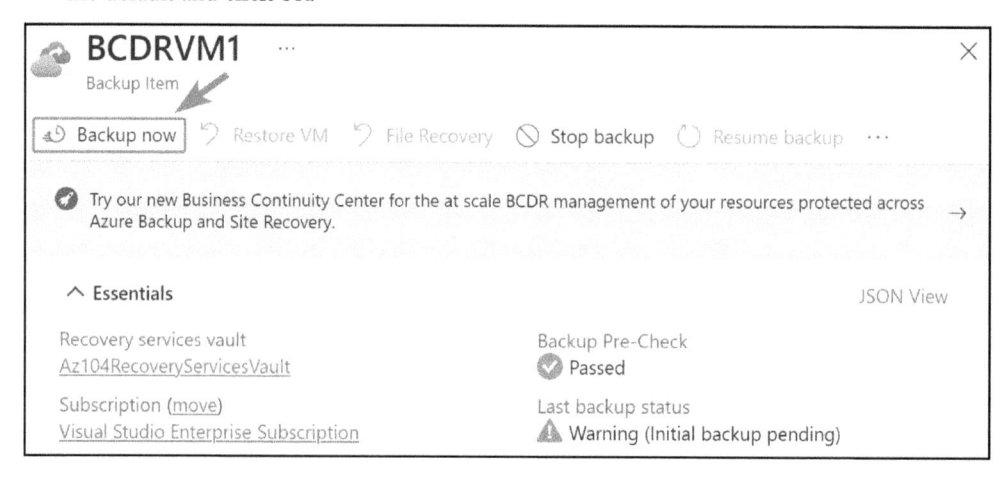

Figure 22.12: On-demand backup of BCDRVM1

Now that you have initiated the first backup of the VM, you will learn how to restore the backup via the Azure portal. Give the backup about 10 minutes to complete.

Restoring a Backup via Azure Backup Center

One of the most important parts of backup operations is to ensure that the resource gets backed up and then that it can be restored. To evaluate whether the resource was backed up correctly, you should assess the backup by doing a restore.

Follow these steps to restore a backup via Backup center:

1. Shut down and deallocate the BCDRVM1 VM.
2. Navigate to Backup center on the Azure portal.
3. Under the Manage context on the left menu, select Backup instances. On the right pane, select the BCDRVM1 resource by clicking on it.
4. At the top of the screen, click Restore VM.

Figure 22.13: Restore VM

5. You will be prompted to select a valid restore point. Click the `Select` text.

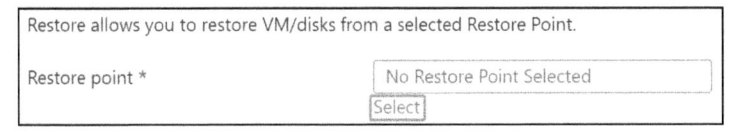

Figure 22.14: Select a restore point

6. Select the first `APPLICATION CONSISTENT` snapshot you see. Then click OK.

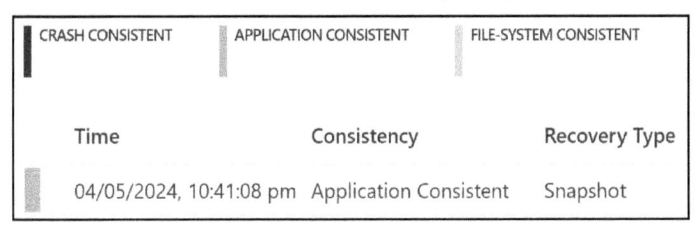

Figure 22.15: Selecting a snapshot

7. Next, under the `Restore configuration` section, you need to choose whether you want to replace the existing VM or create a new VM. For this exercise, you are going to select `Replace existing` and select a storage account for the staging location – you are going to use one of your existing storage accounts that would have spun up with the VMs and click on `Restore`.

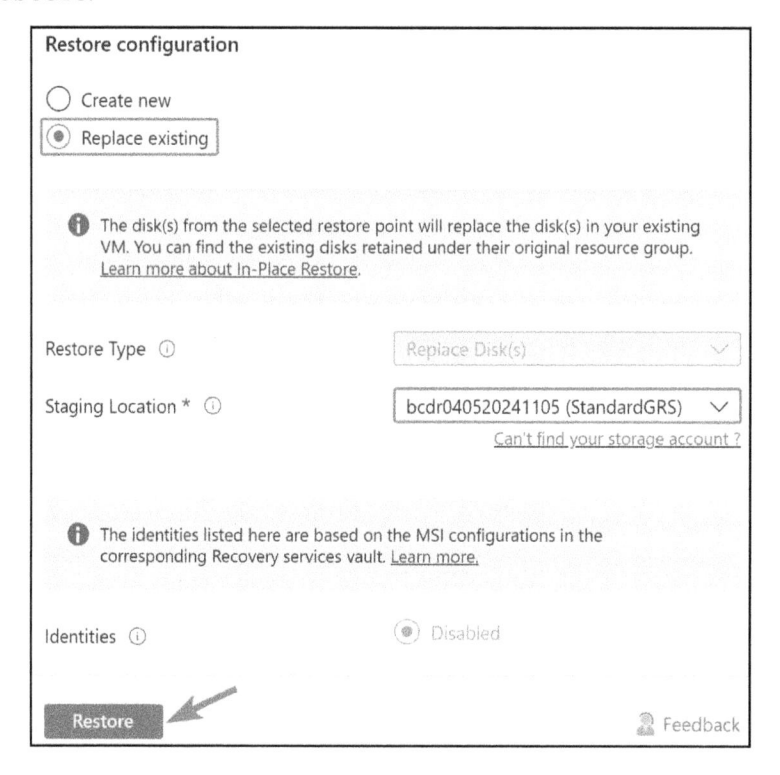

Figure 22.16: Replacing an existing VM

With that, you have successfully restored a VM via Backup center in the Azure portal.

> **Note**
>
> You are encouraged to learn more by going to the following Azure Backup links:
>
> https://learn.microsoft.com/en-us/azure/backup/backup-azure-vms-automation
>
> https://learn.microsoft.com/en-us/azure/backup/backup-center-overview

In this section, you learned how to perform both backup and restore operations via Backup center in the Azure portal. In the next section, you will experience the activities involved in DR with Azure Site Recovery.

Recovering from a Disaster with Azure Site Recovery

Azure Site Recovery is intended to be used as part of an organization's **disaster recovery and business continuity** (**DRBC**) plans, which it does by ensuring applications and workloads are accessible during outages. A simple example of site recovery would be to replicate the storage for a VM from the primary region to the secondary region. If the primary region goes offline, you can fail over to the secondary region without issue. The replication can also occur from on-premises environments to Azure and vice versa. Once the secondary copy is invoked, it then becomes the primary copy and replication will need to be reconfigured again for the reverse direction. Azure Site Recovery creates and orchestrates a complete automated DR plan for your workloads.

> **Note**
> Azure Site Recovery can also be used to migrate on-premises VMs to Azure, although it is preferential to utilize the Azure Migrate service for migrations.

You will now go ahead and perform a site recovery by completing the steps that follow:

1. Navigate to the Azure portal by opening a web browser and going to `https://portal.azure.com`.
2. Create a new resource group named `AZ104-BCDR-Recovery` in the `West US 2` region.
3. Navigate to `Az104RecoveryServicesVault`.
4. On the `Overview` pane, click on `Enable Site Recovery`.

Figure 22.17: Enable Site Recovery

Implementing Backup and Recovery Solutions

5. Next, select `Enable replication` under `Azure virtual machines`.

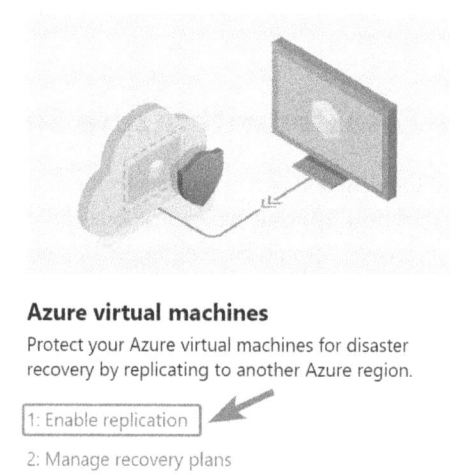

   Figure 22.18: Enable replication

6. For the `Source` tab, configure it as follows and click `Next`:

   - `Region: West US 2`
   - `Resource group: AZ104-BCDR-Recovery`
   - `Virtual machine deployment model: Resource Manager`
   - `Disaster recovery between availability zones?: No`

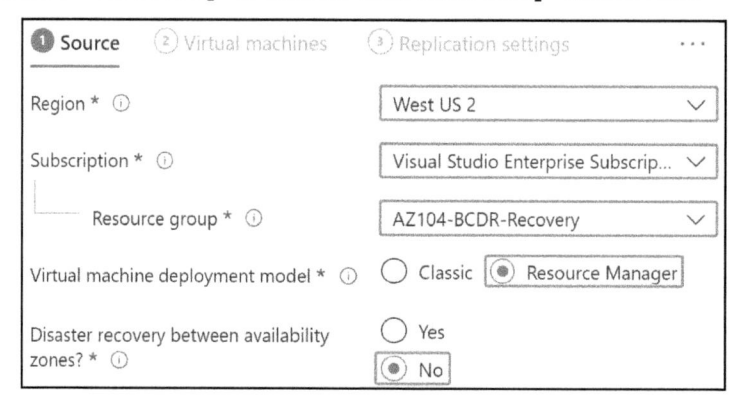

   Figure 22.19: Source settings

7. For `Virtual machines`, select the `BCDRVM2` resource and click `Next`.

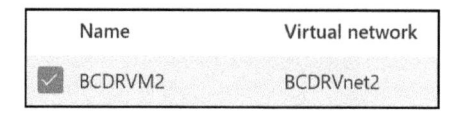

   Figure 22.20: Selecting your VM

8. For the `Location and Resource` group section, configure it as follows:
   - `Target location:` East US
   - `Target resource group:` AZ104-BCDR

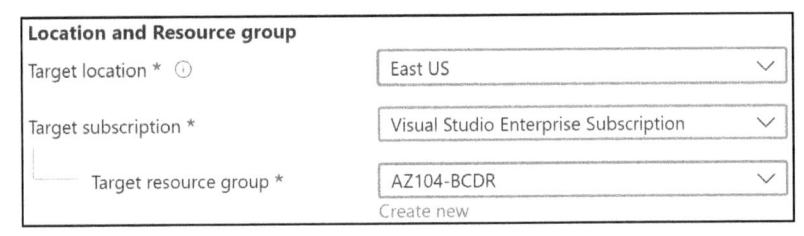

Figure 22.21: Location and Resource group

9. For the `Network` section, configure it as follows:
   - `Failover virtual network:` BCDRVnet
   - `Failover subnet:` BCDRSubnet

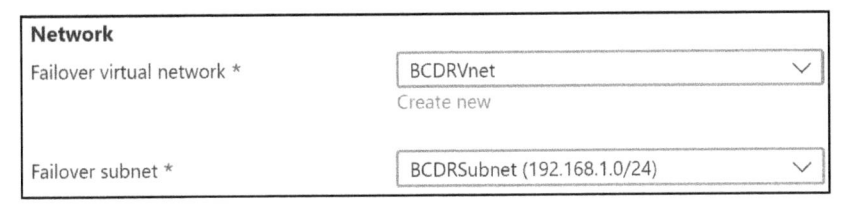

Figure 22.22: Network settings

10. Leave all other settings as the default and click `Next`.
11. On the Manage tab, set `Replication policy` to `24-hour-retention-policy`. Then configure `Update settings` to `Allow ASR to manage`. Click `Next`.
12. Click `Enable replication`.
13. To view the replication status of protected VMs, browse to the `Az104RecoveryServicesVault` resource. On the `Overview` pane, select the `Site Recovery` dashboard from the list of dashboards.

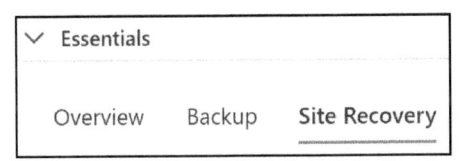

Figure 22.23: Site Recovery dashboard

14. Here, you will see `Replication health` and `Failover health` charts. The following screenshot is an example of an environment with an error state but yours should be green and healthy:

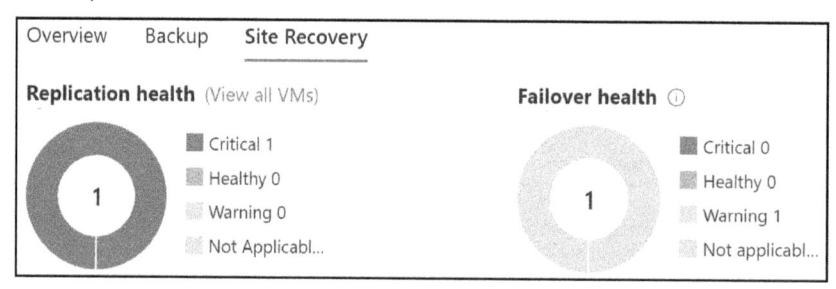

Figure 22.24: Health status

15. Scrolling down the screen, you will be presented with an infrastructure view of the VMs that are replicating to Azure.

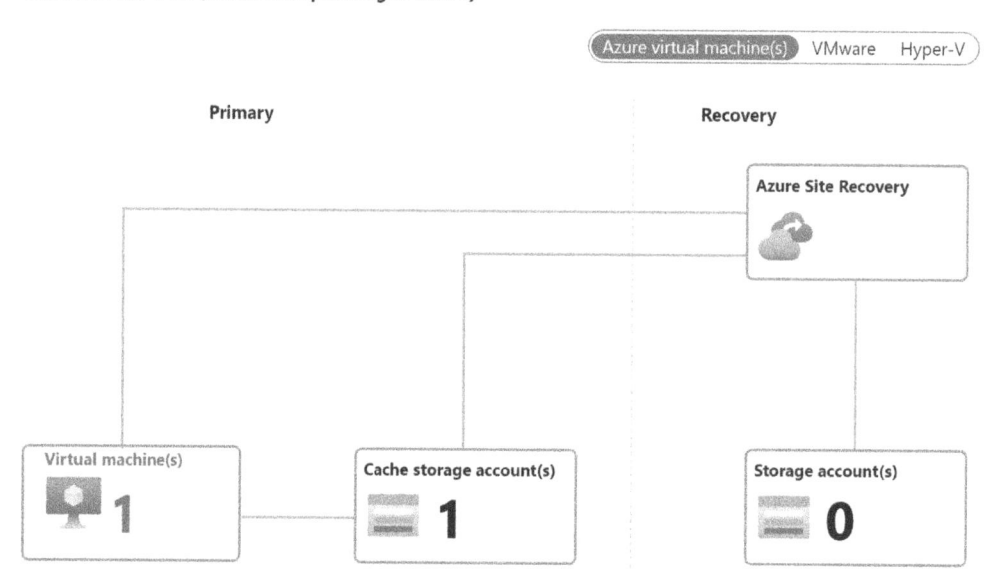

Figure 22.25: Infrastructure view

16. On the left menu, expand the `Protected items` context and click `Replicated items`. On the screen that follows, click the BCDRVM2 resource. You will notice a status under the `Health and status` section. This should show as `Protected`.

Health and status	
Replication Health	-
Status	Protected
RPO	-

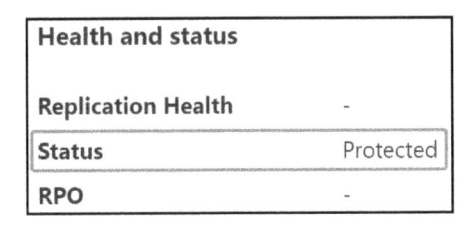

Figure 22.26: Protected status

17. Once the resources have been replicated, you can click on the `Failover` or `Test Failover` button to simulate or start an actual failover. The `Test Failover` choice is great to confirm that your VM can be restored as you expect before the time you need to actually fail over. Actual failover is when you are ready to cut off the resource. Please note that when you perform a failover, you will then need to reactivate replication to restore it in the opposite direction again.

Figure 22.27: Failover options

18. Click `Test Failover`.
19. For `Recovery point`, select `Latest processed` and select BCDRVnet for `Azure virtual network`. Click `Test failover`.

Test failover direction	
Source	West US 2
Destination	East US
Test failover settings	
Recovery point *	Latest processed (lowest RTO) (06/05/2024, ...)
Azure virtual network *	BCDRVnet (mapped)

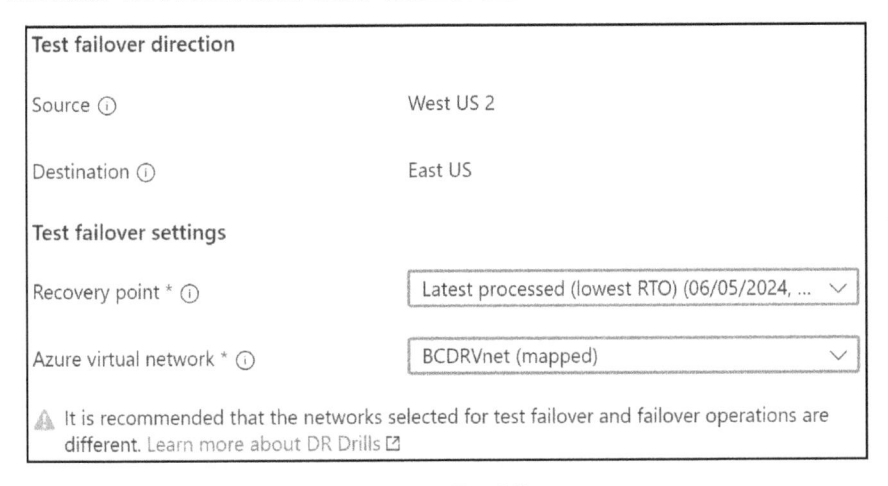

⚠ It is recommended that the networks selected for test failover and failover operations are different. Learn more about DR Drills

Figure 22.28: Test failover

20. You have just run your first test failover.
21. If you would like to clean it up, you can click the `Clean test failover` button.
22. You are now going to perform the failover of your VM to East US. Navigate back to the `AZ104RecoveryServicesVault` resource.

23. On the left menu, click `Replicated items` under the `Protected items` context. Then click on the BCDRVM2 resource.

24. At the top of the `Overview` screen, click `Failover`.

25. Select a recovery point and click `Failover` at the bottom of the page. This will start the failover process.

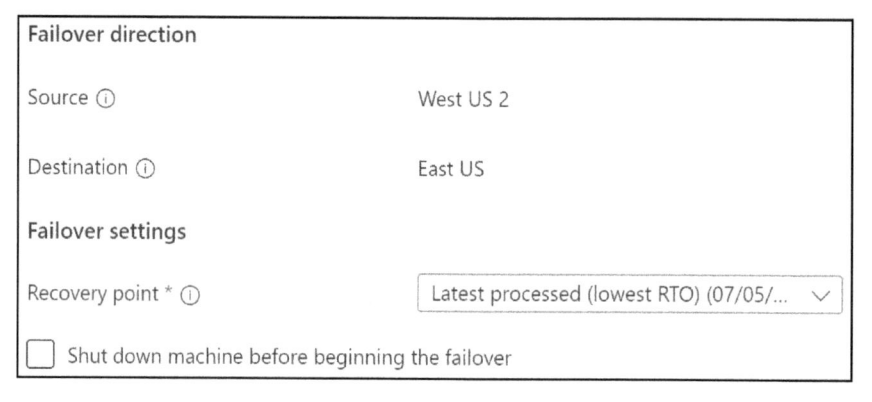

Failover direction	
Source	West US 2
Destination	East US
Failover settings	
Recovery point *	Latest processed (lowest RTO) (07/05/... ∨
☐ Shut down machine before beginning the failover	

Figure 22.29: Failover

26. Replication should take 15 to 20 minutes to complete. Then, click the `Commit` button at the top of the screen. Click `Commit` again on the next screen.

27. At the top of the screen, click the `Re-protect` button to re-enable protection now that the VM is in the `East US` region.

28. Click `Customize`.

29. Change `Cache storage` to New. Click OK to reactivate protection.

30. Navigate back to the `Virtual machines` blade. Note the new BCDRVM2 VM in the East US region.

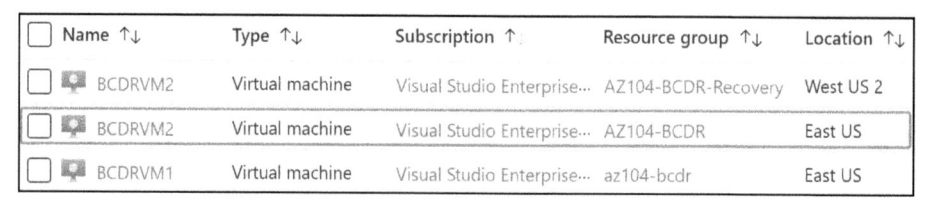

Name ↑↓	Type ↑↓	Subscription ↑	Resource group ↑↓	Location ↑↓
☐ BCDRVM2	Virtual machine	Visual Studio Enterprise...	AZ104-BCDR-Recovery	West US 2
☐ BCDRVM2	Virtual machine	Visual Studio Enterprise...	AZ104-BCDR	East US
☐ BCDRVM1	Virtual machine	Visual Studio Enterprise...	az104-bcdr	East US

Figure 22.30: Replicated BCDRVM2

With that, you have configured Azure Site Recovery and know how to initiate a failover.

In this section, you learned how to activate site-to-site recovery for your VM resources on Azure via the portal. You have also learned how to verify the status of your replication service, learned about some insights you can view, and about your options for failing over your VM.

> **Note**
>
> You are encouraged to read up more on Azure Site Recovery with the following links:
>
> https://azure.microsoft.com/en-us/services/site-recovery/#overview
>
> https://learn.microsoft.com/en-us/azure/site-recovery/site-recovery-overview

Configuring and Reviewing Backup Reports

Earlier in the chapter, you learned how to configure backups using Azure Backup. Now, you are going to learn how to configure backup reports to forecast cloud storage and auditing for backup and restore operations.

In order to provide insights to backup admins about backup data that covers a long period of time, Azure Backup introduced a reporting solution for gaining insights into backup data. The solution includes Azure Monitor logs and workbooks to enhance the presented insight data.

Follow these steps to configure backup reports via Backup center in the Azure portal:

1. Navigate to the Azure portal by opening a web browser and going to https://portal.azure.com.
2. Navigate to the AZ104-BCDR resource group. Click + Create.
3. Search for and select Log Analytics Workspace.
4. Click Create on the screen that follows.
5. Configure the following settings on the Basics tab and click Review and create:
    - Subscription: Select your subscription
    - Resource group: AZ104-BCDR
    - Name: BackupLAW

- Region: East US

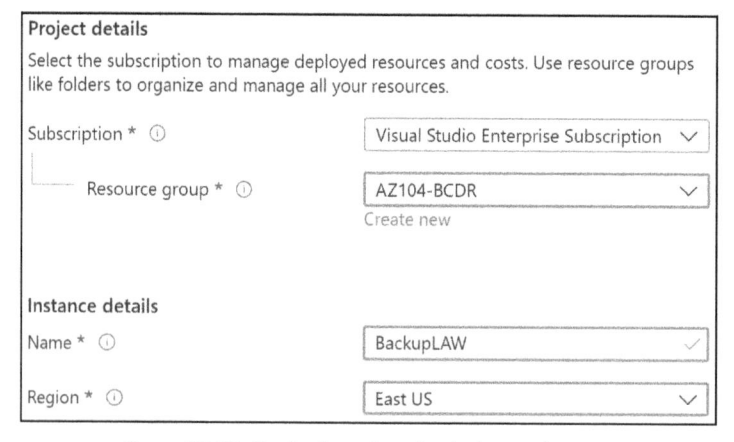

Figure 22.31: Deploying a Log Analytics workspace

6. Click Create.

7. Once your Log Analytics workspace has been created successfully, search for and select Backup center within the Azure portal.

8. Next, from the left menu, select Vaults under the Manage context. Select the AZ104RecoveryServicesVault vault that is used for backups.

9. On the left menu, under Monitoring, select Diagnostic settings and select Add diagnostic setting:

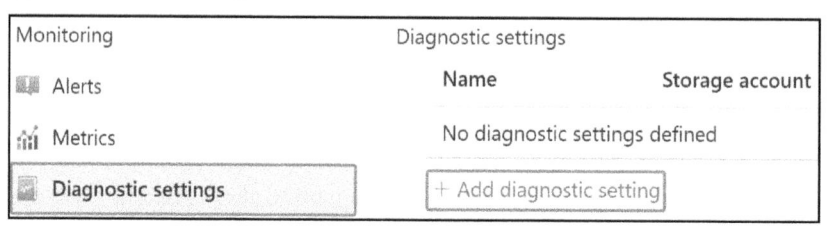

Figure 22.32: Recovery Services vault – Diagnostic settings

10. Give the diagnostic setting a name, such as VaultDiagnostics, and select the following options under Categories:

   - Azure Backup Reporting Data
   - Core Azure Backup Data
   - Addon Azure Backup Job Data
   - Addon Azure Backup Alert Data
   - Addon Azure Backup Policy Data

- `Addon Azure Backup Storage Data`
- `Addon Azure Backup Protected Instance Data`

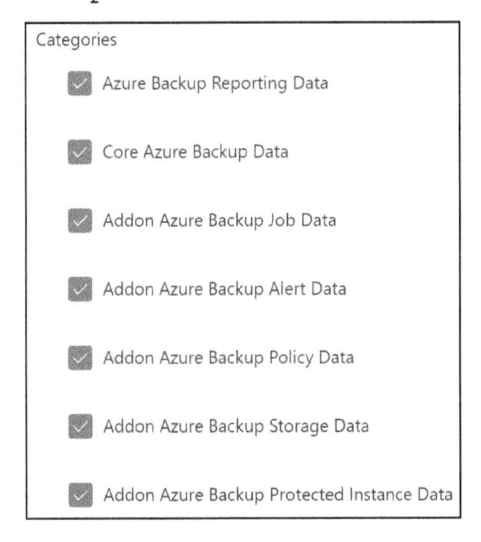

Figure 22.33: Diagnostic settings categories

11. For `Destination details`, select `Send to Log Analytics workspace`. Then, configure as follows:

    - `Log Analytics workspace`: `BackupLAW`
    - `Destination table`: `Resource specific`

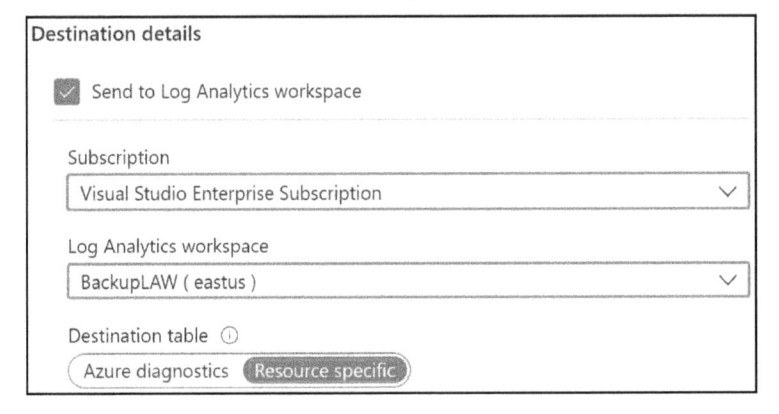

Figure 22.34: Diagnostic settings – Destination details

12. Click on `Save`.

Implementing Backup and Recovery Solutions

13. Navigate back to the `AZ104RecoveryServicesVault` resource. From the left menu, under the `Manage` context, select `Backup reports`.

14. On the `Overview` page, select the subscription and newly created LAW (`BackupLAW`). It will pull all the backup data into the report.

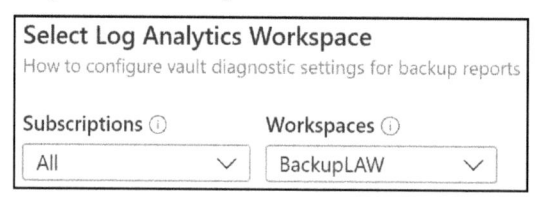

Figure 22.35: Select Log Analytics Workspace

15. The following screenshot shows where you can filter the various report items when they populate after your backups occur and you have data on them.

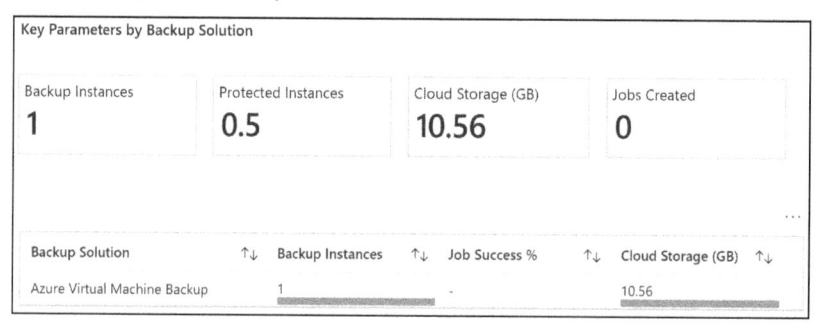

Figure 22.36: Backup report filters

16. Click the `Summary` tab at the top of the screen and you can view some high-level data regarding backups in your environment. Note that since you only have one backed-up workload, you will see this reflected in the data below and see that the expected size of the backup is very limited since nothing has been installed on the VM yet.

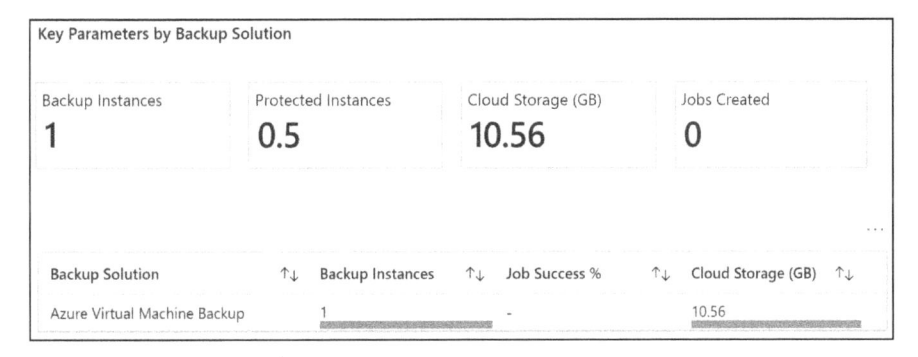

Figure 22.37: Summary backup report data

17. Click the `Backup Instances` tab at the top of the screen to view some more data related to the backed-up instances you have in Azure, such as the count trend and storage usage trend of your backups in Azure.

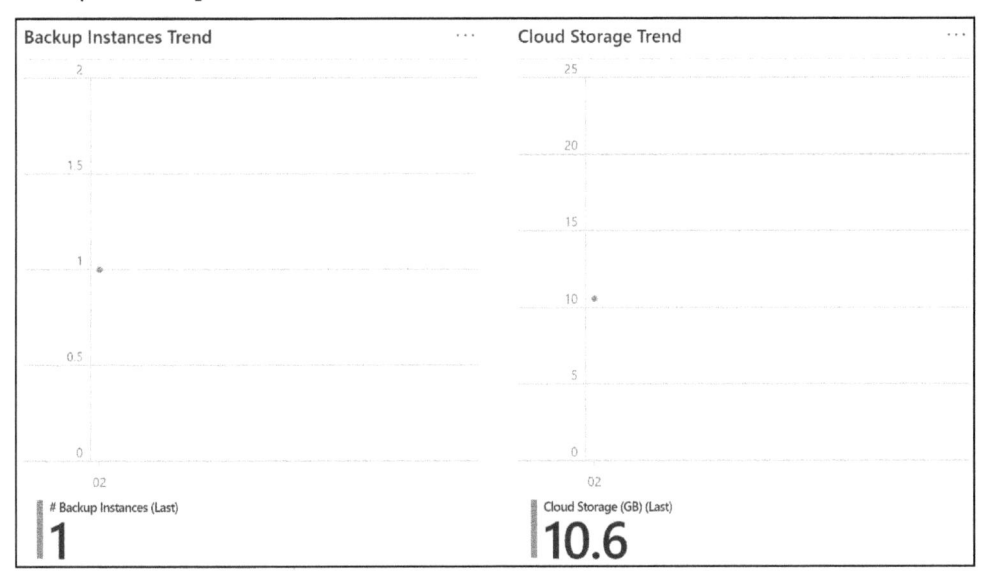

Figure 22.38: Backup Instances report view

18. Have a look through the different tabs to see the different views of data and get more familiar with the type of information you can expect from the reports.

With that, you have learned how to configure Azure Backup reports. In this section, you learned how to create and configure backup reports via the Azure portal, which is incredibly useful in ensuring your BCDR configuration is functioning as expected. These reports can highlight areas of concern that require attention and illustrate the health of your backup environment.

> **Hands-on activities and Further reading**
>
> Reinforce what you learned in *Chapters 21* and *22* by completing the hands-on activities for these chapters. Open the online practice resources using this link: `https://packt.link/az104dash`. Then, from the `Dashboard`, click `Hands-on Activities` and open the menu `Monitoring and Backing Up Azure Resources`
>
> You are encouraged to read up further on Azure Backup reports with the following links:
>
> `https://learn.microsoft.com/en-us/azure/backup/configure-reports`
>
> `https://learn.microsoft.com/en-us/azure/backup/backup-reports-email`

Summary

In this chapter, you learned about Recovery Services vaults, what they are, and how to configure them, as well as what Azure Backup is and how it works, including how to configure a backup policy. You learned how to perform backup and restore operations by using Azure Backup. You also learned how to perform site-to-site recovery via the Azure portal and how to configure backup reports.

Now that you have read this chapter and followed along with the hands-on demos, you should be able to implement backups and recover them and deploy Azure infrastructure.

> **Note**
>
> Remember to delete the resources you created in this chapter to minimize costs.
>
> Run the script in the GitHub repo for the chapter: `Delete_Az104RecoveryServicesVault`.
>
> Remove the resource group and all the corresponding resources with the following:
>
> `Get-AzResourceLock | Where-Object{$_.ResourceGroupName -like "AZ104-BCDR*"} | Remove-AzresourceLock -Force`
> `Remove-AzResourceGroup -Name AZ104-BCDR-Recovery -Force`
> `Remove-AzResourceGroup -Name AZ104-BCDR -Force`

Exam Readiness Drill - Chapters 19-22

Apart from mastering key concepts, strong test-taking skills under time pressure are essential for acing your certification exam. That's why developing these abilities early in your learning journey is critical.

Exam readiness drills, using the free online practice resources provided with this book, help you progressively improve your time management and test-taking skills while reinforcing the key concepts you've learned.

HOW TO GET STARTED

- Open the link or scan the QR code at the bottom of this page
- If you have unlocked the practice resources, already log in to your registered account. If you haven't, follow the instructions in *Chapter 23* and come back to this page.
- Once you log in, click the START button to start a quiz
- We recommend attempting a quiz multiple times till you're able to answer most of the questions correctly and well within the time limit.
- You can use the following practice template to help you plan your attempts :

Attempt	Target	Time Limit
Working On Accuracy		
Attempt 1	40% or more	Till the timer runs out
Attempt 2	60% or more	Till the timer runs out
Attempt 3	75% or more	Till the timer runs out
Working On Timing		
Attempt 4	75% or more	1 minute before time limit
Attempt 5	75% or more	2 minutes before time limit
Attempt 6	75% or more	3 minutes before time limit

The above drill is just an example. Design your drills based on your own goals and make the most out of the online quizzes accompanying this book.

> **First time accessing the online resources?** 🔒
> You'll need to unlock them through a one-time process. **Head to** *Chapter 23* **for instructions**.

Open Quiz

`https://packt.link/az104e3ch19-22`

OR scan this QR code →

23
Accessing the Online Practice Resources

Your copy of *AZ-104 Microsoft Azure Administrator Certification and Beyond* comes with free online practice resources. Use these to hone your exam readiness even further by attempting practice questions on the companion website. The website is user-friendly and can be accessed from mobile, desktop, and tablet devices. It also includes interactive timers for an exam-like experience.

How to Access These Materials

Here's how you can start accessing these resources depending on your source of purchase.

Purchased from Packt Store (packtpub.com)

If you've bought the book from the Packt store (`packtpub.com`) eBook or Print, head to `https://packt.link/az104e3unlock`. There, log in using the same Packt account you created or used to purchase the book.

Packt+ Subscription

If you're a *Packt+ subscriber*, you can head over to the same link (`https://packt.link/az104e3practice`), log in with your `Packt ID`, and start using the resources. You will have access to them as long as your subscription is active.

If you face any issues accessing your free resources, contact us at `customercare@packt.com`.

Purchased from Amazon and Other Sources

If you've purchased from sources other than the ones mentioned above (like *Amazon*), you'll need to unlock the resources first by entering your unique sign-up code provided in this section. **Unlocking takes less than 10 minutes, can be done from any device, and needs to be done only once.** Follow these five easy steps to complete the process:

STEP 1

Open the link `https://packt.link/az104e3unlock` OR scan the following **QR code** (*Figure 23.1*):

Figure 23.1: QR code for the page that lets you unlock this book's free online content

Either of those links will lead to the following page as shown in *Figure 23.2*:

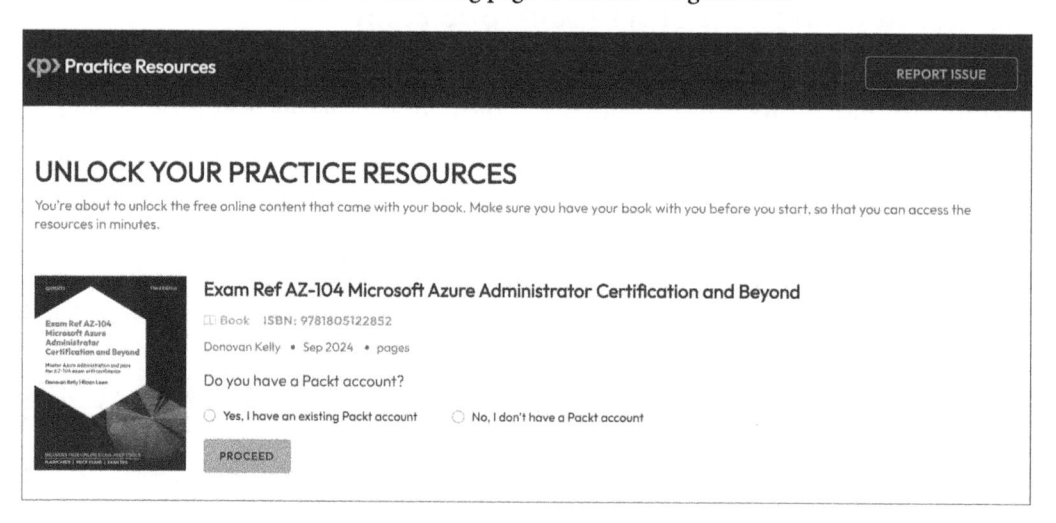

Figure 23.2: Unlock page for the online practice resources

STEP 2

If you already have a Packt account, select the option `Yes, I have an existing Packt account`. If not, select the option `No, I don't have a Packt account`.

If you don't have a Packt account, you'll be prompted to create a new account on the next page. It's free and only takes a minute to create.

Click `Proceed` after selecting one of those options.

STEP 3

After you've created your account or logged in to an existing one, you'll be directed to the following page as shown in *Figure 23.3*.

Make a note of your unique unlock code:

`TBD8974`

Type in or copy this code into the text box labeled 'Enter Unique Code':

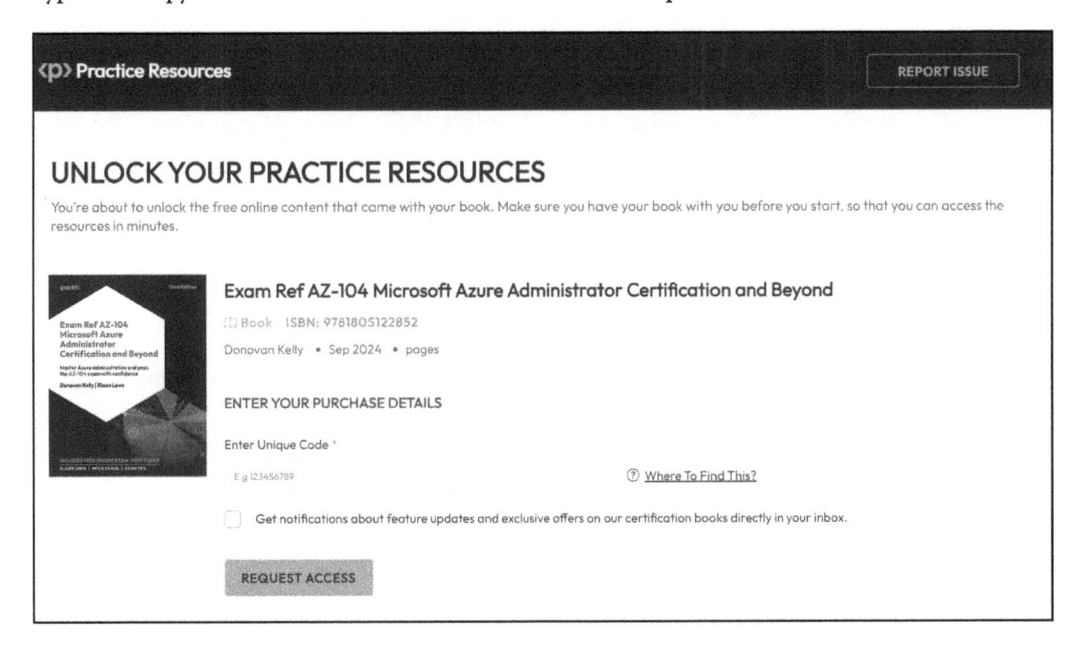

Figure 23.3: Enter your unique sign-up code to unlock the resources

> **Troubleshooting tip**
>
> After creating an account, if your connection drops off or you accidentally close the page, you can reopen the page shown in *Figure 23.2* and select `Yes, I have an existing account`. Then, sign in with the account you had created before you closed the page. You'll be redirected to the screen shown in *Figure 23.3*.

STEP 4

> **Note**
>
> You may choose to opt into emails regarding feature updates and offers on our other certification books. We don't spam, and it's easy to opt out at any time.

Click `Request Access`.

STEP 5

If the code you entered is correct, you'll see a button that says, `OPEN PRACTICE RESOURCES`, as shown in *Figure 23.4*:

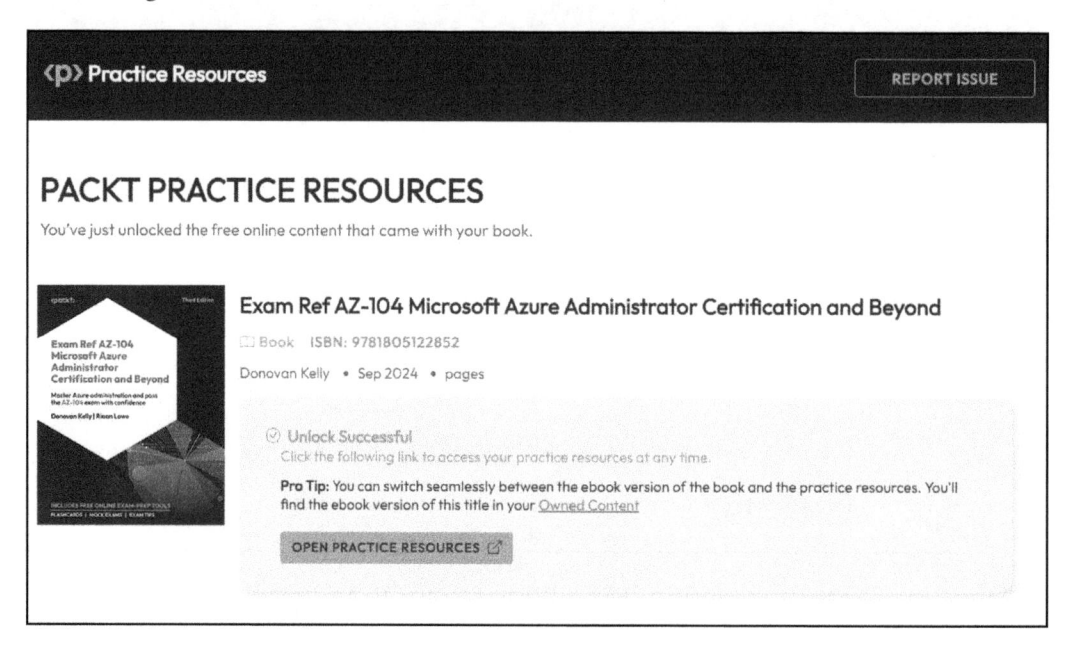

Figure 23.4: Page that shows up after a successful unlock

Click the OPEN PRACTICE RESOURCES link to start using your free online content. You'll be redirected to the Dashboard shown in *Figure 23.5*:

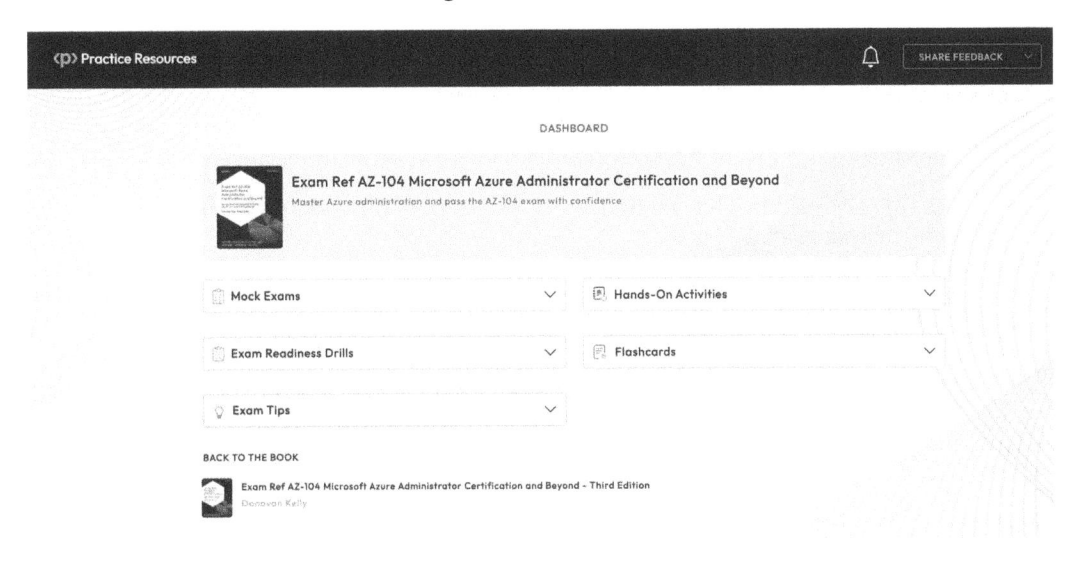

Figure 23.5: Dashboard page for AZ-104 practice resources

> **Bookmark this link**
>
> Now that you've unlocked the resources, you can come back to them anytime by visiting `https://packt.link/az104e3practice` or scanning the following QR code provided in *Figure 23.6*:

Figure 23.6: QR code to bookmark practice resources website

Troubleshooting Tips

If you're facing issues unlocking, here are three things you can do:

- Double-check your unique code. All unique codes in our books are case-sensitive and your code needs to match exactly as it is shown in *STEP 3*.
- If that doesn't work, use the `Report Issue` button located at the top-right corner of the page.
- If you're not able to open the unlock page at all, write to `customercare@packt.com` and mention the name of the book.

Share Feedback

If you find any issues with the platform, the book, or any of the practice materials, you can click the `Share Feedback` button from any page and reach out to us. If you have any suggestions for improvement, you can share those as well.

Back to the Book

To make switching between the book and practice resources easy, we've added a link that takes you back to the book (*Figure 23.7*). Click it to open your book in Packt's online reader. Your reading position is synced so you can jump right back to where you left off when you last opened the book.

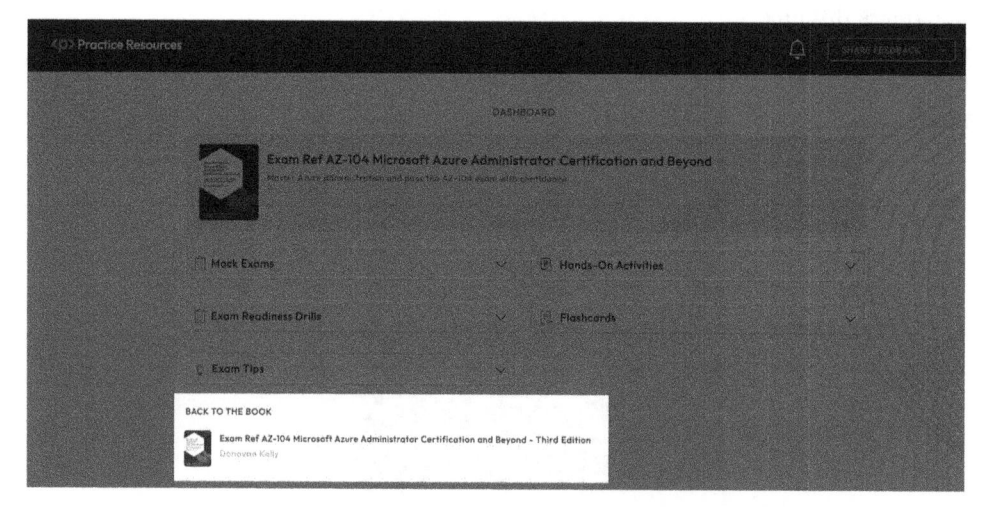

Figure 23.7: Dashboard page for AZ-104 practice resources

> **Note**
> Certain elements of the website might change over time and thus may end up looking different from how they are represented in the screenshots of this book.

Index

A

.net framework 4.7.2: 3, 34, 176, 207, 240, 285, 314, 344, 362, 398, 556, 588, 632, 665, 696

administrative units: 1, 6, 24, 26, 28, 30, 32

application gateway: 507, 523, 585, 587, 588, 590, 591, 593, 618, 619, 620, 621, 622, 623, 624, 625, 626, 627, 628, 631, 666, 674

application rule: 569, 570, 578, 581, 582

archive: 180, 183, 184, 185, 192, 194, 204, 231, 233, 234, 235, 237, 286, 291, 336

area: 24, 68, 70, 156, 314, 341, 360, 430, 485, 730

availability zone: 187, 375, 376, 383, 392, 394, 401, 455, 462, 575, 598, 599, 621, 633, 747, 756

access control lists: 262, 781

account sas: 253, 261

accounting: 127, 588, 590, 781

aci: 427, 430, 434, 436, 438, 442, 444, 454, 456, 457, 459, 460, 461, 464, 473

acls: 262, 282, 781

action: 53, 88, 97, 118, 146, 164, 165, 166, 167, 171, 288, 304, 305, 373, 382, 400, 438, 439, 489, 490, 491, 503, 528, 556, 562, 565, 593, 618, 643, 677, 682, 686, 689, 709, 710, 718, 722, 723, 788

action types: 710

active directory: 5, 11, 13, 15, 35, 36, 44, 48, 69, 239, 261, 274, 279, 430, 513, 781

active events: 710

activity logs: 702

ad hoc sas: 253, 261

ade: 411

ai: 182, 781

aks: 427, 428, 432, 433, 445, 446, 447, 448, 449, 450, 451, 452, 462, 463, 464, 465, 466, 467, 468, 469, 470, 471, 472, 473, 704, 708

alert thresholds: 161

alerts: 70, 133, 160, 161, 168, 169, 170, 171, 173, 379, 465, 575, 593, 669, 670, 695, 698, 704, 706, 708, 709, 710, 712, 713, 715, 717, 719, 720, 721, 723, 725, 727, 728, 729, 734, 742, 746

all azure admins: 20

allocating resources: 378

allowed locations: 104, 110, 112, 119

allowed resource types: 104, 254, 287

allowed virtual machine size skus: 104

an azure file share: 263, 279, 293, 301

analysis: 42, 155, 156, 157, 158, 244, 601, 668, 669, 696, 701, 703, 704, 705, 706, 712, 729, 751, 782, 783, 784 analyze: 42, 160, 292, 597, 668, 696, 698, 704, 705, 708, 713, 720, 724, 728, 729

api: 53, 83, 182, 183, 184, 194, 237, 322, 351, 354, 414, 448, 449, 451, 506, 538, 550, 597, 674, 703, 704, 728, 729, 781

api context: 506

app services: 702

append: 107, 180, 182, 184, 194

append blobs: 180, 182, 184, 194

application security group: 246, 557

application development: 292

application insights: 483, 695, 700, 705, 706, 707, 737, 739, 740, 741

application management: 5, 12

application name: 127

application programming interface: 182, 451, 781

applying tags in powershell: 131

archive storage tier: 185, 233

arm: 106, 154, 236, 270, 293, 313, 314, 315, 316, 317, 318, 319, 320, 321, 322, 323, 324, 325, 326, 327, 328, 329, 330, 331, 332, 333, 334, 335, 336, 337, 338, 339, 340, 341, 343, 344, 345, 347, 348, 352, 353, 355, 356, 357, 358, 359, 360, 361, 384, 394, 397, 413, 414, 415, 416, 417, 419, 421, 423, 424, 437, 451, 456, 457, 458, 459, 538, 550

array: 112, 155, 317, 324, 326, 327, 328, 372, 789

asr: 757

audit: 12, 40, 42, 43, 44, 66, 107, 193, 292, 540, 702, 785, 788

audit logs: 12, 40, 42, 43, 66, 702

auditing and reporting: 5, 12

authentication: 5, 8, 9, 11, 12, 13, 15, 28, 34, 36, 38, 40, 65, 66, 226, 239, 261, 262, 263, 265, 267, 269, 271, 272, 273, 275, 277, 279, 281, 282, 283, 285, 286, 448, 463, 467, 479, 494, 496, 497, 499, 583, 635, 650, 652, 662, 776, 781, 787, 789, 790

auto-instrumentation: 700

auto-scale: 619

automatic scaling: 746

automation: 125, 129, 144, 153, 154, 261, 279, 283, 313, 335, 337, 338, 343, 413, 414, 479, 608, 698, 703, 704, 710, 729, 754

automation of storage access key rotation: 261, 283

autoscale: 376, 377, 393, 464, 469, 470, 478, 488, 491, 492

autoscaling: 446, 464, 491, 493, 621

availability sets: 187, 361, 368, 373, 374, 375, 376, 380

availability zones: 187, 375, 376, 383, 455, 462, 575, 598, 599, 747, 756

average: 489, 490, 493, 670, 692, 721

azcopy documentation: 290

azs: 187, 189, 191, 633

azure active directory: 5, 13, 44, 239

azure ad b2c: 13

azure arm: 344, 424, 538

azure autoscale: 377

azure backup: 291, 743, 744, 745, 746, 747, 748, 750, 751, 752, 753, 754, 761, 762, 763, 766

azure bastion: 523, 555, 576, 577, 579, 581, 583, 584, 585, 587

azure bicep: 341, 343, 344, 345, 346, 348, 350, 352, 354, 356, 358, 360, 413, 538

azure blob storage: 179, 192, 194, 207, 208, 222, 223, 225, 227, 229, 231, 233, 235, 286, 466, 744, 776

azure change analysis: 705

azure cloud shell: 400, 410, 456, 457, 459, 466, 538, 609, 665

azure cni: 450

azure container instances: 427, 430, 434, 460, 473

Index   777

azure container networking interface: 450
azure container registry: 427, 438, 439, 446, 452, 453, 455, 465
azure cost management + billing: 155
azure disk encryption: 410, 411, 412
azure data box: 203, 204, 207, 208, 209, 210, 211, 212, 213, 214, 215, 216, 217, 218, 237
azure disk storage: 186, 361, 362, 363, 365, 367, 369
azure file sync: 182, 237, 285, 290, 291, 293, 294, 295, 296, 297, 298, 300, 301, 311
azure files: 175, 176, 181, 182, 192, 193, 198, 204, 207, 208, 222, 223, 225, 226, 227, 229, 231, 233, 235, 239, 272, 273, 278, 281, 290, 291, 301, 311, 368, 496
azure firewall: 448, 449, 507, 523, 555, 567, 568, 569, 570, 571, 572, 573, 574, 575, 576, 577, 579, 580, 581, 582, 583, 584, 585, 587, 657
azure front door: 504, 507, 587, 590, 591, 627, 628
azure identities and governance: 173, 261
azure kubernetes service: 427, 445, 447, 449, 451, 462, 704
azure load balancer: 377, 523, 587, 588, 590, 594, 595, 596, 597, 598, 599, 601, 607, 609, 631
azure load balancer insights: 597
azure logic apps: 164
azure monitor logs api: 729
azure network policies: 450
azure policy: 68, 102, 103, 104, 107, 109, 120, 125, 132, 134
azure queue storage: 180, 181
azure resource manager: 68, 154, 236, 264, 270, 313, 314, 316, 318, 320, 322, 323, 324, 326, 328, 330, 332, 334, 336, 338, 340, 342, 355, 702

azure resource monitoring data: 697
azure storage accounts: 106, 175, 176, 177, 179, 181, 183, 185, 187, 189, 191, 193, 244, 261, 286, 701
azure subscription: 3, 10, 33, 67, 68, 69, 70, 71, 73, 78, 101, 133, 145, 175, 207, 239, 285, 298, 313, 341, 343, 361, 398, 428, 451, 475, 521, 556, 587, 632, 639, 651, 654, 658, 665, 671, 675, 683, 695, 697, 699, 715, 728, 739, 743
azure site recovery: 743, 751, 755, 757, 759, 760, 761, 766
azure tenant monitoring data: 697
azure ultra disks: 187
azure virtual machines: 361, 412, 756
azure vnet integration: 445

B

backup policies: 743, 746, 747, 749
blob access tiers: 194
blob lifecycle management: 285, 290, 291, 304, 309, 311
blob storage: 175, 176, 179, 180, 183, 184, 185, 186, 192, 193, 194, 198, 201, 203, 204, 207, 208, 222, 223, 225, 227, 229, 231, 233, 235, 237, 286, 291, 292, 466, 674, 744, 776
blob versioning: 180, 254, 285, 290, 291, 292, 311
built-in azure policy definitions: 125
command-line interface: 78, 83, 283, 322, 326, 340, 341, 345, 347, 349, 358, 359, 370, 394, 398, 400, 401, 414, 424, 451, 523, 538, 550, 584, 609, 610, 611, 616, 625, 674, 738

C

configuring and managing devices: 33, 34, 35, 37, 39, 41, 43, 45, 47, 66

consumption: 155, 181, 184, 190, 382, 397, 591, 675, 676, 696, 698, 701, 703, 704, 705, 706

cost analysis: 155, 156, 157, 158

cross-site scripting: 593, 783

cached iops: 365, 367

capacity: 171, 178, 187, 208, 316, 382, 383, 389, 468, 658, 671, 685, 701

category: 29, 42, 106, 110, 112, 156, 200, 201, 477, 486, 494, 568, 675, 676

central processing unit: 432

classless inter-domain routing: 452

client-side encryption: 192, 194

cloud service provider: 382

community-managed policy repository: 125

compliance: 5, 28, 34, 37, 42, 48, 68, 79, 102, 103, 107, 120, 122, 123, 124, 125, 126, 127, 185, 189, 192, 193, 194, 287, 292, 311, 379, 450, 777

compliance reporting: 28, 103

confidentiality: 127, 192, 635, 782

configuration: 24, 26, 30, 32, 37, 49, 66, 90, 94, 103, 106, 112, 113, 117, 120, 155, 159, 160, 164, 182, 184, 187, 193, 198, 199, 239, 242, 244, 246, 248, 249, 253, 254, 255, 258, 262, 268, 269, 270, 291, 293, 296, 297, 299, 302, 303, 304, 310, 315, 316, 317, 320, 321, 336, 346, 348, 349, 350, 353, 358, 362, 364, 365, 370, 377, 379, 380, 382, 389, 393, 397, 399, 403, 413, 414, 416, 422, 429, 430, 431, 434, 435, 438, 447, 448, 449, 456, 463, 464, 472, 478, 480, 481, 483, 493, 494, 496, 497, 498, 500, 501, 503, 504, 506, 514, 516, 525, 531, 532, 533, 536, 539, 540, 547, 549, 550, 552, 558, 560, 568, 571, 572, 582, 584, 590, 597, 599, 604, 605, 607, 608, 609, 612, 613, 614, 616, 618, 619, 623, 631, 635, 636, 637, 646, 650, 654, 655, 663, 667, 670, 675, 681, 683, 684, 685, 687, 692, 693, 701, 705, 709, 710, 713, 724, 725, 735, 741, 742, 754, 766, 776, 782, 790

connection string: 255, 256, 257, 288, 322, 334, 352, 493, 494

container: 7, 10, 70, 201, 219, 229, 230, 231, 232, 236, 254, 258, 260, 287, 288, 289, 291, 292, 304, 306, 307, 317, 341, 427, 429, 430, 431, 433, 434, 435, 436, 437, 438, 439, 440, 441, 443, 444, 445, 446, 450, 452, 453, 454, 455, 456, 457, 458, 459, 460, 461, 462, 465, 469, 473, 482, 511, 518, 587, 610, 706, 708, 738

content delivery network: 627

continuous deployment: 479, 483

contributor role: 79, 80, 96, 97, 282

cost management: 70, 125, 126, 133, 155, 160, 161, 168, 170, 171, 172, 173

cross-region restore: 745

cross-regional performance analysis: 668

custom metrics: 704

custom script extension: 414

D

distributed denial of service: 593, 783

domain name system: 434, 550, 578

domain-specific language: 341, 343

dashboards: 125, 698, 704, 705, 706, 708, 718, 728, 729, 757

data analysis: 669, 703

data collection rules: 701

data disk: 175, 183, 188, 364, 365, 366, 367, 368, 369, 388, 397, 401, 402, 403, 411, 416, 424

data encryption: 193, 747
data export: 729
data isolation: 745
data lake storage: 218, 235, 236
data protection manager: 744
data protection overview: 203, 311
default security: 598, 599
device management: 5, 12, 28, 34, 37, 39, 40, 42, 43, 48
diagnostic logs: 676, 702, 705
diagnostics: 389, 598, 599, 600, 666, 671, 672, 673, 687, 693, 702
disabled: 105, 107, 193, 249, 298, 323, 377, 463, 491, 502, 506, 524, 640
disaster recovery: 180, 231, 291, 501, 744, 755, 756, 783
disk throughput: 363, 372, 704
docker images: 438, 443, 444
docker registry: 438
dockerfile: 438, 439

E

effect: 105, 106, 107, 108, 109, 110, 112, 118, 124, 145, 146, 153, 201, 244, 281, 310, 363, 364, 368, 403, 433, 555, 563, 564, 672, 674, 741
effective security rules: 564, 565, 566, 567, 671, 674, 689, 691
enabling ad ds authentication: 283
encryption: 12, 103, 191, 192, 193, 194, 201, 202, 208, 212, 218, 380, 387, 394, 397, 402, 410, 411, 412, 413, 464, 495, 496, 501, 635, 676, 747, 784
endpoints: 235, 236, 240, 241, 244, 246, 248, 250, 257, 283, 298, 322, 352, 448, 451, 504, 512, 513, 521, 540, 541, 543, 544, 545, 547, 548, 553, 588, 589, 596, 597, 599, 602, 635, 667, 670, 671, 674, 681, 784
enterprise: 15, 39, 66, 72, 172, 183, 368, 369, 380, 382, 430, 638, 784
eviction policy: 382

F

fully qualified domain name: 434, 513, 569, 667
faas: 476, 477
file transfer protocol: 198, 290, 494
firewall: 243, 244, 248, 258, 373, 448, 449, 493, 502, 504, 507, 523, 533, 534, 540, 549, 555, 556, 567, 568, 569, 570, 571, 572, 573, 574, 575, 576, 577, 578, 579, 580, 581, 582, 583, 584, 585, 587, 590, 591, 646, 647, 652, 656, 657, 685, 791
firewall policy: 568
flow logs: 666, 671, 676
function as a service: 476
functional: 73, 75, 127, 593, 595

G

geo-redundant storage: 179, 184, 291, 302, 747
geo-zone-redundant storage: 179, 302
graphics processing units: 436
global administrator: 3, 24, 33, 42, 63, 68, 313, 343
global vnet peering: 525, 598, 600
governance and compliance: 125, 287
graphics processing unit: 370, 436

H

high availability: 186, 373, 375, 376, 382, 575, 587
hardware security module: 193, 785
health probes: 587, 595, 596, 598, 599, 606, 617, 625, 628

high performance: 182, 183, 187, 198, 368, 381, 383, 479, 599
high-performance computing: 370
horizontal scaling: 378, 486, 487, 597
hostname resolution between vnets: 550
hot access tier: 183, 185
hybrid: 15, 35, 36, 37, 38, 48, 66, 172, 261, 266, 382, 430, 506, 589, 595, 635, 667, 668, 669, 745
hybrid application performance optimization: 668

I

identity and access management: 445, 785
infrastructure as code: 313, 343, 413, 538
internet of things: 182, 785
iaas: 186, 476, 521, 699, 785
importing data to blobs: 218
importing data to files: 218
improved security for azure service resources: 540
improving maintainability and consistency: 345
information technology: 126, 785
infrastructure as a service: 476, 521, 785
infrastructure encryption: 193, 201
ingress controller: 451
input/output: 182, 363, 466, 704, 785
insights: 42, 81, 155, 156, 172, 360, 483, 597, 618, 669, 670, 674, 692, 695, 696, 698, 700, 702, 703, 704, 705, 706, 707, 708, 714, 718, 720, 729, 737, 739, 740, 741, 761, 777
integration: 13, 14, 33, 35, 44, 103, 183, 187, 239, 241, 250, 261, 262, 282, 344, 345, 379, 432, 434, 445, 479, 504, 505, 512, 515, 544, 548, 549, 575, 669, 698, 700, 741, 782
internet key exchange: 635
internet protocol: 434, 635
internet protocol security: 635
intrusion detection and prevention: 567
ip address: 240, 241, 243, 246, 249, 255, 258, 265, 373, 377, 403, 405, 408, 417, 420, 434, 436, 449, 452, 459, 502, 503, 504, 508, 514, 521, 522, 523, 529, 531, 532, 533, 536, 538, 540, 543, 547, 553, 556, 557, 558, 560, 561, 566, 569, 576, 577, 579, 580, 595, 596, 597, 599, 606, 607, 608, 609, 611, 613, 616, 617, 622, 625, 626, 635, 636, 639, 640, 645, 649, 651, 660, 661, 670, 672, 674, 676, 684, 686, 687, 688, 689, 690, 693

J

javascript object notation: 103, 154, 314
json: 90, 91, 96, 97, 103, 104, 110, 111, 112, 131, 153, 154, 270, 306, 307, 308, 314, 315, 317, 318, 321, 322, 323, 326, 328, 334, 336, 344, 345, 349, 352, 358, 359, 416, 423, 456, 457, 459, 640

K

kubenet: 449, 450, 464
key rotation: 193, 250, 252, 261, 283
kib: 182, 367
kibibyte: 182
kilobytes: 182
kusto query language: 704

L

locally redundant storage: 179, 302
logs: 12, 40, 42, 43, 66, 200, 666, 671, 676,

696, 699, 701, 702, 703, 704, 705, 708, 727, 728, 729, 730, 742, 761

latency: 178, 182, 183, 185, 186, 187, 247, 363, 368, 369, 370, 383, 525, 595, 599, 627, 637, 638, 667, 668, 670, 680, 692, 701, 704, 786

lifecycle management: 285, 289, 290, 291, 293, 295, 297, 299, 301, 303, 304, 305, 306, 307, 308, 309, 310, 311

live migration: 374

local accounts with kubernetes role-based access control (rbac): 448

local administrator password solution: 38

log-based metrics: 704

low latency: 178, 182, 183, 187, 368, 383, 525, 595, 599

M

multi-factor authentication: 5, 12, 15, 38, 787

machine learning: 182, 372, 787

managed disks: 121, 183, 188, 362, 363, 370, 388, 466, 744

managed services: 12

management groups: 67, 71, 74, 75, 76, 77, 78, 82

management operations: 598, 599

matrix: 73, 781, 782

mb: 182, 187, 462

metadata: 105, 112, 125, 134, 144, 185, 318, 320, 325, 348, 349, 351, 352, 354, 416, 417, 418, 419, 468

metrics: 292, 488, 597, 599, 666, 669, 675, 695, 696, 699, 701, 702, 703, 704, 708, 709, 712, 713, 714, 715, 716, 717, 719, 720, 721, 723, 724, 725, 727, 737, 739, 742

microservices: 477, 669

microsoft azure policy documentation: 125

microsoft entra directory domain services: 261

microsoft entra ds: 261

microsoft entra id: 1, 2, 3, 4, 5, 6, 7, 8, 9, 10, 11, 12, 13, 14, 15, 16, 17, 18, 19, 20, 22, 23, 24, 25, 26, 27, 28, 30, 32, 33, 34, 35, 36, 37, 38, 39, 40, 41, 42, 43, 44, 45, 46, 47, 48, 50, 52, 53, 54, 56, 57, 58, 59, 60, 61, 62, 63, 64, 66, 68, 73, 82, 91, 93, 262, 266, 273, 290, 313, 343, 445, 463, 498, 697, 776

microsoft entra id account: 10, 63

microsoft entra permissions management: 44

microsoft entra tenant: 10, 61, 72, 73, 78

mobile device management: 37

mode: 105, 106, 112, 323, 364, 366, 392, 432, 464, 488, 515, 640

modularity: 315

modules: 273, 344, 345, 352, 424, 432

monitoring and logging: 449

multi-tier application monitoring: 668

multi-divisional: 73

multiple-site hosting: 619

N

network interface card: 244, 373, 397, 422, 556, 685

network interface cards: 397, 685

network rule: 240, 542, 543, 569, 570, 578, 582

network security group: 244, 373, 388, 397, 416, 538, 555, 556, 557, 559, 561, 562, 563, 565, 613, 671, 677, 702

network virtual appliance: 507, 533, 576, 656, 685

native azure metrics: 704

native integration with arm: 345

network address translation: 449, 504, 540, 569, 595, 596

network file system: 183, 198, 262, 290

network performance: 666, 669, 692, 704

network virtual appliances: 576
network watcher: 564, 565, 566, 665, 666, 667, 669, 671, 672, 673, 674, 675, 676, 677, 678, 679, 680, 681, 682, 683, 684, 685, 686, 687, 689, 690, 691, 692, 693, 694
next hop: 533, 534, 536, 671, 673, 675, 685, 686, 687, 693
node pools: 446, 451, 464, 470, 472
node-image: 447, 472
nsg: 244, 373, 403, 416, 419, 420, 421, 555, 556, 557, 558, 559, 560, 561, 562, 563, 564, 566, 567, 576, 585, 599, 600, 612, 613, 617, 671, 672, 673, 674, 675, 676, 684, 693
nsg diagnostic: 671, 672, 673, 675, 693

O

operating systems: 226, 314, 362, 478, 744
optional decorators: 351
organizational unit: 274
out-of-box experience: 49
outbound connections: 544, 549, 596, 599, 671
outbound connectivity: 595, 599
outbound rules: 598, 599

P

pay-as-you-go: 69, 72, 172
paas: 476, 477, 478, 544, 576, 587, 599, 788
page blobs: 179, 183, 184, 194, 204
path mappings: 494, 496
peering: 521, 522, 525, 526, 527, 528, 530, 553, 598, 600, 654, 656
performance monitor: 669
persistent storage: 183, 184, 433, 445, 465, 466, 469, 473
platform as a service: 544, 576, 587, 788
platform metrics: 701, 704

point-in-time restoration: 201, 203, 511
policy assignment: 103, 104
policy definition: 103, 105, 106, 107, 108, 109, 110, 111, 112, 113, 114, 115, 116, 118, 119, 125
port forwarding: 595, 596
portal: 13, 15, 20, 24, 28, 30, 32, 37, 40, 42, 43, 45, 47, 52, 54, 58, 59, 61, 64, 66, 72, 76, 78, 83, 85, 91, 93, 95, 97, 98, 104, 109, 116, 127, 132, 135, 137, 138, 143, 145, 175, 179, 195, 203, 204, 208, 209, 215, 218, 220, 222, 224, 225, 226, 229, 230, 231, 235, 241, 245, 250, 251, 253, 258, 260, 278, 279, 287, 288, 294, 298, 301, 302, 303, 304, 306, 308, 310, 314, 322, 326, 332, 333, 334, 335, 337, 339, 340, 341, 370, 384, 391, 398, 400, 401, 403, 405, 409, 410, 411, 413, 414, 415, 418, 452, 454, 456, 460, 462, 466, 469, 472, 480, 481, 484, 485, 491, 493, 523, 524, 526, 531, 533, 534, 535, 538, 539, 540, 545, 548, 550, 552, 559, 561, 566, 576, 577, 580, 581, 582, 601, 603, 609, 616, 617, 620, 652, 653, 655, 661, 674, 677, 678, 683, 685, 686, 696, 719, 724, 728, 729, 730, 738, 739, 746, 748, 751, 752, 754, 755, 761, 762, 766
power bi: 676, 706, 729
powershell: 3, 24, 33, 34, 53, 59, 60, 61, 78, 83, 101, 102, 129, 130, 131, 132, 133, 134, 144, 153, 175, 176, 195, 203, 204, 207, 208, 226, 227, 228, 236, 237, 239, 240, 248, 249, 271, 272, 273, 280, 282, 285, 286, 288, 314, 322, 326, 334, 340, 341, 343, 344, 347, 356, 357, 359, 362, 370, 390, 391, 394, 398, 400, 405, 409, 410, 413, 414, 424, 428, 432, 440, 442, 443, 444, 451, 454, 466, 475, 476, 484, 485, 491, 492, 493, 522, 523, 524, 525, 526, 528, 529, 530, 532, 533, 537, 538, 540, 544, 545, 550, 551, 552, 553,

556, 577, 578, 579, 583, 584, 588, 601, 602, 608, 610, 611, 625, 632, 665, 666, 674, 677, 687, 695, 696, 724, 729, 738, 744, 745, 746, 747, 788

private endpoint: 199, 244, 245, 246, 247, 248, 249, 250, 283, 373, 448, 451, 504, 512, 513, 514, 515, 521, 544, 545, 546, 547, 548, 553, 556

private link: 244, 250, 451, 544, 545, 598, 599, 600

privileged identity management: 44

protocol: 12, 106, 182, 198, 224, 226, 229, 262, 290, 373, 408, 421, 434, 437, 494, 495, 556, 558, 559, 561, 566, 581, 582, 593, 594, 595, 596, 606, 607, 612, 613, 618, 623, 624, 625, 628, 635, 652, 669, 670, 672, 674, 676, 681, 689, 690, 693, 725, 782, 784, 785, 786, 789, 790

protocol versatility: 669

public connectivity: 434

public load balancer: 587, 595, 598, 600, 609, 611, 613, 614, 615, 616, 617, 628

Q

queue storage: 176, 180, 181, 235

quota: 38, 223, 382, 383, 675

R

remote desktop protocol: 408, 559, 596, 725

role-based access control: 7, 66, 67, 68, 70, 72, 74, 76, 78, 80, 82, 84, 86, 88, 90, 92, 94, 96, 98, 104, 262, 448, 666, 745, 789

rapid deployment: 340, 429

rbac: 7, 23, 66, 67, 68, 75, 78, 79, 80, 82, 83, 84, 85, 87, 89, 91, 93, 95, 97, 98, 104, 134, 145, 146, 262, 448, 463, 493, 500, 501, 666, 745, 789

read-only: 84, 151, 152, 153, 191, 301, 364, 365, 366, 402

read/write: 364, 365

reader: 2, 69, 79, 80, 81, 83, 84, 145, 262, 282, 774

reader role: 79, 84, 145, 282

recovery services vault: 743, 744, 745, 746, 747, 762, 766

reduced attack surface: 577

reduced instruction set computer: 381

reduced security risks: 7

redundancy: 175, 178, 179, 182, 184, 188, 189, 192, 194, 195, 196, 197, 204, 291, 301, 302, 335, 361, 369, 370, 374, 385, 401, 481, 589, 600, 619, 633, 634, 636, 638, 745

regional: 190, 191, 375, 588, 589, 590, 591, 604, 619, 627, 668, 676, 747

rehydrating: 185, 194, 234

reliability: 172, 189, 190, 231, 362, 363, 369, 373, 413, 479, 575

remediation: 102, 103, 107, 120, 698, 710, 723, 789

remote desktop: 293, 404, 408, 559, 596, 641, 725

reporting and monitoring: 125

resource dependency management: 315

resource functions: 317

resource groups: 10, 71, 74, 82, 91, 92, 94, 95, 103, 104, 125, 129, 133, 134, 135, 137, 138, 139, 140, 141, 143, 144, 145, 154, 168, 326, 330, 331, 332, 334, 337, 338, 394, 397, 405, 407, 408, 667, 683

resource logs: 702, 704

rest: 83, 182, 183, 184, 194, 237, 240, 414, 439, 477, 538, 539, 550, 624, 674, 695, 703, 704, 729, 749, 781, 783

restrict access: 10, 241, 255, 285, 499

reusable pieces of code: 345

rewrite http headers and urls: 620
role definition: 80, 81, 82, 83, 84
role-based access control (rbac): 7, 66, 67, 78, 104, 262, 448, 745
round-trip time: 670

S

server-side encryption: 192, 411
single sign-on (sso): 10, 34
standard general-purpose v2: 176, 179
standard hdd: 186, 204, 367, 369, 402
standard hdd (s series): 186
standard ssds: 369
s2s: 280, 631, 632, 633, 634, 635, 636, 637, 639, 640, 650, 652, 653, 656, 657, 659, 662, 688
software as a service (saas): 44, 476
sas tokens: 239, 252, 253, 255, 257, 258, 259, 261, 283, 285, 287
scalable vector graphics (svg): 684
scale out: 464, 486, 487, 490, 491, 493
scale sets: 361, 376, 377, 380, 391, 393, 595, 668, 670, 674
scale up: 433, 479, 486, 512, 595
secure shell (ssh): 576, 596
secure sockets layer (ssl): 590
security advisories: 711, 712
security group: 7, 30, 64, 244, 246, 373, 388, 397, 416, 445, 538, 555, 556, 557, 559, 561, 562, 563, 565, 587, 613, 671, 677, 702
server message block (smb): 224, 290, 433
service-level agreement (sla): 127, 185, 374, 598
service endpoints: 235, 540, 541, 543, 544, 548, 599
service-managed keys: 192, 193
simplified syntax: 344
site recovery: 368, 743, 744, 745, 751, 755, 757, 759, 760, 761, 766
site-to-site (s2s): 631
sku: 172, 188, 320, 350, 351, 353, 355, 356, 362, 365, 366, 378, 398, 399, 400, 417, 418, 419, 420, 424, 451, 455, 464, 478, 479, 482, 486, 496, 512, 532, 571, 572, 573, 574, 576, 579, 597, 598, 599, 600, 601, 603, 604, 611, 612, 619, 620, 633, 634, 639, 654, 657
sla: 127, 185, 186, 187, 194, 374, 478, 479, 598, 599, 600
soft delete for blobs: 203, 292
software development kit (sdk): 698
source port: 558, 562, 595, 618, 693
sql databases: 367, 540, 544, 702
ssh file transfer protocol (sftp): 198
static: 106, 235, 236, 417, 522, 523, 531, 532, 576, 579, 620, 649, 662, 721
static website: 235, 236
stock-keeping unit (sku): 172, 362, 597
stored access policy: 253, 258
storage access keys: 239, 250, 251
storage access tiers: 175, 180, 184, 186, 237
storage accounts: 105, 106, 145, 175, 176, 177, 178, 179, 180, 181, 182, 183, 184, 185, 186, 187, 188, 189, 190, 191, 192, 193, 194, 195, 196, 197, 198, 199, 200, 201, 202, 203, 204, 218, 222, 236, 237, 239, 240, 241, 242, 243, 244, 245, 247, 248, 249, 250, 257, 258, 261, 283, 285, 286, 288, 291, 303, 310, 311, 322, 341, 356, 362, 370, 435, 701, 754
storage redundancy: 179, 194, 197, 291, 301, 302
storage rehydration: 237
streamlined monitoring: 669
string: 81, 105, 255, 256, 257, 288, 316, 317, 318, 319, 320, 322, 325, 334, 348, 349, 350, 353, 354, 355, 356, 416, 417, 418,

419, 423, 485, 492, 493, 620, 641, 731
strong type-checking: 344
subscription: 3, 10, 28, 30, 33, 44, 68, 69, 70, 71, 72, 73, 74, 75, 76, 78, 81, 82, 83, 85, 86, 89, 91, 94, 95, 101, 104, 110, 113, 118, 124, 133, 136, 138, 140, 142, 143, 144, 145, 153, 154, 156, 160, 161, 164, 169, 170, 172, 175, 207, 210, 215, 219, 220, 222, 239, 242, 243, 245, 273, 274, 285, 294, 296, 298, 313, 326, 341, 343, 348, 361, 382, 383, 384, 387, 391, 398, 401, 428, 439, 451, 475, 485, 492, 513, 521, 523, 556, 578, 587, 602, 610, 620, 621, 632, 639, 651, 654, 658, 665, 666, 675, 679, 680, 683, 687, 691, 695, 697, 698, 702, 709, 712, 715, 721, 728, 735, 739, 743, 761, 764, 769

T

tenant ID: 10, 59, 130, 274
tenant root group: 77, 78
tebibytes (TiB): 179
template file: 314, 315, 321, 326, 331, 332, 336, 337, 355, 358
test configurations: 670
test groups: 670, 680
the azure CLI: 78, 83, 398, 400, 538, 550, 609, 616, 625, 674, 738
the azure portal: 15, 20, 24, 28, 30, 32, 37, 40, 42, 43, 45, 47, 52, 54, 58, 61, 64, 66, 76, 78, 83, 85, 91, 93, 95, 98, 135, 137, 175, 179, 195, 203, 204, 208, 209, 215, 220, 222, 224, 225, 226, 229, 230, 231, 241, 245, 250, 251, 253, 258, 260, 278, 279, 287, 288, 294, 298, 301, 302, 303, 304, 306, 310, 314, 322, 326, 332, 334, 335, 337, 339, 370, 384, 391, 398, 400, 401, 403, 405, 409, 410, 411, 413, 414, 415, 418, 452, 454, 456, 460, 462, 466, 469, 472, 480, 481, 484, 491, 493, 523, 524, 526, 531, 533, 534, 535, 538, 539, 540, 545, 552, 559, 561, 576, 577, 580, 581, 582, 601, 603, 609, 616, 617, 620, 652, 653, 661, 674, 677, 678, 683, 685, 686, 696, 719, 724, 728, 729, 738, 739, 746, 748, 751, 752, 754, 755, 761, 762, 766
time to live (TTL): 510
time-based retention: 201, 292
time-based retention policies: 292
traffic analytics: 666, 671, 676
transmission control protocol (TCP): 594
transport layer security (TLS): 571, 591

U

ultra disk: 186, 187, 204, 367, 368, 369, 387
unexpected downtime: 374
unlimited data transfer: 747
user and group management: 5, 12, 44

V

virtual machines (VMs): 103, 134, 175, 361, 427, 522, 667
virtual network (VNet): 241, 373, 434, 483, 560, 666
virtual networks (VNets): 397, 521, 588
virtual private network (VPN): 576, 631, 645, 649, 661
versioning: 180, 184, 200, 254, 285, 290, 291, 292, 311, 315, 316, 321
vertical scaling: 378, 398, 486
virtual appliance: 507, 533, 534, 576, 600, 656, 685
virtual network integration: 504, 505, 548, 549
VNet flow logs: 671, 676
VNet gateway: 525, 534, 637, 638, 671, 674

VNet peering: 522, 525, 526, 530, 553, 598, 600, 656

VPN troubleshoot: 671, 674, 685, 687, 688, 689

W

write once, read many (WORM): 292

web application firewall (WAF): 502, 591

Windows Subsystem for Linux 2 (WSL 2): 440

Z

zone-redundant storage (ZRS): 179, 291, 302, 370

Zero Trust model: 502

zone-resilient storage (ZRS): 187

zone-redundancy: 619

<packt>

www.packtpub.com

Subscribe to our online digital library for full access to over 7,000 books and videos, as well as industry leading tools to help you plan your personal development and advance your career. For more information, please visit our website.

Why subscribe?

- Spend less time learning and more time coding with practical eBooks and Videos from over 4,000 industry professionals
- Improve your learning with Skill Plans built especially for you
- Get a free eBook or video every month
- Fully searchable for easy access to vital information
- Copy and paste, print, and bookmark content

At www.packtpub.com, you can also read a collection of free technical articles, sign up for a range of free newsletters, and receive exclusive discounts and offers on Packt books and eBooks.

Other Books You May Enjoy

If you enjoyed this book, you may be interested in these other books by Packt:

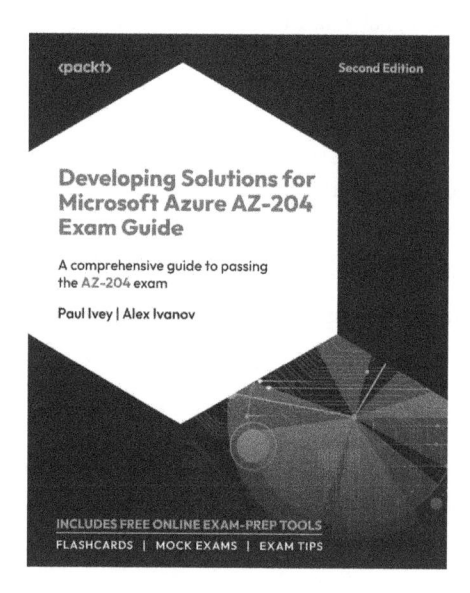

Developing Solutions for Microsoft Azure AZ-204 Exam Guide

Alex Ivanov and Paul Ivey

ISBN:978-1-83508-529-5

- Identify cloud models and services in Azure
- Develop secure Azure web apps and host containerized solutions in Azure
- Implement serverless solutions with Azure Functions
- Utilize Cosmos DB for scalable data storage
- Optimize Azure Blob storage for efficiency
- Securely store secrets and configuration settings centrally
- Ensure web application security with Microsoft Entra ID authentication
- Monitor and troubleshoot Azure solutions

Microsoft Azure Fundamentals Certification and Beyond

Steve Miles

ISBN: 978-1-83763-059-2

- Become proficient in foundational cloud concepts
- Develop a solid understanding of core components of the Microsoft Azure cloud platform
- Get to grips with Azure's core services, deployment, and management tools
- Implement security concepts, operations, and posture management
- Explore identity, governance, and compliance features
- Gain insights into resource deployment, management, and monitoring

Share Your Thoughts

Now you've finished *Exam Ref AZ-104 Microsoft Azure Administrator Certification and Beyond, Third Edition*, we'd love to hear your thoughts! Scan the QR code below to go straight to the Amazon review page for this book and share your feedback or leave a review on the site that you purchased it from.

`https://packt.link/r/1805122851`

Your review is important to us and the tech community and will help us make sure we're delivering excellent quality content.

Download a Free PDF Copy of This Book

Thanks for purchasing this book!

Do you like to read on the go but are unable to carry your print books everywhere?

Is your eBook purchase not compatible with the device of your choice?

Don't worry, now with every Packt book you get a DRM-free PDF version of that book at no cost.

Read anywhere, any place, on any device. Search, copy, and paste code from your favorite technical books directly into your application.

The perks don't stop there, you can get exclusive access to discounts, newsletters, and great free content in your inbox daily.

Follow these simple steps to get the benefits:

1. Scan the QR code or visit the link below:

   `https://packt.link/free-ebook/9781805122852`

2. Submit your proof of purchase.
3. That's it! We'll send your free PDF and other benefits to your email directly.

www.ingramcontent.com/pod-product-compliance
Ingram Content Group UK Ltd.
Pitfield, Milton Keynes, MK11 3LW, UK
UKHW051918220425
457753UK00011B/247

9 781805 122852